textbook*plus*

**Equipping Instructors and Students with
FREE RESOURCES for Core Zondervan Textbooks**

Available Resources for Evangelical Theology

Instructor Resources

- Instructor's manual
- Presentation slides
- Chapter quizzes
- Midterm and final exams
- Sample syllabus
- Chapter summaries

Student Resources

- Videos
- Quizzes
- Flashcards
- Exam study guides

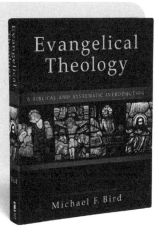

*How To Access Resources

- Go to www.TextbookPlus.Zondervan.com
- Click "Register Now" button and complete registration process
- Find books using search field or "Browse Our Textbooks" feature
- Click "Instructor Resources" or "Student Resources" tab once you get to book page to access resources

▶ **www.TextbookPlus.Zondervan.com**

Evangelical Theology

A BIBLICAL AND SYSTEMATIC INTRODUCTION

Michael F. Bird

We want to hear from you. Please send your comments about this book to us in care of zreview@zondervan.com. Thank you.

ZONDERVAN

Evangelical Theology
Copyright © 2013 by Michael F. Bird

This title is also available as a Zondervan ebook. Visit www.zondervan.com/ebooks.

Requests for information should be addressed to:

Zondervan, *Grand Rapids, Michigan* 49530

Library of Congress Cataloging-in-Publication Data

Bird, Michael F.
    Evangelical theology : a biblical and systematic introduction / Michael F. Bird.
       p. cm.
    Includes bibliographical references and index.
    ISBN 978-0-310-49441-6
    1. 1. Evangelicalism. 2. Theology, Doctrinal. I. Title.
BR1640.B527 2013
230'.04624—dc23   2013005674

All Scripture quotations, unless otherwise indicated, are taken from The Holy Bible, *New International Version®, NIV®*. Copyright © 1973, 1978, 1984, 2011 by Biblica, Inc.™ Used by permission. All rights reserved worldwide.

The Scripture quotations from the Apocrypha are from the *New Revised Standard Version of the Bible*, copyright © 1989 by the Division of Christian Education of the National Council of Churches of Christ in the United States of America, and are used by permission. All rights reserved.

Any Internet addresses (websites, blogs, etc.) and telephone numbers in this book are offered as a resource. They are not intended in any way to be or imply an endorsement by Zondervan, nor does Zondervan vouch for the content of these sites and numbers for the life of this book.

All rights reserved. No part of this publication may be reproduced, stored in a retrieval system, or transmitted in any form or by any means — electronic, mechanical, photocopy, recording, or any other — except for brief quotations in printed reviews, without the prior permission of the publisher.

Cover design: Tammy Johnson
Cover photography: Bridgeman Art Library
Interior design: Matthew Van Zomeren and Ben Fetterley

Printed in the United States of America

To Jim Gibson, Pastor, Evangelist, Theologian, and Gospelizer

CONTENTS

Acknowledgments 11
Abbreviations 13
Preface: "Without the Gospel" (John Calvin) 16
Why an Evangelical Theology? 19

PART 1
PROLEGOMENA: BEGINNING TO TALK ABOUT GOD 27

§ 1.1 What Is Theology? 29

§ 1.2 What Do You Have to Say before You Say Anything? 32

§ 1.3 What Is the Gospel? 47

§ 1.4 The Necessity and Goal of Theology 55

§ 1.5 Is Theology Possible? 60

§ 1.6 Sources for Theology 62

§ 1.7 Toward a Gospel-Driven Theological Method 77

§ 1.8 A Final Word 84

PART 2
THE GOD OF THE GOSPEL: THE TRIUNE GOD IN BEING AND ACTION 87

§ 2.1 God and the Gospel 89

§ 2.2 Getting an Affinity for the Trinity 92

§ 2.3 What Is God Like? 126

§ 2.4 The God Who Creates 140

§ 2.5 The God Who Reveals Himself 164

§ 2.6 God's Purpose and Plan 214

PART 3
THE GOSPEL OF THE KINGDOM: THE NOW AND THE NOT YET..................233

§ 3.1 Gospel and Kingdom...................................235
§ 3.2 Apocalypse Now ... and Not Yet!......................244
§ 3.3 The Return of Jesus Christ...........................258
§ 3.4 Millennium and Tribulation...........................274
§ 3.5 The Final Judgment...................................301
§ 3.6 The Intermediate State: What Happens When You Die?...309
§ 3.7 The Final State: Heaven, Hell, and New Creation......326

PART 4
THE GOSPEL OF GOD'S SON: THE LORD JESUS CHRIST...................341

§ 4.1 The Gospel of God's Son..............................343
§ 4.2 Christological Method................................346
§ 4.3 The Life of Jesus....................................357
§ 4.4 The Death of Jesus...................................385
§ 4.5 The Resurrection of Jesus............................435
§ 4.6 The Ascension and Session of Jesus...................449
§ 4.7 The Story of Jesus and the Identity of God...........460

PART 5
THE GOSPEL OF SALVATION........................489

§ 5.1 Saved by the Gospel..................................491
§ 5.2 Redemptive History: The Plan for the Gospel..........496
§ 5.3 Order of Salvation: The Logical Working of the Gospel....513
§ 5.4 Images of Salvation: The Result of the Gospel........548
§ 5.5 Scope and Security: How Wide and How Certain a Salvation?....580

PART 6
THE PROMISE AND POWER OF THE GOSPEL: THE HOLY SPIRIT 609
§6.1 God's Spirit: The Breath of the Gospel.....................611
§6.2 Person of the Holy Spirit................................615
§6.3 Work of the Holy Spirit.................................621

PART 7
THE GOSPEL AND HUMANITY.....................649
§7.1 Sons and Daughters of the King.........................651
§7.2 Image of God 657
§7.3 What Is Humanity? The Human Constitution..............662
§7.4 What Is the Problem with Humanity?....................666
§7.5 The Odyssey of Theodicy................................684

PART 8
THE COMMUNITY OF THE GOSPELIZED..........697
§8.1 The Evangelical Church.................................699
§8.2 Biblical Images of the Church...........................713
§8.3 The Shape of the Church................................728
§8.4 The Marks of the Church...............................735
§8.5 Governance of the Church..............................745
§8.6 Emblems of the Gospel: Baptism and Lord's Supper............757

Epilogue: Urgent Tasks for Evangelical Theology in the 21st Century 807
Select Bibliography...813
Scripture and Apocrypha Index...................................853
Subject Index...880
Author Index...905

ACKNOWLEDGMENTS

This book was written for one reason. There are a lot of good theology textbooks written by evangelicals, but I do not believe that there is yet a genuinely evangelical theology textbook—a theology textbook that has its content, structure, and substance singularly determined by the evangel. This volume is an attempt at such an exercise. I have found many inspiring dialogue partners along the way: Kevin Vanhoozer, John Webster, Peter Jensen, N. T. Wright, D. A. Carson, and Alister McGrath. My goal has been to construct a theology of the gospel for people who identify themselves as gospel people, namely, the evangelical churches. Though obviously the term *evangelical* means different things to different people, I intend it as designating those faith communities who hold to the catholic and orthodox faith and who possess a singular religious affection for the Triune God, combined with a zealous fervor to proclaim the gospel to the ends of the earth.

Many people must be thanked for what has appeared here. The usual suspects are my wife, Naomi, and my children, Alexis, Alyssa, Markus, and Theodore—they encourage me, support me, inspire me, and keep me accountable. I received help from friends who read portions of the manuscript in draft and final stages, including Michael Allen, Gerald Bray, Rhys Bezzant, Graham Cole, Jason Hood, Michael Jensen, Weber Hsu, John MacClean, Ben Myers, Michael Williams, and Trevin Wax. Their advice and corrections were crucial, but all faults remain my own.

My arrival back in Australia meant a transition from teaching exclusively New Testament to teaching theology and New Testament across two colleges, Crossway (Brisbane) and Ridley (Melbourne). This has been a beneficial experience as it has enabled me to finally concretize proposals and plans that have been simmering away in my mind for over ten years. I've been consumed with *what* evangelicals believe as well as *how* and *why* they believe it. Recently, my poor students in Brisbane and Melbourne have had to put up with my attempt finally to verbalize those thoughts about the nature and goals of evangelical theology. The notes prepared for those classes, which ranged considerably in unity and coherence, formed the basis of the chapters that appear here. I'm grateful for the willingness of my students to listen and question me in the journey we took together.

I'm also grateful to my colleagues at Crossway College and Ridley College for fellowship along the way as this volume was produced. Stephen Morton chased

Acknowledgments

up several volumes that I needed to read in order to complete this project, and I am grateful to him for his excellent library support. My student Mr. Ovi Buciu chased up several obscure references for me and compiled my abbreviations list. Miss Kirsten Mackerras made some creative diagrams for me about christological heresies. David Byrd provided timely help with compiling a bibliography. I have to thank "Special K," being none other than the indefatigable Katya Covrett, my editor at Zondervan, for her enthusiasm on this project, especially when it meant deferring other Zondervan projects I was doing.

Finally, a major inspiration of this book was my former lecturer and friend Rev. Jim Gibson (Malyon College and Salisbury Baptist Church). Jim is a remarkable chap as a lecturer, pastor, and theologian. He brings a wonderful mix of theological depth, evangelistic fervor, and pastoral sensitivity to his teaching ministry. His introductory course to theology and his concept of discipleship as "gospelizing" were formative to my own theological thinking as will be clear from what follows. I always carried with me the idea of evangelical theology as a consistent application of the gospel, thanks to Jim. Our families have spent much time together and they are among our closest friends. So to Jim this book is dedicated in gratitude for his friendship to me and my family.

Michael F. Bird, 1 April 2012
Holy Feast of St. Boschlavich of Guarderloopu

ABBREVIATIONS

Note: The standard abbreviations for classical Greek and Latin works as well as those of the church fathers will not be listed here. They can be found in *The SBL Handbook of Style*. Any that are not in that style manual will be spelled out in full.

AB	Anchor Bible
ABD	*The Anchor Bible Dictionary*
ABRL	Anchor Bible Reference Library
ACCS	Ancient Christian Commentary on Scripture
ACD	Ancient Christian Doctrine
ACT	Ancient Christian Texts
ANF	Ante-Nicene Fathers
AOTC	Abingdon Old Testament Commentary
ATLAMS	American Theological Library Association Monograph Series
ATR	*Australasian Theological Review*
BBR	*Bulletin for Biblical Research*
BDAG	*A Greek-English Lexicon of the New Testament and Other Early Christian Literature* (3rd ed.)
BECNT	Baker Exegetical Commentary on the New Testament
Bib	*Biblica*
BIS	Biblical Interpretation Series
BNTC	Black's New Testament Commentaries
BSac	*Bibliotheca sacra*
BST	The Bible Speaks Today
BTCB	Brazos Theological Commentary on the Bible
CCC	Catechism of the Catholic Church
CD	*Church Dogmatics* (Karl Barth)
CEB	Common English Bible
CGNTC	Cambridge Greek New Testament Commentary
CITM	Christianity in the Making
COQG	Christian Origins and the Question of God
DNTB	*Dictionary of New Testament Background*
DPL	*Dictionary of Paul and His Letters*

Acknowledgments

DTIB	*Dictionary for the Theological Interpretation of the Bible*
EBC	*The Expositor's Bible Commentary*
EDB	*Eerdmans Dictionary of the Bible*
EDEJ	*Eerdmans Dictionary of Early Judaism*
EDNT	*Exegetical Dictionary of the New Testament*
EDT	*Evangelical Dictionary of Theology*
EJTh	*European Journal of Theology*
ERT	*Evangelical Review of Theology*
ESV	English Standard Version
EvQ	*Evangelical Quarterly*
GPP	Gorgias Précis Portfolios
Herm	Hermeneia
ICC	International Critical Commentary
IJST	*International Journal of Systematic Theology*
ISBE	*International Standard Bible Encyclopedia* (rev. ed.)
Int	*Interpretation*
Institutes	John Calvin, *Institutes of the Christian Religion*
JEH	*Journal of Ecclesiastical History*
JETS	*Journal of the Evangelical Theological Society*
JSNT	*Journal for the Study of the New Testament*
JSNTSup	Journal for the Study of the New Testament Supplement Series
JSPSup	Journal for the Study of the Pseudepigrapha and Related Literature Supplement Series
JTI	*Journal of Theological Interpretation*
JTS	*Journal of Theological Studies*
LAE	*Light from the Ancient East* (ed. A. Deissmann)
LBC	London Baptist Confession (1689)
LNTS	Library of New Testament Studies
LXX	Septuagint
NAC	New American Commentary
NACSBT	New American Commentary Studies in Biblical Theology
NASB	New American Standard Bible
NCBC	New Century Bible Commentary
NCCS	New Covenant Commentary Series
NDBT	*New Dictionary of Biblical Theology*
NDIEC	*New Documents Illustrating Early Christianity*
NET	New English Translation
NIB	*The New Interpreter's Bible*

NIBC	New International Biblical Commentary
NICNT	New International Commentary on the New Testament
NICOT	New International Commentary on the Old Testament
NIGTC	New International Greek Testament Commentary
NIV	New International Version
NJB	New Jerusalem Bible
NovT	*Novum Testamentum*
NRSV	New Revised Standard Version
NSBT	New Studies in Biblical Theology
NTC	New Testament Commentary
NTM	New Testament Message
NTS	*New Testament Studies*
PBM	Paternoster Biblical Monograph Series
PNTC	Pillar New Testament Commentary
ProEccl	*Pro ecclesia*
QR	*Quarterly Review*
RSV	Revised Standard Version
RTR	*Reformed Theological Review*
SBET	*Scottish Bulletin of Evangelical Theology*
SBHT	Studies in Baptist History and Thought
SBJT	*Southern Baptist Journal of Theology*
SBT	Studies in Biblical Theology
SJT	*Scottish Journal of Theology*
SNTSMS	Society for New Testament Studies Monograph Series
STI	Studies in Theological Interpretations
SWBJT	*Southwestern Baptist Journal of Theology*
TDNT	Theological Dictionary of the New Testament
Them	*Themelios*
TNIV	Today's New International Version
TOTC	Tyndale Old Testament Commentaries
TrinJ	*Trinity Journal*
TS	*Theological Studies*
TynBul	*Tyndale Bulletin*
UBT	Understanding Biblical Themes
VE	*Vox evangelica*
WBC	Word Biblical Commentary
WCF	Westminster Confession of Faith
WTJ	*Westminster Theological Journal*
WUNT	Wissenschaftliche Untersuchungen zum Neuen Testament

WITHOUT THE GOSPEL[1]

Without the gospel
>everything is useless and vain;

without the gospel
>we are not Christians;

without the gospel
>all riches is poverty,
>all wisdom folly before God;
>strength is weakness,
>and all the justice of man is under the condemnation of God.

But by the knowledge of the gospel we are made
>children of God,
>brothers of Jesus Christ,
>fellow townsmen with the saints,
>citizens of the Kingdom of Heaven,
>heirs of God with Jesus Christ, by whom
>>the poor are made rich,
>>the weak strong,
>>the fools wise,
>>the sinner justified,
>>the desolate comforted,
>>the doubting sure,
>>and slaves free.

It is the power of God for the salvation of all those who believe.

It follows that every good thing we could think or desire is to be found in this same Jesus Christ alone.

For, he was
>sold, to buy us back;

---

1. Posted by Tullian Tchividjian and arranged by Justin Taylor at The Gospel Coalition website from John Calvin's preface to Pierre Robert Olivétan's French translation of the New Testament (1534): http://thegospelcoalition.org/blogs/tullian/2011/06/06/gospel-gold-from-john-calvin/.

Without the Gospel

  captive, to deliver us;
  condemned, to absolve us;
he was
  made a curse for our blessing,
  [a] sin offering for our righteousness;
  marred that we may be made fair;

he died for our life; so that by him
  fury is made gentle,
  wrath appeased,
  darkness turned into light,
  fear reassured,
  despisal despised,
  debt canceled,
  labor lightened,
  sadness made merry,
  misfortune made fortunate,
  difficulty easy,
  disorder ordered,
  division united,
  ignominy ennobled,
  rebellion subjected,
  intimidation intimidated,
  ambush uncovered,
  assaults assailed,
  force forced back,
  combat combated,
  war warred against,
  vengeance avenged,
  torment tormented,
  damnation damned,
  the abyss sunk into the abyss,
  hell transfixed,
  death dead,
  mortality made immortal.

In short,
  mercy has swallowed up all misery,
  and goodness all misfortune.
For all these things which were to be the weapons of the devil in his battle

against us, and the sting of death to pierce us, are turned for us into exercises which we can turn to our profit.

If we are able to boast with the apostle, saying, O hell, where is thy victory? O death, where is thy sting? it is because by the Spirit of Christ promised to the elect, we live no longer, but Christ lives in us; and we are by the same Spirit seated among those who are in heaven, so that for us the world is no more, even while our conversation is in it; but we are content in all things, whether country, place, condition, clothing, meat, and all such things.

And we are
- comforted in tribulation,
- joyful in sorrow,
- glorying under vituperation,
- abounding in poverty,
- warmed in our nakedness,
- patient amongst evils,
- living in death.

This is what we should in short seek in the whole of Scripture: truly to know Jesus Christ, and the infinite riches that are comprised in him and are offered to us by him from God the Father.

WHY AN EVANGELICAL THEOLOGY?

The purpose of this volume on Christian theology is to produce a textbook for Christians that represents a biblically sound expression of the Christian faith from the vantage point of the evangelical tradition. It is intended to be a book about theological doctrine that is accessible to laypeople, seminary students, and leaders in the evangelical churches. That statement, of course, implies a question: What is an evangelical? The term *evangelical* can be used in diverse ways. For some it is a pejorative term meaning basically the same as *fundamentalist*. For others it is largely a cultural term describing those aligned with a particular social, political, and moral bent associated with conservative American politics. When I refer to *evangelicalism*, I am referring to a historic and global phenomenon that seeks to achieve renewal in Christian churches by bringing the church into conformity to the gospel and by promoting the gospel in the mission of the church.[1]

In my reckoning, six key factors led to the formation of modern evangelicalism.

1. The Protestant Reformation with the rediscovery of the doctrines of grace over and against medieval Catholic notions of salvation through merit and penance.
2. The convergence of Puritanism and Pietism in North America and the British colonies that brought together diverse groups in shared social and religious causes like seeking revival and working for the abolition of slavery.
3. The missionary movements of the last two centuries with newly planted churches established in the Majority World.
4. The liberal versus fundamentalist controversies of the early twentieth century over core Christian doctrines.

---

1. See further David F. Wells and John D. Woodbridge, *The Evangelicals: What They Believe, Who They Are, Where They Are Changing* (Nashville: Abingdon, 1975); Leonard I. Sweet, ed., *The Evangelical Tradition in America* (Macon, GA: Mercer University Press, 1984); David Bebbington, *Evangelicalism in Modern Britain: A History from the 1730s to the 1980s* (Grand Rapids: Baker, 1989); Mark A. Noll, David W. Bebbington, and George A. Rawlyk, eds., *Evangelicalism: Comparative Studies of Popular Protestantism in North America, the British Isles, and Beyond 1700–1900* (Oxford: Oxford University Press, 1994); Timothy R. Phillips and Dennis L. Okholm, *A Family of Faith: An Introduction to Evangelical Christianity* (Grand Rapids: Baker, 2001); Randall Balmer, *The Making of Evangelicalism: From Revivalism to Politics and Beyond* (Waco, TX: Baylor University Press, 2010); D. A. Carson, *Evangelicalism: What Is It and Is It Worth Keeping?* (Wheaton, IL: Crossway, 2012).

5. The separation of "evangelicals" from the fundamentalist movement in the mid-twentieth century.[2]
6. In the last quarter of the twentieth century there has been a steady decline of Christianity in the West and a surge of evangelical Christianity in Asia, Africa, and South America. This surge has led to increasing interaction between the Western and Majority World churches through more affordable international travel and because of increasing access to the Internet, so that churches and organizations are becoming more readily aware and influenced by what is happening in other parts of the world. The international representation in the World Evangelical Alliance and Lausanne Covenant shows that evangelicalism is a truly global phenomenon.[3]

Evangelicalism as a theological ethos can be defined by a number of cardinal points. One way of summarizing these points is the "Bebbington Quadrilateral":[4]

- *conversionism*, the belief that human beings need to be converted to faith in Jesus Christ
- *activism*, the belief that the gospel needs to be proclaimed to others and expressed in a commitment to service
- *biblicism*, a particular regard for the Bible as inspired and authoritative
- *crucicentrism*, a focus on the atoning work of Christ on the cross

I think Bebbington's scheme holds true enough, though I would want to add a few nuances, such as that "biblicism" is not bibliolatry, and "crucicentrism" does not mean ignoring the resurrection. We also need to add something on respect for historic Christian orthodoxy (what I call the "catholic" dimension of evangelicalism).[5]

Another summary of the cardinal points of evangelicalism is given by Alister McGrath:

- the supreme authority of Scripture for knowledge of God and as guide to Christian living
- the majesty of Jesus Christ as incarnate God and Lord, and the Savior of sinful humanity
- the lordship of the Holy Spirit
- the need for personal conversion

---

2. The separation between evangelicals and fundamentalists was hastened by a number of factors. Foremost was the rise of a number of Christian leaders who retained belief in the fundamentals of the faith but rejected the separatist ethos and legalistic subculture of fundamentalism. This was led through the ecumenical efforts of Billy Graham in his evangelistic crusades and by other leaders like Carl F. Henry, J. I. Packer, John R. W. Stott, and Henry H. Ockenga.

3. See Timothy C. Tennent, *Theology in the Context of World Christianity: How the Global Church Is Influencing the Way We Think and Discuss Theology* (Grand Rapids: Zondervan, 2007).

4. Bebbington, *Evangelicalism in Modern Britain*, 1–17.

5. See Roger Olson, "Postconservative Evangelicalism View," in *The Spectrum of Evangelicalism: Four Views* (ed. Andrew D. Naselli and Collin Hansen; Grand Rapids: Zondervan, 2011), 175–78.

- the priority of evangelism for both individual Christians and for the church as a whole
- the importance of Christian community for spiritual nourishment, fellowship, and growth[6]

I have written this volume in the first place for the benefit of evangelical churches who embrace this general pattern of belief and practice. It is a gospel-centered theology for Christians who seek to define themselves principally by the gospel. What we need, as a matter of pastoral and missional importance, is an authentically evangelical theology—that is, a theology that makes the evangel the beginning, center, boundary, and interpretive theme of its theological project. Such a project is justified by the observation that the gospel is the cause and criteria of authentic evangelical existence.

So I intend to undertake this theological exercise of constructing an evangelical theology by putting the "evangel" at the helm. That is because I unabashedly believe that the good news of Jesus Christ is the most important doctrine of them all. The gospel is the "canon within the canon" simply because the biblical canon is the scriptural expression of the "rule of faith,"[7] which itself is an exposition of the gospel. Furthermore, the gospel permeates all other doctrines, it defines the church's mission, and it constitutes our identity as followers of the Lord Jesus Christ.

In terms of Christian theology, the gospel is the glue between doctrine, experience, mission, and practice. I submit that an authentic evangelical theology should be a working out of the gospel in the various loci of Christian theology (i.e., the topics in theology like the nature of God, the person and work of Christ, the church, last things, etc.) and then be applied to the sphere of daily Christian life and the offices of Christian leaders. The gospel is the fulcrum of Christian doctrine. The gospel is where God meets us and where we introduce the world to God. So my task is to lay out what a theology driven and defined by the gospel looks like. I will defend the view that at its essence theology is the art of *gospelizing*, that is, making the gospel shape our thinking, praying, preaching, teaching, and ministering in relation to God.

A second reason I have written this book is to try to strike a balance between biblical exposition and engagement with contemporary theological debates. On the one side, there are those theological books that invest so much time documenting what a certain theologian of the past believed on a given issue that they never seem to get around to asking as to what Scripture actually says on the topic. If a theological textbook has more references to Anselm and Barth than to the Major Prophets and

---

6. Alister E. McGrath, *Evangelicalism and the Future of Christianity* (Leicester, UK: Inter-Varsity, 1995), 51.

7. The "rule of faith" (*regula fidei* in Latin) is a short summary of the basic tenets of the ancient church's faith, covering creation and salvation, and was important to many of the church fathers like Irenaeus and Tertullian.

the Gospels, you've got some serious problems. That's not to say that we shouldn't earnestly study the theology of an Augustine or a Luther, for theologies of "retrieval" are important, but at the end of the day retrieving the voices of the past for the present must be married to, rather than be a replacement for, good biblical theology.[8]

On the other extreme are those theological textbooks that are so biblical that they are basically doing theology armed with nothing more than a concordance and ignore every other voice in Christian tradition. For such authors, church history is something that happened to other people. I have a hard time learning from anyone who thinks we have little to learn from our forefathers in the faith. I reckon, in contrast to all this, that a good theology textbook should not simply be a commentary on other theologians. Nor should a decent theology textbook be an exercise in compiling an avalanche of proof texts. Thus, this modest contribution to evangelical theology endeavors to be *canonical* by accepting the Holy Scriptures as the normative guide for the faith and life of the church. It is also attempts to be *creedal* and *confessional* by taking into account the witness of the ancient church and the Reformation into the process of how we think about living a Godward life.

A third reason I have written this book is to avoid two encroaching extremes in the evangelical scene. As I look on the evangelical churches in the West, I see some disturbing trends. On the extreme left of the spectrum are those who want to find ways of speaking about Jesus Christ to a postmodern, post-Christian, and pluralistic world. That is all well and good, except that the way that certain chaps go about that is by assimilating to the culture around them, trying to renegotiate nonnegotiable doctrines like the Trinity and the atonement, replacing the boundaries of the faith with a conversation, buying into the postmodern mantra of "there is no god but pluralism and diversity is his prophet," and holding up doubt as the key virtue rather than faith, love, and hope.

On the extreme right of the theological spectrum are those who care deeply about doctrine and upholding Christian morality. Yet luminaries in this quarter are defined mostly by what they are against rather than what they are for. They labor to impose Christian ethics on people who are not Christians, proudly draw the boundaries of the faith around themselves and their clientele of admirers, and invent shibboleths and code words that one must utter in order to be one of the accepted few. One gets the impression from them that their zeal for doctrines about Jesus has almost eclipsed Jesus himself as the center of faith.

In contrast to all this, I want to advocate that the most central thing in evangelical theology is *the evangel*. A gospel-driven approach will not force us into a

---

8. For a good example of this, see Oliver D. Crisp, *Retrieving Doctrine: Essays in Reformed Theology* (Downers Grove, IL: InterVarsity Press, 2011).

dichotomy of orthodoxy (truth) pitted against orthopraxy (love); instead, we will find the courage to guard the good deposit of the gospel while loving our neighbor as ourselves. The gospel is an expression of the truth of God and the love of God, so it is the best platform on which to integrate a Christian love ethic and Christian creedal convictions.

Before I go any further, I must lay my ecclesial and theological cards on the table. On the church side of things, I did not grow up in a Christian home, but I came to Christ through a Baptist church in Sydney, Australia. I also attended a Baptist seminary (Malyon College) and have been a pastoral intern and itinerant preacher in Baptist churches. I taught for five years in an interdenominational theological college committed to the Reformed tradition in Scotland (Highland Theological College); more recently I spent three years teaching at an interdenominational college in Brisbane while being on the preaching team of a Presbyterian church (Crossway College). I am now a lecturer in theology at an Anglican College (Ridley Melbourne). Strange as it sounds, I would describe myself as an ex-Baptist post-Presbyterian Anglican.

I love the Baptist tradition as it has a rich heritage of being the church of believers and for believers, and I am most grateful for that heritage (indeed, its enduring influence will be obvious in the following pages). In my theological journey, I eventually came to feel that the Baptist way was somewhat lacking when it came to an understanding of the sacraments. I also think Baptists could use a lot more catholicity in their understanding of the church.[9] I find the Presbyterian tradition full of a rich theological heritage that I admire, and I think that the Westminster Confession of Faith is one of the best Protestant expressions of the Christian faith. Yet I find myself now amidst the Anglican tradition because the genius of Anglicanism is in being able to be both Protestant and Catholic at the same time. I have learned to love the *Book of Common Prayer* and appreciate the liturgies in the Anglican tradition. Most of my favorite theologians are Anglican, and I have enjoyed seeing Anglican leaders in Africa defend the gospel against their liberal European and American counterparts.

As for my theological leanings, first and foremost I am a follower of Jesus; second I consider myself an evangelical; and third, I identify with the Reformed tradition. As a self-identified Reformed type, I thereby gravitate toward the Calvinistic scheme of theology. I am a Calvinist because I think it is broadly biblical and because it corresponds with my experience of slavery in sin and receiving God's efficacious

---

9. On proposed correctives to these deficiencies in the Baptist tradition, see Anthony R. Cross and Philip E. Thompson, eds., *Baptist Sacramentalism* (SBHT 5; Milton Keynes, UK: Paternoster, 2003); idem, *Baptist Sacramentalism 2* (SBHT 25; Milton Keynes: Paternoster, 2008); Steve R. Harmon, *Towards Baptist Catholicity: Essays on Tradition and the Baptist Vision* (SBHT 27; Milton Keynes: Paternoster, 2006).

grace in salvation. Calvinism often gets a bad rap as being a cold, wooden, and unfeeling system of doctrine. So when I explain Calvinism to people, I usually say this: "People suck, they suck in sin, they are suckness unto death. And the God who is rich in mercy takes the initiative to save people from the penalty, the power, and even the presence of this sin. This is Calvinism, the rest is commentary." I am more than willing to part company with Calvin and the Reformers when I feel compelled to in the light of biblical evidence and Christian tradition. That happens often, but generally the Reformed tradition is a fallible system of Christian thought that I think is as best on target as we can be.

I do not generally like tags or labels for one's position since they are by nature limiting and open to misunderstanding. Still, I rather like C. S. Lewis's description of "mere Christianity." I would like to think of myself, then, as a "mere evangelical" in that I belong to the big tent that is the evangelical church where Presbyterians, Anglicans, Methodists, Lutherans, and Baptists go for fellowship and share in a common mission. It is a place where we can disagree about the six literal days of creation, baptism, church government, women in ministry, or the millennium, because we are united in the one holy catholic and apostolic church by our common profession of faith in Jesus as Lord.

That said, denominations are good because truth matters: truth about baptism, church government, ministry, and so forth. However, there is one Lord who is Lord over all the churches, and we all confess that Lord and partake of one Holy Spirit. As John Wesley said, "If your heart is the same as my heart, you can hold my hand." There is no denying the differences in doctrine among evangelicals, and the differences are not always insignificant. Still, I like to think that the things that unite us like the gospel are ultimately far stronger than anything that might drive us apart.

J. I. Packer (a Calvinist Anglican) and Thomas Oden (an Arminian Methodist) joined together to write a book called *One Faith: The Evangelical Consensus*, which shows the agreement between a number of evangelical statements of faith written between 1950 and 2000 on key doctrines. The book shows just how much shared belief there is in the evangelical family.[10] Whatever differences and diversity there is within the evangelical house, we can still speak authentically of one evangelical faith.

Next to "mere evangelical," what is probably the label I like to describe myself with the most would have to be "catholic evangelical." For me this means reading Scripture not in the isolation of my study, but as part of the "communion of the saints" that includes my local church and the departed saints of the past as well. The best definition of this "catholic evangelical" is given by Kevin J. Vanhoozer:

---

10. J. I. Packer and Thomas C. Oden, *One Faith: The Evangelical Consensus* (Downers Grove, IL: InterVarsity Press, 1999).

"Catholicity" signifies the church as the whole people of God, spread out over space, across cultures, and through time. "We believe in one ... *catholic* church." The evangelical unity of the church is compatible with a catholic diversity. To say that theology must be catholic, then, is to affirm the necessity of involving the *whole* church in the project of theology. No single denomination "owns" catholicity: catholicity is no more the exclusive domain of the Roman Church than the gospel is the private domain of evangelicals. *Catholic* and *evangelical* belong together. To be precise: "catholic" qualifies "evangelical." The gospel designated a determinate word; catholicity, the scope of its reception. *"Evangelical" is the central notion, but "catholic" adds a crucial antireductionist qualifier that prohibits any one reception of the gospel from becoming paramount.*[11]

Another confession that I have to make is that I am not by specialty a systematic theologian. I cut my scholarly teeth in the realm of biblical studies. I've worked in areas as diverse as the historical Jesus, Synoptic Gospels, the life of Paul, New Testament theology, Second Temple literature, and textual criticism, and I have even written a commentary on 1 Esdras based exclusively on codex Vaticanus. Not exactly the standard training ground for a systematician, who is supposed to do a mandatory PhD on Karl Barth and thereafter write a postdoctoral tome on something like divine aseity and divine freedom, enhypostasis versus anhypostasis, or sexual repression in Augustine's sermons (not my bag unfortunately).

But this book was not something I dreamed up one Sunday afternoon. The first essay I ever published was on systematic theology.[12] I have also spent the better part of ten years trying to figure out how to integrate systematic and biblical theology as well as musing over the nature of evangelical theology.[13] In all of my scholarly ventures, be they historical critical inquiries or biblical theological surveys, I have always tried to be conscious of the big picture and the big questions that go with it. Simply asking, "So what?" can help the most myopic of textual hacks look at the world beyond their own microscopic postage-stamp-sized field on inquiry.

What is more, traversing biblical and theological studies is all the fashion these days. Many theologians are writing biblical commentaries, as in the Brazos Theological Commentary on the Bible series. Meanwhile several biblical scholars are trying to be theologians in the Two Horizons series of biblical commentaries. If theologians can write commentaries, why shouldn't a biblical scholar write a systematic theology? What is more, I would point out that John Calvin wrote his famous

---

11. Kevin J. Vanhoozer, *Drama of Doctrine: A Canonical Linguistic Approach to Christian Theology* (Louisville: Westminster John Knox, 2005), 27 (italics in original); see also Markus Bockmuehl, *Seeing the Word: Refocusing New Testament Study* (STI; Grand Rapids: Baker, 2006), 158–59; Robert Jenson, *Creed and Canon* (Louisville: Westminster John Knox, 2010).

12. Michael F. Bird and James Gibson, "Quest for an Authentically Evangelical Prolegomena to Theology," in *Proclaiming Truth, Pastoring Hearts: Essays in Honour of Deane J. Woods* (ed. R. Todd Stanton and Leslie Crawford; Adelaide, Aus: ACM Press, 2004), 95–106.

13. See esp. Edward W. Klink and Darian R. Lockett, *Understanding Biblical Theology: A Comparison of Theory and Practice* (Grand Rapids: Zondervan, 2012).

Institutes of the Christian Religion primarily as a way of clarifying disputed matters that he never had time to engage in his various biblical commentaries. Great Christian thinkers like B. B. Warfield and Leon Morris taught and wrote in the fields of New Testament and systematic theology. I contend that systematic theology should, in its ideal state, be an aid and clarification to exegesis and be undertaken by those with a solid grasp of biblical studies.

Finally, I would point out that American Orthodox Theologian David Bentley Hart regards a breadth of knowledge as the best qualification for any theologian. He writes:

> Theology requires a far greater scholarly range than does any other humane science. The properly trained Christian theologian, perfectly in command of his materials, should be a proficient linguist, with a mastery of several ancient and modern tongues, should have a complete formation in the subtleties of the whole Christian dogmatic tradition, should possess a considerable knowledge of the texts and arguments produced in every period of the Church, should be a good historian, should be thoroughly trained in philosophy, ancient, medieval and modern, should have a fairly broad grasp of liturgical practice in every culture and age of the Christian world, should (ideally) possess considerable knowledge of literature, music and the plastic arts, should have an intelligent interest in the effects of theological discourse in areas such as law or economics, and so on and so forth.[14]

I do not presume to think that I have all of these qualifications and proficiencies; only a polymath could. I hope that my biblical background and periodic forays into the church fathers and systematic theology will make me a well-equipped theologian—surely it cannot hurt—but how capable I am as a theologian will have to be decided by others. In addition, after seeing a few of the things that systematicians do with Scripture, I have generally believed that some theologians should be routinely slapped in the face with a soggy fish in order to try to smack some exegetical sense into them. You can only watch someone struggling to push a round peg into a square hole for so long before you finally snatch the peg from them and say, "Just give it here; I'll do it for you."

It is rather embarrassing, then, when you discover that pushing the pieces through the holes was in fact a lot harder than it first looked. As a New Testament scholar now taken to teaching theology, I have learned that systematic theology is easy to criticize from a distance, but harder to actually do when you are a practitioner. It is my intention to engage in the task of constructing an evangelical theology, with a breadth of exegetical experience, in dialogue with theologians of the past and present, soaked in Scripture, with an ear to the door of current debates, in order to present to evangelical churches and students a faith seeking understanding.

---

14. David Bentley Hart, *In the Aftermath: Provocations and Laments* (Grand Rapids: Eerdmans, 2009), 177–78.

PART ONE

Prolegomena: Beginning to Talk about God

§1.1 What Is Theology?
§1.2 What Do You Have to Say Before You Say Anything?
§1.3 What Is the Gospel?
§1.4 The Necessity and Goal of Theology
§1.5 Is Theology Possible?
§1.6 Sources for Theology
§1.7 Toward a Gospel-Driven Theological Method
§1.8 A Final Word

Prolegomena is where you clear the deck on preliminary issues and show how you intend to set up a system of theology. It is what you say before you say anything about theology—in other words, a type of pre-theology, or a first theology. Topics dealt with here include defining theology, giving a definition of the gospel, stating the purposes and goals of theology, and outlining a theological method. These chapters lay the foundation for the rest of the volume that will explore the subject of God according to the gospel of God with its accompanying witness of the Holy Scriptures and Christian tradition.

> "We have been studying cheerfully and seriously. As far as I was concerned it could have continued in that way, and I had already resigned myself to having my grave here by the Rhine!... And now the end has come. So listen to my piece of advice: exegesis, exegesis, and yet more exegesis! Keep to the word, to the scripture that has been given to us."[1]

> "Where exegesis is not theology, Scripture cannot be the soul of theology, and conversely, where theology is not essentially the interpretation of the Church's Scripture, such a theology no longer has a foundation."[2]

> "An evangelical theology is one which is evoked, governed and judged by the gospel."[3]

---

1. Karl Barth on the occasion of his farewell to his students in Bonn prior to his expulsion from Germany in 1935. Cited in Gordon D. Fee, *New Testament Exegesis: A Handbook for Students and Pastors* (rev. ed.; Louisville: Westminster John Knox, 1993), 6.

2. Benedict XVI, *Verbum Domini*, §35.

3. John Webster, *Word and Church* (London: T&T Clark, 2001), 191.

§ 1.1 WHAT IS THEOLOGY?

What exactly is theology? If the question is posed in a multiple-choice format, we could choose from the following options.

> a. The name of the eighth full-length album by Sinead O'Connor, released in 2007.
> b. What my father tells me to stop doing and to get a real job.
> c. The study of God.
> d. All of the above.

The answer is option (d), "All of the above." However, option (c), "The study of God," is technically the more correct answer, and we can unpack that a bit more. *The Compact Macquarie Dictionary* defines theology this way: "The science which treats God, His attributes, and His relations to the universe; the science or study of divine things or religious truth."[4] Saint Augustine in the fifth century defined theology as "rational discussion respecting the deity."[5] Charles Ryrie, a dispensationalist theologian, says theology is "thinking about God and expressing those thoughts in some way."[6] According to Baptist theologian Robert Culver, "Christian theology is study or organized treatment of the topic, God, from the standpoint of Christianity."[7] The Anglican theologian Alister McGrath asserts that "theology is reflection upon the God whom Christians worship and adore."[8] The Swiss theologian Karl Barth contended: "Dogmatics is the self-examination of the Christian Church in respect of the content of its distinctive talk about God."[9] All of these

---

4. Arthur Delbridge and J. R. L. Bernard, eds., *The Compact Macquarie Dictionary* (Macquarie, NSW: Macquarie Library, 1994), 1045.

5. Augustine, *Civ.* 8.1.

6. Charles Ryrie, *Basic Theology* (Wheaton, IL: Victor, 1986), 9.

7. Robert Culver, *Systematic Theology: Biblical and Historical* (Fearn, Ross-Shire: Mentor, 2005), 2.

8. Alister McGrath, *Christian Theology: An Introduction* (Oxford: Blackwell, 2001), 137.

9. Karl Barth, *Church Dogmatics: The Doctrine of the Word of God* (trans. G.W. Bromiley; London: Continuum, 2004 1932.), I/1:11 (hereafter: *CD*).

definitions are generally correct; however, a more precise and robust definition of theology is given by Jaroslav Pelikan, who regarded theology as, "What the church of Jesus Christ believes, teaches and confesses on the basis of the word of God: this is Christian doctrine."[10]

To put things simply, theology is the study of God. It comes from the word *theos*, which is Greek for "God," and from *logos*, which is Greek for "word."[11] It is the attempt to say something about God and God's relationship to the world. It is thinking about faith from faith. In a sense, theology is very much akin to the study of philosophy, worldview, religion, ethics, or intellectual history; it is a descriptive survey of ideas and the impact of those ideas.

But there are at least two key differences that distinguish theology from other intellectual disciplines like philosophy and religion. The first difference is that theology is not the study of *ideas* about God; it is the study of the *living God*. Christian theology, then, is different from the study of seventeenth century French literature, ancient Greek religion, and medieval philosophers because the Christian claims that he or she is in personal contact with the subject of study. It is one thing to discuss William Shakespeare in the classroom, but it would be quite another thing to do that if Shakespeare was standing in the classroom with you. Theology, then, is not an objective discipline (i.e., a detached study of an object) like the physical sciences, nor is it a descriptive discipline like the social sciences. Theology is speaking about God while in the very presence of God. We are intimately engaged with the subject of our study.

Second, theology is studied and performed in a *community of faith*. Theology is something that is learned, lived, sung, preached, and renewed through the dynamic interaction between God and his people. Theology is the conversation that takes place between family members in the household of faith about what it means to behold and believe in God. Theology is the attempt to verbalize and to perform our relationship with God. Theology can be likened to the process of learning to take part in a divinely directed musical called "Godspell."[12] To do theology is to describe the God who acts, to be acted upon, and to become an actor in the divine drama of God's plan to repossess the world for himself.

Evangelical theology, then, is the drama of *gospelizing*. By "gospelizing" I mean trying to become what the gospel intends believers to be: slaves of Christ, vessels of grace, agents of the kingdom, and a people worthy of God's name. Dedication

---

10. Jaroslav Pelikan, *The Christian Tradition: A History of the Development of Doctrine* (Chicago: University of Chicago Press, 1971), 1:1.

11. Note that "theology proper" is discussion of the Doctrine of God, whereas general "theology" is the discussion of all matters in relation to God.

12. Here I am playing on the Stephen Schwarz musical also called *Godspell* (1970). On theology as "drama," see Kevin J. Vanhoozer, *Drama of Doctrine: A Canonical Linguistic Approach to Christian Theology* (Louisville: Westminster John Knox, 2005).

to the art of gospelizing is crucial because "evangelicals need to recapture a passion for biblical formation: a desire to be formed, reformed and transformed by the truth and power of the gospel."[13] To pursue Kevin Vanhoozer's image, the task of theology is to enable disciples to perform the script of the Scriptures, according to advice of the dramaturge the Holy Spirit, in obedience to the design of the director, Jesus Christ, with the gospel as the theme music, and performed in the theater of the church. The company of the gospel shows what they believe in an open-air performance staged for the benefit of the world. The purpose of gospelizing is to ensure that those who bear Christ's name walk in Christ's way.[14] Consequently, theology is the task for disciples of Jesus to begin excavating the manifold truth of the gospel and to start reflecting the spiritual realities that the gospel endeavors to cultivate in their own lives.

---

13. Kevin J. Vanhoozer, "Evangelicalism and the Church: The Company of the Gospel," in *The Futures of Evangelicalism: Issues and Prospects* (ed. C. Bartholomew, R. Parry, and A. West; Leicester, UK: Inter-Varsity Press, 2003), 72.

14. Vanhoozer, *Drama of Doctrine*, 16, 102, 442.

§ 1.2 WHAT DO YOU HAVE TO SAY BEFORE YOU SAY ANYTHING?

1.2.1 INTRODUCTION TO PROLEGOMENA

1.2.1.1 DEFINITION AND TASK

For Christians, theology is studying God as he is known according to the perspective of the church's faith. Now if you are going to engage in a study of God, before you formally begin, you need to say something about how you intend to undertake such a study. This is what theologians call "prolegomena." The designation "prolegomena" derives from the Greek word *prolegō,* which means "things spoken in advance." So theological prolegomena is what you say before you begin to say anything about God.

Prolegomena is a type of pre-theology theology. It lays the groundwork for engaging in a systematic study of God. The task of developing a prolegomena has a long and distinguished history. When many of the Christian apologists in the second and third centuries tried to talk about Jesus and God to Greeks, they did so by appealing to a shared theory of knowledge in philosophy in order to commend the Christian faith. Justin Martyr appealed specifically to Plato and Stoic philosophers as containing wisdom that agreed with Christian beliefs.[15] This established a common ground for a discussion about God between a Christian leader and a philosophically minded pagan. For many early Christian thinkers their main task was apologetic,

---

15. Consider this statement from Justin: "I both boast and strive with all my strength to be found a Christian. Not because the teachings of Plato are different from those of Christ, but because they are not totally identical. The same applies to the Stoics, poets and historians. For each man spoke well, in proportion to the share that he had of the seminal Word, seeing what was related to it.... Whatever things were rightly said by any man, belong to us Christians.... For all those writers were able to see reality darkly through the seed of the implanted Word within them" (Justin, *2 Apol.* 13). For Justin, all truth is Christian truth, whether you find it on the lips of Jesus or in the books of Plato. Because philosophers like Plato taught the truth about certain things, even imperfectly, they had an implanted Word within them that gave rise to this truth.

defending and commending the faith, rather than constructing a preface to a system of doctrine. Yet the idea of establishing a theory of knowledge, often called "epistemology" (i.e., the study of knowledge and knowing), has remained at the forefront of prolegomena. A prolegomena ordinarily addresses questions like "Is there a God to be known?" and "How do we know God?"

1.2.1.2 PROLEGOMENA IN CHURCH HISTORY

The form and function of prolegomena has usually been driven by the reigning philosophical framework of the day. For instance, in the Middle Ages, Thomas Aquinas (1224–1275) held to a view about there being "portals of the faith" in philosophy, which gave access to Christianity, and dealt with "the Nature and Domain of Sacred Doctrine."[16] Aquinas was writing at a time when Europe was experiencing a fresh encounter with Aristotle's philosophy. Aquinas's ideas were built on that philosophy, and by switching the default background philosophy from Plato to Aristotle, Aquinas precipitated the need for a different prolegomenon couched in the terms of the new philosophy. For example, Aquinas used philosophical proofs taken from Aristotle to argue for the existence of God. Philosophy established that there was a God to be known; Christian theology then explained what this God was like.

During the Reformation there was a concerted effort to make Scripture the bedrock of all knowledge of God rather than to rely on philosophical specters or humanly devised systems of thought. Martin Luther spoke ferociously against any reliance on philosophy in Christian theology. John Calvin began his theological textbook with an account of the "knowledge of God." The first thing Calvin did in his *Institutes of the Christian Religion* was to ascertain how it is that persons can actually know God. His answer referred to the revelation of God through nature, Scripture, and the testimony of the Spirit.[17] Calvin emphasized, predictably, the Scriptures: "If true religion is to beam upon us, our principle must be, that it is necessary to begin with heavenly teaching, and that it is impossible for any man to obtain even the minutest portion of right and sound doctrine without being a disciple of Scripture."[18]

The key Reformation contribution to the subject of theological prolegomena was the assertion that theology should commence with a description of the mode of God's self-communication of himself to his creatures. We have to remember that the Reformers themselves were not immune from the philosophical currents washing over Europe at that time. The return to Scripture as an authority was

---

16. Thomas Aquinas, *Summa Theologica*, I. Q2. Art. 2; II. Q1. Art. 2.
17. John Calvin, *Institutes* 1.1–7.
18. Ibid., 1.4.2.

possible only amidst the politics of emerging city-states, was indebted to budding rationalistic philosophies, grew out of a new humanism with its penchant for critical history, and was arguably an acute expression of medieval nominalism that was skeptical toward religious authority.

While the Reformers claimed to have thrown off the weighty yoke of medieval philosophy (esp. Platonic and Aristotlean realism), they had done so only by smuggling in a more anthropocentric philosophy that would eventually flower into a refined philosophical rationalism. While exposing the weaknesses of making ecclesiastical authority the ultimate ground of truth and moving religious authority to the sphere of inscripturated revelation, the Reformers paved the way for the same attacks on ecclesiastical authority to be leveled at Scripture as part of the questioning of religious authority. Thus the Reformers' return to Scripture did not remove the problem of philosophical imposition on theology; in fact, it eventually yielded an even more antireligious philosophy in succeeding centuries.

Although the Reformation brought about a spiritual renewal in both the Protestant and Catholic churches, it was largely based on a crisis of authority, specifically, religious authority. Earlier, the Renaissance had been a movement of cultural rebirth within segments of medieval Europe, where new intellectual forces in science, literature, and art began to flourish. The explosion of learning combined with new discoveries in science led to a questioning of the source of intellectual authority. One feature of the "Northern Renaissance," in contrast to the "Italian Renaissance," was that it was interested in deepening religious convictions. The intellectual tools of the burgeoning humanities were rigorously applied to religious matters, which led to a questioning of religious authority with specific skepticism leveled at many claims of the Roman Catholic Church. The most immediate result was, of course, the Protestant Reformation. However, post-Reformation intellectuals began not just questioning the claims of religious institutions like the Catholic Church, but they started questioning the very notion of a religion of revelation. Beliefs that did not purportedly align with the scientific method or looked as if they were rooted in myth and superstition were regarded as unreasonable. This "Age of Reason," otherwise known as the "Enlightenment," marked a period characterized by rationalism, empiricism, the advance of human learning, and the questioning of religious dogma.

The Enlightenment eventually established the intellectual period that is commonly called "Modernity." We could say that Modernity lasted from the fall of the French Bastille in 1789 to the Fall of the Berlin wall in 1989.[19] Modernity had several

---

19. Thomas C. Oden, "The Death of Modernity and Postmodern Evangelical Spirituality," in *The Challenge of Postmodernism: An Evangelical Assessment* (ed. D.S. Dockery; Wheaton, IL: Victor, 1995), 23.

philosophical characteristics.[20] First, reason itself was viewed as universal and unassailable. Truths ascertained by way of reason—as opposed to beliefs derived from tradition or superstition—were universally and incorrigibly true.

Second, the two main schools of thought within Modernity were "rationalism" (knowledge is arrived at by building on self-evident truths) and "empiricism" (knowledge is attained by building on sense data). Both schools assumed a certain foundation for all knowledge. It was on the basis of these foundations that one could establish further truths.

Third, there was a large emphasis on intellectual and cultural progress. It was thought that the world could be made better through reason. Once we got the foundations right, once we refined our methodology, there would be no limits to what humanity could discover or achieve. This could be seen in the way that people spoke of the "assured results" of science, philosophy, medicine, and so on. Progress was the great "meta-narrative" or big story of Modernity that saw itself as leading Europe out of the so-called darkness of the Middle Ages and into a time of intellectual light.

Fourth, Modernity also led to "naturalism," which is distinguished by the rejection of all supernatural explanations and the belief that the universe is a closed system of cause and effect. The upshot of Modernity was that it resulted in religious skepticism, deism, and atheism. Symbolic of this age is that during the French Revolution, Notre Dame was rechristened as the "temple of reason" and a Parisian courtesan was enthroned as the goddess of reason. God had been displaced by a human-centered reason. Ironically, Christian theology, once queen of the sciences in the great universities of Europe, now struggled to sustain its existence in the wake of criticism and neglect.

In the post-Enlightenment era, Christian theology had to find a way to do theology in light of the modernist critique of religion based on divine revelation. Before theologians could even begin to do theology, they had to establish that there was a God to know, that Christianity was reasonable, and that Christianity was scientific. Many theologians retreated from the challenge and embraced the modernist perspective in relation to religion. It was possible to salvage Christianity by adopting basically one of two options.

First, one could become a deist and believe that God created the world but thereafter left it to its own devices thereby eliminating the supernatural altogether. Or, second, one could adopt a more "liberal" approach, where Christian theology was the attempt to provide a grammar and philosophical explanation for the religious feelings that people experienced. That led to a denial of key doctrines like

---

20. D. A. Carson, *The Gagging of God: Christianity Confronts Pluralism* (Grand Rapids: Zondervan 1996), 57–64.

the incarnation, it required a reinterpretation of miracles as symbolic myths, and it altered what was meant by redemption. Not all theologians bowed the knee to Modernity. Some theologians attempted to meet the challenges of Modernity by using the very weapons that Modernity was employing against Christianity. It is here that we enter the golden age of the prolegomena, when theologians in the modernist era strove to demonstrate the rationality of Christian theism as part of their preface to Christian theology.

A good example of a systematic theology written amidst Modernity is that by the Princeton theologian Charles Hodge (1797–1878). Hodge's introduction is both a reaction to Modernity, yet also an appropriation of it.[21] Hodge began his *Systematic Theology* by describing theology as a science in a manner similar to astronomy, chemistry, or history. The realm of nature contains facts, and those facts are to be discovered by science. What is true of other sciences is true of theology. The Bible contains facts, ideas, and principles. It is the task of the theologian to collect, authenticate, arrange, and exhibit these facts and to show their relationship to each other.

Scientific facts are discovered by a method, so one must get the methodology right. Charles Hodge rejected the speculative and mystical methods used in theology in favor of the inductive method. In this method, one assumes the competency of one's own powers of observation and the lucidity of one's mental faculties, and then proceeds to discover the facts of the Bible. The collection is undertaken carefully and comprehensively just as it would be for any scientific field. Hodge also found it necessary in his introduction to discredit other worldviews that inhibit theology: rationalism, mysticism, and Romanism. Thereafter, Hodge endeavored to show the superiority of the Protestant doctrine of Scripture over the Roman doctrine of church tradition. When he gets into the doctrine of God, Hodge establishes how God is known as something innate, by way of reason, and in the supernatural. You can see the basic outline of Hodge's prolegomena:

Establish theology as science
⇨ Show that theology has a scientific method
⇨ Define theology and show its necessity
⇨ Criticize competing options
⇨ Establish bases for beliefs

Charles Hodge's introduction to theology is a defense of theology as a scientific discipline on par with other scientific disciplines. Hence his words: "The Bible is

---

21. Charles Hodge, *Systematic Theology* (3 vols.; London: James Clarke & Co., 1960 [1841]), 1:1–188.

to the theologian what nature is to the man of science. It is his storehouse of facts; and his method of ascertaining what the Bible teaches, is the same as that which the natural philosopher adopts to ascertain what nature teaches."[22] Hodge legitimizes theology against the modernist critique by using the philosophical framework of Modernity.

1. Hodge assumes fixed laws of nature that contain facts that can be excavated. The facts of nature are acquired when a person of sound observational skills constructs the proper methodology for the investigation.
2. God has implanted certain "first principles" into the human constitution, such as a capacity for moral and intellectual reasoning. These first principles are the beginning point of knowledge. They are not arbitrary; rather, they are tested by universality and necessity. These first principles enable someone to investigate sources of nature and revelation in the first place.
3. For Hodge belief in God is intuitional and self-evident, and thus one may reject atheism, polytheism, and pantheism from the outset.
4. The Bible is authenticated by its inspiration through the Holy Spirit. The task of theology is to unearth facts and ideas from the Bible.
5. The reason why other theologies or philosophies do not work is because they reject the source of theology, that is, the Bible, or because they have an erroneous methodology, for example, Roman Catholicism with its affinity for tradition.

Consequently, Hodge imbibes several modernist impulses even when his theology is defined over and against Modernity.

It might seem clever to try and outplay Modernity at its own game. It is perhaps a necessity to take captive the usable elements of modernist philosophy and to press them into the service of Christian theology. Charles Hodge and others made a jolly good attempt at precisely this kind of theological project. He and others tried to walk the line between being in Modernity but not of Modernity. The problem is that they allowed Modernity to define the rules of the game. They enabled Modernity to set the agenda for theology, including its beginnings, task, and method. They also ran the risk that the failings of Modernity with its claim to unbridled access to absolute truth could also become the failings of Christian theology. By showing that the Word of God aligned with "reason," they were in the end subjecting the Word of God beneath reason.

But whose "reason" is authoritative in the end? Whose "science" is the benchmark for all truth: an atheist scientist like Richard Dawkins or a theistic scientist like

---

22. Ibid., 1.10.

John Polkinghorne? Reason and science are not religiously neutral fields. One can believe in reasonable beliefs and one can believe in scientific pursuits. I only wish to point out that what is considered reasonable and what is considered scientific are debated, constantly in flux, and often freighted with other "Trojan" beliefs.

This brings us to another response to Modernity in the theology of Karl Barth. Barth began his *Church Dogmatics* by discussing the topic of "Church, Theology, Science." Barth was ambivalent as to whether theology actually is a science. On the one hand, theology does not have the same subject-object relationship as you find in the natural sciences. Yet on the other hand, theology may prove to be a science, perhaps even more scientific than the other sciences, because theology is concerned with the pursuit of truth and protests against secular definitions of what constitutes science.[23]

Nonetheless, Barth is clear in his rejection of modernist prolegomena for three reasons.

1. We should not assume that the modernist objection to Christian belief is any more vociferous than pagan critiques of Christianity encountered by the ancient church.
2. The church measures its talk about God by way of reference to divine revelation and not by the standard of "godless reasons."
3. Prolegomena makes theology hostage to "relevance" and becomes reducible to theological polemics or theological apologetics. Although the conflict of faith and unbelief is significant, theology must be grounded in its own discourse about God.[24] Our response to unbelief is not apologetics but declaring the revelation of God.

There is a theological prolegomenon, but it is not what one does *before* theology; rather, it is what one does *first in* theology. According to Barth: "In the prolegomena to dogmatics, therefore, we ask concerning the Word of God as the criterion of dogmatics." By this he means that the first thing that you should do in theology is to establish the doctrine of the Word of God as the grounds for dogmatics (i.e., you identify the Triune God as the God who speaks).[25] Winfried Corduan aptly summarizes Barth: "Therefore, prolegomena does not prepare the way for theology but is the first part of theology itself. It does not lay the groundwork for content: it already consists of content. Prolegomena, for Barth, describes the initial contact of God with man."[26]

The shape of prolegomena began to change again with the advent of Postmodernity. The intellectual and cultural edifice called Postmodernity is notoriously

---

23. Barth, *CD*, I/1.3–11.
24. Ibid., I/1.25–31.
25. Ibid., I/1.43.

26. Winfried Corduan, *Handmaid to Theology: An Essay in Philosophical Prolegomena* (Grand Rapids, Baker: 1981), 75.

hard to define. In one sense it is a rejection of Modernity, but in another sense it is the intensification of Modernity. Postmodernity eschews the modernist claim to absolute knowledge, while magnifying the notion that man is the measure of all things. Modernity constructed a certain metanarrative and developed a particular epistemology. That large-scale narrative was about the gradual advance of Western civilization from the darkness of the Middle Ages through its scientific and cultural achievements. Yet this created a certain cultural hegemony and arrogance that was self-serving and self-authenticating. The optimism of progress ended with World War I, and the aftermath of World War II left people searching for a new basis for values other than science.

At the same time, there was a crisis of knowledge in twentieth-century philosophy. Modernity maintained that you know things either one of two ways. Either all knowledge is self-evident (like 2 + 2 = 4) or acquired through sensory perception and inference (like kicking the stone in front of you to know that it is there). This was the foundation for all knowledge. However, people began to point out that this theory of knowledge was itself neither self-evident nor empirically verifiable. Therefore, by its own criteria, foundationalism was not actually true! Intellectual leaders began then to speak of being "postfoundationalist" and advocated instead that the legitimacy of truth claims did not rest on a correspondence of a truth claim to any single reality (whose reality?), but truth claims were true if they were internally consistent and had pragmatic value for a given community.

French philosophers like Michel Foucault and Jacques Derrida became the philosophical high priests of this new intellectual climate. Foucault argued that all claims to truth were not neutral but were de facto claims to power. Derrida asserted that there is no single interpretation of a text, only interpretations, as one can use a text for anything or one can expose the ideology behind a text. Hence a new and more self-critical rationalism was needed—enter stage left, Postmodernity.

Postmodernity is the ultimate synthesis of the philosophical skepticism of all knowledge claims by Immanuel Kant and the anthropocentric nihilism of Friedrich Nietzsche. No one has a God's-eye view of reality. We see reality not as it is, but only as it appears. There are realities that are perceived or constructed, but no single reality. Truth in Postmodernity is not the correspondence of ideas to reality, but is the coherence of a proposition to other propositions. Truth becomes relative to its own circle of claims and constituents. Absolute truth is absolutely dead. The absoluteness of truth is replaced by a view of truth as pluralistic and relativistic, regardless of whether the truth claims put forward are religious, political, economic, or ethical.

Communities create meaning by the stories, language, myths, and symbols of their linguistic frameworks. When applied to theology, this means that theology is nothing more than a language game. Theology is doing things with words that make sense in a faith community, but it has no truth value outside that community. The confession that "Jesus is Lord" is to orientate oneself toward an experience of Jesus Christ as a sovereign master, but it has no meaning outside that linguistic frame of reference.

Postmodern theology tends to reject any prolegomena. For postliberal theologians like George Lindbeck and Hans Frei, Christian theology is a language, and you either speak it or you don't; thus, there is no need for any attempt to justify theology with a prolegomena. Evangelicals have responded to this in several ways. Some, like Stanley Grenz, attempt to use Postmodernity as best as they could to structure and inform a generous Christian orthodoxy.[27] Kevin Vanhoozer has taken postmodern literary theory seriously and attempted to set up a theology by establishing a theory of hermeneutics and divine speech-acts that adequately allows for a theory of revelation.[28] Alister McGrath has recently attempted to reinvigorate the idea of theology as science. This is not a return to the modernist naiveté that scientific truth gives a God's-eye view of reality. McGrath is a chastened foundationalist (i.e., truth can be objectively known, but never known apart from the knower!), so he is well aware of the shortcomings of science. McGrath's project involves identifying nature as a crucial locus for theology; he opts for a "critical realist" approach to epistemology, where we can know an objective reality but never independently of ourselves, and he draws parallels between the pursuit of reality in science and theology.[29]

1.2.1.3 DO WE NEED A PROLEGOMENA?

What shall we say about prolegomena—yea or nay? And if there should be a prolegomena, what should it be? I think that prolegomena has a place in theology if only for the purpose of orientating ourselves to the theological task. Prolegomena is a bit like a map at a shopping mall that says, "You are here." Knowledge of God must begin with knowledge of where we are and how we got here. Consequently, I reject the modernist approach to prolegomena of justifying theology as a science and establishing the existence of a God to be scientifically studied. In the place of philosophical justification, I prefer the Barthian approach of asserting the fact of divine revelation as the counterpoint to unbelief.[30] If prolegomena is concerned with orientating ourselves to the theological task and setting forth the divine revelation,

---

27. Stanley J. Grenz, *Renewing the Center: Evangelical Theology in a Post-Theological Era* (Grand Rapids: Baker, 2000).

28. Kevin J. Vanhoozer, *Is There a Meaning in This Text? The Bible, the Reader, and the Morality of Literary Knowledge* (Grand Rapids: Zondervan, 1998); idem, *Drama of Doctrine*.

29. Alister E. McGrath, *A Scientific Theology: Volume 1—Nature* (Grand Rapids: Eerdmans, 2001); idem, *A Scientific Theology: Volume 2—Reality* (Grand Rapids: Eerdmans, 2001); idem, *A Scientific Theology: Volume 3—Theory* (Grand Rapids: Eerdmans, 2003).

30. Though Barth himself was influenced by Anselm in this regard as the crucial element in Anselm's proofs for God's existence was the event of the Word of God that came to Anselm as God's name lodged in his mind.

then the primary function of an evangelical prolegomena should be a setting out of the gospel. The gospel explains why we are in the theological race in the first place, and the gospel is the nexus into the reality of the God who has revealed himself.[31]

Evangelicalism is defined theologically by the gospel, and it has always been concerned with spiritual and missional renewal through the gospel. That is hardly a new agenda for Christian churches. The Reformation was concerned with restoring the gospel to the church. The magisterial Reformers linked the christological foundations of the church with its gospel message, since it was the preaching of the gospel that mediated the saving presence of Jesus Christ. The Reformation bound the gospel to the center of the church as the ever-present and effervescent force within the church united by Spirit, Word, and Sacrament. That is why evangelicals, as the heirs to the Reformers, take their name from the very *evangel* that brought them into the experience of redemption. Therefore, we need a gospel-driven theology in order to yield a gospel-soaked piety and gospel-acting church. As Grenz wrote:

> To be "evangelical" means to be centered on the gospel. Consequently, evangelicals are a gospel people. They are a people committed to hearing, living out, and sharing the good news of God's saving action in Jesus Christ and the divine gift of the Holy Spirit, a saving action that brings forgiveness, transforms life, and creates a new community. As a gospel people, evangelicals continually set forth the truth that the center of the church is the gospel and that the church, therefore, must be gospel centered.[32]

To set forth the gospel in our prolegomena is to establish the beginning, center, and boundary of evangelical theology. An evangelical theology begins with the gospel because the gospel establishes the hermeneutical horizons for its talk about God and constitutes the purpose or raison d'être of the church's existence. As Andrew McGowan points out, the gospel is not just "caught"; it is genuinely "taught" as the most elementary statement of the Christian faith, just as the Colossians were taught the gospel by Epaphras (Col 1:6–7).[33] The gospel is the driving force behind doctrine and its actualization within the Christian community. Theology has its agenda and energy derived from the good news of Jesus Christ. It is, dare I say, the beauty of the gospel that matures our theological reflection on who God is toward us in Jesus Christ. As John Webster puts it:

> The best evangelical theological work emerges from the delight in the Christian gospel, for the gospel announces a reality which is in itself luminous, persuasive, and infinitely satisfying. That reality is Jesus Christ as he gives himself to be an object for creaturely

---

31. Some theologies (e.g., Ryrie, *Basic Theology*, 335–39; Wayne Grudem, *Systematic Theology* [Grand Rapids: Zondervan, 1995], 694–95) leave defining the gospel until relatively late in their theological system.

32. Grenz, *Renewing the Center*, 337.

33. A. T. B. McGowan, *The Divine Authenticity of Scripture: Retrieving an Evangelical Heritage* (Downers Grove, IL: InterVarsity Press, 2007), 45.

knowledge, love, and praise. To think evangelically about this one is to think in his presence, under the instruction of his Word and Spirit, and in the fellowship of the saints. And it is to do so with cheerful confidence that his own witness to himself is unimaginably more potent than any theological attempts to run to his defense.[34]

1.2.2 AN EVANGELICAL PROLEGOMENA

The evangelical theological project is to construct and live out a theology that is defined by the good news of Jesus Christ. If we accept the premise that the gospel is the most significant story in the life of the church, then evangelical theology should accordingly be a theology of the gospel.[35] Peter Jensen explores this theme further:

> Responsible theologians ought to order their teaching by the gospel, and also to ensure that whatever else their theologies may contain, the reader can see what the essence of the gospel is. The failure to make the subject of the gospel explicit in some theologies means that the reader may not know in the end what the heart of the Christian message is. It is by an exposition of the gospel that the theologian earns the right to proceed, since the gospel is the most significant revelation of all.[36]

Consequently, we need to set out the gospel at the beginning of an evangelical theology for several reasons:

1. A theology that begins with the gospel will be defined and shaped by the gospel. Harry Emerson Fosdick famously said: "He who chooses the beginning of a road chooses the place it leads to. It is the means that determines the end."[37] The beginning point of theology is so crucial because where one starts determines where one ends up. If we begin with the gospel and proceed to unpack its significance in all that follows, we are set for developing a theology that allows the gospel to inform and drive all aspects of Christian belief and practice.

2. The gospel possesses an experiential and logical priority over all other doctrines. Our reception of the gospel is the point where we first experience the salvific benefits of being in a redemptive relationship with God. Theology should begin at the point where faith itself begins, with the gospel of salvation. The gospel is the point where experience and theology first meet. Additionally, the gospel possesses a natural, logical priority in systematic theology since

---

34. John Webster, "Jesus Christ," in *The Cambridge Companion to Evangelical Theology* (ed. T. Larsen and D. Treier; Cambridge: Cambridge University Press, 2007), 60.

35. Kevin J. Vanhoozer, "The Voice and the Actor: A Dramatic Proposal about the Ministry and Minstrelsy of Theology," in *Evangelical Futures: A Conversation on Theological Method* (ed. John G. Stackhouse; Regent, BC: Regent College Publishing, 2000), 61.

36. Peter Jensen, *The Revelation of God* (Downers Grove,

IL: InterVarsity Press, 2002), 33. Also, according to Robert Jenson (*Systematic Theology* [New York: Oxford, 1997], 1:11): "The church has a mission: to see to the speaking of the gospel, whether to the world as message of salvation of to God as appeal and praise. Theology is the reflection internal to the church's labor on this assignment."

37. *The Truth in Words: Inspiring Quotes for the Reflective Mind* (compiled by Paras; Lincoln, NE: iUniverse, 2002), 106.

it explains why we have other doctrinal loci for investigation. The subfields of theology—Christology, eschatology, ecclesiology—must all spring in some sense from the gospel. In regards to the priority of the gospel, Peter Jensen comments:

> The gospel stands at the beginning of the story that explains why there are Christians at all, on the boundary between belief and unbelief—often, for the hearer, prior to a knowledge of the Bible itself. For the person entering from the outside, the gospel is the introduction to the faith, the starting-point for understanding. It then rightly becomes the touchstone of the faith. Since this is where faith begins, it is essential that faith continues to conform to it.[38]

3. Commencing with the gospel will hopefully inoculate us early on against unwholesome deviations of Christian belief caused by either liberalism (a compromised gospel) or fundamentalism (a legalistic gospel) that might infiltrate our theological thinking.[39] As such, an evangelical theology should be a theology that is from the outset vigilant in guarding the good deposit of the gospel by sounding out the gospel as the overture to the theological opera that follows (1 Tim 6:20; 2 Tim 1:12–14). Donald Bloesch commented: "A renewed theology will be evangelical, that is, centered on the gospel of reconciliation and redemption as attested in Holy Scripture."[40]

4. The gospel naturally lends itself to being the integrating point of Christian theology. There are indeed a number of proposals for the integrative motif or organic principle on which a theology is to be based. For Luther this was justification by faith. John Calvin focused on the glory of God. John Wesley was captivated by God's universal grace. Karl Barth saw the coherence of theology in the self-disclosure of the Triune God. Reformed systems emphasize the "covenant" as the center, while Dispensationalists find primacy in the "kingdom." More recently, Millard Erickson posited the integrating motif of his theology as the "magnificence of God," and Stanley Grenz regarded it as the "community of God."[41]

5. On a robustly evangelical reading, the contours of the New Testament point

---

38. Ibid., 32.

39. Though it is common to call someone "liberal" if they are less conservative than thou, when I say "old liberalism," I mean the set of theological commitments than runs roughly from Friedrich Schleiermacher (1768–1834) to the First World War (1914–18). Note this definition of "old" or "classical" liberalism: "In theology, the term *liberalism*, especially when joined with the term *classical*, refers to the post-Enlightenment orientation that sought to reconstruct Christian belief in light of modern knowledge. To be relevant, liberalism wanted to adapt itself to the new scientific and philosophical mind-set. Like the Enlightenment, it championed freedom of the individual thinker, Christian theologians included, to criticize and reformulate beliefs free of authorities" (Veli-Matti Kärkkäinen, *Christology: A Global Introduction* [Grand Rapids: Baker Academic, 2003], 95).

40. Donald G. Bloesch, *A Theology of Word and Spirit: Authority and Method in Theology* (Downers Grove, IL: InterVarsity Press, 1992), 124.

41. Millard J. Erickson, *Christian Theology* (2nd ed.; Grand Rapids: Baker, 1998), 82; Stanley J. Grenz, *Theology for the Community of God* (Grand Rapids: Eerdmans, 1994), 23–24.

to the gospel as the integrative core to Christian belief. Theology proper seeks to understand the God revealed in "the gospel of God" (Rom 1:1; 15:16; 2 Cor 11:7; 1 Thess 2:8–9). As Karl Barth commented: "What the word 'evangelical' will objectively designate is that theology which speaks of the *God of the Gospel.*"[42] Christology is unpacking the manifold significance of the life and work of Christ as narrated in the four Gospels and taught in the one apostolic gospel of Jesus Christ (e.g., Rom 1:3, 9; 15:19; 1 Cor 9:12; 2 Cor 2:12; 9:13; 10:14; Gal 1:7; Phil 1:27; 1 Thess 3:2). Christian ethics mean living a life "worthy of the gospel" (Phil 1:27) and exercising obedience that accompanies "confession of the gospel" (2 Cor 9:13). According to Oliver O'Donovan: "The foundations of Christian ethics must be evangelical foundations; or, to put it more simply, Christian ethics must arise from the Gospel of Jesus Christ. Otherwise it could not be Christian ethics."[43]

6. The study of the Holy Spirit focuses on new birth as the promise of the gospel (Acts 2:38; Rom 5:5). The study of salvation seeks to unpack the polyphonic richness of the gospel of salvation (Rom 1:16; Eph 1:13). Apologetics is the "defense of the gospel" (Phil 1:16). The study of the church is the doctrine of the gospelized community, while missiology is the art of "gossiping" the gospel. Theology and mission are weaved together, so much so that for Barth, "the object and activity with which dogmatics is concerned" is none other than "the proclamation of the Gospel."[44] In terms of applied theology, Derek Tidball writes: "The gospel determines everything about the pastor—his motives, authority, methods, and character are all governed by the good news of Jesus Christ."[45] The gospel links together the various subfields of Christian theology. The scarlet thread running through an evangelical theology is the gospel of Jesus Christ.

7. The Christian canon is gospel-shaped. The canon is enclosed by the gospel. At the beginning of the canon we find the *protoevangelium* of Gen 3:15, where the off-spring of Eve will crush the head of the serpent that typologically prefigures the birth and victory of Jesus Christ. Then at the back end of the Bible, there is the announcement of the "eternal gospel" in the Apocalypse of John, which is heralded to every person in creation (Rev 14:6). The New Testament itself begins with four books called "Gospels." Paul's epistle to the Romans, his most systematic letter, starts with a statement of the gospel in

---

42. Karl Barth, *Evangelical Theology: An Introduction* (trans. Grover Foley; New York: Holt, Rinehart and Winston, 1963), 11.

43. Oliver O'Donovan, *Resurrection and the Moral Order: An Outline for Evangelical Ethics* (Leicester, UK: Inter-Varsity Press, 1986), 11.

44. Karl Barth, *Dogmatics in Outline* (trans. G. T. Thomson; London: SCM, 1949), 9–10.

45. Derek Tidball, *Skillful Shepherds: Explorations in Pastoral Theology* (Leicester, UK: Apollos, 1997), 120.

46. James D. G. Dunn, *The Theology of Paul the Apostle* (Edinburgh: T&T Clark, 1998), 25–26; Sheila E. McGinn, ed., *Celebrating Romans: Template for Pauline Theology* (Grand Rapids: Eerdmans, 2004).

Rom 1:3–4. In this light, Romans sets up a template to follow in doing theology, a theology that originates with the gospel itself.[46] The gospel opens and closes the Christian canon, so our theology should also reflect a gospelesque architecture.

8. The gospel is also a hermeneutical lens through which we read Scripture. Because the gospel is "according to the Scriptures," we must read the Scriptures "according to the gospel." As Francis Watson declares: "To be 'evangelical' is to read Scripture in the light of the *euangelion* that lies at its heart."[47] We learn about the gospel from Scripture, but we also go back and read Scripture in light of the gospel.[48]

In the end, evangelical theology is a *theologia evangelii*—a theology of the gospel. The gospel comprises the beginning point, boundary, and unifying theme for all theology. It is also the interpretive grid through which our reading of Scripture takes place. The first "word" in theology should be the "word of the gospel" (Acts 15:7 RSV). Perhaps our chief example is Irenaeus, who regarded the gospel "handed down to us in the scriptures, to be the ground and pillar of our faith."[49] Similar also is the Heidelberg Catechism, which asks and answers:

> **Question 22.** What is then necessary for a Christian to believe?
> **Answer:** All things promised us in the gospel, which the articles of our catholic undoubted Christian faith [as in the Apostles' Creed] briefly teach us.

Doctrine is that which springs from the word of the gospel and provides the basis for the core teachings of the faith shared by all major Christian groups. Obviously an evangelical theology is one that lunges, leaps, works, worships, prays, and preaches from the gospel itself. Where a theology cannot trace its trajectory back to the gospel, there it is not evangelical. The gospel is the rule of faith for the evangelical churches as it provides the lens through which we understand the mission of the Triune God and his work for us in salvation.

FURTHER READING

Barth, Karl. *Church Dogmatics: The Doctrine of the Word of God*. Trans. G. W. Bromiley; London: Continuum, 2004 [1932], I/1.3–44.

Bavinck, Hermann. *Reformed Dogmatics. Volume 1: Prolegomena*. Ed. J. Bolt; Trans. J. Vriend; Grand Rapids: Baker, 2003.

---

47. Francis Watson, "An Evangelical Response," in *The Trustworthiness of God: Perspectives on the Nature of Scripture* (ed. Carl Trueman and Paul Helm; Grand Rapids: Eerdmans, 2002), 287.

48. Cf. esp. Graeme Goldsworthy, *Gospel-Centered Hermeneutics: Foundations and Principles of Evangelical Biblical Interpretation* (Downers Grove, IL: InterVarsity Press, 2007).

49. *Against Heresies* 3.1.1; cf. 1.10.1.

Berkhof, Hendrikus. *Christian Theology: An Introduction to the Study of the Faith.* Trans. S. Woudstra; Grand Rapids: Eerdmans, 1979, pp. 1–6.

Campbell, Ted A. *The Gospel in Christian Traditions.* Oxford: Oxford University Press, 2009.

Carson, D. A., and Timothy Keller, eds. *The Gospel as Center: Renewing our Faith and Reforming our Ministry Practices.* Wheaton, IL: Crossway, 2012.

Gibson, Jim, and Michael Bird. "Quest for an Evangelical Prolegomena to Theology." Pp. 95–106 in *Proclaiming Truth, Pastoring Hearts: Essays in Honour of Deane J. Woods.* Ed. R. T. Stanton and L. J. Crawford; Adelaide, Aus: ACM Press, 2003.

Lints, Richard. *The Fabric of Theology: A Prolegomenon to Evangelical Theology.* Grand Rapids: Eerdmans, 1993.

Taylor, Iain, ed. *Not Evangelical Enough: The Gospel at the Centre.* Carlisle, UK: Paternoster, 2003.

Vanhoozer, Kevin J. *First Theology: God, Scripture, and Hermeneutics.* Downers Grove, IL: InterVarsity Press, 2002.

§1.3 WHAT IS THE GOSPEL?

The thesis of this book is that the first task in an evangelical theology is to set out the content of the evangelical message of the church, namely, the gospel of Jesus Christ. So what is the gospel? How do you exactly define the gospel? N. T. Wright defines the gospel as follows:

> The gospel is the royal announcement that the crucified and risen Jesus, who died for our sins and rose again according to the Scriptures, has been enthroned as the true Lord of the world. When this gospel is preached, God calls people to salvation, out of sheer grace, leading them to repentance and faith in Jesus Christ as the risen Lord.[50]

This is a cogent definition, but we can perhaps go a little deeper by looking at the various contours of the gospel in the Scriptures. There are several features in the biblical testimony to the gospel that we should consider.

1. *The gospel is the message of the kingdom of God.* Closely connected to gospel is the "kingdom of God." The kingdom of God is best understood as the reign or rule of God that breaks into the world through the dramatic intervention of Israel's God in events like the Exodus or the future "day of the Lord." In the prophetic oracles of Isaiah we read:

> How beautiful on the mountains
>   are the feet of those who bring good news,
> who proclaim peace,
>   who bring good tidings,
>   who proclaim salvation,
> who say to Zion,
>   "Your God reigns!" (Isa 52:7)

---

50. Cited in Trevin Wax, "The Justification Debate: A Primer," *Christianity Today* 53.6 (2009): 34–35. See also John Dickson, *The Best Kept Secret of Christian Mission: Promoting the Gospel with More Than Our Lips* (Grand Rapids: Zondervan, 2010), 22 : "The gospel is the announcement that God has revealed his kingdom and opened it up to sinners through the birth, teaching, miracles, death and resurrection of the Lord Jesus Christ, who will one day return to overthrow evil and consummate the kingdom for eternity." See also Scot McKnight, *The King Jesus Gospel* (Grand Rapids: Zondervan, 2011).

Here the prophet announces the good news that Yahweh reigns and is going to show his kingly power by delivering Israel from the plight and shame of the exile. The designation "gospel [good news] of the kingdom" is found in several places in the Gospels, and it stands as an abbreviation for Jesus' preaching (Matt 4:23; 9:35; 24:14; Luke 4:43; 8:1; 16:16; Acts 8:12). A summary of Jesus' proclamation is that he announced the nearness of the kingdom of God as part of the good news and called for faith and repentance (Matt 4:23/Mark 1:15). The kingdom of God was a cipher for a constellation of hopes, such as the return of the dispersed Jewish tribes to Palestine, the pilgrimage of the Gentiles to Jerusalem to worship Yahweh, the renewal of the covenant, vindication for those who suffered, forgiveness of sins whether personal or national, the rebuilding of the proper temple, and a general fecundity of blessings for God's people. By announcing the kingdom, Jesus was implying that those hopes were now being realized.

What is more, the kingdom is near by virtue of the presence of the messianic king, who is the instrument through which the deliverance wrought by the covenant God is being and will be actualized (see Matt 12:28/Luke 11:20). In the Matthean version of the Olivet Discourse, Jesus declares that "this gospel of the kingdom will be preached in the whole world as a testimony to all nations" (Matt 24:14) as a precursor to the final consummation. When Jesus' followers proclaim a gospel, they do so in continuity with Jesus' own message, by declaring how the saving reign of God has been manifested in Jesus' life, death, resurrection, and exaltation.

In Acts we find exactly that message where Philip announced the "good news [gospel] of the kingdom of God and the name of Jesus Christ" to the Samaritans (Acts 8:12). When Paul arrived in Rome he preached among the Jews, "explaining about the kingdom of God, and from the Law of Moses and from the Prophets he tried to persuade them about Jesus," and "he proclaimed the kingdom of God and taught about the Lord Jesus Christ" (Acts 28:23, 31). In the preaching of Jesus and the apostles, the gospel is set in coordinates relating to the saving reign of God and how that reign is manifested in and through Jesus the Messiah.

2. *The gospel includes the story of Jesus' life, death, resurrection, and exaltation.* The gospel is not a deductive argument that reasons from God's holiness to human sin to an incarnate Savior whom we universally need. The gospel is fundamentally a story about how salvation comes through the life, death, and resurrection of Jesus the Messiah. The gospel does not announce a twelve-step plan to salvation. It narrates the story of salvation that pertains to events in the life and work of Jesus. That story begins with the deeds of "Jesus the Messiah" (Mark 1:1) and climaxes with the Messiah who "suffers these things" and "enters his glory" (Luke 24:26). This is why the books that we call "the Gospels" include the beginnings of Jesus' ministry,

his teaching, his journey to Jerusalem, and his arrest, crucifixion, and resurrection as part of their story.

The evangelistic speeches in Acts frequently follow a similar pattern as evidenced by Peter's sermons that overview Jesus' life, the circumstances of his death, resurrection, exaltation, and the forgiveness of sins offered in Jesus' name—all announced in the context of its fulfillment of Israel's Scriptures (Acts 2:22–24; 10:36–48). In many instances, the accent obviously falls on the death and resurrection as the fulcrum of the redemptive event. Paul himself focuses on the death and resurrection of Jesus Christ as the crux of the gospel (e.g., Rom 4:25; 8:34; 1 Cor 15:3–5; 2 Cor 5:15; 1 Thess 4:14, etc.). The gospel of Paul and the four Gospels all climax in Jesus' death and resurrection as the most singularly important events in the redemptive plan of God. The cross and the empty tomb are where wrath and mercy meet, where God's verdict against us becomes God's verdict for us, where our old selves are crucified with Christ and we are raised with Christ, and where sin is cleansed and new creation begins.

It is equally true, however, that persons would never have reached the conclusion that Jesus died for their sins unless he actually was the promised Messiah, the anointed one as attested by his royal birth, his preaching of the kingdom, his ministry in Palestine, and his confession at the trial before Pilate. Paul does not say a lot about Jesus' life in his letters, but he did regard the crucifixion as a historical event that could be almost acted out in preaching (Gal 3:1). Paul knew of Jesus' Last Supper with his disciples that instituted the new covenant in his sacrificial death (1 Cor 11:23–25). According to Luke, the account of Jesus' life and ministry was part of Paul's preaching of the gospel as well (Acts 13:13–39). In sum, the gospel is not simply an atonement theology, a system of salvation; it is news of events. The gospel includes a narrative unity between the mission, passion, resurrection, and session of the Lord Jesus Christ.[51]

3. *The gospel announces the status of Jesus as the Son of David, Son of God, and Lord.* The authenticity of any reproduction of the gospel depends on the identity of the Jesus preached in that gospel.[52] That is because the gospel is fundamentally christological as it declares that the crucified Nazarene is the Son of David, the Son of God, and the Lord of glory. In Peter's Pentecost sermon he declares to the Jerusalem populace: "Therefore let all Israel be assured of this: God has made this Jesus, whom you crucified, both Lord and Messiah" (Act 2:36).

The gospel announces that the verdict of the Judean people about Jesus, that he was a false prophet and messianic pretender, has been falsified by the verdict of God,

---

51. Dickson, *The Best Kept Secret of Christian Mission*, 115–23.

52. Jensen, *Revelation of God*, 57.

who has designated Jesus as Lord and Messiah by raising him up and exalting him to his right hand. In the opening verses of Romans, Paul defines the gospel of God as "the gospel he promised beforehand through his prophets in the Holy Scriptures regarding his Son, who as to his earthly life was a descendant of David, and who through the Spirit of holiness was appointed the Son of God in power by his resurrection from the dead: Jesus Christ our Lord" (Rom 1:2–4). Similarly, Paul says almost in passing: "Remember Jesus Christ, raised from the dead, descended from David. This is my gospel" (2 Tim 2:8). Martin Luther described the gospel this way:

> The gospel is a story about Christ, God's and David's Son, who died and was raised and is established as Lord. This is the gospel in a nutshell.... And I assure you, if a person fails to grasp this understanding of the gospel, he will never be able to be illuminated in the Scripture nor will he receive the right foundation.[53]

The Roman empire had its own "gospel," found in its propaganda and media that asserted that Caesar was the Lord and Savior of the world. What is more, subjects of the empire could, by devoting themselves to his patronage and power, experience the benefits of obediently living under his imperial jurisdiction. The early Christians didn't steal the idea of a "gospel" from the imperial rhetoric of the Roman empire; instead, they were exposing it as a perverse parody and as a counterfeit fraud of the real gospel about the Lord Jesus Christ. The gospel issues forth in a challenge: Who is the real Lord of the world: the Son of David or the son of Augustus (see Luke 2:1–20; Acts 17:7)? The gospel is a royal announcement that, regardless of what the world may think of Jesus, God has validated him as Israel's Messiah and installed him as the rightful Lord of the world.

4. *The gospel proclaimed by the apostles is intimated in the Old Testament.* In the discussion on the nature of the resurrection body in 1 Corinthians 15, Paul prefaces his arguments by referring to the gospel and its conformity to the Old Testament Scriptures: "that Christ died for our sins *according to the Scriptures*, that he was buried, that he was raised on the third day *according to the Scriptures*" (1 Cor 15:3–4, italics added). Paul does not say here which particular Scriptures he has mind. Still, from his comments elsewhere in the letter we can infer that he has in mind Jesus' death as a type of Passover sacrifice (1 Cor 5:7 = Exod 12), and Jesus' reign over all of creation as God's vicegerent is reminiscent of the divine role given to humanity as custodians of creation (1 Cor 15:27 = Ps 8:6).

Similarly, in the first few verses of Romans, Paul writes that the gospel is something God "promised beforehand through his prophets in the Holy Scriptures

---

53. Martin Luther, "A Brief Instruction on What to Look for and Expect in the Gospels," in *Luther's Works* (ed. Helmut T. Lehmann; Philadelphia: Fortress, 1960), 35:118–19.

regarding his Son" (Rom 1:2–3). The fact that Abraham's faith was credited to him as righteousness in Genesis 15:6 proves for Paul that "Scripture foresaw that God would justify the Gentiles by faith, and announced the gospel in advance to Abraham" (Gal 3:8). Paul does not regard the gospel as a recent invention, but as something that is testified to in Israel's Scriptures. In the resurrection narrative of the gospel of Luke, the risen Jesus says:

> "Did not the Messiah have to suffer these things and then enter his glory?" And beginning with Moses and all the Prophets, he explained to them what was said in all the Scriptures concerning himself....
>
> He said to them, "This is what I told you while I was still with you: Everything must be fulfilled that is written about me in the Law of Moses, the Prophets and the Psalms." (Luke 24:26–27, 44)

Here we are likely to imagine passages like Deuteronomy 18:18, which refers to God's sending Israel another prophet like Moses; the book of Isaiah with its references to the Suffering Servant (Isa 53) and the anointed prophet (Isa 61); and the Psalms about the righteous who suffer unjustly and are afterward vindicated by God (Pss 16; 17; 22). The writer to the Hebrews reminds his audience of those "who spoke the word of God to you," which undoubtedly contains the same manner of argumentation that he himself employs earlier in the letter (Heb 13:7). In a series of intricate arguments the author of Hebrews lays out how the Old Testament points ahead to Jesus Christ, who represents a better covenant, a better tabernacle, a better priesthood, a better sacrifice, and a better mediator than that found under the old covenant.

In Paul's speech in the synagogue in Pisidian Antioch he declared: "We tell you the good news: What God promised our ancestors he has fulfilled for us, their children, by raising up Jesus" (Acts 13:32–33). The gospel is part of a story line of promise and fulfillment. That story reaches back into the Hebrew Scriptures and finds its climax in Jesus the Messiah.

5. *The response that the gospel calls for is faith and repentance.* The gospel offers an invitation for persons to respond to the message. The prescribed responses to the message of salvation announced in the gospel are to repent and believe. Jesus urged his audience to repent and believe the good news of the kingdom (Mark 1:15). Paul summarized his message to the Ephesians elders: "I have declared to both Jews and Greeks that they must turn to God in repentance and have faith in our Lord Jesus" (Acts 20:21; we will explore the terms "repentance" and "faith" later). As an initial summary, we could say that repentance involves (a) changing one's verdict about Jesus and expressing contrition for one's sins that are an offense to God; and (b) entrusting oneself to the faithfulness of God, seen in the faithfulness of Jesus Christ. Together this signifies following Jesus and becoming his disciple.

6. *Salvation is the chief benefit of the gospel.* The gospel brings salvation (Rom 1:16; Eph 1:13). The biblical words for "salvation" in Hebrew and Greek are broad and include healing, forgiveness, restoration, rescue from danger, and eternal life. If we look at the beginning of the biblical story, salvation could be described as the reverse of the fall and being restored to relational harmony with God. If we look at the end of the biblical story, salvation could be expressed as sharing in the new heaven and the new earth, which await God's people. In the Scriptures there is a rich and varied array of images that describe salvation, including the forgiveness of sins, justification, reconciliation, adoption, redemption, renewal, cleansing, and more. At the center of salvation is the promise that God in Christ and through the Holy Spirit ends the alienation and hostility between himself and his creatures so that he draws them into a new relationship with himself, a relationship that will last for all of eternity.

In light of those theological fixtures I define the gospel of Jesus Christ as follows:

> The gospel is the announcement that God's kingdom has come in the life, death, and resurrection of Jesus of Nazareth, the Lord and Messiah, in fulfillment of Israel's Scriptures. The gospel evokes faith, repentance, and discipleship; its accompanying effects include salvation and the gift of the Holy Spirit.

Here we find the major themes of kingdom, the fulfillment of Scripture, Jesus as Messiah and Lord, the call for faith, and bestowal of the Holy Spirit all interwoven together. All of these must be worked into our definition of gospel in order to be a summary that is suitably broad to encompass all of the key elements, but also sufficiently focused on the saving plan of God revealed in Jesus Christ.

The New Testament expresses a concern about the dangers of preaching "another Jesus" or "another gospel" (2 Cor 11:4; Gal 1:6). Consequently, we should be vigilant about truncated or distorted gospels ever getting a foothold in the church. Obviously legalism remains a constant danger, as ego-charged leaders will constantly tell their followers that they need to build their own Babel of works to reach up to God; or else they make up lists of rules upon rules in order to be recognized as a true insider, rather than rest on the abounding grace of Jesus Christ.

To pick up another false gospel, I would mark out the social gospel for special attention. The saving message of the gospel cannot be reduced to the call for economic justice and liberation from poverty. The social gospel of the old liberal theology in the early twentieth century and some strands of emergent theology in the early twenty-first century both make the mistake of translating the gospel into economic categories concerned with the improvement of social conditions in society.[54]

That is not to say that pursuing justice and helping the poor is not an important task for God's people; it is part of our mission to be salt and light! God's concern for justice, helping the poor, and showing compassion lies at the heart of the Mosaic legislation, it permeates the prophets, and it is key in the Sermon on the Mount. The prophet Micah summed up God's will for his people in the prophetic announcement: "He has shown you, O mortal, what is good. And what does the LORD require of you? To act justly and to love mercy and to walk humbly with your God" (Mic 6:8).

Jesus preached good news to the poor, following the script for the Anointed One from Isaiah 61:1–2, as part of the liberating power that operated through his ministry (Matt 11:5; Luke 4:18; 7:22). The biblical concept of salvation includes a rich array of references to eternal life, healing from sickness, inclusion in God's covenant family, a reversal of status, and economic relief. A gospel that promises eternal life as our ultimate spiritual state should not breed indifference to the physical needs of people (see Jas 2:15–17). Christians have always been at the forefront of work for those in need. From the call to end gladiatorial contests in ancient Rome, to the beginnings of the hospices in the Middle Ages, to the founding of orphanages in Africa, to the abolishment of slavery in industrialized Europe, to those who fight for the end to sexual trafficking in Asia in the twenty-first century—Christians have always been at the forefront of such charitable work.

When the Jerusalem pillars of Peter, John, and James met with Paul and Barnabas, the trio validated Paul's gospel that he preached to the Gentiles and gave him the exhortation that he should also remember the poor, precisely what Paul was eager to do (Gal 2:7–10). Social action and caring for the poor is not, however, the gospel; it is simply what Christians are expected to do alongside the gospel. Showing compassion and pursuing justice are implications of the gospel, implications of the fact that Christians belong to a kingdom, not simply share a final heavenly destination. As Christians confess the lordship of Jesus Christ, they begin to order their lives according to the story, symbols, and summons of their exalted Master, and that will inevitably impact, often abrasively, the world around them.

Christians show their family likeness with Christ Jesus by their care for the poor, the marginalized, and the vulnerable. They declare to the despots and dictators of the world that they know what real power lies behind them and that the day of their reckoning approaches. However, a truncated gospel that includes only social

---

54. Cf. Walter Rauschenbusch, *Theology for the Social Gospel* (New York: Abingdon, 1917); Brian MacLaren, *A New Kind of Christianity: Ten Questions That Are Transforming the Faith* (San Francisco: HarperOne, 2010).

programs and economic policies as its contents strips the gospel of its powerful message of how sinful men and women can be reconciled to God through the cross of Jesus Christ. The gospel of old liberalism ends up with "a God without wrath [that] brought men without sin to a kingdom without judgment through the ministration of a Christ without a cross."[55] That is no gospel at all.

FURTHER READING

Bock, Darrell L. *Recovering the Real Lost Gospel of Jesus.* Nashville: Broadman & Holman, 2010.

Carson, D. A. "The Biblical Gospel." Pages 75–85 in *For Such a Time as This: Perspectives on Evangelicalism, Past, Present, and Future.* Ed. S. Brady and H. Rowdon. London: Evangelical Alliance, 1996.

Dickson, John. *The Best Kept Secret of Christian Mission: Promoting the Gospel with More Than Our Lips.* Grand Rapids: Zondervan, 2010, pp. 111–40.

Gilbert, Greg. *What Is the Gospel?* Wheaton, IL: Crossway, 2010.

McKnight, Scot. *The King Jesus Gospel: The Original Good News Revisited.* Grand Rapids: Zondervan, 2011.

Olson, Roger E. *The Westminster Handbook to Evangelical Theology.* Louisville: Westminster John Knox, 2004, pp. 191–93.

Packer, J. I., and Thomas C. Oden, *One Faith: The Evangelical Consensus.* Downers Grove, IL: InterVarsity Press, 1999, pp. 187–91.

Wax, Trevin. *Counterfeit Gospels: Rediscovering the Good News in a World of False Hope.* Chicago: Moody Press, 2011.

---

55. Richard Niebuhr, *The Kingdom of God in America* (New York: Harper, 1937), 193.

§1.4 THE NECESSITY AND GOAL OF THEOLOGY

Why do we need a thing called "theology," let alone a "systematic theology"? Isn't a "biblical theology" eminently preferable if we are people of the Bible? Doesn't systematic theology become speculative, esoteric, and even irrelevant to daily Christian life? Do I really need to know the difference between infralapsarianism and supralapsarianism in order to be a trained missionary or a good pastor or a faithful Christian? Does not theology create more divisions over minute details than it is actually worth?

These are good questions and many people often ask them. Indeed, theology can become dry, cerebral, academic, and elitist, if divorced from the life of faith and if not undertaken with a spirit of charity and humility. However, theology is crucial to the life and witness of the church. It is an important vehicle to take us to the appointed goal in our walk in the Christian life, namely, maturity in Christ. Theology is necessary, and its practice has much needed benefits for practitioners.

1.4.1 THE NECESSITY OF THEOLOGY

Theology is far from a tertiary exercise or a purely academic pursuit, and it is necessary for a number of cogent reasons.

1. *Theology is necessary to provide clarification and unity to the diverse body of biblical materials.* If someone asked you, "What must I do to be saved?" what would you say? Would you reply with, "Well, Isaiah said X, Jesus said Y, and Paul said Z—take the one you like and just run with it"? Or would you want to say something that adequately summarizes the complete witness of the entire counsel of God? Karl Barth wisely distinguished between the task of exegesis to explore the biblical text and the task of theology to engage in consistent exegesis across the breadth of the whole of Scripture. He stated: "Dogmatics as such does not ask what the apostles

and prophets said but what we must say on the basis of the apostles and prophets."[56] Theology is what we say on the basis of the entire witness of Scripture.

2. *Theology is necessary to respond to the ever-evolving challenges of being a Christian in our contemporary culture.* If you were faced with the question from a friend about genetic engineering or experimental use of stem cells, what Bible verse would you cite to give your answer? The fact is that the Bible is not Wikipedia with a hyperlink available to answer every possible question we might face. It takes some effort to work out how God's Word and its reception in the church can be applied to questions, issues, and subjects that did not confront the original recipients.

3. *Theology is a necessary part of discipleship in the church and an important element of our witness to the world.* The Christian community is a teaching community. The early church devoted itself to the teaching of Jesus and the apostles (Acts 2:42; 2 Thess 3:6; 1 Tim 4:6; 6:3; 2 Tim 1:13; 2 John 9). Christians should be able to "instruct one another" (Rom 15:14). They are commanded to "let the message of Christ dwell among you richly as you teach and admonish one another with all wisdom" (Col 3:16). Christians must strive to move beyond the elemental teachings that are like milk and to press onto the more mature items of the faith that are like solid food (1 Cor 3:2; Heb 5:12–14). Believers are also commanded to "always be prepared to give an answer to everyone who asks you to give the reason for the hope that you have" (1 Pet 3:15).

4. *Theology is necessary to maintain the integrity of the faith that we profess against incursions from both inside and outside the church.* In a world where people who profess to be Christians have very different ideas about what that faith is, how do you distinguish the essential and nonessential elements of the Christian faith? How do you discern the difference between true and false teachings about Christian faith? What brings unity and coherence to the Christian faith?

Paul knows that some beliefs are more important than others, and some beliefs can be held as a matter of conscience even when they are not held uniformly (Rom 14–15). Perspectives on eating meat and drinking alcohol, for instance, are not as important as the incarnation and the atonement. Some doctrines are relatively important, like baptism, but beliefs about baptism (i.e., infants vs. believers) do not determine one's salvation. The gospel will always remain of "first importance" (1 Cor 15:2–3), while other doctrines will be for our instruction and edification (Heb 6:1–2), and still others a matter of conscience and conviction (Rom 14:1–23). Theology helps us to understand which beliefs matter most, which theological hills we should be willing to die on, and which doctrines can be left to personal liberty.

The New Testament is replete with instances where the church is called to defend the didactic content of faith in terms of what it teaches us about God, humanity, and

---

56. Barth, *CD*, I/1.16.

salvation. In the epistle of Jude there is an exhortation to "contend for the faith ... once for all entrusted to God's holy people" (Jude 3). Paul exhorts Timothy, "What you heard from me, keep as the pattern of sound teaching, with faith and love in Christ Jesus. Guard the good deposit that was entrusted to you — guard it with the help of the Holy Spirit who lives in us" (2 Tim 1:13–14). The danger of error and heresy is ever on the horizon as the words of Scripture are twisted by those who seek to add to Scripture mere human philosophy or to make the faith more palatable to the world around them by contorting the gospel.

We can embrace theological diversity as a norm; the evangelical church is a broad church after all, though its boundaries are not nebulous. For a true evangelical church can only be as a broad as the gospel. Both heresy and immorality are real, and Christians are not to permit them to gain a foothold in the church. According to Richard Hays: "The Christian community as a community of love is not infinitely inclusive: those who reject Jesus are not and cannot be part of it. There is great danger to the church, in Paul's view, when some people represent themselves as Christians while rejecting the apostolically proclaimed gospel."[57]

The other thing that theology does is to demonstrate the interconnectedness of Christian beliefs. We can understand how the doctrine of humanity relates to our doctrine of sin, and sin to the atonement, and atonement to the Trinity, and Trinity to the church, and so forth. According Irenaeus, one of the major errors of the Gnostic sect of Valentinians was that "they disregard the order and the connection of the Scriptures, and so ... dismember and destroy the truth."[58] The Valentinians not only distorted Scripture (exegesis), but they also rejected the apostolic tradition (hermeneutics), the order of Scripture (biblical theology), and the connection of Scripture (systematic theology). Systematic theology prevents error by drawing out the connections in Scripture through expounding the redemptive-historical story line of Scripture.[59]

Thus, theology is necessary because it enables us to develop a triage with respect to which beliefs are weightier than others, to define and defend orthodoxy against heresy, and to demonstrate how the web of beliefs relate and hold together.

5. *Theology is necessary because it is our task to tell the story of God, to show where we fit into that story, and to decide how to live out that story appropriately.* Ultimately, theology is a story about God. It is a story that has several acts:

---

57. Richard Hays, *First Corinthians* (Interpretation; Louisville: John Knox, 1997), 291–92.
58. Irenaeus, *Haer.* 1.8.1.
59. Notice how, contra much Jewish exegesis of the Old Testament, Paul points out that Abraham was justified by faith *before* he was circumcised, which means that justification cannot be based on works of law (Rom 4). Moreover, the law was introduced 430 years after the Abrahamic promise, which means that law does not nullify the promise (Gal 3). There are examples of Paul's using a redemptive-historical argument, reading the Bible in narrative order, to undermine the arguments of his critics.

Act 1: Creation and Fall
Act 2: Patriarchs and Israel
Act 3: Jesus
Act 4: The Church
Act 5: The Consummation

As we pray, read Scripture, sing, work, live, and die, we are asking, answering, and acting on what that story *means* for us individually and corporately. We are the protectors, the promoters, and the performers of the story of God. So as we read Scripture together while we look to our traditions and our liturgy, we have to confess what it is that we believe and how that makes a difference in how we live.

1.4.2 THE GOAL OF THEOLOGY

A more significant reason why theology is necessary is that theology has a particular benefit for believers and their communities. In the lavish and poetic opening of Paul's letter to the Ephesians, the apostle prays for them: "I keep asking that the God of our Lord Jesus Christ, the glorious Father, may give you the Spirit of wisdom and revelation, so *that you may know him better*" (Eph 1:17, italics added). Notice that the goal of our instruction in the Scriptures and the purpose of our exploration of the Christian faith is to know God better, so that we may grow in our knowledge of God and abound in insight and intimacy. This was expressed most aptly by Anselm, who spoke of a "faith seeking understanding" (*fides quaerens intellectum*). That does not mean trying to replace faith with doctrine; rather, it means something like seeking a deeper knowledge of God through faith informed by learning—not a purely cognitive knowing, but a growing into a closer relationship with someone who loves us.

Theology, then, is our attempt to deepen our relationship with God by having a more profound knowledge of his person and workings. By engaging in concerted theological study we aspire to become "mature and fully assured" (Col 4:12) and thus "truly [understand] God's grace" (Col 1:6). Ignatius of Antioch, the bishop and martyr of the church, instructed believers in Magnesia with these words: "Be eager, therefore, to be firmly grounded in the precepts of the Lord and the apostles, in order that in whatever you do, you may prosper, physically and spiritually, in faith and love, in the Son and the Father and in the Spirit, in the beginning and at the end."[60] If we want to prosper and thrive spiritually, it is necessary to be grounded, rooted, and anchored in the teachings given by Jesus and the apostles.

---

60. Ignatius, *Magn.* 13.1.

FURTHER READING

Grenz, Stanley J., and Roger E. Olson. *Who Needs Theology? An Invitation to the Study of God.* Downers Grove, IL: InterVarsity Press, 1992.

McGrath, Alister E. *The Passionate Intellect: Christian Faith and Discipleship of the Mind.* Downers Grove, IL: InterVarsity Press, 2010.

Migliore, Daniel. *Faith Seeking Understanding: An Introduction to Christian Theology.* Grand Rapids: Eerdmans, 1991, pp. 2–7.

Welker, Michael, and Cynthia A. Jarvis, eds. *Loving God with Our Minds: The Pastor as Theologian.* Grand Rapids: Eerdmans, 2004.

§ 1.5 IS THEOLOGY POSSIBLE?

J. C. Ryle once said: "I have long come to the conclusion that men may be more systematic in their statements than the Bible, and may be led into grave error by idolatrous veneration of a system."[61] Often theologians look as if they are trying to force the round peg of Scripture into the square hole of a system. Truth be told, systematic theology is a fallible attempt to systematize the central tenets of the Christian faith. To say that more fully, systematic theology constitutes the endeavor to lay out methodically the sum of Christian beliefs with special attention given to their unity and interrelatedness—in other words, what the doctrines are and what holds them together. There are, of course, several inherent obstacles in attempting to organize the panoply of Christian beliefs into a logical and hierarchical order.

1. The very choice of loci (e.g., Doctrine of God, Person and Work of Christ, Doctrine of the Church, etc.) requires pressing the biblical materials into several synthetic categories that might not represent the most comprehensive way of organizing the biblical materials. There is the danger that the content of the Bible is forced onto a procrustean bed of classifications that are not themselves drawn from the Bible.

2. An additional problem is that the Bible contains a diversity of authors, a diversity of genres, and a diversity of cultural and historical locations. For instance, salvation for eighth-century Isaiah is principally about the survival of Israel from exile, while salvation in the gospel of John written at the end of first century is principally concerned with eternal life. Consequently, it is challenging to come up a theology that adequately reflects the particularity of each book or corpus, while simultaneously drawing them together in order to establish a doctrinal core. The dangers are that one flattens out the distinctive contribution of each author, or else one retreats to statements that are little more than self-evident platitudes, such as both Isaiah and John agreeing that God saves.

---

61. J. C. Ryle, *Expository Thoughts on the Gospels* (Grand Rapids: Baker, 1979), 3:157.

3. Systematic theology tends to be conditioned by the prevailing philosophy of the day. Much patristic theology, for example, was indebted to neo-Platonism; medieval theology was built on the twelfth-century rediscovery in the West of Aristotle, and even Protestant scholasticism gradually fell under the spell of philosophical rationalism. More recently, late twentieth-century theology has been influenced by the postmodern literary theory about the ideology behind texts and by the post–World War II experiences of religious pluralism.

These challenges are real and should give us pause for thought; but all is not lost. We can offset these challenges in a number of ways. First, we can recognize that systematic theology is indeed selective and limited in its scope. It does not say everything that can possibly be said about what has been revealed in the biblical revelation and received in Christian tradition. The loci are chosen in order to give the biggest payoff by covering the most material with a limited number of categories. Theology is an attempt to say what we can, the most we can, and in the best way we can.

Second, if we allow systematic theology to be informed by biblical theology, we will allow the text to set the agenda for theology more often than not. Ultimately theology is an exercise of "consistent exegesis" (to follow Karl Barth) or "biblical reasoning" (to quote John Webster).[62]

Third, recognition of our own historical situatedness and awareness of the potential influence of our cultural setting on us will make us sufficiently self-critical as we engage in the task of doing theology. Our word is not the last word on theology, but it is an attempt to express "a faith seeking understanding" in the context in which God has put us.

---

62. Barth, *CD*, I/1.3–11; John Webster, "Biblical Reasoning," *ATR* 90 (2008): 733–51. A valuable read also is Michael Williams, "Systematic Theology as a Biblical Discipline," in *All for Jesus: A Celebration of the 50th Anniversary of Covenant Theological Seminary* (ed. R. A. Paterson and S. M. Lucas; Fearn, Ross Shire: Christian Focus, 2005), 167–96.

§1.6 SOURCES FOR THEOLOGY

Theology does not simply happen. Theologians engage in their craft by working through a number of specific sources out of which they construct a theology. The number of the sources, the nature of the sources, and how the sources should be used are all disputed. For example, the protest of the Reformation was against Catholic dogma that merged Scripture and tradition together into one authority. The Reformers insisted on the primacy of Scripture in the doctrine of the church. That left undefined the question as to what role, if any, tradition should have in theology. We could ask the same thing of experience, reason, and culture. It is my contention that an evangelical theology should proceed by taking into account four primary sources of authority: Scripture, tradition, nature, and experience.

1.6.1 SCRIPTURE

As evangelical theologians we look to the gospel as the source of our faith. If our faith is elicited by the gospel, then so is our theology. Consequently we must take seriously the Scriptures that present the gospel message to us. Although we will get into the nitty-gritty of terms like "revelation" and "inspiration" soon, for now it is enough to note the paramount importance that Scripture has for theology.

Theology first emerges from our encounter with God through the gospel. As those who have experienced the gospel, we must take notice of God's self-disclosure in the book that singularly attests to his character and recounts his mighty deeds. We are interested in the trajectory of proclamation that carries the story of God's saving acts across the history of Israel, to Jesus, and into the nascent church.[63] The story of God's saving acts culminating in the gospel is given to us in the Christian Scriptures. Therefore, the primary source for theology is God's revelation of himself in the Holy Scriptures comprised of the Old and New Testaments of the Christian Bible.

Scripture is included in theology because it is part of God's Word to us. The Word

---

63. Grenz, *Theology for the Community of God*, 17.

of God exists in three forms. (1) There is the eternal Word of God, Jesus Christ, who in his incarnation was the "Word made flesh"; (2) there is the spoken prophetic word for admonishing Israel and the apostolic word of the gospel; and (3) there is the inscripturated revelation of the writings of the Old and New Testaments that make up the Word of God in written form. The gospel testifies to the incarnate Word of God, the gospel's proper proclamation is the actual Word of God, and the gospel is preserved in the inscripturated Word of God. God's Word is always a gospel-word, and this is the Word that creates faith (Rom 10:17).

The Bible is the Word of God because it is inspired by the Holy Spirit. (1) We believe this on the basis of the gospel that testifies to the Scriptures as the interpretive framework for understanding Jesus' life, death, and resurrection. In a loop of authority, because we believe the gospel, we believe in the Bible, and because we believe in the Bible, we believe the gospel!

> As a matter of clarification the terms "Bible," "Scripture," and "canon" are not synonymous. The "Bible" is a published collection of holy writings for Christians, but there are different publications, translations, and editions of this book. The "Scriptures" indicate a body of writings regarded as being religiously significant for a certain community, whereas a "canon" is a uniformly recognized register of scriptural writings. In other words, not all "Scripture" is canon (i.e., some in the early church accepted the *Didache* as Scripture), but all "canon" is Scripture (i.e., every book in the canon has the same status as Scripture).

(2) The inner witness of the Holy Spirit convicts us that the words we are reading are not simply human words, but the words of God wrought by the Holy Spirit operating through human authors (John 16:13; 1 Cor 2:10–12; 1 John 2:20).

(3) We may add the testimony of Scripture to itself where we are told that "all Scripture is God-breathed and is useful for teaching, rebuking, correcting and training in righteousness" (2 Tim 3:16). Moreover, "prophecy never had its origin in the human will, but prophets, though human, spoke from God as they were carried along by the Holy Spirit" (2 Pet 1:21). "God-breathed" (*theopneustos*, sometimes translated "inspired by God," RSV) does not mean inspirational, nor does it presuppose a mechanical view of God dictating words to the authors. Rather, inspiration is God's superintending of the sources and authors of the biblical texts in order to reflect the form and content of the revelation that he intended the church to receive.[64] Theologians often try to prove the inspiration of the Bible by referring to miracles, to the Bible's spiritual and moral qualities, or to its consistency and historical reliability.

---

64. There is a more detailed discussion of this topic in part 6 on the person and work of the Holy Spirit, in a section entitled "Inscripturating." Moreover, there is a section in part 2 on "The God Who Reveals Himself" (§ 2.5).

A better approach is simply to recognize that the Bible is the community-forming document of the Christian church. Scripture is the source of the apostolic *kerygma*, the gospel proclamation, in the early communities and in our own contemporary communities as well.[65]

Scripture is the *ultimate norm* for theology; that is, it establishes what is authoritative for Christian belief and practice. As people of the book, our identity, doctrine, and practice are bound up with the belief that God has spoken to us in our Scriptures. It is not simply Scripture itself that is authoritative, but God speaking in the Scriptures through the Holy Spirit that is the standard of all truth. As the Westminster Confession of Faith (1.10) says: "The supreme judge by which all controversies of religion are to be determined, and all decrees of councils, opinions of ancient writers, doctrines of men, and private spirits, are to be examined, and in whose sentence we are to rest, can be no other but the Holy Spirit speaking in the Scripture."[66]

1.6.2 TRADITION
1.6.2.1 EVANGELICALS AND TRADITION

One area that evangelicals have generally been weak on is that of tradition. Strangely enough this is probably one area where liberals and evangelicals actually have something in common. Some more ardently liberal theologians look back on tradition as the primitive and antiquated residue of a naive and superstitious period of history, at least when compared to their own progressive and enlightened selves. Conversely, many evangelicals have tended to fear tradition as something that is cold, stale, and purely of human origin.

Ironically, the mantra of "No creed but Christ, no book but the Bible" is not actually found in the Bible; yet it virtually has canonical status in some churches. They do not seem to realize that the New Testament itself is the written product of a long traditioning process (Luke 1:1–2; 1 Cor 11:23–25), where traditions were passed on in the early church (Rom 6:17; 1 Cor 11:2; 15:1–3; 2 Thess 2:15; 2 Tim 1:13). In response to the threat of Gnosticism in the second century, patristic authors like Irenaeus appealed to an authorized way of reading Scripture that went back to the apostles themselves. For the early church, Scripture was not to be read in an arbitrary, introspective, or esoteric way; rather, Scripture was to be read, interpreted, and applied in continuity with the apostolic explanation of the story line of Scripture.

It was the Gnostics who read Scripture on their own and in isolation from the

---

65. Grenz, *Theology for the Community of God*, 17.
66. See www.reformed.org/documents/wcf_with_proofs/. Any subsequent quotes from the Westminster Confession can be found here.

testimony of the wider church. And it was abandonment of the apostolic tradition of reading Scripture that led the Gnostics into heresy by marrying their biblical interpretation to a particular adaption of platonic cosmology, whereby the world was created by a wicked demiurge from whom Jesus came to save us. Lest we think that problem unique, I would point out that some eighteenth-century English Baptists, through a mix of biblicist and unitarian tendencies, regarded the Trinity as a nonessential element of the faith. Here is the warning: if you disregard Christian tradition, you can end up becoming either a Gnostic or a Unitarian!

1.6.2.2 RETHINKING SCRIPTURE AND TRADITION FROM AN EVANGELICAL PERSPECTIVE

I would point out that there is a symbiotic relationship between Scripture and tradition. The Bible did not fall out of the sky, bound in leather, with words of Jesus in red, written in King James English, and complete with Scofield footnotes! It came to us through the church—through its theologians, bishops, and councils. There were different canonical lists drawn up in the early centuries of the church. Some people wanted to include books like the *Didache* or the *Shepherd of Hermas*, while others had reservations about books like 2 Peter and Revelation. Ultimately the consensus reached was that the sixty-six books of the Old and New Testaments as we have them were regarded as the authoritative register of sacred books for the church.

But how did the church decide which books to include in the canon and which books to exclude? Bishops and elders did not roam the land with an "inspiration-o-meter" searching for books that garnered a high reading. The canonization of the Old and New Testament was a process that took several centuries. While I think that the basic building blocks of the canon were in place by the mid to late second century, it took time for the biblical canon to be formally identified and promulgated.

The church received the Greek translation of the Hebrew Bible as its own account of the Jewish Scriptures, and it would later be identified as the "Old Testament." A Jewish canon consisting of the Law, the Prophets, and the Writings seems to have been accepted by a large number of Jews before the time of Jesus, and such a collection was inherited by the church. In regards to the admission of Christian books into a collection of authoritative books, the criteria for inclusion of a book in the New Testament canon were:

1. *apostolicity*—was it written by an apostle or an associate of an apostle?
2. *orthodoxy*—did it conform to the pattern of Christian teaching?
3. *antiquity*—was it dated to the apostolic era?
4. *usage*—was it accepted and used in the churches in liturgy and preaching?

As such, the Christian Bible was breathed out by the Holy Spirit through the Israelite people and the Christian church.[67]

An urgent qualification is needed here. The Word of God created the church; the church did not create the Word. Nonetheless, the church did create the biblical canon in the sense of being charged with the task of putting the inscripturated Word of God into its canonical form. The canonical process was itself a long and complex affair affected by matters internal and external to the life of the church. Yet the Christian Scriptures exist only because Christians first wrote it, preserved it, transmitted it, preached from it, argued about it, and interpreted it within the context of their own faith communities. Furthermore, the Apostles' Creed precedes the existence of a biblical canon. The word *canon* actually means "rule." The selection of books into the biblical canon was itself driven by its conformity to the "rule of faith." Thus, in historical sequence, the "canon of Scripture" is a written expression of the church's "canon of faith."

1.6.2.3 THE REGULA FIDEI: THE ORIGINAL EVANGELICAL TRADITION

The "rule of faith," usually called by its Latin name *regula fidei*, refers to the general outline of Christian beliefs that circulated in the second-century church. It was also called the "rule of truth" or the "canon of truth." It was not a precise creedal statement, but more of a summary of the narrative of Scripture. Irenaeus (d. ca. AD 202) refers to the "tradition of the truth" that is venerated in the apostolic churches. This faith has been received among the nations:

> carefully preserving the ancient tradition, believing in one God, the Creator of heaven and earth, and all things therein, by means of Christ Jesus, the Son of God; who, because of His surpassing love towards His creation, condescended to be born of the virgin, He Himself uniting man through Himself to God, and having suffered under Pontius Pilate, and rising again, and having been received up in splendour, shall come in glory, the Saviour of those who are saved, and the Judge of those who are judged, and sending into eternal fire those who transform the truth, and despise His Father and His advent. Those who, in the absence of written documents, have believed this faith, are barbarians, so far as regards our language; but as regards doctrine, manner, and tenor of life, they are, because of faith, very wise indeed; and they do please God, ordering their conversation in all righteousness, chastity, and wisdom. If anyone were to preach to these men the inventions of the heretics, speaking to them in their own language, they would at once stop their ears, and flee as far off as possible, not enduring even to listen to the blasphemous address. Thus, by means of that ancient tradition of the apostles, they do not suffer their mind to

---

67. Cf. F. F. Bruce, *The Canon of Scripture* (Downers Grove, IL: InterVarsity Press, 1988); Lee Martin McDonald, *The Biblical Canon: Its Origins, Transmission, and Authority* (Peabody, MA: Hendrickson, 2007).

conceive anything of the [doctrines suggested by the] portentous language of these teachers, among whom neither Church nor doctrine has ever been established.[68]

Note how the *regula fidei* is an exposition of the biblical story line. What is more, those who have had the gospel preached to them, but do not yet have copies of the Scriptures, still hold to the *regula fidei* because they faithfully keep to the tradition of apostolic teaching about Jesus. It is the *regula fidei* that preserved the often simple and unlearned tribes from heretical beliefs by keeping them fastened to the apostolic gospel. Similar to Irenaeus is Tertullian (ca. AD 160–225):

> Now, with regard to this rule of faith—that we may from this point acknowledge what it is which we defend—it is, you must know, that which prescribes the belief that there is one only God, and that He is none other than the Creator of the world, who produced all things out of nothing through His own Word, first of all sent forth; that this Word is called His Son, *and*, under the name of God, was seen "in diverse manners" by the patriarchs, heard at all times in the prophets, at last brought down by the Spirit and Power of the Father into the Virgin Mary, was made flesh in her womb, and, being born of her, went forth as Jesus Christ; thenceforth He preached the new law and the new promise of the kingdom of heaven, worked miracles; having been crucified, He rose again the third day; (then) having ascended into the heavens, He sat at the right hand of the Father; sent instead of Himself the Power of the Holy Ghost to lead such as believe; will come with glory to take the saints to the enjoyment of everlasting life and of the heavenly promises, and to condemn the wicked to everlasting fire, after the resurrection of both these classes shall have happened, together with the restoration of their flesh. This rule, as it will be proved, was taught by Christ, and raises amongst ourselves no other questions than those which heresies introduce, and which make men heretics.[69]

Tertullian regarded the *regula fidei* as the narrative summary of the faith that goes all the way back to Jesus. That sounds like an outrageous claim, but if Jesus was the first person to describe how the story of Israel's Scriptures was fulfilled in his own messianic mission, then Jesus is the originator of the *regula fidei*. A direct line between Jesus to the apostolic testimony to the church is established; this validates the narrative structure and christological focus on the church's summary of its faith.[70]

The *regula fidei* was not an oral tradition that existed parallel to Scripture. The *regula fidei* was what emerged out of the preaching and teaching of Scripture in the early church. The *regula fidei* was both derived from Scripture and was the interpretive lens through which Scripture was to be understood. In this perspective, Scripture and tradition mutually reinforce each other. The *regula fidei* was the attempt to

---

68. Irenaeus, *Haer.* 3.4.2; cf. 1.10.1
69. Tertullian, *Praescrip.* 13.
70. Vanhoozer, *Drama of Doctrine*, 195.

safeguard the authority of Scripture by adopting an interpretive framework sanctioned by Scripture. That took the form, not of a creed, but a general narration of the Christian story as it had been handed on in the early church.

Later the rule was expanded to include reading the Scriptures in light of the Niceno-Constantinopolitan and Chalcedonian clarifications of Christian doctrine. The apostolic teaching gave us the Scriptures, the Scriptures gave us the *regula fidei*, the *regula fidei* defined the theological hermeneutics for the canon, and the canon provided the grounds for the subsequent creeds and confessions of the church. Cyril of Jerusalem taught new believers the Jerusalem Creed because it represented an epitome of the entire Bible:

> Learn the faith and profess it; receive it and keep it—but only the creed which the church will now deliver to you, that creed is firmly based on Scripture.... For the articles of the creed were not put together according to human choice; the most important doctrines were collected from the whole of Scripture to make up a single exposition of the faith.[71]

In light of the *regula fidei*, Christian interpretation of Scripture takes place in the way of Jesus Christ, empowered by the Spirit to transform God's people into Christ's image, anticipating a transformative vision of the Triune God.[72]

1.6.2.4 EMBRACING TRADITION IN EVANGELICAL THEOLOGY

In light of the above, we should be positively disposed toward the idea of tradition informing our theology. However, tradition is a double-edged sword and can be grievously misused. During the Middle Ages there emerged a different view of tradition as something apart from Scripture that was considered as authoritative as revelation. A stream of unwritten sources was vocal where the Bible was silent and provided the authoritative source of God's will revealed through the church fathers, councils, popes, and magisterium. In Catholic teaching, the tradition of the Roman Church was said to be handed on by the apostles themselves and had been faithfully transmitted thereafter. The problem for the Catholics has been that they claimed that the faith was always the same, while introducing doctrinal innovations that were clearly secondary, late, and of questionable theological legitimacy (e.g., the immaculate conception and assumption of Mary; papal infallibility; penance and purgatory, etc.).

In response to this, the Reformers had a slogan of *sola scriptura* ("scripture alone") as the ultimate authority in the churches. Yet when the Reformers spoke of *sola scriptura*, they meant the Bible illuminated by the Spirit in the matrix of the church. *Sola scriptura* is not *nuda scriptura* ("the bare scripture"). The Protestant confessions are

---

71. Cyril of Jerusalem, *Catechetical Lectures* 5.12.
72. J. Todd Billings, *The Word of God for the People of God: An Entryway to the Theological Interpretation of Scripture* (Grand Rapid: Eerdmans, 2010), xiv.

indebted to the ecumenical councils and patristic theologies in every respect. Thus the Reformers' use of Scripture is more tantamount to *suprema scriptura*. This means that the Bible is our primary authority, but not our only authority.[73]

In the evangelical churches that esteem the gospel, the Word of God dominates their teaching and preaching. Scripture is the guarantee of the apostolicity of their message and the authorizer of their ministerial orders. The reading and teaching of Scripture in the church is what guides it back to its apostolic foundation and keeps it genuinely catholic. Yet all churches, even evangelical churches, approach Scripture through the grid of their own traditions and histories. Ultimately, what unites Christian canon and Christian tradition together is the testimony to Jesus Christ emitted in their discourse and the creative work of the Holy Spirit in binding both together.

At the end of the day, engaging with tradition is both unavoidable and necessary. Tradition is a lot like a nose. Everybody has one; even if you cannot see your own, it is still there. We all read Scripture in the context of a "tradition" of some kind even if we do so unconsciously at first. As A. N. S. Lane puts it: "It is impossible to read scripture without tradition, save in the rare examples of those with no prior contact with the Christian faith who pick up a portion of scripture. We bring to the Bible a pre-understanding of the Christian faith that we have received from others, thus by tradition."[74] Even while the pulpit-pounding fundamentalist may preach the authority of the text, in practice he appeals to the consensus of a community and its history of reading Scripture as the basis for his claims to apprehend biblical truth. If we assert that we believe the Bible, we must state somewhere what we think the Bible actually says. As soon as we say it, teach it, and write it down, we are creating a tradition. It is important to recognize that we are all shaped by traditions, and we are all likewise shapers of tradition to some degree or other.

We need to adopt what I call a *believing criticism* as a posture for evaluating tradition. The traditions embedded in the creeds, confessions, and liturgies of our churches should be afforded the opportunity to inform us as to what it means to believe in God and to worship God. Thereafter, we can assess them critically in light of Scripture so that they can be reinterpreted or corrected as required.

To sum up, we should read Scripture in light of tradition for several reasons. (1) We value the testimony of our forefathers in the faith who ran the race ahead of us and in some cases paid for it with their lives. We may not always agree with them, but we ignore them to our peril. (2) The New Testament itself is both a product of the church's tradition about Jesus and also generated a tradition as to how Scripture should be read and understood. (3) The *canon of scripture* is ultimately an expression of the *rule of faith*. (4) The Reformation slogan of *sola scriptura* does not mean only

---

73. Bloesch, *A Theology of Word and Spirit*, 193.
74. A. N. S. Lane, "Tradition," in *DTIB* (ed. K. J. Vanhoozer; Grand Rapids: Baker, 2005), 811.

Scripture, but calls for the primacy of Scripture in our theology. (5) Everybody has a tradition, whether they recognize it or not, and we should test our traditions to see if they are biblical and utilize our traditions to help us understand the Bible.

Tradition, therefore, is the *consultative norm* for theology. Ultimately, tradition is a tool for reading Scripture. Tradition is what the church has learned by reading Scripture. We should read Scripture in light of tradition, and in reflex we must test tradition against the grain of Scripture. In the end we are not slavishly bound by tradition, but we are foolish if we completely ignore it.

I am not calling for *traditionalism*, by which I mean the veneration of rituals, doctrines, and liturgies without submitting them to the test of Scripture, simply because they have always been there. I am advocating an approach to biblical interpretation that places Scripture and tradition in a continuous spiral of listening to the text and listening to our forefathers in the faith. As Jaroslav Pelikan put it: "Tradition is the living faith of the dead; traditionalism is the dead faith of the living."[75]

1.6.3 NATURE

The natural world has long been identified as a source of theology. The biblical materials provide evidence of what is called *natural revelation* or *general revelation*. That natural revelation is God's imprint of himself through the created order of things. Psalm 19 famously reads: "The heavens declare the glory of God; the skies proclaim the work of his hands. Day after day they pour forth speech; night after night they reveal knowledge" (Ps 19:1–2). Paul's speeches to Gentiles in Lystra (Acts 14:15–17) and at the Areopagus in Athens (17:22–32) indicate that God has universally made known his divine goodness and divine power to all of humanity through the created order. What is more, in Romans Paul writes: "what may be known about God is plain to them, because God has made it plain to them. For since the creation of the world God's invisible qualities—his eternal power and divine nature—have been clearly seen, being understood from what has been made, so that people are without excuse" (Rom 1:19–20).

Along these lines the Belgic Confession asks: How do we know God? It answers, first, "by the creation, preservation, and government of the universe, since that universe is before our eyes like a beautiful book in which all creatures, great and small, are as letters to make us ponder the invisible things of God: God's eternal power and his divinity, as the apostle Paul says in Romans 1:20."[76]

Theologians sometimes go so far as to speak of a "natural theology" derived from this natural revelation—a theology about the knowledge of God as he is known from human constitution, nature, and history. That includes knowledge that God

---

75. Pelikan, *The Christian Tradition*, 1:9.
76. Belgic Confession Art. 2. See the translation of the Christian Reformed Church in North America, www.crcna.org/welcome/beliefs/confessions/belgic-confession.

exists, that he is all-powerful, and that he is an intelligent designer, personal and relational. Frequently, natural theology is used to provide arguments for God's existence, such as the ontological (God is by definition a necessary being), cosmological (God is the cause of the universe), teleological (God is the designer of the universe), and moral (God is the origin of ethical obligations) arguments.[77] However, Romans 1:18–25 explicitly states that knowledge of God through creation is suppressed and denied by unregenerate persons, which means that it is sufficient to illuminate our minds for accountability but inadequate to impart a saving knowledge of God because humans suppress the truth in unrighteousness and exchange it for a lie.

Consequently, Calvin claimed that all human beings have a "sense of divinity" (*sensus divinitatis*), which results in the universal phenomena of religion, a troubled conscience, and a fear of God. They also have a sense of awe at the magnitude and design of the created order. But because of sin, they have an inability to respond appropriately to natural revelation—hence the need for special revelation. The basic idea for Calvin is that a knowledge of God as creator may be gained through experience and observation of nature with special revelation confirming, clarifying, and extending what may be known of God through nature.

There have been adverse reactions against the idea of a natural theology. Emil Brunner argued that natural theology was necessary in order to provide a starting point for the Holy Spirit to prepare for God's special revelation to come to us. Karl Barth responded that the Holy Spirit needs no point of contact with creation since God is entirely "other" than creation and does not need nature to make himself known. Faith is evoked by the Word of God and not by daffodils.

Reformed epistemologists like Alvin Plantinga have rejected natural theology on the grounds that it makes the success of theistic proofs necessary to believe in the existence of God. According to Plantinga, belief in God is not an evidentially derived belief but a properly basic belief as it is self-evident and incorrigible—humans are simply wired to believe in God wholly apart from rational proofs for his existence. To ground our belief in God on some other belief is to make the other belief the most epistemologically significant one. For Plantinga, a distinctively Christian approach is to affirm that belief in God is itself basic and does not require justification with reference to other beliefs. That said, Plantinga believes that there is a place for theistic arguments, but only as confirmations of our knowledge of God and not as the grounds of our knowledge of God.[78]

The other thing to remember is that appeal to nature is often a rhetorical argument. It was common in the nineteenth century to argue that certain things were

---

77. Cf. William Lane Craig, *Reasonable Faith: Christian Truth and Apologetics* (Wheaton, IL: Crossway, 1994), 77–125.
78. See Alvin Plantinga, "Two Dozen (or so) Theistic Arguments," in *Alvin Plantinga* (ed. Deane-Peter Baker; New York: Cambridge University Press, 2007), 203–27.

"in accordance with nature," ranging from capitalism, Marxism, democracy, patriarchy, feminism and a lot more. Nature has become a quasi authority. The very concept of "nature" is not neutral because "nature" is constructed differently by artists, scientists, explorers, tribal people, city folk, and so on.[79] For one person, the ocean may be a thing of peace and serenity; for others it is a thing of uncontrollable power and sheer terror. In other words, there is no universal and uniform definition of nature and how we relate to it. When discussing "natural theology," we must be careful not to use nature as an authority.

Nature, or more properly natural revelation, indeed has an important place in theology. Its significance will be felt especially in the particular areas of the doctrines of creation and humanity. The qualification we need to make is that sinful persons suppress the knowledge of God as it has been made known through creation, and the concept of "nature" as a thing is hardly neutral or self-evident. If natural revelation were so clear and effective, we would not need a special revelation through God's actions in history, in Jesus Christ, and in Scripture. Nature is a perhaps not so much a "source" for theology as it is an "inspiration" for theology. Therefore, I propose that nature is a *stimulus* for theology.

1.6.4 EXPERIENCE

"Experience" is a slippery term. It can mean the activation of our sensory receptors or a kind of inward illumination. When I refer to experience as a source of theology, I mean the acquisition of knowledge and relational intimacy through an encounter with the living God. I want to advocate that our encounter with God in prayer, worship, sacraments, Scripture, mission, and Christian fellowship provides a genuine source for theology.

That assertion is legitimated on several grounds. First, I would point out that one of the unifying elements in a New Testament theology is the common experience of the risen Lord in the life and worship of the New Testament authors.[80] Ben Witherington points out that in the New Testament,

> what we are dealing with ... is a group of people who had profound religious experiences that they interpreted as encounters with the living Lord—that is, with Jesus the Christ. To be sure, some of their leaders, such as Paul or the author of Hebrews or the Beloved Disciple, could match wits with many of the great minds of their age. But it was their religious experiences with Christ that they had in common. And it was their com-

---

79. Alister McGrath, *The Open Secret: A New Vision for Natural Theology* (Oxford: Blackwell, 2008), 115–39.

80. Cf. James D. G. Dunn, *Unity and Diversity in the New Testament* (2nd ed.; London: SCM, 1990), 174–202; Luke Timothy Johnson, *Religious Experience in Early Christianity* (Philadelphia: Fortress, 1998).

munities of worship and fellowship, which came into being because of these experiences, that provided the matrix for the reflection about the meaning of the Christ event.[81]

Second, doctrines themselves are built on particular experiences. The doctrines of grace only develop after we have experienced grace as an event.[82]

Third, certain experiences are even revelatory, such as visions, dreams, and gifts of knowledge when God sovereignly bestows them. All theological statements are undergirded by some kind of religious experience.

We must also recognize the real dangers in making experience a source of theology. The statement "I feel that God is telling me X" is open to all sorts of abuses. How do you actually know that? How do you distinguish between valid and invalid experiences? How do you test that a God-given experience has taken place as opposed to an interior psychological event in someone's life? What is the difference between a heartwarming experience of God's love during worship and a bit of heartburn from eating too much chili at the church potluck dinner? As such, religious experiences must be interpreted and authenticated in order to be a legitimate source for theology. Scripture and the wisdom of other Christians are two obvious criteria for evaluating experiences.

Religious experience genuinely informs our theology. You cannot write a doctrine of eschatology without being touched by the horror of death and the beauty of the new heavens. But experience can only be secondary and confirmatory, not primary and absolute. The primary contribution of experience is to inspire our descriptions of doctrine based on how it impacts us and to shape our imagination according to the pattern of God's glory. Therefore, religious experience, when consistent with Scripture, is a *validating norm* for theology. According to Peter Jensen: "Experience intimates, the gospel enlightens; the gospel interprets, experience confirms."[83] To put it in other words, experience is a bit like a practicum, a seminar, or a workshop where our theology is tested, screened, stretched, poked, and prodded. Our theology influences our experience, and in turn our theology is influenced by our experience.

1.6.5 WHAT ABOUT CULTURE?

Should we include culture as a source of theology? Theologians have always looked to the categories of culture for the concepts in which to express their understanding

---

81. Ben Witherington III, "Jesus as the Alpha and Omega of New Testament Thought," in *Contours of Christology in the New Testament* (ed. R. N. Longenecker; Grand Rapids: Eerdmans, 2005), 44–45.

82. On grace as an event, see Rudolf Bultmann, *Theology of the New Testament* (trans. K. Grobel; 2 vols.; London: SCM, 1952), 1:288–92.

83. Jensen, *Revelation of God*, 108. Cf. Stephen E. Fowl (*Engaging with Scripture* [Oxford: Blackwell, 1998], 114): "Experience of the Spirit shapes the reading of scripture, but scripture most often provides the lenses through which the Spirit's work is perceived and acted upon."

of the Christian faith. In order to fulfill our evangelistic mandate and to find some kind of relevance in our own context, we have to be both an interpreter of Scripture and an interpreter of culture. The community of faith forms its identity only in the context of a particular social location that makes use of language, symbols, stories, and worldviews in which they are immersed. Grenz comments: "The message of the action of God in Christ is concerned with the creation of a new identity, namely, the redeemed person participating in the reconciled society, enjoying fellowship with all creation and with the Creator."[84] Thus for Grenz, culture impacts the grammar of our theology and the social context in which its meanings are defined and applied.

There is a constellation of things to consider on the subject of theology and culture. While Grenz views culture as something that is fairly positive, there is a myriad of ways of defining culture and a spectrum of ways that Christian faith can be related to culture. During my undergraduate days I interviewed a theologian for an assignment, who told me in no uncertain terms that "culture is the devil's whore" because "culture is the attempt to create meaning and value without reference to God." Those were weighty words that I spent much time pondering.

H. Richard Niebuhr said that culture is the "artificial, secondary environment" that human subjects superimpose on the natural. Culture is comprised of language, habits, ideas, beliefs, customs, social organization, inherited artifacts, technical processes, and values. It was partly what the New Testament means by *kosmos* ("world"). So, what relationship does culture have to the church? Niebuhr identified five different models as to how Christians have related to culture over the centuries.[85]

1. *Christ against culture.* Allegiance to Christ's lordship means rejection of the values of the culture around us (e.g., 1 John 2:15). Here Christians are independent of the surrounding culture. For Christians of this type (e.g., Tertullian, Tolstoy, the Amish), history is the story of a rising church and a dying pagan civilization. This view results in separatism from the culture around us, which is not conducive to the fulfilling the Great Commission; it naively thinks that we are not affected by the culture around us and requires that in the incarnation Jesus adopted no culture at all.
2. *Christ of culture.* Christ is the highest aspiration of culture. Here persons interpret culture through Christ and esteem those elements of culture that are most congruent with Christ's teaching and person. In addition, they understand Christ through culture, selecting from the Christian doctrine about him such

---

84. Grenz, *Theology for the Community of God*, 19–20.
85. H. Richard Niebuhr, *Christ and Culture* (New York: Harper, 1951).

points as seem to agree with what is best in civilization. This leads to accomodationism as the attempt to show the parity of Christ with the values of the surrounding culture. Typically this results in a liberal-leaning theology, which erases the distinction between church and culture. For these cultural Christians, history is the story of the Spirit's encounter with the world and the absorption of the church into the world.

3. *Christ above culture.* On this viewpoint, what is needed is a synthesis of Christ and culture with the church in the world, but also beyond the world. God's grace is manifested in the church and in the culture around it. Good works are done in the culture that the church exists in and for the benefit of those in the culture. Only by grace can we love our neighbor, but we can only do that in the culture around us. The problem is that this approach can simply support the status quo and relativize what is absolute in Christian teaching.

4. *Christ and culture in paradox.* Although Christ and culture claim our allegiance, there is no way of synthesizing the two together. We must simply live with the dualistic tension of being a citizen of the world and a citizen of heaven.

5. *Christ transforming culture.* While culture can be a hostile thing, it is the duty of the Christian to try to transform the culture around them into conformity with the gospel. There is something to be said for Christians working to bring kingdom values and vision into the secular and even mundane areas of human existence. If the gospel can transform people, it can also transform places. The problem is that this can create a Christendom that is filled with cultural Christians. This amounts to imposing Christian values on people who are not Christians. In effect, Christians become the moral Taliban and become known for all the things that they are against. For instance, I once heard an American evangelist say that he wanted all of America converted, baptized, and enrolled to vote, with the emphasis on "vote"!

How we view culture will be much determined by where we find ourselves living. If we live in a culture that is Christian, nominally Christian, or post-Christian, we will be more inclined to view a positive relationship between the values of Christ and the values of culture. If, however, we live in a culture that is hostile to Christian values and beliefs—politically, religiously, or socially—we will be more inclined to define Christian values in opposition to the dominant culture around us. Yet we may not have to choose between entirely positive and entirely negative conceptions of culture. D. A. Carson writes:

> Instead of imagining that Christ *against* culture and Christ *transforming* culture are two mutually exclusive stances, the rich complexity of biblical norms, worked out in the Bible's story line, tells us that these two often operate simultaneously.... To pursue with passion the robust and nourishing wholeness of biblical theology as the

controlling matrix for our reflection on the relation between Christ and culture will, ironically, help us to be far more flexible than the inflexible grids that are often made to stand in the Bible's place. Scripture will mandate that we think holistically and subtly, wisely and penetratingly, under the Lordship of Christ—utterly dissatisfied with the anesthetic of culture.[86]

Can we do theology wholly apart from our culture? Absolutely not! Culture shapes our language, our heritage, and our frame of reference. It influences us, but hopefully that influence won't be total or received uncritically. Culture is also part of our mission field, and we have to translate doctrine into categories that Christians, who are themselves the product of their cultural context, can understand and be fruitful in. Rather than regard culture as a source of theology, culture is more of an embedded context in which theology takes place.

FURTHER READING

Allert, Craig D. *A High View of Scripture: The Authority of the Bible and the Formation of the New Testament Canon*. Grand Rapids: Baker, 2007.

Bird, Michael F. "From Manuscript to MP3." Pp. 1–18 in *The Sacred Text: Excavating the Texts, Exploring the Interpretations, and Engaging the Theologies of the Christian Scriptures*. Ed. M. Bird and M. Pahl. Piscataway, NJ: Gorgias, 2010.

Grenz, Stanley E. *Theology for the Community of God*. Grand Rapids: Eerdmans, 1994, pp. 16–20.

McGrath, Alister E. *Christian Theology: An Introduction*. 3rd ed. Oxford: Blackwell, 2001, pp. 159–99.

Williams, D. H. *Evangelicals and Tradition: The Formative Influence of the Early Church*. Grand Rapids: Baker, 2005.

———. *Retrieving Tradition and Renewing Evangelicalism: A Primer for Suspicious Protestants*. Grand Rapids: Eerdmans, 1999.

---

[86]. D.A. Carson, *Christ and Culture Revisited* (Grand Rapids: Eerdmans, 2008), 227 (italics original).

§ 1.7 TOWARD A GOSPEL-DRIVEN THEOLOGICAL METHOD

Methodology is a genuinely important element of Christian theology. Methodology is a net, and it catches what it is made to catch. *How* you decide to do theology will inevitably impact *what kind* of theology that you come up with. I have already stated the crucial importance of setting out the evangel as the starting point for an evangelical theology. So we begin with the gospel in order to make sure that our theology is utterly pervaded and distinctly defined by the good news of Jesus Christ. I have some suggestions on how to perform a gospel-driven theology, and I intend to unpack that below. But before I do that, we must look at what is for many evangelicals their default way of constructing theology.

1.7.1 NAIVE BIBLICISM

I lament that most evangelical Christians have a theological method that amounts to a type of naive biblicism. That is, the way that many evangelicals do theology is basically the same way that a butcher makes a sausage. In fact, I would label their method the "Theological Sausage Maker 3000."

Instructions for Theological Sausage Maker 3000
1. Put Bible into Theological Sausage Maker
2. Turn handle of sausage maker grinding Bible into propositions
3. Out comes pristine and pure theological doctrine
4. Eat with Catholic Carrots or Protestant Peas as preferred

The problem here is the assumption that all you need for theology is the Bible, and all you want to get out of theology is creating propositions to be affirmed.

First, with respect to what you need in order to create a theology, I have already demonstrated that the Scriptures are the single most important source for theology, but they cannot be the only source. We should also accept natural revelation, tradition, experience, and even to a degree culture as dialogue partners for theology.

In what is in many respects a fine theology textbook, Wayne Grudem's *Systematic Theology* espouses a theological method that epitomizes the concerns I have about the dangers of biblicism. Grudem describes his theological method as follows: (1) find all relevant verses with a concordance; (2) summarize points made in each verse; (3) summarize all the verses together by making one or two points of what is affirmed; and (4) find a way to harmonize the passages that do not fit your summarizing statement.[87]

Grudem's approach is robustly biblical, which is both its strength and weakness. It is rooted in Scripture, but it is reduced to a theology derived from a concordance.[88] The canonical, hermeneutical, cultural, and historical factors simply do not figure in it. For example, Grudem rejects divine impassibility since the Bible says that God has emotions.[89] But this glosses over all too easily centuries of theological debate that concluded that God does not have "passions" (i.e., emotions) in the same way that human beings do.

We can consider here the idea of divine suffering as an example. Christian theology has traditionally maintained that during the incarnation, God the Son suffered in his human nature but not in his divine nature. There is a reason for this. Divine passibility (i.e., the notion that God suffers) compromises divine perfection and divine immutability. Divine immutability is not the depiction of a God who is unrelational, cold, removed, and distant from human experiences; rather, divine immutability is the grounds for the constancy of his love and the basis for his unwavering faithfulness. That is the position of historic Christian orthodoxy. Thus, the "Bible and me" approach to theology is the recipe for a theology that is somewhat naive and lacking in depth. There is a "cloud of witnesses" from other theological subdisciplines that need to be heard in the conversation.

Second, with respect to what we want to get out of theology, it is far more

---

87. Grudem, *Systematic Theology*, 35–37.

88. Vanhoozer ("The Voice and the Actor," 62–63) writes: "If theology is to be more than a rag-bag collection, it must demonstrate the deeper connections *among* x, y, and z. Theologians need not begin from scratch every time they confront a new problem.... Moreover, is it really the case that one can come to an appropriately theological understanding of birth control and gun control [examples Grudem uses] by exegeting the relevant portions of Scripture? Studying biblical words and concepts takes us only so far. It is one thing to know how a biblical author spoke or thought about a particular issue in the context of ancient Israel or the early church, quite another to relate those words and thoughts about a particular issue to the message of the Bible as a whole and to the significance of the Bible's teaching for us today." For similar concerns, see Kevin Giles, *The Eternal Generation of the Son: Maintaining Orthodoxy in Trinitarian Theology* (Downers Grove, IL: InterVarsity Press, 2012), 38–62; Williams, "Systematic Theology as a Biblical Discipline," 208–9.

89. Grudem, *Systematic Theology*, 165–66.

than a list of theological propositions for our assent. Yet some theologians talk as if God did us a disfavor by giving us the Bible in the form that we have it. Because of the variegated shape of Scripture, one has to reorganize the Bible into a list of propositions to be affirmed. One theologian goes so far as to state: "The Bible is to the theologian what nature is to the scientist, a body of unorganized or only partly organized facts. God has not seen fit to write the Bible in the form of a systematic theology; it remains for us, therefore, to gather together the scattered facts and to build them up into a logical system."[90] I submit that this depicts God like some kind of messy teenager incapable of writing a coherent term paper and it is the theologian's job to bring order to it.

But perhaps Scripture is given in the form exactly as God intended it and given in the form that will have the maximal impact on God's people. Perhaps also the goal of theology is not simply drawing up a list of propositions, but for us to engage in a performance of the divine drama and to experience the transformation of our imaginations so that we can know God better. Consider the comments of Kevin Vanhoozer:

> Once upon a time, if asked what in the New Testament was authoritative, I would have replied, "Revelation." (On this point, Thomists, evangelicals, and Barthians all agree, though they parse "revelation" differently.) Theology's task, I thought, was the extraction of propositional revelation or truth from Scripture and its consequent organization into a consistent conceptual system. Two pictures—one of Scripture as revelation and one of theology as a two-stage process, from descriptive exegesis ("what it meant") to a normative dogmatics ("what it means")—held me captive. Scripture is not simply a propositional shaft to be exegetically mined and theologically refined like so much textual dross to be purified into systems of philosophy or morality. On the contrary, both the form and content of the New Testament are elements in the divine drama of revelation and redemption.[91]

I concur with Vanhoozer. Some theologians have drunk at the well of rationalism and proceed in the theological task as if God, by either folly or weakness, mistakenly gave us revelation in the most confusing mass of genres: law code, narrative, prophecy, proverbs, gospels, epistles, and an apocalypse. Our task is to navigate our way around this unfortunate circumstance by translating this revelation through various genres into propositional statements of truths to be believed. However, an evangelical theology should take into account not only the propositional content of *what* God says in Scripture, but also *how* God has revealed himself in Scripture.

---

90. Henry C. Thiessen, *Lectures in Systematic Theology* (Grand Rapids: Eerdmans, 1977 [1949]), 5.

91. Kevin J. Vanhoozer, "The Apostolic Discourse and Its Developments," in *Scripture's Doctrine and Theology's Bible: How the New Testament Shapes Christian Dogmatics* (ed. M. Bockmuehl and A.J. Torrance; Grand Rapids: Baker, 2008), 193–92.

In other words, the content and genre of revelation are equally important in our analysis of the divine revelation.

On top of that, it is not the formation of doctrinal statements that we are to be exclusively concerned with in theology. A propositional content to theology follows on from the nature of the gospel since it is based on the apostolic testimony to what they "have seen and heard," where truth claims about Jesus and God are asserted (Acts 4:20; 1 John 1:1–3).[92] But it is not only facts and propositions that are to keep our attention. The goal of our instruction is to know God better, which involves renewing the heart and transforming the mind in conformity to Christ.

Note that John Calvin did not call his theology textbook the *Institutes of Christian Theology*; rather, he called it *Institutes of the Christian Religion*. In our time we tend to think of religion as cold rituals, stale beliefs, outdated practices, and even hypocrisy. Yet for Calvin *religion* was a positive word that denoted piety, prayer, service, devotion, and love. The chief end of theology is not the accumulation of theological propositions. Instead, it is equipping of the hands to serve, the warming of the heart to love, and the arming of the mind to engage. Let us then celebrate the "various ways" (Heb 1:1) that Scripture speaks to us in all its genres. Let us learn in "knowledge and depth of insight," so that we might "discern what is best," be "pure and blameless for the day of Christ," and be "filled with the fruit of righteousness" (Phil 1:9–11).

An evangelical theology should not be naively biblicist. We take Scripture with the utmost seriousness, but we do Scripture a disservice if we attend only to it. It is Scripture understood in light of the *regula fidei* that will enable us to bring together the Christian canon and the Christian community in a fruitful exchange. Similarly, we need to believe propositions about God, but our theology is about more than propositions, for it encompasses our relationship with God, our mission in the world, and our performance of the drama that we find ourselves in as Christians.

1.7.2 A GOSPEL-DRIVEN THEOLOGY

There are different ways to skin a fish and different ways to do theology. There is *apologetic theology*, which proceeds by answering questions that present themselves for answer. Thomas Aquinas pursued this path in his *Summa Theologica*, where each subject area is prefaced with several questions, such as "Whether God is the efficient cause of all things?" and is followed by a series of objections and counter-objections. In the apologetic theology of Paul Tillich, the symbols of Christian revelation were to be employed to answer the questions of human existence posed by existential philosophy. Whereas the philosopher generates questions, it is the task of the theo-

---

92. Vanhoozer, *Drama of Doctrine*, 88–91.

logian to try to answer them. That answer is derived from the Bible, church history, history of religions, and culture.

Then there is *dialectic theology*. Key exponents were Karl Barth, Rudolf Bultmann, and Emil Brunner, who emphasized the infinite tensions, paradoxes, and basic ambiguities inherent in Christian faith. It is from the tension of seemingly paradoxical positions, such as how the Jesus of history can be the Son of God of eternity, that one finds angst and then an answer.

There is the *Wesleyan Quadrilateral*, built on the practices and theology of John Wesley.[93] "Wesley believed that the living core of the Christian faith was revealed in scripture, illumined by tradition, vivified in personal experience, and confirmed by reason. Scripture [however] is primary, revealing the Word of God 'so far as it is necessary for our salvation.'"[94] The Wesleyan Quadrilateral is more of a framework than a method, but it has been influential especially in Anglican and Methodist circles.

Discussions on method could go on forever. Discussing method is a bit like clearing your throat before a speech. You can only do it for so long before the audience gets bored. So I will jump into how I think an evangelical theology should be done.

1. *Define the gospel.* The first task in theology, one we have already undertaken in §1.3, is to define the gospel. This establishes the foundation and integrating theme for all the theological discussion that follows.
2. *Identify the relationship of the various loci to the gospel.* The traditional loci of systematic theology are God, the person and work of Christ, salvation, the person and work of the Holy Spirit, humanity, the church, and the last things. In each case, all of these subfields can be ordered and related to the gospel. The starting point for the discussion of each of the loci is to situate it in proximity to the gospel. For instance, what does the gospel say about Christology, and how does Christology illuminate the gospel? The gospel provides a framework through which the various subjects of theology are explored.
3. *Embark on a creative dialogue between the sources of theology.* The primacy of Scripture will be foremost in an evangelical theology. We are interested in what God has said, how he has said it, and what effect his message was intended to have. In combination with that, it is also necessary to explore natural revelation and tradition, and even to reflect on our experience as we investigate specific topics. In most cases it is logical to start with Scripture, as in the case of the nature of God. In other instances, it might be better to start with creeds

---

93. The term "Wesleyan Quadrilateral" was first coined by Albert Outler's introduction, *John Wesley* (New York: Oxford University Press, 1964). Though whether this is the best way to actually describe Wesley's theological method is a point of recent debate among Methodist theologians.

94. *The Book of Discipline of the United Methodist Church* (Nashville: Abingdon, 2004), 77.

> ### COMIC BELIEF
>
> Karl Barth, Emil Brunner, and Rudolf Bultmann were out fishing one morning. As it got hotter, Barth left the boat, walked across the water, grabbed some cool drinks, and walked back across the water and into the boat. A few hours later, everyone was hot and thirsty again, so Brunner got out of the boat, walked across the water, grabbed some drinks, and came back. A few hours later they were sweating pretty heavily, and Bultmann was looking more and more nervous. Barth said, "Come on. Emmy and I got the drinks once already. Now it's your turn." Bultmann nervously got out of the boat and went straight into the water. As he was thrashing about trying to get back into the boat Brunner whispered to Barth, "Do you think we should have told him where the stepping stones were?" Barth replied, "What stepping stones?"

and confessions and work our way back to Scripture when dealing with a subject like the Trinity. The dialogue between the sources of theology is a bit like dancing. Different partners lead in different dances. Sometimes the dance calls for specific steps to be performed, sometimes there is a great amount of freedom in which direction you can move. The challenge is to be careful and comprehensive in our analysis of the sources and in the way we synthesize them together.

4. *Describe what the loci look like when appropriated and applied in light of the gospel.* There is a simple question that every theologian must learn to ask after their study: So what? What does this matter? What difference does it make? What is the significance of this or that? Theology is not simply to be believed; it is something that we are to live. Theology is about engaging with the biblical script that Christians are to perform in their daily lives. We must deliberately concern ourselves with what happens when the rubber of doctrine finally hits the road of real life.

5. Although practical theology is a legitimate discipline in its own right, systematic theology must ask itself the question as to what array of behaviors, activities, applications, and consequences follow on from its findings. Let me emphasize as well that this is not a static one-off event. The move between theology and practice is a continuous cycle. We learn things about God, Christ, or the church, and then we apply them. In the application we learn more, think things over, act it out, and pray about it, and from that we come

up with more questions, fresh convictions, and innovative proposals. So we go back to Scripture, listen to our traditions and teachers, and do some more theology. Thereafter, we go back again into applying what we have learned, and the same thing happens all over again. New questions arise, our beliefs are reshaped, and we try pioneering some new things. The spiral between theology and practice must continue if we are to grow as theologians and ministers of the gospel. What I am offering in this book is not the final and definitive application for each subject area. This volume is simply the first steps toward thinking aloud about how we perform the divine drama in the communities of faith that we find ourselves in.

FURTHER READING

Clark, David K. *To Know and Love God: Method for Theology.* Wheaton, IL: Crossway, 2000.

Stackhouse, John G., ed. *Evangelical Futures: A Conversation on Theological Method.* Grand Rapids: Baker, 2000.

Thorsen, Donald A. *The Wesleyan Quadrilateral: Scripture, Tradition, Reason, and Experience as a Model for Evangelical Theology.* Lexington, KY: Emeth, 1990.

§1.8 A FINAL WORD

Before we undertake a study of theology, one final caveat is needed. Paul says in 1 Corinthians 8:1 that "knowledge puffs up while love builds up." In the gospel of John, Jesus indicts the scribes: "You study the Scriptures diligently because you think that in them you have eternal life. These are the very Scriptures that testify about me, yet you refuse to come to me to have life" (John 5:39–40). The pursuit of theological knowledge is necessary and valuable for individuals and churches. I hope that is clear. However, theology can promote arrogance and disunity when it is disengaged from love for God and love for others. Theology is not a substitute for faith or an excuse for failing to cultivate the fruit of the Spirit. The task of theology demands humility and charity by its practitioners, or else we become living parables of hypocrisy and liable to judgment (see Jas 3:1).

To be worthy of the name "Christian," a Christian theology must bring us closer to Christ and draw us into Christlikeness. Theology should drive believers into a deeper commitment to *orthodoxy* ("right belief"). Theology ideally equips believers to properly apply their faith in life and ministry as *orthopraxy* ("right practice"). Finally, theology should also foster godliness and Christlikeness as *orthokardia* ("right heartedness"). Therefore, I leave you, young theologians, with the words of Mark Allan Powell to contemplate.

> We cannot have a relationship with our *Christology*, but we can have a relationship with our Christ.
> Our *soteriology* cannot save us from our sins, but our Savior can.
> And no matter how much we love *theology*—it will never love us back.[95]
>
> In view of that, let the gospelizing begin in earnest!

---

95. Mark Allan Powell, *Loving Jesus* (Minneapolis: Fortress, 2004), 52 (italics original).

WHAT TO TAKE HOME?

- Theology is the study of the living God undertaken in communion with God and in the context of the community of faith.
- Prolegomena is a pretheology: theology that clears the deck on issues like the method, sources, and the purpose of theology. Our prolegomena stated here is to identify the gospel as the beginning, center, and boundary of evangelical theology.
- The gospel is the announcement that God's kingdom has come through the life, death, and resurrection of Jesus Christ.
- The goal of theology is know God better and to have a faith seeking understanding.
- Theology is necessary for believers to articulate and live out a Christian worldview. Theology is possible because there is a single composer behind the symphony of Scripture.
- The sources for theology are Scripture as the ultimate norm, tradition as the consultative norm, nature as the stimulus, and experience as the validating norm, with culture as the embedded context of theology.
- Evangelicals should not engage in a naive biblicism and do theology armed with nothing more than a concordance. Rather, we view doctrine through a gospel lens, we organize the topics around the gospel, and we thereafter engage in a dramatic interplay between tradition and Scripture as we seek to know the Triune God.

STUDY QUESTIONS FOR INDIVIDUALS AND GROUPS

1. Why are you reading a theology book or taking a theology course?
2. How would you generally characterize your own view or your church's view about the value of theology?
3. Before reading this part, where did you think theology should start?
4. Define in your own words what the "gospel" is.
5. In what way should the gospel shape evangelical theology? Do you think that theology should be built around an alternative theme (e.g., God's covenants, God's sovereignty, kingdom of God)?
6. How do you think theology will impact your discipleship, ministry, and beliefs?
7. How would you describe the role of Scripture, tradition, experience, and culture as sources for theology?
8. Is it possible to do good evangelical theology armed with nothing more than a Bible and a concordance? Why or why not?
9. What can you do to maintain humility as you learn theology?

PART TWO

The God of the Gospel: The Triune God in Being and Action

Part Two • The God of the Gospel: The Triune God in Being and Action

§2.1 God and the Gospel
§2.2 Getting an Affinity for the Trinity
§2.3 What Is God Like?
§2.4 The God Who Creates
§2.5 The God Who Reveals Himself
§2.6 God's Purpose and Plan

The doctrine of God is "theology proper" and concerns the person and purposes of God. Since the gospel is fundamentally the "gospel of God," any theology must be theocentric and seek to understand God as he has made himself known in the gospel of Jesus Christ. To that end, the first point of call is to briefly outline the doctrine of the Trinity, its basis in Scripture and tradition, and explore its meaning and relevance. Thereafter, the subsequent units proceed to describe the various attributes of God and to identify God as the God who creates and reveals. Finally, attention is given to God's purpose and plan as he has made it known to his people.

> The ultimate good of the gospel is seeing and savoring the beauty and value of God. God's wrath and our sin obstruct that vision and that pleasure. You can't see and savor God as supremely satisfying while you are full of rebellion against Him and He is full of wrath against you. The removal of this wrath and this rebellion is what the gospel is for. The ultimate aim of the gospel is the display of God's glory and the removal of every obstacle to our seeing it and savoring it as our highest treasure. "Behold Your God!" is the most gracious command and the best gift of the gospel. If we do not see Him and savor Him as our greatest fortune, we have not obeyed or believed the gospel.[1]

> For who is the Lord except our Lord?
> Who is God except our God?
> The highest.
> The most good.
> The most mighty.
> The most omnipotent.
> The most merciful, yet most just.
> The most hidden, yet the most present.
> The most beautiful, yet the strongest.[2]
>
> And they were calling to one another:
> "Holy, holy, holy is the Lord Almighty;
>   the whole earth is full of his glory."[3]

---

1. John Piper, *God Is the Gospel: Meditations on God's Love as the Gift of Himself* (Wheaton, IL: Crossway, 2005), 56.
2. Augustine, *The Confessions of Saint Augustine: Modern English Version* (Grand Rapids: Baker, 2005), 1.
3. Isaiah 6:3.

§ 2.1 GOD AND THE GOSPEL

In the New Testament the gospel is often described as the "gospel of God" (Rom 1:1; 15:16; 2 Cor 11:7; 1 Thess 2:8–9; 1 Pet 4:17). The meaning of that phrase is, I think, deliberately ambiguous. The gospel is both *from* God and also *about* God. The gospel is God revealing the mystery of himself to his people. In the gospel, God himself draws the curtain back so we see into the mysterious things of God: his person, perfections, power, and plan. The events of the gospel—Jesus' birth, his life, his cross, his empty tomb, his ascension, and even Pentecost—reveal the Triune God.

The gospel tells us not only what God has done for our salvation and how he has done it in Christ and through the Spirit; the gospel also tells us something about God's being and his attributes, actions, plan, and purpose. All Christian theology, all God-talk, and everything we infer of things divine, is really an attempt to work backward from the revealing and redeeming action of God as declared in the gospel. The gospel constitutes our window into the inner being, the divine work, and eternal plan of God, wherein our attention lies. As John Webster states: "The matter to which Christian theology is commanded to attend, and by which it is directed in all its operations, is the presence of the perfect God as it is announced in the gospel."[4] Thus, an evangelical theology is really a mix of extrapolation and exposition of the gospel of God. Such a study of a God-shaped gospel will magnetically draw us toward a study of God's triune nature, his manifold attributes, his creative and revealing works, as well as his ultimate purposes.

First, *the gospel draws us into the mysterious reality of God's triune being*. If we are going to study the God of the gospel, we must study God as he is to us in the gospel: a triune being comprised of Father, Son, and Holy Spirit. In fact, I contend that the gospel itself establishes our primary contact with the doctrine of the Trinity. The operation of God as he is described as acting in the gospel intimates the triune nature of God. Only a triune God can do what is done in the gospel. Think about

---

4. John Webster, *Confessing God: Essays in Christian Dogmatics II* (London: T&T Clark, 2005),

what actually happens in the events narrated in the gospel. The different persons of the Godhead each perform significant roles in executing the divine plan to bring salvation to the world. God the Father sends the Son, the Son ministers in the power of the Spirit, the Father hands him over to the cross, the Father by the Spirit raises the Son up, after his ascension the Father and the Son dispense the Spirit to the church, and the Spirit gives glory to the Father and the Son.

The sequence of events described in the gospel is the work of Father, Son, and Holy Spirit. This is hardly my own discovery. Consider this statement from the *Martyrdom of Polycarp* 22.1: "We wish you well, brothers and sisters, while you walk according to the doctrine of the gospel of *Jesus Christ*; with whom be glory to God the *Father* and the *Holy Spirit*, for the salvation of His holy elect." The early church recognized that the saving event announced in the gospel was the combined and unified effort of all three members of the Godhead. The Father chooses, the Son redeems, and the Spirit sanctifies. Indeed, apart from a triune God, the gospel does not make a lot of sense. Walter Kasper was right to say that the Trinity is "the summation of the entire Christian mystery of salvation and, at the same time, its grammar."[5]

Second, *the gospel provides the best means to answer the question: What is God like?* For in the gospel, God's character and qualities are on display. We learn about the severity of God's judgment and the depth of divine grace and even more. Consequently the gospel is the surest place to sample the many attributes of God. From God's glory to his grace, from his benevolence to his beauty, the gospel enables us to describe God as much as it leads us to ascribe praise to God.

Third, *the gospel is a story about Jesus set within a larger story of creation, redemption, and new creation.* The gospel is like an act within a play, a sequential and logical element of a continuous narrative. The gospel presupposes previous divine acts such as God's actions in the creation of the world and God's revelation of himself to Israel. The gospel is not an abrupt breakaway from those prior scenes, like some kind of theatre of the absurd, where plots and characters are deliberately disjointed. God's prior work of creation establishes a worldview in which the gospel makes sense and God's prior revelation of himself provides the narrative in which the gospel, with its central actor Jesus, enters onto the stage. Viewed this way, the gospel requires us to investigate God as both creator and revealer since the gospel points to a God who made the world and who has been laying out his plan to put this world to rights.

Fourth, *like all stories there is an ultimate aim, and like all stories there is an underlying unity.* The gospel momentarily gives us insight into what God's final objective is, what holds his plan together, and what goal the divine mind has in store by sending his Son and by one day raising up the children of the resurrection. In the gospel,

---

5. Walter Kasper, *The God of Jesus Christ* (trans. J. J. O'Connell; New York: Crossroads, 1986), 311.

the mystery of the ages is revealed to be how the one true God, in his only Son, has effected his ultimate purpose to bring glory to himself by the effusion of his holy love in uniting the world with the Logos. In such a manner as this, the gospel of God's glory leads us to contemplate the moment when we, the church, will be to the praise of his glorious grace.

In sum, to study the God of the gospel—the God who handed over his Son, who raised him up again, and who sent his Spirit into our hearts—is to be propelled toward the study of God's triune being, his divine attributes, his actions of creation and revelation, as well the divine purpose and plan for all things. In the gospel we do not find a catalogue of human religious sentiments offered up for our perusal, no buffet of philosophical theories for us to snack on. In the gospel there is no unearthing of relics and ritual to ponder like broken pottery pieces from a dead civilization, nor are we offered merely modern mantras promising nice things for nice people. To the contrary, the gospel offers us much more, something much better than anyone could envision: the gospel is the offer of God himself. For in the gospel, God is the giver and gift all at once, a gift of life and love that comes by sharing in the life and love that is in his Son. This is the God of the gospel, the God who commands the attention of our intellects, the God who pushes the boundaries of our imagination, the God who stimulates our creative energies in art and music and literature, and the only God worthy of singing or studying about.

FURTHER READING

Bloesch, Donald. *God the Almighty: Power, Wisdom, Holiness, Love.* Downers Grove, IL: InterVarsity Press, 1995.

Bray, Gerald. *The Doctrine of God.* Downers Grove, IL: InterVarsity Press, 1993.

Frame, John. *The Doctrine of God.* Philadelphia, NJ: Presbyterian & Reformed, 2002.

Piper, John. *God Is the Gospel: Meditations on God's Love as the Gift of Himself.* Wheaton, IL: Crossway, 2005.

§ 2.2 GETTING AN AFFINITY FOR THE TRINITY

The God we are confronted with in the gospel is the Triune God. The gospel and the Trinity are internally configured toward each other because the saving acts of God point to a God who exists as Father, Son, and Holy Spirit. The salvation that the gospel promises portrays the Father as choosing, Christ as redeeming, and the Spirit as renewing—all in a unified work by distinct persons in a single Godhead. As Kevin Vahoozer puts it: "The very logic of the gospel—the declaration that God enables believers to relate to God the Father in Jesus Christ through the Spirit— implies the divinity of the Son and Spirit as well."[6] Vanhoozer rightly claims that the "integrity of the gospel is fatally compromised if either the Son or the Spirit is not fully God. If the Son were not God, he could neither reveal the Father nor atone for our sin. If the Spirit were not God, he could unite us neither to the Father and Son nor one another. The gospel, then, requires a triune God."[7]

What is more, the Trinity is not an esoteric doctrine forged in an unholy marriage of Greek metaphysical speculation and dodgy biblical interpretation. Rather, to experience the salvific blessings of the gospel is to be immersed in a Trinitarian reality. The gospel invites us to faith, a faith where we call God our Father, Christ our brother, and the Spirit our comforter. Our experience of God in gospel, prayer, and worship is not unitarian or tritheistic, but authentically Trinitarian. The Trinity is a corollary of our gospel experience[8]—so much so that Fred Sanders is correct that Christians "as gospel people are by definition Trinity people."[9]

If the gospel is the anchor point for our study of God, we must start with the Trinity. We do not commence theology with apologetic arguments and theistic

---

6. Kevin J. Vanhoozer, "The Triune God of the Gospel," in *The Cambridge Companion to Evangelical Theology* (ed. T. Larsen and D. J. Treier; Cambridge: Cambridge University Press, 2007), 17.

7. Kevin J. Vanhoozer, *Drama of Doctrine: A Canonical Linguistic Approach to Christian Theology* (Louisville: Westminster John Knox, 2005), 43.

8. Cf. further Fred Sanders, *The Deep Things of God: How the Trinity Changes Everything* (Wheaton, IL: Crossway, 2010), 1–26.

9. Ibid., 10.

§ 2.2 Getting an Affinity for the Trinity

> **SOME COMIC BELIEF**
>
> What is the Trinity?
> a. The name of the lead female character in the Matrix movie triology.
> b. Something only Catholics believe in.
> c. The name of several girls-only Episcopal Colleges.
> d. All of the above.

proofs that seemingly prove God's existence since we are not going to let skeptics set the agenda for the order of our study. We do not open our theological project with bibliology or a doctrine of Scripture since that would make reasoning from Scripture our foundation, whereas the foundation for our knowledge of God is God himself as revealed in the gospel.[10] Theology is about God; therefore, we must begin with the person of God as we encounter him in the gospel through his operations as Father, Son, and Holy Spirit.[11]

The Trinity is hard to understand, and people struggle with its meaning and its relevance, so much so that Tertullian wrote:

---

10. Whereas the medieval theological tradition began with the Triune God as the starting point for theology, it was the Second Helvetic Confession (followed by the Irish Articles and Westminster Confession) that broke the mold by putting the doctrine of Scripture first in the order of topics covered in theology. This Protestant move is understandable, opposing as it does the medieval Roman Catholic view of authority; yet it was a misstep that ultimately led to a shift from theology beginning with God-in-himself to theology beginning with human reception/perception of revelation. It was inevitable that Protestant theology, in some quarters, would move from theology to anthropology as the measure of religious truth.

11. In support of my thesis about putting the doctrine of God ahead of the doctrine of Scripture, note the superb commentary by D. A. Carson and Tim Keller (*Gospel-Centered Ministry* [Wheaton, IL: Crossway, 2011], 6), which I quote *in extenso*: "We also thought it was important to begin our confession with God rather than with Scripture. This is significant. The Enlightenment was overconfident about human rationality. Some strands of it assumed it was possible to build systems of thought on unassailable foundations that could be absolutely certain to unaided human reason. Despite their frequent vilification of the Enlightenment, many conservative evangelicals have nevertheless been shaped by it. This can be seen in how many evangelical statements of faith start with the Scripture, not with God. They proceed from Scripture to doctrine through rigorous exegesis in order to build (what they consider) an absolutely sure, guaranteed-true-to-Scripture theology. The problem is that this is essentially a foundationalist approach to knowledge. It ignores the degree to which our cultural location affects our interpretation of the Bible, and it assumes a very rigid subject-object distinction. It ignores historical theology, philosophy, and cultural reflection. Starting with the Scripture leads readers to the overconfidence that their exegesis of biblical texts has produced a system of perfect doctrinal truth. This can create pride and rigidity because it may not sufficiently acknowledge the fallenness of human reason. We believe it is best to start with God, to declare (with John Calvin, *Institutes* 1.1) that without knowledge of God we cannot know ourselves, our world, or anything else. If there is no God, we would have no reason to trust our reason." On the place of a doctrine of Scripture in systematic theology, see John Webster, *Holy Scripture: A Dogmatic Sketch* (Cambridge: Cambridge University Press, 2003), 12; Timothy Ward, *Words of Life: Scripture as the Living and Active Word of God* (Nottingham, UK: Apollos, 2009), 11–18; Andrew T. B. McGowan, *Divine Spiration of Scripture* (Nottingham, UK: Apollos, 2007), 26.

> The simple, (indeed, I will not call them unwise and unlearned), who always constitute the majority of believers, are startled at the dispensation [of the Three], on the ground that the very rule of faith withdraws them from the world's plurality of gods to the one only true God. They do not understand that although he is the one only God, he must yet be believed in with his own order of things.[12]

You can understand why the "simple" (the ancient equivalent of seminary students, I'm guessing) preferred just one God with one person over one God with three persons — it's easier! After all, doesn't the Apostles' Creed begin, "I believe in one God, the Father Almighty the maker of heaven and earth"?

The Trinity is a misunderstood doctrine. Even worse, many Christians make no attempt to even try to understand it. That is a travesty because the Trinity is arguably the most distinctive doctrine of Christianity as it distinguishes Christianity from other monotheistic faiths like Islam and Judaism. I remember once talking about the Trinity to some students; afterward one student approached me and made a rather troubling statement: "I didn't think we believed in that Catholic stuff about the Trinity." To which I responded that we most certainly did! The student's objection to the Trinity was rooted in a particular logic: Catholics believe in the Trinity; Catholics are bad; therefore, we do not believe in the Trinity. Unfortunately the (il)logic of this order is not uncommon. It is based on an ignorance and prejudice against the traditions of the ancient church.

If ignorance of our theological heritage is bad enough, I sometimes encounter another objection in that some students simply do not see what the point of the Trinity even is. They cannot perceive any possible application, relevance, or significance that the doctrine of the Trinity might have for them. As such, they consign the doctrine of the Trinity to the theater of intellectual gymnastics. Dorothy Sayers poignantly summarized what many Christians believe about the Trinity: "The Father incomprehensible, the Son incomprehensible, and the whole thing incomprehensible. Something put in by theologians to make it more difficult—nothing to do with daily life or ethics."[13] Inevitably, every year I usually have an argument with a student about the Trinity that goes something like this:

> Student: "Hey, Professor Egghead, why do you have to make it so darned complicated? There's one God, Jesus and the Father are God, stuff the math, that's good enough for me. It's good enough for Pastor Bob at my church who never preaches on the Trinity. It's good enough for my youth leader who cannot even spell 'Trinity.' It is good enough for my cell group and even for my dog Frodo — we just don't care,

---

12. Tertullian, *Prax.* 3.
13. Dorothy L. Sayers, "The Dogma is in the Drama," in *The Whimsical Christian: 18 Essays by Dorothy L. Sayers* (New York: Collier, 1987), 25.

so just gimme Jesus. And while you're at it, nerd-boy, stop messing with me and getting all up in my business with this Trinity tripe. I mean, really, who worries about what the Logos is—hello—the last time I checked the Logos was a missionary boat! And what's up with this homooiousoiousness, the third century Council of 'No-flipping-idea,' and a list of dead guys like Nectarines, Eutickme, and Apillowatmyplace? I mean, how is that gonna turn me into a mega-church pastor?"

Lecturer: "Well, then, my happy lil'o'heretic, how do you affirm the divinity of Father, Son, and Spirit without being a tritheist (with three gods) or a modalist (a single god with three masks)?"

Student: "I don't know, but this is way too complicated to be of any use."

Lecturer: "Or maybe it is a mystery that has many profound and important implications that you just do not know yet because you have not bothered trying to grapple with it!"

Student: "Well ... um ... I guess ... maybe you're right.

Lecturer: "Darn tootin I'm right, my young padawan!"

At the end of the day, if we are going to try to know God better, we have to learn about the Trinity. We have to delve into how the church has explained who God is in light of its Scriptures and through its controversies and creeds. Only when we know who God is can we properly pray to him, worship him, proclaim him, imitate him, and serve him! This isn't easy. It means trying to penetrate into what is an impenetrable mystery, catching a glance of it, and being left in wonder. It will take patience and hard work. You might feel like it is over your head, so lift up your head in order to understand. Once the study is done, the implications and applications will hopefully flow like milk and honey in the promised land of theological labor. As Augustine said: "There is no subject where error is more dangerous, research more laborious, and discovery more fruitful than the oneness of the Trinity [*unitas trinitatis*] of the Father, the Son, and the Holy Spirit."[14]

2.2.1 THE TRINITY IN CREED AND CONFESSION

I have already made it clear that the gospel not only implies but necessitates the triune nature of God, given that the Father is the *author* of salvation, the Son is the *actor* of salvation, and the Holy Spirit is the *applier* of salvation. In want of establishing the Christian doctrine of the tri-unity of Father, Son, and Holy Spirit as three equal yet

---

14. Augustine, *Trin.* 1.3.5.

SOME KEY THEOLOGICAL TERMS

Adoptionism. This view contends that Jesus was a human being who was chosen to be God's Son at his baptism.

Arius/Arians. Arius was a fourth-century Christian presbyter in Alexandria known for his Christology that regarded the Son as a created being inferior to the Father. The Arians, so named after Arius, were the party who argued for the ontological subordination of the Son to the Father.

Consubstantial. This term indicates that the Father, Son, and Spirit share one being and one divine essence. Jesus is consubstantial with the Father as to divinity and consubstantial with us as to humanity.

Eternally begotten/proceeding. The Son is eternally the Son; he was not adopted as God's Son; he was not created to be God's Son. He eternally relates to the Father as Son and is therefore "begotten, not made." The Spirit is eternally the Spirit and is not created or made by the Father. The Spirit eternally proceeds from the Father through the Son. The language of "begotten" and "proceeding" is relational rather than causal; it describes how the three members of the Godhead relate to each other.[15]

Gnosticism. This was a religious philosophy that developed from post–135 AD Judaism and was absorbed into early Christianity. It combined theism with a Neo-Platonic philosophy that regarded the world as created by a wicked demiurge and the Christ came to save people from the material world by imparting knowledge of their true self to them.

Hypostasis. From a Greek word that means the essential nature of something as distinguished from its attributes. In Trinitarian thought it describes the three distinct persons in the Trinity, especially God the Son in his divine and human natures.

Logos Christology. This view exploits the idea of the "Logos" extant in Stoic and Middle Platonic philosophy that attributes the ultimate source of all human knowledge to the "Word." The idea was used by the Jewish philosopher Philo to describe God's wisdom and by the evangelist John to describe the incarnation. Jesus as the "Logos" was an important part of patristic Christology from Justin Martyr to Origen. In Origen's view the Logos was united to the human soul of Jesus so that Jesus' soul took on the properties of the Logos.

---

15. Gerald Bray, *God Is Love: A Biblical and Systematic Theology* (Wheaton, IL: Crossway, 2012), 116.

§ 2.2 Getting an Affinity for the Trinity

> *Modalism.* This is the view that each person of the Trinity is merely a mode of God's activity as opposed to a distinct and independent person.
>
> *Monad.* This entity denotes a simple and indivisible divine essence. In Gnosticism the monad is the supreme being who emanated aeons, which are lesser beings. In Monarchianism the monad is the single and simple divine principle that is the source of the Son and Spirit.
>
> *Subordinationism.* The belief that the Son is inferior in essence and in status to the Father, or sometimes that the Spirit is inferior in essence and status to the Father and the Son. This should be distinguished from functional subordination, whereby the Son and Spirit share the same substance as the Father, but take on a submissive role in the operation of their ministries.
>
> *Substance.* The full nature of what God is. This includes God's ontology or the form and essence of his divine being. The sharing of one substance or essence is called "consubstantial."

distinct persons, it is tempting to leap to the story of Jesus' baptism, to analyze Jesus' farewell discourse in the gospel of John, or even to examine Paul's famous benediction at the end of 2 Corinthians, all in order to give the Trinity biblical warrant. Yet this approach will not do for several reasons. First, I imagine that most readers of this book are people who already believe in the Trinity and are not interested in asking "if" the Trinity has biblical warrant, but are probably keener on grasping the scriptural coherence of the Trinity within the Christian mosaic of beliefs.

Second, the Trinity cannot be established by proof texting, because it is a doctrine that did develop and crystalize into its mature form in the ecumenical creeds. It took time for the ancient church to reason from Scripture, in light of its various debates about God's nature and Christ's person, and, experiencing trial and error along the way, to come up with a theological lexicon and philosophical framework to describe God coherently as a triune being. So rather than work our way up from the Bible to the creeds, a better approach is to start with the creeds and confessions, look at what they say about God as Trinity, and then figure how we found our way here.

Third, before asking if the Trinity is "biblical," it is more appropriate first to enquire as to what Christians mean when they confess that God is Trinity, which necessitates delving into the creeds and confessions as a first port of call.

A good definition of the Trinity is given in first article of the thirty-nine articles of the Anglican Church: "There is but one living and true God, everlasting, without body, parts, or passions; of infinite power, wisdom, and goodness; the Maker, and Preserver of all things both visible and invisible. *And in unity of this Godhead there be three Persons, of one substance, power, and eternity; the Father, the Son, and the Holy Ghost.*"[16] Here the unity of the persons of the Godhead is explicitly given in the threefold description of one "substance, power, and eternity." That means that Father, Son, and Holy Spirit comprise the same essence, there is no inferiority of being among them, and one person did not exist before the others.

A fuller statement of the Trinity is given in the Athanasian Creed (inspired by him rather than written by him), which is a fifth-century statement of faith (see sidebar).

The Athanasian Creed addresses the doctrine of the Trinity in lines 1–28, while lines 29–44 address the doctrine of Christ. With respect to the three persons of the Trinity, the first section ascribes divine attributes to each person, specifying that each person of the Trinity is uncreated (*increatus*), limitless (*immensus*), eternal (*aeternus*), and omnipotent (*omnipotens*). The purpose of ascribing these attributes to all three persons is to avoid subordination, but it also stresses the unity of the three persons in one being, thus avoiding anything resembling tritheism.

Furthermore, the three persons in the one God (consisting of the Father, Son, and Holy Spirit) are explicitly said to be distinct from each other. They are not modes or masks of one person taking on three different forms. The three-in-oneness also includes different roles within the Godhead and different types of relationships between the members of the Godhead. For the Father is neither made nor begotten; the Son is not made but is eternally begotten from the Father; the Holy Spirit is neither made nor begotten but proceeds from the Father and the Son. The question is: How did we get here?

2.2.2 THE MAKING OF THE TRINITY

God is a Triune God and always has been a Triune God—a God who is three-in-one, consisting of Father, Son, and Holy Spirit, all equally divine but fully distinguished persons. But God's revelation of himself as triune unfolds progressively in redemptive history and culminates in the incarnation of the Son and in the pouring out of the Holy Spirit. The early church arrived at the doctrine of the Trinity out of their reflection on Scripture, thinking about God's nature in relation to God's actions, striving to find language to distinguish and correlate the three persons, and attempting to give verbal expression to their experience of God. The Trinitarian doctrine partly demystifies the mystery of God's tripartite being and gives us a way of describing the

---

16. See www.thirtyninearticles.org/religion/.

THE ATHANASIAN CREED (LINES 1–28)

Whosoever will be saved, before all things it is necessary that he hold the catholic faith. Which faith except everyone do keep whole and undefiled, without doubt he shall perish everlastingly. And the catholic faith is this: That we worship one God in Trinity, and Trinity in Unity, neither confounding the persons, nor dividing the substance.

For there is one Person of the Father, another of the Son, and another of the Holy Spirit. But the Godhead of the Father, of the Son, and of the Holy Spirit, is all one, the glory equal, the majesty coeternal.

Such as the Father is, such is the Son, and such is the Holy Spirit.

The Father uncreated, the Son uncreated, and the Holy Spirit uncreated.

The Father incomprehensible, the Son incomprehensible, and the Holy Spirit incomprehensible.

The Father eternal, the Son eternal, and the Holy Spirit eternal. And yet they are not three eternals, but one Eternal.

As also there are not three incomprehensibles, nor three uncreated, but one Uncreated, and one Incomprehensible. So likewise the Father is Almighty, the Son Almighty, and the Holy Spirit Almighty. And yet they are not three almighties, but one Almighty.

So the Father is God, the Son is God, and the Holy Spirit is God. And yet they are not three gods, but one God.

So likewise the Father is Lord, the Son Lord, and the Holy Spirit Lord. And yet not three lords, but one Lord.

For as we are compelled by the Christian verity to acknowledge each Person by Himself to be both God and Lord, so we are also forbidden by the catholic religion to say that there are three gods or three lords.

The Father is made of none, neither created, nor begotten. The Son is of the Father alone, not made, nor created, but begotten. The Holy Spirit is of the Father, neither made, nor created, nor begotten, but proceeding.

So there is one Father, not three fathers; one Son, not three sons; one Holy Spirit, not three holy spirits.

And in the Trinity none is before or after another; none is greater or less than another, but all three Persons are coeternal together and coequal. So that in all things, as is aforesaid, the Unity in Trinity and the Trinity in Unity is to be worshipped.

He therefore that will be saved must think thus of the Trinity.

God who has revealed himself as the Father, Son, and Holy Spirit, in both his essence and in his operations. The affirmation that God is triune became the cornerstone of Christian theology that distinguished it from paganism and from other monotheisms.

The doctrine of the Trinity, mapped historically or articulated in the present, requires all the theological disciplines working in unison including exegesis, biblical theology, systematic theology, and philosophical theology. The complexity of the subject means that the Trinity is not strictly a biblical doctrine, as there is no "Trinity" in any biblical concordance.[17] You cannot derive the Athanasian Creed merely from exegesis of the biblical texts, nor can you proof-text orthodox statements about the Son being a separate *hypostasis* (person) with the same *ousia* (essence) as the Father.

Instead, the Trinity is a theological inference that is drawn out of the biblical materials. The Trinity is no mere abstract speculation, but is a theological attempt to provide coherence to the scriptural narrative about God. The Trinity is "so clearly implied by all that Scripture says and by the logic of the incarnation of God in Jesus Christ that it is a necessary implication of and protective concept of the Christian gospel itself."[18] Or, in the words of the Westminster Confession of Faith (1.6), the Trinity is among those things that "by good and necessary consequence may be deduced from Scripture." The important thing to note is that our "deduction" is not based on abstract or culturally dominating views of deity, but deduced from nothing other than the scriptural narrative of God's own revelatory and redemptive acts.[19] Our deducing from Scripture is a genuine exercise in systematic theology as we have to follow the trajectory of biblical pressures that shape our conception of God into Trinitarian categories.[20]

2.2.3 BIBLICAL ROOTS OF THE TRINITY

1. It is emphatic in Scripture that God is "one" and there is only "one God." The opening words of Genesis refer to the beginning, when "God created the heavens and earth" (Gen 1:1). This terse sentence presents God as the single author and architect of creation. The most basic tenet and most important confession of Israel's

---

17. The *Comma Johannaeum* in 1 John 5:7, "For there are three that bear record in heaven, the Father, the Word, and the Holy Ghost: and these three are one" (KJV), is textually spurious. The verse is found in only eight manuscripts. Four of those manuscripts contain the verse as a variant reading recorded in the margin. The verse probably originated from a late textual recension of the Latin Vulgate. None of the Greek Fathers quoted the passage. The verse is absent from all versions including Syriac, Coptic, Armenian, Ethiopian, Slavonic, and Arabic. It is even absent from the Old Latin witnesses. The biggest reason why the text is clearly late and secondary is because no one quoted this text in debates about Arianism or Sabellianism in the early church. See Bruce M. Metzger, *A Textual Commentary on the Greek New Testament* (2nd ed.; Stuttgart: Deutsche Bibelgesellschaft 1994), 647–49.

18. Roger Olson and Christopher Hall, *The Trinity* (Grand Rapids: Eerdmans, 2002), 2.

19. Vanhoozer, "The Triune God of the Gospel," 26.

20. According to Donald G. Bloesch (*God the Almighty: Power, Wisdom, Holiness, Love* [Downers Grove, IL: InterVarsity Press, 1995], 167): "The doctrine of the Trinity is both an analytical development of the central facts of divine revelation (as Barth maintained) and a synthetic construction drawn from the church's reflection upon this revelation."

faith is found in the *Shema*: "Hear, O Israel: The Lord our God, the Lord is one" (Deut 6:4). Although "monotheism" is a somewhat more slippery and plastic concept than people often realize, the faith of Israel had as its rubric the belief that their covenant God was also the creator God. He was not a territorial or tribal deity. He was not the head of a pantheon of lesser deities. He was the one and only divine reality behind the universe.

This God of heaven and earth had chosen to place his unique personal presence in the Jerusalem temple (Ezra 5:11). Isaiah polemicizes against idol worship with the oracle: "This is what the Lord says—Israel's King and Redeemer, the Lord Almighty: I am the first and I am the last; apart from me there is no God.... Is there any God besides me? No, there is no other Rock; I know not one" (Isa 44:6–8). Isaiah also testifies to the "one true God" as the divine sovereign power over the new heavens and the new earth (Isa 65:16–17). Jesus himself affirmed the *Shema* of Deuteronomy 6:4–6 (Mark 12:29–30) and exemplified Israel's monotheistic faith by praying to God and proclaiming the kingdom of God (e.g., Matt 6:9–13).

Paul also alludes to the *Shema*, albeit with a christocentric pike-half-twist, when he refers to "one God" the Father and to "one Lord" Jesus Christ (1 Cor 8:6). Paul is emphatic in Romans about the oneness of God: "Since there is only one God, who will justify the circumcised by faith and the uncircumcised through that same faith" (Rom 3:30). The doxology of Romans gives praise to the "only wise God" (16:27), and the doxology of Jude exults the "the only God our Savior" (Jude 25). Thus, the biblical faith is a thoroughly monotheistic faith.

2. In the Old Testament we find several intimations of the Trinity. In the opening chapter of Genesis we read:

> Then God said, "*Let us make* mankind in *our image*, in *our likeness*, so that they may rule over the fish in the sea and the birds in the sky, over the livestock and all the wild animals, and over all the creatures that move along the ground." (Gen 1:26, italics added)

Concerning the creation of humankind, the descriptions "let us make," "in our image," and "in our likeness" are notoriously ambiguous. The question is: Who are the persons that constitute the plural pronouns "us" and "our"? Similar inclusive plurals are used in reference to God elsewhere in the Old Testament (e.g., Gen 3:22; 11:7; Isa 6:8). It is plausible that the "us" and "our" designates a heavenly council of angelic beings who are in God's company during his creative actions. Alternatively, the plural pronoun "us" could signify a deliberative dialogue within God himself. That possibility is enhanced when we remember that God's creative act included no cooperation from angelic beings. What is more, human beings reflect the image and likeness of God, not the image and likeness of angels. Thus when humanity is made in "our" image, it is God's own image that they are imprinted with, not the image of angelic creatures. According to K. A. Matthews:

> The interpretation proposed by the Church Fathers and perpetuated by the Reformers was an intra-Trinity dialogue. However, this position can only be entertained as a possible "canonical" reading of the text since the first audience could not have understood it in the sense of a Trinitarian reference. Although the Christian Trinity cannot be derived solely from the use of the plural, a plurality within the unity of the Godhead may be derived from the passage.[21]

To this can be added the testimony of Jesus in John 10:34–36:

> Jesus answered them, "Is it not written in your Law, 'I have said you are "*gods*"'? If he called them 'gods,' to whom the word of God came—and Scripture cannot be set aside—what about the one whom the Father set apart as his very own and sent into the world? Why then do you accuse me of blasphemy because I said, 'I am God's Son'?"

In response to a charge of blasphemy for claiming to be God, Jesus appeals to Psalm 82:6 with its mention of "gods" in the distinctive plural: "I said, 'You are "gods"; you are all sons of the Most High.'" Jesus claims that the Scriptures prove that the word "god" can legitimately be applied to figures other than God himself. D. A. Carson summarizes the logic of Jesus' argument:

> If there are others whom God (the author of Scripture) can address as "god" and "sons of the Most High" (*i.e.* sons of God), on what biblical basis should anyone object when Jesus says, *I am God's Son*? The argument gains extra force when it is remembered that Jesus is *the one whom the Father set apart as his very own and sent into the world*.[22]

The epithet "god" was an ancient Near Eastern title for a monarch as mediator between God and the people (see Ps 45:6), so the application of the title "god" to human beings in 82:6 indicates their special status before God. Originally the psalm probably referred to Israel at Sinai, who received the status of divine sonship, but they failed to apply the law to create a just and caring covenant society (see Exod 4:21–22; Hos 11:1). Jesus is the exemplary model of divine sonship and rightfully claims the title of "Son of God" and "God" by virtue of his unique relationship to his heavenly Father.

Another angle to be pursued is the references in the Old Testament to the "angel of the Lord," "Spirit of the Lord," "Wisdom," and "Word" with their significance for understanding God's nature from God's communication of himself. In several

---

21. K. A. Mathews, *Genesis 1–11:26* (NAC; Nashville: Broadman & Holman, 2001), 162–63.

22. D. A. Carson, *The Gospel according to John* (PNTC; Grand Rapids: Eerdmans, 1991), 397 (italics original).

places, the "angel of the Lord" is a messenger of God and yet is also closely identified with God. In Genesis an angel spoke to Hagar and said, "I will surely increase your descendants," and after hearing the promise Hagar gave a name to "the Lord" who spoke to her as "the [God] who sees me" (Gen 16:7–13; see too 21:17–18). Similarly, when Abraham intended to offer Isaac on the altar, the "angel of the Lord" called from heaven and swore by himself to bless Abraham for his obedience by giving him descendents and land, a promise that recalls the words of God's covenant with Abraham in 12:1–3 (22:11–18). Later in Genesis, the angel of the Lord spoke to Jacob in a dream and identified himself as the God of Bethel (31:10–13).

In Exodus, the angel of the Lord appeared to Moses in the flames of fire within a burning bush (Exod 3:2–6). In Judges, the angel of the Lord addressed Israel and spoke in the first person with words that exhibit God's own perspective: "I brought you up out of Egypt and led you into the land I swore to give to your ancestors. I said, 'I will never break my covenant with you'" (Judg 2:1). The angel of the Lord who appeared to Gideon in Judges 6 is also identified with the Lord in a special way (6:12, 23–24). The identification of the angel of the Lord with the God of Israel in terms of prerogatives and presence is all the more stunning when Jewish and Christian traditions explicitly denounced the worship of angels as an affront to monotheism (e.g., Col 2:18; Rev 19:10; 22:8–9).

Clearly in the cases listed above it is hard to distinguish the angel of the Lord from the Lord himself, but likewise it is impossible to absolutely equate them together. People saw an angel, not God, and yet it was God's prerogative that they heard from the angel. Paradoxically, the angel of the Lord was both God and was not God. The angel is clearly theophanic, and the angelic form enables humans to look on the God who is un-imag(in)able (Exod 20:4) and even unlook-on-able (33:20). The angelic theophany bridges the divide between Creator and creation but remains simultaneously mysterious. The angelic manifestation of the Lord was God's manifesting his immanence to people (i.e., his closeness) without compromising his transcendence (i.e., his otherness). The angel is an "appearance" of God in angelic form, yet it is something other than God-in-himself that is visibly displayed.[23] The theophanic character of the angel of the Lord establishes that God can manifest himself in forms that take on physical characteristics and inhabit limited space.

Also, we are left wondering, in light of the fourth man who looked like a "son of the gods" in Nebuchadnezzar's fiery furnace and who was walking about with the three friends (Dan 3:25), if we are dealing with a christophany, that is, an appearance of the preincarnate Son in angelic form. Justin Martyr identified Jesus with the

---

23. James D. G. Dunn, *Did the First Christians Worship Jesus? The New Testament Evidence* (Louisville: Westminster John Knox, 2010), 67–68.

angel of the Lord because it safeguarded the invisible transcendence of the Father and expressed the Son's mediatorial role.[24]

In the Old Testament the Spirit appears as God's manifested power and presence in the world. That is seen above all in creation, where God's "Spirit" hovered over the waters as a precursor to God's calling creation into being (Gen 1:2). In fact, the work of the Spirit in imparting breath to humankind and in creating them is attributed to none other than Yahweh (Ps 104:29–31). Elsewhere the Spirit is the primary means by which God indwells and empowers his people for various feats of service (e.g., Num 27:18; Judg 3:10; 1 Sam 6:13; Isa 61:1). The departure of the Spirit from King Saul (1 Sam 16:14) was also a departure of the Lord from Saul (18:12). Elsewhere the "Spirit of God" is identified with the "breath of the Almighty" (Job 33:4; 34:14; Ps 33:6). In Ezekiel, the Spirit is equivalent to the "hand of the Lord" (Ezek 3:14; 8:1–3; 37:1). This Old Testament portrayal of the Spirit does not quite bring us to the New Testament conception of the Spirit as a distinct person. But the equation of the work of the Spirit with the work of the Lord is heading toward the same depiction we find in Paul, where "the Lord is the Spirit" (2 Cor 3:17–18).

The Wisdom of God appears as a personalized entity and becomes increasingly prominent in biblical wisdom literature. In Proverbs 8, Wisdom is depicted as a person exhorting the Jewish king to adhere to his instructions. Wisdom is a created, yet preexistent entity, who was present with God in the dawn of creation. Yet Wisdom offers what God offers in terms of promising blessings for obedience, she loves as God loves, and she encourages subjects to have a fear of the Lord. Wisdom is clearly distinct from God, but she is also a personalized effluence of God's workmanship in creation and a personalized exhortation to Israelite rulers. Analogous to God's Wisdom is also his Word. God creates by divine fiat. He speaks, and things come into being; he utters and things transpire immediately. On one occasion, the psalmist presents the creative Word of the Lord as parallel to the work of the Spirit of God in creation (Ps 33:6–9).

In sum, the biblical materials in the Old Testament present to us the possibility that there is a plurality within the Godhead (Gen 1:26). As noted above, Jesus legitimized the application of the title "God" to others based on Psalm 82, since it typologically points to his own divine sonship (John 10:34–36). In addition, the angel of the Lord, God's Word and Wisdom, and the Spirit of the Lord all demonstrate personifications of God's presence, prerogatives, and power. This is not a full-blown doctrine of the Trinity. Even so, we have here the theoretical basis for divine personifications to be divine persons and the possibility of a switch from theophany to

---

24. Gerald O'Collins, *The Tripersonal God: Understanding and Interpreting the Trinity* (London: Geoffrey Chapman, 1999), 88–89.

incarnation as the mode of God's self-revelation. The plurality within God and the diverse agents through whom God acts are anticipations of the triune nature of God.

3. Early Christian worship was largely binitarian in content as it was focused on God the Father and his Son, and their worship was charismatic in character as it was animated by the Holy Spirit. Veneration of Jesus beside the Father can be seen in prayers offered to Jesus (Acts 7:59), thanksgiving offered to God through Jesus (Rom 1:8; Eph 5:20; Col 1:3; 3:17), baptism in his name (Acts 2:38; 8:16; 10:48; 19:5), benedictions involving Father/Son/Spirit (2 Cor 13:14; 1 Thess 5:23), confession of Jesus as "Lord" (Rom 10:9; 1 Cor 16:22; Phil 2:11), hymns or confessions about Jesus (John 1:1–18; Phil 2:5–11; Col 1:15–20), doxologies to Jesus in the New Testament letters (Rom 16:27; Eph 3:21; 2 Pet 3:18; Jude 25), and celebration of his death and exaltation at the Lord's Supper (1 Cor 11:23–25). Thus, the worship of the first Christians, within a few years of Jesus' death, was already edging in a Trinitarian direction. In the words of Larry Hurtado:

> The struggle to work out doctrinal formulations that could express in some coherent way this peculiar view of God (as "one" and yet somehow comprising "the Father" and Jesus, thereafter also including the Spirit as the "third Person" of the Trinity) occupied the best minds in early Christian orthodox/catholic tradition for the first several centuries. But the doctrinal problem they worked on was not of their own making. It was forced upon them by the earnest convictions and devotional practices of believers from the earliest observable years of the Christian movement.[25]

The Trinity is not a doctrinal innovation but constitutes an explanation of the God whom Christians experienced in proclamation, worship, fellowship, communal meals, and prayer. The doctrine of the Trinity is grounded in an experience—an experience of the Spirit of sonship and the Spirit of the Son.[26] The devotional life of the first Christians made it clear that they stood in a triadic relationship to God— God as he was known through the Spirit of holiness, in sonship to the Father, and in service to the Lord Jesus Christ (Rom 8:15–16; 1 Cor 12:3). The Trinity is the theological implication that emerges from the Christian experience of God in the Spirit, through the Son, and before the Father.

4. There are statements in the New Testament about the personhood and divinity of the Father, Son, and Spirit. I will address the personhood and deity of both Jesus Christ and the Holy Spirit later. For the moment we can note: (1) The Father is God; indeed, he is the person revealed as Yahweh in the Old Testament (e.g., Exod 3:14; Deut 1:31; Isa 63:16; 64:8; Mal 3:17; Matt 6:8–9; 7:21; Gal 1:1; 1 Pet 1:3). (2) Jesus of Nazareth is the eternal Word of God made flesh (John 1:1–18; 8:58; 20:28;

---

25. Cf. Larry Hurtado, *Lord Jesus Christ: Devotion to Jesus in Earliest Christianity* (Grand Rapids: Eerdmans, 2003), 651.

26. James D. G. Dunn, *Jesus and the Spirit* (London: SCM, 1975), 326.

Rom 9:5; Titus 2:13). (3) The Spirit is a person as he can be grieved (Isa 63:10; Eph 4:30), and his divinity is implied in several instances (e.g., Mark 3:29; 1 Cor 3:16; 6:19; Acts 5:3–4).

5. There is an *incipient* Trinitarianism in the New Testament where key moments in redemptive history and the application of salvation to believers involve the triadic operation of all three persons of the Godhead. We also find that the identity of God is defined as a sending Father, a sent Son, and a Spirit bestowed by the Father through the Son. This hints in the direction of later Trinitarian thought as the grounds for their coherence as to how the three persons relate to each other in their operation and being.

First, the baptism of Jesus is Trinitarian.[27] In Matthew's account we read, "As soon as Jesus was baptized, he went up out of the water. At that moment heaven was opened, and he saw the Spirit of God descending like a dove and alighting on him" (Matt 3:16). Similar is Peter's speech to Cornelius, where he says: "God anointed Jesus of Nazareth with the Holy Spirit" (Acts 10:38). The baptism of Jesus marks out his commissioning as the messianic Son and his anointing as God's servant (Ps 89:20; Isa 42:1). His baptism was an act of submission to his Father and a reliance on the Holy Spirit to achieve God's redemptive mission.[28]

The baptism of Jesus marks a cosmic rendezvous of Son and Spirit, who come together for the Father's redemptive mission. In this union, the Spirit was the dominant partner, ushering in God's kingdom through Jesus (Matt 4:1/Mark 1:12/Luke 4:1; Matt 12:28; Luke 4:14; 10:21). Ephraem the Syrian considered all members of the Trinity involved in Jesus' baptism and all three were manifested to the senses with "the Father by his voice to the sense of hearing, the Son by his power to the sense of touch, and the Holy Spirit by his descent as a dove to the sense of sight—all three baptized Jesus in the Jordan."[29]

Second, Matthew's gospel climaxes in a resurrection story that includes a baptismal formula for disciples to be baptized "in the name of the Father and of the Son and of the Holy Spirit." I would preface this by saying that the gospel of Matthew accents Jesus' divine status and divine identity, which is why he is called "Immanuel (which means 'God with us')" (1:23) and why female disciples worshiped the risen Lord when they meet him near the empty tomb (28:9). That all "authority in heaven

---

27. Cf. Irenaeus (*Haer.* 3.18.3): "For in the name of Christ is implied, He that anoints, He that is anointed, and the unction itself with which He is anointed. And it is the Father who anoints, but the Son who is anointed by the Spirit, who is the unction, as the Word declares by Isaiah, 'The Spirit of the Lord is upon me, because He hath anointed me,'—pointing out both the anointing Father, the anointed Son, and the unction, which is the Spirit."

28. Cf. Michael F. Bird, "John the Baptist," in *Jesus Amongst His Friends and Enemies* (ed. L Hurtado and C. Keith; Grand Rapids: Baker, 2011), 76.

29. Ephraem the Syrian, *Hymns on Faith* 51.7–8, cited in Everett Ferguson, *Baptism in the Early Church: History, Theology, and Liturgy in the First Five Centuries* (Grand Rapids: Eerdmans, 2009), 504.

and on earth" has been given to Jesus implies that he is installed with the authority over the earthly and heavenly order that most Jews thought were the unique possession of God. On the Trinitarian baptismal formula, John Meier aptly comments:

> Certainly, one could hardly imagine a more forceful proclamation of Christ's divinity—and incidentally, of the Spirit's distinct personality—that this listing together, on a level of equality, of Father, Son, and Spirit. One does not baptize in the name of a divine person, a holy creature, and an impersonal force.[30]

Third, Paul's letter to the Romans contains a few curious Trinitarian threads. For a start, the gospel that Paul annunciates at the head of the letter involves all three persons of the Godhead (Rom 1:1–4). The "gospel of God" concerns the Davidic status of the one who was declared to be the Son of God by the power of the Spirit of holiness. At the end of the letter we observe the same trend again. Paul states that God's grace was given to him in order "to be a minister of Christ Jesus to the Gentiles. He gave me the priestly duty of proclaiming the gospel of God, so that the Gentiles might become an offering acceptable to God, sanctified by the Holy Spirit" (15:16). He also exhorts his readers with these words: "I urge you, brothers and sisters, by our Lord Jesus Christ and by the love of the Spirit, to join me in my struggle by praying to God for me" (15:30). The theocentric framework of Romans expresses salvation through the triadic elements of God, Messiah, and Spirit.[31]

Fourth, by far the most trinitarianesque letters of Paul are the two Corinthian letters. Paul deals with issues such as sexual ethics, church discipline, idol food and pagan temples, the resurrection body, Eucharistic meals, ministry, finances, worship, spiritual gifts, and church unity. All of these topics touch on the nature of God as the Corinthians were taught about him and had experienced him.

> And so it was with me, brothers and sisters. When I came to you, I did not come with eloquence or human wisdom as I proclaimed to you the testimony about *God*. For I resolved to know nothing while I was with you except *Jesus Christ* and him crucified. I came to you in weakness with great fear and trembling. My message and my preaching were not with wise and persuasive words, but with a demonstration of the *Spirit's power*. (1 Cor 2:1–4, italics added)

Paul's apostolic word about "the message of the cross" (see 1 Cor 1:18–21) was not a rhetorically frivolous display of verbal diarrhea. Instead, it was "the testimony about God," because it proclaimed the identity and crucifixion of the Lord Jesus Christ as a saving event enacted by God. The testimony of God/word of the cross, of which Paul is a custodian, was also animated by the visible presence of the Spirit's power. The apostolic proclamation in content and action is determined by three

---

30. John P. Meier, *Matthew* (NTM 3; Wilmington, DE: Liturgical, 1980), 371–72.

31. C. K. Barrett, *The Epistle to the Romans* (BNTC; 2nd ed.; London: A&C Black, 1991), 252, 256.

distinct entities of God, Jesus Christ, and the Holy Spirit. "And that is what some of you were. But you were washed, you were sanctified, you were justified in the name of the *Lord Jesus Christ and by the Spirit of our God*" (6:11, italics added).

This verse is probably contrasting the Corinthians' former life as pagans with their conversion/initiation into the Christian faith. Their washing away of sins, consecration to God, and being declared to be right with God has happened through the agency of the "Lord Jesus Christ" and the "Spirit of our God." Their experience of God's salvation comes through God's agents of Christ and Spirit set in coordinate to each other:

> Therefore I want you to know that no one who is speaking by the *Spirit of God* says, "Jesus be cursed," and no one can say, "*Jesus is Lord*," except by the *Holy Spirit*.
> There are different kinds of gifts, but the *same Spirit* distributes them. There are different kinds of service, but the *same Lord*. There are different kinds of working, but in all of them and in everyone it is the *same God* at work.
> Now to each one the manifestation of the Spirit is given for the common good. (1 Cor 12:3–7, italics added).

This text focuses on the unity between Jesus and the Spirit when it comes to confession of Jesus' lordship and how the spiritual gifts distributed among the Corinthians all stem from the same Spirit. The spiritual gifts are used in devotion to the *same* Lord and are workings of the *same* God. Athanasius cited this passage in order to showcase the lack of division in the Trinity and to highlight their oneness in holiness, eternity, and immutability. Athanasius also argued from this text that the Holy Spirit is not a created being, but has unity with the Father and the Son. This is because:

> What the Spirit gives to each individual is furnished by the Father through the Word. For everything that belongs to the Father belongs to the Son. Thus the "spiritual gifts" given by the Son in the Spirit are gifts of the Father. And when the Spirit is in us, the Word who gives the Spirit is also in us, and the Father is in the Word.... Thus the spiritual "gifts" are given by the Trinity. For in the "variety" of these, as Paul writes to the Corinthians, is "the same Spirit" and "the same Lord" and "the same God who inspires them all in everyone." The Father himself works through the Word and in the Spirit in giving all these gifts.[32]

No surprise, then, that the spiritual gifts are really Trinitarian gifts.

Moving now to 2 Corinthians, concerning the validation of the apostolic office, Paul is confident that God will enable himself and his audience to stand firm in Christ because they have been anointed and sealed by the Spirit: "Now it is *God*

---

32. See Judith L. Kovacs, *1 Corinthians: Interpreted by Early Christian Commentators* (Grand Rapids: Eerdmans, 2005), 200.

who makes both us and you stand firm in *Christ*. He anointed us, set his seal of ownership on us, and put his *Spirit* in our hearts as a deposit, guaranteeing what is to come" (2 Cor 1:21–22, italics added). God acts in believers through Christ and the Spirit for his redemptive purposes that express his own faithfulness (see 1:18–20). Ambrosiaster commented:

> Paul is also saying that the work of the Father and the Son is one, because he says that it is both Christ who establishes God. For whomever the Son establishes, the Father establishes too, because the Holy Spirit comes from both of them.... He mentions the Trinity here because he has been speaking about the perfecting of mankind, and the whole sum of perfection is to be found in the Trinity.[33]

Perhaps the most famous Trinitarian text in Paul's letters is the benediction at the end of 2 Corinthians: "May the grace of the *Lord Jesus Christ*, and the love of *God*, and the fellowship of the *Holy Spirit* be with all of you" (2 Cor 13:14, italics added). If we read this benediction in an Arian sense, it becomes an impoverished blessing, in that the favor and fellowship of two created semidivine beings (Jesus Christ and the Spirit) are oddly made coordinate with the love of God. It is better to read grace, communion, and love as resulting from the one God in equal measure through the threefold agents nominated.

The Corinthian letters address a variety of subjects detailing the apostle's struggle with this belligerent and taxing cluster of Corinthian house churches. In many cases, he addresses the presenting issues by way of reference to the foundational reality of the God, who is known and experienced as Spirit, Lord, and God.

Overall, the primary contribution of the Pauline letters to the formation of the Trinity might be seen in Paul's "economic Trinitarianism," derived from his christological and pneumatological affirmations. For Paul, Jesus is preexistent and part of the divinity identity. The Holy Spirit is personal and applies the redeeming work of the Father and the Son. The Father and Son are somehow equal, but distinct, with the Son freely yielding himself to the Father and the Father in turn exalting the Son to the highest place. We can add to that the triadic nature of the gospel event whereby salvation is effected through the *united* work by Father, Son, and Spirit, whereby believers attain *communion* with God in Christ through the Holy Spirit (see 2 Cor 3:1–4:6; Gal 4:4–6; Eph 1:3–14; 2 Thess 2:13; Titus 3:4–7).

Paul was not a speculative theologian concerned with "God in himself," but rather focused on "God as Savior." Yet God's acting and being cannot be separated. Paul had enough theological *nous* to comprehend that his Damascus road experience

---

33. Gerald L. Bray, *Commentaries on Romans and 1–2 Corinthians by Ambrosiaster* (ACT; Downers Grove, IL: InterVarsity Press, 2009), 211.

and his divinely revealed gospel held implications for one's understanding of the nature of God. It is certain that Paul would not know the meaning of the word "Trinity" if someone had said it to him, but I think it highly probable that he would not have objected to its explanation if one was provided.[34]

Fifth, further Trinitarian trappings can be found elsewhere in the New Testament. As examples, consider two texts from the Johannine and Petrine letters.

> This is how you can recognize the *Spirit of God*: Every spirit that acknowledges that *Jesus Christ* has come in the flesh *is from God*, but every spirit that does not acknowledge Jesus *is not from God*. This is the spirit of the antichrist, which you have heard is coming and even now is already in the world. (1 John 4:2–3)

> … who have been chosen according to the foreknowledge of *God the Father*, through the *sanctifying work of the Spirit*, to be obedient to *Jesus Christ* and sprinkled with his blood: Grace and peace be yours in abundance. (1 Pet 1:2, italics added in both cases)

The first letter of John sets forth a clear litmus test for determining the presence of the Spirit of God in the teaching of certain persons. The person who acknowledges the God-in-the-flesh incarnation of Jesus Christ and recognizes that he was sent from God exhibits the marks of authentic teaching imparted by the Spirit. Only the Spirit *from* God recognizes that Jesus Christ is *from* God. The opening of 1 Peter presents a beautiful collage of the Father's foreknowledge, the Spirit's sanctifying work, and Jesus' atoning blood. Karen Jobes comments:

> This triadic structure describes the relationship of the Christians to whom Peter writes to each member of the Godhead, particularly in reference to their conversion. The order—Father, Spirit, Christ—perhaps reflects the logical *ordo salutis* [order of salvation] of conversion that finds its ultimate origin in the heart of God, is made operative in human lives by the Holy Spirit, and is evidenced through personal expressions of faith in Jesus Christ. Although it would be anachronistic to call this a reference to the Trinity, surely such verses as this one later issued in the orthodox doctrine of the Trinity at the First Council of Nicaea (AD 325), which was located in Bithynia, one of the regions to which Peter writes.[35]

All these passages addressed above point to an *incipient Trinitarianism*. That is true insofar that they contain the building blocks for later Trinitarian thought. It is equally valid to say that when these texts are read through a Trinitarian lens, they take on a new degree of coherence and depth that appears to be consistent with their theological structure and canonical context.

---

34. Cf. Gordon Fee, "Paul and the Trinity: The Experience of Christ and the Spirit for Paul's Understanding of God," in *The Trinity: An Interdisciplinary Symposium on the Trinity* (ed. S. T. Davis, D. Kendall, and G. O'Collins; Oxford: Oxford University Press, 2002), 49–72 (esp. 71).

35. Karen H. Jobes, *1 Peter* (BECNT; Grand Rapids: Baker, 2005), 68.

§ 2.2 Getting an Affinity for the Trinity

Sixth, there is a strong *proto*-Trinitarianism in the gospel of John, where the relationship between the persons is the foundation for later Trinitarian thinking.[36] What is implicit in the rest of the New Testament about the Trinity becomes more explicit in the Fourth Gospel concerning the unity of the Father, Son, and Holy Spirit. The gospel of John creates *pressure* on later commentators to account for the distinct personhood and divinity of the Father, Son, Spirit without compromising the unity of God.[37]

In the gospel of John, the Father, Son, and Spirit are presented as three identities bound up in a mutually constituting way. The Fourth Gospel is resolutely monotheistic and ascribes important attributes and unique prerogative to God. The Johannine Jesus, though he is "with God" and "was God" (John 1:1), intends to make known to the disciples that the Father is "my God and your God" (20:17).

The discourses frequently portray the unique Father-Son relationship in terms of Jesus being the delegated agent of the Father. The filial relationship includes subordination to the Father who sent him (John 5:17, 26–27; 6:44, 57; 8:16–18, 42; 10:36; 12:49; 14:24; 17:21, 25; 20:21) and equality and oneness with the Father as well (5:18; 10:30; 14:9–10; 17:11, 21–23). That relationship cannot be adequately accounted for by an Arian or Sabellian Christology.

The Spirit becomes increasingly prominent in the later stages of the Fourth Gospel. The Spirit is the "Spirit of truth" (John 14:17; 15:26; 16:13) and the "Advocate" (14:16, 26; 15:26; 16:7) sent from the Father after the Son's ascension to empower the disciples in their mission (20:22–23). The Spirit's personal identity is not so much revealed in divine activities he has in common with Father and Son. Instead, the Spirit's personal identity is revealed in the characteristic ways in which he relates to the Father and the Son. In the narration of the Fourth Gospel, the Spirit descends from the Father to rest on the Son so that through the Son, the Spirit may come to rest on the disciples and bring them life and light. The Spirit effects things so that "the Father may be glorified in the Son" (John 14:13).[38]

Arguably the most Trinitarian passage in the Fourth Gospel, or even in the entire New Testament, is the farewell discourse of John 14–16 and the high priestly prayer in John 17. Millard Erickson detects a swell of Trinitarian themes in the farewell discourse:

> The Son is sent by the Father (14:24) and comes forth from him (16:28). The Spirit is given by the Father (14:16), sent from the Father (14:26), and proceeds from the

---

36. Cf. R. G. Gruenler, *The Trinity in the Gospel of John: A Thematic Commentary on the Fourth Gospel* (Grand Rapids: Baker, 1986); Andreas J. Köstenberger and Scott R. Swain, *Father, Son and Spirit: The Trinity and John's Gospel* (NSBT 24; Downers Grove, IL: InterVarsity Press, 2008).

37. C. Plantinga, "The Fourth Gospel as Trinitarian Source Then and Now," in *Biblical Hermeneutics in Historical Perspective* (ed. M. S. Burrows and P. Rorem; Grand Rapids: Eerdmans, 1991): 303–21 (esp. 305); C. Kavin Rowe, "Biblical Pressure and Trinitarian Hermeneutics," *ProEccl* 11 (2002): 295–312.

38. Köstenberger and Swain, *Father, Son and Spirit*, 135–36, 148.

Father (15:26). Yet the Son is closely involved in the coming of the Spirit: he prays for his coming (14:16); the Father sends the Spirit in the Son's name (14:26); the Son will send the Spirit from the Father (15:26); the Son must go away so that he can send the Spirit (16:7). The Spirit's ministry is understood as a continuation and elaboration of that of the Son. He will bring to remembrance what the Son has said (14:26); he will bear witness to the Son (15:26); he will declare what he hears from the Son, thus glorifying the Son (16:13–14).[39]

Concerning John 17, Walter Kasper has stated that "the high-priestly prayer contains the entire doctrine of the Trinity in basic form and in a nutshell."[40] The Father glorifies the Son so that the Son may glorify the Father (17:1, 4–5). Eternal life consists of knowing the "only true God" in the sending of Jesus Christ (17:2–3). The incarnation is a revelation that Jesus comes from the Father (17:6–8). Believers belong simultaneously to the Son and to the Father (17:9–12). The disciples are sanctified by the Father through Jesus' revealing and redeeming work (17:17, 19). The disciples are also said to share in the unity of Father and Son (17:21–23). Though the Spirit is noticeably absent from the prayer, he may be presupposed as the means by which believers enter into fellowship with Father and Son. The Spirit is the mode of their sanctification and their glorification as promised by the Father by sending the Son. From all of this Köstenberger and Swain rightly identify this teaching in the Fourth Gospel: "The triune plan of salvation, the *pactum salutis*, flows from, through and to the Father's eternal love for the Son in the Spirit."[41]

The beloved disciple is the closest we come in the New Testament to a Trinitarian theologian prior to Tertullian. By labeling the Fourth Evangelist as *proto-Trinitarian*, I mean that the interrelations between Father, Son, and Spirit are already on a trajectory toward the Trinity. Reading the gospel of John in light of later Trinitarian perspectives also illuminates rather than obscures the theological texture of the book.

The revelation of God as Trinity is part of the progressive nature of God's self-disclosure in the Holy Scriptures. As the story of redemption moves ahead chapter by chapter, we are slowly and cautiously given clear indications as to who God actually is. The triune nature of God is a mystery that is made manifest in God's revelation of himself through his operations in creation, Israel's history, in the incarnation of Jesus Christ, and in the sending of the Spirit. Gregory of Nazianzen provides a superbly appropriate summary of God's progressive presentation of himself as Trinity through the Scriptures:

> The Old Testament proclaimed the Father openly, and the Son more obscurely. The New manifested the Son, and suggested the deity of the Spirit. Now the Spirit himself dwells among us, and supplies us with a clearer demonstration of himself. For it was not safe, when the Godhead of the Father was not yet acknowledged, plainly to

---

39. Millard Erickson, *Christian Theology* (2nd ed.; Grand Rapids: Baker, 1998), 357.

40. Kasper, *The God of Jesus Christ*, 303.

41. Köstenberger and Swain, *Father, Son and Spirit*, 178.

> ## JONATHAN EDWARD'S A PRIORI ARGUMENT FOR THE TRINITY
>
> Jonathan Edwards attempted to establish the triune nature of God based on *a priori* reasoning (i.e., a deductive argument about God's nature independent of the revelation contained in Scripture). His argument can be schematized as follows:
> (1) God is a perfect and loving Father.
> (2) God has a perfect idea of himself—the Son.
> (3) God has a perfect love for himself—the Spirit
> See Jonathan Edwards, "Discourse on the Trinity," *The Works of Jonathan Edwards* (ed. S. H. Lee; New Haven, CT: Yale University Perss, 2003), 109–44.

proclaim the Son; nor when that of the Son was yet received to burden us further ... with the Holy Spirit.... It was necessary that, increasing little by little, and, as David says, by ascensions from glory to glory, the full splendor of the Trinity should gradually shine forth.[42]

2.2.4 THE TRINITY IN THE PATRISTIC ERA

In the immediate postapostolic period, Christian leaders did not instantly develop a doctrine of the Trinity as eventually blossomed in the fourth century. However, we do find evidence that second-century Christian authors were already wrestling with the implications of the Hebrew Scriptures, apostolic testimony, and the church's worship in order to make sense of God's person and being in triune terms.[43] For example, the bishop Clement, writing from Rome in the late first century, encourages his Corinthian readers with the words: "Have we not one God and one Christ and one Spirit of grace poured out upon us? And have we not one calling in Christ?" (*1 Clem.* 46.6). In the early second century, the Syrian bishop of Antioch, Ignatius, on the way to his execution in Rome, wrote to the church in Ephesus, "There is one physician who is both flesh and spirit; both born and unborn; God in man; true life in death; both from Mary and from God; first subject to suffering and then beyond it, Jesus Christ our Lord" (Ign. *Eph.* 7:2). Ignatius goes on to refer to the church as

---

42. Gregory Nazianzen, *Or. Bas.* 31.26, as cited from Robert Letham, *The Holy Trinity: In Scripture, History, Theology, and Worship* (Phillipsburg, NJ: Presbyterian & Reformed, 2004), 33.

43. Olson and Hall, *The Trinity*, 16.

"the building of God the Father, hoisted up on high by the crane of Jesus Christ, which is the cross, using the Holy Spirit as a rope" (ibid., 9:1). Thus, we have two Christian bishops between 90–110 AD, in Rome and Antioch, both continuing the apostolic message of the incarnation and expressing afresh the triadic nature of God's saving actions.

The second-century apologists contributed further to the development of the doctrine of the Trinity. Justin Martyr (ca. AD 110–165) wrote significant works responding to Jewish, Greek, and Roman objections to Christianity. In the process, he made important contributions to the Christian conception of God.[44] Justin believed that one could establish Christ's divinity from the Hebrew Scriptures. Yet Justin also realized that asserting the divinity of Christ led to several subsequent problems. If Jesus is God, in what sense can Christians still claim to believe in one God? Is Jesus God in the same manner that the Father is God, or is Jesus a kind of lesser deity? If the Father, Son, and the Spirit are all God, in what way are they distinct or equal?

Justin's solution to this conundrum was to identify Jesus as the Logos. Jesus is present in the Old Testament as the Word, Wisdom, and Power of God.[45] He presented his readers with an affirmation of an unbegotten Father and a begotten Son, through whom the Father made the world and whom he anointed as the Messiah.[46] Regarding the Father–Son relationship, Justin used a number of images. To interpret the relationship of the Word from the Father, Justin employed the image of the sun emitting its rays or a fire kindling another fire. He made the incarnation equivalent to "Light from Light," a metaphor that found its way into the Nicene Creed. The implication of the light metaphor was that the product of light had the same qualities as the source of light so that there was no difference or division in the substance of the Father and the Son.

On the Trinitarian relations, Justin appears to refer to an ordering of persons: first is the "Creator of the universe," second is the "Son of the true God," and in the third place is the "Spirit of prophecy."[47] What is not clear is whether this ordering is in terms of superiority or priority as this issue had not presented itself to Justin. Elsewhere drawing on the language of prayer and worship, Justin routinely referred to the "Father of the universe," "his Son," and the "Holy Spirit."[48] The chief contribution of Justin to Trinitarian thought was his affirmation of the divinity and shared essence of the Son with the Father. He identified the Son with mediatorial figures in the Hebrew Scriptures such as God's Wisdom in Proverbs 8:22.

Discussions about how to affirm the triune nature of God with equally divine

---

44. See discussion in O'Collins, *The Tripersonal God*, 87–96.
45. Justin, *Dial.* 61, 129; *1 Apol.* 12, 23.
46. Justin, *2 Apol.* 5.
47. Justin, *1 Apol.* 13.
48. Ibid., 65, 67.

and consubstantial persons were advanced by theologians in the West and the East. Irenaeus of Lyons argued, against the Gnostics, for the unity of the Creator God with the Father of Jesus Christ. Irenaeus also affirmed the Son's eternal existence when he declared that the Son "did not begin to be; he existed always with the Father."[49] Irenaeus rejected the Gnostic concept of emanations and productions from some cosmic monad that brought spiritual beings into existence. In contrast, he used a psychological model to describe the eternal generating of the Son, where the Son is likened to "a thought emerging from our mind or a word from our lips."[50] He also gave the analogy of the Son and Spirit as being like the "two hands" of God who were "carrying out his intended work of creation."[51]

In a fuller Trinitarian statement Irenaeus writes: "The Spirit prepares human beings for the Son of God; the Son leads them to the Father; the Father gives them immortality.... Thus God was revealed: for in all these ways God the Father is displayed. The Spirit works, the Son fulfills his ministry, the Father approves."[52] Irenaeus's account of the *regula fidei* is also thoroughly Trinitarian by referring to the "faith in one God the Father almighty, who made the heaven and the earth and the seas and all things in them; and in one Christ Jesus the Son of God, who was made flesh for our salvation; and in the Holy Spirit, who through the prophets proclaimed the saving dispensations."[53]

Tertullian is by far the grandfather of Trinitarian thought. He developed a Trinitarian basis for understanding God in his criticism of Praxeas, who advocated monarchial theology, whereby it was the Father, not a distinct Son, who was incarnated and crucified. Tertullian developed a model where God was of one substance (*substantia*) with three distinct persons (*persona*) as part of his counterresponse to both modalism and Gnosticism.

Hippolytus rejected modalism with the objection, "See, brothers, what a rash and audacious dogma they have introduced, when they say without shame, the Father is Himself Christ, Himself the Son, Himself was born, Himself suffered, Himself raised Himself." Alternatively, Hippolytus maintained, "We accordingly see the Word incarnate, and we know the Father by Him, and we believe in the Son, (and) we worship the Holy Spirit. Let us then look at the testimony of Scripture, with respect to the announcement of the future manifestation of the Word." Furthermore:

> For the Father indeed is One, but there are two Persons, because there is also the Son; and then there is the third, the Holy Spirit. The Father decrees, the Word executes, and the Son is manifested, through whom the Father is believed on. The

---

49. Irenaeus, *Haer.* 3.18.1.
50. Ibid., 2.28.6.
51. Ibid., 4.20.1.
52. Ibid., 4.20.4, 6.
53. Ibid., 1.10.1.

economy of harmony is led back to one God; for God is One. It is the Father who commands, and the Son who obeys, and the Holy Spirit who gives understanding: the Father who is above all, and the Son who is through all, and the Holy Spirit who is in all. And we cannot otherwise think of one God, but by believing in truth in Father and Son and Holy Spirit.[54]

Against the Arians, Athanasius asserted the full divinity of the Son with the Father on the grounds that one created being cannot redeem another created being. Athanasius also helped to establish the conviction that believers cannot know or speak of the Son apart from his relationship with the Father and the Spirit.[55] Gregory of Nyssa wrote a treatise called *On "Not Three Gods"* to Ablabius, which maintained that the Trinity is not tritheism. The unity of the Godhead is not established by their shared essences since the gods of the Greek pantheon share a similar nature. Rather, their unity is established by the union of their operations that act in complete and perfect harmony.

However, it would be naive to think that the journey toward a full-fledged Trinitarian understanding of God was smooth sailing. For instance, a popular second-century Christian writing from Rome called the *Shepherd of Hermas* committed what would be, in the minds of later theologians, some serious theological errors. It is not clear if this document considered the Son to be an angel or chief angel.[56] Justin Martyr referred to the Logos as "a second god," who was "distinct in number but not in mind" from the Father.[57] This leaves us potentially with either di-theism (two gods) or else a subordinationism (Jesus is a lesser god than the Father). Though Justin affirmed the divinity of the Son and the shared essence of Father and Son, he was still struggling to find a grammar to preserve the unity of the three. What is more, the Shepherd and Justin both appear to conflate the Son and the Spirit together.[58] Given that Son and Spirit are the chief agents of God in creation and redemption, that is understandable, but it is unforgivable by the standards of later Christian orthodoxy. The third-century Christian scholar Origen also regarded the Trinity as a hierarchy of persons:

> The God and Father, who holds the universe together, is superior to every being that exists, for he imparts to each one from his own existence that which each one is; the Son being less than the Father, is superior to rational creatures alone (for he is second to the Father); the Holy Spirit is still less, and dwells within the saints alone.[59]

For Origen, the Son and the Spirit are lesser beings than the Father. Later on major conflicts in the church revolved around the Son's relationship to

---

54. Hippolytus, *Noet.* 2, 12, 14.
55. O'Collins, *The Tripersonal God*, 129.
56. *Herm. Sim.* 5.5.3; 5.6.7.
57. Justin, *Dial.* 50, 56.
58. *Herm. Sim.* 5.5.2; 5.6.5; Justin, *1 Apol.* 33.
59. Origen, *First Principles*, 1.3.5.

the Father and the relation of Christ's human and divine natures. (1) Concerning the Son's relationship to the Father, the Arians held that the Son was a semidivine being, inferior in status to the Father. The Son was created by the Father and subordinate to him. Monarchianism attempted to uphold the unity of God by avoiding tritheism, though at the expense of becoming unitarian. Monarchianism took two distinct forms. Dynamic monarchianism espoused the view that Jesus received the Logos at his baptism and went on to achieve full divinity and saviorhood (Paul of Samosata). Modal Monarchianism taught that the Trinity was a manifestation of three different forms of a single divine monad rather than three persons sharing one essence. Such a perspective exchanges three persons for three manifestations of God, i.e., the Father in the Old Testament, the Son as the Redeemer, and the Holy Spirit after the resurrection (Sabellius). The resolution of these matters was heated, gradual, and intensely political. Eventually several creeds and councils (Nicaea in 325, Constantinople in 381, Toledo in 589) established that the Son shared the same essence as the Father, was coequal with the Father, and was coeternal with the Father.

(2) On the relation of Christ's human and divine natures, the dangers were of overstressing either Jesus' humanity (generally the Antioch tradition) or Jesus' deity (generally the Alexandrian tradition). Apollinarius taught that Christ had a true body and spirit but that the soul in him was replaced by the Logos. The Logos was the active divine element that dominated the passive elements of his body and spirit. Jesus' humanity was absorbed into the divine Logos. His views were condemned at the council of Constantinople in 381. In contrast, Nestorius maintained that that Christ was a perfect man morally linked to the deity. The two natures were combined in his person but not organically united. Christ was a God-bearer rather than a God-man. Nestorius's views were rejected at the Council of Ephesus in 431, but the followers of Nestorius took their views east and established churches from Iraq to China.

The monk Eutyches advocated that after the incarnation the two natures of Christ, the human and divine, were mixed into one new nature. Eutyches's views were refuted in the *Tome* of Leo I and denounced by the Council of Chalcedon in 451, but they continued to have adherents in the Monophysite churches of the Middle East (Coptic churches of Egypt, Ethiopia, Lebanon, Turkey, and Russia). The position reached at the Council of Chalcedon affirmed a hypostatic union of the two natures in one person, unmixed, undivided, and in perfect harmony.

Most of these debates centered on the Father–Son relations and not so much on the Holy Spirit. However, Macedonius, a bishop of Constantinople (341–60), appears to have taught that the Holy Spirit was a servant of God on a par with the angels. He thereby made the Holy Spirit subordinate to Father and Son. The Council of Constantinople (381) condemned his views for demoting the Spirit. In the later

Council of Toledo (589) the phrase *filioque* was added to the Nicene Creed, which means "and the Son." This was added to affirm that the Holy Spirit "proceeds from the Father *and the Son*." This ruled out Arianism and Macedonianism that subordinated the Spirit and Son to the Father.

The ancient church has generally maintained the full deity and the personality of the Holy Spirit as coequal, coeternal, and consubstantial with the Father and the Son. In the Niceno-Constantinopolitian Creed (381) we find an addition to the Nicene Creed (325) that the Holy Spirit is "the Lord and Giver of life, who proceeds from the Father, who with the Father and the Son together is worshiped and glorified, who spoke by the prophets." The Council of Constantinople gave a definition of the Godhead as including one substance (*ousia*) and three persons (*hypostasis*) and formally established the Trinity as the official position of the Eastern and Western churches. This had its roots in the work of several thinkers like Tertullian and Irenaeus, who emphasized an economic view of the Trinity (i.e., the way in which God was manifested in creation and redemption), and the theological work of Athanasius and the Cappadocian Fathers on the immanent view of the Trinity (i.e., the eternal relations of the persons within the Godhead including their deity, unity, and personhood).

2.2.5 INTRA-TRINITARIAN RELATIONSHIPS

Trinitarian thought did not end in 381. Medieval theologians like Augustine and Aquinas, Reformers such as John Calvin, and modern theologians such as Karl Rahner, Karl Barth, and John Zizioulas have all made contributions to how Christians articulate the Trinity.[60] Thinking and writing about the Trinity continues, because the subject is such a mystery and because we are still left with many questions about how the persons within the Godhead relate to each other. Three examples follow.

1. *Perichoresis*. In light of the economic Trinity, how do the persons in the Godhead relate to one another in terms of sharing in their attributes and activities? For instance, how can it be that Jesus says to Philip, "Anyone who has seen me has seen the Father.... Don't you believe that I am in the Father, and that the Father is in me?" (John 14:9–10), and that the Holy Spirit is called the "Spirit of Christ" (Rom 8:9; 1 Pet 1:11)? One way of maintaining the unity-in-variety, without lapsing in modalism, is through *perichoresis*, otherwise known as interpermeation or coinherence.

Perichoresis is our way of describing how the life of each divine person flows through each of the others, so that each divine person infuses the others and each has direct access to the consciousness of the others. It implies that the three persons of the Trinity exist only in a mutual reciprocal relatedness to each other. Colin Gunton put it like this: "God is not God apart from the way in which Father, Son, and

---

60. See the overview in Bloesch, *God the Almighty*, 177–84.

Spirit in eternity give to and receive from each other what they essentially are."[61] This forces us to think clearly about the oneness of God, a oneness in Trinity. The oneness of God is not a oneness of three isolated persons, but the oneness of three persons who permeate and pervade each other's being. One cannot *believe* in the Father without believing in the Son and the Spirit. One cannot *cleave* to the Son without cleaving to the Spirit and the Father. One cannot *receive* the Spirit without also receiving the Father and the Son.

2. *Functional subordination*. The Father and Son are equal in that they share the same essence (*homoousious*). However, during the incarnation the Son submitted to the authority of the Father. Now if the economic Trinity (the operation of the Godhead in creation and redemption) tells us something about the immanent Trinity (the interpersonal relationships within the Godhead in eternity past), does that mean that the Son, though equal in being to the Father, eternally subordinates himself to the Father in terms of his rank? There has been a huge debate within evangelicalism on this very topic. The debate is in fact motivated by gender issues such as male headship and women in ministry. Grudem argues:

> Just as God the Father has authority over the Son, though the two are equal in deity, so in a marriage, the husband has authority over the wife, though they are equal in personhood. In this case, the man's role is like that of God the Father, and the woman's role is parallel to that of God the Son. They are equal in importance, but they have different roles.[62]

In contrast, egalitarians have argued that any form of subordination, ontological or functional,[63] is tantamount to Arianism, so the Trinity is not a good analogy to deny women access to ministerial offices.[64] On the egalitarian side one could point to the Second Helvetic Confession (ch. 3): "We also condemn all heresies and heretics who teach that the Son and Holy Spirit are God in name only, and also that there is something created and subservient, or subordinate to another in the Trinity." The debate has become a somewhat messy affair with the doctrine of the Trinity becoming the battleground for a gender war.[65]

---

61. Colin Gunton, *The One, the Three and the Many* (Cambridge: Cambridge University Press, 1999), 164.

62. Wayne Grudem, *Systematic Theology* (Grand Rapids: Zondervan, 1995), 459-60.

63. R. C. Kroeger and C. C. Kroeger ("Subordinationism," in *Evangelical Dictionary of Theology* [ed. W.A. Elwell; Grand Rapids: Baker, 1984], 1058) define subordinationism as: "A doctrine that assigns an inferiority of being, status, *or role* to the Son or the Holy Spirit within the Trinity" (italics added). They add: "The Nicene fathers ascribed to the Son and Spirit an equality of being or essence, but a subordination of order, with both deriving their existence from the Father as a primal source."

64. Cf., e.g., Kevin Giles, *The Trinity and Subordinationism* (Downers Grove, IL: InterVarsity Press, 2002); idem, *Jesus and the Father: Modern Evangelical Reinvent the Doctrine of the Trinity* (Grand Rapids: Zondervan, 2006); Gilbert Bilezikian, "Hermeneutical Bungee-Jumping: Subordination in the Trinity," *JETS* 40 (1997): 57–68.

65. Cf. Craig S. Keener, "Is Subordination within The Trinity Really Heresy? A Study of John 5:18 in Context," *TrinJ* 20 (1999): 39–51; Stephen Kovach and Peter Schemm, "A Defense of the Doctrine of the Eternal Subordination of the Son," *JETS* 42 (1999): 461–76; Peter Bolt, "Three Heads

My response to this debate is twofold. (1) I do not think that the Trinity should be used to establish the proper relations between men and women, simply for the fact that the Trinity is unique and does not translate well as a model for relations between two persons of separate genders.[66] (2) I think that functional subordination with ontological equality is indeed consistent with historic orthodoxy, although the word "subordination" does make me nervous since it has Arian connotations. Instead, I prefer Wolfhart Pannenberg's model that sonship implies the Son's obedient self-distinction from the Father.[67] To put it another way, Jesus' obedience to the Father's mission in his earthly ministry is itself a revelation of the Son's eternal relationship to the Father—a relationship that is always characterized by sending and being sent.

Thus the incarnation is "fitting" as a historical expression of who the Son always is in his relation to the Father. As J. S. Horrell argues, "if one demurs that all biblical revelation is economic and thus inadequate alone as a *framework* to contemplate infinite God, then on what basis do we have knowledge of the immanent Trinity?"[68] Karl Barth asked a similar question: "If His economy of revelation and salvation is distinguished from His proper being as worldly, does it bring us into touch with God Himself or not?"[69] Because the New Testament speaks about Jesus' submission to his Father during the incarnation (John 5:19; 14:28; 1 Cor 11:3; Phil 2:5–7) and even postascension as God's vice-regent (Acts 2:33; 5:31; Rom 8:34; 1 Cor 15:28; Col 3:1; Heb 1:13; 10:12; 12:2; Rev 3:21), we have to propose that the Son's submission demonstrates something of the eternal relationships within the Godhead.

3. *Primacy*. Do any members of the Godhead have priority in origins and primacy in being? If the Father eternally begets the Son and if the Spirit eternally proceeds from the Father, does that make the Father the cause of the divinity of the Son and Spirit? Such language is common among Catholic and Orthodox theologians since Origen, and they have routinely referred to the Father as *autotheos* ("God in himself"), who is the cause of the divinity of the Son and Spirit. Yet to affirm the

---

in the Divine Order: The Early Church Fathers and 1 Corinthians 11:3," *RTR* 64 (2005): 147–61; Bruce Ware, *Father, Son, and Holy Spirit: Relationships, Roles, and Relevance* (Wheaton, IL: Crossway, 2005); Millard Erickson, *Who's Tampering with the Trinity: An Assessment of the Subordination Debate* (Grand Rapids: Kregel, 2009); Michael F. Bird and Robert Shillaker, "Subordination in the Trinity and Gender Roles: A Response to Recent Discussion," *TrinJ* 29 (2008): 267–83; idem, "The Son Really, Really Is the Son: A Response to Kevin Giles," *TrinJ* 30 (2009): 257–68; Kevin Giles, "Michael Bird and Robert Shillaker: The Son Is Not Eternally Subordinated in Authority to the Father," *TrinJ* 30 (2009): 237–56.

66. 1 Cor 11:3 ("But I want you to realize that the head of every man is Christ, and the head of the woman is man, and the head of Christ is God") does indicate that men and women should both respect their respective heads, but it does not imply that man is the head of women *because* God is the head of Christ.

67. Wolfhart Pannenberg, *Systematic Theology* (trans. G. W. Bromiley; 3 vols.; Edinburgh: T&T Clark, 1991 [1988].), 1:308–17.

68. J. Scott Horrell, "Towards a Biblical Model of the Social Trinity: Avoiding Equivocation of Nature and Order," *JETS* 47 (2004): 416.

69. Barth, *CD*, 4/1:196.

> ## IN A NUTSHELL: THE ESSENTIAL ELEMENTS OF THE DOCTRINE OF THE TRINITY
>
> If we had to summarize what are the critical and salient features of Trinitarian belief, they could be summarized as follows:
>
> 1. The unity of one God in three persons.
> 2. The eternity of the three persons.
> 3. The shared and equal deity of the three persons.
> 4. The shared and equal essence of the three persons.
> 5. The Trinity includes distinction in roles and relationships within the Godhead.
> 6. The Trinity will always be an ineffable mystery.

Father's priority as a source of being for the Son and Spirit can easily lend itself to the Father's ontological superiority over the Son and Spirit and thus bring us into a form of subordinationism. John Calvin argued that each of the persons is *autotheos*, that is to say, God in his own right, and not simply divine by appointment. The French Reformer wrote:

> For though we admit that, in respect of order and gradation, the beginning of divinity is in the Father, we hold it a detestable fiction to maintain that essence is proper to the Father alone, as if he were the deifier of the Son. On this view either the essence is manifold, or Christ is God only in name and imagination.[70]

Calvin here is targeting monarchian tendencies in several contemporary anti-Nicene Italians. He seeks to refute the view that Son and Spirit are equal with the Father in person but not in divine essence. By claiming that each person of the Godhead is *autotheos*, Calvin also ensured that the relations between the persons must be voluntary, since no one person can claim authority to impose his will on the others.[71] Hence it is wiser to affirm a relationship of dependence between the three persons than to refer to one as the source of the other. A better way to state the matter is that the Father is the presupposition of the Son and the Spirit rather

---

70. Calvin, *Institutes*, 1.13.24.
71. Cf. Gerald Bray, *The Doctrine of God* (Downers Grove, IL: InterVarsity Press, 1993), 201–4; Letham, *The Holy Trinity*, 256–57.

than possessing a form of ontological priority over them. The Father is not over and above the Son and the Spirit, but is in, with, and for the Son and the Spirit.[72]

2.2.6 PRACTICAL IMPLICATIONS OF THE TRINITY

If the gospel is where we first experience God, then our primal experience of God is a Trinitarian experience.[73] A Trinitarian theology articulates what it means to "be saved by God through Christ in the power of the Holy Spirit."[74] Although we may not understand the nature of the relationship between Father, Son, and Spirit immediately following conversion, we begin to experience their presence, power, and purpose in the gospel from the outset. According to Fred Sanders: "A Christian, and especially an evangelical Christian, is somebody who is already immersed in the reality of the Trinity, long before beginning to reflect on the idea of the Trinity."[75] Prayer, worship, Eucharist, and preaching are all soaked and pervaded by the triune reality of the Christian God even if Christians themselves do not fully understand the nature of the triune relations. Consequently getting into the Trinity is crucial for Christians to worship God, follow Jesus, and be led by the Spirit. As Charles Sherlock comments: "The churches have discovered this time and again. When we retreat from the task of coming to grips with the doctrine of God, practical Christian life suffers. Spirituality becomes vague and mushy."[76] No surprise, then, that there are several practical implications to a Trinitarian faith.

1. *Prayer and worship.* The only reason why prayer is possible is because God is triune. We cannot pray to the Father except through the mediator, Jesus Christ (1 Tim 2:5; Heb 7:25; 12:24), which is why we petition the Father in Jesus' name (John 14:13–14; 16:23–26). And it is the Spirit who guides us in prayer, and he is even the sphere in which our prayer begins (Rom 8:26–27; Jude 20). Tim Chester writes, "True prayer is Trinitarian and can only be Trinitarian. The Father invites us to call upon him through the Son by the Spirit."[77]

Furthermore, a distinctive aspect of Christian worship should be its focus and locus in the Triune God. Whereas much of what passes off as worship in some evangelical churches is a hybrid between unitarian and christomonistic tendencies, the Triune God is both the subject and sphere of authentic Christian worship. If we want to worship God as he *is*, we must worship God *as* Trinity. We should be exhibiting a conscious regard for the relations of Father, Son, and Holy Spirit in the

---

72. Bloesch, *God the Almighty*, 174–87.
73. T. F. Torrance, *The Trinitarian Faith* (Edinburgh: T&T Clark, 1995), 28.
74. Catherine Mowry LaCugna, "The Trinitarian Mystery," in *Systematic Theology: Roman Catholic Perspectives* (ed. Francis Schüssler Fiorenza and John P. Galvin; Minneapolis: Fortress, 1991), 1:153.
75. Sanders, *The Deep Things of God*, 26.
76. Charles Sherlock, *God on the Inside: Trinitarian Spirituality* (Wanniassa, Aus.: Acorn, 1991), 181.
77. Tim Chester, *The Message of Prayer* (BST; Leicester, UK: Inter-Varsity Press, 2003), 64.

manner in which we sing and serve, confess the creed or recite the confession, pray and preach, give and greet, commemorate and congregate. Worship must extol the grace and glory of the Godhead known to us as Father, Son, and Holy Spirit. Every Sunday should in some sense be "Trinity Sunday."

On top of that, Christian worship even experiences the Triune God as we are drawn to the Father, through the mediatorship of the Son, and in the power of the Holy Spirit. Worship is an intimate engagement with the Triune God, who seeks to meet us and satisfy the longings of our hearts with the joy that only the Father, Son, and Spirit can impart. Worship becomes a moment where we are taken up into the divine life of the Trinity. Viewed this way, "Trinitarian worship is the gift of participating through the Spirit in the incarnate Son's communion with the Father."[78]

2. *Ministry*. The incarnation provides the model of servant ministry. The sending of the Son in his act of voluntary self-humiliation in his passion and crucifixion is a model for believers to follow (Mark 10:41–45; John 13:1–17; Phil 2:5–11). However, humility and service are not limited to the Son, but characterize the entire Godhead because "God exists as Father, Son, and Spirit in a community of greater humility, servanthood and mutual submission."[79] The Holy Spirit does not glorify himself but the Son (John 16:14), just as Jesus glorifies the Father (John 13:31–32; 17:1) and the Father also glorifies the Son (Mark 9:2–9; Matt 3:17; John 8:54; 12:28; Phil 2:5–11). So too must Christians seek the glory of God (Ps 57:5, 11; 1 Cor 10:31) and the honor of fellow Christians (Rom 12:10; Phil 2:3).

3. *Missions*. The quintessential example of mission derives from the Trinity. The Father offers up the Son to be broken, rejected, and bear his wrath. The Son leaves the perfect fellowship of the triune communion to be broken, deserted, and forsaken on earth. The Spirit is poured on the earth to lead and guide believers, never exalting himself but always pointing to the Son. Christian mission imitates the Trinitarian model because just as the Father sends the Son, so does the Son send us (Matt 28:19–20; John 20:21; Acts 1:8). The sending of the church is a continuation of the sending of the Son and the giving of the Spirit, where God's salvific purposes are realized. Indeed, the church is the instrument of God's eschatological repossession of the world to radiate his glory. Ultimately the church can only comprehend its missionary purpose within a Trinitarian framework of sending and being sent.[80]

4. *Community*. The Triune God is an intrapersonal community united in being and will among the persons who love each other in eternal communion. God exists only within the scope of this reciprocal and relational love between the three persons. To say that "God is love" (1 John 4:8) is not to define God as an emotional

---

78. Brian Edgar, *The Message of the Trinity* (BST; Leicester, UK: Inter-Varsity Press, 2004), 23.

79. John Ortberg, "The Shyness of God," *Christianity Today* 45 (2001): 66.

80. Lesslie Newbigin, *The Trinitarian Faith and Today's Mission* (Richmond: John Knox, 1963), 31.

presence but to recognize that love defines God's relationality, internally with himself and externally toward others. The triune nature of the Godhead implies a loving communion between Father and Son and Spirit, so much so that this inner-Trinitarian love is the ground and possibility for God's love toward humankind. The Trinity does not remain within its own harmonious existence but attempts to express its internal love externally.[81]

What is more, as bearers of the divine image, humans reflect their divine image most acutely by imitating and projecting divine love among themselves. Human beings are at their most human when they express the divine love that is hardwired into their being. Thus, inner-Trinitarian love is the pattern for human communities. The church can model Trinitarian love by loving others and so pose an alternative to the self-serving and self-gratifying ethos of secular society. Christians reflect the image of God by imaging the Trinitarian communion, where there is love, fellowship, and equality. The church can offer a countercultural model of being humans-in-community based on the Trinitarian model of reciprocal and self-giving love.[82]

2.2.7 CONCLUSION

The Trinity matters! In the words of Fred Sanders: "Trinitarianism is the encompassing framework within which all Christian thought takes place and within which Christian confession finds its grounding presuppositions."[83] The Trinity is not simply a convoluted debate about theology but comprises the essential fabric of Christian talk about God. The meaning of salvation, the identity of Jesus Christ, the nature of the church, and a whole lot more stuff rides on the operation and being of God as Trinity. So it is crucial that Christians get some kind of grip on the Trinity as part of their faith in God and as part of their attempt to know God better.

We must remember that the Trinity has antecedents in the biblical materials and that these were teased out and developed in the early church. We might say that the Old Testament intimates the Trinity and the New Testament authors are aware of the triadic nature of God's work as Father–Jesus Christ–Holy Spirit: there is an incipient Trinitarianism in the Pauline letters, and the gospel writer John is a proto-Trinitarian theologian. The essential element of the doctrine of the Trinity is that there are three coequal, coeternal, and consubstantial divine persons. Lastly, the Trinity has important ramifications for how we understand salvation, worship, ministry, missions, and community.

---

81. Millard Erickson, *God in Three Persons: A Contemporary Interpretation of the Trinity* (Grand Rapids: Baker, 1995), 333.
82. Leonardo Boff, *Trinity and Society: Theology of Liberation* (Maryknoll, NY: Orbis, 1988), 149–51.
83. Sanders, *The Deep Things of God*, 46.

FURTHER READING

Gunton, Colin E. *The Promise of Trinitarian Theology.* Edinburgh: T&T Clark, 1991.

Hurtado, Larry. *Lord Jesus Christ: Devotion to Jesus in Earliest Christianity.* Grand Rapids: Eerdmans, 2003.

Köstenberger Andreas J., and Scott R. Swain. *Father, Son and Spirit: The Trinity and John's Gospel.* NSBT; Downers Grove, IL: InterVarsity Press, 2008.

Letham, Robert. *The Holy Trinity: In Scripture, History, Theology, and Worship.* Phillipsburg, NJ: Presbyterian & Reformed, 2004.

O'Collins, Gerald. *The Tripersonal God: Understanding and Interpreting the Trinity.* London: Geoffrey Chapman, 1999.

Olson, Roger, and Christopher Hall. *The Trinity.* Grand Rapids: Eerdmans, 2002.

Sanders, Fred. *The Deep Things of God: How the Trinity Changes Everything.* Wheaton, IL: Crossway, 2010.

§ 2.3 WHAT IS GOD LIKE?

All Christian theology is about God as he is known to us in the gospel of Jesus Christ. Perhaps most important, the God of the gospel is a personal God. The God who was in Christ, who is the Father of Christ, and who raised Christ is a personal being with a will, and he works out that will in his personal relations with others. God is not the projection of our existential angst as to why we exist and for what purpose we are here. God is not the verbal expression that we give to the source of our religious consciousness. God is not the "vibe" in the bees, seas, and trees. God is the supernatural being revealed through creation, manifested in Israel's history, testified in the Scriptures, incarnated in Jesus of Nazareth, and experienced in the Holy Spirit. The God of the gospel has a purpose, a plan, and a capacity to relate to others.

This God is the one who called the universe into being, who called Abraham out of idolatry, who chose Israel to be his people, who sent his Son into the world because he loved the world, and who called Gentiles into the family of the Messiah. He is the source of all life in the universe. God is the one who is, who was, and who will always be (Rev 1:4; 4:8). God is the "I am" (Exod 3:14; John 8:58), the self-existent one who creates and covenants. God is the reason why there is "something" rather "nothing" and why the universe exhibits any rational intelligibility at all.

Ironically many people in our secular Western cultures still claim to believe in God, and yet only a limited number are actively involved in Christian churches. The reason for this is because what the masses mean by "God" is not necessarily what evangelical theology has always meant by God. Ask Joe Bloggs or Mary-Joe Biggins what they mean by God and you'll hear something amounting to an old granddad who lives in the clouds, made the universe pretty, sends good people to heaven and bad people to hell, does the odd miracle here and there, and pretty much leaves everyone be.

Now I probably wouldn't get out of bed on Sunday morning to worship that kind of God either, so I don't blame them for staying away from church if that is the only God available to worship. Nevertheless, the Christian God is not a benign geriatric old man up in the nether regions of the cosmos, wagging his finger from afar at a bunch of mischievous mortals frolicking about and having too much fun. The God of Christians is known through the wonder and glory of creation, in his special revelation to Israel, in the incarnation of his Son, and in the presence and power of his Holy Spirit; most importantly, he is known in the gospel. This is a God of justice, love, mercy, jealousy, and power.

2.3.1 THE ATTRIBUTES OF GOD

The study of God attempts to address the question, "What is God like?" The God we immediately encounter in the gospel shows us that he is loving by setting forth Jesus to die for sinners (Rom 5:8). He is good like a shepherd who lays down his life to protect the flock from danger (John 10:11). God is also just by satisfying his wrath against sin in the death of Jesus (Rom 3:21–26; Heb 6:10). The resurrection shows us the goodness of God's power and the power of God's goodness (Acts 2:25–28; 1 Cor 6:14; 15:43).

Yet there are even more facets of God's character for us to consider too. These facets of God's being are ordinarily called *divine attributes*. The divine attributes pertain to those qualities that are found wherever God is revealed. They are those reliable patterns of character that belong to God as God.[84] In the Reformed tradition, God's attributes are usually divided into two categories: incommunicable and communicable.[85] The incommunicable attributes of God refer to those elements of God's being and character that are unique to himself and cannot be shared with others. The communicable attributes of God designate those elements of God's being and character that are transferable and shareable with others in limited degrees. In many cases, the list of attributes in both categories could be multiplied endlessly. What follows below are the primary attributes relating to God's character and actions as we know in Scripture.

2.3.1.1 THE GOD WHO IS UNLIKE US: THE INCOMMUNICABLE DIVINE ATTRIBUTES

God is unique in ways that human minds can scarcely imagine or explain. We often lack analogies to express the full extent and true nature of God's being. The reason why "there is none like [God]" (Isa 46:9) is because God alone possesses particular attributes that cannot be shared with any other creature.

1. *Eternity*. The eternity of God means that God exists without beginning or end. He is, in the language of Revelation, the Alpha and the Omega of all things, before

---

84. Thomas C. Oden, *Systematic Theology* (3 vols.; Peabody, MA: Hendrickson, 1998), 1:35.

85. Cf., e.g., Louis Berkhof, *Systematic Theology* (Grand Rapids: Eerdmans, 1949), 57–81; Hermann Bavinck, *Reformed Dogmatics. Volume 2: God and Creation* (ed. J. Bolt; trans. J. Vriend; Grand Rapids: Baker, 2004), 148–255.

them and after them (Isa 41:4; Rev 1:8; 21:6; 22:13). As the psalmist says, "Before the mountains were born or you brought forth the whole world, from everlasting to everlasting you are God" (Ps 90:2). God existed before the world (Gen 1:1; John 1:1; 17:5, 24), and the number of his years are unsearchable (Job 36:26). He is the one who lives forever (Isa 57:15) and is immortal (Rom 1:23; 1 Tim 6:16).

The question of God and time is a tad more complex than you might first think. If we say that God is "timeless," that means he knows neither past nor future but is completely outside of a space-time limitation. God experiences all of time simultaneously, and there is no gap between God's plan and his execution of it precisely because he stands outside of it. Or, we could say that God is "everlasting" in the sense that he exists within time at every single point so that he is spatially present within every space-time location. In either case, God's experience of time is different from our own experience. That is why one day is like a thousand years and a thousand years are like a day to God (Ps 90:4; 2 Pet 3:8). As the eternal "I am," God stands above the limitation of temporal sequences and beyond the limitations of successive moments. Nevertheless, God's eternity is not a static and entrenched dislocation from time; God is not only eternal; he is his own eternity. God sustains time and God pervades time so that every second throbs with the heartbeat of divine eternity.[86]

2. *Self-sufficiency.* To say that God is self-sufficient is to say that God's being and existence are not contingent on anything else in the universe. God is not served by human hands as if he needed anything (Acts 17:24–25), and no one has even given something to God that God might feel the need to pay them back (Job 41:11). God does not have a parasitic or symbiotic relationship with any other being, force, or agency in heaven or on earth. God does not have needs that have to be met in order to exist or to exist happily. It is not that God does not need anyone; the point is that God *could not* need anyone else. If he did, the difference between Creator and creature would be lessened.

God exists in an infinitely superior capacity to our own as he is the Creator of all things and all things endure only because of his will (Rev 4:11). God's self-sufficiency implies his self-satisfaction with his own glory, a glory that radiated before the foundation of the world. Jesus refers to the glory he shared with the Father before the creation of the world (John 17:5, 24). God's act of creation, redemption, and new creation are, therefore, the means of expressing his glory in a loving relationship with others. It was always God's plan to glorify himself by loving others as the Creator, Redeemer, and Lord. Theologians call this aspect of God's being *aseity*, which means God's all-sufficient greatness as himself without being tied to anything

---

86. Bavinck, *Reformed Dogmatics*, 2:163–64.

else. As the "I am," God's existence and character are determined by himself alone and not derived from anyone else. God's existence is what he eternally and essentially always is and will always be.

3. *Immutable*. Divine immutability is the doctrine that God is characteristically changeless in his character (the tautology is deliberate). Scripture itself is clear in urging our belief in God's changelessness as a constituent element of his person (e.g., Ps 102:26–28; Mal 3:6; Jas 1:17). The psalmist declares: "God, who is enthroned from of old, who does not change" (Ps 55:19). According to the prophet Malachi, Israel's rescue is rooted in God's unchanging nature: "I the LORD do not change. So you, the descendants of Jacob, are not destroyed" (Mal 3:6).

Consequently, God has no duplicity, capriciousness, or fickleness. According to Moses, "God is not human, that he should lie, not a human being, that he should change his mind. Does he speak and then not act? Does he promise and not fulfill?" (Num 23:19). The immutability of God's being establishes the certainty of God's gospel plan (Matt 13:35; 25:34; Eph 1:4, 11; 3:9–11; 2 Tim 2:19; 1 Pet 1:20; Rev 13:8). When Jesus Christ is said to be "the same yesterday and today and forever" (Heb 13:8), it means that faith rests on the unchanging plan centered on Jesus Christ as an eternal being (1:8), with an eternal priesthood (5:6; 6:20; 7:17, 21, 28) to bring eternal salvation (5:9; 7:24–25; 9:12) through the eternal Spirit (9:14). The eternal and unchangeable nature of Jesus Christ holds true also for God's plan for redemption.[87]

Depictions in Scripture of God's changing his mind, repenting, or relenting (e.g., Gen 6:6; Exod 32:9–14; Isa 38:1–6; Jonah 3:10) are anthropomorphic depictions of God—that is, the perception of God from a human vantage point describing his actions in a humanlike way. These anthropomorphisms express the prerogative of God with respect to a specific situation. They employ the imagery of human emotions as the means of emphatic description, like showing God's displeasure with something that is akin to attitudes like "regret."[88] They prove that God is not mystically removed or vaguely aloof from life in creation; he interacts with his creatures, and the anthropomorphisms are the attempt of biblical authors to say what these interactions look like from the human side. These anthropomorphic depictions should not be glibly explained away as if God's inner being is really somehow different from his actions as revealed in Scripture. More likely, as J. I. Packer wisely put it: "The anthropomorphisms are there to show us why God acted as he did in the biblical story, and how therefore he might act towards us in our own personal stories."[89]

---

87. Peter T. O'Brien, *The Letter to the Hebrews* (PNTC; Grand Rapids: Eerdmans, 2010), 517–19.
88. Grudem, *Systematic Theology*, 165.
89. J. I. Packer, "What Do You Mean When You Say God?" *Christianity Today* 30 (September 1986): 30.

It is unfortunate that divine immutability is frequently rejected because it is erroneously thought to imply a God who is impersonal, relationally distant, and unrelated to the dynamics of the world. The assumption here is that for relationships to be meaningful, God himself must be subject to constant change and open to revision. However, divine immutability is not some kind of intrinsic immobility, but the moral constancy of his character: God acts and does as he is and chooses to be. Immutability does not insist that God does not interact with the world, but only that his interactions remain consistent with his purpose and person. Divine immutability is not the construct of an unloving God imported from Greek philosophy; rather, divine immutability is the grounds for the constancy of his love, the surety of his faithfulness, and the triumph of his purposes precisely because he is the God who does not change.

When God the Son became incarnate, there was a real change in that the Son became something that he was not before: a human being. However, the incarnation of the Son and the sending of the Spirit were a part of how God had always intended himself to be. The incarnation was a humble act of God to take on human nature, not as limiting his divinity but as expressing it in a new form outside the sphere of divine timelessness. We must note, however, that the character of God as Father, Son, and Spirit remained the same before, during, and after the incarnation.

If God is the being of all perfections in his purpose, promises, and person, then change is strictly impossible for him—if we assume, of course, that change is construed as correction or coercion to his character. Process theologians suppose that God is like a flowing river, constantly moving, always in flux, so that just as one never steps into the same river twice because it is perpetually in motion, God himself is never unchanged but always in a state of flux. The biblical testimony and that of Christian orthodoxy gravitates to a different metaphor. He is not like a river; rather, he is the Rock: "He is the Rock, his works are perfect, and all his ways are just. A faithful God who does no wrong, upright and just is he" (Deut 32:4), and "Truly he is my rock and my salvation; he is my fortress, I will never be shaken" (Ps 62:2). Indeed, the immutability of God is an anchor for the soul (Heb 6:19).

4. *Impassible.* Divine impassibility means that God cannot be affected by anything such as emotions or events that are external to himself. This does not mean that God does not have emotions like love or joy or grief, for he clearly does; indeed, they even define his character. More properly, impassibility means that God is not affected or changed by anything outside of himself. The main point is that God is not *affected* rather than lacking *affection*! Divine immutability, then, requires divine impassibility.

Now in the incarnation, Jesus experienced grief, pain, joy, and frustration—in his hypostatic union of divinity and humanity—but they did not mark a fundamental change in his personality or purpose. That is what divine impassibility means.

To quote the venerable J. I. Packer again, historically, what divine impassibility means is:

> Not impassivity, unconcern, and impersonal detachment in the face of the creation. Not inability or unwillingness to empathize with human pain and grief. It means simply that God's experiences do not come upon him as ours come upon us. His are foreknown, willed, and chosen by himself, and are not involuntary surprises forced on him from outside, apart from his own decision, in the way that ours regularly are.[90]

However, a number of theologians of many stripes have denied impassibility on the grounds that God is a suffering God and that he is affected by his relationship with us (e.g., Jürgen Moltmann, Karl Barth, Dietrich Bonhoeffer, D. A. Carson, John Stott). Mark Baddeley jokes that "impassibility is the ugly duckling in theology today" because the trend is to posit a God in tune with his emotions and shares the emotional impact of our lives.

Baddeley goes on to argue that impassibility is what makes the gospel good news.[91] First, impassibility proves that God acts out of love and in grace because it is only his own being that motivates him to be so. God is not persuaded to be loving and gracious because of his experience of suffering. Rather, God acts lovingly and graciously toward us because he eternally and unchangeably is so. Second, the incarnation and cross were not simply a manifestation of what was always true, namely, that God suffers and empathizes with human tragedy. No, the incarnation was a fundamentally new event whereby the Son became incarnate and suffered for us. Therefore, things previously not possible for God's Son, such as the experience of suffering and death, became possible when the Son took on flesh and blood. Impassibility establishes that God relates to us in a fully emotional way, grounded in his own nature; accordingly, he is able to act in love and grace toward us. Furthermore, the man Jesus Christ can authentically sympathize with our weaknesses because only God cannot be emotionally pressed to acting in compassion toward us.

So, then, does God suffer? Indeed he does. But his suffering is not surprisingly imposed; it does not move him to be something other than he is or to do something other than he intended to. God chooses to be the God who suffers with and for human creatures. Indeed, according to Packer, "a totally impassive God would be a horror, and not the God of Calvary at all. He might belong in Islam; he has no place in Christianity. If, therefore, we can learn to think of the *chosenness* of God's grief and pain as the essence of his impassibility, so-called, we will do well."[92]

---

90. Packer, "What Do You Mean When You Say God?" 31.
91. Mark Baddeley, "Does God Feel Our Pain?" *The Briefing* 384 (2010): 12–17.
92. Packer, "What Do You Mean When You Say God?" 31 (italics original).

5. *Omnipresence.* The omnipresence of God designates that God is not limited or confined with respect to spatial locations. As Creator he pervades his creation. That is why the God of Israel was not a tribal or territorial God. God's presence cannot be spatially compressed or geographically confined, which is why Solomon prayed, "The heavens, even the highest heaven, cannot contain you. How much less this temple I have built" (1 Kgs 8:27; 2 Chr 6:18), and why Paul insisted that God cannot dwell in idols and temples (Acts 17:24). His speech at the Areopagus translates God's omnipresence into the all-sustaining, life-giving power: "in him we live and move and have our being" (17:28).

In addition, the psalmist states that he cannot escape the Spirit of God, either in heaven, Sheol, or in the uttermost parts of the sea. Everywhere he goes, God is there to lead him (Ps 139:7–10). Jeremiah declared, "'Who can hide in secret places so that I cannot see them?' declares the Lord. 'Do not I fill heaven and earth?' declares the Lord" (Jer 23:24).

Yet we have to ask one peculiar question. Is God in hell? If hell is the absence of God and if God is omnipresent, then either God is in hell or else God is not omnipresent. My own suggestion to this conundrum is that hell is indeed an absence of God, but hell is characterized by the absence of his providence, grace, and goodness. Since God is an omnipresent being, he cannot not be omnipresent by necessity, so that God's presence in hell is a given, but it is perhaps expressed there in terms of his justice and lament for these creatures and their fate.

There are layers of God's presence and his absence.[93] God is present in different places in creation in a different degree and a different manner. That is why some places (heaven, Bethel, Jerusalem) and some persons (Israel in the wilderness, anointed figures, the incarnation, indwelling believers) can express particular modes of God's presence. Unlike panentheism, which proposes that God lives in everything, the biblical testimony is that God exists everywhere in creation while remaining distinct from creation. Finally, divine omnipresence is the presupposition for divine providence as expressed in God's continuing care and concern for creation.

6. *Omnipotence.* The victory declared in the gospel is contingent on a God who cannot be thwarted in what he intends to do. We might even say that Paul is not ashamed of the gospel because it is the *omnipotence of God* for the salvation of Jews and Greeks (Rom 1:16). The power of God knows no limit, no condition, and no contingency other than being expressed in accordance with his own character. Thus God is omnipotent in the sense that he can achieve all that he determines in his holy will. If it were not so, the gospel would not be good news.

---

93. Terence Fretheim, *The Suffering of God: An Old Testament Perspective* (Minneapolis: Fortress, 1984), 60–78.

That God is "almighty" (2 Cor 6:18; Rev 1:8) is shorthand for "he has all might and all power." The rhetorical question, "Is anything too hard for the LORD?" (Gen 18:14; Jer 32:27) must be answered in the negative. Job tells the Lord: "I know that you can do all things; no purpose of yours can be thwarted" (Job 42:2). The angel Gabriel tells Mary that "nothing will be impossible with God" (Luke 1:37 NRSV), and Jesus affirms that "with God all things are possible" (Matt 19:26).

Closely related to God's infinite power is his *sovereignty* and *freedom* in all things. By his sovereignty we mean the authority of his power over creation, and by his freedom we mean the unconstrained application of his power to achieve his will. Of course there is the philosophical objection to omnipotence: "Can God make a rock so heavy that he cannot lift it?" Yet the question is an absurdity itself. As C. S Lewis said:

> Meaningless combinations of words do not suddenly acquire meaning simply because we prefix to them the two words "God can." It remains true that all *things* are possible for God: the intrinsic improbabilities are not things but non-entities. It is no more possible for God than for the weakest of His creatures to carry out both of two mutually exclusive alternatives; not because His power meets an obstacle but because nonsense remains nonsense, even when we talk it about God.[94]

7. *Omnibenevolence*. The goodness of God is that quality of God that lacks any kind of malice and promotes the well-being of others with whom God enters into a covenant relationship. Divine goodness is the glue between God's glory (his transcendent magnificence) and God's holiness (his transcendent otherness). The goodness of creation ("God saw all that he had made, and it was very good" [Gen 1:31]) derived immediately from the goodness of the Creator himself. Just as God's creative word was "good," so too is his redemptive word good since Christians taste "the goodness of the word of God" when they believe the word of the gospel (Heb 6:5). Furthermore, 2 Peter 1:3 states that God called the elect by his own "glory and goodness," which means that God's goodness permeates his person and drives his plan in redemptive history. God's revelation of salvation is motivated by his own goodness and love (Pss 109:21; 142:7). Indeed, God's visible presence can be understood as the displaying of his goodness (Exod 33:19). God's goodness is cause for rejoicing since it is always for the benefit of his people (2 Chr 6:41; Pss 116:12–13; 145:7). Communion with God can be conceived of as experiencing his love and goodness (Pss 23:6; 69:16) even for all eternity (27:13). God's goodness is a place of refuge (31:19) and a sign of divine favor (86:17).

There is, however, the "Euthyphro dilemma": Is something good because God

---

94. C. S. Lewis, *The Problem of Pain* (New York: Macmillan, 1962), 28.

commands it, or does God command something because it is good? In other words, is God arbitrary in what he decrees as good? Could he, for instance, decree at a whim that murder and theft are good? Or is goodness a virtue itself independent of God, which God himself is bound by? We split the horns of the dilemma by saying that God's character is intrinsically good; therefore, God's goodness is an expression of his character, so that whatever he does and says will be necessarily good.

8. *Omniscience.* The absolute knowledge of God over all things, past and present, possible and actual, is called his omniscience. God has knowledge of all things (1 John 3:20), and God is the one "who has perfect knowledge" (Job 37:16). The extent of God's knowledge is boundless, and God uses his knowledge perfectly. God even *foreknows* things in advance, like the destiny of nations and the salvation of individuals (Isa 44:7–8, 25–28; Rom: 8:29). God not only knows all things—past, present, and future—but God also knows all possibilities. That is God's middle knowledge of all potentialities. When God promises not to remember the sins of his people (Isa 43:25), it does not entail that God somehow wipes his own mental hard drive. The point is that God will not let his knowledge of such sins play a part in how he relates to people.

2.3.1.2 THE GOD WE CAN BE LIKE: THE COMMUNICABLE DIVINE ATTRIBUTES

There are a number of qualities that God possesses that can be replicated in human beings. If we are to be "imitators of God" (Eph 5:1 NIV [1984]), it is helpful to know which divine attributes we are to actually imitate in our lives.

1. *Personal.* The God of the gospel brings us into a personal relationship with himself. God is a personal being, a triune being no less, subsisting as Father, Son, and Holy Spirit. God is not simply a "force" or the "ground of being," as in pantheism or deism. God is living and active and enters into relationships with others. That there are personal relationships within the Godhead means that relationality is essential for what it means for God to be God.

God also enters into a relationship with creation and creatures. God's relationship is expressed in specific covenantal relationships defined by promises that are often conditional or unconditional. God has a covenant with creation (Gen 9:9–10), Abraham (15:18), Israel (Exod 19:5), and the new Israel (Matt 26:28). By virtue of creation in the divine image, human beings are also personal beings with cognition, self-awareness, and a capacity for relationships. This relational quality is communicated to them from their Creator. Humans, just like the Trinity, are persons-in-community.

2. *Faithful.* The gospel announces the event through which God's divine faithfulness is enacted by providing the salvation that his covenantal promises bind on

him (e.g., Deut 7:9; Pss 31:5; 145:13). God's faithfulness means that he is true and trustworthy and that his Word can be taken as reliable (Pss 33:4; 145:13; 2 Cor 1:18; 1 Pet 4:19). God's faithfulness guarantees that his plan and promise about the future will come to fruition (1 Cor 1:9; 10:13; 1 Thess 5:24; 2 Thess 3:3; Heb 10:23). The faithfulness of God is expressed in the faithfulness of Christ (Phil 3:8; Heb 3:5–6; Rev 1:5). Human beings can be praised for their faithfulness before God (e.g., Rom 4; Heb 11), and faith is the appropriate response to divine faithfulness (Ps 18:25; Rom 1:17). God creates faith in persons so that their faithfulness reflects God's own fidelity to his creation (Phil 1:29). Faithfulness remains a cardinal virtue of the Christian life since it expresses a key trait of God's own character (1 Cor 4:2; Col 1:5; 2 Tim 2:22).

3. *Loving.* According to Karl Barth, "God is the One who loves in freedom."[95] God's love is closely related to his goodness, mercy, and faithfulness. His special covenant love is uniquely expressed in his devotion to Israel, Jesus, and the church (e.g., Exod 15:13; 34:6; Deut 7:9; Ezra 3:11; John 3:35; 5:20; 2 Thess 2:16; 1 John 3:1). Love prompts God's redemptive acts of atonement and forgiveness (Pss 51:1; 98:3; John 3:16; Rom 5:8). God's love for his people can be seen in the allegories of the rescue of an exposed infant (Ezek 16) and the marriage of Hosea and Gomer (Hos 1–3). God is the "God of love" (2 Cor 13:11) and "God is love" (1 John 4:8).

Divine love is also the example that we are to emulate in terms of loving one another. The greatest commandments according to Jesus are love for God and love for neighbor (Matt 22:36–39). Love is the highest virtue (1 Cor 13:13). Love is the mark of true discipleship (John 13:34–35). God communicates his love by pouring his love into our hearts through the Holy Spirit (Rom 5:5). The connection between God and love is not one made by inference or abstraction, but primarily out of experience of the God who loves his children.

4. *Holy.* The gospel reconciles sinners with a holy God. Now God's holiness is rather hard to define. Several suggestions are often given, such as God's moral uprightness, integrity, set-apartness, or transcendence. God's holiness encompasses all of these, but somehow is even more than all of them put together. God's holiness is the single attribute that distinguishes him most of all from everything else in heaven and on earth. Holiness is the only attribute that is used of God three times with "holy, holy, holy" (Isa 6:3). I suspect that God's holiness is arguably a synonym for God and denotes the sheer God-ness of God himself. God's holiness is God's state of being that is entirely removed from anything that is contrary to him.

According to Wolfhart Pannenberg, God's holiness motivates his judgment and his salvation.[96] Joshua admonishes the people with the words: "You are not able to

---

95. Barth, *CD* II/1:84.   96. Pannenberg, *Systematic Theology*, 1:399.

serve the LORD. He is a holy God; he is a jealous God. He will not forgive your rebellion and your sins. If you forsake the LORD and serve foreign gods, he will turn and bring disaster on you and make an end of you, after he has been good to you" (Josh 24:19–20). Isaiah announces a divine lawsuit against the nation brought against them by "the Holy One of Israel" (Isa 1:4; 5:24; 31:1). At the same time, God's holiness is a source of salvation. Hosea states: "I will not carry out my fierce anger, nor will I devastate Ephraim again. For I am God, and not a man—the Holy One among you. I will not come against their cities" (Hos 11:9). Isaiah also regards "the Holy One of Israel" as the guarantor of the exiles' hope of liberation (Isa 41:14; 43:3, 14; 48:17; 49:7). Pannenberg states: "Thus the holiness of God both opposes the profane world and embraces it, bringing it into fellowship with the holy God."[97]

Since God elects his people in holiness and for holiness, their standing in the world is meant to be a living parable of divine holiness. Objects of the cultus, ministries, persons, and groups can be holy in the sense of being consecrated to God and being set apart from their environment in reflecting the characteristics of God. The holiness of God's people is positional in that believers are uniquely devoted to God (e.g., Lev 11:44; 20:7; Deut 7:6; 26:16; Josh 3:5; John 17:19; Rom 15:16; 1 Cor 1:2; 6:11; 7:14) and ethical as they are set apart from the world and commanded to live uprightly (Exod 19:6; Matt 5:48; 1 Thess 4:3, 7; Heb 12:14; 2 Pet 3:11). God mediates his holiness through Jesus Christ and by the sanctifying work of the Spirit.

5. *Wise.* The gospel is the summit of the wisdom of God as it reveals the folly of human religion and the bankruptcy of worldly philosophy. Divine wisdom means that God consistently selects the best goal and the best way to achieve that goal in his plans. The psalmist exclaims "How many are your works, LORD! In wisdom you made them all; the earth is full of your creatures" (Ps 104:24), and Paul acclaims "the only wise God" (Rom 16:27). The ascription of wisdom to God is a human recognition of the consistency, honor, goodness, and effectiveness of God's knowledge and its workings.

From a christocentric point of view, Jesus is the incarnation of God's wisdom (1 Cor 1:30). John refers to the Word that was made flesh and dwelt among us, which is analogous to the Jewish author Jesus Ben Sirach who said something similar about wisdom coming to dwell among Israel (Sir 24:1–17). The manifold wisdom of God revealed in Christ was made known to the rulers and authorities in the heavenly realm (Eph 3:10). God's wisdom given to human beings is likewise theocentric in that it begins with fear for the Lord (Ps 111:10; Prov 9:10). We do not share in God's wisdom, but God can impart wisdom to his people so that they live appropriately

---

97. Ibid.

and safely in the world. That is why Solomon asked God for the gift of wisdom (1 Kgs 3:29; 2 Chr 1:11) and why James counsels believers to ask for wisdom (Jas 1:5).

6. *Glorious.* God's glory is the infinite and radiant magnificence of God. The only other words that come close to describing it are "splendor" and "majesty." God's purpose to glorify himself is to enable his creatures to magnify and enjoy the glory of his being. Thus, closely related to God's glory is God's reputation and faithfulness (e.g., Exod 14:4). As the incarnate manifestation of the glorious God, Jesus is the "Lord of glory" (1 Cor 2:8). Jesus receives glory from the Father (John 1:14; Acts 3:13; Phil 2:10–11; 1 Pet 1:21) and from Christians because of his self-giving work on the cross (1 Thess 2:19). A key promise of the gospel is that humans will share in the glory of the Lord Jesus Christ (2 Thess 2:14), and Christians will themselves be glorified on the last day (Rom 8:30).

2.3.2 DOES GOD HAVE A GENDER?

Does the fact that God is depicted as male in the Scriptures create an androcentric conception of God that is oppressive to women? Is God really male in his essence? Are men more in the image of God than women because they are male? Does describing God as male provide religious sanction to patriarchal oppression and cultural imperialism? These are the questions about God and gender raised by feminist theologians. A few thoughts to consider here.

We can readily admit the sociolinguistic link between language and power. We can also recognize the injustices and inequalities in society perpetuated by gender discrimination. Yet retaining the maleness of God language as given in Scripture is not an automatic validation of an oppressive and abusive patriarchalism. The God who reveals himself as Father is the loving Father of all men and women. Those who receive Jesus Christ as Savior become "sons of God" (Rom 8:14, 19; Gal 3:26; 4:6 NIV [1984]) but also more generally "children of God" (John 1:12; Rom 8:16–17, 21; Phil 2:15; 1 John 3:10; 5:2). God will always remain a "he," since God is a personal being, and the substitution of the noun "God" for the personal pronoun inevitably makes him impersonal in his speech and actions. The fact that God is described as "he" does not mean that God is intrinsically male, but he relates to us primarily in the masculine mode, as Father, Son, and Lord.[98]

It is notable that it is *maleness and femaleness* that constitutes the image of God according to Genesis 1:26–27. It is humanity created as male and female that marks the image and likeness of God. That means that God's being cannot be confined to masculine qualities. Our humanity has a divine character expressed in the union

---

98. Cf. Bloesch, *God the Almighty*, 25–26.

of male and female. God is the sum of both genders because humanity as male and female are equally rooted in God's divine being.

What is more, God is also described with maternal language and feminine imagery at several points in Scripture. Moses indicts the Hebrews for their rebellion in the wilderness: "You deserted the Rock, who fathered you; you forgot the God who gave you birth" (Deut 32:18). God is depicted like a nurse or mother in his care for his people (Ps 131:2). The love of God is compared to the love of a mother for her child (Isa 49:15; 66:13). God's wisdom is considered one of the primary personifications of his work in the world (e.g., Prov 8:1–12; Jer 10:12; 51:15), and it is expressed in words that are grammatically feminine in both Hebrew (*ḥokmâ*) and Greek (*sophia*). Jesus could even depict himself like a mother hen protecting her chicks from a barnyard fire (Matt 23:37).

In the biblical witness, God's fatherhood is not an oppressive or authoritarian persona that he adopts to force his will on others. Instead, we are to see the imagery of a father's deep love for his children. Jesus taught his disciples to pray to the Father with the intimate term of *abba* (Matt 6:9; Mark 14:36; Rom 8:15; Gal 4:6). Jesus declared that God's fatherhood is why he is so eager to answer prayer (Matt 7:9–11), for God's love is like a father's love for his children. And this is why the image of being "children of God" is so powerful. The God from whom we were formerly estranged on account of our sin has adopted us into his own family (John 1:12–13; Rom 8:13–17; Gal 3:26). If there is something good about a human father's love for his children, then there is something infinitely good about the heavenly Father's love for his children too.

I think it worth pointing out as well that all theological language is analogical since the finiteness of human language cannot contain the entirety of God in all his infinite being. Human language for God brings us only partial and incomplete analogies, parables, similes, and images of what God is like. All God language, including that freighted with connotations of human gender, male or female, and sonship, is only analogous to God's being and not an absolute description of his person. Shirley Guthrie writes:

> With respect to the doctrine of the Trinity ... when we speak about God as "Father," when we speak about the eternal "Son" who comes to us in the man Jesus (who taught us to call his Father "our Father"), and when he speaks about the "Spirit" who is the Spirit of the Father and of the Son, we are not talking about the *gender* of God (for God is neither male nor female). We are using analogical language from human experience to talk about the *kind of relationship* that exists between the members of the Trinity and between the triune God and us human beings—a relationship that is like the intimate relationship between parents and their children.[99]

---

99. Shirley C. Guthrie, *Christian Doctrine* (rev. ed.; Louisville: Westminster John Knox, 1994), 74.

2.3.3 THE ESSENCE OF GOD: GLORIOUS, HOLY, LOVING

Barth said that when God comes to us, there is "an overflow of his essence."[100] What is this essence and how is it displayed in God's attributes? Is there any single attribute that captures the essence of God's character and being? Theologians have made a number of proposals as to which single attribute best accounts for the magnificence, might, and majesty of God. In light of the gospel, we can infer that the seat of God's being—almost like a soul—is his glory, holiness, and love. For in the gospel a holy God reveals the glorious Christ in the loving act of setting him forth as a sacrifice for our sins. These three traits summarize the magnificence and the mercy of God as we describe him in the gospel.

Beyond that, these three attributes of glory, holiness, and love stand out for at least two reasons. First, these three traits are all employed to describe the superlative qualities of God's character. God's glory is the only divine attribute that is so radiant that it fills heaven and earth (Num 14:21; Pss 8:1; 57:5, 11; Isa 6:3). Only holiness is ascribed to him thrice (Isa 6:3). Only love is predicated of God in an absolute way (1 John 4:8, 16).

Second, these facets of God's being blend together very naturally. As a glorious being, God's passion for his glory appears paramount (Isa 42:8; 48:11). But that glory is expressed most profoundly in his love for others. There is a glorious love expressed within the Godhead (John 3:35; 5:20; 2 Pet 1:17) and shown toward his chosen people (Deut 3:25; Pss 98:3; 115:1; John 16:27; Eph 1:4). That is why salvation is a display of God's glory because it is a display of the magnificence of his love (1 Chr 16:25; Ps 106:47; Isa 44:23). What is more, God's love is also permeated by his holiness. God's love is a holy love, a love unlike any other. Therefore, if we were to try to identify the essence of God's character as it is given to us in revelation, we could surmise that it is God's glorious-holy-lovingness that is the most definitive aspect of his character. In other words, God glorifies himself through the expression of his holy love.

---

100. Barth, *CD*, II/1:273.

§ 2.4 THE GOD WHO CREATES

2.4.1 THE GOSPEL AND THE CREATOR

The gospel declares that God has been faithful to Israel by bringing to fruition the prophetic promises for a renewed covenant and a restored Israel. In this renewed covenant, God has launched the new creation through the resurrection of Jesus Christ and in the vitalizing work of the Holy Spirit. Thus, God's act of creation is the presupposition of the gospel, while new creation is the ultimate goal of the gospel. Albert Wolters demonstrates that "creation regained" is an underlying theme of the gospel. The gospel envisages a comprehensive restoration of the created order so that the relational disruption between God and creation caused by the intrusion of evil can be finally resolved.[101] Or, as N. T. Wright says, "the purposes of God in the gospel are focused on God's longing to put the world to rights, and to put people to rights is part of that work."[102]

The gospel is umbilically connected to the wider concepts of covenant and creation. God's intent to establish his reign throughout the entire universe—that is, to conform the cosmos to his sovereignty—was to be achieved through his covenants with Abraham, Israel, and the church. God's saving power is deployed through the covenantal economies in order to restore humanity and to bring creation back to its pattern of Edenic harmony. The Noachian covenant marked God's promise to flood the world with grace rather than to submerge it again beneath the waters of judgment (Gen 9:1–17). The Abrahamic covenant had as part of its terms that Abraham would be the father of many nations (17:4–5; Rom 4:17–18). God made a covenant with Israel so that they would be a "kingdom of priests" (Exod 19:5–6) and a "light to the Gentiles" (Isa 42:6; 49:6).

The return and restoration of Israel from exile in Babylon would be marked by the advent of a new heaven and a new earth (Isa 65–66) and be accompanied by a

---

101. Albert Wolters, *Creation Regained: Biblical Basics for a Reformational Worldview* (2nd ed.; Grand Rapids: Eerdmans, 2005), 121–22.

102. N. T. Wright, *Hebrews for Everyone* (London: SPCK, 2004), 54.

§ 2.4 The God Who Creates

new covenant with renewed hearts as its concomitant proof (Jer 31:31–40; Ezek 16:60–63; 37:26–27). Israel serves as the divine witness to redemption on the international stage, and God's people are the divinely ordained vehicles for mediating God's mercy to the nations. What God does for Israel is a microcosm for what he intends to do within the entire created order.[103] The renewal of Israel's covenant is indelibly connected, then, to the renewal of creation.

The gospel announces that God recompenses and redeems, that he judges and justifies, that he destroys and delivers; but that requires an explanation of God as the author and authority of the created order. The creatorship of God could be assumed in Christian preaching to the Jewish people, since they were custodians of the sacred story of how the Creator God chose and covenanted with the Hebrew people. However, in preaching to pagans, it was often necessary for evangelists and apostles to set forth a monotheistic creation story over against the narratives of paganism as a preface to the gospel. This is exactly what Paul does in his sermons in Lystra (Acts 14:15–17) and at the Athenian Areopagus (17:14–34). Such a move is necessary because the story of the gospel only has intelligibility as part of the story of creation, fall, and the hope of restoration. Consequently, an exposition of the gospel requires an exposition of the Creator God.

2.4.2 GOD AS CREATOR

The Nicene Creed begins, "We believe in one God, the Father Almighty, Maker of heaven and earth, and of all things visible and invisible." Placing this statement at the head of this creed "signifies to us that the doctrine of the Creator belongs to the heart and substance of the Gospel, so that such belief in him is appropriately formulated within the evangelical interrelations of the economic Trinity."[104] It is no surprise, then, that confessing God as Creator has consistently been a mainstay of Christian doctrine.

The Thirty-Nine Articles refer in Article 1 to God as "the Maker, and Preserver of all things both visible and invisible." A fuller statement is given the Westminster Confession (4.1): "It pleased God the Father, Son, and Holy Ghost, for the manifestation of the glory of His eternal power, wisdom, and goodness, in the beginning, to create, or make of nothing, the world, and all things therein whether visible or invisible, in the space of six days; and all very good." The creeds and confessions concur that neither the world nor anything therein is self-existent or eternal. Everything material and temporal owes its existence to God as the one fashioning it. Creation is the theater of God's glory and the medium that expresses his infinite

---

103. Michael Williams, *Far as the Curse Is Found: The Covenant Story of Redemption* (Phillipsburg, NJ: Presbyterian & Reformed, 2005), 121.

104. T. F. Torrance, *The Christian Doctrine of God: One Being Three Persons* (Edinburgh: T&T Clark, 1996), 203.

power, wisdom, and goodness. God is moved to create for no other reason than his glory and his goodness, that is, his love.[105]

The confession of God as Creator is thoroughly attested in the biblical testimony. A panoramic display of Yahweh's majestic power and sheer worshipability as life-giver is offered by Nehemiah, "You alone are the Lord. You made the heavens, even the highest heavens, and all their starry host, the earth and all that is on it, the seas and all that is in them. You give life to everything, and the multitudes of heaven worship you" (Neh 9:6). Jesus prayed to his "Father, Lord of heaven and earth" as a model for Christian prayer that recognizes God as Creator (Matt 11:25/Luke 10:21). We find the common reference in the Scriptures to God Most High, who is the "Creator/Lord/God of heaven and earth" (e.g., Gen 14:19–22; 24:3; Josh 2:11; 2 Kgs 19:15; Pss 115:15; 121:2; 124:8; 134:3; Isa 37:16; Acts 14:15). We could borrow the image used in Job and think of God as a master builder of the universe (Job 38:4–7).

As the Creator, God is the source of all things. Humans are entirely dependent on him for their well-being. His mastery over creation extends to everything in heaven, on earth, or under the earth. The qualities of God's power, wisdom, and majesty are even imprinted on the created order itself. Anyone who has walked under the beauty of a night sky or stood on the heights of a great mountain can relate to the words of Paul: "For since the creation of the world God's invisible qualities—his eternal power and divine nature—have been clearly seen, being understood from what has been made" (Rom 1:20). This has naturally led people to praise God as a response to the majesty and beauty of his creation (Pss 8:1–3; 19:1–6; Rev 4:11). As Isaac Watts wrote:

> The heavens declare thy glory, Lord!
> In every star thy wisdom shines;
> But when our eyes behold thy word,
> We read thy name in clearer lines.[106]

First, confession of God as Creator was accompanied by affirmation of his unique identity as the Lord and a concurrent denial of any comparable being to rival him. That is why references to God as Creator are frequently joined with statements asserting the inimitability of his being. We see that in statements like "there is no other" God (Deut 4:35, 39; 1 Kgs 8:60; Isa 44:8; 45:5, 14, 22; 46:9; Joel 2:27; Acts 4:12) and "there is no God like you" (1 Kgs 8:23; 2 Chr 6:14; cf. Deut 3:24). In the stipulations of the Sinaitic covenant, Israel is accordingly forbidden from worship-

---

105. Cf. John Calvin, *Institutes*, 1.5.6: "Moreover, if it be asked what cause induced him to create all things at first, and now inclines him to preserve them, we shall find that there could be no other cause than his own goodness."
106. See www.cyberhymnal.org/htm/h/e/heavendt.htm.

ing other gods (Exod 20:3; 23:24; 34:14; Deut 12:31; Judg 6:10; 1 Kgs 9:6–7; 2 Kgs 17:35–38; Jer 25:6)—not because God is some kind of jealous narcissist, but because of God's passion for his own glory (Deut 4:24) and because of the dehumanizing effects of idolatry (12:31). In other words, the biblical materials witness to an *exclusive monotheism*.

Second, it notable as well how God's identity as Creator is often associated with his authority over all earthly kingdoms. Hezekiah prayed, "Lord, the God of Israel, enthroned between the cherubim, you alone are God over all the kingdoms of the earth. You have made heaven and earth" (2 Kgs 19:15). Similarly the psalmist declared, "The Lord has established his throne in heaven, and his kingdom rules over all" (Ps 103:19). That is derivative of the fact that God reveals himself as king of creation: "I am the Lord, your Holy One, Israel's Creator, your King" (Isa 43:15). "Yours, Lord, is the greatness and the power and the glory and the majesty and the splendor, for everything in heaven and earth is yours. Yours, Lord, is the kingdom; you are exalted as head over all" (1 Chr 29:11).

This kingship is often described with spatial imagery, with heaven as God's throne and the earth as his footstool (Isa 66:1; Acts 7:49; cf. 1 Kgs 22:19/2 Chr 18:18; Isa 63:15; Matt 5:34; 23:22). This same God also executes his reign through specifically anointed human kings, particularly those associated with the Davidic lineage (1 Sam 2:10; 2 Chr 12:12; Ezra 1:2). On top of that we can note that all things were created by God and for God (Isa 43:7; Col 1:16; Heb 2:10). This act of reigning, ruling, and judging over creation indicates a *regal monotheism* whereby God is sovereign over his creation.

Third, God remains distinct from and other than his creation; yet he is also intimately and constantly at work within creation. In other words, God displays transcendence *from creation* and immanence *within creation*. God is particularly concerned with the well-being of humanity as they are the summit of his creating activity (Gen 1:26–27; Ps 8:4–6). God sends rain for the sustenance of all peoples (Job 5:10; 37:13; Ps 135:7; Zech 10:1; Matt 5:45). Human beings have the spheres of their existence fixed by the Lord (Acts 17:26). God determines the constancy of the universal laws of nature that govern the earth and seas: "I have ... made my covenant with day and night and established the laws of heaven and earth" (Jer 33:25).

Repeatedly it is said that the entire earth is filled with his love (Pss 33:5; 119:64). In Psalm 104 there is a lavish description of how every sphere of creation is filled with his wisdom and workings. God is frequently praised as Creator of heaven and earth and worshiped as its sustainer (Deut 33:25–28; 1 Sam 2:6–9; Neh 9:6). The scope of God's preservation includes natural cycles and seasons in the physical world (Job 37:5, 10; Pss 104:14; 135:6; Matt 5:45), flora and fauna (Ps 104:21, 28; Matt 6:26; 10:29), and even the affairs of nations (Job 12:23; Ps 22:28; Acts 17:26).

What is more, God sustains all things through his Word; that is to say, the world is christologically held together as Christ "holds together" or "sustains" all things (Col 1:17; Heb 1:3). God's continuing care and concern for creation is the substance of his providence. The doctrine of providence "encapsulates the conviction that God sustains the world that he has created and directs it to its appointed destiny."[107] Providence communicates God's enduring love for creation through his sovereign preservation of the created order; it depicts his persistent intervention on behalf of his creatures and discloses God's direction of history and his assurance that his purpose will be attained. Providence is the surest indication of God's faithfulness.[108] Thus, we can also describe God's creatorship in terms of a *providential monotheism*.

Fourth, the creation of humanity is the climax of creation on the sixth day (Gen 1:26–27). Humankind is not simply another animal within creation endowed with higher powers of reasoning; rather, they are image bearers of the Creator God and the stewards of the divine masterpiece. God enters into a relationship with these creatures where there is a mutual obligation between them. The first two primal humans are given a task in the garden to tend to it and hear stipulations with respect to what they are not to do. A successful adherence to these conditions in this probationary period will result in immortality and the perpetuation of paradise. Yet there is also a dire warning if they should disobey, including the threat of exile and death.

The tragic story of Genesis 2–3 shows us that our primordial parents disobeyed God, and the curses and judgments promised to them were therein invoked. The origin and intrusion of evil into God's good creation are a mystery, one we will discuss later. What is important here is that the Creator God has no intention of leaving creation in its state of deprivation and depravation. An increasing cycle of sin, curse, death, and exile will not be the ultimate end of creation. Precisely because God has covenantally bound himself to creature and creation, he intends to restore its inhabitants through forgiveness, blessing, life, and homecoming.

The unfolding drama of redemption from Adam to Abraham to Israel to Messiah is all part of God's plan to repossess the world for himself. God and evil cannot coexist because God is both infinitely holy and infinitely God. In other words, God plus the presence of evil results in eschatology. God purposes to use his covenant partners as his instrument to forgive sin and vanquish evil throughout the world. The corruption of creation through the entrance of evil implies a *covenantal monotheism* whereby the God of creation will put creation itself to rights.

Taken together, exclusive monotheism, regal monotheism, providential monotheism, and covenantal monotheism can all be regarded as constituent parts of the

---

107. S. N. Williams, "Providence," *NDBT*, 711.
108. John Webster, "Providence," in *Mapping Modern Theology: A Thematic and Historical Introduction* (ed. Kelly M. Kapic and Bruce L. McCormack; Grand Rapids: Baker, 2012), 203–7.

one overall heading of *creational monotheism*.[109] This scheme of creational monotheism is what fashioned distinctively Christian views of God, creation, evil, and salvation. Creational monotheism creates a system of values, forms certain ideological fixtures, and implies a story about God's dealings with the world. Creational monotheism has two sets of implications.

The first set of implications yields negative ones. The worldview fostered by creational monotheism eliminates several other models for understanding how creation relates to the divine realm. In societies, ancient and modern, there have been a number of ways of imagining how the transcendent realities of god(s) and the heavens relate to the terrestrial realities of the earth.

1. *Deism* proposes that God created the universe, but thereafter does not interfere with it. You can find this view in Epicurean philosophers, seventeenth-century English deists, and even among twenty-first-century Episcopal bishops. However, creational monotheism stipulates that because of God's providence and covenantal promises, he is intimately concerned with and involved in creation, even to the point of miraculously intervening within it.

2. *Pantheism* is the view that God literally is the universe, while *Panentheism* is the claim that God inhabits the universe much like a soul inhabits a body. These views find advocacy from Stoic philosophers to New Age religions whereby the gap between god and the world is essentially eliminated. By contrast, creational monotheism proposes that God is distinct from the universe and not part of it. Humanity should not worship the stars but the one who made the stars. The forces of nature are not personifications of divine power; rather, they are simply earthly forces themselves subject to their Creator. God can part seas, flatten mountains, put out fires, and still winds. To identify God with a tree, bee, or sea is ultimately the attempt to domesticate him and to confine him to the created order that humans believe that they can control.

3. *Henotheism* is the belief in a supreme god among a pantheon of lesser gods, while *paganism* is the belief in many gods and spirits with varied degrees of interest and concern over human beings. Time and time again Israel struggled against a disposition toward idolatry (worship of graven images of God) and polytheism (worship of many gods). Paganism provided a license for sexual immorality, offered an apparent shortcut way of guaranteeing fertility, and legitimized the rights of ancient Near Eastern monarchs.

The story of the Old Testament is one of Yahweh versus paganism. The Hebrews who departed Egypt and built a golden calf were forced to drink and then excrete

---

109. Cf. N. T. Wright, *The New Testament and the People of God* (COQG 1; London: SPCK, 1992), 248–59.

their god (Exod 32). Yahweh proved the sham of Baal worship through Elijah on Mount Carmel (1 Kgs 18). Isaiah refers to the stupidity of idolatry by asking what kind of fool uses some wood for firewood and carves a god from the rest (Isa 44:9–20). Jeremiah indicts the foreign gods on these grounds: "Tell them this: 'These gods, who did not make the heavens and the earth, will perish from the earth and from under the heavens.' But God made the earth by his power; he founded the world by his wisdom and stretched out the heavens by his understanding" (Jer 10:11–12).

The Jewish polemic against idolatry and paganism continued in the intertestamental period, as in the Wisdom of Solomon 13, which appears to have influenced Paul's remarks in Romans 1:18–31 about the inhumanity and irreligion of idol worship. Paul also tells the Corinthians that idol worship is nothing; nonetheless demonic forces can use idols to lead people astray (1 Cor 8:4–5; 10:20–21). The fact that there is "one true God" and there is "no other" and "none like you" means that there can only be worship of the one God of creation and covenant. Creational monotheism suggests that God intends to expose paganism and idolatry for the sham that it is. God objects to paganism and idolatry because it is the ultimate act of antiworship, where humans create a god in their own image, or else humans create manageable gods that they think they can manipulate or control, or humans use the pantheon to legitimate the malevolence and machinations of mischievous monarchs.

4. *Gnosticism.* Gnosticism is the view that a wicked demigod created the world and that another benevolent god is responsible for salvation. Contrary to common opinion, the essence of Gnosticism is not knowledge, but a demiurgic creationism that separates the God of creation from the God of salvation. What drives Gnosticism is largely theodicy, an attempt to provide a rational explanation for evil in the world, to insulate God against the charge of being the author of evil, and to marry the Christian Scriptures with a Platonic cosmology that postulated several heavens and several tiers of semidivine beings.

The origins of Gnosticism are widely disputed, especially whether its origins are in paganism, in Judaism, or in Christianity. I tend to think that after the destruction of Jerusalem in AD 70 and after the expulsion of the Jews from Palestine in AD 135, Judaism basically went in two directions. The rabbinic schools attempted to create a manufactured micropiety to guide God's people without the temple and without any territory, while other Jews tried to turn Judaism into a pagan philosophy by reinterpreting the Old Testament in a hyper-Hellenistic fashion. The Christian appropriation of this second option became Gnosticism. However, since God made creation good, that means that evil is an intrusion into the divine creation and was not part of its original properties. Christians did not consent to partitioning off the God of creation from the God of salvation. Christians insisted that the God of creation was also the God of the new creation, which implied an intractable link between creation and salvation. The original goodness of creation combined with God's covenant plan to save creation disqualifies Gnosticism as a viable worldview option for believers.

The second set of implications deriving from creational monotheism relates to the specific way that Christians relate to God as the author of the world and the agent of its redemption.

1. Concerning God and creation, God is not to be identified with creation, inside creation, or as creation. Instead, creation owes its existence to God, and he is still benevolently active on creation in his providence and common grace. Creational monotheism commits believers to God's otherness from creation but in the context of his intense care and devotion to its final rescue.

2. The divide between heaven and earth or between spiritual and material realities is a further implication of creational monotheism. This is because creational monotheism posits the existence of two parallel but interlocking realities consisting of an unseen realm and a visible realm. In some instances, the material realities are themselves a visible counterpart to heavenly realities. The heavenly visions granted to Isaiah (Isa 6), Ezekiel (Ezek 1), Paul (2 Cor 12), and John the Seer (Rev 4–5) all demonstrate the interconnecting relationship between what transpires in heaven with what takes place on earth.

3. The existence of suffering and rebellion implies two sets of dualities in terms of good and evil and also present and future. The world currently languishes in the throes of evil; yet this is not the intended plan of God for his creation. God has it in mind to eliminate evil through his plan of cosmic redemption. That means that evil is not a matter of philosophical opinion (moral relativism), an illusion created by the pursuit of pleasure (Buddhism), but is a tyrannical invasion of God's realm that needs to be defeated. In the Christian narration of creational monotheism, it is by Christ and the Spirit that God has and will yet save humanity from the penalty, power, and presence of evil. Because of Easter and Pentecost, Christians live between the old age and the future age, between the "now" and the "not yet." We have received the deposit of our deliverance through the indwelling of the Spirit and await the consummation of our salvation at the Lord's return. We stand in the midst of the old world dying and a new world being born anew.

When we encounter the God of creation, it means that we are laid before the God "who brings order to chaos and sees all of creation as good, who rests on the seventh day so as to not make slaves of creatures and creation, who makes humanity in the divine image and likeness, who enthrones humanity as kings and queens of the animal world, who is in union with creation and gives the original blessing."[110] Recognition of God as Creator entails that we live in our Father's world, we dwell amidst the beauty and majesty of his divine architecture, and we place our hope in God's plan for the restoration of the world from its current travails.

2.4.3 A DISTINCTIVELY CHRISTIAN VIEW OF CREATION

A belief in monotheism, and even a creational monotheism, could be shared, in varying degrees, with other monotheistic faiths like Judaism and Islam. Here I intend to show a distinctively Christian view of God as Creator by way of reference to (1) the triune act of creation, and (2) the new creation.

2.4.3.1 TRIUNE ACT OF CREATION

God the Father is the Creator. Malachi rhetorically asks, "Do we not all have one Father? Did not one God create us?" which demands an affirmative answer (Mal 2:10). The church accordingly confesses the Father as Creator while also taking into account the roles of the Spirit and the Son as God's agents in creation. In the analogy of Irenaeus, Son and Spirit were the gloves that the Father used in the formation of the world.[111] Such an analogy is warranted by Scripture, which attributes the creative act as occurring instrumentally through Spirit and the Son.

> In the beginning God created the heavens and the earth. Now the earth was formless and empty, darkness was over the surface of the deep, and *the Spirit of God was hovering over the waters.* (Gen 1:1–2)
>
> By his power he churned up the sea;
>   by his wisdom he cut Rahab to pieces.
> *By his breath the skies became fair;*
>   his hand pierced the gliding serpent. (Job 26:12–13)
>
> *The Spirit of God has made me;*
>   *the breath of the Almighty gives me life.* (Job 33:4)
>
> When you send your Spirit,
>   *they are created,*
>   and you renew the face of the ground.
> May the glory of the LORD endure forever
>   may the LORD rejoice in his works—
> he who looks at the earth, and it trembles,
>   who touches the mountains, and they smoke. (Ps 104:30–32)

---

110. Arthur E. Zannoni, *Tell Me Your Name: Images of God in the Bible* (Chicago: Liturgy Training, 2000), 32.

111. Irenaeus, *Haer.* 2.30.9; 4.20.1.

> Who has measured the waters in the hollow of his hand,
>> *or with the breadth of his hand marked off the heavens?*
> Who has held the dust of the earth in a basket,
>> or weighed the mountains on the scales
>> and the hills in a balance?
> *Who can fathom the Spirit of the LORD,*
>> or instruct the LORD as his counselor? (Isa 40:12–13, italics added in all cases)

As creation results in the formation of the world and the impartation of life, it is naturally associated with the role of the Spirit as the one who gives life. The Spirit is the source of all energy, movement, and vitality in the universe.

The Son also inhabits a central role in the formation and sustenance of the universe. This role is signified chiefly by the title *Logos* assigned to him in the Fourth Gospel and taken up in the Antiochene school of theology that posited the mediation of creation and salvation through the Word of God.

> Yet for us there is but one God, the Father, from whom all things came and for whom we live; and there is but one Lord, Jesus Christ, *through whom all things came and through whom we live.* (1 Cor 8:6)

> He was with God in the beginning. *Through him all things were made; without him nothing was made that has been made.* (John 1:2–3)

> *For in him all things were created*: things in heaven and on earth, visible and invisible, whether thrones or powers or rulers or authorities; *all things have been created through him and for him.* He is before all things, and *in him all things hold together.* (Col 1:16–17)

> In the past God spoke to our ancestors through the prophets at many times and in various ways, but in these last days he has spoken to us by his Son, whom he appointed heir of all things, and *through whom also he made the universe.* The Son is the radiance of God's glory and the exact representation of his being, *sustaining all things by his powerful word.* (Heb 1:1–3, italics added in all cases)

Jesus Christ is allocated a role in creation as the chief agent who fashioned the created order. The church arrived at this conclusion out of an inference from Jesus' nature miracles and his preexistence. If the Messiah was sovereign over the elemental forces and if he existed before creation itself, then it must have always been the case that God the Father created the world through him. As Sean McDonough writes:

> The mighty works of Jesus, his proclamation of the kingdom of God, and the climatic events of the crucifixion and resurrection, clearly marked him as the definitive agent of God's redemptive purposes. But these mighty works could scarcely be divorced from God's creative acts. The memories of Jesus preserved in the gospels depict a man who brings order to the threatening chaotic waters, creates life out of death, and restores people to their proper place in God's world....

Reflections of these memories of Jesus, coupled with the experience of forgiveness and renewal on the part of the early Church, led to a startling but elegant (theo-)logical conclusion: If the one true God had sent Jesus the Messiah as the definitive agent of redemption, and if this redemption was at one level simply the outworking of the project of creation (a view with ample precedent in the Hebrew Bible and the Ancient Near East in general), it must be that the Messiah was the agent of creation as well.[112]

Given this picture in Scripture, it is inaccurate to say that the Father is the Creator, the Son is the Redeemer, and the Spirit is the Renewer without paying respect to the triunity of God's action in creation, redemption, and renewal as well. We are right to identify the persons of the Godhead with specific roles and against a particular intraTrinitarian order where persons have primacy—the Father is sender, not the Son; the Son dies, not the Father; the Spirit vivifies, not the Father nor the Son—but without limiting the persons into singular modes of action. We cannot reduce divine fatherhood to the mode of Creator, or reduce divine sonship to the mode of Redeemer, or reduce the divine Spirit to the mode of Renewer. That is because of the mutual interpermeation of the persons within the Godhead (i.e., perichoresis) so that all persons share in the act of creation, redemption, and renewal.

The appropriation of specific roles within the Godhead is essential if we are to maintain their distinction as Father, Son, and Spirit. However, these roles of Creator, Redeemer, and Renewer cannot be isolated from the mutuality, shared essence, and cooperative work of the Father, Son, and Spirit.[113]

The mutually shared actions of the Triune God are especially clear when it comes to creation. The Father is confessed as Creator because he eternally begets the Son and eternally breathes out the Spirit. Yet Son and Spirit participate in the Father's work of creation. The Catholic Catechism states:

> The Old Testament suggests and the New Testament reveals the creative action of the Son and the Spirit, inseparably one with that of the Father. This creative cooperation is clearly affirmed in the Church's rule of faith: "There is but one God... he is the Father, God, the Creator, the author, the giver of order. He made all things by himself, that is, by his Word and by his Wisdom," "by the Son and Spirit" who, so to speak, are "his hands." Creation is a common work of the Trinity.[114]

Thomas Torrance is even more specific in recognizing the triune nature of creation:

> Since the Father is never without the Son and the Spirit, all that the Father does is done in, through, and with the Son and the Spirit, and all that the Son and Spirit

---

112. Sean McDonough, *Christ as Creator: Origins of a New Testament Doctrine* (Oxford: Oxford University Press, 2010), 2–3.

113. Cf. Barth, *CD*, I/1:394–98; Pannenberg, *Systematic Theology*, 2:27–31.

114. *Catechism of the Catholic Church* (London: Burns & Oates, 1999), 68.

do is coincident with what the Father does. It is, then, of God the Father in this full sense, in his mutually homoousial and completely perichoretic relations with the Son and the Spirit that we are to think of him as the Sovereign Creator.[115]

The Father has chosen to be "Almighty," not by solely creating but by eternally begetting and breathing the Son and Spirit, who freely create with the Father as much as for the Father.[116]

The doctrine of the Trinity accordingly provides the foundation for the doctrine of creation. God freely chooses to create the world for the purpose of magnifying the love within the Godhead by creating creatures to share in that love. By doing so God brings surpassing glory to his holy name. Since the Father creates the world through the Son and by his Spirit, we may signify the unique and specific roles of each Trinitarian person in the act of creation.[117]

THE ROLE OF THE FATHER

- He is the constitutive grounds for all that exists in creation.
- The Father is directly active in creation with reference to his divine will being the grounds for creation.
- The Father is the author of creation with reference to its goal to glorify himself.
- The Father generates the Son whom he loves and thereby eternally shares his deity with the Son; so also the Father freely makes the world and shares his existence with it.

2.4.3.2 THE ROLE OF THE SON

- Whereas the Father is the grounds of creation, the Son is the principle of creation.
- The role of the Son is analogous to that of Wisdom in Proverbs 8, i.e., "the artisan at his side" (NIV text note).
- As the Logos, the Son is the organizing and unifying principle of the created order.
- According to Colossians 1:16, the Son is the unitive principle and goal of the created world.
- The incarnate Son exemplifies the proper relationship of humanity to God by obeying his Father.

---

115. Torrance, *Christian Doctrine of God*, 206.
116. Hans Urs von Balthasar, *Theodrama: The Last Act* (San Francisco: Ignatius Press, 1998), 66.
117. Stanley E. Grenz, *Theology for the Community of God* (Grand Rapids: Eerdmans, 2000), 102–6.

2.4.3.3 THE ROLE OF THE HOLY SPIRIT

- Whereas the Father is the grounds of creation and the Son is the principle of creation, the Spirit is the divine power active in creation.
- The Spirit is the creative power of God to will, act, and effect creation.
- The Spirit is the power that binds together Father and Son, God and creation together.

2.4.3.4 SUMMATION

Along this line it was Thomas Aquinas who wrote: "Thus God the Father effects creation by his Word, who is the Son, and by his love, who is the Holy Spirit. Thus it is the procession of Persons that cause the generation of creatures, to the extent that they include attributes of being, namely, knowing and willing."[118] I would note here one implication that follows on from the triune act of creation. The procession of Word and Spirit from the Father to fashion the cosmos requires the continuing relationship of God with creation because God creates in love and for love. If God's will is to love creation, then the Triune God is committed to ensuring the triumph of that love over all adversity through the same agents that brought creation into being. In other words, *procession* implies *mission*, as the God who freely creates also freely loves through Word and Spirit. The immanent procession of Son and Spirit from the Father results in the economic mission of Son and Spirit in redemption.

2.4.4 NEW CREATION

An additional characteristic of a Christian view of creation is that it must also incorporate the notion of "new creation." The created order is now marred by sin, death, alienation, evil, exile, and suffering, but this was neither its original state nor its intended state. The God of creation, for the manifestation of his holy love and the pursuit of his surpassing glory, commits himself to re-create the world and to conform it to the pattern of his own goodness and glory.

Isaiah explains that the *new exodus* that awaits the exiles in Babylon will be on such a scale of grandeur that the only way to properly describe it is with the imagery of a *new creation*. This is why Isaiah is often touted as the "Fifth Gospel."[119] Isaiah 40–66 announces the good news that Yahweh's reign will again come to Zion and bring with it a display of his covenant faithfulness and re-creating power (40:9; 41:27; 52:7). This is not simply a return to the old order of things before the fall; rather, it will be an entirely new and unprecedented event. Hence the prophetic

---

118. Aquinas, *Summa Theologica* 1a, 45, 6c.
119. John F. A. Sawyer, *The Fifth Gospel: Isaiah in the History of Christianity* (Cambridge: Cambridge University Press, 1996), 30.

oracle: "Forget the former things; do not dwell on the past. See, I am doing a new thing! Now it springs up; do you not perceive it? I am making a way in the wilderness and streams in the wasteland" (Isa 43:18–19).

Isaiah contains a dynamic interplay between the binary themes of judgment and salvation in the cosmic theater. God's judgment against human sin carries consequences for the natural world and in kind the restoration of humanity also carries over into the natural realm. That is because God's first purpose in election was to reach the world through his chosen people. Israel was the elect nation for the sake of the other nations. Israel was a kingdom of priests (Exod 19:6), a light to the nations (Isa 42:6; 49:6); their worship was to have a kerygmatic character in heralding God to the nations (e.g., Pss 67:2–7; 96:3–10; 117:1), and the end of exile marks the time for the Gentiles to stream toward Zion (Isa 2:2–4; Mic 4:1–3; Zech 8:23). As Julius Wellhausen said: "There is no God but Yahweh and Israel is his prophet."[120]

The story of Israel could not be told without reference to the rest of the world and vice versa. The Abrahamic and Sinaitic covenants had as their goal the restoration of humanity to its original place as children of God and custodians of creation. The fate of humanity and the cosmos hinges on Israel's fulfilling its covenantal mandate. Thus, the new saving event signifies that the debilitating effects of Israel's sin are atoned for, and the pagan nations that mistreated Israel would be accordingly judged and then be drawn to Israel's worship like moths to a flame.[121] In this narrative, the advent of the "new heavens and a new earth" becomes the ultimate expression of redemption from the corruption of human sin that has plagued the elect people and even infected the cosmic order (Isa 65:17; cf. 66:22).

The interlocking destinies of Israel and the world demonstrate that the Isaianic new creation is simultaneously anthropological and cosmological. It encompasses God's people and God's world. A transformed people (Isa 40–55) share in a transformed cosmos (Isa 65–66).[122] Indeed, creation groans and awaits the final revelation of the children of God because it stands next in line to experience liberation from corruption in advent of the new creation (Rom 8:20–23). The glorious freedom of the children of God entails the redemption of their earthly bodies and thereafter the redemption of the cosmic bodies as well. We must emphasize that this new creation cannot be viewed in isolation; it is bound up with a constellation of other prophetic hopes, such as the expectation of a new Davidic king (Isa 11:1–6; Ezek 34:23; Mic 5:1–5), a new covenant (Jer 31:31–34), and an outpouring

---

120. Cited in Robert M. Achard, *A Light to the Nations: A Study of the Old Testament Concept of Israel's Mission to the World* (trans. J. P. Smith; Edinburgh: Oliver & Boyd, 1962), 9.

121. On Israel and the nations see Michael F. Bird, *Jesus and the Origins of the Gentile Mission* (LNTS; London: T&T Clark, 2007), 26–45.

122. Moyer V. Hubbard, *New Creation in Paul's Letters and Thought* (SNTSMS 119; Cambridge: Cambridge University Press, 2002), 17.

of God's Spirit (Ezek 11:19–20; 36:26–27) as instruments of renewal. In all cases, God makes his people new from the inside out, and a world dies and is born anew around them.[123]

Israel's return from the Babylonian exile meant the partial fulfillment of the Isaianic promises. A remnant of Jews returned to the land, but God's reign was not yet fully realized; the new heavens and new earth had not yet materialized, the coming Davidic king was still to appear, and the covenant was still awaiting renewal. It is in this context of impending hopes for national restoration that Jesus of Nazareth appeared in Israel. His message of the kingdom invoked a constellation of stories and expectations about what a rescued Israel would look like, what it would be like, and who would be in it.

As the divine Son, Jesus regathered and restored Israel and undid the sin of Adam through his obedience to his messianic task in going to the cross. The community of believers that Jesus formed around himself has become the nucleus of a new covenant community that now carries with them the embryonic experience of the new creation. As Jesus has completed the role of the Davidic King, Suffering Servant, and Son of Man, the promise of a new heaven and a new earth is then brought to fruition in two stages. These two stages comprise of Jesus' resurrection and the gift of the Spirit in the first stage and the consummation of all things at his return in the second stage.

1. In the first stage, Jesus was not resuscitated after his crucifixion; rather, he was raised into an immortal and glorious body. This was not a return to an old form of life, but the beginning of the new creation. That is why the risen Jesus is called the "firstborn from among the dead" (Col 1:18; Rev 1:5) and the "firstfruits" of the resurrection (1 Cor 15:20–23). Many Jews thought that one day God would set the world aright by raising up the righteous from the dead at the end of history (e.g., Dan 12:1–2; 2 Macc 7:14; 12:43). That would be Israel's vindication as the true people of the Creator God. Yet God had done for one man in the middle of history what many Jews thought he would do for all of Israel at the end of history: resurrection.

Thus, Jesus' resurrection meant the embryonic fulfillment of the prophetic hopes for new creation. Jesus' resurrection signaled the arrival of the new eschatological epoch. The God who created all that existed had now started to transform all that exists into a new creation where death and suffering can no longer be experienced. The kingdom of God expressed in the raising of the Son will produce children of God who are "children of the resurrection" and who "can no longer die" (Luke

---

123. T. Ryan Jackson, *New Creation in Paul's Letters: A Study of the History and Social Setting of a Pauline Concept* (WUNT 2.272; Tübingen: Mohr/Siebeck, 2010), 18–32.

20:36).[124] Jesus' resurrection is both the provision and prototype of the future resurrection of believers. In Jesus' resurrection, God quashes the verdict of condemnation against sinners and transforms it into a verdict of acquittal (Rom 4:25; 1 Cor 15:17). Furthermore, what happened to Jesus—resurrection by the Spirit—also becomes a model for believers who will experience the same transformation (Rom 8:11; 1 Cor 15:51–54; Phil 3:21; 1 Pet 3:18).

The pouring out of the Spirit represents a further element in the first stage of the new creation. Instrumental in the actual transformation of believers and the cosmos is the Spirit. The Spirit has always been associated with creating life, giving life, imparting life, and breathing out life in the Scriptures (Ps 104:30; Job 33:4; John 6:63; Rom 8:2; 2 Cor 3:6). Appropriately the Spirit is called in the Nicene Creed "he who gives life."

I maintain that regeneration is found in the Old Testament. Nonetheless, the indwelling of the Spirit is a genuinely new experience in the new covenant. The Spirit is given in a unique way so as to be a "deposit" or "down payment" of the eternal life that will be bestowed at the consummation (2 Cor 5:5; Eph 1:14). The current experience of life in this Spirit is what enables believers to do what humans beings had hereto been unable to do: to live obediently to God, to deprive flesh and desire of their power in sin, to be authentically human, and to abide in holiness, love, and peace (Rom 8; Gal 5). We note, however, the christocentric dimension of the Spirit, for the Spirit was poured out only subsequent to Jesus' exaltation (John 14:16, 26; 15:26; 16:7; Acts 2:38; Gal 3:14; Eph 1:13). The gift of the Spirit is the eschatological gift of the risen Lord, who continues the work of new creation in the hearts of his people.

2. The second stage in the new creation is the consummation of creation itself. At his second coming, Jesus will be by might what he is by right: the Lord of all. This is the day when "God [will] be all in all" (1 Cor 15:28); the unimaginable image of lions and lambs lying down together becomes real (Isa 11:6; 65:25); the earth is filled with God's *shalom* or peace (Ps 85:8; Isa 52:7; Luke 2:14); all earthly cities are replaced by the heavenly city (Rev 21:2–3); there is no more crying or mourning or pain (21:4); and the new heavens and the new earth are fully revealed (Isa 65:17; 66:22; Rev 21:1). Among the final words of the risen Lord in the Revelation of John is the claim, "I am making everything new" (Rev 21:5), which is a christological appropriation of the "new things" from Isaiah 42:9; 43:19. That new work of creation has already begun as evidenced by the miracle of "new birth" (John 3:3–8; Jas 1:18; 1 Pet 1:3, 23; 1 John 2:29; 3:9; 4:7; 5:1, 4, 18) and "new creation" (2 Cor 5:17; Gal 6:15) that characterize believers.

---

124. D. A. Hagner, "Gospel, Kingdom, and Resurrection in the Synoptic Gospels," in *Life in the Face of Death: The Resurrection Message of the New Testament* (ed. R.N. Longenecker; Grand Rapids: Eerdmans, 1998), 119.

It is paramount to note the unity across God's work in creation, reconciliation, and new creation. For the God who said in creation, "Let light shine out of darkness," is the same God who "made his light shine in our hearts to give us the light of the knowledge of God's glory displayed in the face of Christ" in the gospel (2 Cor 4:6). Knowledge of God's glory is what the Pauline gospel is all about.[125] The problem with creation that even the law could not solve has been made right by the Spirit of life and the Lord of glory. The coordinated work of the Son and Spirit lift the old creation into the embryonic new creation, through the ministry the new covenant with its message of reconciliation. In the Christ Hymn of Colossians, Jesus is both the "firstborn over all creation" (Col 1:15) and the "firstborn from among the dead" (1:18). The author of the original creation reconciles it to God "through his blood, shed on the cross" and by doing so attains supremacy in the new creation (Col 1:18, 20).[126] Unlike Marcion, who attributed creation to a wicked god and credited salvation to a "new and alien god," the God of creation and new creation is the one true God operating in the Son and Spirit.

It follows, then, that attention must be given to the christocentric and pneumatic dimension of creation and new creation. Christ becomes the Creator of the new order only because he was already the Creator of the original order. He is the eternal Logos (John 1:1–3), who in the beginning laid the foundations of the world (Heb 1:10). His exaltation as head of the new creation is a direct a result of his messianic obedience as the true Adam and the true Israel amidst the old creation. The redeemer of the original order is now the author of a new order that has already begun in believers individually and in the church corporately.[127]

Similarly, the Spirit that moved over the primeval chaos in the old creation now moves in the hearts of men and women in the new creation. The Spirit participates in Jesus' messianic mission of redemption from the moment of Jesus' baptism through to his resurrection (Matt 3:16; 12:28; Rom 8:11; Heb 9:14), while also applying Christ's saving work in new birth and new creation as the "Spirit of Christ" (Rom 8:9; 1 Cor 6:11; Phil 1:19). What Paul finally gets at in 2 Corinthians 3–5 is how incorporation into Christ and the new covenant is simultaneously incorporation into the new creation, where the transforming power of the Spirit is operative (esp. 2 Cor 3:6–8, 17; 4:6; 5:17–21).

Taken together, the unity of creation and new creation as well as its christological and pneumatic actualization in the church carries immense missiological significance. The drama of creation, redemption, and new creation becomes the very story we live by, as Lesslie Newbigin wrote:

---

125. Ralph P. Martin, *2 Corinthians* (WBC; Dallas: Word, 1986), 80.

126. Cf. Michael F. Bird, *Colossians and Philemon* (NCCS; Eugene, OR: Cascade, 2009), 51–59.

127. Paul K. Jewett, *God, Creation, and Revelation: A Neo-Evangelical Theology* (Grand Rapids: Eerdmans, 1991), 449.

This presence of a new reality, the presence in the shared life of the Church of the Spirit who is the *arrabōn* [deposit] of the kingdom, has become possible because of what Jesus has done, because of his incarnation, his ministry as the obedient child of his Father, his suffering and death, his resurrection, his ascension into heaven, and his session at the right hand of God. When the apostles are asked to explain the new reality, the new power to find joy in tribulation, healing in sickness, freedom in bondage, life in death, this is the explanation they give. It follows that the visible embodiment of this new reality is not a movement that will take control of history and shape the future according to its own vision, not a new imperialism, not a victorious crusade. Its visible embodiment will be a community that lives by this story, a community whose existence is visibly defined in the regular rehearsing and reenactment of this story which has given it birth, the story of the self-emptying of God in the ministry, life, death, and resurrection of Jesus. Its visible centre as a continuing social entity is that weekly repeated event in which believers share bread and wine as Jesus commanded, as his pledge to them and their pledge to him that they are one with him in his passion and one with him in his victory. Instead of the celebration of the sabbath as the end of God's old creation, they celebrate the first day of the week, the Lord's Day, as the beginning of the new creation. In this they find enacted and affirmed the meaning and goal of their lives as part of the life of the cosmos, their stories part of the universal story. This story does indeed lead to a glorious end and is therefore filled with meaning, but the end is not some far distant date in terrestrial history. The end is the day when Jesus shall come again, when his hidden rule will become manifest and all things will be seen as they truly are. That is why we repeat at each celebration of the Lord's Supper the words which encapsulate the whole mystery of the faith: "Christ has died, Christ has risen: Christ shall come again."[128]

2.4.5 GOODNESS OF CREATION

Another characteristic of creation is its intrinsic goodness. In the opening creation story we find emphasis placed on the fact that God regarded his creation as "good" (Gen 1:4, 10, 12, 18, 21, 25) and creation plus humanity was "very good" (1:31). The goodness of creation is ultimately part of God's goodness communicated to his creation. As the Catholic Catechism puts it:

> Because creation comes forth from God's goodness, it shares in that goodness — "And God saw that it was good ... very good" — for God willed creation as a gift addressed to man, an inheritance destined for and entrusted to him. On many occasions the Church has had to defend the goodness of creation, including that of the physical world.[129]

---

128. Lesslie J. Newbigin, *The Gospel in a Pluralistic Society* (Grand Rapids: Eerdmans, 1989), 120–21.

129. *Catechism of the Catholic Church*, 70–71.

One implication is that creation should not be regarded as antithetical to God. God is not at war with creation. Creation is his piece of artistry, he uses it for his purposes, and it displays his character. A further implication is that sin, evil, and rebellion are not intrinsically part of creation, nor are they forces that God himself has eternally been struggling against; rather, they are intrusions into the created realm. Evil is a corruption of something that was originally good. The new creation will ultimately testify to the creative goodness of God's power over evil and sin. The new creation will finally demonstrate the goodness of God's power and the power of God's goodness when evil and sin are finally vanquished from creation.

2.4.6 CREATIO EX NIHILO

What is arguably an implication of the creation story in Genesis 1 is that God created the world *ex nihilo* (i.e., "from nothing").[130] The Fourth Lateran Council (1215) declared: "We firmly believe and simply confess that there is only one true God ... the Creator of all things visible and invisible, spiritual and corporeal; who from the very beginning of time by His omnipotent power created out of nothing [*de nihilo condidit*] both the spiritual beings and the corporeal." The Westminster Confession of Faith (6.1) upholds the notion that God's creative action took place *ex nihilo*: "It pleased God ... in the beginning, to create or make out of nothing the world, and all things therein." The doctrine was expressed as a way of affirming God's freedom in creation, saying that God's creation was neither constrained nor contingent on anything other than himself. Colin Gunton summarizes this point:

> The teaching that creation was "out of nothing" affirms that God, in creating the world, had no need to rely on anything outside himself, so that creation is an act of divine sovereignty and freedom, an act of personal willing. It further implies that the universe, unlike God who is alone eternal and infinite, had a beginning in time and is limited in space. Here Christian teaching is in contradiction of almost every cosmology that the world has known. The biblical stress on the sovereignty of God, allied with the demonstration of that sovereignty in the resurrection of Jesus from the dead, led in due time to the realization that to attribute eternity to anything other than God was to make that in effect divine.[131]

It surprises many students to learn, however, that the doctrine of creation *ex nihilo* was not universal in the early church. The Greek philosopher Plato had argued that the world was created "out of formless matter," which was followed by Justin; in fact Justin thought that Plato got the idea from Moses.[132] Other Christian authors

---

130. What follows is heavily indebted to Paul Copan, "Is *Creatio Ex Nihilo* A Post-Biblical Invention? An Examination of Gerhard May's Proposal," *TrinJ* 17/1 (1996): 77–93.

131. Colin E. Gunton, "The Doctrine of Creation," in *The Cambridge Companion to Christian Doctrine* (ed. C. E. Gunton; Cambridge: Cambridge University Press, 1997), 141–42.

132. Justin, *1 Apol.* 59; *Discourse to the Greeks* 29.

like Clement of Alexandria and Basil of Caesarea also accepted the Platonic premise of God's forming the world out of preexistent matter.

Coming to more recent times, philosopher of science Ian Barbour goes so far as to say that creation *ex nihilo* is not a biblical concept, but it only developed in the patristic period to defend the notion of God's goodness and absolute sovereignty over against Gnostic ideas that regarded all matter as the product of a malevolent and inferior demiurge.[133] Along similar lines, Arthur Peacocke argues that the Jewish and Christian doctrine of creation only implies that the world owes its existence to God, which would not contradict science if it were to discover that the cosmos is in fact eternal.[134]

Two key questions present themselves for examination. First, is *creatio ex nihilo* an authentically biblical concept? Second, is *creatio ex nihilo* essential for a Christian view of creation? Before that, however, we must establish what is precisely meant by *creatio ex nihilo*. First, *creatio ex nihilo* implies that all things are ontologically dependent on God and that the universe did have an absolute beginning. Augustine argued that since God alone is the source of all being, he willed to exist what formerly did not exist. So he is not a mere shaper of formless and eternal matter: "You did not work as a human craftsman does, making one thing out of something else as his mind directs.... Your Word alone created [the heaven and earth]."[135] As such, *creatio ex nihilo* refers to the ontological origination of the material world by divine decree. God is the reason why there is a "something" rather than "nothing."

We can seize the jugular and get to the core of the matter with a glance at Genesis 1:1–2:

> In the beginning God created the heavens and the earth. Now the earth was formless and empty, darkness was over the surface of the deep, and the Spirit of God was hovering over the waters.

We are confronted with what God actually did when he made the universe. In Genesis 1:2 the earth is described as "formless" (TNIV) or "without form and void" (ESV). In Hebrew, the word *tōhû* means "formless, confusion, wasteland, unreality, non-entity," and the word *bōhû* means "empty." These words (and the comparable ones in the LXX) are ambiguous terms, but you get the impression that God created the world from a mass of imageless, substanceless nothingness.

In contrast to ancient cosmogonies, Genesis points to an absolute beginning to the universe. God was not limited by chaos when creating, as in the Babylonian cosmogony, but is sovereign over the elements only because he brought them into

---

133. Ian Barbour, *Issues in Science and Religion* (New York: Harper & Row, 1971), 384.
134. Arthur Peacock, *Creation and the World of Science* (Oxford: Clarendon, 1979), 78–79.
135. Augustine, *Confessions* 11.5.7.

being. Nor did God simply bring order to a material chaos; rather, Genesis 1:1–2 implies the beginning of everything. Genesis 1 stands as an independent assertion, claiming that God created the entire cosmos in a speech-act: he spoke, and the universe instantly came into being. R. K. Harrison contends that while *creatio ex nihilo* was "too abstract for the [Hebrew] mind to entertain" and is not stated explicitly in Genesis 1, yet "it is certainly implicit in the narrative."[136]

It is striking, however, that many biblical texts are somewhat ambiguous in how they describe God's act of creation. For instance, in Isaiah 40:21–22 we read:

> Do you not know?
> > Have you not heard?
> Has it not been told you from the beginning?
> > Have you not understood since the earth was founded?
> He sits enthroned above the circle of the earth,
> > and its people are like grasshoppers.
> He stretches out the heavens like a canopy,
> > and spreads them out like a tent to live in.

These verses hark back to Genesis 1:1–2 and envisage God as establishing the foundations of the universe and forming the heavens like someone putting up a tent. But the author does not say that God created the tent from, literally or metaphorically, nothing.

In the New Testament, thankfully, there are a number of clear statements that do ascribe the universe's existence to the creative action of God alone. God is reckoned to be the ultimate source of all existing things. The totality of creation is contingent on God's free and creative work, since God is named as "God, who created all things" (Eph 3:9), and John the Seer records the heavenly adulation to God because he "created all things, and by your will they were created and have their being" (Rev 4:11). In a doxology in Romans, Paul declares that all things are "from him [God] and through him [God]" (Rom 11:36). The implication of Yahweh's title "the first and ... the last" (Isa 44:6) and its rehearsal in Revelation as "the Alpha and the Omega" (Rev 1:8) is that the Lord is the ultimate originator and the only eternal being.

In addition, the instrument for God's free and creative action is not preexisting matter but Christ. The New Testament authors consistently ascribe a determinative role in creation to Christ. John unambiguously announces that "*through him* all things"—that is, the material world—"were made," and "without him nothing was made that has been made" (John 1:3). Paul, in a christocentric interpretation of the

---

136. R. K. Harrison, "Creation," in *The Zondervan Pictorial Encyclopedia of the Bible* (ed. M.C. Tenney; 5 vols.; Grand Rapids: Zondervan, 1975), 1:1022.

Shema, says that there is "one Lord, Jesus Christ, *through whom* all things came and *through whom* we live" (1 Cor 8:6). The Christ Hymn of Colossians states that "*in [by] him* all things were created" (Col 1:16, italics added in all passages). Jesus is the organizing principle that God uses to bring a rational intelligibility to the universe.

Two further texts that arguably support the idea of *creatio ex nihilo* are Romans 4:17 and Hebrews 11:3. In Romans, Paul refers to God's imparting life into Sarah's womb; God is there described as "the God who gives life to the dead and calls into being things that were not" (Rom 4:17). Obviously this is not a direct analogy to *creatio ex nihilo* since God created life in Sarah's already existing womb. However, God's ability to create life in lifeless conditions is set in parallel to his absolute power to bring things into existence from their absence and without material assistance. In the context of Romans 4, resurrection and creation stand in parallel: God brings life from death just as God brings things into being from nonbeing.

In the "Hall of Faith" in Hebrews 11:3 we read: "By faith we understand that the universe was formed at God's command, so that what is seen was not made out of what was visible." Strictly speaking it is possible that the author thinks that God made the world out of invisible and formless matter. More convincing is Ben Witherington, who comments on this verse: "Our author here indicates that we understand and accept this idea of God's word creating something out of nothing only by faith, since we were not there to see, though the Son was there and was part of it."[137]

It is entirely correct to say that *creatio ex nihilo* certainly did develop in Christian thought in the patristic era. The gradual crystallization of this teaching was necessitated by the encounter with Gnosticism with its emphasis on emanations and Middle Platonism with its belief in eternally preexistent matter. The doctrine of *creatio ex nihilo* established the freedom, self-sufficiency, and absolute sovereignty of God over the created order. It was against these views that Irenaeus said:

> The things which have been made by Him have received a beginning.... He indeed who made all things can alone, together with His Word, properly be termed God and Lord; but the things which have been made cannot have this term applied to them, neither should they justly assume that appellation which belongs to the Creator.[138]

So the doctrine *creatio ex nihilo* did not emerge *ex nihilo*. It was shaped in the second and third centuries by Christian leaders who sought to affirm the biblical concept of God as Creator over against those who had married their cosmologies to Platonic metaphysics. However, the doctrine itself is solidly rooted in the Scriptures, which emphasize God's supreme role as the originator of the all things.

---

137. Ben Witherington III, *Letters and Homilies for Jewish Christians: A Socio-Rhetorical Commentary on Hebrews, James and Jude* (Nottingham, UK: Apollos, 2007), 301–2.

138. Irenaeus, *Haer.* 3.10.3.

Several corollaries follow from *creatio ex nihilo*. We might note, with Karl Barth, that creation has its basis in Jesus Christ, the Word of God, and in nothing else. Since creatures are not self-created nor contribute anything to their own coming-into-being, God in Christ creates out of sheer grace, and his creative work presupposes nothing but a free act of God's love.[139] Likewise, Hermann Bavinck writes that "the doctrine of creation out of nothing teaches the absolute sovereignty of God and man's absolute dependence; if only a single particle were not created out of nothing God would not be God."[140] Similar to Bavinck is Emil Brunner, for whom *creatio ex nihilo* means that God is the sole determiner of all things and is himself undetermined by any existing thing: "The Creation has its foundation and its origin in God alone."[141] With Bavinck, Brunner, and Barth in unison, we proffer this thought: *creatio ex nihilo* is the quintessential example of the freedom of God's love and the limitless nature of his sovereignty. Finally, *creatio ex nihilo* is an essential doctrine to maintain, if only to uphold God's sovereignty over creation, for if any molecule in the cosmos is coeternal with God, then it would be either an impersonal deity or a personless demiurge.

2.4.7 IMPLICATIONS OF GOD'S ACT OF CREATION

Several corollaries follow on from God's act of creation.

1. The most obvious implication of creation is its contribution to the formation of a distinctly Christian worldview. Creational monotheism makes clear that God is distinct from creation and so prevents us from worshiping created things rather than the Creator (Rom 1:25). At the same time, God remains active on his creation through his common grace and in his providence for his people (Job 5:10; Matt 5:45; 6:25–28). By virtue of their status as part of creation, human beings are thereby obligated to recognize their creatureliness and their utter dependence on the one giving life to them. Humanity is designed to delight in their Creator, and they achieve that end when they recognize the God-centered nature of the reality around them.
2. In the Old Testament the place where God is recognized as Creator most frequently is in the context of worship (e.g., 2 Chr 2:12; Ps 69:34; Rev 4:11). Recognition that God is our Creator should naturally lead us to worship him as our Father, who brought us into being, and as our Provider, who continually cares for us in his mercies that are renewed daily (Lam 3:22–24).
3. Humanity's role in creation is to be the custodians of the earth (Gen 2:15).

---

139. Karl Barth *CD*, 3/1:102–16.
140. Bavinck, *Reformed Dogmatics*, 2:420–21.
141. Emil Brunner, *The Christian Doctrine of Creation and Redemption* (London: Lutterworth, 1952), 2:10.

Consequently the assignment of this role to humanity undergirds the need for a Christian view of ecology and environmental care to carry out this important task. The heavenly good of earthly work undertaken in this creation will be forwarded and rewarded in the new creation.
4. Creation exhibits signs of order that derive from the divine mind that so beautifully fashioned it together. This orderliness of creation establishes the possibility of science for understanding creation and implies the necessity of science for gaining mastery over creation. Although science and religion proffer a huge mountain of debate that I have no interest in scaling here, I submit that the metaphysics of theism, that is, the reality created by God, is the grounds on which scientific inquiry can proceed.

FURTHER READING

Bockmuehl, Markus. "*Creatio Ex Nihilo* in Palestinian Judaism and Early Christianity." *SJT* 65 (2012): 253–70.

Copan, Paul. "Is *Creatio Ex Nihilo* A Post-Biblical Invention? An Examination of Gerhard May's Proposal," *TrinJ* 17.1 (1996): 77–93.

Copan, Paul, and Willian Lane Craig. *Creation out of Nothing: A Biblical, Philosophical, and Scientific Exploration*. Grand Rapids: Baker, 2004.

Grenz, Stanley. *Theology for the Community of God*. Grand Rapids: Eerdmans, 2000, pp. 99–106.

Helm, Paul. *The Providence of God*. Nottingham, UK: Inter-Varsity Press, 1993.

McGrath, Alister. *Christian Theology: An Introduction*. 3rd ed. Oxford: Blackwell, 2001, pp. 296–307.

Walton, John. *The Lost World of Genesis One: Ancient Cosmology and the Origins Debate*. Downers Grove, IL: InterVarsity Press, 2009.

§ 2.5 THE GOD WHO REVEALS HIMSELF

2.5.1 THE GOSPEL AND REVELATION

The good news of Jesus presupposes two crucial things: (1) God has acted (so there is something to report); and (2) God has spoken (so the news is from God and the message is trustworthy). The gospel implies an acting and speaking God, and the ultimate synthesis of divine work and divine word is the message of Jesus Christ.[142] The gospel of Jesus Christ stands as a centerpiece of divine revelation. The gospel springs from the *prior* revelation of God in Israel's history. The gospel itself comprises a *public* revelation of Jesus of Nazareth as Lord and Messiah and declares how salvation comes through faith in him. The gospel also facilitates a *personal* revelation of God as Savior as the gospel brings one into a vivid encounter with the exalted Lord.

The way we understand revelation, God's self-disclosure of himself, will be evangelically shaped because it is *the gospel* that constitutes the organic unity between God's revelation of himself in redemptive-historical, christological, and experiential modes. Indeed, the gospel is so paramount for knowledge of God that we may properly regard the gospel as the paradigm of true revelation. The gospel teaches us what revelation is and what it achieves.[143]

The gospel is revealed truth, not human wisdom.[144] That comports with Paul's testimony that "the gospel I preached is of human origin. I did not receive it from any man, nor was I taught it; rather, I received it by revelation from Jesus Christ" (Gal 1:11–12). The risen and exalted Lord imparted his gospel to Saul of Tarsus in order for Saul to make Christ Jesus known among the Gentiles. The gospel is for all intents and purposes one of the loftiest heights of God's revelation. The gospel brings us to the fullness of Christ, who embodies the fullness of God. The gospel becomes a speech-act whereby God acts in and through the words of proclamation

---

142. Vanhoozer, "The Triune God of the Gospel," 17.
143. Peter Jensen, *The Revelation of God* (Downers Grove, IL: InterVarsity Press, 2002), 31–37.
144. Leon Morris, *The Epistle to the Romans* (PNTC; Grand Rapids: Eerdmans, 1988), 546.

about his Son to bring us to faith. As Klyne Snodgrass writes, "Revelation does not merely bring the gospel: the gospel *is* revelation."[145]

The gospel is a theocentric revelation. It is a pronouncement, a proclamation, a publication of good tidings about God. The "gospel of God" is good news from God and about God. It is news in the sense of reporting the events of Jesus' life, death, and resurrection. However, it does not simply state facts about Jesus; it also tells us what those facts mean in the context of God's purposes in redemptive history.

What is more, the good news is new news. The gospel tells us something that was otherwise unknown but now made known. Because the gospel tells us something about God, it is didactic in nature and propositional in content. Because the gospel is the place where we encounter God, it is also profoundly personal. The gospel mediates the presence and power of God and imparts the promise of the Holy Spirit. The gospel shows—and we will explore this further—that God's unveiling of himself is both propositional and personal.

The gospel is the "word of God," God-words disclosed in the story of Jesus, a divine discourse about judgment (Rom 2:16; 1 Pet 4:17) and salvation (Rom 1:16; Eph 1:13; 2 Tim 1:10). This is made explicit in several places in the New Testament. Peter and John proclaimed the "word of the Lord" in Samaria, which is identical to "preaching the gospel" (Acts 8:25). Paul says to the Corinthians that "the word I preached to you" is the "gospel" by which they were saved (1 Cor 15:2). In Colossians and Ephesians there is a close correlation between the "message [word] of truth" and the "gospel" (Eph 1:13; Col 1:5). To the Thessalonians, Paul wrote that the "gospel" that came to them and which they received was "the word of God" (1 Thess 1:5; 2:13). Finally, in 2 Corinthians 4:1–6, Paul used a number of phrases to describe his ministry of apostolic instruction that includes "the word of God," "gospel," "what we preach," and "the knowledge of God's glory." Evidently knowledge of God begins with knowledge of the gospel.

While the gospel says something genuinely new, it is not foreign to God's prior presentation of himself. The gospel is not a ball hit out of left field (to use baseball language) or a ball bowled under arm (to use cricket language). The gospel gains its currency from the fact that it stands in continuity with God's prior revelation of himself to Israel as laid out in Israel's Scriptures. That is why in the passion predictions and post-resurrection sayings Jesus refers to the necessity and predictability of his death and resurrection (esp. the Lucan versions of the sayings, Luke 9:22; 18:31–34; 22:22; 24:7, 44–47). On the road to Emmaus, again recorded by Luke, the risen Jesus engages the two travelers: "Beginning with Moses and all the Prophets, he explained to them what was said in all the Scriptures concerning himself" (Luke 24:27).

---

145. Klyne Snodgrass, "The Gospel in Romans: A Theology of Revelation," in *Gospel in Paul* (ed. L. Ann Jervis and Peter Richardson; JSNTSup 108; Sheffield: Sheffield Academic, 1994), 108.

In apostolic preaching, what God previously promised is said to be made good in the event of Jesus' passion, resurrection, and exaltation (Acts 13:33–34; 2 Cor 1:20). Paul says that in the covenant God made with Abraham, God had in fact "announced the gospel in advance to Abraham" (Gal 3:8). The gospel is that which God "promised beforehand through his prophets in the Holy Scriptures" (Rom 1:2) and transpires "according to the Scriptures" (1 Cor 15:3–4). Peter goes so far as to say: "They [the prophets] were shown that they were serving not themselves but you, in regard to the things now announced to you through those who proclaimed the gospel to you by the Holy Spirit sent from heaven" (1 Pet 1:12 NET). The prophets were anxiously looking ahead and searching for the revelation of the Messiah and his passion. The "Spirit of Christ" already bore witness within them to the Messiah's sufferings and glory, the advent of grace, and the salvation of our souls. The prophets saw far enough ahead to know that their message would provide the formative groundwork for the preaching of the gospel about the Messiah (1 Pet 1:9–11). According to John the Seer, the fulfillment of the "mystery of God" in the kingdom of Christ was announced (*euangelizō*) long ago to the prophets (Rev 10:7). The gospel is a shorthand summary for the coming of the eschatological salvation that was at the heart of the prophetic writings. In sum, the gospel is validated by its agreement with God's revelation of his saving plan as given in "the Law of Moses, the Prophets and the Psalms" (Luke 24:44).

The gospel demystifies the mysterious plan of God. Paul testified to the "mystery of the gospel" (Eph 6:19) as the disclosure of God's plan to indwell believers with Christ for the hope of glory (Col 1:27) and through the gospel to make "the Gentiles ... heirs together with Israel" (Eph 3:3–6). The one plan of God, intimated in the Scriptures and announced in the gospel, is to "to bring unity to all things in heaven and on earth under Christ" (Eph 1:10). Paul also composed a benediction at the end of Romans with the words:

> Now to him who is able to establish you in accordance with my gospel, the message I proclaim about Jesus Christ, in keeping with the revelation of the mystery hidden for long ages past, but now revealed and made known through the prophetic writings by the command of the eternal God, so that all the Gentiles might come to the obedience that comes from faith. (Rom 16:25–26)

What Paul envisages seems something like this:

mystery ⇨
    prophetic writings ⇨
        gospel
        proclamation of Jesus Christ ⇨
            obedience of faith among the Gentiles

Evidently the substance of the mystery is how it was always God's plan, as laid up in the prophets, to bring Gentiles to the obedience of faith through the preaching of Jesus in the gospel.

The continuity between the gospel and the prophets is not in the sense that the gospel is married to a random series of proof texts and spiritual stories. Rather, the prophetic writings mediate the mystery of God that the gospel climactically reveals. Importantly, the revelation of the gospel also gives new insight into the prophets. The revelation of the gospel reveals that the prophets were pointing all along to the mystery as to how God would bring the Gentiles into the family of faith through the Messiah (see Rom 15:7–8; Gal 3:13–14). The Old Testament pointed ahead to the gospel, while the gospel reveals that God's secret plan was there in the prophets the whole time. The prophets intimate the gospel and the gospel illuminates the prophets. Thus, there is a prophetic gospel that announces the mysterious plan of God concerning salvation of Jews and Gentiles.[146]

As we begin to work through the concept of divine revelation, the gospel reminds us that God has always been a revealing God, the summit of his revelation is Jesus Christ, and God desires a personal encounter with each and every one of us.

2.5.2 REVELATION AS GOD'S SELF-DISCLOSURE

How is God known to us? The Christian tradition has maintained that God is transcendent, invisible, hidden, and completely "other." We cannot reach him or beseech him, nor can we adore him or implore him without God first introducing himself to us. Knowledge of his person and plan cannot be arrived at by mere deduction or by gut intuition. If we are to have knowledge of God, we are entirely dependent on God making himself known to us.

That is what we find in Scripture. According to the prophet Amos, the God of creation is the God of revelation who made himself known to human beings: "He who forms the mountains, who creates the wind, and who reveals his thoughts to mankind, who turns dawn to darkness, and treads on the heights of the earth—the Lord God Almighty is his name" (Amos 4:13). In Deuteronomy, God's hiddenness must be balanced with the fact that he has revealed himself to his people: "The secret things belong to the Lord our God, but the things revealed belong to us and to our children forever, that we may follow all the words of this law" (Deut 29:29).

The apostle Paul loosely cites Isaiah 64:4 when he writes to the Corinthians: "What no eye has seen, what no ear has heard, and what no human mind has conceived—the things God has prepared for those who love him" (1 Cor 2:9). Paul

---

146. Cf. Thomas R. Schreiner, *Romans* (BECNT; Grand Rapids: Baker, 1998), 814.

here affirms the inscrutable mystery of God and the chasm between God and our knowledge of him. But Paul then adds:

> These are the things God has revealed to us by his Spirit.
>
> The Spirit searches all things, even the deep things of God. For who knows a person's thoughts except their own spirit within them? In the same way no one knows the thoughts of God except the Spirit of God. What we have received is not the spirit of the world, but the Spirit who is from God, that we may understand what God has freely given us. (1 Cor 2:10–12)

In other words, the unknowable God had made himself known by his Spirit.

Scripture abounds in examples of God breaking into human lives and making himself known. The effects that follow include blessing, commission, salvation, and judgment. God spoke to Abraham, called him out of Ur, and made a covenant with him (Gen 12:1–10). Jacob met God in a wrestling match at Peniel (Gen 32:24–32). God appeared to Moses in the burning bush and revealed his name that even Abraham, Isaac, and Jacob did not know (Exod 3:15; 6:3). Isaiah and Ezekiel had visions where they were summoned to a heavenly service (Isa 6; Ezek 1). It was revealed to Simeon that he would not die before he saw the Lord's Messiah (Luke 2:26). Peter encountered a Jewish rabbi on a fishing boat and became aware of his sinfulness (Luke 5:1–11). Saul of Tarsus was confronted by the risen Jesus on the road to Damascus so that the persecutor of the faith became its most ardent proclaimer (Acts 9:1–22; Gal 1:12). The Fourth Evangelist and the author of Hebrews both believed God has given a definitive revelation of himself in Jesus Christ (John 1:18; Heb 1:2).

There are two more aspects of revelation we must consider. First, God's revealing of himself is at his own initiative. Isaiah writes, "I revealed myself to those who did not ask for me; I was found by those who did not seek me. To a nation that did not call on my name, I said, 'Here am I, here am I'" (Isa 65:1). God does not wait to be asked before he reaches down to humanity. God does not stand on ceremony in asking for a formal invitation. God freely presents himself as the one who is mighty to save. God's self-communication is, then, entirely gracious.

It naturally follows, then, that God's revelation of himself is chiefly redemptive.[147] The revelation of God is the revelation of a Redeemer (Job 19:25; Pss 19:14; 78:35; Isa 41:14; 43:14; 44:6, 24; 47:4; 48:17; 49:7, 26; 54:5; 59:20; 60:16; 63:16; Jer 50:34). Once more Isaiah epitomizes this truth: "'I have revealed and saved

---

147. Cf. Clark Pinnock (*The Scripture Principle* [Vancouver, BC: Regent College Publishing, 2002], 7): "For my part, I cannot see how any revelation from the God of the gospel can be other than saving in its basic significance if it is truly to be a revelation of him"; Colin Gunton (*A Brief Theology of Revelation* [Edinburgh: T&T Clark, 1995], 111): "While it is undoubtedly true that God identifies himself through the action of the Spirit to be the Father of our Lord Jesus Christ, the focus of that action ... is the salvation brought by Jesus of Nazareth. The centre is not divine self-identification but divine saving action"; Louis Berkhof (*Systematic Theology* [Grand Rapids: Eerdmans, 1949], 137): "Special revelation is a revelation of salvation, and aims at redemption of the entire man, both in his being and in his consciousness."

and proclaimed—I, and not some foreign god among you. You are my witnesses,' declares the Lord, 'that I am God'" (Isa 43:12). In the New Testament we find the eschatological "now" that signifies a revelation of God's grace even when it was undeserved (Rom 3:21; 6:22; 7:6; 16:26; Gal 4:9; Eph 2:13; 5:8; Col 1:22; 2 Tim 1:10; 1 Pet 2:10). The incarnation, as an act of revelation, is salvific as well. In the "good shepherd" discourse, the purpose of Jesus' visitation is this: "I have come that they may have life, and have it to the full" (John 10:10). Paul states that Jesus Christ "appeared" as Savior for the people (Titus 3:4–6). The revelation of Jesus Christ is the revelation of God as Savior.

What should be clear by now is that divine revelation is necessary if human beings are to have knowledge of God. That includes knowledge of his existence, attributes, and purposes. Without revelation the best that humanity could do was to build an altar "TO AN UNKNOWN GOD" (Acts 17:23), assuming that the Athenians were even led to that conclusion. Consequently, a Christian doctrine of "revelation" maintains that humans need to be told who God is by none other than by God himself.

Revelation is also necessary if the alienation and enmity between the Creator and his creatures are to be overcome. It is not enough for people to know that there is a God. Mere assent to monotheism, even a creational monotheism, is not enough to restore humanity to a relationship with God. The chief end of God's revelation is the restoration of humanity back to fellowship with their Lord and Creator. Unless God saves, any revelation he gives will be bad news. Yet if there is a God who is mighty to save, then his revelation will be good news.

If God is a revealing God, we are led to explore "what" God has said and "how" God has said it. On the matter of "how," several models of revelation have been proposed by theologians. Avery Dulles presented a taxonomy of models of revelation, which include:

1. *Doctrine*. Revelation is principally communicated in clear propositional statements that can be developed into doctrinal statements. The appropriate response is assent to a divinely revealed body of truths.
2. *History*. Revelation refers to the deeds of God to which Scripture witnesses; these acts bring God's self-disclosure into human history. The prescribed response on this model is trust and hope in the God who has shown his power, goodness, and faithfulness to his promises.
3. *Experience*. Revelation occurs in the immediate and interior religious experience where one encounters God as he lovingly communicates himself to the soul that is open to him. The response to this experience is a pious affection for God.
4. *Dialectic encounter*. Revelation is the communication of God in paradoxes (e.g., Jesus is Judge and Justifier), whereby the living God is encountered between

the poles of mystery and unveiling. The response to God is an obedient faith that issues forth in a new understanding of God and a new understanding of self.

5. *New awareness.* Revelation is God's breaking into human consciousness and being mysteriously immanent within the creative work of people to provide answers to the question of human existence. The human response is to correlate revelation with cultural and historical questions.[148]

A quick assessment of these views is required. To begin with, the description of divine revelation as a "new awareness" is correct on the existential level. But I would point out that revelation does not rest purely in the fallible subjectivity of human consciousness; its center of gravity is divine action and divine speech. The "dialectic" model rightly captures the inherent tension in key theological themes such as that God is both gracious and just, yet it makes revelation sound rather bipolar. In addition, the coherence of God's revelation is its christological content and evangelical framework, namely, that God tells us who he is principally when he reveals his Son as Savior—a revelation that is direct and not dialectic. Accordingly, I lean then more toward "history," "doctrine," and "experience" as the primary models of revelation as these have more biblical traction and far greater currency in historical theology. What is more, the gospel contains all of these elements. The gospel is *historically referential* in its testimony to Jesus, clearly *propositional* in its affirmation about Jesus, and intensely personal in bringing us to *experience Jesus*.[149]

Dulles himself believed that all five models were not totally disparate, and he gives a fairly holistic definition of revelation: "Revelation is God's free action whereby he communicates saving truth to created minds, especially through Jesus Christ as accepted by the apostolic Church and attested by the Bible and by the continuing community of believers."[150] Note that Dulles includes two important elements here: Jesus Christ and the church. Jesus Christ is the incarnate Word and he is, therefore, the most definitive revelation of God. At the same time, God's Word is never divorced from the people to whom he has spoken his Word, which means that the people of God must also figure in any model of revelation.

That is all well and good, but what is crucially missing on Dulles's definition is the Holy Spirit. The Holy Spirit is not simply a translator enabling God to speak in human language. The Holy Spirit becomes the speaker and actor in God's revelation. It is the Spirit who was involved in creation, a creation that expresses God's

---

148. See Avery Dulles, *Models of Revelation* (Dublin: Gill & MacMillan, 1983).

149. See esp. Jensen, *Revelation of God*, 31–144.

150. Dulles, *Models of Revelation*, 117. See also Webster (*Holy Scripture*, 130: "revelation is the self-presentation of the Triune God, the free work of sovereign mercy in which God wills, establishes and perfects saving fellowship with himself in which humankind comes to know, love and fear him above all things."

divine attributes (e.g., Gen 1:2; Rom 1:19–20). God speaks in prophecy and Scripture by the Holy Spirit, who spirates human subjects to speak forth God's words (2 Tim 3:16; 2 Pet 1:20–21). The Spirit was the means by which the incarnation took place as Mary was overshadowed by the Holy Spirit and became pregnant with the Son of God (Matt 1:18, 20; Luke 1:35). What is more, because revelation is the Holy Spirit speaking and effecting God's self-communication, it means that revelation also provides a personal encounter with God. So I define revelation this way: *Revelation is the self-presentation of the Triune God, who through the Holy Spirit communicates saving truth about himself and draws humankind into a community in fellowship with his Son, so that they might know him, experience his mercy, and enjoy him forever.*

2.5.3 MODES OF REVELATION: NATURE

The modes through which God makes himself known to human beings are intimated in Psalm 19:1–8:

> The *heavens* declare the glory of God
>   the skies proclaim the work of his hands.
> Day after day they pour forth speech;
>   night after night they reveal knowledge.
> They have no speech, they use no words;
>   no sound is heard from them.
> Yet their voice goes out into all the earth,
>   their words to the ends of the world.
> In the heavens God has pitched a tent for the sun.
>   It is like a bridegroom coming out of his chamber,
>   like a champion rejoicing to run his course.
> It rises at one end of the heavens
>   and makes its circuit to the other
>   nothing is deprived of its warmth.
> The *law* of the Lord is perfect,
>   refreshing the soul.
> The statutes of the Lord are trustworthy,
>   making wise the simple.
> The precepts of the Lord are right,
>   giving joy to the heart.
> The commands of the Lord are radiant,
>   giving light to the eyes. (italics added)

God speaks through the created order (i.e., the heavens) and in the law of the Lord (i.e., Scripture). God's revelation is a book in two volumes: nature and Scripture, the natural and the supernatural, the world and the word. According to the Belgic Confession (Article 2):

> We know God by two means: First, by the creation, preservation, and government of the universe, since that universe is before our eyes like a beautiful book in which all creatures, great and small, are as letters to make us ponder the invisible things of God: his eternal power and his divinity, as the apostle Paul says in Romans 1:20. All these things are enough to convict humans and to leave them without excuse. Second, God makes himself known to us more clearly by his holy and divine Word, as much as we need in this life, for God's glory and for our salvation.[151]

It is possible to extrapolate these further. First, there is a *natural revelation*—the disclosure of God's existence and attributes as discerned through nature. The natural order of things points to a Creator and a Designer of the universe. As noted in the previous section, God is the first cause of the universe. God is also the explanation as to why there is a rational intelligibility to the universe. The issue that emerges, however, is its clarity in nature and humanity's ability to perceive this natural revelation in light of the effects of sin on their noetic faculties.

Second, there is *special revelation*, which comprises God's unique and supernatural communication of himself. That takes place through revelatory historical events like the exodus and the resurrection of Christ. It is seen also in the inspired proclamation of the prophets and apostles, who addressed their audiences with a message from God. Then there is inscripturated revelation, understood as the spiration of God's Word through human authors to produce written texts. In addition, there is divine illumination, whereby the Holy Spirit brings understanding to believers about his Word. These are all "special" in the sense that they are communicated directly from God and not mediated through natural processes.

Third, there is *christological revelation*, which refers to the incarnation of Jesus Christ. Ordinarily this gets lumped in with special revelation.[152] In a sense, this equation is valid as the Word made flesh and the Word of Scripture are both particular revelations of God. However, there is something extra-extra special about the incarnation. The incarnation is a revelation of a quality that far surpasses the revelation of Scripture. For the incarnation is a direct and unmediated communication of God. Jesus of Nazareth is not the reality pushed in front of God; he is the reality of God. The incarnation is no convergence of ideas or words about God, but the union of humanity and divinity in one being. None of these affirmations can be said of Scripture. In addition, while Scripture tells us about salvation, the incarnation is salvation. While Scripture teaches us the way to God, Jesus is the way to God. For this reason we put the incarnation into its own category of revelation.

These are worth exploring further since the clarity and impact of these spheres of revelation can be teased out further.

---

151. See www.crcna.org/welcome/beliefs/confessions/belgic-confession.

152. Cf. e.g., Erickson, *Christian Theology*, 215–16.

2.5.3.1 NATURAL REVELATION

The created realm can leave human beings with a sense of awe and wonder at its magnitude and beauty. Therefore, in virtual reflex, those who know him ascribe majesty and might to their Maker. We find this in Psalm 19:1–4, which we cited above. The inanimate objects of the cosmos are animated with testimony to their Creator. The heavens "declare" the glory of God, which radiates through the cosmos. The skies "proclaim" the work of his hands that fashioned the world like a potter making a clay jar. The scope of this speech is universal. It occurs throughout the day and the night. The voice that heralds God's authorship of creation "goes out into all the earth" and "their words to the ends of the world." The metaphorical way in which nature reveals God is underscored: "They have no speech, they use no words; no sound is heard from them." So it is not a literal word that is given in creation. It is a meeting of God through his handiwork. Yet this meeting of God through creation is so real and so powerful that the psalmist likens it to speech being poured out into the all the earth.

Paul's speech to the Athenians in the Areopagus makes clear reference to natural revelation. Paul uses natural revelation as a bridge between the polytheism of his Greek audience and the gospel. In Luke's digest of the sermon, Paul says:

> People of Athens! I see that in every way you are very religious. For as I walked around and looked carefully at your objects of worship, I even found an altar with this inscription: TO AN UNKNOWN GOD. So you are ignorant of the very thing you worship—and this is what I am going to proclaim to you.
>
> The God who made the world and everything in it is the Lord of heaven and earth and does not live in temples built by human hands. And he is not served by human hands, as if he needed anything. Rather, he himself gives everyone life and breath and everything else. From one man he made all the nations, that they should inhabit the whole earth; and he marked out their appointed times in history and the boundaries of their lands. God did this so that they would seek him and perhaps reach out for him and find him, though he is not far from any one of us."For in him we live and move and have our being." As some of your own poets have said, "We are his offspring."
>
> Therefore since we are God's offspring, we should not think that the divine being is like gold or silver or stone—an image made by human design and skill. In the past God overlooked such ignorance, but now he commands all people everywhere to repent. For he has set a day when he will judge the world with justice by the man he has appointed. He has given proof of this to everyone by raising him from the dead. (Acts 17:22–31; cf. earlier Acts 14:15–17)

The Athenians recognized that they had not exhausted knowledge of the pantheon of gods. They wanted to honor all gods, even those as yet unknown to them—hence the altar. Their admitted ignorance gives the occasion for Paul's speech. The god who is unknown to them is *the* God of heaven and earth; as such he cannot be restricted to temples or idols. Indeed, by his very nature this God is self-sufficient just as he is benevolent by imparting life to human races and administrating their times and place. This is the one God who made the nations and determined the times of all people. He did this in the hope that his creatures would seek after their Creator.

Paul even invokes pagan poets and philosophers to indicate recognition within their own cultural setting that all persons are children of God and live in the presence of God. The corollaries that follow from God's fatherhood of humanity and from his sovereignty over creation are that idolatry is an ignorant impiety. This knowledge of God through creation and attested in their own literature implies their culpability for committing worship that is so antithetical to God's nature. Reiterating the point he had made at Lystra, Paul says that God has mercifully overlooked such ignorance, but he now commands people to repent of their idolatry because he intends to judge the world through the appointed judge: Jesus Christ. The proof of this—and this is what seems to have turned off Paul's audience—is that God raised Jesus from the dead. Paul's speech presumes recognition of God's providence and the impropriety of iconic worship of God as the *appropriate implications* from the Athenians' own religious culture.

While many see Paul's speech in Acts 17:22–31 as a model apologetic discourse, it is strictly speaking a challenge to pagan religion and a proclamation of the gospel.[153] Paul appeals to principles current in Stoic and Epicurean philosophy in order to establish the doctrine of creation. Thereafter, he announces divine judgment and the resurrection of Jesus Christ in order to marry natural revelation with special revelation. Paul can connect the God of heaven and earth with religious sentiments extant in their culture. But he also condemns them for idolatry because they have not appropriately engaged the implications that follow on from God's fatherhood of all people and from his common concern for humanity. In other words, the Athenians show they have knowledge of the God of heaven and earth, yet at the same time they equally demonstrate that they have not responded to him in a way befitting the nature of his divine being.

Paul offers a similar thought in Romans 1:18–25, where God's natural revelation is given to humanity, though it does not have a positive effect in the end.

> The wrath of God is being revealed from heaven against all the godlessness and wickedness of people, who suppress the *truth* by their wickedness, since *what may be known about God* is plain to them, because God has made it plain to them. For since the creation of the world God's invisible qualities—his eternal power and divine

---

153. Simon J. Kistemaker, *Exposition of the Acts of the Apostles* (NTC; Grand Rapids: Baker, 1990), 640.

nature — *have been clearly seen, being understood from what has been made*, so that people are without excuse.

For although *they knew God*, they neither glorified him as God nor gave thanks to him, but their thinking became futile and their foolish hearts were darkened. Although they claimed to be wise, they became fools and exchanged the glory of the immortal God for images made to look like mortal human beings and birds and animals and reptiles.

Therefore God gave them over in the sinful desires of their hearts to sexual impurity for the degrading of their bodies with one another. They exchanged the truth about God for a lie, and worshiped and served created things rather than the Creator — who is forever praised. Amen.

The flip side to the revelation of God's righteousness in the gospel is the revelation of God's wrath against sin (Rom 1:16–18). God's punitive judgment, his wrath, is manifested against human beings "who suppress the truth by their wickedness, since what may be known about God is plain to them, because God has made it plain to them" (1:18–19). All human beings are culpable before God because they suppress the truth about God (1:18) and distort the knowledge of God that he has made manifest to all of them (1:19–23). But how has God manifested this truth and knowledge about himself to all of humanity for which they are liable for rejecting?

According to Paul, "since the creation of the world God's invisible qualities — his eternal power and divine nature — have been clearly seen, being understood from what has been made" (Rom 1:20). Observing the world around us imparts an awareness of a Creator who is distinct from creation and responsible for its existence. The visible things of the world point to an invisible Creator who possesses "eternal power" (*aidios dynamis*) and a "divine nature" (*theiotēs*). Creation mediates knowledge of God. Human beings have been wired up to know him and to believe in him so that when they observe the wonder of creation, they should, all things being equal, identify creation as the work of a grand and good Creator. As Schreiner comments: "God has stitched into the fabric of the human mind his existence and power, so that they are instinctively recognized when one views the created world."[154]

The tragedy is that rather than appropriate this knowledge of God as their Creator with worship, humanity reasons their way from God. Sin turns their minds away from God and even against God. This is called the "noetic effects of sin." Sin infects the mind to such a degree that human reasoning assumes a default position that is anti-God. That is why people "suppress the truth," why they have not "glorified him" or given "thanks to him." The "wickedness" of human beings has led

---

154. Schreiner, *Romans*, 86.

them to become "futile" in their thinking, their foolish hearts "were darkened," they "became fools," and "they ... worshiped and served created things rather than the Creator." At the root of the problem is the idea of exchange. Humanity has "exchanged" the glory of the immortal God for inglorious things made in the image of creatures. Humanity "exchanged" the truth of God for a lie. On account of sin, humanity has become doxologically challenged.

If we take all of these texts together (Ps 19:1–14; Acts 14:15–17; 17:22–32; Rom 1:18–25), the knowledge of God manifested in creation includes evidence of God's existence, authority, benevolence, providence, omnipresence, self-sufficiency, power, transcendence, immanence, invisibility, and glory. Creation communicates something of God. Creation is a divine speech-act that uses nonverbal forms of communication to announce God's own person and power. By creating, God speaks. The word of God encoded within creation activates our innate ability to decode God's handiwork. Thereafter, we are able to attribute this marvelous work to the divine being who fashioned it. We might use the following analogy to explain this further. The Locard principle in forensic science states that when one substance touches another, it indelibly leaves traces of itself onto the other material it came into contact with (e.g., fingerprints). As God created the universe, he left an imprint of himself upon it. Human beings, created in the *image of God*, are able to discern that imprint.

The truth and knowledge of God mediated through creation are real and discernible. All humanity knows something of God innately and experientially. His existence and being are understood. However, the presence of sin in the human heart means that this knowledge becomes traumatic because it implies God's authority over them and their accountability to God. People pretend not to hear this natural revelation, and they deactivate their inward mechanism for receiving the message. Therefore, this knowledge of God is suppressed, denied, or exchanged by all human beings in order to escape the consequence that humanity owes God their obedience and praise. The sin of the human heart will give glory to none but its own. The earth is filled with self-made people who love to worship their self-creator. That includes false gods who are carefully crafted so as to keep any divine entity domesticated under the convention of human authority. People will become atheists, pantheists, or polytheists rather than submit themselves to the one true God of the universe. They shift from knowledge to ignorance to idolatry in the course of their thinking. This occurs to the point that Paul can say elsewhere that the Gentiles do not know God (Gal 4:8–9; 1 Thess 4:4–5; 1 Cor 1:21). As a result, God's wrath is inflicted on the world because God is not prized, esteemed, and glorified.[155]

A good summary of natural revelation, including its efficacy and limitations, is

---

155. Ibid., 89.

given by John Calvin. Calvin argued that two types of knowledge may be acquired through natural revelation. The first form of knowledge is our natural sense of divinity (*sensus divinitatis*), which is implanted in every human being. The French Reformer held that we possess a "seed of religion" in that a sense of God is "indelibly engraven on the human heart."[156] The consequences that follow from this include the universality of religion, a troubled conscience from our sin, and a servile fear of God. If uninformed by the Christian revelation, these degenerate into idolatry and a desperate attempt to win favor with gods formed in the image of human failings.

The second form of knowledge that Calvin speaks about refers to our experience and reflection of the world that manifest God's divine perfections. Our observation of the "whole structure of the universe" means that "we cannot open our eyes without being compelled to behold him."[157] For Calvin this is primarily the "creative wisdom" of God that is evident in creation as well as his attributes of self-sufficiency and eternality perceived in the created order.[158]

Calvin is fully aware of the epistemic distance between God and humanity. This divide is accentuated on account of sin. Natural revelation is effective to guarantee human culpability before God, but it is still inadequate to show God's special purposes. Calvin stated: "In vain for us, therefore, does Creation exhibit so many bright lamps lighted up to show for the glory of its Author. Though they beam upon us from every quarter, they are altogether insufficient of themselves to lead us into the right path."[159] Sin renders us like an elderly person who, on account of fading of eyesight, is now unable to see the glory of God in creation. God's special revelation of himself—in Scripture, Christ, and gospel—is like a set of glasses that enables us to finally see what was otherwise obscure. To quote Calvin again: "Scripture, gathering together the impressions of Deity, which, till then, lay confused in their minds, dissipates the darkness, and shows us the true God clearly."[160]

The problem that natural revelation presents for Reformed theologians is well summarized by G. C. Berkouwer: "If, however, the revelation of God in the works of his hands can be known only by illumination of Scripture, then the question arises whether there is any sense to speaking of such a general revelation."[161] The best solution to that problem is probably the one that Berkouwer himself offered—that is, that the relationship between natural and special revelation is not a competitive one. The salvation that God provides calls for hymns of praise for the work of God's hands. The universal actions of God in the creation, preservation, and governance of the universe prepares for the revelation of Jesus Christ, while the Christian revelation of

---

156. Calvin, *Institutes*, 1.3.1, 3; 1.4.1; 1.5.1.
157. Ibid., 1.5.1.
158. Ibid., 1.5.1–8.
159. Ibid., 1.5.14.
160. Ibid., 1.6.1.
161. G. C. Berkouwer, *General Revelation* (Grand Rapids: Eerdmans, 1955), 285.

the cross becomes an epistemological principle for understanding creation. Faith does not create natural revelation, but it enables one to properly perceive it.[162]

I would add that natural revelation is not salvific. Natural revelation does not impart knowledge of God's plan for salvation. It grants a minimal knowledge of God that makes us culpable for our actions before God, but it is insufficient for a redeeming knowledge of God. Natural revelation does not have a saving effect because the knowledge given in natural revelation is inevitably rejected by humanity. I would speculate (and it is no more than that) that if a person were to recognize the glory of God from the grandeur of creation and to cast themselves upon his mercy, even without a special revelation of God, in theory God could look down on them in grace as they have appropriated natural revelation in the best way they could. However, I surmise that because of the universality of sin—universal both in the sense that it is ubiquitous in human societies and that it completely pervades human reasoning—people simply do not respond to God in such a fashion. Therefore, if there is to be salvation, there must also be a special revelation.

2.5.3.2 NATURAL THEOLOGY

Before we come to special revelation, we must first explore the concept of "natural theology." Natural theology is the study of what can be understood about God through human constitution, history, and nature independently of special revelation. It is the systematic exploration of the proposed link between everyday experience of the world and the transcendent reality of God.[163] Natural theology can be approached in two main ways. First, entirely apart from the fall and without the noetic effects of sin, what would human beings normally know about God? Second, what can human beings know about God even in their fallen condition? It is this second area that occupies the subject of natural theology for the most part.

Here we encounter the theology of Thomas Aquinas. The angelic doctor argued that the world bore the imprint of God's signature. Specifically, God's beauty and perfection were evident in the created realm. Using Aristotelian logic, Aquinas came up with "five ways" or five arguments for the existence of God (unmoved mover, first cause, contingency and necessity of objects, gradation of things, and appearance of design).[164] Aquinas was attempting to establish rational grounds for belief in God that any person (Christian, Jew, or Muslim) could agree on. For Aquinas, natural theology informed by reason established the existence of God. Thereafter, special revelation unaided by reason, accepted on the church's authority, established what this God was like.

---

162. Ibid., 285–332.
163. Alister McGrath, *The Open Secret: A New Vision for Natural Theology* (Oxford: Blackwell, 2008), 2.
164. Aquinas, *Summa Theologica*, 1.Q2.

Natural theology does not mean that reason has replaced grace. The goal of natural theology is to establish by universally shared perceptions the specific truth relating to the existence of God. If the arguments of natural theology are accepted, the revealed truths become far more reasonable to maintain. The primary contributions of natural theology are that they establish the following:

1. People are created with the faculties and cognitive abilities to believe in God.
2. People have an endowed sense of God's existence and power.
3. People enjoy God's common grace in its natural and providential forms.
4. People can infer God's existence and attributes from the immensity, beauty, and rational intelligibility of the world around them.

However, in the Reformed tradition there has been some hesitancy about natural theology and even a rejection of it in some quarters.[165] Such objections have taken on numerous forms, including the assertion that natural theology fails to reckon with the noetic effects of sin and natural theology lends itself to an abstract notion of deity altogether removed from special revelation.

Karl Barth rejected both natural revelation and natural theology. According to Barth, "natural theology is the doctrine of a union of man with God existing outside God's revelation in Jesus Christ."[166] To put things in perspective, Barth lived at a time in Germany when theologians and philosophers were arguing that God was working immanently through German culture and politics. Segments of the German church sided with both Kaiser Wilhelm and later with Adolf Hitler and gave theological sanction to German aggression in the two world wars of the twentieth century. Liberalism had long since abandoned Scripture for a natural theology. In its German incarnation, liberalism had claimed that God was at work in the German people to inaugurate the kingdom of God. God was at work in the natural orders of family, church, and state. The immanence of God in nature was transposed into the immanence of God in state affairs. Subsequent political developments show that Barth was right to reject liberalism's assertion that German culture was a revelation of God in history. It led him also to reject the notion of God's revelation in nature for the same reason.

Another important factor for Barth is that revelation is redemptive in nature. To know God is to know him as Savior. That is a traditional Protestant claim that knowledge of God means knowledge of his benefits in salvation. In a debate with Emil Brunner, Barth complained: "How can Brunner maintain that a real knowledge of the true God, however imperfect it may be (and what knowledge of God

---

165. Cf. Michael Sudduth, *The Reformed Objection to Natural Theology* (Farnham, UK: Ashgate, 2009).

166. Barth, *CD*, II/1:168.

TRADITIONAL PROOFS FOR THE EXISTENCE OF GOD

Argument: *Ontological*

Description

The argument for the existence of God based on the necessity of his being.

Example

Anselm of Canterbury (1033–1109) in his *Prologium* developed the "ontological argument" (ontology is the "study of being").

1. God is the being greater than which none can be conceived.
2. But if God does not exist, then one could conceive of a still greater being that does exist.
3. Therefore, God must exist.

In other words, the very definition of "God" requires that God must necessarily exist. We cannot conceive of God not existing. Put another way:

1. God has all perfections.
2. Existence is a perfection.
3. Therefore, God exists.

Objections

One of Anselm's own contemporaries, a monk named [Gaunilo] proposed a counter-argument. Gaunilo posited an "island greater than any which can be conceived," and he wondered whether this island also "must" exist; otherwise a greater island, one that actually does exist, can be conceived of. This is a *reductio ad absurdum* (he pushed the logic of the argument to the point of absurdities). Aquinas responded that concepts in the mind only imply mental existence, not existence in reality. There is no rationale for making a jump from "mind" to "reality." Our intuition is that things we can conceive of like leprechauns or unicorns do not actually exist beyond our conception of them. Therefore, our conceiving of something with necessary existence does not make its existence necessary in the real world.

Immanuel Kant objected to such arguments because "existence" is not one of God's attributes or properties. If God exists, then he does, but he cannot be said to exist necessarily.

Evaluation

The ontological argument is appealing at one level because it posits "necessity" as a predicate of God's being. It also identifies God as the perfect being who must exist if the world is to have values like truth, beauty, and goodness, etc. While the argument sounds fallacious, demonstrating exactly where the fallacy lies has proven quite difficult. However, at the end of the day, you cannot help but get the impression that the ontological argument is little more than a game of words with "God."

Argument: *Cosmological*

Description

The argument for the existence of God based on a first cause of the cosmos.

Example

The cosmological argument has found advocates in Plato, Aristotle, Aquinas, Leibniz, and many others. Arguably the most compelling version of the cosmological argument is the *kalām* version (*kalām* is Arabic for "word"):

1. Whatever begins to exist has a cause.
2. The universe began to exist.
3. Therefore, the universe must have a cause.

The first premise is evidently true since we observe things beginning to exist and know of nothing eternal. The second premise is supported by scientific arguments (e.g., Big Bang cosmology) and philosophical arguments (e.g., against the possibility of an actual infinite regression). The universe began and therefore it has a cause.

It is possible to extrapolate from that the cause of the universe must have several inherent qualities as well as being powerful and even personal.

Objections

Some object to premise #1 on the grounds that an infinite regression of causes is not impossible. The universe may simply be part of an infinite series of causes and effects that are beyond our scientific purview. Some also object to premise #2, positing that the universe is eternal in the sense that it eternally oscillates (it expands and recontracts forever).

Establishing a finite beginning to the universe and a first cause is one thing. To demonstrate that this first cause is God, a personal God, or even the God of Jesus Christ is quite another thing.

Evaluation

Our basic intuition is that the processes of cause and effect are part of reality as we know it. Things do not pop into existence at random. Likewise an infinite regression of events is conceivable conceptually, but not in any mathematical reality. The absolute beginning of the universe requires the postulation of an absolute creative force to explain its existence. Theism remains one of the best explanations to account for the universe's existence.

	Argument: *Teleological*
Description	The argument for the existence of God based on the appearance of design and order in the universe.
Example	Aquinas's "fifth way" for showing God's existence was as follows: *The fifth way is taken from the governance of the world. We see that things which lack intelligence, such as natural bodies, act for an end, and this is evident from their acting always, or nearly always, in the same way, so as to obtain the best result. Hence it is plain that not fortuitously, but designedly, do they achieve their end. Now whatever lacks intelligence cannot move towards an end, unless it be directed by some being endowed with knowledge and intelligence; as the arrow is shot to its mark by the archer. Therefore some intelligent being exists by whom all natural things are directed to their end; and this being we call God.* A popular version of this argument was promulgated in England in the nineteenth century by William Paley. In his book on *Natural Theology*, he wrote: *In crossing a heath, suppose I pitched my foot against a stone, and were asked how the stone came to be there; I might possibly answer, that, for anything I knew to the contrary, it had lain there forever: nor would it perhaps be very easy to show the absurdity of this answer. But suppose I had found a watch upon the ground, and it should be inquired how the watch happened to be in that place; I should hardly think of the answer I had before given, that for anything I knew, the watch might have always been there. There must have existed, at some time, and at some place or other, an artificer or artificers, who formed [the watch] for the purpose which we find it actually to answer; who comprehended its construction, and designed its use. Every indication of contrivance, every manifestation of design, which existed in the watch, exists in the works of nature; with the difference, on the side of nature, of being greater or more, and that in a degree which exceeds all computation.* A modern example of the teleological argument is that from proponents of "Intelligent Design" who argue that the universe is wired up for life or at least is rationally intelligible. For instance, if the earth were slightly closer to the sun the heat would make carbon-based life impossible, equally so if the earth were slightly further away from the sun the cold would make carbon-based life impossible too. At the level of molecular and cosmological observation, it is argued, that design by an intelligent being explains the complexity of things around us.
Objections	Scientists and philosophers have pointed to the seeming errors and horrors in nature that would make the designer to be the author of much suffering and evil (e.g., why design a world full of deformity, short life spans, imperfections, etc.). Biological evolution also maintains that the complexity of living organisms derives from a series of seeming random developments from simplicity to complexity within a species enabling it to survive or to have enhanced survivability. Some cosmologists also posit the existence of a "multiverse," i.e., an infinite number of universes that exist, so that sooner or later one had to come into being that could support life.
Evaluation	The teleological argument is once more intuitively compelling. Design implies a designer. Objections based on evolution can be sidelined by responding that evolutionary processes themselves may require intelligence and ordering since amino acids cannot turn into astronauts at random. Likewise, postulating the existence of a multiverse to escape a theistic explanation is empirically impossible to verify and driven by a desire to escape a theistic explanation for the fact that the universe is wired up to produce intelligent life.

Argument: *Moral*

Description

The argument for the existence of God based on the existence of objective moral values.

Example

The moral argument for the existence of God proposes that God is the ground of objective moral values. The philosopher Immanuel Kant did not accept the standard proofs for the existence of God. Nonetheless, he did regard God as a necessary postulate for a sense of moral duty. For Kant we can only undertake duty if there is a "highest good" (*summum bonum*) for which we pursue it, and there can only be a highest good if there is a divine lawmaker. Accordingly, morality only makes sense if we have freedom, if there is an ultimate state of happiness, and if there is a God who can grant immortality and happiness. Viewed this way, for morality to work, God is the practical necessity.

C. S. Lewis in his book *Mere Christianity* proposed a more theoretical form of the moral argument.

1. Everyone knows, and so believes, that there are objective moral truths.
2. Objective moral laws are peculiar in that they are quite unlike laws of nature and "natural" facts.
3. The hypothesis that there is an intelligence behind, or beyond, the natural facts that implants the knowledge of right and wrong in us and serves as the foundation for the objectivity of such judgments is the best (or a good) explanation of our intuitions of objective moral facts.
4. Therefore, the existence and nature of objective moral facts supports the existence of an intelligence behind them serving as their basis and foundation.

Objections

The objections to the moral argument are that there are no "objective" values. Moral values are created by individuals, societies, groups, etc. Morality is just a form of sociology that enables communities to survive by developing codes of practice and conduct that maximize the happiness and survivability of creatures. What is more, there is no universal morality as moral norms vary from culture to culture. Morality is constructed, not given by divine decree. Also, the Bible commands things like genocide, which are morally abominable; therefore God's decrees are hardly a guide for ethics.

Evaluation

The moral argument must reckon with the social nature of ethics. Yet even once that recognition is made, we can agree that all human societies, however developed, possess an innate sense of "oughtness" and an inherent belief that they are somehow accountable for their actions to a supreme being. Moreover, the existence of evil in the world requires the postulation of God; otherwise, there would be no absolute standard to decide what is good and what is evil.

is not imperfect?), does not bring salvation?"[167] For Barth, if God can be known any other way, then the revelation of Jesus Christ was not necessary and the principle of grace is compromised. A good example of Barth's christocentric doctrine of revelation can be seen in an anecdote narrated by Elizabeth Achtemeier:

> Barth's dedication to the sole authority and power of the Word of God was illustrated for us ... while we were in Basel. Barth was engaged in a dispute over the stained glass windows in the Basel Münster. The windows had been removed during World War II for fear they would be destroyed by bombs, and Barth was resisting the attempt to restore them to the church. His contention was that the church did not need portrayals of the gospel story given by stained glass windows. The gospel came to the church only through the Word proclaimed ... the incident was typical of Barth's sole dedication to the Word.[168]

Barth is forced into a somewhat labored exegesis of Psalm 19 and Romans 1:18–32 in order to show that there is no knowledge of God through the created order other than that which is referred to first in the law (Ps 19) or the gospel (Rom 1).[169] For Barth, the only reason why people can find God in the universe is because special revelation first points them toward it. Barth was willing to admit the existence of lesser lights that display God's glory in creation, yet they do not compromise the fact that Jesus Christ is the one true light of life.[170]

Richard Bell takes a Barthian approach to Romans 1:18–25 and provides a little more exegetical credence to Barth's objections.[171] Yet Bell acknowledges that Paul does speak of a natural revelation in these verses. The qualification Bell makes is that even in natural revelation the preexistent Christ is revealed in creation as its instrument (e.g., 1 Cor 8:6). He writes: "Christ is both the *object* of natural revelation and the *means* of revelation."[172] Concerning natural theology, Bell points out that for Paul, people do not move from natural revelation to natural theology. There is no

---

167. Karl Barth, "No!" in Emil Brunner and Karl Barth, *Natural Theology* (trans. P. Fraenkel; London: Centenary, 1946), 62.

168. Elizabeth Achtemeier cited at http://narrativeandontology.blogspot.com/2007/12/eleven-funky-barth-quotes.html (accessed 15 August 2011).

169. Barth, *CD*, II/1:107–26. For a critique of Barth's exegesis see James Barr, *Biblical Faith and Natural Theology* (Oxford: Clarendon, 1993).

170. According to George Hunsinger (*How To Read Karl Barth* [Oxford: Oxford University Press, 1993], 274–75): "A major reason why Barth rejects both natural and apologetic theology is that he seems to see them as severing this unity [between reconciliation and revelation]. That is, he seems to see each of them as offering some version of objectivism without personalism. His objection to natural theology, as it emerged in the discussion, was not only that it put forward falsifying abstractions and nonexistent capacities, but also that it put forward neutral generalizations. Natural theology, we might say, offended not only against the motifs of particularism and actualism, but also against the motifs of personalism. It obscured not only the mode of God's concrete particularity and the mode by which God is made known, but also the mode by which God is truly apprehended as God. God is not truly apprehended as God, Barth seems to be saying, without our personal conversion, renewal and commitment. From this point of view what natural theology seems to offer is at once the absence of personalism in conjunction with a spurious objectivism (spurious, because it makes no reference to the mediation of Jesus Christ)."

171. Richard H. Bell, *No One Seeks God: An Exegetical and Theological Study of Romans 1.18–3.20* (WUNT 1.106; Tübingen: Mohr/Siebeck, 1998), 90–118.

172. Ibid., 92 (italics original).

logical move from knowledge of God to acknowledgment of God. Quite the opposite takes place. People move from knowledge to ignorance. This marries up with Paul's assertion of the inability of worldly wisdom to know God (1 Cor 1:18–25). The Lystran and Athenian speeches in Acts stress the audience's ignorance, not the basis for a natural theology. If natural theology for those in Adam leads anywhere, it leads to idolatry. In Bell's reading of Paul (or perhaps Bell's reading of Barth's reading of Paul), idolatry is the natural result of a natural theology.[173]

American Presbyterian theologian Cornelius Van Til rejected natural theology chiefly from the motivation that it was a Roman Catholic doctrine that underestimated sin and overestimated the human ability to perceive God apart from special revelation. The Reformed faith, as Van Til wanted it expressed, could give no ground to natural theology without surrendering divine sovereignty to human autonomy as far as the necessity of divine revelation was concerned. In terms of his precise arguments against natural theology, Van Til held that since theistic arguments are restricted to probabilities, they are insufficient to yield knowledge of God, and the natural man rebels against that knowledge. Yet God's revelation of himself is always clear, lucid, cognitive, and propositional. Knowledge of God is based on facts expressed in propositions. The only way that one could ascertain facts about God from the created order is to begin first with God's propositional self-disclosure in Scripture.[174]

Van Til maintained that one could only argue for God's existence presuppositionally.[175] That is because all argumentation and reasoning are bound up with certain preconceived conceptions. There is no intellectual objectivity, neutrality, or common ground. There are only two kinds of epistemologies: Christian and non-Christian. If a person wants to know God, they must adopt the correct framework of reference by presupposing the God revealed in Scripture. Van Til rejected trying to prove God's existence with theistic arguments because a person's presuppositions will determine if they would find those arguments plausible. "To argue by presupposition is to indicate what are the epistemological and metaphysical principles that underlie and control one's method."[176] The key presupposition for the Reformed adherent is the Triune God. What is needed, therefore, is to show the logical absurdity of a person's presuppositions apart from God—like materialism, pantheism, atheism, etc.—and to show the consistency of the Christian's presuppositions. This is what Van Til called the "Transcendental Argument." The believer endeavors to

---

173. Ibid., 93–100.
174. Cornelius Van Til, *Christian Theory of Knowledge* (Phillipsburgh, NJ: Presbyterian & Reformed, 1969), 221–29; idem, *In Defense of the Faith* (3rd ed.; Philadelphia, NJ: Presbyterian & Reformed, 1967), 175–80.
175. See esp. Van Til's *In Defense of the Faith* and the discussion in Greg L. Bahnsen, *Van Til's Apologetic: Readings and Analysis* (Phillipsburg, NJ: Presbyterian & Reformed, 1998).
176. Van Til, *Defense of the Faith*, 99.

show that morality, logic, and science only make sense on the presupposition of a theistic worldview.

Van Til's epistemology and apologetic methodology have come under intense criticism.[177] First, theistic proofs do not demand the autonomy of the mind or deny the noetic effects of sin. The traditional arguments for God's existence attempt to connect natural revelation with the experiential and cognitive capacity for perceiving God that people innately possess. If evidential arguments for theism do not work because of sin, the same must hold for presuppositional arguments for a Triune God as well.

Second, Van Til's epistemology implies that non-Christians do not actually know anything or know anything justifiably within their own worldview. Yet our ability to discuss anything with people from science to theology is premised on the observation that we have a shared propensity for rational discourse independently of one's religious convictions. It is probably better to affirm that the ontological fact of God's existence is necessary grounds for knowledge as opposed to saying that epistemological awareness of God's being is the necessary prerequisite for knowledge.[178]

Third, in terms of his apologetic methodology of presupposing God, several problems follow. For a start, what happens if someone asks, "Why should I adopt your presuppositions?" It would seem that Van Til would have to provide "reasons" for doing so. What is more, though it is a caricature, the presuppositionalist system becomes reduced to the syllogism: God exists; therefore, God exists. It is a circular argument. Van Til's response is that all reasoning is circular. However, that is hardly a convincing counterresponse. While all rationalities—cultural, scientific, or philosophical—are bounded within a self-contained system of thought, they still have to be evidentially convincing within their own system in order to be persuasive. Other presuppositionalists, like John Frame, permit a role for traditional proofs for God's existence on the proviso that we admit that all such arguments presuppose God.[179]

Philosopher Alvin Plantinga is an advocate of "Reformed epistemology." Put simply, Reformed epistemology maintains that belief in God is justified and warranted on its own terms. Belief in God does not depend on other contingent beliefs in order to be reasonable. Belief in God is regarded a "properly basic," which is a variation on Calvin's idea of a *sensus divinitatis*. It is not a matter of religion within the limits of reason, but reason within the limits of religion. Accordingly the onus is on the denier of God's existence rather than on the claimer.

Plantinga's approach is to say that belief in God is not evidentially held; that is, it is not based on prior beliefs that give warrant to belief in God. Instead, belief in

---

177. Cf. esp. R. C. Sproul, John H. Gerstner, and Arthur Lindsley, *Classical Apologetics: A Rational Defense of the Christian Faith* (Grand Rapids: Zondervan 1984), 183–338.

178. Kelly James Clark, "Reformed Epistemologist's Response," in *Five Views on Apologetics* (ed. Steven B. Cowan; Grand Rapids: Zondervan, 2000), 258.

179. John Frame, "Presuppositional Apologetics," in *Five Views on Apologetics*, 220–21.

God is itself properly basic and does not require additional justification.[180] Plantinga believes that "it is entirely right, rational, reasonable, and proper to believe in God without any evidence at all; in this respect belief in God resembles belief in the past, in the existence of other persons, and in the existence of material objects."[181] Plantinga's take on natural theology is that it attempts to show that theistic beliefs are rational when they are derived from propositions that are self-evidently or necessarily true. Plantinga strenuously rejects the view of that the rationality of belief in God is contingent on evidences for his existence, since many of those evidences fail to establish what they claim. He contends:

> There is no reason at all to think that Christian belief requires argument or propositional evidence, if it is to be justified. Christians—indeed, well educated, contemporary, and culturally aware Christians—can be justified ... even if they don't hold their beliefs on the basis of arguments or evidences, even if they aren't aware of good arguments for their beliefs, and even if, indeed, there aren't any.[182]

That is because belief in God—or more properly, certain beliefs that entail God's existence, such as the fact that this vast and intricate world was created by God—can be properly basic. The belief is not arbitrary. For according to Plantinga, belief is warranted when there are grounds for beliefs (note that "grounds" is different from "evidence"). The grounds for belief in God are the realized conditions that give rise to belief in God when our rational faculties are functioning properly.

In his later works, Plantinga has no problem with admitting the cogency of some theistic arguments in providing support for religious beliefs. Yet such arguments are not the grounds for religious belief.[183] Theistic proofs can confirm belief in God, but they cannot establish the rational grounds of belief in God. Belief in God is rational in and of itself.

Several criticisms of Reformed epistemology in general and Plantinga in particular have been raised. In some cases, it appears that Reformed epistemology is a sophisticated form of fideism. Fideism is the reliance on faith rather than reason. Plantinga rejects that criticism since he believes that theistic beliefs are rationally warranted and justified. Yet in his view the rationality of theistic belief is permissive rather than prescriptive, which is a fairly weak claim in the end. Additionally, while it is difficult to dispute the claim that other minds exist, it is possible to dispute the existence of God. If a belief can be challenged, we have to ask if it is properly basic.

---

180. Alvin Plantinga, "Reason and Belief in God," in *Faith and Rationality* (ed. A. Plantinga and N. Wolterstorff; Notre Dame, IN: University of Notre Dame Press, 1983), 16–93; idem, *Warrant: The Current Debate* (Oxford: Oxford University Press, 1993); idem, *Warrant and Proper Function* (Oxford: Oxford University Press, 1993); idem, *Warranted Christian Belief* (Oxford: Oxford University Press, 2000).

181. Plantinga, "Reason and Belief in God," 17.

182. Plantinga, *Warranted Christian Belief*, 93.

183. Cf. Alvin Plantinga, "Two Dozen (or so) Theistic Arguments," in *Alvin Plantinga* (ed. Deane-Peter Baker; Cambridge: Oxford University Press, 2007), 203–28.

Or in the least it is not properly basic in the same way that other basic beliefs might be. Perhaps it is the case that belief in God is bound up with a web of basic beliefs and evidentially derived beliefs. Also, Plantinga's reading of Calvin is often tendentious. It is not clear that Calvin repudiated natural theology or foundationalist epistemology as is claimed.[184] Another problem is whether only belief in the Christian God is properly basic. The same argument about basic beliefs could be mounted to establish that the God of Islam, Jehovah's Witnesses, or Mormons is properly basic.

In light of all of these Reformed objections to natural theology, I wish to set forth four theses concerning natural theology from a neo-Reformed perspective.

1. God's otherness and transcendence do not mean that he has cordoned himself off from creation. Creation remains a witness to God, even if the witness is ignored, rejected, or disbelieved. Emil Brunner was right to insist that there was a "point of contact" (*Anknüpfungspunkt*) between God and humanity through creation.[185] There is a natural revelation that yields knowledge of God. It is not that nature *is* revelation. It is more accurate to say that nature mediates revelation. It shows traces of God's authorship and artistry in creation. However, human reasoning, impaired by sin, suppresses this truth and exchanges that knowledge for idolatry. The natural person who is not indwelt by the Spirit of God will not construct or accept a natural theology. Carl F. Henry was right:

> God's universal disclosure in nature, history, and to the human mind and conscience is not in dispute.... What is rejected rather is the expectation that fallen man will translate general revelation into a natural theology that builds a secure bridge to special revelation; in that event special revelation has significance only as a crown that caps off natural theology elaborated by man in sin.[186]

People will not arrive at an effective knowledge of God by reasoning from natural revelation to natural theology to special revelation to salvation. This is because the mental motherboard in people has been infected by the sin virus and the natural revelation program won't load. Or, to use a different metaphor, the gap in our knowledge of God is like a river. Natural revelation is a bridge. Natural theology is like the cart that goes over the bridge. But the bridge has been burned by sin so that no one is going to even contemplate getting into a cart to get across the river. Consequently, if we are to have knowledge of God, God himself must first come over to our side of the river bank and speak to us. There is no way over the river from the human side. Men and women will not reason their way to God of their own free will and by open-minded discussion.

---

184. Cf. Paul Helm, *Faith and Understanding* (Edinburgh: Edinburgh University Press, 1997), 179–201.

185. Brunner, *The Christian Doctrine of Creation and Redemption*, 234–35.

186. Carl F. Henry, *God, Revelation, and Authority* (Waco, TX: Word, 1976), 2:117.

2. Despite the noetic effects of sin, it is possible to argue for the value of natural theology as a task within Christian theology. If we identify two types of knowledge of God—a natural knowledge of God as per Calvin's *sensus divinitatis* and an inferential knowledge consisting of the development of theistic arguments—we could say that the latter is rooted in the former. In other words, natural theology is grounded in a natural knowledge of God. The innate sense of God in a person, when stupefied by the majesty of creation and when cultivated by the Holy Spirit, provides the framework in which natural theology can be accepted as rational explanations of God's relation to creation. This means that theistic arguments presented in natural theology emerge from a Christian framework of scriptural revelation and the subjective condition of regeneration, rather than in some purportedly autonomous and neutral field of shared philosophical assumptions. As Michael Sudduth puts it:

> On the Reformed view, the project of developing theistic arguments is best understood as a multi-tiered rational exploration of God's general revelation of Himself in both the Universe and the intellectual and moral constitution of the human person. Such a project is driven by the same goals as dogmatic theology: clarity, systematicity, and completeness. If we take seriously the biblical idea that there is a general revelation in the natural order, one of the tasks of the Christian is to provide a rational account of this revelation. An account of general revelation that is developed with the order of nature itself both confirms the confession of the biblical data concerning general revelation and translates it into understanding.[187]

The objective of natural theology is to describe how nature enables us to discern the truth, beauty, and goodness of God in the world. It is not a matter of proving God's existence to unbelievers through a shared philosophical discourse (who of us shares the presuppositions of David Hume or Immanuel Kant?). Instead, natural theology concerns itself with elucidating God's self-disclosure in nature and the mechanism for its human perception.[188] Natural theology of this species is a theological task, not a secular one. As Stanley Hauerwas stresses: "Natural theology divorced from a full [Christian] doctrine of God cannot help but distort the character of God and, accordingly of the world in which we find ourselves.... I must maintain that the God who moves the sun and the stars is the same God who was incarnate in Jesus of Nazareth."[189] Consequently, natural theology is a helpful clarification of God's relationship to the world, but only faith can identify the God of rational demonstration with the God of divine revelation.[190]

3. Natural theology, in arguing for the evidential plausibility of the existence of God based on the traditional proofs, is a way in which we can fulfill the command

---

187. Sudduth, *Reformed Objection to Natural Theology*, 227.
188. McGrath, *The Open Secret*, 5.
189. Stanley Hauerwas, *With the Grain of the Universe: The Church's Witness and Natural Theology* (London: SCM, 2002), 15–16.
190. Bloesch, *God the Almighty*, 66.

in 1 Peter 3:15 to provide a reason for the hope that is within us. God may use those reasons to lead people to faith. The qualification I would make is that we do that from a theistic perspective rather than from a position of purported epistemological neutrality. We don't adopt a "for-sake-of-argument" position of neutrality, any more than we expect other people to adhere to our presuppositions. We do not pretend to be unbelievers or expect unbelievers to pretend to be believers. Instead, we are up-front with our presupposition that traditional proofs support theistic belief rather than establish the warrant for holding those beliefs.

4. The epistemic justification for belief in God is not dependent on the cogency of natural theology or traditional proofs for God's existence. Belief in God is established and warranted on the grounds of God's revelation of himself in the gospel and by the inner testimony of the Holy Spirit.

Perhaps a fuller solution is to understand natural revelation in relation to the gospel. Strictly speaking, natural revelation is there independent of human acknowledgment of it. God is revealed in the natural order as the Creator and Provider of all humanity. This holds true even if humanity's epistemic antennae do not receive the message because of sin's distortion of our reasoning. Therefore, natural revelation is only properly received after one has formally believed in Christ through the gospel. Nonetheless, the natural revelation prepares for special revelation. That is seen in Psalm 19, where the initial verses focus on God's word in creation (19:1–6) and then move on to God's word in the law (19:7–14). The Pauline speeches in Acts move from nature (Acts 14:15–17; 17:22–29) to gospel (14:21; 17:30–31).

I am not suggesting that these passages constitute an *ordo evangelium*, that is, the sequence of events for preaching the gospel. A preacher does not have to take his audience from the starry constellations to the heavenly Christ in every evangelistic sermon. Yet in these passages there is a perceptible and logical order that shifts from news about creation to news about Jesus Christ. So natural revelation is not the gospel. More likely, however, natural revelation is a *preparatio evangelium*, a preparation for the gospel. Natural revelation does not bring a saving knowledge of God, but it can establish a beachhead on the shores of belief so that the rapid march of gospel preaching can break out from there. Sometimes you can parachute the gospel into enemy territory and win your audience over if the Spirit is blowing in your parachute. At other times, establishing the theocentric story of creation, or just arguing for the plain fact that *God is*, to use Francis Schaeffer's terminology,[191] is the preliminary landing we must first undertake before the gospel can plough ahead and do its work.[192]

---

191. Francis A. Schaeffer, *The God Who is There* (Downers Grove, IL: InterVarsity Press, 1968).

192. For a good example of explaining the story of creation as part of redemptive history within an evangelistic presentation of the gospel, see D. A. Carson, *The God Who Is There: Finding Your Place in God's Story* (Grand Rapids: Baker, 2010).

EVANGELICALS AND KARL BARTH

You may have noticed that we've been talking a lot about this "Karl Barth" chap (pronounced "Bart," not "Barth"!). For many Protestant theologians Karl Barth simply is modern theology. For some Barthian acolytes everything that we say about theology now is really just a footnote to Karl Barth. When I was teaching in Scotland, I learned that at Aberdeen University there were more people writing doctoral theses on Karl Barth than writing doctoral studies on Jesus and Paul combined![193] For many evangelicals, however, Karl Barth is the bogeyman. The initial reception of Barth by American theologians such as J. G. Machen, Cornelius Van Til, and Carl F. Henry was far from positive. In fact, when I began doctoral studies at university, my pastor prayed that I would not come under the influence of the neoorthodox! I can honestly say that given the many weirdos and whackos that I met in the religious studies department of a secular university, sharing an office with a Barthian postgrad student would have been an absolute delight.[194]

There are four things young evangelicals need to know about Karl Barth.[195] (1) Karl Barth was not an evangelical. He was a European Protestant wrestling with how to salvage Protestant Christianity in the wake of World War I, which exposed the debacle of liberal theology. Barth was not an inerrantist or a revivalist, and he was wrestling with a different array of issues than the "battle for the Bible."

(2) Karl Barth is on the side of the good guys when it comes to the major ecumenical doctrines about the Trinity and the atonement. Barth is decidedly orthodox and Reformed in his basic stance, though he sees the councils and confessions mainly as guidelines rather than holy writ.

(3) Karl Barth arguably gives evangelicals some good tips about how to do theology over and against liberalism. Keep in mind that Karl Barth's main sparring partner was not Billy Graham or the Chicago Statement on Biblical Inerrancy, but the European liberal tradition from Friedrich Schleiermacher to Albert Ritschl. For a case in point, whereas Schleiermacher made the Trinity an appendix to his book on *Christian Faith*

---

193. No doubt attributable to the presence of the brilliant professor John Webster, who is a recognized expert in Karl Barth and Protestant scholasticism.

194. During my time at university one chap wrote his thesis on "Gay Spirituality," which is fair enough and a valid PhD topic. However, while he was there, he also published a book attempting to prove Jesus was gay, using astrology. Another guy wrote his thesis on the religious significance of vampire myths. Then there was the option of taking a class on religion and body art. It was a top university, but filled with more nuts than Brazil.

195. I am indebted to Prof. Bruce McCormack for several of these thoughts, based on his 2005 lecture at the Edinburgh Dogmatics Conference.

because it was irrelevant to religious experience, Barth made the Trinity first and foremost in his *Church Dogmatics*, which was Barth's way of saying, "Suck on that one, Schleiermacher!"

(4) Evangelicals and the neoorthodox tend to be rather hostile toward each other. Many evangelicals regard the neoorthodox as nothing more than liberalism reloaded, while many neoorthodox theologians regard evangelicals as a more culturally savvy version of fundamentalism. Not true on either score. Evangelicalism and neoorthodoxy are both theological renewal movements trying to find a biblical and orthodox center in the post-Enlightenment era. The evangelicals left fundamentalism and edged left toward a workable orthodox center. The neoorthodox left liberalism and edged right toward a workable orthodox center. Thus, evangelicalism and neoorthodoxy are more like sibling rivals striving to be the heirs of the Reformers in the post-Enlightenment age.

There is much in Karl Barth that evangelicals can benefit from. His theology is arguably the most christocentric ever devised. He has a strong emphasis on God's transcendence, freedom, love, and "otherness." Barth stresses the singular power and authority of the Word of God in its threefold form of "Incarnation, Preaching, and Scripture." Barth strove with others like Karl Rahner to restore the Trinity to its place of importance in modern Christian thought. He was a leader in the Confessing Church until he was expelled from Germany by the Nazi regime. He preached weekly in the Basel prison. His collection of prayers contain moving accounts of his own piety and devotion to God. There is, of course, much to be critical of as well. Barth's doctrine of election implied a universalism that he could never exegetically reconcile. Barth never could regard Scripture as God's Word *per se* as much as it was an instrument for becoming God's Word. He never took evangelicalism all that seriously, as evidenced by his famous retort to Carl Henry that *Christianity Today* was *Christianity Yesterday*.

Barth's theology, pro and con, is something that we must engage if we are to understand the state of modern theology. The best place to start to get your head around Barth is his *Evangelical Theology*, but note that for Barth, "evangelical" (*evangelische*) means basically "not Catholic" rather than something like American evangelicalism. Going beyond that, his *Göttingen Dogmatics* or *Dogmatics in Outline* is a step up where Barth begins to assemble a system of theology based on his understanding of the Word of God. Then one might like to launch into his multivolume *Church Dogmatics* with the kind assistance of Geoffrey Bromiley's *Introduction to the Theology of Karl Barth*, which conveniently summarizes each section of *Church Dogmatics*.

> **FURTHER READING**
>
> Barth, Karl. *Dogmatics in Outline.* Trans. G. T. Thomson. London: SCM, 1949.
> ———. *Evangelical Theology: An Introduction.* New York: Holt, Rinehart, & Winston, 1963.
> ———. *The Göttingen Dogmatics: Instruction in the Christian Religion.* Grand Rapids: Eerdmans, 1991.
> Berkouwer, G. C. *The Triumph of Grace in the Theology of Karl Barth.* Grand Rapids: Eerdmans, 1956.
> Bromiley, Geoffrey W. *An Introduction to the Theology of Karl Barth.* Grand Rapids: Eerdmans, 1979.
> Chung, Sung Wook, ed. *Karl Barth and Evangelical Theology: Convergences and Divergence.* Grand Rapids: Baker, 2006.
> Gibson, David, and Daniel Strange, eds. *Engaging with Barth: Contemporary Evangelical Critiques.* New York: T&T Clark, 2008.
> McCormack, Bruce, and Clifford Anderson, eds. *Karl Barth and American Evangelicalism.* Grand Rapids: Eerdmans, 2011.

Paradoxically, natural revelation sometimes prepares for the gospel, while the gospel in turn makes natural revelation intelligible. Or perhaps we could say that the gospel enables us to move from natural revelation to a natural theology and so rationally connect God to the world via the gospel.

2.5.4 MODES OF REVELATION: SPECIAL REVELATION

God's *special revelation* is comprised of his unique communication of himself through history, proclamation, Scripture, and illumination. The special revelation of God is necessary because natural revelation imparts enough knowledge to make a person culpable before God, but on account of sin, it does not yield a saving knowledge. If there is to be reconciliation between God and humanity, God has to manifest himself to humanity and act to deliver them from the consequences of their rebellion against him.

2.5.4.1 REVELATION AND HISTORY

In some religions, if certain persons never existed, their religious system would not radically change. So, for example, if it turned out that the Buddha never existed, the four noble truths of Buddhism would still be noble and the eightfold path to nirvana would still be the eightfold path. Buddhism could survive if Buddha was not a historical figure. In contrast, Christianity claims to be a historical religion and that God acts in the sphere of history. That God did something miraculous in the exodus, at the tomb of Jesus, and at Pentecost shows that God works in historical events to reveal his saving power.

Indeed, Christianity stands or falls with its historical character. That is why Paul says that if Christ has not been raised, "we are of all people most to be pitied" (1 Cor 15:19). The Petrine testimony about Jesus is this: "For we did not follow cleverly devised stories when we told you about the coming of our Lord Jesus Christ in power, but we were eyewitnesses of his majesty" (2 Pet 1:16). The Christian message does not offer a newly discovered path to enlightenment; rather, it is a testimony to the God who reaches down into human history so that the future of humanity will be different from what it currently is now.

That God operates in the mode of "history" is a given. But what does that exactly mean? There are several models that explain how God's revelation relates to historical sequences of events.[196] On one view, such as that of G. Ernest Wright, Scripture is a historical recital of the acts of God in history and the human response to those acts. The Bible is a record of revelation, not the revelation itself. Biblical doctrine is inferred from the historical recital of the events of *revelation in history.*

Others such as Emil Brunner and Karl Barth contend that God works within history to manifest himself. The qualification made is that it is not in events per se that God is revealed, but in the personal encounter enmeshed within those events. For instance, the Pharisees who saw Jesus' miracles did not have a revelation because they did not believe in him. Yet those people in the crowd who saw and believed in him did have a revelation. While God reveals himself through historical events, his revelation is not coterminous with that event.

Consequently for these theologians, the Bible is not revelation. It is the words of Isaiah, Ezekiel, Paul, and John, and it only becomes the Word of God when God speaks to us through it. Bultmann even went so far as to say that while the New Testament's proclamation refers to historical events, revelation is not "in" those events, but the historical events create a new understanding of God, and it is in that new awareness that the locus of revelation occurs. So, for example, grace is not a historical event, but an existential moment created by the recital of the past. On this perspective, a revelation occurs when the atemporal realities of God and grace are manifested through the temporal world. This view thus emphasizes *revelation through history* in a personal encounter rather than in objectified events and artifacts.

---

196. Erickson, *Christian Theology*, 209–12.

A third approach is that associated with Wolfhart Pannenberg, who regards revelation as a public and universal event in history that is recognized and interpreted as an "act of God." Revelation is not a disclosure of truths about God; it is the self-revelation of God. God's actions in history are not inferred or allegorical; they are literal actions that would have been observable to anyone. For Pannenberg, the key historical event that reveals God is the resurrection of Jesus Christ, which is the climax of God's *revelation as history*.

I think Pannenberg's approach is the most compelling perspective on revelation and history. God's revelation is not reducible to human reflection on historical events, nor is it human experience of God facilitated by historical events. God acts in history, and that history communicates something of God. Such a perspective is demanded by nothing less than the incarnation. The incarnation was a revelation of God enfleshed in the domain of historical events and was completely observable. It can also be said that God's revelation of himself in history is heading toward a certain climax. God's revelation is embedded in the historical sequence and involves progress toward a certain goal.[197] History as divinely ordained is moving toward the consummation of all things. That "end" will constitute the ultimate verification of God's acts in history. The proof of God's call of Israel, the miracle stories, the experience of new birth, and more, will be cosmically confirmed at the full arrival of the eschaton. As Pannenberg noted:

> As the revelation of God in his historical action moves towards the still outstanding future of the consummation of history, its claim to reveal the one God who is the world's Creator, Reconciler, and Redeemer is open to future verification.[198]

2.5.4.2 INSPIRED PROCLAMATION

God speaks through the inspiration of prophets, apostles, and messengers, who set forth the "word of the Lord" or the "gospel of our Lord" to people. That is seen in the Old Testament when it is said that "the word of the Lord came to me" or "the word of the Lord came to X" (e.g., 1 Sam 15:10; 1 Chr 22:8; Isa 38:4; Jer 1:4, 11, 13; 2:1; 13:3, 8; 18:1, 5; Ezek 12:1, 8, 17, 21, 26; Hos 1:1; Joel 1:1; Hag 2:20; Zech 1:1; 4:8). Importantly, this "word" is something that is revealed. In reference to Samuel, we read: "Now Samuel did not yet know the Lord: The word of the Lord had not yet been revealed to him" (1 Sam 3:7). The prophetic word is not something that is arrived at by mere intuition or from an extrapolation of one's religious feelings. The word of God is disclosed and declared to people. The Hebrew word *gālâ* implies uncovering what was concealed. According to Jeremiah, there are three channels

---

197. Graeme Goldsworthy, *Preaching the Whole Bible as Christian Scripture* (Grand Rapids: Eerdmans, 2001), 22.

198. Pannenberg, *Systematic Theology*, 1:257.

of revelation in Israel's community (Jer 18:18): instruction in Torah by the priests (law of Moses), the wise who offered counsel on how to live a God-centered life (Wisdom Literature), and the prophets, who delivered messages that disclosed God's purposes for the people (prophecy).

Closely aligned with the divine word is the divine Spirit in the delivery of the message. People are often filled with the Spirit in order to execute a particular ministry, especially a prophetic ministry (e.g., Deut 34:9; Mic 3:8; Luke 1:15, 41, 67). In fact, the prophetic word is the word of the Spirit operating through the human subject. That is evident in the prophetic word of David ("The Spirit of the LORD spoke through me; his word was on my tongue" [2 Sam 23:2]) and in the words of Jesus ("The Spirit gives life; the flesh counts for nothing. The words I have spoken to you—they are full of the Spirit and life" [John 6:63]). In the early church, we find people being filled with the Holy Spirit to speak forth the Word of God in boldness (Acts 4:8, 31; 7:55).

The unity of God's Word with God's Spirit is underscored further in the preaching of the gospel. Jesus only began preaching the gospel of the kingdom once he had received the Holy Spirit (e.g., Mark 1:9–15; Luke 4:14–21). Paul's preaching of the gospel is animated by and accompanied with demonstrations of the Holy Spirit's power (Rom 15:19; 1 Cor 2:4; 1 Thess 1:5). Peter declares that messengers to the Asian churches "preached the gospel to you by the Holy Spirit sent from heaven" (1 Pet 1:12). The Word that is proclaimed is done so in the power of the Spirit so that it is not accepted "as a human word, but as it actually is, the word of God" (1 Thess 2:13). That is why the Second Helvetic Confession (art. 1) declares that "the preaching of the Word of God is the Word of God."

2.5.4.3 INSPIRED INSCRIPTURATION

God communicates through the inspiration of authors who compose writings that transmit his message to people (1 Tim 3:16; 2 Pet 1:20–21). In Scripture, God invests himself in the written Word and he even identifies with it, to the point that Scripture becomes a mode of God's own presence.[199] In my thinking, a doctrine of Scripture should not be a locus of its own. Such a doctrine stands somewhere between ecclesiology and pneumatology, or between church and Spirit, in terms of its appropriate place in a Christian theology. God breathes out Scripture through the canon of the believing community. I intend to deal with the doctrine of Scripture more fully as part of the "Work of the Holy Spirit."[200] Here we are restricted to the concept of Scripture *as revelation*. Yet it is disputed by some, if Scripture is indeed a revelation, in what way Scripture can be a revelation, and whether that revelation is propositional or personal.

---

199. Ward, *Words of Life*, 29.
200. Cf. Webster, *Holy Scripture*, 12–14, 39–40, 54; McGowan, *Divine Spiration of Scripture*, 28–31.

§ 2.5 The God Who Reveals Himself

First, many thinkers have questioned whether Christianity is a revelatory religion and if the Bible can be regarded as a genuine revelation. For instance, James Barr stated that Scripture is not revelation as a word revealed from God. Rather, it is the word of people about their experience of God. Barr (though he has probably changed his mind on the matter since his death in 2006) wrote:

> My account of the formation of the biblical doctrine is an account of a *human* work. It is *man's* statement of his beliefs, the events he has experienced, the stories he has been told, and so on. It has long been customary to align the Bible with concepts like the Word of God, or revelation, and one effect of this has been to align the Bible with a movement *from God to man*. It is man who developed the biblical tradition and man who decided when it might be suitably fixed and made canonical. If one wants to use the Word-of-God type of language, the proper term for the Bible would be Word of Israel, Word of some leading early Christians.[201]

The problem here is that one either accepts the Bible's testimony to itself or one does not. Scripture does not present itself as the recollections of religious people about God. Rather, Scripture is written as the words God spoke to and through human subjects. Scripture is not a report from persons who *generated* words about God; instead, Scripture is filled with the story of God *giving* words to people. That is why it is treated as an authoritative and trustworthy message, because it comes from God. What is more, Jesus regarded the Old Testament as the word of God (e.g., Matt 4:4; 15:6/Mark 7:13; John 10:35), and his own teaching was also the word of God (Luke 5:1; 8:11; 11:28). A disciple of Jesus can hardly have a view of Scripture altogether at odds with that of Jesus himself.

Second, we need to explore exactly how revelation is contained in Scripture. The center of gravity in revelation can be pushed into one of three spheres.

Type of Revelation	Where God Speaks	Example
Is the Bible a *record* of revelation?	God spoke back then at the event.	The events at Sinai
Is the Bible the *content* of revelation?	God spoke in the Bible.	The book of Exodus
Is the Bible the *means* of revelation?	God speaks through the Bible.	Illumination gained by reading the exodus story

God undoubtedly acted and spoke in past historical events. This is seen in the

---

201. James Barr, *The Bible in the Modern World* (London, 1973), 120 (italics original); see also John Macquarrie, *Principles of Christian Theology* (London: SCM, 2003), 9–11.

two most momentous events in the Christian Scriptures, namely, the exodus event and the Easter story. History bears witness to the acts of God, and these acts are recorded for us in the Scriptures. Scripture is a revelation on the grounds that it is a *record* of the events whereby God did mighty and amazing things in the past.

Yet the Scriptures are not simply the record of events that happened in the past; it is also the interpretation of those events. The exodus was not a circumstantial migration of refugees; instead, it was an act of deliverance where God called Israel to be his son (Exod 4:22–23; Hos 11:1). The death of Jesus was not an execution of a Jewish martyr; it was a sacrifice for human sins (Rom 3:25; Heb 9:14; 1 Pet 2:24). The Bible is the *content* of revelation because it records what God did and informs us what God intended to communicate by it. In Scripture, God tells us what God meant when he did X, Y, or Z.[202] The Scriptures do not merely point to a prior revelation; they are revelation.

A further thought to consider here is that the Scriptures are also a *means* of revelation. Scripture is the instrument through which God continues to speak to his people. Here we must access the experiential component to a theology of Scripture. As we hear Scripture read to us or when we take it up and read it ourselves, we are moved, challenged, grieved, rebuked, and encouraged. Reading Scripture is spiritually nourishing and noetically enriching. God speaks to us through Scripture, not in the sense of new revelation, but in the sense of addressing us with the true meaning of his Word for our particular circumstance. To draw near to God in Scripture is to allow the wisdom and power of God's Word to dwell in you richly. Gordon Smith states: "There is no reading of Scripture that is not in some way or another informed by experience; and the ideal of course is that as we continue to experience the grace of God we will continue to allow the text to inform and reform our experience."[203]

Viewed this way, the revelation of God in the Scriptures is historical, textual, and experiential.

Third, another unhelpful bifurcation is often made about revelation as something that is either propositional or something that is personal. John Macquarrie wrote: "The Christian revelation comes in a person, not in a book."[204] Yet this is a false dichotomy, and we may safely declare the revelation of Scripture to be both propositional and personal.[205]

In light of rationalistic critiques of Scripture as revealing truths about God, Prot-

---

202. Leon Morris, *I Believe in Revelation* (Grand Rapids: Eerdmans, 1976), 43–44, 110–11.
203. Gordon T. Smith, *Beginning Well: Christian Conversion and Authentic Transformation* (Downers Grove, IL: InterVarsity Press, 2001), 52.
204. Macquarrie, *Principles of Christian Theology*, 10.
205. To give a conservative example of this unhelpful dichotomy, the preamble to the *Baptist Faith and Message* of 1963 stated: "This faith is rooted and grounded in *Jesus Christ*.... Therefore, the sole authority for faith and practice among Baptists is Jesus Christ whose will is revealed in the Holy Scriptures." However, the preamble to the *Baptist Faith and Message* of 2000 changed this to read: "Our living faith is established upon *eternal truths*." You can see the problem. The *BFM* 2000 has replaced the person of Jesus Christ with doctrinal propositions as the foundation for faith. Can you replace Jesus with doctrine as the foundation of your faith?

estant theologians began to react in one of two ways. Some theologians retreated from criticism of revealed religion by seeking refuge in the towers of experience. By contrast, conservatives reacted by fortifying their bibliology around the concept of propositional revelation and plenary inspiration. On the more liberal perspective, revelation is what happens when one encounters God through Scripture, not God speaking in Scripture per se. On a more conservative perspective, revelation is characterized as a series of revealed facts about God that are to be translated by the theologian into doctrinal propositions (e.g., God is good, he sent Jesus to be our Savior, etc). The Bible becomes, to quote Carl Henry, "referential information about the nature of God."[206] Scripture becomes a deposit of facts to be excavated and ordered. Todd Billings describes the unfortunate result of what happens with a narrow focus on Scripture as containing propositions:

> The propositions in Scripture are facts that need organization, and the system of the theology provides that organization. In a sense, we already know the extensive meaning of Scripture; our system of theology tells us that. There is thus no need to look into history, or other cultures, to see how others "hear" Scripture. Instead, the task of interpreting Scripture is to discover where in our theological system this particular Scripture passage goes.[207]

Without diminishing the truth content of Scripture, we should affirm the christocentric power and charismatic energy that inhabits the word of God in Scripture. The Westminster Confession 1.10 says: "The supreme judge by which all controversies of religion are to be determined, and all decrees of councils, opinions of ancient writers, doctrines of men, and private spirits, are to be examined, and in whose sentence we are to rest, can be no other but the *Holy Spirit speaking in the Scripture.*" Scripture is the instrument for how the Spirit addresses the people with the words of the living Christ. However, conservative Protestant theologians abbreviated "Holy Spirit speaking in the Scripture" to just "Scripture." This led to an emphasis on the Bible as a plenary, verbal, and propositional form of revelation that *is* fully identical to the revelation itself. Yet it bracketed out the redemptive events behind Scripture and the personal encounter with God at the front of Scripture.

There are a number of shortcomings in a strictly propositional approach.

1. An overemphasis on propositions fails to note the distance between language and personality. Words cannot encompass all that God is. Human words can only ever be analogous to divine words. Propositional revelation will always be restricted by the limitation of language.
2. A heightened propositional approach makes revelation a thing that is "there,"

---

206. Cited in Alister McGrath, *Christian Theology: An Introduction* (3rd ed.; Oxford: Blackwell, 2001), 154.
207. J. Todd Billings, *The Word of God for the People of God: An Entryway to the Theological Interpretation of Scripture* (Grand Rapid: Eerdmans, 2010), 5.

rather than something more dynamic, including the message, the medium, and the effect. It might be better to say that revelation is not simply a revealed fact, but a divine speech-act. God speaks the truth and the truth sets us free.

3. Post-liberal theologians have a point when they allege that a strictly propositional approach makes it impossible to show how doctrines like the Trinity developed or how doctrines can be reinterpreted, such as whether women need to wear head coverings. If revelation simply contains propositions, then why did it take so long to develop a doctrine of the Trinity? Are all propositions revealed in Scripture timeless, or are they culturally bound like certain aspects of male-female relationships in the New Testament that pertain only to the culture of Greco-Roman urban centers? We can answer this with reference to the progressive nature of revelation. God progressively revealed more and more of himself. Concurrently, the Holy Spirit was gradually working in the church through the Scriptures to develop a fully orbed doctrine of the Trinity when the church finally needed to know its own mind on the matter. Also, God speaks the truth, but some truths have different applications in different cultures (who greets each other with a kiss these days as in Rom 16:16?).

4. If Hebrews 1:1–2 is to be believed, God speaks at various times and in various ways, such as law code, narrative, proverbs, psalms, prophecy, gospels, letters, and apocalypse. The Westminster Confession 1.1 captures this same thought when it states that "it pleased the Lord, at sundry times, and in diverse manners, to reveal himself." This is a short yet profound statement. It illustrates that Scripture contains a diverse array of literary forms that provide a self-communication of God. So it is more proper to say that special revelation has a *canonically* shaped content that brings a divine disclosure of God's person.

5. The penchant for propositions demonstrates an Enlightenment bias that prefers propositions over other literary forms. For example, Thomas Hobbes regarded "metaphor" as a deceitful means of communication because it obscured the propositional nature of truth. In *Leviathan* he wrote: "But for metaphors, they are in this case utterly excluded. For seeing they openly profess deceit, to admit them into council, or reasoning, were manifest folly."[208] If one were to apply Hobbes's view of truth to divine revelation, one could infer that the parables of Jesus are subrevelatory compared to propositions about redemption found in Paul's letter to the Romans. An unqualified preference for proposi-

---

208. Thomas Hobbes, *Leviathan: Parts I and II* (ed. A. P. Martinich; Peterborough, ON: Broadview, 2005), 55.

tions is evidence for buying into the Enlightenment view that *real* truth is propositional and all other forms for expressing truth are inferior.[209]

So if by propositional revelation one means that certain propositions have been divinely revealed and laid up in a book and that is the end of the story, that concept is to be utterly rejected.[210] Edward Carnell went so far as to say: "To conceive of the Bible as the primary revelation [i.e., mere communication of facts] is heresy."[211] That is because it denies the epochal events behind Scripture and the personal encounter with God in front of Scripture.

Yet we can fully hold to a propositional revelation as long as it is properly nuanced. Propositional revelation means only that there is a conceptual side to revelation. It means that when God comes to us, he comes to us with the truth.[212] The propositional nature of revelation in Scripture can be resolutely affirmed because Scripture indeed states true things about God. We must hold to a propositional revelation simply because the gospel has propositional content in recounting past events (see esp. 1 Cor 15:3–5).[213] The gospel poses propositions about God, Israel, Jesus, and God's kingdom. Yet the gospel is not merely propositional data, but an encounter, even a confrontation, with the royal figure announced as Lord and Messiah in the gospel, namely, Jesus of Nazareth. Let us reflect on what the Westminster Shorter Catechism 86 asks, "What is faith in Jesus Christ?" to which it answers: "Faith in Jesus Christ is a saving grace, whereby we receive and rest upon him alone for salvation, as he is offered to us in the gospel." The Westminster divines did not regard assent to propositions as the sum of our faith; rather, they regarded faith as resting or trusting in the person we meet in the gospel.[214]

Thus, we can wholeheartedly affirm that special revelation is propositional; that is, it contains true ideas, words, and statements about God. However, it is better to say that special revelation is *canonically factual* and comes to us in diverse forms within the Christian canon. Our authority is not the propositions of Scripture. Our authority is the Holy Spirit speaking in Scripture as a testimony to the living Lord. Recognizing the Spirit as the one who breathes out Scripture enables us to bridge the gap between the propositional and personal nature of revelation. That is because revelation contains the propositions of a divine person speaking, so that there is no divide between personal and propositional revelation.[215] The special revelation

---

209. By the same token, those who entirely eschew propositions in favor of narrative and experience sacrifice the notion of God's speaking the truth to us in his self-communication.
210. Morris, *I Believe in Revelation*, 113.
211. Edward Carnell, *The Case for Orthodox Theology* (Philadelphia: Westminster, 1959), 49.
212. Bernard Ramm, *Special Revelation and the Word of God* (Grand Rapids: Eerdmans, 1961), 154–55.
213. Cf. Jensen, *Revelation of God*, 87–90.
214. Paul Helm, *The Divine Revelation: The Basic Issues* (Vancouver, BC: Regent College Publishing, 2004), 42.
215. Ibid.; Kevin Vanhoozer, *First Theology: God, Scripture, and Hermeneutics* (Downers Grove, IL: InterVarsity Press, 2002), 131.

sealed for us in Scripture is designed to function beside the Holy Spirit, beside the presence of the living God, beside the presence of the risen Lord, and dwell among the people of God.[216]

When we confess that revelation is personal, we mean that when we hear the gospel proclaimed or when Scripture is read, we are not only hearing facts about God, but we are genuinely encountering God. If misunderstood, propositional revelation could imply that we are hearing only raw data and concepts about God. But through the event that is the Word of God, we are encountering God wherever that Word is present: in the gospel, in Scripture, in sacrament, or in a confession of faith. The Spirit actualizes the Word in terms of its propositional content and brings about a transforming existential effect. To read that "Jesus Christ is Lord" is not only to become aware of Jesus' authority, but also to experience the effects of his lordship. As Donald Bloesch has put it, revelation is an "event in which God personally confronts his people with a message that both enlightens and redeems" and is "an act of communication by which God confronts the whole person with his redeeming mercy and glorious presence." Consequently, "revelation is being grasped by the power of the resurrected Christ and set in a completely new direction."[217]

Karl Barth argued that revelation was not only personal, but in fact tri-personal. Revelation is a triune act as it has a sender, a content, and an effect (what Grenz called Barth's "Revelational Trinitarianism"). That corresponds to Father, Son, and Holy Spirit. God is the "Revealer, the revelation, and the revealedness."[218] John Webster similarly identifies revelation with God's triune being in its active self-presence. He writes: "As Father, God is the personal will or origin of this self-presence; as Son, God actualizes his self-presence, upholding it and establishing it against all opposition; as Holy Spirit, God perfects that self-presence by making it real and effective to and in the history of humankind."[219] The unity of Word and Spirit—with divine sender, christological content, and charismatic affect—entails that revelation is shaped by a Trinitarian God.

If special revelation is construed this way, the theological task is not to extract propositions from the morass of genres in Scripture and to file them away in some darkened recess of our minds. Rather, the goal of theology is to translate divine speech-acts into human responses that lead to an increased knowledge of God, an increasing participation in the mission of God, and an increasing Christlikeness in the believer. As such, study of the doctrine of revelation is incomplete unless it results in theological transformation, undertaking mission, and pursuing holiness; only then has a revelation been truly received.

---

216. Ramm, *Special Revelation*, 98–99.
217. Donald Bloesch, *Holy Scripture: Revelation, Inspiration and Interpretation* (Downers Grove, IL: InterVarsity Press, 1994), 48–49.
218. Barth, *CD*, I/1:400–4.
219. Webster, *Holy Scripture*, 14.

2.5.4.4 DIVINE ILLUMINATION

God reveals knowledge of himself through the Holy Spirit, who brings understanding of God to the hearts and minds of believers. Illumination refers to the divine enlightening of the mind to grasp the beauty of God's being and the meaning of God's Word. The gospel brings us to an encounter with God's Word and God's Spirit, and in that encounter we are not only informed but also illuminated. As Ramm wrote: "The word of God, crystallized as gospel, concentrated as gospel is that word used by the Holy Spirit as his instrument for our regeneration and for his illuminating work issuing in the internal witness of the Spirit."[220]

Some models of revelation practically collapse revelation and illumination together. This is apparent chiefly in neoorthodoxy. For Barth, the Bible is not God's Word per se; it only becomes God's Word when God speaks to people through it. The scriptural words are those of Isaiah, Jeremiah, Matthew, Paul, or Luke. When God speaks through them, then and only then are the words a revelation. So for Karl Barth, the Bible is "God's Word to the extent that God causes it to be His Word."[221]

Barth was concerned that equating the Bible as God's Word would lead to a domestication of the Bible to human reason, result in a virtual bibliolatry, and lessen the uniqueness of the incarnation by ascribing divine qualities to Scripture. But if we identify God with his own Word, as Scripture clearly does, we are compelled to regard Scripture as the mode of divine speech that is sanctified and personified in such a way as to convey the wisdom and will of God.[222] Scripture is not an incarnation of God's Word, not a hypostatic union of divine being and human flesh; instead, it is an inspired inscripturation of God's Word that operates through human authors. Rightly understood, there is no reason to engage in a Barthian retreat from identifying God with his inscripturated Word.

Illumination is revelatory because if God has spoken, he needs to ensure that it is heard and understood. After all, if God speaks and if no one understands it, has there really been a revelation from God? I say, "No!" Thus special revelation, to be effective, must include God's illuminating work through the Holy Spirit to provide people with a transformed awareness of God. Whereas it is the Holy Spirit speaking through the Scripture that makes Scripture authoritative, it is the Spirit's continuing work in bringing understanding to the reader of Scripture that makes Scripture an effective medium of divine revelation. In a nutshell, illumination relates to the ministry of the Holy Spirit that enables believers to understand the truth of God's Word. So revelation relates to God's unveiling of himself, inspiration concerns the process by which this revelation is infused into human authors, and illumination

---

220. Ramm, *Special Revelation*, 58–59.
221. Barth, *CD*, I/1:109.
222. Cf. Ward, *Words of Life*, 62–69.

refers to the ministry of the Spirit by which the meaning of revelation is appropriately grasped by the believer.

Illumination is necessary because ordinary people are deprived of the truth about God as a result of their depraved state of mind (John 3:5; 14:17; 1 Cor 2:14). Giving a revelation to men and women alienated from God is a bit like trying to insert a DVD into a video cassette player; it won't load. Thus, the people sin for lack of knowledge (Hos 4:6), they do not know either Scripture or the power of God (Matt 22:29), and they are mystified by the mystery of God (Job 11:7; Dan 2:26–27; Mark 4:11–12). Revelation requires not only information but transformation in order to be effective.

So it is that the revealing God not only speaks but also gives insight into the wonder and wisdom of his own Word. For example, the bestowal of the Spirit of God in the Old Testament was so that a person would have wisdom, understanding, and knowledge with respect to a particular task (Exod 31:3; 35:31; Deut 34:9; Isa 11:2). Daniel was given supernatural understanding of the events that he had to decipher in Babylon (e.g., Dan 1:20; 2:21; 5:11, 14). The Spirit granted to believers in Christ imparts wisdom so that they may possess special spiritual insight even into the mysterious things of God (1 Cor 2:9–13; 12:8; Eph 1:17; Col 1:9; 3:16; Jas 3:13). Maturity in the Christian faith comes through the experience of being enlightened about the hope, riches, and mystery of God (Eph 1:18; 3:9).

The best example of illumination as revelation comes from the resurrection narrative in gospel of Luke. Illumination, a divinely given ability to understand what has exactly happened, appears in the women's remembrance of Jesus' passion prediction (Luke 24:8) and in the recognition of the risen Jesus amidst the breaking of bread by the two travelers to Emmaus (24:31–32, 35). The risen Jesus imparts to his disciples a resurrection hermeneutic so that they can finally perceive how Israel's Scriptures point to the passion and glory of the Messiah: "Then he opened their minds so they could understand the Scriptures" (24:45). In other words, a christocentric reading of Scripture is not merely an exercise in exegesis, but it is something sovereignly bestowed so that one can detect and discern in Scripture the promises that Jesus fulfills.

A similar equation of divine illumination as a mode of divine revelation is found in the Fourth Gospel. In Jesus' farewell discourse recorded in John 14–16, the Spirit plays a key role in enabling his followers to learn and discern the truth (14:26; 16:13). Jesus promised his followers that when the Spirit came, he would lead them into the truth (14:16–17; 16:13–16). The "Spirit of truth" is welded to the revelation of God in Jesus Christ and ensures its enduring effect among Jesus' followers (14:17; 15:26; 16:13; cf. 4:23–24; 1 John 4:6). The Spirit testifies to the truth of Jesus and effects the knowledge of that truth in his universal disciples.[223]

---

223. Saeed Hamid-Khani, *Revelation and Concealment of Christ: A Theological Inquiry into the Elusive Language of the Fourth Gospel* (WUNT 2.120; Tübingen: Mohr/Siebeck, 2000), 337–45.

The evangelically structured revelation of God manifests itself in historical events, the Word of God proclaimed, the Word of God inscripturated, and the illuminating work of the Spirit. With respect to the gospel, the revelation of God is manifested in the historical event of Jesus' death and resurrection, in the apostolic testimony to the gospel event, in the Scriptures that narrate the gospel, and in the effectual call and regenerating work of the Holy Spirit who communicates the truth of the gospel to people.

2.5.5 MODES OF REVELATION: CHRISTOLOGICAL REVELATION

A final mode of revelation to consider is "christological revelation," by which I mean the incarnation of the eternal Son as the man Jesus of Nazareth. Strictly speaking the incarnation is a form of special revelation. However, I contend that the incarnation is qualitatively above and beyond all other forms of special revelation by virtue of the immediacy, clarity, and personality of its revelation.[224] When the Fourth Evangelist wanted to describe the single greatest act of God's self-revelation, he did not say, "The Word became a book"; instead he wrote, "The Word became flesh" (John 1:14).[225]

Incarnation is the most efficacious revelation that God has ever made. The incarnation is not mediated through nature; it not a word spoken through human agents; it is not given in the pages of a scroll; and it is not a word activated in the human mind. The incarnation is God-in-the-flesh. It is the perspicuous and powerful revelation of God as a human being—not God in human words, but God with a human face. Even though Scripture sometimes gets described in terms analogous to an incarnation, as a theoanthropic book, the Bible is not an incarnation of God's Word.[226] That is why I call the incarnation extra-extra special revelation. This needs to be explored further.

Now one might object to placing Christology over bibliology in the revelation stakes on the grounds that our knowledge of the incarnation is largely communicated through Scripture. We only know about the incarnation because Scripture tells us about it. Of course, from our vantage point that is basically true. The Scriptures testify that Jesus is the Son of God and stands within the divine identity. This

---

224. This was arguably along the lines of what Ignatius (*Phld.* 8.2) said: "For I heard some saying, 'If I do not find it in the archives [i.e., Old Testament], I will not believe it in the gospel.'... But for me, the 'archives' are Jesus Christ, the unalterable archives are his cross and death and his resurrection, and the faith that comes through him."

225. N. T. Wright, *The Last Word* (San Francisco: HarperOne, 2005), 23.

226. Cf. Peter Enns, *Inspiration and Incarnation: Evangelicals and the Problem of the Old Testament* (Grand Rapids: Baker, 2005). Cf. Webster, *Holy Scripture*, 22–23, who thinks to regard the Scripture as an incarnation is "christologically disastrous, in that it may threaten the uniqueness of the Word's becoming flesh by making 'incarnation' a general principle or characteristic of divine action in, through or under creaturely reality." See also Ward, *Words of Life*, 79–80.

could be said to put Scripture and incarnation on the same playing field or, in some extreme cases, subordinate the incarnation to Scripture in terms of the epistemological priority of knowing about the incarnation.

However, I would point out, terribly obvious as it might seem, that the incarnation actually occurred prior to the canonization of the Old and New Testaments in the church. What is more, before the age of the printing press, at a time when most people were illiterate, or even in places where the Bible was not yet translated, it was still possible to know about Jesus through the teaching and preaching of Christians. Moreover, if you had met Jesus in Capernaum or had seen the risen Jesus in Jerusalem, you would have experienced a genuine revelation of God, even if the meaning of Jesus' mission as narrated in the Gospels was not yet available to you.

I am not denying the supremacy of Scripture as our witness to Jesus. Jesus himself said that the Scriptures testify to him (e.g., John 5:36–39; 7:38). Nor do I want minimize the necessity of Scripture for knowing Jesus. Yet the Bible does not have a monopoly for giving us access to knowledge about the incarnation and the salvation that it brings. You can apprehend knowledge of Jesus Christ through the proclamation of the gospel, by the experience of him in baptism and Eucharist, and through catechisms and creeds that summarize the teaching of Scripture.

In addition, Scripture itself points to the incarnation as the definitive revelation of God. The identity of the God of heaven and earth is bound up with the identity of Jesus Christ. The story of Jesus is the human history of God. In that story, God is identified in a way that is both continuous with the identity of God in the Old Testament and also radically novel. The Johannine prologue concludes with the words, "No one has ever seen God, but the one and only Son, who is himself God and is in closest relationship with the Father, has made him known" (John 1:18). Moses did not see God's face, only his glory (Exod 33–34). Yet witnesses to Jesus behold God's glory when they behold the one-of-a-kind Son, who mediates divine grace and truth by dwelling among the people as "the Word [made] flesh" (John 1:14).

In addition, the Greek word for "made him known" in John 1:18 is *exēgeomai*, which means to set forth and expound; it is where we get our word "exegesis" from. In other words—and don't push the etymology too far—Jesus is an exegesis of God.[227] Perhaps a better way to put that is to say that Jesus tells the whole story of God the Father.[228] Carson states the significance of the text this way: "The emphasis of the Prologue [of John], then, is on the revelation of the Word as the ultimate disclosure of God himself."[229]

Another important text about the uniqueness of the incarnation is Hebrews

---

227. Cf. George R. Beasley-Murray, *John* (WBC; Dallas: Word, 1999), 16.
228. Andreas J. Köstenberger, *John* (BECNT; Grand Rapids: Baker, 2004), 50.
229. Carson, *Gospel According to John*, 135.

1:1–2, which reads: "In the past God spoke to our ancestors through the prophets at many times and in various ways, but in these last days he has spoken to us by his Son, whom he appointed heir of all things, and through whom also he made the universe." Whereas God formerly spoke to the people in diverse forms through the prophets, there is now a definitive revelation of God communicated in the Son, who is the chief agent of creation and redemption.

Irenaeus wrote: "The mystery of God who uses the mouth and words of the prophets is the mystery of God beginning his apprenticeship as Word incarnate among men."[230] That is, everything that God said prior to his self-revelation in the incarnation was an apprenticeship, a preparation for the coming of Jesus Christ. That apprenticeship ends in the incarnation, where the definitive manifestation of God's Son as mediator publicly begins. When God reveals himself in the incarnation, through the Son operating in the power of the Spirit, what more could God possibly say to make himself known? The incarnation is the ultimate revelation, not merely because of the human manner in which God's presence was manifest, but also because all the sway of redemptive history had been preparing itself and getting reading for the unveiling of God-in-the-flesh.

This is what God's plan was working toward from the moment of the expulsion of the first couple from the garden: the offspring of Eve coming to crush the head of the snake (Gen 3:15). The whole movement of creation was directing itself toward the climactic inbreaking of God into human affairs by taking on human form and being made in human likeness. Whatever God says after the incarnation can be treated as mere footnotes to the fact that God has dwelt and died among us for the salvation of the world.

We need to mention here Karl Barth's view of Jesus Christ as the primary manifestation of the Word of God. Barth believed in a threefold form of the Word of God in incarnation, proclamation, and Scripture. Not three different words of God, but one Word in three forms! In terms of this structure, revelation is identified with the incarnation: "Revelation in fact does not differ from the person of Jesus Christ nor from the reconciliation accomplished in him."[231] In other words, Jesus Christ is *the* revelation of God. Consequently, Scripture and proclamation are the word of God when and only when they provide an encounter with God and testify to God's divine action. The Bible and proclamation must continually become the word of God insofar as they are freely used by God to reveal himself.[232]

Barth rejects any distinction of value between the three forms and posits a unity between them. Yet he maintains: "The first revelation [incarnation] is the form that underlies the other two."[233] By implication, the incarnation is revelation while

---

230. Irenaeus, *Haer.* 4.12.4.
231. Barth, *CD*, I/1:119.
232. Ibid., I/1:117.
233. Ibid., I/1:121.

Scripture and preaching are the attestation to it. To put this in context, Barth broke with the Protestant tradition that believed that the unknown and inscrutable God stood behind his revelation in Jesus Christ. For Reformers like Melanchthon, we do not see God's essence but only his benefits toward us in salvation. Yet Barth maintained that we really know the hiddenness of God in Jesus Christ. What God is in himself, he is unto us in the revelation in Jesus Christ—not a direct knowing of God's inner being, but an indirect knowledge through the sign and work of his revealing acts in history.[234] On this latter point we may agree with Barth. The incarnation rolls back the curtain of the mystery of God, if only for a moment, and gives us a glimpse into the inner being of God.

The Christian tradition maintains that Jesus forms an intricate part of the identity of the God of Israel. Not that Jesus merely taught about God, or that he was God-like, or that he was intensely conscious of God—but that God must be defined in reference to the life, death, resurrection, and exaltation of Jesus the Messiah. The incarnation is not simply about God hopping down to earth like an angel on a tourist visit. It's about God coming to accomplish God's purpose to redeem God's people.

It is astounding to note that when the early Christians mentioned God the Father, they felt compelled to discuss Jesus; and when they taught about Jesus, they had to teach about God the Father as well. Just look at Paul's letter openings, which constantly speak of prayer and thanksgiving to God the Father and the Lord Jesus Christ (Rom 1:1–4; 1 Cor 1:1–3; Gal 1:1–4; etc.). Jesus Christ is the embodiment of the divine plan for creation and its already inaugurated future salvation. We may legitimately speak of the self-revelation of God by this Word insofar as the Word shares the same divine identity of God the Father.[235] Bernard Ramm captures the uniqueness of the revelation of the incarnation with the following description:

> The New Testament in a special manner calls Jesus Christ the Word of God. As the Word of God in Person he is the Sower of the word of the kingdom, the Teacher of the Word of God, and the Speaker of the Word of God. He is the gospel in Person; he is the Word of God become flesh (John 1:14); and he is the Word of God in a touchable, perceptible manifestation (1 John 1:1–3). Thus Jesus Christ is the supreme Word of God above all other forms of the Word of God.[236]

The incarnation, as a mode of extra-extra special revelation, carries several important implications. The incarnation reveals the compatibility between divine and human spheres of existence, it is the validation of God's covenant plan, it points to Jesus' unique role in salvation, and the incarnation emphasizes the gracious attributes of God.

---

234. Karl Barth, *The Göttingen Dogmatics: Instruction in the Christian Religion* (ed. H. Reiffen; trans. G. W. Bromiley; Grand Rapids: Eerdmans, 1991), 1:361.

235. Pannenberg, *Systematic Theology*, 1:257.
236. Ramm, *Special Revelation*, 59.

First, the ontological compatibility between human and divine spheres of existence is a corollary of the incarnation. The fact that the Logos was able to take on human form suggests that divinity and humanity are not mutually exclusive modes of being. Adam was created with immortality in mind, and God created humanity in his own image. The incarnation is not simply God *assuming human form*, as if human flesh were a mask over his real nature. Rather, the incarnation is God *as a human being* and completely sharing in human properties. The incarnation shows us what God intended humanity to be and what it finally will be. To quote Athanasius (based on 2 Pet 1:3): "God became what we are, so that we might become what he is."[237]

So the transcendence and otherness of God from humanity must be balanced against the ability of human existence to be a mode of God's self-communication. Thus the incarnation is a revelation about the relatedness of humanity to God and how God intends humanity to exist for all eternity. The ontological compatibility of divine and human existence demonstrates the certainty of God's saving plan as well. The fact that God took on human flesh means that the redemption and resurrection of the entire earthly order are not only possible, but a reality.[238]

Second, the incarnation validates God's covenant plan by fulfilling it. All four Evangelists introduce Jesus in the context of Israel's covenant history (Matt 1:1–17; Mark 1:1–5; Luke 1:1–2; John 1:1–18). So the incarnation could not have happened in the far-off land of Madagascar just as long as Jesus had a sinless birth and a sin-bearing death. Jesus had to come to Israel (Matt 10:5–6; 15:24; 23:37–39/Luke 13:34–35). That is because God's plan to undo the fall of Adam occurs through the Abraham-Israel story, which is executed in the work of Jesus Christ and in the mission of the church. The eternal purposes of God are anticipated in the old covenant and applied in the new covenant.

That is why Jesus focuses so much on fulfilling the Scriptures. It is not a list of prophetic proof texts that Jesus needs to cross off to prove he is who he says he is; rather, Jesus was rehearsing themes, lines, motifs, and plots from Israel's Scriptures that indicate that the day of salvation had arrived. In the aftermath of Easter and Pentecost, it is Jesus' own affirmation of Israel's past as the anticipation of his work that led the early church to ransack their Scriptures in search of images, types, and patterns that helped illuminate their understanding of him. That is why the first Christians regarded the events of Jesus' life, passion, and resurrection as being "according to the Scriptures" (1 Cor 15:3–8; cf. Rom 1:3–4).

Third, the incarnation marks out Jesus as the ultimate mediator. In the incarnation we see that God is with us and God is for us, but only because God was

---

237. Athanasius, *Inc.* 54.
238. Hans Urs von Balthasar, *The Scandal of the Incarnation: Irenaeus against the Heresies* (trans. John Saward; San Francisco: Ignatius Press, 1990), 9.

one of us. The New Testament underscores that Jesus is unique in terms of his identity, task, and being. He is the only mediator who can reconcile God and humanity together (1 Tim 2:5; Heb 8:6; 9:15; 12:24). The exclusive claim of the all-inclusive Savior is that he is the way, the truth, and the life, and no one comes to the Father except through him (John 14:6).

In apostolic proclamation, salvation is available only in Jesus' name (Acts 4:12). In Paul's discourse, reconciliation happens through the God-in-Christ event, and this extends not only to Israel but also to the whole world (2 Cor 5:21). The writer to the Hebrews stated: "For this reason *he had to be made like them, fully human in every way*, in order that he might become a merciful and faithful high priest in service to God, and that he might make atonement for the sins of the people" (Heb 2:17, italics added). Jesus is not the mere means of salvation, but the personal mediator of salvation.[239]

The incarnation was, therefore, completely necessary for reconciliation between God and humanity. As Athanasius saw, the problem was not simply human disobedience as that could have been remedied with repentance. Instead, humanity had fallen into such a state of corruption and rebellion that it would result in humanity's inevitable annihilation by its own debasement and as the consequence of divine judgment. The incarnation was necessary because only the Logos who created humanity from nothing could rescue humanity and unite them with their divine maker.[240]

Fourth, the incarnation is a further revelation of the divine attributes, especially the faithfulness of God. That God is faithful is a common refrain in Israel's worship. For example, Psalm 145:13 says, "Your kingdom is an everlasting kingdom, and your dominion endures through all generations. The LORD is trustworthy in all he promises and faithful in all he does." We see that God's faithfulness is expressed in his providing salvation for Israel and the Gentiles by setting forth Christ. God's faithfulness is even identified with the faithfulness of Jesus the Messiah (see Heb 3:6; Phil 3:9). God's faithfulness pertains to what he did in Jesus Christ for humans—hence Paul's remarks to the Corinthians:

> God is faithful, who has called you into fellowship with his Son, Jesus Christ our Lord. (1 Cor 1:9)

> But as surely as God is faithful, our message to you is not "Yes" and "No." For the Son of God, Jesus Christ, who was preached among you by us—by me and Silas and Timothy—was not "Yes" and "No," but in him it has always been "Yes." For no matter how many promises God has made, they are "Yes" in Christ. And so through him the "Amen" is spoken by us to the glory of God. (2 Cor 1:18–20)

---

239. Walter Kasper, *Jesus the Christ* (trans. V. Green; New York: Paulist, 1976), 209.

240. Jaroslav Pelikan, *The Christian Tradition: A History of the Development of Doctrine* (Chicago: University of Chicago Press, 1971), 1:285.

The "Yes" of God's faithfulness is uttered in the sending of Jesus and in the preaching of Jesus Christ. As God was faithful in the past, he was faithful in Christ, and he will therefore be faithful in the future (see 1 Thess 5:24; 2 Thess 3:3). *In light of the incarnation, God's faithfulness is his "Yes" to sinners in Jesus Christ.*

The incarnation also demonstrates God's love for the whole world. In the gospel of John we find the famous verse: "For this is how God loved the world: he gave his only Son, so that everyone who believes in him may not perish but may have eternal life" (John 3:16 [NJB]). Note that the NJB treats the adverbial *houtōs* as instrumental rather than causative (i.e., "this is how God loved" rather than "For God so loved"). The incarnation is an expression of not just the *fact* that God loves the world, but the way in which God loves the world: by sending his only Son.

Elsewhere, the apostle Paul writes: "But God demonstrates his own love for us in this: While we were still sinners, Christ died for us" (Rom 5:8). It is Christ's dying for sinners, not for the righteous, that shows God's love for them. The love of the Father is made known in the love of Christ and the love of the Spirit. This triune love is the anchor of Christian hope (Rom 8:30, 35–39).

Prior to the incarnation, there was ample testimony to God's love for his people (i.e., God's love is not limited to the New Testament). But the incarnation shows that that divine love has been configured and conveyed through, of all things, the cross of Christ. So intense is the love of God in Christ that it leads the apostle John to say that "God is love"; such a statement is blasphemous apart from the incarnation. Richard Bauckham writes: "Only because the incarnation *is* this unique act of God's love does Jesus reveal God as the love which takes this step of radical self-identification with humanity."[241] *So the incarnation is a revelation of the triune love of God embodied in Jesus that avails for all of humanity who need to be restored to communion with God.*

God's grace did not begin with the incarnation. God's special covenant love was always with his people, even in the Sinaitic covenant (e.g., Deut 9; Ezek 16; Dan 9). Yet in Christ we experience grace upon grace (John 1:16). As Paul says: "I always thank my God for you because of his grace given you in Christ Jesus" (1 Cor 1:4). And Peter writes in his first letter: "And the God of all grace, who called you to his eternal glory in Christ, after you have suffered a little while, will himself restore you and make you strong, firm and steadfast" (1 Pet 5:10). What is new is not the fact of grace, but the locus of God's grace and the supereffective power of grace abounding. In Christ we experience what I call über-grace (see Rom 5:15, 17). *The incarnation testifies that God's grace is mediated through Christ, where it abounds to others as never before.*

---

241. Richard Bauckham, "Jesus the Revelation of God," in *Divine Revelation* (ed. P. Avis; Grand Rapids: Eerdmans, 1997), 180.

> ## TALKING POINT
>
> The parable of the three blind men and the elephant is often used to justify why there are so many religions and to prove that each religion is equally (or partly) true.
>
> The story runs: Three blind men were asked what an elephant is like. Each in turn went up to the elephant and investigated the elephant for himself by inspecting it with his sense of touch. Each in turn then described what the elephant was like. The first blind man felt the ear of the elephant and said that the elephant is like a hand fan. The second blind man felt the belly of the elephant and said that the elephant is like a wall. Then the third blind man touched the tusk of the elephant and said that the elephant is like a solid pipe.
>
> So who was right? A wise man explained to them: "All of you are right. The reason every one of you is telling it differently is because each one of you touched a different part of the elephant. So, actually the elephant has all the features you mentioned."
>
> Given the Christian doctrine of revelation, why should we reject this parable?

Finally, the truth of God is revealed in a new way in Christ Jesus (John 1:17; 14:6). Even Jesus' opponents recognized that he taught things according to the truth, albeit a startling truth (e.g., Matt 22:16). In the major confrontation discourse in the gospel of John, Jesus emphasizes that he teaches the truth about God in the face of opposition and recalcitrance (John 8–9). Paul reports that Christ became a servant of Israel "on behalf of God's truth" (Rom 15:8; i.e., his promises, which were true). *The incarnation confirms God's prophetic truth and authorizes the truth of the apostolic gospel. Truth can be identified not only with canonical propositions, but with the activity of the Spirit of truth and with Jesus as the way of truth.*

2.5.6 FINAL THOUGHTS ON SPECIAL REVELATION

Our study of God's revelation of himself can end by affirming the unity of special revelation and its redemptive nature.

First, as for the unity of special revelation, we can aver that history is the theater of God's revelation. It is like the stage on which God unveils his masterpiece as the director of the redemptive drama. History is where God reveals himself, and anyone who beholds the stage may look on the acts of God. In this theater, the Word of God comes to us. It comes to us in its threefold forms of the Word of proclamation, the

Word of Scripture, and in the Word incarnate. What is more, God's illuminating work through the Holy Spirit ensures the reception and recognition of his Word. The summit of revelation is the incarnation of Jesus Christ, who is the definitive Word of God. Put together, God's revelation of himself is historically rooted, evangelical at heart, covenantal by nature, scriptural in form, and christological by design.[242]

Second, concerning the redemptive nature of special revelation, to separate Scripture from redemption is to make Scripture like the Koran, a sheer communication of divine facts about how to live.[243] Rather, when God reveals himself, it is always as the God-who-saves. To know God is to know about a God who loves, is merciful, and reaches out to others. Because God is a saving God, it means that divine revelation will always be tied to divine redemption.

FURTHER READING

Avis, Paul, ed. *Divine Revelation*. Grand Rapids: Eerdmans, 1997.
Erickson, Millard. *Christian Theology*. 2nd ed. Grand Rapids: Baker, 1998, pp. 177–223.
Jensen, Peter. *The Revelation of God*. Downers Grove, IL: InterVarsity Press, 2002.
McGrath, Alister E. *The Open Secret: A New Vision for Natural Theology*. Oxford: Blackwell, 2008.
Morris, Leon. *I Believe in Revelation*. Grand Rapids: Eerdmans, 1976.
Sudduth, Michael. *The Reformed Objection to Natural Theology*. Farnham, UK: Ashgate, 2009.

---

242. Jensen, *Revelation of God*, 94.   243. Ramm, *Special Revelation*, 80.

§ 2.6 GOD'S PURPOSE AND PLAN

Why did God make the universe? Why did God call Abraham? Why did God rescue the Hebrews from Egypt? Why did God send his Son? Why did God become a man? Why does God wait so long for the consummation? When we ask questions like these, we are inquiring about God's ultimate *purposes*. What is more, God's overarching purpose must be distinguished from the precise way that he intends to achieve that purpose, namely, through his *plan*.

We will see in this section, among other things, that God's purposes are primarily doxological; that is, God is concerned with his glory, and the gospel reveals the various tiers of God's plan. The primary interface of glory and gospel can be found in the Fourth Gospel, where Jesus' death and resurrection amount to his glorification and thus the glorification of the Father (see John 12:16, 23, 28, 41; 13:31–32; 14:13; 17:1–5). When the one who came from glory glorified his Father by his obedience to his messianic task, divine glory is increasingly ascribed to the Son by his resurrection and ascension, and the Son in turn shares his glory with others. In other words, the evangelical story of Jesus explains how God glorifies himself by glorifying the messianic Son and by sharing his glory with his followers. God's purpose is a divine glory that flows through the Son and fills all of creation. The gospel provides the funnel through which that glory flows. God's intention is that we would be for the praise of his glory through the gospel of Jesus Christ (see Eph 1:11–12).

Consequently, we will consider the chief end of God's purposes, how those purposes are manifested in the plan of God found in redemptive history, the logical order within that plan, and the theological unity of that plan.

2.6.1 GOD'S PURPOSE

The gospel is a story that narrates how Jesus fulfills God's purposes for our world. Peter's Pentecost sermon announced that Jesus was not a victim of circumstances when he was crucified; rather, the events that transpired did so according to "God's deliberate plan and foreknowledge," to bring salvation to Israel and beyond (Acts

2:23). Pauls regards God's predestined decree to conform the elect to the image of the Son as purposed in order to create a Christ-shaped family in the new creation (Rom 8:29–30). The goal of setting forth Christ was "salvation," but salvation itself points to a larger aim and bigger project in God's design. The sending of the Savior, the advent of salvation, and the collection of the saved creates a theater in which the glory of God would abound for all ages. This thought is adequately captured in the Pauline doxology: "to him be glory in the church and in Christ Jesus throughout all generations, for ever and ever!" (Eph 3:21).

In speaking of God's purpose(s) we are looking at God's ultimate intention in creation and redemption. These are not ends in and of themselves, but they serve some superior goal in the mind of God. God's creative and redemptive tasks are placed in service of a higher aim that is associated with God's self-delight, that is, his satisfaction with his own glory. Along this line, Question 7 of the Westminster Shorter Catechism asks:

> Q: What are the decrees of God?
> A: The decrees of God are, his eternal purpose, according to the counsel of his will, whereby, *for his own glory*, he hath foreordained whatsoever comes to pass. (italics added)

According to the catechism, God's eternal and determined purpose is to bring glory to himself. That notion is safely embedded in biblical testimony, where God's glory represents the chief end of God's action. In Isaiah we observe that the saving work of God is rooted in his glory, yet is also somehow identified with it (Isa 40:5; 44:23; 48:9–11; 66:18–19). The reason why the surrounding nations will set the Israelite exiles free is because God elected Israel on the basis his glory (43:5–7). The same idea occurs later in Isaiah, only now God's intention is to glorify himself by delivering Israel from his anger:

> For my own name's sake I delay my wrath;
>> for the sake of my praise I hold it back from you,
>> so as not to destroy you completely.
> See, I have refined you, though not as silver;
>> I have tested you in the furnace of affliction.
> For my own sake, for my own sake, I do this.
>> How can I let myself be defamed?
> I will not yield my glory to another. (Isa 48:9–11)

Here the purpose of God is to save Israel from the sin that occasioned the Babylonian exile, and this deliverance is a manifestation of God's glory.

Indeed, throughout the Old Testament, the Israelites appealed to God's glory as the basis for God's saving works:

> Not to us, LORD, not to us
>   but to your name be the glory,
>   because of your love and faithfulness. (Ps 115:1)
>
> Help us, God our Savior,
>   for the glory of your name;
> deliver us and forgive our sins
>   for your name's sake. (Ps 79:9)
>
> All the nations you have made
>   will come and worship before you, Lord;
> they will bring glory to your name. (Ps 86:9)

We observe here how God's faithfulness and love are the application of his glory to salvation. God's glory is exalted, his name is honored, and his reputation upheld when God delivers Israel from the nations or even when he brings the nations to share in the heritage of Israel. I would provocatively add that God is glorified when he saves, not just when he looks in a mirror.

In the New Testament, God's glory, the magnificent radiance of his saving power, is manifested supremely in Jesus Christ. Ephesians opens with the poignant words: "In him [i.e., in Christ] we were also chosen, having been predestined according to the plan of him who works out everything in conformity with the purpose of his will, in order that we, who were the first to put our hope in Christ, *might be for the praise of his glory*" (Eph 1:11–12, italics added). Paul is here referring to Jewish Christians, who were the first to put their hope in the Messiah. Their election in Christ was purposed for God's own glory. This status of being elected for God's glory is confirmed when God is honored by Jews and Gentiles who live in accordance with his will and display their family likeness, which seals them as his children.[244] Their election is doxologically driven, foreordained as they are to be praisers of God's glory, by putting their hope in Christ, and God's glory abounds from the divine faithfulness that elicits human faith. Christ becomes the choir leader for the redeemed people, who will praise God's unsurpassable glory.

Later in Ephesians the celebration of God's saving plan to reveal salvation in the united commonwealth of Jews and Gentiles leads to an outburst of praise: "Now to him who is able to do immeasurably more than all we ask or imagine, according to his power that is at work within us, to him *be glory in the church and in Christ Jesus* throughout all generations, for ever and ever! Amen" (Eph 3:20–21, italics added). Peter O'Brien comments on this verse: "God's glory *in the church* cannot be separated

---

244. Peter T. O'Brien, *The Letter to the Ephesians* (PNTC; Grand Rapids: Eerdmans, 1999), 118.

from his glory *in Christ Jesus*. This expression of incorporation signifies that believers are able to ascribe glory to God because they are in Christ Jesus."[245] Note the provocative point here. The summit of God's glory is the union of Jews and Gentiles in communion with God's Messiah.

Finally, we can also consider the doxology of Romans 16:

> Now to him who is able to strengthen you according to my gospel and the preaching of Jesus Christ, according to the revelation of the mystery that was kept secret for long ages but has now been *disclosed* and through the prophetic writings has been made known to all nations, according to *the command of the eternal God*, to bring about the obedience of faith—to the only wise God *be glory forevermore through Jesus Christ*! Amen. (Rom 16:25–27 ESV, italics added)

Here God's purpose, his eternal command that was hidden in eternity past, concerns how Jews and Gentiles would be praisers and participants in God's own glory through Jesus Christ. When God's plan to save the world through Israel and her Messiah happens, it is absolutely, utterly, and completely glorious, and the only response one can make to it is to strike up a symphony of praise in every language imaginable. So note this: God's glory is an all-merciful-infinite-love-in-action-saving glory.

To drive that point home again, the biblical revelation shows that God is ultimately concerned with glorifying himself in Christ and through the Spirit.[246] The qualification we must make is that God's glory is intimately bound up with his rescuing love. Note the link between God's glory and his covenant love in the Psalter: "Not to us, Lord, not to us but to your name be the glory, because of your love and faithfulness" (Ps 115:1). And love, if it is authentic love, must be a love for others, both within the Trinity and external to it. God's highest act of glorifying himself, then, is to be the lover of his creation. The eternal decision of God to be God-in-Christ-for-the-sake-of-others and to make inglorious beings partakers of the exclusive glory is God's final purpose. God's magnifies himself in his self-giving love for his creatures.

Thus, in the Fourth Gospel, God's glory is manifested most supremely in the self-giving love of Father and Son for the world. If we believe the testimony of the Beloved Disciple, Golgotha reveals God's glory, not because of what it does for God, but because of what God does for others. God's glory is revealed in paradoxes of grace. God's indescribable glory and redeeming love invade a world that rejected his glory and spurned his love. God's greatness is manifested in his self-humiliation, not his self-exaltation. God's glory is found in his self-divestment, not his self-interest. God's glory is God's own god-ness as it is revealed to others, so that they participate in the glorious divine life. This is not just Johannine theology; someone

---

245. Ibid., 268 (italics original).
246. Thomas Schreiner, *New Testament Theology: Magnifying God in Christ* (Grand Rapids: Baker, 2008), 13–14.

once summarized Paul in this way: "For St. Paul the most sovereign thing in God, divinest of the Divine, is the sacrificial sin-bearing love revealed in the Cross. God's glory is displayed in his mercy."[247]

God's driving purpose, then, is to glorify himself through his rescuing love. God pursues his own glory through the salvation of his people. In the end, the display of God's glory is the revelation of his salvation. If God were not a Savior, we would not consider him glorious. Divine glory and divine love meet, mix, and mingle because the highest doxology ascribed to God is that he is our Savior, who loves us in his beloved Son, and the Spirit is the very presence of his divine affection for us. How he works that salvation out in the radiant effusion of his grace and glory is the next matter for discussion.

2.6.2 GOD'S PLAN IN REDEMPTIVE HISTORY

What is God's exact plan to achieve his purpose? What is God's modus operandi for glorifying himself by rescuing his people? In the Old Testament, God's plan is often connected with the Hebrew word *'ēṣâ*, meaning "decision, plan" concerning the foreordained purposes of God (e.g., Pss 106:13; 107:11; Isa 5:19; 14:26; 25:1; 28:29; Jer 49:20; Mic 4:12). In the New Testament, the primary word for "plan" is *boulē*, which describes God's saving intent that is fulfilled in the gospel of Christ (Luke 7:30; Acts 2:23; 13:36; 20:27; Eph 1:11; Heb 6:17). In that sense, salvation is God setting out to do what God had already intended to do in Christ.

This perspective is wonderfully laid out in 2 Timothy 1:9–10, where Paul writes that God "has saved us and called us to a holy life—not because of anything we have done *but because of his own purpose and grace*. This grace was given us in Christ Jesus *before the beginning of time*, but it has now been revealed through the appearing of our Savior, Christ Jesus" (italics added). Salvation rests not on the merits of the individual, but in the christological revelation of divine grace that was planned before the beginning of time. Expounding the same theme, Irenaeus said that God has always had a rescue plan:

> Thus it was, too, that God formed man at the first, because of His kindness; but chose the patriarchs for the sake of their salvation; and prepared a people beforehand, teaching the headstrong to follow God; and raised up prophets upon earth, accustoming man to bear His Spirit [within him], and to hold communion with God: He Himself, indeed, having need of nothing, but granting communion with Himself to those who stood in need of it, and sketching out, *like an architect, the plan of salvation* to those that pleased Him.[248]

---

247. R. Law, "Glory," in *Hastings Dictionary of the Apostolic Church* (New York: Scribner's & Sons, 1914–18), 1:452.

248. Irenaeus, *Haer.* 4.14.2.

If we focus on God's "plan" as the scheme by which God's purposes are worked out, we can say several things about that plan.[249]

1. The *eternity* of God's plan as God ordained things in eternity past and determined to execute them in human history (Isa 22:11; 1 Cor 2:7; Eph 1:4; 3:11)
2. The *unity* of God's plan, implying the consistency and coherence of his actions (Prov 16:4; Isa 46:10–11; Luke 24:26–27; Acts 2:23; 4:28; Eph 2:5–10)
3. The *priority* of God's plan in the relationship between God and humanity, where the plan is divinely initiated (Isa 14:26; 23:9; Acts 2:23; 2 Tim 1:9)
4. The *immutability* of God's plan as rooted in the immutability of God himself, which implies that the plan does not change; rather, it is certain (Isa 46:10–11; Luke 4:43; 22:22; 24:26; John 3:14–15)
5. God's plan as *revealed to the prophets and apostles* (Deut 29:29; Amos 3:7; 1 Cor 4:1; Eph 1:9)
6. The *revelation of Jesus Christ* as central to God's plan (Gen 3:15; Luke 24:26; Acts 2:23; Gal 4:4)
7. The *victory* of God's plan as God will triumph over the terrible enemies of sin, death, and evil (Prov 19:21; Isa 14:27; 28:29; John 16:33; 1 John 5:4)
8. The *end state* of God's plan as a place, the new creation, where God dwells fully with his people amidst his radiant glory (Exod 29:45; Isa 66:22–24; Ezek 36:28; Zech 8:8; 1 Cor 15:28; Rev 21:3). God intends to repossess and recreate the world to reflect his glory with his people in it. This is where God is "all in all" in the new heavens and new earth (Isa 66; Rev 21). New creation is the goal where God's plan for salvation finally achieves God's purpose to glorify himself.

Like a three-legged stool, we can say that God's plan has three elements. First, it focuses on a key person, namely, the Son. God plans to unite himself with creation through the sending of the Logos. Second, the plan focuses on a people, the elect, as God eternally decrees to save his elect, who believe in the Son. Third, God will transform the corrupted Eden into a heavenly Eden, with the climactic revelation of the new creation. Thus, God's purpose to glorify himself is worked out in his eternal plan, which is to save his people through the Logos and to bring them into the splendor of the new creation.

2.6.3 THE UNITY OF THE PLAN

If God has *one purpose* to glorify himself through his love for others, and if God has *one plan* to bring men and women into the new creation through Jesus Christ the Logos, we may legitimately ask: What is the unity of that plan as it is laid out in the

---

249. Largely following Erickson, *Christian Theology*, 372–81.

biblical canon? There have been different ways of understanding the unity of God's plan. For the sake of simplicity we will define them into two categories: dispensational and covenantal theologies.

2.6.3.1 DISPENSATIONAL THEOLOGY

Dispensational theology is a brand of theology popular in North America and has gained prominence since the nineteenth century. It emphasizes a literal reading of Scriptures and, in so doing, looks forward to a rapture of the church prior to a time of global tribulation, followed with Christ's return to establish a millennial kingdom on earth. As a theological system, dispensationalism focuses on the uniqueness of the particular "dispensations" or the administrations of God's dealings with his people. Adherents of dispensationalism generally refer to six dispensations: Eden, Noah, patriarchs, Israel, church, and the millennium. The true essence of dispensational theology is the distinction between Israel and the church. God has two plans for salvation: one plan for the salvation of Israel and another plan for the salvation of the church.

It is also important to note that there are different types of dispensational theology: classic (C. I. Scofield, L. S. Chafer), revisionist (C. Ryrie, J. Walvoord), and progressive (D. Bock, C. Blaising), and they do not agree on all things. The most mature manifestation of dispensational theology is the progressive variety, which avoids many of the excesses and eccentricities of its forbearers. Progressive dispensationalists see the kingdom of God as the central theme of God's revelation, but they recognize the christological unity of revelation as well. As Craig Blaising states: "The unity of divine revelation, of the various dispensations, is found in the goal of history, the kingdom of God. And since this kingdom is centered in the person and work of Jesus Christ, the dispensational unity of Scripture and of history is christological as much as it is eschatological."[250]

Dispensationalism has as its chief benefit a willingness to take the diversity of Scripture seriously through its plain-sense reading of the Bible. Dispensationalism posits a thematic unity to the biblical revelation, whereby all of God's works ultimately bring glory to God. Dispensationalism also has a forward-looking orientation that eagerly awaits the arrival of our "blessed hope," which we can likewise affirm (Titus 2:13). However, dispensational theology has several serious errors.

1. Dispensationalism envisages too much discontinuity between the epochs of redemptive history concerning the scope and means of salvation. There is a tendency to overemphasize what was true of the Israelite age and what is true of the church age.

---

250. Craig A. Blaising, "Dispensationalism: The Search for a Definition," in *Dispensationalism, Israel and the Church: The Search for a Definition* (Grand Rapids: Zondervan, 1992),

33. On the clash between the revisionists and the progressives see Herbert W. Bateman, ed., *Three Central Issues in Contemporary Dispensationalism* (Grand Rapids: Kregel, 1999).

2. The sine qua non of dispensationalism is the distinction between Israel and the church, even though that distinction is varyingly understood within dispensationalism.[251] What is more, the salvation provided for Israel and the church is often differentiated in terms of its mode, form, and end state. However, this is untenable because the story of Israel is continued in the story of the church. Thus, you cannot have two peoples of God anymore than you can have two modes of salvation separated along the lines of political and spiritual. Galatians and Ephesians rule out any kind of dichotomy between Israel and the church or between a Gentile church and a messianic church. The Israel of the messianic age is a commonwealth of Jews and Gentiles united in Christ by the Spirit (Eph 2:11–3:21). Language used to describe Israel is applied to Christians in the New Testament (e.g., Gal 6:16; Phil 3:3; 1 Pet 2:9–10). The Old Testament promises to Israel are fulfilled in the death and resurrection of Jesus Christ (Acts 13:33–34; 2 Cor 1:20). There remains a hope for national Israel to respond one day to the gospel of the Messiah (see Rom 11), but there is no exegetical basis for the view that the future promises about a kingdom will be fulfilled exclusively by ethnic Israel. God's promises have their fulfillment in the gospel of Jesus Christ among those who believe in his name.

3. Dispensationalism has had bad consequences for Jewish evangelism and for Palestinian Christians. Some extreme dispensationalist groups believe that the Jews will be saved during a period of apocalyptic tribulation. Therefore, we should not preach the gospel to the Jewish people, only help them to return to the land of Israel and to drive out the Palestinians, as this will hasten the second coming. Yet this means conveniently explaining away passages that promote evangelism toward the Jewish people, such as is reflected in Paul's words to the Ephesian elders: "I have declared to both Jews and Greeks that they must turn to God in repentance and have faith in our Lord Jesus" (Acts 20:21). What is more, Palestinian Christians in the Holy Land are sometimes regarded as obstacles to the second coming. Some American dispensational churches even write letters to these Palestinian Christians urging them to leave Israel because they are preventing the second coming, despite the fact they and their ancestors have been in that land for nearly two thousand years.[252] In other words, some forms of dispensationalism can inhibit Jewish evangelism and promote unjust treatment of our fellow Christian brothers and sisters in Palestine.[253]

---

251. Charles Ryrie, *Dispensationalism Today* (Chicago: Moody Press, 1965), 47.

252. Cf. Gary M. Burge, *Whose Land? Whose Promise? What Christians Are Not Being Told about Israel and the Palestinians* (Cleveland: Pilgrim, 2003); idem, *Who Are God's People in the Middle East?* (Grand Rapids: Zondervan, 1993).

253. For a moderate dispensational view of the Palestinian issue, see Darrell L. Bock, "Some Christians See a 'Road Map' to the End Times," *LA Times* (18 June 2003). http://articles.latimes.com/2003/jun/18/opinion/oe-bock18. Accessed 1 Aug 2011.

2.6.3.2 COVENANT THEOLOGY

Covenant theology was one of the major spin-offs from the Reformation and developed through the teachings of Zacharias Ursinus (1534–83) and Johannes Cocceius (1603–69). Covenant theology sees the relationship between God and humanity as mediated through divinely instituted "covenants," where God's purposes and obligations to his people are set down. There are also intra-Trinitarian covenants that detail the roles and rewards within the Godhead. In classic Reformed Theology, these covenants are:[254]

> *The covenant of redemption.* This is the eternal pact between God the Father and God the Son concerning the salvation of the elect (*pactum salutis*). Father and Son covenanted together for the redemption of the elect, with the Father appointing the Son to be the mediator, the second Adam, whose life would be given for the salvation of the elect. The Son accepted the commission and agreed to do the work assigned him by the Father. Thus, before the foundation of the world, within the mind of the Triune God, it has been determined that creation would not be destroyed by sin, but that it would be overcome by God's grace and that the Son would be the head of a new humanity, Savior of the world; that is how God would be glorified.
>
> *The covenant of works.* Having created humanity in his own image as a free creature with knowledge of right and wrong, God entered into a covenant with Adam, whereby Adam was promised eternal life upon condition of perfect obedience of the law during a probationary period in the garden of Eden (*foederus naturae*). Adam was also the federal head of humanity, and his violation of the covenant brought down the curses of the covenant not only on himself, but also on all of those whom he represented. This covenant of works was then republished in the Mosaic law, which is why the Mosaic covenant contains a similar scheme of obedience for salvation.
>
> *The covenant of grace.* This is a covenant that God made with humanity, where he offers salvation and life through Christ to all who believe (*foederus gratiae*). The covenant of grace is the application of the covenant of redemption to human subjects. The covenant was first announced in the garden (Gen 3:15), seen again in God's covenant with Noah (Gen 6–9), formally established with Abraham (Gen 15–21), reiterated in the Davidic covenant (2 Sam 7:12–16), and fully realized in the new covenant (Jer 31:31–34; Gal 3:17–18). In the covenant of grace, God restores his new creation that was lost by virtue of the Messiah having fulfilled the covenant of works.

---

254. Cf. Grudem, *Systematic Theology*, 515–22; Michael S. Horton, *God of Promise: Introducing Covenant Theology* (Grand Rapids: Baker, 2006), 77–110.

There is a diversity of views within covenant theology, such as whether grace or law is the priority in any given covenantal economy. The primary benefit of covenant theology is that it posits unity and coherence to the biblical revelation. God has one plan, one people, and one goal in mind. Even so, covenant theology does have several major drawbacks.

1. While God has one purpose in salvation, the multiplication of covenants is unnecessary. What is more, the penchant for unity between the covenants is often overplayed, and the distinctiveness of each particular epoch of God's dealings with his people is sometimes flattened out. For example, the simple equation of circumcision replaced by baptism is contestable.

2. We must question whether there was in fact a covenant between God and Adam in the garden of Eden (no matter how much I try, I cannot find a "covenant of works" in my ESV concordance!). First, there is no explicit reference to a "covenant" in Genesis 1–2. Appeal is often made to Hosea 6:7 for the existence of a covenant with Adam, but the verse can be translated quite differently.[255] While there is some "deal" between God and Adam, it is not described in terms of a covenant, nor is there any law etched out beyond the commands that Adam is given. Second, one prominent Reformed theologian, John Murray, rejects the idea of both an Adamic covenant and a republication of that covenant in the law of Moses:

> Covenant in Scripture denotes the oath-bound confirmation of promise and involves a security which the Adamic economy did not bestow.... The view that in the Mosaic covenant there was a repetition of the so-called covenant of works, is a grave misconception and involves an erroneous construction of the Mosaic covenant, as well as fails to assess the uniqueness of the Adamic Administration. The Mosaic covenant was distinctly redemptive in character and was continuous with and extensive of the Abrahamic covenants. The Adamic had no provision, nor did its promissory elements have any relevance within a context that made redemption necessary.[256]

Granted that Israel in a sense recapitulates the role of Adam, the Mosaic law cannot be a republication of a covenant of works, since there is grace under the Mosaic covenant (see Deut 9:1–19; 26:1–10; Ezek 16:1–63; John 1:16). The Mosaic covenant was given to cocoon God's promises around Israel until the promised seed came and was a temporary administration of God's grace to govern God's people. It taught the Israelites about God's holiness and severity of sin, prolonged their

---

255. Contrast the NIV: "*As at Adam*, they have broken the covenant; they were unfaithful to me there"; and the ESV: "*But like Adam* they transgressed the covenant; there they dealt faithlessly with me" (italics added).

256. John Murray, "The Adamic Administration," in *Collected Writings of John Murray* (Edinburgh: Banner of Truth, 1977), 2:49–50.

capacity to worship God in a pagan environment, pointed to the coming of a messianic deliverer, and was prefatory for Israel's role to extend salvation to the world.[257]

3. The scheme of salvation in some covenant theologies, when reduced to its basic tenets, is essentially Pelagian. By this I mean that in some construal of covenant theology, salvation is tied to the accrual and imputation of meritorious law-keeping. Thus, Adam was put in the garden with a divinely given law, and he failed to obey the law. What we need now is someone to keep God's law on our behalf and to impute the merit of his law-keeping to us. This is Pelagianism in the sense that salvation is indeed by meritorious works, and grace is present in the sense that such an accrual is possible. One could say, with a degree of hyperbole, that the only difference between traditional covenant theology and the British monk Pelagius is the question of who actually does the law-keeping. Whereas Pelagius thought that all people were able to keep God's commands to the point of being able to earn salvation, some covenantal schemes emphasize the pattern of obedience for salvation in such a way that Jesus becomes our vicarious Pelagian, who keeps the law for us and imputes his obedience to us. As Peter Leithart comically puts it: "Adam was created Catholic [he was created to earn salvation by works], but became a Protestant after he fell [he thereafter needed salvation by grace]."[258]

But what if the problem occasioned by Adam's disobedience was not a failure to accrue merit by keeping an eternal law? What if the problem was the rupture in a divine-human relationship? There is a tremendous difference between conceiving of salvation as a contract to be fulfilled as opposed to a relationship that needs to be restored. Granted that covenants are essentially relational pacts, God's covenanting work can emit a range of promises and obligations that ensure that his grace manifested in Christ is the ultimate cause of salvation. I would contend that Jesus does not fulfill a covenant of works by his life and death, but that he fulfills the roles given to Adam and Israel in completion of his messianic task. By virtue of his faithfulness in his messianic ministry and messianic death, he achieves a messianic victory over evil and sin so that he is able to reconcile humanity to God and to reconstitute a new humanity and a new Israel in his own person.

2.6.3.3 A MODIFIED COVENANT THEOLOGY

We can safely reject the dispensationalist approach to the unity of God's plan since it posits a fundamental disjunction between Israel and the church. At the same time,

---

257. Despite our rejecting a covenant of works, we can say that God does have a covenant relationship with creation insofar that he has bound himself to act for the renewal of creation. God's covenantal relationships with the cosmos are implied in Gen 9:9 and Jer 33:20–26. See further Paul R. Williamson, *Sealed with an Oath: Covenant in God's Unfolding Purpose* (NSBT 23; Downers Grove, IL: InterVarsity Press, 2007), 52–58.

258. Peter J. Leithart, "Adam the Catholic? Faith and Life in the Adamic Covenant," in *A Faith That Is Never Alone: A Response to Westminster Seminary California* (ed. P. Andrew Sandlin; LaGrange, CA: Kerygma, 2007), 187. The bracketed parentheses are my own explanations of Leithart's point!

> ## SOME COMIC BELIEF
>
> How many dispensationalists does it take to change a light bulb? One. But we are now living in the dispensation of fluorescent lights, so he'll have to switch the bulbs accordingly.
>
> How many covenant theologians does it take to change a light bulb? One. There has only been only one light socket throughout history with the promise of applying light to all bulbs, and whether they were part of the socket of works or under the socket of grace, all bulbs now enjoy in the one light socket of God.

covenant theology postulates the existence of covenants that appear to have disputed exegetical warrant, and sometimes their construal of the interrelationships between these covenants is not always convincing.

Those qualifications aside, I lean toward a covenantal view because "covenant" is a biblical way of describing the formal and material unity of redemptive history. God's saving action is always mediated through his covenanting relationships with Abraham, Israel, David, and the church. What is more, I think that continuity between the Old and New Testaments is far more predominant than patterns of discontinuity.

Two examples from church history underscore this. First, the *Epistle to Diognetus* (ca. AD 150) testifies that in the message of the Son, "the fear of the law is sung, the grace of the prophets is known, the faith of the Gospels is established, the tradition of the Apostles is preserved, and the joy of the church springs forth" (*Diogn.* 11.6). The author, whoever he was, believes that the law, prophets, Gospels, and church tradition are fundamentally united in their witness to the incarnation of God the Son. Second, the Swiss reformer Heinrich Bullinger (1504–75) wrote:

> In brief, I find that the New Testament is nothing but the interpretation of the Old. Except that I saw that what the Old promises, the New teaches as having been exhibited; the Old is more concealed, the New is more revealed openly; the Old has to do with veils and figures, the New with clear evidences and the very things themselves.[259]

---

259. Heinrich Bullinger, *Werke Dritte Abteilung: Theologische Schriften—Band 2: Unveröffentlichte Werke aus der Kappeler Zeit* (Zürich: Theologischer Verlag Zürich, 1991), 25 (I owe the translation to Rev. Dr. Joe Mock).

That is a standard line in Reformed teaching and one that resonates well with the promise-fulfillment theme of Luke–Acts and the picture of shadows and realities in Hebrews.

There are two main platforms on which I intend to build a modified covenant theology. First, I posit a covenant of grace as the premise behind God's plan to offer salvation through Jesus Christ and so unite humanity to him in the new creation. The covenant of grace may be conceptually correlated with the "eternal covenant" mentioned in Hebrews 13:20. This eternal covenant included the sacrificial "blood" of Jesus, which is an expression of God's plan for Jesus to be the Lamb of God slain before the creation of the world (Rev 13:8). This eternal covenant delivers people from the sins committed under the "first covenant" (i.e., Sinaitic covenant) according to the author of Hebrews and Paul (Heb 9:15; Gal 3:13). Hence, the covenant of grace is the overarching conceptual reality behind the Abrahamic covenant and the new covenant that avails for the redemption of God's people. The covenant of grace is God's rescue plan to turn the corrupted garden of Eden into the garden city of a new Jerusalem.

Second, the key epochs of redemptive history can be defined as an "Adamic administration" and a "messianic administration."[260] The unity of the biblical story line is God's eternal decision to set forth Jesus Christ to undo the effect of Adam's sin and thereby to unite the Logos with his people in the new creation. The contrast between Adam and Jesus is a far more biblical model than the contrast between a covenant of works and a covenant of grace (see Rom 5:12–21; 1 Cor 15:21–22, 45–49). The human problem is that we are identified against and participated in Adam's sin and its condemnation. The divine solution is that we identify with and participate in the Messiah's faithfulness, death, and resurrection. As a result, the covenant of grace takes us from being "in Adam" to being "in Messiah," where we experience life, righteousness, and communion with God.

Jesus fulfils the role of Adam by being the new Adam. Jesus fulfils the role of Israel by being the true Israel. He succeeds where his forbearers failed. He is faithful where they were flawed.[261] By doing so he is able to redeem, restore, and renew a humanity that is finally worthy of the name "the Israel of God." The distinction of this scheme from classic covenant theology can be made in several ways:

1. There is no Adamic covenant based on Adam keeping a law that is a protological Mosaic law. Instead, there is an Adamic administration that was a probationary period rather than a meritorious exercise. Adam could have retained his relationship

---

260. Cf. A. T. B. McGowan, "In Defence of 'Headship Theology,'" in *The God of Covenant: Biblical, Theological, and Contemporary Perspectives* (ed. J. A. Grant and A. I. Wilson; Leicester, UK: Apollos, 2005), 178–99.

261. According to Graham Cole (*God the Peacemaker: How Atonement Brings Shalom* [Downers Grove, IL: InterVarsity Press, 2009], 108): "Jesus is all that Israel should have been as God's Son and all that Adam and Israel should have been as God's sons. In other words, Jesus is the faithful Adam and the faithful Israel."

with God and even gained immortality had he remained obedient to God in the garden during that probationary period in Eden. Adam's failure was not the failure to keep an eternal law; it was the breaking of his relationship with God through his desire for autonomy from God. Salvation will henceforth mean restoring the relationship between Creator and humanity as opposed to accruing the meritorious law-keeping that Adam failed to achieve.

2. The covenant of grace is intimated in the *protoevangelium* stated to Eve in the garden and in the Noachide covenant (Gen 3:15; 9:9–11). The covenant of grace is then formally enacted in the Abrahamic covenant. The Abrahamic covenant is the prototypical declaration of the gospel by promising salvation by faith to those who trust in God's promises (Gal 3:8). The Abrahamic covenant is not abolished by the Mosaic covenant, but telescoped through it. In fact, Exodus 19:4–5 is a virtual restatement of Gen 12:1–3, so that the Mosaic covenant is an expansion of the Abrahamic promises.[262] The Davidic covenant specifies how the seed of the woman, the offspring of Abraham, and a Davidic descendent will bring salvation to God's people. The new covenant is then the eschatological realization of the Abrahamic promises for Jews and Gentiles to which the Mosaic covenant leads people.

3. The Mosaic covenant was not a republication of an Adamic covenant. The Mosaic covenant was a temporary, national, and preparatory covenant. It momentarily cocooned God's purposes around Israel in order to (1) protract Israel's capacity to worship God; (2) use Israel to project God's first order purposes into the world; (3) demonstrate the consequences of sin; and (4) designate Israel as the means for the revelation of the Messiah. The Mosaic law is antithetical to the gospel only when the law is regarded as a means of salvation rather than a messenger of salvation. The law was given to a redeemed people, not to redeem the people. The period of law has its own gospel (Isa 52:7), though its promises were conditional (Lev 18:5). It was our guardian to lead us to Christ (Gal 3:24), and our faith upholds the law (Rom 3:31). Viewed this way, law and gospel are two administrations of the one covenant of grace, one preparatory and provisional, the other climactic and final.

4. The new covenant is the eschatological fulfillment of the Abrahamic and Mosaic covenants by bringing the Abrahamic promises to bear on Jews and Gentiles through faith in Jesus Christ. What is new in the new covenant is the death and resurrection of Jesus as the means of salvation, Jesus as the object of faith, God's people as multiethnic, and the permanent indwelling of the Holy Spirit. The obligations of the new covenant are not the moral law of the Decalogue but the example of Jesus, the teaching of Jesus, and life in the Spirit. Those things represent the "law of Christ" (Gal 6:2) and their performance fulfills the Mosaic law. Nonetheless, the

---

262. William J. Dumbrell, *Covenant and Creation* (Nashville: Nelson, 1984), 89–90.

law remains as a type of wisdom for Christian living, but it no longer defines the constitution or conduct for God's people.

We could diagram this model in this way:

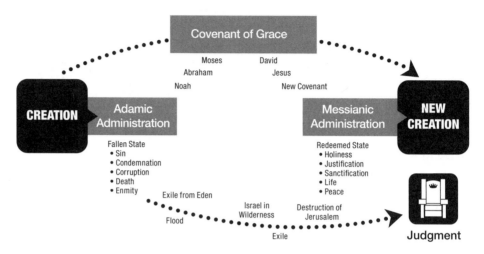

We can summarize this by saying that God has one plan to take people from being "in Adam" to being "in Messiah." We call this plan *the covenant of grace*. Redemptive history is the manifestation of this covenant as it pertains to the progressive revelation of the God who works for the salvation of his people. The covenant history is neither a series of disconnected dispensations nor a binary pairing of covenants defined by grace versus law; rather, each new covenant presupposes and renews what preceded it.[263]

FURTHER READING

Blaising, Craig A., and Darrell L. Bock, eds. *Dispensationalism, Israel, and the Church: The Search for a Definition*. Grand Rapids: Zondervan, 1992.

Goldsworthy, Graeme. *According to Plan: The Unfolding of God in the Bible*. Leicester, UK: Inter-Varsity Press, 1991.

Grant, Jamie A., and Alistair I. Wilson, eds. *The God of Covenant: Biblical, Theological, and Contemporary Perspectives*. Leicester, UK: Apollos: 2005.

Horton, Michael S. *God of Promise: Introducing Covenant Theology*. Grand Rapids: Baker, 2006.

Williams, Michael. *Far as the Curse is Found: The Covenant Story of Redemption*. Phillipsburg, NJ; Presbyterian & Reformed, 2005.

---

263. Michael Williams, *Far as the Curse Is Found: The Covenant Story of Redemption* (Phillipsburg, NJ; Presbyterian & Reformed, 2005), 51.

WHAT TO TAKE HOME?

- God's attributes can be categorized into communicable and incommunicable varieties.
- God reveals himself predominantly in the male forms of Father, Son, and Lord, but masculinity is not part of the essence of God's being, since God also describes himself in maternal imagery. All theological language for God, including that involving gender, is analogical and describes the relationship between members within the Godhead and illustrates the relationship of believers to God as a parent-child relationship.
- The essence of God's nature is a combination of his glory, holiness, and love.
- God as Creator is the presupposition for the gospel of God.
- The Bible teaches a creational monotheism—that is, an exclusive monotheism, a regal monotheism, a providential monotheism, and a covenantal monotheism.
- The Christian creation story eliminates several alternative worldview options, including deism, pantheism, panentheism, henotheism, paganism, and Gnosticism.
- The distinctive elements of a Christian view of creation are the triune nature of the act of creation and the salvation of creation through new creation.
- The goodness of creation derives from the goodness of the Creator.
- Despite the ambiguity of Genesis 1:1–2, Christian and Jewish traditions attest to God's creative act as occurring *ex nihilo*.
- The doctrine of God as Creator is the basis of the Christian worldview; it establishes the grounds for a Christian ecological ethic and provides the grounds for scientific inquiry of nature.
- Revelation can be defined as God's free action where he communicates saving truth about himself and the very presence of himself to humanity, especially through Jesus Christ, who is the incarnate Word of God, as testified by the apostles and attested by the Holy Scriptures and received by the community of believers.

- Revelation is at God's own initiative and redemptive by design.
- God's revelation is evangelical in that it is aimed at and structured around the person and work of Christ.
- The three modes of revelation are natural, special, and christological.
- Natural revelation is the communication of God's power and attributes in nature. Sadly, this knowledge is largely rejected by human beings and leaves them culpable for rejecting natural revelation.
- Natural theology is possible, not as an exercise of neutral rationality, but under the aegis of a theistic worldview to connect God to creation.
- Special revelation is God's unique communication of himself through history, proclamation, Scripture, and illumination.
- The incarnation is the fullest revelation of God in both its human immediacy and redemptive effect.
- God has *one purpose*: to glorify himself through his love for others.
- God has *one plan*: to bring men and women into the new creation through Jesus Christ.
- There are different ways to understand the unity of God's plan—in covenantal and dispensational theologies.
- The unity of Scripture can be organized around a single divine purpose for salvation called the covenant of grace.

STUDY QUESTIONS FOR INDIVIDUALS AND GROUPS

1. What do you think of Augustine's statement that "whoever denies the Trinity is in danger of losing his salvation; whoever tries to understand the Trinity is in danger of losing his mind"?
2. If being Trinitarian was a crime, what evidence would there be to convict you?
3. Describe what is the most distinguishing attribute or set of attributes describing God's character.
4. Identify what makes a Christian view of God as Creator different from Jewish or Islamic perspectives on God as Creator.
5. Why is revelation necessary?
6. What does nature tell us about God? What is the limitation of nature for the knowledge of God?
7. Is there something extra special about the incarnation as a mode of divine revelation?
8. Is it possible to understand God's glory without understanding his love?
9. How would you describe God's purpose and God's plan?

PART THREE

The Gospel of the Kingdom: The Now and the Not Yet

Part Three • The Gospel of the Kingdom: The Now and the Not Yet

§3.1 Gospel and Kingdom
§3.2 Apocalypse Now ... and Not Yet!
§3.3 The Return of Jesus Christ
§3.4 Millennium and Tribulation
§3.5 The Final Judgment
§3.6 The Intermediate State: What Happens When You Die?
§3.7 The Final State: Heaven, Hell, and New Creation

The study of the last things is called *eschatology*. The gospel of the kingdom announces the dramatic and apocalyptic invasion of God's saving power into our world through Christ and operating in the sphere of the Holy Spirit. God's plan to recapture the world for himself and to put it to rights is disclosed in the prophetic writings and effected in Christ; it is the substance of Christian hope. Along the way we must discuss the nature of biblical language about the end times, the return of Jesus Christ (i.e., the *parousia*), evaluate the various options relating to a period of tribulation and a millennial reign of Christ, identify the nature of the final judgment, look at what Scripture says about what happens between death and resurrection, and examine final states of heaven, hell, and the new creation.

> Then the end will come, when he hands over the kingdom to God the Father after he has destroyed all dominion, authority and power. For he must reign until he has put all his enemies under his feet. The last enemy to be destroyed is death.[1]

> Christian eschatology speaks of Jesus Christ and his future. It recognizes the reality of the raising of Jesus and proclaims the future of the risen Lord. Hence the question whether all statements about the future are grounded in the person and history of Jesus Christ provides it with the touchstone by which to distinguish the spirit of eschatology from that of utopia.[2]

> The only philosophy that can be practiced responsibly in the face of despair is the attempt to contemplate all things as they would present themselves from the standpoint of redemption. Knowledge has no light but that shed on the world by redemption: all else is reconstruction, mere technique. Perspectives must be fashioned that displace and estrange the world, that reveal its fissures and crevices, as indigent and distorted as it will one day appear in the Messianic light.[3]

---

1. 1 Corinthians 15:24–26.
2. Jürgen Moltmann, *Theology of Hope* (trans. J. W. Leitch; New York: Harper & Row, 1967), 17.
3. Theodor W. Ardo, *Minima Moralia*, 247, cited in Joseph D. Lewandowski, *Interpreting Culture: Rethinking Method and Truth in Social Theory* (Lincoln, NB: University of Nebraska Press, 2001), 80.

§ 3.1 GOSPEL AND KINGDOM

Normally eschatology (i.e., the study of the last things) is placed at the end of a systematic theology textbook. It is understandable to put "last things" last in the teaching schedule. However, I am strongly convinced that a study of eschatology, with its emphasis on the final kingdom of God, needs to be pushed up much earlier in the theological curriculum for a couple of reasons.

First, "kingdom of God" stands as an extremely important motif in biblical theology. The kingdom is not something that appears just at the end of time; rather, the whole sweep of redemptive history is driven by the conception of God as both king and yet becoming king. God shows his kingly power by redeeming his creation from the evil that has infected it, and he redeems it specifically through the work of King Jesus. As such, the biblical story is told in such a way that we are constantly confronted, from Genesis to Revelation, with the theme of God's reign over God's people in God's place.[4] Thus, eschatology is not an afterthought but is one of the main building blocks in constructing an evangelical theology from the outset.

Second, we cannot help but notice that the kingdom of God figured prominently in Jesus' gospel. Hence the summaries we find in the Gospels about Jesus' preaching and activities: "'The time has come,' he said. 'The kingdom of God has come near. Repent and believe the good news!'" (Mark 1:15), and "Jesus went through all the towns and villages, teaching in their synagogues, proclaiming the good news of the kingdom and healing every disease and sickness" (Matt 9:35). In Jesus' gospel, he announces that the covenantal promises of God—those made with Abraham and David and those given to the prophets—are coming to fruition. The shot clock has wound down to zero and God is acting with kingly power through the liberating work of Jesus' healings and exorcisms, and especially in his passion and resurrection. Indeed, "the kingdom of God" can even stand as a shorthand

---

4. Cf. Graeme Goldsworthy ("Kingdom of God," in *NDBT*, 620): "The entire biblical story, despite its great diversity of forms and foci, is consistent in its emphasis on the reign of God over his people in the environment he creates for them. The kingdom depicted in Eden is lost to humankind at the beginning of the biblical account. The history of redemption begins immediately when the kingdom is lost, and tells of the way the kingdom of God will finally be established as a new people of God in fellowship with him in a new Eden, a new Jerusalem, a new heaven and a new earth."

for Christian preaching about God, Jesus, salvation, and the future (e.g., Acts 8:12; 14:22; 19:8; 28:23, 31; 1 Cor 4:20; Col 4:11).

This means that eschatology provides the framework for Christian theology but also comprises the essential nucleus of the Christian gospel. Thus, an evangelical theology should be one that is colored, flavored, saturated, and pervaded by eschatology: God is king and becoming king in the reign of the Lord Jesus Christ.

It cannot be emphasized enough how vital eschatology is for theology. Ernst Käsemann went so far as to say that "apocalyptic [eschatology] was the mother of all theology."[5] That is completely true. For instance, what we say about Jesus Christ must be determined by who he was, who he is, and who he yet will be on the final day of history. We can only speak of Jesus as Judge if we look ahead to the future. Christian redemption is a present experience and yet is also something we still anxiously await. Our justification is both declared in the present and enacted in the resurrection of our bodies. The church at present is a community of exiles, to use the language of 1 Peter and Hebrews, but we are journeying on toward the heavenly Jerusalem. The reason for this is because all Christian theology is based on God's promise to put the world to right, to unite himself to creation through the Logos, and to usher in the new creation. What we call "eschatology" represents the constellation of hopes and expectations for the transformation of the cosmos into the new creation. In the words of Jürgen Moltmann:

> From first to last, and not merely in the epilogue, Christianity is eschatology, is hope, forward looking and forward moving, and therefore also revolutionizing and transforming the present. The eschatological is not one element of Christianity, but it is the medium of the Christian faith as such, the key in which everything in it is set.... Hence eschatology cannot really be only a part of Christian doctrine. Rather, the eschatological outlook is characteristic of all Christian proclamation, and of every Christian existence and of the whole Church.[6]

Furthermore, this eschatology is not just pie in the sky. There is a deeply practical side here, for how we act in the present is deeply impacted by what we think of the future. What we think about evangelism, justice, ecological responsibility, pastoral care, budgets, the church, and ethics is based on what God *has done* and *will yet do* for his people *through Jesus Christ*. If our actions echo into eternity, if we contribute something to God's coming kingdom, we will be constrained to operate with a kingdom perspective. Thus Barth was correct to note that "eschatology, rightly understood, is the most practical thing that can be thought."[7]

---

5. Ernst Käsemann, "The Beginnings of Christian Theology," in *New Testament Questions of Today* (London: SCM, 1969), 102. See also I. Howard Marshall, "Is Apocalyptic the Mother of Christian Theology?" in *Tradition and Interpretation in the New Testament* (ed. G. F. Hawthorne and O. Betz; Grand Rapids: Eerdmans, 1987), 33–42.

6. Moltmann, *Theology of Hope*, 16.

7. Karl Barth, *Dogmatics in Outline* (trans. G. T. Thomson; London: SCM, 1949), 154.

§ 3.1 Gospel and Kingdom

Christian eschatology is a key marker that distinguishes Christianity from other worldviews. So, for instance, in the New Testament age of the Roman empire, the dominant eschatology was an imperial one. The pantheon of gods had chosen toga-wearing Romans and Augustus to bring peace and prosperity to the world by conquering with all the might of their armies. As long as Augustus or one of his heirs was on the throne, there was nothing to fear from the Germanic tribes in the north or the Parthians in the east, and the Roman empire would continue its onward march of conquering and civilizing the barbarian tribes on the outskirts of Europe. Foreign gold and foreign slaves would continue to flow into Rome, and there would be bread and circuses for everyone. Just read the poetry of Virgil or Horace to get a load of Roman propaganda with its own eschatological story.

However, when the Emperor Constantine's soldiers started putting the sign of the cross on their shields at the battle of Milvian bridge in 312, it meant the end of that story; it was the triumph of Christ over Caesar. Any further pretensions to the Roman empire's co-opting God's kingdom were finally eviscerated when King Alaric I of the Goths sacked Rome in 410.

Then there are contemporary eschatologies like modernity and postmodernity. The Enlightenment, with its self-assured confidence in "Reason," rejected Christianity as a leftover relic of the superstitious beliefs of the Middle Ages. Now that we have "Reason," it was said, we can advance in knowledge, science, and learning and create a human-centered utopia. The belief in the progress of Western civilization was the eschatological story from 1789 with the fall of the Bastille to 1989 with the fall of the Berlin Wall. Some of the revolutionaries even installed a Parisian woman as the "goddess of reason" on the altar in the Notre Dame de Paris. "Reason is god" was the effective catch cry!

The problem was, however, that what was "reasonable" kept changing with every new discovery. Reason, it turned out, was not a neutral sphere. Indeed, Reason was used as a license to persecute minorities like the European Jews; it gave us weapons of mass destruction like nuclear bombs; it masked covert claims to power, and it disempowered dissenters as irrational. Ironically Reason claimed absolute authority but could find no basis for absolute value. The great myth of the triumph of European progress collapsed under the weight of two world wars in the twentieth century. The modernist myth of progress, utopia, and an age of reason ends just like the T. S. Eliot poem "The Hollow Men": "This is the way the world ends / Not with a bang but a whimper." Not the explosion of victory by Guy Fawkes blowing up the English Parliament, but with the sound of torment with Guy Fawkes dying at the hands of his executioners. Or, even worse, modernity becomes the very thing it feared: irrationality and destruction. Hence the grim words of

Robert Oppenheimer, inventor of the nuclear bomb, who quoted the Bhagavadita: "I am become death, the destroyer of worlds." The modernist dream had become a nightmare.

Postmodernity was in many ways a critical response to modernity. It rejected the modernist claim to absolute truth and the contention that anyone can have a purely "rational" perspective, and it unmasked the underlying power ploys in all claims to truth. Yet postmodernity is really the intensification of Modernity — a hyper-modernity in fact. Postmodernity accentuates the claim that man is the measure of all things, and it allows for the use of religious language on the proviso that the language has no referent to any reality other than the language of the users who utter it. In postmodernity, pluralism is god and diversity is his prophet.

In the postmodern era, the overarching story is that our world is heading for political, economic, and ecological oblivion. The only way we can save it is through a rescue; we need a savior, a state, who will end discrimination by enforcing diversity, who will deliver our economy by neo-Marxism, and who will rescue our environment with eco-legislation. Then we will have complete equality, true diversity, and authentic community. Just read philosophers like Peter Singer, Alain Badiou, or Slavoj Žižek, and you get themes like this coming through. Here religion, as an ideology of resistance to hyper-secularism, stands in the way of diversity and eco-responsibility; therefore, it must be exiled out of the public sphere. Sex can be publicized, but religions must be interiorized. Tolerance is not a respect for the beliefs of others; it is the abandonment of beliefs that offend. I suspect that, when all is said and done, the postmodern vision will collapse in on itself in nihilism. Its hope for a global community-in-diversity can only be achieved by forcing faith communities to forfeit their truth claims, to deny the finality of their hopes, and to expunge themselves of anything offensive to others. The irony of postmodernism is that its quest for absolute diversity can only be achieved by crushing dissenters.

In contrast to all this, Christian theology claims that history is about the mission of God working out his purposes. These purposes were promised to the patriarchs and to Israel, were summed up in Christ, flow into the church, and will climax at the appointed day. We know how the story goes, we know who it is about, and we even know how it all ends — not with a whimper but a new creation. We do not die; rather, we become alive at the great resurrection. Christian eschatology represents a competing story, a story that dares to challenge the dehumanizing ideologies of secularism and nihilism, for it tells us of a world without end, a benevolent Lord, a never-ending peace, and time without tears. What is more, it is a world that has already begun in the context of this world, for that is the eschatological horizon of the gospel.

The gospel constitutes a keyhole through which we glance into God's new world. This gospel imparts to us a vision of the future by warning us of the final judgment, giving us hope of eternal life, previewing the new creation and resurrection of the dead, and heralding the triumph of God over sin and suffering. The gospel functions much like the program one receives at the beginning of a musical drama. We learn the characters and the plot, and we are told how the story will dramatically end. We discover also, much to our surprise, that we are characters in the story. The gospel calls us to sing and act amidst the melodies and motifs of God's kingdom and its king.

The eschatological horizon to the gospel is summarily announced to the world in the "gospel/good news of the kingdom" (Matt 4:23; 9:35; 24:14; Luke 4:43; 8:1; 16:16; Acts 8:12). God acts with kingly power to effect his redeeming reign over Israel and finally over all creation. The kingdom of God is not a single place; rather, it is divine dominion over the entire world.[8] It has two key moments: a fulfillment of Old Testament promises in the historical mission of Jesus, and a future consummation at the end of the age that inaugurates the coming age.[9] That the kingdom is both "already" and "yet to come" is, in the words Herman Ridderbos, "one of the fundamental presuppositions for understanding the gospel."[10] The gospel thus *announces* that God's reign is already bursting into our world, and it *invites* persons to enter into the rule of God for a future consummation of its saving power. Peter Jensen writes:

> The future of God's dealings with the whole world—and especially his judgment—may be regarded as essential to the framework of the gospel, without which it cannot be properly understood. The gospel locates us in a time that God is unfolding: historical time, but with a present meaning revealed by the promised future. Thus the form of the gospel is eschatological. In accordance with the teaching of the New Testament we recognize that the gospel announces that the eschaton has arrived, although it awaits its consummation in a further decisive universal revelation of Christ.[11]

The gospel is the announcement that God's kingdom is advancing, not in the sphere of human progress, but in the person and work of Jesus Christ and the mission of the church. It is Christ who brings the kingdom because he is its king and the harbinger of a royal redemption (see esp. Matt 12:28; Luke 11:20). The kingdom is

---

8. For a list of kingdom of God references in the New Testament and early Christian literature, see N. T. Wright, *Jesus and the Victory of God* (Minneapolis: Fortress, 2002), 663–70.

9. G. E. Ladd, *A Theology of the New Testament* (Grand Rapids; Eerdmans, 1974), 90. He prefaces his statement with this definition of the kingdom (89–90): "The Kingdom of God is the redemptive reign of God dynamically active to establish his rule among human beings, and that this Kingdom, which will appear as an apocalyptic act at the end of the age, has already come into human history in the person and mission of Jesus to overcome evil, to deliver people from its power, and to bring them into the blessings of God's reign."

10. Herman Ridderbos, *The Coming of the Kingdom* (trans. H. de Jongste; Philadelphia: Presbyterian & Reformed, 1962), 104.

11. Peter Jensen, *The Revelation of God* (Downers Grove, IL: InterVarsity Press, 2002), 51.

so intimately bound up with Jesus Christ that Origen called Jesus the *autobasileia*, the "kingdom in himself"! Tom Schreiner comments on the connection between Christ and kingdom: "When we speak of the kingdom, inevitably we are introduced to Christology, for Jesus does not merely speak abstractly about the coming kingdom. He invariably considers his own role as paramount in the eschatological kingdom. The most remarkable feature of the kingdom is the role of Jesus Christ himself."[12] Jesus is the anointed king who brings deliverance to Israel, who embodies the reign of God, and who will establish God's rule over all the earth.

Consequently, eschatology, as the study of the "last things," is not just about the final chapter of the book of history. No, eschatology is an invasive story, about how God's promises to bring justice, reconciliation, and peace to earth have *already* invaded this age—even if unexpected in timing and means—so that the plan and purposes of God will ebb *toward* a dramatic final moment in the divine plan. That plan, of course, is union between the Logos and the Lost in a new creation where God reigns, over God's people, in God's place. The rescue is a form of recovery of the old order of creation; but more than that, the old order is transfigured into a more glorious state than the original creation. In that end state "God [will] be all in all" with his rule over all things and in every way (1 Cor 15:28).

The primary tasks in mapping eschatology are to demonstrate how we live between the ages, discuss the continuities between this age and the coming age, and describe what the future state of the kingdom will look like for both the individual and the cosmos. More specifically, there are several questions that come up for discussion:

1. To what extent is the kingdom both "now" and "not yet"?
2. What is Jesus' second coming, i.e., the *parousia*?
3. What are the tribulation and the millennium?
4. What is the nature of the final judgment?
5. What is the intermediate state?
6. What will the new creation look like?

---

12. Thomas Schreiner, *New Testament Theology: Magnifying God in Christ* (Grand Rapids: Baker, 2008), 51.

WHY ESCHATOLOGY MATTERS!

People can debate, conjecture, and argue a great deal about "last things." Many seminaries in North America explicitly align themselves with certain eschatological schemes and make it an article of faith to which faculty, staff, and students must subscribe. The unhealthy theological divisions created by eschatology combined with fantastical books like Hal Lindsey's *The Late Great Planet Earth* and Jerry Jenkins and Tim LaHaye's *Left Behind* series might make it prudent for us to retreat from the business of eschatology and distance ourselves from the controversy and lunacy that seem to go with the field. We could substitute the ardor and arguments for simple affirmations that we can all agree on, like "Jesus wins in the end."

Now while "Jesus wins in the end" is certainly true, it is a rather terse and vague slogan and does not capture the full breadth of what eschatology means. Jesus wins because he is winning and has already won! The "end" matters not merely because it is the future, but in Christian theology we have a future that already shapes the present. What is more, this Christian eschatology is "apocalyptic," in that it reveals several dualisms, like those between the present and the future, between earthly events and heavenly realities, and between good and evil. Richard Hays lists seven reasons why the church needs apocalyptic eschatology:[13]

1. *The church needs apocalyptic eschatology to carry Israel's story forward.* Without a future-oriented hope one cannot affirm God's faithfulness to Israel, and God's covenantal promises become unintelligible. Or even worse, a faithless God means we have a fickle deity on whom we cannot rely. God intends to vindicate his people (Deut 32:36) at the appointed time when the Redeemer comes to Zion (Isa 59:20). These promises find their proleptic fulfillment in Jesus Christ in the church as a prefiguration of the eschatological people of God, which is a sign in itself of the full divine embracing (*proslē mpsis*) of eschatological Israel.
2. *The church needs apocalyptic eschatology for interpreting the cross as a saving event for the world.* If we are to grasp the centrality of the cross, we must see it as more than a propitiatory sacrifice for the forgiveness of the sins of all believers. The cross should be interpreted as an atoning event within a larger apocalyptic

---

13. Richard B. Hays, "'Why Do You Stand Looking Up toward Heaven?' New Testament Eschatology at the Turn of the Millennium," in *Theology at the Turn of the Millennium* (ed. L. G. Jones and J. J. Buckley; Oxford: Blackwell, 2001), 123–29.

narrative where God destroys the powers of the old order and inaugurates the new creation (Gal 6:14–16).

3. *The church needs apocalyptic eschatology for the gospel's political critique of pagan culture.* The biting edge to Christian eschatology is that Jesus is the Lord to whom every leader and government will one day bow (Phil 2:9–11). Christian apocalypticism reminds us that Caesar's power (in whatever form it takes) might claim to be comprehensive, but in fact it is transient. Christian loyalty to the Lord means resistance to the power, politics, and pantheon of the world around us. If we train our eyes on the ultimate reversal of fortunes, we will never become accommodated or complacent with the status quo in an unjust world.

4. *The church needs apocalyptic eschatology to resist ecclesial complacency and triumphalism.* The looming reality of a final judgment—a judgment that begins with the church—strikes a chord because it prevents the church from having grandiose concepts of its own importance (see 2 Cor 5:11–6:2). The church is a provisional servant of God, a lifeboat between shipwreck and salvage, and so must avoid becoming fat, sleepy, or abusive.

5. *The church needs apocalyptic eschatology in order to affirm the body.* Apocalyptic eschatology is in one sense dualistic between certain temporal and spatial entities (e.g., heaven vs. earth, future vs. present, etc.). However, that dualism is never portrayed as a radical rejection of the material world *in toto*. Apocalyptic eschatology looks forward to the Creator's redemption of the created order and his refusal to abandon it to decay. God redeems what he creates. That is why Christians look forward to the resurrection of the flesh and not to the immortality of the soul (1 Cor 15:35–58).

6. *The church needs apocalyptic eschatology to ground its mission.* The resurrection and ascension of Jesus was a sign that Israel's restoration was indeed at hand (Acts 1:11). Yet it was also a call to engage in witness to the expanding kingdom. That witnessing inevitably brings the witnesses into conflict with a world hostile to the message of the lordship of Jesus Christ. The Holy Spirit empowers the church and forms the community as a missional organism that works out God's purposes for redemption and judgment. Without this end-time perspective the content and urgency of the Christian mission is greatly retarded.

7. *The church needs apocalyptic eschatology to speak with integrity about suffering and death.* Those armed with an apocalyptic eschatology need not live in denial

> of the sufferings of this age and the groaning that accompanies it. Neither cynicism nor despair takes over Christians because they know that their *telos* is the resurrection of their body assured by the resurrection of Jesus' body. Christians therefore know how to grieve with hope in the face of the horror of death, knowing that every tear will one day be wiped away from their eyes in the new creation.
>
> Recognizing that we are "not there yet" is a sobering reminder that our world is far from redeemed. Since we are still very much part of that world, individual salvation is incomplete until the redemption of all things. Moreover, the salvation of the church is ultimately bound up with the restoration of the universal order itself. The fate of the universe hangs on the revelation of the children of God at the *parousia* (Rom 8:18–23; 1 Cor 15:28). That hope impinges on the present and directs our sense of identity and mission away from a dualistic escapism in the meantime. The Spirit-filled church is the global billboard declaring the good things that God has prepared for the restoration of all things. Therefore, "hope for the future coming of the crucified and risen Christ has continually served to counter Christian tendencies to pietism and quietism, spiritualization and privatization, because it has opened the church to the world and the future, to the universal scope of God's purposes in Jesus the Messiah."[14]
>
> ---
>
> 14. Richard Bauckham, "The Future of Jesus Christ," in *The Cambridge Companion to Jesus* (ed. M. N. Bockmuehl; Cambridge: Cambridge University Press, 2001), 268.

§ 3.2 APOCALYPSE NOW ... AND NOT YET!

3.2.1 BIBLICAL ESCHATOLOGY IN HISTORICAL THOUGHT

Biblical scholarship has generally wrestled with the temporal nature of the kingdom of God and gravitated toward an emphasis on the kingdom as either present or future, especially in relation to the preaching of Jesus.[15] In response to the idealism of European Protestant liberalism, Johannes Weiss and Albert Schweitzer both emphasized consistent eschatology. This model regarded Jesus as an apocalyptic seer who proclaimed the imminent arrival of the kingdom of God, within a matter of months, which would bring about a dramatic change in the sociopolitical affairs of Judea. The climax of the end would be in the revelation of a heavenly figure called the Son of Man, not Jesus, another figure, a semidivine being who would usher in God's kingdom (particularly important for Schweitzer was Matt 10:23, "When you are persecuted in one place, flee to another. Truly I tell you, you will not finish going through the towns of Israel before the Son of Man comes"). It was the nonoccurrence of this portentous event that led Jesus to go to Jerusalem in order to die as a martyr and to force God to bring the kingdom forward—but he failed; the kingdom never came. The rest of the history of Christianity can be seen as a response to the failure of the *parousia* to materialize, with the result that eschatological hopes were consequently reshaped and progressively abandoned.[16]

Problems abound with this "consistent eschatology model."[17] First, the view that many of the Son of Man sayings refer to a future figure other than Jesus has been largely abandoned. The designation "Son of Man" is primarily a circumlocution

---

15. D. E. Aune, "Eschatology (Early Christian)," *ABD*, 2:599–600.

16. Johannes Weiss, *Jesus' Proclamation of the Kingdom of God* (trans. R. H. Hiers and R.L. Holland; Philadelphia: Fortress, 1971); Albert Schweitzer, *The Quest of the Historical Jesus* (New York: Macmillan, 1961); see more recently Dale C. Allison, *Jesus of Nazareth: Millenarian Prophet* (Minneapolis: Fortress, 1998); idem, *Constructing Jesus: Memory, Imagination, and History* (Grand Rapids: Baker, 2010), 31–220.

17. What follows is adapted from Michael F. Bird, "Parousia," in *Encyclopedia of the Historical Jesus* (ed. C. Evans; New York: Routledge, 2008), 439–40.

for Jesus in his role as the eschatological representative of Israel. It is more of a role than a title and is an encoded description of his messianic task.[18] The so-called "Son of Man concept" (*Menschensohnbegriff*) involving a primordial myth of a heavenly redeemer appropriated by Jesus or others is equally mythical in its content. As Paul Winter wrote, "the place of origin of the Son of Man myth must be sought neither in Iran, nor in Judea, not even in Ugarit, but in German universities."[19]

Second, unlike other apocalyptic seers, Jesus did not set a timetable for the end, and so the kingdom's final consummation was indeterminate (see Matt 24:36; Mark 13:32). Moreover, the imminence of the kingdom must be understood in conjunction with other complexes in which Jesus entertains the possibility of the delay of the kingdom's final manifestation. The trial or testing (*peirasmos*) has not yet occurred (Matt 6:13/Luke 11:4), the prospect of persecution implies a further period of activity (Matt 16:25–27/Mark 8:35–38/Luke 9:24–26; Matt 10:16–25; Luke 11:49–50), the parable of the unjust judge exhorts disciples to wait patiently for vindication (Luke 18:7), and at the Last Supper Jesus refused to drink from the fruit of the vine "until that day when I drink it new in the kingdom of God," which means that the kingdom was still to come at an unspecified date (Mark 14:25; cf. Matt 26:29; Luke 22:18).

Similarly, the parables of growth, which refer to the kingdom progressively growing (Matt 13:1–32/Mark 4:1–32/Luke 13:18–19), and the parable of ten talents, where a nobleman goes to a distant country to become king (Luke 19:11–27), appear to entertain some notion of delay in the kingdom's final advent. The paradox between Jesus' proclamation of both the imminence and presence of the kingdom is resolved when it is realized that Jewish thinking could accommodate the arrival of the kingdom as extending over time, in and through a series of events that could invade the present (e.g., *Jub.* 23; *1 En.* 91.12–17). What is more, some of these purportedly imminent sayings can arguably be identified with events other than a "cosmic meltdown," including Jesus' death and resurrection (Mark 9:1), the destruction of Jerusalem (Matt 10:23; Mark 13:30), or the exaltation of Jesus (Mark 14:62). These were all crucial events in the kingdom story that Jesus was announcing. Consequently, the reference to the kingdom's imminence does not necessarily entail the imminence of the entire eschatological scenario.[20]

Third, the notion that the failure of the *parousia* to occur was the single greatest force in Christian theology is blandly overstated. For a start, the question of "why the delay" was not unique to Christianity; it was inherited from Judaism, which

---

18. Michael F. Bird, *Are You the One Who Is to Come? The Historical Jesus and the Messianic Question* (Grand Rapids: Baker, 2009), 78–98.

19. Cited in Simon Gathercole, *The Preexistent Son: Recovering the Christologies of Matthew, Mark, and Luke* (Grand Rapids: Eerdmans, 2006), 255.

20. Ben Witherington III, *Jesus the Seer* (Peabody, MA: Hendrickson, 1999), 261–65.

had long wrestled with the apparent delay in God's salvation since the Babylonian exile. This is reflected in texts such as Habakkuk 2:3 and seen in appropriation of these texts by Judean groups of the first century like the Qumranites (e.g., 1QpHab 7.6–14).[21] In addition, if the early church was disappointed by the failure of Christ to return, such a disappointment is not reflected in the key texts. The intensity of hope for Christ's return fluctuated in some contexts. There was no definite tendency toward diminished eschatological enthusiasm since Matthew actually intensifies rather than downplays Mark's eschatological material. If the delay of the *parousia* was so detrimental to early Christian belief, one must wonder why the church of the second century did not find the predictions inherently embarrassing.[22]

Another school of eschatological thought, which emphasized the presence of the kingdom, is the realized eschatology of scholars such as C. H. Dodd. He believed that Jesus taught the essential presence of the kingdom of God. In this case, the kingdom of God is "the manifest and effective assertion of divine sovereignty against all the evil of the world," and Dodd maintained that "history had become the vehicle for the eternal."[23] Obviously there are texts that emphasize the presence of the kingdom, such as "the kingdom of God has come near" (Mark 1:15) and "the kingdom of God is in your midst" (Luke 17:21). Dodd knew that some kingdom sayings referred to the future and that Christianity began to quickly develop an apocalyptic expectation of Jesus' return. He was open to a kingdom consummation "beyond history,"[24] but in the main he interpreted the kingdom as being transcendent in character and wholly "other" in nature, and it had broken in through Jesus.

On a different tack, other researchers have attempted to deemphasize eschatology in Jesus' message and aligned Jesus with Greek philosophical traditions that rendered the kingdom a matter of wisdom traditions, countercultural ethos, and egalitarian practice rather than eschatological hope (e.g., John D. Crossan, Marcus Borg). They claimed to find textual support for their view in the allegedly authentic teachings of Jesus embedded in the sayings-source (Q) and in the *Gospel of Thomas*, which supposedly preserve Jesus' "real" teachings.[25] According to Crossan, Jesus' kingdom is the promotion of a radical egalitarianism of unmediated physical and spiritual access between God, people, and each other. Jesus "announced, in other words, the brokerless kingdom of God."[26]

The problem for the "realized" and "egalitarian" kingdom views are multiple. First, it should be admitted that the general impression created by the Gospels is that

---

21. Richard Bauckham, "The Delay of the Parousia," *TynBul* 31 (1980): 3–36.

22. N. T. Wright, *The New Testament and the People of God* (COQG 1; London: SPCK, 1992), 342–43, 459–64.

23. C. H. Dodd, *The Parables of the Kingdom* (New York: Scribner, 1961), 35, 169.

24. C. H. Dodd, *The Founder of Christianity* (New York: Macmillan, 1970), 115.

25. See survey in Wright, *Jesus and the Victory of God*, 44–78.

26. J. D. Crossan, *The Historical Jesus* (San Francisco: Harper, 1991), 422.

Jesus was remembered as an eschatological prophet who proclaimed the kingdom of God. John P. Meier writes: "A completely un-eschatological Jesus, a Jesus totally shorn of all apocalyptic traits, is simply not the historical Jesus, however compatible he might be to modern tastes, at least in middle-class American academia."[27]

Second, if Jesus did not have a strong eschatological message for the future, we are at somewhat of a loss to explain how such strong eschatological hopes for his return emerged in early Christianity. Continuity between John the Baptist–Jesus–the early church centers on a deep sense of expectation that God's "day" is coming.

Third, the de-eschatologized Jesus becomes tantamount to a de-judaized Jesus. He is artificially removed from the Hebrew Scriptures, insulated from the apocalypticism that liberal theologians find so distasteful. This Jesus is forcibly conscripted into the cause of Hellenistic philosophy, and he is concerned with social equality rather than with saving a world from its final judgment. Jesus becomes an icon of liberal dissent against the Holy Scripture and a protest against apocalyptic hopes. Such a Jesus is most definitely not a Galilean prophet announcing that God is becoming king. Gerd Theissen rightly comments: "The 'non-eschatological Jesus' seems to have more Californian than Galilean local colouring."[28] Ouch! And rightly so!!

A third option for eschatology is the inaugurated or proleptic position. This view, with many antecedents in the church fathers and modern scholarship, sees the kingdom of God as *both* a present reality and a future expectation (primary proponents include Joachim Jeremias, Oscar Cullmann, W. G. Kümmel, G. E. Ladd, G. R. Beasley-Murray). Jesus was promoting an eschatology in the process of realizing itself.[29] It is this perspective that I now intend to defend and expound.

3.2.2 BIBLICAL ESCHATOLOGY

There are various elements that feature largely in the hope for Israel in the Old Testament: survival in the aftermath of suffering, a coming Davidic deliverer, freedom from pagan oppressors, end of exile/new exodus, reconstitution of the twelve tribes, judgment for the wicked, a new covenant, a new temple, and so on. Although there are few references to "God's kingdom" in the Old Testament, yet God as King is the presupposition of the Old Testament witness. As Graeme Goldsworthy states: "The idea of the rule of God over creation, over all creatures, over the kingdoms of

---

27. John P. Meier, *A Marginal Jew: Rethinking the Historical Jesus* (ABRL: New York: Doubleday, 1991), 2:317. Cf. Henry Cadbury (*The Peril of Modernizing Jesus* [London: SPCK, 1962], 26): "Thus the apocalyptic element in the gospels has been frequently laid almost exclusively to the account of the evangelists, not because there is any real evidence that Jesus also did not share it, but mainly because it is uncongenial to the present day critic."

28. Gerd Theissen and Annette Merz, *The Historical Jesus: A Comprehensive Guide* (trans. John Bowden; Minneapolis: Fortress, 1998), 11.

29. Joachim Jeremias, *The Parables of Jesus* (New York: Scribners, 1963), 21, 230.

the world and in a unique and special way, over his chosen and redeemed people, is the very heart of the Hebrew scriptures."[30] Put simply, Jewish hopes focused on God's restoration of Israel to rule, like Adam, over a new creation as God's viceroy.

A shared and central conviction of the New Testament authors is that "the Old Testament prophecies of the great tribulation, God's deliverance of Israel from oppressors, God's rule over the Gentiles and the establishment of His kingdom have been set in motion by Christ's life, death, resurrection and the formation of the Christian church."[31] This is seen particularly in the reference by some New Testament authors to the "last days." Whereas Joel prophesied that in the "afterward" (i.e., after God restores his people), God will pour out his prophetic Spirit on all people, Peter announced at Pentecost that those "days" had arrived. At Pentecost, God had poured out his Spirit, not merely on prophets and priests, but on all people (lit., "all flesh"). Similarly, Paul believed that the Old Testament was written in order to guide Christians about how to live in the "end times" since Christians are those on whom "the culmination of the ages has come" (1 Cor 10:11).

The author of Hebrews declares in the opening of his letter that God spoke to the people in various ways through the prophets, but "in these last days he has spoken to us by his Son" (lit., "in Son"). James admonishes the rich who have "hoarded wealth in the last days," as they have amplified suffering in the "day of slaughter" and so bring destruction on themselves (Jas 5:3–5). Peter's first letter proclaims that the sacrificial death of Christ and his resurrection have been "revealed in these last times for your sake" (1 Pet 1:20). This theme is recurrent in 2 Peter, which identifies the anticipated detractors of the Christian message arriving; "in the last days scoffers will come, scoffing and following their own evil desires" (2 Pet 3:3). The same idea is rehearsed in the Johannine letters, "Dear children, this is the last hour; and as you have heard that the antichrist is coming, even now many antichrists have come" (1 John 2:18). In other words, the "last days" began with Jesus' first day on earth.

The dialectic tension between the kingdom as both now and not yet pervades the entire New Testament. In the Synoptic Gospels, Jesus began his Galilean ministry by proclaiming the "kingdom of God" (or "kingdom of heaven" in Matthew"),[32] which is summarized with the description that the "time has come [*peplērōtai*]" and "the kingdom of God has come near [*engiken*]" (Mark 1:15; cf. Matt 4:17). The significance of the perfect verbs is not of a past event with enduring significance, but of the heightened states of "fulfillment" and "nearness" to the audience, who share in

---

30. Goldsworthy, "Kingdom of God," 618.

31. Greg K. Beale, "The Eschatological Conception of New Testament Theology," in *The Reader Must Understand: Eschatology in Bible and Theology* (ed. M. Elliott and K. E. Brower; Leicester, UK: Apollos, 1997), 14.

32. On the specific nuance of Matthew's "kingdom of heaven," see Jonathan T. Pennington, *Heaven and Earth in the Gospel of Matthew* (Grand Rapids: Baker, 2009). According to Pennington, "Kingdom *of* Heaven" is not merely a circumlocution for "Kingdom *of* God," rather, it is part of a highly developed cosmological discourse about the heavens and the earth in relation to God, Jesus, and the church.

the events forecast simply by hearing the announcement. Jesus announces the beginning of the day of reckoning and the coming day of deliverance at the same time.

Elsewhere Jesus rejected the scribal habit of trying to "observe" the kingdom through calendrical calculations and conjectures, because "the kingdom of God is in your midst" (Luke 17:21). Though older translations translate *entos hymōn* as "within you" (KJV, NIV 1984), more accurate are other translations (e.g., NIV 2011) that render it as "in your midst" (NRSV, "among you"), since Jesus indicts the Pharisees for not seeing what is right in front of them: Jesus' kingdom ministry. The enigmatic saying about the kingdom of God suffering violence or violent persons trying to force their way into it is probably an affirmation that the kingdom of God has arrived, but not through the means of violent revolution by which some thought it would come (Matt 11:12/Luke 16:16). The exorcisms of Jesus are signs that the kingdom "has come upon you [*ephthasen eph' hymas*]" as God invades demonic spaces and cleanses it by force (Matt 12:28/Luke 11:20). What is present is not the eschaton but the kingly power of God over demonic forces as a foretaste of the eschaton.

Yet Jesus also shows a sharp future expectation for the kingdom in several places. The Lord's Prayer is for a kingdom yet to come on earth (Matt 6:10/Luke 11:2). Jesus looks ahead to the great eschatological banquet (see Isa 25:6–8), where a restored Israel and Gentile guests will recline with the patriarchs (Matt 8:11–12/Luke 13:28–29). There are abundant warnings about a future judgment, though it is not always clear if this is a judgment within this age or at the end of it, but a judgment to be earnestly avoided (e.g., Matt 5:21–22; 10:15; 12:41–42; 25:1–26). There are also exhortations to "enter" the kingdom at a future point (e.g., Matt 5:20; 7:21; 18:3; 19:23–24; 23:13; Mark 9:47; 10:15). Jesus was the prophet, teacher, and Messiah of God's kingdom. In story, symbol, praxis, and preaching, he referred to the dominion of God that was shining its light on a shadowy world as his kingship began to manifest itself once and for all through his present work—a declaration to which Israel had to quickly respond for their own sakes.

The Fourth Gospel clearly favors the realized component of Jesus' work. John sees in Jesus the coming of God's revelatory light, the incarnation of divine glory, and the life of heaven made manifest (John 1:3–4, 14; 3:31). The final resurrection expected at the end of the age (see 11:24) is burgeoning in the spiritual life that Jesus imparts to his followers (5:25; 11:25–26). Eternal life becomes intractably bound up with, almost collapsed into, the act of knowing and believing in the God who sent Jesus (17:3). The Johannine Jesus can even aver that "now is the time for judgment on this world" by virtue of the presence of the Judge (12:31; cf. 5:22, 27, 30; 8:15–16; esp. 9:39).

Still, John has not forfeited all sense of the future as he refers to a judgment and resurrection still to come (John 5:28–29; 6:39, 40, 44, 54; 11:23–26). The demonic "prince of this world" must yet be fully driven out (12:31). The kingdom of God is something that one must still enter into (3:3–5). The Fourth Evangelist also knows that Jesus is preparing a place for his disciples and will one day return to take them there (14:1–3). Putting this together, in the gospel of John, an absolute distinction between this age and the coming age has become fluid so that believers can experience real blessings, even eternal life, in the here and now.

The Johannine Jesus brings a "rift" between evil and good, darkness and light, belief and unbelief, future and present. John knows of the cosmic "hour" that already has come and is yet to be, an hour that brings condemnation as well as life, unity as well as division, salvation as well as judgment (John 5:25). Contra much scholarship, John does not endorse the abandonment of a future apocalyptic kingdom for an existential present experience; rather,

> John's sense of time—his eschatology—is shaped by his recognition that in the coming of Jesus the light has made a decisive difference between the past and present. But John also knows that the present is the scene of conflicting claims. True life is a current reality, yet so is death; some people can now see; yet others have become blind. These truths grate against each other like a dissonant sound pressing for resolution. The Gospel assumes that there is no going back, as if Jesus never came. There can only be going forward to the point where the dissonance resolves into harmony.[33]

For John that harmony transpires at the future judgment. He offers a summons to believe in Jesus as the light, life, and judge of the present hour and so avoid condemnation "at the last day" (John 12:44–50).

Shifting to Paul, Jesus Christ is the one through whom "the culmination of the ages has come" as his resurrection and the giving of the Spirit marks the partial arrival of the future age in the here and now (1 Cor 10:11). What many Jews thought God would do for Israel at the end of history (i.e., resurrection), God did for Jesus in the middle of history, and he will do exactly the same for believers at the final day. The resurrection of Christ is the firstfruits of the future age (15:20, 23), and he is the firstborn of the general resurrection (Rom 1:4; 8:29; Col 1:15, 18). His resurrection is the prototype of the resurrection of believers (Rom 8:11; 1 Cor 15:48–58; Phil 3:10–11).

Similarly, the gift of the Spirit is the deposit and guarantee of the new age yet to come in its fullness (2 Cor 1:22; 5:5; Eph 1:13–14), and it is given to strengthen believers until the *parousia* of the Lord (1 Cor 1:7). The new creation that Isaiah looked ahead to (Isa 32:14–18; 65:17; 66:22) is embryonically present in believers

---

33. Craig R. Koester, *The Word of Life: A Theology of John's Gospel* (Grand Rapids: Eerdmans, 2008), 176.

(2 Cor 5:17; Gal 6:15) as a sneak preview of the recreated cosmos (Rom 8:20–23). While Paul knows the difference between the present age and the one to come (Eph 1:21), he also knows that the two ages now overlap. Paul can say in Romans 6:4 that believers have been crucified and buried with Christ so that they may walk in the newness of life (in the present), and yet in the future they will be united with him in a resurrection like his. More acutely, in Ephesians and Colossians, Paul can regard believers as *already* raised and reigning with Christ in spiritual unity with the risen and exalted Savior (Eph 2:5–6; Col 2:12; 3:1). The dynamic interface of the now and not yet influences Paul's understanding of salvation. Redemption, freedom, inheritance, and righteousness can be spoken of as something that believers participate in during the present time, but also as something they still anticipate for the future.

Elsewhere, the concept of the kingdom of God in Paul is most of the time a future object of hope (1 Cor 6:9–10; 15:24, 50; Gal 5:21; 1 Thess 2:12; 2 Thess 1:5; 2 Tim 4:1, 18; though see Rom 14:17 and Col 1:13, which connote present experiences of God's kingship). In the scenario Paul envisages, he sees the end as involving the salvation of "all Israel" (Rom 11:25) and finds its apex in the "day of the Lord" (1 Cor 1:8; 5:5; 2 Cor 1:14; 1 Thess 5:2; 2 Thess 2:2).[34] Paul's eschatology is at its root apocalyptic since the death and resurrection of Jesus mean that the clocks have been switched forward and Paul calls people to read the sign of the times and to prepare for the final eschatological showdown. Ahead of that day the saving power of God is already expressing itself in the Son and the Spirit, so that God's people are anticipating the verdict and vindication of the final judgment and looking forward to the renewal all things.

Revelation, the most forward-looking book of the New Testament, has a surprising amount of attention given to the present experience of its audience. This book, with symbols resting upon symbols and metaphors piled upon metaphors, narrates an enigmatic and encoded story of the triumph of God through his Messiah over Satan. John the Seer reiterates the struggle of God's people in their witness against compromise and persecution. He knows that Satan, the beast, and the false prophet will be consigned to the "lake of burning sulfur" (Rev 19:20; 20:10); Babylon the Great will be thrown down (17:1–19:5); and John looks ahead to a glorious day when the kingdoms of this world are supplanted by the kingdom of the Lord and his Messiah (11:15–19). All of this introduces the consummation of a new heaven and a new earth, where God dwells with his people forever (21:1–22:5).

Yet ahead of those events much can still be said. Believers have already been liberated from their sins by the blood of the Lamb and formed into a kingdom of priests (Rev 1:5–6; 5:9–10; 12:11). God has expelled Satan from heaven (12:9),

---

34. Michael F. Bird, *A Bird's-Eye View of Paul: The Man, His Mission and His Message* (Nottingham, UK: Inter-Varsity Press, 2008), 114–23.

and though he scours the earth to attack believers, the faithful must endure torrid trials (3:10; 13:10; 14:12) and persevere to receive their reward (2:7, 11, 17, 26; 3:5, 12, 21; 15:2, 21:7). In the end, "the cross of Christ is the fulcrum of history; he has redeemed believers from sin. Still, they must suffer and endure until Jesus returns and recompenses their enemies."[35]

Thus the "last days" do not refer to the final period before a tribulation or the final moments preceding the *parousia*. The "last days" began with the first advent of Jesus. At the same time, the future element remains constant throughout. There will be a final judgment, and believers look forward to a bodily resurrection. There (probably!) awaits a messianic reign of Christ over the earth where he subjugates his enemies, followed by a new heaven and a new earth.

The best analogy of how Christians live between the "now" and the "not yet" is that given by Oscar Cullmann. Christians stand metaphorically between "D-Day" and "VE-Day" of World War II. Jesus' first coming was like the allied landing at Normandy (D-Day), where Jesus defeated Satan by his death and resurrection, while his second coming will be like the formal surrender of Germany to the allies ("VE-Day"), when Jesus subjugates all hostile forces to God's reign. As Cullman put it: "The hope of the final victory is so much more vivid because of the unshakably firm conviction that the battle that decides the victory has already taken place."[36] An inaugurated scheme of eschatology can be pictorialized as follows:

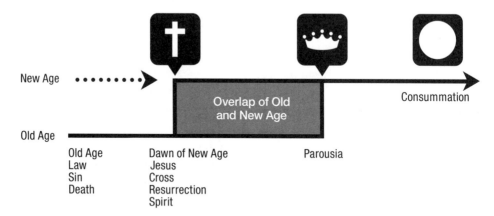

In eschatology it is possible to overemphasize either the present or future aspect. We see there are warnings about both extremes in apostolic instruction. To begin with, in the Pastoral Letters, we are told about Hymenaeus and Philetus, who

---

35. Schreiner, *New Testament Theology*, 113.
36. Oscar Cullmann, *Christ and Time* (trans. Floyd V. Filson; Philadelphia: Westminster, 1950), 84.

departed from the truth by saying that "the resurrection has already taken place, and they destroy the faith of some" (2 Tim 2:17–18). Given Paul's statements that believers are already "raised with Christ" in the sense of sharing new life (Eph 2:5–6; Col 2:12; 3:1), one can conceive how the inference of Hymenaeus and Philetus came about. The same proclivity to collapse future expectations into present experiences occurred in later literature like the ascetic *Acts of Paul and Thecla* ("The resurrection ... has already taken place; it has come about in the children we have, and knowing the true God we are risen" [14]), and the Gnostic tract *Treatise on the Resurrection* ("The Apostle said, 'We suffered with him, and we arose with him, and we went to heaven with him'" [45]).

According to Irenaeus, the second-century teacher Menander taught that "his disciples obtain the resurrection by being baptized into him, and can die no more, but never grow old and are immortal."[37] The problem here is that some people overemphasized the present experience of faith and were led to abandon belief in a future resurrection by reinterpreting key doctrines on the basis of an internal, individual, and veridical experience. Paul countered this with the "trustworthy saying" that "if we died with him, *we will* also live with him" (2 Tim 2:11, italics added), and he will not surrender the future horizon to the reinterpretation of spiritual enthusiasts because the resurrection of Christ is the brick in the wall of his gospel (2:8).[38]

Somewhat similarly in Thessalonica were reports that "the day of the Lord" (i.e., the *parousia*) had already occurred. Paul writes to them, "Concerning the coming of our Lord Jesus Christ and our being gathered to him, we ask you, brothers and sisters, not to become easily unsettled or alarmed by the teaching allegedly from us—whether by a prophecy or by word of mouth or by letter—asserting that the day of the Lord has already come" (2 Thess 2:1–2). Evidently some prophetic utterance or spurious text had led persons in Thessalonica to think that "the day" had come and gone and they had missed the glorious train. Paul again responds by affirming that the gospel has a future hope to share in the glory of the Lord Jesus Christ, which they do not yet have but will certainly have. What they have is the "firstfruits," not the full harvest. In the interim they need to be encouraged, should keep their hope sure, and be strengthened as they look ahead to that day—a strength that will be needed as the "the lawless one" must first be revealed before the end of all things (2:3–17).

Reinterpreting doctrines of the resurrection and the return of the Lord as having already taken place were not the only eschatological problems encountered in the early church. Whereas some early Christians *inferred* that the future hopes were

---

37. Irenaeus, *Haer.* 1.23.5.
38. Philip H. Towner, *The Letters to Timothy and Titus* (NICNT; Grand Rapids: Eerdmans, 2006), 526–29.

in fact reducible to internalized and individual experiences, other Christians simply *deferred* the future hopes altogether. In 2 Peter there is the report of certain mockers of the faith: "They will say, 'Where is this "coming" he promised? Ever since our ancestors died, everything goes on as it has since the beginning of creation.' But they deliberately forget that long ago by God's word the heavens came into being and the earth was formed out of water and by water" (2 Pet 3:4–5). This group of persons, probably related to the church in some way, scoff at the second coming because death continues and the current manner of the world persists. They mock at the promise of Jesus' "coming" because they are ignorant of the power of God to create a new heaven, they have forgotten the patience of God in giving time for repentance, and they do not comprehend the inscrutability of God's own plan (3:5–13).

It is often alleged that one of the many problems in Corinth that Paul had to deal with was an overrealized eschatology. This apparently explains the denial of the resurrection in 1 Corinthians 15 and why some of the Corinthians had such high opinions of themselves as "already" rich and reigning in 1 Corinthians 4:8–13. So the problem of the spiritual enthusiasts is likened to the case of Hymenaeus and Philetus, who say that the resurrection has already happened.

However, this interpretation will not do. The problem in Corinth was, in fact, not enough eschatology. Some of the Corinthians rejected the resurrection of the body probably because of typical Greek detestation at the prospect of an embodied postmortem afterlife. More acutely, others probably rejected the idea of a future bodily resurrection because resurrection would imply a radical reordering of power that certain influential and socially advanced persons in the church were far from enthusiastic about. The boasting of the Corinthians that Paul ridicules in 1 Corinthians 4:8 ("Already you have all you want! Already you have become rich! You have begun to reign—and that without us! How I wish that you really had begun to reign so that we also might reign with you!") is not about too much eschatology; rather, it repeats the common Greco-Roman maxim that the wise and philosophically savvy are rich, royal, and transcend normal human limitations.

Indeed, 1 Corinthians 1–4 is about the wisdom of the world versus the foolishness of the cross. Some of the Corinthians were puffed up by self-estimates of their own wisdom and knowledge and looked down on other less fortunate people like Paul. To combat this, it is Paul who keeps bringing the apocalyptic worldview and the shadow of the *parousia* to bear against their arrogant boasting, social inequalities, moral deviancy, and theological errors (e.g., 1:8; 11:26; 15:1–58). In terms of application, Richard Hays states:

> Pastors and teachers in our time have the same task that Paul had. We must analyze the ways in which our congregations are linking the gospel with the beliefs and aspirations of surrounding culture and—where this is being done in inappropriate

ways—provide sharply focused critiques and alternatives. Paul models what every pastor must do; he encounters people in a given cultural situation and tries to get them to reshape their lives in light of the gospel by reframing the story within which they live and move.[39]

An overrealized eschatology is ecclesially and ethically unhealthy. It collapses the future revelation of God's coming glory in Jesus Christ into an inward set of experiences that represent a withdrawal of the gospel from the world and a retreat into the emotional space of one's interior existence. It is dangerous because it makes one think that one already has the blessings that God has promised. It is like believing that one already has all the oxygen one needs before plunging into the depths of the ocean without a scuba diver's air tank.

Even more disturbing, I once heard the story of an American church where there were rumors of endemic sexual impropriety among the pastoral staff. The bishop of the congregation called a press conference where he did not deny the allegations; in fact, he celebrated them by telling the journalists that in coming age, "people will neither marry nor be given in marriage; they will be like the angels in heaven" (Matt 22:30). Since he and fellow pastors already live in this promised age, they are no longer bound by the laws of marriage tied to the old age.

Similarly, abandoning the future view of the coming kingdom and trying to bring in the kingdom by social progress will mean the deification of human effort and the exchange of good news for good programs. Let me be clear: it is not that Christians should be uninterested in good works about ending poverty and injustice and in promoting reconciliation and peace. After admonishing the Corinthians about the denial of a resurrection body, he extols them to commit themselves to Christian labor, knowing that what we do is not in vain and will carry over into eternity (1 Cor 15:58). These are *basileianic* acts as they bring the justice and liberation of heaven to bear on earthly circumstances. Yet they are anticipations of the kingdom, cosmetic preparations for something cosmic, and the final dénouement will execute a fundamental and final change in the affairs of the world.

The new Jerusalem will not be brought to us by the same people who gave us New York. There is continuity and discontinuity between the ages, and overplaying the continuity card will lead to an evaporation of the future promises on which we set our hopes. It will also retard our ability to speak prophetically to a culture about the God who will judge the world in righteousness.

The reverse side, of course, is the eschatomaniacs, who plot dates, make calendars, write apocalyptic soap opera novels, and predict the precise time of Christ's

---

39. Richard B. Hays, *First Corinthians* (Interpretation; Louisville: John Knox, 1997), 71.

return. Daniel and Revelation are all they know for preaching material, and they constantly find in these apocalyptic books the presence of contemporary persons that they so brazenly read into the texts. One only has to visit the website called the "Rapture Index" (which gives daily calculations on how close we are to the *parousia* based on the number of natural disasters, apostasy, and left-wing political wins on any given day) to see the danger of too much futurist eschatology. Paul warns about this in 2 Thessalonians 3, where he admonishes those who are so apocalyptically minded that they have ceased to be of any earthly good.

If our Lord returns tomorrow, so be it; let him find us here busy at work as good and faithful servants rather than speculating about dates and arguing over anachronistic interpretations of symbology. Let us not be ignorant of the end (Rom 11:25; 1 Thess 4:13), but let's not be lazy in the interim either (2 Thess 3:6–15). Rather than being obsessed with those who get "left behind," it is better to "encourage one another—and all the more so as [we] see the Day approaching" (Heb 10:25).

3.2.3 SUMMARY OF BIBLICAL ESCHATOLOGY

In sum, the gospel is a kingdom story, a story where God's saving reign is revealed in the lordship of Jesus Christ. To put that simply: God has launched his rescue mission through his Son, and the Son will put the world to right, beginning with his people, and then the whole universe. For God has promised to put all things in subjection to Jesus. And yet, "we do not see everything subject to them. But we do see Jesus, who was made lower than the angels for a little while, now crowned with glory and honor because he suffered death, so that by the grace of God he might taste death for everyone" (Heb 2:8–9).

The final pages in a story of rebellion and death have been torn up and replaced with a different ending written by the Father, who is the author; Jesus is the protagonist, who saves his bride in the tale, and the Holy Spirit is the ink on the page. We read the story, and yet we are the story. For Christians stand straddled between an age of infamy and an age of glory. We live our lives flanked by horror and hope, misery and majesty, destruction and creation. We dwell amidst the death throes of an evil world dying and amidst the birth pains of a new world being reborn. Like pilgrims we continue to make our way toward the heavenly city, inviting others to join the journey with us, and together we long to see paradise containing the good things that God has already been working out and is prepared to give to those who love him (Rom 8:28; 1 Cor 2:9).

SOME KEY TERMS

Apocalypticism: A sociological phenomenon where a group embraces an apocalyptic eschatology and defines themselves as "insiders" and everyone else as "outsiders." They believe themselves to be the chosen recipients about divinely revealed information concerning the true nature of current affairs and the future course of events.

Apocalypse: A literary genre with a narrative framework in which a revelation is mediated through intermediary beings to a human subject, which discloses a transcendent reality. An apocalypse is distinguished by several types of dualism: this age/coming age, heaven/earth, good/evil, and light/darkness. An apocalypse normally includes several literary traits like journeys to heavenly planes and angelic visits, and it provides insights into the heavenly realm and the future.

Apocalyptic eschatology: A worldview that envisages God's plan to interrupt history because it is currently contrary to God's intended purposes. In contrast, *prophetic eschatology* declares the activity of God within human history and ensures the continued preservation of his people in this age. Thus, while everything apocalyptic is eschatological, not all eschatology is apocalyptic.

Eschatology: The study of last things pertaining to the coming age.

Millennium: The belief that Christ will reign for a thousand years prior to the consummation.

Preterism: An approach to New Testament eschatology that holds that most or all of the scriptural prophecies concerning the end times refer to events in the first centuries of the Common Era.

Tribulation: A period of suffering and testing that will come upon the church ahead of Jesus' second coming.

FURTHER READING

Collins, John J. *The Apocalyptic Imagination: An Introduction to the Jewish Matrix of Christianity*. Los Angeles: Crossroad, 1984.

Morris, Leon. *Apocalyptic*. Grand Rapids: Eerdmans, 1972.

Murphy, Frederick J. "Introduction to Apocalyptic Literature." Pages 1–16 in volume 8, *NIB*.

§ 3.3 THE RETURN OF JESUS CHRIST

3.3.1 THE GOSPEL OF THE *COMING* KINGDOM

The gospel narrates the story of Jesus as the mediator of God's kingdom. Like all good stories it has a gripping conclusion. The final chapter in redemptive history is the one associated with the glorious return of Jesus Christ to establish his kingdom fully and finally. That is why the Nicene Creed affirms that: "He will come again in glory to judge the living and the dead, and his kingdom will have no end." The return of Jesus is not a dispensable part of the Christian faith; it was embedded into Christian creeds because it is so intrinsic to what it means to believe in God and to hope in Jesus. Article 15 of the Lausanne Covenant expounds this tenet of the faith as follows:

> We believe that Jesus Christ will return personally and visibly, in power and glory, to consummate his salvation and his judgment. This promise of his coming is a further spur to our evangelism, for we remember his words that the gospel must first be preached to all nations. We believe that the interim period between Christ's ascension and return is to be filled with the mission of the people of God, who have no liberty to stop before the end. We also remember his warning that false Christs and false prophets will arise as precursors of the final Antichrist. We therefore reject as a proud, self-confident dream the notion that people can ever build a utopia on earth. Our Christian confidence is that God will perfect his kingdom, and we look forward with eager anticipation to that day, and to the new heaven and earth in which righteousness will dwell and God will reign forever. Meanwhile, we rededicate ourselves to the service of Christ and of people in joyful submission to his authority over the whole of our lives.[40]

That is as good a statement as any about the nature and purpose of Christ's second coming. The return of the Lord Jesus will consummate what he began at his

---

40. See http://www.lausanne.org/en/documents/lausanne-covenant.html.

first coming. He will be by might what he is by right: the Cosmocrator, the King of kings, the Lord of the universe. The Lausanne Covenant reiterates here what the ancient creeds have affirmed—that the show is not over yet and Jesus still has one vital act left to perform.

There is ample biblical witness to the reality and nature of Jesus' return. The Apocalypse of John culminates in the return of Jesus to bring in a new heaven and a new earth, which is described as a wedding banquet (Rev 21–22). Paul in several of his letters (esp. 1–2 Thess), spends much time explaining the Lord's return and its various corollaries. The gospel of John, for all its personal and realized eschatology, does not lose sight of the fact that Jesus made a promise to his disciples (and by implication to *all* disciples): "If I go and prepare a place for you, I will come back and take you to be with me that you also may be where I am" (John 14:3).

In addition, although the gospel proclamation focuses on Jesus' life, death, and resurrection, it also includes a future element. The gospel announces how the appointed Judge becomes our appointed Savior. The gospel declares a word about a future judgment (Rom 2:16), and it offers a hope of sharing in the glory of the Lord Jesus at his return (2 Thess 2:14). The gospel presupposes that all humanity will face the Lord Jesus at his return and meet him either as Judge or as Savior. What happens immediately before and after the second coming will be discussed later. It is the nature of the return that we intend to explore here.

3.3.2 BIBLICAL WITNESS

The hope for Jesus' return was uniform among the Christian groups who contributed to the formation and canonization of the New Testament. The phrases "second coming" or "second advent" are not found in the New Testament. The earliest reference to a first and second coming appears in the mid-second century with Justin Martyr, who differentiated Jesus' "first coming" from "his second coming."[41] Roughly contemporary with Justin, the Muratorian fragment refers to "his double advent: the first in the humiliation of rejection, which is now past, and the second in the glory of royal power, which is yet in the future."[42] The eschatological structure of early Christian eschatology was two-staged: Christ has come and is coming again.

In the New Testament, the second coming is described with several words and phrases. (1) *Parousia* means, literally, "presence after absence" or "arrival." In the Hellenistic world, this word referred to an epiphany of a god or to the visitation of a ruler to a city.[43] *Parousia* can be used in this noneschatological sense in the New

---

41. Justin Martyr, *Dial.* 14, 40, 54.
42. This translation is by Roberts-Donaldson in ANF vol. 5; see www.earlychristianwritings.com/text/muratorian.html.
43. Deissmann, *LAE*, 368–72.

Testament of someone's visit (1 Cor 16:17; 2 Cor 7:6–7; 10:10; Phil 1:26; 2:12), though generally it is used "of [Jesus'] Messianic Advent in glory to judge the world at the end of this age" (1 Cor 15:23; 1 Thess 2:19; 3:13; 4:15; 5:23; 2 Thess 2:1, 8; Jas 5:7; 2 Pet 1:16; 3:4, 12; 1 John 2:28).[44] The *parousia* is the royal visitation of Jesus to his people as their King and Savior.

(2) *Epiphaneia* means "manifestation" or "appearance." It is used of the incarnation (2 Tim 1:10) and of Christ's return (2 Thess 2:8; 1 Tim 6:14; 2 Tim 4:1, 8; Titus 2:13). The image is chiefly focused on the appearance of salvation with the advent of the Savior. In the case of 2 Thessalonians 2:8, Paul refers to the "appearance of his coming" (ESV; *epiphaneia tēs parousias autou*). The combination of *epiphaneia* and *parousia* is not redundant, for *epiphaneia* refers to the salvation that goes into effect when the *parousia* takes place.[45]

(3) *Apokalypsis* is translatable as "revelation" and "revealing" and signifies the divine disclosure of Jesus on the last day (1 Cor 1:7; 2 Thess 1:7; 1 Pet 1:7, 13; 4:13).[46] The book of Revelation titles itself "The Apocalypse of Jesus Christ" (*Apokalypsis Iēsou Christou*) in Revelation 1:1; this identifies the book as a prophetic unveiling of truth from and about Jesus Christ and his future.

(4) Finally, *hē hēmera tou kuriou* is "the day of the Lord." This phrase is taken up from the Old Testament (e.g., Amos 5:18, 20; Obad 15; Zeph 1:7, 14; Zech 12:4) and is linked to Christ's advent in several passages, principally in the context of judgment (1 Cor 1:8; 5:5; 2 Cor 1:14; Phil 1:6, 10; 2:16; 1 Thess 5:2; 2 Thess 2:2).[47]

The Old Testament has much to contribute to eschatology in general with its emphasis on God's covenantal purposes, the manifestation of God's kingdom, the promise of redemption from sins, the coming of a new Davidic king, hope for a new covenant, a renewed Israel, a day of judgment, and a restored creation.[48] Yet because of the progressive nature of God's revelation, the Old Testament contributes virtually nothing to our knowledge of the second coming. The messianic elements of the Old Testament point almost exclusively to the first coming of Christ through prophecy and typology. However, there are seeming anticipations of God's everlasting kingdom to be established over the earth and intimations of a human ruler over it. The book of Daniel looks ahead to the universal and everlasting dominion of God that encompasses the entire earth (Dan 2:44; 6:26; 7:27), and other passages foresee a specially designated ruler to reign over it (Gen 49:10; Ps 110:1–2; Isa 9:7).

Even so, the fact remains that no Old Testament text refers to a second visitation of the Lord's anointed to establish a messianic kingdom. Moreover, the Old

---

44. BDAG, 781.
45. Ibid., 386.
46. See also the verb *apokalyptō* (Luke 17:30; Rom 1:17–18; 1 Cor 3:13; 1 Pet 5:1).
47. Bird, "Parousia," 439.
48. Cf. A. A. Hoekema, *The Bible and the Future* (Grand Rapids: Eerdmans, 1979), 3–12.

Testament texts thought to allude to the second coming most probably do not. The book of Daniel contains court narratives from the Babylonian and Persian periods and a series of eschatological visions that achieved their final form during the Maccabean crisis of 164–67 BC.[49] Interestingly enough, several early Christian Syrian commentators, who knew the history of Palestine better than their Western counterparts, identified the Maccabean revolt as the context for understanding Daniel's visions.[50]

In the vision of Daniel 7, the four beasts represent Babylon, Media, Persia, and Greece (7:1–8). The "one like a son of man," who receives authority, glory, and power over the nations in 7:13–14, is symbolic for God's people, God's kingdom, and God's anointed king over and against the pagan kingdoms, pagan people, and pagan kings (esp. the arrogant "horn" in 7:8, 11, 20–21).[51] Dan 7:13 is not about the *parousia* of Jesus Christ, but it is richly laden imagery for the vindication and enthronement of God's people in the aftermath of oppression (see 7:18). The "one like a son of man" comes before the "Ancient of Days" and receives a kingdom, but the direction of his coming is rather ambiguous. Although many evangelical commentators read this as a *descent* from heaven to earth by Jesus, it is just as well an *ascent* from earth to heaven. As we will soon see, Daniel 7:13 was used in the New Testament primarily with reference to Jesus' ascension and enthronement rather than to his *parousia*.

Coming to Daniel 9:24–27, the angelic report pertains to events that belong to the Maccabean period with the desecration of the temple ordered by Antiochus Epiphanes IV and his persecution of the Jewish way of life. Endless speculations about the "seventy 'sevens'" (9:24) that correlate the restoration of Jerusalem with the establishment of the modern secular state of Israel (9:25), an identification of the death of the "Anointed One" with the crucifixion of Jesus (9:26), and placing the whole narrative within an apocalyptic tribulation of the last days are about as convincing as vows of fidelity in a Hollywood wedding ceremony.[52]

I understand the appeal of reading Jesus into this text by Christian authors, but the literary and historical context mitigate against such a reading. If we read Daniel in its Second Temple Jewish context and look at how New Testament authors appropriate the imagery, we will get a good picture of how the book of Daniel shaped future hopes verbalized by Jesus and was appropriated in early Christian

---

49. For evangelical Old Testament scholars who take this approach, see John E. Goldingay, *Daniel* (WBC; Dallas: Word, 1989); Ernest C. Lucas, *Daniel* (AOTC; Leicester, UK: Apollos, 2002); and R. Glenn Wooden's forthcoming commentary on Daniel in the NICOT series.

50. On Christian Syrian interpretation of Daniel, see P. M. Casey, *Son of Man: The Interpretation and Influence of Daniel 7* (London: SPCK, 1979), ch. 3.

51. Bird, *Are You the One Who Is to Come?* 78–87.

52. For a typical example of the problem I am talking about see Charles Ryrie, *Basic Theology* (Wheaton, IL: Victor, 1986), 465–66. For a better reading of Dan 9:24–27, see Lucas, *Daniel*, 240–54.

eschatologies. For a case in point, the "abomination that causes desolation" (Dan 9:27; 11:31; 12:11) caused by Antiochus IV Epiphanes's putting a statue of Zeus in the Most Holy Place is an act that Jesus believed would be replicated before the destruction of the Jerusalem temple in his own generation (Matt 24:15/Mark 13:14). Similarly, Antiochus IV Epiphanes is the arrogant "horn" (Dan 7:8, 11, 20–21; 8:9) who persecuted God's people and serves as the prototype of "the lawless one" (2 Thess 2:2–3) and the "beast" of Revelation who opposes the church (esp. Rev. 13).

Furthermore, we need only examine Daniel 12:1–2 to see that the Maccabean emergency was not the end of the show as a final resurrection is still to take place. Jesus and the first Christian generation happily affirmed this Danielic narrative of suffering and vindication. But Daniel does not provide a front row seat for the second coming or a timetable for a tribulation; rather, he tells a story of how God's people shift from defeat to dominion and how they recapture their Adamic vocation as master and commander of creation through their arch-representative, the mysterious "son of man." That story gave hope to Judeans facing religious and ethnic annihilation under the Seleucids, and it shaped the language of Jesus' teachings about his role and mission in relation to God's kingdom.[53]

On the back of that—I know the claim is controversial—is the contentious issue of what is meant in the Gospels when Jesus refers to the *parousia* of the Son of Man (Matt 10:23; 16:27–28 [Mark 9:1/Luke 9:26]; Matt 24/Mark 13/Luke 21 [Luke 12:40; 17:22]; Matt 25:31; Luke 18:8; Matt 26:64/Mark 14:62/Luke 21:27). While it is traditional to identify them as predictions of Jesus' return, I'm persuaded that they refer to the destruction of the temple in AD 70. It seems to me that on close inspection, the *coming* of the Son of Man sayings refer to a significant stage in the ushering in of the kingdom and the vindication of Jesus as the prophet sent to Israel. My take is that most, if not all, of the Son of Man *parousia* sayings predict the vindication of Jesus and his followers in their opposition to the temple establishment when the temple fell to the Romans forces in AD 70. This proved that Jesus was a true prophet and Jesus' followers were the new temple of God's Spirit.

Obviously what stands in the background of these sayings is Daniel 7. Now if we read this vision about the Son of Man as a cipher for the vindication of God's people rather than the prediction of the cosmic return of an individual from heaven, we can make a lot more sense of the material before us in the Gospels. Daniel 7 sets forth a well-worn biblical pattern of suffering and vindication situated in corporate terms, where the Son of Man's exaltation and enthronement can be understood as the vindication of the saints. When this interpretation is applied to the Gospels,

---

53. Cf. Wright, *New Testament and People of God*, 291–97; idem, *Jesus and the Victory of God*, 360–67; Craig A. Evans, "Defeating Satan and Liberating Israel: Jesus and Daniel's Visions," *JSHJ* 1 (2003): 161–70.

the picture that emerges is that Jesus pronounced judgment against faithless Israel and the wicked Judean leadership. Also this judgment would be manifested in the destruction of the temple, which would constitute the vindication of Jesus himself and his followers. Let me give three examples of three difficult texts that underscore what I am saying.

First is the enigmatic pronouncement by Jesus in Matthew's missionary discourse: "When you are persecuted in one place, flee to another. Truly I tell you, you will not finish going through the towns of Israel before the Son of Man comes" (Matt 10:23). Jesus exhorts the disciples to proclaim the gospel to their fellow Judeans, and before they are finished the Son of Man will come. If we take this as a straight-out *parousia* reference, as many do, we are faced with a small but significant problem: Jesus was wrong! Moreover, if Matthew is writing around the 80s of the first century, then he, his audience, and his subsequent readers know full well that Jesus did not return in the limited time span nominated. One can compensate for this by thinking that it refers to Jewish evangelism throughout the centuries, but that would hardly come to the mind of Jesus' disciples or even to Matthew's readers. More probable is that it refers to some other event that transpired after a concerted mission to the Jews in Palestine. In support we can note that the "coming of the Son of Man" in Matthew seems to bear the same conceptual domain as the "coming of the kingdom," and for that reason has an indeterminate point of reference.[54]

In addition, we can point to another Matthean saying that is similarly enigmatic as it is problematic. At the end of the Caesarea Philippi scene, Jesus states: "Truly I tell you, some who are standing here will not taste death before they see the Son of Man coming in his kingdom" (Matt 16:28). Notably Matthew changes Mark's "kingdom of God has come with power" (Mark 9:1) to "the Son of Man coming in his kingdom." We are left asking, what exactly is being spoken about here? If we take this to be a *parousia* reference, Jesus was obviously wrong because the disciples did die before the event and nothing more need be said. Then again, given that the transfiguration story follows immediately after, perhaps the transfiguration, as a glorious foretaste of the kingdom, could be the intended referent. However, the disciples did not exactly face death in the mere six days that separated the pronouncement from the transfiguration.

More likely, therefore, Matthew 16:27–28 involves another event or sequence of events, including Jesus' crucifixion, given the context of passion predictions running from Matthew 16:21–17:13.[55] Furthermore, the word "power" is suggestive of something beyond Jesus' death and could include resurrection, exaltation, and

---

54. D. A. Carson, "Matthew," in *EBC* (1985), 8:235.
55. Cf. Michael F. Bird, "The Crucifixion of Jesus as the Fulfilment of Mark 9:1," *TrinJ* 24 (2003): 23–36.

maybe even something retributive like the destruction of Jerusalem. The point of 10:23 is that those persecuted for their missionary endeavors in Jesus' name will experience vindication at the Son of Man's coming. The point of 16:27 is that those who remain loyal to Jesus as he turns his face to go to Jerusalem will see the Son of Man's kingdom in all its power. Whatever we think of these sayings, we must identify their fulfillment within the lifetime of the original audience.

That brings us now to the Olivet Discourse of Matthew 24:1–36/Mark 13:1–37/Luke 21:5–36. Since the Markan version is the earliest, I'll concentrate on his account. To begin with, I and many others consider strange the popular understanding where Jesus' disciples brag about the adornments of the temple, Jesus responds that every stone of this great religious monument will be thrown down, and the disciples follow up by asking what will be the sign that such things are about to happen, that Jesus then responds in effect, "Forget that; let me tell you about my second coming!" (Mark 13:1–5). More likely, the speech is an exposition of their initial question, namely, when will the temple be destroyed. The content of Mark 13:5–23 concerns the tumultuous events leading up to the sacking of Jerusalem, including rumors of war, war itself, earthquakes, famine, persecution of missionaries by authorities, beginnings of the Gentile mission, familial discord, desecration of the temple, messianic pretenders, false prophets, and the flow of refugees.

The subject of Mark 13:24–28 is the coming of the Son of Man (esp. v. 26). The accompanying language about the sun and moon being darkened, stars falling, and heavenly bodies shaken is not literal, as it invests a sociopolitical disaster with cosmic imagery in order to underscore its catastrophic significance. We are not meant to hear this as a weather report about Jerusalem that is followed with "and the rest of Galilee and Judea can expect scattered showers with light to moderate northeasterly winds." All in all, these are the portentous events surrounding the destruction of Jerusalem (something Luke makes even clearer in Luke 19:42–44; 21:30). It is not the end of *the* world, but the end of *a* world, the symbolic universe of first-century Judaism connected with the temple. All that the temple stood for is out, and the Son of Man is in.[56]

Now it may be possible to take the exhortations about watchfulness in Mark 13:32–37 as referring to Jesus' subsequent *parousia*, which occurs at a later day,[57] or to detect a merging of historical and eschatological referents throughout the speech,[58] but this is far from certain. The most natural point of reference is that the entire speech signifies the destruction of Jerusalem, which is a vindication of Jesus

---

56. R. T. France, *The Gospel of Mark* (NIGTC; Grand Rapids: Eerdmans, 2002), 501.

57. Cf. ibid., 501, 541–46.

58. As arguably happens in Matt 24:1–25:46. Note how Matthew changes the disciples' question in Matt 24:3 to "what will be the sign of your coming and of the end of the age" rather than to the simple destruction of the temple as in Mark 13:4. See R. T. France, *Gospel of Matthew* (NICNT; Grand Rapids: Eerdmans, 2005), 889–94; also James R. Edwards, *The Gospel according to Mark* (PNTC; Grand Rapids: Eerdmans, 2002), 383–409.

as the prophet who opposed the temple. That is confirmed by the allusion in Mark 13:28 back to Jesus' teaching about the fig tree in 11:12–23, which intimated the destruction of the temple. Another confirmation is the mention of "this generation" in Mark 13:30, who are not those alive at the *parousia*, but are those alive when the destruction of the temple takes place, because "this generation" in Jesus' teaching always refers to his recalcitrant and unbelieving Judean contemporaries (see Matt 11:16; 12:41–32, 45; 23:36; Mark 8:12, 38). I conclude, therefore, that the Olivet Discourse does not *directly* involve events beyond AD 70.[59]

Andrew Perriman has composed a "Titanic" parable about how Jesus' followers might have regarded Jesus' prophecy of the destruction of the temple and the overthrow of the religious structures that went with it:

> Let us imagine first-century Judaism as a ship—a splendid but badly run ship in which the officers and crew mistreat the passengers and squabble and fight over who should have control of the vessel. Blinded by their obsessions and jealousies, no one on the bridge notices that the ship is drifting towards a ferocious eschatological storm. When one or two men raise the alarm, they are seized as trouble-markers, brutally beaten, and thrown overboard. As the winds tear at the rigging and waves wash across the deck, a few brave souls decide to heed the warnings; they lower a lifeboat and take their chances on the rough seas. To the passengers and crew who stay on board this seems a reckless and disloyal move—and at times those clinging desperately to each other in the belly of the small boat, as it pitches and rolls, wonder if they have made the right choice. Some are swept overboard, some die from exposure and hunger. They cry out to the dark heavens, praying that the storm would cease. But they do not give up hope; they believe that they have done the right thing. Then from a distance they watch in horror as the ship strikes rocks and sinks with massive loss of life—they are appalled, but they also feel vindicated. Eventually the wind drops, the waves subside. The lifeboat runs ashore on a sandy beach. They have come to the end of the end; they have survived. This is the beginning of a new age.[60]

Another key text to examine is Jesus' answer to Caiaphas's question whether he is the Messiah, the Son of the Blessed One: "'I am,' said Jesus. 'And you will see the Son of Man sitting at the right hand of the Mighty One and coming on the clouds of heaven'" (Mark 14:62). The words here are a conflation of Psalm 110:1 and Daniel 7:13; both refer to the enthronement of a figure beside God. Ordinarily, Mark 14:62 is taken as a *parousia* prediction, whereby Jesus retorts to Caiaphas that he is the appointed judge who will bring judgment at the last day. However, despite a few dissenters,[61] the vast majority of commentators now regard this passage as an

---

59. Scot McKnight, *A New Vision for Israel: The Teachings of Jesus in National Context* (Grand Rapids: Eerdmans, 1999), 130–39.

60. Andrew Perriman, *The Coming Son of Man: New Testament Eschatology for an Emerging Church* (Milton Keynes, UK: Paternoster, 2005), 224.

allusion to Jesus' exaltation to the right hand of the Father.[62] Much like Mark 13:26, the "Son of Man" is enthroned and given authority by God for judgment.

What matters here is not the direction of the Son of Man's coming, but the transfer of sovereignty, the display of judgment, and the enthronement of the Son of Man beside God.[63] This meshes comfortably with the framework of ascent and enthronement in Daniel 7, upon which Jesus' words are indebted. Moreover, the parallels in Matthew 26:64 ("*from now on* [*ap' arti*] you will see the Son of Man sitting at the right hand of the Mighty One") and Luke 22:69 ("*from now on* [*apo tou nun*] the Son of Man will be seated at the right hand of the mighty God," italics added in both cases) are even more clearly understood as references to enthronement rather than to a future return from heaven.

I have to acknowledge objections to the preterist interpretation of Mark 13 that I have just given. Douglas Moo, an exegete I tremendously respect, writes:

> First, the association of Jesus' 'coming' with clouds (dependent on Dan. 7:13) always has reference to the Parousia in the New Testament. Second the cosmic signs of Mark 13:24–25 are held by the author of Revelation to be future (6:14–17)—and he is probably writing *after* A.D. 70.[64]

The problem is that Moo's first point is obviously false in light of our discussion of Mark 14:62 and parallels that can be located against Jesus' exaltation. Second, identifying Mark 13 as relating to the destruction of Jerusalem does not mean that all eschatological hopes were exhausted by that date. The destruction of Jerusalem is itself the beginning of the final judgment, a judgment that will encompass the whole world, not just one city.

Furthermore, the imagery of Mark 13, like much prophetic eschatology and apocalyptic visions, is allusive and is open to reapplication to a wider and more comprehensive scenario. Matthew arguably converges the destruction of Jerusalem with the second coming in his version of the Olivet Discourse, whereas Luke makes it even clearer that AD 70 is in view. Yet even Luke cannot resist looking a bit farther ahead. He knows that Jerusalem will be trampled "until the times of the Gentiles are fulfilled" (Luke 21:24), and he sees ahead to a judgment that will come upon "the face of the whole earth" (21:35). George Caird comments:

> Luke made his own peculiar contribution to New Testament eschatology, by distin-

---

61. Cf., e.g., Robert H. Gundry, *Mark: A Commentary on His Apology for the Cross* (Grand Rapids: Baker, 1993), 886–87.

62. Cf. France, *Gospel of Mark*, 611–13.

63. Perriman, *The Coming Son of Man*, 55, 61.

64. Douglas J. Moo, "The Case for the Post-Tribulation Rapture Position," in *Three Views of the Rapture: Pre-, Mid-, Or Post-Tribulation?* (ed. S. N. Gundry; Grand Rapids: Zondervan, 1984), 192. See also George R. Beasley-Murray, *Jesus and the Future* (London: Macmillan, 1954), 167–71; Wayne Grudem, *Systematic Theology: An Introduction to Biblical Doctrine* (Grand Rapids: Zondervan, 1994), 1126; Michael S. Horton, *The Christian Faith* (Grand Rapids: Zondervan, 2011), 939–40.

guishing those parts of the Church's expectation which had already been fulfilled in his day from those that remained outstanding. The crisis which Jesus had predicted would happen within a generation, bring death to himself, persecution to his disciples, and destruction to Jerusalem was now accomplished; Luke and his contemporaries were living in a period of indeterminate length, the times of the Gentiles, during which God's judgment on Jerusalem must run its course, and only after that would the End come and with it the consummation of the kingdom.[65]

Don't be confused; I'm not saying that the whole eschatological scenario was wrapped by AD 70—I am not hyper-preterist![66] In the teaching of Jesus and the early church there is ample evidence of a perspective beyond AD 70. Jesus taught that the kingdom of God had a future installment with a consummation at the "renewal of all things" with himself installed as king (Matt 19:28/Luke 22:29–30). A lot in Jesus' teaching focuses on the theme of judgment and hell that requires a futurist orientation (e.g., Matt 23:33; Mark 9:45–47; Luke 12:5). The clearest reference to the second coming on the lips of Jesus appears in the Fourth Gospel: "If I go and prepare a place for you, I will come back and take you to be with me that you also may be where I am" (John 14:3), where Jesus promises to return to take his disciples into his heavenly state. Among the final words of Jesus in this gospel are "until I return" (21:23). According to Peter's speech in Solomon's Colonnade: "Heaven must receive him *until the time comes* for God to restore everything, as he promised long ago through his holy prophets" (Acts 3:21, italics added).

Thus, early Christian readings of the Old Testament looked forward to a renewal of all things that would take place when Jesus returned to finish his kingdom work. That article of faith was umbilically connected to Jesus' teaching, but for the most part Jesus' return appears to be a corollary of his ascension. The angelic witnesses inform the disciples: "'Men of Galilee,' they said, 'why do you stand here looking into the sky? This same Jesus, who has been taken from you into heaven, will come back in the same way you have seen him go into heaven'" (Acts 1:11). If Jesus is exalted to God's right hand, surely he will be the one who comes again to put the kingdom into full effect.

The New Testament letters provide further insight into Jesus' return. Paul refers to the *parousia* on several occasions. Within the Thessalonian correspondence, he mentions in passing that the Thessalonian believers are "our hope, our joy, or the crown in which we will glory in the presence of our Lord Jesus when he comes

---

65. George B. Caird, *Saint Luke* (London: Penguin, 1963), 229.

66. Cf. N. T. Wright (*Surprised by Hope* [New York: HarperOne, 2008], 127): "Nor will it do to say, as do some who grasp the point but have not worked it through, that the events of A.D. 70 were themselves the second coming of Jesus so that ever since then we have been living in God's new age and there is no further coming to await ... Jesus' vindication—in his resurrection, ascension, and judgment on Jerusalem—requires still a further event for everything to be complete."

[*parousia*]" (1 Thess 2:19). Paul hopes they will be "blameless and holy in the presence of our God and Father when our Lord Jesus comes with all his holy ones" (3:13). Paul appeals to "the Lord's word"—either a saying from Jesus or a prophetic utterance about Jesus—that those who have already died will not miss out on the *parousia*. Thereafter, "the Lord himself will come down from heaven, with a loud command, with the voice of the archangel and with the trumpet call of God, and the dead in Christ will rise first" (4:16).

In Philippians we read, "we eagerly await a Savior from there [heaven], the Lord Jesus Christ, who, by the power that enables him to bring everything under his control, will transform our lowly bodies so that they will be like his glorious body" (Phil 3:20–21). Similar ideas are found in Colossians: "When Christ, who is your life, appears, then you also will appear with him in glory" (Col 3:4). Paul also contemplates the "blessed hope—the appearing of the glory of our great God and Savior" (Titus 2:13). Joseph Plevnik summarizes Paul's teaching on the *parousia*:

> The parousia is the culmination of Christ's present rule, the beginning of God's kingdom, and the moment for the resurrection of the dead. The Lord's coming is thus the moment for the resurrection of the dead. The Lord's coming is thus the culmination of Christ's own resurrection and of his lordship, which began with that event. Christ was raised as the first of many and as the one through whom all others will be brought to life. And he was made Lord so that he may put everything under his feet. The parousia is also the culmination of the present existence "in Christ." Those who belong to Christ will be with Christ at his coming.[67]

Outside of Paul, the author of Hebrews states that Christ "will appear a second time, not to bear sin, but to bring salvation to those who are waiting for him" (Heb 9:28). A beautiful description of the second coming is offered by John in 1 John 3:2: "we know that when Christ appears, we shall be like him, for we shall see him as he is."

Revelation is strangely silent about the actual circumstances surrounding Christ's return, owing to the fact that Jesus' return is a transcendent reality that comes to history rather than merely a historical occurrence. In fact, the word *parousia* does not even occur in the book! Instead, in the initial vision report, the audience is exhorted: "'Look, he is coming with the clouds,' and 'every eye will see him, even those who pierced him;' and all peoples on earth 'will mourn because of him'" (Rev 1:7). The most vivid description of the event is 19:10–21, which depicts "heaven standing open" and Jesus appears as a mighty warrior to destroy his enemies. Revelation is emphatic that Jesus' coming is imminent (1:7; 2:5, 16; 3:3,

---

67. Joseph Plevnik, *Paul and the Parousia: An Exegetical and Theological Investigation* (Peabody, MA: Hendrickson, 1997), 328.

> # IN A NUTSHELL: THE RETURN OF JESUS
>
> - As Millard Erickson writes: "Jesus' return will be personal and bodily, and thus perceivable and unmistakable" (Acts 1:11).[68]
> - His return will be accompanied with angels (1 Thess 3:13; Jude 14; cf. Zech 14:5).
> - Reference to a trumpet at his return is symbolic for the royal nature of the event (Isa 27:13; Joel 2:1; Zeph 1:14–16; Matt 24:31; 1 Cor 15:52; 1 Thess 4:16; Rev 11:15). The trumpets mark the arrival of the day of the Lord and are a rallying sound for the gathering of God's people.
> - Around the time of Jesus' return "all Israel" will be saved, meaning a large segment of ethnic or empirical Israel (Rom 11:26).
> - Jesus' return will involve a resurrection of believers (1 Cor 15:20–23, 52; Phil 3:21; 1 Thess 4:14–17; Rev 20:4).
> - At his return Jesus will judge and subjugate all of his enemies (1 Cor 15:24–28; Rev 19:11–21).

11; 16:15; 22:7, 12, 20), and Jesus repeatedly declares "I am coming" (2:5, 16; 3:11; 16:15; 22:7, 12, 20).

The *parousia* is predicated on the promise for an eschatological fulfillment to union with Christ through communion with God in a new creation. The return of Christ is not a repetition of his original coming, nor an addendum to his earthly work; rather, it is the completion of his work of reconciliation. The divide between heaven and earth is melted down at Christ's second advent. Two worlds collide, and the terrestrial world is changed as heaven is permanently imprinted on it. It is the final stage for God to dwell with his people, in his reign, in his place. As C. S. Lewis said, when the author steps onto the stage, the play is over.

3.3.3 ABSENCE MAKES THE HEART GROW FONDER

It is interesting that Paul concludes his description of the Lord's Supper with the words: "For whenever you eat this bread and drink this cup, you proclaim the Lord's

---

68. Millard J. Erickson, "Second Coming of Christ," in *EDT*, 993.

death until he comes" (1 Cor 11:26). The meal that believers regularly celebrated was not just a celebration of Jesus' death and resurrection; it looked forward to his return. Though Christ is "spiritually" present at the meal, he was "physically" absent from the church. When the risen Jesus said to his disciples, "I am with you always, to the very end of the age" (Matt 28:20), his presence is mediated through the Spirit who indwells the church, who are themselves the physical representatives of Christ on earth. Jesus remains united with his people by the Spirit, and he even indwells his people; yet there is still an anticipation for a fuller and physical communion between Christ and the church that is yet to come. That "day" is the return of Christ to bring judgment, raise believers to life, and establish an everlasting kingdom.

Salvation is past, present and ... future. The kingdom is now and ... not yet. Thus, the gospel of the kingdom orientates us toward the future day when Christ fulfills the work he began in his earthly life. That is why believers are constantly exhorted to "wait for" the return of the Lord Jesus Christ, who will bring hope, glory, light, mercy, praise, salvation, redemption, rescue, and righteousness to believers in their fullest sense (1 Cor 1:7; 4:5; Phil 3:20; 1 Thess 1:10; Titus 2:13; Heb 9:28; Jas 5:8; Jude 21; Rev 6:11). This is the prayer of all Christians in every generation, amidst the trials and tribulations of life and death: *marana tha*, "Come, Lord" (1 Cor 16:22; Rev 22:20; *Did.* 10.6). Such a prayer recognizes that this world is not our home. Though we colonize it now with the life of heaven for the king-in-waiting, it is his last battle that we so desperately look for, so that at that time "God may be all in all" (1 Cor 15:28).

What I think is perhaps the most joyous image of the second coming is the "wedding supper of the Lamb" (Rev 19:9). This is identical to the feast in the messianic kingdom that Jesus referred to (Matt 26:29/Mark 14:25/Luke 22:18). It is one and the same with the great banquet that will feature Jews and Gentiles breaking bread with the patriarchs (Matt 8:11–12/Luke 13:28–29). The new creation becomes the holy mountain of the Lord, where Gentiles come to dine with God (Isa 25:6–8). Indeed, one of the most blessed words of Scripture comes from Exodus 24:11, where it is reported that the Israelites "saw God, and they ate and drank."

At this heavenly wedding, the church—made up of people from every tribe, language, people, and nation—is received by Jesus Christ, the bridegroom. A wedding feast is a powerful image because it conveys notions of celebration and consummation as well as feasting, family, festivity, and fellowship all rolled in one. In rabbinic teaching and in Middle Eastern village life, it was customary for a bridegroom to spend a great deal of time preparing the bridal chamber and making ready the preparation for the wedding day. When his father was satisfied with the preparations, the bridegroom was permitted to go and "fetch" his bride. On the evening of the wedding day, a band of groomsmen would make a noisy and joyous procession with music and merriment across the village toward the bride's house, where the bride and bridesmaids would be ready and waiting. The procession would carry the bride across the village and arrive back at the house of the bridegroom's father. Then the bridegroom would receive the bride, there would be a blessing of the union, the marriage would be consummated, and several days of feasting would begin (see Matt 25:1–13).[69] The second coming is the bridegroom receiving the bride. The church waits in purity and with purpose for the bridegroom to take her into his home. Then the celebrations can really begin.

The second coming of the Lord warrants consideration of several implications concerning the spirituality of believers and the mission of the church.

(1) *Evangelize*. In view of the imminence of Jesus' coming, believers are to set themselves to the task of announcing the good news that the Lord Jesus has died and risen and will come again as judge. In Jesus' name, the church is to preach the forgiveness of sins, and to declare that the sufferings and injustices of this age are set to end. In Matthew's Olivet Discourse, which blends the historical and eschatological together, "this gospel of the kingdom will be preached in the whole world as a testimony to all nations, and then the end will come (Matt 24:14). Paul's conviction that "time is short" (1 Cor 7:29) arguably urged him on in intense evangelistic fervor to proclaim the gospel (9:16). Hence eschatology is the engine for mission. And mission is an apocalyptic event that advances the gospel through the church's evangelical proclamation and merciful action.[70]

(2) *Endure*. In the parable of the sower, Jesus taught that the seed that landed on the good soil stood for people who, by endurance, produce a fruitful crop (Luke 8:15). Paul constantly exhorted his network of house churches to "endure" their trials because they had assurance that their God would vindicate them from accusation and take them into his presence. He tells the Corinthians that both he and they must show "patient endurance," and they do so knowing that they have the Spirit, which is a deposit "guaranteeing what is to come" (2 Cor 1:6–22). He reminds the Thessalonians of their "endurance inspired by hope in our Lord Jesus Christ" (1 Thess 1:3). These believers are even a model to others: "Therefore, among God's churches we boast about your perseverance and faith in all the persecutions and trials you are enduring. All this is evidence that God's judgment is right, and as a result you will be counted worthy of the kingdom of God, for which you are suffering" (2 Thess 1:4–5).

Endurance under intense duress—from religious, social, and political pressures—is paramount in Revelation. John describes himself as a "brother and

---

69. Cf. Craig S. Keener, "Marriage," in *DNTB*, 685–87; Klyne Snodgrass, *Stories with Intent: A Comprehensive Guide to the Parables of Jesus* (Grand Rapids: Eerdmans, 2008), 510.

70. Cf. Michael F. Bird, "Mission as an Apocalyptic Event: Reflections on Lk. 10:18 and Mk. 13:10," *EvQ* 76 (2004): 117–34.

MOLTMANN AND THE "COMING OF GOD"

Jürgen Moltmann has perhaps done more than any other contemporary theologian to bring eschatology back to the heart of theology. In the mid-1960s, he famously said:

> Christian eschatology does not speak of the future as such.... Christian eschatology speaks of Jesus Christ and *his* future.... Hence the question whether all statements about the future are grounded in the person and history of Jesus Christ provides it with the touchstone by which to distinguish the spirit of eschatology from that of utopia.[71]

Moltmann's "theology of hope" asserts that eschatology is not the last chapter of theology, but the perspective in which all theology is to be understood and assigned its proper meaning. Moltmann's experience as a prisoner of war in Britain (1945–47) shaped him significantly in terms of a coming to faith, and he observed that fellow prisoners who had hope faired the best. In Moltmann's scheme, the coming kingdom creates a confronting and transforming vision for the mission of God's people, who contest and criticize all man-made securities that attempt to erect barriers between people and the reality that is to be manifested in Jesus Christ.

In contrast to Karl Barth, who reduced the *parousia* to an unveiling of what is already true or to a revelation already given in the past history of Jesus, Moltmann objected that this reduced the eschaton to a present sense of eternity, whereas the *parousia* brings a genuine *novum*: something new, something glorious. In *The Coming of God*, Moltmann advocates that "the eschaton is neither the future of time nor timeless eternity. It is God coming and his arrival." Furthermore:

> *The God of hope* is himself *the coming of God* (Isa. 35.4; 40.5). When God comes in his glory, he will fill the universe with his radiance, everyone will see him, and he will swallow up death forever. The future is God's mode of being in history. The power of the future is his power in time. His eternity is not timeless simultaneity; it is the power of his future over every historical time. It is therefore logical that it was not only God himself who was experienced as "the Coming One," but that the conveyers of hope who communicate his coming and prepare men and women for his parousia should also be given this title: the Messiah, the Son of Man, and Wisdom.... If God's being is in his coming, then the future that comes to meet us must become the theological paradigm of transcendence.[72]

---

71. Jürgen Moltmann, *Theology of Hope*, 17.
72. Jürgen Moltmann, *Coming of God* (trans. M. Kohl; London: SCM, 1996), 22, 24 (italics original).

> **FURTHER READING**
>
> Bauckham, Richard (ed.). *God Will Be All in All: The Eschatology of Jürgen Moltmann*. Edinburgh: T&T Clark, 1999.
> Moltmann, Jürgen. *Theology of Hope*. Trans. J. W. Leitch. London: SCM, 1967.
> ———. *The Coming of God*. Trans. M. Kohl. London: SCM, 1996.
> Smith, S. M. "Hope, Theology of," in *EDT*, 532–34.

companion in the suffering and kingdom and patient endurance that are ours in Jesus" (Rev 1:9). Twice the Seer repeats the exhortation: "This calls for patient endurance and faithfulness on the part of God's people" (13:10; 14:12). The word *hypomonē* indicates, passively, a patient fortitude, and actively, a determined will for perseverance. In addition, to be "steadfast" is both God's demand (Isa 26:3) and a gift from God (1 Pet 5:10). We become steadfast in our faith by abiding, remaining, and keeping ourselves in the love of God.

(3) *Encourage*. One of the purposes of prophecy in the early church was so that everyone would be "instructed and encouraged," especially if that prophecy had a forward-looking element toward Christ's return (1 Cor 14:31). Notably after detailing the events set to transpire at the Lord's *parousia* (1 Thess 4:15–17), Paul immediately tells the Thessalonians: "Therefore encourage one another with these words" (1 Thess 4:18). In Hebrews, the audience is told: "And let us consider how we may spur one another on toward love and good deeds, not giving up meeting together, as some are in the habit of doing, but encouraging one another—and all the more as you see the Day approaching" (Heb 10:24–25). As Christians live under the thunderous clouds of mortality and persecution, they keep each from falling or failing as they set their faces toward the rising sun of the east, from whence Christ will come.

Perhaps a fitting note to end on is some pastoral words from *2 Clement* 12.1: "Let us expect, therefore, hour by hour, the kingdom of God in love and righteousness, since we know not the day of the appearing of God." We are not to set a date for the *parousia* since nobody knows when Jesus is returning. Instead, we wait with evangelistic energy, endurance, and encouragement. In the interim, we are called to imitate the one whom we anticipate, and we are to remain ever watchful for the dawn that will one day break upon us. We may hope for many things to come: graduation, marriage, children, or retirement. Yet our deepest longings should be for intimate and instant communion with the Triune God for all eternity. For where our deepest longings are, there our heart is also.

§ 3.4 MILLENNIUM AND TRIBULATION

I remember several years ago walking through the mall at Surfers Paradise on the Gold Coast in Queensland, Australia (kind of like West Palm Beach in Florida or Brighton in the UK) when I saw a rather confused lady standing with a sign around her neck that said: "Ross Perot is the Antichrist." Here I was in the southern hemisphere, 10,000 kilometers from the USA, and an Australian woman, albeit not in complete control of her mental faculties, was announcing that some third-tier American presidential candidate was the figure of evil prophesied in the Bible. She claimed to know the details and was eager to tell everyone else. Time has proven her wrong (apparently the *real* Antichrist is currently the Secretary of State according to one chap I met in a hotel lobby in Rhode Island).

But people do want to know the details. The world is going to end. Even secular atheists believe that the world will indeed end one day. The question is how. Will it end with an ecological catastrophe or with a zombie apocalypse? According to the Scriptures, the world will end in an act of glorious new order where heaven comes to earth. This transformed world will radiate the glory of its Creator and the peace of God will reign in all its fullness. At this mother-of-all-endings, Christ returns to establish his kingdom and consummate the new creation.

The two events often said to precede this apocalyptic re-creation are the tribulation and the millennium. However, millennial and tribulation views are disputed among theologians as to what they are and in what order they will occur. If we are to understand the pattern of events that occurs immediately before and immediately after Christ's *parousia*, we must examine these topics afresh. Before we do that, one crucial caveat must be stated. Beliefs about the millennium and tribulation are second order matters of faith and doctrine. They are not as important as the gospel, nor should they be the basis for fellowship (or getting tenure!). One should afford a degree of liberality and charity to believers with whom one disagrees. For at the end of the day our "blessed hope" is not the millennium; our hope is the Lord Jesus Christ. According to Louis Berkhof, "the doctrine of the millennium has never yet been embodied in a single Confession, and therefore cannot be regarded as a dogma of the Church."[73]

3.4.1 THE MILLENNIUM: THE MESSIANIC INTERREGNUM

The word *millennium* means one thousand years. Those who believe that Christ will return to establish a millennial kingdom are called either *chiliasts* or *premillennialists*. Such a view is derived principally from Revelation 20:4–8, which describes an apparent millennial reign of Christ on earth:

> I saw thrones on which were seated those who had been given authority to judge. And I saw the souls of those who had been beheaded because of their testimony about Jesus and because of the word of God. They had not worshiped the beast or its image and had not received its mark on their foreheads or their hands. *They came to life and reigned with Christ a thousand years.* (The rest of the dead did not come to life until the *thousand years* were ended.) This is the *first resurrection*. Blessed and holy are those who have part in the *first resurrection*. The second death has no power over them, but they will be priests of God and of Christ and will reign with him for a *thousand years.*
>
> When the *thousand years* are over, Satan will be released from his prison and will go out to deceive the nations in the four corners of the earth—Gog and Magog—and to gather them for battle. In number they are like the sand on the seashore. (italics added)

The dispute centers on these issues: (1) Should the thousand years be taken literally or metaphorically? (2) What does the millennium actually signify? The options are postmillennialism, amillennialism, and premillennialism.

POSTMILLENNIAL

The "post" in "postmillennial" means "after." So on this view, Christ will return *after* the millennium. Postmillennialists advocate that the kingdom of God is presently being extended in the world through the proclamation of the gospel and in the saving work of the Holy Spirit.[74] The world will eventually be Christianized and experience a period of unprecedented peace and righteousness called the millennium. After that, Christ will return with the general resurrection, final judgment,

---

73. Louis Berkhof, *The History of Christian Doctrines* (Grand Rapids: Baker, 1975), 264.

74. Cf. Loraine Boettner, *The Millennium* (Philadelphia, PA: Presbyterian & Reformed, 1957); idem, "Postmillennialism," in *The Meaning of the Millennium: Four Views* (ed. R. G. Clouse; Downers Grove, IL: InterVarsity Press, 1977), 115–41; Kenneth L. Gentry, "Postmillennialism," in *Three Views on the Millennium* (ed. D. L. Bock; Grand Rapids: Zondervan, 1999), 11–57; Keith Mathison, *An Eschatology of Hope* (Phillipsburg, NJ: Presbyterian & Reformed, 1999).

and introduction of heaven and hell. The postmillennial view can be depicted as follows:

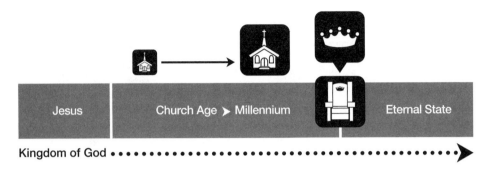

To describe this more fully, the advance of the gospel and the triumph of the church will gradually increase so that a large proportion of the world's population become Christians. Society will become more Christian as biblical values are progressively ingrained into civic laws. The millennium refers to a golden age of Christian evangelization and social progress—not necessarily a full thousand years, but an era typified by a glorious Christendom that is at once religious, political, and social. Life will carry on as normal with births, deaths, and marriages; sin won't be eliminated entirely either; but the moral and spiritual tenor of the world will be predominantly Christian. At the end of this millennium, Christ will return to earth and judge believers and unbelievers. This will be followed by a final judgment and the eternal state of a new heavens and a new earth. The motto of Wheaton College, "For Christ and His Kingdom," is based on a postmillennial belief that the church can advance Christ's kingdom in their revivalist crusades and social work until the present age becomes a millennium of Christ reigning on earth through the church militant.[75] Ken Gentry avers: "The historical prospect of gospel victory bringing blessing on all nations comes *by gradualistic conversion*, not by catastrophic imposition (as in premillennialism) or by apocalyptic conclusion (as in amillennialism)."[76]

The postmillennial position rests on a series of arguments. First, the Great Commission (Matt 28:19–20) declares that the church has the task of evangelizing the nations in the name of Jesus Christ, who has all authority in heaven and earth invested in him. Christ will extend his reign over all the nations by reigning in the hearts of the regenerated peoples of the earth.

---

75. Wheaton College was founded by Jonathan Blanchard (1811–92), postmillennialist social reformer, who gave the school its motto in the hope that its graduates would go out and transform the world and usher in the kingdom. It was not until the 1920s that Wheaton College adopted a premillennial statement of faith. See Timothy Larsen, *Christabel Pankhurst: Fundamentalism and Feminism in Coalition* (Woodbridge, Suffolk, UK: Boydell, 2002), 33–36.

76. Gentry, "Postmillennialism," 29–30 (italics original).

Second, the parables of growth are thought to denote the gradual forward movement of the kingdom that will finally bud into a period of spiritual victory over spiritual darkness (e.g., Matt 13:31–32).

Third, postmillennialists point to the success of Christianity in the world with the frequency of conversions, the multiplication of theological colleges, the number of missionaries sent out, and the proliferation of Christian media on radio, television, and the internet.

Fourth, concerning Revelation 20:4–6, A. A. Hodge wrote:

> Christ has in reserve for his church a period of universal expansion and of preeminent spiritual prosperity, when the spirit and character of the "noble army of martyrs" shall be reproduced again in the great body of God's people in an unprecedented measure, and when these martyrs shall, in the general triumph of their cause, and in the overthrow of that of their enemies, receive judgment over their foes and reign in the earth; while the party of Satan, "the rest of the dead," shall not flourish again until the thousand years be ended, when it shall prevail again for a little season.[77]

Postmillennialism is based on the present reality of the kingdom combined with an optimism of the work of God in the world through the church.

Out of the three millennial options, the postmillennial is the one easiest set aside. First, although the risen Christ has all authority, he does not use that authority to bring about the conversion of all or even most of the nations. The church is a witness to his authority, but nothing is said in the Great Commission about how that authority is used and manifested in the proclamation of the gospel. A mission to the nations does not mean that all of the nations will embrace the good news. In fact, history has shown us otherwise.

Second, the parables of growth—specifically the sower, mustard seed, and leaven—demonstrate that the kingdom does grow and advance, and it becomes almost viral in its effusion into the world. But this tells us nothing about the extent to which the kingdom will grow until the consummation.[78] Moreover, in the case of the parable of the sower, most of the seed scattered proves fruitless, and relatively few seeds grow up to bear fruit.

Third, the notion that society is gradually getting better and more Christian can be easily refuted by merely picking up a newspaper or by clicking on CNN.com. There were more martyrs in the twentieth century than in the previous nineteen centuries of the church. We have also seen two world wars that have ravaged the

---

77. A. A. Hodge, *Outlines of Theology* (London: Banner of Truth, 1860), 570–71.

78. I would add that biblical texts that refer to God's rule on earth or Edenic conditions on earth can be related to the inauguration of the kingdom during the new covenant period or else refer to the consummated state in the new creation (e.g., Gen 12:2–3; Pss 2:8; 22:27; Isa 2:2–4).

globe. The advent of the nuclear age brought us nuclear disaster and weapons of mass destruction. The Cold War was replaced with the Global War on Terror. My own country, Australia, now has more Buddhists than Baptists! Religious pluralism and antidiscrimination laws threaten religious freedom. Europe cannot eject Christianity quickly enough for some European intellectuals.

The church is assailed by Islamic fundamentalism in the East and secular fundamentalism in the West. I hate going into book stores because the religion section is soiled with volumes filled with ultraliberal, antiorthodox propaganda, wishy-washy nonsense of spiritual fuzzy-wuzzy feelings, biographical ramblings of Christian apostates, and greedy charlatans promising wealth and prosperity as if God were some kind of slot machine. I'm not bothered so much that people write these books, but I'm deeply troubled by the fact that so many people buy them. The world is cold, brutal, and dark, and it is only getting worse. If this is the hour approaching the millennium, I tremor to think what a tribulation might be like! Evidently post-millennialists do not receive email updates from Christian parachurch groups that minister to the persecuted church like *Voice of the Martyrs* and *Barnabas Fund* because Christians in Sudan, Iran, and North Korea know full well that the millennium ain't getting closer from their point of view.

Fourth, I find Hodge's reading of Revelation 20:4–6 unconvincing because he treats the martyrs as character types that are imitated during a millennial period. While the martyrs of the late first century like Antipas (2:13) might like to think of themselves as role models for others, I think it is a safe bet that to say that they also looked forward to a real resurrection after suffering for their faith; that is arguably what John the Seer is talking about in Revelation 20. What is more, there is nothing *gradual* about the millennium in 20:4–6.

Fifth, whatever optimism one can glean from the biblical materials is quickly nullified by biblical forecasts of tribulation set to come on the church in the last days (2 Thess 2:1–12; 2 Tim 3:1–13; 2 Pet 3:2–14).

3.4.1.1 AMILLENNIAL

The *a* in *amillennial* designates "no millennium." But this is a misnomer because amillennialism does not actually deny that a millennium exists; more accurately, it regards the millennium as a present reality with a future consummation. Greg Beale labels amillennialism more precisely as "inaugurated millennialism."[79] On this view the church age is the millennium because this is where and when Christ reigns over his people as their Lord. Unlike the postmillennial position, the millennium here is

---

79. Gregory K. Beale, *The Book of Revelation* (NIGTC; Grand Rapids: Eerdmans, 1999), 973.

not a golden age that transpires as the church age gets progressively better. Instead, the church age is identical to the millennium itself, and there is a period of persecution at the end of the church age, usually called the tribulation; thereafter Christ returns to bring in the eternal state of a new heaven and a new earth.[80] We can show this scheme diagrammatically as follows:

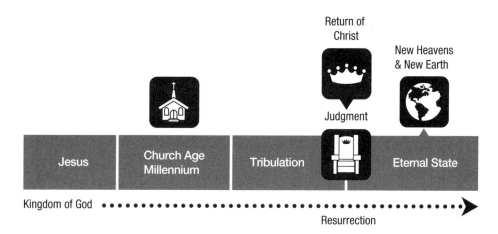

To unpack the amillennial view further, the final eschatological events mentioned in the Bible are regarded as an overall unity. The *parousia*, the resurrection, and the final judgment all occur at the same time with no intervening raptures, no multiple resurrections, and only one judgment. Moreover, the Old Testament promises concerning a chapter of earthly harmony and bliss should be relegated to the new creation, not to a millennium that ends in rebellion against its Lord (e.g., Isa 11:6–9). Anthony Hoekema puts it this way: "Amillennialists therefore feel no need for positing an earthly millennium to provide for the fulfillment of prophecies of this sort; they see such prophecies as pointing to the glorious eternal future which awaits all the people of God."[81] The new creation is the culmination of the covenant of grace that effects an eternal dwelling place for the redeemed people of God on a renewed earth. While recognizing the tension of the "now" and "not yet," the amillennialist scheme refuses to divide that tension into a series of dislocated events. Horton comments: "Premillennialism fails adequately to appreciate the 'already,' while postmillennialism undervalues the 'not yet' of Christ's kingdom."[82]

---

80. Anthony A. Hoekema, *The Bible and the Future*; idem, "Amillennialism," in *The Meaning of the Millennium: Four Views* (ed. R.G. Clouse; Downers Grove, IL: InterVarsity Press, 1977), 155–87; Kim Riddlebarger, *A Case for Amillen-* *nialism* (Grand Rapids: Baker, 2003); Horton, *Christian Faith*, 919–56.

81. Hoekema, "Amillennialism," 185.

82. Horton, *Christian Faith*, 936.

In regard to Revelation 20:1–6, amillennialists first of all claim that the binding of Satan took place during Jesus' ministry. In Luke 10–11 are two stories in close proximity that indicate Jesus' victory over Satan. Jesus announced: "I saw Satan fall like lightning," which implies the defeat of Satan in his ministry and in that of his disciples (10:18). Jesus retorts to his objectors that he is not in league with Satan; rather, he performs exorcisms only because he is the "strong man" who has bound and plundered the satanic realm (11:1–26). As a result, and as Revelation 12 states, Satan is cast out of heaven and is impotent in his endeavors to inhibit God's redemptive plan for the saints.

Second, the resurrection of believers in Revelation 20:6 is not an actual physical resurrection; rather, either it refers to a spiritual resurrection understood as regeneration (see John 5:25; 11:26) or else it denotes the souls of the martyred believers coming into the presence of God (see Rev 6:10). Further confirmation is that the rest of the New Testament teaches only one resurrection, not two split by a millennium (John 5:28–29; Acts 24:15; cf. Dan 12:2).

Third, amillennialists raise objections against a literal millennium, such as how could glorified and nonglorified bodies coexist together? They contend that Revelation 20 should be regarded as symbolic like the rest of the book. Ultimately, on the amillennialist account, Revelation 20 describes the entire history of the church, beginning with the first coming of Christ and ending in the consummation.

I would seriously like to be amillennial. It is so much simpler. It recognizes the "already" and "not-yet" of biblical eschatology and avoids the eccentricities of postmillennialism and dispensational premillennialism. The *parousia*, general resurrection, and final judgment are united in a narrative coherence. Jesus comes back and it is game-set-match, thank you ball boys and ball girls, chik chik boom, Elvis has left the building, the fat lady is singing up a storm, and tha-tha-tha-that's all folks! My point of contention is with its reading of Revelation 20.[83] I confess, as G. E. Ladd did a generation ago, that if it were not for Revelation 20, I would be amillennial (and I nearly changed my mind when writing this).[84]

A first criticism is that the binding of Satan in Revelation 20:2–3 is not simply an inhibition of his work like a junkyard dog tied up with a long chain so that it can still snarl and bite at those in its reach (see Luke 22:31, 53; 2 Cor 4:4; Eph 4:27; 1 Thess 2:18; 2 Thess 2:9; 2 Tim 2:26; Jas 4:7; 1 Pet 5:8; Rev 2:13). Instead, the angel "threw him into the Abyss, and locked and sealed it over him, to keep him from deceiving the nations anymore," which indicates a far more restrictive

---

83. My good friend Craig S. Keener (Asbury Seminary) once told me: "Theologically I am amillennial, but exegetically I am premillennial"—a sentiment I agree with.

84. I remain intrigued by I. Howard Marshall's view that the millennium is another image for the glorious end-state and symbolizes the endless character of the kingdom of God (I. Howard Marshall, "The Christian Millennium," *EvQ* 72 [2000]: 217–36). That makes sense if Revelation 20:4–6 intimates 22:5.

containment (Rev 20:3). Yes, this could be no more than the hyperbole of the imagery, but then again, it might also suggest that Christ's return curtails Satan's power in an entirely unprecedented way. More grievous for the amillennial position is that we can hardly say that the current age reflects an absence of satanic deception over the nations.

Second, amillennialists take the description that "they came to life and reigned with Christ a thousand years" (Rev 20:4) to refer to the reign of Christ over his church in the church age. The problem is that this appears to be a future promise and therefore a means of encouragement for those who endure a great ordeal of persecution. On the amillennialist scheme, the specific promise given to the martyrs is generalized and even deapocalypticized of its radical reversals in order to make it relevant to all believers in all ages. In contrast, although believers in the present time share in Christ's reign by virtue of their union with the exalted Lord (see Eph 2:6; Col 3:1), they still anticipate a future and earthly implementation of that corule in the future.

Third, on the "first resurrection," it is most unlikely that this is anything other than a physical resurrection. The word *zaō* can mean "living" in the sense of existence or being alive (Rev 3:1; 4:9–10; 7:2; 10:6; 13:14), but it is also used to refer to a physical resurrection in several places (Matt 9:18, Rom 14:9; 2 Cor 13:4). The same word describes the resurrection of Jesus (Rev 1:18; 2:8) and those at the second resurrection after the millennium (20:5). Moreover, and what I think is critical against the amillennial position, those who partake of the first resurrection *do not* partake of the second resurrection ("The *rest of the dead* did not come to life *until* the thousand years were ended" [20:5, italics added]). So the first resurrection cannot be regeneration or coming into God's presence at death because the first resurrection is something that is not true of all persons. The grist for the mill in the amillennial view is not the millennium but the two resurrections mentioned in Revelation 20.[85]

3.4.1.2 PREMILLENNIAL

Premillennialism proposes that Christ returns before (*pre*) the millennium. There are two varieties of premillennialism. Dispensational premillennialism is typified by a sharp Israel and church contrast and the advocacy of a pretribulation rapture. Historical or classical premillennialism holds to continuity between Israel and the church and believes in a posttribulation return of Christ. Historic premillennialism looks like this:

---

85. That said, I find no evidence to believe that John 5:29 or Phil 3:11 teach a double resurrection, against Millard Erickson, *Christian Theology* (2nd ed.; Grand Rapids: Baker, 1998), 1223–34; Grudem, *Systematic Theology*, 1119–20; and with Horton, *Christian Faith*, 940–41.

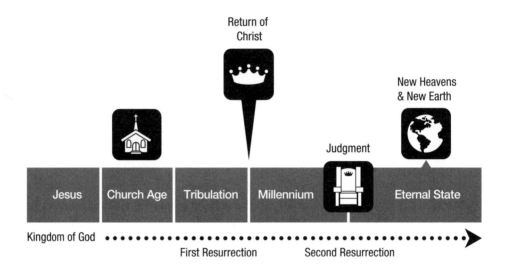

In premillennialism, the second coming of Christ will usher in a reign of Christ on earth ahead of the final consummation of God's redemptive purposes in the new heavens and the new earth.[86] The view is based, first, on the observation that biblical prophecies look forward to a time of blessing and fecundity to transpire on the earth, and second, on its exegesis of Revelation 20. I should note that historic premillennialists don't necessarily believe that the millennium will be a literal thousand years, but it will mark a period of Christ's reign on the earth with his people for a time. For this reason, I prefer to call the millennium a *messianic interregnum* since it demonstrates the penultimate stage of the realization of the kingdom ahead of the new heavens and new earth.

Sung Wook Chung argues that Reformed theology has overemphasized the soteriological dimension of the covenant of grace at the expense of the kingdom dimension to God's work within history.[87] Assuming the unity of the covenant of grace from Genesis 3:15 to Revelation 22:21, one can still see an anticipation of the millennial reign of Christ in the covenantal architecture of the biblical promises. Genesis 1:27–28 ("So God created mankind in his own image, in the image of God he created them; male and female he created them. God blessed them and said to them, 'Be fruitful and increase in number; fill the earth and subdue it. Rule over the fish in the sea and the birds in the sky and over every living creature that moves on the ground'") can be interpreted as the archetype of the covenants of promise and

---

86. Cf. G. E. Ladd, "Historic Premillennialism," in *The Meaning of the Millennium: Four Views* (ed. R. G. Clouse; Downers Grove, IL: InterVarsity Press, 1977), 15–40; Erickson, *Christian Theology*, 1215–24; Grudem, *Systematic Theology*, 1127–31.

87. Sung Wook Chung, "Toward the Reformed and Covenantal Theology of Premillennialism: A Proposal," in *A Case for Historic Premillennialism* (ed. C. L. Blomberg and S. W. Chung; Grand Rapids: Baker, 2009), 133–46.

blessings found in later sections of the Old Testament. God blesses Adam and Eve and gives them a kingdom that represents the manifested reign of God on earth. As vice-regents of creation, they are commissioned to represent the king and his attributes in their ruling over creation. What Reformed theologians call a "cultural mandate" is in fact a "kingdom mandate," which gives humanity dominion over the created order. Adam had the role of king and priest by reigning over the whole world and leading it in submission to God. The command given in 2:16–17 about not eating from the tree was the constitution for the kingdom in Eden and the condition for continued blessing of the Edenic paradise.

According to Greg Beale, God's penultimate purpose was to make creation a livable place for human inhabitants in order to achieve the grand purpose of glorifying him. Beale goes on to state: "God's ultimate goal in creation was to magnify his glory throughout the earth by means of his faithful image-bearers inhabiting the world in obedience to the divine mandate."[88] The fall meant a loss of that dominion and a forfeit of that priestly prerogative. Both the penultimate and ultimate purposes of God were, temporally, thwarted as sin entered the creation. In light of that, and though Beale would probably himself object, I would be prepared to argue that God's plan to restore creation will also include a two-stage renewal: a penultimate stage, where people dwell in God's presence to worship him, and then an ultimate stage of glorified human-divine fellowship. This two-stage process is a corollary that emerges out of the covenantal framework of Scripture. In eschatology these two stages, penultimate and ultimate, are the millennium and the new creation.

In addition, Jesus, the second Adam, by his faithfulness and obedience to God, fulfills the kingly and priestly roles given to Adam and reestablishes the kingdom of God on earth in a staged delivery. First, God inaugurates the kingdom in the life, death, resurrection, and exaltation of Jesus Christ. Second, he establishes a millennial kingdom where Christ restores the priestly and regal roles of humanity in a new Adamic kingdom—hence the promise that resurrected saints will "be priests of God and of Christ and will reign with him for a thousand years" (Rev 20:6). Third, as Lord, Jesus hands over this kingdom to his Father and establishes the glory of the new heavens and new earth in its full consummated state (1 Cor 15:24). This is where the earthly millennial kingdom gives way to a geocosmic reality: "God's dwelling place is now among the people, and he will dwell with them. They will be his people, and God himself will be with them and be their God" (Rev 21:3). Chung cogently puts it:

> Since the Edenic covenants of blessing and the law were given in the context of this earth, they must be fulfilled on this earth before its entrance into the eternal and

---

88. Greg Beale, *The Temple and the Church's Mission* (NSBT 17; Downers Grove, IL: InterVarsity Press, 2004), 82.

transformed state of the new heavens and earth. The major difference between the millennial kingdom and the new heavens and earth is that the millennial kingdom is not an eternal kingdom whereas the new heavens and earth are eternal in character. The major continuity between the millennial kingdom and the new Jerusalem in the new heavens and earth is that both will have priest-kings who will reign with Jesus Christ. In this sense, we may say that the millennial kingdom is the penultimate realization of the kingdom promise/blessing in the context of the current world, whereas the new Jerusalem in the new heavens and earth is the ultimate realization of the kingdom promise/blessings in the context of the eternally transformed cosmos.... In sum, the covenantal unity of the Bible demands that the millennial kingdom should be materialized on this earth before the beginning of the new heavens and earth.[89]

This point can be reinforced further by several passages that predict God's reign over the earth, sometimes through a Davidic king and characterized as an age of peace, blessing, and prosperity (e.g., Ps 72:8–14; Isa 2:2–4; Dan 2:28–45; Mic 4:1–3; Zech 14:5–17). The most explicit imagery of a messianic kingdom is in Isaiah 11:1–10:

> A shoot will come up from the stump of Jesse;
>> from his roots a Branch will bear fruit.
> The Spirit of the Lord will rest on him—
>> the Spirit of wisdom and of understanding,
>> the Spirit of counsel and of might,
>> the Spirit of the knowledge and fear of the Lord—
> and he will delight in the fear of the Lord.
> He will not judge by what he sees with his eyes,
>> or decide by what he hears with his ears;
> but with righteousness he will judge the needy,
>> with justice he will give decisions for the poor of the earth.
> He will strike the earth with the rod of his mouth;
>> with the breath of his lips he will slay the wicked.
> Righteousness will be his belt
>> and faithfulness the sash around his waist.
> *The wolf will live with the lamb,*
>> *the leopard will lie down with the goat,*
> *the calf and the lion and the yearling together;*
>> *and a little child will lead them.*
> *The cow will feed with the bear,*
>> *their young will lie down together*
> *and the lion will eat straw like the ox.*

---

89. Chung, "Reformed and Covenantal," 143–44. Cf. D. J. McCartney, "*Ecce Homo*: The Coming of the Kingdom as the Restoration of Human Vice-regency," *WTJ* 56 (1994): 1–21.

> *Infants will play near the hole of the cobra;*
> > *young children will put their hands into the viper's nest.*
> *They will neither harm nor destroy*
> > *on all my holy mountain,*
> *for the earth will be filled with the knowledge of the* LORD
> > *as the waters cover the sea.*
>
> In that day the Root of Jesse will stand as a banner for the peoples; the nations will rally to him, and his resting place will be glorious. (italics added)

I think it certainly possible that this type of bliss and peace transpires during the new creation (Isa 65:17; 66:22), but it is likewise possible that it transpires at the penultimate stage envisioned above.

Furthermore, the Scriptures look ahead to the reign of humanity as God's vice-regent at a future juncture. Humanity is created to reign, which is clear from Genesis 1:26–28. The same point is affirmed in Psalm 8:4–6: "What is mankind that you are mindful of them, human beings that you care for them? You made them a little lower than the angels and crowned them with glory and honor. You made them rulers over the works of your hands; you put everything under their feet." It is interesting how Hebrews 2:6–10 cites Psalm 8 in regards to the incarnation and exaltation of Christ with a forward glance toward his subjugation of all things.

The call of Israel was meant to carry forward this task of being the custodian of the Adamic kingdom. Israel was a kingdom of priests (Exod 19:6) and was meant to lead the nations in worshipping God (e.g., Isa 42:6; 49:6). Israel's covenant with God was the means by which the Creator God would bless the world. Israel's place in the world takes its direction from the pattern that God marked out for Adam. What is more, in the period roughly contemporary with the New Testament, we see Jewish interpreters finding in Scripture an Adam–Israel connection. The Qumranites believed that "all the glory of Adam shall be theirs" (1QS 4.22; CD 3.19–20; 1QH 17.14–15; 4QpPs37, 3).[90] In *4 Ezra* (a post-AD 70 Jewish apocalypse extant with Christian touches), the Seer complains to God:

> On the sixth day you commanded the earth to bring forth before you cattle, wild animals, and creeping things; and *over these you placed Adam, as ruler over all the works that you had made; and from him we have all come, the people whom you have chosen.* All this I have spoken before you, O Lord, *because you have said that it was for us that you created this world.* As for the other nations that have descended from Adam, you have said that they are nothing, and that they are like spittle, and you have compared their abundance to a drop from a bucket. And now, O Lord, these nations, which are reputed to be as nothing, domineer over us and devour us. But we your people, whom you have called your firstborn, only begotten, zealous for you, and most

---

90. Wright, *New Testament and the People of God*, 262–72.

dear, have been given into their hands. If the world has indeed been created for us, why do we not possess our world as an inheritance? How long will this be so? (*4 Ezra* 6.53–59, italics added)

The Seer opines that Israel stands in the line of Adam, and it is their job to rule over creation. In fact, the world was made for them, and yet the beasts of the field are trampling over the Adamic custodians as if they were nothing. Early Christian authors believed that this Adamic authority had been invested in Christ—hence the hymn in Colossians 1:16 that says: "All things have been created through him and for him." This is why Christians have celebrated Christ's kingdom by way of reference to Psalms 2 and 110, because they identified in the messianic kingdom the realization of the Adamic kingdom that God had intended for Israel.

Later Christian authors looked forward to God, the Messiah, and the redeemed people reigning over the earth in an eschatological triumvirate. Contrast the vision of *4 Ezra* with the vision of an early Christian apocalypse the *Shepherd of Hermas* (probably written in Rome in the early second century):

As I slept, brothers and sisters, a revelation was given to me by a very handsome young man, who said to me, "Who do you think the elderly woman from whom you received the little book was?" I said: "The Sibyl." "You are wrong," he said. "She is not." "Then who is she?" I said. "The church," he replied, "she was created before all things; therefore she is elderly, and *for her sake the world was formed*." (*Herm. Vis.* 2.4.1, italics added)

Whereas the author of *4 Ezra* thought that the world was created for Israel, the Shepherd declares that the world was created for the church. He believes that the church, as the new Israel, is the renewed Adamic race, and they are the custodians of the created order. That stands at a piece with what we see gradually unfolding in the Scriptures: the democratization of the messianic idea, with God's king and God's people reigning together. Bear in mind that the "one like a son of man" in Daniel 7 receives an everlasting kingdom at his exaltation (7:13–14), but his enthronement beside God is in fact symbolic for the kingdom being handed over to the saints (7:27). According to James Dunn: "The implication is clear: that as 'man' = the human being was climax to creation and given dominion over the rest of creation, so Israel was the climax of God's universal purpose and would be given dominion over all other nations."[91]

When we read about new covenant believers being a royal priesthood (1 Pet 2:9) and a kingdom of priests (Rev 1:6; 5:10), we are to see this as the eschatological fulfillment of Israel's (Exod 19:5–6) and Adam's (Gen 1:26–28) vocation to be

---

91. James D. G. Dunn, *Jesus Remembered* (CITM 1; Grand Rapids: Eerdmans, 2003), 729.

priest kings. Reigning with Christ is intimated widely in the New Testament. Jesus told the disciples that "at the renewal of all things, when the Son of Man sits on his glorious throne, you who have followed me will also sit on twelve thrones, judging the twelve tribes of Israel" (Matt 19:28; cf. Luke 22:30). In a hymnic fragment, Paul states: "if we endure, we will also reign with him" (2 Tim 2:12). Well before Revelation 20, the reign of Christ with his people is disclosed in the vision of the heavenly throne room: "You have made them to be a kingdom and priests to serve our God, and they will reign on the earth" (5:10). The believers who "came to life and reigned with Christ" at the dawn of the millennium (20:4) constituted the penultimate stage in God's plan to fill the world with human viceroys reigning with the Messiah. Later, they reign with him also in the ultimate stage of the new creation, where "they will reign for ever and ever" amidst divine glory (Rev 22:5).

To recap the story so far: (1) God has delegated a special authority to humanity to reign on the earth as kings and priests in a *penultimate* stage of the kingdom in the context of the present world, and then (2) God has also intended for humanity to rule over the world in the *ultimate* stage of the kingdom characterized by everlasting glory. This role of reigning over the earth was given to Adam, rehearsed in Israel, fulfilled in Christ, and then shared with the church. In the era of the new covenant, Christ's kingdom is inaugurated, and its future consummation consists of a penultimate stage where Messiah and church reign in the millennium, and then in an ultimate stage where Messiah and church reign in the new creation.

Shifting attention to Jesus, we ask: Did Jesus in any way intimate a millennial kingdom as an intermediate phase ahead of the new creation? The fact is that apart from affirming the "already" and "not-yet" nature of the kingdom, it is difficult to map an actual timetable for the end in Jesus' teaching because that is not what his message was focused on. Resurrection and final judgment are affirmed, but no details beyond that general orientation are given. However, the Lord's Prayer could be called the "millennium prayer" since it petitions God, "your kingdom come, your will be done, on earth as it is in heaven (Matt 6:10/Luke 11:2 [though Luke omits "earth"]). The prayer that all Christians pray—Catholic, Orthodox, or Protestant—looks ahead to the reign of God on the earth and its recognition and reverence around the world.

Paul the apostle has nothing as complex as Revelation 19–20 when it comes to the actual events that transpire in the future. We are left to sieve information from his passing remarks about the kingdom, *parousia*, resurrection, and judgment from his letters, primarily from the Thessalonian and Corinthian correspondence. One passage in Paul might well intimate a messianic interregnum:

> But in this order: Christ, the firstfruits; *then* [*epeita*], when he comes [*parousia*], those who belong to him. *Then* [*eita*] the end will come, when he hands over the

kingdom to God the Father after he has destroyed all dominion, authority and power. For [*gar*] he must reign until he has put all his enemies under his feet. The last enemy to be destroyed is death. For he "has put everything under his feet." Now when it says that "everything" has been put under him, it is clear that this does not include God himself, who put everything under Christ. (1 Cor 15:23–27)[92]

This passage can be broken down into three stages: (1) Jesus' resurrection; (2) *then* the resurrection of believers at the *parousia*; and (3) *then* the end. An undefined interval falls between Christ's resurrection and his *parousia*, and a second implied interval falls between the *parousia* and the end, when Christ subjugates his enemies.[93] This arguably corresponds to the eschatological scenario that can be mapped from Paul's letters:

1. The sudden *parousia* (Phil 3:20; 1 Thess 5:1–4)
2. The resurrection of deceased and living believers (1 Cor 15:51–52; Phil 3:21; 1 Thess 4:13–17; 5:1–4)
3. A messianic interregnum with a struggle against angelic powers at the end (Rom 16:20; 1 Cor 15:22–24)
4. A general resurrection of all (1 Cor 6:3)
5. A final judgment (Rom 14:10; 2 Cor 5:10)
6. The transformation of creation (Rom 8:19–20)

I admit this is subject to dispute, and some scholars maintain that "in Pauline thought there is an unforeseen interval only between the resurrection and Parousia of Christ."[94] Even so, the materials set forth above are coherent and correspond remarkably well with a millennial interpretation of Revelation 20:4–6.

That brings us to Revelation 20 itself. In support of a millennial interpretation,[95] consider the following:

1. The sequence of preliminary judgment, millennium, final judgment, and new heavens and new earth must be taken seriously.
2. The reference to a millennium stands at a piece with other Jewish apocalypses that envision an earthly reign by a messianic figure in an interim messianic kingdom (*1 En.* 91.1–10; 93.12–17; *4 Ezra* 7.26–44; 12.31–34; *2 Bar.* 29.3–30.1; 40.1–4; 72.2–74.3). If John the Seer intended something other

---

92. Contrast exegesis of this passage by C. E. Hill, "Paul's Understanding of Christ's Kingdom in 1 Corinthians 15.20–28," *NovT* 30 (1988): 297–320, and by Seth Turner, "The Interim, Earthly Messianic Kingdom in Paul," *JSNT* 25 (2003): 323–42.

93. Cf. Ladd, "Historic Premillennialism," 38–39; Erickson, *Christian Theology*, 1223; Grudem, *Systematic Theology*, 1130; Turner, "Messianic Kingdom in Paul," 335–38.

94. Aune, "Eschatology (Early Christian)," 2:603.

95. For a few commentaries that support a millennial interpretation (sensibly argued!), see G. R. Beasley-Murray, *Revelation* (NCBC; Grand Rapids: Eerdmans, 1974), 284–92; Robert H. Mounce, *The Book of Revelation* (NICNT; Grand Rapids: Eerdmans, 1977), 354–59; Ben Witherington III, *Revelation* (CGNTC; Cambridge: Cambridge University Press, 2003), 239–52.

than a Jewish messianic age to be signified, we are at a loss as to why he chose the imagery of a messianic age in the first place.

3. No matter how many flashbacks or disruptions of sequence there are in Revelation, it makes no sense to place one between Revelation 19 and 20.[96] Revelation 19 narrates the destruction of the beast and the false prophet, while Revelation 20 concerns the destruction of the Satan—the third member in the unholy trinity of Revelation. Similarly, the role of the martyrs in 20:4 is very different from that in 6:9–11. In Revelation 6, the martyrs are told to wait and receive their robes while Satan continues engineering his schemes, while in Revelation 20, the martyrs reign with Christ and Satan is shut up and sealed from them.

4. The mixing of resurrection bodies among nonresurrection bodies during the millennium is no more a problem for the millennium than the resurrection of Jesus was for the Easter narratives where the risen Jesus walked among his disciples.[97]

5. In terms of literary function, the martyrs and the millennium constitute one of the key means of exhortation in the book and have stronger persuasiveness if the imagery is in some sense literal: "This is a scene of role reversals. The martyrs have had to stand before the imperial throne (at least figuratively) and receive the sentence of death. Now they are the ones who are seated on thrones and deliver judgment.... The millennium is John's way of offering encouragement to the martyrs. Those who have paid the greatest price receive the greatest reward."[98]

6. We must also consider the reception history of Revelation 20. Many of the early church fathers, such as Papias, Melito of Sardis, Justin Martyr, Irenaeus, and Tertullian, were chiliasts. Not everyone was a chiliast, and there were orthodox and nonorthodox versions of nonchiliasm.[99] By the time one reaches Eusebius (third century) and Augustine (fourth century), chiliasm has lost the day and seceded ground to amillennialism.[100] Chiliasm was even condemned

---

96. Craig L. Blomberg, "The Posttribulationism of the New Testament: Leaving 'Left Behind' Behind," in *A Case for Historic Premillennialism* (ed. C. L. Blomberg and S. W. Chung; Grand Rapids: Baker, 2009), 67–68.

97. Ibid., 85.

98. M. G. Reddish, *Revelation* (Macon, GA: Smyth & Helwys, 2001), 394–95.

99. Cf. Charles E. Hill, *Regnum Caelorum: Patterns of Millennial Thought in Early Christianity* (2nd ed.; Grand Rapids: Eerdmans, 2001); Andrew Chester, *Messiah and Exaltation* (Tübingen: Mohr/Siebeck, 2007), 423–30.

100. Hill (*Regnum Caelorum*, 20) tries to make a case that belief in a millennium was tied to belief in a subterranean intermediate state between death and resurrection, so that a millennium is an improvement on the postmortem condition, but still an interim point prior to the new heavens and new earth. Yet I would argue that the apostle Paul and John the Seer are two examples of persons who believed in a heavenly intermediate state (2 Cor 5:1–9; Phil 1:23; Rev 6:9–11) as well as a terrestrial kingdom established on the earth ahead of the consummation. Contra Hill, heaven is not the ultimate home of humanity, and therefore a millennium is not an anticlimactic appendage of salvation history or an unconscionable digression.

at the Council of Ephesus in 431 AD, and the First Helvetic Confession states, "We also reject the Jewish dream of a millennium, or golden age on earth, before the last judgment" (art. 11).

My own estimation is that chiliasm fell out of favor when the Roman empire converted to Christianity. Thereafter, as Christianity was gradually disengaged from its Jewish roots and as it became comfortable with the political status quo, it abandoned the idea of a radical rapture in the present order of things. After all, one is hardly going to look for a messianic kingdom to replace the present one if the present order of things is turning out rather spiffy for the church. Chiliasm thrives under circumstances of pain and persecution where believers hope for a kingdom of a different order to the present one in order to vindicate the faithful. The Apocalypse was written under such circumstances, but its vision inevitably did not capture the imagination of those who would later live under the sponsorship of the very empire that John the Seer hoped would one day burn under the weight of divine judgment. The fact that the Apocalypse uses millennial imagery found in contemporary apocalyptic Jewish literature and the fact that the earliest Christian authors of the second century were chiliasts seem to place Revelation 20 in a literary chain that supports a millennial interpretation.

I readily admit that this is not the only way to read Revelation 20. Greg Beale writes: "Life and rule are the primary themes in 20:4–6. This means that the primary point of the millennium is to demonstrate the victory of suffering Christians."[101] Gordon Fee contends that John's point is not a literal millennium, but the passage is best understood as "an interlude between the divine overthrow of the unholy triumvirate (Satan, the Empire, the cult of the emperor) delineated in the preceding section (19:11–21), and the final judgment of all evil, both demonic and human, in 20:7–15."[102] Loren Stuckenbruck concludes: "The impression is left that John, rather than being concerned with the order of events ... was attempting to draw attention to the ultimate destinies of the righteous and the wicked, that is, to show in sharpest relief that God will vindicate the faithful ones and annihilate those who are allies of Satan."[103] For Richard Bauckham, "The theological point of the millennium is solely to demonstrate the triumph of the martyrs: that those whom the beast put to death are those who will truly live—eschatologically, and that those who contested his right to rule and suffered for it are those who will in the end rule as universally as he—and for much longer: a thousand years!"[104] Those

---

101. Beale, *Revelation*, 991.

102. Gordon D. Fee, *Revelation* (NCCS; Eugene, OR: Wipf & Stock, 2011), 280.

103. Loren Stuckenbruck, "Revelation," in *Eerdmans Commentary on the Bible* (ed. J. D. G. Dunn and J. W. Rogerson; Grand Rapids: Eerdmans, 2003), 1567.

104. Richard Bauckham, *The Theology of the Book of Revelation* (Cambridge: Cambridge University Press, 1993), 107.

are serious alternatives, but I find none of them (for the moment) outweighing the scheme exposited above.

3.4.1.3 COOL INTERNET RESOURCES

- Audio: Thomas R. Schreiner's sermon entitled "The Millennium," preached at Clifton Baptist Church on 4 June 2009, provides a detailed description of his shift from amillennial to historic premillennial with some groovy exegesis of Revelation 20: http://cliftonbaptist.org/sermons-and-audio/?sermon_id=241. Accessed 5 April 2011.
- Video: Desiring God Ministries at Bethlehem Baptist Church had a panel discussion on the millennium that took place on 27 September 2009 entitled, "An Evening of Eschatology" (chaired by John Piper). It featured Doug Wilson (postmillennial), Sam Storms (amillennial), and Jim Hamilton (historic premillennial). Excellent discussion. http://www.desiringgod.org/resource-library/conference-messages/an-evening-of-eschatology. Accessed 5 April 2011.

3.4.2 THE TRIBULATION: THE RAGE OF SATAN AGAINST THE CHURCH

A shared tenet of Jewish and Christian eschatologies is that before the final consummation, things on earth will get progressively worse rather than better for the people of God, in a period known as the "birth pangs of the Messiah."[105] This time of "tribulation" (*thlipsis*) is characterized chiefly by persecution of the faithful and apostasy by the faithless. The persecution of Judeans under the Seleucid ruler Antiochus IV Epiphanes in the mid-second century BC was the quintessential model of the type of sufferings that would fall on God's people (read 2 Macc 7 about the martyrs to see what I'm talking about).

Likewise, the Jewish war between Judea and Rome (AD 66–70) that climaxed in the destruction of the Jerusalem temple was one of the many tribulations to fall on God's people, both Jews and Christians, at that time (see Matt 24:21; Mark 13:19). We can also

---

105. Cf. "At that time Michael, the great prince who protects your people, will arise. There will be a time of distress such as has not happened from the beginning of nations until then. But at that time your people — everyone whose name is found written in the book — will be delivered" (Dan 12:1). "The great day of the LORD is near — near and coming quickly. The cry on the day of the LORD is bitter; the Mighty Warrior shouts his battle cry. That day will be a day of wrath — a day of distress and anguish, a day of trouble and ruin, a day of darkness and gloom, a day of clouds and blackness" (Zeph 1:14–15). "And there will come upon them … punishment and wrath such as has never happened to them from the creation till that time when he stirs up against them a king of the kings of the earth" (*T. Mos.* 8.1). "In the first part there shall be the beginning of commotions.... For some shall leave out some of their own, and receive (in its stead) from others, and some complete their own and that of others, so that those may not understand who are upon the earth in those days that this is the consummation of the times" (*2 Bar.* 27.1, 15). "Then shall the creation of men come into the fire of trial, and many shall be made to stumble and shall perish; but they that endure in their faith shall be saved from under the curse itself" (*Did.* 16.5).

look back to the Roman persecutions of Christians by Nero, Decius, and Diocletian as instances of heightened attacks against the church. Evidently the people of God have faced tribulation in every age, in various forms, depending on their circumstances.

What is more, the New Testament sees the advance of the kingdom and the coexistence of tribulation together. Tribulation is something that all believers can experience (see Matt 13:21; John 16:33; Acts 14:22; Rom 12:12; 1 Thess 3:4; Rev 2:9–10).[106] However, it is prophesied that before the *parousia* that there will be a "great tribulation" (*thlipsis megas*, Rev 7:14; cf. 3:10). That tribulation existed partly in John's own day, but it will be extended and escalated in the future. The great tribulation is presented as a time of severe persecution of God's people and a time of God's judgment against the world.

The prayer that Jesus taught his disciples includes the petition to the Father: "And lead us not into *temptation*" (Matt 6:13/Luke 11:4, italics added). This "temptation" (*peirasmos*) may not simply be a propensity to moral failure under enticement, but the eschatological trials widely expected to precede the age to come. Paul also teaches that the *parousia* will not happen "until the rebellion occurs and the man of lawlessness is revealed, the man doomed to destruction" (2 Thess 2:3). The apostle envisages a rebellion against God at the end of the age, described in the language of a political revolt and widespread religious apostasy combined together.

In some amillennial schemes, tribulation simply coexists with kingdom until the *parousia* (though some allow for a final tribulation toward the end of the church age). That is true to a point as Satan rages against the church in every age (see Rev 12). However, the Lord's Prayer, Paul's teaching in 2 Thessalonians 2, and the futuristic orientation of the book of Revelation do look ahead to a climactic time of trial to fall on God's people as a prelude to the final consummation.

Among premillennial commentators the question remains as to the exact time of the tribulation in relation to the *parousia*.[107] The belief that Christ will return and take the church to himself before the tribulation is called the *pretribulation* view. The belief that Christ will return after the church has gone through the tribulation is called the *posttribulation* view. Bound up with this debate also is the question of the "rapture" and whether there will be a separate coming to remove the church from tribulation and another coming with the church for judgment.

3.4.2.1 PRETRIBULATIONISM

Among the presuppositions of the pretribulation (henceforth "pretrib") position is that Daniel 9:24–27 (esp. v. 27) provides a future forecast of an unprecedented

---

106. Beale, "Eschatological Conception," 15; Horton, *Christian Faith*, 940.

107. Cf. Gleason L. Archer et al., *The Rapture: Pre-, Mid-, or Post-Tribulation?* (Grand Rapids: Zondervan, 1984).

WRAPPING UP THE RAPTURE

The rapture (from the Latin verb *rapto*, which means "to snatch up") is the sudden taking away of believers to be with the Lord (on whether the rapture means to be with the Lord and whether it is different to what happens to believers at the *parousia* of the Lord, see below on the differences between pretribulationism and posttribulationism). What exactly is the rapture and what does the Bible say about it?

In Matthew we read: "Two men will be in the field; one will be taken and the other left. Two women will be grinding with a hand mill; one will be taken and the other left" (Matt 24:40–41; cf. Luke 17:34–35). Many dispensational commentators have taken this passage as a reference to the rapture, the sudden disappearance of one person while another person is "left behind." There are other options to consider. To begin with, this might be more akin to someone being dragged away by local authorities. It is the picture of secret police, mob violence, and loud knocks on the door at midnight where people are taken away without warning. Or it may be an army raiding a village and catching by surprise those having a noonday siesta or working at the mill, which makes a lot of sense for Judean and Galilean villages between AD 66 and 70.[108] There again, if this refers to the *parousia*, perhaps one person is taken in judgment, while the other is left in peace. Perhaps those left behind are Christians, who are unscathed by the final judgment and are free to enjoy Christ's millennial reign.[109] No rapture required here!

The Thessalonian correspondence has further descriptions of the return of Christ. Paul writes: "Concerning the coming of our Lord Jesus Christ and our *being gathered to him* [*episynagōgēs ep' auton*], we ask you, brothers and sisters ..." (2 Thess 2:1, italics added). Unfortunately, this is a terse description about being gathered to the Lord and does not provide much information other than a general affirmation that believers are assembled toward him. More explicit detail is provided in 1 Thessalonians 4:14–17:

> For we believe that Jesus died and rose again, and so we believe that God will bring with Jesus those who have fallen asleep in him. According to the Lord's word, we tell you that we who are still alive, who are left till the coming of the Lord, will certainly not precede those who have fallen asleep. For the Lord himself will come down from heaven, with a loud command, with the voice of the archangel and with the trumpet call of God, and the dead in Christ will rise first. After that, we who are still alive

---

108. Cf. further Caird, *Saint Luke*, 197–200.
109. Robert H. Gundry, *Matthew: A Commentary on His Handbook for a Mixed Church under Persecution* (Grand Rapids: Eerdmans, 1995), 494.

and are left *will be caught up together* [*harpagēsometha*] with them in the clouds *to meet the Lord in the air* [*eis apantēsin tou kuriou eis aera*]. And so we will be with the Lord forever. (italics added).

Here the coming of the Lord is the *parousia*, a full descent to earth, not a partial descent to pick up Christians who have been launched into the sky like bottle rockets. This is confirmed by the background to the imagery. During Hellenistic times, when a regent paid an official visit to a city (called a *parousia*, meaning "royal presence" or "royal visitation"), leading citizens would go out to meet him and escort him on the final stages of his journey to the city. This "meeting" was called the *apantēsis*, which is the same word we find in 1 Thessalonians 4:17. As F. F. Bruce comments: "These analogies (especially in association with the term *parousia*) suggest the possibility that the Lord is pictured here as escorted on the remainder of his journey to earth by his people—both those newly raised from the dead and those who have remained alive."[110]

In other words, those who come with Jesus at his *parousia* are the dead in Christ, proving that they don't miss out (1 Thess 4:14). Note also that the dead do not actually descend with Jesus from heaven; rather, they are raised up at Christ's return ahead of those who are alive at the time (4:16). The point is not that some people are descending and others ascending; what happens is the resurrection of the body (1 Cor 15:51–52; Phil 3:20–21; Rev 20:4). Rather than referring to a "rapture," we are perhaps better served to use biblical language of resurrection and transformation. So that's a wrap on the rapture!

---

110. F. F. Bruce, *1–2 Thessalonians* (WBC; Dallas: Word, 1982), 103.

---

seven-year tribulation that will precede the kingdom and that the judgments that make up Revelation 6–18 are future and chronological as opposed to symbolic for what happens in church history.[111] Overall, the idea behind the pretrib view is that Christ will come at the beginning of the great tribulation and remove the church from the world. It is a secret coming, not all the way to earth, just far enough to rapture the church up into the air to meet the Lord (1 Thess 4:17). Then, after the tribulation, Christ will come again, this time the whole way to earth with the

---

111. For discussion of mediating positions such as "midtribulation" and "partial rapture" see Erickson, *Christian Theology*, 1239; Robert H. Gundry, *The Church and the Tribulation: A Biblical Examination of Posttribulationism* (Grand Rapids: Zondervan, 1973), 200–201.

church and establish a millennial kingdom. On top of that there will be three resurrections. The first will be a resurrection of the departed saints at the rapture before the tribulation, the second at the end of the tribulation for believers who died during the tribulation, and the third of unbelievers at the end of the millennium for a final judgment. The scheme looks as follows:

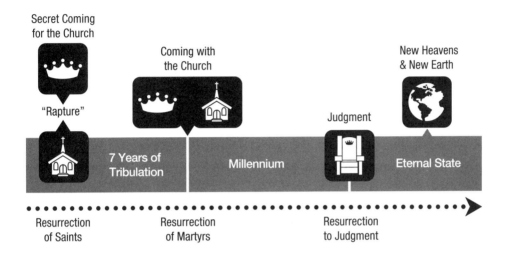

Several arguments are adduced in favor of the pretrib view.[112] First, it is explicitly said that the church is saved from God's wrath: "Jesus ... rescues us from the coming wrath" (1 Thess 1:10), and "God did not appoint us to suffer wrath but to receive salvation through our Lord Jesus Christ" (5:9). Therefore, believers are delivered from God's wrath poured out on the world during the great tribulation (see Rev 6:16–17; 11:18; 14:10, 19; 15:1, 7; 16:1, 19). This deliverance occurs at the rapture, where Christ takes the church out of the world (1 Thess 4:17). The reference to the "elect" who undergo the tribulation in Mark 13 and Matthew 24 refers to Jews and not to Christians. In dispensational theology there is a sharp distinction between Israel and the church. Though the church is taken from the earth, the Jewish people must suffer under the reign of the Antichrist, who attacks the Jews and any others who convert to Christ during that time. Moreover, at the end of the tribulation, all Israel is converted to faith in Jesus (Rom 11:26).

Second, concerning the absence of the church from the tribulation, appeal is also made to Revelation 3:10: "Since you have kept my command to endure patiently, I will also keep you from the hour of trial that is going to come on the whole world

---

112. Cf. John F. Walvoord, *The Rapture Question* (Findlay, OH: Dunham, 1957); Paul D. Feinberg, "The Case for the Pretribulation Rapture Position," in *The Rapture* (Grand Rapids: Zondervan, 1984), 45–86; Gordon R. Lewis and Bruce A. Demarest, *Integrative Theology* (3 vols.; Grand Rapids: Zondervan, 1987–94), 3:369–444.

to test the inhabitants of the earth." In other words, believers will be exempted from undergoing a worldwide affliction by their rapture to the Lord. On the pretrib view, Jesus' return is thus imminent, and he may come any time like a thief in the night—something for which believers must be prepared for (Matt 24:43; 1 Thess 5:2). Paul Feinberg concludes:

> For me at least, the church will not go through the Tribulation because of the character of that entire period as a time of outpouring of penal, retributive, divine wrath, as well as the promises of God to the church that exempt it from both the time and experience of wrath. Further, it is necessary to separate the Rapture of the church from the Second Advent of Christ because of the need for an interval for people to be saved, so that they can enter the kingdom age in natural non-glorified bodies. Finally, the differences between Rapture passages and Second Coming passages lead me to believe that there are two separate events referred to in the passages.[113]

The pretrib position, however, suffers from several rather devastating criticisms. First, if (as argued above) Mark 13 is Jesus' prophecy about the destruction of Jerusalem at AD 70 rather than a prediction of the end times, a whole sway of biblical material immediately is removed from the pretrib/dispensationalist grasp.[114] For Jesus, the great tribulation denotes neither the events of the second century BC (i.e., the Maccabbean crisis) nor the distress immediately preceding his return; rather, it describes the destruction of Jerusalem with its razing of the temple.[115] As D. A. Carson notes, "That Jesus in v. 21 [of Matt 24] promises that such 'great distress' is never to be equaled implies that it cannot refer to the Tribulation at the end of the age, for if what happens next is the Millennium or the new heaven and the new earth, it seems inane to say that such 'great distress' will not take place again."[116]

Second, though God's wrath can be revealed in the present time (Rom 1:18) or identified with particular local and temporal punishments (1 Thess 2:16), in the New Testament God's wrath from which believers are delivered always refers to God's judgment against sin at the final judgment, not to the wrath of the tribulation (see Matt 3:7/Luke 3:7; John 3:36; Rom 2:5; 5:9; Col 3:5–6).

Third, there is little chance that Revelation 3:10 supports the pretrib argument.[117] Here's why: (a) This text refers to a persecution affecting just the Philadelphian church. As David Aune comments: "The promise made here pertains to Philadelphian Christians *only* and cannot be generalized to include Christians in other churches of Asia much less all Christians in all places and times."[118] What

---

113. Feinberg, "Pretribulation Rapture," 86.

114. Matthew 24 converges the two events, destruction of Jerusalem and Jesus' *parousia* together, but only insofar as the destruction of Jerusalem is typological of the *parousia* rather than a detailed description of its events.

115. Blomberg, "Posttribulationism," 73.

116. Carson, "Matthew," 8:501.

117. Contrast the perspectives in Grant R. Osborne, *Revelation* (BECNT; Grand Rapids: Baker, 2002), 192–94; Beale, *Revelation*, 289–92.

118. David E. Aune, *Revelation* (WBC; 3 vols.; Dallas: Word, 1997–98), 1:240 (italics original).

comfort or solace would Christians in Philadelphia take if John's point was that in two thousand years or so, the believers alive at the rapture will be spared tribulation while the Philadelphians themselves are now left to suffer the merciless persecution of Roman authorities based on slanderous accusations from local Jewish communities in the late first century? Ironically, whereas pretrib/dispensational interpreters strongly advocate the literal approach to Revelation, here they must understand the Philadelphians as symbolic for faithful believers across history; otherwise the promise is irrelevant to the initial audience.

(b) In addition, the letters to the seven churches in Revelation 2–3 exhort the churches to persevere under duress; they do not promise them an escape route from trial. That the Philadelphians are kept "from" (*ek*) the "hour of trial" means that they are preserved *within* it and not *removed from* it (see John 17:15, "My prayer is not that you take them out of the world but that you protect them from the evil one").

(c) The trial about to transpire, much like the ten-day affliction in Smyrna (Rev 2:10), is temporary. The extent of this tribulation as coming upon the "whole world" (*oikoumenē*) to test those who "live on the earth" obviously has a universal character, but the "world" here is probably limited to the known world of the author and encompasses regions of Asia Minor (see the use of *oikoumenē* in Luke 2:1; Acts 11:28). Moreover, given the anticipation of the second coming in Revelation 3:11, it is possible to see the tribulation here in the context of a wider narrative about the judgment and the *parousia*, so that there is an organic unity between the localized tribulation confronting the Philadelphian church and the escalating tribulation preceding Christ's return.

Fourth, and finally, the pretrib position eccentrically breaks up the second coming into a secret coming for the church (i.e., *rapture*) and a visible coming with the church (i.e., *parousia*); this division has no analogy or warrant in Scripture other than being an inference from the dispensational scheme. Yet 1 Thessalonians 4:13–17; 5:1–10; and Revelation 19–20 depict the same event of Christ's one and only return to earth.[119]

3.4.2.2 POSTTRIBULATIONISM

The posttribulation view (henceforth "posttrib") is that the church will undergo the great tribulation and afterward be resurrected at the *parousia*.[120] The gist of the posttrib position is that the church will go through a period of trial before the second coming, which also precedes the millennial reign of Christ on earth. There

---

119. What is more, those who accompany Jesus at his coming in 1 Thess 3:13 and Rev 19:14 are angels, not the raptured church.

120. Most posttrib advocates also include Dan 9:24–27 and Matthew 24/Mark 13 as part of their evidence as well.

is a resurrection concurrent with Jesus' return and another resurrection of the rest of humanity at the end of the millennium.[121] During the tribulation, the unbelieving world experiences God's wrath in the form of natural and supernatural disasters, while believers experience the wrath of Satan, the Antichrist, and the wicked against God's people.[122] Unlike the dispensational scheme, there is no absolute bifurcation between Israel and the church, nor are the rapture and the *parousia* regarded as separate events. On this scheme, the return of the Lord is "impending" rather than "imminent."[123] This can be diagrammed as follows:

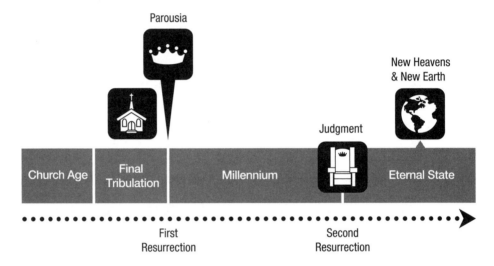

Several arguments can be adduced in support of the posttrib view.[124] First, there are many exhortations in the New Testament to believers to endure under adversity and fidelity in the face of compromise. These warnings intensify in passages that anticipate a particularly difficult period of trial that will come upon the world (see John 16:33; 1 Thess 5:2–12; 2 Thess 2:9–10; Rev 13:10; 14:12). In one sense, the end-time "messianic woes" began with Jesus' death, but subsequent believers can also participate in them in some form. Jesus' Olivet Discourse states plainly that the elect will experience the "days of distress" as a cataclysmic event approaches (Mark 13:19–25; cf. Matt 24:21–29). Though I think that this warning refers specifically to the Jewish war of AD 66–70, it is also typological for any further period of distress that God's people will experience thereafter. Paul tells the Colossians: "Now I rejoice in what I am suffering for you, and I fill up in my flesh what is still lacking

---

121. Many posttribers do not like using the word "rapture" since it is not found in Scripture.
122. Gundry, *The Church and the Tribulation*, 49.
123. Ibid., 29–43.

124. Robert H. Gundry, *The Church and the Tribulation*; Douglas J. Moo, "Posttribulation Rapture Position," in *The Rapture* (Grand Rapids, MI: Zondervan, 1984), 169–211; Blomberg, "Posttribulationism," 61–87.

in regard to Christ's afflictions, for the sake of his body, which is the church" (Col 1:24). The point here is that Paul's apostolic sufferings are also part of the end-time affliction, and Paul soaks up more than his fair share.[125]

John the Seer refers to himself as "your brother and companion in the suffering and kingdom and patient endurance that are ours in Jesus" (Rev 1:9); this shows that kingdom and tribulation coexist across church history. God's people have been experiencing tribulation ever since the arrival of the "last days" in Jesus' first advent. It is hardly surprising, then, that the church will have to patiently endure distress when this affliction is intensified at the great tribulation rather than expect to be removed from it.

Second, Paul's narration of events in 2 Thessalonians 2:1–12 makes it clear that the *parousia* of Jesus will occur after the rebellion takes place and after the man of lawlessness is revealed (see esp. 2 Thess 2:3, "Don't let anyone deceive you in any way, for that day will not come until the rebellion occurs and the man of lawlessness is revealed"). On the fairly safe assumption that Paul's description of the *parousia* as "we who are still alive and are left will be caught up together with them in the clouds to meet the Lord in the air" (1 Thess 4:17) is the same as "the coming of our Lord Jesus Christ and our being gathered to him" (2 Thess 2:1), then a period of rebellion (*apostasia*) immediately precedes the second coming (2:3). This "man of lawlessness" can be correlated with the "antichrist" (1 John 4:3; 2 John 7) and "the beast" (Rev 13–17). This figure, resembling a mixture of Antiochus IV Epiphanes and Nero, opposes God, persecutes God's people, and leads nations astray.[126] He is revealed, then comes the tribulation, and only after that does Christ return.

Third, there is another clear indication of a posttrib perspective in Revelation. The sequence that runs through Revelation 6–17 contains a series of images about seals, trumpets, and bowls that unleash God's fury against the unbelieving world (with an interlude in Revelation 12–14) and concurrently narrates the persecution of God's people by the beast and his forces. In Revelation 7, there is a further vision of the throne room, and one of the elders asks John about the identity of those in the white robes who are gathered around the throne. John replies: "I answered, 'Sir, you know.' And he said, 'These are they who have come out of the great tribulation; they have washed their robes and made them white in the blood of the Lamb'" (Rev 7:14). These people are not just Jews, but Christians, because earlier they are described as coming "from every nation, tribe, people and language" (7:9), which is the same designation used for the church in 5:9.

What is more, the 144,000 described in Revelation 7:1–8 are identical to the great multitude in 7:9–17. It is the church of Jesus Christ, symbolically depicted as

---

125. Michael F. Bird, *Colossians and Philemon* (NCCS; Eugene, OR: Cascade, 2009), 64–66.

126. Cf. Geert W. Lorein, *The Antichrist Theme in the Intertestamental Period* (London: T&T Clark, 2003).

Israel, who comes through the tribulation. The description "they who came out of the great tribulation" (7:14) reads most naturally as designating people who had been in some sense exposed to it but have now come to safe quarters. That is confirmed by the observation that they were sealed so as to be preserved from God's judgments against the world, so they must have lived through the tribulation before coming out of it.[127]

Fourth, the posttrib view is eminently preferable to the pretrib view because the latter did not appear on the scene of church history until J. N. Darby in the 1830s (perhaps inspired by a spiritual enthusiastic teenage girl from Glasgow [all the more harrowing for me since I know some Scottish teenage girls from Glasgow]).[128] Donald Fairburn surveys the historical evidence and concludes:

> From this discussion, it has become clear that among early patristic writers who deal with the great tribulation, there is no evidence of a belief that the rapture of the church would be before the tribulation. The patristic identification of the Old Testament and New Testament people of God, coupled with the early church's attitude toward suffering, predisposes the fathers against such a view. More important, the early church saw the tribulation as the final proving ground for the saints and thus indicated that the church would be present on earth at that time.... The premillennialism of the early church was posttribulational, and in substance it was very different from dispensational premillennialism even though there were some noteworthy points of contact.[129]

The differences between pretrib and posttrib are not incidental. It matters a great deal if we are going to disciple people to endure trials and tribulations—especially the "great tribulation"—or tell them that they can expect to be delivered from it. Though we are urged to pray to our Father to spare us from the *peirasmos* (the "trial"), we are also exhorted many times to be alert and prepared for the ordeal that may follow.

In summary, from all of this discussion, I conclude that the biblical eschatology is best described as historic premillennialism.

---

127. Blomberg, "Posttribulationism," 75–77.

128. Cf. Ben Witherington III, *The Problem with Evangelical Theology: Testing the Exegetical Foundations of Calvinism, Dispensationalism, and Wesleyanism* (Waco, TX: Baylor University Press, 2005), 94–96.

129. Donald Fairburn, "Contemporary Millennial/Tribulational Debates: Whose Side Was the Early Church On?" in *A Case for Historic Premillennialism* (ed. C. L. Blomberg and S. W. Chung; Grand Rapids: Baker, 2009), 128.

§ 3.5 THE FINAL JUDGMENT

The Christ of God and the judgment of God are both features of the Christian gospel. Jesus Christ is appointed as both *Savior* and *Judge* (John 5:27; Acts 10:42; 17:31; Rom 2:16; 2 Tim 4:1). The gospel *announces salvation* and *declares judgment* as it specifically warns of the grave consequences for rejecting the gospel, much like someone refusing the desperate plea to board a lifeboat from a sinking ship (Rom 2:16; 10:16–21; 2 Thess 1:8; 1 Pet 4:17). The Apostles' Creed summarizes a New Testament theme with its brief affirmation that Jesus "will come again to judge the living and the dead." The whole world, the righteous and the unrighteous, will stand before the judgment seat of Christ (Rom 14:10; 2 Cor 5:10). However unpleasant the thought of divine judgment may be, salvation is ultimately a deliverance from judgment. The task now is to unpack the meaning of "judgment" and to explore questions like what judgment actually is and how divine judgment functions.

3.5.1 JUDGMENT AS FACING GOD WITHOUT THE CROSS

The final judgment is an extension of the judgment of God executed at the cross. It was on the cross that God meted out his wrath, displeasure, grief, and pain at the morass of human evil. There, Jesus underwent the darkness and forsakenness of judgment: "From noon until three in the afternoon darkness came over all the land. About three in the afternoon Jesus cried out in a loud voice, *'Eli, Eli, lema sabachthani?'* (which means 'My God, my God, why have you forsaken me?')" (Matt 27:45–46, quoting Ps 22:1). As he bore the sins of humanity—past, present, and future—Jesus experienced separation from God, which is the essence of hell—a full partitioning from the divine presence of love and peace. In the words of Isaiah, the crucifixion visibly disfigured Christ as he bore the shame, impurity, and malevolence of humanity: "His appearance was so disfigured beyond that of any human being and his form marred beyond human likeness" (Isa 52:14). Jesus bore the weight of human evil and set aside the beauty of God's glory for the ugliness of human transgression.

At the cross, Christ is judged in the place of humanity. As Paul says, "God made him who had no sin to be sin for us" (2 Cor 5:21). Jesus was "made" (*poieō*) sin in the sense of carrying and identifying with our sin while yet being sinless himself. Jesus' atoning death, as we will see, is made immediately effective for the elect and conditionally effective for all of humanity. Judgment against human wickedness can be absorbed in the flesh of Christ on the cross or in the flesh of the wicked who will be resurrected at the final judgment. There are no alternatives. People sin in the flesh, and the fleshly nature that causes sin must receive its due penalty.

Yet those who bind themselves to Christ in faith have no fear of the final judgment. Hear the promise of Jesus in the gospel of John: "Very truly I tell you, whoever hears my word and believes him who sent me has eternal life and *will not be judged* but has crossed over from death to life" (John 5:24, italics added). Or in the words of the Heidelberg Catechism Q. 52:

> Question: How does Christ's return "to judge the living and the dead" comfort you? Answer: In all distress and persecution, with uplifted head, I confidently await the very judge who has already offered himself to the judgment of God in my place and removed the whole curse from me. Christ will cast all his enemies and mine into everlasting condemnation, but will take me and all his chosen ones to himself into the joy and glory of heaven.[130]

This is because, first, believers have died with Christ and have already been through judgment with Christ as their representative, and they do not need to go through it again (see Rom 6:4–8; Gal 2:20; Col 2:20; 3:3). Second, Christ as their substitute died in their place for their sins, and the penalty cannot be applied again. Thus, no wrath and condemnation remain for them, for Christ has drained it all away like poison sucked clean from a wound. The cross of Christ is like the wings of a hen that shields its young from the flames of a barnyard fire (see Matt 23:37; Luke 13:34).

The tragedy of the final judgment is that men and women will stand before the judgment of God without the shield of the cross to protect them, because they do not carry the insignia of the cross, namely, faith in the crucified and risen Lord.

3.5.2 JUDGMENT AND THE JUDGED

Who will be judged? First, it is unbelievers. The secret things of every human heart will be exposed for all to see (Luke 8:17; Rom 2:16; 1 Cor 4:5). The final judgment is impartial and judicial as God distributes justice to each as they deserve. That includes distributing both degrees of punishment and rewards to all persons. Paul, quoting Psalm 62:12, declares: "God 'will repay everyone according to what they have done'" (Rom 2:6). John the Seer records the words of Jesus: "I am coming

---

130. See www.crcna.org/welcome/beliefs/confessions/heidelberg-catechism.

soon! My reward is with me, and I will give to each person according to what they have done" (Rev 22:12). Unbelievers can expect their good deeds to be universally acknowledged and praised. The problem is that the wickedness that permeates every facet of their being, even the good they did, will be exposed and receive its due penalty as well.

Second, believers are also subjects of judgment. This is clear in two Pauline texts: "For we will all stand before God's judgment seat" (Rom 14:10); "For we must all appear before the judgment seat of Christ, so that each of us may receive what is due us for the things done while in the body, whether good or bad" (2 Cor 5:10). In the section on justification (see §5.4) I will argue that the apparent tension between being justified by faith and judged according to works is resolved when we remember that God works his works in us so that his declarative verdict of acquittal has parity with his work of renewal in us. Good works are not the cause of salvation, for that is exclusively the work of Christ; rather, good works demonstrate the necessary evidences of a saving faith in the Savior. The final judgment shows that God himself has produced in believers the necessary evidences of authentic faith; moreover, God assigns degrees of reward on the basis of how successfully believers have cooperated with his grace of renewal.[131]

Third, angels will also be judged. According to Peter, "God did not spare angels when they sinned, but sent them to hell, putting them in chains of darkness to be held for judgment" (2 Pet 2:4). Similar also is Jude 6, "And the angels who did not keep their positions of authority but abandoned their proper dwelling—these he has kept in darkness, bound with everlasting chains for judgment on the great Day." The angels who rebelled with Satan in his war against the heavenly host (Rev 12:7–9; cf. Luke 10:18) and the "sons of God" who lusted for beautiful women (Gen 6:2) will be subject to judgment on the last day. What is more, many angels are already bound in the dark prison (*tartarus*, cf. 2 Pet 2:4), a Greek word that denoted a subterranean place lower than Hades and taken up in Jewish apocalyptic thought as the darkest caverns of the waiting place of the dead.[132] Paul also adds that believers will participate in the work of judgment by judging the angels. If they are going to judge the angels, how much more, then, are Christians competent to adjudicate between one another rather than leave matters to civil and secular courts (1 Cor 6:2).

3.5.3 JUDGMENT AS THE VICTORY OF CHRIST

A number of judgments have already been meted out in biblical history. Individuals like David experienced judgment for their sins. Israel suffered judgment in the

---

131. Cf. Grudem, *Systematic Theology*, 1143–45.
132. BDAG, 991.

Assyrian and Babylonian exiles because of their idolatry and wickedness. Jerusalem underwent judgment for rejecting Jesus as the Son of God. The nations in the book of Revelation undergo judgments because of their continued rebellion against God and mistreatment of his people. These judgments are temporary and local. The final judgment, however, is everlasting, transhistorical, and universal. Revelation 20:11–15 describes judgment in this way:

> Then I saw a *great white throne* and him who was seated on it. The earth and the heavens fled from his presence, and there was no place for them. And I saw the dead, great and small, standing before the throne, and books were opened. Another book was opened, which is the book of life. The dead were judged according to what they had done as recorded in the books. The sea gave up the dead that were in it, and death and Hades gave up the dead that were in them, and *everyone was judged according to what they had done*. Then death and Hades were thrown into the lake of fire. The lake of fire is the second death. All whose names were not found written in the book of life were thrown into the lake of fire. (italics added)

Judgment is more than a distribution of rewards and punishments. Judgment is the vindication of Christ and his people. The destruction of Jerusalem in AD 70 was the coming of the Son of Man in judgment and the vindication of Jesus as the prophet, who spoke up against the temple establishment (esp. clear in Mark 11–13). At his trial before Caiaphas, Jesus responded that he would be enthroned beside God and, therefore, be the agent of God's judging and saving work (Mark 14:62). When people stand before the Great White Throne, before Jesus the Judge, it is the eschatological proof that he is who he claimed to be. He was not a religious fanatic, a false prophet, or a messianic pretender; he was in fact the Son of God, and before him every knee will bow. The one condemned by a human court now presides over the heavenly court.

Similarly, judgment against the wicked is solace for God's people who go through tribulation, or even through *the* tribulation, since they will see God's justice visibly executed in their favor. According to John 3:19–20: "This is the verdict: Light has come into the world, but people loved darkness instead of light because their deeds were evil. Everyone who does evil hates the light, and will not come into the light for fear that their deeds will be exposed." The final judgment proves that Christians are of the light while the world is in darkness. The church is the sheep and the rest of the world are the goats (Matt 25:31–46). Despite what others said about them, and even did to them, the church is the children of God. Though they are hated by the world, they are honored by God and will enjoy their reward with him forever. The final judgment reveals the true status of believers before the cosmos. It is a demonstration that believers are more than conquerors through the Messiah who loved them (Rom 8:37).

3.5.4 JUDGMENT AS RETRIBUTION AND RESTORATION

A common theme in recent theological work is to stress God's justice as restorative rather than retributive. The underlying assumption is that retribution is mean, nasty, not nice, and therefore unworthy of a God of love, grace, and mercy. For instance, Tom Smail comments: "God's justice is concerned less with punishing wrong relationships than with restoring right ones. Like the heroes of the Book of Judges, Jesus is concerned with freeing the land from the evil forces that have infested it and setting our humanity free from the personal and social twistedness that is corrupting and destroying it."[133] Stephen Travis believes:

> Retributive concepts are forced toward the edges of New Testament thought by the nature of the Christian gospel. It is a gospel that proclaims Christ as the one through whom people are invited into a relationship with God. Once the relationship to Christ and to God is seen as central, retributive concepts become inappropriate. The experience described by such terms as forgiveness, love, grace and acceptance overrides them. And the experience of those who refuse to respond to this gospel is not so much an experience of retributive punishment as the negation of all that is offered in Christ.[134]

Travis goes on to point out that the biblical imagery for justice contains warnings of retribution against the wicked, but they are largely metaphors for exclusion from God's presence rather than speculative descriptions of postmortem torments like that found in some Jewish apocalyptic literature. Moreover, retributive judgment is frequently juxtaposed with wider visions of the triumph of God's glory and love. In his conclusion, he asks whether "retributive language should be displaced from Christian vocabulary" in favor of "the language of a relationship to Christ."

Now I can genuinely sympathize with a desire to escape the Western captivity to a contractual understanding of divine-human relationships and the limitation of justice to a recompense of deeds. Aristotle and Anselm have set the agenda and grammar for theology for too long. So it is tempting to ask God to give us a covenant relationship rather than a contract. May his justice be transformative rather than punitive.

But the more I think about this, the more the old saying about the baby and the bath water comes to my mind. God's covenants are intimately relational, but they are also legally binding—hence the lawsuit motif one finds in the Pentateuch and Prophets. God's justice will transform the world, but a transformed world must be one where the most insidious of evils and their perpetrators are not lightly rinsed

---

133. Tom Smail, *Once and For All: A Confession of the Cross* (Eugene, OR: Wipf & Stock, 1998), 95.

134. Stephen H. Travis, *Christ and the Judgment of God: The Limits of Divine Retribution in New Testament Thought* (2nd ed.; Milton Keynes, UK: Paternoster, 2008), 325, 327.

with a perfume of goodness. Evil is such that it must be destroyed or quarantined if the goodness of God has utter supremacy in the new creation. That is why the psalmist says that creation rejoices in the coming of the Lord to judge the earth, because creation will then be cured of evil (Ps 96:13). Precisely because God is love, he must not allow evil to have the last enduring word in any corner of the galaxy.

We do not have to choose between retributive and restorative schemes of divine justice. The righteousness that brings judgment also fills the universe with God's *shalom*. For "the fruit of that righteousness will be peace; its effect will be quietness and confidence forever" (Isa 32:17; cf. Ps 85:10; Isa 9:7; Heb 12:11). There can be no reconciliation without recompense; otherwise the disorder, destruction, and decay of evil prevent peace from lasting. The incarnation and the cross achieve both: juridical judgment and relational peace are wrought in the atonement. As Henri Blocher comments: "Retribution and restoration are not mutually exclusive; the good news is the retribution, and the basis of restoration is in the person of the head and substitute."[135]

Theologians will protest that this is divine violence, and it sanctions human violence rather than preventing it. Yet God's justice is about vindication, not vindictiveness. The "vengeance" (*ekdikēsis*) of God is not his unbridled and disproportionate violence unleashed through an unchecked hatred of his opponents. It is more properly his righteous decision to be the God who vindicates those who suffer and to avenge their pain with an appropriate action that holds the subjects of evil responsible for their actions (see esp. Deut 32:43; Luke 18:3, 5; Rom 12:19; Rev 6:10). Divine vengeance — like it or not, there is such a thing — is not a license for human violence, but rather the grounds for the end of it. As Miroslav Volf states: "The certainty of God's judgment at the end of history is the presupposition for the renunciation of violence. The divine system of judgment is not the flip side of the human reign of terror, but a necessary correlate of human nonviolence."[136]

3.5.5 JUDGMENT AS THE TRIUMPH OF GRACE

Donald Bloesch subtitles his section on the final judgment as "The Triumph of Grace."[137] We might think of judgment as the antithesis of grace; judgment is about punishment while grace is about mercy, is it not? Scripture is clear that in the end, light triumphs over darkness, good over evil, and holiness over corruption. What will abide forever is not God's wrath, but his mercy: "You do not stay angry forever but delight to show mercy" (Mic 7:18). God's mercies "never fail" because they

---

135. Henri Blocher, "God and the Cross," in *Engaging the Doctrine of God: Contemporary Protestant Perspectives* (ed. B. L. McCormack; Grand Rapids: Baker, 2008), 140 (125–41).

136. Miroslav Volf, *Exclusion and Embrace: A Theological Exploration of Identity, Otherness and Reconciliation* (Nashville: Abingdon, 1996), 302.

137. Donald Bloesch, *The Last Things: Resurrection, Judgment, Glory* (Downers Grove, IL: InterVarsity Press, 2004), 213.

are rooted in his steadfast love (Lam 3:22). James the Just writes: "Mercy triumphs over judgment" because "the Lord is full of compassion and mercy" (Jas 2:13; 5:11). When God's judgment falls on rebellious humanity, it reveals that at his essence God is love rather than wrath. God will be all in all, and all things will be united to him.

But not all will be united to God in the same way.[138] In other words, some will be united to God by way of experiencing his discipline and displeasure with evil. That itself is a measure of mercy because it demonstrates the error of their ways, it prevents the perpetuation of evil in its earthly state, and God abstains from annihilation as a form of punishment as he counts them worthy of an eternal existence; thus even hell, in a sense, is a form of mercy, albeit one embedded with punishment. As C. S. Lewis proposed, hell is the means by which God sets a limit on how terrible people can be. It is God's last mercy to those who will let him do no other.[139] Then there are others who will be drawn into the glory and beauty of God's eternal dwelling because of their union with Christ and vivification by the Spirit. Their eternal communion with God rests in the unmerited mercy of God planned since eternity past that is to be made manifest in the new heavens and the new earth.

3.5.6 JUDGMENT AND THE GLORY OF GOD

God's purpose is to glorify himself in his rescuing love for others. God's plan to achieve that purpose is to unite creation to himself through the Logos. The unity of that plan is the covenant of grace, and the substance of the covenant is worked out in the unfolding narrative of redemptive history. What has glory to do with judgment? Toward the end of Revelation, when Babylon the Great falls, we hear an oracle of celebration: "After this I heard what sounded like the roar of a great multitude in heaven shouting: 'Hallelujah! Salvation and glory and power belong to our God, for true and just are his judgments. He has condemned the great prostitute who corrupted the earth by her adulteries. He has avenged on her the blood of his servants'" (Rev 19:1–2). The powers that oppressed have been disempowered. The "powers that be" are the "powers no more." Those who denied justice and inflicted injustices receive justice at the end. God's people rejoice, the nations worship God, and the entire universe gives God glory.

This dramatic scene is part of a larger narrative whereby Jesus defeats his enemies (Rev 19:11–21), establishes a messianic kingdom (20:1–6), puts down a final rebellion (20:7–10), enacts a final judgment (20:11–15), and rules with God and the saints in a new heaven and a new earth (chs. 21–22). God's glory is revealed when

---

138. Ibid., 214–15.
139. C. S. Lewis, *Pilgrim's Regress* (London: Geoffrey Bles, 1965), 180.

creation is purified from evil and the exile from Eden comes to an end.[140] This corresponds to the main theme of Revelation, which Greg Beale rightly captures: "The main idea of the entire book may be roughly formulated as follows: *The sovereignty of God and Christ in redeeming and judging brings them glory, which is intended to motivate saints to worship God and reflect his glorious attributes through obedience to his word.*"[141] God's glory comes by redemption and renewal, and that means putting the world to right, giving evil its due, destroying the weed of sin at its root, and obliterating the spiritual cancer of rebellion at the level of its DNA.

3.5.7 HOW ETERNAL JUDGMENT AFFECTS THE HISTORICAL PRESENT

"God wins" is the theme of Revelation. It is not just that God wins, but we win with him. God's victory at the cross is put into effect at the final judgment, and God's people reign with the Lord forever. Once the wrongs have been righted, once sin is dealt with, and once death dies, then comes the new creation. A garden city is purified of the weeds of evil that destroyed the first garden. The tears of sorrow give way to trumpets of joy. Then God's people dwell in God's place under God's reign in God's presence. We are heading toward a world of justice and peace. So we are waiting for it.

But not just waiting. The church is meant to be a showroom for the new creation. The church is meant to be a place where reconciliation, peace, love, and mercy are modeled in front of a world that knows only strife, confrontation, hatred, and abuse. The church is meant to be the billboard for the world to come. Now that is not always the case. Obviously a kitchen showroom at a home renovation exhibition can sometimes have the wrong color tiles or not enough space for a fridge, and be missing a few shelves. Similarly, the church does not always constitute the best advertisement for the product it is pointing to. But let's face it, what advertisement is ever the same as the real thing? The life of the church is to hint at what the world would look like in a redeemed state: righteousness flowing like a river, lions lying down with lambs, swords beaten into plowshares, and grace and mercy mingling together. We can work for justice in this world as part of our preparations for the next world. Advocating for the defenseless and the oppressed is an act of worship that reminds the world that the just judge is ready to make his final entrance.

---

140. James M. Hamilton, *God's Glory in Salvation through Judgment: A Biblical Theology* (Wheaton, IL: Crossway, 2010), 549.

141. Beale, *Revelation*, 151 (italics original).

§ 3.6 THE INTERMEDIATE STATE: WHAT HAPPENS WHEN YOU DIE?

Thus far we have dealt with cosmic eschatology, examining the momentous topics of the second coming, the millennium, the tribulation, and the final judgment. It should be clear by now that the final state of the church is deeply connected with the final state of the universe. The new humanity will dwell in the fullness of the new creation in full communion with their Creator and Redeemer. Zeroing in on something more specific, we will now engage the topic of individual eschatology, which concerns the fate and future of the individual person. Within the domain of Christian theology, individual eschatology must be understood in relation to (1) a redemptive-history that narrates the fall and the subsequent entrance of spiritual and physical death into creation; and (2) the intermediate state, which the believer experiences upon death but before the final resurrection. Our individual experience of grave and glory is ultimately part of a wider story of God's intention to destroy death and to return creation to its vitalizing beauty.

The subject of the intermediate state is important for several reasons. First, we have to wrestle with our own mortality. I am now thirty-seven years of age, and I have reached the point where the naive feelings of invincibility and immortality associated with youth are beginning to recede quicker than my hairline. My strawberry and cream-colored beard is beginning to show more cream than strawberry these days. Death approaches me ... and you. What will become of me? I must ask.

Second, we must consider how to minister to the dying and the bereaved. Only yesterday, the day before I wrote this section, I visited a dying woman in a hospital and did my best to comfort her and her son. "What will happen to me?" and "What happened to my mother?" are questions that all Christians need to able to answer with confidence and clarity. Thankfully we are not underresourced to respond, and we can do so with theological integrity and pastoral sensitivity because Scripture has something to say to these issues.

The gospel holds out the promise of eternal life because it brings good news of God's victory over death. The Christian testimony to the gospel is one of hope for those who die in the Lord. Let us remember, too, that what we think about death and its aftermath will ultimately be determined by what we think about God, Jesus Christ, the communion of the saints, and the resurrection of the dead. Dealing with death forces us to engage the seriousness of the sin that caused death and the brightness of the hope that overcomes it. The gospel is a word of hope that our life is hidden in Christ (Col 1:5, 23; 3:3) and that life and immortality are brought to light through the gospel (2 Tim 1:10). It is the details of that hope for the future of the believer that individual eschatology is concerned with.

3.6.1 THE FINAL ENEMY: DEATH

In the movie *Bill and Ted's Excellent Adventure* (directed by Stephen Herek [1989]) the Grim Reaper makes a colorful announcement: "You can be a king or a street sweeper, but sooner or later you dance with the Reaper." Death, like taxes, is unavoidable. In Hebrews we read, "People are destined to die once, and after that to face judgment" (Heb 9:27). There is a whole industry related to death in our society, including its prevention, preparation, and posthumous care for the bereaved. There is a peer-reviewed journal called *Death Studies*, which provides an "international interdisciplinary forum in which a variety of professionals share results of research and practice, with the aim of better understanding the human encounter with death and assisting those who work with the dying and their families." Death has fascinated people from Homer to Shakespeare to today and is portrayed in literature, art, music, and drama. Death is big business; it is artistically captivating, philosophically fascinating, and existentially haunting. But it is real, universal, and inevitable.

But death is not the way it always was. In the Christian story, humanity was created to dwell with God in paradise and was made for immortality. Human beings were brought to life in order to know God and to enjoy him forever. The opening narratives of Genesis 1–3 show that sin and death were intrusions into this paradise, not part of its original design; they are intruders into a habitat that is not rightly theirs. Death was a threat as to what would happen to humanity if they disobeyed God's commandments (Gen 2:17; 3:3). If Adam and Eve had obeyed God in their probationary period, they would have perpetuated the Edenic condition for eternity.

Yet humanity refused to believe the threat; they subsequently disobeyed God, and thus death came and reigned over them. Adam and Eve's exile from the paradise of Eden meant subservience to the power of death and living under its tyranny (Gen 3:19–24). That is why in Genesis 5 we are given a genealogy that is characterized by the formula "X lived a total of Y years, and then he died," and the refrain continues with "he died" and then "he died" and "he died" and so on. Death begets death, and a cycle of decay is passed on through sharing in the sin and fate of fallen humanity. Paul puts it this way: "sin entered the world through one man, and death through sin, and in this way death came to all people, because all sinned" (Rom 5:12). In other words, by the disobedience of Adam, sin came and death followed, and now sin and death reign over us. Also, we learn that the fleetingness of human mortality is often likened to "dust," from which humanity was taken and to which it returns (Gen 3:19; Job 7:21; 17:16; Pss 22:29; 30:9). Or else human life is like grass that grows briefly and then withers permanently (Job 8:12; Pss 37:2; 102:11; Isa 40:7–8; 1 Pet 1:24).

The sin–death nexus is what holds humanity in its bonds, producing both a physical death (separation of soul from body) and a spiritual death (separation of humanity from God). In the Christian scheme, death is multifaceted. First, death is a present experience caused by sin. Paul says that believers, before their conversion, were "dead in your transgressions and sins" (Eph 2:1, 5). People are spiritually dead to God, as evidenced by sinful behavior, rebellion against God, and a coldness toward spiritual things. This is why they need the miracle of regeneration to be made spiritually alive; thereafter, they need resurrection to make their bodies alive.

Second, sin is also tied to physical death. We have already seen that in Genesis 1–3 and in Paul's words in Romans 5:12–21. The point is accentuated in the biblical testimony: "The earnings of the wicked are sin and death" (Prov 10:16); "you wicked person, you will surely die" (Ezek 33:8); "the wages of sin is death" (Rom 6:23); "after desire has conceived, it gives birth to sin; and sin, when it is full-grown, gives birth to death" (Jas 1:15). Death is God's judgment against sin and meted out with the full punishment it deserves.

Third, there is a postmortem death to be feared. Jesus taught: "Do not be afraid of those who kill the body but cannot kill the soul. Rather, be afraid of the One who can destroy both soul and body in hell" (Matt 10:28). Even after physical death, people are warned of the prospect of another death where soul and body perish in hell. This is what John the Seer calls "the second death" (Rev 2:11; 20:6; 21:4). The second death is what believers are saved from, but something that unbelievers and the wicked are destined for.

But death does not have the last word, much less the last laugh. The gospel declares God's last word on the matter and that word is "life." God acts, through Christ and in the Spirit, to bring life to those living under the reign of death—not an extended period of earthly life in our mortal coil, not another round of reincarnation, not a cryogenic slumber where only our minds survive, but a full and bodily everlasting life in God's new creation.

Admittedly, some of the biblical authors could be quite pessimistic about death and the afterlife of the individual (Job 7:8–9; Ps 6:5; Eccl 5:18). But as revelation progresses, we see glimpses of a hope beyond the grip of the grave for the covenant community. The psalmist believes that, in contrast to the fate of the wicked, God will redeem him from the power of Sheol and take him into his presence: "They are like sheep and are destined to die; death will be their shepherd ... their forms will decay in the grave, far from their princely mansions. But God will redeem me from the realm of the dead; he will surely take me to himself" (Ps 49:14–15). A similar thought is proffered by the psalmist who appeals to the power of God's love to rescue him from the depths of death: "We are brought down to the dust; our bodies cling to the ground. Rise up and help us; rescue us because of your unfailing love" (Ps 44:25–26). When combined with hints (e.g., Job 19:25–26; Isa 25:8; 53:11; Hos 13:14) and explicit affirmations of resurrection (Dan 12:2–3), we see that death is not how the story will end for God's people. He is preparing a dwelling place for them so that they can find rest in the heavenly city that is made in advance for them (Heb 11:16; 12:22; Rev 21:2).

Although death reigns and falls on everyone through the disobedience of Adam, Paul teaches that through the obedience of Jesus Christ, righteousness will reign in life for everyone (Rom 5:15–21; 1 Cor 15:21–22). The reign of sin and death is dethroned by the abounding grace of God exercised in the righteousness and eternal life that comes in Christ Jesus (Rom 5:21). What is more, in the teaching of Jesus, believers are "children of the resurrection," and they "can no longer die" (Luke 20:36). There is a reason for this. Moses calls the Lord "the God of Abraham, the God of Isaac, and the God of Jacob." He can only be their God if the patriarchs still are with him. For "he is not the God of the dead but of the living." The logic of Jesus' response to the Sadducees is that if God is the covenanting God who freely binds himself to his people, even death itself cannot prevent his communion with them from prevailing forever (see Matt 22:23–33; Mark 12:18–27; Luke 20:27–39).

So physical death is not the end for believers or the wicked. There is a second death at the final judgment to be avoided and hope for a resurrection of the dead to be attained. What happens in between is called the "intermediate state." To this we now turn.

3.6.2 THE INTERMEDIATE STATE

There are a number of options for what, where, and when the intermediate state takes place. We will survey these options and then examine the biblical materials.

3.6.2.1 IMMORTALITY OF THE SOUL

Among the Jewish people in the first century, hope for a future resurrection was merely one view among many options. Obviously the Maccabean martyrs did believe in the resurrection of the body (2 Macc 7:1–29; 12:43), and perhaps the Qumranites did as well (4Q521 2.1–13). For Jews like the Sadducees, the best one might hope for was some kind of shadowy postmortem existence in Sheol, while others believed in the immorality of the soul (Josephus, *Ant.* 17.354; 18.18; *War* 3.372; 7.340, 348); for others all that one leaves behind is a good memory (Sir 45:1; 46:11; 49:1).

The pervasiveness of belief in the immortality of the soul in Judaism entered by means of Hellenistic influences. In Plato's *Phaedo*, Socrates, facing imminent execution, discourses on the immortality of the soul and discusses the afterlife as a blessed return of the soul to the immaterial world of ideas from which it came. In Platonic thought, humanity is dualistic and comprised of body and soul, and the two are essentially alien to each other. For Plato, the soul was even "imprisoned" in the body. The immortality of the soul flows out of the cyclic character of nature. The soul preexists the body; therefore, the soul must survive the body's dissolution. It was a philosophical attachment to this type of Platonic cosmology and anthropology that led the Athenians to reject Paul's message of the resurrection (Acts 17:32) and even some of the Corinthian Christians to abandon it (1 Cor 15:12–58).

Platonic and Neo-Platonic ideas continued to have varied degrees of intellectual influence on Christian authors in the patristic era. Justin Martyr lamented to Trypho: "For if you have fallen in with some who are called Christians, but who do not admit this ... who say there is no resurrection of the dead, and that their souls, when they die, are taken to heaven, do not imagine that they are Christians."[142] Justin is right to object so fully. Though Christians believe that the soul is immortal, a disembodied eternity as a soul residing in heaven is not the end state for the saints. Christians "look for the resurrection of the dead and the life of the world to come," as the Nicene Creed says (cf. also the Apostles' Creed).

I lament that many Christians today think of the afterlife more in line with Plato than with Jesus or Paul. Some devout Christians are captured with a vision that when they die, they will float about heaven like Caspar the friendly ghost, play volleyball with the angels on the clouds, and glide between stars like a mannequin in outer space. To which we say, "No," for the resurrection of the body and dwelling in a terrestrial and glorified new creation are our destiny. Though the soul or the spirit may depart to be with the Lord—more on that in a minute—it is only an interim arrangement. One goal of contemporary Christian theology, then, should be to deplatonize and reapocalypticize Christian hopes for the future—to bring our congregations back to the language of resurrection, new creation, a unity of body and soul, and an end state in order show that the inherent goodness of creation carries over into a new heaven and a new earth. As Horton notes: "The pagan idea of

---

142. Justin Martyr, *Dial.* 80.

the immortality of the soul and the Christian doctrine of the gift of everlasting life issue in radically different worldviews."[143]

3.6.2.2 SOUL SLEEP

Soul sleep (or "psychopannychy") is the doctrine that the soul is unconscious between death and resurrection. This position has popped up throughout church history and has been a minority view. Martin Luther held to it as did some of the Anabaptists and Socinians. More recently, it is held by Seventh-day Adventists and Jehovah's Witnesses. Those who hold to a monistic understanding of human constitution also adhere to this view because they insist that human existence requires a bodily mode, and if we do not have a bodily state, we cannot exist.

This view rests on a couple of arguments: (1) Human existence is a unity of body and soul. So if the body ceases to function, so must the soul. (2) In Scripture the word "sleep" is used as a euphemism for death and implies a cessation of consciousness after death (2 Sam 7:12; 1 Kgs 2:10; 11:43; 22:50; Job 14:12; Ps 13:3; Dan 12:2; Matt 9:24; John 11:11; Acts 7:60; 13:36; 1 Cor 15:51; 1 Thess 4:13). One can grant the unity of body and soul, but it is a conditional unity, a unity dependent on the bond of the material and the immaterial being united by God's power. Death introduces a temporary disunity that is resolved at the resurrection.

In any case, the body-soul unity does not necessitate that the soul cannot survive independently of the body. There is ample biblical evidence that the departed are conscious and joyous in their postmortem disembodied state (see 2 Cor 5:8; Phil 1:23). In addition, the euphemism for death as "sleep" is not a literal description of the person's state, but a phenomenological description of their physical position at death. The body sleeps in death and awakes at resurrection. Sleep is a figure of speech for death, not an ontological mode of hibernation. Though soul sleep is not heretical, it was condemned in the 42 Articles of England's Edward VI, which stated in Article 40: "They which say that the souls of those depart hence do sleep being without all sense, feeling or perceiving till the Day of Judgment, do utterly dissent from the right belief disclosed to us in Holy Scripture."[144]

Of course, we should point out an interesting corollary of the conscious existence of the soul postmortem. Placing the soul in a state of consciousness beyond death means that the disembodied soul acquires new experiences outside of the body (i.e., memories, feelings, interaction with God and other souls). Therefore, the resurrected person who meets God at the judgment is not experientially identical with the earthly person of former bodily existence.[145]

---

143. Horton, *Christian Faith*, 908.
144. Cited in E. F. Harrison, "Soul Sleep," in *EDT*, 1037–38.
145. Stanley E. Grenz, *Theology for the Community of God* (Grand Rapids: Eerdmans, 1994), 592.

3.6.2.3 PURGATORY

In the Roman Catholic tradition, saints at death are transported to heaven, while lesser souls must experience the cleansing of purgatory before entering the blessed state. According to the Catholic Catechism: "All who die in God's grace and friendship, but still imperfectly purified, are indeed assured of their eternal salvation; but after death they undergo purification, so as to achieve holiness necessary to enter the joy of heaven." As such, "the Church gives the name *Purgatory* to this final purification of the elect, which is entirely different from the punishment of the damned." Purgatory is a place where one can be cleansed of venial sins rather than mortal sins. Aquinas taught that if purity cannot be attained by works of satisfaction in this life, it is necessary to "posit a purgatory or place of cleansing" for this to occur.[146] The Roman Catholic Church also commands "almsgiving, indulgences and works of penance undertaken on behalf of the dead."[147] The primary "scriptural" justification for this comes from 2 Maccabees 12:43–45, where Judas takes a collection as an offering that benefits the dead:

> He also took up a collection, man by man, to the amount of two thousand drachmas of silver, and sent it to Jerusalem to provide for a *sin offering*. In doing this he acted very well and honorably, taking account of the resurrection. For if he were not expecting that those who had fallen would rise again, it would have been superfluous and foolish to pray for the dead. But if he was looking to the splendid reward that is laid up for those who fall asleep in godliness, it was a holy and pious thought. Therefore *he made atonement for the dead, so that they might be delivered from their sin*. (italics added)

This passage is important in establishing the tradition for memorializing the martyrs and explaining how believers in this life can perform deeds that benefit departed saints in the next life. It was a view common in the church fathers and ratified at the Councils of Florence and Trent.[148]

Several things can be said by way of response to the doctrine of purgatory. First, there is no evidence in Old or New Testament that the intermediate state is a place of cleansing or that its punitive effects can be lessened by the performance of good deeds by the living. It is undoubtedly true that human beings need to be cleansed from their sin; however, cleansing and purification are one of the achievements of the cross and received by faith. The joy of the psalmist who confesses his transgressions and sins before God is that while he knows his sin stems all the way back to his birth, he also knows that God can and will cleanse him: "Cleanse me with hyssop, and I will be clean; wash me, and I will be whiter than snow" (Ps 51:7).

---

146. Aquinas, *Summa contra Gentiles* 4.91.
147. *CCC*, 1030–32.
148. Some Roman Catholic commentators have tried to reexpress the doctrine of purgatory in new ways that break from the notion of a lasting penal intermediate state. Karl Rahner thought of purgatory as the place where souls at death become bounded to the cosmos and become aware of their sin as they await resurrection. Joseph Ratzinger (aka Pope Benedict XVI), building on 1 Cor 3, regards purgatory as the final moments of judgment where one is purged and cleansed by the Lord Jesus, who is the fire of judgment (see Wright, *Surprised by Hope*, 166–67).

What is more, the author of Hebrews teaches that Jesus' death is *better* than the Old Testament sacrifices: "How much more, then, will the blood of Christ, who through the eternal Spirit offered himself unblemished to God, cleanse our consciences from acts that lead to death, so that we may serve the living God!" (Heb 9:14; cf. 10:1–22). And in 2 Peter 1:9, believers are reminded that "they have been cleansed from their past sins." The definitive work of sanctification gives us the position of holiness despite the fact that we are not always holy. The definitive declaration of justification means we are entirely just, not because our deeds are just but because Christ is the source of our holiness, righteousness, and redemption (1 Cor 1:30; 6:11). If we have the cross of Christ, we don't need purgatory.

Second, other texts thought to imply a postmortem absolution of sins do not say so. In the case of Matthew 12:32 ("anyone who speaks against the Holy Spirit will not be forgiven, either in this age or in the age to come"), the point is the irreversible effect of committing blasphemy against the Holy Spirit, not the notion, however odd, that even those who commit such blasphemy in the intermediate state will not be forgiven despite the fact that forgiveness in the intermediate state is normally possible. Similarly, 1 Corinthians 3:15 ("If it is burned up, the builder will suffer loss but yet will be saved — even though only as one escaping through the flames") is not talking about escaping purgatory by the skin of one's teeth, but that the final judgment will show the true character of one's ministry, and some Christian workers will find that their ministerial houses of straw are burned up by the judgment while they themselves are barely lucky to escape.

Third, the authority of the Apocrypha is contested by Protestant and evangelical churches. Evangelicals should recognize the historical worth of the Apocrypha for its information about Judaism and the Jewish people and honor it as a text that held genuine religious significance for many of the church fathers. These writings are, as the Article 6 of the Anglican 39 Articles, state: "The other Books (as Hierome [Jerome] saith) the Church doth read for example of life and instruction of manners; but yet doth it not apply them to establish any doctrine." That is slightly more generous than the Westminster confession 1.3, which states: "The books commonly called Apocrypha, not being of divine inspiration, are no part of the canon of the Scripture, and therefore are of no authority in the Church of God, nor to be any otherwise approved, or made use of, than other human writings."

Objections to the canonicity of the Apocrypha are based on their exclusion from the Hebrew canon. New Testament authors never cite them as *graphē* ("Scripture"), and their teaching of doctrines, such as we find in 2 Maccabees 12:43–45, seems to contradict what the more universally recognized Scriptures teach about judgment and rewards. Moreover, although Jerome included the Apocrypha in his

Latin Vulgate, he made the Apocrypha a corpus on its own with a particular preface detailing its status and significance vis-à-vis the other writings.[149]

3.6.2.4 THE INTERMEDIATE STATE ACCORDING TO SCRIPTURE

The place of the dead is described with two mains words in Scripture: Sheol in the Old Testament and Hades in the New Testament. Unfortunately the Greek word *hadēs* is erroneously translated as "hell" in some English versions of the New Testament (on Matt 16:18, compare the following: "gates of hell" (ESV); "gates of Hades" [NRSV, NIV]; "gates of the underworld" [NJB]; "gates of death" [TNIV]). The words Sheol and Hades refer to the abode of the dead, but not necessarily the final place of torment for the wicked.

In Hellenistic religious thought, Hades was the Greek god of the underworld, but Hades commonly referred to the realm of the underworld itself, where the souls of the dead endured a shadowy existence. Eventually the idea of postmortem rewards and punishments in Hades entered Greek thought, probably through Homer. Jewish views of the afterlife most likely developed independently of Greek thought, but Greek-speaking Jews did take on similar words and concepts from Greek and Roman views of Hades and the afterlife. The Hebrew concept of the place of the dead is called *šeʾôl*; it is a place of darkness and gloom with a fading existence (see, e.g., Job 7:9; 17:13; Pss 6:5; 16:10; 49:14; 55:15; 116:3; Hos 13:14). The Hebrew word *šeʾôl* was translated as *hadēs* in the LXX, which explains the ten occurrences of *hadēs* in the New Testament (Matt 11:23; 16:18; Luke 10:15; 16:23; Acts 2:27, 31; Rev 1:18; 6:8; 20:13–14).

Jewish beliefs about a future day of judgment and the resurrection of the dead began to impact ideas about Sheol and Hades. Resurrection was a divine act of God bringing the dead in Hades back to life. Jewish writings are fairly consistent about Sheol and Hades as the place to which the dead depart (e.g., 2 Macc 6:23; *1 En.* 102.5; 103.7; *2 Bar.* 23.4), but the ultimate distinction between the righteous and the wicked at the final judgment could be anticipated during the temporary mode of existence in Hades. The best examples of this are *1 Enoch* 22.1–14 and *4 Ezra* 7.75–101, where the righteous and wicked are separated in Hades until the final judgment, with mixed fortunes for each group ahead of that day.

This provides the context for understanding several texts about "Hades" and the "imprisoned spirits" in Luke 16:19–31 and 1 Peter 3:19–20. The New Testament teaches that the kingdom of God will advance in such a way that the "gates of Hades/death" will not be able to break it (Matt 16:18). Moreover, the gates of

---

149. Cf. D. A. Carson, "The Apocryphal/Deuterocanonical Books: An Evangelical View," in *The Parallel Apocrypha* (ed. John Kohlenberger; Oxford: Oxford University Press, 1997), xliv–xlvii; Henri Blocher, "Helpful or Harmful? The 'Apocrypha' and Evangelical Theology," *EJTh* 13 (2004): 81–90.

Hades/death were thought to keep the dead imprisoned in its realm and only God can open the gates ("For you have power over life and death; you lead mortals down to the gates of Hades and back again" [Wis 16:13]); yet the risen Lord says to John the Seer: "I am the Living One; I was dead, and now look, I am alive for ever and ever! And I hold the keys of death and Hades" (Rev 1:18); this text means that he has acquired the divine power to release people from the realm of the dead.[150]

A number of Lucan texts provide information about a possible intermediate state. The most controversial is the parable of the rich man and Lazarus in Luke 16:19–31:

> There was a rich man who was dressed in purple and fine linen and lived in luxury every day. At his gate was laid a beggar named Lazarus, covered with sores and longing to eat what fell from the rich man's table. Even the dogs came and licked his sores.
>
> The time came when the beggar died and the angels carried him to *Abraham's side*. The rich man also died and was buried. In *Hades*, where *he was in torment*, he looked up and saw Abraham far away, with Lazarus by his side. So he called to him, "Father Abraham, have pity on me and send Lazarus to dip the tip of his finger in water and cool my tongue, because I am in agony in this *fire*."
>
> But Abraham replied, "Son, remember that in your lifetime you received your good things, while Lazarus received bad things, but now he is comforted here and you are in agony. And besides all this, between us and you a *great chasm* has been set in place, so that those who want to go from here to you cannot, nor can anyone cross over from there to us."
>
> He answered, "Then I beg you, father, send Lazarus to my family, for I have five brothers. Let him warn them, so that they will not also come to this place of torment.
>
> Abraham replied, "They have Moses and the Prophets; let them listen to them."
>
> "No, father Abraham," he said, "but if someone from the dead goes to them, they will repent."
>
> He said to him, "If they do not listen to Moses and the Prophets, they will not be convinced even if someone rises from the dead." (italics added)

The key thing to remember about this passage is that it is a fictive narrative designed to reinforce the point made in Luke 16:14–18 about the terrible dangers of the love of money. It is the ancient equivalent to vignettes about "St. Peter's Gate" or the "Pearly Gates," where the meaning is moral rather than literal. So although this parable refers to the intermediate state, personal eschatology is not its main point.

With that caveat in mind, we can conclude the following: (1) The story corresponds with what we saw above, where the concept of Hades developed in Jewish thought so that the division of the final judgment between the righteous and the wicked was already anticipated in the abode of the dead. (2) It also reflects the view found in the *Testament of Abraham* 20.14, which refers to a "paradise" in the afterlife where there is the

---

150. Richard Bauckham, "Hades, Hell," *ABD*, 3:14–15.

"bosom of Abraham," and how Abraham's descendents there enjoy "peace and rejoicing and life unending." Luke's parable is a hyperbolic depiction of an existence in the afterlife that affirms an intermediate state in Hades prior to the final resurrection, but its major concern is Abraham's refusal to the rich man's request to send a messenger, and so it highlights the inexcusable behavior of the rich and the penalty that awaits them.[151]

Also in the gospel of Luke, there is a curious remark uttered by Jesus on the cross. When one of the bandits crucified with Jesus asks him, "Remember me when you come into your kingdom" (Luke 23:42), Jesus replies with the promise, "Truly I tell you, today you will be with me in paradise" (23:43). The saying is problematic because the other two appearances of *paradeisos* in the New Testament both refer to heaven (2 Cor 12:4; Rev 2:7). Yet Jesus did not go to heaven between the cross and resurrection. We find this clearly in the Johannine resurrection narrative, where the risen Jesus tells Mary: "Do not hold on to me, for I have not yet ascended to the Father. Go instead to my brothers and tell them, 'I am ascending to my Father and your Father, to my God and your God'" (John 20:17). So if Jesus was not in "heaven," then where did he go? What is this "paradise" he promised the bandit?

Most likely, "paradise" here denotes the intermediate state and is another way of referring to Hades. This comports with the biblical teaching that when Jesus died, he went to the waiting place of the dead (Acts 2:27, 31; 1 Pet 3:19–21). The Greek word *paradeisos* was a Persian loanword that denoted an enclosed park surrounded by a wall. It was known to Hellenistic authors like Xenophon and adopted by Jewish authors to refer to Eden in the creation account in Genesis 2:8–10, 16 (LXX). It was also used to describe the future state so that the future city of Jerusalem will be like the garden of Eden (Ezek 36:35; cf. 28:13; 31:8–9). In subsequent Jewish thought, paradise also referred to the present abode of departed patriarchs, the elect, and the righteous (*1 En.* 60.7–8, 23; 61.12; 70.4; *2 En.* 8.1–8; 9.1; 42.3; *Apoc. Mos.* 37.5). Paradise here is an intermediate state that is neither heaven nor hell; it is the waiting place of the dead, the blissful location within *šeʾôl* or *hadēs*.[152]

Shifting to Luke's second volume, the Acts of the Apostles, Stephen is stoned for his testimony to Jesus' exaltation to the right hand of God (Acts 7:55–60). As he is bludgeoned with stones, Stephen exclaims, "Lord Jesus, receive my spirit'" (7:59). This mirrors the words of Jesus himself at his crucifixion, "Father, into your hands I commit my spirit" (Luke 23:46). It is christologically significant that while the Lucan Jesus prays to the Father to receive his spirit at his crucifixion, Stephen

---

151. Cf. Richard Bauckham, "The Rich Man and Lazarus: The Parable and the Parallels," *NTS* 37 (1991): 225–46. See also Joel B. Green, *Body, Soul, and Human Life: The Nature of Humanity in the Bible* (Grand Rapids: Baker, 2008), 165, who rejects using Luke 16 to construct an idea of an intermediate state.

152. See J. Jeremias, *TDNT*, 5:765–73; Grant Macaskill, "Paradise in the New Testament," in *Paradise in Antiquity: Jewish and Christian Views* (ed. M. Bockmuehl and G. G. Stroumsa; Cambridge: Cambridge University Press, 2010), 64–81.

prays that Jesus would receive him beyond his martyrdom. What Luke presents to his readers is not a platonizing of the afterlife; more likely these three texts (Luke 16:19–31; 23:43, 46; Acts 7:55–60) exhibit belief in an intermediate state located in Hades before the resurrection and then in heaven after the resurrection.

References to an intermediate state were not a mainstay of Paul's eschatological teachings that focused primarily on Christ's *parousia*, the resurrection, and the final judgment. Information about an intermediate state must be inferred from Paul's remarks elsewhere. Paul writes to the Philippians from Ephesus about his imprisonment and possible execution:

> I eagerly expect and hope that I will in no way be ashamed, but will have sufficient courage so that now as always Christ will be exalted in my body, whether by life or by death. For to me, to live is Christ and to die is gain. If I am to go on living in the body, this will mean fruitful labor for me. Yet what shall I choose? I do not know! I am torn between the two: I desire to depart and be with Christ, which is better by far; but it is more necessary for you that I remain in the body. (Phil 1:20–24)

Paul contrasts "living in the body" with departing to "be with Christ, which is better by far." Paul provides no data about the nature of this state, where it takes place, or what form he exists in there, and we can only assume that death entails a removal from his body and transportation to instant intimacy with the Savior.

The place where Paul discourses specifically about the postmortem fate of the individual, starting with himself, is 2 Corinthians 5:1–10:

> For we know that if the *earthly tent* we live in is destroyed, *we have a building from God, an eternal house in heaven, not built by human hands*. Meanwhile we groan, longing to be clothed instead with *our heavenly dwelling*, because when we are *clothed*, we will not be found *naked*. For while we are in this **tent**, we groan and are burdened, because we do not wish to be *unclothed but to be clothed instead with our heavenly dwelling*, so that what is mortal may be swallowed up by *life*. Now the one who has fashioned us for this very purpose is God, who has given us the Spirit as a deposit, guaranteeing what is to come.
>
> Therefore we are always confident and know that as long as we are at *home in the body we are away from the Lord*. For we live by faith, not by sight. We are confident, I say, and would prefer to be *away from the body and at home with the Lord*. So we make it our goal to please him, whether we are at *home in the body or away from it*. For we must all appear before the judgment seat of Christ, that everyone may receive what is due them for the things done while in the body, whether good or bad. (italics added)

It is often alleged that in these verses Paul has abandoned the apocalyptic eschatology of 1 Corinthians 15, with its future resurrection of the body, for a resurrection into a spiritual body into God's presence immediately after death.[153] But this

---

153. Cf. e.g., W. D. Davies, *Paul and Rabbinic Judaism* (2nd ed.; London: SPCK, 1955), 310–18.

is hardly likely since Paul's reference to "we know" (5:1) introduces a rehearsed doctrine rather than a newly fashioned one. Second, Paul has intimated earlier in the letter his continued affirmation of the resurrection (1:9–10; 4:14) and affirms it again a few sentences later (5:15). Third, 1 Corinthians 15 and 2 Corinthians 5 share a lot of vocabulary, such as "unclothed" and "earthly." Paul's teaching on the future remains consistent, though in 2 Corinthians 5 he does begin to talk about the immediate postmortem fate of the individual, starting with himself.[154]

The most likely scenario as to what Paul means here is that he contrasts two phases of being in the body with being clothed in a heavenly dwelling ahead of the *parousia*.

Present State	Postmortem State
earthly tent	building from God
naked	eternal house
unclothed	heavenly dwelling
home in the body	clothed
away from the Lord	away from it [body]
in the body	at home with the Lord
destroyable	immortal

Paul had intimated an interval between death and resurrection that was a bodiless one (1 Cor 15:35–38) and a temporary state (15:32–44). Now as he faces the expectation of death *ahead of the parousia*, he turns his mind to what lies in store for him. If Paul expected to receive a spiritual resurrection body after his death, it leads one to wonder why he would still anticipate the Lord's return in the future since resurrection and *parousia* have been consistently bound together in his eschatology across the Thessalonian and Corinthian correspondences and also later in Philippians and Romans. What Paul appears to envisage immediately upon death is not a spiritual resurrection, but a future spiritual mode of existence that is transcendent, yet not fully actualized until the *parousia*. There is a transition from the sarkic (fleshly) and somatic (bodily) form of existence into a heavenly dwelling in the company of the Lord, characterized by a heightened form of interpersonal communion with Christ.[155]

Yet this state is clearly something that is prior to Christ's *parousia* and the

---

154. Cf. Paul Barnett, *The Second Epistle to the Corinthians* (NICNT; Grand Rapids: Eerdmans, 1997), 269–70; Richard N. Longenecker, "Is There Development in Paul's Resurrection Thought," in *Life in the Face of Death: The Resurrection Message of the New Testament* (ed. R. N. Longenecker; Grand Rapids: Eerdmans, 1998), 171–202; Paul Woodbridge, "Did Paul Change His Mind?—An Examination of Some Aspects of Pauline Eschatology," *Themelios* 28 (2003): 5–18.

155. Murray J. Harris, *The Second Epistle to the Corinthians* (NIGTC; Grand Rapids: Eerdmans, 2005), 401.

resurrection because it is ahead of the judgment of believers when their resurrection will take place. Paul hopes to please the Lord in both his bodily state and in his heavenly dwelling, knowing that he will stand before Christ at the final judgment. In any case, the promise of the Spirit and the object of faith is such that he looks forward to leaving his body, imagining a time away from the body in this eternal dwelling, and then *presumably* being raised to stand at the final judgment.

The book of Revelation focuses attention on the events leading up to the final state of a new heaven and a new earth (Rev 22:1–5). Still, John makes some comment about a possible intermediate state for believers after death and before their resurrection. First, when John the Seer refers to the state of the martyrs, it is clear that they exist in a heavenly dimension that is at once both blissful and yet not entirely satisfying.

> When he opened the fifth seal, I saw under the altar the *souls of those who had been slain because of the word of God and the testimony they had maintained.* They called out in a loud voice, "How long, Sovereign Lord, holy and true, until you judge the inhabitants of the earth and avenge our blood?" *Then each of them was given a white robe, and they were told to wait a little longer,* until the full number of their fellow servants and brothers and sisters were killed just as they had been. (Rev 6:9–11)

> Then one of the elders asked me, "These in white robes—who are they, and where did they come from?" I answered, "Sir, you know." And he said, "These are they who have come out of the great tribulation; they have washed their robes and made them white in the blood of the Lamb. Therefore, *"they are before the throne of God and serve him day and night in his temple; and he who sits on the throne will shelter them with his presence. Never again will they hunger; never again will they thirst. The sun will not beat down on them, nor any scorching heat. For the Lamb at the center of the throne will be their shepherd; he will lead them to springs of living water. And God will wipe away every tear from their eyes."* (Rev 7:13–17, italics added in both cases)

In Revelation 6, the martyrs cry out for vindication and look forward to the judgment and wrath that are set to follow upon those who mistreated and murdered them. In Revelation 7, the martyrs enter into the presence of the throne room of heaven and engage in heavenly worship and enjoy heavenly peace, and they are shepherded by the Lamb, who comforts them. This penultimate stage depicts departed saints as being in the presence of God in heaven.

Another thing to note from Revelation is the relationship between "Hades" and "hell." In Revelation, Hades is closely related to "death" and thus stands for the waiting place of the dead rather than the final place of the condemned (Rev 1:18; 6:8; 20:13–14).[156] Though the Greek word for "hell" (*geenna*) does not occur in

---

156. The state of people in Sheol/Hades is peculiar because although they are somehow stuck there, there are indications of persons leaving there ahead of the final consummation. For instance, the witch of Endor is able to summon the "spirit" of Samuel (1 Sam 28:7–25). Also, at the transfiguration Jesus talks to Moses and Elijah (Matt 17:1–8 and par.). Moses died a normal death (Deut 34:5–7), but Elijah was assumed into heaven (2 Kgs 2:11–12).

§ 3.6 The Intermediate State: What Happens When You Die?

Revelation, there is mention of a "lake of fire/burning sulfur" that amounts to the same thing (19:20; 20:10, 14–15; 21:8). Note that "death and Hades were thrown into the lake of fire. The lake of fire is the second death" (20:14). That is, Hades is thrown into hell. That would mean that no one is in hell yet, and the contents of Hades will be dumped into hell at the final judgment. In view of all of this, I would represent the intermediate state as follows:

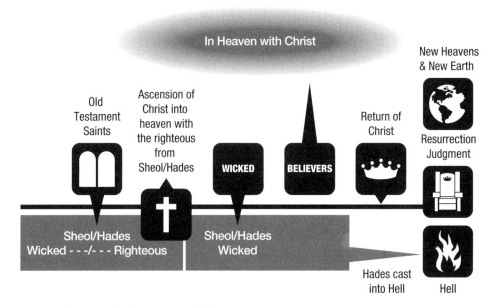

According to the scheme sketched above:
1. Prior to Christ's ascension, all who died descended to Sheol/Hades, which was divided into two parts, one for the wicked and one for the righteous.[157]
2. At Christ's ascension, he went into heaven and took with him all of the saints in the paradisal part of Sheol/Hades, while the wicked remain in Sheol/Hades, waiting for judgment.[158]
3. Upon death new covenant believers go to be with Christ in heaven ahead of the general resurrection, while the wicked descend to Sheol/Hades waiting for judgment.
4. Eventually Sheol/Hades will be thrown into hell and all believers will share in the new heavens and new earth.

---

157. Contra Grudem (*Systematic Theology*, 821–22), who thinks that Old Testament saints went to heaven upon death. This is true of only Enoch (Gen 5:24) and Elijah (1 Kgs 2:11–12).

158. The ascension of Old Testament saints with Jesus is an implication that follows from (1) the affirmation of Sheol as the place of the dead in the Old Testament (e.g., Gen 37:35; 1 Sam 2:6; Job 7:9); (2) part of Jesus' descent into Hades (Acts 2:2,31) and ascent into heaven (Eph 4:8–10) meant leading captives free; and (3) Hebrews 12:1, 22–24, which implies that Old Testament saints, the great cloud of witnesses, are now in heaven as "the spirits of the righteous made perfect." What enabled the Old Testament saints to shift from Sheol to heaven has probably something to do with Jesus' ascension.

Some scholars, nobly desirous to avoid any connotations of Platonistic heritage and wary of a soul/body dichotomy, have expressed reluctance about affirming an intermediate state. Joel Green leans this way in his approach that he calls "christological intermediacy." For Green, after death "our lives are hid with Christ in God." So although we are "dead" in ourselves, we still remain "alive" to God in Christ, awaiting the final resurrection.[159] Similarly Wolfhart Pannenberg's intention to reinforce belief in a future resurrection led him to deny any intermediary existence for the believer because it would somehow impinge on the reality of resurrection and imply a notion of the immortality of the soul: "The so-called 'life after death' can no longer be thought of as immortality of the soul, but only as another mode of existence of the *whole* man. However, that is the content of the picture of a resurrection of the dead."[160]

However, an affirmation of a future resurrection does not demand that there is no conscious existence in a nonbodied, postmortem state ahead of the resurrection. When Paul dies, he intends to be with Christ, which is better than his current bodily existence (Phil 1:23); yet he also thinks of the immediate postmortem state as something temporary, like a car on loan from a mechanic, waiting for the original vehicle to be renewed (cf. 1 Cor 15:35–38). So it seems that upon death, the separation of body and soul is both blessing and a bummer, something enjoyable but also somewhat ephemeral. The unity of the material and immaterial parts of one's being are the norm, but death ruptures that norm ahead of the resurrection. Yet, despite the awkward disunity of body and soul at death, believers still enjoy God's presence and look forward to the day when they will be raised in a psychosomatic unity of body and soul in God's everlasting kingdom.[161]

3.6.3 CHRIST IS THE PLACE OF REST

It is difficult to plot the exact place and type of existence in the intermediate state. No text, save perhaps 2 Corinthians 5, discourses on it at length. But overall it seems that Joachim Jeremias was correct when he writes: "The NT consistently represents fellowship with Christ after death as the distinctively Christian view of the intermediate state."[162] The intermediate state has to be articulated primarily in christological terms. Paul is clear that one departs to be with Christ (Phil 1:23), and according to John the Evangelist, where Christ is, there believers will also be (John 14:3). For nothing, not even death or demons, will separate believers from the love of God that is in Christ Jesus our Lord (Rom 8:38–39). The intermediate state brings fellowship with Christ, and in him we find also the continued fellowship of believers ahead of

---

159. See Green, *Body, Soul, and Human Life*, 178–80.
160. Wolfhart Pannenberg, *Jesus: God and Man* (2nd ed.; Philadelphia: Westminster John Knox, 1968), 87 (italics original).
161. Horton, *Christian Faith*, 910.
162. J. Jeremias, *TDNT*, 5:771.

the final consummation (Heb 12:23). Death does not eradicate the believer's union with Christ or communion with fellow believers. Whatever life is ahead in the eschatological future, interim and final, it can only be a "life in Christ."[163]

FURTHER READING

Edgar, Brian. "Biblical Anthropology and the Intermediate State." *EvQ* 74 (2002): 27–45, 109–21.

Green, Joel B. *Body, Soul, and Human Life: The Nature of Humanity in the Bible*. STI. Grand Rapids: Baker, 2008, esp. pp. 140–80.

---

163. Markus Bockmuehl, *The Epistle to the Philippians* (BNTC; London: Black, 1998), 88.

§ 3.7 THE FINAL STATE: HEAVEN, HELL, AND NEW CREATION

3.7.1 THE GOSPEL AND THE HOPE OF GLORY

The gospel is a message of hope that this world is not all that there is. God's kingdom is everlasting, and the church will reign with Jesus Christ in a new heaven and a new earth. This perspective bursts forth beautifully in Colossians 1:5, where the apostle Paul reminds the believers about the "hope stored up for you in heaven and about which you have already heard in the true message of the gospel." He tells them that the riches of the great mystery is "Christ in you, the hope of glory" (1:27). In fact, "hope" and "glory" go together like peanut butter and jelly, beer and baseball, wine and cheese, or marmite and toast. For by grace and standing in faith, we gain access to God so that we may boast in the hope of glory (cf. Rom 5:2). Christ is the faithful Son of God, who builds God's own house, the church, established with the mortar and tar of the hope of glory (Heb 3:6).

Such a hope is focused on Jesus Christ and the consummation of his kingdom in the future. This is not an escapist theology that looks for something radically different to the present reality we experience. For the renewed creation will be a resurrection of the present order of things. There will be a continuity between this world and the next one. Thus, what we do in this world and in this life will carry over into the future realm of a transformed heaven and earth. That's why the church is busy with mission rather than being bored with waiting. As the people of God shine like stars (Dan 12:3; Phil 2:15), they radiate before the world a glimpse of what the coming glory will be like. The church, as God's children indwelt by the Holy Spirit and living under the lordship of Jesus Christ, is a living preview of the final state of the universe: glory.

Central to Christian visions of the future are the notions of heaven and hell. Normally people think of these in terms like good people go to heaven and bad people go to hell. Heaven is a bright shiny place with clouds and angels, where everyone wears white, and it seems to be characterized by a blissful boredom. Hell, however, is a subterranean cavern with fire, burning lakes, demons with pitch forks, and untold misery combined with riotous partying. This is understandable if you look at heaven and hell in popular culture like media, songs, advertisements, and movies. Good grief! I've seen bikini-clad women on TV trying to sell an ice cream called "Heaven" that had as its tag line, the treat is "positively sinful." And I've seen a Pizza shop called "Hell" that had as its motto, "Hungry, then go to Hell!" (I am glad the franchise near where I live went bust!) But if we get away from the media stereotypes that have even filtered their way into Sunday School lessons, if we remember that the final volume of the *Left Behind* series is not a Discovery Channel documentary on the afterlife, and if we think about heaven and hell based around the key nodes of Christ, kingdom, and consummation, we will get a more theologically nuanced picture of what is truly meant by heaven and hell.

3.7.2 HEAVEN AND *THEN* THE NEW CREATION

In biblical language "heaven" (*šāmayim* in Hebrew and *ouranos* in Greek) refers to the cosmological world above and beyond earth (e.g., Gen 1:1; Matt 5:18). Heaven can even be a circumlocution for God (e.g., Matt 21:25; John 3:27), and heaven is the abode of God (e.g., Deut 4:39; Matt 6:9). At his ascension, Jesus was taken up to heaven to share the throne of God in his incarnate, glorified, and exalted human state (Luke 9:51; John 20:17; Acts 1:11; Heb 9:24). It is also from heaven that Jesus will be revealed (1 Thess 1:10; 4:16; 2 Thess 1:7). Heaven is the place of our treasure (Matt 6:19–21; 19:21), our citizenship (Phil 3:20), our inheritance (1 Pet 1:4–5), and the place where our hope is laid up (Col 1:5).

That does not mean, however, that we have go to heaven in order to get them any more than we have to crawl into the fridge to get the beer kept in refrigeration for us.[164] The heavenly realities have earthly anticipations in the here and now. Moreover, when "heaven" is mentioned in Scripture, it is not described primarily as a destination—complete with stars, angels playing harps, and celebrities who snuck passed St. Peter; it is rather the hidden dimension of ordinary life, God's dimension, the control room of the universe, where God's plans are laid bare like a map on a table.[165] When John the Seer receives a vision of heaven in Revelation 4–5, it is like he's summoned to a cross between a military headquarters and the throne room of a monarch. It's a mixture of planning for the full-scale invasion of this world, combined with worship that abounds in symbols, metaphors, and visions that language stretches to properly describe.[166]

---

164. N. T. Wright, *The Resurrection of the Son of God* (COQG 3; London: SPCK, 2003), 368; idem, *Surprised by Hope*, 151–52.

165. Wright, *Surprised by Hope*, 19.

166. G. B. Caird, *A Commentary on the Revelation of St. John the Divine* (London: Black, 1966), 60–61.

Remember also Revelation 21–22 and the glorious picture of a new Jerusalem coming down from heaven to earth. Though God made heaven and earth, he intends in the end to remake both and to join them together forever.[167] So there's more to heaven than clouds, angels, and elevator music. Heaven is the source of the hope we possess now and the seat of God's authority. So although heaven might be a rewarding and blessed state for departed saints to be with Christ, it is certainly not the final state.

The intermediate state means going to be with Christ; Christ is in heaven, so believers go to heaven upon death (e.g., John 14:2–3; Phil 1:23). For our departed saints, as Sunday school children rightly sing, "heaven is a wonderful place filled with glory and grace" because one is transported to the presence of the Lord Jesus Christ. Heaven is not a dreamlike place of disembodied bliss; rather, it is a place of both longing for the future state (Rev 6:10–11) and a place of worship (7:13–17). The heavenly state is like being wrapped in a blanket of joy, free from the sadness of this age, but still anticipating through worship the full blessings yet to come.

The immediate postmortem experience of heaven is eschatologically intermediate; that is, it is a glorious interlude, not the final destination. That is because heaven is a transitional mode of existence until the resurrection and the new creation. Millard Erickson is not quite right when he says that "as God's abode, heaven is obviously where believers will be for all eternity."[168] It is the coming together of heaven and earth in union with Christ that is the ultimate goal of God's plan and the final destination of God's people. Paul declares that God's purpose is "to bring unity to all things in heaven and on earth under Christ" (Eph 1:10). The final state is a new creation created in Christ and under Christ and even for Christ. God unites himself to creation through the Logos, and the glory of God effuses into the new creation through Son and Spirit.

The final state is a heaven that descends to earth and an earth that receives the heavens, so that both heaven and earth are transformed into something other than what they were before. Heaven and earth are changed into the new creation. Heaven does not swallow up earth and earth does not simply absorb heaven. The earth is transfigured and transformed into a heavenly plane of existence, and the dividing line between heaven and earth is obliterated. Heaven becomes earthly and earth becomes heavenly. Though heaven is life after death, the new creation is life after life after death.[169]

We first read about a new heaven and a new earth in Isaiah 65–66. Those who remain faithful to the one true God will forget their past troubles when Yahweh

---

167. Wright, *Surprised by Hope*, 19.
168. Erickson, *Christian Theology*, 1234.
169. Wright, *Surprised by Hope*, 148.

§ 3.7 The Final State: Heaven, Hell, and New Creation

brings his new world into being (Isa 65:17). According to Walter Brueggemann, this means that the audience is "about to be inducted into a gospel newness."[170] The image is described by Isaiah like this:

> See, I will create *new heavens and a new earth*. The former things will not be remembered, nor will they come to mind. But be glad and rejoice forever in what I will create, for *I will create Jerusalem* to be a delight and its people a joy. I will rejoice over Jerusalem and take delight in my people; the sound of weeping and of crying will be heard in it no more. (Isa 65:17–19, italics added)

The picture Isaiah imparts to us is one of the absolute and inscrutable reign of Yahweh, who sovereignly renews the cosmos, and this new place is characterized by intense eschatological joy. The old earth, infested with hatred and violence, gives way to the dynamic *shalom* of the covenant God. Importantly, the centerpiece of the new heaven and new earth is a remade Jerusalem. In Isaiah, Jerusalem remains the special location of God's power and his law as it is the mountain of the Lord that draws the nations like a magnet (Isa 1:26–27; 2:2–4). The new creation will give people an everlasting life that is juxtaposed with the judgment of those who rebelled against God (66:22–24).

In Revelation, John describes the final state as a new heaven and a new earth in Revelation 21:1, but then switches to a new Jerusalem in 21:2, 10–21. Rather than a two-staged revelation of the end through a new heaven and new earth followed by a new Jerusalem, these images are for the one and same new creation. The vision represents a merging of the new heaven and earth from Isaiah 65–66 with the new temple from Ezekiel 40–48 in order to display the transcendent abode of God and his people at the very end. In Revelation 21:1–22:5 is a convergence of the scriptural themes of new covenant, new temple, new Israel, new Jerusalem, and new creation.[171]

This new Jerusalem is a place of God's presence and peace that comes down from heaven to the earth:

> The one who is victorious I will make a pillar in the temple of my God. Never again will they leave it. I will write on them the name of my God and the name of *the city of my God, the new Jerusalem, which is coming down out of heaven from my God*; and I will also write on them my new name. (Rev 3:12)

> Then I saw "a new heaven and a new earth," for the first heaven and the first earth had passed away, and there was no longer any sea. *I saw the Holy City, the new Jerusalem, coming down out of heaven from God*, prepared as a bride beautifully dressed for her husband. And I heard a loud voice from the throne saying, "Look! God's dwell-

---

170. Walter Brueggemann, *Isaiah 40–66* (Louisville: Westminster John Knox, 1998), 245.

171. Beale, *Revelation*, 173.

ing place is now among the people, and he will dwell with them. They will be his people, and God himself will be with them and be their God....

And he carried me away in the Spirit to a mountain great and high, and showed me the *Holy City, Jerusalem, coming down out of heaven from God.* (Rev 21:1–3, 10, italics added in both cases)

A city is not simply a maze of malls, boulevards, and buildings. In the ancient world, a city offered security as its walls protected its inhabitants from marauding animals and invading armies. A city was also a community of citizens, under a king, sharing a common purpose, citizenship, culture, and cultus. Jerusalem was the city of God (Pss 46:4–7; 48:1–8; 87:1–3) and the city of David (2 Sam 5–6). It was a place of geography and cosmology; it was where the God of heaven touched earth. It was where God placed his king to instruct Israel and to subdue the nations (see Ps 2:6). Jerusalem, as the place of God's temple, was the seat of divine worship. Jerusalem, really a temple city, was the abode of God's glory where God had his earthly dwelling (1 Kgs 8:10–11; Pss 9:11; 74:2; 135:21). It was seemingly invincible, not because it was strategically well located, but because God was its defender.

One of the prayers of ancient Israel for Jerusalem was that there would be "no breaching of walls, no going into captivity, no cry of distress in our streets" (Ps 144:14). This would be because "we have a strong city; God makes salvation its walls and ramparts" (Isa 26:1). The tragedy is that such confidence led to a mistaken false trust in Zion as a kind of magical talisman (see Jer 7:4). God's protection of the city would depend on the people's faithfulness toward him in the worship and life that the covenant people were called to display (see 1 Kgs 9:4–8). The temple became tainted with corruption, and the glory of the Lord departed before its destruction by the Babylonians in 586 BC (Ezek 10:18).

Thereafter, the prophets looked forward to a new, rebuilt, and glorious temple. A new city of God would arise, the throne of God would be established there, and the glory of the Lord would return. A vision of a new temple is given in great detail in Ezekiel 40–48. In lavish language, Isaiah presents the rebuilding of the temple as the high point of the end of exile (Isa 54). The prophet Haggai said the new temple would be more glorious than the former one (Hag 2:9). The programs of Ezra, Nehemiah, and later even Herod the Great were aimed at returning the temple to its former glory as in the age of Solomon.

As time passed, however, it was recognized that the temple establishment could be corrupt, the city could be easily destroyed, and the sanctuary was liable to desecration. Some Jews began to set their hopes on a heavenly city, a future dwelling place, one beyond this world. In Galatians 4, Paul contrasts the present Jerusalem (symbolizing the Sinai covenant and slavery) with the Jerusalem that is above (symbolizing the new covenant and freedom), and the latter is the mother of believers

(4:26). The point of Paul's allegory is, in good apocalyptic fashion, that the people of God, despite suffering and adversity in the present age, are the children of a heavenly Jerusalem that will one day be eschatologically revealed.[172]

Hebrews utilizes a similar theme of Christians on a journey toward a heavenly city. In the rhetorical climax to the letter, the author declares that believers have not entered a revelation like the one given at Mount Sinai; rather: "You have come to Mount Zion, to the city of the living God, the heavenly Jerusalem. You have come to *thousands upon thousands of angels* in joyful assembly, to the *church of the firstborn*, whose names are written in heaven. You have come to *God*, the Judge of all, to the *spirits of the righteous made perfect*, to *Jesus* the mediator of a new covenant" (Heb 12:22–24, italics added). What the author means by "the city of the living God" and "the heavenly Jerusalem" is more than a piece of cosmic real estate. It is defined by what follows: angelic worship, communion of the saints, and eternal fellowship with Jesus and the Father.

That means that this place comprises a redeemed people in worshipful communion with Jesus and the Father. This is the eschatological kingdom of God that the writer to the Hebrews speaks of (see Heb 11:10, 16; esp. 13:14). Yes, heaven is the goal of the Christian pilgrimage (4:1; 13:14), but the idea of the heavenly world is shaped by Psalm 110, which refers to the exaltation of Jesus to the right hand of God, from whence he exercises his priestly and royal prerogatives (Heb 1:3, 13; 8:1; 12:2). Jesus is not a heavenly property developer looking for tenants; he is instead the priest-king of God's holy kingdom that will envelop God's people. As such, the heavenly Jerusalem in Hebrews 12 presupposes an apocalyptic viewpoint whereby the new Jerusalem is the transcendent reign of God over God's people rather than a metaphysical dualism between the earthly and the heavenly.[173]

Returning now to the vision of the new Jerusalem by John the Seer in Revelation 21, we notice that this city defines what John means by "a new heaven and a new earth." The first and last mentions of heaven in Revelation are focused on the Holy City coming down from heaven (Rev 3:12; 21:10). In this city, there is an end to the old order and all things are made new (21:1, 4–6). Here God dwells with his people, and this is the hope for them to inherit if they remain faithful (21:3, 7–8). The physical description of the city is richly embedded with Old Testament symbols like the repeated use of "twelve" to signify the twelve tribes of Israel, its walls are impregnable like Zion, it is guarded by angels just like Eden, it contains the wealth of the nations, and it has no temple because the Lord Almighty and the Lamb are its temple (21:10–27).

---

172. Richard Hays, "The Letter to the Galatians," in *NIB*, 11:304.

173. Kiwong Son, *Zion Symbolism in Hebrews: Hebrews 12:14–24 as a Hermeneutical Key to the Epistle* (Milton Keynes, UK: Paternoster, 2005), 91–93.

The imagery of the new Jerusalem as both a temple and a garden is significant.[174] The eschatological goal of the garden of Eden, which was a temple in its own right,[175] was to fill the whole creation by becoming coequal and coextensive with it. But sin desecrated the garden of Eden. The Israelite temple was an interim entity designed to embody the presence of God and was given to symbolize the same goal of making the earth radiate with divine glory. The new Jerusalem fulfills this role so that eschatology not only recapitulates the protology of Eden but even escalates it. The new Jerusalem is the celestial city in the form of a garden temple that constitutes the renewed cosmos. Being in the new heaven and new earth means sharing in the "tree of life" and the "Holy City." It is, in the Miltonian sense, paradise regained.[176]

Life in the new creation will have a number of distinct features. First, it is characterized by peace and joy—the absence of hostilities and the intimate enjoyment of God (Isa 65:17–25; Rev 21:4; 22:2–4). Second, the fundamental task is worship as believers will serve and praise God (Rev 22:3). As Augustine wrote: "Certainly that city shall have no greater joy than the celebration of the grace of Christ, who redeemed us by His blood."[177] Wright thinks that far from sitting on clouds playing harps, "the redeemed people of God in the new world will be the agents of his love going out in new ways, to accomplish new creative tasks, to celebrate and extend the glory of his love."[178] Third, glorified humanity will possess transcendent and somatic qualities in the sense they will have resurrection bodies, but they will be become like the angels and be without certain procreative functions (Matt 22:30). We will be a glorified humanity, dwelling in the glory of God's own presence, fully and finally free from the penalty, power, and presence of sin.

The new heaven and new earth are presented as a new Jerusalem, an arboreal city-temple with Edenic qualities. This new world materializes the pervasive presence of God over the whole earth and brings with it a triumphant joy for those who had long waited for it.[179] At its center is the unity between the church and Christ. Notably Jerusalem is closely identified *with* and even *as* the temple (e.g., 2 Kgs 21:4, 7; Ezra 7:16–17; Ps 79:1; Isa 44:28; 66:20). Christians are called God's temple (1 Cor 3:16; Eph 2:19–21; 1 Pet 2:5–9; Rev 3:12) and so is Christ himself (John 2:21; esp. use of Ps 118:22 in Matt 21:42; Acts 4:11; Eph 2:20). Thus, the new Jerusalem is not simply people in a place, but place and people are actually, dare I say, mystically

---

174. The temple aspect is highlighted by the fact that nothing unclean shall come into it (Rev 21:27), which was similar to commandments about impurity and the temple in the Old Testament (Num 19:13, 20; 2 Chr 23:19; 29:16). Also, the city is the dwelling of God (Rev 21:3) just as the temple was the dwelling of God (Lev 26:11–12; Ezek 37:27). Earlier in Revelation, heaven is described as a temple as well (Rev 3:12; 7:15; esp. 11:19; 14:15–17; 15:5–8; 16:1, 17). Also, the heavenly temple and new Jerusalem are equated in 3:12. The new Jerusalem as a new Eden is clear in 22:1–3, where the city has the water of life and trees of life, and there is no curse (as opposed to the cursing of Adam, Eve, and the serpent).

175. Cf. Beale, *The Temple and the Church's Mission*, 65–80.

176. Ibid., 365–73; idem, *Revelation*, 1039–46.

177. Augustine, *Civ.* 22.30.

178. Wright, *Surprised by Hope*, 105–6.

179. Alister McGrath, *A Brief History of Heaven* (Oxford: Blackwell, 2003), 12.

§ 3.7 The Final State: Heaven, Hell, and New Creation

> **COMIC BELIEF**
>
> "When we speak of heaven and the joys of this life, let your face light up, your smile shine, your eyes twinkle. When you speak of hell, your ordinary face will do."
>
> — Charles Spurgeon

merged (see Rev 3:12). The scene is figurative for the full fellowship of God with his people in the new cosmic order. Or, as Augustine eloquently put it:

> Wherefore it may very well be, and it is thoroughly credible, that we shall in the future world see the material forms of the new heavens and the new earth in such a way that we shall most distinctly recognize God everywhere present and governing all things, material as well as spiritual, and shall see Him, not as now we understand the invisible things of God, by the things which are made, and see Him darkly, as in a mirror, and in part, and rather by faith than by bodily vision of material appearances, but by means of the bodies we shall wear and which we shall see wherever we turn our eyes. As we do not believe, but see that the living men around us who are exercising vital functions are alive, though we cannot see their life without their bodies, but see it most distinctly by means of their bodies, so, wherever we shall look with those spiritual eyes of our future bodies, we shall then, too, by means of bodily substances behold God, though a spirit, ruling all things. Either, therefore, the eyes shall possess some quality similar to that of the mind, by which they may be able to discern spiritual things, and among these God,—a supposition for which it is difficult or even impossible to find any support in Scripture,—or, which is more easy to comprehend, God will be so known by us, and shall be so much before us, that we shall see Him by the spirit in ourselves, in one another, in Himself, in the new heavens and the new earth, in every created thing which shall then exist; and also by the body we shall see Him in everybody which the keen vision of the eye of the spiritual body shall reach.[180]

3.7.3 HELL

The famous bronze and marble sculpture commonly called *The Thinker* depicts a man sitting, leaning forward, fist planted under his chin, and deep in thought. But the sculpture is not about the human struggle for knowledge.[181] In fact, the

---

180. Augustine, *Civ.* 22.30.
181. The artist was Auguste Rodin and the sculpture was made in 1902.

sculpture was originally called *The Poet*, and the figure is meant to depict Dante in front of the gates of hell pondering his great poem! Like Rodin's sculpture of Dante, such despondent reflection is our task now. To systematize biblical instruction about hell, to conceptualize its existence and state, to meditate on its profound punishment, and to reflect on a God who would consign people there, is not the most uplifting topic of Christian theology. However, any theology that takes the glory of God seriously must set itself the task of showing how the abounding glory of God is made known even in the enduring vestiges of his judgment. If God is God, the God we know in Jesus Christ and in the Holy Spirit, then no matter what our doubts about the suitability of hell, we cannot doubt his goodness, mercy, and justice. Let that be our rule as we approach the topic of hell.

In biblical witness "hell" is called *gê'-hinnōm* or *geenna* and takes its name from the Wadi er-Rababi or "Valley of Hinnom" on the southwest side of Jerusalem. It was a terrible place because it was remembered as the location where child sacrifices had been made to Moloch (2 Kgs 16:3; Jer 7:31). It had judgment pronounced on it, and the wicked would be buried there (Jer 7:32). In intertestamental literature, hell was the place of the fiery abyss and the final judgment (e.g., *1 En.* 90.26).

The New Testament distinguishes *hadēs* (waiting place of the dead) from *geenna* (judgment place for the dead). The former is temporary, while the later is final; *hadēs* is for the soul, while *geenna* is for a reunited body and soul. Seven out of twelve occurrences of *geenna* occur in Matthew's gospel. Insulting a brother makes one liable to the fires of hell (Matt 5:22). Hyperbolically it is better to cut out an eye or cut off a hand than to be thrown into hell (Matt 5:29–30; 18:9; cf. Mark 9:43–47). Soul and body can perish in hell (Matt 10:28; cf. Luke 12:5), and the Pharisees make their converts twice the sons of hell as themselves (Matt 23:15). Jesus sees little prospect for the Pharisees escaping the "judgment of hell" (Matt 23:33). Outside of the Gospels, James, whose teaching bears great similarities to that of Jesus, says that the tongue itself is "set on fire by hell" (Jas 3:6).[182]

Evidently judgment by hell was a consistent theme in Jesus' preaching. Jesus used images, concepts, and motifs found in Scripture and known in contemporary usage—examples both historical and about the eschatological hereafter—to underscore the dire state of those who refuse God. Importantly, the judgment oracles in the Gospels about hell are not the rants of a man who looks forward to seeing sinners tormented for their sins, but they are urgent warnings calling people to repent. Let us remember that to preach a warning of judgment so that people can avoid it is really an act of mercy.[183]

The place of the final judgment is described with numerous phrases. Hell is the

---

182. J. Jeremias, *TDNT*, 1.657–58.
183. On Jesus and judgment, see Marius Reiser, *Jesus and Judgment: The Eschatological Proclamation in Its Jewish Context* (trans. Linda M. Maloney; Minneapolis: Fortress, 2007), esp. 302–23.

fiery abyss after the general resurrection, "where the fire never goes out" (Mark 9:43). For the wicked and unbelieving it is an "eternal fire," "eternal punishment," (Matt 25:41, 46), and "into the darkness" (8:12; cf. Jude 13). In Revelation, the final state of the wicked is expressed as "the Abyss" (Rev 9:1–2, 11) or "bottomless pit" (ESV), which can be locked forever; it is the place of "torment" (14:10–11), a "second death" (21:8); it is imagined as a "lake of burning sulfur" (14:10; 19:20; 20:10; 21:8). This shows that Jonathan Edwards was right about at least one thing: it is a terrible thing to fall into the judgment of God.

But what is the actual nature of hell, what is its essence, and what is so terrible about hell? The biblical witness suggests that "hell" is both reality and metaphor. The visibly confronting images for hell in the New Testament are imaginative descriptions of the full brunt of divine justice. Hell is not literally a place of fire, sulfur, and brimstone. If it was, how could Jesus say that people will be thrown into the "outer darkness"? You can't have roaring fires and total blackness at the same time. If hell is not literally a fiery abyss, then how do we conceive of it?

Christopher Marlowe wrote in his *Doctor Faustus*: "When all the world dissolves, And every creature shall be purified, All places shall be hell that are not heaven." Is that what hell is, simply the absence of heaven? It sounds a bit vague if you ask me. That's almost like saying that boredom is defined by the absence of Euro Disney. Now one could say that hell is the absence of God, or at least the absence of his goodness. It could also be said that hell consists in an acute awareness of the failure to attain the bliss and happiness that was offered humanity through Jesus Christ. Those are true I think, but they are probably not the essence of hell.

Hell is a punishment as all impositions of justice are in some way penalties. But do not be confused by the word "punishment." I do not mean that hell is something like God's own little Siberian Gulag or Guantanamo Bay located in the basement of the new heavens where criminals are tortured for the amusement of their captors, who look down at them through a glass flooring. Hell is more like a heavenly Hague where the inhumanity of humanity is laid before a tribunal and fitting recompenses are carried out toward those who sinned against an infinitely holy God and who sinned against other human beings who bear God's image. Hell is about justice, not torture. Perhaps we could say that hell will be that dimension of the future reality that quarantines evil much like the last traces of smallpox being locked in a secured laboratory so that it can never escape. I suspect that those in hell will mourn their bitter state, but they will still rage against the one who put them there.

What is more, some might still prefer in the end to reign in hell rather than to serve in heaven, for in hell they still may be able to enjoy their defiance against God. Hell is the place for creatures who have rejected God's revelation of himself in both nature and in the gospel, who refuse to bow the knee to the one true Lord, and who would rather live in darkness than in the light that exposes them. I surmise, following Tom Wright, that such persons have entered a posthuman state; they became what they worshiped—greed, lust, power—and they ceased to reflect the divine image in any meaningful sense. They arrived at a state beyond hope and beyond pity.[184] Hell, then, is the eternal and punitive quarantining of a humanity that has ceased to be human.

If you haven't noticed, not everybody likes hell. Rob Bell has a humorous little book endeavoring to show that the "eternal" in "eternal judgment" does not really mean "eternal." He cites a couple of verses from the Old Testament that show that "eternal" or "forever" can be temporary, so when Jesus said that hell was "forever," it was not literally "forever."[185] This is so lexically fallacious I won't even bother to refute it, except to say that this might sound attractive concerning "eternal judgment" so that the odium of the hell is downplayed. I wonder, however, if Bell would say that same thing about "eternal life"! Is eternal life not really forever? Despite the occasional hyperbole about "eternal" in the Bible (*'ôlām* [Hebrew]; *aiōnion* [Greek]), the words are overwhelming used in the sense of a period of unending duration (see esp. Matt 25:46).[186] Forget Bell and go for Wright instead, who states: "The traditional view of hell is clear: human beings will be punished in an endless time."[187]

There are other ways of trying to avoid the prospect of hell as an eternal state. One approach is annihilationism, sometimes called "conditional immortality," the view that those who are not saved will be eliminated and cease to exist. God will inflict a punishment against sin, but it will not be everlasting; subjects will eventually be annihilated. A number of ancient authors and modern evangelicals have given tacit approval to this view or have forthrightly endorsed it.[188] Advocates maintain a notion of judgment but see that judgment is fundamentally about "destruction" (see 2 Thess 1:9, "eternal destruction" [*olethron aiōnion*]). Ralph Bowles contends that "the doctrine of eternal torment, applied as a[n] interpretative grid, compels a particular, metaphorical view of all the texts that deal with 'death' and 'destruction' as the ultimate penalty for sin. It is hard for those texts that do indeed speak of 'destruction' to be heard over the noise of this doctrinal grid."[189]

The problem is that this "doctrinal grid," which refers to an eternal, conscious punishment of the wicked in hell, is itself not a metaphor taken too seriously but part of the fabric of the biblical warnings about judgment. Daniel contrasts "everlasting life" with "everlasting contempt" (Dan 12:2), and Paul similarly contrasts "death"

---

184. Wright, *Surprised by Hope*, 182–3.
185. Rob Bell, *Love Wins* (New York: HarperOne, 2009), 91–93.
186. BDAG, 32.
187. Wright, *Surprised by Hope*, 180.
188. Cf. e.g., John Wenham, "The Case for Conditional Immortality," in *Universalism and the Doctrine of Hell* (ed. Nigel Cameron; Grand Rapids: Baker, 1992), 161–91.
189. Ralph G. Bowles, "Does Revelation 14:11 Teach Eternal Torment? Examining a Proof-text on Hell," *EvQ* 73 (2001): 34 (21–36).

with "eternal life" (Rom 6:23). The final state is described as "eternal fire" (Matt 18:8; 25:41; Jude 7), and "eternal judgment" (Heb 6:2). Concerning the destruction of God's enemies, John says that the "smoke of their torment will rise for ever and ever" (Rev 14:11; cf. 19:3). It seems, then, that conditionalists disparage those scriptural passages that speak clearly of a never-ending state for those who reject the worship of the true God and the way of humanness that follows from it.[190] Eternal punishment is not injurious to God's justice and love; rather, it upholds it, as Robert Gundry writes:

> The NT doesn't put forward eternal punishment of the wicked as a doctrine to be defended because it casts suspicion on God's justice and love. To the contrary, the NT puts forward eternal punishment as right, even obviously right. It wouldn't be right of God not to punish the wicked, so that the doctrine supports rather than subverts his justice and love. It shows that he keeps faith with the righteous, that he loves them enough to vindicate them, that he rules according to moral and religious standards that really count, that moral and religious behavior has consequences, that wickedness gets punished as well as righteousness rewarded, and that the eternality of punishment as well as of reward invests the moral and religious behavior of human beings with ultimate significance. We're not playing games. In short, the doctrine of eternal punishment defends God's justice and love and supplies an answer to the problem of moral and religious evil rather than contributing to the problem.[191]

I am very conscious of reducing evangelism to some kind of offer of fire insurance for young people. Sign this card, walk down this aisle, or say this prayer, and you won't suffer the flames of hell. But something has to be said about the exhortation to "save yourselves from this corrupt generation" (Acts 2:40). If salvation is from judgment, and if the final judgment is meted out in hell, then salvation is from hell—pure and simple. A gospel that does not warn of a final judgment is like telling the citizens of ancient Pompeii that an umbrella made of straw will be sufficient enough to protect them should Mount Vesuvius erupt.

FURTHER READING

Crockett, William V., ed. *Four Views on Hell*. Grand Rapids: Zondervan, 1992.

Powys, David. "*Hell: A Hard Look at a Hard Question: The Fate of the Unrighteous in New Testament Thought*. PBM; Milton Keynes, UK: Paternoster, 2007.

---

190. Wright, *Surprised by Hope*, 182.
191. Robert H. Gundry, "Pastoral Pensées: The Hopelessness of the Unevangelized," *Themelios* 36 (2011). See www.gospelcoalition.org/themelios/archive (accessed 14 June 2012).

WHAT TO TAKE HOME?

- All theology is driven by eschatology since theology is the attempt to identify what happened when God's plan for the future began to invade the present age.
- Biblical eschatology is inaugurated eschatology so that the kingdom of God is both present and future, both now and not yet.
- The return of Jesus will be bodily, personal, and visible and will result in the final consummation of the kingdom of God.
- The main millennial views are postmillennial, amillennial, dispensational premillennial, and historic premillennial.
- The main tribulation views are pretribulation and posttribulation.
- The intermediate state means going to be with Christ in heaven, but the final state is a new heaven and a new earth.
- The new creation will be a city temple with Edenic qualities.
- Hell is a state of everlasting punishment for the wicked that is eternal and final.

STUDY QUESTIONS FOR INDIVIDUALS AND GROUPS

1. Explain how the kingdom is both a present experience and a future hope. What do we already have and what do we still hope for?
2. What do you think the book of Daniel and the Olivet Discourse contribute to our understanding of Jesus' second coming?
3. What view of the millennium do you find the most persuasive and why?
4. If someone asked you, "What happens to believers after they die?" what would you say?
5. Is "hell" a place, a state, or a metaphor?
6. Describe in your own words what the new creation will be like.

PART FOUR

The Gospel of God's Son: The Lord Jesus Christ

Part Four • The Gospel of God's Son: The Lord Jesus Christ

§4.1 The Gospel of God's Son
§4.2 Christological Method
§4.3 The Life of Jesus
§4.4 The Death of Jesus
§4.5 The Resurrection of Jesus
§4.6 The Ascension and Session of Jesus
§4.7 The Story of Jesus and the Identity of God

Study of the person and work of Christ is called "Christology." The gospel declares what God has done in his Son, and thus we look to Jesus Christ as the climax of God's revelation and as the primary actor in the drama of redemption. The work of Christ is announced summarily in the gospel and can be unpacked by expositing the redemptive significance of his life, death, resurrection, and ascension in God's plan. Furthermore, the person of Jesus Christ must be studied with a view to what Jesus tells us about the identity of God.

> It is one and the same Son of God who exists in both natures, taking what is ours to himself, without losing what is his own.[1]

> For Judah's lion bursts his chains
> Crushing the serpent's head;
> And cries aloud through death's domain
> To wake the imprisoned dead.
> Devouring depths of hell their prey
> At his command restore;
> His ransomed hosts pursue their way
> Where Jesus goes before.[2]

> So when the devil throws your sins in your face and declares that you deserve death and hell, tell him this: "I admit that I deserve death and hell, what of it? For I know One who suffered and made satisfaction on my behalf. His name is Jesus Christ, Son of God, and where He is there I shall be also!"[3]

---

[1] Pope Leo the Great, cited in Donald G. Bloesch, *Jesus Christ: Savior & Lord* (Downers Grove, IL: InterVarsity Press, 1997), 1.

[2] Fulbert of Chartres (ca. 970–1028), "You Choirs of New Jerusalem," cited in Alister E. McGrath, *A Brief History of Heaven* (Oxford: Blackwell, 2003), 89–90.

[3] Movie *Luther* (2003), directed by Eric Till.

§ 4.1 THE GOSPEL OF GOD'S SON

The centerpiece of the gospel is Jesus the Messiah. Jesus is so identifiable with the gospel that there can be no gospel without him. His identity as the Messiah and Lord, the redemptive significance of his death and resurrection, set in the coordinates of God's kingdom, constitute the core of the gospel message (Rom 1:3–4; 1 Cor 15:3–5; 2 Tim 2:8). In other words, the gospel sets before us both the *work* of Jesus Christ and the *person* of Jesus Christ. George W. Peters puts it this way: "The deity-humanity mystery and the cross-resurrection event are inseparably linked in the foundational message of the New Testament, the gospel of God and the gospel of our salvation."[4] A gospel-driven Christology entails a bifocal approach on a study of both salvation and the Savior. Therefore, explorations in Christology are attempts to penetrate into the mystery of Jesus' identity, while simultaneously expounding the significance of his career, crucifixion, and resurrection.

It is crucial that we also remember that the gospel is the story about Jesus set in the wider narrative of the story of God. The gospel includes a theology of atonement, but it also touches on the plan of God to save the world through Israel's deliverer. The triune architecture of the gospel means that the proclamation is based on the supporting beams of Israel's Messiah, a sending Father, and a promised Spirit. Consequently, our study of Jesus must be more than merely affirming his human and divine natures, more than affirming what his death achieved, and more than affirming his second coming. A Christology rooted in the gospel is going to redefine the very meaning of "God" (e.g., Phil 2:5–11) and exposit the story line of what it means to say that God was in the Messiah reconciling the world to himself (2 Cor 5:19). That caveat is important because it forces us to place our Christology in the context of God's mission, God's triune nature, and God's redemptive-historical purposes.

The centrality of Jesus can be tied to every subsection of theology and every subspecies of Christian thought. God is known to us most profoundly in the media-

---

4. George W. Peters, *A Biblical Theology of Missions* (Chicago: Moody Press, 1974), 310.

torship of Jesus Christ, and it is through the economic relationships of Father–Son and Son–Spirit that we can glimpse into the Trinity. In creation, God makes the universe in, through, and for Jesus Christ. In revelation, Jesus Christ unveils the mystery of God, executing the divine covenant for redemption, hidden in ages past but unveiled in these last days. In eschatology, the end of all things involves every man and woman appearing before the judgment seat of Christ and Christ himself consummating the Father's purposes in the new creation.

On the Holy Spirit, Jesus is the bearer of the Spirit and the dispenser of the Spirit; only through him is the Spirit given. The church is a community called and commissioned by Jesus to represent him before the world. Ethics is the practical discipline of learning to walk in Christ's steps behind him and showing our likeness to him in our behavior. I have labored the point, but at least it should be clear. If theology were a maze, every corner and every turn would lead to Jesus. If anything does not, it is not worthy of the name "Christian Theology." In theology, "no one can lay any foundation other than the one already laid, which is Jesus Christ" (1 Cor 3:11).

What the gospel announces is the most important claim in the history of the universe, that Jesus Christ is Lord and Savior, and that claim must not be compromised by any wayward or well-intentioned moves in the theological project. Contemporary theologies of Christ have often blunted the supremacy of his Lordship, diminished the glory of his person, or even denied the absolute necessity of his death for salvation—all in order to accommodate the Christian faith to the pluralistic *zeitgeist* of the day. Like Dostoyevsky's Grand Inquisitor, they command Jesus to leave, to drift away into the night, while they themselves remain behind, burdened and confused.

But conservatives are not immune from this temptation either. In some evangelical theologies, the Bible has eclipsed Christ as the center and lifeblood of faith. To be sure, Scripture is the authoritative testimony to Jesus; it is inspired and infallible. But the locus of our theology must be the person of Jesus, not our holy book. Our trust and hopes are invested in Christ, not in our sacred book. This is not a uniquely American or even Western problem. The danger is that some theologies, whether liberal or conservative, can be insufficiently christocentric. According to Timothy Tennent, writing about the church in India, but true enough elsewhere: "The liberal view is rejected because it tends to relativize and downplay the uniqueness and centrality of Jesus Christ in the Christian message. The conservative extreme is rejected because it tends to lock Jesus Christ up inside the covers of a book."[5]

Such extremes can be avoided if we make central what the gospel makes cen-

---

5. Timothy C. Tennent, *Theology in the Context of World Christianity: How the Global Church Is Influencing the Way We Think about and Discuss Theology* (Grand Rapids: Zondervan, 2007), 69.

tral: Jesus Christ, crucified and risen, Son of Man and Son of God. To speak of the centrality of Christ is at once to affirm the scriptural testimony to him; but it is more than that, more than propositional assent. It is to imply that the coherence of Christian beliefs are determined by our quest to articulate and enact the Lordship of Jesus Christ in our own spiritual journey, worship, confession of faith, and corporate mission. The gospel calls us to follow Christ our Redeemer, and the task of Christology is to describe, in all the beauty and majesty worthy of his person, whom it is we are following and why he is worthy of our worship.

§ 4.2 CHRISTOLOGICAL METHOD

Having established that Christology is the study of the person and work of Christ, we still have to inquire as to the best way to go about that task. Method in Christology is a notoriously disputed affair. How do you teach someone about Jesus? Do you start with the person of Christ or with the work of Christ? Do you start with the Gospels or the epistles? If Gospels, would you start with Mark or with John? Should we begin with a full-blown Nicene Christology or work our way up from the historical Jesus? Do we study Jesus based on titles given to him, like "Son of God" and "Son of Man," or should we prioritize things Jesus did and accomplished, like his miracles and teaching? These are the issues.[6]

4.2.1 QUESTS FOR THE HISTORICAL JESUS

The debate about the method for Christology is often posed in terms of "Christology from Below" versus "Christology from Above." A "Christology from Below" attempts to anchor the Christian teaching about Jesus in history. In this vein, the "Quest for the Historical Jesus" was the attempt to get behind the layers of Christian doctrine and dogma and discover the "real Jesus."[7] The many Jesuses that this quest spawned, at least in Germany, presented little more than an artificially constructed figure who was human and not divine, and yet romantically likeable as a religious genius, carefully displaced from Catholic dogma (which was so reprehensible), and had an uncanny resemblance to the liberal Protestants who wrote about him.

For instance, Adolf von Harnack described the essence of Jesus' teaching as the love of God and the brotherhood of man, and he completely de-eschatologized Jesus from any hopes of an apocalyptic deliverance.[8] Albert Schweitzer was one of the first who exposed the quest for the historical Jesus as the attempt to domesticate Jesus to modern

---

6. Although the "titles" approach is common in the study of New Testament Christology, I point to the words of Leander E. Keck ("Towards the Renewal of NT Christology," *NTS* 32 [1986]: 368): "To reconstruct the history of the titles as if this were the study of christology is like trying to understand the windows of Chartres cathedral by studying the history of coloured glass."

7. Cf. N. T. Wright, "Quest for the Historical Jesus," in *ABD*, 3:796–802; James H. Charlesworth, *The Historical Jesus: An Essential Guide* (Nashville: Abingdon, 2008), 1–14.

8. Adolf von Harnack, *What Is Christianity?* (3rd ed.; London: Williams and Norgate, 1904).

sensibilities. The Jesus of European thought was "'a figure designed by rationalism, endowed with life by liberalism, and clothed by modern theology in an historical gab."[9] Similarly, George Tyrrell criticized the Jesus of Adolf von Harnack: "The Christ that Harnack sees, looking back through nineteen centuries of Catholic darkness, is only the reflection of a liberal Protestant face, seen at the bottom of a deep well."[10] The first quest ended with a bit of a whimper, but it still set up the questions about Jesus, the Jesus tradition, history versus theology, the genre of the Gospels, the Synoptic Gospels versus John's gospel, and similar issues that would dominate discussion for the next century.

In the aftermath of the failed quest, many retreated from a historical approach. For Rudolf Bultmann and Karl Barth, a historical quest for Jesus was illegitimate. For a start, such a quest was methodologically impossible since the Evangelists were not interested in a Jesus "according to the flesh" but only the Christ of faith (with some text twisting here of 2 Cor 5:16). Moreover, the quest was theologically improper since it sought to ground faith in historical evidence rather than in trust of God's revelation. It was not the Jesus of history, but the Jesus of the church's proclamation that mattered.

Still, not everyone followed that course. While certain pockets of Christian scholarship gave up on historical Jesus research, others pressed on with renewed vigor. In Britain, New Testament scholars like F. C. Burkitt, C. H. Dodd, and T. W. Manson all wrote significant works about Jesus' teaching, words, parables, ethics, and eschatology. On the continent, Joachim Jeremias and Otto Betz went against the grain by continuing to treat the Gospels as reliable sources of information about Jesus. Still, those in the Barthian and Bultmannian camps denied that the historical Jesus was part of faith, dogmatics, or even New Testament theology. In fact, Bultmann went so far as to affirm that "personal decision cannot be dependent upon a historian's labor" and "the message of Jesus is a presupposition for the theology of the New Testament rather than a part of that theology itself."[11]

Then in 1953, Ernst Käsemann, a former student of Bultmann, presented a lecture at the University of Marburg on "The Problem of the Historical Jesus."[12] Käsemann's contention was that Easter did not totally eradicate the continuity between Jesus and the early church. The primitive church never lost its interest in the life history of Jesus as being properly basic for faith. As long as the one called "Lord" was also known as the "crucified one," it was impossible to eviscerate history from the Christian *kerygma*. This led to a new impetus in Jesus research, which

---

9. Albert Schweitzer, *The Quest of the Historical Jesus* (trans. W. Montgomery; New York: Macmillan, 1961), 396.

10. George Tyrrell, *Christianity at the Crossroads* (London: Longman Green, 1909), 49.

11. Rudolf Bultmann, *Theology of the New Testament* (2 vols.; trans. K. Grobel; London: SCM, 1952), 1:3, 26.

12. Ernst Käsemann, "The Problem of the Historical Jesus," in *Essays on New Testament Themes* (trans. W. J. Montague; London: SCM, 1964), 15–47.

has subsequently become known as the "New Quest" for the historical Jesus.[13] Its notable proponents have included James Robinson, Günther Bornkamm, Norman Perrin, Eduard Schweizer, Ernst Fuchs, and Eduard Schillebeeckx.

The New Questers felt a little more confident about outlining a life of Jesus by use of form-critical tools. Yet they remained skeptical about the majority of material ascribed to Jesus in the Gospels and did not really extend our understanding of Jesus very far. When you introduce your book on Jesus with the words, "No one is any longer in the position to write a life of Jesus,"[14] you don't really have far to go. Despite constructing a more historically convincing portrait of Jesus, the resultant product was a Jesus who often looked far more like a twentieth-century Jewish existential philosopher than a first-century Jewish Messiah. So this New Quest did not get far, primarily because its main criterion for historical veracity was to isolate sayings of Jesus that did not resemble anything a Jew or Christian could possibly believe (the so-called criterion of double dissimilarity).

The New Quest did receive a shot in the arm from the North American Jesus Seminar in the late 1980s, where a band of scholars attempted to reconstruct Jesus by voting on materials in the Gospels that they thought were authentic. They also posited wider Hellenistic and Mediterranean social and intellectual currents rather than Judaism or the Hebrew Bible as the main locus for Jesus' teachings. They also focused on the hypothetical source Q (traditions common to Luke and Matthew) and the *Gospel of Thomas* as their primary sources. But in the end this new-new quest—I call them the neo-Bultmannians strike back—ended up giving us a "California Jesus." Richard Burridge noted that the Jesus Seminar "produced a Jesus who is not Jewish in his teaching, but more like a Greek wisdom teacher or philosopher, and he's against sexism, imperialism and all the oppressiveness of the Roman empire. In other words, he's a Californian."[15]

In retrospect, when one looks at both the First and, to a much lesser extent, the Second Quest for the historical Jesus, the results appear to resemble a line from the opening song of Jesus Christ Superstar, "I remember when this whole thing began. No talk of God then, we called you a man. And believe me, my admiration for you hasn't died." Following the lyrics of Tim Rice, some scholars claim that they can see clearly through the corridors of history, they can see around the naiveté of dogma, they can see beyond the fog of faith, and the Jesus they see is not the orthodox one. Jesus is a man, a brilliant man, a religious genius even, a man also worthy of imitation, but he is not the same

---

13. See James M. Robinson, *A New Quest for the Historical Jesus* (SBT 25; London: SCM, 1959).

14. Günther Bornkamm, *Jesus of Nazareth* (trans. I. Mcluskey, F. Mcluskey, and J. Robinson; New York: Harper & Row, 1960), 13.

15. Richard A. Burridge and Graham Gould, *Jesus Now and Then* (Grand Rapids: Eerdmans, 2004), 32; cf. Gerd Theissen and Annette Merz, *The Historical Jesus: A Comprehensive Guide* (trans. John Bowden; Minneapolis: Fortress, 1998), 11; Michael F. Bird, "The Peril of Modernizing Jesus and the Crisis of Not Contemporizing the Christ," *EvQ* 78 (2006): 293–97.

man as we find in the Gospels. For the Gospels have so radically reworked the tradition that there remains only but the faintest whisper of the authentic voice of Jesus.[16]

This brings us to the "Jesus Quest Episode III: A New Hope." The Third Quest for the historical Jesus had antecedents in those many scholars who tried to study Jesus in his Jewish context.[17] Yet it was Ben F. Myers and E. P. Sanders, writing in the late 70s and early 80s, who really got the ball rolling here in their respective works that situated Jesus in terms of first-century Judaism and setting his message within Jewish eschatological hopes. Researchers here were far more willing to regard Jesus as formally Jewish and not completely disengaged from the later church. Catholic scholar John P. Meier lists what he thinks are the present gains from the Third Quest: (1) the ecumenical and international dimension to the scholars involved in the research (as opposed to a band of Continental Lutherans); (2) a reexamination of various texts as reliable sources for the quest; (3) new insights from archaeology, philology, and sociology in the illumination of Jesus and his context; (4) a more accurate picture of the diverse and variegated nature of Palestinian Judaism; (5) clarification of the criteria of historicity, which has led to a more balanced appreciation of the historical traditions underlying the Gospels; (6) a more positive treatment of the miracle traditions in the Gospels; and (7) taking the Jewishness of Jesus with seriousness.[18]

Even so, as I write this in the first quarter of the twenty-first century, the Third Quest appears to have run out of steam. Not much now is left to be said: we have a better methodology, we have a Jewish Jesus, and he's thoroughly eschatological, but the doubt persists that this historical Jesus is still something of a mirror who reflects the biases and tastes of his biographers. In other words, historical Jesus research remains a great place to go and try to get your theological parking historically validated.[19]

4.2.2 THEOLOGY FROM BELOW AND THEOLOGY FROM ABOVE

Pannenberg's appropriation of Christology from Below is perhaps the most helpful articulation of such an approach.[20] According to Pannenberg:

> To test and justify christological statements about Jesus, christology must get behind the confessional statements and titles of the primitive Christian tradition, reaching the foundation to which these point, which underlies faith in Jesus. This foundation

---

16. Michael Bird, "Should Evangelicals Participate in the 'Third Quest for the Historical Jesus'?" *Them* 29 (2004): 6–7.

17. Cf. Ben Witherington III, *The Jesus Quest: The Third Search for the Jew of Nazareth* (2nd ed.; Downers Grove, IL: InterVarsity Press, 1997); Mark Allan Powell, *The Jesus Debate: Modern Historians Investigate the Life of Christ* (Louisville: Westminster John Knox, 1998); Michael F. Bird, "Is There Really a 'Third Quest' for the Historical Jesus," *SBET* 24 (2006): 195–256.

18. John P. Meier, "The Present State of the 'Third Quest' for the Historical Jesus: Loss and Gain," *Bib* 80 (1999): 459–87.

19. Cf. Dale C. Allison, *The Historical Christ and the Theological Jesus* (Grand Rapids: Eerdmans, 2009).

20. Wolfhart Pannenberg, *Systematic Theology* (3 vols.; trans. G. W. Bromiley; Edinburgh: T&T Clark, 1991), 2:278–97.

is the history of Jesus. Christology must ask and show how far this history of Jesus is the basis of faith. It does so by inquiring into the actual inner necessity of christological development in the NT and the continuation of this logic in the christology of the early church.[21]

This does not rule out a classic Christology of the incarnation. Rather, it is the presupposition for it, given that revelation as its manifestation is an action of God in human history. Furthermore, a Christology from Below enables us to critically differentiate between the essential content of christological dogma based on the New Testament witness and its secondary features in the early church that resulted in either clarification or distortion.[22]

So one approach to Christology, a Christology from Below, is to begin with the historical Jesus, then describe how this person impacted the origins and shape of the early church, look at how the early church developed its doctrines about Jesus, and trace the development historically through to our contemporary period. It sounds like a noble approach. This method is behind N. T. Wright's *Christian Origins and the Question of God* project and Wolfhart Pannenberg's paradigm of Christology built on God's revelation in history. Christology from Below takes seriously the notion that God reveals himself in history, that Jesus was a historical figure, and the resurrection was a historical event.

However, the problem will always remain that the historical Jesus is a scholarly construct, not an article of faith. The scholar's Jesus will always be, to some degree, subjective and artificial. Furthermore, the historical Jesus risks becoming more "canonical" than the Jesus of the canonical Gospels themselves. We are left wondering what role the Jesus of the canon and creeds plays in theology if they are just the *festschrift* to the historical Jesus. Are we to try to look behind the veil of the canonical Jesus, like Dorothy peering behind the curtain in the city of Oz, or is the real Jesus experienced in canon, creed, Eucharist, prayer, and worship?[23]

This objection is not new. Martin Kähler in the late nineteenth century argued similarly when he advocated that it is the biblical Christ that matters, the Christ of faith, and not the historical Jesus of the scholars.[24] Personally, I am quite committed to the historical Jesus as a necessary field of study because as a follower of Jesus, I am following a historical person.[25] But I am not quite so certain that historical study of Jesus is going to give us all the fuel we need to ascend to the heights of the risen and exalted Lord.

---

21. Ibid., 2:282.
22. Ibid., 2:288–89.
23. Cf. Luke Timothy Johnson, *The Real Jesus: The Misguided Quest for the Historical Jesus and the Truth of the Gospels* (San Francisco: HarperOne, 1996).
24. Martin Kähler, *The So-called Historical Jesus and the Historic, Biblical Christ* (trans. Carl E. Braaten; Philadelphia: Fortress, 1964); cf. also Paul Tillich, *Systematic Theology* (3 vols.; London: SCM, 1951–63), 2:101–6.
25. Bird, "Should Evangelicals Participate," 8–15; idem, "Peril," 302–12.

The alternative track of "Christology from Above" begins not with historical investigation of Jesus from a state of purported intellectual neutrality, but in the church's proclamation of who Jesus was, is, and will yet be. Rather than move from Jesus as a human figure to a divine being, the Christology from Above perspective begins with Jesus as divine and human, especially accenting the divine side. Methodologically it favors the Fourth Gospel and Pauline letters as the primary ingredients for a high Christology of Jesus' person and work.

Christology from Above found its primary twentieth-century exponents in theologians like Rudolf Bultmann and Karl Barth, to name a couple. These theologians emphasized the priority of faith in the church's proclamation about Jesus. The proper method for doing Christology is heaven to earth, not earth to heaven. It privileges divine speech over human inquiry. The history of Jesus, though tacitly acknowledged at points, was not as important as the event of the incarnation. It is not a mere human being but the exalted Lord that we meet in faith. Jesus comes to us in worship, not in the study of past relics. The incarnation is not something to be established by historical examination; rather, it is to be believed and embraced as an article of faith.

In the case of Bultmann, the mere fact of Jesus' historical existence would have sufficed for faith to be valid. Christology arises from the revelatory movement of Christ making himself known through the proclamation of the church, which is then apprehended by faith. Bultmann naturally gravitated toward the gospel of John, and his favorite designation for Jesus in his commentary on John was the "Revealer." The prologue of John's gospel is not a historical witness to the incarnation. Rather, the Johannine prologue, laden as it was in Gnostic mythology, attests the truth that Jesus is known in faith. In the Word becoming flesh, Bultmann believed that the Gnostic redeemer myth had been applied to the incarnation of the Logos: "The redeemer is in truth no specific historical figure.... Thus the place and time of his appearance are in effect of no importance; the [Gnostic] myth can attach itself to any savior figure, and let the historical tradition be submerged." The claim that "we have seen his glory" is, for Bultmann, "neither sensory nor spiritual, but it is the sight of *faith*."[26]

Concerning the resurrection, Bultmann believed that Jesus did not physically rise from the dead; rather, he rose into the *kerygma*. For it is in the preaching *about* Jesus that one encounters the *risen Jesus*. Bultmann wrote: "The real Easter faith is faith in the word of preaching which brings illumination. If the event of Easter is in any sense an historical event additional to the events of the cross, it is nothing else

---

26. Rudolf Bultmann, *The Gospel of John: A Commentary* (trans. G. R. Beasley-Murray et al.; Philadelphia: Westminster, 1971), 65, 69 (italics original).

than the rise of faith in the risen Lord, since it was this faith that led to the apostolic preaching."[27]

Karl Barth's christological approach is distinctly from Above as well. Barth's Christology commences with the decision of the Triune God to send the preexistent Son into the world as Savior. Barth assumes the divinity of Jesus and follows his movement from eternity to temporality in the incarnation. Jesus' humanity is then evaluated from the standpoint of his divinity.[28] Christology begins with the prophetic and apostolic witnesses that "Jesus Christ is very God and very Man," which constitutes the assumption on which all further reflection must proceed. The incarnation is a mystery that "can be contemplated, acknowledged, worshipped and confessed as such, but it cannot be solved, or transformed into a non-mystery."[29] That is why Barth engages in such a lengthy exposition of John 1:14, "The Word became flesh," as part of his christological study.[30]

More recently some scholars have proposed that the genesis of Christology lies not in the excavation of history beneath the Gospels, but in (1) the experience of Jesus in the life of the church and (2) the scriptural narrative about Jesus and its exposition in the early church. As an example of the first option, Luke Timothy Johnson writes:

> Jesus is best learned through the practices of faith in the church: through prayer, worship, the reading of Scripture, and encounters with saints and strangers. This position is based on the premise that Jesus is not a dead man of the past but a living Lord of the present. Furthermore, the tradition of the church, beginning with the Gospels, was right when they viewed Jesus from the perspective of his resurrection and exaltation, for he can be only understood as the risen Lord. Accordingly, the real Jesus on this perspective is not a figure of the past but of the present, not an object of scholarly investigation but the subject of obedient faith.[31]

The "Identity of Jesus Project" at the Center of Theological Inquiry in Princeton embarked on its christological quest with the assumption that

> Jesus is best understood not by separating him from canon and creed but by investigating the ways in which the church's canon and creed provide distinctive clarification of his identity. The church's ancient ecumenical creeds are not artificial impositions on Scripture but interpretative summaries of biblical narratives. There-

---

27. Rudolf Bultmann, "New Testament and Mythology," in *New Testament and Mythology and Other Basic Writings* (trans. S.M. Ogden; Philadelphia: Fortress, 1984), 42.

28. Cf. Mark L. Y. Chan, *Christology from Within and Ahead: Hermeneutics, Contingency, and the Quest for the Transcontextual Criteria in Christology* (BIS 49; Leiden: Brill, 2000), 64.

29. Barth, *CD*, I/1:122–32.

30. Ibid., I/1:134–71. I would note that Hans Vium Mikkelsen (*Reconciled Humanity: Karl Barth in Dialogue* [Grand Rapids: Eerdmans, 2010], 147–48) points out that Barth's Christology is perhaps more balanced than it appears to be. Although Barth operates first and primarily with a Christology from Above, he also operates with a Christology from Below, where the latter explains the meaning of Jesus as the elected human being.

31. Luke Timothy Johnson, "Learning the Human Jesus: Historical Criticism and Literary Criticism," in *The Historical Jesus: Five Views* (ed. J. K. Beilby and P. R. Eddy; Downers Grove, IL: InterVarsity Press, 2009), 154–55.

fore, they offer us an overarching sense of the meaning of the whole Bible, and of Jesus' place within that story.[32]

Thus, Christology, the meaning of who Jesus is, is not anchored primarily in the history of Jesus, but in the church's continuing witness to who Jesus is, was, and will yet be.

There are a number of factors that favor a Christology from Above—not the least of which is the beginning of the Fourth Gospel, which begins: "In the beginning was the Word, and the Word was with God, and the Word was God" (John 1:1). The Johannine model of Christology starts with the preexistence of the Logos, his taking on flesh, and his redemptive mission to bring salvation to the world. Likewise, the Nicene Creed's christological affirmations do not mess around with historical questions but move straight to confession: "We believe in one Lord, Jesus Christ, the only Son of God, eternally begotten of the Father." It makes sense: Christology should begin with God telling us who Jesus is.

Yet the Christology from Above approach is not without its detractors. For a start, the Gospels are not simply deposits about what people believed about Jesus, but they are actual testimonies and memories of Jesus of Nazareth. The Gospels are not narrative commentaries on the church's faith; they are genuine historical sources (e.g., Luke 1:1–4; John 20:31). Although they admittedly use a postresurrection hermeneutic that is pronounced at certain points, they are concerned with pointing back to the past of Jesus, a past different from the time of the Evangelists as they are writing.

Perhaps the most substantial objection is that the "Above" method leaves us with a question mark as to whether the Christ of faith is the same as the Jesus of history. While some might not care and even prefer a separation between the two, that is ultimately unsatisfying for those of us who believe in a God who acts in history. What is more, while the creeds provide a superb clarification of Jesus' identity and saving work in relation to the Father, the creeds completely omit any reference to his mission to Israel and his teaching. That omission is not an insignificant one as it means that the most basic Christian confessions have no immediate way of linking Jesus to the history of Israel and their Scriptures.

What is more, moving from Creator to Christ and bypassing redemptive history leaves us without tangible evidence of explaining the relationship between Jesus' message of the kingdom and the church's message of the cross. The incarnation becomes abstracted from both the redemptive-historical story of Scripture and from the sociohistorical context of first-century Palestine. Berkhof opines that in

---

32. Beverly R. Gaventa and Richard B. Hays, "Seeking the Identity of Jesus," in *Seeking the Identity of Jesus: A Pilgrimage* (ed. B. R. Gaventa and R. B. Hays; Grand Rapids: Eerdmans, 2008), 5.

theological study, "there is hardly room and interest for God's history with Israel. The impression is given that after a long period of divine inactivity, Jesus drops out of heaven."[33] This is perhaps the most fundamental problem with popular level evangelical theology: God's relationship with Israel becomes irrelevant to evangelical concepts of Christ and salvation.

The differences between Christology from Below and Christology from Above can be tabulated below:

	Christology from Below	**Christology from Above**
Starting Point	Jesus of History	Christ of Faith
Gospel	Synoptic Gospels	John's Gospel
Methodology	Rationalistic	Fideistic
Emphasis	Humanity	Deity
Precedents	Antiochene	Alexandrian
Dangers	Ebionite	Docetism

To sum up, Christology from Below begins with the Jesus of history. As such, it naturally favors the Synoptic Gospels as the primary historical portraits of Jesus. It leans toward the historical-critical method of interpretation by isolating what is historical in the Gospels and then by plotting the history of ideas about Jesus. Due emphasis falls on the humanity of Jesus: Jesus the prophet, rabbi, sage, and martyr. It has antecedents in the Antiochene interpretation of Christology that emphasized a plain sense reading of the Gospels and their historical context. The danger is, however, that it could descend to Ebionism, where Jesus is simply a human being who has a special relationship with God but is not identified with God in any serious way.

In contrast, Christology from Above begins with the Christ of the church's faith and proclamation, since that is where we first meet Jesus. It leans toward John's gospel since that is the gospel where the spiritual depth and theological breadth of Jesus' person is most pronounced. It tends towards fideistic emphases pertaining to faith and creed as the primary hermeneutical keys. Emphasis is given to Jesus' deity; his humanity, though not denied, takes a backseat. It has antecedents in the Alexandrian tradition, which reckoned with the spiritual nature of the Gospels and their testimony to heavenly realities. The danger is, of course, Docetism, where Jesus is so divine that he can scarcely be regarded as genuinely human.

---

33. Cf. Hendrikus Berkhof, *The Christian Faith: An Introduction to the Study of the Faith* (Grand Rapids: Eerdmans, 1979), 221.

§ 4.2 Christological Method

What are we to make of this? In regards to Christology, do we go below or do we try on high? Well, I concur with Martin Hengel: "This is a false alternative that goes against the course of New Testament christology, which develops in an indissoluble dialect between God's saving activity and man's answer."[34] Dissolving the dichotomy is justified when we remember that the two primary axes in biblical Christology are: (1) the narrative unity between Jesus of Nazareth and the risen and exalted Lord; and (2) the identification of the Lord Jesus with the God of Israel. Members of the EHCC (Early High Christology Club), including Martin Hengel, Richard Bauckham, and Larry Hurtado, have been quick to point out that in terms of the development of the church's Christology, more happened in the first twenty years than in the succeeding centuries of development of christological doctrine![35] Thus, a high Christology is one of the earliest recoverable Christologies of the early church.

Not only that, but the gospel cannot be strictly tied to a Christology from Above or to a Christology from Below. The gospel presupposes a divine action in a particular agent who mediates *between* the heavenly and earthly realms in order to achieve God's purposes. In addition, the canonical shape of the four Gospels takes us from the infant Jesus as "Immanuel" in Matthew 1, to the risen Jesus confessed as "my Lord and my God" by Thomas in John 20—all set in the context of the Messiah's historical mission to redeem Israel. Consequently, Jesus as the Messiah is a historical fact and an article of faith in the believing community. One cannot speak the truth about the one without the other in Christian discourse about Jesus Christ.[36]

Furthermore, to try to state the doctrine of Christ purely in substantive or ontological terms without adequate attention to his earthly life and saving mission will not do justice to the New Testament witness to Christ. On such a path, the dynamic christological revelation of Jesus Christ in history is replaced by static dogma. Similarly, to engage in christological study in strictly historical terms, cordoned off from Christ's eternity, which is equally attested in the New Testament, will replace the Christ of faith with the Jesus of scholarly historical construct.[37]

That means that Christology is not top down or bottom up. Rather, we do Christology from behind, below, above, and before.[38] In terms of the tactics of armored warfare, this is a quadruple envelopment as we look at Jesus from behind (Old Testament), below (historical Jesus), above (Jesus of divine speech), and before (creedal and confessional testimonies to Christ). Thus, we study Jesus according to

---

34. Martin Hengel, *The Cross of the Son of God* (trans. J. Bowden: Philadelphia: Fortress, 1976), 92.

35. Cf., e.g., Martin Hengel, *Studies in Early Christology* (Edinburgh: T&T Clark, 1995), 383.

36. Tillich, *Systematic Theology*, 2:98; Cf. also Millard Erickson, *Christian Theology* (2nd ed.; Grand Rapids: Baker, 1998), 689–91.

37. Thomas F. Torrance, *Incarnation* (Milton Keynes, UK: Paternoster, 2008), 182–83.

38. Berkhof, *Christian Faith*, 267–68.

the Old Testament Scriptures, in the history delivered in the Gospels, through gospel message about Jesus, and amidst the christological faith as it has been received in the church.[39]

FURTHER READING

Crisp, Oliver. *God Incarnate: Explorations in Christology.* London: T&T Clark, 2009.

Lash, Nicholas. "Up and Down in Christology." Pp. 31–46 in *New Studies in Theology*, eds. S. Sykes and D. Holmes; London: Duckworth, 1980.

Pannenberg, Wolfhart. *Jesus: God and Man.* 2nd ed. Philadelphia: Westminster John Knox, 1968, esp. pp. 33–37.

---

[39]. This model will hopefully relieve us of other dichotomies like a functional vs. titular Christology or person vs. work of Christ.

§ 4.3 THE LIFE OF JESUS

The life of Jesus does not feature prominently in evangelical theology. As long as Jesus was born of a virgin and as long as he died on the cross, it doesn't seem to matter much what else he did or where he did it. In other words, as long as he had a sinless birth and a sin-bearing death, he could have lived among the Eskimos for all it really matters. Some may tip the hat to Jesus' life and admit that his teaching has some value for helping to prepare Sunday school lessons. Jesus told cute earthly stories with heavenly meanings about how to get to heaven, and he gave quaint advice about how to be a nice Christian. The sad fact is, though, that for many Christians, Jesus' life is really just the warm-up act to Paul's atonement theology.

This is not a recent failure limited to evangelical or Reformed churches in the twenty-first century. Christian statements of faith such as the Apostles' Creed, Westminster Confession, and Lausanne Covenant do not resource Jesus' life and teaching much in their doctrinal affirmations.[40] Christian theologians have been overwhelmingly concerned in their Christology with the human and divine natures of Christ and with the saving benefits of Christ's death. But what is the theological significance of his life and teaching?

To begin, we must remember that our New Testament canon opens up with four books called "Gospels," recounting the "the beginning of the good news about Jesus the Messiah" (Mark 1:1). I don't know why in God's providence the canon is ordered the way that it is, but the fact that you have to read four biographies of Jesus before we get to the epistles means God might be trying to tell us something, namely, that the life of Jesus matters!

Unsurprisingly the apostolic preaching in Acts makes much of Jesus' life. Peter even presents a précis of Jesus' career in his preaching to the household of Cornelius (Acts 10:34–43). Though Paul does not mention much in way of Jesus' life, he does spasmodically refer to and echo Jesus' teachings on occasion (e.g., Rom 14:14; 1 Cor

---

40. On this complaint, see N. T. Wright, *Jesus and the Victory of God* (COQG 2; London: SPCK, 1996), 14; Douglas Kennard, *Messiah Jesus* (New York: Peter Lang, 2008), 1–3; Berkhof, *Christian Faith*, 221–22.

7:12–13; 1 Thess 4:15), and Paul is aware of a basic outline of his life (e.g., 1 Cor 15:3–4; 2 Cor 8:9; Gal 4:4–5; Phil 2:5–11). The gospel of Christian proclamation is incomplete unless it references the gospel story of Jesus' life.

If you do not believe me, consider the following. In our various manuscripts of the New Testament, there are more copies of the Gospels than any other New Testament books. The Apostolic Fathers and the apologists quoted from the Gospels more than any other New Testament writing. The Apostolic Fathers were in effect "red letter Christians," who frequently quoted the words of Jesus as their first grounds of appeal and exhortation. These first theologians found their main theological impetus from the Gospels.

One thing I love about the Book of Common Prayer is that every day there is at least one reading from the Gospels, usually from the words of Jesus. And rightly so, because Christian theology will be deficient if it neglects the deeds and words of the Lord to whom it is committed to following. In order to be theologians of the gospel, we must be theologians of the Gospels! Before we can box with Paul, fence with Hebrews, or dance with Revelation, we must wrestle with Jesus. J. I. Packer also gives us cause for thought:

> Finally, we could then correct the wooliness of view as to what Christian commitment involves, by stressing the need for constant meditation on the four gospels, over and above the rest of our Bible reading; for gospel study enables us both to keep our Lord in clear view and to hold before our minds the relational frame of discipleship to him. The doctrines on which our discipleship rests are clearest in the epistles, but the nature of discipleship itself is most vividly portrayed in the gospels. Some Christians seem to prefer the epistles to the gospels and talk of graduating from the gospels to the epistles as if this were a mark of growing up spiritually; but really this attitude is a very bad sign, suggesting that we are more interested in theological notions than in fellowship with the Lord Jesus in person. We should think, rather, of the theology of the epistles as preparing us to understand better the disciple relationship with Christ that is set forth in the gospels, and we should never let ourselves forget that the four gospels are, as has often and rightly been said, the most wonderful books on earth.[41]

Below we will explore the life of Jesus as a theological subject with focus on: (1) Jesus and the Old Testament; (2) the birth of Jesus; and (3) the ministry of Jesus.

---

41. J. I. Packer, *Keep in Step with the Spirit: Finding Fullness in Our Walk with God* (Downers Grove, IL: InterVarsity Press, 2005), 61. See also Emil Brunner, *The Christian Doctrine of Creation and Redemption* (London: Lutterworth, 1952), 283: "The view that because our one aim is to proclaim 'Christ Crucified' the story of His life does not actually belong to the Gospel, is equally mistaken. The Early Church, rightly, held the opposite opinion, when she called the four books which tell the story of the life of Jesus, 'the Four Gospels.' As the life of Jesus can only be rightly understood from the point of view of the cross—the object of the Fourth Gospel to show this—so, conversely, the Cross of Jesus can only be understood in light His life, as its culmination."

4.3.1 JESUS AND THE OLD TESTAMENT

What is basic to the gospel message is that the events surrounding Jesus of Nazareth occurred "according to the Scriptures." That is affirmed in gospel summaries given by Paul (Rom 1:2; 1 Cor 15:3–4), in the apostolic preaching summarized in Acts (e.g., Acts 2:22–36), and in seeing how the Gospels themselves are pervaded with Old Testament imagery (e.g., Matt 2:15, 17–18, 23; 13:14–16, 35; 26:54–56). We might even say that the Old Testament formed the script for Jesus' ministry and passion. The Jesus of the Gospels asserts that the Jewish "Scriptures ... testify about me" (John 5:39), and the risen Jesus, in his encounter with the two travelers to Emmaus, began "with Moses and all the Prophets ... [and] explained to them what was said in all the Scriptures concerning himself" (Luke 24:27). As C. H. Dodd saw long ago, the Old Testament provided the substructure to New Testament theology.[42]

There are manifold issues that could be discussed here, such as the way that New Testament authors cite the Old Testament, how much Old Testament authors actually knew about Jesus and the future, and text-critical issues concerning what versions of the Old Testament are cited by a New Testament author. Those issues are beyond our scope here and belong to the task of New Testament studies.[43] The question before us is this one: *How* is Christ present in the Old Testament and *what* does that contribute to Christology?

As for the manner in which Christ is present in the Old Testament, I propose the following four ways.

1. *Prophetically.* Jesus is the Messiah because he is the one prophesied about in the Old Testament. The claim that Jesus' coming was foretold in the Old Testament was a basic element of apostolic preaching. The church's only "Bible" at this time was what we now call the Old Testament, and the Christian believers argued that the prophetic words in these texts pointed ahead to Jesus. These are prophetic in the sense that the Old Testament contains promises that find fulfillment in Jesus Christ.

We must remember that not every prophetic promise is messianic and not every eschatological deliverer is a Messiah.[44] To give a few highlights, we would have to say that Jesus is: the promised seed of Eve who will crush the head of the serpent (Gen 3:15); the promised seed of Abraham (Gen 15:3–4); the ruler who comes forth

---

42. C. H. Dodd, *According to the Scriptures: The Substructure of New Testament Theology* (London: Nisbet, 1953).

43. Cf. E. Earle Ellis, *The Old Testament in Early Christianity: Canon and Interpretation in the Light of Modern Research* (WUNT 54; Tübingen: Mohr/Siebeck, 1991); Peter Enns, *Inspiration and Incarnation: Evangelicals and the Problem of the Old Testament* (Grand Rapids: Baker, 2005); D. A. Carson and Greg Beale, eds., *Commentary on the New Testament Use of the Old Testament* (Grand Rapids: Baker, 2007); Kenneth Berding and Jonathan Lunde, eds., *Three Views on the New Testament Use of the Old Testament* (Grand Rapids: Zondervan, 2008); Larry W. Hurtado, *Lord Jesus Christ: Devotion to Jesus in Earliest Christianity* (Grand Rapids: Eerdmans, 2003), 564–78.

44. On what counts as a messianic text in the Old Testament, see Michael F. Bird, *Are You the One Who Is to Come? The Historical Jesus and the Messianic Question* (Grand Rapids: Baker, 2009), 31–62.

from the tribe of Judah (Gen 49:10); the future prophet like Moses (Deut 18:15); the new Davidic leader who leads Israel out of exile (2 Sam 7:11–14; Pss 89; 132; Isa 16:5; Jer 33:17–26; Ezek 34:23–24; 37:24–25; Mic 5:1–4), and the Suffering Servant who redeems the elect by his suffering (Isaiah 52–53).

2. *Typologically.* Typology is a hermeneutical approach that "sees in persons, events or places the prototype, pattern, or figure of historical persons, events or places that follow it in time."[45] Jesus' life and work rehearse several patterns or types from the Old Testament.[46] In Romans 5:12–21, Adam is a "type" or "pattern" of the one to come, who is Christ. Several of the Old Testament citations in the infancy narrative of the gospel of Matthew are typological rather than prophetic. For example, the citation of Hosea 11:1 in Matthew 2:15 ("out of Egypt I called my son") to describe the flight of the holy family to Egypt, is not a messianic prophecy. Rather, Hosea's words were meant to remind Israel that God intended to carry out a new exodus for them modeled on the former exodus. Matthew cites Hosea 11:1 to show that this same pattern is recapitulated in Jesus' own history as God is beginning a new exodus with the new David.[47]

In 1 Corinthians 10:1–11, Paul illustrates a number of types intended to be recognized by Christians who understand themselves to be living in the age of eschatological fulfillment. Paul's exhortation, drawn from the story of Israel's wanderings in the wilderness, narrates how believers' own journeys toward the future are similar to the Israelites' journey toward Canaan with similar pitfalls to be avoided along the way. Typology was used by New Testament authors to explain how the key nodes of redemptive history, from Adam through to David, prefigured the nature of Christ's person and work.

3. *Christophany.* Another approach to finding Jesus in the Old Testament asserts that certain theophanies (appearances of God) in the Old Testament were in fact christophanies (appearances of the preincarnate Jesus). A good example is the "angel of the LORD," who appears at several places and speaks with an immediate divine authority (e.g., Gen 16:7–13; 21:17–21; 31:10–13; Exod 3:2–6; Judg 2:1). What comes to mind as well is Daniel 3:25, where Nebuchadnezzar puts the three friends into the furnace and then exclaims: "Look! I see four men walking around in the

---

45. Michael Fishbane, *Biblical Interpretation in Ancient Israel* (Oxford: Clarendon, 1985), 350.

46. Cf. Leonhard Goppelt, *Typos: The Typological Interpretation of the Old Testament in the New* (Grand Rapids: Eerdmans, 1982), esp. 225–29; John Goldingay, *Models for Interpretation of Scripture* (Grand Rapids: Eerdmans, 1994), 61–70.

47. According to James Hamilton ("The Virgin Will Conceive: Typological Fulfillment in Matthew 1:18–23," in *Built upon the Rock: Studies in the Gospel of Matthew* (ed. J. Nolland and D. Gurtner; Grand Rapids: Eerdmans, 2008], 243): "Matthew cites these words because just as the nation, the collective son of God, was led out of Egypt by a pillar of fire and cloud to failure in the desert, so Jesus the singular Son of God, was summoned out of Egypt and then led out to the desert by the Spirit to succeed against temptation (Matt. 4:1–11). The historical circumstances correspond to one another, but the stakes are higher and Jesus is found faithful where the nation grumbled and rebelled. The fulfillment of Hosea 11:1 in Matthew 2:15 is typological, as the elements of historical correspondence and escalation show."

fire, unbound and unharmed, and the fourth looks like a son of the gods."[48] Justin Martyr regarded the Old Testament theophanies as appearances of the Son rather than the Father.[49] A. T. Hanson goes so far as to ascribe a "real presence" to Jesus in the Old Testament and not exclusively a deposit of typological imagery.[50] This is not purely speculative exegesis by second- and third-century Christians. The belief in Jesus as the preexistent Son, who was present in creation and Israel's history, goes back as far as the first-century New Testament authors (1 Cor 8:4–6; Phil 2:6–8; Col 1:15–17; Heb 1:1–3; John 1:1–2).

4. *Allegorically.* Because of wide-scale abuses of allegory by the church fathers, we are accustomed to exegetical revulsion at the thought of allegory. You only have to read Augustine's allegorical gymnastics on the parable of the good Samaritan to realize that allegory is more painful to listen to than nails on a blackboard. Yet we must countenance our revulsion with the fact that New Testament authors do use allegory, both explicitly and implicitly, in their expositions of Scripture. It is explicit in the case of Paul in Galatians, who says concerning the present Jerusalem and the Jerusalem that is above, "Now this is an allegory" (Gal 4:24 NRSV). Despite the best efforts of commentators to deny that the word *allēgoreō* means "allegory," the lexical meaning of the word makes the connection plain and simple.[51]

Allegory is a legitimate interpretation with apostolic precedent and a long history of usage in the early church. Allegory is a fine interpretive vehicle as long as you have a hermeneutical seat belt. Allegory is the canvas for a canonically shaped imagination to find Jesus in places we never saw him before. Allegory, when framed within a redemptive-historical story line, spurs us on to creative ways of thinking about how the Old Testament rehearses, recapitulates, and interprets the story of Jesus.

The most obvious example would have to be the Song of Songs. This is a decidedly nontheistic romance story between a king and his concubine that can be preached as an allegory between Christ and the people of God. That is not part of its authorial intent, yet it makes sense canonically and preaches well to believers. An allegorical reading of the Song of Songs was developed with great pathos and power by patristic writers, including Hippolytus, Origen, Augustine, and Gregory of Nyssa, and even by Reformers such as Luther and Calvin.[52]

---

48. On Jesus and angels, I would point out that in Revelation Jesus is portrayed with angelic characteristics, he sends his "angel" as a messenger, and yet it is basically himself who speaks (Rev 1:1; 22:16).

49. Cf. Justin, *Dial.* 56–62, 126–29.

50. A. T. Hanson, *Jesus Christ in the Old Testament* (London: SPCK, 1965), 172.

51. Cf. BDAG, 46; *EDNT*, 1:62–63.

52. On nonliterary approaches to the Song of Songs, see Daniel C. Fredericks and Daniel T Estes, *Ecclesiastes and the Song of Songs* (AOTC; Nottingham, UK: Apollos, 2010), 275–80; Barry Webb, *Five Festal Garments: Christian Reflections on the Song of Songs, Ruth, Lamentations, Ecclesiastes, Esther* (NSBT 10; Downers Grove, IL: InterVarsity Press, 2000), 34–35. For a "canonical" reading of Song of Songs, see James Hamilton, "The Messianic Music of the Song of Songs: A Non-Allegorical Interpretation," *WTJ* 68 (2006): 331–45.

It was the intertextual connections between the Old Testament and Christian discourse about Jesus that led Paul to tell the Jews in Pisidian Antioch: "We tell you the good news: What God promised our ancestors he has fulfilled for us, their children, by raising up Jesus" (Acts 13:32–33). This is why the Old Testament was regarded as a "shadow" of the realities that were realized in Christ (Col 2:17; Heb 8:5; 10:1). It explains how Luke could refer to the things that have been "fulfilled among us" in his introduction (Luke 1:1). The Mosaic law provided the scaffolding for God's intention to build a people of God with Jesus as the cornerstone. The scaffolding pointed ahead to that future but was not part of it.

The point of debate between the New Testament authors and their Jewish contemporaries was that many Jews believed that the scaffolding was permanent, whereas the first Christians believed it was a necessary though intermediate step until the revelation of the Messiah. This is why Jesus Christ is "the culmination [or 'goal'] of the law" (Rom 10:4). This christocentric hermeneutic ultimately derived from Jesus himself, who deliberately lived out patterns and provocatively acted out prophecies from the Old Testament so that the Scriptures would be fulfilled (see Matt 26:53–56; Luke 4:21; 18:31; 22:37; 24:44; John 19:28).

Augustine's well-known adage was that the New Testament lies hidden in the Old and the Old Testament is unveiled in the New. Christ is there in the Old Testament. Yet this does not set aside the genuinely new nature of the incarnation and the disclosure of a divine mystery about Jesus in the gospel. As Ignatius of Antioch wrote:

> [He] himself is the door of the Father, through which Abraham, and Isaac, and Jacob, and the prophets, and the apostles, and the Church enter in. All these come together in the unity of God. But the gospel possesses something distinctive, namely, the coming of the Savior, our Lord Jesus Christ, his suffering and the resurrection. For the beloved prophets preached in anticipation of him, but the gospel is the imperishable finished work. All these things together are good, if you believe in love.[53]

Much of the Old Testament is prospectively christological, in that certain Old Testament texts clearly point ahead to a future figure who would be God's agent of deliverance for Israel. Whether any person could legitimately lay claim to actually fulfilling those prophecies by his words and actions was another matter. Jesus set out to fulfill the prophecy of Zechariah 9 in the way that he entered Jerusalem on a donkey, but not all onlookers thought that he was the Shepherd King of Israel. Yet the church's testimony to Jesus assures us that he is the one spoken about in those prophecies because of the divine validation of his ministry by his miracles and by his resurrection.

---

53. Ign. *Phld.* 9.1–2.

On the reverse side, much of this Old Testament material is retrospectively christological. Jesus is present in the Old Testament, but only when viewed from the vantage point of New Testament faith. Identifying Jesus in the Old Testament in this fuller sense depends not on good exegesis, but on a revelation (Luke 24:45), new birth (John 3:5–10), the illuminating work of the *Paraclete* (John 14:26), and the veil being taken away (2 Cor 3:12–18). That the Old Testament teaches the crucifixion and resurrection of the Messiah is not anywhere explicit. Yet when one assembles the pieces in a certain way and views it through a certain lens, it becomes clear that this always was God's plan for the Messiah.

This plan is discernible in Scripture through the suffering righteous one of the Psalms, the Suffering Servant of Isaiah, and the Son of Man in Daniel 7. The gospel becomes the hermeneutical lens that allows us to see Jesus present in the Old Testament. The Spirit cures our myopia so that we can see beyond the surface of the text and delve into its inner substance. Through the Spirit's illuminating work, we apprehend the mysterious things of God manifested in Israel's Scriptures concerning the revelation of Jesus Christ.

A core claim of Christian proclamation was that the story of Jesus completes the story of Israel about God's intention to repossess the world for himself and to draw the nations into the family of Abraham. The late Martin Hengel wrote: "In view of the use of the Old Testament in early Christianity, one could speak, if one wished, of a—tacitly assumed—eschatologically determined 'centre of the Scriptures' [*Mitte der Schrift*], that of fulfilment in the gospel."[54] A central platform for any biblical theology, then, is that what was promised in the old covenant is fulfilled in the gospel of the new covenant.

That carries two significant corollaries. First, that the Old Testament is not a dispensable prologue to Jesus, but contains the first vital scenes of the one theodrama.[55] Second, the Old Testament is legitimately identified as Christian Scripture that is canonically unified with other Christian writings around Christ. The Old Testament is not merely *christological* but *christotelic* in that Jesus is the goal and climax of Israel's revelation (see Rom 10:4; Heb 1:2; 7:28).[56]

So what does the Old Testament say about Jesus? One can detect revelations of Christ in places such as the "angel [of the Lord], who spoke to [Moses] on Mount Sinai" (Acts 7:38), or even the moveable rock that accompanied the Israelites in

---

54. Martin Hengel, *The Septuagint as Christian Scripture: Its Prehistory and the Problem of Its Canon* (trans. M. E. Biddle; London: T&T Clark, 2002), 108.

55. Cf. Goldingay (*Models*, 62): "Each individual biblical story belongs in the setting of the story as a whole, stretching from the Beginning to the End, with the Christ event at the center. The Second Testament story has to be read in light of the story related in the First and vice versa. The two Testaments are like the two acts of the one play. People cannot expect to understand Act II if they miss Act I, nor Act I if they leave at the intermission; neither act can be understood independently of the other."

56. On the Old Testament as "christotelic" see Enns, *Inspiration and Incarnation*, 152–60.

the wilderness (1 Cor 10:4). Indeed, it was often said that the Old Testament saints received the gospel in advance about Christ and even from Christ (Rom 10:16; Gal 3:8; Heb 4:2; 1 Pet 3:19–20). In many ways, identifying Jesus within these episodes is simply the logical outworking of the doctrines of Jesus' preexistence and Jesus' mediatorship. If Jesus is God's ultimate agent of revelation and redemption as the gospel claims, presumably he has always had this role. That is what motivated Christians to go to the Old Testament to search for him.

In any case, what matters most is not the presence of Christ in this Old Testament story or that one, but the christological macrostructure of the Old Testament. I surmise that the primary contribution of the Old Testament to Christology is to intimate the nature of his threefold office as prophet, priest, and king. From Justin Martyr to John Calvin the *munus triplex Christi* ("threefold office of Christ") has been used to show that Jesus consummates the promises of salvation in Israel's Scriptures.[57] As Eusebius wrote:

> All these [prophets, priests, kings] have reference to the true Christ, the divine heavenly Word, the only High Priest of the universe, the only King of all creation, and of the prophets the Father's sole supreme Prophet. Of all who in former times were anointed with chrism as a type, whether of priests or kings or prophets, no one until now received such power of divine virtue as our Savior and Lord Jesus Christ demonstrates, who is the only and true Christ.[58]

So when Jesus begins his public ministry in Galilee by saying that "the time has come ... the kingdom of God has come near" (Mark 1:15), we are to hear that message against the backdrop of the complex political history of Jews in the ancient world and within the story of the Scriptures for the covenant God to redeem his people from their plight. Indeed, the fate of not only Israel but the whole world hangs on the shoulders of a young Galilean prophet bearing a message that God is at last becoming king. The offices of prophet, priest, and king are climatically fulfilled in the ministry of the one who would reveal, redeem, and reign on God's behalf. In reflection on Jesus' preexistence and redemptive mission, it is no wonder that the prologue to the Fourth Gospel identifies Jesus in these roles (John 1:1–18). Jesus is the witness who makes God known (prophet), the one who mediates adoption into God's family (priest), and the one who rules over the creation that he coauthored (king).

FURTHER READING

Borland, James. *Christ in the Old Testament*. Fearn, UK: Christian Focus, 2010.
Greidanus, Sidney. *Preaching Christ from the Old Testament*. Grand Rapids: Eerdmans, 1999.

---

57. Cf., e.g., Justin, *Dial.* 86; Calvin, *Institutes* 2.15.1.

58. Eusebius, *Hist. Eccl.* 1.3.8–9.

Hanson, A. T. *Jesus Christ in the Old Testament*. London: SPCK, 1965.
Wright, Christopher J. H. *Knowing Jesus through the Old Testament*. Downers Grove, IL: InterVarsity Press, 1992.

4.3.2 THE BIRTH OF JESUS

It was Martin Luther who said: "No other God have I but Thee, born in a manger, died on a tree." Jesus, the baby in the manger, was born to the Virgin Mary. He entered our world as "Immanuel" ("God with us") and was named "Jesus" because he was born to "save his people from their sins" (Matt 1:21–23). Luke celebrates the saving significance of Jesus' birth to the maiden Mary in the three songs of the *Magnificat* (Luke 1:46–55), *Benedictus* (Luke 1:68–79), and *Nunc dimittis* (Luke 2:29–32) that announce the dawn of the messianic age of redemption and its accompanying effusion of joy.

The virgin birth (or more properly, the virgin conception) is part of the story line of Matthew and Luke and is enmeshed in the creeds and confessions of orthodox Christianity. However, the historicity and significance of the virgin conception are disputed. Did it really happen and what does it mean? In what follows, I will (1) outline the biblical materials about the birth of Jesus, (2) defend the historical reality of the event, and (3) demonstrate the significance of the virgin conception.[59]

1. *Biblical testimony to the birth of Jesus.* Outside of Matthew and Luke, there are perhaps some implicit references to Jesus having a special or enigmatic birth. Paul refers in passing to Jesus as "born of a woman" (Gal 4:4), and though it might mean no more than Jesus was born in the ordinary way, it could echo a known tradition about Jesus' birth. In Mark 6:3 Jesus is called "Mary's son," not the son of Joseph, which may reflect a particular jibe about Jesus' paternal origins being unknown or questionable. Interesting also is that a well-known Jewish polemic that Jesus was a *mamzer* or illegitimate child. Such an accusation presupposes that there was something thought to be suspicious about the circumstances surrounding his birth (see John 8:41; *Gos. Thom.* 105; Tertullian, *Spect.* 30.6; *Prot. Jas.* 13–16; *Acts Pil.* 2.3).

In the Matthean birth story, Mary, though pledged to Joseph, was "found to be pregnant through the Holy Spirit" (Matt 1:18). Joseph's unsurprising suspicions are assuaged by a dream that confirms that the child Mary carries is "from the Holy Spirit" (1:20). Matthew implies a supernatural event in Mary's conceiving a child prior to her union with Joseph.

---

59. What follows is largely derivative from my earlier work on this subject, Michael F. Bird and James G. Crossley, *How Did Christianity Begin? A Believer and Non-Believer Examine the Evidence* (London: SPCK, 2008), 18–21; Michael F. Bird, "Birth of Jesus," *Encyclopedia of the Historical Jesus* (ed. Craig A. Evans; New York: Routledge, 2008), 71–75.

Luke's account emphasizes the virginity of Mary at several points, which further indicate the nonnatural means of conception (Luke 1:27, 34). Luke describes how an angel reports to Mary that she will conceive through the Holy Spirit, who "will come on you," and the power of the Most High "will overshadow you" (Luke 1:35). The verb *episkiazō* is ordinarily translated "overshadow" and means to interpose something like casting a shadow.[60] The image is somewhat reminiscent of how the glory of God "settled" on the tabernacle in Moses' day (Exod 40:35; the LXX uses *episkiazō*).

In these two infancy stories it is clear that this isn't IVF with God as their gynecologist and the Holy Spirit as a sperm donor. The actual "how" remains mysterious to us. What is clear is that God's Spirit miraculously imparts divine life into Mary's human womb. There is also an allusion to new creation as the Spirit, who created something from nothing in the beginning of creation, now creates something from nothing in Mary's womb in the beginning of the gospel. We are arguably led to think here that God's new creation has begun.

Despite the differences between the Matthean and Lucan accounts, they agree on the following details:

1. Jesus' birth is set in relation to the reign of Herod the Great (Matt 2:1; Luke 1:5).
2. Mary is a virgin, betrothed to Joseph, but their relationship is not yet consummated (Matt 1:18; Luke 1:27, 34; 2:5).
3. Joseph is of Davidic descent (Matt 1:16, 20; Luke 1:27; 2:4).
4. The birth is announced by angels (Matt 1:20–23; Luke 1:26–35).
5. Jesus is the Son of David (Matt 1:1; Luke 1:32).
6. Jesus is conceived by the Holy Spirit (Matt 1:18, 20; Luke 1:35).
7. Joseph plays no role in the conception (Matt 1:18–25; Luke 1:35).
8. The name "Jesus" is divinely given (Matt 1:21; Luke 1:31).
9. An angel refers to Jesus as "Savior" (Matt 1:21; Luke 2:11).
10. Jesus is born after Mary and Joseph have come to live together (Matt 1:24–25; Luke 2:4–7).
11. Jesus is born in Bethlehem (Matt 2:1; Luke 2:4–7).
12. Jesus' family settles in Nazareth (Matt 2:22–23; Luke 2:39).

2. *The reality of the virgin conception.* A number of objections typically get raised at the possibility of Jesus being born of a virgin. First, it is often alleged that the virgin birth has been fabricated on the back of some bad proof texting derived from a misreading of Isaiah 7:14 ("The virgin will conceive and give birth to a son"). It

---

60. BDAG, 378–79.

SOMETHING ABOUT MARY?

What is the evangelical view of Mary? In the Catholic tradition, Mother Mary was born of an immaculate conception, she was sinless, she abstained from sexual relations all of her life, she was assumed into heaven, she is a mediator, and she is coredemptrix alongside Christ. She is revered as "Advocate, Helper, Benefactress, and Mediatrix."[61] It is safe to say that the doctrines of her immaculate conception and heavenly assumption are legendary accretions to the tradition, are not biblically defensible, and therefore may be easily set aside. The fact that Mary rejoices in "God my Savior" means she is fully aware of her own need for the wondrous salvation that she so beautifully sings about (Luke 1:47).

What is more, while Catholics root Mary's mediation in the mediation of Christ from which it draws its power, the point of the biblical teaching is that there is no mediator needed beyond Jesus Christ (see 1 Tim 2:5; Heb 8:6; 9:15; 12:24). Jesus is not simply the mother of all mediators, ranging from St. Aaron to St. Zoticus with Mother Mary at top of the pack. The *solus Christus* of the Reformation (i.e., Christ alone) perfectly summarizes the biblical faith that identifies Jesus as the eschatologically absolute and final go-between between God the Father and humanity. Jesus is the only being in all of creation who could ascend the throne of the Father, open the scroll, and execute the divine plan for redemption (Rev 5).

That said, there is indeed a mediator between the church and Christ and that is the Holy Spirit, who continues the work of Christ in the world. That is not apart from Christ since the Spirit is the "Spirit of Christ" (Rom 8:9–11; Phil 1:19; 1 Pet 1:11) and is sent in the name of Christ and by Christ (John 14:26; 15:26). It is the doctrine of Christ as mediator and the Holy Spirit as advocate that rules out a doctrine of Mary as mediator and redemptrix for evangelicals. Still, what can we say positively about a doctrine of Mary? I propose several points:

1. We can and should call Mary "blessed" (Luke 1:48). She was elected to take on one of the most important tasks in the history of the cosmos, to be the human carrier of God incarnate in her womb, to nurture him, to love him, and to raise him into manhood. She showed her worthiness for that role throughout her life, and though far from perfect (e.g., Matt 12:47–50), she remains a paragon of humility, virtue, godliness, and dedication. What is more, the Lord Jesus retained a special affection for her (John 19:26–27), so should not the followers of Jesus share his affection?

---

61. *CCC*, 220–23.

2. In Christian tradition, Mary is called *theotokos* or "God-bearer." This is an important title (over and against *Christotokos* or "Christ-bearer") since it affirms that Mary was the bearer of God incarnate and not simply the mother of a man who became God. As Gregory of Nazianzus said against Apollinarianism: "If anyone does not believe that Mary is *Theotokos*, they will be cut off from the deity.... If anyone asserts that humanity was created and only afterwards endued with divinity, they also will be condemned.... If anyone brings in the idea of two sons, one of God the Father, the other of the mother, may they lose their share in the adoption."[62] For a real humanity Jesus must have had a real birth, which is why it was necessary that Mary be the *theotokos*.

3. Mary can be understood as the antitype to Eve. Irenaeus draws on a contrast of two "virgins" to highlight the role of Mary in God's saving plan: "For just as the former [woman Eve] was led astray by the word of an angel, so that she fled from God when she had transgressed His word; so did the latter, by an angelic communication, receive the glad tidings that she should sustain God, being obedient to His word. And if the former did disobey God, yet the latter was persuaded to be obedient to God, in order that the Virgin Mary might become the patroness of the virgin Eve. And thus, as the human race fell into bondage to death by means of a virgin, so is it rescued by a virgin; virginal disobedience having been balanced in the opposite scale by virginal obedience."[63] Mary is a symbol for humanity receiving the grace of God in faith in contrast to the old humanity symbolized by Eve, who rejected it. Hence Mary can be a suitable symbol of the church in its relation to God.[64] Let us not forget that it is through Mary as the human receptacle for the incarnation that God is able to rescue the sons of Adam and Eve. Without Mary as a new Eve, we could not have Jesus as a new Adam.

FURTHER READING

McKnight, Scot. *The Real Mary: Why Evangelical Christians Can Embrace the Mother of Jesus*. Brewster, MA: Paraclete, 2007.

Parker, David. "Evangelicals and Mary: Recent Theological Evaluations." *ERT* 30 (2006): 121–40.

Perry, Tim. *Mary for Evangelicals: Toward an Understanding of the Mother of Our Lord*. Downers Grove, IL: InterVarsity Press, 2006.

---

62. Cited from Alister E. McGrath, *The Christian Theology Reader* (3rd ed.; Oxford: Blackwell, 2006), 270.
63. Irenaeus, *Haer.* 5.19.1 (see also 3.22.4).
64. Wolfhart Pannenberg, *Jesus: God and Man* (2nd ed.; Philadelphia: Westminster John Knox, 1968), 145.

should be agreed that the birth narratives have evidently been shaped by precedents in the Jewish Scriptures. The Lucan annunciation narratives in particular are heavily influenced by Old Testament prototypes of godly women who give birth to national heroes (e.g., Gen 17:15–21; Judg 13:2–7; 1 Sam 1–3). Matthew's depiction of Herod the Great parallels the Pentateuchal account of Pharaoh's cruelty to the Hebrews and Moses' birth as national deliverer (Exod 1–2).

While it might be possible that early Christians created the birth narratives out of their reflection of certain scriptural passages in order to develop their Christology, this is not generally how primitive Christian exegesis operated. Instead, the Old Testament functioned as the hermeneutical grid through which they interpreted traditional material rather than comprising the creative pool from which it was formulated. Matthew's citation of Isaiah 7:14 in Matthew 1:23 is often attacked as a poor hermeneutical exercise. The problem is that in its original context the prophecy refers to an infant born during the time of Ahaz and Isaiah, not to a divine messianic deliverer to be born some seven hundred years later. Moreover, the Hebrew word ʿalmâ means a woman of marriageable age, not necessarily a virgin. The notion of virginity is probably imported from the LXX through the word *parthenos*, which was used to translate ʿalmâ, and *parthenos* more explicitly implies a "virgin." Even so, while ʿalmâ is not a technical term for *virgo intact*, the idea of virginity could be connoted, depending on the context.

In any case, a virgin conception is clearly not predicted in the Hebrew text of Isaiah 7:14. Yet Matthew's citation does not demand an exact correspondence of events as much as it postulates a correlation of patterns or types between Isaiah's narrative and the birth story Matthew narrates. The coming of God's anointed one, the manifestation of God's presence, and the rescue of Israel through a child born to a young girl bring to Matthew's mind Isaiah 7 as an obvious prophetic precedent again repeated at a new juncture of redemptive history.

Second, tales of divine-human intercourse that produce the offspring of pagan demigods, political heroes, and oriental sages were common in the ancient world. Virgin births have been ascribed to people from Krishna in India to Anakin Skywalker on Tatooine. According to Suetonius, the birth of Augustus came about by his mother being impregnated by the god Apollo.[65] You can guess what ammunition this gives the skeptics: the birth of Jesus is an early Christian plagiarism of pagan mythology, blah, blah, blah ... Jesus never existed ... blahcetera, blahcetera.

In response, we should point out that analogy does not mean genealogy. There is no indication that Luke and Matthew are dependent on Greco-Roman or oriental birth stories as their source. To the contrary, the birth narratives are saturated

---

65. Suetonius, *Aug.* 94.4.

with Old Testament themes and possess a distinctive Jewish character that reflects the piety of Jewish Christianity (esp. the Lucan hymns). Additionally, other mythic birth stories like that of Augustus imply some human-divine sexual union that is entirely absent from the Gospels.[66] I would add that there is no reason for taking the birth narratives as being altogether different from the rest of the Gospels, which contain historical narratives set in the parameters of a Greco-Roman biography.

Third, it is often asserted that the virgin conception is not mentioned in Mark, John, Paul, the preaching of Acts, or the Catholic Epistles; therefore, it is relatively insignificant in the overall witness of the New Testament. In response we can say that general absence does not mean specific insignificance. There is a paucity of references to an intermediate state in the Bible (i.e., the state of believers after death), yet it is no less significant for that reason. The absence of references to the virgin conception is perhaps explainable on the grounds that it refers to second order instruction. The virgin conception is not part of the core gospel message. Yet it is part of the gospel, which explains the identity of Jesus of Nazareth, his human birth in relation to his divine person, his coming to fulfill Jewish hopes, and his bond with humanity.

At the end of the day we cannot prove that Jesus was born of a virgin just as Luke and Matthew narrate. What we can say with a good degree of historical probability is that Jesus' paternity was enigmatic from the start—hence the taunts about his illegitimacy.[67] Such a claim does not prove the virgin conception, but it is at least consistent with it. Whether one chooses to accept the virgin conception will ultimately depend on one's theological and philosophical convictions as well as one's willingness to embrace the testimony of the ancient church.

3. *The theological meaning of the virgin conception.* Did Jesus *need* to be born of a virgin? Given the parallels with pagan mythology and questions raised by modern biology, would it have been much easier if Jesus were perhaps born in the usual way? If not, what is the core importance of the virgin conception? Mark Strauss helps us out with a good answer:

> What is the theological significance of the virginal conception? Some have argued it was necessary to protect Jesus' sinless nature, but the narratives themselves do not indicate this purpose. The Messiah could have entered human life free from sin with or without a virginal conception. Nor is Scripture explicit on the details of the conception. Did God create the sperm for Mary's egg? Did he create a fertilized embryo? The latter question raises questions about how Jesus could have been fully human if he had no physical connection to Mary or Joseph. The former raises the question of

---

66. For early Christian responses to pagan myths about parallels between the birth of Jesus and similar stories in pagan mythology, see Justin, *Dial.* 67–70; 1 *Apol.* 33; Origen, *Cels.* 1.37.

67. Markus Bockmuehl, *This Jesus: Martyr, Lord, Messiah* (London: T&T Clark, 1994), 33.

how Jesus could have avoided Mary's sinful nature. The Roman Catholic answer is the immaculate conception, whereby Mary herself was born free from sin. But this doctrine has no basis in Scripture. In the final analysis, the details remain a mystery. What is certain from the text is that the conception of Jesus was a supernatural act of God, confirming that God himself was about to accomplish the salvation which no human being could achieve.[68]

Strauss is correct. Historically speaking, biology has often been stated as the main reason for the virgin conception. But we know from genetics that we inherit genes from both our mother and our father. So a virgin birth would not protect Jesus from Adamic DNA. We also know from the history of religions that claims to a virgin conception are not unique and form no trump card proving his divinity. I suggest that we can appreciate the theological import of the virgin conception only when we examine why it has sometimes been denied in church history.

The orthodox affirmation of the virgin birth in the second century took place amidst other so-called Christian groups who postulated either a purely human birth for Jesus (i.e., the Ebionites, Cerinthus, Carpocrates) or those who denied that Jesus had a human birth at all (i.e., Marcion). What is at stake here is nothing less than the identity of Jesus in relation to God the Father. Was Jesus a normal human being who was adopted as God's Son at his baptism? Was Jesus a heavenly revealer sent to impart esoteric truths to receptive minds? Or was Jesus the figure promised in Israel's Scriptures, who came to rescue the world beginning with the rescue of God's covenant people?

The Gnostic objection to the virgin conception is easy to understand. If you rip out the virgin birth from the Jesus story, you can rip out Jesus from the story of Israel and so divorce Jesus from the Jewish people—a divorce that suited the racial and religious prejudices of Rome's cultural elite. Yet time and time again the church has rightfully put down its foot against the Gnostic incursion. Whether that is ancient Gnosticism or modern Ivy League Gnosticism, both prefer Jesus the talking-head who leads us into a journey of self-discovery and redeems us from our bodies. This Jesus teaches that we had the power to get home all along—for "home" read self-fulfillment, the mothership "pleroma," spiritual nirvana, or whatever—just by clicking our intellectual shoes together and by repeating three times, "I can be all that I want to be."

The virgin conception means that Jesus was not simply a holy man whom God honored with divine status. It means Jesus was not a cosmic ghost disguised as a man dispensing philosophically savvy self-help advice to be true to ourselves. The virgin birth means that God's deliverance comes through the people, the story, and

---

68. Mark Strauss, *Four Portraits, One Jesus: An Introduction to Jesus and the Gospels* (Grand Rapids: Zondervan, 2007), 415.

the covenants of Israel. The infancy story is indelibly part of God's mission to bring the children of Adam into a relationship with himself through the children of Israel. That plan is executed, in fact, through the one very *special son of Israel*, the messianic seed of Abraham, a special Son of David, a new Son of Adam, and the true Son of Israel's God.

There is something else as well. The virgin conception means that God's new world was at last becoming a reality. The virgin conception means that the coming kingdom with a renewal of creation had already started. N. T. Wright comments:

> Actually, the strange story of Jesus' being conceived without a human father is so peculiar, particularly within Judaism, and so obviously open to sneering accusations on the one hand and the charge that the Christians were simply aping the pagans on the other, that it would be very unlikely for someone to invent it so early in the Christian movement as Matthew and Luke. But there's more to it than just that. The virginal conception speaks powerfully of new creation, something fresh happening within the old world, beyond the reach and dreams of the possibilities we currently know. And if we believe that the God we're talking about is the creator of the world, who longs to rescue the world from its corruption and decay, then an act of real new creation, anticipating in fact the great moment of Easter itself, might just be what we should expect, however tremblingly, if and when this God decides to act to bring this new creation about. The ordinary means of procreation is one of the ways, deep down, in which we laugh in the face of death. Mary's conception of Jesus has no need of that manoeuvre. "In him was life, and the life was the light of all people." The real objection to the virginal conception is not primarily scientific. It is deeper than that. It is the notion that a new world really might be starting up within the midst of the old, leaving us with the stark choice of birth or death; leaving us, like the Magi, no longer at ease: leaving us, in other words, as Christmas people faced with the Herods of the world.[69]

There's one additional thing that the birth of Jesus teaches us about, namely, the triumph of God over evil—the victory of God and the vanquishing of the Satan. Think of your standard nativity scene. I'm sure you can imagine a sign saying "Bethlehem Holiday Inn: No Vacancy,"[70] with a ten-year-old girl playing Mary, an eleven-year-old boy uncomfortably dressed as Joseph, plastic baby in the manger, some donkeys for realism, a few bundles of hay for effect, three cute little toddlers playing the three wise men, and everyone in the audience singing "Away in the Manger" while photos are taken. Well, here is another nativity scene for one, one that I'm sure you would seldom see. Imagine a woman in the throes of childbirth, screaming in

---

69. N. T. Wright, "Power to Become Children: Isaiah 52:7–10 and John 1:1–18," Sermon preached at Cathedral Church of Christ, 25 December 2007. http://www.ntwright-page.com/sermons/Christmas07.htm. Accessed 24 Dec 2010.

70. I should point out that the word *katalyma* in Luke 2:7 more properly means "guest room" rather than "inn" (rightly NIV). Thus, Jesus was probably born in the house of a family related to Joseph in an indoor stable.

pain, with her legs spread apart. Imagine also that standing over the woman is a seven-headed dragon, who is crouched, poised, salivating, and ready to devour the child as soon as it is expelled from the birth canal. It reads like a nativity scene directed by Quentin Tarrantino, doesn't it? But cast your eyes over Revelation 12:1–11:

> A great sign appeared in heaven: a woman clothed with the sun, with the moon under her feet and a crown of twelve stars on her head. She was pregnant and cried out in pain as she was about to give birth. Then another sign appeared in heaven: an enormous red dragon with seven heads and ten horns and seven crowns on its heads. Its tail swept a third of the stars out of the sky and flung them to the earth. The dragon stood in front of the woman who was about to give birth, so that it might devour her child the moment he was born. She gave birth to a son, a male child, who "will rule all the nations with an iron scepter." And her child was snatched up to God and to his throne. The woman fled into the wilderness to a place prepared for her by God, where she might be taken care of for 1,260 days.
>
> Then war broke out in heaven. Michael and his angels fought against the dragon, and the dragon and his angels fought back. But he was not strong enough, and they lost their place in heaven. The great dragon was hurled down—that ancient serpent called the devil, or Satan, who leads the whole world astray. He was hurled to the earth, and his angels with him.
>
> Then I heard a loud voice in heaven say:
>
> "Now have come the salvation and the power
>   and the kingdom of our God,
>   and the authority of his Messiah.
> For the accuser of our brothers and sisters,
>   who accuses them before our God day and night,
>   has been hurled down.
> They triumphed over him
>   by the blood of the Lamb
>   and by the word of their testimony;
> they did not love their lives so much
>   as to shrink from death."

The scene depicts the cosmic battle between the forces of evil and the hosts of heaven as the context for the birth of Jesus. The woman in question is not Mary; rather, she is the messianic community through whom Jesus is birthed. The child is obviously the Messiah—hence the citation of Psalm 2:9 and his rule over the nations with an iron scepter. The messianic child is removed by God from the malevolent grasp of the red dragon. The removal is allusive of Jesus' ascension and exaltation. What is important here is that Jesus' birth and the blood he sheds constitute the victory of God over the evil one. God's plan to repossess the world from the dominion of darkness is launched in the birth of a child who is destined to defeat the dragon that rages against the people of God.

This triumph of God over evil begins in the unlikely place of a child born in the midst of all the vulnerabilities of infancy. The Christmas miracle is God's answer to all the evil, injustice, brutality, suffering, and death that we see around us. Justin Martyr said: "And by her [Mary] has he been born, to whom we have proved so many Scriptures refer, and by whom God destroys both the serpent and those angels and men who are like him; but works deliverance from death to those who repent of their wickedness and believe upon Him."[71]

The annual celebration of the birth of the Savior that Christians around the world commemorate year after year is a bold profession that the despots of this age, political or spiritual, are living on borrowed time. What is more, the victory of God's Messiah in Bethlehem and Calvary is replicated in the triumph of God's people, who conquer evil through the strength of their testimony. The birth of Jesus is God reaching down into human life so that humanity can become the fist that shatters the dynasty of evil, once and for all. To quote Eugene Peterson:

> It is St. John's genius to take Jesus in a manger attended by shepherds and wise men and put him in a cosmos attacked by a dragon.... Our response to the Nativity cannot be reduced to shutting the door against a wintry world, drinking hot chocolate, and singing carols. Rather we are ready to walk out the door with ... high praises of God in our throats and two-edged swords in our hands.[72]

We might ask now: Is the virgin conception one of the essential elements of the faith? I don't want to contradict myself here since I believe in the virgin conception and have outlined its manifold significance. Affirmation of the virgin conception was vitally important in the debates against Docetists in the second century and against old liberalism in the twentieth century. The Apostles' Creed has only seventy-five Latin words, and it dedicates ten words to describing the virgin conception.

That said, I wouldn't put the virgin conception in my top five doctrines. For a start, only two Gospels refer to the virgin conception, Paul refers to Jesus' birth but not explicitly to a miraculous birth, and it is nowhere made a crucial doctrine in the church fathers prior to the christological heresies. In fact, there may have been Christians in the first century who did not know anything about Jesus' birth (which perhaps explains some of the problems that emerged in the second century). I suggest that the chief significance of the virgin conception rests not in its confessional import as a test case for orthodoxy, but in its christological meaning that the Word was made flesh in one of the most bodily events of human existence, namely, childbirth.

The virgin conception is necessary for there to be an incarnation as opposed to a transmutation of the Word into human form. Jesus did not float down from

---

71. Justin, *Dial.* 100.4.
72. Eugene Peterson, *Reversed Thunder: The Revelation of John and the Praying Imagination* (San Francisco: Harper & Row, 1988), 121–22.

heaven and morph into a man. He came through the same processes as the rest of us, including birth, childhood, adolescence, and adulthood. Jesus was made lower than the angels so that we might rise above the angels (Heb 2:7). The virgin conception is of crucial importance if Christian theology was to take the shape that it did, that is, declaring that in the midst of Israelite history God became a man in order to rescue people from the powers of the present evil age. On the import of the virgin conception Karl Barth stated:

> In this connexion we may reply briefly to the question of popular theology, whether in order to believe in a really Christian way "one" would have to believe fully in the Virgin birth. We must answer that there is certainly nothing to prevent anyone, without affirming the doctrine of the Virgin birth, from recognising the mystery of the person of Jesus Christ or from believing in a perfectly Christian way. It is within God's counsel and will to make this possible, just as it cannot be at all impossible for Him to bring anyone to the knowledge of Himself even beyond the sphere of the Church visible to us. But this does not imply that the Church is at liberty to convert the doctrine of the Virgin birth into an option for specifically strong or for specially weak souls. The Church knew well what it was doing when it posted this doctrine on guard, as it were, at the door of the mystery of Christmas. It can never be in favour of anyone thinking he can hurry past this guard. It will remind him that he is walking along a private road at his own cost and risk. It will warn him against doing so. It will proclaim as a church ordinance that to affirm the doctrine of the Virgin birth is a part of real Christian faith.[73]

We might summarize this thought with the words of J. Gresham Machen, "Even if the belief in the virgin birth is not necessary to every Christian, it is certainly necessary to Christianity."[74]

4.3.3 THE MINISTRY OF JESUS

Most theologies seem to move from a sinless birth to a sin-bearing death, and most ignore all that lies in between. This is a terrible misstep since Jesus' ministry, beginning in Galilee with his baptism by John and ending in Jerusalem with his crucifixion, puts into motion crucial events in the divine drama of redemption. Let us remember that the books we call "Gospels" narrate Jesus' redemptive death as the climax to his messianic career, and that career should be part and parcel of our study.

The prologue to the gospel of John introduces the incarnation with the remark that "the Word became flesh" (John 1:14), yet the rest of the gospel highlights that Jesus was sent by the Father as a testimony to Israel (e.g., John 5). Paul's reference to

---

73. Barth, *CD*, I/2:181.
74. J. G. Machen, *The Virgin Birth of Christ* (New York: Harper, 1930), 396. Cf. Berkhof, *Christian Faith*, 293.

BARTH AND PANNENBERG ON THE VIRGIN CONCEPTION

Karl Barth deals with the virgin birth under the heading "The Miracle of Christmas."[75] For Barth the virgin conception is the event that describes how "in Jesus Christ God comes forth out of the profound hiddenness of His divinity in order to act as God among us and upon us."[76] Barth is aware of the historical and theological objections, but in his view the mystery of the incarnation is indicated by the miracle of Christmas. While the virgin conception is a sign that signifies the incarnation, it is not for that reason a merely dispensable sign that can be relegated to legend as long as one retains the reality to which it points. Much like the resurrection, there is an intrinsic link between the sign and the thing signified. If one rejects the sign of the incarnation, one is forced into a different understanding of the mystery of the event itself. Thus one cannot affirm that Jesus was "conceived by the Holy Spirit" without being "born from the virgin," as the Creed suggests. Ultimately for Barth the virgin conception ensures that Jesus is "truly God and truly Man."

Wolfhart Pannenberg defines his view of the virgin birth over against Karl Barth, whom he judges to be guilty of edging into "Mariolatry."[77] According to Pannenberg, the virgin birth is a "legend" that developed relatively late in circles associated with the Hellenistic Jewish Christian community. He regards the virgin birth as standing "in an irreconcilable contradiction to the Christology of the incarnation of the preexistent Son of God found in Paul and John.... Sonship cannot at the same time consist in preexistence and still have its origin only in the divine procreation of Jesus in Mary." It is a "legend that has been constructed out of an [a]etiological interest, namely in order to illustrate the title 'Son of God.'"[78] Pannenberg thinks it tolerable to retain the virgin birth in Christian confessions because of the antidocetic and antiadoptionistic function it possesses.

In response to Pannenberg, however, we can proffer the following thoughts. (1) The virgin conception did not originate from later Jewish Hellenistic circles; rather, stories of Jesus' birth emerged from the Jewish Christian community, probably in Jesus' own family—hence the Jewish character of the infancy narratives. (2) The virgin conception is far from a contradiction to Christ's preexistence, for the virgin birth

---

75. Barth, *CD*, I/2:172–202.
76. Ibid., I/2:182.
77. Pannenberg, *Jesus: God and Man*, 141–50.
78. Ibid., 143, 149.

nowhere imagines the temporal beginnings of Jesus' sonship as much as it sets forth the beginnings of his humanity. One would expect a supernatural being to enter the human realm in a supernatural manner. Furthermore, it is impossible to force a divide between the virgin conception and preexistence when Luke and Matthew affirm both without hesitation.[79] (3) The virgin conception is useful for far more than rejecting docetic and adoptionistic christologies. On the contrary, it becomes a fundamental way of expressing the reality of the incarnation and the nature of God's grace given to humanity.

FURTHER READING

Bloesch, Donald. *Jesus Christ: Savior and Lord*. Downers Grove, IL: InterVarsity Press, 2005, pp. 80–106.

Brown, Raymond. *The Birth of the Messiah*. ABRL; New York: Doubleday, 1993.

Cranfield, C. E. B. "Some Reflections on the Subject of the Virgin Birth." Pp. 151–66 in *On Romans: And Other New Testament Essays*. Edinburgh: T&T Clark, 2001.

Labooy, Guus. "The Historicity of the Virginal Conception. A Study in Argumentation." *EJTh* 13 (2004): 91–101.

Lincoln, Andrew. "'Born of the Virgin Mary': Creedal Affirmation and Critical Reading." Pp. 84–103 in *Christology and Scripture: Interdisciplinary Perspectives*. Ed. A. T. Lincoln and A. Paddison. London: T&T Clark, 2008.

von Campenhausen, H. *The Virgin Birth in the Theology of the Ancient Church*. Trans. F. Clarke. London: SCM, 1964.

---

79. Cf. Simon Gathercole, *The Preexistent Son: Recovering the Christologies of Matthew, Mark, and Luke* (Grand Rapids: Eerdmans, 2006), 285.

Jesus as one "born of a woman, born under the law" presupposes his human life as a faithful Israelite (Gal 4:4). Peter's speech to the Jerusalemites emphasize that "this Jesus," whom God accredited by signs and wonders and whom the Judean leaders crucified, is both Lord and Messiah (Acts 2:22–36). No theology based on the gospel can jump from a stable in Bethlehem to a public execution on Golgotha without serious injury to the whole layout of Christology. The mediation of Jesus only makes sense as the end result of his ministry to inaugurate the kingdom.

After Jesus' birth and childhood, the next important event was his baptism by

John (Mark 1:9–11). If John's baptism was a baptism of repentance, obviously we need to ask why Jesus had to be baptized (see how the tension is worked out in Matt 3:13–17). Most likely, Jesus' baptism was an act of solidarity with the oppressed and exiled nation that needed to repent and enter into the new exodus that the waters symbolize. What is more, the baptism functions as a kind of commissioning service where Jesus is anointed with the Holy Spirit, is publicly identified as the messianic "Son," and is then ready to begin his ministry to call Israel to enter the kingdom of God. The baptism of Jesus comprises a cosmic rendezvous with the union of Son and Spirit united together to usher in the kingdom. Jesus as the bearer of the Holy Spirit will also be the dispenser of the Holy Spirit as John the Baptizer predicted. He will baptize with "the Holy Spirit and fire" (Matt 3:11/Luke 3:16), which means that he will kick off the final judgment and plunge people into the fiery breath of God as an act of preparation for it.[80]

Jesus was a charismatic figure who drew crowds with his teaching. He especially chose twelve disciples to form part of his inner circle (Mark 3:13–16). The number twelve was symbolic of the twelve tribes of Israel. However, everyone knew that the Jewish tribal league had long since been gone. The ten northern tribes were taken away into exile by the Assyrians in the eighth century, and the two remaining tribes had gone into Babylon in the sixth century and only a remnant had returned to Judea. In fact, 70 percent of all Jews in the ancient world lived outside of Palestine in the Diaspora. A major hope was that when the age of deliverance dawned, it would be accompanied by a rejoining of the twelve tribes together in a renewed Jewish kingdom (e.g., Isa 34:10; 43:5; 56:8).[81] In many cases, when Israel returned to God and the exiles returned to the land, the Gentiles would also be brought into this restoration event (e.g., Isa 2:2–5; 55:5; Mic 4:1–4; Zech 8:23). The restored Israel would be a beacon to the nations (Isa 60) and comprise the penultimate state before the advent of a new creation (Isa 65–66)

By choosing twelve disciples, who heralded the signs of restoration like healings and preaching good news to the poor, Jesus was in effect saying that the restoration of Israel had now begun around him and his twelve followers. They were the vanguard for the new Israel. That is why Jesus chose twelve disciples to reign over a renewed nation (Matt 19:28/Luke 22:30), why he focused his ministry exclusively on Israel (Matt 10:5–6; 15:24), and why he declared that many were soon to come from east and west to join in this momentous event (Matt 8:10–12/Luke 13:28–30). Yet this news came with a warning as well. If Israel would not be Israel-for-the-sake-of-the-world, trusting instead in their own power to defeat Rome, Jesus and

---

80. Bird, "John the Baptist," in *Jesus Among Friends and Enemies* (ed. L. Hurtado and C. Keith; Grand Rapids: Baker, 2011), 65, 76.

81. Cf. further Bird, *Jesus and the Origins of the Gentile Mission* (LNTS 331; London: T&T Clark, 2006), 29–38.

his followers would be for the sake of the world, and the rest of Israel would face the consequences for its obstinacy.

The central thread of Jesus' preaching was the message of the kingdom of God. Older scholarly debates were largely divided over what the kingdom actually was and whether the kingdom was future or present (see "Gospel and Kingdom" in part 3). The scholarly equilibrium achieved in the mid-twentieth century was the consensus that the kingdom denoted God's dynamic reign and was inaugurated in Jesus' ministry. In other words, the kingdom of God was the saving power of God's authority that was both present and future, both now and not yet.[82]

Though the phrase "the kingdom of God" is relatively rare in the Old Testament (see Obad 21; Dan 2:44; 6:26), the notion of God as King is widespread. The narrative tension of Israel's story is that God is king ("the LORD reigns," Pss 93:1; 97:1; 99:1) and will yet show himself to be king (Isa 24:23; Amos 9:11–15; Zeph 3:15; Zech 14:9). Jesus' proclamation of the kingdom was the announcement that God was at last becoming king of Israel. This was evidenced by the presence of the Spirit with Jesus (Luke 11:20/Matt 12:28), exorcisms that plundered Satan's kingdom (Mark 3:23–27), various miracles that prove the presence of Israel's Lord with his people (like the feeding miracles in John 6 and Mark 6, 8), and the healing of the sick (Matt 11:4–5/Luke 7:22). The kingdom of God was not to be found in timetables or calendars since the kingdom was in their very midst (Luke 17:20–21).

The "Nazareth Manifesto" of Luke 4:18–21 asserts that the Isaianic signs of deliverance were at hand, as evidenced by the publication of good news for the poor, prisoners, and the blind. Jesus claimed that he was anointed with the eschatological Spirit, and the release from exile was being realized through him (Isa 44:3; Ezek 11:18–19; 36:26–27; Joel 2:28). God's favor and mercy were at hand—not in the distant future but in the present moment of his listeners. At the same time, this kingdom is still something to be "entered" as Jesus anticipated a future period in which the saving promises would be fully realized (Matt 5:20; 7:21; Mark 10:15, 23–25; John 3:5).

Jesus' teaching was primarily about how people should understand his message of the kingdom and Israel's restoration and how to avoid the coming judgment. The parables are not earthly stories with heavenly meanings; rather, they are subversive stories that turn the presuppositions of his audience on their head. The parables are centered on God, God's people, and God's word and set forth a pressing challenge as to whether Israel will respond appropriately to the message and the messenger.[83] On most occasions the parables of Jesus take place in the context of controversy or

---

82. Cf. G. E. Ladd, *A Theology of the New Testament* (ed. D. A. Hagner; Grand Rapids: Eerdmans, 1993), 68–78; Thomas R. Schreiner, *New Testament Theology: Magnifying God in Christ* (Grand Rapids: Baker, 2008), 41–116.

83. Markus Bockmuehl, *Seeing the Word: Refocusing New Testament Study* (Grand Rapids: Baker, 2006), 216.

opposition. Jesus' parable about the tenants (Mark 12:1–12 and par.) is a story that presents himself as God's Son while the Judean leaders are the wicked tenants who have their place taken away and given to others. The parables of the lost sheep, the lost coin, and the lost son defend Jesus' table fellowship with sinners and reflect the outrageous joy of God at the repentance of sinners (Luke 15:1–32). The parable of the mustard seed disparages militaristic interpretations of the kingdom's entrance in favor of a model that seems almost inert when compared to human activism (Mark 4:30–32). In contrast to militaristic views of the kingdom, Jesus taught that the kingdom grows like a pugnacious weed taking over a garden. Stick that in your zealot pipe and smoke it!

The Sermon on the Mount (Matthew 5–7) and the Sermon on the Plain (Luke 6) are good test cases for any theological system. Contra *some* Reformed theologians, Jesus is not teaching people the law so they can see how they don't measure up, wail for their sinful hearts, and realize their need for the imputation of Jesus' righteousness. Contra *some* dispensational theologians, Jesus is not teaching what kind of law the Jews will keep in a post-rapture millennium. The Sermon on the Mount is Jesus' manifesto for the kingdom. It is the ethical vision for God's people if they are to live out the covenantal righteousness that comes from experiencing the kingdom's saving power. This is what the new Israel of the new age is supposed to look like. Not the elitist micropiety of Pharisaic leaders who claim their tradition represents the true measure of righteousness, nor the compromised Jewishness of the Herodians who dress up Hellenistic values in a Jewish garb. The sermon is about new law for the new age.

Jesus' final week in Jerusalem brings several running themes of his ministry—kingship, kingdom, and salvation—to their gripping conclusion. Joel Green writes:

> Everything—his interpretation of Israel's Scriptures, his practices of prayer and worship, his astounding choice of travel companions, his crossing of the boundaries of clean and unclean, his engagement with children, his miracles of healing and exorcism—leads to the cross. Calling twelve disciples as representative of a restored Israel, weaving the hopes of a new exodus and the eschatological era into his ministries of word and deed, speaking of fulfillment of God's promises to Israel, his prophetic action in the temple in anticipation of a temple not made by human hands—in all of these ways and more....
>
> This led him to a form of execution emblematic of a way of life that rejected the value of public opinion in the determination of status before God and inspired interpretations of his death that accorded privilege to the redemptive power of righteous suffering. The way was opened for Jesus' followers to accord positive value to his shameful death, and thus to learn to associate in a meaningful way what would otherwise have been only a clash of contradictory images: Jesus' heinous suffering and his messianic status....

Thus, Jesus was able to gather together Israel's history and hopes and from them a view of himself as the one through whose suffering Israel, through Israel the nations, would experience redemption.[84]

What unites Jesus' ministry and death is his messianic vocation to inaugurate the kingdom of God. We see this in Jesus' triumphal entry, the temple episode, teaching on the "end," and his trial. Jesus enters Jerusalem as the Shepherd King whom Israel had hoped for (Mark 11:1–10 and par.). He goes to the root of Judaism's problem in the corruption of the temple with its exploitation of the poor and violent nationalism (Mark 11:15–17; John 2:12–25). He teaches about the destruction of Jerusalem by the Romans in the Olivet Discourse (Mark 13 and par.),[85] and several other topics, such as the identity of the Messiah (Mark 12:35–37 and par.). The final meal Jesus held with his disciples interpreted his forthcoming death as a covenant-instituting sacrifice that seals the redemptive effect of the kingdom (Mark 14:22–26 and par.).

Jesus will be the smitten shepherd whose death protects his disciples from the coming wrath like a mother hen that uses its wings to protect her chicks from a barnyard fire (Mark 14:27; cf. Matt 23:37/Luke 13:34). Jesus is arrested, falsely accused, and then tried on a political charge for claiming to be the Messiah—a charge he enigmatically affirmed (Mark 14:62). Then Jesus was crucified, but unbeknownst to the Judean and Roman authorities, this was not to be the last of him or his followers.

If we had to summarize Jesus' ministry and message, we could perhaps quip that "Aslan was on the move"! In Jesus' work, God was finally becoming king of Israel, bringing a new exodus, establishing a new covenant, teaching the way of covenantal righteousness, calling Israel to its appointed vocation, defining law by love rather than by debate about legal minutia, reminding people of God's special concern for the poor, calling the religious leaders to account, and finally dying as the martyred messiah.[86]

The contribution of Jesus' life to theology lies in three main areas. First, Jesus himself must be seen as the primary theologian for the early church. The big questions about "Who is God?" or "What does God require of people?" must as part of their answer refer to the words and actions of the Master himself. In fact, we could comically divide the New Testament into "Gospels" and the "Jesus Festschrift."[87] By this I mean that the Gospels are about Jesus, while the rest of the New Testament is largely a response to him: his teaching, death, resurrection, and exaltation. The direction for all later theology is embryonically pregnant in Jesus' ministry. The life

---

84. Joel Green, "Kaleidescopic View," in *The Nature of the Atonement* (ed. J. Beilby and P. R. Eddy; Downers Grove, IL: InterVarsity Press, 2006), 163–65.

85. Here I am assuming a "preterist" interpretation of Mark 13; see part 3.

86. Cf. Brunner (*Creation and Redemption*, 282): "The whole life of the historical Jesus is the Way to the Cross."

87. A "Festschrift" is an academic book written in honor of an esteemed friend, mentor, researcher, and teacher that largely interacts with their intellectual legacy.

and passion of Jesus of Nazareth are the genetic protein from which later theological cells of the early church emerged.

What is more, if any Christian theologian is to be worthy of the name *Christ*ian, surely he or she must look first to Jesus, Lord and Savior of the church, for truth and wisdom. Jesus is rightly venerated in the Matthean tradition as the "one Teacher," and his instruction and authority are therefore entirely unique within the New Testament (Matt 23:8–10). True, some will use this prioritization of Jesus' teaching as license to play Jesus off against Paul (i.e., Paul was a homophobic, misogynistic bigot, while Jesus taught an ethic of love and inclusiveness, so let's just run with that). But such a misappropriation of Jesus' authority will be dismissed by anyone with an ounce of canonical consciousness. Ultimately discipleship, both in belief and behavior, can be summed up in terms of trying to attain the "mind of Christ" (1 Cor 2:16; Phil 2:5).

Second, Jesus is the glue that connects Israel's hopes with the church's faith. As long as Jesus is the Jewish Messiah, a circumcised Judean male, a servant to Israel, Gnosticism is off the table as a theological option. But most importantly, Jesus' life means that we are dealing with one continuous story that runs from Genesis through Revelation. It is one story, not two separate ones, for the one God of Israel does in Jesus for the world what he had said he would do through Israel.

This is made explicit in Peter's speech in Acts 3, where Peter proclaims Jesus as the appointed Messiah who will bring Israel's "universal restoration"—the Messiah who is the instrument to make good the Abrahamic promise, "through your offspring all peoples on earth will be blessed" (Act 3:20–25). The one God of Israel's faith is the God *of* Jesus and the God revealed *in* Jesus. It is this God-in-the-Messiah who achieves his purposes through a renewed Israel. While many facets of contemporary understandings of the Jewish story are challenged and redefined by Jesus, it remains nonetheless a Jewish story all the same. Jesus' identification with Israel, his reverence for the Hebrew Scriptures, and his love for the Jewish people constitute worldview-making events that establish the identity and mission of God's people.

Third, we could say that a historical Jesus rules out the possibility of a docetic Jesus. I do not just mean a hard Docetism in terms of denying Jesus' physical humanity and making him out to be some kind of phantasm. I also mean ruling out a soft Docetism that often posits a Jesus who wanders around Galilee and Judea and is so heavenly minded with his reminiscences of the angels playing their harps in heaven that he is of no earthly good. Jesus addressed real-life issues such poverty, taxes, death, and divorce because he was a real-life person. Jesus was, as the writer to the Hebrews says, "fully human in every way" and thus shares the complete human experience (Heb 2:17). Jesus did not transcend the mundane elements of human existence. Jesus cannot be the mediator unless he shared in the experience of pain, laughter, sweat, tears, touch, taste, thirst, and even the sexual drive of humanity.

4.3.4 CONCLUSION

What can we conclude about the historical Jesus and Christology? In the end the historical Jesus is not a *presupposition* to Christology; rather, the historical Jesus is a *prolegomena* to Christology. All theologians from St. Paul to Paul Jewett have had to engage the subjects of the mission and identity of the man Jesus as part of their theological system. First, the mission of the church is a sequel to the ministry of Jesus. What begins in the waters of the Jordan is continued in the Pentecostal experience in Jerusalem. What is taught on the hills of Galilee is recalled in a lecture hall in Ephesus. The openness of Jesus to sinners in Capernaum is applied in the openness of the church to receive Gentiles in Antioch. The mission of the historical Jesus to restore Israel is extended in the mission of the church to be the people of God of the messianic age. The meal consumed in an upper room in Jerusalem is later rehearsed in an atrium in Corinth. What happened one dark Friday at Golgotha is proclaimed every Sunday in Gaul. The theology, symbols, and praxis of the church is only valid as an appropriation of the ministry of Jesus. Accordingly, any theological loci should have to deal with what Jesus, in light of the Old Testament, taught about a given subject.

Second, it is impossible to theologize about the one called the Lord of glory and the Word made flesh without first clearing the deck on the identity of Jesus of Nazareth. "Who is this man?" is the question raised before and after Easter. The mystery of Jesus in relation to Israel's hopes, the God of Israel, and the Spirit of God calls for clarification and explanation. The explanation began before Easter and has continued ever since in light of God's revelation about his Son to the apostles. Within the early church the identity of God was redefined in light of the life and exaltation of Jesus. Christology moved in a binitarian and then finally a Trinitarian direction. The continuity is of vital importance. For unless Jesus of Nazareth is one and the same as the risen and exalted Lord, all christological talk is a chimera. As German theologian Gerhard Kittel said:

> The Jesus of History is valueless and unintelligible unless He be experienced and confessed by faith as the living Christ. But, if we would be true to the New Testament, we must at once reverse this judgment. The Christ of faith has no existence, is mere noise and smoke, apart from the reality of the Jesus of History. These two are utterly inseparable in the New Testament. They cannot even be thought of apart.... Anyone who attempts first to separate the two and then to describe only one of them, has nothing in common with the New Testament.[88]

I hope it is clear by now that the life of Jesus has the utmost theological significance. Everything—and I mean *everything*: kingdom, church, and salvation—rides

---

88. Gerhard Kittel, G. K. A. Bell, and A. Deissman, eds., *Mysterium Christi* (London: Longmans & Green, 1930), 49.

on the singular fact that the eternal Son became a human being. The significance is not simply the *fact* of God taking on humanity per se. The true import is in God's becoming a man at a particular juncture in Israel's history with a particular mission. God's plan to unite the world with his glory through the Logos takes place in a single story that runs from Adam to Abraham to Israel to Jesus.

Jesus as the new Adam and the true Israel is obedient and faithful whereas those before him failed. Jesus called Israel to be what it was always meant to be: a light to the nations, a kingdom of priests, and a city on a hill. That is why he preached repentance, announced a national referendum on Israel's future, warned of judgment, embraced sinners and tax collectors, healed the sick, cleansed the temple, and taught about covenant justice and God's love. The shot clock had wound down to zero; it was now time for Israel, in whole or in part, to become a kingdom community or to face judgment if it refused. For it is through a renewed Israel that God brings the nations into the covenant promises made to Abraham—promises that will eventually flower into a new creation.

In this story, Jesus' life and death can be put properly together. Jesus' death was the culmination of one who will be the mistreated Son of Man, the stricken Shepherd, and the Suffering Servant, for in this role he was being what Israel aspired to be but never became: a mediator between God and creation. For this reason it is crucial that our gospel presentation get past the syllogism of "God is holy, man is sinful, therefore ..." and instead situate the death and resurrection of Jesus as part of a redemptive historical story about paradise lost and paradise regained. The gospel indicates that Jesus was a human being, sent by God, in fulfillment of Israel's hopes; he was the Messiah who proclaimed the kingdom of God, and yet the proclaimer soon became the proclaimed in the preaching of the early church. The reason for this transition is his death and resurrection, to which we now turn.

FURTHER READING

Kinlaw, Dennis F. *Let's Start with Jesus: A New Way of Doing Theology.* Grand Rapids: Zondervan, 2005.

Tilley, Terence W. "Remembering the Historic Jesus—a New Research Program?" *TS* 68 (2007): 3–35.

Wright, N. T. *The Challenge of Jesus.* London: SPCK, 2000.

§ 4.4 THE DEATH OF JESUS

Evangelicals have a crucicentric gospel and for good reasons. To begin with, Jesus knew what destiny lay ahead of him in Jerusalem, and yet he believed that his death would not be the end of his kingdom message; rather, it would actually inaugurate the very kingdom he was proclaiming (e.g., Mark 9:1; 14:22–25). Early Christian preaching identified the cross as part of God's design for the renewal of Israel and for the salvation of all peoples (Acts 3:18–21; 13:24–30). Primitive hymns and confessions of the early church demonstrate that the death of Christ was a key article of faith and determinative for salvation in the early church (Rom 4:25; 1 Cor 15:3–5; 2 Cor 5:15; Phil 2:5–11; 1 Thess 4:14). The two emblems of the gospel, baptism and Eucharist, were reminders of believers identifying with and participating in the death and resurrection of Jesus (Rom 6:3–4; 1 Cor 10:16; 1 Pet 3:21).

The message of the cross was central to the preaching of Paul (1 Cor 1:18–2:5; Gal 2:19–21; 3:1, 13). For the apostle to the Gentiles, the cross was the cosmic event that defined a people and purchased salvation (Gal 3:28; Col 3:11). All the canonical Gospels emphasize the crucifixion of Jesus as the climax of his kingdom ministry (Matt 27; Mark 15; Luke 23; John 19). The Catholic letters, especially Hebrews and 1 Peter, give significant attention to the death of Jesus as a sacrificial act that effects the salvation of those who trust in him. It is not too much to say that the first Christians preached, remembered, and ordered their lives around the story of the cross.

Unsurprisingly Christian leaders over the centuries have spent much of their time preaching, interpreting, and meditating on the death of Jesus. The second-century author of the *Epistle to Diognetus* sounds much like Paul when he wrote: "He took upon himself our sins; God himself gave up his own Son as a ransom for us, the holy one for the lawless, the guiltless for the guilty, the just for the unjust, the incorruptible for the corruptible, the immortal for the mortal" (*Diogn.* 9.2). According to Cyril of Jerusalem: "Every deed of Christ is a cause of glorying to the universal church, but her greatest of all glorying is in the cross"; and "He stretched out His hands on the cross, that He might embrace the ends of the world; for this

Golgotha is the very center of the earth."[89] John Chrysostom described what the cross achieved with these poignant words:

> For the cross destroyed the enmity of God towards man, brought about the reconciliation, made the earth Heaven, associated men with angels, pulled down the citadel of death, unstrung the force of the devil, extinguished the power of sin, delivered the world from error, brought back the truth, expelled the Demons, destroyed temples, overturned altars, suppressed the sacrificial offering, implanted virtue, founded the Churches. The cross is the will of the Father, the glory of the Son, the rejoicing of the Spirit, the boast of Paul, "for," he says, "God forbid that I should boast save in the cross of our Lord Jesus Christ" [Gal 6:14]. The cross is that which is brighter than the sun, more brilliant than the sunbeam: for when the sun is darkened then the cross shines brightly: and the sun is darkened not because it is extinguished, but because it is overpowered by the brilliancy of the cross. The cross has broken our bond, it has made the prison of death ineffectual, it is the demonstration of the love of God.[90]

The centrality of the cross was a *leitmotif* of the Reformation. For the German Reformer Martin Luther, true Christian theology was not a theology of glory (*theologia gloriae*) but a theology of the cross (*theologia crucis*). In his Heidelberg Disputation Luther wrote: "He deserves to be called a theologian, however, who comprehends the visible and manifest things of God seen through suffering and the cross," and "a theologian of glory calls evil good and good evil. A theologian of the cross calls the thing what it actually is."[91] For Luther, it was not just a matter of setting before God your virtue and hoping he would crown it with salvation. Rather, for Luther, the cross meant that one had to lay one's own sin and inability at the foot of the cross and beg for forgiveness from the God who is rich in mercy.[92]

Liberal theologies of the late nineteenth century reduced the cross to an example of divine love given to spur men and women on to loving deeds. This not only evacuated the cross of any objective achievement, but it supposed that a sincere suicide was God's answer to the evils of this world. The theological bankruptcy of liberalism was evident to many. In the early twentieth century Peter T. Forsyth, in the tradition of the Reformers, wrote: "Christ is to us what his cross is. All that Christ was in heaven or on earth was put into what he did there.... Christ, I repeat, is to us what his cross is. You do not understand Christ till you understand his cross."[93] Neoorthodox and evangelical believers have genuinely agreed on the centrality of the cross though often differing on what the cross achieved.

---

89. Cyril, *Catechetical Lectures* 13.1, 28.
90. John Chrysostom, *Against the Marcionites and Manichaeans* 2.
91. Heidelberg Disputation, 20–21.
92. Cf. Alister McGrath, *Luther's Theology of the Cross: Martin Luther's Theological Breakthrough* (Oxford: Blackwell, 1995).
93. Peter T. Forsyth, *The Cruciality of the Cross* (London: Hodder & Stoughton, 1909), 44–45.

Neoorthodox theologians labored to move beyond the subjective atonement theories of old liberalism and to recapture a theocentric vision of the cross. Emil Brunner accented the notion that Jesus' death was a "must," a divine necessity: "If man is to be brought back into contact with God, if he is to be able to receive the salvation which God has provided for him, then the Cross of Jesus Christ 'must' happen." For Brunner, the cross is a revelation of the "incomprehensible, unconditional love of God" and "the revelation of righteousness is combined with love." The atonement is both objective and subjective. The cross is an objective sign of God's right judgment against sin, but only effective when people identify themselves with Christ and comprehend that Christ suffers and bears the penalty that they deserve.[94]

Karl Barth's volume on reconciliation in *Church Dogmatics* made a resolute emphasis on the vicarious nature of Jesus' death. Barth weaved together the various themes of his theology: election, fulfillment of the covenant, threefold offices of Christ, and Jesus as the God-man. In the end, Barth regards Christ as the judge, who is judged in our place and establishes judgment and justice thereafter: "Man's reconciliation with God takes place through God's putting Himself in man's place and man's being put in God's place, as a sheer act of grace. It is this inconceivable miracle which is our reconciliation."[95]

The cross has been no less significant for modern evangelicalism, with several significant works written on the cross and several edited collections that tirelessly assert the centrality of penal substitution. David Bebbington points out that in nineteenth-century British evangelical churches, the verse that inspired the most sermons was Galatians 2:20, "I have been crucified with Christ and I no longer live, but Christ lives in me. The life I now live in the body, I live by faith in the Son of God, who loved me and gave himself for me."[96] John Stott speaks for much of evangelicalism when he says, "There is then, it is safe to say, no Christianity without the cross. If the cross of Jesus is not central to our religion, ours is not the religion of Jesus."[97] The cross is the *crux* of the gospel and also impacts discipleship to the point that following Jesus entails *cruciformity* or being conformed the pattern of the cross (see Luke 9:23–24; Phil 2:5–11; Heb 12:3; 1 Pet 2:21).[98]

But the neoorthodox and evangelical focus on the cross is simply an outflow of an ancient theological phenomenon. Christian theologians over the ages have bound themselves to the cross. The sign of the cross has been made in prayers, hymns, and baptisms. Paintings and icons of the crucified Jesus have adorned the walls of

---

94. Brunner, *Creation and Redemption*, 286, 295–96.
95. Karl Barth, *Dogmatics in Outline* (trans. G. T. Thomson; London: SCM, 1949), 115.
96. David W. Bebbington, "The Gospel in the Nineteenth Century," *VE* 13 (1983): 24.

97. John Stott, *The Cross of Christ* (Downers Grove, IL: InterVarsity Press, 1986), 71.
98. Cf. esp. Michael J. Gorman, *Cruciformity: Paul's Narrative Spirituality of the Cross* (Grand Rapids: Eerdmans, 2001).

churches for centuries. But what is the problem that the cross solves and what type of remedy is offered?

In the Christian story, God, at the cross, deals with the problem of sin, Satan, and humanity's separation from himself through a redemptive action that draws together the offender and the offended party in reconciliation. The traditional theological code word used to describe God's response to the problem of evil in the world is "atonement," which derives from the Old English "onement," meaning to unite or to attain a state of "at-one-ness."[99] There are a variety of images in the New Testament for what the cross achieved in terms of salvation; these will be explored more fully in part 5. Here we will focus more specifically on the various modes of the atonement that have been proposed. Nobody doubts that Jesus' death "achieves" something beneficial, but the questions are: what, how, and for whom?

4.4.1 WHAT THE CROSS ACHIEVED

There a variety of ways in Scripture for describing the achievement of the cross, and there are several ways of describing the overall biblical presentation of what the cross accomplished. Clement of Alexandria (ca. 155–220) said: "The Savior uses many tones of voice and many methods for the salvation of humanity."[100] Often these various "voices" are called "theories," "models," or "metaphors" of the atonement. I balk at this language because "theory" sounds like an abstraction; "model" sounds overly theoretical; and even "metaphor" could perhaps be misunderstood to remove the event from reality. Consequently, I prefer the term "mode," since it spells out the contingent form, manner, and method that speaks to the reality of the atonement. However, the language of "theories" and "models" is so widespread in the literature that is hard to engage the topic without using them. We now discuss the various modes of the atonement.

4.4.1.1 RECAPITULATION

In the Gospels, Jesus is depicted as the representative of humanity in general and Israel in particular. Adam and Israel both held the title "Son of God," and Jesus is *the* eschatological Son of God who embodies their role in his own person. Luke emphasizes this in his genealogy, where Jesus is related to the "Son of David" and "Son of Adam" in his family line (Luke 3:31, 38). Matthew typologically connects the flight of the holy family to Egypt to escape the evil designs of Herod the Great with Hosea 11:1 ("Out of Egypt I called my son"; see Matt 2:15). In this way, Jesus' own biography recapitulates similar events in Israel's exodus story. Whereas Adam

---

99. Graham A. Cole, *God the Peacemaker: How Atonement Brings Shalom* (NSBT; Downers Grove: InterVarsity Press, 2009), 20, 24.

100. Clement of Alexandria, *Protr.* 1.

and Israel disobeyed God when faced with temptation, Jesus was obedient and faithful, as seen in the temptation narratives, where he resists the devil (Matt 4:1–11/ Luke 4:1–13).

Paul identified the risen Jesus as the glorified humanity that God had always intended the human race to be (1 Cor 15:45–49). Jesus was the new Adam, who undid all that went wrong with the first Adam (15:22; see also Rom 5:12–21). This story of Jesus as the new Adam found a natural home in the church fathers, who saw the cross as the moment where the story of the two Adams collided and brought with it salvation for all humanity.

Irenaeus saw the story of salvation as consisting of fallen human beings being removed from the corruption of the first Adam and becoming partakers of the salvation of the second Adam. Irenaeus called this a "recapitulation" (*anakephalaiōsis*), whereby God's purpose was to sum up all things in Christ. Adam was a historical person who disobeyed God, and humanity thereafter participated in Adam's sin and shared his guilt. When the Son of God became a human being, he gathered to himself the whole of humanity, the entire human race, and he stands as their new representative. According to Irenaeus: "He became incarnate, and was made man, He commenced afresh [Latin: *in seipso recapitulavit*, "summed up in himself"] the long line of human beings, and furnished us, in a brief, comprehensive manner, with salvation; so that what we had lost in Adam—namely, to be according to the image and likeness of God—that we might recover in Christ Jesus."[101]

The incarnate Christ recapitulated or replayed over the sequence of human existence. He passed through all of the stages of life, including birth, manhood, and even death, and he sanctified human life in the process. Jesus recapitulated in his own person all that Adam should have been. Yet unlike Adam, Jesus lived out a truly faithful human life.[102] Irenaeus puts it into these words: "God recapitulated in Himself the ancient formation of man, that He might kill sin, deprive death of its power, and vivify man; and therefore His works are true."[103] As a result, just as Adam was the originator of a race of that was disobedient and doomed to death, so now Christ created in himself a new and redeemed humanity that could live before God in holiness and life.

In this recapitulated narrative, humans are saved by the obedience of Jesus that overturns Adam's disobedience and by the blood of Jesus that redeems believers from the devil.[104] Irenaeus draws a parallel between two trees: the tree that brought disobedience in the garden of Eden and the tree that Jesus was hanged on. The first tree symbolized disobedience and death, while the second tree symbolized

---

101. Irenaeus, *Haer.* 3.18.1.
102. Ibid., 3.18.2.
103. Ibid., 3.18.7.
104. Ibid., 3.18.1–2, 7; 3.18.22; 5.20.2.

obedience and life.[105] Elsewhere Irenaeus does refer to Jesus' death as an act of sacrifice for redemption, God reconciling believers through Christ's death, and Jesus' death propitiating the Father.[106] But these are minor themes in the major key of Jesus' life as a climactic replaying of the story of Adam, but with better results. Viewed this way, Jesus' incarnation itself is the means of atonement, the means of putting the world to rights.

A cursory glance at the temptation narratives in Matthew 4:1–11/Luke 4:1–13 as well as Paul's Adam and Christ comparison in Romans 5:12–21 indicates that Irenaeus was onto something.[107] The incarnation was itself a redemptive event, and Jesus' entire life was oriented toward salvation. As the new head of the human race, Jesus is able to save humanity because he reconstitutes humanity in himself and brings it to its appointed goal: a glorified state, in a glorified place, dwelling with the glorious God.

There is, however, one slight problem with the recapitulation theory. While it shows how the cross fits into the dramatic story of Adam, Israel, and Christ, it fails to show the *necessity* of the cross in that story. What is necessary on this presentation is the complete obedience of Jesus to his task as the messianic Son. Jesus' willingness to go to the cross is regarded as the most supreme display of his obedience to the Father. But the question looms: Could Jesus' obedience have saved humanity without going to the cross? Was Jesus' obedience in the wilderness enough, or his obedience in his preaching in Galilee, or his obedience in the garden of Gethsemane? For the cross is not simply an example of Jesus' obedience; instead, it is the necessary obedience that Jesus exercises so that he can redeem humanity from the clutches of sin and death.

In the story of salvation, the fall of Adam is undone by the obedience of Christ. Believers shift from being under the jurisdiction of the old Adam to being under the jurisdiction of the new Adam. If one is united to Christ, one is identified with the obedient and glorified Son of God. But this new reality that God creates for us in Christ only comes about because of Jesus' death, resurrection, and ascension. It would have been no good for Jesus to be an obedient person living among the Eskimos of northern Canada. He had to be obedient—obedient to death on a cross. Only then could we share in this new humanity that is constituted in his own person.

---

105. Ibid., 5.16.3.

106. Cf. "He became 'the mediator of God and men' [1 Tim 2:5], propitiating for us the Father against whom we had sinned, consoling Him for our disobedience by His obedience [on the cross], granting us the grace of conversion and submission to our Creator" (Irenaeus, *Haer.*, 5.17.1 cited from Hans Urs von Balthasar, *The Scandal of the Incarnation: Irenaeus Against the Heresies* [San Francisco: Ignatius, 1990], 47).

107. N. T. Wright (*Climax of the Covenant: Christ and the Law in Pauline Theology* [Edinburgh: T&T Clark, 1991], 144–48 [esp. 146]) regards Jesus becoming "accursed" on the cross in Gal 3:13 as an example how Jesus' death recapitulates Israel's exile and restoration.

4.4.1.2 RANSOM

A common mode of atonement popular in the early church was the "ransom" view. Its biblical roots lie in the references to Jesus' death and blood possessing redemptive significance (see Mark 10:45; Rom 3:24; 8:23; Gal 3:13–14; 1 Cor 1:30; 6:20; Eph 1:7; Col 1:14; Titus 2:14; Heb 9:12; 1 Pet 1:18). The innovative event is that Jesus' death is reckoned to be a ransom from the devil. This perspective was popular in both the east and the west with various ancient supporters.

Its first clear advocate was Origen, but later adherents included Chrysostom, Gregory of Nyssa, Hilary, Ambrosiaster, and especially Augustine. Exponents who took this view typically asserted that the disobedience of Adam and Eve caused God to abandon humankind to the devil, or that Adam and Eve sold humankind to the devil, or that through sin humanity passed into the jurisdiction of the devil. In any case, the devil then exerted his power and authority over humanity and locked them in the prison of sin, death, and hell. God thereafter decided to redeem humanity from the devil. Accordingly, he agreed to pay Satan a ransom; the agreed payment was Jesus' death on the cross. After the crucifixion, Satan kept his part of the bargain by releasing humanity from the grip of his power. But God then pulled a fast one on the devil by raising his Son from the dead.

Origen (ca. AD 185–254) asked the question: To whom was the ransom paid? Origen denies that it was paid to God; rather, it was paid to the devil:

> But to whom did He give His soul as a ransom for many? Surely not to God. Could it, then, be to the Evil One? For he had us in his power, until the ransom for us should be given to him, even the life of Jesus, since he [the Evil One] had been deceived, and led to suppose that he was capable of mastering that soul, and he did not see that to hold Him involved a trial of strength greater than he was equal to. Therefore also death, though he thought he had prevailed against Him, no longer lords over Him, He [Christ] having become free among the dead and stronger than the power of death, and so much stronger than death that all who will amongst those who are mastered by death may also follow Him, death no longer prevailing against them. For every one who is with Jesus is unassailable by death.[108]

Gregory of Nyssa (ca. AD 330–395) agreed that the devil had a legitimate claim over humanity, since through the fall all humans had voluntarily placed themselves under the devil's power. In order to set humanity free from the devil, God paid the devil a ransom price for his property. The devil was dazzled by Christ's miracles, but, Gregory said, the devil was deceived because the deity of Christ was veiled in the flesh of Jesus. Gregory compared the devil to a hungry fish who swallowed the bait of Jesus' humanity but got caught on the hook of Christ's deity.[109]

---

108. Origen, *Comm. ser. Matt.* 16.8.

109. Gregory of Nyssa, *Religious Instruction*, 24.

The most consistent usage of the ransom mode for understanding the atonement derives from Augustine. According to Augustine:

> In this redemption, the blood of Christ was given, as it were, as a price for us, by accepting which the Devil was not enriched, but bound: that we might be freed from his bonds, and that he might not with himself involve in the meshes of sins, and so deliver to the destruction of the second and eternal death, any one of those whom Christ, free from all debt, had redeemed by pouring out His own blood.[110]

The African bishop also wrote:

> Anyone can buy his servant, create him he cannot; but the Lord has both created and redeemed His servants; created them, that they might be; redeemed them, that they might not be captives forever. For we fell into the hands of the prince of this world, who seduced Adam, and made him his servant, and began to possess us as his slaves. But the Redeemer came, and the seducer was overcome. And what did our Redeemer do to him who held us captive? For our ransom he held out His Cross as a trap; he placed in it as a bait His Blood.[111]

Augustine was aware of the tensions that this mode of atonement created, and he nuanced its description in places. J. N. D. Kelly summarizes Augustine's expression of this view:

1. The devil owned no rights, in the strict sense, over mankind; when men sinned, they passed inevitably into his power, and God permitted rather than enjoined this.
2. No ransom as such was therefore due Satan; on the contrary, when the remission of sins was procured by Christ's sacrifice, God's favor was restored and the human race might well have been freed.
3. God preferred, however, as a course more consonant with his justice, that the devil should not be deprived of his dominion by force, but as the penalty for abusing his position.
4. Hence Christ's passion, the primary object of which was quite different, placed the Son of God in Satan's hands, and when the latter overreached himself by seizing the divine prey, with the arrogance and greed that were characteristically his, he was justly constrained, as a penalty, to deliver up mankind.[112]

The ransom view attempts to bring together two images of the cross in Scripture: Jesus' death as a ransom and Jesus' conquest over the devil. These are both valid images, but when synthesized this way the ransom theory creates two problems. First, did the devil really own humanity? To be under the power or persuasion of

---

110. Augustine, *Trin.* 13.15.19.
111. Augustine, *Serm.* 80.2.
112. J. N. D Kelly, *Early Christian Doctrines* (London: Adam and Charles Black, 1958), 392.

the devil is one thing, but to belong to him is quite another. There is nothing in Scripture that indicates that humanity was ever an official possession of the devil. As bearers of the divine image, humanity, even in its fallen state, still belongs to God.

Second, was it morally right for God to deceive the devil this way?[113] Ancient theologians were aware of this problem and tried to give creative answers as to why God was justified in deceiving the devil. For instance, Gregory of Nyssa claimed that God was paying the devil back for the deception he committed in the garden of Eden. Even so, if God cannot lie or deceive (Num 23:19; Heb 6:18), can we really expect the greatest salvific event in the history of the cosmos to be based on God duping a wicked angelic being? Gregory of Nazianzus (ca. 330–389) contested the ransom theory when he wrote:

> Admittedly we were held in captivity by the Devil, having been sold under sin and having abdicated our happiness in exchange for wickedness. But if the ransom belongs exclusively to him who holds the prisoner, I ask to whom was it paid, and why? If to the Devil, how shameful that that robber should receive not only a ransom from God, but a ransom consisting of God Himself, and that so extravagant a price should be paid to his tyranny before he could justly spare us![114]

4.4.1.3 CHRISTUS VICTOR

Another perspective common in the early church viewed Jesus' death as a victory over death, the devil, and evil. Here the significance of Jesus' death is cosmic as it produces a victory over the dark powers—personal or impersonal, angelic or political—that enslave the people of God. The preponderance of such a model in the early church is comprehensible once we familiarize ourselves with the theme of Jesus' death as a victory in the Scriptures.

To begin with, the Gospels portray Jesus as engaged in a battle with Satan from the beginning. There is an initial victory over him in the temptation narratives, where Jesus withstands the seductive enticements set before him (Matt 4:1–11/Luke 4:1–13). Interestingly enough, John Milton's poem *Paradise Regained* is set in the temptation story, not on the cross. Rightly so, because this is where Jesus launches the first major offensive against the Satan's estate. Later Jesus' disciples report to him

---

113. According to Gregory Boyd ("Christus Victor View," in *The Nature of the Atonement: Four Views* [ed. J. Beilby and P. R. Eddy; Downers Grove, IL: InterVarsity Press, 2006], 37): "As I see it, the truth embodied in the most ancient ways of thinking about the atonement was that God did, in a sense, deceive Satan and the powers, and that Jesus was, in a sense, 'bait.' But that there was nothing duplicitous or unjust in God's behavior. To the contrary, God was simply acting in an outrageously loving way, knowing all the while that his actions could not be understood by the powers whose evil blinds them to love. Like an infinitely wise military strategist, God knows how to get his enemies to use their self-inflicted blindness against themselves and thus use their self-chosen evil to his advantage. He wisely let evil implode on itself, as it were, and thereby freed creation and humanity from evil's oppression."

114. Gregory of Nazianzus, *Orations* 45.22, cited in Kelly, *Early Christian Doctrines*, 383.

their success in expelling demonic spirits in their mission and Jesus tells them: "I saw Satan fall like lightning from heaven" (Luke 10:18). Jesus' exorcisms indicate that he is the strongman who binds the Satan and plunders the satanic kingdom, bringing release to the captives (Matt 12:29; Mark 3:27). In the gospel of John, we learn that the Holy Spirit's ministry of bringing conviction of sin is only possible because "the prince of this world now stands condemned" (John 16:11). Yet these are little more than preliminary skirmishes until the real battle with the devil, evil, and death that Jesus wages at Golgotha.

Paul accentuates the achievement of Jesus' death as a divine victory over the evils of the cosmos. The commission Paul receives from the exalted Jesus is given in the words: "I will rescue you from your own people and from the Gentiles. I am sending you to them to open their eyes and turn them from darkness to light, and *from the power of Satan to God*, so that they may receive forgiveness of sins and a place among those who are sanctified by faith in me" (Act 26:17–18, italics added). Here the forgiveness of sins is part of a larger scheme of freeing people from the grip of Satan.

The opening of Paul's letter to the Galatians places the death of Jesus in the context of an apocalyptic triumph as he writes that Jesus "gave himself for our sins to rescue us from the present evil age, according to the will of our God and Father" (Gal 1:4). Toward the end of 1 Corinthians 15, one observes Paul's rather dramatic words:

> When the perishable has been clothed with the imperishable, and the mortal with immortality, then the saying that is written will come true: 'Death has been swallowed up in victory.' 'Where, O death, is your victory? Where, O death, is your sting?' The sting of death is sin, and the power of sin is the law. But thanks be to God! He gives us the victory through our Lord Jesus Christ. (1 Cor 15:54–57)

To the Colossians Paul writes: "God made you alive with Christ. He forgave us all our sins, having canceled the charge of our legal indebtedness, which stood against us and condemned us; he has taken it away, nailing it to the cross. And having disarmed the powers and authorities, he made a public spectacle of them, triumphing over them by the cross" (Col 2:13–15).

Let's get Paul right here. Jesus' death is not *only* a transaction of my sin being placed into Jesus' account; there's much more to it. Jesus lets the powers do their worst to him, he takes the full brunt of sin, he drinks the dregs of judgment, and he allows death to hold him in its clutches. Then in the midst of a powerless death emerges a divine saving power to forgive, redeem, and renew. The festering cancer of sin has at last heard news of its cure. In the apex of death, life rises with healing in its wing. Satan's force is spent and his worst was no match for the best of the Son of God. The fatal wound of Jesus deals a fatal blow to death. The powers of this present darkness shiver as the looming tsunami of the kingdom of God draws ever nearer. The despots of the world live in denial as much as they live on borrowed time. This is Paul's atonement theology; this is the victory of God.

In the Catholic Epistles and in the Apocalypse, the same emphasis on Jesus' death as a divine triumph appears. In Hebrews we read: "Since the children have flesh and blood, he too shared in their humanity so that by his death he might break the power of him who holds the power of death—that is, the devil—and free those who all their lives were held in slavery by their fear of death" (Heb 2:14–15). According to John the Elder: "The reason the Son of God appeared was to destroy the devil's works" (1 John 3:8). The death of Jesus conquers all in Revelation:

> Now have come the salvation and the power
>   and the kingdom of our God
>   and the authority of his Messiah.
> For the accuser of our brothers and sisters,
>   who accuses them before our God day and night
>   has been thrown down.
> They triumphed over him
>   by the blood of the Lamb
>   and by the word of their testimony;
> they did not love their lives so much
>   as to shrink from death. (Rev 12:10–11)

The cross is a kingdom event that forever shakes the spiritual forces of this age with the power of the age to come.

Exegesis of these texts is found abundantly in the early church, who drew on such biblical images to show the saving power of Jesus' death over the devil. John Chrysostom commented on Colossians 2:15:

> Never yet was the devil in so shameful a plight. For while expecting to have him, he lost even those he had; and when Christ's body was nailed to the cross, the dead arose. At the cross death received his wound, having met his death stroke from a dead body. And as an athlete, when he thinks he has hit his adversary, himself is caught in a fatal grasp, so truly does Christ also show, that to die with arrogance is the devil's shame.[115]

Augustine's exposition is similar:

> The devil received outwardly the power of slaying the Lord in the flesh, but in so doing, his inward power, by which he held us in prison was slain.... In this way, by

---

115. Cited in Peter Gorday, ed., *Colossians, 1–2 Thessalonians, 1–2 Timothy, Titus, Philemon* (ACC 9; Downers Grove, IL: InterVarsity Press, 2000), 35.

a most just right, He overcame the devil, and so led captive the captivity brought about through sin. He freed us from a just captivity on account of sin, by blotting out the handwriting, and through His own righteous blood unrighteously shed He redeemed us—us who were to be justified although we were sinners.[116]

On the same passage Calvin spoke equally eloquently:

Hence it is not without cause that Paul magnificently celebrates the triumph which Christ obtained upon the cross, as if the cross, the symbol of ignominy, had been converted into a triumphal chariot. For he says, that he blotted out the handwriting of ordinances that was against us, which was contrary to us, and took it out of the way, nailing it to his cross.[117]

A search on the word "cross" in the Ante-Nicene Fathers shows time and time again how Jesus' death was part of a narrative of victory, triumph, and the defeat of sin and death. Jesus takes on the real enemy of Israel: the evil age, the hostile angelic powers, the accuser, the sin they are accused of, and the tyranny of death. The Son of God becomes the hammer of God against these inhuman powers that have kept humanity enslaved in their grasp.

This perspective of Christ's death as a divine victory was popularized in the twentieth century by Gustaf Aulen in his famous little book *Christus Victor*. For Aulen, the crucial element is "the idea of the Atonement as a Divine conflict and victory; Christ—Christus Victor—fights against and triumphs over the evil powers of the world, the tyrants under which mankind is in bondage and suffering."[118] Aulen showed the prominence of this perspective in the early church and set it up as an alternative to "objective" and "subjective" theories of the atonement that had polarized modern Protestant dogmatics. After surveying various authors in the Eastern and Western church fathers, Aulen concluded:

But in truth the idea of the Atonement, as it is set forth in the Fathers, is both clear and monumental. It sets forth God's coming to man, to accomplish His redemptive work; Incarnation and Redemption belong indissolubly together; God in Christ overcomes the hostile powers which hold man in bondage. At the same time these hostile powers are also the executants of God's will. The patristic theology is dualistic, but it is not an absolute Dualism. The deliverance of man from the power of death and the devil is at the same time his deliverance from God's judgment. God is reconciled by His own act in reconciling the world to Himself. Thus the power of evil is broken; that is to say, not that sin and death no longer exist, but that, the devil having been once for all conquered by Christ, His triumph is in principle universal, and His redemptive work can go forward everywhere through the Spirit who unites

---

116. Augustine, *Trin.* 4.17 (cited in N. R. Needham, *The Triumph of Grace: Augustine's Writings on Salvation* [London: Grace Publications Trust, 2000], 139).

117. Calvin, *Institutes* 2.16.6.

118. Gustaf Aulen, *Christus Victor* (London: SPCK, 1953), 4.

men with God and "deifies" them; and in regard to death, Athanasius can say that the disciples of Christ no longer fear death, since death has no more dominion over them, but "by the sign of the cross and by faith in Christ they trample death to the ground as itself dead" [*The Incarnation* 27].[119]

Perhaps the best way to summarize the Christus Victor view is with a line from the wonderful modern hymn "In Christ Alone" by Stuart Townshend and Keith Getty: "And as he stands in victory, Sin's curse has lost its grip on me."

Although the Christus Victor view rightly emphasizes the cosmic nature of Jesus' death as a victory over evil, a further explanation is required to detail precisely how this victory is achieved. Thus, the Christus Victor view cannot stand alone.[120] The victory of God in Jesus' death needs to be explained with some other mode of the atonement that shows how Jesus' death cancels sin, overcomes death, and vanquishes Satan. More likely, the victory of Jesus' death is achieved because his death is an atonement for sin, it is a substitutionary death, and it renders the devil's work of accusation as impotent (see Zech 3:4; Rev 12:10).[121]

4.4.1.4 SATISFACTION

St. Anselm of Canterbury (1033–1109) recognized the inherent shortcomings of the ransom view of the atonement and suggested another theory based on the idea of "satisfaction."[122] The satisfaction theory identifies Jesus' death as a means by which restitution is made as an alternative to punishment. Anselm suggested that the problem is that human beings owe God a debt of honor: "This is the debt which man and angel owe to God, and no one who pays this debt commits sin; but everyone who does not pay it sins. This is justice, or uprightness of will, which makes a being just or upright in heart, that is, in will; and this is the sole and complete debt of honor which we owe to God, and which God requires of us."[123]

This debt creates a moral rupture in the universe that God cannot allow to continue indefinitely. In Anselm's view, the only possible way of repaying the debt was for a being of infinite greatness to live as a person on behalf of human beings and

---

119. Aulen, *Christus Victor*, 75–76.
120. Cf. Thomas R. Schreiner, "Penal Substitution View," in *The Nature of the Atonement* (ed. J. Beilby and P. R. Eddy; Downers Grove, IL: InterVarsity Press, 2006), 68; Henri Blocher, "*Agnus Victor*: The Atonement as Victory and Vicarious Punishment," in *What Does It Mean to Be Saved?* (ed. J. G. Stackhouse; Grand Rapids: Baker, 2002), 67–91.
121. Cf. D. B. Knox ("Some Aspects of the Atonement," in *Selected Works: Volume 1 — The Doctrine of God* [Kingsford, NSW, Aus: Matthias Media, 2000], 256): "At one stroke the wiles of Satan, begun in Eden, by which men were set at enmity with their Creator, and which were to lead to their eternal perdition, were overthrown. The work of the devil was pulverized. Forgiveness was provided in place of wrath, and the sovereignty of God over evil was matchlessly vindicated. The very centre of this victory was that Christ underwent the curse which was ours. God made Christ to be sin for us. He laid on him the iniquity of us all."
122. For a good summary, see David Brown, "Anselm on Atonement," in *The Cambridge Companion to Anselm* (ed. Brian Davies and Brian Leftow; Cambridge: Cambridge University Press, 2005), 279–302.
123. Anselm, *Cur Deus Homo?* 1.9.

to repay the debt of honor that was owed to God. As such, Jesus' death was indeed a payment, but it was not the payment of a debt to the devil, but to God the Father.

According to Anselm, a person who sins against another person owes that person a form of recompense, a "satisfaction" for their misdeed. What is owed is a restoration of what has been taken from the victim, such as the honor denied God by the performance of human sin. The perpetrator of sin needs to be punished if the debt or "satisfaction" for sin cannot be paid. So in Anselm's presentation, Jesus is not punished in our place; rather, Jesus voluntarily pays the satisfaction that we are incapable of paying, which is why nobody needs to be punished for the crime. Although Anselm's view is periodically connected to penal substitution, this is a misnomer. What Anselm advocated was not penal, since the exchange that Anselm envisaged was not punitive but a restitution of honor that was owed.[124]

Anselm gave one of the first systematic treatments of the atonement and tied the atonement to the event of the incarnation.[125] Anselm was one of the first defenders of an "objective" view of the atonement, whereby the atonement changed God's disposition toward sinners rather than changing the inward disposition of sinners toward God. He also recognized that what was satisfied was not only divine honor but divine justice as well. I might add, following Graham Cole, that there is a biblical concept of "satisfaction" insofar as divine standards need to be met and the cross satisfies God's justice.[126]

However, there are points of criticism worth noting. First, Anselm's model for the atonement is indebted to the medieval feudal system with a reciprocal system of rights and obligations within a strict hierarchy. Anselm presents God as a type of feudal lord who has been wronged and needs to have his honor upheld. While this is probably the only Christian society that Anselm knew, it hardly models the divine attributes of justice and mercy in God's character, nor does it explain why God's character required atonement for sin. Second, it is not altogether clear how the benefits of Jesus' death come to believers in terms of what happens to them once satisfaction is rendered.

4.4.1.5 MORAL INFLUENCE

Some theologians, medieval and modern, have argued that the primary effect of Christ's death is not to change the *objective* state of humanity's relationship with God. Rather, the chief effect is to change the *subjective* state of a person's being. The cross demonstrates divine love and kindles a corresponding love in ourselves. The chief proponent of this theory in the medieval church was Peter Abelard, who saw the

---

124. Colin Gunton, *The Actuality of Atonement* (Grand Rapids: Eerdmans, 1989), 91.

125. Ibid., 87–88.
126. Cole, *God the Peacemaker*, 130–32.

death of Christ as achieving an inward effect on the attitude of the sinner. Abelard taught that when people look at the cross, they behold the greatness of divine love, a love that delivers them from fear and produces in them an unwavering love in return. Abelard tried to base this on texts like Luke 7:47, where Jesus says to the sinful woman: "Her many sins have been forgiven—as her great love has shown." Thus the atonement awakens love in believers, and this love is treated as a form of merit that enables them to have a relationship with God.

Faustus Socinus (1539–1604), the progenitor of the non-Trinitarian "Socinians," also rejected the idea of Jesus' death as a satisfaction for sin and emphasized that the cross was the perfect example of sacrificial devotion to God. Socinus declared: "Jesus Christ is our savior because he announced to us the way of eternal salvation, confirmed, and in his own person, both by the example of his life and by rising from the dead, clearly showed it, and will give that eternal life to us who have faith in him."[127] That the atonement causes a change in the believer can be grounded in Romans. Paul wrote, "God's love has been poured out into our hearts through the Holy Spirit, who has been given to us" (Rom 5:5). The atonement and its accompanying justification of the believer result in a love from and for God permeating the believer.

There are several of problems with this view.[128] First, while we can grant that one purpose of Christ's death is to restore humankind to a position of holiness as they enter into communion with a holy God, it is impossible to reduce the achievement of the cross to a mere change of a person's inward disposition. This view overlooks the objective alienation between God and humanity on account of the evil that must be dealt with. Or, in the words of Anselm to Boso, "You have not yet considered the seriousness of sin."[129] That is why we need not just a teacher but a Savior, not merely an influencer but a Redeemer, not merely a lover but a Deliverer.

Second, the cross of Christ is a revelation of both the "justice" (Rom 3:25–26; Rev 16:7) and the "love" of God (John 15:13; Rom 5:8). The Scriptures nowhere regard as contradictory the notion that God's justice and love are equally manifested in the cross of Jesus Christ.

Third, imagine if someone went running down the street and blew kisses to us as he yelled out, "I love you all, I love you all, I love you all." Then to demonstrate that love for us, this person he threw himself off the end of a jetty and was drowned in its deep waters. Would you feel loved or motivated go and love others? I don't know about you, but I certainly would not. Jesus' death can only be loving if it objectively changes something in our relationship with God. Jesus himself saw his

---

127. Cited in Robert Culpeppar, *Interpreting the Atonement* (Grand Rapids: Eerdmans, 1966), 104.

128. Alister E. McGrath, "The Moral Theory of the Atonement: An Historic and Theological Critique," *SJT* 38 (1985): 205–20.

129. Anselm, *Cur Deus Homo?* 1.20.

death as being like a mother hen who uses her feathers to protect her chicks from a barnyard fire (Matt 23:37/Luke 13:34). His blood was poured out like a sacrificial victim in the making of a covenant (Matt 26:28). He was like a shepherd about to be struck down to protect the flock under his care (Matt 26:31). His death was like a kernel falling to the ground from which wheat could grow and sustaining bread be made (John 12:24). Jesus could regard his death as the greatest loving act that one could do for one's friends *only because he entered into the terror of judgment, sin, and death on their behalf* (John 15:13).

An anecdote from Scottish theologian Thomas Torrance's student days at Edinburgh shows the theological impoverishment of the moral influence view:

> One day a student called Harold Estes came into my rooms in the Dormitory to discuss an essay he had written on the atonement. He was a very gentle kindly person. It is he had spoke of the death of Christ simply as a demonstration of the love of God. He had been expounding something like what was known as a "moral influence theory" of the atonement favoured by liberal thinkers but theologically quite inadequate, as H. R. Mackintosh had shown us in Edinburgh. To help Harold I showed him a reproduction which I had of Grünewald's famous painting of the Crucifixion, at Colmar, which is incredibly starkly vivid. I also showed him some of the enlargements of the painting, reproduced in a book I had with me, which focused on the fearfully lacerated flesh of Jesus which he suffered from the flagellation with thorns inflicted on him by the soldiers, deep wounds now blackened by the sun. Harold shrank back in horror at what he saw. I said to him: "Harold, you have written about that as a picture of the love of God. It is certainly a picture of the fearful sin and hatred of mankind, but if you can tell me WHY Jesus was crucified, WHY he endured such unbelievable pain and anguish, then you will be able to say something of the real meaning of the atonement, and about why the crucifixion of Jesus was and is indeed a revelation of the love of God—Christ was crucified like that FOR our sakes, to save us from sin and judgment. The meaning of the atoning death of Christ is expressed in that word FOR—Jesus died for you and for me, and for all people. It is only in the light of that FOR that the death of Jesus is a picture of the love of God. And what a wonderful picture it is of the infinite love of God who so loved us that 'he did not spare his only Son but freely delivered him up for us all, that we might be saved.'"[130]

The moral influence theory does not deal with the problem of guilt. A guilt that is glossed over will produce only greater guilt. The guilt that separates humanity from God must be removed.[131] Furthermore, as G. W. Bromiley observed, "Apart from existential variations, more recent subjective statements have been little more than stale and platitudinous repetitions that answer to the biblical data only by discarding the biblical norm."[132]

---

130. Cited in Alister E. McGrath, *T. F. Torrance: An Intellectual Biography* (Edinburgh: T&T Clark, 1999), 54–55.

131. Brunner, *Creation and Redemption*, 291.

132. G. W. Bromiley, "Atone," in *ISBE*, 1:359.

4.4.1.6 EXEMPLARY

The old hymn by Cecil Frances Alexander, "There Is a Green Hill Far Away," contains this lyric: "He died that we might be forgiven, *He died to make us good*, that we might go at last to heaven, Saved by His precious blood." The hymn announces that the Lord Jesus was crucified to save sinners from sins; yet it also adds that Jesus' death was to somehow make Christians good persons. The idea that Christ died in order that we become good is thoroughly biblical. According to Paul's letter to Titus, Jesus is the one "who gave himself for us to redeem us from all wickedness and to purify for himself a people that are his very own, eager to do what is good" (Titus 2:14). That is, Jesus' death has both a redemptive and transformative effect on believers.

This comes out clearly in Romans 6, where Paul tells believers that since they have died with Christ, they are liberated from the effects of sin: "For we know that our old self was crucified with him so that the body ruled by sin might be done away with, that we should no longer be slaves to sin—because anyone who has died has been set free from sin" (6:6–7). As such, believers need not offer their bodies to evil desires; instead, they can offer their bodies up as instruments of "righteousness" (6:13) and so "bear fruit for God" (7:4). This is known as the indicative and the imperative of biblical ethics. Because Christ did *this* for you, now go and *live obediently* for him.

While Jesus' death is an atoning sacrifice for sins, it is also an example that Christians are to emulate. The majestic Christ Hymn of Philippians 2:5–11 about the incarnation and crucifixion of Christ is a kerygmatic summary of the church's story of Jesus. Even so, the hymn is principally an exhortation to follow Christ's example in cultivating humility and in self-giving in corporate church life. In Hebrews, Jesus' endurance under temptation to the point of shedding blood is an example for all believers to follow (Heb 12:3–4). The example of Jesus' self-giving death is the model for how husbands are to love their wives (Eph 5:25–26). First Peter clearly affirms a substitutionary model of the atonement (1 Pet 2:24), yet Peter also contains the clearest reference to Jesus' death as an example for others to follow: "To this you were called, because Christ suffered for you, leaving you an example, that you should follow in his steps" (2:21).

In the ancient church, Pelagius made much of the death of Jesus as an example for believers to follow in living a noble and righteous life before God. There is nothing wrong with that unless you think that Jesus' death is *only* an example to be followed. For Pelagius our problem was not that we received a corrupt nature or a deadly verdict on us through Adam; rather, it was that Adam was a bad example. Jesus' death on the cross provided a better example that we should follow. The problem with this view, of course, is that it did not take seriously the impact of Adam's sin on humanity in giving us both an inherited guilt and an innate propensity to sin. We are not able to live a righteous life before God; therefore, we need more than a good example to imitate; indeed, we need someone to take away our sin.[133]

4.4.1.7 GOVERNMENT

In response to the views of the Socinians who held to the moral influence theory of the atonement, the Dutch jurist Hugo Grotius (1583–1645) developed Anselm's satisfaction theory of the atonement further in his work *Defensio Fidei Catholicae de Satisfactione Christi* (1617). Grotius attempted to defend the rationality of the atonement in light of the jurisprudence of his day. The model that Grotius put forward has been called the "governmental theory" of atonement, and its influence extended to both Calvinists like Richard Baxter and Arminians like Philip Limborch.

The governmental theory of atonement contends that Jesus Christ's death was a genuine substitution for the punishment that humans themselves deserved. However, this punishment did not consist of Christ's receiving the exact same punishment due to sinful people. Instead, God publicly demonstrated his disapproval with sin through the death of his own sinless Son as a propitiation. Christ's death served as a substitute for the punishment humans might have received. On this basis, God is able to extend forgiveness while maintaining divine order and divine justice. On the cross, God demonstrated the seriousness of sin and its consequences, so God thus allows his wrath to "pass over" the sins actually committed. With the law satisfied, the threat of the law can be relaxed, where sinners show penitence and remorse for their sins.

For Grotius, the cross is not about retributive justice but public justice. God shows his displeasure at sin so he can acquit the repentant. The inadequacies of the governmental model are fairly easy to identify. The most devastating is that Grotius replaced the sacrificial idea of Scripture with utilitarian ideas of punishment as a deterrent. Moreover, if the punishment inflicted on Jesus is not the same as that deserved by sinners, it seems hard to say that atonement for their sins has really been made.

4.4.1.8 PENAL SUBSTITUTION

According to John Stott, "evangelical Christians believe that in and through Christ crucified God substituted himself for us and bore our sins, dying in our place the death we deserved to die, in order that we might be restored to his favor and adopted into his family."[134] Jesus' death bears God's wrath against our sin (i.e., it is penal),

---

133. The main difference between the moral influence theory and the exemplary theory is that the moral influence theory says that Christ's death teaches us how much God loves us and the exemplary theory says that Christ's death teaches us how to love.

134. Stott, *The Cross of Christ*, 7. Another definition (Stephen Jeffery, Michael Ovey, and Andrew Sach, *Pierced for Our Transgressions: Rediscovering the Glory of Penal Substitution* [Wheaton, IL: Crossway, 2007], 21) is: "The doctrine of penal substitution states God gave himself in the person of his Son to suffer instead of us the death, punishment and curse due to fallen humanity as the penalty for sin."

and Jesus dies in our place (i.e., it is a substitution). This model of the atonement is a "dramatic, kerygmatic picturing of divine action" whereby God brings about reconciliation by punishing Christ in the stead of sinful men and women.[135] Thus, the penal substitutionary view maintains that Jesus' death was a sacrifice for sins in our place as our representative.[136]

In the sacrificial system described in Leviticus, the offerer of a sacrifice would lay hands on the sacrificial animal before the sacrifice was made (Lev 4:15; 16:21; Num 8:12). The laying of hands on the victim was a practice that suggests not merely identification or ownership, but that the victim was a vicarious substitution for the offerer himself. The worshiper's sins were transferred or credited to the victim.[137] The sacrificial system provided a provisional means for God to deal with the uncleanness of Israel's sin in relation to his holiness. The sacrifices, especially the scapegoat in Leviticus 16, were a means of expiation of the nation's sins when an animal died in the stead of people.

Jesus' death is described in terms indicative of the Old Testament sacrifices concerning the removal of sin from the sinner by the shedding of blood (Lev 17:11)—hence the appeal to the "blood" of Jesus (Matt 26:28; Rom 3:25; Eph 2:13; Heb 9:14; 1 Pet 1:2, 9; 1 John 5:6; Rev 1:7). Christ's death is also described as a Passover sacrifice (1 Cor 5:7). That is important because the lamb that died on the first Passover died in place of the firstborn of each Hebrew family. When the blood was smeared on the door of a house, the Lord passed over that house (Exod 12:13). As David Garland avers: "As God saved Israel in Egypt through the sacrifice of the Passover lamb, God now saves all people through the sacrifice of Jesus."[138]

The image of the Suffering Servant of Isaiah 53 appears to have had a monumental influence on the New Testament, even though the extent and shape of that influence is disputed. This section is located within Isaiah 40–55 concerning the new exodus that God will bring for the exiles and how he will set up a renewed Israelite kingdom. Note the following about the Suffering Servant:

1. He is explicitly said to die for others because "he took up our pain," "bore our suffering," and "he was pierced for our transgression, he was crushed for our iniquities" (53:4–5).
2. Other benefits from his sufferings are peace, healing, and justification (53:5, 11).
3. He was a willing victim and not a victim of circumstances as "he poured out his life unto death" and "was numbered with the transgressors" (53:12).

---

135. James I. Packer, "The Logic of Penal Substitution," *TynBul* 25 (1974): 3–45.

136. For three recent collections of essays arguing for penal substitution, see David Peterson, ed., *Where Wrath and Mercy Meet* (Waynesboro, GA: Paternoster, 2001); Charles E. Hill and Frank A. James, eds., *The Glory of the Atonement* (Downers Grove, IL: InterVarsity Press, 2005); Jeffery, Ovey, and Sach, *Pierced for Our Transgressions*.

137. Charles Scobie, *The Ways of Our Lord: An Approach to Biblical Theology* (Grand Rapids: Eerdmans, 2003), 585.

138. David E. Garland, *1 Corinthians* (BECNT; Grand Rapids: Baker, 2003), 180.

4. It was God who laid the people's sins on the Servant since "the Lord has laid on him the iniquity of us all" and "it was the Lord's will to crush him and cause him to suffer" (53:6, 10).
5. The Servant himself was righteous, evidenced by the fact that he "had done no violence, nor was any deceit in his mouth," and he was "my righteous servant" (53:9, 11).[139]

This passage is used frequently in the New Testament in relation to Jesus' death. For example, Mark probably alludes to it in Jesus' words that "this is my blood of the covenant, which is poured out for many" (Mark 14:24 = Isa 53:12). Luke 22:37 explicitly cites Isaiah 53:12 about Jesus' being numbered among transgressors in relation to Jesus' death. The traditional material that Paul cites in Romans 4:25 ("delivered over to death for our sins and was raised to life for our justification") is likely based on the pattern of death and resurrection in Isaiah 53:11–12. Peter makes a long allusion to Isaiah 53 in his remarks about the cross in 1 Peter 2:22–25 (Isa 53:7–12). The net impression gleaned is that the Servant is the representative of the people of God who dies as one bearing the penalty that was theirs.

Routinely students run to Paul's letters or to Hebrews in search of proof texts for penal substitution. They completely bypass the Gospels like tourists from Florida detouring around Philadelphia on their way to New York. How much I enjoy the surprise when students learn that the gospel of the cross actually begins with the gospel according to the Evangelists. Even more gobsmacking is when they learn that you actually can preach the gospel from the Gospels! Who would have imagined!

Beyond his passion predictions, Jesus taught a great deal about what his death would achieve. He yearned to take up the children of Jerusalem as a mother hen uses her wings to protect her chicks from a barnyard fire so that though the hen dies, the chicks live (Matt 23:37/Luke 13:34). In the famous ransom logion, Jesus gives his life as a "ransom for many" (Matt 20:28/Mark 10:45). A ransom was the price paid for redemption from captivity or slavery. In the Old Testament, the image is related to freeing slaves (Lev 19:20; 25:51–52) and redeeming land (Lev 25:26). The meaning of "for" (*anti*) in the ransom is "a ransom in substitution for many."[140] Just like the Servant of Isaiah 53, the Son of Man gives his life as a ransom in place of others and so achieves the redemption of the new Isaianic exodus.

---

139. Jeffery, Ovey, and Sach, *Pierced for Our Transgressions*, 54–61.

140. Robert H. Gundry (*Mark: A Commentary on His Apology for the Cross* [Grand Rapids: Eerdmans, 1993], 588–91): "Since the price of ransom in substitution for many consists in the Son of Man's giving his life, substitutionary death is hard to avoid" (591). Peter G. Bolt (*Cross from a Distance: Atonement in Mark's Gospel* [NSBT; Downers Grove, IL: InterVarsity Press, 2004], 72): "At the heart of the ransom idea is the concept of exchange. This is highlighted strongly in Jesus' saying, in which the death of the Son of Man would be a ransom *anti pollōn*—instead of, in the place of many." I. Howard Marshall (*Aspects of the Atonement: Cross and Resurrection in the Reconciling of God and Humanity* [London: Paternoster, 2007], 47): "The price is a substitute for the person redeemed, and in that the price is costly it is, we might say, painful. Hence the concept of substitution is present and the cost may be regarded as a penalty in the broad sense."

The substance of the ransom logion is reinforced by the words of institution at the Last Supper: "This is my blood of the covenant, which is poured out for many" (Mark 14:24). The saying connects with Isaiah 53:12 about the vicarious nature of the Servant's death. Yet the language also recalls the language of the cultus and its sacrifices (Lev 4). The proximity of "blood" and "covenant" means that Jesus' death is a covenant-inaugurating event; it brings in the new covenant where there would be the forgiveness of sins (Jer 31:31–34), and the blood of the covenant rescues God's people from the pit of the underworld (Zech 9:11).[141]

When Jesus cried on the cross from Psalm 22, "My God, my God, why have you forsaken me?" (Matt 27:46; Mark 15:34), it was not a cry of defeat as one who had pinned his hopes on the advent of God's kingdom only to be disappointed at the end. Rather, it was a cry of abandonment. Jesus was abandoned by God because he bore the sins of others and God could no longer look upon his Son with love. Jesus made that cry of God-forsakenness so that no child of God would ever be God-forsaken. Jesus became a cosmic sponge that absorbed the evil of humanity and the wrath of God against it. He absorbed the wrath with such perfection and such finality that no wrath remains on those for whom his sacrifice is effected. He drank the dregs of God's judgment so that not a drop remains for his followers. In the cry of dereliction, we hear Jesus crying out in solidarity with our own God-forsaken mortality. It is a cry from *within* the Trinity as the Father must abandon the Son and God must experience his own wrath on behalf of many.[142]

Three texts from the epistles clearly imply that Jesus bears the divine judgment against our sins in our place. First, "for what the law was powerless to do because it was weakened by the flesh, God did by sending his own Son in the likeness of sinful flesh to be a sin offering [*peri hamartias*]. And so *he condemned sin in the flesh*" (Rom 8:3, italics added). The law was powerless to acquit us from the penalty of sin or to liberate us from the power of sin. God achieved justification *from sin's condemnation* and liberation *from sin's power* by sending his own Son. The phrase *peri harmatias* does not mean "concerning sin," but is idiomatic for "sin offering," since the prepositional phrase is used to refer to a sin offering in forty-four of its fifty-four occurrences in the LXX (see too Heb 10:6, 8; 13:11).[143] N. T. Wright comments:

> No clearer statement is found in Paul, or indeed anywhere else in all early Christian literature, of the early Christian belief that what happened on the cross was the judicial punishment of sin. Taken in conjunction with 8:1 and the whole argument of the passage, not to mention the partial parallels in 2 Cor 5:21 and Gal 3:13, it is clear that Paul intends to say that in Jesus' death the damnation that sin deserved was

---

141. Bolt, *Cross from a Distance*, 105.
142. Ibid., 141.
143. N. T. Wright, *The New Testament and the People of God* (COQG 1; London: SPCK, 1992), 220–25.

meted out fully and finally, so that sinners over whose heads that condemnation had hung might be liberated from this threat once and for all.[144]

Second, "Christ redeemed us from the curse of the law by *becoming a curse for us*, for it is written: 'Cursed is everyone who is hung on a pole'" (Gal 3:13, italics added). This passage is on top of the A-list of penal substitution texts. The logic of Paul's argument is that the law requires obedience, and it results in curses for disobedience. People who disobey the law, accordingly, fall under the penalty of covenantal curses. In particular, Jewish contemporaries of Paul associated crucifixion with the accursedness of one who was hanged on a tree (Deut 21:23). The strange fact is that believers are redeemed from this curse because their accursedness is taken away by Christ, who has taken the curse on himself.

Paul tells us here what we are being saved from—the curse. The only explanation is that the Messiah had willingly taken on himself the dreaded curse that rightly belonged to others. This takes us to the heart of Pauline soteriology.[145] As Timothy George comments:

> For this reason the doctrine of atonement can never be merely a matter of cool theologizing or dispassionate discourse. *For us* the Son of God became a curse. *For us* he shed his precious blood. *For us* he who from all eternity knew only the intimacy of the Father's bosom came "to stand in that relation with God which normally is the result of sin, estranged from God and the object of his wrath."[146]

Despite some protests to the contrary, we cannot imagine a clearer affirmation of penal substitutionary atonement.[147]

Third, "'*he [Jesus] himself bore our sins' in his body on the cross*, so that we might die to sins and live for righteousness; 'by his wounds you have been healed'" (1 Pet 2:24, italics added). Much neglected are what the Catholic Epistles contribute to the doctrine of the atonement. Here I'll focus on just one important text from 1 Peter. In this verse, Peter uses Isaiah 53:4–5 to make the point that Jesus bore the punishment due our sins in his body. He carries our sin away by bearing the brunt of its punishment. In making note of Jesus' body, Peter underscores the redeeming quality of Christ's humanity as he suffered unjustly and for those who deserved to suffer as sinners.[148]

The common refrain that "Jesus died for our sins" does not mean *for the benefit of*

---

144. N. T. Wright, "The Letter to the Romans," in *NIB*, 10:574–75. How can one read this statement by Wright and then say, as I heard one "theologian" declare on a weekly podcast show, that N. T. Wright does not know "what to do with the cross"? That simply baffles me.

145. Timothy George, *Galatians* (NAC; Nashville: Broadman & Holman, 2001), 240.

146. Ibid., 242 (with quotation from C. K. Barrett, *The Second Epistle to the Corinthians* [London: Harper & Row, 1957], 180) and italics original.

147. Marshall (*Aspects of the Atonement*, 53 n. 32 [see too 45–46]): "Jesus bears the curse of God on our behalf. If that is not penal substitution I do not know what it is." Jeffery, Ovey, and Sach (*Pierced for our Transgressions*, 89): "It is hard to imagine a plainer statement of the doctrine of penal substitution."

148. Cf. Ben Witherington III, *Letters and Homilies for Hellenized Christians: A Socio-Rhetorical Commentary on 1–2 Peter* (Downers Grove, IL: InterVarsity Press, 2007), 157.

our sins, but in the sense of removing them and their punitive effects. A presenting issue is the exact mechanics as to how Jesus' death removes sin or obviates the need for punishment. In the mid-twentieth century several publications focused on the meaning of one obscure word, *hilastērion*, and whether it means "propitiation" as the appeasement of wrath or "expiation" as the removal of sin. The noun *hilastērion* only occurs in Romans 3:25 and Hebrews 9:5. In Hebrews 9:5 it obviously refers to the "mercy seat," the lid on the ark of the covenant as the place where the blood of a bull and a goat was sprinkled on the Day of Atonement (Lev 16:1–15).

In the case of Romans 3:25, Paul writes that "God presented Christ as a [*hilastērion*], through the shedding of his blood—to be received by faith." Some translations take this also as a reference to the mercy seat, the lid of the ark of the covenant, denoting the place of atonement (NET; CEB); but more likely it is the means of atonement that is being described, given the reference to Jesus' blood (see 4 Macc 17.22; Josephus, *Ant.* 16.182). Accordingly some translations opt for a sacrificial meaning of "expiation" (RSV), others for propitiation (KJV, NASB, ESV), and the NIV and NRSV have a bet both ways with "sacrifice of atonement" (see NJB, "sacrifice for reconciliation"). Now "expiation" means the removal of sin, while "propitiation" means the appeasement of wrath.

Commentators are bitterly divided over which image Paul meant when he called Jesus' death a *hilastērion*. C. H. Dodd argued that propitiation was a concept in pagan religions where the capricious gods needed to be placated by sacrifice in order to assuage their temperamental anger and win their favor. The God of the Bible did not sink to the level of pagan deities as an angry deity having his tantrums cooled by sacrifice. So Dodd argued strenuously for "expiation" in the cancellation of sin.[149] In response, Leon Morris and Roger Nicole pointed out that *hilastērion* occurs in the LXX most frequently in contexts pertaining to God's wrath.[150] Moreover, given the context of Romans 1:18–3:20 (esp. "wrath" in 1:18; 2:5, 8; 3:5), *hilastērion* surely refers to the appeasement of divine wrath against humans, both Jews and Gentiles, who sin and rebel against God (i.e., propitiation). At the same time, I would add that we do not have to choose absolutely between expiation and propitiation because both are true of Jesus' sacrificial death. We might say that when sin is *expiated*, then God's wrath is *propitiated*. When sin is removed, God's wrath is appeased.[151]

It is important to balance the *substitutionary* and *representative* natures of Jesus' death. Obviously Jesus dies in our place so that we do not have to die and face the

---

149. C.H. Dodd, "*hilastērion*, Its Cognates, Derivatives and Synonyms in the Septuagint," *JTS* 32 (1931): 352–60.

150. Roger Nicole, "C. H. Dodd and the Doctrine of Propitiation," *WTJ* 17 (1954–55): 117–57; Leon Morris, *Apostolic Preaching of the Cross* (Grand Rapids: Eerdmans, 1955), 135–56.

151. Cole, *God the Peacemaker*, 143–48; James D. G. Dunn, *Romans 1–8* (WBC; Dallas: Word, 1988), 171; D. A. Carson, "Atonement in Romans 3:21–26," in *The Glory of the Atonement* (ed. C. E. Hill and F. A. James; Downers Grove, IL: InterVarsity Press, 2005), 130; Marshall, *Aspects of the Atonement*, 42.

effects of sin's penalty. But Jesus' death is also representative and vicarious so that we experience judgment and death through him, but without suffering its final consequences. Representation assumes the notion of being identified with and incorporated into a person who is able to stand for them, with them, and instead of them![152]

Paul makes this point in several places where he points out that we have died with Christ and been crucified with him (Rom 6:1–7; Gal 2:19–20; Col 2:20). We enter into the experience of judgment, but we emerge from it unscathed because Christ was our covering. Because we have been through it once, we cannot go through it again. But because we have been through it, we have been changed. Our old self was crucified, killed, and destroyed, so the state we survive in is no longer our original state; instead, it is a renewed and revived person who emerges from the cross of Christ.

In a fine study, Daniel Bailey notes that the discussion of Jesus' death as vicarious and substitutionary is often confused by the terms and freighted with certain presuppositions. He suggests adopting the German word *Stellvertretung* (lit., "place-taking"). Jesus *inclusively* takes the place of other persons in that he is one of them and shares solidarity with them. Only as a human being and only as an Israelite can Jesus take their place because he stands as one of them. The people of the Messiah are included in him and therefore benefit from the salvation bound to him. Jesus *exclusively* takes the places of others when he suffers for them in their place, as their substitute, so that they need not suffer.[153] Importantly, only because Jesus represents humanity as one of them (inclusive, representative) can he stand in their place in their absence (exclusive, substitutionary).

The criticism that penal substitution was a latecomer on the scene in Christian theology is profoundly false. It was not necessarily the most popular model for the atonement in the church fathers and among medieval theologians, but it was apparent to many. For example, among the Apostolic Fathers, Clement wrote: "In love the Master has received us. Because of the love that he had for us, Jesus Christ our Lord, in accordance with God's will, gave his blood for us, and his flesh for our flesh, and his life for our lives."[154] The second-century author of the *Epistle to Diognetus* expressed these poetic words: "O the sweet exchange, O incomprehensible work of God, O the unexpected blessings that the sinfulness of many should be hidden in one righteous person, while the righteousness of one should justify many sinners."[155] Then there is Augustine:

> But the Catholic faith affirms this exclusively of the one and only Mediator between God and mankind, the man Christ Jesus, who for our sake stooped down to undergo death—that is, the penalty of sin—Himself being without sin. As He alone became

---

152. Scot McKnight, *A Community Called Atonement* (Nashville: Abingdon, 2007), 107–10.

153. Daniel P. Bailey, "Concepts of *Stellvertretung* in the Interpretation of Isaiah 53," in *Jesus and the Suffering Servant: Isaiah 53 and Christian Origins* (ed. W. H. Bellinger and W. R. Farmer; Harrisburg, PA: Trinity, 1998), 223–50. See also Scot McKnight, *Jesus and His Death: Historiography, the Historical Jesus, and Atonement Theory* (Waco, TX: Baylor University Press, 2005), 346–47; Bolt, *Cross from a Distance*, 70–72.

154. *1 Clem* 49.6.

155. *Diogn.* 9.5.

the Son of Man in order that we might become through Him sons of God, so He alone, on our behalf, undertook punishment without deserving it, that we through Him might obtain grace without deserving it.[156]

Penal substitution was at the heart of the atonement according to the Reformers. Calvin stated:

> Scripture teaches, that [humanity] was estranged from God by sin, an heir of wrath, exposed to the curse of eternal death, excluded from all hope of salvation, a complete alien from the blessing of God, the slave of Satan, captive under the yoke of sin; in fine, doomed to horrible destruction, and already involved in it; that then Christ interposed, took the punishment upon himself and bore what by the just judgment of God was impending over sinners; with his own blood expiated the sins which rendered them hateful to God, by this expiation satisfied and duly propitiated God the Father, by this intercession appeased his anger, on this basis founded peace between God and men, and by this tie secured the Divine benevolence toward them.[157]

In the modern period, substitution was vitally important to Karl Barth's doctrine of reconciliation. In Barth's articulation the atonement is about "The Judge Judged in our Place." To say that God is "for us" means, not simply "with us," but that Jesus dies for us as the judge condemned in our stead. Barth identified at least four aspects of Jesus' substitution: (1) Jesus takes the place of believers as the judge whereby he displaces others from judgment and so liberates them. (2) He takes the place of the judged and so becomes sin in a genuine exchange of places. (3) Jesus takes our place in judgment as the Father's act for us that brings reconciliation. (4) He establishes the justice of God that assures the conformity of the action with God's freedom and character. Ultimately, the Judge, the Judging, and the Judgment are expressions of the justice of God as the Just One vicariously takes the place of sinners.[158]

In Barth's estimation, what happened at the cross is that "the Son of God fulfilled the righteous judgment on us men by Himself taking our place as man in our place undergoing the judgment under which we had passed." Answering Anselm's question *Cur Deus homo*? (*Why Did God Become Human?*) Barth replied: "In order that God as man might do and accomplish and achieve all this for us wrong-doers, in order that in this way there might be brought about by Him our reconciliation with Him and conversion to Him."[159]

Penal substitution must be central to any account of the atonement for it demonstrates how the penalty due sinners is borne away by Jesus Christ.[160] What also needs to be said, however, is that substitutionary atonement must be integrated within a

---

156. Augustine, *Two Letters of the Pelagians* 4.6 (cited in Needham, *Augustine*, 147).
157. Calvin, *Institutes* 2.16.2.
158. Barth, *CD* IV.1:211–83.
159. Ibid., IV.1:222–23.
160. Cf. Leon Morris, *The Cross in the New Testament* (Grand Rapids: Eerdmans, 1965), 404–19.

comprehensive biblical theology and correlated with the doctrine of God as the one who judges, is judged, and justifies. Or else the atonement becomes abstracted from the story line of Scripture and is artificially removed from the character of God. What is more, the atonement should not be described in language that is inappropriate, such as that God gets "revenge" on Jesus. God does not get revenge on himself. More properly, God propitiates his own wrath by becoming the object of his own wrath for the benefit of his chosen people.

Models of the Atonement			
	View	Description	Advocates
Historical	Recapitulation	Jesus' death replays the story of Adam except that unlike Adam, Jesus is successful over sin and obedient to death on the cross.	Irenaeus
	Ransom	Jesus paid the price for the release of humanity from Satan.	Church Fathers
	Victory	Jesus' death is a triumph over evil and the devil.	Church Fathers
Subjective	Moral Influence	Jesus' death changes our inward disposition and enables us to love others.	Peter Abelard
	Exemplary	Jesus' death provides an example of love for believers to emulate.	Pelagius
Objective	Satisfaction	Jesus' death satisfies the debt of God's honor that our sins affronted.	Anselm
	Governmental	Jesus' death shows God's displeasure with sin and Jesus' death takes the debt caused by our transgression of God's justice.	Hugo Grotius
	Penal Substitution	Jesus dies as our representative and substitute and takes away the penalty meant for us.	Martin Luther, John Calvin, Charles Hodge, J. I. Packer.

4.4.2 WHAT IS THE MOST CENTRAL IMAGE OF THE ATONEMENT?

Most of the atonement modes described above have some scriptural warrant for their assertions. In particular, we can affirm that the recapitulation, Christus Victor, exemplary, satisfaction, and penal substitution models can all be safely traced back to Scripture to varying degrees. Indeed, there is a rich variety of images for describing how Jesus' death makes atonement for sin and delivers believers from death and

IS THE CROSS "DIVINE CHILD ABUSE"?

A recent criticism of the atonement, especially penal substitution, is leveled by postmodern, emergent, and feminist theologians who regard the atonement as a form of "divine child abuse." Stephen Chalke and Alan Mann describe penal substitution as:

> a form of cosmic child abuse—a vengeful Father, punishing his Son for an offence he has not even committed. Understandably, both people inside and outside of the Church have found this twisted version of events morally dubious and a huge barrier to faith. Deeper than that, however, is that such a concept stands in total contradiction to the statement that "God is love." If the cross is a personal act of violence perpetrated by God towards humankind but borne by his Son, then it makes a mockery of Jesus' own teaching to love your enemies and to refuse to repay evil with evil.[161]

Dem dere be fightin words! The problem is that this argument is filled with so much straw that you could literally take that argument, put a costume on it, and audition it for the role of the scarecrow in a new Broadway production of the *Wizard of Oz*. This pejorative criticism against orthodox atonement doctrine can be deflected by recognizing the triune nature of the atonement. As Henri Blocher has noted, the only God capable of achieving what the cross achieved is the God of Trinitarian and christological orthodoxy.[162] The Father sends the Son, and the Son goes voluntarily to the cross. The Spirit empowers the Son to suffer and withdraws at the final moment, only to raise the Son back to life. God does not inflict suffering on an unwilling Son who is sacrificed for a wrath devoid of love, a justice motivated by hatred, and a disproportionate display of divine rage. Nor does Jesus persuade a blood thirsty Father to be merciful. According to Bruce McCormack:

> If the Father were not mercifully inclined toward the human race all along, why would he have sent his only Son into this world in the first place? Surely, a determination to be merciful and forgiving must precede and ground the sending of the Son into the world to die in our place. Surely forgiveness is not *elicited* from the Father (grudgingly?) by what Christ did on our behalf; it is rather *effected* by the Father in and through Christ's passion and death. So the picture of an angry God the Father and a gentle and

---

161. Stephen Chalke and Alan Mann, *The Lost Message of Jesus* (Grand Rapids: Zondervan, 2003), 182. Cf. Brian McLaren, *The Story We Find Ourselves in: Further Adventures in a New Kind of Christian* (San Francisco: Jossey-Bass, 2003), 102–4.

162. Henri Blocher, "God and the Cross," in *Engaging the Doctrine of God: Contemporary Protestant Perspectives* (ed. B. L. McCormack; Grand Rapids: Baker, 2008), 138.

self-sacrificial Son who pays the ultimate price to effect an alteration in the Father's "attitude" fails to hit the mark.[163]

The atonement is a triune action as Jesus Christ is both subject and object of the atonement. He was the one, in union with Father and in cooperation with the Spirit, who determined to bear the outpouring of divine wrath against sin. He is the one, as judge and justifier, who mediates for sinners that the Spirit draws and the Father accepts. To be sure, there is no patricide here; that is, the Father does not die on the cross for sins, but the Father sends and the Son willingly goes, the Spirit willingly withdraws, all in order that the Triune God would make atonement for the evil of humanity. We might say, with Graham Cole, that the Father is the architect of the atonement, the Son is the accomplisher of the atonement, and the Holy Spirit is the applier of the atonement.[164]

It is irresponsible, as Scot McKnight comments, for critics to depict penal substitution as divine child abuse because the atonement is prompted by the loving grace of the Father. That said, it would be wise for advocates of penal substitution to listen to their critics and ensure they are not theologically bankrolling an atonement theory that legitimates violence or a brutal patriarchy.[165] Neither is it helpful to inflate the biblical language for substitutionary judgment by saying things like at the cross God "hates" Jesus or gets "revenge" on him. Jesus certainly "becomes" sin by bearing it; yet he does not literally become sin and cease to be the Son. Jesus suffers the wrath of the Father, but what makes it so dramatic is that the Father simultaneously loves the Son! In our atonement theories let us not go beyond what is written.[166]

FURTHER READING

Gathercole, Simon. "The Cross and Substitutionary Atonement." *SBET* 21 (2003): 152–65.

McKnight, Scot. *A Community Called Atonement*. Nashville: Abingdon, 2007.

Morris, Leon. *The Cross in the New Testament*. Grand Rapids: Eerdmans, 1965.

Packer, James I. "The Logic of Penal Substitution." *TynBul* 25 (1974): 3–45.

---

163. Bruce L. McCormack, "The Ontological Presuppositions of Barth's Doctrine of the Atonement," in *The Glory of the Atonement* (ed. C. E. Hill and F. A. James; Downers Grove, IL: InterVarsity Press, 2004), 366 (italics original).
164. Cole, *God the Peacemaker*, 88–89.
165. McKnight, *Community Called Atonement*, 41.
166. Cf. Grudem (*Systematic Theology*, 575), who writes: "God ... poured out on Jesus the fury of his wrath: Jesus became the object of the intense hatred of sin and vengeance against sin which God had patiently stored up since the beginning of the world." The concepts here are not entirely wrong, but where does Scripture say that at the cross God hates Jesus or gets revenge on him? Grudem's view becomes liable to some of the criticisms that postconservative, emergent, and liberal theologians raise against penal substitution. More carefully nuanced language should be used.

evil. The $64,000 question is, which one is of these images is the first among equals? Which one ring will rule them all, or who is the big kahuna in this theological tribe?

Normally evangelicals have maintained that the primary, and therefore, most important mode of the atonement is penal substitution. Tom Schreiner maintains:

> Penal substitution is the anchor and heart of the atonement, for it reminds us that God himself is central in the universe. What God has accomplished in Jesus Christ displays both the justice and love of God because God's holiness is vindicated in the cross, while at the same time his love is displayed in the willing and glad sacrifice of his Son. Penal substitution is not all that needs to be said about the atonement, but it is the anchor of all other theories of the atonement precisely because of its God-centered focus.[167]

Sounds good; but there are two problems with this proposal. First, in the apostolic preaching summarized in Acts, the resurrection and exaltation of Jesus feature far more prominently than his death. Moreover, even when Jesus' death is mentioned at certain places in Acts, its penal and substitutionary nature is not emphasized. Now some might resign themselves to saying that Luke is simply a bad historian. His précis of apostolic preaching muddles up the message of Paul in particular, who proclaimed "Jesus Christ and him crucified" (1 Cor 2:2; cf. Gal 3:1). Luke unilaterally presses the apostle's teaching into the service of his own theological ends. In other words, Luke was a naughty boy by not giving penal substitution enough air time!

Now Luke does indeed make reference to the death of Jesus (Luke 22:20; Acts 20:28), but he carefully (and rightly) places it in the broader horizon of the saving acts of God that stretch from the history of Israel to the exaltation and return of the Messiah. Luke is more interested in Jesus' death as part of the plan and purpose of God than he is on the nitty-gritty details of how his death applies to individual believers. Still, we must ask, if penal substitution is so central, then why is it not central in Acts, which contains a Reader's Digest version of apostolic instruction? It is a jolly good question, isn't it, and it often stumps my students![168]

Second, we might also query the place of penal substitution in the theology of church history. A common liberal jibe is that no one believed in penal substitution until Anselm of Canterbury came up with his satisfaction view that he ripped off from the medieval feudal system. Anselm, so the story goes, planted the seeds for penal substitution to flower in later centuries.[169] That is a load of hokum, for, as we have already seen, penal substitution pops its head up at certain points earlier in

---

167. Schreiner, "Penal Substitution View," 93.
168. See discussion in Hurtado, *Lord Jesus Christ*, 185–88.
169. Gerald O'Collins (*Jesus Our Redeemer: A Christian Approach to Salvation* [Oxford: Oxford University Press, 2007], 132) declares: "By his theory of 'satisfaction,' St. Anselm of Canterbury (d. 1109) established an enduringly standard expression for Christ's redemptive work when understood as expiation." But note the words of Peter Schmiechen (*Saving Power: Theories of Atonement and Forms of the Church* [Grand Rapids: Eerdmans, 2005], 196): "I am in basic agreement with these criticisms of transaction theories and have raised these issues when dealing with the theories of sacrifice and penal substitution. But I disagree that Anselm is the origin of these negative values."

church history. However, admittedly, penal substitution was not the front and center of most Christian atonement theology throughout the ages, even though it was always lurking about somewhere to be seen. It was the recovery of the doctrine by the Reformers that placed the death of Jesus as a penal, vicarious, and substitutionary atonement for sins on the center stage of theology (and may I add, rightly so!).

My concern, though, is whether the penal substitutionary model carries the sufficient gravitas needed to be the one doctrine of Jesus' death that can unite the biblical and historical theologies of the atonement together. In other words, does penal substitution have the appeal to be the most centrally agreed doctrine of the atonement that exegetes, systematicians, church historians, and biblical theologians can agree on?

I tentatively propose that the Christus Victor model is the crucial integrative hub of the atonement because it provides the canopy under which the other modes of the atonement gain their currency.[170] The Christus Victor mode enables us to hold together the binary nodes that make up the substructure of the atonement, including its objective and the subjective aspects, the cosmic and the individual constituents, Christ's death and God's dominion, redemption and reprobation, incarnation and redemption, wrath and mercy, sin and salvation, triumph and tragedy, and Jesus' life and death; it also unites Christology and soteriology in the victory of God over evil. Hans Boersma is on the money when he writes:

> Christ's victory over the powers of darkness is the telos and climax of his work of recapitulation. In other words, the victory is the *result* of the entire process of recapitulation. In my understanding of the Christus Victor theme, it does not explain *how* Christ gains the victory. Christ's obedient life and his teaching, as well as his representative punishment on the cross, are what constitute the battle against Satan. It is by this means that Christ brings about the victory. There is a sense, therefore, in which the Christus Victor theme is the ultimate metaphor. Moral influence and penal representation are subordinate to Christus Victor inasmuch as they are the means towards an end.[171]

Is such a claim justified? Well, to begin with, from a canonical standpoint, I find it genuinely compelling that the first and last mention of the atonement in the biblical canon refer to Jesus' triumph over Satan by his death. In Genesis 3:15, often called the *protoevangelium*, we read: "And I will put enmity between you and the woman, and between your offspring and hers; he will crush your head, and you will strike his heel." While this verse reads as a straight-out curse of the serpent for

---

170. Robert Webber (*The Church in the World* [Grand Rapids: Zondervan, 1986], 267) believed that a new theological consensus was emerging with respect to the restoration of the *Christus Victor* model to a place of importance in atonement theology. Gregory Boyd (*God at War: The Bible and Spiritual Conflict* [Downers Grove, IL: InterVarsity Press, 1997]), writing from an open theistic position, has attempted to place the theme of divine warfare, God against evil, as the conceptual framework for understanding the atonement. Hans Boersma (*Violence, Hospitality, and the Cross: Reappropriating the Atonement Tradition* [Grand Rapids: Baker, 2004], 181) believes that *Christus Victor* is the "most significant model of the atonement."

171. Boersma, *Violence*, 181–82 (italics original).

his role in deceiving Eve, it leaves open the identities of the collective offspring of both the serpent and the woman who will be at continual enmity with each other.

Furthermore, the meanings of "crush your head" and "strike his heel" are equally opaque. This ambiguity was exploited by later Christian readers who saw in Genesis 3:15 a promise of the gospel with the text pointing ahead to the crucifixion of Jesus ("strike his heel") and Jesus' victory over Satan in his death ("crush your head"). Traditionally this is where Reformed writers such as Johannes Cocceius and Thomas Goodwin have seen the first intimations of the covenant of grace.

In addition, it is interesting that the last mention of Jesus' death in the New Testament occurs in Revelation 12, which contains a narrative that has Genesis 3:15 at its core.[172] There a woman (signifying the messianic community) gives birth to a child (the messianic deliverer) as a seven-headed red dragon (Satan) is poised to devour the infant (Jesus). Mother and child are supernaturally preserved from the malicious attacks of the dragon. Shortly thereafter, there is enmity between the woman and the dragon, which symbolizes the rage of Satan against the people of God. The dragon is violently thrown down to earth following a battle in heaven, and the dragon continues his pursuit of the woman and her seed only to be defeated by the "blood of the Lamb" (Rev 12:11). In a canonical inclusio we are given the meaning of Genesis 3:15 in Revelation 12. The skull-crushing victory of the woman's seed over the Satan is attained by the blood of Jesus Christ, which was shed for the ransom of humanity from their sins (see Rev 1:5; 5:9). It is no small fact for our evangelical theology that the canon is bracketed, at the beginning and the end, with God's design for the seed of the woman to defeat the evil one. We are told that this victory of crushing the serpent's head takes place by the blood of the Lamb.

A second factor for us to consider in favor of the Christus Victor model as the integrative motif of atonement theology is the popularity of the doctrine in Christian history. While the church fathers were far from monolithic in their atonement theology, the dominating idea seems to have been something along the lines of the Christus Victor model. Medieval theologians rehearsed the same ideas, but they also wrestled with whether the atonement had an effect that was subjective (in changing a person's inward disposition) or objective (in changing a person's status before God). It should not be forgotten that Calvin, who championed the view of Jesus' death as penal and substitutionary, also had room for the cross as a divine victory. The French Reformer commented:

> Finally, since as God only he could not suffer, and as man only could not overcome death, he united the human nature with the divine, that he might subject the weakness of the one to death as an expiation of sin, and by the power of the other, maintaining a struggle with death, might gain us the victory.... But special attention

---

172. Cf. further James Hamilton, "The Skull Crushing Seed of the Woman: Inner-Biblical Interpretation of Genesis 3:15," *SBJT* 10 (2006): 30–54 (esp. 42).

must be paid to what I lately explained, namely, that a common nature is the pledge of our union with the Son of God; that, clothed with our flesh, he warred to death with sin that he might be our triumphant conqueror.[173]

If we identify sin, death, and evil as that which believers are redeemed from, then regarding the cross as a redemptive victory enables us to construct a view of the atonement that is simultaneously catholic in breadth and Reformed in emphasis.

Third, the Christus Victor model provides a way of uniting the theme of the kingdom of God and the cross of Christ. In Isaiah, the reign of Yahweh and the salvation it brings (Isa 52) are intimately bound up with the death and vivification of the Servant of the Lord (Isa 53). In Psalms 20–22 is a compressed précis of God's victory, God's anointed king, and the vindication of the suffering righteous. Jesus proclaimed the kingdom of God and enacted it in his exorcisms and preaching (Matt 12:29; Luke 10:18). Indeed, the ruler of the world is cast out and condemned as Jesus ebbs closer and closer toward Golgotha (John 12:31; 16:11).

Yet what we find placarded on the cross at the end of the passion story is a mocking statement about the kingship of the crucified (Matt 27:37; John 19:19). The perennial problem of aligning the messages of Jesus and Paul can be resolved when we remember that the "kingdom of God" and the "righteousness of God" both denote the *victory of God* in the life, death, and resurrection of the Lord Jesus. In Revelation 5, the Lion of Judah who triumphs is none other than the Lamb who was slain. A victory–cross nexus explains the pastoral exhortations in the New Testament about resisting conformity to the pattern of this world. We overcome the world only because Jesus first overcame the world (John 16:33; 1 John 2:14; 4:4; 5:4). Christians are more than conquerors because death has been swallowed up in victory through Jesus' resurrection (Rom 8:37; 1 Cor 15:54–57). Jesus shared in our humanity so that by death he would break the power of him who holds the power of death, the devil, and so has freed us from the fear of death (Heb 2:14–15). Thus, the Christus Victor model demonstrates the unity of soteriology and eschatology in Christology.

We might also consider the dimension of new creation in the Christus Victor model in light of the remarks of Timothy Gombis:

> Paul tells the story in Ephesians 2 of God beginning to fulfill his promises to reclaim and redeem his creation, restoring his world and humanity to their original condition. The whole world was meant to be God's temple, according to the biblical narrative, as God dwelled with humanity and delighted in humanity's enjoyment of creation. After the fall and the tragic corruption of creation, God promises to make

---

173. *Institutes* 2.12.2–3. Calvin also wrote: "And so, by fighting hand to hand with the power of the Devil, with the horror of death, he won the victory over them and triumphed, so that now in our death we should not fear those things which our Prince has swallowed up" (*Institutes* 2.16.11). See Robert A. Peterson, *Calvin's Doctrine of the Atonement* (Phillipsburg, NJ: Presbyterian & Reformed, 1983), 46–54.

all things new and to return with his life-giving presence. These promises are now being fulfilled in the church and will one day be fulfilled creation-wide. This is why Paul quotes Psalm 110 in Ephesians 1:22. God has installed his King on his heavenly throne, and Jesus Christ has begun his work of reclaiming his world. The powers and authorities had rebelled, hijacking God's good world, and have held it in their oppressive and enslaving grip. But God has broken their hold in Jesus Christ and is magnifying his victory through the church. God has triumphed by opening up a sphere within creation that is the beginning of God's work of making all things new.[174]

Fourth, Paul provides a standing template for how victory and sacrifice go together. His major eschatological discourses in Romans 8 and 1 Corinthians 15 both begin by highlighting the saving significance of Jesus' death in the gospel, but he then proceeds to the climactic announcement that God's victory has been given to his people.

Romans 8	1 Corinthians 15
[1]Therefore, there is now no condemnation for those who are in Christ Jesus, [2]because through Christ Jesus the law of the Spirit who gives life has set you free from the law of sin and death. [3]For what the law was powerless to do because it was weakened by the sinful flesh, God did by sending his own Son in the likeness of flesh to be a sin offering. And *so he condemned sin in the flesh*, [4]in order that the righteous requirement of the law might be fully met in us, who do not live according to the flesh but according to the Spirit....	[2]By this gospel you are saved, if you hold firmly to the word I preached to you. Otherwise, you have believed in vain. [3]For what I received I passed on to you as of first importance: that *Christ died for our sins according to the Scriptures*, [4]that he was buried, that he was raised on the third day according to the Scriptures, [5]and that he appeared to Cephas, and then to the Twelve....
[35]Who shall separate us from the love of Christ? Shall trouble or hardship or persecution or famine or nakedness or danger or sword? [36]As it is written: "For your sake we face death all day long; we are considered as sheep to be slaughtered." [37]*No, in all these things we are more than conquerors through him who loved us.* [38]For I am convinced that neither death nor life, neither angels nor demons, neither the present nor the future, nor any powers, [39]neither height nor depth, nor anything else in all creation, will be able to separate us from the love of God that is in Christ Jesus our Lord.	[54]When the perishable has been clothed with the imperishable, and the mortal with immortality, then the saying that is written will come true: "Death has been swallowed up in victory." [55]"Where, O death, is your victory? Where, O death, is your sting?" [56]The sting of death is sin, and the power of sin is the law. [57]*But thanks be to God! He gives us the victory through our Lord Jesus Christ.* [58]Therefore, my dear brothers and sisters, stand firm. Let nothing move you. Always give yourselves fully to the work of the Lord, because you know that your labor in the Lord is not in vain. (italics added in both columns)

---

174. Timothy Gombis, *The Drama of Ephesians: Participating in the Triumph of God* (Downers Grove, IL: InterVarsity Press, 2010), 105.

The Christus Victor model places Jesus' death in its proper coordinates as an apocalyptic event that reveals God's rescue plan against the evil powers (see Gal 1:4). Evidently Jesus' substitutionary death constitutes the basis and center of the divine victory—a victory not only against sin but also against Satan. Henri Blocher points out that "accusation" is the devil's chief weapon; so once the sacrifice is paid, once justice is satisfied, and once sin is expiated, Satan is deprived of his power to accuse the saints (Rev 12:10).[175] I would add that in Colossians 2:13–15 the victory of the cross over the powers is achieved by the forgiveness of sins from the written charge against believers. Thus Jesus' substitutionary death for sinners is the means to the cosmic triumph of God's purposes for God's people leading to God's new creation.

This seems to mesh with the theological contours of Romans 8 and 1 Corinthians 15 that move from atonement to triumph. To put that differently, because Jesus is the *Agnus Dei* ("Lamb of God"), he is also the *Christus Victor* ("Christ Victorious"). To appeal to a different genre, in the movie *Transformers* (2007 [directed by Michael Bay]) the motto of the film is, "No victory without sacrifice." That is true of the gospel as well, with the qualification that Jesus' sacrifice constitutes the basis of the divine victory. The divine victory is the goal of the atonement and Jesus' sacrificial death is the means to it. As John Murray wrote:

> Redemption from sin cannot be adequately conceived or formulated except as it comprehends the victory which Christ secured once for all over him who is the god of this world, the prince of the power of the air.... It is impossible to speak in terms of redemption from the power of sin except as there comes within the range of this redemptive accomplishment the destruction of the powers of darkness.[176]

I do not wish to disparage Jesus' death as an atoning, vicarious, substitutionary, and penal sacrifice for sin. However, I am convinced that Jesus' death for sinners on the cross is part of a bigger picture that is laid out in redemptive history, visible in the very shape of our canon, apparent in biblical theology, ubiquitous in historical theology, and explicit in Pauline theology. The doctrines of penal substitution and Christus Victor do not compete against each other, for the former is clearly the grounds for the latter. Athanasius combined the two perspectives when he referred to the marvel of the cross, where Jesus offered up his body in the place of everyone and for everyone, and thereby brought the devil's power to ruin (*Incarnation* 20.5–6). What binds together new exodus, new creation, Jesus' ministry, the cross, and the mission of God's people in the world is the victory of God in the substitutionary death of Jesus. Graham Cole said in an online interview:

---

175. Henri Blocher, "The Sacrifice of Jesus Christ: The Current Theological Situation," *EJTh* 8 (1999): 31.

176. John Murray, *Redemption Accomplished and Applied* (Grand Rapids: Eerdmans, 1955), 50.

> It seems to me that following the biblical plotline, the first note struck is the Christus Victor one (i.e., the defeat of evil) in the *protevangelium* (first gospel) set out in Genesis 3:15. But how is the evil one defeated? The grounds of accusation need to be removed that stand against us, and the fear of death that is the devil's tool needs to be addressed as well. The cross of Christ disarms the evil one by removing the grounds of accusation against us (Col 2). Christ died in our place (1 Pet 2), experienced the righteous divine wrath that we deserve (Rom 5) and so, if we are in Christ, there is no condemnation (Rom 8). Because we stand clothed in Christ's righteousness we will not face the divine judgment of the great white throne for our sins (Rev 20). Our names are in the Lamb's book of life. The fear of death, which lies in judgment, is thereby addressed (Heb 2). Evangelicals in my view need to do more justice to the Christus Victor theme and in so doing find that penal substitution is integral or central to it.[177]

The worship of the believing community recites the "victories of the LORD" (Judg 5:11), and in the new covenant context that takes the specific shape of remembering Jesus' death and resurrection (Luke 22:19; 1 Cor 11:24–25). On that doctrine we may bind up the loincloths of our mind, put on the apron of a servant, and get busy exemplifying a faith that, in the words of the author of Hebrews, conquers kingdoms, dispenses justice, and gains what is promised (Heb 11:33).

Let us remember too that the Lordship of Jesus Christ is the Lordship of the crucified Nazarene. For John Stott, although Jesus was "crushed by the ruthless power of Rome, he was himself crushing the serpent's head.... The victim was the victor, and the cross is still the throne from which he rules the world."[178] At the heart of our hopes for the future, what drives our concept of theodicy, and what motivates a Christian political theology is the belief that the cross is the triumph of God. The death of the slaughtered lamb is a strange victory; yet on it hangs the final sentence against evil, the vanquishing of injustice, and the redemption of sinners. I can think of no better conclusion to a chapter on the atonement other than John Chrysostom's famous Paschal Homily. It is a sermon that is read every Easter in Orthodox churches to this day:

> He has destroyed death by undoing death.
> He has despoiled hell by descending into hell.
> He vexed it even as it tasted of His flesh.
> Isaiah foretold this when he cried:
> Hell was filled with bitterness when it met Thee face to face below;
> Filled with bitterness, for it was brought to nothing;
> Filled with bitterness, for it was mocked;

---

177. Andy Naselli, "Graham Cole's Book on the Atonement," *The Gospel Coalition*. 5 Aug 2009. http://thegospelcoalition.org/blogs/justintaylor/2009/08/05/graham-coles-book-on-atonement/. Accessed 5 April 2011.

178. John Stott, *Why I Am a Christian* (Leicester, UK: Inter-Varsity Press, 2003), 61.

> Filled with bitterness, for it was overthrown;
> Filled with bitterness, for it was put in chains
> Hell received a body, and encountered God.
> It received earth and confronted heaven.
> O death, where is your sting?
> O hell, where is your victory?[179]

4.4.3 THE EXTENT OF THE ATONEMENT

The final question we face here is not *how* Jesus' death effects atonement, but for *whom* his death avails. One might appeal immediately and sensibly to John 3:16 and say that Jesus died for the sins of the whole world since the entire world is the object of God's love in the Son. Alas, all is not so simple. The logic of the atonement according to the Reformed scheme is that Jesus died, not for the whole world, but exclusively for the elect. That "logic" is contested by Arminian, Wesleyan, and Pietist theologians, who stress the universality of God's love and the universal availability of redemption through the offer of the gospel. In fact, the question "for whom did Christ die?" has been a divisive topic between churches:

- It separated Lutherans from the Reformed churches in Protestant countries.
- It separated the Remonstrants (Arminians) from the Reformed churches in the Netherlands.
- It separated the Amyraldians from the Reformed churches in France.
- It separated the Particular Baptists from the General Baptists in Britain.
- It has also been an issue associated with hyper-Calvinism and prompted debates about whether you should only preach the gospel to people who show signs of election.

The fact is, however, that everyone believes in some kind of limitation to the atonement. The atonement is limited either by effect or by design, what it achieves or for whom it achieves it. Consider the following two questions:

1. Was the purpose of the atonement to make salvation
   a. possible for everyone?
      or
   b. actual for some?

If we adopt (a), we would say that the atonement makes salvation a potentiality for everyone but is absolutely certain for no one unless the atonement is received with faith and repentance. If we accept (b), we could surmise that the atonement

---

179. Cited in McKnight, *Community Called Atonement*, 105.

> ## IN A NUTSHELL: WHAT DID THE CROSS ACHIEVE?
>
> - A ransom for sins (Matt 20:28; Mark 10:45)
> - Protection from the tribulation and future judgment (Matt 23:37–39)
> - Institution of the new covenant (Mark 14:22–25 and par.)
> - Restoration of Israel and drawing the nations into the family of Abraham (Mark 9:12; Luke 1:68; 2:38; John 11:51–52; Acts 3:18–21; 13:25–29; Gal 3:13; Rev 5:9–10)
> - Rescue from the kingdom of darkness and the present evil age (Gal 1:4; Col 1:13)
> - Reconciliation (Rom 5:10–11; 2 Cor 5:18–20; Eph 2:16; Col 1:20, 22)
> - Redemption (Rom 3:24; 8:23; 1 Cor 1:30; 7:23; Gal 3:13; 4:5; Eph 1:7, 14; Col 1:14; Heb 9:12; Titus 2:14; 1 Pet 1:18; Rev 5:9)
> - Justification (Rom 3:24; 5:9; Gal 2:21)
> - Forgiveness of sins (Matt 26:28; Luke 1:77; 23:24; Acts 2:38; 5:31; 10:43; 13:38; 26:18; Eph 1:7; Col 1:14; 3:13; Heb 9:22; 1 John 1:9; Rev 1:6)
> - Peace (Isa 53:5; Acts 10:36; Rom 5:1; Eph 2:14–17; Col 1:20)
> - Healing (Exod 15:26; Isa 53:5; Mal 4:2; 1 Pet 2:24)
> - Cleansing (1 Cor 6:11; Titus 2:14; Heb 1:3; 9:14–22; 10:2, 22; 1 John 1:7, 9; 2 Pet 1:9; Rev 7:14)
> - An example to be followed (Phil 2:5–11; 1 Pet 2:21; Heb 12:1–4)
>
> In light of this, we can say that the atonement is the climax of God's project to put the world to right through the cross of Jesus. The atonement brings God's people into God's place under God's reign to share in God's holy, loving glory on account of the love demonstrated in the cross and the justice satisfied on the cross.

guarantees salvation but that salvation would only be for the elect whom God intended to save in the first place. As such we can ask now:

2. Is the atonement limited by
   a. effect?
      or
   b. scope?

Answer 1a implies 2a, whereby the atonement is limited by its effect as it does not guarantee the salvation of anyone but it makes salvation possible for everyone.

Answer 1b implies 2b whereby the atonement is limited in scope as it was not designed to save everyone; only the elect can be saved through the cross, but they definitely will be saved. So which one is it? Well, there are three main views to choose from:

- Limited atonement view: Jesus died for the elect (Reformed)
- Universal atonement view: Jesus died for the entire world (Arminian)
- Armyraldian view: Jesus made atonement possible for all, but effective only for the elect (Calvinist lite)

As will be clear, I stand in the Armyraldian tradition as I opt for a Reformed view of the effectiveness of Christ's death that also accommodates the cosmic scope of what the cross achieves in biblical testimony.

4.4.3.1 LIMITED ATONEMENT VIEW

Limited atonement is the "L" in the acronym TULIP. However, "limited atonement" is a rather negative way of putting it. It is much better to speak of "particular" or "deliberate" redemption by which theologians mean that Jesus' death accomplishes what it set out to achieve, namely, the redemption of the elect. The emphasis is not on exclusion but on the efficacy of the atonement for the elect when they turn to Christ in faith. Limited atonement is said to be the logical outworking of the doctrine of election. Charles Hodge avers:

> If God from eternity determined to save one portion of the human race and not another, it seems to be a contradiction to say that the plan of salvation had equal reference to both portions; that the Father sent his Son to die for those whom He had predetermined not to save, as truly as, and in the same sense that He gave Him up for those whom He had chosen to make the heirs of salvation.[180]

Contrary to widespread assumptions, deliberate redemption was not invented by John Calvin. Basil of Caesarea (330–79) said at one point that the Lord Jesus Christ "poured out His blood for the Churches' sake."[181] Theodoret of Cyrus (393–466), commenting on Heb 9:27–28, said: "It should be noted, of course, that Christ bore the sins of many, not all, and not all came to faith. So He removed the sins of the believers only."[182] Even after Augustine the notion of a limited or deliberate aspect to the atonement restricted in its benefits to the church persisted during the Middle Ages.[183] Yet it is to Calvin that most look to for the mature formation of this doctrine. Despite some ambiguity on the matter that can be exploited in Calvin's com-

---

180. Charles Hodge, *Systematic Theology* (3 vols.; London: James Clarke, 1960 [1841]), 2:538.
181. Basil of Caesarea, *Letters* 229.1.
182. Theodoret, *Interpretation of Hebrews* 9.
183. Cited in Jaroslav Pelikan, *The Christian Tradition: A History of the Development of Doctrine* (4 vols.; Chicago: University of Chicago Press, 1971), 1:320–31.

mentaries on Ezekiel 18:23; John 3:16; Romans 5:10; and 2 Peter 3:9 and his sermons on Isaiah 53; 1 Timothy 2:3–5; and 2 Timothy 2:19,[184] it seems that Calvin held to something akin to deliberate redemption. Hence his words:

> For our present question is, not what the power or virtue of Christ is, nor what *efficacy it has in itself,* but *who those are* to whom he gives Himself to be enjoyed. Now if the possession of Christ stands in faith, and if faith flows from the Spirit of adoption, it follows that he alone is numbered of God among His children who is designed of God to be a partaker of Christ. Indeed the evangelist John sets forth the office of Christ to be none other than that of "gathering together all the children of God" in one by His death. From all which we conclude that, although reconciliation is offered unto all men through him, yet, that *the great benefit belongs peculiarly to the elect,* that they might be "gathered together" and be made "together" partakers of eternal life.[185]

Catching this wave of deliberate redemption, the Westminster Confession 8.8 states: "To all those for whom Christ has purchased redemption, He does certainly and effectually apply and communicate the same." This strongly implies that the benefits of Jesus' death are applied only to the elect. Later the most vocal (and sometimes vitriolic) defender of deliberate redemption was the English Puritan John Owen (1616–83). Owen's book *The Death of Death in the Death of Christ* (1647) is the singularly most potent and popular expression of the doctrine of deliberate redemption.[186] For Owen the atonement was planned, accomplished, and applied by the Triune God for the sake of the elect. Father and Son shared the same mission and will for the atonement, Jesus' death achieved that will, and the divine will pertains to the salvation of the elect. Owen sets forth the logic of deliberate atonement, exegetes key texts, attacks the notion of general atonement, and answers objections. Perhaps a good example of his argumentation is with these words:

> If Christ died in the stead of all men, and made satisfaction for their sins, then he did it for all their sins, or only for some of their sins. If for some only, who then can be saved? If for all, why then are all not saved? They say it is because of their unbelief; they will not believe, and therefore are not saved. That unbelief, is it a sin, or is it not? If it be not, how can it be a cause of damnation? If it be, Christ died for it, or he did not. If he did not, then he died not for all the sins of all men. If he did, why is this an obstacle to their salvation? Is there any new shift to be invented for this? Or must we be contented with the old, namely, because they do not believe? That is, Christ did not die for their unbelief, or rather, did not by his death remove their unbelief,

---

184. Cf. R. T. Kendall, *Calvin and English Calvinism to 1649* (Carlisle, UK: Paternoster, 1997), 13–18.

185. John Calvin, *A Treatise on the Eternal Predestination of God* (trans. H. Cole; London: Sovereign Grace Union, 1927), 165–66 (italics added); see www.reformed.org/documents/calvin/calvin_predestination.html.

186. John Owen, *The Death of Death in the Death of Christ* (with preface by J. I. Packer; London: Banner of Truth, 1959). Citations are from *Works of John Owen* (ed. William H. Goold; Carlisle, PA: Banner of Truth, 1967).

because they would not believe, or because they would not themselves remove their unbelief; or he died for their unbelief conditionally, that they were not unbelievers. These do not seem to me to be sober assertions.[187]

Owen's arguments are fairly cogent most of the time, though he does have a propensity to engage in strong polemics. For example, he wrote that universal atonement "seems to us blasphemously injurious to the wisdom, power, and perfection of God, as likewise derogatory to the worth and value of the death of Christ."[188] Truth be told, his verbose rant is not always the best billboard for deliberate redemption.[189] A much warmer and pastoral approach to deliberate redemption, though no less forthright, is that given by Charles Spurgeon:

> We are often told that we limit the atonement of Christ, because we say that Christ has not made satisfaction for all men, or all men would be saved. Now, our reply to this is that, on the other hand, our opponents limit it, we do not. The Arminians say, Christ died for all men. Ask them what they mean by it. Did Christ die so as to secure the salvation of all men? They say, "No, certainly not." We ask them the next question — Did Christ die so as to secure the salvation of any man in particular? They say, "No." They are obliged to admit this if they are consistent. They say, "No; Christ has died so that any man may be saved if" — and then follow certain conditions of salvation. We say then, we will just go back to the old statement — Christ did not die so as beyond a doubt to secure the salvation of anybody, did He? You must say "No"; you are obliged to say so, for you believe that even after a man has been pardoned, he may yet fall from grace and perish. Now, who is it that limits the death of Christ? Why you.... We say Christ so died that He infallibly secured the salvation of a multitude that no man can number, who through Christ's death not only may be saved, but are saved, must be saved, and cannot by any possibility run the hazard of being anything but saved. You are welcome to your atonement; you may keep it. We will never renounce ours for the sake of it.[190]

Deliberate redemption has not lacked contemporary advocates.[191] The question is whether it has biblical support. Advocates usually point to a cohort of texts in defense of its position. Beginning with the Old Testament one could point out that the goat sacrificed on the Day of Atonement was for the sins of the elect nation and not for the sins of the whole world, which suggests that atonement from the beginning has been for the elect and is not universal in its design (Lev 16:21–22; cf. Deut 21:8; 1 Chr 6:49; Neh 10:33; Ezek 45:17). The problem, however, is that the sacri-

---

187. Owen, *Death of Death*, 249.
188. Ibid., 159.
189. For an excellent survey, analysis, and response to Owen, see the sympathetic treatment by Andrew D. Naselli, "John Owen's Argument for Definite Atonement in *The Death of Death in the Death of Christ*: A Summary and Evaluation," *SBJT* 14 (2010): 60–83. Available on-line at http://andynaselli.com/wp-content/uploads/2010_Owen.pdf.
190. Cited in James Montgomery Boice and Philip Ryken, *The Doctrines of Grace* (Wheaton, IL: Crossway, 2009), 117.
191. Grudem, *Systematic Theology*, 594–603; Horton, *Christian Faith*, 516–20; Jeffery, Ovey, and Sach, *Pierced for Our Transgression*, 271–78.

fices of the Old Testament were inferior to and preparatory for the death of Christ, so we should not expect an exact correlation between the two. What is more, non-Hebrew people in the midst of the Israelites (e.g., aliens and slaves) could partake of the festivals that involved sacrifices like Passover.

In the Gospels, we read that an angel reported to Joseph, "She will give birth to a son, and you are to give him the name Jesus, because *he will save his people from their sins* (Matt 1:21, italics added); this passage suggests that Jesus' mission is to save a particular people. Again, in counterpoint, by the time we get to the end of Matthew, Jesus' death has certainly transcended the ethnic boundaries of Israel's election and his saving work can embrace "all nations" (Matt 28:19–20).

Another favorite text of limited atonement advocates is where Jesus said: "For even the Son of Man did not come to be served, but to serve, and to give his life as a ransom for *many*" (Mark 10:45, italics added; cf. Matt 20:28). It is emphasized that "many" is not "everyone." Yet "many" is an inclusive Semitism for "all Israel" derived from the background in Isaiah 53:11 and should not be violently juxtaposed with "a ransom for all" in 1 Timothy 2:6. The main point is the effectiveness of Jesus' death as a ransom, not on a limitation on those for whom it is effective for. R. T. France states: "A Theology of 'limited atonement' is far from the intention of this passage and would be anachronistic in this context."[192]

Much is also made of Jesus' intercession for the elect according to John's Gospel: "I pray for them. I am not praying for the world, but for those you have given me, for they are yours" (John 17:9). Though this certainly indicates Jesus' priestly intercession for his chosen ones, it is hardly restricts the effects of his death to a few or denies that others are included within the orbit of its saving power. For Jesus is the one mediator between God and all "mankind" (1 Tim 2:5).

In Paul's speech to the Ephesian elders, he exhorts them: "Keep watch over yourselves and all the flock of which the Holy Spirit has made you overseers. Be shepherds of the *church of God, which he bought with his own blood*" (Acts 20:28, italics added throughout this paragraph). Similarly in his letter to Ephesians, Paul writes: "Husbands, love your wives, *just as Christ loved the church and gave himself up for her*" (Eph 5:25). These Pauline materials are similar to the gospel of John, which includes the words: "I am the good shepherd; I know my sheep and my sheep know me—just as the Father knows me and I know the Father—and *I lay down my life for the sheep*" (John 10:14–15). In the farewell discourse, Jesus says: "Greater love has no one than this: *to lay down one's life for one's friends*" (John 15:13). Here Jesus clearly dies for the church; even so, none of these texts say that he dies *only and exclusively* for the

---

192. R. T. France, *The Gospel of Matthew* (NICNT; Grand Rapids: Eerdmans, 2007), 763.

church.¹⁹³ But even if Jesus died only for the church, the church and the elect are not exact equivalents if you believe, as many do, that the church is an *ecclesia mixta* that includes both the regenerate and the unregenerate in its ranks.

So what do advocates of deliberate redemption do with texts that provide a universal scope to the atonement? Passages like "God so loved the world that he gave his one and only Son" (John 3:16); "he is the atoning sacrifice for our sins, and not only for ours but also for the sins of the whole world" (1 John 2:2); and Christ "gave himself as a ransom for all" (1 Tim 2:6). Deliberate redemption proponents explain these texts in several ways. (1) The "world" means "sinners generally," so Jesus is the Lamb of God who takes away the sin of sinners in general (John 1:29). But this needlessly generalizes what is a specific propositional claim that Jesus' death encompasses the entire world.

(2) That Christ died "for" the whole world is understood to mean that Jesus died so that the free offer of the gospel can be made to all people (John 6:51; 1 John 2:2). That is a half truth. Jesus died so that an offer can be made, but it is only a genuine offer if people can actually receive its benefits. Yet if Jesus' death is designed for no one else beyond the elect, the universal offer of the gospel is a bit pointless, like offering a guy with no teeth a prime rib steak.

(3) Passages that refer Jesus' death for "all" are taken to mean "all without distinction" or "all kinds of people" (2 Cor 5:14–15; 1 Tim 2:6; 4:10).¹⁹⁴ Here "all" is reinterpreted to mean all subclasses within the world, which stretches the meaning of "all" to the breaking point. Given these failings, I think that D. B. Knox was right when he called limited atonement "a textless doctrine" since it lacks biblical justification, and such a state is "a fatal defect for any doctrine for which a place in Reformed theology is sought."¹⁹⁵

Now there is something resolutely right about deliberate redemption. Christ came to save sinners, and he actually saves them. He does not throw a rope to people sinking in a swamp and invite them to take hold of the rope; no, he jumps into the swamp, ties the sinking wretches to himself, and he drags them out of the swamp with him. I do not imagine that after ascending to heaven, Jesus took his seat next to the Father and said, "Okay Dad, I did my bit, I hope this works." Jesus came to make salvation actual for the elect, not just possible for all; this is a key tenet of evangelical theology because it assures us that God's saving purposes will be achieved.

At the same time, however, there is something suspiciously wrong here. There is a piece of the puzzle that doesn't seem to fit. One of the keys on the piano is slightly

---

193. Contra Grudem (*Systematic Theology*, 600), who says such texts are not "naturally interpreted in this way," by which he means a particularizing of redemption.

194. Grudem, *Systematic Theology*, 598–600; Jeffery, Ovey, and Sach, *Pierced for Our Transgression*, 274–75.

195. D. B. Knox, "Some Aspects of the Atonement," 263, 266.

out of tune. Proponents of deliberate redemption have not sufficiently explained the universal dimension of the atonement beyond vague platitudes that it might somehow benefit others in theory, though not in reality. Their explanation of "all people" as "all kinds of people" does not stand in coherent alignment with biblical references to Christ's work as including the entire world in its scope. Yes, Jesus executed the eternal will of the Triune God to save the elect; however, there is also a desire to unite God with creation through the Logos, so that God is all in all.

4.4.3.2 UNIVERSAL ATONEMENT VIEW

The view called universal atonement declares that Jesus died for the sins of every person who has lived and will ever live. Moreover, Jesus died for all in the same way and to the same extent. The atonement, however, only becomes effective for a person when they choose to believe in Jesus for salvation. A large number of texts are often paraded out to support universal atonement:

> The next day John saw Jesus coming toward him and said, "Look, *the Lamb of God, who takes away the sin of the world!*" (John 1:29)

> For Christ's love compels us, because we are convinced that *one died for all, and therefore all died*. And he died for all, that those who live should no longer live for themselves but *for him who died for them and was raised again*. (2 Cor 5:14–15)

> All this is from God, who reconciled us to himself through Christ and gave us the ministry of reconciliation: that *God was reconciling the world to himself in Christ*, not counting people's sins against them. And he has committed to us the message of reconciliation. (2 Cor 5:18–19)

> This is good, and pleases God our Savior, who *wants all people to be saved* and to come to a knowledge of the truth. For there is *one God and one mediator between God and mankind*, the man Christ Jesus, *who gave himself as a ransom for all people*. This has now been witnessed to at the proper time. (1 Tim 2:3–6)

> That is why we labor and strive, because we have put our hope in the living God, *who is the Savior of all people, and especially of those who believe*. (1 Tim 4:10)

> For the grace of God has appeared that *offers salvation to all people*. (Titus 2:11)

> But we do see Jesus, who was made lower than the angels for a little while, now crowned with glory and honor because he suffered death, so that *by the grace of God he might taste death for everyone*. (Heb 2:9)

> He is the atoning sacrifice for our sins, and *not only for ours but also for the sins of the whole world*. (1 John 2:2)

> And we have seen and testify that the Father has sent his Son *to be the Savior of the world*. (1 John 4:14, italics added in all cases)

This view is one that had widespread support in the church fathers. Let me give a few examples: Cyril of Jerusalem (315–386) taught: "And wonder not that the whole world was ransomed; for it was no mere man, but the only-begotten Son of God, who died on its behalf."[196] Gregory of Nazianzus (324–389) wrote about Jesus' death: "He sets us free, who were held captive under sin, giving Himself a Ransom for us, the Sacrifice to make expiation for the world."[197] Finally, Basil of Caesarea (330–379) noted: "The Lord was bound to taste of death for every man—to become a propitiation for the world and to justify all men by His own blood."[198]

Fundamental to universal atonement is the notion of divine love. God sets forth Christ to be a sacrifice for the sins of the world only because God loves the world (John 3:16). Now if Christ is the perfect incarnation of the character of God, the answer to the question, "For whom did Christ die?" becomes theologically self-evident: Jesus died for the world whom God created and loves.[199] Now real love must be freely given and freely received. The love of Christ shown on the cross must be appropriated if it is to be effected. Charles Ryrie gives a cute illustration of how universal atonement must be particularly appropriated.

> An illustration: In one school where I have taught, the student aid was handled in this way. People make gifts to the student aid fund. Needy students apply for help from that fund. A committee decided who will receive aid and how much. But when the actual money is distributed, it is done by issuing a check to the student who then is expected to endorse it back to the school which will then place the credit on his account. The money was not moved directly from the aid fund to the individual student's account. The student had to receive it personally and place it on his account. Let us suppose you gave a gift to cover one student's tuition for one year. You could properly say that his tuition was fully paid. But until the selection is made by the committee, and until the student receives the gift and places it on his account, his tuition is not paid. If he fails to endorse the check, it will never be paid even though it has been paid! The death of Christ pays for all the sins of all people. But not one individual has his own account settled until he believes. If he never believes, then even though the price has been fully paid, his sins will not be forgiven. The death of Christ is like some benefactor paying the tuitions of all students in all schools everywhere. If that could be true, what should we be telling students? The good news that their tuitions are paid. Christ died for all. What should we be telling the world?[200]

There are, however, some problems with universal atonement. First, as we saw earlier, there are some texts that refer to the benefits of Christ's death being applied specifically to his friends, followers, sheep, and church. That might be because

---

196. Cyril of Jerusalem, *Catechetical Lectures* 13.2.
197. Gregory Nazianzus, *Orat. Bas.* 30.20.
198. Basil of Caesarea, *Letter* 260.9.
199. I owe this point to a blog exchange with Ben Witherington III.
200. Charles Ryrie, *Basic Theology* (Wheaton, IL: Victor, 1986), 323.

believers are simply part of the world for whom Christ died. We must ask, however, if God knew who would believe in him, by divine election or by foreknowledge, would he not therefore design to make the atonement effective for such people as opposed to simply possible for everyone? The tension here is how we integrate God's universal love with his specific purposes for the atonement. The Arminian view runs the danger of overemphasizing divine love at the expense of divine purpose.

Second, there is also an accounting problem. If Jesus died for the sins of the world, then regardless of whether people believe it or not, the debt has been paid and the sinner is free from sin's penalty. How can God threaten anyone with judgment if their sin has been paid in full? Universal atonement could imply universalism. Christ died for all and so all will be saved — the exact argument that universalists use and one that has a logical consistency. Arminians respond that the atonement must be appropriated by faith in order to be effective. But if I pay someone's mortgage for them, the bank cannot demand payment from that person regardless of whether they know that their mortgage has been paid and irrespective of whether they thank me for it. How can a subjective response trigger the objective reality of a debt being paid?

In addition, if God does punish sinners with eternal judgment despite the fact that Christ died for all sinners, it seems that we have double payment. God is punishing sin twice, once in the death of Christ, and then again at the final judgment. Thus, critics of universal atonement have pointed out that universal atonement leads logically to universalism, or else they suggest it makes God unjust by extracting payment against sin twice. As a result Arminian theologians must affirm that the atonement is limited in some sense in order to avoid universalism and double payment. Normally they argue that the atonement is sufficient for all but efficient only for the elect — the elect being those who freely chose to believe. While the atonement is indeed universal, its application is conditional upon faith and repentance.[201]

4.4.3.3 AMYRALDIAN VIEW

The Amyraldian view attempts to combine a Calvinist view of election with a universal view of the atonement. The view is named after Moyse Amyraut (1596–1664), who was professor of theology at the Academy of Saumer in France. This academy was the most influential school of French Protestantism of the day. Amyraut was committed to the Calvinist doctrines, but he wanted to soften the harshness of predestination and imbibe into Reformed theology a concern for God's universal grace to all mankind.

---

201. Paige Patterson, "The Work of Christ," in *A Theology for the Church* (ed. D. L. Atkin; Nashville: Broadman & Holman, 2007), 584–87.

His contemporaries accused him of heading toward Arminianism, a charge that Amyraut denied, and he was tried for heresy three times but never actually condemned.[202]

Amyraut's views are set out in his *Eschantillon de la doctrine de Calvin touchant la predestination* (1636), where he developed a system of covenant theology beyond the normal covenant of grace and covenant of works scheme. Amyraut argued for a tripartite covenantal structure ordered around God's covenant of nature with creation, God's covenant of works with Israel, and the covenant of grace between God and humanity. The covenant of grace had two parts: a conditional covenant of universal grace and an unconditional covenant of particular grace. The actualization of the universal grace covenant required the condition of faith. The covenant of particular grace did not simply call for faith; rather, in God's good pleasure, he created faith in the elect.

Hence, Amyraldianism implies a twofold will of God, whereby he wills both the salvation of all people on condition of faith, but he also wills the salvation of the elect by imparting faith. The theological conundrum of God's will having been seemingly frustrated by the fact that not all are saved is met by the response that God only willed their salvation on the condition of faith. Where a person has no faith, God has not willed the salvation of that person.[203] Positing a universal dimension to God's covenanting activity meant that Amyraut was able to make a provision for universal atonement. According to Roger Nicole:

> Amyraut held that God, moved by compassion for the plight of fallen mankind, designed to save all men and sent His Son Jesus Christ as a substitutionary offering for the sins of all men and of every man—this is Amyraut's *universalism*. This sacrifice is not effectual unto salvation, however, unless God's offer of grace is accepted by man in repentance and faith, which acceptance is the fruit of God's special grace, conferred on those only whom He has chosen—this is the *hypothetical* aspect of Amyraut's view.[204]

The Anglican tradition has been Amyraldian in the sense of affirming both divine predestination and universal atonement (The Thirty-Nine Articles, §§17 and 31). Great leaders such J. C. Ryle, Charles Simeon, and John Newton advocated a view of universal atonement in conjunction with a deeply rooted Calvinism. D. B. Knox, a much-neglected Australian Anglican theologian, stands in this tradition of

---

202. Cf. B. A. Demarest, "Amyraldianism," in *EDT*, 41–42.

203. Andrew McGowan, "Amyraldianism," in *The Dictionary of Historical Theology* (ed. T. Hart and R. Bauckham; Grand Rapids: Eerdmans, 2000), 12.

204. Roger Nicole, "Moyse Amyraut (1596–1664) and the Controversy on Universal Grace, First Phase (1634–1637)" (PhD diss., Harvard University, 1966), 3–4. Oliver D. Crisp (*God Incarnate: Explorations in Christology* [London: T&T Clark, 2009], 44) summarizes the Amyrialdian (Saumerian) view this way: "God ordains an initial universal election of all human beings that is conditional upon each human being responding to the divine call by faith and appropriating the means of salvation. However, foreseeing that this decree would fail, on account of the fact that not all fallen human beings will respond to the universal call to salvation, God subsequently decrees the salvation of some particular number of fallen persons whom he effectually calls through the work of the Holy Spirit. The latter decree is unconditional and effectual."

Anglican Amyraldians.[205] For Knox, the work of Christ extends uniformly to the whole of humanity, and this is clear when based around certain theological heads.

1. *Incarnation.* When Christ took on human nature, he assumed the nature that all people share, not just the nature of the elect.
2. *Christ's perfect righteousness.* When Christ perfectly obeyed the law of God, he fulfilled the obligation that rests on all people equally, not just the obligations of the elect alone.
3. *Christ's victory.* When Jesus defeated Satan on the cross, he defeated the enemy of all humanity, not just the enemy of the elect.
4. *Christ's bearing of the curse.* On the cross, Jesus bore the curse that God threatens against all the breakers of his covenant, not the curse that is applicable only to the elect.

In other words, the work of Christ, apart from its application, is coextensive with humanity and it is sufficient for all.[206]

For Knox, therefore, the preacher is perfectly justified to tell his audience that "Christ died for you." Everyone has an equal interest in the death of Christ. If it were not so, it would be impossible for there to be a universal offer of the gospel. For the offer to be universal, it must rest on equally universal and adequate grounds for those to whom the offer is made. The gospel is offered to all because Christ died for all. The Arminian and Calvinist are right in what they affirm, but wrong in what they deny. The Arminian is right that Christ renders all people savable, but denies that he actually saves any. The Calvinist is right that God saves the elect, but speaks as if the atonement in no apparent way affects the savableness of others. However, the elect and nonelect are made savable by Christ's death for humanity, but only the elect receive the necessary grace for the work of Christ to be applied to them.[207] Knox concludes:

> The object of the doctrine of limited atonement is to ensure the truth that Christ's death saves his people effectively, as against the Arminian doctrine of general redemption, which holds that by the atonement Christ redeems all men, without necessarily effecting the salvation of any. But while rightly stressing that the atonement saves those whom God intends it to save, we should not speak of the substitution of Christ on Calvary in such a way as to overthrow other Scriptural points of view. Limited atonement as commonly propounded, introduces unscriptural concepts into the doctrine of God's relation to the world, and may prove an Achilles' heel for the revival of Reformed theology.[208]

I suspect that the Reformed view can be stretched to accept a universal dimension to the atonement. Let us consider what John Owen said, that Jesus' death has

---

205. Knox, "Some Aspects of the Atonement," 260–66.
206. Ibid., 260.
207. Ibid., 261.
208. Ibid., 266.

"infinite worth, value, and dignity" and is "sufficient in itself" to save all persons without exception. Jesus' death is infinitely sufficient for universal evangelism even "if there were a thousand worlds."[209] Think about that last quote. If we established a wormhole to another world or a stargate to another solar system, we can send John Piper to tell them that "Christ died for you."

A chief issue is the design and application of the atonement. If we root the atonement in God's eternal plan of redemption and his sovereign predestination of all things, we discover that his plan is about the effect of salvation and not merely its possibility. God sets forth Christ to save, not simply to offer salvation. Yet countenanced with that must be some provision to incorporate the biblical materials that present the work of Christ as somehow universal and even cosmic (see 2 Cor 5:15, 21). God's love for his divine image bearers and his redemptive purpose to unite creation with himself through the Logos, while indeed telescoped in his elect people, inevitably flows beyond them in some sense, just like a light shone into a dark shack can pierce through the cracks in the wall and shine beyond the murky shack.

Our challenge, then, is to hold together both the sovereignty of God's predestination of the elect and the universality of the atonement to make provision for all people.[210] That challenge can be successfully met if we posit that God's decree to designate Christ as Savior logically precedes God's decision to save the elect.[211] To that it might be objected that the Amyraldian makes election subordinate to salvation.[212] To which we might respond, *mē genoito*, "may it never be." Election is anchored in the sovereign pleasures of God and executed in Christ (Eph 1:5).

Be that as it may, it is God's purposes in the Son that shape election, rather than election that shapes God's purposes in the Son. It should be obvious that God cannot elect humans to salvation unless he has first elected a Savior.[213] In addition, the biblical

---

209. Owen, *Death of Death*, 295–98.

210. The debate about the order of the decrees can be seen in the confessions of the Swiss Reformed churches. In the First Helvetic Confession (1536) it says about election (art. 10): "God has from eternity predestinated or freely chosen, of his mere grace, without any respect of men, the saints whom he will save in Christ.... We are to hear the gospel and believe it, and be sure that if we believe and are in Christ, we are chosen. We must listen to the Lord's invitation, 'Come unto me' (Matt. xi. 28), and believe in the unbounded love of God, who gave his own Son for the salvation of the world, and will not that 'one of these little ones should perish.'" The same confession then adds (art. 11): "We believe and teach that the Son of God, our Lord Jesus Christ, was from eternity predestinated by the Father to be the Saviour of the world.... We believe and teach that Christ is the only Redeemer of the whole world, in whom all are saved that were saved before the law, under the law, and under the gospel, or will yet be saved to the end of the world." In the First Helvetic Confession is a strong insistence on the predestination of the elect and the predestination of Jesus to be Savior! The question of the order of these predestinations was not given. It was the Helvetic Consensus (1675), authored principally by Francis Turrentin and in response to the Saumer academy, that rejected the hypothetical universalism of Amyraldianism in canons 4–6.

211. Cf. Augustus H. Strong, *Systematic Theology* (Old Tappan, NJ: Revell, 1977), 777–79; Erickson, *Christian Theology*, 849–52; Crisp, *God Incarnate*, 46–52.

212. Hodge, *Systematic Theology*, 2:546–47; G. C. Berkouwer, *Studies in Dogmatics: Divine Election* (Grand Rapids: Eerdmans, 1960), 135. Note the Helvetic Consensus (canon 6): "The appointment, also, of Christ, as Mediator, equally with the salvation of those who were given to him for a possession and an inheritance that cannot be taken away, proceeds from one and the same election, and does not form the basis of election." See Martin I. Klauber, "The Helvetic Formula Consensus (1675): An Introduction and Translation," *TrinJ* 11 (1990): 103–23.

213. A significant point raised by Crisp, *God Incarnate*, 47–52.

DID JESUS DESCEND INTO HELL?

Where was Jesus between his death and resurrection? Some English translations of the Apostles' Creed state: "He [Christ] descended into hell."[214] Since the sixteenth century some have objected to this line of the creed because Christ did not descend to "hell" but to "paradise" (Luke 23:43) or to "the realm of the dead" (Acts 2:27–32 [= Ps 16:10]; cf. Matt 12:40; 27:52–53; Eph 4:9) ahead of his resurrection. Though Calvin rejected the notion that Christ descended into hell, he still urged people to keep this line in the Apostles' Creed because "the place which it holds in a summary of our redemption is so important, that the omission of it greatly detracts from the benefits of Christ's death." Calvin affirmed the Creed because "it furnishes us with a full and every way complete summary of faith, containing nothing but what has been derived from the infallible word of God."

Calvin instead took the line about Christ's descent as referring to the torment that Christ suffered on the cross; that is, on the cross Christ descended into hell. It is the point where Jesus experienced at close quarters "the powers of hell and the horrors of eternal death" and "bore in his soul the tortures of condemned and ruined men."[215] In other words, Jesus did not literally go down to hell; rather, he experienced the agonies of hell on the cross as part of the penalty for our sins that he suffered on the cross. Calvin thus recasts its meaning to fit with biblical materials.[216] But for some, this reinterpretation of the creed is an unnecessary stretch of the imagination. Would it not be better to drop this line from the creed if it is so unbiblical?[217]

The problem is that this whole debate is misguided. The Latin creed does not say that Christ descended into hell. This wrong "tradition" is based on a mistranslation of the Latin. The Latin *ad inferos* found in the creed means "to the grave, the place of the dead" (i.e., *hadēs*).[218] It does not say *ad infernum*, meaning "to hell," the place of punishment after death (i.e., *Gehenna*).[219] The biblical background for this line in the creed is not 1 Peter 3:18–21 ("he went and made proclamation to the imprisoned spirits—to those who were disobedient long ago"), but Acts 2:31 ("Seeing what was to come, he spoke of the resurrection of the Messiah, that he was not abandoned to the realm of

---

214. Cf. a short history of the doctrine in Hurtado, *Lord Jesus Christ*, 628–35.
215. Calvin, *Institutes* 2.16.8–10.
216. R. Michael Allen, *Reformed Theology* (London: Continuum, 2010), 154.
217. For case in point, see Wayne Grudem, "He Did Not Descend Into Hell: A Plea for Following Scripture instead of the Apostles's Creed," *JETS* 34 (1991): 107–112; idem, *Systematic Theology*, 586–94.
218. The Greek version of the Apostles' Creed has *ta katō tata* (lit., "the lower depths").
219. An observation I owe to Richard Bauckham.

> the dead"). A better English translation of the creed, which is used in the Church of England, is this: "He descended to the dead." In other words, the wrong "tradition" about a descent into hell is really a wrong translation of the Latin perpetuated by the Reformers, who did not differentiate "hell" from "Hades."[220] They then worked out a needless correction to make *ad inferos* the experience of Jesus on the cross (now Jesus did experience separation from the Father and undergo judgment on the cross, but that is not what this line from the Creed says!). So the Reformed reinterpretation of the Apostles' Creed needs to be reformed in order to recover the proper meaning of the *descendit ad inferos* (Gk. *katelthonta eis ta katō tata*).[221]
>
> ---
>
> 220. For instance, on Matt 16:18, see "gates of hell" in the KJV compared to the "gates of Hades" in the NIV.
> 221. Granted that *descendit ad inferos* was not in the original or earliest versions of the creed, nonetheless, it is part of the creed as it is confessed universally in the Catholic, Orthodox, and Protestant churches for over a millennium.

evidence shows a mixture of inclusivity and particularity when it comes to the saving scope of Jesus' death. Israel, the elect, and the church are the specifically named beneficiaries of Jesus' death. However, since Christ's death contains an infinite power, the saving event's scope cannot be exhausted or confined to the elect. That is why there is a universal offer of salvation and a universal impact of Jesus' death.[222] Jesus' death and resurrection will inevitably effect the whole universe as it ushers in the new creation. Jesus' death and resurrection lead to the transformation of God's people and even to God's world (see Rom 8:18–30). Therefore, the death of Jesus is *efficient* for the salvation of the elect, but remains *sufficient* for the salvation of everyone. Jesus' death is *purposed* for the salvation of the elect, yet it creates the *possibility* of the salvation of everyone.[223]

4.4.3.4 SUMMARY

The extent of the atonement is a controversial area when it need not be. Everyone believes in the universal offer of the gospel. Everyone affirms the universal love of God for the lost. Everyone can affirm *in their own way* that Jesus' death is sufficient for all but efficient only for the elect. Despite differences between Reformed, Arminian, and Amyraldian views, we can all affirm as much.[224]

---

222. On Calvin's attempt to reconcile election and the universal offer of the gospel see his *Institutes* 3.24.17. See also Berkouwer, *Divine Election*, 218–53.

223. Hence the Latin formula "*sufficienter pro omnibus, sed efficaciter tantum pro electis*" ("sufficent for all, but efficient for only the elect").

224. Cf. the exemplary treatment in Grudem, *Systematic Theology*, 601–3.

§ 4.5 THE RESURRECTION OF JESUS

Evangelicals are crucicentric. Like Paul they preach "Jesus Christ and him crucified" (1 Cor 2:2). Worship music from Isaac Watts' "When I Survey the Wondrous Cross" to Keith Getty and Stuart Townshend's "In Christ Alone" demonstrates that the cross has been the center of evangelical worship. The cross-centered vision of evangelicalism is captured perfectly by John Piper:

> All exultation in anything else should be exultation in the cross. If you exult in the hope of glory, you should be exulting in the cross of Christ. If you exult in tribulation because tribulation works hope, you should be exulting in the cross of Christ. If you exult in your weaknesses, or in the people of God, you should be exulting in the cross of Christ.[225]

Christian discipleship is cruciformity, being conformed to the pattern of the cross, dying to self in service to God. That is what it means to take up your cross and follow Jesus *daily* (Luke 9:23) and to be crucified to the world (Gal 6:14).

In light of this cross-centered faith, the resurrection has been regarded largely as a confirmation of what the cross achieved and as proof of life after death. John Stott speaks for many when he writes: "What the resurrection did was to vindicate the Jesus whom men had rejected, to declare with power that he is the Son of God, and publicly to confirm that his sin-bearing death had been effective for the forgiveness of sins."[226] On the apologetic frontier, Gary Habermas says: "Jesus' resurrection is an actual *example* of our eternal life. It is the only miracle that, by its very nature, indicates the reality of the afterlife."[227]

All of this is indeed true. But if we regard the resurrection as simply a kind of certificate of authenticity for the atonement and sterling evidence for life beyond

---

225. John Piper, "Boasting in the Cross," preached at the Passion OneDay 2000 Conference. Cited http://cruciform-life.wordpress.com/2010/02/25/only-in-the-cross/. Accessed 21 May 2011.

226. Stott, *The Cross of Christ*, 238.

227. Gary Habermas, *The Risen Jesus and Future Hope* (Lanham, MD: Rowman & Littlefield, 2003), 163 (italics original).

the grave, we have sold the resurrection short. As Markus Barth and Verne H. Fletcher noted: "Western theological thought, while affirming that 'on the third day he rose again from the dead,' has nonetheless given relatively more weight to the crucifixion as the primary expression of the Christ event."[228] If our gospel begins and ends on Good Friday, it is impoverished. If our gospel reduces the resurrection to a footnote, it is not telling the full story of the Easter message. Strange as it may sound to our ears, I agree with Ross Clifford and Philip Johnson: the cross is not enough![229]

We must remember that the cross and resurrection form an indissoluble unity. The cross without the resurrection is just martyrdom—at the most an act of solidarity with the persecuted nation, and at worst a wrongly calculated disaster. Conversely, the resurrection without the cross is a miraculous intrusion into history, a redemptive-historical enigma, and a paranormal freak show with indeterminable significance. But together the cross and resurrection constitute the fulcrum on which God's intention to recapture the world for himself is launched and enacted.[230]

The four Gospels climax in Jesus' death *and* resurrection. The preaching of Jesus' resurrection is arguably more pervasive than the cross in the book of Acts (Acts 2:31; 3:26; 4:2, 33; 10:41; 13:33; 17:18). The Old Testament texts most often cited in the New Testament are Psalms 2 and 110, which focused on Jesus' resurrection and exaltation (e.g., Acts 2:34; 13:33; 1 Cor 15:25; Heb 1:2–3,5). Primitive confessional materials known to Paul emphasize that Jesus died *and* rose again (see Rom 4:25; 1 Cor 15:3–8; 2 Cor 5:15; 1 Thess 4:14). The resurrection figures prominently in Paul's concise summaries of the gospel (Rom 1:3–4; 10:9–10; 1 Cor 15:3–8; 2 Tim 2:8). The presupposition behind the prophecy of Revelation are the words of Jesus to John: "I am the Living One; I was dead, and now look, I am alive for ever and ever! And I hold the keys of death and Hades" (Rev 1:18).

I like the comment of Cyprian: "I confess the Cross, because I know of the Resurrection; for if, after being crucified, He had remained as He was, I had not perchance confessed it, for I might have concealed both it and my Master; but now that the Resurrection has followed the Cross, I am not ashamed to declare it."[231] Let's explore, then, the meaning of "resurrection."[232]

---

228. Markus Barth and Verne H. Fletcher, *Acquittal by Resurrection* (New York: Holt, Rinehard and Winston, 1964), v.

229. Ross Clifford and Philip Johnson, *The Cross Is Not Enough: Living as Witnesses to the Resurrection* (Grand Rapids: Baker, 2012).

230. Michael F. Bird, *The Saving Righteousness of God: Studies in Paul, Justification and the New Perspective* (PBM; Carlise, UK: Paternoster, 2007), 57–58.

231. Cyprian, *Sent.* 13.4.

232. Wolfhart Pannenberg (*Jesus: God and Man*) argued that the resurrection should be the starting point for theology since the resurrection authenticated the message of Jesus, it grounded the confession of the church in revelation, and it established the unity of Jesus and God.

THE HISTORICITY OF THE RESURRECTION

The historicity and reality of the bodily resurrection of Jesus is frequently assailed by atheists, agnostics, critics, and liberal Christians. However, the physical resurrection of Jesus rests on a bedrock of historical evidence that renders it more probable than any alternative thesis.[233]

1. *Jesus was buried by Joseph of Arimathea*. According to the Gospels (Matt 27:57–61; Mark 15:42–47; Luke 23:50–55; John 19:38–42) and Paul (1 Cor 15:4), Jesus was buried after his death. Moreover, the Gospels tell us he was buried by a sympathetic member of the Sanhedrin, Joseph of Arimathea, who placed Jesus' body in his own personal tomb. This burial is highly probable because we have multiple attestation through the early tradition that Paul cites, Synoptic sources (Mark seems to be citing an early source), and John's testimony. That Jesus was interred by Joseph of Arimathea is also probable since a Christian fictive account would be unlikely to depict a member of the Jewish Sanhedrin as undertaking this generous act for Jesus when Christian authors had a tendency to vehemently criticize and condemn the Judean leadership for their part in Jesus' death (e.g., John's version states that Joseph was a disciple "secretly because he feared the Jewish leaders").

2. *Jesus' tomb was found empty*. The empty tomb is narrated in all four Gospels, and it is impossible to invent the story on the back of Old Testament texts (Matt 28:1–8; Mark 16:1–8; Luke 24:1–10; John 20:1–2). The empty tomb is strongly implied in Paul's account in 1 Corinthians 15:4 because you can't move from "buried" to "raised" without a body vacating the tomb. Moreover, women are invoked as eyewitnesses to the empty tomb; in the ancient world a woman's testimony did not carry legal weight. If someone were going to manufacture a miraculous story such as this, I sincerely doubt that person would make the truth of this incredible tale rest on the testimony of a few grief-stricken and frightened Jewish women whose report would most likely be cast aside as a womanish fantasy (as happened according to Luke 24:11, "they did not believe the women, because their words seemed to them like nonsense").

On top of that, the primitive Jewish polemic against the resurrection proclamation actually presupposes that the tomb was empty. The Jewish counterclaim that the disciples stole the body (Matt 28:13; Justin, *Dial.* 108.2; *Gos. Pet.* 30) assumes that Jesus' body had somehow vacated the tomb. Furthermore, early Christian preaching in Jerusalem sometime after Jesus' crucifixion would have been problematic if the whereabouts of Jesus' body were known to the Jewish authorities.

---

233. What follows is based on Bird and Crossley, *How Did Christianity Begin?* 38–50, 64–69.

3. Jesus was seen alive after his death. According to Paul (1 Cor 15:3–8), the risen Jesus was seen by individuals and groups that included Jesus' followers, skeptics, unbelievers, and even enemies. This early tradition interlocks with the multiple accounts in the Gospels that narrate persons seeing, hearing, and touching the resurrected Jesus. That includes individuals, couples, groups, and even five hundred people who saw Jesus at a single time. There are clear divergences in the details provided by the Evangelists that do not appear to add up at first reading. Indeed, we can speak of an excited bewilderment as to exactly where, when, and who saw the risen Jesus and in what order, but this only adds to the realism. In the words of E. P. Sanders: "Calculated deception should have produced greater unanimity. Instead, there seems to have been *competitors*: 'I saw him first!' 'No! I did.' "[234] As we investigate the various stories of the appearances at the tomb, in a locked room, on a road out of Jerusalem, in Galilee, and by the Lake of Tiberias, we can only conclude that several individuals and groups believed that they had genuinely seen Jesus alive in a physical mode of existence after his death.

4. Jesus' resurrection is the best cause for the origin and shape of early Christianity. It boggles the minds of historians and sociologists how a Galilean movement in some backwater Roman provenance with a crucified leader soon became a religion that eventually dominated the Roman empire. What drove the mission, preaching, hopes, symbols, and story of the first Christians was their belief that the God of Israel had raised Jesus from the dead, and this meant the launch of a new world in the midst of an old one. Resurrection signified that the new creation had begun, and those who had seen Jesus were the custodians of a message that proclaimed justice, life, and hope to the world around them.

But what gave them that idea? Their leader was dead, they were regarded as schismatic or even apostate by their Jewish contemporaries, and they were regarded as religious rabble from the east by the Romans. Yet they remained steadfast in their conviction that Israel's Messiah had risen from the dead, and that meant the transformation of the entire Jewish worldview. I think Paul Barnett hits the nail on the head:

> In short, the logic of history, when applied to the study of Jesus means that the existence, momentum and direction of the early church are most plausibly explained by a powerful teacher who had a close relationship beforehand with his immediate circle, an influence radically reinforced by the confirmatory event of his resurrection from the dead.[235]

From time to time people will put forward alternative "theories" that Jesus swooned, the disciples stole the body, his followers had grief-induced hallucinations, or

---

234. E. P. Sanders, *The Historical Figure of Jesus* (London: Penguin, 1993), 280.
235. Paul Barnett, *Jesus and the Logic of History* (NSBT; Downers Grove, IL: InterVarsity Press, 1997), 35.

§ 4.5 The Resurrection of Jesus

the whole thing was a fraud. Yet these fanciful theories fall and break on the bedrock of evidence. How do five hundred people have the same hallucination? How does a subjective vision eat fish? How do you survive crucifixion and burial? Once the critics have stated their case, once the skeptics have had their rant, once the liberals have tried to water down the truth, and once the rhetoric has been aired, the testimony of the first Christian remains: "You are looking for Jesus the Nazarene, who was crucified. He has risen!" (Mark 16:6). John Updike wrote in a poem:

> Make no mistake: if He rose at all
> it was as His body;
> if the cells' dissolution did not reverse,
> the molecules reknit, the amino acids rekindle,
> the Church will fall....
> Let us not mock God with metaphor,
> analogy, sidestepping, transcendence;
> making of the event a parable, a sign painted in the faded
> credulity of earlier ages:
> let us walk through the door.[236]

To be sure, there is no absolute "proof" of the resurrection; we can deal only with probabilities. People will always find excuses and reasons not to believe. At the end of the day, belief in the risen Lord is an expression of faith and not simply a matter of the intellect. It comes down to whether one trusts in the early church's witness to Jesus mediated through Scripture.

I confess the resurrection of Jesus because it has inherent meaning, personally and theologically. Some years ago I began an experiment in the laboratory of life that Jesus is the risen Lord. That experiment is not yet complete, but I do have some preliminary results. In August of 1994, I died to the world; through the gift of faith I thereafter considered myself to be crucified with Christ, and now I live on by some strange and wonderful quickening whereby I exist in union with that same Jesus who could not be shackled by death and is exalted to God's right hand. From this union flows an unspeakable joy, an urge to worship, a sense of mission, and an odd feeling that I live in a world partially reborn.

---

236. "Seven Stanzas at Easter" from *Collected Poems*, 1953-1993 by John Updike, copyright © 1993 by John Updike. Used by permission of Alfred A. Knopf, and imprint of the Knopf Doubleday Publishing Group, a division of Random House LLC. All rights reserved.

> **FURTHER READING**
>
> Craig, William Lane. *The Son Rises: The Historical Evidence for the Resurrection of Jesus.* Chicago: Moody Press, 1981.
>
> Licona, Michael R. *The Resurrection of Jesus: A New Historiographical Approach.* Downers Grove, IL: InterVarsity Press, 2010.
>
> Wright, N. T. *The Resurrection of the Son of God.* COQG 3. London: SPCK, 2003.

4.5.1 JESUS' IDENTITY AND THE BEGINNING OF THE FUTURE AGE

So what does the resurrection mean? It is not just a rubber stamp for an atonement theology, and it is more than a sneak preview of life after death. I want to suggest five things.

First, *the resurrection is a revelation of Jesus' identity, and it marks the beginning of the future age.* Let us remember that many Jews thought that God would resurrect everyone at the end of history. The final vision of Daniel includes the report that "multitudes who sleep in the dust of the earth will awake: some to everlasting life, others to shame and everlasting contempt" (Dan 12:1–2). When Jesus told Martha that her dead brother, Lazarus, would live again, she assumed Jesus was referring to the end of the age: "I know he will rise again in the resurrection at the last day" (John 11:24). The second blessing of the Jewish *Amidah* includes the words: "[You] keep faith with those who sleep in the dust. Who is like you, O doer of mighty acts? Who resembles you, a king who puts to death and restores to life, and causes salvation to flourish? And you are certain to revive the dead. Blessed are you, O Lord, who revives the dead."

Now given that background, the shocking thing about Jesus' resurrection was that God brought that day of resurrection forward in the resurrection of Jesus. In other words, what most Jews hoped God would do for Israel at the end of history, God had done for Jesus in the middle of history, namely, to raise him from the dead. This was the sign that Jesus had been given all authority in heaven and on earth (Matt 28:18), was vindicated from false accusations (1 Tim 3:16), was marked out as God's Son (Rom 1:4), was designated the heir of all things (Heb 1:2), and was installed as Messiah and Lord (Acts 2:36). God's covenant with creation and Israel must now be interpreted in light of the fact that the resurrection designated Jesus as the Son of God.

What this means is that Jesus was the real deal; but not only that, God's whole deal with the world had changed. The new age that began as Jesus' resurrection was the firstfruits of the future resurrection, and he was the firstborn of the new creation (Rom 8:29; 1 Cor 15:20, 23; Col 1:15, 18; Heb 12:23; Rev 1:5). So when the first Christians proclaimed Jesus' resurrection to outsiders, it wasn't a case of, "Well, chaps, you'll never guess what happened last Sunday, our dear friend Yeshua ben Joseph, who got a raw deal at his trial, came back to life after his horrible execution. Isn't God really nice!" The resurrection meant that Jesus was the climax of God's plan.

What God was going to do for Israel and for the world he was beginning to do through Jesus, Israel's Messiah, the Son of God! Israel's promises were embodied in the crucified and risen person of Jesus of Nazareth. It meant also that the clocks had been moved forward. The D-Day of salvation had arrived in Jesus' resurrection and the V-Day would be completed at his return. Note how eschatology and Christology are intertwined in this apocalyptic story of God's action that brings historical fulfillment to scriptural promises. That is because resurrection means that God invades and disrupts the present order of things by bringing life in the face of death, justification in the midst of condemnation, and rays of hope in the caverns of fear. God's new day arises in the raising of his Son.

4.5.2 THE INAUGURATION OF THE NEW CREATION

Second, *the resurrection constitutes the inauguration of the new creation*. Jesus' resurrection also brings with it the beginnings of a new world. The raising of Jesus implies an ultimate state with a renewed heavens and earth. Resurrection is really an act about and for creation. God made the world, he made it good, it has gone bad, and so God intends to renew creation through a cosmic resurrection. That cosmic vivification was intimated in Jesus' own resurrection, and its fulfillment will mark the end of dystrophy, death, and decay in the created world. Resurrection means we witness the goodness of God's power and the power of God's goodness as it applies to material existence.[237] The tragic travails of creation are not terminal, and it is those very travails that will be terminated in a cosmic transformation at the ushering in of new heavens and a new earth. That is what Jesus' resurrection points ahead to. Listen to the words of Paul:

> I consider that our present sufferings are not worth comparing with the glory that will be revealed in us. The creation waits in eager expectation for the children of God to be revealed. For the creation was subjected to frustration, not by its own

---

237. Leander E. Keck, *Who Is Jesus? History in Perfect Tense* (Columbia: University of South Carolina Press, 2000), 129.

choice, but by the will of the one who subjected it, in hope that the creation itself will be liberated from its bondage to decay and brought *into the freedom and glory of the children of God.*

We know that the whole creation has been groaning as in the pains of childbirth right up to the present time. (Rom 8:18–22, italics added)

Like a birthing mother groaning for the delivery of her child, creation is desperately waiting for the resurrection of the children of God, for their glory to be publicly revealed at the appointed day. On that day, the whole created order will be set free from slavery to the curse and will share in the glorious freedom of God's children. Note this: the fate of the universe hangs on the destiny of God's people. Their glorification will mean a transformative liberation for the world. Oliver O'Donovan puts in this way:

> In proclaiming the resurrection of Christ, the apostles proclaimed also the resurrection of mankind in Christ; and in proclaiming the resurrection of mankind, they proclaimed the renewal of all creation with him. The resurrection of Christ in isolation from mankind would not be a gospel message. The resurrection of mankind apart from creation would be a gospel of a sort, but of a purely Gnostic and world-denying sort, which is far from the gospel that the apostles actually preached.[238]

That new creation is here already in the deposit of the Spirit in believers, which marks them out as the new humanity created to live in this soon-to-be new world (2 Cor 5:17; Gal 6:15; Col 3:10). The creative power of God to make alive, to renew, and to transform is fired through a trajectory of Christ ⇨ Church ⇨ Creation. Resurrection means that the curse of creation and the nexus of sin and death have been broken and will be swept aside. God's new creation is launched upon a surprised and unsuspecting world where new hopes are buoyed among oceans of terror, and the stories of Jesus' followers are billboards in the global metropolis of things soon to come upon the world. In the words of N. T. Wright: "What creation needs is neither abandonment nor evolution but rather redemption and renewal; and this is both promised and guaranteed by the resurrection of Jesus from the dead."[239]

Resurrection as the first installment of the new creation gives us a platform for developing a distinctive Christian ecological ethic. God's intention to transform creation should inform Christian attitudes toward the created order. The renewal of the image of God in human beings means a reissuing of the Adamic task to be responsible custodians of creation (Gen 1:28). Although creation has been tainted by corruption, it is not destined for destruction but for renewal. As creation has suffered

---

238. Oliver O'Donovan, *Resurrection and Moral Order: An Outline for Evangelical Ethics* (Leicester, UK: Inter-Varsity Press, 1986), 31.

239. N. T. Wright, *Surprised by Hope* (New York: HarperOne, 2008), 107.

the effects of human sin, so will it also participate in the fruits of human deliverance. When the church is resurrected and glorified, creation's bondage to corruption will end, and it will participate in the glorious freedom of the children of God. Thus, when Christians take an interest in the preservation of the environment, in which God has an interest, they are revealing their identity as the children of God, the new Adam, and are proving their worth as future stewards of a renewed creation.[240]

4.5.3 THE OBJECTIVE GROUNDS OF SALVATION

Third, *the resurrection is the objective grounds of salvation*. Ordinarily folks think of the cross as the means of salvation, and resurrection is proof that the cross redeems believers from the penalty of sin. No, we are saved by, in, and through the resurrection of Jesus Christ. Consider what Paul says: "He was delivered over to death for our sins and *was raised to life for our justification*" (Rom 4:25). "*If Christ has not been raised*, your faith is futile; *you are still in your sins* (1 Cor 15:17, italics added in both cases).

Hang on; doesn't Paul say we are justified and forgiven on account Jesus' death? Yes, he does (see Rom 3:24–25; 5:9; Eph 1:7), but obviously he also says that believers are justified and forgiven on account of Jesus' resurrection. How so?[241] In short, God executes his verdict of condemnation against sin on the cross, and then he issues another verdict of justification in the resurrection. By raising Jesus up in the power of the Spirit, God vindicates Jesus as the faithful Son and as the righteous sin-bearer (see Rom 1:4; 1 Tim 3:16).

Keep in mind that death and resurrection are representative acts; the Messiah undergoes them on behalf of his people. Thus, God's verdict against us is transposed into God's verdict for us. Jesus is justified by God, and because we are united to him in his resurrection, we share in that verdict of justification. We are justified because we participate in the justification of the Messiah. And what is true of him is reckoned to be true of his people. Resurrection is part of the story of how God proves his faithfulness to his covenant promises by vindicating those who trust in him. So God's raising of Jesus from the dead was the act in which the justification of all God's people was contained in a nutshell.

That is why believers are reconciled to God through Jesus' death and will be saved through Jesus' life (Rom 5:10). Baptism into Jesus' death also entails union with his resurrection, which is why believers are transferred from being under the power of sin and death to being under the power of righteousness and life (6:1–12).

---

240. Cf. Douglas J. Moo, "Nature in the New Creation: New Testament Eschatology and the Environment," *JETS* 49 (2006): 449–88.

241. Cf. Grudem, *Systematic Theology*, 615; Bird, *Saving Righteousness*, 48–53; N. T. Wright, *The Resurrection of the Son of God* (COQG 3; London: SPCK, 2003), 247–48.

The Spirit that raised Jesus will also raise believers up at the final day (8:10–11). What is more, "Christ died and returned to life so that he might be the Lord of both the dead and the living" (14:9); thus, resurrection draws people under the redemptive reign of Jesus' lordship. On this brief reading of Romans alone, it is clear that resurrection brings believers into a new objective state of salvation.

Faith in Christ means we participate in the covenant promises that Christ embodies as the risen one—we are placed in him and adopted into his family, bearing the fruit of righteousness, and we are made right with God. So union with Christ is the means of justification from sin, putting us right with God in the raising of the Son. Resurrection also marks a transfer of authority. Believers shift from being captive under the tyranny of evil and death to living under the Lordship of Jesus the Christ in whom is found life and glory.

Resurrection and salvation are not Pauline hobby horses. A similar perspective emerges in 1 Peter. In the opening prayer of the letter we read: "Praise be to the God and Father of our Lord Jesus Christ! In his great mercy he has given us new birth into a living hope *through the resurrection of Jesus Christ from the dead*" (1 Pet 1:3, italics added). Later, comparing the story of Jesus to the story of Noah's ark, Peter writes: "This water symbolizes baptism that now saves you also—not the removal of dirt from the body but the pledge of a clear conscience toward God. *It saves you by the resurrection of Jesus Christ*" (3:21, italics added).

The new birth and new life that belong to God's people are apprehended only in connection with the Messiah's resurrection. Baptism is a sign of grace and the pledge of fidelity to God. But baptism draws its power from the cross and resurrection so that baptism both signals and communicates something of the saving event. It is not water, but the torrents of resurrection life that impart salvation to the believer. The wider context of these passages from 1 Peter also suggests that Peter is laboring the point that readers ought to prepare themselves to share in the sufferings of Jesus in order thereby to share in his glory. In the midst of that suffering, in the world with its dark powers, the life of the risen Christ is revealed in their weakness.

Resurrection is also an indicator of the Trinitarian nature of salvation. The Father hands over the Son to the cross; then the Father raises the Son by the Spirit; afterward the Son dispenses the Spirit to believers, and the risen Son continually mediates between humanity and God the Father. Hans Urs von Balthasar commented, "Without the resurrection the whole Trinitarian salvific plan would be incomprehensible, and the work begun in the life of Jesus would remain incomprehensible."[242] To experience the vivifying power of God is to be caught up into the life of the Triune God and to share in his glory. God has life in himself, and

---

242. Cited in Cole, *God the Peacemaker*, 152.

he communicates that life to believers through the resurrection of Christ, which results first in regeneration and later in a resurrection of the body. Resurrection is the creative power of God that imparts life to soul and body.

4.5.4 ANASTASITY

Fourth, *an integral feature of discipleship is anastasity*. By the neologism *anastasity*, I mean experiencing the power of Christ's resurrection flowing into our lives ("anastasity" is based on the Greek word ***anastasis***, which means "resurrection"). Now the cross looms large as a symbol and example of Christian discipleship (see, e.g., Luke 9:23; Phil 2:5–11). The cross is determinative because it bankrupts our boasting in human trinkets, it sobers our minds when we become full of ourselves, and it pulls the plug from any naive triumphalism (see esp. Mark 10:35–45; 1 Cor 1–4). The imitation of Christ is the imitation of the way of the cross.

However, the resurrection is equally prominent in what it means to be a follower of Jesus and to be part of God's people. A spirituality that meditates only on the cross could potentially reduce us to self-loathing, spiritual insecurity, and an unhealthy fixation on our own pathetic wormliness—as if we remain pathetic lowly sinners, miserable wretches, unable to do one good thing for God, and beyond the prospect of a heavenly afterlife, so that not much has really changed (the Reformed tradition can sometimes edge in this direction). But because of the resurrection, we are "saints," the "elect," the "church of God," and the "bride of Christ"—and this a big deal. In what can only be described as the greatest reversal of fortunes since Cinderella, believers have gone from condemnation-death-poverty-grief-shame to righteousness-life-riches-joy-glory.

Some people pride themselves on their self-deprecation to the point that the more they tell everyone that they are a pathetic worm, the holier they must be! Let it not be so! Do not think less of yourself than what God thinks of you. And if he thinks well of his Son, he thinks well of you. If God loves his Son, he loves you. For you are one with his Son—sharing in his sufferings, partaking of his glory, and already raised to the heights of his throne. Who can condemn the Christian? There is only one man, Christ Jesus, and how will he condemn us when he commits himself to interceding for us (Rom 8:34)?

That anastasity of the Christian life is evident in several ways. (1) For the believer resurrection life has begun in our spiritual life. Paul says that "God ... made [believers] alive with Christ" (Eph. 2:4–5; cf. Eph 2:6; Col 2:12; 3:1). In Romans we read that believers were "buried with him through baptism into death in order that, just as Christ was raised from the dead through the glory of the Father, *we too may live a new life*" (Rom 6:4). In the gospel of John, Jesus teaches that "a time is coming and *has now come* when the dead will hear the voice of the Son of God and those who hear will live" (John 5:25). These texts all show that in the here-and-now, Christians already experience the life-giving power of God in the vitalizing work of the Spirit. While their outer nature is wasting away, their inner nature is being renewed (2 Cor 4:16). The challenge is to live a life that emits the fragrance of resurrection life.

(2) The resurrection imparts hope to Christians. In an age when most people ebb between the fear of death and the futility of life (see Heb 2:14–15), Paul can say that the cornerstone of Christian hope is the future resurrection of believers (Rom 8:24–25). Christian hope is not a placebo in the face of certain death, but it has real substance and is confirmed by Christ's own resurrection as the prototype of what will happen to us (1 Cor 6:14; 2 Cor 4:14). If there is no resurrection, then Christians are the most pitiable of people (1 Cor 15:19). But if Christ has been raised, then Christians look forward to the final victory over death and evil.

(3) Resurrection imparts a new ethical paradigm and kingdom perspective—hence Paul's words: "Since, then, you have been *raised with Christ*, set your hearts on things above, where Christ is seated at the right hand of God. Set your minds on things above, not on earthly things" (Col 3:1–2, italics added). Paul is not bidding people to become so heavenly minded that they cease to be of any earthly good. The reality of who they are *in Christ* and where *Christ is seated* must surely impact their perspective and praxis in the present. All of Colossians 3 works out what it means in practice to be raised with Christ. The heavenly perspective on which they are to fix their minds is the truth pertaining to Jesus' exaltation as Lord and the fact that they themselves are bonded to him.

(4) The resurrection is a motivation to press on toward the goal for which Christ has called believers. Paul states: "I want to know Christ—yes, to know the power of his resurrection and participation in his sufferings, becoming like him in his death, and so, somehow, attaining to the resurrection from the dead. Not that I have already obtained all this, or have already arrived at my goal, but I press on to take hold of that for which Christ Jesus took hold of me" (Phil 3:10–12).[243] Resurrection becomes the goal, the *telos*, and the prize of our journey. Resurrection encourages us to finish the race even as we share in Christ's sufferings and follow his example. God calls us to struggle, strive, and run to win the prize (Phil 3:14; Heb 12:1–2). Beyond the paths of suffering lies the heavenly city, the new Jerusalem, where God will raise up believers in glorious and immortal bodies. The risen Christ made us his own so that we would run toward our glorious home.

---

243. Cf. Michael F. Bird, *A Bird's-Eye View of Paul: The Man, His Mission and His Message* (Nottingham, UK: Inter-Varsity Press, 2008), 166–68.

4.5.5 INSPIRATION FOR KINGDOM MINISTRY

Finally, *resurrection is an inspiration for kingdom ministry.* The resurrection is not simply an amazing fact that God brings dead people to life. It has a host of consequences. Jesus is risen; therefore God's new world has begun. Jesus is risen; therefore the tyrants and despots of the world should tremble and quiver—because God has exalted Jesus and every knee will bow before him. Jesus is risen; therefore Israel has been restored and the plan for the nation is fulfilled in him. Jesus is risen; therefore death has been defeated. Jesus is risen; therefore creation groans in anticipation of its renewal. Jesus is risen; therefore we will be raised also to live in God's new world. Jesus is risen; therefore go and make disciples in his name. The resurrection means that God's new world has broken into our own world, and we are heirs and ambassadors of the king that is coming.

But the resurrection implies something else. It means we have the task of proclaiming and embodying before the world exactly what this new creation is and what it looks like. We are a resurrection people, and we demonstrate how resurrection—as both a present experience and a future hope—impacts people when it is worked out in daily life, family life, and community life. If we are "children of the resurrection" (Luke 20:36), we show the suitability of this name when we are committed to talking, taking, and turning our lives into a means of life-giving grace to those around us.

In 1 Corinthians 15, Paul writes his most extensive discourse on the resurrection—that it is intrinsic to the gospel, what the resurrection body looks like, and how it is part of God's victory. Yet we must take to heart the application that the apostle makes at the end: "Therefore, my dear brothers and sisters, stand firm. Let nothing move you. *Always give yourselves fully to the work of the Lord, because you know that your labor in the Lord is not in vain*" (15:58, italics added). Here Paul is telling the Corinthians that despite the world around them, pagan and promiscuous as it is, they must hold their ground, not let up, and not shut up, because they are the vessels of the same divine power exercised in the resurrection of Christ. The future horizon of resurrection gives purpose and drive to Christian living in the present.

If you're contemplating missionary service, adding your name to rosters at church, learning to preach, becoming a Sunday school teacher, wondering what you can do to stop sex-trafficking, then do it. Here's why: the resurrection moves us to take risks for God because the resurrection proves that God is behind us, before us, and with us. Our labor in the Lord in this life plants seeds that will sprout forth in the resurrection life; thus, what work we do in this age will flower in the coming age of new creation.

Furthermore, if the resurrection drives us to do anything, it must surely be worship. Look what happened when the women at the empty tomb met the risen Lord:

"Suddenly Jesus met them. 'Greetings,' he said. *They came to him, clasped his feet and worshiped him*" (Matt 28:9, italics added). Their first thought was not to hold a colloquium on the nature of the resurrection body or reconcile scientific notions of personal identity with molecular biology. I imagine that their knees bent with awe, their mouths opened with joy, and their arms were raised in adoration. Resurrection bids us to cling to Christ in joyous and exulting worship.

If our theology is gospel-driven, the resurrection will permeate every facet of Christian thought. We can contemplate Christ only as the risen Lord. We may speak of God's kingdom only as it enters our world through resurrection power. We imagine the Spirit not as an impersonal force, but as the personal instrument of inward regeneration and physical resurrection. The church exists only upon the premise and in the power of resurrection. Indeed, we can only view the world around us through the lens of resurrection faith. John Chrysostom's famous paschal homily speaks of the all-encompassing transformation of reality wrought by Christ's resurrection:

> Christ is risen! And you, O death, are annihilated!
> Christ is risen! And the evil ones are cast down!
> Christ is risen! And the angels rejoice!
> Christ is risen! And life is liberated!
> Christ is risen! And the tomb is emptied of its dead;
> For Christ having risen from the dead,
> Is become the firstfruits of those who have fallen asleep.
> To Him be glory and power, now and forever, and from all ages to all ages.
> Amen.[244]

FURTHER READING

Clifford, Ross., and Philip Johnson. *The Cross Is Not Enough: Living as Witnesses to the Resurrection*. Grand Rapids: Baker, 2012.

Davis, Stephen T. *Risen Indeed: Making Sense of the Resurrection*. Grand Rapids: Eerdmans, 1993.

Gaffin, Richard B. *The Centrality of the Resurrection: A Study in Paul's Soteriology*. Grand Rapids: Baker, 1978.

Haire, James, Christine Ledger, and Stephen Pickard, eds. *From Resurrection to Return: Perspectives from Theology and Science on Christian Eschatology*. Adelaide, Aus.: ATF Press, 2007.

Pannenberg, Wolfhart. *Jesus: God and Man*. 2nd ed. Philadelphia: Westminster John Knox, 1968, pp. 66–73.

---

244. Cited from McKnight, *Community Called Atonement*, 106.

§ 4.6 THE ASCENSION AND SESSION OF JESUS

If the resurrection has been relatively neglected in evangelical theology, the ascension of Jesus Christ has been neglected even more. The ascension is the poor cousin in the family of the work of Christ. Evangelicals celebrate Christmas and Easter, sometimes even Pentecost, but Ascension Sunday is pretty much a nonstarter in the evangelical liturgical calendar (and yes, I'm aware that "evangelical liturgy" is an oxymoron). Yet the ascension of Jesus, including his exaltation to the right hand of God, is a significant element of the work of Christ. It is arguably the *real* fulfillment of the rejoicing in the Psalms about the exaltation of God's kingship and his being anointed as king (see Pss 24; 47; 68; 110).

It is recorded in the short confessional piece in 1 Timothy that Jesus "appeared in the flesh ... [was] taken up in glory" (1 Tim 3:16). The Apostles' Creed, the Nicene Creed, and the Athanasian Creed all affirm that Jesus ascended to heaven and now sits at the right hand of God the Father. Bishop Maximus of Turin explained the ascension this way:

> The mystery of the Lord's Ascension, dear brothers, has ordained today's festival. Let us rejoice that the Only-begotten of God came to earth for the redemption of all and let us be glad that He entered heaven for our immortality. For this is the truth of our saving faith that we believe in His Passion and do not deny His glory. Nor indeed is the essence of the miracle such that He who came from heaven returned to heaven, but that He brought to the Father the manhood which he had assumed from the earth.... The earth rejoices when it sees its Redeemer reigning in the heavens; heaven is glad because it has not lost its God which it had, and has received the manhood which it had not.[245]

As we have noted above, when Jesus died, he went neither to heaven nor to hell, but descended to Hades, the waiting place of the dead (see Acts 2:27, 31). That is

---

245. Cited in Peter Toon, *The Ascension of Our Lord* (Nashville: Nelson, 1984), 131–32.

evident not only from Jesus' words to the bandit on the cross that both of them would soon be in "paradise" (Luke 23:43), but also from his words to Mary Magdalene at the tomb, "Do not hold on to me, for I have not yet ascended to the Father" (John 20:17). Jesus only returns to heaven at his ascension; this is recorded twice within Luke–Acts.

Luke 24:49–53	Acts 1:9–11
"I am going to send you what my Father has promised; but stay in the city until you have been clothed with power from on high." When he had led them out to the vicinity of Bethany, he lifted up his hands and blessed them. While he was blessing them, he left them and was taken up into heaven. Then they worshiped him and returned to Jerusalem with great joy. And they stayed continually at the temple, praising God.	After he said this, he was taken up before their very eyes, and a cloud hid him from their sight. They were looking intently up into the sky as he was going, when suddenly two men dressed in white stood beside them. "Men of Galilee," they said, "why do you stand here looking into the sky? This same Jesus, who has been taken from you into heaven, will come back in the same way you have seen him go into heaven."

What actually happened at the ascension is a bit of a puzzle. I've heard an atheist speaker refer to the ascension as "the launching of the Lord." Yet Jesus did not fly up to heaven, which was only several miles or so up in the sky just above the clouds. The ascension is not making a statement about cosmology in the scientific sense. Jesus is taken into heaven much as biblical figures such as Enoch and Elijah were taken away to be with the Lord (Gen 5:24; 2 Kgs 2:11).

What we have in the ascension is a mixture of visual marvel, strange metaphor, and utter mystery. Yet Jesus is taken away in such a manner as to leave clear in the minds of observers that he has been taken up into heaven where God is. Ascension marks the end of the resurrection appearances and the beginning of Jesus' session as the Father's vice-regent. Just as the ascension is differentiated from resurrection, so too is the ascension differentiated from Jesus' session.[246] The ascension happened as a historical event when he was assumed into heaven. The session is what Jesus is doing now as he sits at God's right hand in glory until the day of his return to earth.[247]

The ascension carries significance, but discerning that significance is a little tricky. The most important thing here is not that Jesus went to a *place* rather than merely entered into some kind of heavenly *state*. True though that may be, Luke hardly narrates the ascension story twice because he's rather keen on his share in heavenly real estate as opposed to states of heavenly consciousness. Nor is the key

---

246. Scholars frequently refer to Christ's twofold state as consisting of his humiliation (incarnation, suffering, death, burial, and descent to the underworld) and his exaltation (resurrection, ascension, session at God's right hand, and return in glory). See Grudem, *Systematic Theology*, 620; Horton, *Christian Faith*, 483–547.

247. Toon, *The Ascension of Our Lord*, 128.

§ 4.6 The Ascension and Session of Jesus

> **SOME COMIC BELIEF**
>
> Why does God always have to use his left hand?
> Because Jesus is sitting on his right hand!

point to reassure us that our final home will be in heaven, because our final home is definitely not heaven; rather, it is the renewed creation of a new heaven and a new earth.[248] Instead, I suggest several implications of the significance of Jesus' ascension.

First, *Jesus ascends to heaven so that he can send the Holy Spirit to his followers.* In the gospel of John, Jesus taught at the Feast of Tabernacles that rivers of living water would flow from within those who believed in him, and the Evangelist informs us: "By this he meant the Spirit, whom those who believed in him were later to receive. Up to that time the Spirit had not been given, since Jesus had not yet been glorified" (John 7:39). In Jesus' farewell discourse in John, there is a strong emphasis on his departing so that the "advocate" (*paraklētos*) will come:

- I will ask the Father, and *he will give you another advocate* to help you and be with you forever—the Spirit of truth. (14:16–17)
- But the Advocate, the Holy Spirit, whom *the Father will send in my name*, will teach you all things and will remind you of everything I have said to you. (14:26)
- When the Advocate comes, whom *I will send to you from the Father*—the Spirit of truth who goes out from the Father—he will testify about me. (15:26)
- Unless I go away, the Advocate will not come to you; but if I go, *I will send him to you.* (16:7, italics added in all cases)

The ministry of the Advocate will continue the witness of Jesus in the witness of the disciples.

In Luke–Acts there is a similar emphasis on Jesus' departure to heaven resulting in his giving of the Spirit to the disciples (see Luke 9:51; Acts 1:2). In Luke's gospel, the Father intends to give the Holy Spirit to those who ask him (Luke 11:13), and the Holy Spirit will teach Jesus' followers what to say when they are on trial (12:12). Prior to his ascension, Jesus promised the disciples that they will receive what the

---

248. Contra Grudem, *Systematic Theology*, 617, 619.

Father has promised them, namely, that they will be clothed with "power from on high" (24:49). The purpose of such "power" is disclosed in the opening verses of Acts where Jesus told the disciples: "But you will receive power when the Holy Spirit comes on you; and you will be my witnesses in Jerusalem, and in all Judea and Samaria, and to the ends of the earth" (Acts 1:8). What the disciples received was empowerment for mission through the Spirit's enabling.

Later in Peter's Pentecost speech, the giving of the Spirit is equated with the fulfillment of Joel's prophecy, where God said through Joel, "I will pour out my Spirit on all people" (Acts 2:17; cf. Joel 2:28). The visible and spectacular outpouring of the Holy Spirit is proof of three things. (1) The "last days" have arrived with the sending of the Holy Spirit in a qualitatively new way (Acts 2:17). (2) The time for salvation has come, for "everyone who calls on the name of the Lord will be saved" (2:21). (3) Jesus in his earthly life was the anointed Spirit-bearer, and in his exalted state Jesus is the Spirit-giver: "Exalted to the right hand of God, he has received from the Father the promised Holy Spirit and has poured out what you now see and hear" (2:33).

Christology, eschatology, and pneumatology merge together. The last days are here because the fresh winds of the Holy Spirit are blowing like never before. However, the Spirit is only poured out anew because Jesus, whom the Judean leaders crucified, has been raised and exalted by God, and it is he who sends the Spirit.

Second, *after Jesus' ascension there is an expectation for the worship of Jesus and the witness to Jesus by the disciples.* The ascension of Jesus indicates the beginning of a Trinitarian worship focused on the Lord Jesus and God the Father, operating in the power of the Spirit.[249] The risen Jesus was immediately worshiped as someone who has overcome death and transcends the heaven–earth divide after the resurrection (Matt 28:9, 17). The ascension meant that Jesus was not only assumed to heaven like Enoch and Elijah, but also exalted and enthroned beside God and was therefore worthy of similar honors given to God. That is why immediately after the ascension the disciples genuinely worshiped him (Luke 24:52) and why prayers, baptisms, and healings were performed in his name (Acts 2:38; 3:6, 16; 4:18, 30; 5:40; 8:12, 16). These were forms of devotion to Jesus and the means of receiving benefits from God through Jesus.

In addition, the ascension also marks the commissioning of the disciples as witnesses to Jesus. During his prophetic career, Jesus promised that the Spirit would be given to his followers so that they would know what to say when they stood before governors and rulers (Matt 10:18–20; Mark 13:9–11; Luke 12:11–12). That is, the Spirit would provide forensic testimony to Jesus through his disciples.

What now links the Lucan and Johannine teaching about Jesus' ascension and the dispensing of the Spirit is the fact that the disciples are given the Spirit in order to testify to Jesus. When the Spirit is sent, says Jesus, "he will testify about me"; and

---

249. Cf. Hurtado, *Lord Jesus Christ*, 177–206.

because the disciples receive this Spirit, "you also must testify" (John 15:26–27). The ascension in the gospel of Luke narrates how the disciples are "witnesses of these things" (i.e., the death and resurrection of the Messiah according to the Scriptures); therefore they must preach to all nations, beginning from Jerusalem (Luke 24:46–48). Then in Acts, baptism in the Holy Spirit imparts to them a power that enables them to witness to all nations in Jerusalem, Judea, Samaria, and the ends of the earth (Acts 1:8). To put it simply, the ascension means that the Christian community will always be a worshiping and witnessing community, with Jesus as the object of marvelous adoration and the subject of missionary action.

Third, *Jesus' ascension means that he is exalted to God's right hand and is invested with divine authority.* The most commonly cited Old Testament chapter in the New Testament is Psalm 110.[250]

> *Of David. A psalm.*
> The Lord says to my lord:
> "Sit at my right hand
>   until I make your enemies
>   a footstool for your feet."
> The Lord will extend your mighty scepter from Zion, saying,
>   "Rule in the midst of your enemies."
> Your troops will be willing
>   on your day of battle.
> Arrayed in holy splendor,
>   your young men will come to you
>   like dew from the morning's womb.
> The Lord has sworn
>   and will not change his mind:
> "You are a priest forever,
>   in the order of Melchizedek."
> The Lord is at your right hand;
>   he will crush kings on the day of his wrath.
> He will judge the nations, heaping up the dead
>   and crushing the rulers of the whole earth.
> He will drink from a brook along the way,
>   and so he will lift up his head.

---

250. Cf. citations, allusions, and echoes of Ps 110:1 in Matt 22:44/Mark 12:36/Luke 20:42; Matt 26:64/Mark 14:62/Luke 22:69; Acts 2:33–35; 5:31; Rom 8:34; 1 Cor 15:25; Eph 1:20–22; 2:6; Phil 2:9–11; Col 3:1; Heb 1:3, 13; 5:6; 7:17, 21; 8:1; 10:12–13; 12:2; 1 Pet 3:22; Rev 3:21; Mark 16:19. For a good survey of these texts see Aquila H. I. Lee, *From Messiah to Preexistent Son: Jesus' Self-Consciousness and Early Christian Exegesis of Messianic Psalms* (WUNT 2.192; Tübingen: Mohr/Siebeck, 2005), 202–39.

The important thing to remember here is that David is the speaker of this psalm. So he refers to the Lord (Yahweh) as speaking speaks to his Lord (Adoni); this means that David looks ahead to a future king whom the Lord of Israel will make Lord of the nations—a king other than himself, but from the Davidic line.

Psalm 110 was employed in Judaism in two main ways: (1) envisaging a figure who combines priestly and royal roles, as in the depiction of Melchizedek in 11Q13 from Qumran; and (2) the expectation for an exalted eschatological deliverer as found in Isaiah 52; Daniel 7; and *1 Enoch*. Jesus appears to have used Psalm 110 in both senses. In his debate with the scribes in Jerusalem, Jesus conflated the Davidic and priestly qualities of the Messiah and asserted that the coming Son of David was more than a human descendent of David (e.g., Matt 22:44–45). He also announced at his trial that he would be enthroned beside the God of Israel and vindicated in glory (Matt 26:64).

Concerning early Christian usage of Psalm 110, three texts clearly demonstrate how the first Christians used it to show that Jesus was exalted to a state of lordship after his ascension:

For David did not ascend to heaven, and yet he said, "The Lord said to my Lord: 'Sit at my right hand until I make your enemies a footstool for your feet.'" Therefore let all Israel be assured of this: God has made this Jesus, whom you crucified, both Lord and Messiah. (Acts 2:34–36)	Then the end will come, when he hands over the kingdom to God the Father after he has destroyed all dominion, authority and power. For he must reign until he has put all his enemies under his feet. (1 Cor 15:24–25)	The Son is the radiance of God's glory and the exact representation of his being, sustaining all things by his powerful word. After he had provided purification for sins, he sat down at the right hand of the Majesty in heaven. (Heb 1:3)

The testimony of Peter in Acts, the apostle Paul in 1 Corinthians, and the writer to the Hebrews is that after Jesus' death and resurrection, he was seated beside God and is thereafter invested with divine authority. Jesus is raised to reign with God. Jesus is taken into heaven to take control of the affairs of the universe. Jesus is elevated to heaven to be enthroned as God's vice-regent. The person whom Christians worship and to whom they witness is the one the God of Israel has marked out as Lord of the universe, and he is thus the key agent in its redemption.

Not only that, but by applying the image of Psalm 110 to Jesus, the New Testament authors were implying Jesus' preexistence, because in this psalm the Lord speaks to the priest-king in the Psalm as if he were already living (on preexistence, note also the echoes of Ps 110:1 in Phil 2:9–11)! As for what Jesus' exaltation means for discipleship, hear the words of the martyr Polycarp in his letter to the Philippians (Pol. *Phil.* 2.1):

> Therefore, prepare for action and serve God in fear and truth, leaving behind the empty and meaningless talk and the error for the crowd, and believing in the one who raised our Lord Jesus Christ from the dead and gave him glory and a throne at his right hand. To him all things in heaven and on earth were subjected, whom every breathing creatures serves, who is coming as judge of the living and the dead.

To use a meteorological pun, to be a follower of Jesus means to walk in the "reign" of Jesus Christ. It entails that believers order their lives, story, symbols, worship, preaching, finances, relationships, ambitions, and hopes around the most important confession of the faith: Jesus is Lord (see Rom 10:9).

Fourth, *the ascension demonstrates that God has placed a human being as vice-regent of the universe.* Jesus was the preexistent Son of God and was incarnated as a human being. When he was resurrected, he was still God incarnated as a human being, except now he had a glorified human body. When he ascended into heaven, he did not cease to be human, though he does remain the second person of the Trinity. Jesus ascended as a human being, and he remains in this glorified humanity for all of eternity. Hence the one enthroned beside God is a human being. In other words, it is human person who is at the helm of the universe.[251]

The commission given to Adam in Genesis 1:28 demonstrates that humanity's first task was to rule over creation on behalf of God. The image of God means to royally rule as God does. Psalm 8 picks up this theme when it says about human beings: "You have made them a little lower than the angels and crowned them with glory and honor. You made them rulers over the works of your hands; you put everything under their feet" (Ps 8:5–6). In fact, for the author of Hebrews, Psalm 8 shows that Jesus is "the human being" par excellence, whom God crowns with glory and honor because he qualified himself for exaltation by his salvific death for others (Heb 1:5–11). The enthronement of Jesus constitutes the restoration of the task that God had always intended for humanity: to reign over a created world on behalf of God.

Fifth, *believers embryonically share in the reign of Christ by virtue of their union with Christ.* Believers are united with Jesus in his death, resurrection, and exaltation. We find progressively revealed in Scripture the democratization of the messianic idea. On this perspective, God's people reign both under God's anointed king and with God's anointed king. We find this first announced in Daniel 7, where the enthronement of the "one like a son of man" beside God is interpreted as a symbolic image for the future moment when "the holy people of the Most High will receive the kingdom and will possess it forever—yes, for ever and ever" (Dan 7:13–14, 18). Jesus told his twelve disciples that when the Son of Man was enthroned in his glory,

---

251. Wright, *Surprised by Hope*, 114–16.

they would "sit on twelve thrones, judging the twelve tribes of Israel" (Matt 19:28; Luke 22:30). In the Lucan version of the saying, it is prefaced with the promise: "I confer on you a kingdom, just as my Father conferred one on me" (Luke 22:29). In the New Testament, reigning with Christ is still held out as an impending hope to be consummated in a future moment (2 Tim 2:12; Rev 2:26–27; 3:21; 5:10; 20:6; 22:5).

However, in Ephesians and Colossians, believers are in a sense already seated with Christ: "God raised us up with Christ and seated us with him in the heavenly realms in Christ Jesus" (Eph 2:6); "since ... you have been raised with Christ, set your hearts on things above, where Christ is, seated at the right hand of God" (Col 3:1). Obviously this "already" aspect of eschatology, whereby believers can already count themselves as reigning with Christ, can lead to an unhealthy spiritual triumphalism. We are not on the throne yet, but our Man is, our Messiah is, our Master is; and where he is, we shall also be! That fact should not lead to triumphalistic self-assurance nor to a disdain for all other earthly authorities. Rather, the prospect of reigning with Christ should cultivate a deep desire to live lives worthy of our royal calling (see Col 3:2). It should promote a sense of awe at the grace of God, which has turned rebellious sinners who raged against the kingdom into royal heirs of the glorious king (see Eph 2:7).

Sixth, *Jesus' work of intercession continues in his heavenly session.* The priestly office of Christ is expressed in his mediation between God and humanity. That mediation is demonstrated supremely in his atoning death but is not limited to it. The ascended Jesus is the mediator who gives us access to God, and he continues to make intercession for his people.

Jesus has reconciled humanity to himself through his obedience, death, and resurrection. He put us in a right relationship with God. He brought us out of the exile of sin and back into the family of God's covenantal promises. Remember the lament of Job: "If only there were someone to mediate between us, someone to bring us together, someone to remove God's rod from me, so that his terror would frighten me no more. Then I would speak up without fear of him, but as it now stands with me, I cannot" (Job 9:33–35). The answer to Job's lament is Jesus. In the words of Paul, "For there is one God and one mediator between God and mankind, the man Jesus Christ, who gave himself as a ransom for all people" (1 Tim 2:5–6). Because the Son became incarnate and died a redemptive death, Job and all others like him have someone who is standing between God and them to remove any contention and to bring peace with God.

When Jesus died, the curtain of the temple was torn in two, symbolizing that the way to God was no longer restricted to the mediation of the Jerusalem priesthood and cultus, but was opened up to everyone in every place (Matt. 27:51/Mark 15:38/

Luke 23:45). The salvation mediated through Jesus is superior to the law because the law was put into effect through angels (Acts 7:53; Gal 3:19), but Jesus is the divine-human mediator of a new covenant that is based on a better promise, a better sacrifice, and a better priesthood (Luke 22:20; Heb 8:6; 9:15; 12:24). The exaltation of Jesus completes this work of mediation because the *ascension* of Jesus into heaven means the *acceptance* of those for whom he died and rose. This is expressed beautifully in Hebrews:

> We have this hope *as an anchor for the soul*, firm and secure. It enters the inner sanctuary behind the curtain, *where our forerunner, Jesus, has entered* [heaven] on our behalf. He has become a high priest forever, in the order of Melchizedek. (Heb 6:19–20) Therefore, brothers and sisters, *since we have confidence to enter the Most Holy Place by the blood of Jesus*, by a new and living way opened for us through the curtain, that is, his body, and since we have a great priest over the house of God, *let us draw near to God with a sincere heart with the full assurance that faith brings*, having our hearts sprinkled to cleanse us from a guilty conscience and having our bodies washed with pure water. Let us hold unswervingly to the hope we profess, for he who promised is faithful. (10:19–23, italics added in both cases)

Jesus has entered the heavenly sanctuary ahead of us as our forerunner, and we have assurance that we too will be accepted there. If there are two Greek words to teach our congregations, it would have to be *parrēsia* ("confidence") and *prosagōgē* ("access").[252] Paul puts it this way: "In him and through faith in him we may approach God with freedom and confidence" (Eph 3:12). Because Jesus is the exalted Lord, we have a means to approach God, for our mediator is enthroned beside the Father. As a result, "this is the confidence we have in approaching God: that if we ask anything according to his will, he hears us" (1 John 5:14). With the ascension of Jesus, the door into the presence of God is permanently open for us. Believers have a brazen confidence to presume upon God's favor and a shameless sense of security that God's door to them always stands open.

Another aspect of the postresurrection priestly work of Jesus is his intercession. The high priestly prayer of John 17 shows the beginning of Jesus' work of interceding for his disciples. Jesus was already praying for his disciples even before he ascended. Concerning the intercessory work of Christ, Romans and Hebrews are our key witnesses: "Who then is the one who condemns? No one. Christ Jesus who died—more than that, who was raised to life—is at the right hand of God and is also interceding for us" (Rom 8:34). "Therefore he is able to save completely those who come to God through him, because he always lives to intercede for them"

---

252. Cf. Rom 5:2; Eph 2:18; 3:12; Heb 4:16; 1 John 3:21; 4:17; 5:14.

(Heb 7:25). This intercession is achieved partly by virtue of Jesus' presence in the courtroom of heaven. His presence there proves that our rightful place belongs in the throne room of heaven.

In his ascension, "Jesus Christ is the living guarantor of the believer's justification from Easter until the end of this world."[253] On top of that, it is not just his presence in heaven but his prayers in heaven that constitute his intercession.[254] Jesus lives in the presence of God to petition him to act in our favor. That is why we are committed to praying to God the Father in Jesus' name (John 14:13–14; 15:16; 16:23–26).

Intercession is not Jesus' constantly begging a reluctant Father to help us. Our heavenly Father is already disposed to provide good things for his creatures (see Matt 6:8; 7:11). The prayers of Jesus are part of the communion between Father, Son, and Spirit, so that Jesus' petitions are part of the work that the Triune God effected in the world. The prayers of the church are mediated through the Son in order to show that God answers prayer because of the Son. Above all, in his ascension Jesus' humanity is raised to the heights of heaven to present requests to God, and this provides assurance that God is for his people and will always hear them.

Finally, *Jesus will return in the same manner that he left*. The certainty of Jesus' future *parousia* is anchored in the reality of his ascension into heaven. Hence the words of the angels to the disciples: "This same Jesus, who has been taken from you into heaven, will come back in the same way you have seen him go into heaven" (Acts 1:11). Jesus will return *in the same way*, but more importantly, it is the *same Jesus*. In whatever mysterious way Jesus ascended into heaven, in the same mysterious way he will return to reign over the earth and consummate his kingdom. It certainly appears that for Luke the ascension and *parousia* of Jesus belong together, not as two ends of the one pole but as an organic unity. As J. A. T. Robinson said, the ascension is "the advance notice of the end."[255]

Many churches follow a liturgical calendar or use a lectionary that includes events like celebrating Ascension Day. I imagine that for some folks this might seem stale and constrictive (esp. when the pastor wants to preach on things like "Twelve Steps to Being a Better Pet Owner," which is not found in the lectionary). Lectionaries aren't perfect because sometimes they selectively omit some unpopular readings (e.g., Revelation). But one good thing about a lectionary is that you get a regular diet of preaching and readings from the "whole counsel of God" rather than whatever the preacher feels like doing on a given day.

If nothing else, I would love to see churches return to celebrating Ascension Day

---

253. Peter Stuhlmacher, *Revisiting Paul's Doctrine of Justification: A Challenge to the New Perspective* (Downers Grove, IL: InterVarsity Press, 2001), 58–59.

254. Cf. rightly Grudem, *Systematic Theology*, 627–28.

255. Cited in Arie W. Ziep, *The Ascension of the Messiah in Lukan Christology* (Leiden: Brill, 1997), 196.

next to Christmas, Easter, Trinity Sunday, and Reformation Sunday. As to why, consider the words of the great textual critic Bruce Metzger:

> Ascension Day proclaims that there is no sphere, however secular, in which Christ has no rights—and no sphere in which his followers are absolved from obedience to him. Instead of it being a fairy tale from the pre-space age, Christ's ascension is the guarantee that he has triumphed over the principalities and powers, so that at his name "every knee should bow, in heaven and on earth and under the earth, and every tongue confess that Jesus Christ is Lord, to the glory of God the Father" (Phil. 2:10–11).[256]

FURTHER READING

Dawson, Gerrit. *Jesus Ascended: The Meaning of Christ's Continuing Incarnation.* London: T&T Clark, 2001.

Farrow, Douglas B. *Ascension and Ecclesia: On the Significance of the Doctrine of the Ascension.* Grand Rapids: Eerdmans, 1999.

Toon, Peter. *The Ascension of Our Lord.* Nashville: Nelson, 1984.

---

256. Bruce M. Metzger, "The Meaning of Christ's Ascension," in *Search the Scriptures: New Testament Studies in Honor of Raymond T. Stamm* (ed. J. M. Myers, O. Reimherr, and H. N. Bream; Leiden: Brill, 1969), 128.

§ 4.7 THE STORY OF JESUS AND THE IDENTITY OF GOD

The gospel preaching in the New Testament nowhere makes explicit that Jesus is a divine person, coequal with the Father in being from all eternity, sharing in one divine substance. What the gospel does make clear is that the epochal saving action of God is executed in his Son in such an intense way that the identity of God must now be (re)defined in light of the mission of the messianic Son. The gospel is a story about God, and the story within the story is Jesus the Messiah. In our God-storied gospel, Jesus is not a human being who was commissioned to speak and act on behalf of God; rather, Jesus speaks and acts from a viewpoint that represents God from the inside.

The logic of the gospel leads us inevitably toward an affirmation of the deity of Christ. This is not as an inference from the titles used to describe him; rather, the narrative climax of the gospel points us toward Jesus as the full-bodied fullness of the divine person. God's reign and redemption are tied up with the gospel of Jesus as Messiah and Lord. In that story we are confronted with a mediator who represents both parties; in that story we properly grasp the divine personhood of Christ. All in all, the testimony of the Christian tradition, based on its exegesis and experience, is that Jesus Christ is both fully God and fully human. In other words, Jesus is God with a human face.

John the Evangelist anchors the story of Jesus in the primeval origins of the cosmos. In the universe's beginning was the Word, and what was true of this Word was also true of God (John 1:1). Then the Word became flesh; he pitched his tent in the midst of humanity; he took on human existence (1:14). This affirmation is not a Johannine innovation, for traditions earlier than the Fourth Gospel had already begun to posit Jesus as a preexistent being and to incorporate Jesus into patterns of devotion normally reserved for the worship of Yahweh.[257] John is merely the apex of the New Testament tradition where Jesus is invested with divine attributes and even worshiped.

---

257. Cf. Hurtado, *Lord Jesus Christ*; Richard Bauckham, *Jesus and the God of Israel* (Grand Rapids: Eerdmans, 2008).

In the early second century, Ignatius of Antioch summarized the widespread belief of Christians in his day that Jesus Christ is both "the Son of Man and the Son of God" (Ign. *Eph.* 20.2), indicating that he possessed divine and human natures. The "how" and "in what sense" Jesus is both human and divine are questions that were explored later, and we too will visit them. For the time being, we can merely note that the double affirmation of Jesus' deity and humanity carried over from the New Testament into creedal statements. The classic confession of Christology is the Nicene-Constantinopolitan Creed, which includes the words:

> We believe in one Lord, Jesus Christ,
> the only Son of God,
> eternally *begotten* of the Father,
> God from God, light from light,
> true God from true God,
> begotten, not made,
> of one Being with the Father;
> through him all things were made.
> *For us and for our salvation*
> *he came down from heaven,*
> was *incarnate of the Holy Spirit* and the Virgin Mary
> and *became truly human.*

Note first of all that Jesus is "eternally begotten ... not made," nor did he emanate. The Johannine language of Jesus as being "begotten" is rooted in his divine nature and is not extrinsic to it. There was no time when he was not. Jesus is the one-of-a-kind-Son, who shares in the Father's eternity. He is eternally begotten, "which is to say that he is not only the product of the Father's eternal love but also in some way defines that love."[258] He shares in the same substance as the Father, not merely a similar substance.

The language of "light from light" is drawn from biblical language about the radiance of God's glory (e.g., Pss 4:6; 104:2; Isa 9:2). It intends to define the relationship of the Son to the Father in terms akin to the glory of God radiating in the person of the Son. Furthermore, the language for the incarnation is vivid. The Son is, through the agency of the Spirit, literally "enfleshed" or "enhumanized." Jesus is not made, adopted, or elevated to divine sonship; rather, he is eternally the Son, who takes on humanity into his own person.

In the Nicene Creed, incarnation and redemption are also bound up together.

---

258. Colin Gunton, *Father, Son, and Holy Spirit: Essays Toward a Fully Trinitarian Theology* (London: T&T Clark, 2003), 62.

Hence the words, "For us and for our salvation, he came down from heaven." In Christian theology, the economy of salvation and the identity of Jesus Christ are intertwined. As such there is an indissoluble unity between the person of Christ and the work of Christ.

The New Testament demonstrates that the incarnation is purposed for the task of redemption. In Matthew's birth narrative, an angel tells Joseph that Mary "will give birth to a son, and you are to give him the name Jesus, because *he will save his people from their sins*" (Matt 1:21, italics added). Immediately following, the Evangelist puts this in a redemptive-historical perspective by identifying in Isaiah 7:14 a typology of the incarnation: "'The virgin will conceive and give birth to a son, and they will call him Immanuel' (which means 'God with us')" (Matt 1:23). The mission of Jesus to save people from their sins rests exclusively on the fact that he is "God" coming to dwell with the people. Jesus was not a tourist from heaven who decided to save some folks while he was on earth. No, he came for the specific purpose of securing the salvation of God's people.

An almost identical point is made in Hebrews: "Since the children have flesh and blood, *he too shared in their humanity so that by his death he might break the power of him who holds the power of death*—that is, the devil.... For this reason *he had to be made like them, fully human in every way*, in order that he might become a merciful and faithful high priest in service to God, and that *he might make atonement for the sins of the people*" (Heb 2:14–17, italics added). Jesus began to share fully the nature of those whom he chose to redeem. The incarnation itself brought victory over the devil and liberation from sin and death.

Moving to the church fathers, we see a lucid awareness that incarnation and redemption are welded together. It was Irenaeus who said:

> For it was incumbent upon the Mediator between God and men, by His relationship to both, to bring both to friendship and concord, and present man to God while He revealed God to man.... For it behooved Him who was to destroy sin, and redeem man under the power of death, that He should Himself be made that very same thing which he was, that is, man; who had been drawn into bondage, but was held by death, so that sin should be destroyed by a man, and man should go forth from death.[259]

Redemption requires incarnation because only a mediator who shares the characteristics of both parties—human and divine—can reconcile the two parties together. In the Christology of the fourth century, the Eastern church fathers such as Athanasius and Gregory of Nazianzus crafted a response with the short sharp phrase: "What is not assumed cannot be redeemed." Only if Jesus has taken on a fully orbed humanity can humanity be fully redeemed. Neither a demigod nor an

---

259. Irenaeus, *Haer.* 3.18.7.

§4.7 The Story of Jesus and the Identity of God

angel can be a savior. It was such a link between incarnation and redemption that made Anselm famously ask, "Why Did God Become Man?" (*Cur Deus Homo?*). Anselm's reply was:

> For, as death came upon the human race by the disobedience of one man, it was fitting that by another man's obedience life should be restored. And, as sin, the cause of our condemnation, had its origin from a woman, so ought the author of our righteousness and salvation to be born of a woman. And so also it was proper that the devil, who, being man's tempter, had conquered him in eating of the tree, should be vanquished by man in the suffering on the tree which man bore. Many other things also, if we carefully explain them, give a certain *indescribable beauty to our redemption* as thus procured.[260]

The Reformation was primarily over debates about church authority and soteriology (with sundry political factors also weighing in). The Reformers maintained the high Christology of the medieval church that was based on the Nicene and Chaledonian formulations. Although the Lutherans and the Reformed differed over the communication of divine attributes in the person of Jesus,[261] they were nonetheless united in affirming Jesus' full humanity and deity. In a subsequent generation this is evident in both the Westminster Confession and Thirty-Nine Articles.

Westminster Confession 8.2	Article 2 of Thirty-Nine Articles
The Son of God, the second person of the Trinity, being very and eternal God, of one substance and equal with the Father, did, when the fullness of time was come, take upon Him man's nature, with all the essential properties, and common infirmities thereof, yet without sin; being conceived by the power of the Holy Ghost, in the womb of the virgin Mary, of her substance. So that two whole, perfect, and distinct natures, the Godhead and the manhood, were inseparably joined together in one person, without conversion, composition, or confusion. Which person is very God, and very man, yet one Christ, the only Mediator between God and man.	The Son, which is the Word of the Father, begotten from everlasting of the Father, the very and eternal God, and of one substance with the Father, took Man's nature in the womb of the blessed Virgin, of her substance: so that two whole and perfect Natures, that is to say, the Godhead and Manhood, were joined together in one Person, never to be divided, whereof is one Christ, very God, and very Man; who truly suffered, was crucified, dead, and buried, to reconcile His Father to us, and to be a sacrifice, not only for original guilt, but also for all actual sins of men.

These christological affirmations of Jesus' coequal deity with the Father, worked out in the church fathers and maintained by the Reformers, are not mindless

---

260. Anselm, *Cur Deus Homo?* 1.3.

261. Cf. Horton, *Christian Faith*, 477–79.

philosophical speculations that have overstretched the pure and primitive Christology of the early church. Rather, there is biblical pressure to define the nature of Jesus' relationship to the God the Father and to develop an appropriate understanding of his agency in creation and redemption.

All of this emerges out of two key axioms of biblical Christology. First is the identification of Jesus of Nazareth as the exalted Lord. This is exemplified by Peter's speech in Acts 2, where he announces that "God has made *this Jesus* [i.e., the historical figure], whom you crucified, both Lord and Messiah" (Acts 2:36, italics added). In light of later debates, this ruled out the view that the Logos came upon the man Jesus and replaced his soul, or that the Logos was joined to the man Jesus who was born of woman. Rather, "he who was made flesh and became man is the one, selfsame Jesus Christ our Lord, the Word of God."[262]

Second is the identification of the exalted Jesus as the Lord of Israel. This is made explicit in the ascription of Old Testament language for Yahweh being applied to Jesus in places like Philippians 2:5–11 (= Isa 45:23) and 1 Corinthians 8:6 (= Deut 6:4). The one God of Jewish monotheism must be defined by way of the exaltation of Jesus to the Father's right hand. Thus, it was a real human being who was revealed as "Lord," and this "Lord" is defined in relation to the God of Israel. The God who creates, covenants, redeems, and re-creates is the God revealed in and through Jesus Christ. There is a unity between what God does in creation and redemption and what is attributed to Jesus Christ in these same roles. That is what we will explore further in this part: the man Jesus is the God of Israel incarnated in human flesh.

Before we move on, a tantalizing subject is the relevance of the incarnation for gospel proclamation. Let us remember that the first Christians were not given a private revelation of the Nicene and Chalcedonian Creeds in advance. The evangelistic sermons of the early church did not begin with Four Spiritual Laws about the holiness of God, the sinfulness of humanity, and the need for an incarnated Savior to bear the sins of the world. The Christology of the first decades and even the first two centuries of the church was a work in progress, and a messy one at that. The mind of the church came to the conclusion that the biblical materials are best explained by way of affirming Jesus' preexistence, coequality, and comajesty with the Father. I do not doubt that the apostles and early leaders knew that Jesus was from God and shared an existence with God in some form, but I do not think that they necessarily had the same theological precision in their thinking that we find in the later creeds.

---

262. Second Council of Constantinople (553) anathema 3, cited in John Anthony McGuckin, *We Believe in One Lord Jesus Christ* (ACD 2; ed. T. C. Oden; Downers Grove, IL: InterVarsity Press, 2009), 4.

§ 4.7 The Story of Jesus and the Identity of God

In light of that, I often ask my students the provocative question: "Do we have to tell people that Jesus is God in our evangelistic proclamation?" Normally they say, "Yes, of course!" and I can hardly blame then. But as we look at the classic summaries of the gospel in Romans 1:3–4; 1 Corinthians 15:2–4; 2 Timothy 2:8; and in the speeches in Acts, we observe that the affirmation of Jesus' sonship pertains not to his ontological status as the second person of the Trinity as much as it applies to his salvific agency and messianic office. Jesus is sent from God to enable us to be reconciled to God, but the gospel itself does not require an explicit statement of Jesus' coequal deity with the Father.

In other words, incarnation is the presupposition of the gospel, not its content. But the incarnation is no less significant for that fact. For if there were no incarnation, there would be no good news for which we can speak. The proclamation of the gospel (except in the case of Muslim evangelism and in dealing with cults like Jehovah's Witnesses) does not have to include a theology of incarnation. Rather, it is the subsequent exposition of the gospel, the reading of the Gospels, and the further exploration of the identity of the one crucified that leads us to affirm the deity of Christ in catechetical instruction for the converted.

4.7.1 THE PREEXISTENT SON

The doctrine of Christ's preexistence as the second person of the Trinity is affirmed in creedal and confessional statements because preexistence is thought to be explicitly present in biblical materials. Christ's preexistence could be expressed this way: the Son of Mary is the incarnation of the eternal Son of God, who became something that he was not, that is, human, and he was a conscious personal being before he took on flesh. Yet not all theologians accept it.[263] John Macquarrie contends that if Jesus had a conscious and personal preexistence, then the incarnation is mythological, and preexistence is grossly injurious into the humanity of Jesus.[264] Concerning the nature of Christ, John Knox believes that we can have humanity without preexistence and we can have preexistence without humanity, but there is no way to have them both.[265] Robert Jenson thinks of Jesus as preexistent in a logical sense concerning Jesus' divine identity, but there was no "before" for the child born to Mary.[266] However, the biblical evidence clearly undermines such denials of Christ's preexistence.

We begin with the earliest data, hymnic and creedal material, attested in Paul.

---

263. Cf. survey of modern theology in Douglas McCready, *He Came Down from Heaven: The Preexistence of Christ and the Christian Faith* (Downers Grove, IL: InterVarsity Press, 2005), 257–307.

264. John Macquarrie, *Jesus Christ in Modern Thought* (London: SCM, 1990), 57.

265. John Knox, *The Humanity and Divinity of Christ* (Cambridge: Cambridge University Press, 1967), 106.

266. Robert W. Jenson, *Systematic Theology* (2 vols.; New York: Oxford University Press, 1997–1999), 1:141.

Philippians 2:6–11	Colossians 1:15–20
Who, *being in very nature God*, did not consider equality with God something to be used to his own advantage; rather, he *made himself nothing* by taking the *very nature of a servant, being made in human likeness.* And being found in appearance as a man, he humbled himself by becoming obedient to death—even death on a cross! Therefore God exalted him to the highest place and gave him the name that is above every name, that at the name of Jesus every knee should bow, in heaven and on earth and under the earth, and every tongue acknowledge that Jesus Christ is Lord, to the glory of God the Father.	The Son is the image of the invisible God, the firstborn over all creation. *For in him all things were created*: things in heaven and on earth, visible and invisible, whether thrones or powers or rulers or authorities; all things have been created through him and for him. *He is before all things*, and in him all things hold together. And he is the head of the body, the church; he is the beginning and the firstborn from among the dead, so that in everything he might have the supremacy. For God was pleased to have all his fullness dwell in him, and through him to reconcile to himself all things, whether things on earth or things in heaven, by making peace through his blood, shed on the cross. (italics added in both columns)

Philippians 2:6–11 is most likely a pre-Pauline hymn developed by Greek-speaking Christians in the early years of the church. A straightforward reading of the hymn suggests three states of Christ, including preexistence, humiliation, and exaltation. However, several scholars deny, or else minimize, any notion of preexistence and divine Christology in the hymn. For instance, James Dunn contends that what we have here is not so much preexistence as an Adam-Christology, where Jesus has a metaphorical prehistory, but only in the second Adam's decision to become human.[267]

Though one might detect echoes of Genesis 1–3 in the Christ hymn in Philippians 2, especially in the contrast of obedience and disobedience, an Adam-Christology is an insufficient explanation of the content of the hymn. That Jesus was "in very nature God" is not strictly the same as saying that he was in the "image of God." Adam's failure, or Eve's actually, was aspiring to be "like God" in knowledge of good and evil, not pursuing "equality" with God. Nowhere in extant ancient literature is Adam ever called "equal with God," and the phrase appears elsewhere in a pejorative sense to describe the vain efforts of human beings to attain divine status for themselves

---

267. James D. G. Dunn, *Christology in the Making* (2nd ed. Grand Rapids: Eerdmans, 1996), 113–21; idem, *Theology of Paul the Apostle* (Edinburgh: T&T Clark, 2003), 286–88.

(cf., e.g., John 5:18; 2 Macc 9:12; Philo, *Leg.* 1.49).[268] Furthermore, Christ's attitude to divine equality is exhibited prior to taking on human form, not after it. So the focus of this Christ Hymn is not on a replication of the Adam story in Jesus' humanity.

The phrases "form of God" and "equality with God" are mutually interpretive. They identify Jesus with the glory and authority of Israel's God prior to his humiliation on the cross. The fact that Jesus shifts from the "nature" of God to the "nature of a servant" implies a movement from one state to another state, divided by his taking on "human likeness" and his appearance as a "man." What is envisaged in this preexistence is, according to N. T. Wright, "no mere personification, then, but a person, a conscious individual entity."[269] If that is the case, then Christ did not regard his equality with God as excusing him from the task of redemptive suffering; on the contrary, it uniquely qualified him for it.[270]

The emptying of Christ himself (*kenoō*) is not the grounds for a so-called kenotic Christology, whereby Christ left behind certain attributes such as his glory, omniscience, or powers, like someone stripping off before climbing into a dirty pit. The emptying occurred not by what he left behind but through what he took on, humanity—humanity in humiliation no less. Philippians 2:5–11 is about the preexistent Son, who is equal with God, who voluntarily takes on human form, and is finally acknowledged as "Lord" at the end of his redemptive mission.

The hymn in Colossians is equally forthright in asserting Christ's preexistence. The Colossian hymn appears to be based on a christological reading of Genesis 1, supplemented with motifs drawn from Jewish wisdom traditions. That Jesus is the firstborn is not to make him a created being. To call someone "firstborn" is to say something of their primacy in rule, preeminence in role, and priority in rank. As "firstborn," Jesus is the appointed authority over creation and the head of a new eschatological humanity. Jesus is explicitly said to have existed "before all things." He is the creator, sustainer, and redeemer of the universe. While Colossians 1:15–20 gave Arians ammunition for their view that Jesus as the "firstborn" was a created, subordinated, semidivine being, it also provided ample grounds to refute them.[271]

If the hymns of Philippians 2 and Colossians 1 are pre-Pauline and early, then—and this is what keeps scholars of Christian Origins up at night—within twenty years of Jesus' death, people were revering him as a preexistent being, active in both creation and redemption and ascribing to him the title "Lord."

Numerous other texts clearly demand that Jesus is a preexistent person within the Godhead. Paul identifies Christ as active with the Israelites in the wilderness through the rock that followed them (1 Cor 10:4, 9). Jude, depending on textual

---

268. Hurtado, *Lord Jesus Christ*, 122–23.
269. Wright, *Climax of the Covenant*, 97.
270. Ibid., 83–84.
271. Michael F. Bird, *Colossians and Philemon* (NCCS; Eugene, OR: Cascade, 2009), 47–59.

variants, sees "Jesus" as delivering the people from Egypt (Jude 5).[272] In 2 Corinthians 8:9 ("For you know the grace of our Lord Jesus Christ, that though he was rich, yet for your sake he became poor, so that you through his poverty might become rich"), the incarnation and cross are telescoped into a single action that reinforces the point that preexistence shows the gracious work of Christ on the cross.[273] That Jesus is from "heaven" is the clear teaching of both Paul (1 Cor 15:47–48) and John (John 3:13). The Johannine Jesus refers to the "the glory I had with you [i.e., the Father] before the world began" (John 17:5).

In 1 Peter 1:20, Jesus was "chosen" before the creation of the world, but only "revealed" in the last days. The language of Christ as preexistent permeates the entire letter to the Hebrews. In Hebrews 1, the Son is appointed the "heir of all things"; he is the one through whom God made universe and was designated as "Son" prior to a human birth, and he is greater than the angels. Lastly, the Pauline notion of the "sending" of Jesus (Rom 8:3; Gal 4:4) stands in analogy to the "I have come" logia in the Gospels that depict Jesus coming from A to B, with A being heaven and B being earth (e.g., Matt 5:17; Mark 2:17; Luke 12:49; John 5:43).

Jesus has a personal and conscious preexistence as the Son of God. The significance of Jesus' preexistence is twofold. First, incarnation and redemption are merged together. Jesus *comes* from heaven in order to *redeem* his people. In fact, his role as mediator is then retrojected across redemptive history and even into creation. If Jesus is God's agent of redemption and creation, presumably he has always been so. Second, the incarnation was a voluntary act of the Son. It was not forced or imposed. The Son wills to be incarnate, in obedience to the Father, in the power of the Spirit, in order to execute the divine plan for salvation.[274]

FURTHER READING

Gathercole, Simon G. *The Preexistent Son: Recovering the Christologies of Matthew, Mark, and Luke*. Grand Rapids: Eerdmans, 2006.

McCready, Douglas. *He Came Down From Heaven: The Preexistence of Christ and the Christian Faith*. Downers Grove, IL: InterVarsity Press, 2005.

4.7.2 JESUS AND THE GOD OF ISRAEL

Jesus was a monotheist. He proclaimed the kingdom of God and the gospel of God (e.g., Mark 1:14–15). He prayed to God as Father (Mark 14:36; Luke 11:1–4/Matt 6:9–13; John 11:41–42). He affirmed the Jewish confession of one God in the *Shema*

---

272. The Editio Critica Maior prefers the reading "Jesus" over "Lord" in v. 5 of Jude.

273. Gathercole, *The Preexistent Son*, 26.

274. Cf. ibid., 289–91.

(Deut 6:4–5; Mark 12:29–30), and he called for steadfast devotion to God (Luke 16:13/Matt 6:24). Yet Jesus also expressed a sense of unmediated divine authority that led the Judean leaders to query him about the origin of his authority (Mark 11:27–33), and public opinion was that he spoke with a *unique* authority that set him apart from the teachers of the law (Mark 1:22, 27). Jesus also reconfigures divine commandments based on his own authority (e.g., Matt 5:21–22, 27–28, 33–34, 38–39, 43–44). In the Johannine witness, Jesus repeatedly affirms that he was "sent" by the Father, and yet there is also an intimate unity between Father and Son. This culminates in his implicit claim to be "equal with God" and to be "one" with the Father (John 5:18; 10:30; 14:7–9). In Jesus' ministry, the authority of the sender and the sent becomes blurred as Jesus acts in effect as if he holds the weight of divine authority.

Jesus and the apostles were devout monotheists. They believed in one God alone. Jesus never claimed to be a second god and never said, "Behold, I am the Father." The best category to explain how Jesus relates to God is through what Richard Bauckham calls "divine identity." That is, the one God of Israel is understood and defined in relation to the person and work of Jesus Christ. The very meaning of "God" is redrawn around the life, death, resurrection, exaltation, and subsequent worship of Jesus Christ.[275] This can be demonstrated from how several Yahweh texts from the Old Testament are applied to Jesus.[276]

"I will send my messenger, who will prepare the way before me. Then suddenly the *Lord* you are seeking will come to his temple; the messenger of the covenant, whom you desire, will come," says the LORD Almighty." (Mal 3:1)	And you, my child, will be called a prophet of the Most High; for you will go on before the *Lord* to prepare the way for him. (Luke 1:76)
A voice of one calling: "In the wilderness prepare the way *for the* LORD; make straight in the desert a highway for our God." (Isa 40:3)	John replied in the words of Isaiah the prophet, "I am the voice of one calling in the wilderness, 'Make straight the way *for the Lord.*'" (John 1:23)
Hear, O Israel: The LORD our God, the LORD is one. (Deut 6:4)	For even if there are so-called gods, whether in heaven or on earth (as indeed there are many "gods" and many "lords"), yet for us there is but *one God, the Father*, from whom all things came and for whom we live; and there is but *one Lord, Jesus Christ*, through whom all things came and through whom we live. (1 Cor 8:5–6)

---

275. Bauckham, *Jesus and the God of Israel*, x.
276. Cf. further ibid., 182–232.

By myself I [Yahweh] have sworn, my mouth has uttered in all integrity a word that will not be revoked: *Before me every knee will bow; by me every tongue will swear.* (Isa 45:23)	Therefore God exalted him to the highest place and gave him the name that is above every name, that at the name of Jesus every *knee should bow, in heaven and on earth and under the earth, and every tongue acknowledge that Jesus Christ is Lord*, to the glory of God the Father. (Phil 2:9–11)
In the beginning *you* [Yahweh] laid the foundations of the earth, and the heavens are the work of your hands. They will perish, but you remain; they will all wear out like a garment. Like clothing you will change them and they will be discarded. But you remain the same, and your years will never end. (Ps 102:25–27)	He also says, "In the beginning, *Lord*, you laid the foundations of the earth, and the heavens are the work of your hands. They will perish, but you remain; they will all wear out like a garment. You will roll them up like a robe; like a garment they will be changed. But you remain the same, and your years will never end." (Heb 1:10–12, italics added in all cases)

These passages present a consistent pattern of explicitly depicting Jesus in light of Old Testament texts that refer to the Lord of Israel. John the Baptist prepares the way for the Lord, and yet the Lord who comes is none other than Jesus. Paul develops a christological monotheism by taking up the confession of God's exclusive oneness in the *Shema* and the monotheistic theology of Isaiah, and then redefining it around the identity of Jesus Christ as Lord in direct contrast to pagan polytheism. The writer of Hebrews switches from speaking about the "Son" to the "Lord" and describes his work in creation in terms normally applicable only to Yahweh. The implication should be clear: the one and only Lord of Israel is uniquely known, experienced, and revealed in the Lord Jesus Christ.

One could possibly work through the New Testament one book at a time, weighing up where, how, and with what degree of certainty the relevant passages identify Jesus as God.[277] A more dynamic approach is used by Robert Bowman and Ed Komoszewski, who demonstrate the deity of Jesus in the New Testament by expositing the acronym HANDS, which I will now loosely follow.[278]

H: Jesus shares the *honors* due to God. In the gospel of John, honor given to Jesus is treated as honor given to the Father. The Father entrusts judgment to the Son so that "all may honor the Son just as they honor the Father," and "whoever does not honor the Son does not honor the Father, who sent him" (John 5:23). Many doxologies in the New Testament are a straightforward exulting of God's honor and glory; however, several doxologies have a christocentric element, so that the glory of God

---

277. Cf. Murray Harris, *Jesus as God: The New Testament Use of Theos in Reference to Jesus* (Grand Rapids: Baker, 1992).

278. Robert M. Bowman and J. Ed Komoszewski, *Putting Jesus in His Place: The Case for the Deity of Christ* (Grand Rapids: Kregel, 2007).

the Father and Jesus Christ are intrinsically connected (e.g., Rom 11:36; Gal 1:4–5; Phil 4:20). Glory ascribed to God is mediated *through* Jesus Christ (Rom 16:27; Heb 13:20–21; 1 Pet 4:11; Jude 25). In 2 Peter, glory is ascribed to Jesus without any reference to the Father: "Grow in the grace and knowledge of our Lord and Savior Jesus Christ. To him be glory both now and forever! Amen" (2 Pet 3:18). Importantly, in Revelation, there is a great deal of overlap between the doxologies and praise ascribed to God and the doxologies and praise ascribed to Jesus. Honor and glory are given to God and extended to the Lamb (Rev 4:11; 5:12–13).

A: Jesus shares the *attributes* of God. The shared likeness of Jesus and God is suggested initially by the fact that Jesus is the "image of the invisible God" (Col 1:15), "God's glory [is] displayed in the face of Christ" (2 Cor 4:6), and the "Son is the radiance of God's glory and the exact representation of his being" (Heb 1:3). To see Jesus is to see the Father, since Father and Son mutually permeate each other (John 14:7–10). In the testimony of the Fourth Gospel, Jesus had a preexistent glory because Isaiah "saw Jesus' glory and spoke about him" (John 12:37–41; cf. Isa 6:1–10). In the book of Revelation, attributes are shared between God and the Lamb: "To him who sits on the throne and to the Lamb be praise and honor and glory and power, for ever and ever" (Rev 5:13). There is clear avowal that God is changeless (Num 23:19; 1 Sam 15:29; Mal 3:6; Jas 1:17), while according to Hebrews "Jesus Christ is the same yesterday and today and forever" (Heb 13:8).

N: Jesus shares the *names* of God. The designations for Jesus in the New Testament indicate that his origins and authority are bound up with the God of Israel. The most obvious of these is that Jesus is repeatedly designated with a combination of "God," "Lord," and "Savior" (John 20:28; Titus 2:13; 2 Pet 1:1, 11). As the "Lord Jesus," there is an immediate rehearsal of the *kyrios* from the LXX that translated the Hebrew tetragrammaton for God, Yahweh. As the "Lord," Jesus brings a redefinition of Israel's God in virtue of his life, death, and resurrection (Rom 10:16; 1 Cor 8:6; 16:22). The name of God was always something to be revered (Exod 20:7; Lev 19:12; 22:32; Deut 5:11; Matt 6:9/Luke 11:2), and Jesus' name becomes efficient in baptism (Acts 2:38; 8:16; 10:48; 19:5), prayer (John 14:13–14; 15:16; 16:23–26), and even salvation (Luke 24:47; Acts 2:21; 4:12; 1 John 2:12). The reverence for Jesus' name is also seen by what Christians do in the name of the Lord Jesus (Col 3:17) and their willingness to suffer for his name (1 Pet 4:14).

In the gospel of Matthew, Jesus is called "Immanuel," meaning "God with us." What is a regal ancient Near Eastern name in Isaiah 7:14 becomes a reality for the son of Mary in Matthew 1:23. In the gospel of John, Jesus is named as the eternal "Word" that preexisted and tabernacled among Israel (John 1:1, 14). Then, at the end, Thomas addresses him as "my Lord and my God" (John 20:28). Similarly, Jesus is explicitly addressed as "God" in Romans 9:5 ("Theirs are the patriarchs, and from them is traced the human ancestry of the Messiah, who is God over all, forever praised!") and Hebrews 1:8 ("But about the Son he says, "Your throne, O God, will last for ever and ever; a scepter of justice will be the scepter of your kingdom"). Israel's God is the God of gods and Lord of lords (Deut 10:17; Ps 136:3; 1 Tim 6:15), which is taken up and applied to the reign of Jesus (Rev 17:14; 19:16). Finally, God is described as the "first and the last" (Isa 41:4; 44:6; 48:12), which is applied to Jesus in Revelation (Rev 1:17–18; 2:8) and even the Alpha and Omega in 1:8; 21:6; and 22:13.

D: Jesus shares the *deeds* of God. The works ordinarily attributed to Yahweh are said in the New Testament to be executed by, in, and through Jesus. Axiomatic in the Old Testament is that Yahweh is the creator of all things (Gen 1:1; Neh 9:6; Pss 95:5–7; 100:3). This creation takes place *through* Jesus as "the world was made through him" (John 1:10), the one "through whom all things came and through whom we live" (1 Cor 8:6); "all things have been created through him and for him" (Col 1:16), and "through [him] also he made the universe" (Heb 1:2). In these passages, Jesus is not a subordinate figure to whom creation is delegated like a subcontractor. A comparison of Romans 11:36 and 1 Corinthians 8:6, with the prepositional phrase "through him," indicate that the instrumental cause of creation is attributed in identical ways to both God the Father and the Lord Jesus.

Another role jointly shared by God and Jesus is that of Redeemer. The God of Israel is the Savior of Israel (e.g., Deut 32:15; 2 Sam 22:3; Ps 18:46; Isa 43:3; Hab 3:18), while Jesus is the Savior of the new Israel (e.g., John 4:42; Acts 5:31; 13:23; Phil 3:20). Obviously the Father remains as Savior "through" Jesus (Titus 3:4–6; 1 John 4:14; Jude 25), but Jesus becomes the instrumental cause by which salvation is put into effect. Finally, Jesus is appointed as "judge" (John 5:22; Acts 17:31; Rom 2:16; 2 Tim 4:1), even though judgment is frequently predicated of God elsewhere in the Bible (e.g., Gen 16:5; Ps 96:10, 13; Isa 11:3–4; 33:22; Rev 6:10).

S: Jesus shares the *seat* of God's throne. A common theme in the New Testament is that Jesus is enthroned beside God and from that throne he exercises divine prerogatives. In his trial before the Sanhedrin, Jesus replied to a messianic charge with a claim that he as the Son of Man will be enthroned at the right hand of God, conflating Psalm 110:1 and Daniel 7:13, which prompts a charge of blasphemy (Matt 26:64–65). In subsequent reflection, God "seated him at his right hand in the heavenly realms, far above all rule and authority, power and dominion" (Eph 1:20–21); "he sat down at the right hand of the Majesty in heaven" (Heb 1:3); and Jesus "has gone into heaven and is at God's right hand—with angels, authorities and powers in submission to him" (1 Pet 3:22).

This point is accentuated in Revelation 4–5, where there is a shift from a visionary report of the heavenly throne room of God and the worship therein, but it is clear that the Lamb of God shares God's throne, he stands in the center of the throne, and he receives the same chorus of heavenly worship. Later in the book is a description of God and the Lamb who sit on the throne (7:10, 17; 22:1, 3). It is what Jesus does from the throne, as giver of the Spirit and Redeemer, that shows he exercises the prerogatives of God and why he receives worship due to God.

The New Testament provides clear accounts of Jesus' deity and intimations of Jesus' coequal authority and majesty with God. But there is still a sense in which Jesus is, functionally at least, subordinate to God. This is evident in 1 Corinthians 15:28, where Paul says, "When he has done this, then the Son himself will be made subject to him who put everything under him, so that God may be all in all." Similar is John's emphasis that Jesus is sent by the Father and delegated authority by the Father; Jesus even says "the Father is greater than I" (John 14:28).

Admittedly, in the early church, some laid the emphasis on this seeming subordination of Jesus in different ways. Some early church fathers regarded Jesus as a human being who was adopted by God as his Son at either his baptism or resurrection. A Jewish Christian group called the Ebionites, who traced their heritage back to the Jerusalem church, seem to have held to an adoptionist Christology (though whether a group called the "Ebionites" actually believed this is itself disputed).[279] James Dunn goes so far as to say that Ebionite Christology had a firm anchor in biblical texts (e.g., Mark 1:11; Acts 2:36; Rom 1:3–4 with influence from Ps 2:7: "You are my son; today I have become your father").

Thus, it is thought that for some Jewish Christians, Jesus was a human Davidide, who ascended into heaven and was appointed by God to a position of authority, so that a Christology later deemed to be heretical was perhaps the earliest Christology of all.[280] The problem is that these texts pertain to enthronement rather than to adoption. Psalm 2:7 certainly includes the refrain, "Today I have become your father," but note the preceding words in 2:6: "I have installed my king on Zion, my holy mountain," which concerns a political appointment from which an honorary filial status flows. The focus of Psalm 2, both its literary content and its Christian appropriation, is messianic—the revelation of God's king to the nations of the world; the focus is not the post-coronation, ontological makeup of Israel's king.

In addition, the New Testament authors do not regard Jesus as a human being adopted into the theocratic heavenly hierarchy. More accurately, Jesus is exalted to a position of royal and divine status, not simply accepted into the heavenly court or transformed into a high-ranking angel. He shares God's throne and is subsequently worshiped. Divine features are attributed to him from the beginning of his ministry and even in his preexistence. While adoptionist christologies may be loosely based on

---

279. See discussion in Timo Eskola, *Messiah and the Throne: Jewish Merkabah Mysticism and Early Christian Exaltation Discourse* (WUNT 2.142; Tübingen: Mohr/Siebeck, 2001), 299–309.

280. James D. G. Dunn, *Unity and Diversity in the New Testament* (2nd ed.; London: SCM, 1990), 258–66.

texts like Psalms 2 and 110, they cannot explain primitive christological confessions of Jesus as enthroned with God, nor do they account for the devotional practices of the early church with the worship of Jesus beside God.[281] Adoptionism, both its ancient and modern varieties,[282] fails to grapple with the christological narrative and worship life of the early church. Irenaus's complaint against adoptionism remains correct: "How can they be saved unless it was God who wrought out their salvation upon the earth? Or how shall a human pass into god, unless God has first passed into a human."[283]

In the third and fourth centuries, the divinity of Jesus was not pursued as a matter of intellectual speculation. Rather, it was undertaken as a way of understanding the purpose and mission of the Son of God. It was a question that the Gnostics had instigated by the mid-second century on account of their identification of Jesus as an emanation from the divine "fullness." Similarly, the Monarchian controversy projected the issue into the wider Mediterranean world with their description of God as one person who either adopted Jesus or appeared as Jesus. By the early third century, it was the Logos Christology, beginning with Justin and climaxing in Origen, that eventually carried the day.

However, even after Origen, the question of Jesus' sonship and status became more acute, especially in terms of the Son's ontology and preexistence. The question of Jesus' deity was strenuously debated in the fourth century, and it came down to whether Jesus Christ was merely one of the angelic powers found worthy of special honors. In the final analysis, Jesus was proclaimed as what the church had always suspected: the Son of God in a unique and fully divine sense.

The zenith of the debates over Christ's deity arrived in the Arian controversy. Arius was a popular Alexandrian preacher who believed that Jesus was preexistent, much like an angel, but not eternal and not coequal with the Father. Jesus had a type of divinity, but not the full deity of the Father. The motto of Arius and his popular movement was: "There was a time when he was not." The Council of Nicea (325) was meant to end the controversy; it did make some headway, but the debate continued, and the Arians even held sway for much of the time. For the Arians, Jesus was "like" (*homoiousios*) the Father in being, while for the Niceans, Jesus was the "same" (*homoousios*) as the Father in substance. In practicality, *homoiousios* meant that God was not always a Father, and the Son was in fact a created being.

While this looks odd to us, the Arian position held several attractions. (1) It made it easier to conceive as to how the Son could suffer and die—something impossible

---

281. Eskola, *Messiah and the Throne*, 321.

282. For a "modern" Christology that countenances adoptionism, see Friedrich Schleiermacher (*The Christian Faith* [ed. and trans. H. R. Mackintosh and J. S. Steward; Edinburgh: T&T Clark, 1928], 385): "The Redeemer, then, is like all men in virtue of the identity of human nature, but distinguished from them all by the constant potency of His God-consciousness, which was a veritable existence of God in Him."

283. Irenaeus, *Haer.* 4.33.4.

for God but quite possible for a creature. (2) It made it easier to understand Jesus' advent from heaven: a heavenly being transformed into a human being but not an incarnation of God-in-the-flesh. (3) It also protected the transcendence and "otherness" of God by distancing God from the earthly work of Jesus.[284] Rowan Williams summarizes Arian theology as follows:

> It is inadmissible to say that God and his Son "co-exist." God must *pre-exist* the Son. If not, we are faced with a whole range of unacceptable ideas — that the Son is part of God, or an emanation of God, or worst of all, that he is, like God, self-subsistent. The Son exists by God's free will, brought into existence by him before all times and ages and existing stably and "inalienably."[285]

The most impassioned defense of a divine Christology against the Arians came from the bishop of Alexandria, Athanasius (ca. 296–373). Athanasius recognized that Arius destroyed the internal coherence of the Christian message by divorcing the person of God from the work of Christ. Athanasius' most compelling attack on Arius took the form of a syllogism:

1. No creature can redeem another creature.
2. According to Arius, Jesus is a creature.
3. Therefore, according to Arius, Jesus cannot redeem humanity.

The chink in Arius's armor was that he affirmed that Jesus was the Savior of humanity and even agreed that Jesus should be worshiped, but he operated with a Christology that could not coherently hold these beliefs and practices together. If Jesus was a created being, then he was part of the created order that needed redemption and was, therefore, unable to be its Redeemer. If Jesus was not in the full sense "God," it was idolatrous to venerate him with sacred honors and religious pageantry. Arius was effectively sawing off the soteriological and doxological branches that the church had been sitting on. For Athanasius:

> You must understand why it is that the Word of the Father, so great and so high, has been manifest in bodily form.... He has been manifested in a human body for this reason only, out of the love and goodness of His Father, for the salvation of us men. We will begin, then, with the creation of the world and with God its Maker, for the first fact that you must grasp is this: the renewal of creation has been wrought by the Self-same Word who made it in the beginning.[286]

What Athanasius advocates here is the exact opposite of what had been set forth by the Gnostics and the Arians, namely, the unity of God in his actions in both creation and redemption. On the worship of Jesus, Athanasius said:

---

284. Gerald Bray, *God Is Love: A Biblical and Systematic Theology* (Wheaton, IL: Crossway, 2012), 209.
285. Rowan Williams, *Arius: Heresy & Tradition* (London: SCM, 1987), 97.
286. Athanasius, *Inc.* 1.

[Jesus Christ] would not have been worshipped or spoken of in this way [Heb 1:6; John 13:13; 20:28] if he belonged merely to the rank of creatures. But as it is, since he is not a creature but the offspring of the God who is worshipped and is believed to be God, and is Lord of hosts, and has authority, and is All-sovereign, just as the Father is ... it is proper to the Son to have all that the Father has and to be such that the Father is beheld in him, and that through him all things were made and that in him the salvation of all is brought about and established.[287]

Arius's attempt to emphasize the unity and oneness of God in many ways resembles a monotheism much like that of the Jehovah's Witnesses or Islam rather than a Trinitarian monotheism. Orthodox Trinitarianism was developed out of the internal debates of the church, which long had to wrestle with the Jewish monotheistic heritage of its faith and Hellenistic models for postulating how God interacts with the physical world. What was rejected in the ecumenical councils is that Jesus was in any sense God's deputy or an inferior being. Such ways of thinking simply did not map into the New Testament witness, nor did they correspond with Christian experience of him in worship.[288]

4.7.3 MADE LIKE HIS BROTHERS

Jesus was human. He had a birth, childhood, adulthood, and death. He had a fully orbed existence at the emotional level with grief, sorrow, joy, and anger, as well as a complete physical existence with tiredness, hunger, and thirst. He even had a spirit and a soul and so shares in the immaterial constituents of humanity. Jesus calls himself the "Son of Man," which as a Semitic term often means "human one" or "son of Adam." The New Testament speaks to the full humanity of Christ. He comes as bone to our bone, flesh to our flesh; he speaks with a human voice; he grows up in a human family, eats, drinks, thirsts, hungers, grows weary, mourns, rejoices, and sheds tears. It is majesty in frailty.[289]

Paul's soteriology depends on the notion that Jesus was a historic human being when he writes: "For if the many died by the trespass of the one man, how much more did God's grace and the gift that came by the grace of the one man, Jesus Christ, overflow to the many!" (Rom 5:15). The grace of God can only come to humanity through a real human being. Only a new Adam can undo the condemnation of the first Adam. Peter has no issue with calling Jesus "a man" in his proclamation to the Jerusalemites: "Jesus of Nazareth was a man accredited by God to you by miracles, wonders and signs, which God did among you through him" (Acts 2:22). Similarly, Jesus defends himself by describing himself as "a man who has told you

---

287. Athanasius, *Apol. sec.* 2.24 (cited in McGuckin, *We Believe in One Lord Jesus Christ*, 24–25).
288. Alister E. McGrath, *Heresy: A History of Defending the Truth* (San Francisco: HarperOne, 2009), 141–42.
289. Torrance, *Incarnation*, 185.

THE SONSHIP OF THE SON

Jesus is the "the Father's Son" (2 John 3). The meaning and mission of his sonship is an enduring matter of theological reflection. What is a "son" after all, and what is a "Son of God"? The New Testament emphasizes at length that Jesus is the "Son," not in a biological sense but in a relational sense. Sonship is the divinely revealed analogy for how Jesus relates to God the Father. What is more, if Jesus Christ is the Son of God for us, he must also be the Son of God for God. As the incarnate Son, his sonship reaches all the way into eternity past and exists eternally within the Godhead. Since he is the Son of God in the incarnation, he is also the Son of God antecedently in himself.[290]

The development of the doctrine of Jesus' sonship endeavored to affirm Jesus' ontological equality with God the Father, while simultaneously affirming that Jesus was not simply a mode of the Father's being. The grammar developed to indicate this was to say that God consists of three *hypostases* ("persons") sharing in one *ousia* ("substance"). This means that what distinguishes the Son from the Father is his particular relationship with Father and Spirit in light of the equality of essence within the Godhead. The Son is not a miniature deity inferior to the Father, nor a mere alternative persona of the Father. Cyril of Jerusalem made a short remark that ruled out both subordinationism and modalism as legitimate christological options:

> The Son then is very God, having the Father in Himself, not changed into the Father; for the Father was not made man, but the Son. For let the truth be freely spoken. The Father suffered not for us, but the Father sent Him who suffered. Neither let us say, "There was a time when the Son was not"; nor let us admit a Son who is the Father: but let us walk in the king's highway; let us turn aside neither on the left hand nor on the right. Neither from thinking to honor the Son, let us call Him the Father; nor from thinking to honor the Father, imagine the Son to be some one of the creatures. But let One Father be worshipped through One Son, and let not their worship be separated. Let One Son be proclaimed, sitting at the right hand of the Father before all ages: sharing His throne not by advancement in time after His Passion, but by eternal possession.[291]

---

290. Torrance, *Incarnation*, 176. 291. Cyril of Jerusalem, *Catechetical Lectures* 11.17.

the truth that I heard from God" (John 8:40). The gospel is incomplete if it speaks only of God's attitude to humanity without detailing that it was through a human being and for human beings that God's salvation is wrought.

The denial that Jesus had a physical body is called "Docetism." The Docetists tried to have a higher Christology by claiming that Jesus Christ never came in the flesh, but only *appeared* to be human (*dokeō* means "to seem"). Human flesh was purportedly beneath a transcendent God. Salvation was escape from the body, not the redemption of it. The problem is that this snaps the lifeline between God and humanity. It destroys the relevance of the divine act in Jesus for men and women of flesh and blood. What is not assumed cannot be redeemed. Only if Jesus was actually "born" (Matt 2:1), had "come in the flesh" (1 John 4:2), partook of "flesh and blood" (Heb 2:14), and was "made like them, fully human in every way" (2:17) could there be atonement and reconciliation. An angel can be a messenger. A mortal man can be a messiah. But the mediator between God and mankind must be both God and Man.

To counter the developing Docetism, even in the first generations, the New Testament authors often stress that Jesus came "in the flesh." Paul cites a traditional formula: "He appeared in the flesh, was vindicated by the Spirit, was seen by angels, was preached among the nations, was believed on in the world, was taken up in glory" (1 Tim 3:16). The point of Jesus' nakedly human and fleshly existence is emphasized even further in the Johannine corpus. Though for us the idea of Christ as a human being might be readily assumed, in John's context it was the touchstone for right belief. Hence he writes, "The Word became flesh and made his dwelling among us. We have seen his glory, the glory of the one and only Son, who came from the Father, full of grace and truth" (John 1:14).

In John's letters, we observe the importance of confessing Jesus' incarnation in the flesh: "This is how you can recognize the Spirit of God: Every spirit that acknowledges that Jesus Christ has come in the flesh is from God" (1 John 4:2). Those who denied Jesus' incarnation in bodily form are denounced in the strongest possible language: "Many deceivers, who do not acknowledge Jesus Christ as coming in the flesh, have gone out into the world. Any such person is the deceiver and the antichrist" (2 John 7). This is no vitriolic overstatement. To deny the real fleshly nature of Jesus is to deny the gospel at a fundamental level, the very truth that John had witnessed, namely, that God became fully human in order to fully reconcile humanity to God.

The humanity of Jesus becomes theologically and pastorally acute in Hebrews, which pins reconciliation on the incarnation:

> Since the children have flesh and blood, he too shared in their humanity so that by his death he might break the power of him who holds the power of death—that is, the devil—and free those who all their lives were held in slavery by their fear of death. For surely it is not angels he helps, but Abraham's descendants. For this reason he had to be make like them, fully human in every way, in order that he might become a merciful and faithful high priest in service to God, and that he might

make atonement for the sins of the people. Because he himself suffered when he was tempted, he is able to help those who are being tempted. (Heb 2:14–18)

This is a wonderfully rich passage about what God incarnate did for lost humanity and how he did it. To redeem these children where they are, the Son had to become what they are. By sharing in their human existence, he was able to destroy the one thing that threatened and frightened them the most: death. As the Greek paschal hymn celebrates, "He has trampled down death by death." This achieves a new exodus, freedom from slavery—not from Pharaoh this time, but liberation from death itself, personified as a wicked tyrant who keeps people in the shackles of its fearful power. That saving event of defeating death is part of the promises made to Abraham, to give life to his children, to make them brothers and sisters of God's own Son in God's own family.

Jesus was constrained, then, to be just like them, so that he could intercede for them and as one of them. This priestly service was carried out in faithfulness to achieve mercy for these children by virtue of his atoning death. Yet the priestly service of Jesus does not finish with his death. Those fighting temptation and suffering under its weight can take genuine sympathy from Christ, who was tempted as we were, yet remained on track to finish the race in faithfulness and persevered under its weight. In this way, he provides an example for us all. Jesus is the humanity of God releasing us from our fears and foe. Jesus is the humanity of God pointing us to the real condition of what our own humanity is supposed to be. It was this thought that led Godfrey Thring to write:

Crown Him the Son of God, before the worlds began,
And ye who tread where He hath trod, crown Him the Son of Man;
Who every grief hath known that wrings the human breast,
And takes and bears them for His own, that all in Him may rest.

We can summarize the significance of Jesus' humanity by noting several points.[292]

1. *Representative obedience.* Jesus is the federal head of humanity, who is obedient to God in contrast to Adam, who was disobedient to God. Jesus' testing in the wilderness was a temptation to rehearse Adam's failure, but he didn't lapse; instead, he was faithful and obedient in his vocation as God's Son as Adam should have been (Luke 4:1–13). Paul also makes overt use of the Adam–Christ contrast in his theology: one man's transgression led to the condemnation of all people (Rom 5:18), and one man's righteous act led to the acquittal for all people (5:19). Jesus takes on

---

292. Adapted largely from Grudem, *Systematic Theology*, 540–42.

the role of Adam, and because he was obedient and faithful where Adam failed, he is uniquely qualified to redeem the sons and daughters of Adam. Therefore, as the *real* human being, Jesus faithfully executed the role of humanity under God, and his obedience undoes the transgression of Adam.

2. *Substitute sacrifice.* Only a fully human Jesus can make full atonement for the sins of humanity. For if Jesus was not really and completely human as we are, his sacrificial death would be inadequate. God could only condemn sin in the flesh, not sin in a phantom (Rom 8:3). In order to take the penalty of sin away, he had to become a person who could suffer the consequences of sin in his body.

3. *Mediator.* As Paul wrote to Timothy: "For there is one God and one mediator between God and mankind, the man Christ Jesus" (1 Tim 2:5). Though it is theoretically possible to fulfill the role of mediator without complete association with both parties (normally by complete impartiality), the perfect mediator is one who completely "connects" with both parties. Jesus makes such a connection as he is fully God and fully human.

4. *Fulfilling the original purpose of God, that mankind should rule over creation.* In Genesis 2 we have the ideal picture of humanity ruling over creation. We see Adam naming the animals and enjoying the fruit of the garden. It's a beautiful picture of humanity's mandate to rule creation as God's vice-regent. Obviously this vocation was marred and corrupted by the fall. However, God's plan to rule the earth through human subjects is not irretrievably thwarted, because in Jesus Christ the role is fully restored. Jesus is given "all authority in heaven and on earth" (Matt 28:18; cf. Eph 1:22; Rev 3:21), and he along with those who reign with him fulfills Adam's mandate to reign as priest-kings over all the earth. Jesus is the second Adam, but he is the first human being to be authentically human. The universe at last beholds a human being who glorifies God. As the late Bishop Stephen Neil wrote:

> When Jesus died, something happened that had never happened before in the whole history of the world. A man had lived the whole of his life in perfect and complete obedience to God. Death really is an end. It marks the end of the chapter. Nothing can now change what has gone before. Through temptation and suffering Jesus has kept His spirit from anger or hate or bitterness. He has given back that spirit in its perfect purity to the Father. This was the purpose for which the whole world was made. The universe had never seen, and so it had lived on through all the centuries in frustration. Now we know what the machine was made for. At last we have seen a man.[293]

5. *An example and pattern in life.* Jesus' humanity is the means of our salvation, but also the model we are to follow in our discipleship. In particular, Jesus' faithfulness in death, his willingness to go to the cross, his life of prayer, his compassion, and his

---

293. Stephen Neil, *What is Man?* (London: Lutterworth, 1960), 37.

preparedness to suffer shame are the quintessential marks of human dedication to the will of God. The imitation of Christ is one of the crucial elements in Christian ethics that is emphasized at many points in the New Testament.[294] The Gospels, like all ancient biographies, demonstrate the virtues of the lead character and show why it is honorable to imitate him. The majestic Christ hymn of Philippians 2:5–11 is not about esoteric kenotic christologies, but principally about having the mind of Christ by way of imitating the humility he showed in his death on the cross. Paul urges the Corinthians: "Follow my example, as I follow the example of Christ" (1 Cor 11:1). He praises the Thessalonians because "you became imitators of us and of the Lord" (1 Thess 1:6).

The amazing claim of 1 John is: "Whoever claims to live in him must live as Jesus did" (1 John 2:6). First Peter 2:24 includes a clear statement of Jesus' substitutionary death, but it also includes a moving exhortation: "To this you were called, because Christ suffered for you, leaving you an example, that you should follow in his steps" (2:21). The author of Hebrews regards Jesus as the quintessential example of the one who overcomes hardship: "Consider him who endured such opposition from sinners, so that you will not grow weary and lose heart" (Heb 12:3). A resource for ethics and the measure of Christian spirituality is likeness to the example of Christ.

6. *A pattern for our redeemed bodies*. If Jesus is the pattern for Christian disciples, he is also the pioneer for our Christian hope. Jesus is the firstborn from among the dead (Col 1:18; Rev 1:5) and the firstfruits of the general resurrection (1 Cor 15:20, 23). What happened to Jesus is the prototype for what will happen to believers at the end of the age. The same Spirit who raised Jesus from the dead will give life to our mortal bodies (Rom 8:11). That is why, "when Christ appears, we shall be like him," because we will experience the same resurrection power in our bodies, whether we are dead or alive at the *parousia* (1 John 3:2). The risen Jesus is the eschatological demonstration of what humanity will look like in its glorified state.

7. *He can sympathize as high priest*. What is arguably the greatest pastoral significance of Jesus' humanity is that God in Christ experienced human life in our fallen world with all of its suffering, grief, fear, and pain. As the author of Hebrews put it: "For we do not have a high priest who is unable to empathize with our weaknesses, but we have one who has been tempted in every way, just as we are—yet he did not sin. Let us then approach God's throne of grace with confidence" (Heb 4:15–16). The God of Christians is not a distant deity who looks down abstractly on the human condition with no thought or care for their plight. No, he cared enough to graciously condescend to the depths of our humanity so that he might draw it up to the heights of heaven.

Lord Anthony Ashley Cooper (a.k.a., the 7th Earl of Shaftesbury) was a nineteenth-century reformer who strove for reform in the areas of child labor in

---

294. Paul claimed that what he teaches agrees with "my way of life in Christ Jesus" (1 Cor 4:17). On imitation more generally see 1 Cor 4:16; 11:1; 1 Thess 1:6; 2:14; 2 Thess 3:9; Eph 5:1; Heb 6:12; 13:7; 1 John 3:16; 3 John 11.

factories and providing housing for the working class. Though he was an aristocrat, at his funeral procession workers of the poorer classes lined the streets respecting him for his work on their behalf, because in popular opinion and despite his privileged life, "he was one of us." That is similar to what the incarnation is about: God is for us, God is with us, because God is one of us!

4.7.4 HYPOSTATIC UNION

I once gave a lecture on the hypostatic union to some students, and several of them found the whole presentation rather dry, cerebral, and academic. Did they really need to know the difference between the *theotokos* and *christotokos*? Should they really care why the views of Apollinarius and Nestorius were rejected by the wider church? Lo and behold, two weeks later, some of the same students found themselves on a mission trip in a Muslim suburb of Sydney, where they were invited into a mosque. During their time there they were quizzed by an imam as to how they could believe that Jesus is both God and man! Suddenly their lecture on the hypostatic union became an invaluable source of information about how to explain the incarnation to Muslims. There actually was some practical benefit from knowing the doctrine of the incarnation—who would ever have guessed?

While the church fathers were successful in showing that Jesus had to be God in order to be a redeemer, it left open the question as to how the divine and human natures coexisted together. Was Jesus more God than human? Which of his two natures dominated? Did one nature absorb the other? Were those natures unified or mixed? Did Jesus have a soul, or did the Logos replace Jesus' soul? Did he have two wills, divine and human? In want of a solution, a common analogy in the ancient church was to describe the union of the two natures with the image of Jesus' divinity saturating his humanity in the same way that heat flows through iron. Such an analogy, however, is open to multiple interpretations and is therefore insufficient.[295]

The doctrine of Christ's divine and human natures developed in several stages:

1. As noted above, the Council of Nicea (325) affirmed that Jesus is "truly God" against the Arians, who regarded Jesus as a created being.
2. The Council of Constantinople (381) affirmed that Jesus was "perfectly" human against the Apollinarians, who impaired the humanity of Christ by teaching that the Logos replaced the soul or mind in a man.
3. The Council of Ephesus (431) affirmed that Jesus Christ was one person, against the Nestorians, who divided Christ into two persons.
4. The Council of Chalcedon (451) provided the mature statement on the union of natures so that Christ's divine and human natures were united "without

---

295. Pannenberg, *Jesus: God and Man*, 297.

§ 4.7 The Story of Jesus and the Identity of God

confusion, without change, without division, or without separation" against the Eutychians and Monophysites, who both regarded Jesus as having only one hybrid nature in the incarnation with his humanity absorbed into his divinity.

5. The Council of Constantinople (680) affirmed the two wills of Christ, human and divine, against the Monothelites, who asserted that Jesus Christ had only one single will.

	Christological Heresies	
Apollinarianism	Apollinarius of Laodicea (310–90 AD) was a friend of Athanasius. He advocated that the Logos took the place of the soul of Jesus. Apollinarius's argument was that the soul is linked to free will and free will was linked to sin. So the Logos replaced the soul of Jesus. The counterargument by Eastern bishops was that which is not assumed by the Logos cannot be healed by the Logos. Only if the Logos assumed human form with a soul could the Logos save the souls of humanity.	
Nestorianism	Nestorius was the patriarch of Constantinople (ca. 428 AD), who rejected the term for Mary of *theotokos* (God-bearer) in preference for *christotokos* (Christ-bearer). While the human element came from Mary, the divine element came from the Father. Nestorius wanted to safeguard the humanity of Jesus, and he spoke of a unity of wills rather than a unity of essences. By refusing to allow a communication between human and divine essences, he was coming close to adoptionism. For Nestorians, the natures are distinct, but not in any way tangibly united, so that the divinity does not overwhelm the humanity. The problem was that this makes Jesus almost schizophrenic. It results in two natures and two persons!	
Monophysites	The Monophysites, typified by the monastic leader Eutyches (374–454 AD), advocated that Jesus had one nature where his divinity was absorbed by his humanity. Jesus had a third kind of nature where divinity and humanity were synergized to create the incarnate nature of Christ. This view survives among Coptic and Ethiopic churches. I call this the "two natures in a blender Christology."	

Divine Nature   Human Nature

The orthodox position of the Christian church regarding the relationship between the divine and human natures of Christ is that of a hypostatic union, whereby Jesus has two natures (*ousia*) in one person (*hypostasis*). He is also of the same substance with the father (*homoousia*) rather than just like God (*homoiousia*). So "hypostatic union" is the *personal union* of Jesus' two natures. Jesus has two complete natures—one fully human and one fully divine. What the doctrine of the hypostatic union teaches is that these *two natures* are united in *one person* in the God-man Jesus. He is not two persons; he is one. The two natures are distinct, yet they concur or coinhere in his person. The hypostatic union is the joining of the divine and the human in the one person of Jesus without their confusion.

The Council of Chalcedon (451) rejected Apollinarianism, Nestorianism, and Monophysitism and summed up its deliberations in this statement:

> We, then, following the holy Fathers, all with one consent, teach people to confess one and the same Son, our Lord Jesus Christ, the same complete in Godhead and also complete in manhood; truly God and truly man, of a reasonable [rational] soul and body; of one substance with the Father as regards his Godhead, and at the same time of one substance with us as regards his Manhood; in all things like unto us, without sin; begotten before all ages of the Father according to the Godhead, and in these latter days, for us and for our salvation, born of the Virgin Mary, the Mother of God, according to the Manhood; one and the same Christ, Son, Lord, only begotten, to be acknowledged in two natures, without confusion, without change, without division, without separation; the distinction of natures being by no means taken away by the union, but rather the property of each nature being preserved, and concurring in one Person [*prosōpon*] and one Subsistence [*hypostasis*], not parted or divided into two persons, but one and the same Son, and only begotten, God the Word, the Lord Jesus Christ; as the prophets from the beginning [have declared] concerning Him, and the Lord Jesus Christ Himself has taught us, and the Creed of the holy Fathers has handed down to us.

Chalcedonian orthodoxy established the reality of the two natures in one person. It affirmed the full humanity and full divinity of Christ. In the Chalcedonian definition, Christ is "complete in Godhead and also complete in manhood," as "truly God and truly man," and being "of one substance with the Father as regards his Godhead." At the same time, Christ is of "one substance with us as regards his manhood." It also defined the relationship between the two natures of Christ as being "without confusion, without change, without division, without separation," while also "concurring in one Person and one Subsistence." By saying that the union of the two natures in Christ was hypostatic (i.e., personal), the Chalcedonian fathers made the natures dependent on the one person, not the person dependent on the two natures.

Thus, the Chalcedonian statement affirmed against Apollinarianism that Jesus had a rational soul just like the rest of humanity. It affirmed against Nestorianism that Jesus was one person, not two persons. It affirmed against the Monophysites that Jesus had two natures, not one hybrid nature. The Chalcedonian statement is mostly an affirmation of what the incarnation is not, rather than what it actually is. What is affirmed, however, is that Christ definitely has two natures, one divine and one human, with the divine nature exactly like the Father and the human nature exactly like the rest of humanity; the natures are united, but unmixed.

Similar debates were played out during the Reformation. Following the ancient belief in a communication of attributes (*communicatio idiomatum*), Lutheran theologians took seriously the claim that the divine attributes were communicated to Jesus' humanity, so even on the cross, Jesus suffered as the God-man. The Lutherans argued for the principle *finitum capax infiniti*, the human Jesus is able to receive and bear the divine attributes, where there is a mutual exchange and participation of Jesus' divine human natures together. In contrast, the Reformed churches, led principally by Calvin and Zwingli, were hesitant about a strictly "realist" communication of the divine attributes to Jesus' humanity, even while maintaining the unity of the two natures in Jesus' person. They argued instead for *finitum non capax infiniti*, whereby Jesus' humanity does not and cannot bear the weight of all of the divine attributes. For the Reformed theologians Jesus' humanity is grounded in his deity, but the two are not confused; the Word assumes flesh, but does not become flesh. To the Reformed thinkers, Luther had come close to the Eutychian heresy where Jesus' humanity was engulfed by his deity. To Lutheran thinkers, the Reformed position appeared to run the risk of the Nestorian heresy, by dividing apart Jesus' human and divine natures.

Finally, we can note that Jesus' assumption of humanity remains permanent. He did not revert back to the heavenly and incorporeal form of the preexistent Son of God after his ascension. The exalted Jesus is repeatedly described and addressed as "Son of Man," indicating his enduring human character even amidst divine glory (Acts 7:56; Rev 1:13). Jesus carries out his offices of prophet, priest, and king as the God-man who intercedes and mediates between heaven and earth because his full human identity remains intact. It is a human being who is now enthroned beside God, who will advocate for them and render judgment on their behalf. Augustine elegantly put it:

> Christ did not take human form for a time, to show himself to be a man in this guise, and an outward appearance that should thereafter be discarded. He took the visible form of man into the unity of his person, the form of God remaining invisible. Not only was he born in that form of a human mother, but he also grew up in it. He ate and drank and slept and was put to death in that form. In the same human form he rose again and ascended into heaven. He now sits at the right hand of the Father in the same human form, in which he is to come to judge the living and the dead.[296]

---

296. Augustine, *Maxim.* 1.19 (cited in McGuckin, *We Believe in One Lord Jesus Christ*, 125–26).

WHAT TO TAKE HOME?

- The best christological method is neither from "above" nor from "below," but integrates both into a holistic way of analyzing the history of Jesus and what the believing community confesses about him.
- The Old Testament points to Jesus prophetically, typologically, christophanically, and even allegorically.
- The virgin conception demonstrates that Jesus is the special Son of God, the seed of Abraham, descended from David, with a historical redemptive mission to the lost sheep of the house of Israel.
- The unity between Jesus' kingdom message and his vicarious death is his messianic vocation to inaugurate the new exodus for the salvation of God's people.
- The primary models for the atonement are: recapitulation, ransom, Christus Victor, satisfaction, moral influence, exemplary, governmental, and penal substitution.
- The three views for the extent of the atonement are limited, universal, and Amyraldian.
- The resurrection of Jesus is indelibly connected to the cross and marks the beginnings of the new age bursting into our current world.
- The ascension marks the enthronement of Jesus and the beginning of his heavenly session.
- Jesus is part of the identity of God and is equal to God in authority, majesty, and substance.
- Prior to his human existence, Jesus had a personal and conscious existence.
- The humanity of Jesus was necessary for his redemptive task.
- Hypostatic union means that Jesus combines two natures in one person.

STUDY QUESTIONS

1. What are the dangers of doing Christology exclusively from below?
2. Why was it necessary for Jesus to be born of a virgin?
3. What is the link between Jesus' preaching of the kingdom and his death on the cross?
4. What is the one model of the atonement that best explains the nature and purpose of Jesus' death?
5. Describe the necessity of the resurrection for salvation.
6. Why is Psalm 110 the most frequently cited Old Testament text in the New Testament?
7. Should we explain to people the incarnation when we proclaim the gospel?
8. Does the New Testament teach an adoptionist Christology?
9. Is it possible to overemphasize the deity of Christ at the expense of his humanity?

PART FIVE

The Gospel of Salvation

§5.1 Saved by the Gospel
§5.2 Redemptive History: The Plan for the Gospel
§5.3 Order of Salvation: The Logical Working of the Gospel
§5.4 Images of Salvation: The Result of the Gospel
§5.5 Scope and Security: How Wide and How Certain a Salvation?

The study of salvation is called *soteriology*. The gospel tells us that God saves in the life, death, and resurrection of Jesus Christ; consequently, salvation is understood as the chief benefit of the gospel. Furthermore, salvation is more than the sojourn of souls into heaven; rather, it is holistic and includes the well-being of body, mind, and soul. Salvation is part of a story (redemptive history) and is applied to the believer in a particular process (order of salvation). These following sections include a brief exposition of the various images for salvation in the Bible. Thereafter follows a discussion about who will be saved and whether one can lose one's salvation. Finally, the center of salvation is articulated in terms of an act of the Triune God that incorporates the work of the Father, the Son, and the Holy Spirit.

> The Gospel speaks of God as He is: it is concerned with Him Himself and with Him only. It speaks of the Creator who shall be our Redeemer, and of the Redeemer who is our Creator. It is pregnant with our complete conversion; for it announces the transformation of our creatureliness into freedom. It proclaims the forgiveness of our sins, the victory of life over death, in fact, the restoration of everything that has been lost. It is the signal, the fire-alarm of a coming, new world.[1]

> The chief task of Christian soteriology is to show how the bruising of the man Jesus, the servant of God, saves lost creatures and reconciles them to their creator.[2]

> Christ alone is our salvation,
> Christ the rock on which we stand;
> Other than this sure foundation
> Will be found but sinking sand.
> Christ, His cross and resurrection,
> Is alone the sinners' plea;
> At the throne of God's perfection
> Nothing else can set him free.[3]

---

1. Karl Barth, *The Epistle to the Romans* (trans. E. Hoskyns; London: Oxford University Press, 1933), 37–38.
2. John Webster, "'It Was the Will of the Lord to Bruise Him': Soteriology and the Doctrine of God," in *God of Salvation: Soteriology in Theological Perspective* (ed. I. J. Davidson and M. Rae; Farnham, UK: Ashgate, 2011), 15.
3. Author Unknown, "Christ Alone Is Our Salvation."

§ 5.1 SAVED BY THE GOSPEL

The gospel is only good news because it first tells us some bad news. It presupposes the story of a world gone wrong, humanity corrupted, and spiritual powers in open revolt against God. The bad news is that our relationship with God has been severed on account of our rebellion against God and that we all stand under divine judgment because of our sinful actions. Adam disobeyed God, and since he was our representative, his disobedience was counted as ours (see Rom 5:12–21). Yet we have each become our own Adam and confirmed our family likeness by our behavior.

This defiance against the deity manifests itself in two ways. First, it is demonstrated by moral evils perpetrated against other human beings; second, it discloses itself in the desperate attempt of people to do almost anything to avoid worshiping the Creator (see Rom 1:18–32). The inhumanity of humanity and the corruption of the human heart are signs and symptoms of this rage against God. The result of our sinful state and guilty status before God is that we are relationally separated from God and God enters into contention against us. The final result is that God intends to prosecute his case against us at the final judgment. Divine judgment is the response of God's infinite justice and holiness to the evil that has infested creation.

Thus, the story in which we find ourselves is that we belong to a world that is broken and corrupted, barbaric and conceited, brutal and condemned. We will have more to say about the state of sin, evil, and depravity in part 7; suffice to say here that the Bible overwhelmingly confirms this picture of humanity as pervaded by sinful desires and culpable for its wicked actions. According to the exilic prophets, "the heart is deceitful above all things and beyond cure. Who can understand it?" (Jer 17:9), and "the one who sins is the one who will die" (Ezek 18:20). The voice of the Evangelist in the Fourth Gospel announces, "This is the verdict: Light has come into the world, but people loved darkness instead of light because their deeds were evil" (John 3:19). Paul's collage of texts about human wickedness in Romans 3:10–18 can be summed up this way: "All have sinned and fall short of the glory of God" (3:23). According to the writer to the Hebrews, "people are destined to die once, and after that to face judgment" (Heb 9:27).

Humanity at its lowest ebb is little more than an intellectually sophisticated beast, controlled by impulses for pleasure and power and contained in a cage of divine providence that prevents it from being as destructive as it could be. The beast resents its confinement, and it barks and growls at its keeper, seemingly unaware that it waits to be destroyed. That is the tragic human story: the sons and daughters of Adam have become little more than another beast of the earth. Can the beast avoid destruction, and will the beast ever become human again?

God's judgment against sin is a motif that runs through the biblical story from Genesis to Revelation. As God is judge of all the earth, he is committed to putting the world aright (Gen 18:25; Pss 58:11; 82:8). One way to do that is obviously through God's distributive justice. Indeed, such justice is demanded by the holiness and righteousness of God's character. God punishes evil and rewards good. At the same time, there is another element of God's justice that we need to account for, namely, his saving justice. God can condemn and destroy, but he also has the power to acquit and give life. This justice is restorative and redemptive. Thus, the full sway of God's justice encompasses his judgment against the wicked (e.g., Eccl 3:17; Isa 11:4; 57:21), but also his deliverance of the ungodly (e.g., Pss 51; 98; Isaiah 55–56).

The difference between God's judging justice and his saving justice is his covenanting activity. God commits himself through his promises—to Noah, Abraham, Israel, David, and the new Israel—to rescue a people from judgment, to rectify their status, to renew their humanity, and to relocate them to his realm and under his reign. The faithfulness of God to his covenants means that justice will be done and yet judgment will not overtake God's people. The satisfaction of God's justice and the manifestation of his mercy will take place in the covenantal economy so that God is both just and the justifier of the wicked (Rom 3:26). This is why the psalmist exclaims: "You answer us with awesome and righteous deeds, God our Savior, the hope of all the ends of the earth and of the farthest seas" (Ps 65:5).

God's project to put the world to right finds its soteric architecture in the covenants. God's promises from Abraham to Israel provided a temporary lifeboat from the flood of judgment. Yet the ultimate realization of these promises was always future oriented. The promises were forward looking, pointing ahead to the day when God would deal with Adam's disobedience and his expulsion from Eden and would deal with Israel's sin and exile from Canaan. The climax of the covenants comes in the incarnation of Jesus Christ and the gospel that announces the news of salvation through him. Jesus' life-death-resurrection-exaltation undoes what has happened to Adam and Israel. God's new world is launched in the midst of the old one. The insidious powers of desire, death, and the devil receive their fatal blow in the cross of Christ and his glorious resurrection. The gospel marks the beginning of

WHAT DOES IT MEAN TO BE "SAVED"?

David Bentley Hart bemoans the "rather feeble and formal way many Christians have habitually thought of [salvation] at various periods in the Church's history: as some sort of forensic exoneration accompanied by a ticket of entry into an Elysian aftermath of sun-soaked meadows and old friends."[4] It should be clear that I've repeatedly referred to God's project to unite himself to creation through the Logos; that is the big picture of salvation. Getting down into the nitty-gritty, there is a kaleidoscope of images for salvation that we will explore (§5.4).

Still, we must address what exactly is the range of referents in the "salvation" that makes up soteriology. At a popular level, and as Hart complains, it seems little more than fire insurance against hell and a ticket to a heavenly paradise. Yet biblical conceptions of salvation are far broader than this. Many students do not know that words ordinarily translated as "healing" are often based on the same Greek words as those for salvation (*sōzō, sōtēria*). To give a couple of examples, when the woman subject to continual bleeding touched Jesus and was healed, "Jesus turned and saw her. 'Take heart, daughter,' he said, 'your faith has healed [*sesōken*] you.' And the woman was healed [*esōthē*] at that moment" (Matt 9:22). Jairus pleaded with Jesus to come and see his daughter, "Please come and put your hands on her so that she will be healed and live [*sōthē kai zēsē*]" (Mark 5:23).

In the Scriptures salvation can mean deliverance from enemies, physical danger, death, disability, demonic powers, illness, poverty, injustice, social exclusion, false accusation, shame, and of course sin and its consequences. Undoubtedly what lies behind the misery and mortality of the human condition is sin—a power that corrupts us as much as it kills us. Be that as it may, salvation consists of more than a spiritual rescue in a postmortem state. If the Old Testament prophets and the ministry of Jesus teach us anything, it is that God profoundly cares about the life of his covenant people and all people in general even ahead of a final judgment. The Scriptures affirm God's desire to save us in our future eternal state as much as it affirms God's desire to save people in their current physical state.

Consequently, when we think of salvation, we should get beyond the thought that it is just about me and the immortality of my wretched soul; rather, we should conceive of God's deliverance as involving the entire person as the full extent of his care and compassion. If we take into account the *whole* biblical witness, we will

---

4. David Bentley Hart, "The Lively God of Robert Jenson," *First Things* 156 (2005): 15.

adhere to a *holistic* understanding of salvation that will shape a *holistic* understanding of mission.

FURTHER READING

Stanley, Alan P. *Salvation Is More Complicated Than You Think: A Study on the Teaching of Jesus.* Colorado Springs, CO: Authentic, 2007.

Wright, Christopher. *Salvation Belongs to Our God: Celebrating the Bible's Central Story.* Downers Grove, IL: InterVarsity Press, 2008, pp. 1–35.

Wright, N. T. *Surprised by Hope.* New York: HarperOne, 2008, pp. 206–13.

---

paradise restored. The good news about Jesus is the story of God's rescue plan and how one can be included in that plan.

The words "gospel" and "salvation" go naturally together. In Isaiah, the good news that God is going to show his kingly power and deliver Israel from exile is given in the jubilant words: "How beautiful on the mountains are the feet of those who bring good news, who proclaim peace, who bring good tidings, who proclaim salvation, who say to Zion, 'Your God reigns!'" (Isa 52:7). Jesus taught that following him meant saving one's life: "For whoever wants to save their life will lose it, but whoever loses their life for me and for the gospel will save it" (Mark 8:35).

Paul's main thesis in Romans is this: "I am not ashamed of the gospel, because it is the power of God that brings salvation to everyone who believes: first to the Jew, then to the Gentile" (Rom 1:16). In Ephesians, the apostle celebrates the evangelical experience of his audience with these words, "And you also were included in Christ when you heard the message of truth, the gospel of your salvation" (Eph 1:13). In the Pastorals, Paul states that the grace appearing in Jesus Christ has made Christ the one who "has destroyed death and has brought life and immortality to light through the gospel" (2 Tim 1:10). In Acts, salvation is linked to gospel preaching (e.g., Acts 2:21, 40, 47; 4:12; 11:14; 16:31), and Paul climactically tells the Corinthians: "By this gospel you are saved, if you hold firmly to the word I preached to you" (1 Cor 15:2).

All of these verses show that our entry point into salvation must pass through Jesus Christ and the gospel that communicates his saving work. The New Testament knows of only one form of salvation: given in Christ, proclaimed in the gospel, and appropriated by faith. The Savior is the content of the gospel and salvation is the goal of the gospel.

§5.1 Saved by the Gospel

The "gospel of salvation" is multifaceted and its touches on the themes of God's kingship, divine covenants, and new creation. In what follows, we will explore the underlying story of salvation (redemptive history), propose the logical sequence of events for when salvation is applied to the individual (order of salvation), survey various images for salvation (what the gospel achieves), and try to identify an organic unity to salvation (the central motif in salvation).

§ 5.2 REDEMPTIVE HISTORY: THE PLAN FOR THE GOSPEL

The gospel is not an innovation; rather, it is the culmination of God's covenanting activity. Salvation is thus indelibly connected to God's prior dealings with the world and is rooted in his eternal decision. We have already seen that God has one *purpose* (to glorify himself through the effusion of his holy love) and one *plan* (to bring people into the new creation through the incarnate Logos). The *unity* of that plan can be conceived by way of inference to the covenant of grace. In that covenant, God acts through a series of covenantal promises to draw his people from being in Adam to being in the Messiah so that they may share in his glory. The *outworking* of this covenantal plan is what we call "redemptive history" or (by others) "salvation history" (*historia salutis*). Redemptive history narrates the key events that take us from Eden to the new Jerusalem and all that lies in between. So where does the gospel of salvation sit in relation to redemptive history?

When we hear that the story of Jesus narrated in the "gospel" transpired "according to the Scriptures," this does not mean that the advent of Jesus can be loosely married up to a seemingly random series of proof texts. Instead, the agreement of the gospel with the Scriptures means the accordance of the gospel with the underlying story of Scripture. The gospel is the next chapter of the story because the story thus far had anticipated the coming of the gospel. While the gospel may be the goal of redemptive history, in a deeper sense, the gospel is also part of its overall unity. The promises given to Adam (Gen 3:15), Abraham (12:1–3), Jacob (49:10), Israel (Deut 9:6), David (2 Sam 7:12–16), the Babylonian exiles (Isa 52:7; Ezek 34), and the Judean remnant (Hos 2:14–23; Zech 6:11–12) are evangelic in character and prepare for the good news about Jesus Christ.

The salvation that the gospel announces must be understood in the context of the redemptive history that discloses God's salvific plan. The gospel assumes an underlying narrative that describes why people need saving in the first place. We must get our heads around this story if we are to come to grips with what it means to be "saved." If we think of redemptive history as a drama, we can say that it takes place in several distinct acts: *Act 1*: Creation and fall; *Act 2*: Patriarchs and Israel; *Act 3*: Jesus; *Act 4*: The church; *Act 5*: The consummation. An exposition of these acts would take a volume of its own. In what follows I will summarize each act, identify the objects and means of salvation, and situate them in relation to God's rule and covenants.[5]

5.2.1 ACT 1: CREATION AND FALL

The Old Testament commences by narrating God's creation of the world. God's creative act brings into being all living creatures and the whole reality of the universe. By creating, God commits himself to be the master and caretaker of creation, and he is thus relationally and even covenantally bound to his creation (see Jer 33:20–21, 25–26). Here God is king and creation is his vassal or servant.

The pinnacle of creation is the creation of the first man and woman, who are formed in God's image. They are divinely blessed, given dominion over the world, and charged with ruling the world in obedience to God (Gen 1–2). They are placed in a "garden," which is a divine sanctuary and constitutes a microcosm of the blessing that God intends for the entire earth (2:8–10).[6] During this time, Adam and Eve know God as their Creator. They are tasked with being God's instrument of blessing for the whole creation.

Their time in the garden is also probationary as they are created for immortality. They will receive immortality if they remain obedient to their mission and do not eat from the tree of the knowledge of good and evil. To disobey will lead to death (Gen 2:17).[7] God's rule in the garden is seen by way of the harmonious order and peaceful fellowship that exists between humanity, creation, creatures, and Creator. Eden is a paradise of divine and human fellowship that exhibits the beauty and goodness of its divine author. We can tabulate the situation in this way:

God	Covenant	People	Place	Promise	Kingdom	Response
Creator	Creation	Adam & Eve	Eden	Immortality	Harmony, order, and fellowship	Obedience

---

5. The tabulation that follows is modified from Graeme Goldsworthy, *According to Plan: The Unfolding of God in the Bible* (Leicester, UK: Inter-Varsity Press, 1991).

6. Paul R. Williamson, *Sealed with an Oath: Covenant in God's Unfolding Purpose* (NSBT 23; Downers Grove, IL: Inter-Varsity Press, 2007), 49.

7. Although Adam's future is determined by his obedience, there is no merit-based salvation scheme here. As Michael Williams (*Far as the Curse Is Found: The Covenant Story of Redemption* [Phillipsburg, NJ; Presbyterian & Reformed, 2005], 72) writes: "Adam's obedience was a necessary condition, not the sufficient condition for life in God's favor. Adam was required to obey the covenant instruction not to eat from the Tree of the Knowledge of Good and Evil, and Adam's failure to obey would bring sin and death. But the sufficient condition for the covenant and Adam's life within it was the fatherly and kingly favor of God. What I am suggesting here is that life in covenant relationship with God was something that Adam enjoyed by God's grace. He possessed it as a gift. He could lose that gift by the misapplication of his responsible freedom, his disobedience, but he could not earn or merit it." In other words, there is grace before the fall.

The garden paradise is fatally disrupted by the strange intrusion of the serpent (whose origins are not explained). The serpent's machinations prove to be sinister when he deceives the woman into eating fruit from the forbidden tree and the woman in turn gives some of the fruit to her husband. As a result, both of them experience the transformative effects of sin, which instill into them a mix of self-awareness and shame that leads them to flee from God's presence (Gen 3). In the words of the Westminster Larger Catechism Q. 21: "Our first parents being left to the freedom of their own will, through the temptation of Satan, transgressed the commandment of God in eating the forbidden fruit; and thereby fell from the estate of innocency wherein they were created." Consequently, the goodness of creation is ruined, the image of God is marred, the male-female union is corrupted, and the harmonious relationship between God and humanity is ruptured. The word of the serpent appears to triumph over the Word of God. God is at enmity with Adam and in full-out hostility against the serpent.

Genesis 3–11 is a tragic tale of paradise lost. Adam and Eve are expelled from the garden and must toil in labor and childbirth (3:14–19). Human rebellion against God intensifies as do the consequences for the rebellion. The descendents of Adam and Eve become progressively more malevolent and commit fratricide (e.g., Cain in 4:1–14) and boast of their vengeful exploits (e.g., Lamech in 4:23–24). The fatal nature of sin is underscored further in Genesis 5, where it is repeated in the genealogy that so and so lived for long, he fathered X, and then "he died." The repetition of the formula always climaxes in the announcement of death: "he died ... and then he died," and so forth. What reigns on the earth are not grace and blessings, but death and decay. Death becomes an intrusive and tyrannical force in God's creation.

The corruption of humanity becomes so terrible that God resorts to judgment through a massive flood. Along the way, God chooses Noah to lead the chosen line through that judgment and to start anew. In the aftermath of the flood, God renews his covenant with creation, and there is hope for a new beginning (Gen 5:32–10:32). Such a hope, however, quickly founders with the sin of Noah and his sons (9:18–29), and Noah also succumbs to death, which means that nothing has really changed (9:29).

Soon after, humanity attempts to construct its own way to the heavens independent of God through the tower of Babel (Gen 11:1–9). From there God scatters the human race and confuses their languages. Judgment strikes again, but before long we are also introduced to another hope on the horizon with Abram (11:27–32).

Yet Genesis 1–11 is not all gloom and judgment. A cycle emerges of sin–judgment–grace. The sin of people occasions God's punitive response, but at the same time there is always an element of grace to ensure that a future hope for the people carries through in the end. The relationship with God is ruptured, but it is not broken beyond repair. God takes the initiative to bridge the gulf between himself and his creatures.

§5.2 Redemptive History: The Plan for the Gospel

Sin	Judgment	Grace
Adam and Eve's disobedience	Exile from the garden of Eden; curses on earth and humanity	God promises a seed to crush the head of the serpent (Gen 3:15). Adam names his wife "Eve" (means "living") because she would become the mother of all living things, which implies that death will not be the end of their family (3:20). God makes garments for Adam and Eve, which suggests that sin is covered by sacrifice (3:21). Exile from the garden is both retributive and remedial. It is remedial in the sense that they must not be allowed to eat from the tree of life and eternally perpetuate their fallen state. That is because God has another plan to redeem them from their fallen state before granting immortality to them (3:22–23).
Cain's murder of Abel	Cain is cursed; his crops will be fruitless; he will be a restless wanderer; he fears for his life.	God marks Cain to protect him from murder (4:15). Adam fathers Seth and Seth fathers Enosh, which implies that Cain's legacy is not the only one set to endure (4:25–26). People begin to call on the name of the Lord and worship is restored to the earth (4:26).
People of earth corrupted	Flood	Noah, a righteous man, is found (6:9). Noah's family survives the flood and God begins with a new family (Gen 6–8). God blesses Noah and his sons, who recover the creation mandate to multiply and fill the earth (9:1–3). God renews his covenant with creation (9:9–17).
Sin by Noah's family	Noah curses his sons.	Noah's family continues to live on (Gen 10).
Nations and the tower of Babel	Scattering of nations; confusion of languages	Introduction of Abram (11:27–32)

The post-fall period in Genesis 3–11 has several characteristics. God remains Creator, though his role as Judge is accentuated in punishing the sins of Adam, Cain, wicked humanity, and even the united nations for their wickedness. God's care rests on a specific line of descendents from Adam through to Seth, Noah, and Shem, who are associated with hope, righteousness, and blessing (Gen 4:25–26; 5:29; 6:9; 9:26–27). The geographical locus of God's dealings with humanity extends from Eden into the wider territory of Canaan and the ancient Near Eastern lands, and even the whole earth is remembered in the covenant renewal under Noah. God's saving plan is affirmed by promising a future seed of Eve, who will crush the snake (3:15); God makes a covenant with Noah to deliver his family (6:18), and then he renews his covenant with creation (8:20–9:17). The reign of God can be discerned in actions that execute his justice against sin and his deliverance of the chosen family of Noah. The key response that individuals make to God is to trust him and to call on the Lord in worship (8:20–21).

God	Covenant	People	Place	Promise	Kingdom	Response
Creator	Creation	Adam & Eve	Eden	Immortality	Harmony, order, and fellowship	Obedience
Creator	Creation	Adam, Eve, descendents	Earth	Seed of Eve	Justice	Worship
Creator	Creation	Noah	Earth	New beginning	Ark	Trust and worship

Despite the tragic picture of fallen humanity, even within the cycle of sin and judgment, the gospel of grace can still be discerned. God promises to Adam that the seed of his wife will destroy the snake, God promises Noah that his family will survive the flood, and God promises creation that it will never again suffer such a colossal disaster. If God is God, the sin that has entered his world will not be the final word. Rather, the saving promises of God's covenants and the saving power of God's reign will yet work for the redemption of humanity and the rescue of creation. The tragedy created in the garden of Eden by the disobedience of one man will be undone by the obedience of another man in the garden of Gethsemane.

5.2.2 ACT 2: THE PATRIARCHS AND ISRAEL

In Genesis 12, Abraham is called to leave his native land and his father's household and to travel to Canaan. He is the recipient of a great promise from God: "I will make you into a great nation, and I will bless you; I will make your name great, and you will be a blessing. I will bless those who bless you, and whoever curses you I will curse; and all peoples on earth will be blessed through you" (12:2–3). These promises mark the undoing of all the turmoil in Genesis 3–11. Abraham will restore the blessing promised to the first man (1:28), and the nation that comes from him will arise to address the plight of the scattered nations (11:1–9).[8] In Genesis 15–22 God formally cuts a covenant with Abraham and reaffirms his promise to give him an inheritance of land, descendents, and blessings.

Although the word "covenant" does not occur in connection with Abraham until Genesis 15:18, Genesis 12:1–3 expresses the heart of the Abrahamic covenant. This is God's new deal with the world. It is a manifestation of the covenant of grace in the form of a promissory covenant with the pagan man from Haran. God's cosmic purpose is telescoped into the Abrahamic covenant. As William Dumbrell states: "What is being written in these few verses is a theological blueprint for the redemptive history of the world."[9]

There is a clear missionary element as the blessing of Abraham's descendents will also result in the blessing of the nations (Gen 12:3; 22:18; 26:4) The promise of descendents is not limited to the birth of Isaac or even to the Jewish nation. It is the promised *seed* of Abraham that will ultimately bring forth the Messiah, the Savior (see Rom 9:4; Gal 3:16).

The promise of *land* is given too, and it is temporarily achieved in the Israelite kingdoms of David and Solomon. Yet for the most part that promise was never really fulfilled. The patriarchs were seminomads in Canaan, and the Israelites were constantly harassed by their neighbors with territories often annexed. But God's plan is not thwarted; instead, the promise of land is eschatologically transposed into an inheritance that extends to all the earth (Matt 5:5) and can "never perish" because it is "kept in heaven" (1 Pet 1:4). In other words, the eschatological fulfillment of the promise of land will be the new creation. That fulfillment does not renege on the original promise; rather, it intensifies it further and places it in a cosmic scope.

The promise of *blessings* pertains to protection and provision for the covenant family. The preservation of the Abrahamic family despite thousands of years of turmoil is a wondrous fact of history. The Abrahamic family is God's chosen instrument to bless all the nations of the world. As a consequence, the Abrahamic covenant marks a crucial stage in the mission of God to bring the world into a redemptive relationship with himself. The conviction of the early church was that inclusion in the Abrahamic family had been opened up by the son of Abraham, Jesus Christ (see Matt 1:1; Rom 4; Gal 3). Abraham was considered a model of faith and obedience for believers to emulate (Rom 4:1–25; Heb 11:8–19; Jas 2:21–23). It is not ethnicity that makes one a child of Abraham (Matt 3:9/Luke 3:8), but faith in God's promises (Rom 4), for Abraham is the "father of us all" (4:16). Believers will one day recline with Abraham in the kingdom of God (Matt 8:11–12; Luke 13:28–29).

---

8. P. E. Satterthwaite, "Biblical History," in *NDBT*, 44.
9. William J. Dumbrell, *Covenant and Creation* (Nashville: Nelson, 1984), 66.

To summarize this epoch of redemptive history, we can say that God reveals himself as the Lord who covenants with his people. The covenant made with Abraham contains promises for an inheritance, descendents, and blessings. Importantly, the blessings will extend to the nations. The Abrahamic covenant enacts the mission of God to reach into the world through his chosen people. Thus, the reign of the Lord is exercised in and through Abraham's family, and the response that is required is principally faith in the promises and obedience to the subsequent commands. Furthermore, as the Lord provided a sheep in place of Abraham's offering up Isaac, one day God will offer up his own Son in the place of the people (Gen 22; Rom 8:32).

God	Covenant	People	Place	Promise	Kingdom	Response
Creator	Creation	Adam & Eve	Eden	Immortality	Harmony, order, and fellowship	Obedience
Creator	Creation	Adam, Eve, descendents	Earth	Seed of Eve	Justice	Worship
Creator	Creation	Noah	Earth	New beginning	Ark	Trust and worship
(Lord)	Abraham	Abrahamic family	Canaan	Land, descendents, blessings	Family	Trust and obey

Eventually Abraham's descendents become a multitude in Egypt. But they are enslaved and cry out to God for deliverance (Exod 1–2). They are then rescued in the exodus and, through Moses' mediation, they enter into a covenant with God at Sinai and become the chosen nation. Israel is to acknowledge the sovereignty of God by obeying his laws. The law (*Torah*) is an expression of the Lord's holiness, and his people are to express that holiness in their corporate life and act as priests between the pagan nations and God the Creator. Hence the words: "You yourselves have seen what I did to Egypt, and how I carried you on eagles' wings and brought you to myself. Now if you obey me fully and keep my covenant, then out of all nations you will be my treasured possession. Although the whole earth is mine, you will be for me a kingdom of priests and a holy nation" (Exod 19:4–6; see Lev 19:1–2; Deut 26:17–18).

The Sinaitic covenant does not annul or cancel the Abrahamic covenant (Gal 3:17); rather, it is the means by which the promise will be advanced through Abraham's national descendents. In fact, the Exodus event and Sinai covenant are launched on the basis of God's remembering his covenant with Abraham, Isaac, and Jacob (Exod 2:23–24; 3:7–8). According to Dumbrell, Exodus 19:4–5 is a basic restatement of Genesis 12:1–3, so that the Sinai covenant is a restatement and expansion of the Abrahamic promises.[10] It is out of slavery and in the wilderness that the great nation promised to Abraham finally emerges (Gen 12:2).

In the exodus, God makes a covenant with the Israelite at Sinai with further conditions and blessings (Exod 19; 24). In the Sinai covenant, God cocoons his promises around the chosen nation by giving them the Torah in order to protract their capacity to serve him and to project his holiness into the surrounding nations. The giving of the Torah does not introduce a works-salvation scheme into the fray. God's grace is presupposed in his unmerited election of the Hebrews (Deut 9:1–6; 10:12–19; Ezek 16). Keep in mind that commandments have already been given to the patriarchs to keep the way of the Lord by doing what was right and just (e.g., Gen 17:1; 18:19; 26:5).

Blessings and obligations are indelibly bound together in God's dealings with his people. Divine grace typically precedes divine commands. God gives his law to a redeemed people, not to redeem the people. As Williams comments, "obedience flows from; it does not buy it."[11] The commands for obedience, expressed in terms of conditions (e.g., Exod 19:5–6; Lev 18:4–5) or with respect to blessings and curses (Deut 28), are primarily revelatory of God's character. The covenantal regulations function to bind the nation to their God, who is like a king over a vassal. The Sinaitic covenant and its accompanying stipulations demonstrate how the great nation promised to Abraham should live before God in Canaan. The theocratic state is to be a role model for God's kingdom on earth; as such it must remain morally, ceremonially, and ethnically distinct.

Importantly there is also a new level of intimacy between God and the people at this juncture of redemptive history. God appears to Moses in the burning bush (Exod 3), he is present in the pillar of smoke that accompanies the Israelites in their sojourn across the wilderness (Exod 13:21–22), and he is encountered in the "tent of meeting" (33:7–11) and in the tabernacle (Exod 25–26). Here is a new vehicle for divine communion—a way of approaching God in holiness and a way for God to communicate his holiness to others. The tabernacle, like the later temple, is a sign of God's presence with Israel. It announces his intention for his glory to dwell among his people. It foreshadows the incarnation of the Logos (John 1:14) and God's majestic presence that will come to earth in the new Jerusalem (Rev 21–22).

Despite God's initiative to establish his covenant with the Israelite nation, the fragility of divine-human relationships continues to persist. No sooner have the people left Egypt and received the Decalogue than a crisis occurs in the golden calf incident (Exod 32–34). Israel deserves to forfeit participation in the covenant even before it has even been properly ratified. Yet on the basis of God's gracious

---

10. Ibid., 89–90.

11. Williams, *Far as the Curse Is Found*, 150.

character, he desists from destroying the Israelites (34:6), and he renews the covenant with them at Moab (Deut 1–29 [esp. 26:16–19]).[12]

Even so, sin continues to plague the covenant people—hence the necessity of the sacrificial system for dealing with sin through offerings and the need for the offices of prophet, priest, and king to mediate between God and the people. The continuing history of Israel from the conquest, to the time of the judges, through the united and divided monarchies, to the Assyrian and Babylonian exiles, and to the return of the remnant to Judea, all show the proclivity of the people to disobey, commit idolatry, oppress the poor, imitate the nations, and ignore their covenantal mandate (see the history of Israel's sin recounted in Ezra 9:1–15; Dan 9:9–19; Acts 7:1–53). This implies that while the Sinai covenant was a step toward fulfilling the Abrahamic promises, it was ultimately ineffective to implement it entirely. Therefore, it was a temporary state, and a new epoch in redemptive history was needed to bring lasting blessing and substantive peace to the nations of the world through the Israel of God.

The new way ahead can be seen in the prophetic books. They warn of judgment for disobedience—principally the destruction of Jerusalem and threat of exile—but they also announce vistas of hope for a repentant Israel. Despite their sin, God will pardon his people (Jer 31:18–20), execute a new exodus (Isa 40–55), or bring a new betrothal between God and his people (Hos 2:14–23), unite the two kingdoms in a purified land (Isa 11:11–16; Jer 3:18; 30:1–11; Ezek 37:15–23; 48:1–29), institute a renewed covenant (Jer 31:31), bestow a new capacity for obedience to God's commands with a new heart (Jer 31:31–34; Ezek 11:16–21; Zeph 3:9–13), rebuild Jerusalem and the temple (Isa 54; Jer 33:1–34; Ezek 40–43), and the nations will flock to Zion to learn the ways of God (Isa 2:2–4; Mic 4:1–4; Zech 8:23).

This restoration of the nation will be a miracle on a par with resurrection (Ezek 37). Indeed, restoration of the nation flows into the restoration of creation with the images of a river that flows from the temple to sweeten the bitter waters of the Dead Sea and even a new heavens and a new earth (Isa 61; Ezek 47; Zech 14). It is important to note that Israel's restoration is ultimately part of a bigger picture seen in the renewing of creation and the rescuing of the nations in fulfillment of God's promises given to Abraham (e.g., Acts 3:19–26).[13]

Three divine agents are central to the realization of this promise of restoration in the Old Testament. First, the king became idealized in ancient Israel, and future hopes began to be invested on a future royal leader to save God's people. God's covenant with David stipulated that God would establish a Davidic dynasty whose

---

12. Cf. later covenant renewals as well in Josh 8:30–35; 24:1–28; 2 Kgs 11:17–18; 22–23; 2 Chr 14–15; Ezra 10:1–5; Neh 8–10.

13. Satterthwaite, "Biblical History," 45.

kingdom would never end, and he would be a son to God (2 Sam 7:12–16). This covenant was important to Israel as it was celebrated in song (Pss 89; 132), and it constituted a large segment of the hope for a new Davidide reigning over a new Davidic kingdom in Israel (Isa 11:1–5; 55:1–13; Jer 33:20–21; Amos 9:11–12; Mic 5:1–8). It was these prophetic hopes for a new David, combined with an apocalyptic worldview and sociopolitical disempowerment, that led to the rise of Jewish messianic expectations.

Second, in Isaiah 40–55, a figure central to Israel's restoration is the "Servant of the Lord." This mysterious agent is Israel (see Isa 49:3, "You are my servant, Israel"), and he fulfills the role of being a light of the nations (42:6; 49:6). Paradoxically the figure is both identified with Israel and is the agent for Israel's deliverance. In language reminiscent of the Levitical sacrificial system, he expiates the sins of the people (53:5–6, 8, 11–12). If one reads Isaiah 53 about the Suffering Servant in tandem with Isaiah 61 about the Spirit-anointed leader and in light of Isaiah 11 concerning the "root/stump of Jesse," one can easily imagine how Isaiah was a major diet of messianic hopes. Such a messianic reading of Isaiah is exactly what we find in *Targum Isaiah* and *1 Enoch* 37–70 from a later period.

Third, the enigmatic "one like a son of man" in Daniel 7:13 provides another scheme for Israel's deliverance. In the aftermath of the pagan empires that follow one after another and that look and act like hybrid beasts, we see that authority, glory, and dominion are given to this heavenly "man." As we read on, it is clear that the "man" is the heavenly counterpart to the blasphemous horn. What is more, the "man" is, in fact, Israel, and it is Israel who receives a kingdom from God (7:18, 27). This picture is that of a restored Israel reigning over the world as God intended Adam (Gen 1:28). Daniel 7 is pregnant with messianic imagery and was taken that way by Jewish and Christian authors.[14] It is these figures—Davidic king, Servant of the Lord, and Son of Man, who were the agents whom God would use to bring his deliverance to Israel and to the world.

The history of Israel is one of call, judgment, and restoration. In many ways, Israel's history can be defined as its attempt, however unsuccessful, to live out the promises given to Abraham in the context of life in Canaan. The turmoil of the Israelite kingdom derived from their failure to appropriately execute their covenantal task caused by either imitating the surrounding nations or by trusting in their own might and wisdom. Yet in each case there is a consistent response of God, who meets his people with mercy and justice and directs them back to the proper path of being his treasured possession. The covenants made at Sinai, renewed at Moab, instituted

---

14. Cf. Michael F. Bird, *Are You the One Who Is to Come? The Historical Jesus and the Messianic Question* (Grand Rapids: Baker, 2009), 78–104.

with David, and hoped for in the new covenant all presuppose the faithfulness of God to his people. Despite their failures, God still intends his people to dwell with him, in his place, under his rule.

God	Covenant	People	Place	Promise	Kingdom	Response
Creator	Creation	Adam & Eve	Eden	Immortality	Harmony, order, and fellowship	Obedience
Creator	Creation	Adam, Eve, descendents	Earth	Seed of Eve	Justice	Worship
Creator	Creation	Noah	Earth	New beginning	Ark	Trust and worship
Lord	Abraham	Abrahamic family	Canaan	Land, descendents, blessings	Family	Trust and obey
Lord	Sinai	Israel	Canaan	Blessings	Nation	Trust and obey
Lord	Davidic	David's line	Israel	King	King	Hope
Lord	Sinai	Remnant	Israel	New exodus	Restored Jewish kingdom	Trust and obey

The economies of the Old Testament are diverse because divine revelation is progressive and God is gradually revealing more and more of himself to the people. In any case, we can speak of a single "salvation" in the Old Testament, understood as entering the promises of God, which consist of God's dwelling with his people, in his especially prepared place and under his reign. The form of that promise can vary from Adam to Ezra, but the substance remains consistent. Israel's "gospel" announces that God's grace precedes human action, faith is the appropriate response to God's promises, obedience to divine commandments permits the perpetuation of divine blessings, and the goal of salvation is the restoration of communion between Creator and humanity through the chosen people. It is from this story, and not despite it, that we encounter the gospel of God, the gospel of Christ, the gospel of the Son, the gospel of the kingdom, the gospel of salvation, and the gospel of peace.

5.2.3 ACT 3: JESUS

From one perspective, Jesus is born in the midst of Judean political history to be the Messiah who will bring sinners into the family of Abraham (Luke 2:1–14; 19:9–10).

From another perspective, Jesus is the eternal Word of God made flesh, who came to be the light of the world and to adopt believers into God's family (John 1:1–14). And from still another point of view, Jesus is born under the law to redeem people from the curse of the law so that believers may receive adoption as sons (Gal 4:4–5). We can summarize this by saying that Jesus brings people into the saving reign of God, which makes them sons and daughters of God's kingdom and so fulfills the promises given to Abraham, David, and expounded by the prophets.

Jesus' life is not an isolated story but stands in organic unity with Israel's story. The life-death-resurrection-exaltation of the Messiah marks the fulfillment of God's promises and the realization of Israel's hope (see Acts 13:32–33). In his roles as the Son of Man, Son of God, and Son of David, Jesus becomes the ultimate mediator between God and humanity. This "ultimacy" is rooted not only in the way he executes his role, but also in the fact that his very being is a union of divine and human natures. Jesus comes to make the prophetic hopes a reality: the end of exile, advent of a new exodus, reconstitution of the twelve tribes, rebuilding the temple, inauguration of the new covenant, calling for a return to covenant righteousness, and blessings for the nations; these terms are the manifesto for Jesus' ministry. The kingdom of God is established by virtue of the presence of the Spirit and the coming of its king. This is the kingdom that will one day be established over all the earth as the prophets foretold.

The good news is that the God who promised covenant love for his people, who acted for them throughout their tumultuous history, and who set before them the vision of his future world has come in Jesus of Nazareth to make those promises good.[15] By his obedience, Jesus is the new Adam and the true Israel, and for that reason he is singularly qualified to be the "great high priest" and "the Lamb of God," who can make expiation for the sins of God's people (John 1:29, 36; Heb 4:14–5:10; 8–9; Rev 5:6; 12:11; 13:8). Through Jesus, the royal seed of Abraham, divine blessings now extend to all the families of the earth. In his own person, he reconstitutes a new humanity, a new Israel, and a new temple that break down the dividing wall between the Jews and Gentiles (Eph 2:11–22).

As a result, the Father of Jesus becomes the Father of all believers. The new covenant is established as a covenant that brings blessings not available under the Sinatic covenant. God's people are those who belong to the Messiah. Jesus is the eschatological Davidic king, and his followers are the subjects of a new Israel within old Israel. In Jesus' ministry, the promise for a new exodus with a future consummation is fully underway, though not completed. The long-awaited kingdom is expressed here by the presence of the Spirit-anointed King and the liberating power that his work achieves. The response of people to this event is to turn from sins and to believe the good news that in and through Jesus, God is becoming king.

---

15. Williams, *Far as the Curse Is Found*, 223.

God	Covenant	People	Place	Promise	Kingdom	Response
Creator	Creation	Adam & Eve	Eden	Immortality	Harmony, order, and fellowship	Obedience
Creator	Creation	Adam, Eve, descendants	Earth	Seed of Eve	Justice	Worship
Creator	Creation	Noah	Earth	New beginning	Ark	Trust and worship
Lord	Abraham	Abrahamic family	Canaan	Land, descendents, blessings	Family	Trust and obey
Lord	Sinai	Israel	Canaan	Blessings	Nation	Trust and obey
Lord	Davidic	David's line	Israel	King	King	Hope
Lord	Sinai	Remnant	Israel	New exodus	Restored Jewish kingdom	Trust and obey
Father	New	Jesus/followers	New Israel	Restoration	Jesus/Spirit	Trust and repent

5.2.4 ACT 4: CHURCH

The church does not replace Israel, nor is it identical to ethnic Israel. Yet the historical and redemptive events manifested in Jesus and the Spirit forever transform and redefine God's people. Jesus becomes the new covenant mediator, himself the true Israel, and so the people of God are constituted as Israel by virtue of their relationship to him.[16] The church represents the goal of Israel's election and intimates the renewed humanity that God was aspiring to create since Adam's fall. The church is God's people in the messianic age, under the design of the new covenant, with a renewed mission from God.

The new covenant expands the old covenant; it does not replace it. Rather, it reaches through the Mosaic covenant back to the Abrahamic covenant. The new covenant is what the Mosaic covenant looks like when it flowers from its Abrahamic roots. The church has a *new scope*, comprising Jews and Gentile rather than being limited to one ethnic group; it has a *new mission*: reaching out to the world rather than simply drawing them in; it has a *new resource* in the Holy Spirit poured out in a qualitatively different way than in the old covenant.[17]

The church age of redemptive history has several distinguishing characteristics. Theologically speaking, the triune nature of God intimated in the Old Testament

---

16. Ibid., 252.

17. Ibid., 255–58.

becomes explicit in the New Testament through the economies of the Father who sends, the Son who redeems, and the Spirit who renews. In regards to the covenantal economy, the Abrahamic and Sinai covenants are essentially renewed and transformed into the new covenant, where God's people are united with Jesus the Messiah. The church comprises those who are adopted into God's family through the Messiah and who partake of the one Spirit (e.g., Gal 3:26–29). The church is the new temple and experiences God's presence in communion with his people (1 Cor 3:16–17).

The promise that the church possesses is that of eternal life and dwelling in the new creation after the final resurrection. Such promises have been proleptically launched in Jesus' own resurrection and joyfully experienced in the gift of the Spirit (Rom 8:29; 1 Cor 15:23; 2 Cor 1:22; 5:5; Eph 1:14; Col 1:18; Rev 1:5). The kingdom of God is expressed in the message of salvation, mediated through the Holy Spirit, and manifested in the life of the church. The church is not identical to the kingdom of God; rather, the church is called to proclaim and live out the kingdom (e.g., Matt 6:33; Acts 14:22; 19:8; 20:25; Rom 14:17; Heb 12:28). The way in which one enters this kingdom is by faith, repentance, and confession that Jesus as Lord (see Acts 20:21; Rom 10:9–11). The fresh tasks for the church include evangelism, disciple making, showing mercy, doing justice, and other kingdom works.

God	Covenant	People	Place	Promise	Kingdom	Response
Creator	Creation	Adam & Eve	Eden	Immortality	Harmony, order, and fellowship	Obedience
Creator	Creation	Adam, Eve, descendants	Earth	Seed of Eve	Justice	Worship
Creator	Creation	Noah	Earth	New Beginning	Ark	Trust and worship
Lord	Abraham	Abrahamic family	Canaan	Land, descendents, blessings	Family	Trust and obey
Lord	Sinai	Israel	Canaan	Blessings	Nation	Trust and obey
Lord	Davidic	David's Line	Israel	King	King	Hope
Lord	Sinai	Remnant	Israel	New exodus	Restored Jewish kingdom	Trust and obey
Father	New	Jesus/ followers	New Israel	Restoration	Jesus/ Spirit	Trust and repent
Trinity	New	Church	Church	Resurrection	Salvation	Fidelity

5.2.5 ACT 5: CONSUMMATION

The hope for a new heaven and a new earth was the climax of Isaiah's prophecy to the exiles in Babylon (Isa 66). In the Gospels, Jesus looks ahead to the day when he will drink the wine at the messianic banquet in the Father's kingdom (Matt 26:29/Mark 14:25/Luke 22:18). In the farewell discourse, the Johannine Jesus promises to prepare a place for his disciples, who will go after him (John 14:2–3). Paul asserts that one day "God [will] be all in all," meaning that he will dwell fully and finally with his people (1 Cor 15:28). John the Seer is granted a vision of a new heaven and a new earth with a new Jerusalem as its centerpiece (Rev 21–22).

At some point in human history, though the day and hour are unknown, the return of the Lord to earth will mark the beginning of God's kingdom on earth and its transformation into the new creation when it is united with heaven. The earth will become the theater for the glorious splendor of God's kingdom (Ps 145:12; 1 Thess 2:12). What hymn writers call "the land beyond the Jordan" and what C. S. Lewis called "Aslan's kingdom" is the beautiful world of God's Edenic paradise.

We discussed the various aspects of eschatology in part 3. Here we can note that in the consummation, after the resurrection and final judgment, the order of things will have several characteristics. The mystery of God as Trinity will no longer be a theological exercise but an experiential one as God dwells among his people. The new covenant will have achieved its appointed goal, and God's unbreakable covenant with creation will be put into permanent effect (Jer 33:20). The church, as the elect, will live forever with the Lord in the new creation (1 Thess 4:17). Humanity will experience a union with divine glory, holiness, and love as they dwell in the midst of God's presence and engage in the heavenly chorus of praise to their Creator and Redeemer (Rev 21). Creation will be rescued and restored. Humanity will be placed once more in their proper position with God as their companion (Gen 1:26–28; Ps 115:16).

God	Covenant	People	Place	Promise	Kingdom	Response
Creator	Creation	Adam and Eve	Eden	Immortality	Harmony, order, and fellowship	Obedience
Creator	Creation	Adam, Eve, descendents	Earth	Seed of Eve	Justice	Worship
Creator	Creation	Noah	Earth	New Beginning	Ark	Trust and worship
Lord	Abraham	Abrahamic family	Canaan	Land, descendents, blessings	Family	Trust and obey

Lord	Sinai	Israel	Canaan	Blessings	Nation	Trust and obey
Lord	Davidic	David's line	Israel	King	King	Hope
Lord	Sinai	Remnant	Israel	New Exodus	Restored Jewish kingdom	Trust and obey
Father	New covenant	Jesus/followers	New Israel	Restoration	Jesus/Spirit	Trust and repent
Trinity	New Covenant	Church	Church	Resurrection	Salvation	Fidelity
Trinity	Creation	Church	New creation	Divine glory	God's presence	Worship

This extended survey of redemptive history has been necessary in order to highlight that the "salvation" preached in the gospel is part of a particular story. To speak of being "saved" apart from this story would reduce the salvation event to a kind of crass individual escapism, where the focus is on my transaction with God and what it does for me alone. However, the meaning of salvation, its scope and substance, can only be understood if we grasp the overarching story in which salvation comes to us.

What is at stake in the gospel is the entire universe, not just my particular soul. The goal of salvation is to return humanity and creation to the state of peace and harmony that it enjoyed with God before the fall. The underlying promise is that in the end (i.e., the eschaton) things will be as they were in the beginning (i.e., the proton), only better. The plan of God, which we call the covenant of grace, is for God's people to dwell in God's place, in God's presence, under God's reign. The Logos redeems humanity and reunites them with their Creator for an everlasting eternity. As an interim report we can say that when we preach the gospel of salvation, we are talking about the culmination of the redemptive drama of God's rescue of humanity in Christ and through the Spirit.

FURTHER READING

Chester, Tim. *From Creation to New Creation: Understanding the Bible Story*. Carlisle, UK: Paternoster, 2003.

Goldsworthy, Graeme. *According to Plan: The Unfolding of God in the Bible*. Leicester, UK: Inter-Varsity Press, 1991.

Roberts, Vaughan. *God's Big Picture: Tracing the Storyline of the Bible*. Nottingham, UK: Inter-Varsity Press, 2002.

Strom, Mark. *The Symphony of Scripture: Making Sense of the Bible's Many Themes.* Downers Grove, IL: InterVarsity Press, 1990.

VanGemeren, William. *The Progress of Redemption: The Story of Salvation from Creation to the New Jerusalem.* Grand Rapids: Zondervan, 1988.

Williams, Michael D. *Far as the Curse Is Found: The Covenant Story of Redemption.* Phillipsburg, NJ: Presbyterian & Reformed, 2005.

Williamson, Paul R. *Sealed with an Oath: Covenant in God's Unfolding Purpose.* NSBT 23; Downers Grove, IL: InterVarsity Press, 2007.

§ 5.3 ORDER OF SALVATION: THE LOGICAL WORKING OF THE GOSPEL

We have just explored in brief the outworking of God's saving plan in redemptive history (*historia salutis*). It now remains to explore how salvation is applied to the individual believer in the order of salvation (*ordo salutis*).

Believing in Jesus as he is proclaimed to us in the gospel is what saves. But *how* does the gospel save? What are the mechanics? We know that a crane can winch us to safety if we are stuck on a cliff. But one might wonder afterward: How did that crane work? Once safely above the cliff, if we opened up the lid of the crane and took a look inside, what would we see and how would we describe the function of its moving parts?

Thus, when we ask, "How does the gospel actually work out salvation?" we are lifting up the hood of the vehicle of salvation and attempting to understand the actual process through which God's saving action is communicated to the believer. What I am referring to is the attempt to describe the sequence and complexity of salvation as it moves from God's eternal decision to save people, to the gospel call that people hear, to the faith and repentance of the individual, followed by their spiritual transformation, and their participation in God's new creation. The sequence of events in salvation takes on a particular order. Consequently, we call this saving sequence the *ordo salutis* ("order of salvation").[18]

The basic outline of an *ordo salutis* is given to us by Paul in Romans 8:29–30, where the apostle writes: "For those God foreknew he also predestined to be conformed to the image of his Son, that he might be the firstborn among many brothers and sisters. And those he predestined, he also called; those he called, he also

---

18. Louis Berkhof (*Systematic Theology* [Grand Rapids: Eerdmans, 1958], 415–16) defines the *ordo salutis* this way: "The *ordo salutis* describes the process by which the work of salvation, wrought in Christ, is subjectively realized in the hearts and lives of sinners. It aims at describing in their logical order, and also in their interrelations, the various movements of the Holy Spirit in the application of the work of redemption."

justified; those he justified, he also glorified." In its context, this tightly knit list of phrases is designed to bolster a sense of assurance for the readers in light of the trials they are facing (see 8:18–39). Paul emphasizes that it has always been God's intention from the beginning to create a Christ-shaped family, a renewed human race modeled on the Son, who are heirs of God and fellow heirs with Israel's Messiah.[19] Christians can take comfort from this, for in the mire of a world gone horribly wrong, God's purposes work for their good, and nothing at all can thwart the certainty of God's salvation. In other words, what God has started in them he will most definitely finish. No wonder this short verse in Romans was nicknamed by William Perkins the "golden chain of salvation."

Understandably the verbs in Romans 8:29–30 (foreknown, predestined, called, justified, and glorified) have proven to be the building blocks for theologians to construct a grand scheme that traces salvation from God's election of believers to their glorification in heaven. Book 3 of Calvin's *Institutes* is arguably an expanded *ordo salutis*, which, though not pursued in a strictly logical fashion, proceeds to map salvation from the initial work of the Spirit to the final resurrection of believers. In more recent times, the second half of John Murray's *Redemption: Accomplished and Applied* describes the process of salvation from effectual calling to glorification.[20] The value of tracing the *ordo salutis* is that it allows us to plot the logical sequence of events in God's application of salvation to the individual. In the *ordo salutis* set forth below we will cover the areas of predestination, calling, regeneration, faith and repentance, justification, transformation, and glorification. Our aim is to explore their order, meaning, and purpose in the overarching grace of God.[21]

5.3.1 PREDESTINATION

Sequence of salvation: *predestination* ⇨ calling ⇨ regeneration ⇨ faith and repentance ⇨ justification ⇨ transformation ⇨ glorification.

The doctrine of predestination is one of the most controversial and heated areas of theological debate. This doctrine proposes God's foreordaining of all events that come to pass. Broken down analytically, it includes God's *election* of some persons

---

19. N. T. Wright, "Romans," in *NIB*, 10:601–2.
20. John Murray, *Redemption Accomplished and Applied* (Grand Rapids: Eerdmans, 1955), 79–181.
21. The sequence I have given is notable because, unlike other accounts of the *ordo salutis*, I have not included "adoption" after "justification." That is a deliberate omission. Whereas some (like Murray, *Redemption*, 132–33) regard adoption as distinct from and in addition to other acts of grace in redemption, I want to argue that adoption is another contingent image for salvation (see John 1:12–13; Rom 8:15–16; Gal 3:26; 4:4–6; Eph 1:5; Rev 2:17; see next section). Furthermore, adoption expresses the corporate element of justification. God's justifying verdict means that we are acquitted from condemnation and are vindicated as members of his covenant family. Justification is vertical and horizontal—hence Paul's remarks about Jews and Gentile being in one body in Gal 3:14, 26–28; Rom 3:27–4:25; and Eph 1–2. See further Michael F. Bird, *The Saving Righteousness of God: Studies in Paul, Justification and the New Perspective* (PBM; Carlisle, UK: Paternoster, 2007), 154, with bibliography.

for salvation and his *reprobation* of others for punishment. In general, all theologians agree that God "elects" people to salvation. The people of God, across both Testaments, are called the "chosen ones" (e.g., 1 Chr 16:13; Pss 105:6, 43; 106:5; Isa 65:22; Luke 18:7; Col 3:12; 1 Pet 2:9) or the "elect" (Matt 24:22–24; Rom 11:7; 2 Tim 2:10; Titus 1:1; 1 Pet 1:1).[22]

The point of contention is the *basis* for this election. Does it lie in God's foreknowledge of persons who would freely choose for themselves to believe in him, or does it pertain to God's free and inscrutable decision to save some but not others? That is the debate![23] Everyone agrees that God elects in grace, in Christ, and for his glory; yet disputation emerges when we try to determine the cause and scope of that grace. In fact, discussions I've had on this topic can quickly become very ungracious. Lynn Cohick writes:

> It is important to keep this picture of the gracious God as central, as some of the discussion surrounding terms such as "predestine" can give rise to images of capriciousness or cavalier flippancy in a modern reader's mind. Either God is presented as fickle, choosing willy-nilly whomever he wants and also choosing to damn the rest, or God is seen as choosing some because in some way, however hidden it may be, they deserved it more than the others. Of course we usually don't voice either of these claims in such bald language, but nonetheless their unsettling presence, like ants at a picnic, intrudes inconveniently.[24]

The doctrine of election is a topic more hairy than a gorilla called "Harry the Hairy Gorilla," but it is a debate we must have if we are to wrestle with the entire counsel of God.

In Scripture there is ample reference to God's determining things ahead of time. According to the psalmist: "All the days ordained for me were written in your book before one of them came to be" (Ps 139:16). Similarly in Isaiah we find: "Have you not heard? Long ago I ordained it. In days of old I planned it; now I have brought it to pass, that you have turned fortified cities into piles of stone" (Isa 37:26). In Peter's speech in Acts, he says that Herod, Pontius Pilate, and the Jerusalemites conspired against Jesus, and they "did what your power and will *had decided beforehand* should happen" (Acts 4:28). In Paul's speech in the Areopagus, he tells his audience that God has "appointed" the times and places of the peoples and nations (Acts 17:26). It seems that God knows the future only because he has preordained it.

---

22. Often signified with the words *eklektos, eklegomai, eklogē* (Greek) and *bāḥir, bāḥar* (Hebrew).

23. There are five types of "election" in the scriptures. (1) Reference to elect angels (1 Cor 6:3; 1 Tim 5:21; 2 Pet 2:4; Jude 6). (2) Election to service, such as God's choice of David to be king of Israel (1 Sam 16:7–12), Jesus' choosing of the disciples (Luke 6:12–16; John 6:70; 15:16; Acts 9:15; 15:7). (3) The election of Abraham's descendents to form the nation of Israel (Deut 4:37; 7:6–7; 10:15; 1 Kgs 3:8; Isa 44:1–2; 65:9, 15, 22; Amos 3:2; Acts 13:17; Rom 9:1–5). (4) The election of the Messiah is implied in several places in Scripture (Isa 42:1; Matt 12:18; 1 Pet 1:20); hence Jesus is called the "chosen" one (Luke 9:35; 23:35). As the chosen one Jesus executes the messianic mission of redemption. (5) Election consists of individuals predestined to salvation (e.g., Acts 13:48); see F. H. Klooster, "Elect, Election," in *EDT*, 348.

24. Lynn H. Cohick, *Ephesians* (NCCS; Eugene, OR: Cascade, 2010), 46.

In addition, there are various references to God's sovereign choice of his people for salvation. In Deuteronomy, there are several mentions of God's choosing of Israel on account of his promises to the patriarchs (Deut 4:37; 7:6–8; 10:15; 14:2). The narration in 9:1–29 states that Israel was not chosen to go into the promised land because of their own merits. In fact, their stubbornness and disobedience meant that God had every reason to reject them. God's gracious choice of Israel is also underscored in the narrative recollection to the Passover celebration, where the descendents of a nomadic pagan become objects of God's rescuing love, who are gifted with an inheritance (26:5–9).

In Isaiah, the exiles are encouraged with the words: "But you, Israel, my servant, Jacob, whom I have *chosen*, you descendants of Abraham my friend, I took you from the ends of the earth, from its farthest corners I called you" (Isa 41:8–9). Also, in Ezekiel 16, the story of the abandoned newborn infant who is rescued and adopted into a royal family is a powerful metaphor for God's election of the nation for no other reason than God's profound mercy. Again, God's plan stated in Hosea to woo adulterous Israel back to the wilderness for a new marriage covenant suggests that God's selection of the nation for salvation is entirely gracious (Hos 2:14–23).

The same pattern of God's gracious choosing of people continues in the New Testament. In the Fourth Gospel, Jesus utters the words, "All those the Father gives me will come to me, and whoever comes to me I will never drive away" (John 6:37). "No one can come to me unless the Father who sent me draws them, and I will raise them up at the last day" (6:44). "Whoever belongs to God hears what God says. The reason you do not hear is that you do not belong to God" (8:47). "You did not choose me, but I chose you and appointed you so that you might go and bear fruit" (15:16). These are explicit mentions of salvation as anchored in God's initiative, expressed in his choosing, and possible only because of his enabling. The references elsewhere to a salvation that embraces the world (3:16) and draws all people (12:32) must be countenanced with God's special election of believers (10:25–26; 12:37–40; 14:17). It is because the world is in bondage to sin, locked in darkness, and trapped in unbelief that God chooses from the world special objects for salvation (1:5; 3:19; 8:34; 12:46; 15:24; 16:8–9; 17:2). The Holy Spirit moves in the hearts of people to bring conviction of sin, draw people to God, and even bring new birth (3:5–6; 6:44, 65; 16:8). In other words, according to John, because of the power of sin it is impossible for anyone to be saved apart from divine enabling and divine election.[25]

---

25. Cf. Robert W. Yarbrough, "Divine Election in the Gospel of John," in *Still Sovereign: Contemporary Perspectives on Election, Foreknowledge, and Grace* (ed. T. R. Schreiner and B. A. Ware; Grand Rapids: Baker, 2000), 47–62. Andreas Köstenberger, *A Theology of John's Gospel and Letters* (Grand Rapids: Zondervan, 2008), 458–64.

§5.3 Order of Salvation: The Logical Working of the Gospel

In Acts there is a clear reference to the election of believers. Luke recounts how Paul and Barnabas ministered in Pisidian Antioch, and many Gentiles came to faith in Jesus. Luke then adds the comment: "When the Gentiles heard this, they were glad and honored the word of the Lord; and all who were *appointed* for eternal life believed" (Acts 13:48).[26] The word for "appointed" is *tassō*, which means to "bring about an order of things by arranging."[27] Its form here is a perfect passive participle *tetagmenoi*, which some try to take as a middle voice to the effect that "all who had appointed *themselves* for eternal life believed."[28] Yet there is no reason to take the verb as a reflexive middle other than for theological inclination. It is a straightforward passive verb that indicates that God does the choosing. Indeed, the perfect tense highlights the state of "chosen-ness" that believers are said to possess. Luke undoubtedly meant "appointed" as a contrast to the more exclusivist attitudes of the Jews to Gentiles. As such, the messianic community accepts as equals those whom Jewish communities rejected as outsiders (pagans) or treated as mere guests (God-fearers). In the words of C. K. Barrett, "The present verse is an unqualified statement of absolute predestination ... as is found anywhere in the NT."[29]

Many of the clearest statements about predestination occur in Paul's letters. In the Thessalonian correspondence Paul writes: "For we know, brothers and sisters loved by God, that *he has chosen you*, because our gospel came to you not simply with words but also with power, with the Holy Spirit and deep conviction" (1 Thess 1:4–5); and, "we ought always to thank God for you, brothers and sisters loved by the Lord, because *God chose you* as firstfruits to be saved through the sanctifying work of the Spirit and through belief in the truth" (2 Thess 2:13).

A more definite reference to God's predetermining of believers is found in Ephesians 1:1–14. In this lavish and poetic eulogy to God's grace, Paul writes: "For *he chose us* in him before the creation of the world to be holy and blameless in his sight. In love *he predestined us* for adoption to sonship through Jesus Christ, in accordance with his pleasure and will" (1:4–5). "In him *we were also chosen, having been predestined* according to the plan of him who works out everything in conformity with the purpose of his will" (1:11). In Ephesians, election is evidently corporate and mediated through Christ, yet it consists of individuals who have been embraced by this display of divine grace. What occasions Paul's eulogy is the gracious and sovereign decision of God to bring believers into a personal relationship with himself, through Christ, and to adopt them as his children.[30]

---

26. Please note that in all Scripture references in this section on the *ordo salutis*, any italics have been added to the text.
27. BDAG, 806.
28. David J. Williams, *Acts* (NIBC; Peabody, MA: Hendrickson, 1985), 239.
29. C. K. Barrett, *Acts 1–14* (ICC: Edinburgh: T&T Clark, 1994), 658. See also discussion on "predestination" in Jaroslav Pelikan, *Acts* (BTCB; Grand Rapids: Brazos, 2005), 159–61.
30. Peter T. O'Brien, *The Letter to the Ephesians* (PNTC; Grand Rapids: Eerdmans, 1999), 102.

The primary arena for battles over election is several texts in Romans. At the end of Romans 8, Paul avers: "For those God *foreknew* he also *predestined* to be conformed to the image of his Son, that he might be the firstborn among many brothers and sisters. And those he predestined, he also called; those he called, he also justified; those he justified, he also glorified" (Rom 8:29–30). The meaning of "predestine" (*proorizō*) here must be defined in light of "foreknowledge" (*prognōsis*) and "foreknow" (*proginōskō*). I submit that divine foreknowledge, properly understood, indicates that predestination rests in God's sovereign choice, not in human initiative.

From Luke we learn that Jesus was handed over according to "God's deliberate plan and *foreknowledge*" (Acts 2:23). Here the divine plan (*boulē*) and divine foreknowledge (*prognōsis*) amount to the same thing: God knows in advance what he has planned to do.

In the opening to 1 Peter 1:1–2, we find more said about divine foreknowledge with reference to God's elect exiles, "who have been *chosen according to the foreknowledge of God* the Father, through the sanctifying work of the Spirit, to be obedient to Jesus Christ and sprinkled with his blood." As Christ himself is foreknown to be Savior (1:20), now the audience is foreknown to be the saved (2:9–10). In Peter's telling, it seems that the cause of their salvation is not that they reached out to a distant God, but that God chose to relate to them and to form the exiles into his people.[31]

Elsewhere divine foreknowledge is a particular intimate knowledge of persons and not simply knowledge of their actions ("you only have I chosen of all the families of the earth" [Amos 3:2], and "whoever loves God is known by God" [1 Cor 8:3]). That coheres with Romans 8:29, where what is foreknown is persons, not their actions or attitudes. In light of that, it looks as if the words for "foreknow" and "foreknowledge" indicate more than precognition, but espouse an intimate knowledge of persons. God's "foreknowledge" is not his prescience as to what certain persons might do under given circumstances, but constitutes a willful choice of a person for a special purpose.

Divine foreknowledge consists of God's plan, and that plan is implemented in divine predestination. This kind of foreknowing is not a neutral advanced knowledge of what a person will decide; rather, it is an affirmative choice of that person. So God does not look ahead into history, seeing who will believe, and then elect them on that basis. Rather, election is part of God's sovereign choice. Tautological as it sounds, God foreknows the elect because he has elected them. In other words, foreknowledge is not the grounds of predestination but a confirmation of

---

31. Peter H. Davids, *The First Epistle of Peter* (NICNT; Grand Rapid: Eerdmans, 1990), 48.

it.[32] Viewed this way, Romans 8:29–30 and Ephesians 1:1–14 exhibit a lucid predestinarian portrait of salvation as being rooted, not in the decision of believers, but in the eternal decision of God himself.

If Romans is the arena of the predestination debate, then Romans 9 is the cage that the gladiators get locked in for their combat. Romans 9–11 is intractably connected to Romans 8. Both sections deal with the subject of God's faithfulness to his promises. Whereas Paul ends Romans 8 on the note of complete assurance in the salvation that God offers through Christ (esp. 8:31–39), Paul cannot escape the obvious question, "Well, what about Israel?" If God's promise of salvation is so inviolable, then why has Israel, for the most part, rejected the message? Thus, in Romans 9–11, Paul deals with the question of Israel vis-à-vis the gospel. To that end, Paul addresses Israel in the past (9:1–29), Israel in the present (9:30–10:21), and Israel in the future (11:1–32). Specifically in Romans 9 the presenting issues for discussion are: (1) Has God's word to Israel failed (9:6)? (2) Who is Israel according to the flesh in contrast to Israel according to the promise (9:8–9)?

It has to be said that the concept of election in Romans 9–11 is fundamentally corporate and ethnic. The subject matter is how Christ-believing Gentiles came to be heirs of the promises given to Israel and what that means for unbelieving Israel in the meantime. Israel's disobedience and hardening has provided the occasion for the in-grafting of Gentiles into the people of God, and that in-grafting is designed to rouse Israel to jealousy (see esp. 11:11). Yet corporate and individual election are by no means mutually exclusive as the flow of argumentation in Romans 9 encompasses discussion of both topics.

1. The heritage of Israel is rich with symbols and signs of God's electing love (9:1–5).
2. God's promises to Israel have not failed because Israel according to the promise has always been a subset within Israel according to the flesh (9:6–8).
3. Individuals from Israel's sacred history indicate how God chooses on the basis of his mercy and not according to human effort (9:9–18).
4. God's electing purposes are not arbitrary, but are purposed to show the riches of his mercy by creating a people who were far from worthy of his affections (9:19–29).[33]

---

32. Millard J. Erickson, *Christian Theology* (2nd ed.; Grand Rapids: Baker, 1998), 939.

33. Paul K. Jewett (*Election & Predestination* [Grand Rapids: Eerdmans, 1985], 47) says: "In the Bible the elect are generally spoken of as a class, not as individuals per se. Yet the implication is plain, especially in the New Testament, that each member who belongs to the fellowship of the elect shares, as an individual, in the election of that people. The doctrine of election, in other words, has not only a corporate but also an individual aspect. The elect are not only all those together whom God has chosen to be the objects of his grace and favor, but each one in particular."

The point is not that the church is elect and one joins the elect by faith. Faith is created by God's word (Rom 10:17). Faith is not the means to election, but the sign of it (see 4:1–25). Furthermore, while the invitation to Jews and Gentiles to believe in Jesus runs through Romans 9–11 (see 9:30; 10:9–13, 17–21), God's sovereign purposes extend to individuals who are the objects of his electing mercy, such as Jacob and Elijah (9:10–13; 11:1–5), and this sovereign purpose includes reprobation in judgment as is the case with Pharaoh (9:17–18). Evidently, Romans 9–11 demonstrates that Gentiles have been brought into the covenantal promises of Israel and are therefore among the "elect" of the messianic age. Yet Paul also argues that God's mercy always precedes both human effort and human decision, for inclusion in the elect is based on God's mercy and nothing more (9:16). God prepared the elect to be the objects of his mercy in advance (9:23), and the messianic remnant is chosen entirely by grace (11:5–6).[34]

The doctrine of predestination has developed over the course of church history. It came to prominence in the debate between Pelagius and Augustine. For Pelagius, human beings enter the world with no disposition toward sin and are unaffected by Adam's fall. Each person has the ability to do good or to do evil, and God does not compel anyone to choose to do good. While grace is freely available to all persons, it is apprehended by the exercise of free will. According to Pelagius, God's moral commands are only comprehensible if he has given humans the ability to actually obey them. In other words, "ought" means "can." As such, God's predestining of persons is based exclusively on his foreknowledge of the moral quality of their lives.

In contrast to Pelagius, Augustine developed his doctrine of predestination in light of the effect of Adam's sin on humanity. All persons born into the world are already marred and corrupted by Adam's sin. Humanity has free will to chose what it desires, but humanity in its fallen state will never choose God because of their rebellious hearts. That is why grace is needed; it restores people to freedom and allows them the proper exercise of human will once grace has set it free. In regards to predestination, then, Augustine taught that if the good we do is entirely derived from God's work in us, our choosing to do good is ultimately a consequence of what God has already chosen to do in us. God's choice of people reaches back into all eternity, and he has elected humans to replace the fallen elect angels.[35] Augustine wrote:

---

34. Cf. further Thomas R. Schreiner, "Does Romans 9 Teach Individual Election unto Salvation?" in *Still Sovereign: Contemporary Perspectives on Election, Foreknowledge, and Grace* (ed. T. R. Schreiner and B. A. Ware; Grand Rapids: Baker, 2000), 89–106; Brian J. Abasciano, "Corporate Election in Romans 9: A Reply to Thomas Schreiner," *JETS* 49 (2006): 351–71; Thomas R. Schreiner, "Corporate and Individual Election in Romans 9: A Response to Brian Abasciano," *JETS* 49 (2006): 373–86.

35. For a compilation of Augustine's teachings on election, see Nick Needham, *The Triumph of Grace: Augustine's Writings on Salvation* (London: Grace Publications Trust, 2000), 206–41.

"You did not choose Me," He says, "I chose you" (John 15:16). Such grace is beyond description. What were we, apart from Christ's choice of us, when we were empty of love?... What were we but sinful and lost? We did not lead Him to choose us by believing in Him; for if Christ chose people who already believed, then we chose Him before He chose us. How then could He say, "You did not choose Me," unless His mercy came before our faith? Here is the faulty reasoning of those who defend the foreknowledge of God in opposition to His grace. For they say that God chose us before the creation of the world, not in order to make us good, but because He foreknew we would be good. This was not the view of Him Who said, "You did not choose Me." For if He had chosen us because He foreknew we would be good, then He would also have foreknown that we would *not* first of all choose Him. There is no other possible way to be good, apart from choosing the good; so what was it that God chose in people who were not good? They were not chosen because of their goodness, for they could not be good without being chosen. Grace is no longer grace, if human goodness comes first. It is God's electing grace that comes first.[36]

Augustine's views prevailed and Pelagius was condemned at the Council in Ephesus in 431. What emerged in the aftermath, however, was not a bonafide Augustinian view of predestination, but a Semi-Pelagianism comprising of a synergistic cooperation of human and divine wills to effect salvation. The semi-Pelagian view was condemned at the Synod of Orange in 529. The synod favored human inability and the efficacy of God's gracious salvation, but it fell short of affirming a decree of predestination about whom God would save in the end.

Predestination continued to find defenders in the Middle Ages. Gottschalk defended a view of double predestination—to salvation and to condemnation—and was condemned at a synod in Mainz in 848. Johannes Scotus Eriugena advocated the view that God, because of his eternity, views all time—past, present, and future—simultaneously; thus it is wrongheaded to speak of divine foreknowledge. Thomas Aquinas advocated a strong form of predestination, where God wills some to be saved but not others, though he distinguished God's general will that all be saved from his special will in electing some and passing over others.

On the eve of the Reformation, the general trend among theologians was a drift back towards Semi-Pelagianism. The Reformers reacted negatively to the moralistic optimism of medieval theology and insisted on a pessimistic view of the human will in its state of sin. Martin Luther and John Calvin both wrote works on the *Bondage of the Will* that emphasized how sin has eradicated free will so that people will not choose God of their own free volition. If people are to be saved, God must enable

---

36. Augustine, *Sermons on John* 86.2–3 (cited in Needham, *Augustine*, 218–19).

them; yet he enables some and not others. Therefore, believing in God is the work of God who activates faith in the believer by his sovereign choice.

Calvin is obviously the best-known advocate of predestination, though it is a misconception to say that predestination was the center of his theological system. Calvin believed that God's choice of persons was rooted in an eternal decision to elect some persons to salvation.[37] By "predestination," Calvin meant "the eternal decree of God, by which he determined with himself whatever he wished to happen with regard to every man."[38] About the doctrine he says: "Paul declares that it is only when the salvation of a remnant is ascribed to gratuitous election, we arrive at the knowledge that God saves whom he wills of his mere good pleasure, and does not pay a debt, a debt which never can be due."[39] The chief characteristics of the Calvinistic scheme are the following:

1. Election is an expression of God's sovereign purposes.
2. Election is efficacious, as those who are elected will certainly come to faith and persevere in faith.
3. Election is from all eternity and was not made at some later point in time.
4. Election is unconditional, not dependent on the inherit qualities of any person.
5. Election is immutable; God does not unelect anyone or elect others thereafter.[40]

Not all Protestants shared the view of divine predestination found in the Lutheran and Reformed churches. Jacob Arminius, a former student of Theodore Beza (Calvin's successor in Geneva) and a popular pastor in Amsterdam, developed doubts about double predestination.

1. For Arminius, God's first decree was the appointment of Jesus Christ as Savior.
2. God then decreed that all who repented and believed would be saved.
3. God granted to all persons a sufficient grace to enable them to believe if they chose to.
4. God predestined persons whom he knew would choose to believe.

Arminius's position was condemned at the Synod of Dort in 1618–19. Still, his views became popular and influenced many Anglican and Wesleyan churches, and there developed a group that followed after him called the Remonstrants. John Wesley even published a magazine called *The Arminian*. The Wesleyan contribution to this theological school was to emphasize God's prevenient grace that supposedly undid the effects of original sin and placed humanity back in a neutral position where they could voluntarily choose God.

---

37. Calvin, *Institutes* 3.21–24.
38. Ibid., 3.21.5.
39. Ibid., 3.21.1.
40. Berkhof, *Systematic Theology*, 114–15.

WAS THE INCARNATION PLAN B?

Medieval theologians wrestled with the topic of whether the incarnation would have happened if Adam had not sinned. Was it only sin that necessitated the incarnation, or was the incarnation something that was foreordained before creation and before the fall? Some, like Thomas Aquinas, regarded the incarnation as a remedy for sin. Thus, if there had been no fall, there would have been no incarnation. Aquinas wrote: "God allows evil to happen in order to bring a greater good there from … a great Redeemer."[41]

Other theologians maintained that the incarnation was always intended. It was part of God's wider project to unite all of creation with himself through the Logos. For Maximus the Confessor the incarnation was purposed as the crown of creation and would have taken place even if humans had never fallen into sin. According to Honorius of Autun, the incarnation was not originally foreordained as a rescue mission for sin, but in order to secure the divinization of humanity. On his view, the incarnation became redemptive because of sin, but the incarnation was always intended because of God's plan to have communion with his creatures.[42]

Calvin on this topic is notoriously inconsistent. On the one hand, Calvin believed that the Son was eternally the mediator. He wrote: "Had man remained free from all taint, he was of too humble a condition to penetrate to God without a mediator." This implies that even without the fall, humanity still needed a mediator to bridge the gap between the infinite God and finite human beings. Also, when Calvin says that the incarnation was the means where "by mutual union his divinity and our nature might be combined,"[43] we are right to think that this could take place without reference to the fall.

On the other hand, when Calvin dealt with objections to Catholic Christology in Andreas Osiander's work, he declared: "The only end which the Scripture uniformly assigns for the Son of God voluntarily assuming our nature, and even receiving it as a command from the Father, is, that he might propitiate the Father to us by becoming a victim."[44] Calvin goes so far as to say that even if Adam had not fallen into

---

41. Aquinas, *Summa Theologica* III, Q.1, A.3.
42. Roger Olson, *The Story of Christian Theology: Twenty Centuries of Tradition and Reform* (Downers Grove, IL: InterVarsity Press, 1999), 298–99; Alister McGrath, *Christian Theology: An Introduction* (Oxford: Blackwell, 2001), 282.
43. Calvin, *Institutes* 2.12.1.
44. Ibid., 2.12.5.

sin, with the angels he would have been like God; and "it would not therefore have been necessary that the Son of God should become either a man or an angel."[45] That means that the Son was contingently cast into incarnation by the intrusion of sin into the world. Calvin seems forced into affirming, then, that a union between God and humanity is contingent on the fall, since that is what provides the necessary condition for the incarnation. So for Calvin, Christ's general mediatorship is not contingent on the fall, but the incarnation is contingent on the fall.[46] The inconsistency in Calvin's position is that his conception of Christ's headship and Christ's eternal mediatorial role requires the incarnation entirely apart from any redemptive function assigned to it. Yet Calvin remains adamant that the incarnation eventuates *only* as a solution to the fall.

In Reformed theology there has never been any question of the incarnation as "Plan B." But the incarnation was held to be contingent on the fall, making the fall a *felix culpa*, or "happy misfortune," since the fall necessitated the incarnation, and the incarnation brought salvation. Reformed theology has attempted to identify a unity to God's plan by focusing on the *logical order* of God's decrees pertaining to creation, permitting the fall, election and reprobation, and appointing the Son to be Savior. Several different ideas developed about the logical order of the decrees in God's plan. They are not insignificant as they impact the shape of salvation as it relates to God's eternal decision. The three main views are:[47]

Infralapsarianism	Supralapsarianism	Sublapsarianism
The decree to create human beings.	The decree to elect some and to reprobate others.	The decree to create human beings.
The decree to permit the fall.	The decree to create both the elect and reprobate.	The decree to permit the fall.
The decree to elect some and to reprobate others.	The decree to permit the fall of both groups.	The decree to provide salvation sufficient for all.
The decree to provide salvation for the elect.	The decree to provide salvation only for the elect.	The decree to elect some and to reprobate others.

---

45. Ibid., 2.12.7.
46. Edwin Chr. van Driel, *Incarnation Anyway: Arguments for Supralapsarian Christology* (Oxford: Oxford University Press, 2008), 173.
47. Erickson, *Christian Theology*, 931.

I do not think anyone can reasonably claim to know the logical order of the decrees in the mind of God with any certainty. What might be a logical order within a system of theology is one thing, but to claim that such a logical order carries over into divine planning is quite another.[48] The best we can do is to infer a possible logic from the economy of salvation about the apparent order that God has enacted his sovereign and saving purposes.

Coming to a solution, there are sufficient reasons to believe that the incarnation is not logically dependent on the decree to permit the fall. First, the incarnation is necessitated by (1) God's intention for humans to have union with him in a perfected creation, i.e., the eschaton; and (2) the nature of the Son as the eternal mediator between God and creation. If God's ultimate end in creation is to be united with his creatures, then the incarnation is necessary for such a goal to be realized independent of the fall.

Second, as proof of the above point, if the incarnation was intended merely to address the problem of sin, there is no reason for Jesus to remain incarnate after atonement has been made, nor is there a necessary reason for God to revamp the universe in a new creation. The fact that the crucified and risen Jesus remains incarnate after Easter, combined with the fact that Easter previews and even propels us toward the new creation, means that it is not redemption from sin, but God's union with his creatures in the eschaton that is the chief end of his purposes.[49]

Third, as many evangelical theologians have recognized, the only way that Jesus Christ can be appointed as the Savior of all people (see John 3:16; 1 Tim 2:4; 2 Pet 3:9; 1 John 2:2; etc.), while maintaining the sovereignty of God's decision in election, is through a scheme that makes the appointment of Christ as Redeemer logically prior to God's decision to provide salvation for the elect. God determines in himself to be the God who would be gracious to humanity and to unite them with himself through the Son.[50]

---

48. To quote Hermann Bavinck (*Reformed Dogmatics: Volume 2: God and Creation* [ed. J. Bolt; trans. J. Vriend; Grand Rapids: Baker, 2004], 391): "Accordingly, neither the supra- nor the infralapsarian view of predestination is able to do full justice to the truth of Scripture, and to satisfy our theological thinking. The true element in supralapsarianism is: that it emphasizes the unity of the divine decree and the fact that God had one final aim in view, that sin's entrance into the universe was not something unexpected and unlooked for by God but that he willed sin in a certain sense, and that the work of creation was immediately adapted to God's redemptive activity so that even before the fall, i.e., in the creation of Adam, Christ's coming was definitely fixed. And the true element in infralapsarianism is: that the decrees manifest not only a unity but also a diversity (with a view to their several objects), that these decrees reveal not only a teleological but also a causal order, that creation and fall cannot merely be regarded as means to an end, and that sin should be regarded not as an element of progress but rather as an element of disturbance in the universe so that in and by itself it cannot have been willed by God." Calvin (*Institutes* 2.12.5; 3.21.1–4) also warned against too much speculation on the decrees of God.

49. Van Driel, *Incarnation Anyway*, 148.

50. Karl Barth, *CD*, II/2.101.

In this case, the incarnation was not an "emergency measure" that God intended to apply to a broken world. Sin was not the "happy misfortune" that occasioned the incarnation. Rather, the incarnation has its grounds in God's decision to make Jesus Christ the "firstborn over all creation" (Col 1:15), while the subsequent decree to permit the fall necessitates that Jesus be the "Lamb who was slain from the creation of the world" (Rev 13:8).

In sum, if we regard God's plan as being to unite creation with himself through the Logos, the divine decree for the incarnation of the Logos must logically precede the decree to permit the fall. I propose, then, that in logical order, God decrees to create, God decrees the incarnation of the Son, God decrees to create human beings, God decrees to permit the fall, God decrees to offer salvation in the Son to human beings, and God decrees to save the elect.

FURTHER READING

Crisp, Oliver D. *Revisioning Christology: Theology in the Reformed Tradition*. Surrey, UK: Ashgate, 2011, pp. 23–42.

Gibson, David A. *Reading the Decree: Exegesis, Election, and Christology in Calvin and Barth*. London: T&T Clark, 2009.

Muller, Richard A. *Christ and the Decree: Christology and Predestination in Reformed Theology from Calvin to Perkins*. Durham, NC: Labyrinth, 1986.

Van Driel, Edwin Chr. *Incarnation Anyway: Arguments for Supralapsarian Christology*. Oxford: Oxford University Press, 2008.

The doctrine of election was invigorated in the mid-twentieth century by Swiss theologian Karl Barth.[51] Barth rejected the traditional Reformed view of predestination as being based on a metaphysical belief about God's inert and static relationship with individuals from eternity past. Barth's doctrine of election encompassed a strong rejection of the notion of an eternal, hidden divine decree that is abstracted from God's self-revelation in Jesus Christ. For Barth, "the election of grace is the whole of the gospel, the gospel *in nuce*."[52] Consistent with his christocentric theological method, Barth argued that to ascribe the salvation or damnation of people to an eternally hidden divine decision is to make God's pretemporal decrees more final

---

51. Ibid., II/2.1–506.

52. Ibid., II/2.13–24.

and determinative for salvation than God's redemptive revelation in Jesus Christ. Thus, for Barth Jesus Christ is the electing God, the elected Savior, and all people are elect in him. Jesus is both the subject and object of election. He writes:

> According to Scripture, the divine election of grace is an activity of God which has a definite goal and limit. Its direct and proper object is not individuals generally, but one individual—and only in Him are the people called and united by Him, and only in that people, individuals in general in their private relationships with God. It is only in that one man that a human determination corresponds to the divine determining. In the strict sense only He can be understood and described as "elected."[53]

The election of Jesus Christ means that God has uttered his "yes" to humanity in the atonement. The whole world is elect in Christ. Consequently, the distinction between the elect and nonelect is obviated. On the cross, God chooses rejection for himself and election for the human race. According to Ben Myers:

> For Barth, predestination is God's choice and determination of his own being. God chooses to be the kind of God he is—he elects to be the gracious God, the *human* God—and he chooses not to be without humanity. God's eternal being is nothing other than this free decision. God *constitutes* himself in this decision. And the name of this decision is Jesus Christ.[54]

In terms of an evaluation, Barth's doctrine of election holds several attractive features. Barth does not think it wise to ground election in the metaphysics of God's nature, but wants election determined by God's action in Christ. That carries weight as both Reformed and Remonstrant theologians believe that Jesus is the foundation of election. One thinks particularly of Ephesians 1, which underscores that election is in and through Christ. Calvin himself seems capable of affirming that Christ is both the author and mediator of election, so in a sense, Jesus is both the electing God and elected mediator. The problem, however, with Barth's view of election is that it seems to imply universalism, and the very concept of election is eviscerated when there is no difference between believers and unbelievers. Furthermore, it is simply impossible to locate Barth's idea of election in the exegetical terrain of Scripture or in the broad Christian tradition.[55]

Popular evangelicalism in the US, Europe, UK, and British colonies has known a variety of views and models about election, grace, and free will ranging from Calvinism (e.g., Charles Spurgeon, J. I. Packer), Calvinism-lite (e.g., Richard

---

53. Ibid., II/2.43.
54. Benjamin Myers, *Faith and Theology*, "Karl Barth's Doctrine of Election": http://faith-theology.blogspot.com/2005/12/karl-barths-doctrine-of-election.html. Posted 20 Dec 2005. Accessed 25 Feb 2011.
55. For evaluation and critique of Barth on election see Emil Brunner, *The Christian Doctrine of God* (2 vols.; trans. O. Wyon; London: Lutterworth, 1949), 1:346–52; Wolfhart Pannenberg, *Systematic Theology* (3 vols.; trans. G. W. Bromiley; Edinburgh: T&T Clark, 1991), 3:457–61; Sung Wook Chung, "A Bold Innovator: Barth on God and Election," in *Karl Barth and Evangelical Theology: Convergences and Differences* (ed. S. W. Chung; Grand Rapids: Baker, 2006), 60–76; Michael S. Horton, *Christian Faith* (Grand Rapids: Zondervan, 2011), 317–23.

Baxter, R. T. Kendall), Arminianism (e.g., Henry Thiessen, Roger Olson), Barthian (e.g., G. Berkouwer, T. F. Torrance), and even Pelagianism (e. g., Charles Finney). I think it safe to say that in evangelical churches the primary competing views are between the Calvinistic and Arminian options. These can be summarized with the acronym TULIP and the palindrome DOGOD.

Calvinist View (TULIP)	Arminian View (DOGOD)
Total Depravity: Sin has effected human beings in their moral and mental faculties. They are not necessarily as bad as they can be, but their free will is enslaved to sin and thus no one is free to choose to believe in God.	**Deprived Ability**: Human beings are impacted by sin but God's prevenient grace enables them to believe in him if they so choose. Humans are in a depraved state, but not a powerless state in sin.
Unconditional Election: God elects people to salvation not because of any quality that makes them worthy, nor because God knows in advance who will choose him. God elects out of his own free decision to give salvation to some who do not deserve it.	**Open Election**: Election is determined by faith for it is faith that incorporates one into the church, the elect people of God. Election is, then, indeterminate or open, and realized by the act of faith.
Limited Atonement: Jesus' death was only for the elect. Jesus did not die for the whole world, only for those predestined to salvation.	**General Atonement**: Jesus died for the sins of the whole world and not just for the elect.
Irresistible Grace: Those whom God elects will come to salvation in the end because God's grace is efficient and effective. It is not that those who are elect cannot resist God's grace, but in the end the elect will always succumb to grace.	**Opposable Grace**: People can and do resist God's grace when they fail to appropriate prevenient grace and disbelieve the message of the gospel.
Perseverance of the Saints: Those whom God has elected will assuredly continue in their faith and live with God forever. It is not the case that the elect cannot backslide or fall into sin, but ultimately they will persevere in their faith due to divine enabling.	**Danger of Apostasy**: It is possible for believers to fall from their state of grace into apostasy, a position from which there is no possibility of restoration.

Many of the issues of TULIP versus DOGOD will be tackled throughout this volume. Suffice it to say that on the issue of predestination, I find the Calvinist scheme to be inherently more plausible than its Arminian counterpart. I regard Arminianism as an understandable theological option within evangelicalism; it is a type of intra-Protestant renewal aimed at countenancing divine sovereignty with divine love,[56] and I appreciate the gravity of some of its objections to the Calvinistic scheme.[57] Calvinists and Arminians can agree that "God is involved in people's lives before they hear and respond to his call."[58]

That said, I have several problems with the Arminian conception of election. First, as we've already shown, in Scripture divine foreknowledge is foreknowledge of persons, not foreknowledge of what those persons might do under given circumstances, with God then electing them on that basis. God's foreknowledge is the application of his preordained purposes in salvation. Second, Calvinists and Arminians agree that the weight of sin indeed restricts the capacity of the will to believe. Yet the Wesleyan way to get around this with a "prevenient grace" fails. The problem is, as Arminian theologian Clark Pinnock has pointed out, that "the Bible has no developed doctrine of universal prevenient grace, however convenient it would be for us if it did."[59] All grace is prevenient in the sense that it precedes human action, but it is also efficacious in that God's grace genuinely saves. Note this: grace does not make salvation possible; it makes salvation actual. Yet salvation becomes actual for some and not for others. Why? Our answer must be that it is because of God's election of persons for salvation.[60]

The Calvinistic scheme does not mean that God has no love for the nonelect. God desires all persons to be saved, and none who come to him will ever be rejected. That is God's general love for all of people. Yet God also has a special love, and he demonstrates that love by choosing a people for salvation even though neither they nor anybody deserved it. God loves generally in his willingness to receive all, and he loves particularly in ensuring that a remnant of humanity will be saved. It is important to remember that God owes humanity justice, not mercy. It is only because mercy is undeserved that it is mercy at all. Rather than ask why God saves only the elect, perhaps we should ask why God saves anyone at all.

If God has determined who will be saved, is there any point in engaging in evangelism? Should we only preach to people who, the hyper-Calvinists say, show signs of election? God's instrument to bring the elect into salvation is the proclamation of the gospel by the church. God has determined not only the end of salvation, but also

---

56. It is important to note that the Remonstrant (Arminians) are not necessarily or always identical in perspective to Wesleyan views. See Roger Olson, *Arminian Theology: Myths and Realities* (Downers Grove, IL: InterVarsity Press, 2006), 44–60.

57. John Wesley in his sermon "A Catholic Spirit" said: "If your heart is as my heart, if you love God and all mankind, I ask no more: give me your hand." Sage advice for anyone regardless of their theological disposition.

58. Brenda B. Colijn, *Images of Salvation in the New Testament* (Downers Grove, IL: InterVarsity Press, 2010), 226.

59. Clark H. Pinnock, "From Augustine to Arminius: A Pilgrimage in Theology," in *The Grace of God and the Will of Man* (ed. C. H. Pinnock; Grand Rapids: Bethany, 1995), 22. See also the critique of prevenient grace from a Wesleyan perspective by Ben Witherington III, *The Problem with Evangelical Theology: Testing the Exegetical Foundations of Calvinism, Dispensationalism, and Wesleyanism* (Waco, TX: Baylor University Press, 2005), 207–9.

60. Cf. further Michael D. Williams and Robert A. Peterson, *Why I am Not an Arminian* (Downers Grove, IL: InterVarsity Press, 2004).

> ## COMIC BELIEF
>
> A Calvinist arrives at St. Peter's gates and sees that there are two queues going in. One is marked "predestined," and the other is marked "free will." Being the card-carrying Calvinist that he is, he strolls on over to the predestined queue. After several moments an angel asks him, "Why are you in this line?" He replies, "Because I chose it." The angel looks surprised, "Well, if you 'chose' it, then you should be in the free will line." So our Calvinist, now slightly miffed, obediently wanders over to the free will line. Again, after a few minutes, another angel asks him, "Why are you in this line?" He sullenly replies, "Someone made me come here."

its means. Far from stifling evangelism, God's predestination of believers motivates evangelism since we know that God's Word does not fail and those whom he elects will be saved through our message. As J. I. Packer wrote:

> While we must remember that it is our responsibility to proclaim salvation, we must never forget that it is God who saves. It is God who brings men and women under the sound of the gospel, and it is God who brings them to faith in Christ. Our evangelistic work is the instrument that He uses for this purpose, but the power that saves is not in the instrument: it is in the hand of the One who uses the instrument. We must not at any stage forget that. First, if we forget that it is God's prerogative to give results when the gospel is preached, we shall start to think that it is our responsibility to secure them. And if we forget that only God can give faith, we shall start to think that the making of converts depends, in the last analysis, not on God, but on us, and that the decisive factor is the way which we evangelize.[61]

FURTHER READING

Boettner, Loraine. *The Reformed Doctrine of Predestination*. Philadelphia: Presbyterian & Reformed, 1932.

Geisler, Norman. *Chosen But Free: A Balanced View of God's Sovereignty and Free Will*. Minneapolis: Bethany, 2010.

---

61. J. I. Packer, *Evangelism and the Sovereignty of God* (Downers Grove, IL: InterVarsity Press, 1961), 27.

Gibson, David. *Reading the Decree: Exegesis, Election and Christology in Calvin and Barth.* London: T&T Clark, 2009.

Klein, William H. *The New Chosen People: A Corporate View of Election.* Grand Rapids: Zondervan, 1990.

O'Neil, M. "Karl Barth's Doctrine of Election." *EvQ* 76 (2004): 311–26.

5.3.2 CALLING

Sequence of Salvation: predestination ⇨ *calling* ⇨ regeneration ⇨ faith and repentance ⇨ justification ⇨ transformation ⇨ glorification.

In Romans 8:30, following predestination, Paul adds that believers are "called." This "call" represents the implementation of God's determined-ahead-of-time-plan (i.e., foreknowledge + predestination) mediated via the summons to believe in the Lord Jesus Christ.[62] As Calvin wrote: "For the elect are brought by calling into the fold of Christ, not from the very womb, nor all at the same time, but according as God sees it [fit] to dispense grace."[63] Those whom "he called" (*ekalesen*) in Romans 8:30 are precisely those in 8:28 who are said to have been "called according to his purpose" (*tois kata prothesin klētois ousin*). The call, then, is the outworking of God's electing purposes.

Importantly, the "call" here is not a general invitation for all people to believe in Jesus Christ (see Matt 11:28; John 3:16; Rev 22:17). Rather, this specific call is what happens when the Holy Spirit moves in the hearts of people as they hear the gospel and are brought to a point of conversion.[64] Accordingly, this call designates God's action whereby he summons and brings people to himself through the gospel.[65] A good example of what this looks like is Luke's account of Lydia's conversion during Paul's ministry in Philippi: "The Lord opened her heart to respond to Paul's message" (Act 16:14). The call of Lydia was effected through the quickening of her heart as occasioned by Paul's preaching of the gospel.

A link between "gospel" and "call" is highlighted elsewhere. Paul reminds the Thessalonian church that God "called you to this through our gospel, that you might share in the glory of our Lord Jesus Christ" (2 Thess 2:14; cf. 1 Thess 1:4–5). Paul emphasizes that this call has gone out to Jews and Gentiles who make up the one new covenant community (Rom 1:6–7; 9:24–29; 1 Cor 1:24). Believers are called "into fellowship with his Son" (1 Cor 1:9); they are called by grace (Gal 1:6, 15) and in hope (Eph 1:18; 4:4). In the Pastoral Epistles there is an exhortation to "take hold of the eternal life to which you were called when you made your good confession in the presence of many witnesses" (1 Tim 6:12).

The call places a person beneath the saving Lordship of Jesus Christ as the writer

---

62. Cf. further Murray, *Redemption*, 88–95; Grudem, *Systematic Theology*, 692–93; Horton, *Christian Faith*, 564–72.

63. Calvin, *Institutes* 3.24.10.

64. Wright, "Romans," 10:603.

65. T. R. Schreiner, *Romans* (BECNT; Grand Rapids: Baker, 1998), 455.

to the Hebrews states: "For this reason Christ is the mediator of a new covenant, that those who are called may receive the promised eternal inheritance" (Heb 9:15). The call shifts persons between realms; hence God's call brings believers "out of darkness into his wonderful light" (1 Pet 2:9; cf. Col 1:13). In the words of 2 Peter 1:3: "His divine power has given us everything we need for a godly life through our knowledge of him who called us by his own glory and goodness."[66]

The call is not an isolated event that occurs when people happen to hear the Christian gospel and decide for themselves to accept it. It is clear in Romans 8:29–30 that "call" is part of the unbreakable chain of events that implements God's saving purposes from election through to glorification. We find this idea in 1 Peter 5:10 as well: "And the God of all grace, who called you to his eternal glory in Christ, after you have suffered a little while, will himself restore you and make you strong, firm and steadfast." Here "call" is a feature of God's initial saving grace and also his sustaining grace that will assuredly bring believers to God's eternal glory in Christ.

Moreover, there is a triune nature to the call. The Father is the "caller," Christ is the "one called about," and the Holy Spirit is the "effecter of the call," who enables us to hear. The call is an event where God communicates something of himself to people so that they participate in the drama of redemption. The call is made in the gospel, through the Spirit, and brings believers into a living hope of eternal glory.[67] God's Word issued in the call simultaneously achieves what it announces, namely, salvation.

Put simply, the word given in divine calling is a salvation-announcing and salvation-creating event. Horton comments: "In effectual calling, the Spirit draws us into the world that the Word not only *describes* but *brings into existence*. Through this Word, the Spirit not only works to propose, lure, invite, and attract, but actually kills and makes alive, sweeping sinners from their identity 'in Adam' to the riches of their inheritance in Christ."[68] In the end, we should understand calling as a triune, effectual, evangelical, and doxological speech-act of God.

5.3.3 REGENERATION

Sequence of Salvation: predestination ⇨ calling ⇨ *regeneration* ⇨ faith and repentance ⇨ justification ⇨ transformation ⇨ glorification.

---

66. I would add that his calling is not coercive since human will is freed from unbelief in order to believe by the efficacy of God's call when it is laid on the unregenerate heart. The Westminster Confession 10.1 states: "All those whom God hath predestinated unto life, and those only, He is pleased, in His appointed time, effectually to call, by His Word and Spirit, out of that state of sin and death, in which they are by nature to grace and salvation, by Jesus Christ; enlightening their minds spiritually and savingly to understand the things of God, taking away their heart of stone, and giving unto them an heart of flesh; renewing their wills, and, by His almighty power, determining them to that which is good, and effectually drawing them to Jesus Christ: yet so, as they come most freely, being made willing by His grace."

67. Cf. Kevin Vanhoozer, *First Theology: God, Scripture, and Hermeneutics* (Downers Grove, IL: InterVarsity Press, 2002), 96–124.

68. Horton, *Christian Faith*, 570 (italics original).

Missing from Romans 8:29–30 is any reference to "regeneration" or "new birth." In the list Paul gives, God's life-creating power is implied in the reference to "calling." This call is made effective by the proclamation of the gospel and through the agency of the Spirit. Here "calling" refers to what happens to the believer from the *divine perspective*, whereby God's ordained plan is brought to pass through the call, and this call actively brings a person to faith. From the *individual perspective*, however, it is the Holy Spirit who brings spiritual life from spiritual death in a moment coincident with faith, and this we call regeneration.[69]

Regeneration refers to the new birth wrought by the Holy Spirit in a person. It involves restoring and recreating a person from spiritual death to spiritual life. It entails cleansing and transforming the human heart so that one may believe in God, enjoy God, and produce fruit for God. Regeneration is God establishing a beachhead of new creation on the shores of the human heart.

The prologue to the Fourth Gospel states explicitly that regeneration is an exclusive work of God as believers are "children born not of natural descent, nor of human decision or a husband's will, but born of God [*ek theou egennēthēsan*]" (John 1:13). Birth into the family of the Messiah is different from natural birth since it is a feature of divine grace. Regeneration is necessary for salvation since Jesus taught that no one can enter the kingdom unless he or she is "born again" (3:3–5, 7). According to Leon Morris: "These solemn words forever exclude the possibility of salvation by human merit. Our nature is so gripped by sin that an activity of the very Spirit of God is a necessity if we are to be associated with God's kingdom."[70]

Regeneration is also true of all believers as stated in 1 John 5:1: "Everyone who believes that Jesus is the Christ is born of God [*ek tou theou gegennētai*]." That in turn leads to a decisive break from sin and sinning. Though we continue to struggle with sin (1:8), we lose the general inclination to sin because we are now born of God (3:9; 5:18). The Johannine teaching on new birth emphasizes the recipient's passivity, its irreversibility, and the ethical activity that accompanies it.

The opening exhortation of 1 Peter includes the remark, "Praise be to the God and Father of our Lord Jesus Christ! In his great mercy he has given us new birth [*anagennēsas hēmas*] into a living hope through the resurrection of Jesus Christ from the dead' (1 Pet 1:3). Here the new birth means consecration by the Spirit and entering into the salvation of God. The resurrection of Jesus Christ has as its sequel the resurrection of the human heart. In Peter's testimony, "the basis for being a

---

69. According to Grudem (*Systematic Theology*, 700): "Effective calling is thus God the Father *speaking powerfully to us*, and regeneration is God the Father and God the Holy Spirit *working powerfully in us*, to make us alive" (italics original). The problem is that I would regard effectual calling and regeneration as different perspectives of the same triune action.

70. Leon Morris, *The Gospel according to John* (NICNT; rev. ed.; Grand Rapids: Eerdmans, 1995), 194.

Christian is not a decision or the appropriation of a commandment, but a second birth established in God's mercy, the manifestation of a new being."[71]

Paul makes mention of new birth in Titus 3:5: "He saved us, not because of righteous things we had done, but because of his mercy. He saved us through the washing of rebirth and renewal by the Holy Spirit [*palingenesias kai anakainōseōs pneumatos hagiou*]." Nonetheless, Paul's preferred image for expressing the reality of new birth comes through his language of "new creation" (Gal 6:15; 2 Cor 5:17). The new spiritual life given to believers occurs through a Spirit-effected vivification wrought in their hearts. Regeneration can also be equated with being "made ... alive with Christ" (Eph 2:5; Col 2:13) and walking in "new life" (Rom 6:4). The way to appropriate regeneration is to "put on the new self" (Eph 4:24; Col 3:10) and to live for God in righteousness (Rom 7:4).

New birth represents the fulfillment of the prophetic promise that God will write his law into the hearts of his people and change their hearts from stone to flesh (Jer 31:33; 32:40; Ezek 11:19; 18:31; 36:25–27).[72] This "circumcision of the heart" hoped for in the Old Testament (cf. Deut 10:16; 30:6; Rom 2:29) is identical with the circumcision effected by Christ and "not performed by human hands" (Col 2:11). The biblical teaching on regeneration assumes the deadness of the human condition and the singular power of God to effect an instantaneous spiritual vivification in a person. It does not amplify spiritual traits in a person, nor is it a drawn-out process leading to spiritual insight. Regeneration is a triune act as one is born of God the Father, by the vivifying work of the Spirit, and in union with Christ, who effects a spiritual circumcision of the heart.

We have to ask: What comes first, regeneration or faith? Nowhere is the causal relationship between "believing" and being "born of God" given in Scripture. Still, some argue that regeneration follows faith.[73] First, appeal can be made to John 1:12–13, where "all who did receive him, to those who believed in his name, he gave the right to become children of God"; that is, so it seems, believing in verse 12 is the basis for being born of God in verse 13. Yet in 1:12–13 we are not told that persons are born of God *because* they believe or that they believe because they are *already* born of God. The Evangelist simply equates the two groups together (i.e., "believers" and "those born of God") without stipulating the temporal relationship between the two.[74] But we can note that since God "gave" the right to become children of God, that new birth is a result of divine initiative, which is at a piece

---

71. Leonhard Goppelt, *A Commentary on I Peter* (trans. J. E. Alsup; Grand Rapids: Eerdmans, 1993), 81.

72. Cf. J.I. Packer, "Regeneration," *EDT*, 924–26; Andrew McGowan, *The New Birth* (Rosshire, UK: Christian Focus, 1999); Grudem, *Systematic Theoloy*, 699–706.

73. Cf., e.g., Charles Ryrie, *Basic Theology* (Wheaton, IL: Victor, 1986), 326; Erickson, *Christian Theology*, 944–45.

74. J. Ramsay Michaels, *The Gospel of John* (NICNT; Grand Rapids: Eerdmans, 2010), 71.

with what we find elsewhere in John's gospel about God actively drawing believers to himself (12:32; 15:16).

Second, reference is often made to Peter's appeal to the Jerusalemites in Acts 2:38, "Repent and be baptized, every one of you, in the name of Jesus Christ for the forgiveness of your sins. And you will receive the gift of the Holy Spirit" (see also 11:17). The problem is that in Acts there are roughly twenty-four conversions, and there are significant differences as to when persons formally receive the Spirit. Some receive the Spirit at their baptism (2:38), others receive the Spirit upon conversion (10:44–46), and for others it is after the laying on of hands (8:14–17). Arguably the best way to understand these passages is that the promise of the Holy Spirit refers to indwelling, not to regeneration. The experience of indwelling is an event where the Holy Spirit is poured into our hearts in a manner that renews and transforms.

I would also maintain that there is good evidence that regeneration logically precedes faith. From the outset, I find it unlikely that the person who is a slave to sin (John 8:34; Rom 7:14, 25) can free themselves to believe in God—note how Paul draws from Psalm 14:1–2 that "there is no one who seeks God" (Rom 3:11). Sin is so traumatic that people suppress the truth about God known to them through natural revelation (1:18), and they love darkness rather than the light because their deeds are evil (John 3:19). Humanity runs from God like cockroaches running from light. Even worse, people are dead in their sins (Eph 2:1); and no altar call, no enticement, no amount of reason and emotion can give life to their dead soul. Wesley was right that in order to believe sinners need a prevenient grace; this glorious grace that brings life to death we call regeneration.[75]

Determinative for a solution is that there is solid biblical evidence that God gives faith as a gift. We read in Romans 10:17: "Faith comes from hearing the message, and the message is heard through the word about Christ." The stress of the passage is that "faith" derives from "hearing," and "hearing" comes from the "word about Christ." That word does not simply provide the opportunity to believe; it is the instrumental cause of belief itself. What is implicit in Romans 10 is explicit in two of the General Epistles. First, according to 1 Peter 1:23, "You have been born again, not of perishable seed, but of imperishable, through the living and enduring word of God." Clearly here the word of God is a primary cause of new birth. Second, according to James 1:18, God "chose to give us birth through the word of truth, that we might be a kind of firstfruits of all he created." This "word planted in you" is able to "save" believers (1:21). Peter and James attest that the proclaimed word is the mother of our faith that brings us into a spiritual rebirth that cleanses and saves.

---

75. Cf. similarly Murray (*Redemption*, 96): "God's grace reaches down to the lowest depths of our need and meets all the exigencies of the moral and spiritual impossibility which inheres in our depravity and inability. And that grace is the grace of regeneration."

We observe an emphasis on divine enabling to believe in several places. Paul states in Romans 10:9–11 that confession of Jesus as Lord secures salvation. And to the Corinthians he says that no one can say that "Jesus is Lord" except by the Holy Spirit (1 Cor 12:3). As such, profession of Jesus' lordship is created by the Holy Spirit. In addition, Luke describes Lydia's conversion with the narration: "The Lord opened her heart to respond to Paul's message" (Acts 16:14). That the "Lord opened her heart" seems a clear indication of divine initiative and not merely divine assistance.

Another important text that indicates the God-given nature of faith is Ephesians 2:8: "For it is by grace you have been saved, through faith—and *this* is not from yourselves, *it* is the gift of God." This passage is slightly deceptive! The closest possible antecedent of the demonstrative pronoun *touto* ("this") is *pisteōs* ("faith"). But *pisteōs* is feminine, while *touto* is neuter. So it is not strictly saying that faith is a gift from God. Rather, "this" is probably an adverbial explication of "by grace you have been saved." Paul is saying that the entire process of salvation is a gift from God. Yet the gift of salvation includes faith, meaning that God is behind everything that brings salvation to its fullest form; otherwise grace is hardly a gift.

God also grants to persons faith and repentance. This is explicit in Philippians 1:29, where Paul says, "For it has been [graciously] granted [*charizomai*] to you on behalf of Christ not only to believe in him, but also to suffer for him." Elsewhere we read that God "gives" (*didōmi*) repentance that leads to life (Acts 11:18) and leads to knowledge of the truth (2 Tim 2:25). In other words, we can say that the faith and repentance that are *granted* are created by the word of God *implanted*![76] Or, to use the words of Martin Luther, "God creates faith the same way that he made the universe, he found nothing and made something!"[77] And, "I believe," wrote Luther, "that by my own reason or strength I cannot believe in Jesus Christ, my Lord, or come to him. But the Holy Spirit has called me through the Gospel, enlightened me with his gifts, and sanctified and preserved me in true faith."[78] So it seems that regeneration creates new life that in turn creates faith, not robotically but

---

76. Cf. the Heidelberg Catechism Q.65: Question: "It is through faith alone that we share in Christ and all his benefits: where then does that faith come from?" Answer: "The Holy Spirit produces it in our hearts by the preaching of the holy gospel, and confirms it by the use of the holy sacraments."

77. Sadly I have not been able to find the source of this quote.

78. *The Book of Concord* (ed. T. G. Tappert; Philadelphia: Fortress, 1959), 345.

79. J. L. Martyn ("The Apocalyptic Gospel in Galatians," *Int* 54 [2000]: 250) tells an interesting story about Karl Barth and the gift of faith: "Oral tradition, which I have not been able to find in print, tells of a priest who made an appointment with K. Barth on a personal matter. Coming after a while to the point, he said, 'The problem, Dr. Barth, is that I have lost my faith.' The response: 'But what on earth gave you the impression that it was yours to lose?'" I am grateful to Ben Myers for bringing this anecdote to my attention.

freeing the will to believe, and thereafter persons receive the gift of the indwelling of the Holy Spirit.[79]

A tertiary issue we must address is whether Old Testament saints were regenerate or if regeneration is a blessing unique to the new covenant.[80] Many theologians believe that something genuinely "new" happened when the Spirit was poured out at Pentecost, including regeneration (Acts 2). In addition, Jesus said that "rivers of living water," a type of spiritual vitality, will pour forth from believers, but this will not occur until after the ascension because "by this he meant the Spirit, whom those who believed in him were later to receive. Up to that time the Spirit had not been given, since Jesus had not yet been glorified" (John 7:39). On that basis, one could infer that regeneration is a unique blessing of the new covenant, available only after the ascension.

In response, I favor continuity between the Old Testament saints and New Testament believers with regards to regeneration. To begin with, the same Spirit is active across both Testaments with the same life-giving power. There is one covenant of grace that ties together the diverse epochs of redemptive history in the old and the new covenants. If the patriarchs or Israelites were to have faith in God, they also needed the same regenerating power we find described in the New Testament. The discourses about the faith of Old Testament figures in Romans 4 and Hebrews 11 are pointless if these paragons of faith were not regenerated similarly to Christians.

Moreover, if there is no regeneration under the old covenant, Jesus can no more expect Nicodemus to understand the concept of spiritual new birth than he could expect him to understand the Internet (John 3:3–5).[81] What is new in the new covenant is not regeneration, but the *permanent* indwelling of the Spirit.[82] The Old Testament saints were born again, but the permanent indwelling the Spirit was contingent on Jesus' return to the Father (John 16:7; see 7:39; 14:17). So there is continuity and discontinuity between the Old and New Testaments. There is regeneration for the all believing people of God through the ages, but the indwelling of the Holy Spirit understood as God's "abiding, positive, covenant presence in believers" occurs only in the era of the new covenant.[83]

5.3.4 FAITH AND REPENTANCE

---

80. For a survey of opinion see James M. Hamilton, "Old Covenant Believers and the Indwelling Spirit: A Survey of the Spectrum of Opinion," *TrinJ* 24 (2003): 37–54.

81. Cf. Daniel P. Fuller (*The Unity of the Bible: Unfolding God's Plan for Humanity* [Grand Rapids: Zondervan, 2000], 229–30): "The only way that depraved people can acquire a heart attitude and behavior pleasing to God is to be indwelt by the Holy Spirit (that is, regenerated) ... to deny that these Old Testament saints were born again, one would have to hold the incredible position that Enoch and Noah walked with God and Abraham was God's friend, even though they were hostile to him."

82. See excellent discussion in James M. Hamilton, *God's Indwelling Presence: The Holy Spirit in the Old & New Testaments* (NACSBT; Nashville: Broadman & Holman, 2006). See also Graham A. Cole, *He Who Gives Life: The Doctrine of the Holy Spirit* (Wheaton, IL: Crossway, 2007), 143–45.

83. Hamilton, *God's Indwelling Presence*, 2–3.

Sequence of salvation: predestination ⇨ calling ⇨ regeneration ⇨ *faith and repentance* ⇨ justification ⇨ transformation ⇨ glorification.

So far we've seen in the *ordo salutis* what God objectively does in terms of predestination, calling, and regeneration. In the process, the human response, or the subjective dimension, includes faith and repentance. In the preaching of Jesus, the Jewish people were called to "repent and believe the good news" (Mark 1:15), and Paul summarizes his message, "I have declared to both Jews and Greeks that they must turn to God in repentance and have faith in our Lord Jesus" (Acts 20:21). Faith and repentance are the instruments of salvation, as persons are saved *through* their trust in the God who saves (e.g., Gen 15:6; Jer 39:18; Hab 2:4; Luke 7:50; Acts 16:31; Rom 5:1; 10:10; 1 Cor 1:21; Eph 2:8; Heb 10:39; 11:7; Jas 2:14; 1 Pet 1:9).

In regards to "faith" the Hebrew words ʾāman, ʾĕmûnâ, ʾĕmet, bāṭaḥ, and qāwâ have a semantic range involving "steadfastness," "trustworthiness," "faithfulness," and "faith."[84] The New Testament vocabulary for faith is largely taken over from the LXX with words such as *pistis* ("faith," "trust"), *pistos* ("faithful"), and *pisteuō* ("believe") standing in for the Hebrew. Though English makes a clear distinction between "faith" as trust and "faithfulness" as promise-keeping, no absolute distinction can be made in the underlying Hebrew and Greek words. It is not that a conceptual distinction is never discernible in Hebrew and Greek, but that the semantic distinctions that we have in English do not carry over into the biblical languages.[85]

The story of Abraham in Genesis 15–22 could be titled, "The Faithfulness of Yahweh Elicits the Faith of a Pagan Man." In 15:6, Abraham "believed" the divine promises and God reckoned it to him as righteousness. Abraham took God at his word and so was reckoned to be a "right" covenant partner. Yet this statement must be related to the wider context of Abraham's decision to leave Haran (12:1–4) and his willingness to offer up Isaac (Gen 22). The Lord eulogizes Abraham to Abraham's son Isaac with the words, "Abraham obeyed me and did everything I required of him, keeping my commands, my decrees and my instructions" (26:5).

Nehemiah (Neh 9:7–8) and James (Jas 2:21–23) remember Abraham explicitly for how his faith was expressed in his faithfulness to Yahweh. Paul can identify Abraham as the prototype of Gentile Christians who have faith in God's life-giving power (esp. Rom 4:19–21); yet faith in Romans is itself broadened out to include the "obedience that comes from faith" (Rom 1:5; 16:26). The writer to the Hebrews emphasizes Abraham's faith by way of reference to his obedience, steadfastness, and hope (Heb 11:8–11).

Faith is one of the cardinal Christian virtues as it is often situated within a tri-

---

84. Benjamin E. Reynolds, "Faith/Faithfulness," *EDEJ*, 627–29.

85. S. S. Taylor, "Faith, Faithfulness," in *NDBT*, 488.

partite virtue list of faith, hope, and love (1 Cor 13:13; 1 Thess 1:3; 5:8, Ign., *Phld.* 11.2; *Barn.* 1.4; 11.8). Faith obviously has a cognitive content as to what is believed (e.g., 1 Cor 16:13; Gal 1:23; Eph 4:5; Jude 3, 20). Faith is linked principally with the hope that is offered in the gospel (Acts 15:7; Col 1:5, 23; on "faith" and "hope" more generally see Rom 4:19–21; 2 Cor 5:7; Heb 11:1).

Faith is the defining characteristic of God's people that marks them out for salvation in the face of judgment. Faith is transformative as it works itself out in love (Gal 5:6) and overcomes the world (1 John 5:4). In light of that, I define "faith" as the act of entrusting oneself to the faithfulness of God. Yet faith goes beyond assent and trust; it keeps faith with God by continual believing and by holding to a disposition of obedience within the parameters of the faith relationship itself; this we call "faithfulness."[86] In the end, as D. B. Knox observed, "The whole of our Christian life is a life of faith."[87]

Turning to repentance (pun intended), we find this act to be equally part of the human response to the divine saving action. God entered into a covenant relationship with his people so that they would reflect his character and project his salvation to the ends of earth (Exod 19:5–6; Lev 19:2; 20:22–26). As such, their turning away in unbelief and unfaithfulness implies a rejection of the covenant and the covenant God (e.g., Deut 4:23; 11:16–17; Jer 11:10). God, therefore, invokes the covenantal curses for such disobedience (e.g., Deut 4:15–28; Ezra 9:7; Dan 9:11–14). The purposes of these curses were not just punitive but also redemptive; they were designed to lead people to repentance (Deut 4:29–30; 1 Kgs 8:33–35, 48). This is why the Israelites were commanded to "turn" (*šûb*) away from their sins and to return to God (e.g., 2 Chr 7:14; Isa 55:7; 59:20; Jer 26:3; Ezek 18:30).[88]

Furthermore, repentance is particularly important in the prophets, as repentance is what Israel needed to do for the exile finally to end.[89] John the Baptist came onto the socioreligious scene of Judea preaching a "baptism of repentance for the forgiveness of sins" (Mark 1:4; Luke 3:3). John the Baptist was inviting people to prepare themselves for entering the eschatological age and to ready themselves for the ministry of the "one who is more powerful than I," who would follow after him (Matt 3:11–12; Mark 1:7–8; Luke 3:16–17).

In the New Testament the Greek words from which we get "repentance" and "repent" are *metanoia* and *metanoeō*. It is closely linked to *epistrephō* ("turn around")

---

86. See the excellent exposition of faith in Graham A. Cole (*God the Peacemaker: How Atonement Brings Shalom* [NSBT; Downers Grove: InterVarsity Press, 2009], 190–204), who notes that faith appreciates the price that was paid, faith lives for Christ, faith walks worthy of the gospel, faith suffers for the name, faith resists the devil, and faith offers a living sacrifice.

87. D. B. Knox, *Justification by Faith* (London: Church Book Room, 1959), 15.

88. J. M. Lunde, "Repentance," in *NDBT*, 726–27.

89. N. T. Wright, *Jesus and the Victory of God* (COQG 2; London: SPCK, 1996), 246–58.

in Acts 3:19 and 26:20. Thus, repentance is more than an expression of sorrow for sins committed; it encompasses a change of verdict and a turning around of one's self to God.[90] Jesus called individuals to repent of their sins and to return to covenant righteousness (Luke 5:32; 15:10). Yet Jesus also called for the Israelites to corporately give up their own kingdom aspirations and to follow him instead (Mark 1:14–15).

In Peter's Pentecost speech, the Jerusalemites are urged to repent, by which Peter meant to change their verdict about who Jesus is and to express sorrow for what they had done to him (Acts 2:36–38). Elsewhere repentance involves turning away from evil (Acts 8:22; 2 Cor 12:21; Rev 2:21–22) and turning toward God (Acts 20:21; 26:20; Rev 16:9). The blessings of repentance are the forgiveness of sins (Luke 24:47; Acts 3:19; 5:31) as well as life and salvation (Acts 11:18; 2 Cor 7:9–10). Indeed, repentance and salvation are synonymous in 2 Peter 3:9, where God is "patient with you, not wanting anyone to perish, but everyone to come to repentance." Overall,

> Jews are presented with a second opportunity to repent of their rejection of God's Messiah and to turn to him in faith; Gentiles are to turn from idols to the living God who will give them life. For both, repentance leads to baptism in Jesus' name, incorporation into the renewed people of God, forgiveness of sins, and the gift of the Spirit.[91]

I should add that the Christian life is one of continual repentance. While repentance as part of conversion is initiatory and final (i.e., one orientates oneself wholly toward God and accepts God's verdict about who Jesus is) — what the writer to the Hebrews calls "the foundation of repentance" (Heb 6:1) — there is an ongoing process of repentance in the Christian life. Christians are called to repent in sundry places in Scripture, often with dire warnings if they do not (2 Cor 7:9–10; 12:21; Rev 2:5, 16; 3:3, 19). Repentance is also the means by which erring believers are to be restored to fellowship (Luke 17:3–4). One student tells me that the word for "Evangelicals" in Romanian translates roughly into "Repenters."

In regards to the relationship between faith and repentance, it is likely that faith has the priority. Only if someone trusts in God will he or she turn from their sin and look to God for deliverance. As Calvin quaintly put it, "repentance not only always follows faith, but is produced by it."[92]

5.3.5 JUSTIFICATION

---

90. As an illustration of "changing one's verdict," in 406 BC the Athenians won a naval victory over the Spartans at the Battle of Arginusae. After the battle a storm arose, and the Athenian generals in command failed to collect survivors: the Athenians tried and sentenced six of the eight generals to death. They tried them together rather than individually (which was illegal), and false evidence was brought against them. The Greek historian Xenophon says that the people later *repented* the executions (i.e., changed their legal verdict) and made up for it by executing those who had accused the generals before them (Xenophon, *Hell.* 1.6.1–34).

91. Frances Taylor Gench, "Repentance in the NT," in *NIB*, 4:763.

92. Calvin, *Institutes* 3.3.1.

Sequence of salvation: predestination ⇨ calling ⇨ regeneration ⇨ faith and repentance ⇨ *justification* ⇨ transformation ⇨ glorification.

The Pauline sequence in Romans 8:30 moves from "called" to "justified." When we mention justification at this point in the *ordo salutis*, we mean it in the broader sense of "reconciliation" and "salvation" (see 5:9–10; 10:10, where reconciliation and salvation are equated with justification). The issue here is the objective state of affairs that changes the relationship between God and the human subject. What was broken is fixed, those exiled are brought near, the condemned are acquitted, the wounded are healed, hostility is pacified, enmity is reconciled, the dying are given life, the impure are cleansed, and inglorious beings are glorified.

The Bible uses a variety of images to describe the process of salvation, including forgiveness, redemption, rescue, reconciliation, justification, peace, adoption, eternal life, and deification. These will be explored later in §5.4. Here we note that God's choosing and regenerating of believers, through faith, restore the sons and daughters of Adam to a relationship with their Creator.[93]

5.3.6 TRANSFORMATION

Sequence of Salvation: predestination ⇨ calling ⇨ regeneration ⇨ faith and repentance ⇨ justification ⇨ *transformation* ⇨ glorification.

Salvation effects the objective state of affairs between God and the believer that we broadly label reconciliation, but the subjective and inward change to the believer we call transformation. In most theologies this is usually called "sanctification." I am hesitant to use that term because of the confusion it fosters. In systematic theology "sanctification" denotes progress in personal holiness, ethical righteousness, godliness, resistance to temptation, and increasing Christlikeness. In the discourse of exegetical studies, however, biblical words for holiness (*qādôš, hagios, hagiazō*) generally reflect positional sanctification in the sense that believers are consecrated and possessed by God in the same way that a tong can be dedicated to divine use at the altar of the temple (see, e.g., 1 Kgs 7:49; Acts 20:32; Rom 1:7; Eph 1:1; 2 Tim 2:21; 1 Pet 1:2).[94]

---

93. Cf. Andrew T. B. McGowan, "Justification and the Ordo Salutis," in *Justification in Perspective: Historical Developments and Contemporary Challenges* (ed. B. L. McCormack; Grand Rapids: Baker, 2006), 147–63.

94. D. A. Carson, "The Vindication of Imputation: On Fields of Discourse and Semantic Fields," in *Justification: What's at Stake in the Current Debates* (ed. M. Husbands and D. J. Treier; Downers Grove, IL: InterVarsity Press, 2004), 47–49. In a most peculiar essay J. V. Fesko ("Sanctification and Union with Christ: A Reformed Pespective," *EvQ* 82 [2010]: 197–214) denies the existence of positional sanctification altogether! His chief objection is that the Reformed standards simply don't know of sanctification as an "act" of God, and such a distinction confuses the transformative and forensic categories together. I submit that exegesis of passages like 1 Cor 1:2 ("To the church of God in Corinth, to *those sanctified in Christ Jesus* and *called to be his holy people*") unequivocally demonstrates that sanctification is both positional and progressive (see also Heb 10:10; 12:14). See further David Peterson, *Possessed by God: A New Testament Theology of Holiness and Sanctification* (NSBT; Downers Grove, IL: InterVarsity Press, 1995).

Both aspects of sanctification are true of believers; they are definitively set apart by God, and they progress in holy living. All this is from Christ, who is the source and fountain of the believer's holiness (1 Cor 1:30). What I designate here as "transformation" encompasses the aspects of regeneration (the impartation of spiritual life), sanctification (positional and effectual holiness), and the beginning stages of glorification (conformity to the pattern of Christ).

Though Christians are reconciled to God, they still wrestle with what Martin Luther called "the trinity of evil," namely, the world, the flesh, and the devil. That struggle is brilliantly illustrated in several texts that talk about Christian resistance to the prevailing cultural ethos, sinful desires, and the evil one (Gal 5:16–26; Heb 12:4; Jas 4:7; 1 Pet 5:8–9; 1 John 2:15–16). Accordingly, the Scriptures are filled with strenuous commands to avoid corruption and contamination from sin (e.g., Ezra 9:11–12; Prov 25:26; Jas 1:27).

Believers are to prosecute their holiness actively in their everyday lives (e.g., Lev 19:2; 20:7, 26; Rom 6:19, 22; 8:1–14; 12:1–2; 2 Cor 7:1; Heb 12:10, 14; 2 Pet 1:5–7). Central to this task is the imitation of God (Lev 19:2; 20:7, 26; Eph 5:1), of Jesus (1 Cor 11:1; Phil 2:5–11; 1 Thess 1:6; Heb 12:3; 1 Pet 2:21), and of Christian leaders (1 Cor 4:16–17; 11:1; Phil 3:17; 1 Thess 1:6; 2:14; 2 Thess 3:7–9; Heb 6:12; 13:7). The divine example is meant to be a mimetic contagion that shapes, forms, and replicates itself in disciples. Second Peter 1:5 urges believers to "make every effort" in pursuing godly behavior. As G. C. Berkouwer commented on this verse: "Everything points to consistent and active endeavour."[95]

What is important to remember is that the divine imperatives (what God commands) follow on from the divine indicative (what God has done for us). Ethics is the "therefore" that follows on from the experience of salvation (see esp. Rom 6:1–2; 8:12; 12:1–2). Galatians, Ephesians, and Colossians are structured generally around this theme of the indicative (Gal 1–4; Eph 1–3; Col 1–2) and the imperative (Gal 5–6; Eph 4–6; Col 3–4).[96] Pursuing holiness and righteousness is not the basis of our salvation; rather, it is the appropriate response to salvation and the outworking of salvation in our character and conduct.[97]

---

95. G. C. Berkouwer, *Faith and Sanctification: Studies in Dogmatics* (Grand Rapids: Eerdmans, 1952), 101.

96. Berkouwer (ibid., 108) notes the shift from Romans 1–11 to Romans 12 and Hebrews 1–12 to Hebrews 13 concerning the move from indicative to imperative. He notes: "Nowhere can we find a break between justification and sanctification. There is only the relationship in which the grace of God admonishes the progressing believer. The proclamation of God's grace which preceded the admonition is never neglected in the admonition but rather applied, and given content, in it."

97. True, Hebrews teaches us, "Make every effort to live in peace with everyone and to be holy; without holiness no one will see the Lord" (Heb 12:14). Though this can hardly mean that we are saved by anything other than faith (Heb 12), it only means that authentic faith will issue forth in holiness. God himself makes us holy by uniting us to Christ (1 Cor 1:2). On top of that, Paul tells the Thessalonians that "God chose you as firstfruits to be saved *through the sanctifying work of the Spirit* and through belief in the truth" (2 Thess 2:13, italics added).

Significantly, sanctification, though needing spiritual discipline, is not entirely a self-effort. The Holy Spirit leads God's people into holiness and transforms them to reflect more and more of God's character in their lives. The Holy Spirit, as the Spirit of holiness, works holiness into people by producing conviction, desire, and reverent fear. Paul exhorts the Philippians to obedience with the words, "work out your salvation with fear and trembling," but he adds, "for it is God who works in you to will and to act in order to fulfill his good purpose" (Phil 2:12–13).

Holiness is apprehended in union with Christ—holy God and holy man—and is imparted to the believer through the Spirit of Christ (1 Cor 1:30). The Spirit produces abundant fruit in the believer in terms of character traits (Gal 5:22; 2 Tim 1:7) and cultivates key virtues (Eph 3:16–19). Believers must, therefore, nourish this spiritual work and give the Spirit more to work with. For that reason, Christians are commanded to keep in step with the Spirit (Gal 5:25) and to be filled with the Spirit (Eph 5:18).

The regenerating work of the Spirit sets the wheels in motion for a new humanity to produce a new obedience.[98] One of the blessings of the new covenant is that God's people receive a new power to obey when they have received a new heart: "I will put my Spirit in you and move you to follow my decrees and be careful to keep my laws" (Ezek 36:27). Paul uses new creation language to spur on the Corinthians to be less like Corinth and more like what the people of God are meant to be: "If anyone is in Christ, the new creation has come: The old has gone, the new is here!" (2 Cor 5:17). The Johannine letters make new birth the indicative that drives the imperative of Christian behavior. Those born anew do what is right (1 John 2:29) and do not languish in sin because of the Holy Spirit that indwells them (3:9; 5:18). They are distinguished by their love (4:7), and they overcome the world (5:4).

The new ethics for the new creation includes putting on "the new self, created to be like God in true righteousness and holiness" (Eph 4:24), and putting on "the new self, which is being renewed in knowledge in the image of its Creator" (Col 3:10). Here we see some eschatological glimpses of the new life: it is Godlike and Christlike. Christian sanctification means "being transformed into his image with ever-increasing glory" (2 Cor 3:18) and being "conformed to the image of his Son" (Rom 8:29). We become, behaviorally at least, like God and Christ. Transformation

---

98. Calvin (*Institutes* 3.3.9) seems to understand regeneration fairly broadly, not just the impartation of new life but the entire process of renewal into righteousness from rebellion. He writes: "This renewal, indeed, is not accomplished in a moment, a day, or a year, but by uninterrupted, sometimes even by slow, progress God abolishes the remains of carnal corruption in his elect, cleanses them from pollution, and consecrates them as his temples, restoring all their inclinations to real purity, so that during their lives they may practice repentance, and know that death is the only terminator to this warfare." Calvin evidently blends regeneration with sanctification.

means what *began* in regeneration and what is *progressively being realized* in sanctification, will climax in our glorification into the image of Jesus Christ.

Though it is common to insist that Christians are merely sinners saved by grace, we should consider a different paradigm. Christians have definitively broken with the old age of sin and evil; they are new creations, and they are more aptly described as saints who sometimes sin.[99] That is because I am no longer who I was, nor will I ever be that person again. That old self is dead, crucified, buried, and raised with Christ. As I live between the ages, between the "now" of what God has already done for me and the "not yet" of what he still intends to do with me, I struggle with the sin that so easily entangles. Indeed, as Calvin saw, there remains in the born-again believer a "moldering cinder of evil."[100]

But sin is no longer my *true* master, and sin is no longer the source of my *true* identity. I am defined by my love for the Father, my union with Christ, and my possession of the Spirit. The continuing struggle with sin is not a case of trying harder, nor of just getting more doctrine under your belt. Holiness happens when I obey God, imitate Christ's example, and let the Spirit lead me into being who I truly am: a new creation.[101]

The good news of the gospel does not allow us to forget the depths of our sin or to forgo the continued struggle to excise it. But neither does the gospel allow us to incessantly bemoan our wretched estate without respect to the joy that washes over it, nor to revile ourselves day by day without mention of the justification that frees us from all condemnation, nor will it allow us to think of ourselves as nothing but wretched worms when God has declared us and even made us something else: light in the world, holy ones, children of God, and the church triumphant. Our gospel faith bids us to think of our sin as nailed to the cross and we bear it no more, for God has made it well with our soul.[102]

5.3.7 GLORIFICATION

Sequence of salvation: predestination ⇨ calling ⇨ regeneration ⇨ faith and repentance ⇨ justification ⇨ transformation ⇨ *glorification*.

---

99. Cf. esp. Robert Saucy, "'Sinners' Who Are Forgiven or 'Saints' Who Sin?" *BSac* 152 (1995): 400–12.

100. Calvin, *Institutes* 3.3.10.

101. In some forms of the Wesleyan/Pentecostal/Holiness tradition it has been often said that "moral perfection" is a possibility in this life. John Wesley taught some form of this doctrine in his short essay "A Plain Account of Christian Perfectionism" (though Wesley did qualify what he meant by "perfection" considerably). Inspiration comes from texts like, "Be ye therefore perfect, even as your Father which is in heaven is perfect" (Matt 5:48 KJV). However, perfectionism appears to rehearse the Pelagian premise that "ought" means "can." That we ought to be perfect does not establish that perfection in this life is really attainable. We all struggle with sin, and it is imperfect to deny it (see Eccl 7:20; 1 John 1:8). For a Wesleyan critique of perfectionism, see Witherington, *The Problem with Evangelical Theology*, 209–16.

102. Echoing Horatio Bonar's famous hymn, "It Is Well with My Soul."

According to Paul's sequence in Romans 8:29–30, persons were predestined in order "to be conformed to the image of his Son." God purposes to imprint all those who belong to Christ with the image of Christ. When this occurs is debated, but the parallel language with Philippians 3:21 (God "*will* transform our lowly bodies so that they will be like his glorious body") and 1 Corinthians 15:49 ("just as we have borne the image of the earthly man, so *shall* we bear the image of the heavenly man") suggests that conforming to Christ's image is a future eschatological event. That is to say, God predestines believers to a future glory, the glory that Christ currently enjoys.[103] Thus, glory is a future hope for the believer to share in Christ's glory after sharing in his sufferings in the present (Rom 8:17; Col 3:4; 2 Thess 2:14; 2 Tim 2:10; Titus 2:13; 1 Pet 4:13; 5:10). The path to glory runs through the shame of the cross. In this sense glorification is really Christification—sharing in the suffering, vindication, and exaltation of the Messiah.[104]

This perspective meshes with the final item mentioned in Paul's sequence in Romans 8:29–30, that those justified are also "glorified." Too much is made of the aorist tense form of *edoxasen*, as if it means a completed or punctiliar event; the main issue is the verbal aspect, which is perfective and so the action is envisaged as a simple whole. Perhaps as a proleptic aorist, the point could be that those whom God justified *he will also glorify*. The aorist is fitting because God has already decreed that it will take place.[105]

Yet in another sense "glory" is a proleptic experience for believers. For Paul, transformation into the glory of the Lord Jesus has already begun: "And we all, who with unveiled faces contemplate the Lord's glory, are being transformed into his image with ever-increasing glory, which comes from the Lord, who is the Spirit" (2 Cor 3:18). Peter informs believers that "the Spirit of glory and of God rests on you" (1 Pet 4:14). Undoubtedly "glorification" is essentially a future hope, but it has proleptically begun through the ministry of the Holy Spirit, who unites us with the Lord of glory.

In sum, glorification represents the culmination of salvation as the "redemption of our bodies" (Rom 8:23) and being "brought into the freedom and glory of the children of God" (8:21). If justification means being freed from the penalty of sin, if transformation means being gradually freed from the power of sin, then glorification means being freed from the presence of sin. This "glory" means entrance into the new creation, to dwell in God's new world, in God's eschatological reign, among the glorified host of God's people. Glorification is coterminus with the advent of the cosmic renewal of creation and has already begun in our life lived in the Spirit.

---

103. Douglas J. Moo, *The Epistle to the Romans* (NICNT; Grand Rapids: Eerdmans, 1996), 534–35.

104. Cole, *God the Peacemaker*, 223.

105. Stanley E. Porter, *Idioms of the Greek New Testament* (Sheffield: Sheffield Academic, 1992), 37.

QUALIFICATIONS TO THE *ORDO SALUTIS*

A couple of final remarks need to be made before we leave the *ordo salutis*. First, we must remember that eschatology is the key to New Testament soteriology. Salvation is past, present, and future. In the opening of 1 Corinthians, Paul says about the Corinthians that in the *past* they have been given God's grace, they were enriched in every way, and they had the gospel confirmed among them (1 Cor 1:4–6). In the *present*, they are amply supplied with spiritual gifts and live in eager anticipation of the return of the Lord Jesus (1:7–8). In the *future*, they will be blameless on the day of Christ Jesus (1:8; cf. 1:10).[106]

The same three tenses can be applied to salvation as a whole.[107] According to oral tradition, B. F. Westcott was asked if he was "saved." The British bishop replied, "I am saved, I am being saved, I will be saved." In a complete sense, salvation refers to "a past event, a present experience, and a future hope."[108] God's saving work in us traverses all three tenses of past, present, and future. Justification is both "now" and "not yet." While God's verdict has already been declared and the verdict is "acquitted," we still wait for that verdict to be enacted at the final judgment (see Rom 2:13; 5:19; Gal 5:5). Glorification is principally future, but it has already begun in union with Christ and communion with the Holy Spirit. The main point is that God's saving work in us begins in eternity past and ends in eternity future. While believers have been redeemed and reconciled, they have not yet been fully released from temptation and suffering, and they are yet to be fully glorified. The *ordo salutis* must be understood in light of this eschatological scheme of "now" and "not yet."

Second, we must also appreciate the importance of union with Christ and the indwelling of the Spirit as the vehicles by which salvation is applied. When it comes to salvation, what matters is "location, location, location."[109] Paul for one places a huge amount of emphasis on being "in Christ."[110] For "whoever is united with the Lord is one with him in spirit" (1 Cor 6:17). Note Calvin's summative remark: "The

---

106. Roy E. Ciampa and Brian S. Rosner, *The First Letter to the Corinthians* (PNTC; Grand Rapids: Eerdmans, 2010), 66.

107. An evangelist in an airport once asked a man, "When did you get saved?" The man paused, thought about it for a moment, and replied: "Two thousand years ago, but I only found out about it recently." Salvation can be viewed as a past event if one considers the eternity of God's saving plan, its execution on the cross and empty tomb, or in our having come to faith.

108. A. M. Hunter, *The Gospel according to Paul* (Philadelphia: Westminster, 1966), 15.

109. Cole, *God the Peacemaker*, 160.

110. Cf. further, Mark A. Seifrid, "In Christ," in *DPL*, 433–36; James D. G. Dunn, *The Theology of Paul the Apostle* (Edinburgh: T&T Clark, 1998), 390–412; Horton, *Christian Faith*, 587–619.

111. *Institutes* 2.16.19. Calvin opens book 3 of the *Institutes* (3.1.1) with the words: "We must now see in what way we become possessed of the blessings which God has bestowed on his only begotten Son, not for private use, but to enrich the poor and needy. And the first thing to be attended to is, that so long as we are without Christ and separated from him, nothing which he suffered and did for the salvation of the human race is of the least benefit to us. To communicate to us the blessings which he has received from the Father, he must become ours and dwell in us."

whole sum of our salvation and all its parts are comprehended in Christ."[111] According to Murray, "union with Christ is really the central truth of the whole doctrine of salvation, not only its application but also in its once-for-all accomplishment.... It is not simply a phase of the application of redemption; it underlies every aspect of redemption."[112] Richard Gaffin rightly comments: "The first and, in the final analysis, the only question for the Pauline *ordo* concerns the point at which and the conditions under which incorporation with [Christ and] the life-giving Spirit takes place."[113] Robert Letham is similar: "Union with Christ is, in fact, the foundation of all the blessings of salvation. Justification, sanctification, adoption and glorification are all received through our being united to Christ."[114]

The roots of union with Christ are in divine election (Eph 1:3–4). The means of union with Christ is faith in his redemptive work and the seal of the Holy Spirit (1:13). Final salvation will involve union with the glory of Christ at the last day (2 Tim 2:10).[115] In our union with Christ, we participate in his obedience, death, resurrection, vindication, exaltation, and future glory. Consequently, justification and transformation can never be conceived in abstraction from union with Christ as they both proceed immediately from that faith union itself. God's salvation revealed as the gospel is apprehended only in union with Christ as applied by the Spirit.[116]

These two qualifications of eschatology and union with Christ mean that the *ordo* is a logical order, not necessarily a temporal one. This stands against some Reformed theologians who wish to treat them as logical and temporal.[117] The state of the union produces a state of peace between the believer and the Lord as salvation is wrought in the believer from conversion to consummation.

---

112. Murray, *Redemption*, 161, 165.

113. Richard Gaffin, *Resurrection and Redemption: A Study in Paul's Soteriology* (Grand Rapids: Baker, 1987), 135.

114. Robert Letham, *The Work of Christ* (Leicester, UK: Inter-Varsity Press, 1993), 80.

115. Horton (*Christian Faith*, 587) puts it these terms: "Believers share in Christ in eternity (by election), in past history (by redemption), in the present (by effectual calling, justification, and sanctification), and in the future (by glorification)."

116. Interestingly enough the Heidelberg Catechism (esp. questions 32, 36, 55–56, 59–61) combines the *ordo salutis* with an emphasis on union with Christ (McGowan, "Justification," 163 n. 61).

117. Cf., e.g., Charles Hodge, *Systematic Theology* (3 vols.; London: James Clarke & Co., 1960 [1841]), 3:172; contrasted with Berkhof, *Systematic Theology*, 450.

§ 5.4 IMAGES OF SALVATION: THE RESULT OF THE GOSPEL

Speaking about the gospel means speaking about salvation. By following Christ and by believing the gospel we are saved (Matt 1:21; 1 Cor 15:2). However, salvation is not a monolithic concept in the scriptural witness. There is no single account of what it means to be "saved." As we have seen, salvation encompasses various elements of the human condition, including physical well-being, mental health, freedom from spiritual oppression, economic needs, honor, and one's relationship with God. In the tenses of past, present, and future, the saving action of God is effected toward his people and the whole sphere of their existence.

At the end of the day, despite the qualifications we must make about the extent of salvation on the human condition, the biblical authors are primarily concerned with the relationship of people toward God. Sin may have horrible horizontal consequences (Rom 1:24–31), but it is fundamentally symptomatic of a vertical rejection of God (1:18–23).

No doubt sin makes humanity less humane, it promotes injustice of the highest order, and it preys on the most vulnerable. Yet we must remember that God is the primary party offended by our sin. All sin represents a defiance of his sovereignty, a deliberate contamination of his holiness, a perversion of his gift, a contempt for his goodness, and an insurrection against his justice. Thus God has a contention to prosecute against humanity, and it is that prosecution that is removed in the event of the gospel. Before there can be a restoration of creation, there must be a reconciliation of creature to Creator. This dramatic redemptive movement that we call salvation finds its unity is the common plot about the God who rescues people to bring them into his new creation. Its contingency is the varied language and conceptual diversity to how that plot is enacted in the drama of the doctrine of salvation. To give an example of what I mean, consider the broad sway of images for salvation in the following two psalms:

§5.4 Images of Salvation: The Result of the Gospel

Psalm 103:2–10	**Psalm 51:1–14**

Praise the LORD, my soul,
    and forget not all his benefits—
who *forgives all your sins*
    and *heals all your diseases*,
who *redeems your life from the pit*
    and *crowns you with love* and
        compassion,
who *satisfies your desires* with good things
    so that *your youth is renewed* like the
        eagle's.
The LORD *works righteousness*
    and *justice for all the oppressed*.
He made known his ways to Moses,
    his deeds to the people of Israel:
The LORD is compassionate and gracious,
    slow to anger, abounding in love.
He *will not always accuse*,
    nor will he harbor his anger forever;
he *does not treat us as our sins deserve*
    or repay us according to our iniquities.
        (italics added in both columns)
	Have mercy on me, O God,
	    according to your unfailing love;
	according to your great compassion
	    blot out my transgressions.
	Wash away all my iniquity
	    and cleanse me from my sin.
	For I know my transgressions,
	    and my sin is always before me.
	Against you, you only, have I sinned
	    and done what is evil in your sight;
	so you are right in your verdict
	    and justified when you judge.
	Surely I was sinful at birth,
	    sinful from the time my mother
	        conceived me.
	Yet you desired faithfulness even in the
	        womb;
	    you taught me wisdom in that secret
	        place.
	Cleanse me with hyssop, and I will be clean;
	    wash me, and I will be whiter than snow.
	Let me hear joy and gladness;
	    let the bones you have crushed rejoice.
	Hide your face from my sins
	    and blot out all my iniquity.
	Create in me a pure heart, O God,
	    and *renew a steadfast spirit within me*.
	Do not cast me from your presence
	    or take your Holy Spirit from me.
	Restore to me the joy of your salvation
	    and grant me a willing spirit, to sustain
	        me.
	Then I will teach transgressors your ways,
	    and sinners will turn back to you.
	Deliver me from bloodguilt, O God,
	    you who are God my Savior,
	    and my tongue will sing of your
	        righteousness.

This rich array of images in these psalms—including forgiveness, cleansing, justice, inner renewal, release from guilt—all show just how broad the range of images for salvation are. God's saving action is so comprehensive that psalmists—as well as the prophets, Evangelists, and apostles—struggle to find enough language in their cultural repertoire to describe the full extent of what God has done for his people. The modest aim of this section is to explore several images from this kaleidoscope.

5.4.1 FORGIVENESS

Forgiveness should be first and foremost in our discussion of the images of salvation. The only reference to a form of salvation in the Apostles' Creed is given in the statement, "I believe ... in the forgiveness of sins." Despite its relative neglect in many systematic theologies,[118] the forgiveness of sins is one of the central benefits of the Mosaic sacrificial system and is a chief benefit of Jesus' death in apostolic preaching. Forgiveness is one of the blessings explicitly named in the new covenant (Jer 31:34); it is the one image that Jesus uses to interpret the achievement of his death at the Last Supper (Matt 26:28); it is part of the missionary command to the disciples (Luke 24:47; John 20:23), and it is the one image found across the various corpora of Torah, Writings, Prophets, Gospels, Epistles, and Apocalypse. Forgiveness indicates a release from guilt and an end to relational estrangement.

In the Old Testament, God is said to "wipe out" the sins of the people when requested (Ps 51:1; Isa 43:25; 44:22; Jer 18:23; Zech 3:9). More commonly, God is often asked to "forgive" (Heb. *nāśā', sālaḥ, kāpar*) the people. Moses pleaded with God, "Although this is a stiff-necked people, forgive our wickedness and our sin, and take us as your inheritance" (Exod 34:9). In the Levitical legislation for the cultus, it is repeated that after offering a sacrifice, "the priest will make atonement for the community, and they will be forgiven" (Lev 4:20; cf. 4:26, 35; 5:10, 13, 16; 6:7; 19:22).

The penitential psalms explore the link between confession of personal guilt and divine mercy where God is implored:

- For the sake of your name, LORD, forgive my iniquity, though it is great. (Ps 25:11)
- Blessed is the one whose transgressions are forgiven, whose sins are covered. (Ps 32:1)
- Help us, God our Savior, for the glory of your name; deliver us and forgive our sins for your name's sake. (Ps 79:9)

In Isaiah 33:24, God is ready to reveal himself as Judge, Lawgiver, and King, and when he does so for Jerusalem, the "sins of those who dwell there will be forgiven." According to Jeremiah 31:34, one of the blessings of the new covenant is this: "I will forgive their wickedness and will remember their sins no more." Daniel pleads with God to forgive and restore the exiles because the honor of God is at stake: "Lord, listen! Lord, forgive! Lord, hear and act!" (Dan 9:19).

The Old Testament demonstrates two great truths about forgiveness: God is a

---

118. It is touched upon only briefly by Grudem (*Systematic Theology*, 386, 695, 740), Erickson (*Christian Theology*, 323, 701, 976), and Horton, (*Christian Faith*, 466, 637). This relative neglect is probably due to a focus on the forensic images in contrast to relational ones. McGrath (*Christian Theology*, 419–25) gives the subject more print space than most. Calvin (*Institutes* 3.3.1) called repentance and forgiveness of sins "the sum of the gospel."

forgiving God, ready to pardon his people's sin (Isa 33:24; Jer 33:8; Dan 9:9), yet his patience has limits and at some points forgiveness is no longer possible (Josh 24:19; 2 Kgs 24:4; Jer 5:7; Hos 1:6). But in contrast to the postmodern stereotypes of the Old Testament with God as some kind of tyrannical monster, we read these words of Micah 7:18–20:

> Who is a God like you,
>   who pardons sin and forgives the transgression
>   of the remnant of his inheritance?
> You do not stay angry forever
>   but delight to show mercy.
> You will again have compassion on us;
>   you will tread our sins underfoot
>   and hurl all our iniquities into the depths of the sea.
> You will be faithful to Jacob,
>   and show love to Abraham,
> as you pledged on oath to our ancestors
>   in days long ago.

In the New Testament the primary words for forgiveness are *aphiēmi* ("to forgive"), *aphesis* ("forgiveness"), *charizomai* ("to grace"), and *apolyō* ("to pardon"). Reference to forgiveness occurs most frequently in relation to sins (e.g., Matt 6:15; 9:2–6; 26:28; Acts 2:38; 5:31; 10:43; Rom 4:7; Eph 1:7; Col 1:14; Heb 8:12; 1 John 1:9; 2:12). In the infancy narrative there is a clear picture of the messianic deliverer who brings forgiveness and salvation from sins. The angel of the Lord tells Joseph in a dream that Mary's child is to be called "Jesus," because "he will save his people from their sins" (Matt 1:21). Zechariah prophesies that John the Baptist will bring God's "people the knowledge of salvation through the forgiveness of their sins" (Luke 1:77). The baptism John administered pertained to the forgiveness of sins as a preparation for the coming judgment (Mark 1:4).

The healings that Jesus performed in his ministry were often accompanied by declarations that the supplicant's sins had also been forgiven (Mark 2:5–12; Luke 7:47–50). Jesus taught about mutual forgiveness and restoration in human relationships in the Lord's Prayer (Matt 6:12/Luke 11:4). He taught the same elsewhere to the point that God's forgiving us is dependent on our forgiving others (Matt 6:14–15; 18:15–25; Luke 7:41–43; 17:3–4). The parable of the lost son is about the eagerness of God to forgive wayward children (Luke 15:11–32).

At the Last Supper, Jesus taught that his death would mark the blood of the covenant poured out for the forgiveness of sins (Matt 26:28). On the cross, Jesus pleaded with his Father to forgive his persecutors (Luke 23:34). The believing community is granted authority by Jesus to administer the forgiveness of sins (John 20:23). The risen Jesus commanded his disciples to proclaim a message about the forgiveness of sins (Luke 24:47). As Robert Yarbrough states: "The story of Jesus' life from infancy to ascension is dominated by the account of his mission to provide forgiveness."[119]

The apostolic preaching recounted by Luke makes forgiveness central in gospel proclamation. In Luke–Acts, forgiveness is a virtual stand-in for salvation language.[120] To Jews, Samaritans, and Gentiles, there is the consistent message of forgiveness of sins through faith in the Messiah (Acts 2:38; 5:31; 8:22; 10:43; 13:38; 26:18). Forgiveness is equated with a number of other images in the New Testament, including the nonreckoning of sin (Rom 4:7–8; Heb 8:12), redemption (Eph 1:7; Col 1:14), cleansing (1 John 1:9), and an atoning sacrifice (1 John 2:2, 12).[121] In Hebrews, the forgiveness of sins explains the necessity of Jesus' death and the end to the sacrificial system: "The law requires that nearly everything be cleansed with blood, and without the shedding of blood there is no forgiveness" (Heb 9:22), and "where these [sins] have been forgiven, sacrifice for sin is no longer necessary" (10:18).

Why did forgiveness have to occur? Calvin wrote: "But if there is anything in the whole of religion that we should most certainly know, we ought most closely to grasp by what reason, with what law, under what condition, with what ease or difficulty, forgiveness of sins may be obtained!"[122] Forgiveness occurs because of Jesus' "name" (1 John 2:12), but primarily because of his "blood" (Matt 26:28; Eph 1:7; Heb 9:22). It is his sacrificial death that makes forgiveness possible, and the preaching of his death must include the preaching of the forgiveness of sins.[123]

Forgiveness has clear blessings in the community of faith. Christians are commanded (not recommended) to forgive others, as is narrated in the Lord's Prayer (Matt 6:12/Luke 11:4). The first mention of forgiveness in Scripture is Joseph's forgiving his brothers for what they did to him (Gen 50:17). Indeed, divine forgiveness is a model for human forgiveness, as Paul tells the Colossians: "Bear with each other

---

119. Robert Yarbrough, "Forgiveness and Reconciliation," in *NDBT*, 501.

120. Joel B. Green, *Salvation* (UBT; St. Louis: Chalice, 2003), 56.

121. In the Reformed tradition it is common to define justification as the forgiveness of sins supplemented by the imputation of Christ's righteousness to the believer (e.g., Calvin, *Institutes* 3.11–2). The logic is that forgiveness clears the slate so to speak and negates guilt. But thereafter persons still need an imputation of righteous law-keeping in order to have a positive legal status before God. That is certainly logical, but it is not biblical. The fact is that the biblical writers use justification and forgiveness as two sides of the same coin and not as two stages in one event (see esp. Acts 13:38–39; Rom 4:7–8). See Brian Vickers, *Jesus' Blood and Righteousness: Paul's Theology of Imputation* (Wheaton, IL: Crossway, 2006), 100–109.

122. Calvin, *Institutes* 3.4.2.

123. Colijn (*Images of Salvation*, 164, 170) notes: "The metaphor of debt forgiveness is one way to describe what happens at the cross: in Christ, God bears the cost of human sin so that human beings can be released from it. That is not the quite the same thing as saying that Jesus pays the penalty for human sin. In the model of penal substitution, for example, God receives his due through the penalty paid by Christ. The debt owed to God is repaid, although not by the debtors. In the metaphor of debt forgiveness, by contrast, God is not repaid. Like the creditor in Luke 7:41–43, God writes off the debt." But she adds: "Like redemption, forgiveness requires a kind of substitution: one must identify with another, even put oneself in the place of the other, in order to set the other free. It is a costly and creative act that involves a kind of death to self."

and forgive one another if any of you has a grievance against someone. Forgive as the Lord forgave you" (Col 3:13; cf. Eph 4:32). Forgiveness does not mean that I do not continue to feel the hurt from someone's sin. No, forgiveness means that I forfeit my right to show my hurt at someone's painful actions. It is the forgiver who must ultimately bear the price for the transgression when he or she would prefer retaliation or recompense, hard as that is to do; that is the divine model that we are to follow.

5.4.2 REDEMPTION

Salvation as "redemption" is a further arrow in our quiver of images. In some cases "redemption" is a metaphor for the completion of salvation (Luke 21:28; Rom 8:23; Eph 1:14; 4:30; Rev 14:3). In the Old Testament, redemption language is employed in commercial and legal contexts. It was an integral part of the covenantal regulations concerning debts and justice. Leviticus 25 contains instructions pertaining to "guardian-redeemers" (cf. Ruth 2:20), who are close relatives who can redeem property sold because of debt and redeem persons sold into slavery. In Exodus 21:28–32 is a redemption scheme pertaining to accidental death and personal injuries. If a bull habitually gores people, if the owner fails to keep the bull penned, and if the bull subsequently kills someone, then "its owner also is to be put to death." A reprieve can be granted, however, if payment is made; then the owner "may redeem his life by the payment of whatever is demanded."

Furthermore, in the Old Testament individuals thank God for redeeming them from sin (Pss 19:14; 103:3–4; 130:8) and death (Job 33:28; Ps 49:15; Hos 13:14). The great act of redemption was, of course, the exodus (e.g., Exod 6:6; Deut 7:8; 9:26; 13:5; 15:15; 24:18; 2 Sam 7:23; 1 Chr 17:21; Neh 1:10; Pss 77:15; 78:42; 11:9; Mic 6:4). This event was the epochal moment where God remembered his promises to the patriarchs and redeemed his people from slavery in Egypt. This was celebrated at every Passover thereafter. What is more, just as God once redeemed Israel from slavery and bondage, so too did the prophets announce that God would *again* redeem Israel in a new exodus from exile (e.g., Isa 43:1–8; 48:20; 51:10–11; 62:12; Jer 16:14–15; 31:11–12; Mic 4:10; Zech 10:8).

In the Greco-Roman context, redemption pertained to the manumission of slaves and the repatriation of prisoners of war when an appropriate price was paid. This underscores that redemption meant freedom from slavery and salvation from death. Importantly, in the Christian scheme, slaves contribute nothing to their redemption. The price is paid by another, not by the enslaved.

In the Gospels, hope for Israel's national restoration is espoused in terms of Israel's redemption (Luke 2:38; 24:21; cf. Acts 1:6). One would naturally think of the sin that caused Israel's sociopolitical misfortunes, so that redemption for the nation is reconciliation with God and rescue from oppression under foreign powers. We must also consider the famous "ransom logion" found Matthew 20:28/Mark 10:45. According to the Matthean version, "the Son of Man did not come to be served, but to serve, and to give his life as a ransom for many." It is probable that that the logion is allusive of Isaiah 43 and 53 and Daniel 7, with connotations of a vicarious death for the benefit of "many," though other Old Testament ransom texts may be echoed too (Job 33:24; Prov 21:18). Jesus redeems a people by his death on the cross.

Paul's makes frequent usage of the redemption theme.[124] Redemption is related to the forgiveness of sins (Eph 1:7; Col 1:14), righteousness, and holiness (1 Cor 1:30). It brings adoption (Gal 4:5); it occurs through Christ's "sacrifice" and "blood" (Rom 3:24–25; Eph 1:7). Christ redeems believers from wickedness (Titus 2:14). Paul can even say that Jesus is a "ransom" for all men (1 Tim 2:6). While it is possible to infer that in redemption Christ pays our *price* rather than takes our *place*, in at least one text Paul states that Christ redeemed us from the curse of the law by becoming "a curse for us," or by enduring the curse in our stead (Gal 3:13). This implies that redemption occurs through substitution.

We must also add a much-neglected aspect that believers are redeemed for the purpose of living a godly life and showing forth righteous behavior. Christ redeems persons so that they are no longer "slaves to sin" (Rom 6:6), "to purify for himself a people that are his very own, eager to do what is good" (Titus 2:14). Finally Paul admonishes the Corinthians: "You are not your own; you were bought at a price. Therefore honor God with your bodies" (1 Cor 6:19b–20; cf. 7:23). For Paul, redemption means becoming a slave of Christ and being dedicated to the purposes and patterns of life that are summed up in Christ. Christians are freed from the old order of service to serve in a new one.[125]

The Catholic Letters show a great interest in the redeeming character of Jesus' death. According to the writer of Hebrews, Jesus' blood obtained "eternal redemption" (Heb 9:12) and died as a "ransom" to set people free "from the sins committed under the first covenant" (9:15). Peter says that believers "were redeemed from the empty way of life handed down to you from your ancestors ... with the precious blood of Christ, a lamb without blemish or defect" (1 Pet 1:18–19). In the cosmic worship of Revelation 5, the elders and living creatures celebrate that the Lamb has "purchased for God persons from every tribe and language and people and nation" (Rev 5:9), and they were "purchased from among mankind" (14:4).

If Jesus' death is a ransom, the question is: To whom is the ransom paid? We have already investigated the "ransom" view of the atonement (see §4.4). Here we merely note that the recipient of the ransom price is never identified; neither God nor Satan

---

124. Michael F. Bird, *A Bird's-Eye View of Paul: The Man, His Mission and His Message* (Nottingham, UK: Inter-Varsity Press, 2008), 106–8.

125. David J. Williams, *Paul's Metaphors: Their Context and Character* (Peabody, MA: Hendrickson, 1999), 116.

is named as receiving payment for sin. What redemption shows is the costliness of human salvation and that Jesus sets human beings free at the expense of his own life. A modern analogy is that of a hostage situation, where the negotiator takes the place of the innocent hostages.[126]

If the New Testament has one witness to Jesus' death, it is that it constitutes a redemptive event. It is a new exodus, a transfer from slavery in sin to service of the risen Lord. It is paid in blood and liberates the lost, and this redemption is apprehended only in the Redeemer. Irenaeus wrote that God offered "His own beloved and only-begotten Son, as a sacrifice for our redemption."[127] According to Cyprian, "Jesus then really suffered for all men; for the Cross was no illusion, otherwise our redemption is an illusion also."[128]

5.4.3 RESCUE

A more general picture of salvation is found in a group of texts that refer to "rescue" from peril. The most basic Hebrew word for this is *yašaʿ*, which means literally "to be roomy, broad" as opposed to constricted and oppressed. In Greek, there are the words *sōzō* ("to save") and *sōtēria* ("salvation"). The basic meaning of salvation is preservation and deliverance from danger.

Walter Brueggemann identifies several words in Exodus used in relation to the idea of "Yahweh, the God Who Delivers." Yahweh delivers in terms of removing people from one place to another (Exod 6:6; 13:3); Yahweh delivers in the sense of powerfully rescuing the Hebrews from danger (3:8; 14:30); Yahweh redeems much like a kinsman redeemer who advocates for oppressed Israel (6:6; 13:15; 15:13); and Yahweh brings up, that is, God leads Israel from the land of slavery to the land of promise (3:8, 17).[129]

Salvation language also features widely in the Psalms and in Isaiah, which occasions praise for God and describes God's plan for the deliverance of Israel. According to Isaiah, God is "mighty to save" (Isa 63:1), and the psalmist extols God with the words, "That I may declare your praises in the gates of Daughter Zion, and there rejoice in your salvation" (Ps 9:14). The reference to a "horn of salvation" mentioned in Luke 1:69 in Zechariah's song is rooted in Old Testament imagery, where the horn amounts to God in strength acting for his people (2 Sam 22:3; Ps 18:2; on "salvation" and "strength," see Exod 15:2; Pss 28:8; 118:14; Isa 12:2; 30:15; 33:2).

As we have already seen (§5.1), salvation can be equated with physical healing, economic liberation, deliverance from demonic oppression, and release from shame.

---

126. Colijn, *Images of Salvation*, 150–51.
127. Irenaeus, *Haer.* 4.5.4.
128. Cyprian, *Sent.* 13.4.
129. Walter Brueggemann, *Theology of the Old Testament: Testimony, Dispute, Advocacy* (Minneapolis: Fortress, 1997), 173–76.

The Gospels testify to a broad and even ambiguous scope to salvation. The name "Jesus" is taken from the Hebrew "Joshua" ("Yeshua" in postexilic Hebrew and Aramaic), meaning "Yahweh saves." That is why the angel tells Joseph to name Mary's child "Jesus," because "he will save his people from their sins" (Matt 1:21). By following Jesus one "saves" their own life (16:25). In the encounter with the rich young man, gaining "eternal life" is equivalent to being "saved" (19:16, 25). In the Olivet Discourse we are told that "the one who stands firm to the end will be saved" (24:13; cf. 10:22). John relates salvation principally to eternal life, and for Luke it is mainly about the forgiveness of sins.

Paul understands salvation in apocalyptic coordinates as a past event, where Jesus "gave himself for our sins to rescue us from the present evil age" (Gal 1:4), and also as a future hope as believers are to "wait for his Son from heaven, whom he raised from the dead—Jesus, who rescues us from the coming wrath" (1 Thess 1:10).

Salvation is also something that is achieved by the cooperation of all members of the Godhead. The triune nature of salvation is aptly summarized by Brenda Colijn:

> Throughout the New Testament, as in the Old, *sōtēria* is regarded as the work of God. It is provided by the Father, accomplished by the Son, and applied by the Spirit. The Father is the source of *sōtēria*; he sends the Son into the world so that it might be saved (Jn 3:17). Jesus is the mediator of *sōtēria*. He came to seek and save the lost (Lk 19:10), and salvation comes only through him (Acts 4:12). Jesus provides *sōtēria* through his healings, forgiveness, his death and his life (Rom 5:10). The power of *sōtēria* is the power of his resurrection (1 Pet 3:21; cf. Rom 1:4). The Holy Spirit makes *sōtēria* actual in the lives of believers by setting them apart for God and making them holy so that they can share in the glory of Christ (2 Thess 2:13).[130]

A "rescue" is what happens at an intersection between grace and faith. It is God reaching down into the human condition, as a human being, to lift people to the heights of divine glory. This rescue has two direction: salvation *from* and salvation *for*. We are rescued from the evil age, sin, death, judgment, and the evil one; and we are saved for good deeds and holy living. Salvation is definitive in the sense that its root lay in the eternal divine decision of God to be Savior, in the event of the cross and resurrection, and in the awakening of faith; but in another sense salvation is conditional and future. Salvation is not a transaction but an ongoing relationship between the rescuer and the rescued. It is steadfast faith and faithfulness that keep us in communion with Christ and his benefits (and it is God who keeps us steadfast [see Ps 51:10; Isa 26:3; 1 Pet 5:10]). I will have more to say about perseverance soon (§5.5); what should be noted here is that the sign of salvation is transformation.

---

130. Colijn, *Images of Salvation*, 137.

That is why we read that we are saved by grace through faith for good works (Eph 2:8–10).

The author of Hebrews refers to Jesus as "the source for eternal salvation for all who obey him" (Heb 5:9) and for those who "show this same diligence to the very end, so that what you hope for may be fully realized" (6:11). Salvation is not based on some kind of easy believism. Salvation in its triune form, in all three tenses, is the means to the ultimate manifestation of God's glory: "Help us, God our Savior, for the glory of your name; deliver us and forgive our sins for your name's sake" (Ps 79:9.) God elects to be Savior because it is the most supreme and lovely display of his glory (see 1 Chr 16:35; Ps 106:47; Isa 44:23; Eph 1:14; Jude 25).

5.4.4 RECONCILIATION

A further image of salvation is that of "reconciliation," which is taken from the world of relationships; it refers to the restoration between persons such as husbands and wives (1 Cor 7:11) and between fellow Israelites (Acts 7:26). Paul speaks of humanity being reconciled to God (Rom 5:10–11; 2 Cor 5:18–21; Eph 2:14–17; Col 1:20–22).[131] The key word here is *katallassō*, which basically means "the exchange of hostility for a friendly relationship."[132] Many New Testament scholars regard "reconciliation" as the center of Paul's theology, or at least of his soteriology.[133] For systematic theologians, the doctrine of reconciliation is the label for the entire field of soteriology itself.[134] Brevard Childs goes so far as to speak of reconciliation as "a broad inclusive theological category ... [that] encompasses the subject matter of atonement, sacrifice, forgiveness, redemption, righteousness and justification."[135] Scot McKnight and Miroslav Volf have recently argued that reconciliation is central to the gospel.[136]

Several Jewish authors also speak of reconciliation. Josephus describes Moses acting as a mediator between God and the people: "When Moses had spoken to them, according to the decision of God, the multitude became grieved in their affliction, and pleaded with Moses to procure their *reconciliation* to God, and to permit them to no longer wander in the wilderness" (*Ant* 3.315). Josephus also gives an account of

---

131. What follows is drawn from Bird, *Bird's-Eye View of Paul*, 104–6.

132. BDAG, 521.

133. Peter Stuhlmacher, *Biblische Theologie des Neuen Testaments* (2 vols.; Göttingen: Vandenhoeck und Ruprecht, 1992–1999), 1:32–33; 2:320–21; Ralph P. Martin, *Reconciliation: A Study of Paul's Theology* (Atlanta: John Knox, 1981); I. Howard Marshall, *New Testament Theology: Many Witnesses, One Gospel* (Nottingham, UK: Apollos, 2004), 440–42, 719–20; idem, *Aspects of the Atonement: Cross and Resurrection in the Reconciling of God and Humanity* (London: Paternoster,

2007), 98–137.

134. Cf., e.g., Karl Barth, *CD*, IV/1–4; James Denny, *The Christian Doctrine of Reconciliation* (Piscataway, NJ: Gorgias, 2010).

135. B. S. Childs, *Biblical Theology of the Old and New Testaments: Theological Reflection on the Christian Bible* (Minneapolis: Fortress, 1992), 486.

136. Miroslav Volf, *Exclusion and Embrace: A Theological Exploration of Identity, Otherness, and Reconciliation* (Nashville: Abingdon, 1996); Scot McKnight, *Embracing Grace: A Gospel for All of Us* (Brewster, MA: Paraclete, 2005).

how a cohort of Roman infantry were foolishly ambushed during the siege of Jerusalem. Titus sought to inflict severe discipline on them because of their foolishness, but at the petition of his commanders he relented in his anger. Josephus wrote that "he was reconciled to the soldiers, but gave them special orders to act more wisely in the future; and he considered with himself how he might get even with the Jews for their stratagem" (*War* 5.129). In 2 Maccabees, one of the martyrs declares: "And if our living Lord is angry for a little while, to rebuke and discipline us, he will again be reconciled with his own servants" (2 Macc 7.33; cf. 1:5). This is the background to what Paul says especially in Romans 5:1–11 and 2 Corinthians 5:14–21.

What is significant, though, as Stanley Porter has argued, is that Paul was the first author to speak of the offended party (God) initiating reconciliation and using the verb *katallassō* ("I reconcile") in the active voice.[137] For Paul, reconciliation starts with God, who reaches out in grace; it does not begin with the offending party reaching out for peace and forgiveness. He spends a lot of time explaining reconciliation. In his perspective, reconciliation has a universal and cosmic scope as the world that is alienated from God is brought back to God: "All this is from God, who reconciled us to himself through Christ and gave us the ministry of reconciliation; that God was reconciling the world to himself in Christ, not counting people's sins against them. And he has committed to us the message of reconciliation" (2 Cor 5:18–19). This global sweep to reconciliation is reiterated at the end of Romans 9–11, where Jewish rejection of the gospel provides occasion for the "reconciliation to the world" (11:15). Yet God is no less concerned with individuals reconciled to him by faith in Christ. Note Romans 5:10–11:

> For if, while we were God's enemies, we were reconciled to him through the death of his Son, how much more, having been reconciled, shall we be saved through his life! Not only is this so, but we also boast in God through our Lord Jesus Christ, through whom we have now received reconciliation.

This reconciliation is available exclusively through the cross. Remember that the word "atonement" comes from "at-one-ment," meaning reconciliation. In Colossians, Paul wonderfully blends together the cosmic and crucicentric mechanism for reconciliation:

> [God was pleased] through him to reconcile to himself all things, whether things on earth or things in heaven, by making peace through his blood, shed on the cross. Once you were alienated from God and were enemies in your minds because of your evil behavior. But now he has reconciled you by Christ's physical body through death. (Col 1:20–22)

---

137. Stanley E. Porter, *Καταλλάσσω in Ancient Greek Literature, with Reference to the Pauline Writings* (Cordoba: Ediciónes El Almendro, 1994).

What accompanies reconciliation is the unity of Jews and Gentiles in one body since the dividing wall between them has been broken down. As such, they are united together so that Christ might "reconcile both of them to God through the cross, by which he put to death their hostility" (Eph 2:16). Reconciliation emerges as a counterpart to justification. It marks the end of alienation and hostilities between humanity and God and restores the rupture to the God-humanity relationship. It occurs through Christ's death; as a result, God no longer reckons sin to sinners but establishes peace.[138]

One of the upshots of reconciliation is that Christians preach a message of reconciliation from God, but they also model reconciliation in a community context. For Jesus, being reconciled to a fellow human being was more important than offering sacrifices at the altar (Matt 5:24). The gospel is lived out when Christians practice reconciliation among themselves and exemplify it before their neighbors. The ambassadors for reconciliation have the opportunity to promote peacemaking in communities rife with factions, distrust, and mutual suspicions. Because we have been comforted we can be a comfort to others (2 Cor 1:4). As John Chrysostom wrote:

> If he who reconciles only is called a son of God, of what shall not he be worthy, who makes friends of those who are reconciled? Let us engage ourselves in this trade, let us make those who are enemies to each other friends, and those who are not indeed enemies, but are not friends, them let us bring together, and before all, our own selves.[139]

5.4.5 JUSTIFICATION

The doctrine of justification is a crucial image for how God's contention against humanity is overturned by Jesus' death and resurrection.[140] Jesus taught a parable in which a penitent publican rather than an über-pious Pharisee "went home justified" after praying in the temple (Luke 18:9–14). The testimony of Paul is that "all have sinned and fall short of the glory of God, and all are justified freely by his grace through the redemption that came by Christ Jesus" (Rom 3:23–24). Paradoxically God does not justify the righteous; rather, he justifies the ungodly (4:5; 5:6)—not because God's justice has been compromised, but because it has been satisfied.

---

138. Cf. Stanley E. Porter, "Reconciliation as the Heart of Paul's Missionary Theology," in *Paul as Missionary: Identity, Activity, Theology, and Practice* (ed. T. J. Burke and B. S. Rosner; LNTS 420; London: T&T Clark, 2011), 169–79.

139. Chrysostom, *Hom. Act.* 37.

140. Cf. Bird, *Saving Righteousness*; idem, *Bird's-Eye View of Paul*, 93–98; idem, "Judgment and Justification in Paul: A Review Article," *BBR* 18 (2008): 299–313; idem, "What if Martin Luther Had Read the Dead Sea Scrolls? Historical Particularity and Theological Interpretation in Pauline Theology: Galatians as a Test Case," *JTI* 3 (2009): 107–25; idem, "Justification: A Progressive Reformed View," in *Justification: Five Views* (ed. P. Eddy and J. Beilby; Downers Grove, IL: InterVarsity Press, 2011).

Through Calvary and the empty tomb, God's verdict against us has been transformed into God's verdict for us. These verdicts have been changed from condemnation to righteousness. It was the rediscovery of justification by faith alone, through grace alone, in Christ alone that constituted the protest of the Reformation against the Semi-Pelagianism of the medieval church, which promoted a teaching of salvation based on a synergy of grace, merits, sacraments, and free will.[141]

In Roman Catholic teaching, justification refers principally to the infusion of grace into a person through the sacraments so that they attain to just behavior. Justification, then, is the *process* of becoming just. This perspective is espoused in the 1993 Catechism of the Catholic Church, where justification is conferred in baptism, conforms persons to the righteousness of God, and imparts the merits of Jesus' passion, by which people may become inwardly renewed through a cooperation between God's grace and human freedom.[142] A short definition of the Catholic view is: "Justification includes the remission of sins, sanctification, and the renewal of the inner man."[143] So in terms of official Catholic dogma, justification is the process of forgiveness and renewal. The Council of Trent produced a series of Counter-Reformation canons that dug in the heels of the Roman Church against the Reformers with a series of affirmations and anathemas:

> Canon 9: If anyone says, that by faith alone the impious is justified; in such wise as to mean, that nothing else is required to cooperate in order to the obtaining the grace of Justification, and that it is not in any way necessary, that he be prepared and disposed by the movement of his own will; let him be anathema.
>
> Canon 12: If anyone says, that justifying faith is nothing else but confidence in the divine mercy which remits sins for Christ's sake; or, that this confidence alone is that whereby we are justified; let him be anathema.
>
> Canon 24: If anyone says, that the justice received is not preserved and also increased before God through good works; but that the said works are merely the fruits and signs of Justification obtained, but not a cause of the increase thereof; let him be anathema.

That is not to say that all Catholics would define justification in these terms. One need only consult Joseph Fitzmyer or Scott Hahn to see how some Catholic scholars can imbibe a bit of good biblical theology in their accounts of justification.[144] What is more, the 1999 Joint Declaration on the Doctrine of Justification by

---

141. On the history of the doctrine see Alister E. McGrath, *Iustitia Dei: A History of the Christian Doctrine of Justification: The Beginnings to the Reformation* (Cambridge: Cambridge University Press, 1986); D. H. Williams, "Justification by Faith: A Patristic Doctrine," *JEH* 57.6 (2006): 649–67; Nick Needham, "Justification in the Early Church Fathers," in *Justification in Perspective: Historical Developments and Contemporary Challenges* (ed. B. L. McCormack; Grand Rapids: Baker, 2006), 25–53.
142. CCC, 1989–95.
143. CCC, 2019.
144. Joseph A. Fitzmyer, *Romans: A New Translation with Introduction and Commentary* (AB; New York: Doubleday, 1993); Scott A. Hahn, *Justification: Becoming a Child of God* (Cassette Recording; Saint Joseph Communications, 1995).

Lutherans and Catholics moved the ecumenical conversation forward in a positive way and broke down some of the misconceptions and caricatures that Catholics and Protestants have had of each other's positions.[145] The document defines justification in this manner:

> Justification is the forgiveness of sins (cf. Rom 3:23–25; Acts 13:39; Lk 18:14), liberation from the dominating power of sin and death (Rom 5:12–21) and from the curse of the law (Gal 3:10–14). It is acceptance into communion with God: already now, but then fully in God's coming kingdom (Rom 5:1f). It unites with Christ and with his death and resurrection (Rom 6:5). It occurs in the reception of the Holy Spirit in baptism and incorporation into the one body (Rom 8:1f, 9f; I Cor 12:12f). All this is from God alone, for Christ's sake, by grace, through faith in "the gospel of God's Son" (Rom 1:1–3).

That sounds *mostly* right. I think that justification does edge toward transformative categories in certain places like in Acts 13:39 and Romans 6:7, which both talk about being "justified from sin" (i.e., declaring *and* making righteous).[146] Yet it remains inescapable for me that justification is essentially and principally a forensic declaration of being in a right relationship with God, a relationship established and sustained by God's saving righteousness. In the Reformed scheme the Christian is *simil iustus et peccator* ("at the same time both justified and a sinner"). Such a claim appears to be irreconcilable with the Catholic scheme.[147]

The Catholic objection to a strictly forensic justification is that it amounts to a "legal fiction," where God *pretends* we are righteous. But nothing could be further from the truth. God does not treat sinners *as if* they were righteous; they are in fact righteous. Through participation in Christ they are genuinely righteous because God has condemned their sin and then acquitted them in the death and resurrection of Jesus Christ. God vindicates Jesus as the faithful Son in the resurrection (Rom 4:25; 1 Tim 3:16), and because they are in the Son, what is true of him is reckoned to be true of them too (Rom 5:18–21).[148] Justification and transformation are linked together logically, not conceptually. They are distinct works of God both apprehended by union with Christ and applied through the Holy Spirit. To collapse justification and transformation together would inevitably lead to justification by works, which is strictly ruled out by biblical teaching (Luke 18:9–14; Rom 3:21–4:25; Gal 2:15–21; Eph 2:8–9; 2 Tim 1:9; Titus 3:5).

---

145. www.lutheranworld.org/LWF_Documents/EN/JDDJ_99-jd97e.pdf (accessed 8 March 2011).

146. Cf. Eberhard Jüngel, *Justification: The Heart of the Christian Faith* (Edinburgh: T&T Clark, 2001).

147. For an assessment of Catholic-Protestant dialogue see Anthony N. S. Lane, *Justification by Faith in Catholic-Protestant Dialogue: An Evangelical Assessment* (London: T&T Clark, 2002); David E. Aune, ed., *Rereading Paul Together: Protestant and Catholic Perspectives on Justification* (Grand Rapids: Baker, 2006).

148. Bird, *Saving Righteousness*, 8–9; G. E. Ladd, *A Theology of the New Testament* (ed. and rev. D. A. Hagner; Grand Rapids: Eerdmans, 1993), 486–87; Dunn, *Theology of Paul*, 385–86.

On the Reformed side, it is important to remember that there was a lot of diversity among the Reformers about justification itself.[149] A summary of what came to be the dominant "Reformed view" is summarized in the Westminster Shorter Catechism Q. 33: "What is Justification?" and it answers: "Justification is an act of God's free grace, wherein he pardoneth all our sins, and accepteth us as righteous in His sight, only for the righteousness of Christ imputed to us, and received by faith alone." The primary contentions of the Reformed view are: (1) the distinction between justification and sanctification; (2) justification based on the imputation of the meritorious law-keeping of Jesus Christ in his life and death; and (3) faith as the single instrument that enables believers to share in the blessings of justification.[150]

I wholeheartedly agree with the Reformed position on justification about a forensic and alien righteousness. Yet I have one primary objection to the Reformed scheme, namely, that the emphasis on the imputation of Jesus' active obedience needs urgent qualification.[151] The underlying scenario is something like this: Adam failed to acquire merit in the garden of Eden and so did not fulfill the covenant of works. Jesus, as the new Adam, acquires merit for us in his life of obedience, his merit is imputed into our account, and this imputation is the basis of our righteousness. The problem is twofold.

(1) We are stuck with the medieval mind-set of a treasury of merits that we somehow have to acquire, and the only options on the table are impartation (Catholic) or imputation (Reformed). I think this whole theology of merit is asking the wrong questions about the text. The problem humanity has is not a lack of moral merits. The problem is a broken relationship. What is needed is not merit, but reconciliation.[152] Jesus takes us from alienation to restoration through

---

149. Note this comment by James R. Payton (*Getting the Reformation Wrong: Correcting Some Misunderstandings* [Downers Grove, IL: InterVarsity Press, 2010], 121–22): "The various Reformers reflected on how the great transaction promised in the gospel 'worked,' and they came to somewhat different insights. These sometimes reinforced each other, but at times they were in conflict. Luther emphasized the 'sweet exchange' between the sinner and Christ and that sinners are united to Christ by that faith impelled in them by the Holy Spirit. Melanchthon's regular stress on divine mercy fits closely with this, although bringing a different accent. Zwingli tied justification to the divine decree of election, with faith the temporal manifestation of what God intended from eternity past from his chosen. Bucer stressed that justification includes the reception of the Holy Spirit, who leads believers to live for God: 'Hence he [St. Paul] never uses the word "justify" in this way without appearing to speak no less of this imparting of true righteousness than of the fount and head of our entire salvation, the forgiveness of sins.' Calvin stepped back from Bucer's declaration when he asserted that justification by faith precludes 'the sense ... that we receive within any righteousness,' but Calvin brought another emphasis when he asserted, 'Christ, therefore, makes us thus participants in himself in order that we, who are in ourselves sinners, may be, through Christ's righteousness, considered just before the throne of God.' But these differences were variant modulations within the Reformers' concerto. The Protestant Reformers agreed in emphasizing justification *sola fide*."

150. Cf. Calvin, *Institutes* 3.11–17; Thirty-Nine Arts. 11–13; WCF 11.1–6; Belgic Confession 22–23. For contemporary restatements of the doctrine see Grudem, *Systematic Theology*, 722–35; Robert L. Reymond, *A New Systematic Theology of the Christian Faith* (2nd ed.; Nashville: Nelson, 1998), 739–58; Horton, *Christian Faith*, 620–47.

151. Note Emil Brunner's (*Dogmatics: The Christian Doctrine of Creation and Redemption* [Philadelphia: Westminster, 1980], 282) objections to distinguishing between Jesus' active and passive obedience.

152. Cf. Norman Shepherd (*The Call of Grace: How the Covenant Illuminates Salvation and Evangelism* [Phillipsburg, NJ: Presbyterian & Reformed, 2000], 61–62): "If we do not reject the idea of merit, we are not really able to challenge the Romanist doctrine of salvation as its very root."

his messianic ministry, by his atoning death and his glorious resurrection. Don't get me wrong. Jesus' obedience matters immensely and without it no one can be saved. But that is not because Jesus was racking up frequent flyer points that can transferred into our account. Jesus' obedience and faithfulness in his vocation as Son enabled him to execute his role as the second Adam and as the new Israel. He was obedient where Adam and Israel failed to be. Jesus' obedience qualified him to be the sacrifice who could redeem Israel and humanity in their alienation from God. Hence the New Testament emphasizes his *passive* obedience, that is, his obedience to death on the cross (Rom 5:19; Phil 2:8; Heb 5:8–9; 12:3).[153] Consequently, believers escape the punishment of their sin when Christ takes the penalty for them, and they experience justification when they participate in the justification of the Messiah, who has fulfilled the role God gave to Adam and Israel as representatives of humanity.

(2) The standard proof texts lined up to prove imputation fail to say exactly what some Reformed theologians think they say. Appeal is often made to a cohort of texts to prove imputation (Rom 4:4–5; 5:17–19; 1 Cor 1:30; 2 Cor 5:21; Phil 3:7–9). Robert Gundry notes that in these texts, "nothing is said about a replacement of believers' sins with the righteousness of Christ."[154] Some texts say something close, similar, or vaguely analogous, but no text explicitly says that the obedience of Jesus is imputed to believers as their righteousness. Upon closer inspection one notices that the emphasis falls squarely on *union with Christ*. For Paul believers are "seeking to be justified *in Christ*" (Gal 2:17); "*in him* we might become the righteousness of God" (2 Cor 5:21), and also "be found *in him*, not having a righteousness of my own that comes from the law, but that which is through faith *in Christ*—the righteousness that comes from God" (Phil 3:9, italics added in all cases).

Rather than imputation, a better description of the biblical materials is *incorporation* into the righteousness of Christ. The verdict that God the Father executes on the Son is shared by those who are united to the risen Jesus. They share in the verdict and, I would add, the basis for the verdict: Jesus' obedience to his messianic task of redemptive suffering. So Jesus' obedience does become ours—but not through artificially dividing Jesus' obedience into active and passive varieties, not through a medieval concept of "merit" that is imputed instead of imparted, not because Jesus is the exemplary Pelagian who earns salvation when we cannot, not by fulfilling a covenant of works that required meritorious fulfillment, not by way of righteousness molecules floating through the air to us; rather, we become "righteous" in

---

153. WCF 11.1 deliberately omits reference to the "active" obedience of Jesus Christ. See discussion in J. R. Daniel Kirk, "The Sufficiency of the Cross," *SBET* 24 (2006): 35–39.

154. Robert H. Gundry, "Why I Didn't Endorse 'The Gospel of Jesus Christ: An Evangelical Celebration' ... Even Though I Wasn't Asked to," *Books and Culture* (Jan-Feb 2001): 6–9.

Christ when by faith we participate in the vicarious death and resurrection of Jesus Christ. We are incorporated into the righteousness of Jesus Christ.

Now imputation is a legitimate concept under this aegis of union and is inferred from the gift of righteousness (Rom 5:17; Phil 3:9), emphasis on Jesus' obedience and faithfulness (Rom 5:17–19; Phil 2:5–11; Heb 3:1–6; Rev 1:5), the representative role of Adam and Jesus (Rom 5:12–21), the language of reckoning and forgiveness (Rom 4:4–5; 2 Cor 5:21), and the forensic nature of righteousness (Rom 5:16; 8:1; 2 Cor 3:9).[155] It is true, then, as N. T. Wright says, that one of the "great truths of the gospel" is that "the accomplishments of Jesus Christ are *reckoned* to all those who are 'in him.' "[156] Yet the accomplishment is the fulfillment of a role, not the acquisition of merit. Believers are justified because they are incorporated into the faithfulness, death, and resurrection of the Messiah so that what is true of the Messiah is true of his people.[157]

We could easily survey more perspectives on justification among Anabaptists views, Protestant scholastics, Wesleyan emphases, Eastern Orthodox, Karl Barth, neo-Barthian postliberals, and the "Federal Vision," but I will only look at one other group: the "New Perspective on Paul" (NPP).[158] Since the Reformation, Judaism has commonly been regarded as a religion of legalistic works righteousness set in antithesis to Christianity. This was largely assumed in the works of New Testament scholars in the twentieth century. However, scholars such as G. F. Moore, S. Sandmel, K. Stendahl, M. Barth, and others began to question this view of Judaism as a proto-Catholic theology of merits. This was spurred on by the discovery of the Dead Sea Scrolls, where we read things like, "As for me, if I stumble, the mercies of God shall be my eternal salvation. If I stagger because of the sin of the flesh, my justification shall be by the righteousness of God which endures forever.... He will draw me near by His grace, and by His mercy will He bring my justification" (1QS 11.11–13). Hard to say how that smacks of legalistic self-righteousness, isn't it?

Then in 1977, E. P. Sanders wrote a book arguing that Palestinian Judaism was not a legalistic religion of works righteousness but instead elaborated a system he

---

155. Bird, *Bird's-Eye View of Paul*, 96–98.

156. N. T. Wright, "Paul in Different Perspective: Lecture 1: Starting Points and Opening Reflections," unpublished lecture delivered at Auburn Avenue Presbyterian Church, Monroe, Louisiana (3 January 2005). http://www.ntwright-page.com/Wright_Auburn_Paul.htm (accessed 1 Dec 2010).

157. On "incorporation," see Bird, *Saving Righteousness*, 60–87; see further Timo Laato, "Paul's Anthropological Considerations: Two Problems," in *Justification and Variegated Nomism: Volume 2—The Paradoxes of Paul* (ed. D.A. Carson, Mark A. Seifrid, and Peter T. O'Brien; Grand Rapids: Baker, 2004), 348–49. My argument has been taken up and furthered (far better than I could have) by Kevin J. Vanhoozer,

"Wrighting the Wrongs of the Reformation? The State of the Union with Christ in St. Paul and Protestant Soteriology," in *Jesus, Paul and the People of God: A Theological Dialogue with N. T. Wright* (Downers Grove, IL: InterVarsity Press, 2011), 251–52, 261. On justification and union with Christ more generally see Leon Morris, *The Apostolic Preaching of the Cross* (Grand Rapids: Eerdmans, 1955), 282; Carson, "Vindication of Imputation," 72–73; Vickers, *Jesus' Blood*, 195; Cole, *God the Peacemaker*, 118.

158. For an introduction see Kent L. Yinger, *The New Perspective on Paul: An Introduction* (Eugene, OR: Cascade, 2011); Bird, *Saving Righteousness*, passim.

called "covenantal nomism." The "pattern of religion" in Palestinian Judaism can be schematized as:

> (1) God has chosen Israel and (2) given the law. The law implies both (3) God's promise to maintain election and (4) the requirement to obey. (5) God rewards obedience and punishes transgression. (6) The law provides for means of atonement, and atonement results in (7) maintenance or re-establishment of the covenantal relationship. (8) All those who are maintained in the covenant by obedience, atonement and God's mercy belong to the group which will be saved. An important interpretation of the first and last points is that election and ultimately salvation are considered to be by God's mercy rather than human achievement.[159]

In a nutshell then: "Covenantal nomism is the view that one's place in God's plan is established on the basis of the covenant and that the covenant requires as the proper response of man his obedience to its commandments, while proving means of atonement for transgression."[160] Thus one gets into the covenant by grace but one stays in by works. The purpose of keeping the law for the Jewish people was to maintain one's salvation, not to earn salvation. Now if Paul's problem with Judaism was not that it was legalistic, then what did he find wrong with Judaism? According to Sanders, Paul advocated that the Abrahamic covenant is fulfilled in Christians: "In short, this is what Paul finds wrong with Judaism: it is not Christianity."[161] Salvation is in Christ alone and therefore not in the law.

Others have found Sanders' view of Judaism as mostly correct, but demur from his reading of Paul (e.g., N. T. Wright; James D. G. Dunn) and argue that what Paul found wrong in Judaism was Jewish exclusivism—that is, the belief that if Gentiles were to be saved, they had to take on the badges of Jewish identity (circumcision, Sabbath observance, dietary laws). Thus the problem was not *legalism*, but *ethnocentricism*. According to Francis Watson, the five cardinal points of the NPP are (in good TULIP fashion):

Total Travesty: The Lutheran view skewed by reading medieval Catholic legalism into Judaism.
Unconditional Election: Palestinian Judaism emphasized grace, not human effort.
Loyalty to the Law: They contained ethnic boundary markers to demarcate Jews from Gentiles.
Inclusive Salvation: Paul's problem with Judaism was its belief that salvation is tied strictly to Israel.
Perseverance: Along with Judaism, Paul emphasized grace to get in and obedience to stay in.[162]

---

159. E. P. Sanders, *Paul and Palestinian Judaism* (London: SCM, 1977), 422.
160. Ibid., 75.
161. Ibid., 552.
162. Francis Watson, "Not the New Perspective," unpublished paper delivered at the British New Testament Conference in Manchester in September 2001. [http://www.abdn.ac.uk/divinity/staff/watsonart.shtml. Cited 9 March 11.]

Neither Dunn nor Wright regard their views as incompatible with the Reformed tradition; nonetheless, they pursue lines of argumentation that are not familiar to most traditional ways of reading Paul.[163] The NPP is largely correct in its position that justification has a social dimension in legitimating Gentile membership in the churches without coming through the route of conversion of Judaism via circumcision. Where they are wrong is in some of the aggravated denials that justification is primarily about how we get right with God. We are now entering a post-NPP era, where the emerging consensus appears to be that justification is both vertical and horizontal.[164] God declares people righteous and declares them members of his people. Whereas the Protestant versus Catholic debates led the evangelical churches to a nuanced understanding of justification and sanctification, the NPP debate is leading to a fruitful dialogue about the relationship between justification and adoption.[165]

If one had to summarize the biblical teaching on justification, it could be put in the following categories:

1. Justification is *forensic* as it denotes one's status, not one's moral state. Debates about whether righteousness is a relational term or adherence to a norm are needless. In the Old Testament *ṣedeq* is a relational term (see Gen 38:26 about Tamar), but that relationship is worked out in the norms of the covenantal relationship since a covenant was a legally binding pact.[166] What is more, the New Testament word for "justify" (*dikaioō*) has a declarative and forensic meaning.[167] The LXX uses this word to describe how judges are to "acquit the innocent and condemn the guilty" (Deut 25:1; cf. Exod 23:7; Prov 17:15; Isa 5:23). In addition, in Paul's letters justification is the opposite of condemnation (Rom 5:16; 8:1; 2 Cor 3:9). If Paul's gospel conflated justification and trans-

---

163. The latter works by Dunn and Wright are much more careful, guarded, and nuanced than their earlier works in this regard. See particularly James D. G. Dunn, *The New Perspective on Paul* (rev. ed.; Grand Rapids: Eerdmans, 2008), and N. T. Wright, *Justification: God's Plan and Paul's Vision* (Downers Grove, IL: InterVarsity Press, 2009).

164. Bird, *Saving Righteousness*, 153; Peter T. O'Brien, "Was Paul a Covenantal Nomist?" in *Justification and Variegated Nomism: Volume 2 — The Paradoxes of Paul* (ed. D. A. Carson, Mark A. Seifrid, and Peter T. O'Brien; Grand Rapids: Baker, 2004), 291; James D. G. Dunn, *Beginning from Jerusalem* (CITM 2; Grand Rapids: Eerdmans, 2009), 489; Wright, *Justification*, 126 – 27; Francis Watson, *Paul, Judaism, and the Gentiles: Beyond the New Perspective* (Grand Rapids: Eerdmans, 2007), 6.

165. Cf. Bird, *Saving Righteousness*, 154; esp. Vanhoozer, "Wrighting the Wrongs of the Reformation?" 254 – 59. See earlier Albrecht Ritschl, *The Christian Doctrine of Justi-*

fication and Reconciliation (Edinburgh: T&T Clark, 1902), 93 – 99, 108 – 14; Donald MacLeod, "How Right Are the Justified? Or, What is a *Dikaios*?" *SBET* 22 (2004): 191 – 95; Guy Prentiss Waters, *Justification and the New Perspectives on Paul: A Review and Response* (Phillipsburg, NJ: Presbyterian & Reformed, 2004), 189 – 90; Michael Theobald, "Rechtfertigung und Ekklesiologie nach Paulus: Anmerkungen zur 'Gemeinsamen Erklärung zur Rechtfertigungslehre,'" in *Studien zum Römerbrief* (WUNT 136; Tübingen: Mohr/Siebeck, 2001), 226 – 40; Henri Blocher, "Justification of the Ungodly (*Sola Fide*): Theological Reflections," in *Justification and Variegated Nomism: Volume 2 — The Paradoxes of Paul* (ed. D. A. Carson, Mark A. Seifrid, and Peter T. O'Brien; Grand Rapids: Baker, 2004), 499 – 500; Horton, *Christian Faith*, 645.

166. Cf. Bird, *Saving Righteousness*, 6 – 39.

167. Cf. Moo, *Romans*, 79 – 80; Anthony Thiselton, *First Epistle to the Corinthians* (NIGTC; Grand Rapids: Eerdmans, 2000), 455.

formation then, the charge of antinomianism would not have emerged against Paul (Rom 3:8; 6:1–2).

2. Justification is *eschatological* in that the verdict of the final judgment has been declared in the present. The verdict is one of acquittal and is assured by the continuing work of Christ and the Spirit. In the mind of many Jews, there would be a final judgment, with rewards for the righteous and punishment for the wicked. This "day of the Lord" would be the vindication of Israel as the people of God. Yet Christians like Paul believed that this verdict had already been declared in advance and it was apprehended by faith. The "but now" on Romans 3:21 introduces the verdict of acquittal that has been revealed through apocalyptic manifestation of God's saving righteousness in the gospel (3:21–26). There is no condemnation for believers because God's verdict has already been passed, and it is assured by the priestly intercession of the Lord Jesus (Rom 8).

3. Justification is *covenantal* since it confirms the promises of the Abrahamic covenant and legitimates the identity of Jews, Greeks, and barbarians as full and equal members of God's people. Let us remember that the primary debate that Paul was having with Jewish Christian proselytizers was not about merit or sacramental grace. No, it was whether Gentiles have to become Jews in order to become Christians (see Gal 2:11–21; 5:1–6). When Paul asks what is the logical alternative to justification by faith, he raises the question: "Or is God the God of Jews only? Is he not the God of Gentiles too? Yes, of Gentiles too" (Rom 3:29). Justification trumps ethnocentrism! Similarly, note the purpose as to why Jesus was cursed on the cross: "He redeemed us in order that the blessing given to Abraham might come to the Gentiles through Christ Jesus, so that by faith we might receive the promise of the Spirit" (Gal 3:14). Justification is God's instrument to realize the redemptive-historical promises given in the Abrahamic covenant. In Ephesians 2:8–9 there is a clear denial as any of a work-for-reward theology, but straight after Paul launches into a majestic celebration of how the dividing wall between Jews and Gentiles has been broken down and the church is a commonwealth of Jews and Gentiles in one body (2:11–3:12; cf. Gal 3:28; Col 3:11). Here we have the best resource for confronting and condemning racism in the church, namely, justification by faith.

4. Justification is *effective* insofar as moral transformation cannot be subsumed under justification, but neither can they be absolutely separated. Justification and transformation are both rooted in the same reality of union with Christ (i.e., Calvin's "twofold grace"). In some cases it is unclear if "righteousness" means a transformative righteousness or a declarative righteousness (e.g., 1 Cor 1:30; Gal 5:5). Paul has no category for an untransformed believer. While we

are justified by faith, faith expresses itself through love (Gal 5:6). The gospel of John is a testament to faith in Jesus as the appropriate response to Jesus; yet love is also the measure of true discipleship in Jesus' commandment to his followers (John 13:34–35).

5. Justification is *Trinitarian* because it is "God who justifies" (Rom 8:33). This is seen in the *Father* handing over the Son to the cross and raising him up for our justification (Rom 4:25). Justification only transpires in the sphere of union with *Christ*, and the only one who can condemn believers is at this moment interceding for them before Father (8:34). The *Spirit* activates justification by creating and supplying faith, and the same Spirit that justified Christ (1 Tim 3:16) also justifies believers (1 Cor 6:11).

In light of that, I define justification as the act whereby the Triune God creates a new people, with a new status, in a new covenant, as a foretaste of the new age.[168] By faith we are united to the Messiah in his condemnation on the cross, and we are also united to his justification at his resurrection. To tease that out, God's verdict of condemnation against our sin at the cross is transformed into God's verdict of righteousness issued in the raising of the Son. We are incorporated into the righteousness of Jesus Christ so that his vindication and his obedient act that were the basis for it are counted as ours. Justification also has vertical and horizontal elements in declaring the sinner to be right with God and also in bringing Gentiles into the family of Abraham. Justification is the answer to two questions: "Who are the people of God?" and "How will God's people be put right with God?" The answer is "justification by faith."

5.4.6 PEACE

What the fall produced was hostility between God and humanity. That is seen in human rebellion against God and divine displeasure against human wickedness. That hostility comes to an end with the coming of God's *shalom*, God's peace, that ends the enmity between Creator and creature. Gideon even built an altar to God and called it, "The LORD Is Peace" (Judg 6:24). The psalmist celebrates that God "blesses his people with peace" (Ps 29:11) and "love and faithfulness meet together; righteousness and peace kiss each other" (85:10).

The Davidic deliverer of Isaiah 9 is called "Prince of Peace," and of his peace "there will be no end" (9:6–7). The gospel of Isaiah declares "peace" because God reigns in Zion (52:7; cf. Nah 1:15). About the Suffering Servant, we are told that

---

168. Bird, *Saving Righteousness*, 4; see approval of this definition by Scot McKnight, *A Community Called Atonement* (Nashville: Abingdon, 2007), 94; Michael J. Gorman, *Inhabiting the Cruciform God: Kenosis, Justification, and Theosis in Paul's Narrative Soteriology* (Grand Rapids: Eerdmans, 2009), 54 n. 41; Vanhoozer, "Wrighting the Wrongs of the Reformation?" 251.

JUSTIFIED BY FAITH AND JUDGED BY WORKS

The only place where the words "by faith alone" occur in the New Testament is in James 2:24, where James explicitly says that faith alone does not justify: "You see that a person is considered righteous by what they do and not by faith alone." In addition, while we are saved by faith, the biblical teaching clearly states that believers will be judged by their works (Matt 12:36–37; 16:27; 25:31–46; John 5:28–29; Rom 14:10–12; 1 Cor 3:10–15; 2 Cor 5:10; 9:6; 11:15; Gal 6:7–8; Eph 2:10; 6:8; Col 3:25; 1 Tim 5:24–25; 2 Tim 4:14; Rev: 20.11–15). So are we saved by faith, faith and works, or what? What are we to make of this anomaly?

First, I think James and Paul are talking about different things. When James says that "faith alone" does not justify, he means faith as mere mental assent. When he says "works," he means loving demonstrations of faith. By contrast, when Paul says "faith," he means trust and a complete reorientation of the self to God, resulting in faithfulness. By "works" he means performance of the Jewish law that satisfies alleged criteria for entrance into the people of God who will be saved at the final day. James and Paul agree that we are saved by faith and called to live lives of faithfulness.

The Reformers were constantly accused of being antinomian and bruising the nerve that connects faith with obedience. In response Calvin wisely said: "We are not saved by works, but neither are we saved without them."[169] The Augsburg Confession points out that God's righteousness produces in believers the power for a "new obedience." As I see it, God the Father, in Christ Jesus and by the Holy Spirit, works his works in us so that we might be blameless and praiseworthy at the final judgment. On that day, God's verdict for us at the cross and the resurrection will have parity with God's work in us from the Spirit-driven life of faith. To quote the Tetrapolitan Confession:

> But since they who are the children of God are led by the Spirit of God, rather than that they act themselves (Rom 8:14), and "of him, and through him, and to him, are all things" (Rom 11:36), whatsoever things we do well and holily are to be ascribed to none other than to this one only Spirit, the Giver of all virtues. However it be, he does not compel us, but leads us, being willing, working in us to both will and to do (Phil 2:12). Hence Augustine writes wisely that God rewards his own works in us. By this we are so far from rejecting good works that we utterly deny that anyone can be saved

---

169. Calvin, *Institutes* 3.16.1.

> unless by Christ's Spirit he be brought thus far, that there be in him no lack of good works, for which God has created in him.[170]
>
> Or, to put it differently, good works demonstrate the integrity of the faith that we profess and we are led into good works by the Holy Spirit.[171]

---

170. See Arthur C. Cochrane, ed., *Reformed Confessions of the Sixteenth Century* (Louisville: Westminster John Knox, 2003), 60.
171. Cf. Bird, *Saving Righteousness*, 155–78; Bird, "Justification: A Progressive Reformed View"; Dane C. Ortlund, "Justified by Faith, Judged According to Works: Another Look at a Pauline Paradox," *JETS* 52 (2009): 323–39.

"the punishment that brought us peace was on him" (Isa 53:5). The restoration of Israel will mean a time of peace for the nation that causes the mountains and hills to burst into song (Isa 55:12). In the new creation, there will even be "peace ... like a river" (66:12). The new covenant that Ezekiel prophesied about would be a "covenant of peace" (Ezek 34:25; 37:26). In Zechariah, when the king comes to Israel, he will proclaim peace to the nations as he extends his reign over the earth (Zech 9:10).

In other words, in the Old Testament peace is among the chief blessings that God provides the nation—peace with himself and peace with the surrounding nations. The hope of Israel was for the eschatological peace of God to dawn in a covenant of peace, through a Davidic ruler who would bring peace—a peace that would spread over the entire earth.

In the gospel of John, when Jesus prepared to leave his disciples, he promised them that he would leave them his peace (John 14:27; 16:33). Note also that the first words the risen Jesus speaks to his disciples in the Fourth Gospel are, "Peace be with you!" (20:19). In the book of Acts, the gospel is called "the good news of peace through Jesus Christ" because Jesus brings peace to the people of Israel (Acts 10:36). Paul writes to the Romans that they have been justified by faith and thus have "peace with God" (Rom 5:1), and the kingdom of God is concerned with "righteousness, peace and joy in the Holy Spirit" (14:17). The benediction of Romans blesses the audience with appeal to the "God of peace" (15:33; 16:20). In Ephesians, Paul writes that Jesus "is our peace" (Eph 2:14) and he himself "preached peace" everywhere (2:17), and the audience is to be ready to announce the "gospel of peace" (6:15).

When we refer to salvation as "peace," we often have in mind not the subjective state of inner tranquility but the absence of hostilities. God does indeed provide solace and satisfaction for his people (see Phil 4:7), but the primary element in divine peace is God's work in pacifying all opposition to himself and bringing a relational peace to those who were formerly estranged from him. Across both Testaments "peace" is a core dividend of what God will establish for his people (Isa 52:7; Nah 1:15; Acts 10:36; Eph 6:15). God brings peace to the individual through various peace dividends such as forgiveness, reconciliation, and redemption, which are achieved by the cross of Christ (Isa 53:5; Col 1:20). God brought peace to Jews and Gentiles and unified them in the commonwealth of a new Israel (Eph 2:11–18). The peace of God brought peace to the cosmos through the pacification of hostile powers (Col 2:15).[172]

According to Leon Morris, "peace means the defeat of evil. Peace means breaking down the barrier between man and God. Peace means the presence of God's rich and abundant blessing.... Peace is the presence, the presence of God. Christ 'is our peace.'"[173] It is peace of this order and magnitude that enables us to sing, as Horatio Spafford composed in the aftermath of great personal tragedy, "It is well with my soul."

5.4.7 ADOPTION

Another image used in the New Testament to describe salvation is that of adoption.[174] In other terms, we could call that attaining sonship in God's family. We can relate this to the big picture of salvation as God's plan is to bring the nations into the Abrahamic family and to make them coheirs with Israel. What God does in the new covenant is to bring Gentiles into the family of Abraham by making them coheirs with the Messiah (Rom 8:17).

The Old and New Testament both refer to believers as "sons" of God in a special relationship with the God of creation who fathered them, called them, and delivered them (Exod 4:22; Deut 1:31; John 1:11–12; 11:52; 1 John 3:1–2). The metaphor of salvation as adoption is, however, unique to Paul and is adapted from Roman law. In Roman society *adoptio* was the process whereby an adoptee shifted from being under the authority of his own family to being under the authority of his adopted father. The adoptee would then become a member of the new household and sometimes even be the sole heir to the father's estate. For Paul, adoption and sonship meant becoming part of God's people. While the Greek word for adoption (*huiothesia*) does not occur in the LXX, the idea of Israel as "sons" of God is present (Exod 4:22; Hos 11:1). The exodus was the great act of redemption and adoption, and the same is no doubt true of the new exodus.

---

172. Cole, *God the Peacemaker*, 157–85.
173. Leon Morris, *The Atonement: Its Meaning and Significance* (Leicester, UK: Inter-Varsity Press: 1983), 143–44.
174. Bird, *Bird's-Eye View of Paul*, 108–9.

It is said in Ephesians that God "predestined us for adoption to sonship through Jesus Christ" (Eph 1:5). In Galatians, Paul states that God sent his Son to redeem those under the law so that "we might receive adoption to sonship" (Gal 4:5). In Romans he writes, "the Spirit you received brought about your adoption to sonship" (Rom 8:15). Because believers "are [God's] sons," they are no longer slaves and have been given the Spirit of God through whom they are able to cry out "*Abba*, Father" (Gal 4:6–7; cf. Rom 8:15–16). They are now part of Abraham's family, which is also Christ's family; consequently they are heirs of God's promises and even coheirs with Christ (Rom 8:17; Gal 3:29). The transfer is a radical one since believers have shifted from being slaves who are heirless and fatherless to coheirs with Christ, who are fathered by the Creator God.

Two further points are noteworthy. First, Paul links adoption closely with redemption (Rom 8:23; Gal 4:4–5). While redemption and adoption are a present experience, they are also something to be awaited more fully in the future. As Christians wait for the "redemption of their bodies," they also "wait eagerly for our adoption to sonship," which gives a wide eschatological span to the act of being and becoming sons of God. Second, adoption occurs in the messianic Son of God, and Jesus is the broker or means through which the former slaves of sin and death are brought into God's family and are granted the blessings that go with being in Christ Jesus.[175]

5.4.8 ETERNAL LIFE

Perhaps the most basic and easily understood concept of salvation is that of "life" and "eternal life." In Acts, the apostles are told by an angel to "tell the people all about this new life," which summarizes the message of salvation in Jesus (Act 5:20). John the Elder summarizes the Christian proclamation as the "Word of life" (1 John 1:1). The life that God offers is the opposite of death; it is free from the decay of evil and undoes the corruption of sin. It is a life that shares in the very life of God, and because God is eternal, the life he gives is eternal. In the words of Brenda Colijn: "Eternal life is the eschatological gift of God, the life of the kingdom of God in the age to come. It is everlasting life."[176]

In the garden of Eden Adam and Eve were not created for death; rather, death was a tyrannical intrusion. They were created for immortality and for eternal fellowship with God. God gave them the "breath of life" (Gen 1:30; 2:7; Job 33:4). Life is thus a gift from God. This gift is lost and is waiting to be restored. The whole sway of redemptive history is about bringing the life of heaven to the earthly garden of death.

---

175. On adoption in the New Testament, see Trevor Burke, *Adopted into God's Family: Exploring a Pauline Metaphor* (Downers Grove, IL: InterVarsity Press, 2006).
176. Colijn, *Images of Salvation*, 99.

§5.4 Images of Salvation: The Result of the Gospel

One of the standard blessings of the Mosaic covenant was "long life" (Deut 6:2; 22:7; Pss 21:4; 61:6; 91:16; 119:88; Prov 4:10). It is God's righteousness and promises that preserve life (Pss 119:40, 50; 143:8, 11). In the covenant stipulations, God sets before the Israelites the choices of "life and prosperity [or] death and destruction" (Deut 30:15), and "life and death, [or] blessings and curses" (30:19). There was a "covenant of life and peace" with the priests that bound them to perform their duties properly (Mal 2:5).

The prophetic warnings of judgment and the promises of salvation could take a similar form as is the case with Jeremiah: "This is what the Lord says: See, I am setting before you the way of life and the way of death" (Jer 21:8). That is why the way of God is the way of life (Ps 16:11), and the psalmist asks God to preserve his life because he loves his precepts (Ps 119:159). In Proverbs, God's wisdom—manifested in the *Torah* and the king's instruction—imparts life to the people (Prov 2:19; 3:2, 16; 4:22; 8:35).

Life, especially its preservation, can be maintained through certain redemptive acts. Atonement through blood sacrifice is predicated on the notion that the life of a creature is in its blood, so that a sacrifice is one life for another (Lev 17:11, 14). The Servant of the Lord gives his life in an exchange for others (Isa 43:4; 53:10–12). In a moment of despair the psalmist complains: "No one can redeem the life of another or give to God a ransom for them—the ransom for a life is costly, no payment is ever enough—so that someone should live on forever and not see decay" (Ps 49:7–9). Yet in counterpoint it can be said that redeeming life is God's exclusive prerogative since God is the one "who forgives all your sins and heals all your diseases, who redeems your life from the pit" (Ps 103:3–4).

We also observe something of a transition in the Old Testament from a focus on earthly life to a future life with God. Though the primary focus was a this-worldly life, many were aware that life with God can continue into the next world. The psalmist believed that his relationship with God would endure eternally: "Surely your goodness and love will follow me all the days of my life, and I will dwell in the house of the Lord forever" (Ps 23:6). In some cases, this even edges toward something akin to resurrection, "Though you have made me see troubles, many and bitter, you will restore my life again; from the depths of the earth you will again bring me up" (71:20). In the final scene in Daniel we read: "Multitudes who sleep in the dust of the earth will awake: some to everlasting life, others to shame and everlasting contempt. Those who are wise will shine like the brightness of the heavens, and those who lead many to righteousness, like the stars for ever and ever" (Dan 12:2–3).

In the Synoptic Gospels, Jesus teaches about a salvation that leads to "life" but without explicating what kind of life it is (Matt 7:14; 18:8–9). There is mention of "eternal life," which is equated with the kingdom of God (19:16–24). The kingdom has many blessings, but the principal one is eternal life. Indeed, eternal life is something to be "entered" or "inherited" by responding rightly to Jesus' message (19:29). Jesus refers to an eternal punishment and eternal life in the Matthean eschatological discourse (25:46). It is clear that this life is bound up with resurrection life. In the dispute with the Sadducees about a future resurrection, Jesus declared: God is "the God of Abraham, the God of Isaac, and the God of Jacob. He is not the God of the dead but of the living" (22:32). If God's people are to have true covenantal fellowship with God, not even death can break the bonds between them.

It is the Johannine corpus that has the most to say about "life" and "eternal life." In John's testimony, the Father has life in himself (John 5:26), and he "raises the dead and gives them life" (5:21). In a christological parallel, the prologue announces about the Word that "in him was life" (1:4). The Son also has life in himself (5:26), and the Father delegates to the Son to raise the dead. Jesus is the way, the truth, and the life of God (14:6); he is the "resurrection and the life" (11:25), and there is "life in his name" (20:31). Peter follows Jesus because he has "the words of eternal life" (6:68). Jesus is, metaphorically, the "bread of life" (6:35, 48). The chief goal of believing is to apprehend "eternal life" (3:15–16; 5:24; 20:31), and to reject the Son is to reject eternal life (3:36). One gets this life by coming to Jesus, who himself came to give life (5:39–40; 6:27; 8:12; 10:10; 17:2–3). In his life "they shall never perish" (10:28). The life that Jesus imparts becomes in believers "a spring of water welling up to eternal life" (4:14).

The Johannine letters and Revelation accentuate the theme of "life." The incarnation of Jesus is described as the moment when "life appeared" and brought "eternal life" (1 John 1:2). Eternal life is the reward for remaining in the Son and the Father (2:24–25). Believers pass over the channel of death to life (3:14; cf. John 5:24). God gives eternal life and this life is in the Son (1 John 5:11–13). The Son "is the true God and eternal life" (5:20). For erring Christians, the faithful are exhorted to pray that "God will give them life" (5:16).

In Revelation, the primary images of life are related to pictures of the tree of life, the Lamb's book of life, and a well of living water. According to John the Seer, victorious believers receive "the right to eat from the tree of life, which is in the paradise of God" (Rev 2:7), and life is the "victor's crown" that believers will receive (2:10). Resurrection entails a return "to life to reign with Christ" (20:4–5). The seer makes reference to those who freely receive the "spring of the water of life" (21:6; cf. John 4:14). The salvation of the new Jerusalem is described as "the free gift of the water of life" (Rev 22:17). By believing in Jesus' victory, one's name is written in the Lamb's "book of life," which destines one to experience the new heavens and the new earth (3:5; 13:8; 17:8; 20:12, 15; 21:27; cf. Ps 69:28; Phil 4:3).

Paul and the authors of the Catholic Epistles do not major on "life" or "eternal life" in the same manner as John. For Paul, justification brings life (Rom 5:17), and in Christ grace reigns through righteousness "to bring eternal life" (5:21). Quite famously Paul writes: "The wages of sin is death, but the gift of God is eternal life in Christ Jesus our Lord" (6:23; cf. Prov 10:16). Salvation as eternal life is mentioned several times in the Pastoral Letters and constitutes the cornerstone of Christian hope (1 Tim 1:16; 6:12; Titus 1:2; 3:7). A better summary of Paul's end state for believers would be "immortality," which connotes eternal life via resurrection (1 Cor 15:53–54). In Jude, the short letter ends with the blessed words: "keep yourselves in God's love as you wait for the mercy of our Lord Jesus Christ to bring you to eternal life" (Jude 21).

The living God is the life-giving God. In the Old Testament it is said that "the LORD is your life" (Deut 30:20) and "the fountain of life" (Ps 36:9). In Acts, Jesus is the "author of life" (Acts 3:15; cf. John 6:33), and the Holy Spirit is the one "who gives life" (Rom 8:2, 10; 2 Cor 3:6). God alone is eternal and immortal (see Rom 16:26; 1 Tim 1:17; 6:16; Heb 6:14), and when united with him through the Son believers experience the eternal glory of God (2 Tim 2:10; 1 Pet 5:10). Eternal life is a life altogether different from mortal life because it is everlasting and participates in a life not of this world. Communion with God means sharing the immortal and imperishable life that is part of his very own essence. The gospel is the good news that the life of God is available to all through faith in Jesus Christ. Jesus has not only destroyed death but also "brought life and immortality to light through the gospel" (2 Tim 1:10). Perhaps a good summary of salvation is that *life wins over death*.

5.4.8 THEOSIS

Theosis, also called "deification," identifies salvation as becoming like God and sharing in the divine life.[177] In recent years there has been a surge of scholarly interest in theosis in what might be called an evangelical discovery of the Eastern Orthodox tradition.[178] It is the Eastern church that has had the most interest in theosis as a theological category for salvation. As for a definition of theosis, the *Orthodox Study Bible* describes it as follows:

> This does not mean we become divine by nature. If we participated in God's essence, the distinction between God and man would be abolished. What this *does* mean is

---

177. What follows is partly drawn from my "Progressive Reformed Response to Theosis," in *Five Views of Justification* (ed. P. R. Eddy and J. Beilby; Downers Grove, IL: InterVarsity Press, 2011), 249–53.

178. Cf. Michael J. Christensen and Jeffery A. Wittung, eds., *Partakers of the Divine Nature: The History and Development of Deification in the Christian Traditions* (Grand Rapids: Baker, 2007); Stephen Finlan and Vladimir Kharlamov, eds., *Theosis: Deification in Christian Theology* (Eugene, OR: Pickwick, 2006); Gorman, *Inhabiting the Cruciform God*.

that we participate in God's energy, described by a number of terms in scripture such as glory, love, virtue, and power. We are to become like God by His grace, and truly be His adopted children, but never become like God by nature.... When we are joined to Christ, our humanity is interpenetrated with the energies of God through Christ's glorified flesh. Nourished by the Blood and Body of Christ, we partake of the grace of God—His strength, His righteousness, His love—and are enabled to serve Him and glorify Him. Thus we, being human, are being deified.[179]

There is some scriptural basis for theosis. We read in 2 Peter, "he has given us his very great and precious promises, so that through them you may *participate in the divine nature [theias koinōnoi physeōs]*, having escaped the corruption of the world caused by evil desires" (2 Pet 1:4). In Romans, Paul states that the purpose of divine predestination is so that believers will be "conformed to the image of his Son" (Rom 8:29). A further destiny of believers is that they will be "glorified" (8:30), presumably with divine glory. Paul also wrote: "And we all, who with unveiled faces contemplate the Lord's glory, are being transformed into his image with ever-increasing glory, which comes from the Lord, who is the Spirit" (2 Cor 3:18). This is certainly the biblical ingredients for a doctrine of theosis or something like it.

Undoubtedly the biblical texts cited above refer to a transformation of believers that brings them into ontological conformity, in some mysterious sense, with God. The concept of becoming united with God and even like God was not far from the minds of some church fathers. "Because of his measureless love," writes Irenaeus, "he became what we are in order to enable us to become what he is."[180] According to Clement of Alexandria, "the Word of God became man that you may also learn from a man how to become God."[181] For Origen it was possible to participate in "holiness, wisdom, and divinity itself."[182] Athanasius memorably wrote that the Word "was made man so that we might be made God."[183] Augustine declared, "Therefore by joining to us the likeness of His humanity, He took away the unlikeness of our unrighteousness; and by becoming sharer of our mortality, He made us sharers of His divinity."[184]

Yet the concept of deification is rather slippery. What precisely is meant by being "made God" not entirely clear. According to Jaroslav Pelikan: "The church could not specify what it meant to promise that man would become divine until it had specified what it meant to confess that Christ had always been divine"; later he adds: "The idea of deification in the Greek fathers had run the danger of obscuring the distinction between Creator and creature."[185]

---

179. *The Orthodox Study Bible: Ancient Christianity Speaks to Today's World* (Nashville: Nelson, 2008), 1691–92.
180. Irenaeus, *Haer.* 5, Preface.
181. Clement of Alexandria, *Protr.* 1.8.
182. Origen, *Princ.* 1.6.2.
183. Athanasius, *Inc.* 54.3.

184. Augustine, *Trin.* 4.2.4 (cited in Needham, *Augustine*, 135).
185. Jaroslav Pelikan, *The Christian Tradition: A History of the Development of Doctrine* (Chicago: University of Chicago Press, 1971), 1:155, 345.

§5.4 Images of Salvation: The Result of the Gospel

Union with Christ is, through the Holy Spirit, union with God. All the same, rather than speak in terms of theosis or deification, I think that *participation* and *transformation* are the more appropriate categories to describe how believers enter into the messianic glory of a consummated salvation. Because believers are united with Christ, co-crucified and co-resurrected with him, they participate in the benefits of his life as the faithful one, his death as the crucified one, his resurrection as the vindicated one, and his ascension as the exalted one. That involves a participation in Jesus' humanity, which transforms them into the body of Christ; a participation in the benefits of Jesus' death, which transfers them from alienation to reconciliation; and a participation in Jesus' divine life, which transmutes their state from death to immortality. In sum, it is participation in the person and work of the Messiah that transforms believers' status from condemnation to righteousness and transforms their state from human death to divine life.

I am happy to use the terms theosis and deification, but only as a shorthand summary for describing how, through Christ's mediation, believers are transformed to *share in the divine life that God has* and are conformed to the pattern of Christ in order to *imitate the righteousness that God is*. Anything beyond that is going to raise more problems than it solves.[186]

Calvin is a particularly helpful resource for considering theosis.[187] There are several texts from Calvin that appear on first glance to support theosis: "The flesh of Christ is like a rich and inexhaustible fountain *that pours into us the life springing forth from the Godhead into itself*. Now who does not see that communion with Christ's flesh and blood is necessary for all who aspire to heavenly life?"[188] And, in their union with Christ, believers are "participants not only in all his benefits but also in himself."[189] Furthermore, a wondrous exchange sees believers share in what Christ has and is:

> Having become with us the Son of Man, he has made us with himself sons of God. By his own descent to the earth he has prepared our ascent to heaven. Having received our mortality, he has bestowed on us his immortality. Having undertaken our weakness, he has made us strong in his strength. Having submitted to our poverty, he has transferred to us his riches. Having taken upon himself the burden of unrighteousness with which we were oppressed, he has clothed us with his righteousness.[190]

Calvin can be regarded as "Eastern" if by that one account Calvin's view of participation in Christ, which envisages the incorporation of believers into the triune

---

186. Origen (*Princ.* 1.6.2) evidently regarded "participation" as the functional equivalent of "imitation" of God.
187. Cf. J. Todd Billings, *Calvin, Participation, and the Gift* (Oxford: Oxford University Press, 2007), 13–14, 51–61, 193; Mark A. Garcia, *Life in Christ: Union with Christ and Twofold Grace in Calvin's Theology* (Carlisle, UK: Paternoster, 2008), 209, 257–58.
188. Calvin, *Institutes* 4.17.9 (italics added).
189. Ibid., 3.2.24.
190. Ibid., 4.17.2.

life, as a legitimate form of theosis. However, if one holds up Calvin to a Byzantine standard, I think he fails.[191]

Bruce McCormack rejects the notion that Calvin's idea of union with Christ can be seriously integrated with the Eastern Orthodox notion of theosis. McCormack notes that Calvin's Christology will not actually allow God's essential life to be communicated to believers (and rightly so, to avoid the error of Andreas Osiander that we share in God's essential righteousness in justification).[192] McCormack argues that Calvin has dispensed with that which made deification theories possible, namely, the idea of an interpenetration of the natures. For Calvin, the believer participates only in the human nature of Christ. Moreover, since there can be no interpenetration of the natures in Christ, participation in the human nature of Christ cannot result in a participation in the divine nature. The upshot is that one simply cannot find the ontological purchase needed for a deification theory in Calvin's Christology. In my mind, Calvin is at best an advocate of a soft form of deification (i.e., participation), but not in the fully orbed Eastern sense.

5.4.9 THE CENTER OF SALVATION

In part 4 we looked at what is the primary model for understanding the achievement of the atonement. I argued that the Christus Victor view is the overarching model that is able to integrate the other models together. While the saving work of God includes the atonement, it is also much broader than this, and it includes Jesus' life, resurrection, and priestly intercession. So what is the unifying image for "the salvation we share" (Jude 3)?

To begin with, we can disqualify justification and theosis as the primary structures for a salvation framework. Justification is limited mostly to the Pauline corpus and is determinative only in Galatians and Romans 1–10. Its importance in the Reformation was primarily out of a polemic against Roman Catholicism. Similarly, theosis is based almost exclusively on 2 Peter 1:4, and though prominent in the Eastern Orthodox tradition, it has never really been a serious contender for the organizing theme of soteriology. Adoption is a serious candidate since it can hold together the relational and forensic aspects of salvation. However, its limitation to the Pauline corpus and its paucity even in those materials counts against it as an integrating force.

---

191. Billings, *Calvin*, 54.
192. Bruce McCormack, "Participation in God, Yes, Deification, No: Two Modern Protestant Responses to an Ancient Question," in *Denkwürdiges Geheimnis: Beiträge zur Gotteslehre: Festschrift für Eberhard Jüngel zum 70. Geburtstag* (ed. Ingolf U. Dalferth, Johannes Fischer, and Hans-Peter Grosshans; Tübingen: Mohr/Siebeck, 2004), 347–74; idem, "Union with Christ in Calvin's Theology: Grounds for a Divinisation Theory?" *Tributes to John Calvin* (ed. David W. Hall; Phillipsburg, NJ: Presbyterian & Reformed, 2010), 504–29.

Forgiveness, peace, and eternal life appear consistently through both Testaments. That God cancels sin, ends enmity, and imparts life is perhaps the most fundamental idea of salvation. Still, popularity does not mean centrality, and there are probably better of ways of unifying all the images together. In many ways, any of the three R's—redemption, rescue, and reconciliation—could easily lend themselves to being the overarching framework as they are common in the biblical corpora and are broad enough to accommodate other images under their heading.

That said, I am more inclined to think that no single image of salvation really has the explanatory power and complexity to constitute the underlying unity for all the other images. In my mind, the center and substance of salvation comes in the gospel announcement of the God who saves. This God is the Triune God. Any attempt to define the center of salvation must accommodate the economic actions of Father, Son, and Spirit in the saving event. If God's plan is to unite himself to creation through the Logos with the Spirit, perhaps we could proffer the suggestion that the center of salvation consists of *communion with God, union with Christ, and life in the Spirit*. That encompasses not only the goal of salvation, but also its instruments and its chief blessings in light of God's plan for the cosmos.

§ 5.5 SCOPE AND SECURITY: HOW WIDE AND HOW CERTAIN A SALVATION?

The gospel provides a promise of salvation, yet that promise is in many ways conditional: upon believing the gospel (e.g., Mark 1:15) and upon continuing in the faith and hope of the gospel (e.g., Col 1:22–23). Hence, in our elaboration of soteriology, we are confronted with the question of who will be saved (the scope of salvation) and how certain that salvation is (the security of salvation). These two questions concern the effectiveness of salvation in terms of its span and sureness. In this section we will explore (1) who will be saved and the fate of those who do not respond to the gospel; and (2) the question as to whether it is possible to lose one's salvation.

5.5.1 THE SCOPE OF SALVATION

Throughout church history the dominant view has been that not everyone will be saved. It is not because many have not wanted to broaden the scope of God's saving mercy, but because Christians have generally found overwhelming evidence in Scripture to the effect that some people will be eternally lost. That said, two things must be noted. First, there have been persons who have conjectured that an eternal punishment for the lost is not God's final plan. Perhaps there is "another way" for people to be saved apart from hearing the gospel. Perhaps persons get a second chance in a postmortem state, or maybe hell is only temporary. Or perhaps God simply annihilates the wicked rather than allowing them to languish forever in torment. These proposals, which have become rather popular in the last 150 years, need to be evaluated against the weight of Scripture and in light of the wisdom of the Christian tradition.

    Second, we must also consider the fate of persons who never had an opportunity to respond to the gospel of grace. What about tribes or civilizations who had never heard of the God of Israel or about Jesus Christ? What about children who die in infancy? What about the mentally disabled or the intellectually handicapped? Are they to be assigned to everlasting perdition even though they never had the chance or in some cases even the ability to respond to the gospel? These are the issues we must address.

5.5.1.1 UNIVERSALISM

Put simply, universalism is the view that, in the end, all human beings will be saved. One might detect the potential for a universal salvation in Irenaeus's doctrine of "recapitulation," where the whole human condition is rehearsed and redeemed in the incarnation.[193] For Irenaeus, the incarnation bridges the gap between Creator and creature, it sums up God's saving purposes, and Christ the second Adam is victorious where the first Adam failed. Accordingly, Christ "recapitulated the long history of humanity in himself and procured salvation for us in a concise way, so that what we lost in Adam, namely, to be according to the image and likeness of God, we recover in Christ Jesus," and "he passed through all the ages of life, restoring thereby all people to communion with God."[194]

The notion of God in Christ bringing salvation to the lost sons and daughters of Adam is a key Pauline theme (see Rom 5:12–21; 1 Cor 15:22). Though Irenaeus himself did not think that the recapitulation of Adam in Christ paved the way for any kind of universalism, it was a logic that was followed by others. Origen, for example, believed that the end will be as the beginning. The unity of the created order will be reflected in the unity of the final state. Human beings will be judged for their failure for not imitating God; however, he avers:

> But those who have been removed from their primal state of blessedness have not been removed irrecoverably, but have been placed under the rule of those holy and blessed orders which we have described; and by availing themselves of the aid of these, and being remoulded by salutary principles and discipline, they may recover themselves, and be restored to their condition of happiness. From all which I am of opinion, so far as I can see, that this order of the human race has been appointed in order that in the future world, or in ages to come, when there shall be the new heavens and new earth, spoken of by Isaiah, it may be restored to that unity promised by the Lord Jesus.[195]

Later he adds:

> So then, when the end has been restored to the beginning, and the termination of things compared with their commencement, that condition of things will be re-established in which rational nature was placed, when it had no need to eat of the tree of the

---

193. Cf. Terence L. Tiessen, *Irenaeus on the Salvation of the Unevangelized* (ATLAMS 31; Metuchen, NJ: Scarecrow, 1993).

194. Irenaeus, *Haer.* 3.18.1, 7.

195. Origen, *Princ.* 1.6.2.

knowledge of good and evil; so that when all feeling of wickedness has been removed, and the individual has been purified and cleansed, He who alone is the one good God becomes to him "all," and that not in the case of a few individuals, or of a considerable number, but He Himself is "all in all." And when death shall no longer anywhere exist, nor the sting of death, nor any evil at all, then verily God will be "all in all."[196]

Judgment for Origen is about purification, not retribution. All humans will be restored and will recover their original unity with God. This led to Origen's doctrine of *apokatastasis*, which designates the restoration of all things back to their original state. Whether Origen consistently taught this is an open question among patristic scholars, and Origen may not have been quite so dedicated to *apokatastasis* as some of the later Origenists were. In any case, *apokatastasis* was condemned at the Synod of Constantinople (543) and the Fifth Ecumenical Council of Constantinople (553).

According to Gregory of Nyssa (332–398), God is just and will recompense the wicked for their deeds. However, God's justice is purifying and restorative rather than punitive and vindictive. He stated:

> The approach of the Divine power, acting like fire, and making that unnatural accretion to disappear, thus by purification of the evil becomes a blessing to that nature.... These and the like benefits the great mystery of the Divine incarnation bestows. For in those points in which He was mingled with humanity, passing as He did through all the accidents proper to human nature, such as birth, rearing, growing up, and advancing even to the taste of death, He accomplished all the results before mentioned, freeing both man from evil, and healing even the introducer of evil himself.[197]

In Gregory's view even the devil himself is redeemed by the work of the cross and included in the salvation it achieves.

Universalism never dominated Christian thought, though it continued to be a point of reflection for many and held attraction for a few. In the Middle Ages figures like Isaac of Nineveh, John Scotus, and Julian of Norwich had universalist leanings. The magisterial Reformers were in full agreement about the destiny of the wicked in everlasting destruction. Yet in the post-Reformation era persons began to express doubts about eternal punishment. In seventeenth-century England, authors such as Gerrand Winstanley, Richard Coppin, Jane Leade, and Oliver Cromwell's chaplain Jeremy White composed works in favor of universal salvation. Universalism came to prominence through the Quakers and Unitarians in England and the American colonies. There even arose Christian Universalist denominations in North America.

In the twentieth century, influential universalists included Karl Rahner and

---

196. Ibid., 3.6.3.

197. Gregory of Nyssa, *Great Catechism* 26.

§5.5 Scope and Security: How Wide and How Certain a Salvation?

Jürgen Moltmann. Rahner developed a concept of "anonymous Christians," who consist of "the pagan after the beginning of the Christian mission, who lives in the state of Christ's grace through faith, hope and love, yet who has no explicit knowledge of the fact that his life is oriented in grace-given salvation to Jesus Christ."[198] This was based on Rahner's conviction that God's supernatural grace will share life with every person and that all other religions are touched by God's grace and truth.

Moltmann's "theology of hope" is expressed through his cosmic Christology. Christ is the *Pantocrator* and will, therefore, restore all things in the new creation. For Moltmann a "universal reconciliation" and "reconciliation of all things" is possible, not despite the cross but precisely because of it. He poignantly said: "God's judgment in the Last Judgment is not God's last word. His last word is: 'Behold, I make all things new.'"[199] Moltmann also writes:

> I am not preaching universal reconciliation. I am preaching the reconciliation of all men and women in the cross of Christ. I am not proclaiming that everyone will be redeemed, but it is my trust that the proclamation will go forward until everyone has been redeemed. Universalism is not the substance of the Christian proclamation; it is its presupposition and goal.[200]

Karl Barth also appeared to be a quasi-universalist. His doctrine of election is certainly set up in such a way as could accommodate universalism; that is, the world is elect in Jesus. His famous maxim about universalism was: "I don't teach it, but I don't not teach it." In several places, Barth suggests that on the cross Jesus Christ has borne God's rejection for the ungodly finally and fully so that no one else can ever be rejected. Reconciliation is not something that is yet to be; it is a *fait accompli*.[201] Even so, Barth expressed some hesitation about universalist salvation, not because it might not be true, but on account of divine freedom:

> If we are to respect the freedom of divine grace, we cannot venture the statement that it must and finally will be coincident with the world of man as such (as in the doctrine of the so-called *apokatastasis*). No such right or necessity can legitimately be deduced. Just as the gracious God does not need to elect or call any single man, so He does not need to elect or call all mankind.[202]

In the last ten years several books advocating universalism have been written. Two Quaker ministers, Philip Gulley and James Mullholland, wrote *If Grace Is True: Why God Will Save Every Person*, which argues for universalism. Their basic premise

---

198. Karl Rahner, "Observations on the Problem of the 'Anonymous Christian,'" in *Theological Investigations* (Baltimore: Helicon, 1979), 14:283.

199. Jürgen Moltmann, *Jesus Christ for Today's World* (Minneapolis: Fortress, 1994), 142.

200. Ibid., 143.

201. Karl Barth, *The Humanity of God* (Richmond: John Knox, 1960), 60–62.

202. Barth, *CD*, II/2:417.

is that if grace is true, it is true for everyone: "All will be redeemed in God's fullness of time, all, not just the small portion of the population who have been given the grace to know and accept Christ. All the strayed and stolen sheep. All the little lost ones."[203] Gregory MacDonald (a.k.a., Robin Parry) attempts to demonstrate the seemingly indemonstrable, namely, the consistency and coherence of evangelical faith with universal salvation in the book *The Evangelical Universalist*.[204]

Then there is the culturally savvy Rob Bell with his book *Love Wins*, who opaquely entertains the universalist position, albeit confusingly, where hell is what you make it and it is only temporary. Bell maintains that belief in hell is "misguided, toxic, and ultimately subverts the contagious spread of Jesus' love, peace, forgiveness and joy that our world desperately needs to hear."[205] This makes one naturally wonder why Jesus spoke so often about it!

There are a variety of universalistic beliefs as to how universalism will be achieved.[206] First, though, I wish to note the legitimate appeal of universalism. At one level, the attractiveness of universalism is easy to understand. Those of us who have had loved ones die without accepting Christ will grieve for their loss and worry about their eternal fate. Biblical images of God tormenting people for eternity are sometimes hard to reconcile with a God of love and mercy (see Matt 25:41; Luke 16:23–31; 2 Thess 1:9; Jude 6). We are left with haunting questions about the fairness of God condemning those who never had the opportunity or the ability to respond to the gospel. In addition, statements about God's universal love, such as God "takes no pleasure in the death of the wicked" (Ezek 33:11) and God our Savior desires "all people to be saved" (1 Tim 2:4), may be convenient biblical hooks for us on which to hang our universalistic hopes. However, at the end of the day, we cannot accept the universalistic option because of the overwhelming testimony of Scripture and because of the character of God's justice.

There are several reasons why a universalist position is biblically inadequate and theologically unsatisfactory.

First, the biblical teaching on judgment and eternal separation is lucidly clear. According to I. Howard Marshall the "uniform assumption and teaching of the New Testament authors is that there will be a final judgment, the outcome of which will be justification for some and condemnation for others, and that there is no indication that these outcomes are anything other than final."[207] In the Synop-

---

203. Philip Gulley and James Mullholland, *If Grace Is True: Why God Will Save Every Person* (San Francisco: HarperSanFrancisco, 2003).

204. Gregory MacDonald, *The Evangelical Universalist* (Eugene, OR: Cascade, 2006).

205. Rob Bell, *Love Wins: A Book about Heaven, Hell, and the Fate of Every Person Who Ever Lived* (New York: HarperOne, 2011), viii.

206. Cf. Erickson, *Christian Theology*, 1025–28.

207. I. Howard Marshall, "The New Testament Does *Not* Teach Universal Salvation," in *Universal Salvation? The Current Debate* (eds. R. Parry and C. Partridge; Carlisle, UK: Paternoster, 2003), 56 (55–76).

tic Gospels, Jesus is portrayed as inviting people to enter the kingdom of God and warns them of dire consequences if they reject the message. He urged people to avoid the way of destruction (Matt 7:13). Jesus exhorted his audience that the fate of Sodom and Gomorrah will be preferable to the destiny that awaits those who do not welcome emissaries of the gospel (Matt 10:15; cf. 11:22–24; 12:41–42). There is an unimaginable fate for those who lead others into sin (18:6). Jesus taught that sin leads to "hell," and one must avoid it at all costs to the point of self-mutilation (5:29–30; 18:8–9; Mark 9:47–48). People should be afraid of "the One who can destroy both soul and body in hell" (10:28).

In some scathing remarks, Jesus admonished the Pharisees, "How will you escape being condemned to hell?" (Matt 23:33). In the Matthean version of the parable of the wedding banquet, the guest who arrived without wedding clothes was to be thrown "outside, into the darkness, where there will be weeping and gnashing of teeth" (22:13). Of those who failed to care for the vulnerable and needy, Jesus said: "Depart from me, you who are cursed, into the eternal fire prepared for the devil and his angels" (25:41). The Johannine Jesus testified that at the final judgment, "those who have done what is good will rise to live, and those who have done what is evil will rise to be condemned" (John 5:29).

Paul saw the world as consisting of two classes, "us who are being saved" and "those who are perishing" (1 Cor 1:18). Paul envisaged a day when all people will stand before the judgment seat of Christ, including believers (Rom 14:10; 2 Cor 5:10). Paul can even say that people's sins reach the place of judgment ahead of them (1 Tim 5:24). The delay of God's judgment is a feature of God's patience (Rom 3:25), but judgment is inevitable, and only Jesus delivers believers from this wrath (1 Thess 1:10).

The writer to the Hebrews shares the same thought as "people are destined to die once, and after that to face judgment, so Christ was sacrificed once to take away the sins of many; and he will appear a second time, not to bear sin, but to bring salvation to those who are waiting for him" (Heb 9:27–28). The fact and nature of divine judgment were evidently items of Christian teaching passed on, as we see in Acts and Hebrews (Acts 24:25; Heb 6:2). Hebrews also refers to a "fearful expectation of judgment and of raging fire that will consume the enemies of God" (Heb 10:27). For John the Elder only believers defined by their love "will have confidence on the day of judgment" (1 John 4:17). Peter pessimistically asks: "For it is time for judgment to begin with God's household; and if it begins with us, what will the outcome be for those who do not obey the gospel of God?" (1 Pet 4:17). Second Peter, Jude, and Revelation are consumed with the theme of God's judgment, which brings vindication for righteous sufferers and justice for the wicked. Overall, the picture we get is that (1) judgment is universal; (2) judgment is punitive for the wicked; and (3) judgment is eternal.

Second, biblical texts used to justify universalism are habitually misunderstood. The universalist can point to a series of texts that give a universal horizon to God's saving purposes, and these must be countenanced within our study. In 1 Timothy we are told that God our Savior "wants all people to be saved and to come to a knowledge of the truth" (1 Tim 2:4). That is at a piece with 2 Peter 3:9, where God is "not wanting anyone to perish, but everyone to come to repentance" (2 Pet 3:9). Here God is wanting or wishing (*thelō, boulomai*) for a universal salvation. Such verses have "always been a conundrum to Augustinian doctrines of predestination and the will of God,"[208] on the assumption that God always gets what God wants or wills — but only on the dubious assumption that God's will or desire here is identical with his eternal decrees, which Reformed theologians would deny.

We can speak legitimately of the two wills of God understood as (1) his desire to provide a salvation sufficient for all, deriving from his merciful character; and (2) his desire to execute salvation for the elect, deriving from his glory. Arminian scholar Howard Marshall comments: "We must certainly distinguish between what God would like to see happen and what he actually does will to happen, and both of these things can be spoken of as God's will."[209]

Several Pauline texts are ordinarily paraded out to support universal salvation. In the Adam-Christ typology of Romans 5, we find the statement: "Consequently, just as one trespass resulted in condemnation for all people, so also one righteous act resulted in justification and life for all people" (Rom 5:18). The condemnation of all humanity in Adam is paralleled by the justification of all humanity in Christ. Jan Bonda infers from this that "the salvation God has realized in Christ encompasses all humanity from the beginning."[210] However, as Robert Jewett points out, "the concern is not so much whether salvation is universal in a theoretical sense, a question shaped by later theories of predestination, but whether all believers stand within its scope."[211]

We must remember as well that Romans 5:18 is an explication of 5:17 concerning how those who receive *through faith* the gift of righteousness and provision of grace will reign in life through Jesus Christ. Elsewhere in Romans we read: "For God has bound everyone over to disobedience so that he may have mercy on them all" (11:32). John Barclay writes about salvation in Romans 9–11: "The purposes of God are reducible to his will, a will that initially appears equally set to harden or to save, but turns out on closer inspection, and in the end, to harden only in order to save, to hate only in order to love, and to consign all to disobedience only in order

---

208. Pelikan, *The Christian Tradition*, 4:237.
209. I. Howard Marshall, "Universal Grace and Atonement in the Pastoral Epistles," in *The Grace of God, the Will of Man* (ed. C. Pinnock; Minneapolis: Bethany, 1995), 56.
210. Jan Bonda, *The One Purpose of God: An Answer to the Doctrine of Eternal Punishment* (Grand Rapids: Eerdmans 1998), 97.
211. Robert Jewett, *Romans* (Herm.; Minneapolis: Fortress, 2007), 385.

to have mercy on all."[212] What eliminates a universalist reading here is that Paul is talking here about two groups, Jews and Gentiles; he is not discoursing on the fate of individuals. While "all Israel" in 11:26 might include all or most Israelites, "the full number of the Gentiles" in 11:25 refers to Gentiles who believe the gospel. The big idea is not universal salvation, but that God will save Jews and Gentiles *sola gratia*, *sola fide*, and *propter Christum*.[213]

Moving to the Corinthian letters, we notice these words: "We are convinced that one died for all, and therefore all died" (2 Cor 5:14). This statement must be situated in its literary context, where believers wait for their future destiny by living by faith rather than by sight (5:7), there is a reference to a final judgment (5:10), and Paul's ministry is to persuade people of this truth (5:11) by urging them to be reconciled to God (5:20).

Much like Romans 5:18, the Adam-Christ contrast is highlighted again in 1 Corinthians 15:22, "For as in Adam all die, so in Christ all will be made alive," which climaxes in the favorite universalist statement that "God may be all in all" (15:28). This Adam-Christ contrast is a typology that indicates the consequences of solidarity with their representative head. Though all in Adam die, all bound to Christ *in faith* will be made alive. To be "made alive" is undoubtedly a reference to resurrection. Yet one receives this blessing only by believing in the gospel, as Paul makes clear at the beginning of the chapter (see 15:2). What is more, between 15:22 and 15:28 is an eschatological narrative that includes the resurrection of Christ, the resurrection of believers, a messianic reign to subjugate enemies, and then handing over the kingdom to the Father. It is only after the enemies have been destroyed that God is thought to be "all in all." That denotes God's rule over all things in every way: God's people, in God's place, under God's reign, in the full and consummated sense. The meaning of this is espoused by Augustine:

> God will be the consummation of all our desiring—the object of our unending vision, of our unlessening love, of our unwearying praise. And in this gift of vision, the response of love, this paean of praise, all alike will share, as all will share in everlasting life.[214]

Finally, we may consider a passage from Titus: "For the grace of God has appeared that offers salvation to all people" (Titus 2:11). The problem with equating "salvation" with universalism here should be obvious. The "all people" cannot mean everyone without exception, for the "grace of God" that appeared is a reference to the incarnation, and that event was beholden by relatively few persons

---

212. John Barclay, unpublished paper presented to the British New Testament Conference in 2009.

213. Richard H. Bell, *Provoked to Jealousy: The Origin and Purpose of the Jealousy Motif in Romans* (WUNT 2.63; Tübingen: Mohr/Siebeck, 1994), 152–53.

214. Augustine, *Civ.* 22.30.

living in Palestinian in the first century. Paul's point is that God's saving grace has appeared not only to Jews but to Jews and Gentiles alike, to slave and free, to male and female, to all without distinction.[215]

Third, universalists overemphasize the objective dimension of salvation and neglect the importance of the subjective appropriation that is required. What one finds repeated in discussions from Barth to Bell is an emphasis on salvation as accomplished in the past, at the cross. Yet that is only half the story. To use John Murray's terms, salvation is something objectively "accomplished" and then subjectively "applied." Salvation is past (divine decrees, divine plan, cross, resurrection), present (conversion, faith, faithfulness), and future (entering the kingdom of God, resurrection, eternal state).

Moreover, there is an overwhelming emphasis in the Scriptures that faith is necessary to enter into God's saving promises. In Isaiah and Habakkuk, it is faith in God in the face of judgment that secures salvation (Isa 7:9; Hab 2:4). Jesus repeatedly taught that it was faith that occasioned healing for a supplicant (Matt 9:22, 29–30; Luke 7:50; 8:48). The gospel of John makes it clear that receiving Christ means believing in Christ (John 1:12). Faith in Jesus effectively brings a new exodus: "Very truly I tell you, whoever hears my word and believes him who sent me has eternal life and will not be judged but has crossed over from death to life" (5:24). The authorial purpose of the Fourth Gospel is that "that you may believe that Jesus is the Messiah, the Son of God, and that by believing you may have life in his name" (20:31).

The call to "believe" in the Lord Jesus is ubiquitous in the apostolic message as Paul told the Philippian jailer: "Believe in the Lord Jesus, and you will be saved" (Acts 16:31). Paul taught the Romans that "for it is with your heart that you believe and are justified, and it is with your mouth that you profess your faith and are saved" (Rom 10:10). Paul tells the Corinthians that the message "was preached to save those who believe" (1 Cor 1:21). And the author of Hebrews declares: "And without faith it is impossible to please God, because anyone who comes to him must believe that he exists and that he rewards those who earnestly seek him" (Heb 11:6). It seems that the norm is that faith in God's work in Jesus Christ is necessary for salvation. It is important to note that in the biblical testimony, we are saved *by grace* and *through faith*. Universalists unfortunately define grace in such a way as to obviate the necessity for faith.

Fourth, universalists also adopt a view of the mechanism of salvation contrary to Scripture. Some in the Calvinist tradition like to tout themselves as holding to

---

215. D. A. Carson, *The Gagging of God: Christianity Confronts Pluralism* (Grand Rapids: Zondervan 1996), 288.

a form of monergism whereby God alone works salvation in the individual, while those dubious Arminians and Catholics purportedly teach a synergism of divine and human wills. The problem is that any scriptural system of theology, including Calvinism, that recognizes a tension between divine sovereignty and human responsibility is going to entertain some form of synergism. Unless humans are nothing more than puppets, there is always going to be the objective work of God countenanced with the subjective response of humanity to the divine work.

In the Reformed scheme, the human will is freed and faith is activated by the regenerating work of the Spirit. God takes the initiative, he is utterly sovereign, and his purposes are assured, though I'd hardly call it monergism in the literal sense. Truth be told, the only true monergism is universalism, since God alone does everything for salvation and no response, not even faith, is required; there simply is no tension about divine sovereignty and human responsibility on the universalist scheme. Understood this way, universalists are the true "Calminians," a hybrid Calvinist-Arminian offspring, as they combine the Calvinistic view of the efficacy of God's saving power with the Arminian view of the universal scope of God's salvation. God's love is universal and his power is limitless; what God desires must effectively come to pass. If his desire is that all people be saved, then all people must be saved.

However, this is a jaundiced view of salvation. God produces the means of salvation and also induces the prescribed response. God determines the end of salvation and also the means for it. God's glory is manifested in the satisfaction of his justice, the exercise of his grace, the protection of his holiness, and the effusion of his love. God gives to each as they deserve, though to some, for reasons ineffable and mysterious to us, he designs to show mercy by bestowing the gift of faith. I would add that the universal offer of the gospel does not require a universal salvation. Irenaeus believed that the incarnation was purposed to unite humanity to the Logos so that they might receive adoption. But he also believed in an eternal punishment for the wicked, for those who failed to embrace the gospel.[216] So there is an objective dimension to salvation, but it needs a subjective appropriation.

Fifth, there is another problem for universalism concerning divine justice. Is it the case that the Pol Pots and the Billy Grahams, the Adolf Hitlers and the William Wilberforces of world history, will share in God's paradise with only a temporary detention for the wicked? Does the depth of depravity perpetrated against other human beings and against the infinite holiness of God not warrant a proportionate punishment? If martyrs for the faith receive the same destiny as those that murdered them, is there any point in suffering for the faith? Do martyrs really receive

---

216. Irenaeus, *Haer.* 1.10.1; 3.19.1; 4.37.1.

a reward that is different from what their murderers receive? Will God not answer their prayer and avenge their blood (Rev 6:10). In the end, I have to agree with Dale C. Allison:

> I do not know what befell Mother Theresa of Calcutta when she died, nor what has become of Joseph Stalin. But the same thing cannot have come upon both. If there is any moral rhyme or reason in the universe, all human beings cannot be equally well off as soon as they breathe their last and wake again.[217]

Though heaven may be the will of God, an eternity without God is the will of fallen humanity. For I believe that many on the last day, though they may regret their sin and the estate it has brought them, they will still loath their Judge, will show contempt for the Savior, and will prefer to reign in hell than to serve in heaven.

There is something magnetic about universalism, but the testimony of Scripture and the witness of the broad Christian tradition suggest that it is not a legitimate theological option. The exegetical gymnastics used to justify universalism will not score high before a panel of exegetes. Universalists misrepresent the meaning of the universalesque New Testament texts (like Rom 5:18; 1 Cor 15:22, 28, etc.); they do not deny judgment, but they postulate a second chance or postjudgment restoration to which Scripture bears no witness. Howard Marshall rightly concludes:

> The major weakness in the universalist view is thus that in attempting to explain the few texts which it interprets to refer to the salvation of all people it has to offer an unconvincing reinterpretation of texts about God's judgement and wrath and to postulate an unattested salvific action of God in the future.... The New Testament does not teach nor imply universal salvation. It teaches the reality of a final judgment on the impenitent and sadly it states that some will be lost. That is why there is such an urgency to proclaim the gospel to all the world.[218]

I agree, universalism is exegetically unsubstantiated. Furthermore, a passion for mission inevitably evaporates in the universalist scheme. If everyone is saved whether they know it or not, does it really matter if we make it known?

In addition, the announcement of judgment is part and parcel of the gospel message (Acts 17:31; Rom 2:16), and judgment is partly deserved for not believing the gospel itself (Rom 10:16–18; 2 Thess 1:8; 1 Pet 4:17). For the universalist, judgment is effectively curtailed by their scheme. Let us remember that the gospel is news about destruction and salvation; it is invitation and warning; it pertains to persons lost and found; it is both gift and demand. A denial of a final separation between God and the wicked tears apart the heart of the salvation that the gospel offers. For

---

217. Dale C. Allison, "The Problem of Gehenna," in *Resurrecting Jesus* (London: T&T Clark, 2005), 99.

218. Marshall, "Universal Grace," 73–74.

if we are not saved from the judgment of God, then what are we saved from? For the universalist, the best he or she can say is that by believing in Jesus one avoids an unfortunate though entirely temporary purgatorial state that cleanses a person before entering paradise.

For the universalist, the gospel is news of salvation for all, not an invitation for the lost to be saved. For the universalist, the good news is so good that it need not be announced, for Jesus Christ and faith in him are not, never were, and never will be the necessary means of salvation. But this is not the gospel we have received in the church. The condemnation resulting from Adam's fall can only be undone by condemning sin in the flesh of the Son of God, so that the sons and daughters of Adam, through faith in the Son, attain to reconciliation with their Creator.

We might also point to the words of the serpent in the garden of Eden, who told Eve that if she were to eat of the tree of knowledge, "you will not certainly die" (Gen 3:4). The gospel was required because the first doctrine denied by anyone was the doctrine of judgment. If a denial of judgment facilitated the fall and necessitated the gospel, if the gospel saves believers from the judgment of God against their sin, then denying judgment can be nothing other than a denial of the gospel story. What universalism offers is a mirage; what the gospel offers is hope.

In the end, hell is the necessary implication of God's love, holiness, and goodness. Hell emerges because of God's purpose to unite himself to creation. The earth must be purified of evil *by his justice* before it can be renewed with glory *by his love*. I find Tom Wright's comment to hold true:

> I find it quite impossible, reading the New Testament on the one hand and the newspaper on the other, to suppose that there will be no ultimate condemnation, no final loss, no human beings to whom, as C. S. Lewis put it, God will eventually say, "*Thy will be done.*" I wish it were otherwise, but one cannot forever whistle "There's a wideness in God's mercy" in the darkness of Hiroshima, of Auschwitz, the murder of children and the careless greed that enslaves millions with debts not their own. Humankind cannot, alas, bear very much reality, and the massive denial of reality by the cheap and cheerful universalism of Western liberalism has a lot to answer for.[219]

5.5.1.2 EXCLUSIVISM (BUT HOW "INCLUSIVE" CAN "EXCLUSIVE" BE?)

By virtue of the gospel we are consigned to being proverbial Jesus-freaks since salvation is found in no other name and in no other way other than Jesus the Christ (John 14:6; Acts 4:12). It seems, then, that only a "few" will be "saved" (Luke 13:23–25;

---

219. N. T. Wright, *Surprised by Hope* (New York: HarperOne, 2008), 180.

1 Pet 3:20). What is more, salvation comes by faith (Eph 2:8–9), faith comes by "hearing" (Rom 10:17), and hearing comes by people being sent (Matt 28:19–20; Luke 24:47–49; Rom 10:14–15). But two questions poke in the back of our minds. What about those who never had the opportunity to hear, and what about those without the ability to respond?

By the end of the second century, many Christian authors argued with rhetorical hyperbole that the gospel had already gone out into the whole world.[220] That was true of the "world" they knew: the Mediterranean basin, parts of Africa and Asia Minor, and as far as India. But it was not the whole world. It would be centuries before the gospel would reach other places in the Far East, the Americas, and the Pacific rim. Christian missionaries did not arrive in Australia and New Zealand until the eighteenth century. Were all the indigenous tribes and populations before that time consigned to damnation even though they never had a revelation of Israel's God or the church's gospel?

Several scholars believe that the content of natural revelation, the universal work of the Holy Spirit, and the limited "light" given in other religions are a way of holding out hope that the unevangelized might be saved. This view is called "inclusivism," which may be defined this way:

> The Father reaches out to the unevangelized through both the Son and the Spirit via general revelation, conscience and human culture. God does not leave himself without witness to any people. Salvation for the unevangelized is made possible only by the redemptive work of Jesus, but God applies that work even to those who are ignorant of the atonement. God does this if people respond in trusting faith to the revelation they have. In other words, unevangelized persons may be saved on the basis of Christ's work if they respond in faith to the God who created them.[221]

It is not that anyone can be saved without the cross, but that the objective work of Jesus can be applied where there is an adequate response to the light that is given. Unlike the universalist scheme, which denies the need for a subjective response, the inclusivist maintains that a response is needed, but the response is appropriate to one's historical and cultural circumstances and does not require explicit faith in Christ.

The obvious place to start is with the saints in the Old Testament. Abraham, Isaac, Jacob, David, and the covenant people were believers in God, and their faith was premessianic even if they looked forward to the hope of God's eschatological

---

220. Cf., e.g., Justin, *1 Apol.* 25, 32; Tertullian, *Apol.* 37.4; Irenaeus, *Epid.*, 86. See Tiessen, *Irenaeus on Salvation*, 64–81.
221. John Sanders, "Inclusivism," in *What About Those Who Have Never Heard? Three Views on the Destiny of the Unevangelized* (ed. J. Sanders; Downers Grove, IL: InterVarsity Press, 1995), 36 (21–55).

deliverer. It is not that they were saved apart from Christ, for the cross of Christ reaches back across history to embrace them in its saving power. Could it be the same for others regardless of whether they are polytheists, pagan monotheists, animists, or even Muslims? Even Paul says in Romans: "To those who by persistence in doing good seek glory, honor and immortality, he will give eternal life" (Rom 2:7). Certainly the faithful saints in the Old Testament are examples of persons who were saved without knowing Christ, but not apart from Christ.

In response, I would advocate the Old Testament saints are the exception because they stood within the covenantal promises that would culminate in the messianic deliverer. Israel's faith was a pre-Christ faith, but it was a faith in the same God. We should not expect that it would normally be true, post-Golgotha, for persons to be saved without explicit knowledge of Christ. Still, I believe it is *theoretically possible* that persons in other places, even in other religions, who express a sincere devotion to God, recognize their accountability to him, seek to live uprightly before him, and simply throw themselves at his mercy, might actually receive mercy! God could conceivably look on them in mercy and accept their limited response to his natural revelation as an element of saving trust.

Yet the sad fact is that humanity never responds to general revelation that way. Yes, Romans 1:19–20 shows that God reveals himself in nature, and this revelation does register with people. However, the same passage teaches that people suppress and deny this truth of God from nature to escape the reality of God. Instead, they build gods in their own image and use them to provide divine sanction to their sinful behaviors. That is why the wrath of God is revealed (1:18), because humans do not appropriate general revelation in a positive way; instead, they misappropriate it and retreat to a subhuman state. General revelation is ineffective for salvation, which necessitates a special revelation to make salvation actual. That is why it is necessary to preach the gospel to every living person.

Let me say also that we should respect the freedom of God and recognize the surprising extent of God's grace, for God will have mercy on whom he will have mercy. Yet there is nothing in Scripture to contest the view that those who die in their sins without turning to God through Christ are headed for a dire state. Michael Horton wisely comments: "Whatever God *might choose to do* in any given case, he has *promised* to save all of those—and only those—who call on the name of his Son."[222]

Another area for consideration is the fate of those who die in infancy and the mentally handicapped. A consistent exclusivist view would be that, in the absence of faith, such persons too are headed for eternal destruction. It is here that I think

---

222. Horton, *Christian Faith*, 983 (italics original).

we find the exception to the rule. It is necessary to bring up this topic because in ministry you will be confronted with this issue, and it is perhaps the most pastorally sensitive element concerning the extent of salvation. The problem is that there are only a few biblical texts that guide us. When David's illegitimate child born to Bathsheba died, David stopped fasting and said, "But now that he is dead, why should I go on fasting? Can I bring him back again? I will go to him, but he will not return to me" (2 Sam 12:23). This could mean no more than that when he himself died, David expected to go to the same waiting place for the dead where the child was, though he might conceivably also have anticipated being reunited to the child in a splendid future state.

Notable also is that Jesus held out a special place for children in his ministry to the point that he said: "'Let the little children come to me, and do not hinder them, for the kingdom of God belongs to such as these. Truly I tell you, anyone who will not receive the kingdom of God like a little child will never enter it.' And he took the children in his arms, placed his hands on them and blessed them" (Mark 10:14–16; cf. also Matt 18:1–4). Jesus also showed great compassion for those with chronic disabilities, and he freely healed them (e.g., Matt 15:30–32).

Theologians have dealt with the salvation of infants and the intellectually handicapped in different ways.[223] For Pelagius, there was no problem with infant salvation because infants don't sin and they have no original sin, so they do not need to be saved. Some Arminians believe that God's grace nullifies the effects of original sin on infants until a later point where they reach an age of accountability. Catholics believe that the grace conferred in infant baptism undoes the effects of original sin, so infants can be saved, but only through baptismal regeneration. Many Calvinists contend that some infants are elect and others are not elect and only the elect infants will be saved. Other Calvinists propose that all children are conditionally elect until an age of accountability.

In want of a clear biblical answer, my suggestion is that all children are conditionally elect and do not have Adam's sin imputed to them until a time of accountability. The only biblical argument we can use to substantiate this is Jesus' special affection for children as models of receiving the kingdom, which indicates their special state before him. Beyond that one can only appeal to the character of God, "who is rich in mercy" (Eph 2:4). Moreover, we expect that "the Judge of all the earth [will] do right" (Gen 18:25). As a father, a theologian, and a follower of Jesus, I entrust the most vulnerable of God's creatures to his mercy and justice, knowing that God will work all things for the greatest good.

---

223. Cf. survey in Millard J. Erickson, *How Shall They Be Saved? The Destiny of Those Who Do Not Hear of Jesus* (Grand Rapids: Baker, 1996), 239–48.

FURTHER READING

Crockett, William V., and James G. Sigountos, eds. *Through No Fault of Their Own: The Fate of Those Who Have Never Heard*. Grand Rapids: Baker, 1991.

Erickson, Millard J. *How Shall They Be Saved? The Destiny of Those Who Do Not Hear of Jesus*. Grand Rapids: Baker, 1996.

MacDonald, Gregory, ed. *"All Shall Be Well": Explorations in Universalism and Christian Theology from Origen to Moltmann*. Eugene, OR: Cascade, 2011.

Parry, Robin, and Chris Partridge, eds. *Universal Salvation? The Current Debate*. Carlisle, UK: Paternoster, 2003.

Peterson, Robert, and Christopher W. Morgan, eds. *Faith Comes by Hearing: A Response to Inclusivism*. Downers Grove, IL: InterVarsity Press, 2008.

Sanders, John, ed. *What about Those Who Have Never Heard? Three Views on the Destiny of the Unevangelized*. Downers Grove, IL: InterVarsity Press, 1995.

Tiessen, Terrance L. *Who Can Be Saved? Reassessing Salvation in Christ and World Religions*. Downers Grove, IL: InterVarsity Press, 2004.

5.5.2 THE SECURITY OF SALVATION

We come now to the issue of the perseverance of the believer and the sense of assurance they may enjoy. The two main options regarding the certainty of salvation may be summarized by way of comparing two pithy slogans. For the Reformed there is the bumper sticker, "Once Saved Always Saved!" while for the Arminian there is the counter-slogan, "No Eternal Security until Securely in Eternity!" To put the question bluntly: Can you lose your salvation?[224]

The Reformed view is summarized in the Westminster Confession 17.1–3, which says in part: "They, whom God has accepted in His Beloved, effectually called, and sanctified by His Spirit, can neither totally nor finally fall away from the state of grace, but shall certainly persevere therein to the end, and be eternally saved." The rationale for this is as follows:

> This perseverance of the saints depends not upon their own free will, but upon the immutability of the decree of election, flowing from the free and unchangeable love of God the Father; upon the efficacy of the merit and intercession of Jesus Christ, the abiding of the Spirit, and of the seed of God within them, and the nature of the covenant of grace: from all which arises also the certainty and infallibility thereof.

Whereas medieval Catholicism taught that assurance can be attained only by cooperating with divine grace and by confidence in the fruit of moral effort, the

---

224. Cf. J. Matthew Pinson, ed., *Four Views on Eternal Security* (Grand Rapids: Zondervan, 2002).

Reformers claimed that the fate of the believer does not remain "in suspense" but is guaranteed. After surveying several texts and climaxing in Jesus' prayer in Luke 22:32 that Peter's faith not fail, Calvin comments: "Hence we infer, that there is no danger of their falling away, since the Son of God who asks that their piety may prove constant, never meets with a refusal. What then did our Savior intend to teach us by this prayer, but to just confide, that whenever we are his our eternal salvation is secure."[225]

The Arminian position, by contrast, emphasizes the conditional nature of salvation contingent upon perseverance.[226] Stephen Ashby suggests:

> Since God has chosen to deal with his human creation in terms of their personhood, by influence and response rather than through cause and effect, he allows us to resist his grace—though he has enabled us to receive it.... If, however, as persons, we exercise our God-given, personal freedom after salvation and reject the Christ who saved us, then logically we must admit that it is possible for one who has been *in Christ* to exit by the same door that God had ordained as being the way into union with Christ.[227]

John Wesley in response to John Gill listed all of the manifold blessings that believers enjoy, like seeing the light of glory in Jesus Christ, being made partakers of the Holy Spirit, witnessing the fruit of the Spirit, living by faith in the Son of God, and being sanctified by the blood of the covenant; and yet he adds that believers "may nevertheless so fall from God as to perish everlastingly."[228] Howard Marshall, in his study of perseverance and apostasy in the Bible, concludes that perseverance is assured only by, well, persevering. In the end, he simply embraces the paradox:

> In short, we cannot go beyond the teaching of the New Testament which places side by side the possibility of failure to persevere and the greater possibility of a confi-

---

225. Calvin, *Institutes* 3.24.6; see 2.3.11; 3.3.40–43.

226. I would point out that the fifth point of the Remonstrant article is actually rather ambiguous on perseverance. On the one hand it declares: "That those who are incorporated into Christ by a true faith, and have thereby become partakers of his life-giving Spirit, have thereby full power to strive against Satan, sin, the world, and their own flesh, and to win the victory; it being well understood that it is ever through the assisting grace of the Holy Ghost; and that Jesus Christ assists them through his Spirit in all temptations, extends to them his hand, and if only they are ready for the conflict, and desire his help, and are not inactive, keeps them from falling, so that they, by no craft or power of Satan, can be misled nor plucked out of Christ's hands," yet then qualifies that statement with, "But whether they are capable, through negligence, of forsaking again the first beginnings of their life in Christ, of again returning to this present evil world, of turning away from the holy doctrine which was delivered them, of losing a good conscience, of becoming devoid of grace, that must be more particularly determined out of the Holy Scripture, before we ourselves can teach it with the full persuasion of our minds." Jacob Arminius himself was uncertain about perseverance since he wrote: "I should not readily dare to say that true and saving faith may finally and totally fall away" (cited in Olson, *Arminian Theology*, 187).

227. Stephen M. Ashby, "A Reformed Arminian View," in *Four Views on Eternal Security* (ed. J. Matthew Pinson; Grand Rapids: Zondervan, 2002), 155–56.

228. Cited in A. P. F. Sell, D. J. Hall, and D. W. Bebbington, *Protestant Non-Conformist Texts: The Eighteenth Century* (Aldershot, UK: Ashgate, 2006), 131.

§5.5 Scope and Security: How Wide and How Certain a Salvation?

dence in God and a continuing faith, which as it is sustained by God, is preserved from the fear of falling away. We must rest content with this twofold emphasis and not try to deny either side of it.[229]

The tension between God's faithfulness to the believer and the believer's obligation to continue in the faith is well represented in the epistle of Jude. In the opening of this short letter, Jude tells his audience that they are those "who have been called, who are loved in God the Father and kept for Jesus Christ" (Jude 1).[230] Later Jude admonishes his audience to "keep yourselves in God's love as you wait for the mercy of our Lord Jesus Christ to bring you to eternal life" (v. 21). Then in the doxology he praises the God "who is able to keep you from stumbling and to present you before his glorious presence without fault and with great joy" (v. 24). Richard Bauckham describes the tension this way:

> Jude knows that the divine action in calling, loving, and keeping safe must be met by a faithful human response, and when he takes up the themes of v 1 in v 21 it is to put the other side of the matter: his readers must *keep themselves* in the love of God as they faithfully *await* the salvation which will be theirs at the Parousia. The divine action does not annul this human responsibility. But in his final doxology Jude will return to the note on which he began: his confidence that the God who is their Savior through Jesus Christ can keep them safe until they come to their eschatological destiny (v 24).[231]

The tension is hardly unique to Jude; it permeates the entire biblical canon with assurances of divine faithfulness matched with warnings against falling away. The election of Israel was inviolable and permanent, yet many within the nation still received the due punishment for their rebellion, and exile was the physical outcome of a covenant they had broken by national disobedience. Paul knows that not all from Israel belong to Israel (Rom 9:6); yet he believes that God's promises to the nation will prove effective in the end for Israel's salvation (11:1–32).

In the gospel of John there are promises for the preservation of believers: "My sheep listen to my voice; I know them, and they follow me. I give them eternal life, and they shall never perish; no one will snatch them out of my hand. My Father, who has given them to me, is greater than all; no one can snatch them out of my

---

229. I. Howard Marshall, *Kept by the Power of God: A Study of Perseverance and Falling Away* (Minneapolis: Bethany, 1969), 208–10. Since I know the author, I will provide some anecdotal information. First, it was this book by Howard Marshall that partly led the Calvinist Clark Pinnock to abandon his Calvinism and to head on a trajectory from Calvinism to Arminianism to Pentecostalism to Open Theism. Second, Marshall's book sold so poorly in the UK that Epworth publishers threw out most copies. The volume only came to prominence when it was published by Bethany House in the USA on the recommendation of Clark Pinnock (see Pinnock, "From Augustine to Arminius," 17–18; Marshall, *Kept by the Power of God*, 12).

230. The perfect participle *tetērēmenois* "expresses the secure state of being in God's safekeeping" (Richard Bauckham, *Jude, 2 Peter* [WBC; Waco, TX: Word, 1983], 26).

231. Ibid., 27 (italics original).

Father's hand" (John 10:27–29). But these are matched with warnings against turning away from the faith: "I am the vine; you are the branches. If you remain in me and I in you, you will bear much fruit; apart from me you can do nothing. If you do not remain in me, you are like a branch that is thrown away and withers; such branches are picked up, thrown into the fire and burned" (15:5–6). The Johannine corpus as a whole anchors salvation in the lavish love of God, but it still adds to that the necessity of obeying, loving, abiding, and persevering in the faith. In light of this tension, Köstenberger concludes:

> Everyone who is truly born of God is assured that "the One who was born of God keeps them safe, and the evil one cannot harm them" (1 John 5:18). Thus 1 John, in further development of Jesus' words of reassurance and exhortation in the gospel, serves as a manifesto of Christian assurance, which paints a realistic, yet supremely hopeful picture of Christian discipleship and perseverance, which is ultimately undergirded, not by human effort, but by the power of God.[232]

The Johannine vision is that God's love will bring his children, his true children, into the blessed state of eternal life.

If we shift to Paul, the Corinthian letters demonstrate the same tension of assurance and obligation, divine faithfulness and human culpability. In the opening of 1 Corinthians the apostle writes: "He will also keep you firm to the end, so that you will be blameless on the day of our Lord Jesus Christ. God is faithful, who has called you into fellowship with his Son, Jesus Christ our Lord" (1 Cor 1:8–9). Yet one must wonder how certain Paul is of this when he uses the example of Israel's idolatry in the wilderness to exhort, "So, if you think you are standing firm, be careful that you don't fall!" (10:12; cf. 9:27). In his estrangement from the Corinthians he warns them, "As God's co-workers we urge you not to receive God's grace in vain" (2 Cor 6:1).

Paul is soberly aware that salvation is conditional upon remaining in the faith (Col 1:23); believers can be tempted to "fall from grace" (Gal 5:4), and by turning to unbelief his converts would prove his apostolic labors to have been "in vain" (Phil 2:16; 1 Thess 3:5). However, Paul has absolute confidence in the saving power of the gospel and the faithfulness of God in the past, present, and future to bring his saving plan to its appointed goal (Rom 8:38–39; Phil 2:13; Eph 1:4–6). Judith Gundry proffers a sound summary of what Paul believed:

> The perseverance which Paul affirms, therefore, can only be "in faith." Only the one who believes in Christ can know assurance of final salvation (Col 1:22–23). Perseverance is not automatic. Estrangement from the gospel through unbelief can

---

232. Köstenberger, *A Theology of John's Gospel and Letters*, 481.

break the continuity in salvation and bring its completion into question—or call the genuineness of a person's conversion itself into question. Nevertheless Paul can view the threat of unbelief from the ultimate perspective of his confidence in God, the gracious and faithful giver and finisher of salvation. This perspective enables Paul to hold onto perseverance in this non-automatic sense, always dependent upon divine intervention.[233]

So far it should be clear that the evidence supports the case for perseverance, and the Calvinistic scheme appears the most compatible with biblical materials. There is, however, one final topic we must deal with, namely, the warning passages in Hebrews about the dangers of abandoning the faith (Heb 2:1–4; 3:7–4:13; 5:11–6:12; 10:19–39; 12:1–29). The gravity, seriousness, and sheer terror of these warnings against falling away must give everyone pause for thought. What is more, they are not isolated verses, for they comport with images elsewhere in the canon about the dangers of abandoning the faith.

For example, because of the Israelites' disobedience and turning away from the Lord in the wilderness, Moses told the people: "And here you are, a brood of sinners, standing in the place of your fathers and making the Lord even more angry with Israel. If you turn away from following him, he will again leave all this people in the wilderness, and you will be the cause of their destruction" (Num 32:14–15). Paul warned Timothy to hold onto the faith that "some have rejected and so have suffered shipwreck with regard to the faith" (1 Tim 1:19). Peter similarly warned of dangerous teachers in the church, whom he described with these words: "If they have escaped the corruption of the world by knowing our Lord and Savior Jesus Christ and are again entangled in it and are overcome, they are worse off at the end than they were at the beginning" (2 Pet 2:20). On face value it appears that falling from grace is a real possibility—one that must be avoided because of its dire consequences.

The significance of the warning passages in Hebrews is that they have been the "Waterloo" and "Armageddon" for so many Calvinist exegetes who cannot match their system with the texts before them in a way that is convincing to others or even to themselves. Moreover, there is the possibility that if the Calvinist can be forced under the weight of evidence of these texts to surrender the "P" of "TULIP," there might be a potential domino effect that will eradicate the entire Reformed system of coherence and evacuate its claims for biblical justification (as happened to Clark Pinnock!). Hebrews is not the battleground of the Calvinists' own choosing, but it is the place on which a battle must be fought if we are to include the witness of Hebrews in a systematic statement of perseverance and assurance.

---

233. Judith Gundry-Volf, "Apostasy, Falling Away, Perseverance," in *DPL*, 44 (39–45).

Part Five • The Gospel of Salvation

> ### The Warning Passages of Hebrews 6 and 10
>
> $^{6:4}$It is impossible for those who have *once been enlightened*, who have *tasted the heavenly gift*, who have *shared in the Holy Spirit*, ^{5}who have *tasted the goodness of the word of God and the powers of the coming age* ^{6}and who *have fallen away*, to be brought back to repentance. To their loss they are crucifying the Son of God all over again and subjecting him to public disgrace. ^{7}Land that drinks in the rain often falling on it and that produces a crop useful to those for whom it is farmed receives the blessing of God. ^{8}But land that produces thorns and thistles is worthless and is in danger of being cursed. In the end it will be burned. ^{9}Even though we speak like this, dear friends, we are convinced of better things in your case—the things that have to do with salvation. (Heb 6:4–9)
>
> $^{10:26}$*If we deliberately keep on sinning* after we have received the knowledge of the truth, no sacrifice for sins is left, ^{27}*but only a fearful expectation of judgment and of raging fire that will consume the enemies of God.* ^{28}Anyone who rejected the law of Moses died without mercy on the testimony of two or three witnesses. ^{29}*How much more severely do you think those deserve to be punished who have trampled the Son of God underfoot, who have treated as an unholy thing the blood of the covenant that sanctified them, and who have insulted the Spirit of grace?* ^{30}For we know him who said, "It is mine to avenge; I will repay," and again, "The Lord will judge his people." ^{31}It is a dreadful thing to fall into the hands of the living God. ^{32}Remember those earlier days after you had received the light, when you endured in a great conflict full of suffering. ^{33}Sometimes you were publicly exposed to insult and persecution; at other times you stood side by side with those who were so treated. ^{34}You suffered along with those in prison and joyfully accepted the confiscation of your property, because you knew that you yourselves had better and lasting possessions. ^{35}So do not throw away your confidence; it will be richly rewarded. ^{36}You need to persevere so that when you have done the will of God, you will receive what he has promised. ^{37}For, "In just a little while, he who is coming will come and will not delay." ^{38}And, "But my righteous one will live by faith. And I take no pleasure in the one who *shrinks back*." ^{39}But we are not of those who shrink back and are destroyed, but of those who believe and are saved. (Heb 10:26–39, italics added in both cases)

There are different views on how to understand the Hebrews warning passages. (1) The hypothetical view advocates that the warnings, while in fact real, do not come to fruition because believers cannot actually fall away. (2) The phenomenological view maintains that the warnings are directed at people who show some signs of faith but are not genuine or bona fide believers. (3) The apostasy view asserts that falling away is a real possibility for believers who turn away from Christ and forfeit their final eternal salvation. (4) The community view suggests that in keeping with the Old Testament background in Hebrews, the author is warning a local community about the perils of abandoning the faith en masse.[234]

On the apostasy view, several scholars maintain that it is not simply a spiritual lethargy but an outright apostasy that is being warned about (e.g., "drift away" [Heb 2:1]; "turn away from the living God" [3:12]; "have fallen away" [6:6]; "crucifying the Son of God all over again" [6:6]; "trampled the Son of God" [10:29], etc.). Moreover, the warnings are addressed to persons who are actual Christians, not merely pseudo-believers, since the author addresses them as "brothers" (e.g., 3:1; 10:19; 13:22), those who had been already sanctified (10:29). The author refers to their reception of the gospel message (2:3–4) and having had their hearts sprinkled and cleansed (perhaps indicating baptism, 10:22); it explicitly says that the audience had "been enlightened" (6:4) with certain knowledge of God. Furthermore, such persons are said to "have tasted the heavenly gift ... shared in the Holy Spirit ... tasted the goodness of the word of God and the powers of the coming age," which are most plausibly to be understood as indicating regeneration (6:4–5).[235] Scot McKnight infers:

> The author of Hebrews make it unambiguously clear that those who do not persevere until the end will suffer eternal punishment at the expense of the wrath of God. There is no escape; like children of Israel who disobeyed, those who shrink back will be destroyed. The consequences for those who apostasize are eternal damnation and judgment; therefore, the author has exhorted his readers to persevere until the end.[236]

I argue that the warnings are real, but they pertain not to elect Christians or to false believers, but to participants in the covenant community, who have a share in the message of the gospel and exhibit a degree of faith, but are at risk of forfeiting what they have set on course for. First, we must consider the corporate nature of the exhortation in the letter. It is not individuals whom the author addresses here, but the believing community as a whole. His warning can be summarized with the words: "You [*echete*] need to persevere so that when you have done the will of God, you will receive [*komisēsthe*] what he has promised" (Heb 10:36). As such, I believe the warnings are ultimately addressed to the community in order to ensure that the whole "body of believers" does not allow their community to spiritually deteriorate

---

234. Cf. Scot McKnight, "The Warning Passages of Hebrews: A Formal Analysis and Theological Conclusions," *TrinJ* 13 (1992): 23–25; Herbert W. Bateman, ed., *Four Views on the Warning Passages in Hebrews* (Grand Rapids: Kregel, 2007).

235. McKnight, "Warning Passages," 43–44; cf. Marshall, *Kept by the Power of God*, 142–44. Reformed scholar Alan Mugridge ("'Warnings in the Epistle to the Hebrews': An Exegetical and Theological Study," *RTR* 46 [1987]: 76) admits that in Heb 6:4–6: "There seems to be no reason to deny that these five phrases describe Christians from various points of view, and focus on the blessings which Christians have experienced as part of God's gift of salvation to them."

236. McKnight, "Warning Passages," 36.

to the point that apostasy becomes possible or even inevitable. This also explains the exhortation, "See to it that no one falls short of the grace of God and that no bitter root grows up to cause trouble and defile many" (12:15).

Because the author of Hebrews is addressing the community as a whole, we can expect that persons in that community will be in different spiritual states. Some will be alive in Christ and alert to the Spirit. Others may be lukewarm and lethargic. Then again some might be cold and stale and look back to where they've been and wonder why they ever joined. The warnings will relate to these people in different ways. The warning of apostasy and condemnation remains for all, but the capacity to commit this horrible sin will depend on one's spiritual state.

The church has always been an *ecclesia mixta*, a visible church comprising of faithful, struggling, potential, fallen, and even unbelievers. Hebrews is case in point. The community must strive to prevent those who participate in its covenantal life, spiritual blessings, and evangelical benefits from wandering off. The warnings are in essence a typological application of Israel's apostasy in Kadesh-Barnea to believers in Rome in the 60s AD (see Num 13–14; Ps 95).[237] While not all persons in the community may be regenerate, they are all believers in some form, and they are all on the road together heading toward the heavenly city. The warnings are addressed to those who are, at least phenomenally speaking, "saved" because they show the covenant sign of faith that will lead to salvation. The question is whether all people in their community, especially those who have not closed the deal (so to speak) in full conversion, will continue in the faith and make it to the final destination.

That leads to my second point: in Hebrews salvation is essentially future.[238] Though the present benefits of salvation are enjoyed by the believers (Heb 2:1–5; 6:4–6; 9:14–15; 10:10), salvation is primarily something that lies ahead (1:14; 7:25; 9:28; 10:36), for these believers must still face death (Heb 2:15; 11:5), still enter God's rest (Heb 3–4), prepare to inherit the kingdom promises (6:12; 10:36; 11:13, 28), and come into the new Jerusalem (11:10–16; 13:14). If we understand Hebrews this way, you cannot lose your salvation because no one in the full sense is saved yet! But the community is being exhorted as a whole to be a place where the grace of God is not received in vain, for it is "impossible" for those who share in its benefits and then go on to denounce them "to be brought back to repentance" (6:4–6). They must therefore encourage one another (10:25)—regardless of where they are in relation to God—and not take their eyes off Jesus in their sojourn toward the heavenly city (12:2). This is why, in addition to warnings of apostasy, the author also imbibes sentiments of assurance, because "even though we speak like this, dear friends, we

---

237. R. C. Gleason, "The Old Testament Background of the Warning in Hebrews 6:4–6," *BSac* 155 (1998): 62–91.

238. David A. deSilva, "Hebrews 6:4–8: A Socio-Rhetorical Investigation (Part 1)," *TynBul* 50 (1999): 43–44 (33–57).

are convinced of better things in your case—the things that have to do with salvation" (6:9), and "we do not belong to those who shrink back and are destroyed, but to those who have faith and are saved" (10:39).

Juxtaposed with the warnings are the affirmations of divine faithfulness and Christian "confidence" in Christ's work (Heb 3:6; 4:16; 10:19, 23, 35; 13:6, 15–16).[239] The combination of the threat of apostasy and the blessings of assurance are only possible in a mixed community, and I think that it is the Reformed model that explains what is going on here: "Covenant theology can integrate both sets of proof texts because it recognizes a third category besides 'saved' and 'unsaved': the person who belongs to the covenant community and experiences thereby the work of the Spirit through the means of grace and yet is not regenerate."[240]

Thus I opt for the Reformed position that those elected to salvation will inevitably, though not necessarily without struggle, persevere in the end. It is not that Scripture teaches "once saved, always saved," for the reality is more complex; instead, perseverance is based on the covenantal promise, "So you will be my people, and I will be your God" (Jer 30:22; cf. Exod 6:7; Lev 26:12; Jer 7:23; Ezek 36:28), and it stems from the engine room of election whereby "those he predestined, he also called; those he called, he also justified; those he justified, he also glorified" (Rom 8:30).

We all know of people who have professed faith for a time and fallen away. For the duration of their faith they were "saved," but their true nature was revealed by their departure from the race. The idea of a "spurious" or "transitory faith" is well-known in the New Testament, as evidenced by the parable of the sower (Matt 13:1–23), and admonitions against superficial belief can be found in every biblical corpus.[241] Many enjoy something of God's grace at the beginning, but without completing the grace of perseverance.[242] As John the Elder wrote, "they went out from us, but they did not really belong to us. For if they had belonged to us, they would have remained with us; but their going showed that none of them belonged to us" (1 John 2:19).[243] However, the covenant of

---

239. Cf. Marshall, *Kept by the Power of God*, 153–57.

240. Michael S. Horton, "A Classical Calvinist View," in *Four Views on Eternal Security* (ed. J. Matthew Pinson; Grand Rapids: Zondervan, 2002), 37. Cf. Mugridge ("Warnings," 81): "Perhaps ... *it is possible for those who claim to have Christian faith to fall away from the faith which they confess, but ... God will keep those whose faith is genuine*" (italics original).

241. D. A. Carson, "Reflections on Assurance," in *Still Sovereign: Contemporary Perspectives on Election, Foreknowledge, and Grace* (ed. T. R. Schreiner and B. A. Ware; Grand Rapids: Baker, 2000), 260–64.

242. Peter T. O'Brien, *The Letter to the Hebrews* (PNTC; Grand Rapids: Eerdmans, 2010), 220.

243. F. F. Bruce (*The Epistle to the Hebrews* [NICNT; rev. ed.; Grand Rapids: Eerdmans, 1990], 144) writes: "The reason why there is no point in laying the foundation over again is now stated: apostasy is irremediable. Once more our author emphasizes that continuance is the test of reality. In these verses he is not questioning the perseverance of the saints; we might say that rather he is insisting that those who persevere are the true saints. But in fact he is stating a practical truth that has verified itself repeatedly in the experience of the church. Those who have shared the covenant privileges of the people of God, and then deliberately renounce them,

grace means that God will ensure that his people successfully make it through this fallen world and safely enter the new creation. As Horton eloquently puts it:

> God cannot cast away those whom he has elected, placed in Christ, redeemed by Christ, and united to Christ without violating his eternal oath. It is not because of the principle of "once saved, always saved," but because of the promise that the God who began the work of salvation will complete it (Phil 1:6; 2:13).... God will see to it that the believer, who is always in this life simultaneously justified and sinful, will persevere, enduring the struggle with sin and suffering, until he or she beholds the Lamb who was slain sitting upon his throne.[244]

In the end, what convinces me is not the impossibility of losing one's salvation. For I think people who abandon their faith do in a sense "lose" their salvation. In such cases, their faith, however incomplete or spurious it was, did set them up for a share in salvation based on God's promises. The problem is that their faith proved to be superficial and they opted out of the race. Instead, I am convinced that we cannot lose our regeneration or forfeit our new creation. You cannot lose regeneration anymore than a butterfly can lose its chrysalis. You can no more lose new creation than you can lose a nuclear explosion. If we are regenerated, if we are new creations, we will inevitably and assuredly be saved.

Consequently, Christians can have complete assurance that the God they trust will bring them into the new heavens and the new earth, provided that they remain in the faith. According to Westminster Confession 18.1, as many as truly believe in the Lord can "be certainly assured that they are in the state of grace, and may rejoice in the hope of the glory of God, which hope shall never make them ashamed." It was this sense of assurance that the Council of Trent found so presumptuous in the Reformers' theology of faith and perseverance (though some in the Reformed tradition tended in effect to reduce faith to little more than assurance!). The grounds for assurance, subjectively, are the inward testimony of the Holy Spirit that we are children of God (Rom 8:16) and the steadfastness of our faith (2 Cor 1:24; Phil 4:1; 2 Thess 2:15; 1 John 2:28). Assurance is objectively grounded in the promises of the gospel (John 5:24; Rom 8:31–35; Heb 6:17–18) and the person of Christ (2 Cor 3:4; Heb 3:6).

---

are the most difficult persons of all to reclaim for the faith. It is indeed impossible to reclaim them, says our author. We know, of course, that nothing of this sort is ultimately impossible for the grace of God, but as a matter of human experience the reclamation of such people is, practically speaking, impossible. People are frequently immunized against a disease with a mild form of it, or with a related but milder disease. And in the spiritual realm experience suggests that it is possible to be 'immunized' against Christianity by being inoculated with something which, for the time being, looks so like the real thing that it is generally mistaken for it. This is not a question of those who are attached in a formal way to the profession of true religion without having experienced its power; it is blessedly possible for such people to have an experience of God's grace which changes what was once a matter of formal attachment into a matter of inward reality. It is a question of people who see clearly where the truth lies, and perhaps for a period to conform to it, but then, for one reason or another, renounce it."

244. Horton, "Classical Calvinist View," 42.

These two elements are important in our preaching, exhortations, rebuke, and encouragement about Christian assurance. We need the subjective element as faith is experiential and faith is necessary to keep us in communion with God. New birth and faith are necessary to have assurance; otherwise, we risk giving a sense of assurance to people who have no right to have it—hence, the necessity of introspection (2 Cor 13:5). But equally important, if not more so, is the objective aspect of assurance. We bind ourselves to Christ who is faithful over God's household, and we are that house (Heb 3:6). If we do not look to Christ for assurance, inevitably we will look to something else, such as our works or religiosity, which can have unhealthy consequences and lead to boasting in ourselves rather than in Christ, who gives us cause for boasting (2 Cor 3:12; Eph 3:12; Heb 4:16). As Calvin said:

> Therefore, if we would know whether God cares for our salvation, let us ask whether he has committed us to Christ, whom he has appointed to be the only Savior of all his people. Then, if we doubt whether we are received into the protection of Christ, he obviates the doubt when he spontaneously offers himself as our Shepherd, and declares that we are of the number of his sheep if we hear his voice (John 10:3, 16). Let us, therefore, embrace Christ, who is kindly offered to us, and comes forth to meet us: he will number us among his flock, and keep us within his fold.[245]

FURTHER READING

Bateman, Herbert W., ed. *Four Views on the Warning Passages in Hebrews*. Grand Rapids: Kregel, 2007.

Carson, D. A. "Reflections on Assurance." Pp. 247–76 in *Still Sovereign: Contemporary Perspectives on Election, Foreknowledge, and Grace*. Ed. T. R. Schreiner and B. A. Ware. Grand Rapids: Baker, 2000.

Gundry-Volf, Judith. *Paul and Perseverance: Staying In and Falling Away*. Louisville: Westminster John Knox, 1990.

Marshall, I. Howard. *Kept by the Power of God: A Study of Perseverance and Falling Away*. Minneapolis: Bethany, 1969.

McKnight, Scot. "The Warning Passages of Hebrews: A Formal Analysis and Theological Conclusions." *TrinJ* 13 (1992): 21–59.

Oropeza, B. J. *Paul and Apostasy: Eschatology, Perseverance, and Falling Away in the Corinthian Congregation*. WUNT 2.115; Tübingen: Mohr/Siebeck, 2000.

Pinson, J. Matthew, ed. *Four Views on Eternal Security*. Grand Rapids: Zondervan, 2002.

Schreiner, Thomas R., and Ardel Caneday, *The Race Set before Us: A Biblical Theology of Perseverance and Assurance*. Downers Grove, IL: InterVarsity Press, 2001.

---

245. Calvin, *Institutes* 3.24.6.

WHAT TO TAKE HOME?

- The gospel is a declaration that the salvation of God is revealed in Jesus Christ and received by faith and repentance.
- Salvation in the Bible is holistic and includes deliverance from many things, including enemies, physical danger, death, disability, demonic powers, illness, poverty, injustice, social exclusion, false accusation, shame, and of course from sin and its consequences at the final judgment.
- The outworking of God's covenantal plan is called "redemptive history"; it consists of several acts: *Act 1*: Creation and fall; *Act 2*: Patriarchs and Israel; *Act 3*: Jesus; *Act 4*: The church; *Act 5*: The consummation.
- The order of salvation (*ordo salutis*) concerns the sequence for the application of reconciliation to the individual, including predestination, calling, regeneration, faith and repentance, justification, transformation, and glorification.
- The kaleidoscope of biblical images for salvation includes forgiveness, redemption, rescue, reconciliation, justification, peace, adoption, eternal life, and theosis.
- The center of salvation consists of communion with God, union with Christ, and life in the Spirit.
- The uniform teaching of the biblical authors is that there will be a final judgment, the outcome of which will be justification for some and condemnation for others; there is no indication that these outcomes are anything other than final.
- Christians can have complete and full assurance in the God who redeems them because of God's unwavering faithfulness toward those who remain faithful to him.

STUDY QUESTIONS FOR INDIVIDUALS AND GROUPS

1. If someone asked you, "What does it mean to be saved?" what would you say?
2. If someone asked you, "What must I do to be saved?" how would you respond?
3. Describe in what sense salvation is past, present, and future.
4. What is the relationship between the *historia salutis* and the *ordo salutis*?
5. What image for salvation do you naturally gravitate toward and why?
6. Identify some of the reasons for and against universalism.
7. Is it possible to be saved without knowledge of Christ as Savior?
8. Is there any such thing as "eternal security"?

PART SIX

The Promise and Power of the Gospel: The Holy Spirit

Part Six • The Promise and Power of the Gospel: The Holy Spirit

§6.1 God's Spirit: The Breath of the Gospel
§6.2 Person of the Holy Spirit
§6.3 Work of the Holy Spirit

The doctrine of the Holy Spirit is "pneumatology"; it describes the person and work of the Holy Spirit. The Holy Spirit is important because he is part of the promise of the gospel and empowers the effusion of the gospel from our churches. We must emphasize that the Holy Spirit is a personal being, not an impersonal force. Among his chief works are applying the work of Christ to the believer, regenerating and baptizing the believer, and inspiring Scripture.

> The coming of Christ was the fulfilling of the Law,
> the coming of the Holy Spirit is the fulfilling of the gospel.[1]

> Come, thou Holy Spirit, come:
> And from thy celestial home send thy light and brilliancy.
> Come, thou father of the poor,
> Come, who givest all our store,
> Come, the soul's true radiancy.
> Come, of comforters the best, of the soul the sweetest guest,
> sweetly and refreshingly.
> Come, in labour rest most sweet,
> shade and coolness in the heat, comfort in adversity.
> Thou who art the Light most blest,
> come, fulfill their inmost breast, who believe most faithfully.
> For without thy Godhead's dower,
> man hath nothing in his power, save to work iniquity.
> What is filthy make thou pure,
> what is wounded work its cure,
> water what is parched and dry.
> Gently bend the stubborn will,
> warm to life the heart that's chill,
> guide who goeth erringly.
> Fill thy faithful who adore,
> and confess thee evermore,
> with thy sevenfold mystery.
> Here thy grace and virtue send,
> grant salvation in the end, and in heaven felicity. Amen.[2]

---

1. Tertullian, cited in Donald G. Bloesch, *The Holy Spirit: Works and Gifts* (Downers Grove, IL: InterVarsity Press, 2000), 78.

2. Latin hymn from the thirteenth century.

§ 6.1 GOD'S SPIRIT: THE BREATH OF THE GOSPEL

The Holy Spirit is the third member of the Triune Godhead. In Christian thought the Holy Spirit is often regarded as the personification of the love between the Father and the Son. In operation the Spirit is the energy and power of God who works in creation, revelation, redemption, and renewal. More specifically, in salvation, the Holy Spirit applies the work of Christ to the believer and thus mediates the work of the mediator. The role of the church is to follow the leading of the Spirit in mission, and the goal of discipleship is to keep in step with the Spirit and bear its fruit.

Tragically, however, the Holy Spirit is largely neglected by many evangelicals. They regard the Holy Spirit as the poor cousin of the Trinity. There is the Father (long grey hair, big white beard, shiny white gown, kinda like an Anglican version of Santa Claus); then there is the Son (hippie long hair, well-trimmed beard, and good Caucasian complexion); finally, there is the Holy Spirit, who is kinda like a "buzz" that sets off good vibrations about God when our favorite hymn is sung at church. The doctrine of the Holy Spirit often ends up becoming an empty affirmation in a theological checklist.

The Holy Spirit is eclipsed partly because evangelicals lay such a high stress on Christology. But some evangelicals are also scared of the Holy Spirit because of a desire to avoid the excesses of Pentecostalism. The result is a virtual pneumaphobia. The other problem is that the Spirit is suspect because he is not a denominational or theological loyalist. Indeed, the Holy Spirit is a maverick. He crosses the floor on many issues, breaks ranks in division, and won't be owned by any party. He is impossible to predict or predetermine and can't be bottled up by doctrine or by denomination. He calls no theologian "master" and lives as a free agent, going and blowing where he wishes. Keeping up with the Spirit is like trying to follow the beat in some syncopated jazz music: there is a rhythm, but you have no idea where it is going. Too many churches are passionate for the glory of the Father, are resolute in their Christ-centered faith, but languish in a spiritual impoverishment by neglecting the Holy Spirit.

Thankfully, other quarters of evangelicalism have given the Holy Spirit his due by focusing on life in the Spirit and the holiness of the Holy Spirit. The charismatic and holiness movements, whatever their shortcomings, have reminded evangelicals that they are meant to be Trinitarian rather than binitarian. The movement of the Spirit in the twentieth century has shown that worship can be and should be scandalously joyous. Doctrinal adherence goes hand in hand with religious affections. Our faith is not purely cerebral, but also experiential. For as we pursue devotion to the Father and adhere to doctrines about the Son, it is surely to our detriment that we ignore our experience of the Holy Spirit, who mediates the presence and power of God.

That is not to say that the Holy Spirit is purely an experiential thing; far from it, the person and work of the Spirit is crucial to the faith that Christians profess. The Nicene Creed includes this affirmation:

> We believe in the Holy Spirit, the Lord, the giver of life,
> who proceeds from the Father and the Son,
> who with the Father and the Son is worshiped and glorified,
> who has spoken through the prophets.

The creed identifies the Holy Spirit as the Lord who is worshiped and glorified alongside the Father and Son. His work of imparting life is his chief action in salvation. It was the Spirit who spoke through the prophets and who inspires Scripture. The Holy Spirit is the divine life and divine word given to humanity so that they might worship God in truth.

The doctrine of the Spirit is a treasure trove of riches for those who take the time to quest after it. The doctrine of the Holy Spirit is important for several reasons:

1. The doctrine intersects with so many other doctrines like the Trinity, soteriology, ecclesiology, sacraments, creation, and bibliology.
2. The Holy Spirit is the person within the Godhead who applies the work of Christ to us and enables us to personally encounter the Triune God.
3. The Spirit's work is prominent as he is the agent by whom God works in his people through their prayers, worship, and ministry.
4. The Holy Spirit is the chief agent who empowers the church for its mission, testimony, and proclamation.
5. The work of the Holy Spirit has taken on renewed importance with the debates and controversies begun with the advent of twentieth-century Pentecostalism about spiritual gifts and baptism in the Holy Spirit.

The Holy Spirit should be all the more prominent in evangelical theology because of the Spirit's unique relation to the gospel. The Holy Spirit acts in gospel preaching to evangelize, to execute God's purposes in our lives, and to impart to us an effervescent spiritual life. Several further corollaries follow from this Spirit–gospel nexus.

First, the Holy Spirit is part of the *promise* of the gospel. In the Fourth Gospel, Jesus taught that the Spirit is the one who brings new birth (John 3:3–5). The Spirit was to be given in a new and amazing way after Jesus was glorified (7:39). Jesus promised his disciples that he would send them "another advocate" to help them (14:16, 26; 15:26; 16:7). Jesus comes to give life, and this life is the spiritual life that pours forth like a fountain (6:63; 7:38; 10:10). The apostle Peter told the Jerusalem crowd: "Repent and be baptized, every one of you, in the name of Jesus Christ for the forgiveness of your sins. And you will receive the gift of the Holy Spirit" (Acts 2:38). The gift of the Spirit authenticates Jesus' ministry and indwells believers to animate their hearts with divine power.

Paul taught that those who have been reconciled to God experience his love being "poured out into our hearts through the Holy Spirit, who has been given to us" (Rom 5:5). He admonishes the Galatians for retreating to the law when they received the Holy Spirit through believing the gospel (Gal 3:1–5). The Spirit is sent into the hearts of believers so that they can address God as "Abba" or "Father" (4:6). To the Ephesians Paul teaches, "When you believed, you were marked in him with a seal, the promised Holy Spirit" (Eph 1:13). The receipt of the Holy Spirit is one of the chief blessings of faith, since he imparts life, quickens the soul, and unites us to God.

Second, the Holy Spirit is the great *liberator* of humanity. He acts to set people free. The end of Israel's exile would be enacted by the Spirit-anointed Servant of the Lord proclaiming freedom to captives (Isa 61:1). Jesus claimed to be fulfilling such a program in his ministry of healing, proclamation, and fellowship with outsiders (Luke 4:18). According to the apostle Paul, it is the Spirit who sets believers free from the law of sin and death (Rom 8:2). He affirms in dramatic fashion that "where the Spirit of the Lord is, there is freedom" (2 Cor 3:17). The Spirit of God is God acting to release and redeem his people from enslaving powers. The Spirit frees us from sin, from guilt, and from human-centered traditions that draw us away from God. The Holy Spirit frees us to call God our Father, Christ our brother, and the Spirit our Comforter.

As Karl Barth put it, the Holy Spirit imparts "freedom, freedom to have a Lord, this Lord, God, as Lord."[3] The Holy Spirit enables us to yield ourselves up to God in obedience and to live as authentic human beings in freedom—a freedom that is apprehended in the free decision of Christ to be Savior and a freedom that is sanctified and offered up in devotion to the Father. According to Barth, the power of the Holy Spirit is "the power of our liberation accomplished already in the freedom of

---

3. Karl Barth, *CD*, I/1:457.

Jesus Christ: our liberation from the compulsion of continuing in our disobedience now that the Son of God has humbled Himself to be one of us and to be obedient in our place; and our liberation for a life as the brother of that royal and exalted man."[4] Precisely because God is the one who loves in freedom—a major motif for Barth—freedom is the outflow of the redeeming love of God.

Third, the Holy Spirit is the *empowerer* of the gospel. When the risen Jesus said to the eleven disciples, "As the Father has sent me, I am sending you," the next thing he did was to breathe on them and say, "Receive the Holy Spirit," in order to parabolically demonstrate that the Spirit would help them in their witness (John 20:21–22). At the beginning of Acts, Jesus promised the disciples that "you will receive power when the Holy Spirit comes on you" for the express purpose to "be my witnesses in Jerusalem, and in all Judea and Samaria, and to the ends of the earth" (Acts 1:8). Throughout the narrative of Acts, the Spirit fills people to proclaim the gospel message about salvation through the Lord Jesus Christ. The Spirit is the director of the dramatic mission of the church (4:8, 31; 6:10; 7:55; 11:24; 13:9).

Paul reminds the Thessalonians how "our gospel came to you not simply with words but also with power, with the Holy Spirit and deep conviction" (1 Thess 1:5). He later describes his ministry as depending on the "power of the Spirit of God" as Paul "fully proclaimed the gospel of Christ" from Jerusalem all the way around to Illyricum (Rom 15:19). In other words, the work of the gospel is achieved through the work of the Spirit. The fruit of the gospel is the harvest of the Spirit's work in the churches. The gospel can be seen as the ultimate union of Word and Spirit in the spheres of proclamation. The Spirit is what makes the proclamation of the "word of the gospel" effective. The Spirit is the magnetism that makes Christians gather, but he is also the propulsion that makes Christians go and proclaim the message of Christ.

FURTHER READING

Bloesch, Donald G. *The Holy Spirit: Works and Gifts*. Downers Grove, IL: InterVarsity Press, 2000.

Cole, Graham. *He Who Gives Life: The Doctrine of the Holy Spirit*. Wheaton, IL: Crossway, 2007.

Ferguson, Sinclair. *The Holy Spirit*. Downers Grove, IL: InterVarsity Press, 1997.

Kärkkäinen, Veli-Matti. *Pneumatology: The Holy Spirit in Ecumenical, International, and Contextual Perspective*. Grand Rapids: Baker, 2002.

McIntyre, John. *The Shape of Pneumatology*. Edinburgh: T&T Clark, 1997.

Schreiner, Thomas R. *New Testament Theology: Magnifying God in Christ*. Grand Rapids: Baker Academic, 2008), esp. 431–506.

---

4. Ibid., IV/2: 311–12.

§ 6.2 PERSON OF THE HOLY SPIRIT

I have to confess I was more than a little alarmed when I once preached about the Holy Spirit and many parishioners told me how mind-blowing it was for them to learn that the Holy Spirit is an actual person—a divine person no less. Before that they had always thought of the Holy Spirit as like "the Force" from *Star Wars*, powerful but impersonal. I have learned that many Christians tend to equate the Holy Spirit with some kind of divine vibe that floats between the Father and the believer. This is most unsatisfactory. We must bring our churches back to their creedal and confessional heritage that the Holy Spirit is of "one substance, power, and eternity" with the Father and Son.[5]

6.2.1 HOLY SPIRIT AS A PERSONAL BEING

Much theological debate has concerned itself with the question of whether the third person of the Trinity is in fact a real person with distinctive traits and character, or whether he/it is simply the action or power of God. The Spirit has been described as "the common Spirit of the Christian society" (Friedrich Schleiermacher), "the principle of evolution" (Jürgen Moltmann), or "serendipitous creativity" (Clark Pinnock).[6] The New Testament does occasionally use impersonal categories for the presence and activity of the Spirit. When Jesus promised the Holy Spirit, he promised his disciples "power from on high" (Luke 24:49; Acts 1:8). On the day of Pentecost, the Spirit's activity was like a "rushing wind" that fell on the disciples, likened to "tongues of fire," and it "filled" them like liquid filling a cup (Acts 2:1–4). In Paul's letters, the Spirit is like the firstfruits of a harvest (Rom 8:23), a seal (Eph 1:13), and a deposit of something yet to come (1:14). So is the Holy Spirit personal or impersonal, a divine person or a divine power?

Well, it comes down to a definition. Personhood is a complex matter, but we are safe to say that a person is a living being (no robot, imaginary friend, or pet rock), who is self-aware, capable of cognition, is able to relate to other beings, and

---

5. Thirty-Nine Articles, art. 1; WCF 2.3. 6. Bloesch, *The Holy Spirit*, 51.

possesses recognizable character traits. A person is someone who can distinguish "I" from "you." God the Father is obviously a person as the great "I am" (Exod 3:14), and Jesus is also a person who speaks in the first person (e.g., Matt 5:22; John 14:6). The Holy Spirit speaks with an "I" on at least one occasion when he spoke through a prophet and said: "Set apart for me Barnabas and Saul for the work to which I have called them" (Acts 13:2).

Elsewhere in the NT we find activities and roles attributed to the Spirit that imply he is a personal agent. Jesus promised to send the Holy Spirit who would come as another *paraklētos*. The translation of *paraklētos* is notoriously complex; it can mean something like "Comforter," "Advocate," or "Helper" (John 14:16, 15:26–27; 16:7). The Holy Spirit is "another *paraklētos*," who continues the ministry of Jesus in the midst of the disciples as sent from the Father (14:16). His role is to witness, convict, guide, hear, speak, glorify, and declare (16:8–15).

Paul's discourse in Romans 8 contains further images of the Spirit as an active person. There is the leading of the Holy Spirit to our becoming sons of God (Rom 8:14), the witness of the Spirit to our own spirit (8:16; cf. Acts 5:32), and the help of the Spirit in prayer (Rom 8:26). The intercessory work of the Spirit is linked to the "mind of the Spirit" (8:27). The Spirit of God knows the thoughts of God (1 Cor 2:11), and it is the Spirit who decides how the grace gifts are to be distributed among the church (12:11).

The Spirit can be insulted (Heb 10:29) and blasphemed (Matt 12:31–32). From the Spirit of God comes encouragement (Acts 9:31), and the "Spirit of Jesus" prevented Paul from going into Bithynia (16:7). Elsewhere Paul speaks of "grieving" the Holy Spirit (Eph 4:30); Isaiah also refers to Yahweh's Holy Spirit being grieved by Israel's rebellion (Isa 63:10). Bruce Milne reminds us that one can resist a power, but you can only grieve a person.[7] Finally, the benediction in 2 Corinthians 13:14 is an "impoverished blessing if interpreted in an Arian or Modalist sense."[8] The unstudied coherence of such texts makes a compelling witness to the divine dignity and personal authority of the Holy Spirit.

The Holy Spirit is not Jesus' vapor trail or a divine fog that descends from heaven. He is a person with personality, purpose, and prerogatives.

6.2.2 HOLY SPIRIT AS GOD

The logic of the gospel is that God is the author, actor, and applier of salvation. The application of salvation to the believer is accomplished by God the Holy Spirit. It must be admitted that it is harder to establish the full and equal deity of the Holy

---

7. Bruce Milne, *Know the Truth* (3rd ed.; Downers Grove, IL: InterVarsity Press, 2009), 222.

8. Sinclair Ferguson, *The Holy Spirit* (Downers Grove, IL: InterVarsity Press, 1997), 31.

Spirit since we have far fewer references to the Holy Spirit in Scripture than to the deity of Christ. Also, in the church fathers, the doctrine of the deity of the Holy Spirit was established relatively slowly, mostly taking a backseat to the christological debates about Jesus' deity and natures. Yet that is not to say that there is no biblical warrant for the doctrine; indeed, there is, and the church fathers prosecuted the logic of Scripture when they identified the Spirit of God as a coequal and coeternal member of the Triune Godhead.

To begin with, there are references to the Holy Spirit in the New Testament that are references to God. For instance, Peter told Ananias that his lying about the property he and his wife sold was a lie to the Holy Spirit; then, in the next verse, Peter adds that Ananias was lying "to God" (Acts 5:3–4). Similarly, Paul told the Corinthians that the body of believers is a "temple of God" (1 Cor 3:16–17), and later the body of believers is referred to as a "temple of the Holy Spirit" (6:19–20). At one point, Paul even says that the "Lord is the Spirit" (2 Cor 3:17). It is commonly said that God raised up Jesus from the dead (Acts 2:24, 32; 3:26; 4:10; 5:30; 10:40; 13:30; 13:37; Rom 10:9; Gal 1:1; 1 Pet 1:21), and yet it is stated elsewhere that the Spirit raised up Jesus (Rom 8:11). In the Gospels it is possible to commit blasphemy against the Holy Spirit; this makes sense only if the Spirit is in some sense God (Matt 12:28–31).

The Holy Spirit also possesses the qualities and attributes of God. The Holy Spirit is omniscient to the point that no one comprehends the thoughts of God except the "Spirit of God" (1 Cor 2:10–11). The Holy Spirit is also regarded as the presence of divine power when described as the "the power of the Most High" (Luke 1:35). The Holy Spirit is described as the "eternal Spirit" (Heb 9:14). The Spirit is also a key agent in the act of creation (Gen 1:2; Job 26:13; 33:4; Ps 104:30). The Holy Spirit is omnipresent and can be found in heaven, earth, and even in Sheol (Ps 139:7–10). God's speaking to and through human subjects is often attributed to the agency of the Holy Spirit as the divine voice heard through speakers (Acts 4:25, 31; 28:25–27).

Just like patristic Christology, the doctrine of the Holy Spirit as a full and equal member of the Godhead had to emerge through a series of polemical debates among the church fathers. The Holy Spirit was often treated as a tertiary character who was subordinated to the Son, who was himself subordinated to the Father. Arius regarded the Holy Spirit as something created by the Son, creating a triarchy of Father, Son, and Spirit, with three tiers of authority, rather than a Trinity comprising three equal persons with a shared divine essence. Bishop Macedonius of Constantinople also believed that the Spirit was a spiritual creature subordinated to the Son.

The deity of the Holy Spirit was affirmed at the Council of Constantinople, where it was added to the Nicene Creed that the Holy Spirit is "the Lord, the giver of life, who proceeds from the Father, who with the Father and the Son is worshiped and glorified." Such a theological claim was justifiable since, as we have seen, there is enough evidence in Scripture for regarding the Holy Spirit as part of the divine identity; that is, the Christian God must be defined in relation to the persons of the Father, Son, and Holy Spirit. What is more, in order for the Spirit to mediate the presence of Christ and the Father, the Spirit must participate in the identity of God. Or else there is a gaping hole between God's saving action and its application to the believer. Only a personal and fully divine Spirit can effect the salvation that is wrought by the Father and the Son and also affect the spiritual disposition of men and women to God. A semi-divine being cannot unite us to the divine any more than a tree can unite us to the stars; an impersonal force cannot unite us to a person any more than a rock can lead us to rabbit.

According to many of the church fathers, the Holy Spirit belongs in a coordinate series with the Father and the Son. It was Clement of Rome, writing in the first century, who said: "Have we not one God, and one Messiah, and one Spirit of grace poured upon us?"[9] Basil of Caesarea (ca. 330–79) wrote an important work *On the Holy Spirit* to defend the deity of the Spirit. Basil assigned distinct operations, also called "appropriations," to the members of the Trinity. The Father is the "original cause of all things made," the Son is the "creative cause," and the Spirit is the "perfecting cause."[10] Though all three persons of the Godhead are involved in creation, redemption, and sanctification, the logic of Scripture assigns a lead role to one person for certain respective tasks: Father: creation; Son: redemption; and Holy Spirit: renewal. Basil also argued that the same glory, honor, and worship given to the Father and the Son must also be given to the Holy Spirit.

---

9. *1 Clem.* 46.6.

10. Basil of Caesarea, *On the Holy Spirit*, 16.38.

FLIPPING OUT ABOUT THE FILIOQUE CONTROVERSY

In order to ensure the conversion of the Goths from Arianism to Catholicism, the Roman church required the Goths to affirm a Latin version of the Niceno-Constantinopolitan Creed that had the Latin word *filioque* added, whereby the Holy Spirit proceeds from the Father *and the Son*, a statement no Arian could affirm. The problem is, who had the authority to change the ecumenical creeds of the church? This addition of the *filioque* clause alarmed Eastern Orthodox Christians, especially when Pope Benedict VIII finally ratified the addition in 1014. This unilateral addition, among other political machinations of the time, led to an eventual split between the Eastern and Western churches in 1054.

The Eastern church took an Irenaean view, where the Son and Spirit are distinguished through their eternal relations with the Father. The Son is distinguished from the Father as the one eternally begotten by the Father, while the Spirit is distinguished from the Father as the one eternally breathed out by the Father. The primary concern on the Eastern view was to uphold the Father "as the sole origin and source of divinity," a conviction that was perceived to be put at risk by the *filioque* addition since it potentially confused the persons of the Father and the Son.[11]

In contrast, the Western church took an Augustinian view, where the Father eternally begets the Son, but the Spirit is jointly and eternally breathed out by them both.[12] From this Augustinian vantage point, it made no sense to say that the Spirit proceeded from the Father alone, given that all members of the Trinity shared the divine nature and shared in the economic operations.[13] Here there is a "double breathing" of the Spirit by the Father and the Son, which ensures that Son and Spirit are not confused.[14] McGrath illustrates the differences between the two positions as follows:[15]

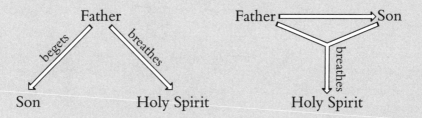

---

11. John S. Feinberg, *No One Like Him: The Doctrine of God* (Wheaton, IL: Crossway, 2001), 485.
12. Graham Cole, *He Who Gives Life: The Doctrine of the Holy Spirit* (Wheaton, IL: Crossway, 2007), 77.
13. Feinberg, *No One Like Him*, 485.
14. Cole, *He Who Gives Life*, 77.
15. Alistair McGrath, *Christian Theology: An Introduction* (Oxford: Blackwell, 2001), 325 (I must thank Ovi Buciu for bringing this diagram to my attention).

Little would be lost to the essence of the Latin version of the Nicene Creed by dropping the *filioque* clause. Generally speaking, no one is in danger of giving it an Arian spin these days. Also, dropping the clause would facilitate closer unity between the Eastern and Western churches. Thus, some would like to repeal the *filioque* clause.

Nonetheless, there are good reasons for keeping the *filioque* clause, especially if we closely correlate the economic Trinity with the immanent Trinity (i.e., what the Triune God does in his operations tells us something about the inner relationships within the Triune God). First, if the Spirit of God proceeds directly from the Father without the Son, there may be a theological argument that this same Spirit may relate adherents of other religions directly to the Father without the need for the mediatorship of the Son. A Father–Spirit procession makes it possible, in theory, to share in the Spirit without the work of the Son.[16]

Second, there is good biblical evidence that the Spirit is christologically endowed. In the Fourth Gospel, the Spirit is sent by the Father in Jesus' name (John 14:26). Jesus even refers to the Advocate "whom I will send to you from the Father—the Spirit of truth who goes out from the Father—he will testify about me" (15:26). Later Jesus tells his disciples that unless he returns to the Father, "the Advocate will not come to you; but if I go, I will send him to you" (16:7). The so-called "Johannine Pentecost," where Jesus breathes on the disciples and says, "Receive the Holy Spirit," is arguably a parabolic action designed to remind the disciples that when they receive the Spirit, they should remember who it was who sent him to them (20:22). This Johannine text was important to Augustine's formulation, and so he wrote:

> Nor do I see what else He intended to signify, when He breathed on the face of the disciples, and said, "Receive ye the Holy Ghost." For that bodily breathing, proceeding from the body with the feeling of bodily touching, was not the substance of the Holy Spirit, but a declaration by a fitting sign, that the Holy Spirit proceeds not only from the Father, but also from the Son.[17]

Burgess, Stanley M. *The Holy Spirit: Eastern Christian Traditions.* Peabody, MA: Hendrickson, 1989.

Bray, Gerald. "The *Filioque* Clause in History and Theology." *TynBul* 34 (1983): 91–144.

———. "The Double Procession of the Holy Spirit in Evangelical Theology Today: Do We Still Need It?" *JETS* 41 (1998): 415–26.

---

16. Cf. Bloesch, *The Holy Spirit*, 16; Cole, *He Who Gives Life*, 78.
17. Augustine, *Trin.* 4.20.

§ 6.3 WORK OF THE HOLY SPIRIT

What the gospel promises, the Holy Spirit actualizes: life, love, and hope. The work of the Holy Spirit is a significant feature of Trinitarian theology because the Holy Spirit is the workhorse of the Trinity. He is the love between Father and Son. He is the grace between Christ and the believer. He is the power of God's presence and the presence of God's power in both creation and redemption. The Holy Spirit turns theology into experience by drawing us into the life of God. The Holy Spirit is the deposit of our hope known in the present and the actualizer of that hope to be realized in the future. If there were no Holy Spirit, there would be nothing to bind us to Christ and to apply his redemptive work to us. There would be no revelation and no way to comprehend it. The Holy Spirit explains how the invisible God works in his creation without becoming confused with it.

6.3.1 SPIRIT AND CREATION

The Holy Spirit is present in God's creative work to bring creation into being and to infuse life into its human subjects. The Old Testament affirms the role of the Spirit for his primeval creative act and for giving "breath" to humanity.

> In the beginning God created the heavens and the earth. Now the earth was formless and empty, darkness was over the surface of the deep, and *the Spirit*[18] *of God was hovering over the waters*. (Gen 1:1–2)

> By his power he churned up the sea; by his wisdom he cut Rahab to pieces. *By his breath the skies became fair*; his hand pierced the gliding serpent. (Job 26:12–13)

> The Spirit of God has made me; the breath of the Almighty gives me life. (Job 33:4)

> *When you send your Spirit, they are created*, and you renew the face of the ground. May the glory of the Lord endure forever; may the Lord rejoice in his works—he who

---

18. On the translation issues related to *rûaḥ*, specifically, whether it means "Spirit," "spirit," "wind," or "breath," see Cole, *He Who Gives Life*, 96–100.

looks at the earth, and it trembles, who touches the mountains, and they smoke. (Ps 104:30–32)

Who has measured the waters in the hollow of his hand, *or with the breadth of his hand marked off the heavens*? Who has held the dust of the earth in a basket, or weighed the mountains on the scales and the hills in a balance? *Who can fathom the Spirit of the* LORD, or instruct the LORD as his counselor? (Isa 40:12–13).

We can gather from this that the Holy Spirit is God's creative self. The Spirit is, dare I say, the artistic side of God. The Holy Spirit is involved in forming the world into being and crafting its various spheres and tiers. The function of the Spirit emerges from his distinctive appropriation within the Trinity. The fellowship between Father and Son funnels a creative yet personal energy that is the Holy Spirit, who makes things so that creation shares in the Father's glory and the Son's love. The dynamic power and creative love of God is actualized in the ordering and design of the cosmos through the Holy Spirit. The Holy Spirit makes the world a piece of organic divine art! The Holy Spirit is also engaged in a further conservationist exercise in preserving the creation from absolute disruption and anarchic disorder. Grenz has noted that whereas the Father is the grounds of creation, the Son is the principle of creation and the Spirit is the divine power active in creation.[19]

Any account of the Spirit and creation is ultimately impoverished if it does not take into account the new creation. The Spirit links the protological (original) creation and the eschatological (final) creation together insofar as both are the work of the one Spirit. In the New Testament, the Holy Spirit acts eschatologically to make all things new. He is the power of new creation and the force behind resurrection. He is the seal of salvation and the pledge of glory. He provides efficacy in the new birth of men and women, who are the first lamps lit in the new creation. While the activity of the Spirit is inward, it points ahead to an outward reality: the kingdom of God in all its fullness. The Spirit that fashioned the first creation (Gen 1:2) will also form the new creation (Rom 8:23).

6.3.2 SPIRIT, ISRAEL, AND MESSIAH

The Spirit did not disappear after the act of creation. God's Spirit had a special relation to God's covenant people. That can be observed in several areas.[20] First, the Spirit was active in empowering Israel's leaders. Many of the judges, such as Othniel (Judg 3:10), Gideon (6:34), Jephthah (11:29), and especially Samson (14:6, 19; 15:14–15), were enabled by the Spirit to lead Israel to victory. Israelite kings were

---

19. Stanley E. Grenz, *Theology for the Community of God* (Grand Rapids: Eerdmans, 1994), 105.

20. Cf. Cole, *He Who Gives Life*, 115–45.

THE HOLY SPIRIT AND GENDER

What gender is the Holy Spirit? The answer is rather interesting if we look at the gender of words used for the Spirit in some ancient languages. The Hebrew *rûaḥ* is feminine, the Greek *pneuma* is neuter, and the Latin *spiritus* is masculine! Several thinkers—ranging from Catholic, to liberal, to new age—have identified the Spirit with the feminine side of God, the divine *Sophia*, the womanly wisdom of the Godhead, a consort and counterpart to the Father. The fact that the Holy Spirit is the chief actor in regeneration or new birth has also led some theologians to think of the Spirit in terms like "the Mother of life."[21] In the second century *Gospel of the Ebionites*, there is an account where Jesus refers to "My Mother, the Holy Spirit." Moltmann stresses the operation of the Spirit in the world with the roles of "Lord, Mother, and Judge."[22] That is not a literal "mother," but he means that the Holy Spirit engages in acts of mothering, not that the Holy Spirit is inwardly feminine.

Given the comforting and birthing roles of the Holy Spirit in Scripture, and with due cognizance of the overly patriarchal perspectives inherent in some theology, is the feminine dimension of the Holy Spirit an opportunity to demasculinize the Trinity? Should we refer to the Holy Spirit as a "she"? I think not! God is beyond gender, and he transcends both masculinity and femininity. Male titles and roles are used analogically for God. Bloesch soberly comments:

> A name is not a simile but a title that God gives himself in his revelation. To refer to the Spirit or the Son as feminine and the Father as masculine creates a bifurcation in the Trinity so that we are pushed into binitarianism: a God partly male and partly female. Orthodox theologian Thomas Hopko argues that we are not at liberty to emend the Trinitarian names for God because this "nameless God" has personally revealed himself ... as Father through the person of Jesus Christ the Son, by the person of the Holy Spirit.[23]

---

21. Cf. Donald Gelpi, *The Divine Mother: A Trinitarian Theology of the Holy Spirit* (Lanham, MD: University of America Press, 1984).
22. Jürgen Moltmann, *The Spirit of Life: A Universal Affirmation* (trans. M. Kohl; Minneapolis: Fortress, 1992), 272–74.
23. Bloesch, *The Holy Spirit*, 61.

uniquely endowed with the Spirit as well for their task of ruling and judging (e.g., 1 Sam 16:13).

Second, the Spirit was responsible for bringing the divine word to Israel. The Spirit impelled the word of God in the prophets. For instance, Micah's ministry of the "word of the Lord" is indebted to his being filled with the Spirit: "I am filled with power, with the Spirit of the Lord, and with justice and might, to declare to Jacob his transgression, to Israel his sin" (Mic 3:8). Word and Spirit have a similar symbiosis in Ezekiel, where the Spirit lifts him up and brings him to the east gate of the temple (Ezek 11:1), and the Spirit falls on him and forces him to speak (11:5–14). Zechariah attributes the exile to Israel's failure to hear the law and the words that the Lord of hosts had sent by his Spirit through the prophets (Zech 7:12).

Third, the Spirit figures prominently in the hope of Israel. The various leaders of Israel's past, such as Moses, the judges, the kings, and prophets, were all animated and guided by the Spirit of the Lord. As the Old Testament looks forward to an ultimate deliverer, there is an increasing focus on the role played by the Holy Spirit in the actions of this deliverer. The Spirit will provide the "root of Jesse" with wisdom, understanding, knowledge, and fear (Isa 11:2). The "Servant of the Lord" is a Spirit-endowed agent for God's redemptive purposes. His ministry, through the Spirit, is one of liberation with a mix of royal, prophetic, and priestly tasks (Isa 42:1; 61:1–4). The Spirit is also important in God's purpose to reconstitute the nation with a new heart and a new law written by the Spirit. The political resuscitation of the exiled kingdom is bound up with their spiritual revivification by the Spirit in Ezekiel 37. The Lord puts his "breath" into the bones of the spiritually dead people via the preaching of the prophetic word (37:7–10). Later in Joel 2:28–32, the aftermath of judgment is followed by the lavish pouring out of God's Spirit.

The Gospels depict the Messiah as the bearer and dispenser of the Spirit. That is why so much in Jesus' life and ministry can be closely connected to the Holy Spirit. For a start, Jesus' birth is regarded as a special act of the Holy Spirit as the Spirit "overshadowed" Mary (Luke 1:35; cf. Matt 1:18, 20). Jesus' baptism occasioned his reception of the Holy Spirit. The tearing of the heavens, the descent of the Spirit, and the voice from above all indicate Jesus' anointing as the messianic Son and his empowering as the eschatological prophet (Matt 3:13–17; cf. Isa 61:1–2). What we have in the baptismal episode is thoroughly Trinitarian. The Father anoints, the Son obeys, and the Spirit is received. The baptism is a cosmic rendezvous between the second and third members of the Godhead united in the redemptive mission to rescue Israel, and then through the renewed Israel, to take salvation to the ends of the earth.

The Holy Spirit can even be considered the dominant partner in their work.[24] That is why Jesus does not do any miracles until he himself receives the Holy Spirit at his baptism. That dominance is expressed when the Spirit "led" Jesus into the

---

24. Irenaeus's account of the *regula fidei* even regards the earthly life of Christ as a subset of the work of the Holy Spirit (*Haer.* 1.10.1)!

wilderness to face the accuser and to win the victory over Satan that Adam and Israel failed to win (Matt 4:1–11/Luke 4:1–13). Jesus engages in his itinerant ministry "in the power of the Spirit" (Luke 4:14). Jesus even experienced "joy through the Holy Spirit" (10:21).

The work of Messiah and Spirit are dynamic expressions of the reign of God. Consequently, Jesus' mighty deeds by the Holy Spirit are as a sign that the kingdom has come (Matt 12:28). J. Rodman Williams cogently writes: "The ministry of Jesus in word and deed was carried forward in the power of the Holy Spirit. In everything He did, Jesus knew in Himself a mighty force working that was beyond Himself.... Jesus lived and moved in the presence of the Holy Spirit."[25] The Spirit is also active in the Messiah's death and resurrection. The Spirit withdraws from Jesus at his death, indicating his abandonment to divine judgment. But later the Spirit is the means by which he rises from the dead (Rom 8:11). All in all, "Jesus was *full* of the Spirit, *led* by the Spirit, *empowered* by the Spirit, and *anointed* with the Spirit. He is clearly the apex and transcendence of all people of the Spirit who have preceded Him."[26]

Williams notes that the Spirit points to Christ, but Christ also points to the Spirit. Prior to the Spirit's work in uniting the believer to Christ is Christ's mediation of the Spirit to others.[27] That is observable when, after the resurrection, Jesus assumes the role of bestower of the Spirit, as is seen in the Johannine and Lucan Pentecosts (John 20:22; Acts 2:1–11). This role was already intimated in John the Baptist's testimony that the Messiah will "baptize with the Holy Spirit (and with fire)" (Mark 1:8/Matt 3:11/Luke 3:16; John 1:33). What does that mean? Is this a baptism for purification or for judgment? It may well be idiomatic for being plunged into the fiery breath of God, which denotes a purification that prepares one to survive the coming judgment of the future.[28] The Messiah brings people to the precipice of judgment, but they are purified rather than destroyed by exposure to the divine eschatological power.

6.3.3 THE HOLY SPIRIT AND THE CHURCH

Central to Christianity is the continual experience of the Spirit in the messianic community. The Holy Spirit is the authenticator of Jesus' message. He is the author of faith. He applies the work of Christ to the believer. He is the agent of resurrection and consummation. The Spirit operates in and through the church to bring

---

25. J. Rodman Williams, *Renewal Theology: Systematic Theology from a Charismatic Perspective* (Grand Rapids: Zondervan, 1996), 2:173.
26. Ibid., 2:171 (italics original).
27. Ibid., 2:207.
28. Cf. James D. G. Dunn, *Baptism in the Spirit* (London: SCM, 1970), 13–14.

BLASPHEMY AGAINST THE HOLY SPIRIT

"And so I tell you, every kind of sin and slander can be forgiven, but blasphemy against the Spirit will not be forgiven" (Matt 12:31).

These are terrifying words from Jesus! Can Christians commit this unforgivable sin of blasphemy against the Holy Spirit? I once had a young man in my youth group tell me that a friend of his had given up going to church because he had committed blasphemy against the Holy Spirit, and since he was damned for all eternity, there was no point going to church any more. Some years ago, I met an associate minister who told me that his senior minister refused to criticize any Christian leader, even televangelists, because if he did, he would run the risk of committing blasphemy against the Holy Spirit. Should Christians be worried about this sin?

To begin with, let us understand what blasphemy against the Holy Spirit actually is. This sin is saying that Jesus casts out demons by the power of Beelzebub. Of course, one might put it more generally as John Piper does: "The unforgivable sin of blasphemy against the Holy Spirit is an act of resistance which belittles the Holy Spirit so grievously that he withdraws for ever with his convicting power so that we are never able to repent and be forgiven."[29] Such blasphemy is to denigrate and deny the work of the Spirit in the Lord Jesus Christ.

So can Christians fall into this heinous sin from which there is no repentance or reprieve? I want to say emphatically "no"! First, Christians are not only saved by grace, but they are sustained in their faith by God's grace. God in his grace prevents Christians from committing such a sin. Salvation is by the power of grace from first to last. Second, one who is born of the Spirit, baptized in the Spirit, filled in the Spirit, and being renewed in the Spirit is unlikely to blaspheme the Spirit. Third, if a Christian is worried about blaspheming the Spirit, that itself is a good sign that he or she has not done so. A person who has blasphemed the Spirit is in such a state of utter rebellion that they are incapable of repentance, remorse, or contrition before God.

---

29. John Piper, "Beyond Forgiveness: Blasphemy against the Spirit," Bethelehem Baptist Church, 1 April 1984. www.soundofgrace.com/piper84/040184m.htm (accessed 21 July 2011).

spiritual life and to make the message of Jesus known to the world. The Spirit is why we have a relationship with God and not simply a religion about God. The Holy Spirit makes the evangel gloriously effervescent by empowering the messengers and instilling an experience of unimaginable joy in the church. The work of the Spirit in the church can be broken down into vitalizing, empowering, purifying, revealing, and unifying.

6.3.3.1 VIVIFYING

The Holy Spirit is called in the creed, "he who gives life"—an apt description given that the role of the Spirit in creating life is seen in the Old Testament with God's giving the "breath of life" to Adam (Gen 2:7). On the national level, there is the dramatic account of the Spirit giving life to exiled Israel like breath coming upon a valley of dry bones (Ezek 37:5). The image of the Spirit as life-giver is even more prominent in the New Testament.

> *The Spirit gives life*; the flesh counts for nothing. The words that I have spoken to you—they are full of the Spirit and life. (John 6:63)

> But if Christ is in you, then even though your body is subject to death because of sin, the *Spirit gives life* because of righteousness. And if *the Spirit* of him who raised Jesus from the dead is living in you, he who raised Christ from the dead *will also give life to your mortal bodies* because of his Spirit who lives in you. (Rom 8:10–11)

> He has made us competent as ministers of a new covenant—not of the letter but of the Spirit; for the letter kills, *but the Spirit gives life*. (2 Cor 3:6, italics added in all cases)

The penultimate participation in the Spirit's life-giving power, second only to resurrection, is regeneration or new birth. Regeneration pertains to the spiritual change wrought in the heart of a person by the Holy Spirit. In this infusion of new life the sinful heart is changed so that a person can respond to God in faith and live in accordance with God's will (Matt 19:28; John 3:3, 5–7; Titus 3:5). It enlightens the blinded mind to discern spiritual realities (1 Cor 2:14–15; 2 Cor. 4:6; Col. 3:10) and liberates the enslaved for obedience to God (Rom 6:14, 17–22; Phil 2:13).[30]

The image of new birth has two important corollaries. First, it denotes something decisive rather than a formative stage of Christian life. The regenerate person has in a sense ceased to be the person they were before; their old life is gone; it is crucified, dead, and buried with Christ forever. While it is the same "I" before and after new birth, the new "I" is one now sharing in the body of Christ through the life-giving energy of the Spirit.

The second element is the sovereignty of God in regeneration. You cannot make it, build it, cultivate it, or invent it. Just as children don't plan or contribute to their own birth apart from being there, so too we contribute nothing to our new birth. What is more, this spiritual vivification is absolutely free; it is a mysterious event, an exercise of

---

30. J. I. Packer, "Regeneration," in *EDT*, 924.

raw divine power. Regeneration is not comprehensible in purely human terms (John 3:6–7), not induced by any human efforts (1:12–13), not earned by human merits (Titus 3:3–7). The Spirit latches onto and launches from the Word in a mysterious way so that the outer call of gospel preaching yields an irresistible inner call placed on the heart by the Spirit. The Word sows, but the Spirit reaps. Therefore, regeneration is not to be equated with, or attributed to, any of the experiences, decisions, and acts to which it gives rise and by which it may be known to have taken place.

One of the distinctive marks of evangelical theology, at least as it has been inherited from the Reformed tradition, is the emphasis on the Holy Spirit as the applier of salvation. Indeed, it is not too much to say that the Roman Church's chief error was replacing the Spirit with the church when it came to the application of salvation to the individual. Reformers like John Calvin laid great emphasis on the Spirit bringing the believer to Christ in order to partake of his benefits from union with Christ. B. B. Warfield was correct to call John Calvin the preeminent "theologian of the Holy Spirit." Calvin's *Institutes* is a treatise on the work of the Holy Spirit in making God's salvation known and effected to sinners and bringing humanity into communion with a holy God. According to Warfield:

> It was he [Calvin] who first related the whole experience of salvation specifically to the working of the Holy Spirit, worked it out into its details, and contemplated its several steps and stages in orderly progress as the product of the Holy Spirit's specific work in applying salvation to the soul. Thus he gave systematic and adequate expression to the whole doctrine of the Holy Spirit and made it the assured possession of the Church of God.[31]

It is for this reason that evangelical theology will rightly have a "Pentecostal soteriology" that sees the work of Christ as worked into the believer via the Holy Spirit. We see this most of all in the work of the Spirit, who brings new life to the believer as designed by the Father and executed through the Son.

6.3.3.2 EMPOWERING

In the Old Testament the Holy Spirit often empowers people for ministries that serve God's purposes. God empowered Joshua with leadership and wisdom (Num 27:18; Deut 34:9) and enabled the judges to deliver the nation from peril (Judg 3:10; 6:34; 11:29; 13:25; 14:6, 19; 15:14). The Holy Spirit was with Saul and David as part of their kingly office (1 Sam 11:6; 16:13). Elijah and Elisha carried out their prophetic vocation through the Spirit, a pattern repeated in John the Baptizer's pro-

---

31. B. B. Warfield, "John Calvin the Theologian," (1909), see http://homepage.mac.com/shanerosenthal/reformation-ink/bbwcalvin1.htm (accessed 20 July 2011).

phetic ministry (2 Kings 2; Luke 1:17). The Holy Spirit was also prophesied to rest on a future king of Israel to help in his royal task (Isa 11:2–3), and the Servant of the Lord is anointed with the Spirit of the Lord for his redemptive mission (Isa 61:1).

Jesus the Messiah was empowered by the Spirit (Luke 4:14) and preached with the Spirit actively upon him (Luke 4:18–19). The prophecy about the abundant fullness of God's Spirit being poured out on "all people" in Joel 2:28–29 is fulfilled at Pentecost. We also find that the Spirit empowered Christians to work miracles, such as Stephen (Acts 6:5, 8), Paul (Rom 15:19; 1 Cor 2:4), and others (Heb 2:4). But what is most noticeable is that the Holy Spirit empowered apostolic preaching of the gospel throughout Acts. The Spirit's empowerment also consists of equipping the church with spiritual offices of pastors, teachers, and evangelists (Eph 4:11) and to fight spiritual battles against the present evil age (6:17). It is true not only of Paul, but of the whole Scriptures, to say that the Holy Spirit is "God's empowering presence" (as Gordon Fee has put as the title of his book on this issue).[32]

The Spirit is the "power" that the church receives for its evangelistic mission (Luke 24:49; Acts 1:8). In fact, the Acts of the Apostles could be called the *Acts of the Holy Spirit through the Apostles and Sometimes Even Despite Them*! One cannot help but notice the repeated references in Luke–Acts to believers being filled with the Spirit. Whenever someone is described as being "filled" with the Spirit, there is always a conjunction "and" that follows as amazing events transpire soon after.[33] John the Baptist, while in his mother's womb, was prophesied as one who would be filled with the Spirit *and* many would turn to the Lord on account of him (Luke 1:15–16). The disciples were filled with the Spirit *and* they spoke in tongues (Acts 2:4). Stephen was full of the Holy Spirit *and* he saw a vision of God's glory with Jesus at God's right hand (Acts 7:55). Saul of Tarsus was filled with the Holy Spirit *and* immediately something like scales fell from his eyes (Acts 9:17–18). Barnabas was a good man, full of the Spirit, *and* many people were brought to the Lord in Antioch (Acts 11:24). When someone is filled with the Holy Spirit, one should take cover and look for a helmet, because something explosive is about to go down.

One of the chief ways that the Holy Spirit equips the church for its mission is through the bestowal of spiritual gifts and ministerial offices. There are different words used to describe the gifts (*charisma, pneumata, dōrea*), but all emphasize the gracious and giving character of the spiritual charism bestowed. Defined properly, a spiritual gift is an empowerment from God for God's people through the Spirit for spiritual work in the church. Some gifts appear to magnify ordinary attitudes and talents (e.g., leadership, generosity, helping), while other gifts are out of the ordinary

---

32. Gordon D. Fee, *God's Empowering Presence: The Holy Spirit in the Letters of Paul* (Peabody, MA: Hendrickson, 1994), 5–9.

33. Cole, *He Who Gives Life*, 218.

and have a supernatural quality (e.g., prophecy, tongues, etc.). We are told that the Spirit distributes gifts "as he determines" (1 Cor 12:11) and "according to his will" (Heb 2:4). Thus, the Spirit is the sovereign author of the power bestowed on the church for its mission and edification. There are several gift lists in Paul's letters:

Romans 12:6–8	1 Corinthians 12:8–10, 28–30	Ephesians 4:11
Prophecy Service Teaching Encouragement Giving Leadership Mercy	Message of wisdom Message of knowledge Faith Healing Miracles Prophecy Discernment of spirits Tongues Interpretation of tongues Apostles Prophets Teachers Miracle workers Healers Helpers Leaders	Apostles Prophets Evangelists Pastors/Teachers

We should note a few important things about the spiritual gifts. First, the burden of Paul's exhortation in 1 Corinthians 12 is to prove to the Corinthians that their spiritual unity-in-diversity is crucial to a healthy body life because the whole body needs the whole cohort of gifts in order to be wholly effective. While some gifts are "greater" (12:31a), all are nonetheless indispensable for the vitality of the body.

Second, the gifts function to build up the household of faith. The spiritual gifts are manifestations given "for the common good" (1 Cor 12:7), they serve to "build up the church" (14:12), and the offices operate so that "the body of Christ may be built up" (Eph 4:12).

Third, a point crucial for the cessationism debate is that the Corinthians "do not lack any spiritual gift as you eagerly wait for our Lord Jesus Christ to be revealed" (1 Cor 1:7). If the spiritual gifts help the church in its life and mission prior to the *parousia*, and if Christ has not yet returned, then it is sensible to think that *some* of the gifts will carry on until Christ's second advent. An apocalyptic hope of Christ's return and a belief that God has not abandoned the church seem to necessitate the view that Spirit remains active in gifting the church to succeed in its mission until the second coming.[34]

---

34. For more on this topic, see Wayne Grudem, ed., *Are Miraculous Gifts for Today? Four Views* (Grand Rapids: Zondervan, 1996).

That said, not all of the gifts and offices have to endure in order to achieve that. For instance, I think it likely that the offices of prophet and apostle, which were eschatological ministries to provide the "foundation" for the church (Eph 2:20), no longer persist because the foundation has been laid, and the apostolic office and prophetic voice is largely subsumed into Christian preaching, witness, and teaching.[35]

6.3.3.3 SANCTIFYING

A major task of the Holy Spirit is to purify, cleanse, and prune God's people. In the lives of unbelievers the Holy Spirit brings the conviction of sin (John 16:8–11; Acts 7:51). When we come to faith, we are washed, sanctified, and justified by the Holy Spirit (1 Cor 6:11). The washing of new birth (Titus 3:5) shows that the sanctifying work of the Spirit is part of our initial salvation (1 Cor 1:2; 2 Thess 2:13). This order of sanctification is positional; that is, we are consecrated to God. The new life is to be a holy life as it is birthed and animated by the Holy Spirit. The Christian life will naturally start to produce the fruit of the Spirit (Gal 5:22–23), and believers become conformed to the image of God's Son (2 Cor 3:18). By the Spirit we put to death the deeds of the body and grow in personal holiness (Rom 8:13). A healthy Christian life is one that begins with the Spirit (Gal 3:3), walks in step with the Spirit (5:25), and cultivates righteousness, peace, and joy in the Holy Spirit (Rom 14:17). Holiness means the Holy Spirit is living in believers, reproducing the life of Christ in them, especially in their community relationships.[36]

6.3.3.4 REVEALING

The God of Christian testimony is a revealing God. In Barthian terms we can say that God is the Revealer (Father), the Revelation (Son), and the effect of this Revelation (Holy Spirit). The Holy Spirit spirates, inscripturates,[37] and illuminates the revelation of God to human beings. He is the material source, preserver, and authority of God's revelation. The Holy Spirit is the mouthpiece by which God speaks his Word into the world, he is the agency by which the Word is made flesh, and he is the chief author of the word of salvation through the church.

In the Old Testament, the prophetic message was a word from God given to the prophets by the Spirit. For instance, Ezekiel writes, "Then the Spirit of the Lord came on me, and he told me to say . . ." (Ezek 11:5; see Num 24:2; Zech 7:12, etc.). This testimony is affirmed in the New Testament that the "prophets . . . spoke from God as they were carried along by the Holy Spirit" (2 Pet 1:21). This prophetic word is carried on into the pre-Pentecost period with Elizabeth (Luke 1:41), Zechariah

---

35. Cf. Fee, *God's Empowering Presence*, 893.
36. Ibid., 881.
37. On inscripturation, see the section below, "Inscripturation."

(1:67), and Simeon (2:25), all speaking prophetically about the events soon to take place. This prophetic ministry is also apparent in the early church with the office of "prophet" (Acts 13:1; 21:10; 1 Cor 12:28–29; Eph 2:20; 3:5; 4:11).

The Holy Spirit reveals himself by guiding God's people. The elders of Israel were led by the Spirit of God (Num 11:25). All of the judges were led by God's Spirit to deliver Israel (e.g., Judg 3:10). The Spirit guided the actions of apostles like Philip to go and speak to the Ethiopian eunuch (Acts 8:29). The Holy Spirit gives people a positive disposition to minister to others, such as what the Jerusalem church did for the Antioch church in not making the believers there take on the yoke of the Torah (15:28). At the same time, the Holy Spirit can inhibit outreach, such as preventing Paul from going to Bithynia (16:7). The Spirit can even constrain people to a course of action like Paul having to go to Jerusalem (20:22–23).

The Holy Spirit performs a didactic and illuminating function. In the Old Testament the psalmist desires the Spirit to lead and teach him (Ps 143:10). The role of the Spirit is to teach Jesus' disciples the things they need to know to follow him (John 14:26; 16:13). He is given specifically so that God's people "may understand what God has freely given us" (1 Cor 2:12). This is why Calvin saw the role of the Holy Spirit as being "to seal on our minds the very doctrine which the gospel recommends" (*Institutes* 1.9.1).

6.3.3.5 UNIFYING

The Holy Spirit is evangelical. He comes to empower gospel preaching, and he himself is the effect of that preaching in the hearts of hearers. What is more, he is ecumenical and interdenominational. The Spirit draws together all who accept the word of Christ irrespective of ethnicity, gender, race, or economic status. He binds people together in one fellowship by uniting them with Christ and with each other. According to Barth, the Spirit lights up the outer structures of the church with an inward spiritual life. Thus, the church is not a human activity; it is the Holy Spirit who gathers the church together as a sign of grace and witness to Christ.[38]

The outpouring of the Spirit at Pentecost did not introduce the Spirit who had been hereto unknown by the people of God. No, the Spirit of God was always with the people, regenerating them and even leading them. However, the qualitative work of the Spirit in the individual believers and in the believing community was intensified at Pentecost. Such intensification brought with it a tightening of the bonds between them. The fresh grace and raw power poured out by the Spirit at Pentecost brought with it the introduction of an iron bond tethering believers together, a bond forged in the fire of baptism in the Spirit.

The early church in Acts was a community bound together by a common mes-

---

38. Barth, *CD*, 4/1:661.

sage, a shared experience, fellowship meals, and one Spirit (Acts 2:44–47). Augustine saw in the Pentecostal blessing of the gift of tongues a parable for the unity of the church through the Spirit: "Just as then, whoever received the Holy Spirit, even as one person, started speaking all languages, so too now the unity itself is speaking all languages throughout all the nations; and it is by being established in this unity that you have the Holy Spirit."[39]

The saints have fellowship together because they have fellowship and single-mindedness in and with the Holy Spirit (e.g., 2 Cor 13:14; Phil 2:1–2). All Christian fellowship must be a spiritual fellowship—not friendship on some social plane, but fellowship animated by the Holy Spirit himself. Paul wrote: "There is one body and one Spirit, just as you were called to the one hope when you were called; one Lord, one faith, one baptism" (Eph 4:4–5). Elsewhere Paul noted: "For we were all baptized by one Spirit so as to form one body—whether Jews or Gentiles, slave or free—and we were all given the one Spirit to drink" (1 Cor 12:13). It is because of this oneness in the Spirit that Christians are "to keep the unity of the Spirit through the bond of peace" (Eph 4:3).

6.3.4 BAPTISM IN THE SPIRIT AND FILLING WITH THE SPIRIT

In recent decades the rise of Pentecostalism and the growth of charismatic churches has led to a resurgent of interest in baptism in the Holy Spirit. The experience of the Jerusalem church at Pentecost, where the church received the Holy Spirit as evidenced by speaking in tongues, is viewed as the normal pattern for all Christians to emulate. This baptism in the Spirit is reckoned to be a secondary and subsequent experience to conversion. In terms of what that means, Pentecostal theologian J. Rodman Williams defines baptism in the Spirit this way:

> It depicts vividly, the idea of being enveloped in the reality of the Holy Spirit. Since to be baptized in waters means literally to be immersed in, plunged under, and even drenched or soaked with, then to be baptized in the Holy Spirit can mean no less than that. In immersion no part of the body is left untouched; everything goes under. So with Spirit baptism the whole being of a person—body, soul, and spirit—is imbued with the Spirit of God. Likewise, the community of those who are so baptized is profoundly affected in its total life. Both individual and community are touched in every area by the presence and power of the living God.[40]

That is a thick and wholesome definition, but when does this Spirit baptism occur? In Pentecostal theology, Spirit baptism refers to a secondary experience subsequent to conversion, whereby a person receives a dramatic infusion of the

---

39. Augustine, *Sermon* 174, cited in Angelo Di Beradino, ed., *We Believe in One Holy Catholic and Apostolic Church* (Downers Grove, IL: InterVarsity Press, 2010), 68.

40. Williams, *Renewal Theology*, 2:199–200.

Holy Spirit evidenced by *glossolalia*, that is, speaking in tongues, often called "the initial physical evidence" of Spirit baptism. This experience has the knock-on effect of empowerment for a triumphant spiritual life. The dispute over Spirit baptism between evangelicals and Pentecostals pertains to whether Spirit baptism is an initial salvific event coterminus with conversion (evangelical view), or whether it is a secondary experiential event later in a Christian's life (Pentecostal view).

The Gospels speak unanimously about the role of the Messiah to baptize with the Holy Spirit, as narrated in the testimony of John the Baptist (Matt 3:11/Mark 1:8/Luke 3:16; John 1:33). Before his ascension, Jesus promised his disciples that they would be baptized with the Holy Spirit (Acts 1:5). What did the disciples get and when did they get it? Many Pentecostals see a two-stage process for being "born again" and then "baptized in the Spirit," with faith as the sign of new birth and speaking in tongues as the sign of Spirit baptism. Pentecostal theologians often argue that the disciples received the Spirit as "new birth" after the resurrection when the risen Jesus "breathed" on them (John 20:22), but then later received a subsequent "baptism in the Spirit" on the day of Pentecost (Acts 2:1–4). Furthermore, they point out that many Samaritans were converted by Philip the evangelist where they presumably received the miracle of regeneration (8:1–13), yet they did not receive the Spirit until Peter and John laid hands on them. The Jerusalem apostles laid hands on the Samaritan believers, and they only then received Spirit baptism in addition to a water baptism (8:14–17). One could also appeal to the subsequent receptions of the Holy Spirit by Cornelius the centurion (10:44–48) and the disciples of John the Baptist at Ephesus (19:1–7) as proof that a secondary experience of the Spirit after conversion is perhaps normative for all Christians.[41]

This order of events, however, where an intermission is posited between new birth by the Spirit and baptism in the Spirit, is contestable.

First, the Johannine Pentecost, "And with that he breathed on them and said, 'Receive the Holy Spirit'" (John 20:22), apparently depicts the disciples receiving the Spirit after Jesus' resurrection, yet ahead of the day of Pentecost. Is this the right order? The Fourth Gospel is clear that the Spirit was not given until Jesus was glorified (John 7:39). So when was Jesus glorified? If Jesus' glory is linked with his ascension (12:16; 17:5; Luke 24:26), the Spirit was not given formally until Pentecost (Acts 1:8; 2:1–4). Alternatively, if the Fourth Evangelist identifies Jesus' glory with his death (John 12:23; 13:31), then perhaps we can allow for an incipient pre-ascension dispensing of the Holy Spirit (20:22).

One explanation is that John might be telescoping the resurrection-ascension-

---

41. Cf. discussion in Allan Anderson, *An Introduction to Pentecostalism: Global Charismatic Christianity* (Cambridge: Cambridge University Press, 2004), 189–95.

Spirit-outpouring. Or perhaps the Johannine Pentecost was a first installment of Pentecost, with the big new covenant event of the outpouring of the Spirit to happen later. Then again—and what I think more likely—is that the Johannine Pentecost is a symbolic act rather than an actual reception of the Spirit. The purpose of Jesus' gesture of breathing on the disciples is to remind them that he is the dispenser of the Spirit and that they receive the Spirit only as Jesus endows them with it. This theme is emphasized at length in the Farewell Discourse, where Jesus promises to send the *paraklētos* (John 14:26; 15:26; 16:7). In other words, the Johannine Jesus is saying, when you get the Spirit, make sure you remember who sent it to you!

Second, we must remember that "baptism" itself is an initiation metaphor. Water baptism is the rite of passage for entry into the church, while Spirit baptism is the point of entry into the Christian life. Baptism is always associated with "beginnings" in the New Testament, not secondary or subsequent events in the life of the believer. If that is the case, then Spirit baptism is coterminus with conversion.

Third, Paul tells the fractious Corinthians, "For we were all baptized by one Spirit so as to form one body—whether Jews or Gentiles, slave or free—and we were all given the one Spirit to drink" (1 Cor 12:13). Moreover, note that Paul says this to a group where not everyone spoke in tongues (12:30). The baptism by one Spirit and the drinking of the one Spirit do not refer to two separate experiences, but in typical Semitic parallelism, they are the one and same event. Since the Corinthians have different experiences of the *charismata*, hence the diversity and divisions evident in 1 Corinthians 12–14, Paul must be referring to a common experience of conversion. What makes the Corinthians one here is their common experience of the Spirit. Indeed, reception of the Spirit is the *sine qua non* of the Christian life and the bond of Christian community. For Paul, it is the Spirit that distinguishes the believer from the unbeliever (1 Cor 2:10–14); the Spirit marks the beginning of the Christian life (Gal 3:2–3), and the Spirit makes a person a child of God (Rom 8:14–17).[42]

Fourth, concerning the conversions and reception of the Spirit in Acts, it seems unlikely that Spirit baptism is normatively a secondary experience for Christians. For a start, there are so many conversions in Acts and so many different instances when people receive the Spirit that it is impossible to determine what exactly is happening and whether it is regeneration, Spirit baptism, indwelling, or empowering. There is no set template as the Spirit blows and goes where, when, and on whom he wishes. Sometimes he comes after water baptism (Acts 2:38), other times before water baptism (10:44–48; 19:5–6).

---

42. Gordon D. Fee, *The First Epistle to the Corinthians* (NICNT; Grand Rapids: Eerdmans, 1987), 603–6.

Regarding specific events, there is probably a good reason for a delay between the Samaritans becoming converted and their later receiving the Holy Spirit (and I think this reception of the Spirit is a filling with the Spirit rather than Spirit baptism). That is, the Samaritans had to learn that they received the Spirit from the Jews, and the apostles had to learn that salvation is for more than ethnic Jews (Acts 8:14–17). "The Spirit as it were indicated in a visible manifestation the divine approval of this new missionary step beyond Judaism."[43]

The story of the baptism of the disciples of John the Baptist, whom Paul met in Ephesus, is equally peculiar. In the exchange, Paul asks them, "Did you receive the Holy Spirit when you believed?" To which they answered, "No, we have not even heard that there is a Holy Spirit" (Acts 19:2). The problem is that these "disciples" knew only the baptism of John. John's baptism was for repentance and preparatory for the Spirit baptizer. That Paul had to explain to these disciples of the Baptist that John "told the people to believe in the one coming after him, that is, in Jesus" (19:4) is a solid indication that these chaps were not properly converted. Thus, their baptism and reception of the Spirit at this point in Acts was part of their full conversion. These twelve men were not far from the kingdom of God, but they needed an apostolic messenger to bring them to Christ and to lay hands on them in order to receive the Spirit.[44]

Therefore, Spirit baptism refers to the initial experience of the Holy Spirit that denotes the rushing and uncontrollable divine power falling on a person at their conversion. Its imagery is akin to standing under a waterfall of the Holy Spirit. The baptism of the Holy Spirit is a genuinely new blessing in the new covenant that has a cleansing and purifying effect on believers as part of their conversion experience.

That does not lessen the significance of Spirit baptism in the Christian life. Darrell Bock wishes that Luke 3:16 was just as well-known and oft-quoted as John 3:16.[45] I agree! Luke 3:16 reports the words of John the Baptist about the coming messianic deliverer: "I baptize you with water. But one who is more powerful than I will come, the straps of whose sandals I am not worthy to untie. He will baptize you with the Holy Spirit and fire." This promise, reminiscent of Isaiah 4:4–5, looks forward to an eschatological baptism by the Messiah that cleanses or consumes all in its path. By undergoing this baptism we enter into the purifying power of God so that we emerge from it as a redeemed and refined new humanity. Barth rightly saw Spirit baptism as a divine action that opens up a new mode of existence by calling people to faith from ignorance and from unfaithfulness to faith.[46]

---

43. J. B. Polhill, *Acts* (NAC; Nashville: Broadman & Holman, 2001), 218.
44. Dunn, *Baptism in the Spirit*, 83–89.
45. Darrell L. Bock, *Recovering the Real Lost Gospel of Jesus* (Nashville: Broadman & Holman, 2010), 12.
46. Barth, *CD*, IV/4:3–40, 101–2.

As to being filled with the Spirit, I maintain that whereas Spirit baptism is a singular, initiatory, and unrepeatable event, filling with the Spirit is a secondary and repeatable experience in the Christian life. In the Old Testament, God "filled" certain people with his Spirit for special tasks (e.g., Exod 31:1–3; 35:30–35; Mic 3:8; cf. Luke 1:15). In the New Testament people are especially "filled" for the purpose of witness and proclamation (Acts 4:8, 31; 9:17; 13:9). God fills people with the Spirit so they can further the announcement of the gospel. If we want to know which church has more of the Spirit blowing in its sails, we need only look at which church is the most active in gospel proclamation — that's the sign of a Spirit-filled church!

Filling with the Spirit brings an inner warmth and a visible joy to the life of a believer. Being filled with the Spirit elicits a delighting in the Lord and a special sense of peace in one's soul. Luke describes how the disciples in Pisidian Antioch were "filled with joy and with the Holy Spirit" (Acts 13:52). Paul also prays for the Romans: "May the God of hope fill you with all joy and peace as you trust in him, so that you may overflow with hope by the power of the Holy Spirit" (Rom 15:13). Like overloading a washing machine with detergent, the believer bubbles over with joy and other aspects of the Spirit's fruit when the Spirit falls on him or her.

Filling with the Spirit is something that one should seek to cultivate. Paul tells the Ephesians to "be filled with the Spirit" (Eph 5:18), and this can be fostered by renewed worship and thanksgiving (5:19–20). The verb "be filled" (*plērousthe*) is an imperative and plural: the church is to strive to be filled with the Holy Spirit. Instead of being intoxicated with wine, they are to be God-intoxicated people. Their inhibitions, apathy, self-doubt, and distractions are overcome by the eruption of God's Spirit within them. Under the influence of this Spirit-inebriation, the church will grow in spiritual understanding (Col 1:9), proclaim the gospel (Rom 15:19; 1 Thess 1:5; 1 Pet 1:12), walk in the Spirit (Gal 5:15, 25), and bear the fruit of the Spirit (5:22–23). Believers together should pray and look for an outpouring of spiritual gifts and spiritual empowerment for service (1 Cor 12:31; 14:1, 12). Individuals and churches should offer themselves to God as an empty cup waiting to be filled with the Spirit of God.

Being filled with the Spirit means to have God's empowering presence fall on you. The purpose of these spiritual fillings is chiefly evangelical; they provide heavenly unction for the task of boldly declaring the gospel when human effort alone cannot succeed. Spirit filling is not a mechanical event like adding fuel to an engine; it is rather more akin to being wrapped in a blanket of heavenly joy. It is something to be energetically sought after, prayed for, and valued in church life.[47]

---

47. On Spirit baptism and Spirit filling, strongly recommended is Wayne Grudem, *Systematic Theology: An Introduction to Biblical Doctrine* (Grand Rapids: Zondervan, 1994), 763–87.

6.3.5 INSCRIPTURATING

The doctrine of Scripture should be a subsection of the doctrine of the Holy Spirit. That is because the Holy Spirit is the one who inspired authors to write Scripture, who preserves the inscripturated revelation, and who brings illumination to those who read Scripture. I would go so far as to say that Scripture is not itself authoritative, but the Westminster divines were correct to affirm that our authority is "the Holy Spirit speaking in the Scripture" (WCF 1.10). The Spirit is not a mere supplement to the Word of God, some kind of spiritual afterthought, but he is the authority that establishes the Word itself.[48] It is the nature of the inspiration of Scripture and the veracity of Scripture that is to be examined now.

6.3.5.1 INSPIRATION

The doctrine of inspiration explains how it is that the words of human authors are also the words of God. If there is a special revelation from God in the biblical canon, we can legitimately ask: How does the canon relate to the voice of God? Inspiration describes how God publicizes and preserves the special revelation of himself through the medium of human authors in what is now the biblical canon.[49]

It is a circular argument to say that the canon is inspired because it claims to be so. Nevertheless, it is legitimate to let the biblical canon speak for itself as to what it claims to be. The testimony of the defendant is still a valid testimony. Whether we believe it or not is another matter, but the defendant must be allowed to speak. Here is what the canon says about itself:

> Above all, you must understand that no prophecy of Scripture came about by the prophet's own interpretation of things. For prophecy never had its origin in the human will, but prophets, though human, *spoke from God as they were carried along by the Holy Spirit*. (2 Pet 1:20–21, italics added)

This text is an outright denial that Old Testament prophecy has a purely human origin. Instead, what the prophets said is that both its origin and its impetus came from God. The prophetic word is reckoned as a divine word on account of the fact that the prophets were carried along or animated by the Holy Spirit. The passive participle *pheromenoi* makes the prophets dependent on and driven by the Spirit concerning the content of their prophecy.

---

48. Bloesch, *The Holy Spirit*, 261.
49. Importantly, inspiration encompasses more than just the composition of the original autographs; it pertains to any subsequent editing of the text by the believing community, the preservation of the text in the community, and the canonization of the text as an authority over the community. See Norris C. Grubbs and Curtis Scott Drumm, "What Does Theology Have to Do with the Bible? A Call for the Expansion of the Doctrine of Inspiration," *JETS* 53 (2010): 65–79. John Webster (*Scripture: A Dogmatic Sketch* [Cambridge: Cambridge University Press, 2003], 17–18) describes the process of the composition of Scripture as a type of "sanctification," which he defines as "the act of God the Holy Spirit in hallowing creaturely processes, employing them in the service of the taking form of revelation within the history of the creation."

> All Scripture is *God-breathed* and is useful for teaching, rebuking, correcting and training in righteousness, so that [all God's people] may be thoroughly equipped for every good work. (2 Tim 3:16–17, italics added)

Here the word "God-breathed" (*theopneustos*) is a neologism and is ambiguous. It could mean that Scripture is simply "life-giving," in the sense that just as God's breath gave life to Adam, so too Scripture is life-giving in character—a genuine word of life. But more likely, the imagery here is analogous to the depictions of the Spirit coming upon a prophet, who then speaks a word from the Lord (e.g., "The Spirit of the Lord spoke through me; his word was on my tongue" [2 Sam 23:2]; "Brothers and sisters, the Scripture had to be fulfilled in which the Holy Spirit spoke long ago through David concerning Judas, who served as guide for those who arrested Jesus" [Acts 1:16]).

What we must remember about 2 Timothy 3:16–17 is that (1) the passage is more concerned about the function of Scripture than its origin; (2) the passage emphasizes soundness of life and doctrine that one may learn through Scripture; and (3) we must be careful of etymological errors that take "God-breathed" as a mechanically literal description of how Scripture was produced. Craig Allert argues that this text primarily indicates that the authority of Scripture is from God and contributes to the plan of salvation; thus, the main point is the usefulness of Scripture in the believing community.[50]

What is clear from both these passages is that the authority of Scripture derives from God and its human agency is animated by God's Spirit. There is a "concursive operation" of God's Word through the free operation of human minds.[51] Thus, the Scriptures are divine-human works, as B. B. Warfield puts it:

> The whole of Scripture is the product of divine activities which enter it, however, not by superseding the activities of the human authors, but confluently with them; so that the Scriptures are the joint product of divine and human activities, both of which penetrate them at every point, working harmoniously together to the production of a writing which is not divine here and human there, but at once divine and human in every part, every word, and every particular. According to this conception, therefore, the whole Bible is recognized as human, the free product of human effort, in every part and word. And at the same time, the whole Bible is recognized as divine, the Word of God, his utterances, of which he is in the truest sense the Author. The human and divine factors in inspiration are conceived of as flowing confluently and harmoniously to the production of a common product. And the two elements are conceived of in the Scriptures as the inseparable constituents of one single and uncompounded product.[52]

---

50. Craig Allert, *A High View of Scripture: The Authority of the Bible and the Formation of the New Testament Canon* (Grand Rapids: Baker, 2007), 148–56.

51. J. I. Packer, *"Fundamentalism" and the Word of God: Some Evangelical Principles* (Grand Rapids: Eerdmans, 1958), 82.

52. B. B. Warfield, *Selected Shorter Writings*, 547, cited in A. N. S. Lane, "B. B. Warfield on the Humanity of Scripture," *VE* 16 (1986): 82 (77–94).

The precise type of agency and animation at work in bringing God's Word into human words has spawned several theories of inspiration.⁵³

1. *Intuition theory.* Common among liberal theologians was the notion that inspiration functions like a gift akin to artistic ability. Certain persons have particular religious aptitude for writing works that people find "inspirational." Here inspiration is a heightened sense of religious experience.
2. *Dictation theory.* Another perspective, popular in the seventeenth century, is that God dictated to authors exactly what he wanted them to say. Human authors were little more than passive receptacles of the divine voice that were used to convey divine words. Here inspiration effectively drowns the human subject.
3. *Dynamic theory.* This view sees a combination of divine and human elements in the process of writing Scripture. The Spirit of God directed the writer's thoughts and concepts, while allowing their respective personality, style, and disposition to come into play with the choice of words and expressions. Here inspiration is largely conceptual.
4. *Verbal theory.* Another approach is to suggest that the Holy Spirit's influence goes beyond the direction of thoughts and ideas, but extends to the very words used. Each word used is exactly the one that God intended. Here inspiration is verbal.

Against the intuition theory, it assumes that anything inspirational is inspired by God. In other words, God does not actually speak through human authors as much as he is the muse from whom human authors find their creative juices to write about transcendent religious subjects.

The problem with dictation theory is that it does not account for the personality, style, and historical contingency of the author. Dictation theory reduces the author to a mechanical machine like a printing press through whom God produces his written Word. Dictation theory was rightly rejected by both B. B. Warfield and J. I. Packer.⁵⁴

While I resonate with the verbal theory, especially in light of the importance that Jesus placed on the words and very minutia of scripture (Matt 5:18; John 10:35–36), it still raises some big problems. First, it is not all that clear exactly how it differs from dictation theory. While dictation theory and verbal theory are not strictly the same, the difference is one of degree rather than mode of inspiration.

Second, if we take 2 Peter 1:20–21 at face value, God inspires persons, not pages,

---

53. The survey that follows is mostly indebted to Millard J. Erickson, *Christian Theology* (2nd ed.; Grand Rapids: Baker, 1998), 231–33.

54. B. B. Warfield, *Inspiration and Authority of the Bible* (London: Epworth, 1956), 421; Packer, *Word of God*, 79.

by the direct agency of the Spirit. Verbal inspiration can too quickly jump from "God" to "Scripture" and bypass the all-important human subject in the process of inscripturating God's Word.

Third, if God inspired "all" words of Scripture, we have to wonder whether he must have inspired the words of sources quoted in Scripture. For instance, portions of the *Assumption of Moses* and *1 Enoch* (pseudepigraphical works) are quoted in Jude 9, 14–15. Paul also quoted the pagan author Aratus in his speech to the Areopagus (Acts 17:28). A whole chapter of the Bible, Daniel 4, was written by the Babylonian King Nebuchadnezzar, a life-long pagan. Verbal inspiration forces us into some peculiar positions, like saying that God inspires noncanonical and even pagan works when it comes to the use of sources since these are part of the "words" of Scripture.

Fourth, it would also seem odd for God to inspire Paul's anacoluthon in 1 Corinthians 1:15–16 with his forgetfulness and last moment remembrance of whom he actually baptized in Corinth; did God make Paul forget whom he baptized?

Fifth, a further factor we have to consider is that when New Testament authors cited the Old Testament, they often did so in a way that was inexact or even different to the original Hebrew. Sometimes this is due to their reliance on the Septuagint rather than the original Hebrew, but on other occasions the citation is almost paraphrastic and resembles no extant version of the Old Testament text (e.g., Joel 2:28–32 = Acts 2:17–21; Ps 68:18 = Eph 4:8) or else minor adjustments are made to the Old Testament text (e.g., Hab 2:4 = Rom 1:17). In citing the Old Testament, the New Testament authors were not so much concerned with reproducing the exact words of an autograph, but with conveying the meaning of the text, and they even felt the liberty at times to render the text more conducive to their interpretive and expository intentions.

Sixth, another comment I have to make, at the risk of sounding irreverent, is that if God inspired all the words of Scripture in their Greek case, order, and syntactical construction, then in the book of Revelation, God needs some remedial training in Greek grammar. That is because the Greek of Revelation, highly Semitized and rough, is poor compared to the polished Greek of Luke and Hebrews.

My suggestion is that if we take into account the *phenomenon* of Scripture as well as its *didactic witness* to itself, the best model for the inspiration of Scripture is the dynamic view. Inspiration takes place *primarily* at the conceptual level. Obviously, you cannot have concepts without words, so there is some overlap with the verbal model. Inspiration tells us, though without giving us a description of the exact cognitive process, that these human *words* can be identified with God's *Word*. Thus we can legitimately say that it is not only Ezekiel, Amos, Jeremiah, Matthew, Paul, or Peter who speak to us, but through them, God is the one speaking to the church. It is God's voice that is heard in the grammar, style, and words of the authors.

However, authors are inspired at the level of concept, framework, worldview, and idea.[55] Their own style, personality, vocabulary, and even their idiosyncrasies come out—not despite inspiration but in tandem with it. As Loraine Boettner wrote:

> Inspiration must have been somewhat like the touch of the driver on the reins of the racing steeds. The preservation of the individual styles and mannerisms indicates as much. Under this providential control the prophets were so governed that while their humanity was not superseded their words to the people were God's words and have been accepted as such by the Church in all ages.... Hence we see that the Christian doctrine of inspiration is not the mechanical lifeless process which unfriendly critics have often represented it to be. Rather it calls the whole personality of the prophet into action, giving full play to his own literary style and mannerisms, taking into consideration the preparation given the prophet in order that he might deliver a particular kind of message, and allowing for the use of other documents or sources of information as these were needed. If these facts were kept more clearly in mind the doctrine of inspiration would not be so summarily set aside nor so unreasonably attacked by otherwise cautious and reverent scholars.[56]

6.3.5.2 VERACITY

Historically, Christians of all stripes have believed that their Scriptures are "true."[57] What God reveals about himself is true because God speaks the truth and he does not lie. But that still leads to the issues such as to what extent is Scripture true? Is it true even on scientific matters? Is it fully accurate on the minutia of historical details? Are its truth claims restricted entirely to theological matters? Does Scripture contain any errors at all, like errors of fact or consistency?

The witness of Scripture is that the Word of God is fully truthful in all that it affirms. In the Psalter we read things like: "The words of the LORD are flawless, like silver purified in a crucible, like gold refined seven times" (Ps 12:6); "the law of the LORD is perfect, refreshing the soul. The statutes of the LORD are trustworthy" (19:7); "the word of the LORD is right and true; he is faithful in all he does" (33:4). In the testimony of the Beloved Disciple, Jesus himself said, "Scripture cannot be set aside" (John 10:35), which means that Scripture cannot prove to be inconsistent with itself. John the Seer constantly emphasizes that the words of his prophecy are "trustworthy and true" (Rev 21:5; 22:6) because they come from Messiah Jesus, who is himself faithful,

---

55. Against Timothy Ward (*Words of Life: Scripture as the Living and Active Word of God* [Nottingham, UK: Apollos, 2009], 87–88) this is more than God giving the biblical authors "clues" and then leaving them "to their own devices." What I envisage is the active power of God enabling the authors to be themselves in their own words, to communicate that which God fully intends, but without overpowering their vocabulary or necessarily improving their grammar.

56. Loraine Boettner, *The Inspiration of the Scriptures* (Grand Rapids: Eerdmans, 1940), 25–27.

57. Cf. especially John Woodbridge, *Biblical Authority: A Critique of the Rogers/McKim Proposal* (Grand Rapids: Zondervan, 1982).

holy, just, and true (3:7, 14; 15:3). The testimony of God's Word to itself is that it is an authentic and authoritative account of everything it declares to have happened, to be, or will yet take place. God speaks to reality as it was, as it is, and as it yet will be.

The language of revelation is accommodated to the worldview and expectations of its audience in matters of cosmology and historiography, but the accommodation is never a capitulation to error. God does not speak erroneously nor does he feed us nuts of truth lodged inside shells of falsehood. G. W. Bromiley put it aptly: "While it is in no doubt a paradox that eternal truth is revealed in temporal events and witnesses through a human book, it is sheer unreason to say that truth is revealed in and through that which is erroneous."[58]

The Christian tradition, in diverse ways, has affirmed the biblical testimony that Scripture is inspired, authoritative, and reliable. The 1689 LBC (1.1) confesses: "The Holy Scripture is the only sufficient, certain, and infallible rule of all saving knowledge, faith, and obedience."[59] In more recent decades, the Lausanne Covenant (par. 2) declares a belief shared by evangelicals around the world: "We affirm the divine inspiration, truthfulness and authority of both Old and New Testament Scriptures in their entirety as the only written word of God, without error in all that it affirms, and the only infallible rule of faith and practice." You can pick up the recurring theme: God reveals truth, contingent and eternal, that corresponds to the God-created reality of the universe.

In North America, amidst the liberal versus fundamentalist debates that raged in denominations from the late nineteenth century on, many Christians began to speak of biblical "inerrancy." According to the Chicago Statement on Biblical Inerrancy, inerrancy means: "Scripture, having been given by divine inspiration, is infallible, so that, far from misleading us, it is true and reliable in all the matters it addresses.... Scripture in its entirety is inerrant, being free from all falsehood, fraud, or deceit."[60] The concept of inerrancy is a thoroughly ancient idea, though the actual word is a relatively new one, as J. I. Packer writes:

> Evangelicals are accustomed to speak of the Word of God as *infallible* and *inerrant*. The former has a long pedigree; among the Reformers, Cranmer and Jewel spoke of God's Word as infallible, and the Westminster Confession of the "infallible truth" of Holy Scripture. The latter, however, seems not to have been regularly used in this connection before the nineteenth century.[61]

The word "infallible" is the more prominent term in historic and global evangelicalism and for that reason is all the more preferable.

---

58. G. W. Bromiley, "The Authority of Scripture," in *The New Bible Commentary* (eds. F. Davidson, A. M. Stibbs, and E. F. Kevan (London: Inter-Varsity Fellowship, 1954), 22.

59. For an online version of the London Baptist Confession of 1689, see www.1689.com/confession.html.

60. Chicago Statement on Biblical Inerrancy, arts. 11–12.

61. Packer, *Word of God*, 94–95.

It is important to remember that many Christians around the world, though holding to an orthodox and high view of Scripture, did not experience the struggle with liberalism in the same way as what took place in North America. The inerrancy debate that came to a head in the late twentieth century is very much an intra-American affair, as Daniel J. Treier comments, "Conflict over scriptural inerrancy has not defined evangelicalism elsewhere as it did in the United States."[62] So outside of America "inerrancy" has never been a mandatory marker for orthodoxy. Instead, global churches have used the language of authority, infallibility, and sufficiency to underscore the claims of Scripture.

Thus, in seeking to define the way in which the Bible is true, or not untrue, there is the danger that one opts for a definition that is detailed and robust, but thereby becomes so specific that it fails to reflect the breadth of the Christian tradition, historical and global. For that reason, I prefer stating the truthfulness of the Christian Bible in positive terms as "veracity." In fact, this is the more "biblical" approach since in the book of Revelation there is a large emphasis on God and God's Word as "trustworthy" (Rev 3:14; 19:9; 21:5; 22:6). Hence, there is merit in Donald Bloesch's advocacy of the "truthfulness or veracity of Scripture" as a preferred point of affirmation. Bloesch proceeds to speak of infallibility "as derivative from the One who alone is infallible." He thinks inerrancy is "not the preferable word" but maintains that "it should not be abandoned, for it preserves the nuance of truthfulness and is necessary for a high view of Holy Scripture."[63]

What is the basis for belief in the Bible as inspired, infallible, veracious, and authoritative? Augustine said: "I should not believe the gospel except as moved by the authority of the catholic church."[64] Obviously the church approves and canonizes Scripture, but only as a way of acknowledging the Word that created the church in the first place. The problem is that while there is a close relationship between God's revelation and those through whom and to whom it was revealed, the church is nonetheless too fallible to be an ultimate judge for authenticating divine revelation. As Webster says, "the authority of scripture is the authority of the church's Lord and his gospel, and so cannot be made an immanent feature of ecclesial existence."[65]

Alternatively, can one rationally prove the inspiration and inerrancy of Scripture? It is tempting to try take on the modernist critique of biblical revelation by using the tools of modernist rationalism. On such a scheme, an apologist might try

---

62. Daniel J. Treier, "Scripture and Hermeneutics," in *The Cambridge Companion to Evangelical Theology* (ed. Timothy Larsen and Daniel J. Treier; Cambridge: Cambridge University Press, 2007), 40.

63. Donald Bloesch, *Holy Scripture: Revelation, Inspiration and Interpretation* (Downers Grove, IL: InterVarsity Press, 1994), 116.

64. Cited in Webster, *Scripture*, 61.

65. Ibid., 56.

to turn the rationalist assault against the Christian faith into an apologetic boomerang that returns to clobber the critic by exposing the inconsistency and illogic of their position with their own methods. That would mean showing by means of rational evidences that the Bible is God's inspired and inerrant Word. Such a strategy seeks to establish the existence of God by rational proofs, prove the historicity of the Bible's miracles, and then demonstrate the reliability of Jesus' claims as narrated in the Bible.

I have no problem with apologetic approaches to the historical character of God's Word and its reliability when measured by canons of historical study. Christianity is a historical religion based on a historical revelation; thus to historical study it must go![66] However, I think that ultimately, if the Word of God is God's own Word, then its veracity is safeguarded not by our efforts to harmonize any apparent inconsistencies or even by our sophisticated arguments for inerrancy, but by divine fidelity.[67] That is to say, the truthfulness of Scripture is secured by the faithfulness of God to his own Word. The veracity of Scripture is established by the integrity of God and is not dependent on our abilities to demonstrate the absence of error in every case that could be thrown in our face by non-Christian critics. Unsurprisingly, Psalm 119 and Revelation 21–22 anchor the trustworthiness of God's Word to the very faithfulness of God.

Furthermore, epistemologically speaking, the way that we know Scripture is true (not the basis on which it is true, which is God's faithfulness) is not the testimony of the church or our best apologetic arguments, but it is primarily due to the Spirit's testimony. As the Westminster Confession 1.5 declares: "Our full persuasion and assurance of the infallible truth and divine authority thereof, is from the inward work of the Holy Spirit bearing witness by and with the Word in our hearts." That derives from Jesus' words that the Holy Spirit "will guide you into all the truth" (John 16:13).

Scripture is authenticated through the witness of God's Spirit. The Bible is God's Word not because we have "evidence that demands a verdict" or because any church council said so, but on account of the witness of the Holy Spirit to our spirit that we are reading the words of a Holy God in our Holy Scripture. All other evidence, from apologetics or historical theology, though having a valid place, is secondary to the work of the Holy Spirit in authoring and authenticating Scripture.

I suggest that the base plate for our doctrine of Scripture is not infallibility or inerrancy, important though they may be, but it is the matter of biblical authority.

---

66. Hence my own forays into historical apologetics in Michael Bird and James Crossley, *How Did Christianity Begin? A Believer and Non-Believer Examine the Evidence* (London: SPCK, 2008).

67. Cf. Carl Trueman and Paul Helm, eds., *The Trustworthiness of God: Perspectives on the Nature of Scripture* (Grand Rapids: Eerdmans, 2002), and Ward, *Words of Life*, 132.

If God's Word is true, it must be obeyed, simple as that. However, Scripture is not authoritative in and of itself, as if its pages have some kind of magical theological quality. Its authority is mediated from elsewhere. That authority is not derived from the church, but from God. The risen Jesus did not say to his disciples that all authority in heaven and earth has been given to the books they were going to write. No, he said, "All authority in heaven and on earth has been given to me" (Matt 28:18).[68]

Authority is mediated from God the Son to Scripture via the Holy Spirit so that it will authoritatively testify to God. Going further, we could say that the authority of Scripture must be conceived in Trinitarian terms. The authority is God the Father revealing the Son for whom the Holy Spirit speaks in Scripture. If that is the case, then the claims of Scripture are not negotiable. For it is in the Scriptures that the Holy Spirit speaks to us![69]

FURTHER READING

Allert, Craig D. *A High View of Scripture: The Authority of the Bible and the Formation of the New Testament Canon.* Grand Rapids: Baker, 2007.

Bird, Michael B., and Michael Pahl, eds. *The Sacred Text: Excavating the Texts, Exploring the Interpretations, and Engaging the Theologies of the Christian Scriptures.* GPP 7; Piscataway, NJ: Gorgias, 2010.

Henry, Carl F. *God, Revelation, and Authority.* 6 vols. Wheaton, IL: Crossway, 1999.

Ward, Timothy. *Words of Life: Scripture as the Living and Active Word of God.* Nottingham, UK: Apollos, 2009.

---

68. N. T. Wright, *The Last Word* (New York: HarperCollins, 2005), xi.

69. A tertiary matter to mention is the "clarity" of Scripture. Exactly how clear is it and on what topics? Both the WCF 1.7 and 1689 LBC 1.7 state that the clarity of Scripture is actually limited: "All things in Scripture are not alike plain in themselves, nor alike clear unto all: yet those things *which are necessary* to be known, believed, and observed *for salvation* are so clearly propounded, and opened in some place of Scripture or other, that not only the learned, but the unlearned, in a due use of the ordinary means, may attain unto a sufficient understanding of them." Some things in Scripture are easy to understand (like the gospel), while other things are rather hard (like certain tricky passages, e.g., Mark 4:11–12). I rather like the definition of the clarity of Scripture given by Vanhoozer (*Is There A Meaning in This Text?* [Grand Rapids: Zondervan, 1998], 315): "Clarity means that the Bible is sufficiently unambiguous in the main for any well-intentioned person with Christian faith to interpret each part with relative adequacy." See further, Mark D. Thompson, *A Clear and Present Word: The Clarity of Scripture* (NSBT; Downers Grove, IL: InterVarsity Press, 2006); Ward, *Words of Life*, 117–29.

WHAT TO TAKE HOME?

- The gift of the Holy Spirit is part of the promise of the gospel and also the power for gospel proclamation.
- The Holy Spirit is a personal being, not an impersonal force or energy from God.
- The Holy Spirit is equal in deity and majesty with the Father and the Son.
- The work of the Holy Spirit includes creating, vivifying, empowering, sanctifying, revealing, and unifying.
- Baptism in the Holy Spirit happens at conversion, though filling with the Holy Spirit is a repeatable experience throughout the Christian life.
- The Holy Spirit inspires Scripture through a synthesis of divine and human minds to create God's Word in written form.
- Scripture is authoritative because it is the Holy Spirit speaking in it, and Scripture is true because of God's own faithfulness to his Word.

STUDY QUESTIONS FOR INDIVIDUALS AND GROUPS

1. Do people in your churches think of the Holy Spirit as an impersonal power?
2. What have been the blessings and drawbacks of the Pentecostal/charismatic movement?
3. Do you think we should worship the Holy Spirit?
4. Does the Holy Spirit still reveal new truths?
5. How does the doctrine of the Holy Spirit affect the way you attempt to live a Spirit-filled life?
6. What does the Spirit-filled church look like?
7. What is meant by the "veracity of Scripture"?

PART SEVEN

The Gospel and Humanity

§7.1 Sons and Daughters of the King
§7.2 Image of God
§7.3 What Is Humanity? The Human Constitution
§7.4 What is the Problem with Humanity?
§7.5 The Odyssey of Theodicy

The study of humanity is called "anthropology." Our mediator is "the man Christ Jesus," who saves men and women in the gospel of grace. Study of humanity covers the topics of the image of God, the constitution of humanity, and the nature of sin. The main theme is that of the royal nature of humanity in the plan of God.

> What is man that you are mindful of him,
>   and the son of man that you care for him?
> Yet you have made him a little lower than the heavenly beings
>   and crowned him with glory and honor.[1]

What a figment of the imagination human beings are! What a novelty, what monsters! Chaotic, contradictory, prodigious, judging everything, mindless worm of the earth, storehouse of truth, cesspool of uncertainty and error, glory and reject of the universe. Who will unravel this tangle?[2]

> A paradox, this man: both son of God
> And rebel, stellar powers bursting out
> Through spirit mean and shoddy, cloaked about
> With fine creative genius, yet a clod
> Of dirt, compounded equally of sod
> And everlasting consciousness, a lout
> With moral aspirations, clutching clout
> In empty power scrambles, sordid, odd.
> Reflecting the Creator, given high
> Preferment, ever served by angel hosts,
> This son of wrath, preferring darkness, died,
> His true paternity a barren boast.
> God spoke: in his own image he made man;
> And blemished though that image be, it stands.[3]

---

1. Psalm 8:4–5 (ESV).
2. Blaise Pascal, *Pensées and Other Writings* (Oxford: Oxford University Press, 2008), 41,
3. D. A. Carson, *Holy Sonnets of the Twentieth Century* (Grand Rapids: Baker, 1994), 17.

§7.1 SONS AND DAUGHTERS OF THE KING

According to Answers.com, a human being consists of the following elements: oxygen (65%), carbon (18%), hydrogen (10%), nitrogen (3%), calcium (1.5%), phosphorus (1.0%), potassium (0.35%), sulfur (0.25%), sodium (0.15%), magnesium (0.05%), along with copper, zinc, selenium, molybdenum, fluorine, chlorine, iodine, manganese, cobalt, iron (0.70%), plus trace amounts of lithium, strontium, aluminum, silicon, lead, vanadium, arsenic, and bromine. In an atheistic conception of human beings, they are nothing more than a mass of elements that has slowly evolved into a living organism through seemingly random and purposeless forces. On such an account of humankind, existence is accidental and meaningless, life is meaningless, death is meaningless, and all attempts to find or create meaning prove to be in the end, well, meaningless. Whether it is ethics, art, or religion, these are all feeble attempts to identify value in an existence that is inherently valueless.

In this view, one can pretend that human life has worth, a goal, or even intrinsic rights, but such statements have the same metaphysical truth value as saying, "I think that the stars are pretty." They are nothing more than constructs of a mind desperately trying to find significance in its otherwise insignificant existence. All human talk of value, purpose, or transcendence is just as meaningless as the soulless and senseless universe that accidentally brought those humans into being. It is truly a cruel irony of human existence that humans have evolved to a point of such cerebral complexity where they are able to understand and enjoy the universe, can love "others," and can even create works of beauty, only to learn that all their emotion and energy are nothing more than an evolutionary mechanism; they are an illusion of value, a mirage of meaning, designed to enhance their survival by tricking them into thinking that who they are and what they do actually matter. These pitiable creatures reach the precipice of knowledge only to learn that all knowledge is void of any truth and value other than what they created for themselves.

This plight, this "human condition," is bleak. Albert Camus famously said, "He who despairs of the human condition is a coward, but he who has hope for it is a fool." Article 11 of the Humanist Manifesto I (1933) proffers this advice:

> Man will learn to face the crises of life in terms of his knowledge of their naturalness and probability. Reasonable and manly attitudes will be fostered by education and supported by custom. We assume that humanism will take the path of social and mental hygiene and discourage sentimental and unreal hopes and wishful thinking.[4]

I find the words "social and mental hygiene" disturbing, as they presume the need and legitimacy of cleansing society and deprogramming people's minds of belief in anything nonmaterialist or transcendent. One need only read the chilling accounts of the cruelty done to religious minorities by atheistic regimes in Asia, Africa, South America, and Europe to know how this works out in practice.[5] The humanist can become utterly inhumane when it comes to forcing their ideology onto others. But this itself we are told is part of an evolutionary process of bringing humanity to a higher plane of consciousness and is thus legitimate. So it seems that one must descend into primal, animal-like violence in order to save the world from primitive superstitions, though we should hardly be surprised, after all, if human life is marred by *insignificance* that it can easily be treated with *indifference*.

Jared Diamond in his book *The Third Chimpanzee* refers to humans as "little more than glorified chimpanzees."[6] Diamond actually gets something right here. There is something absolutely "glorious" about human beings. There is something about humanity that is different from the animal world. We walk upright, we have opposable thumbs and a large brain, and we even invented fire and X-Box 360! The "design" of the human body, from the eye to the brain, is truly a feat of biological engineering. It was the marvel of the human constitution that led the psalmist to praise God because "I am fearfully and wonderfully made" (Ps 139:14).

It is not just that human life is complex, but it appears to be both complex and good when it need not be. Arguments for theism and debates over creation aside, Christians confess that this sense of awe at human life and its order, goodness, and value is possible only because of a divine Creator who gives life to humanity as the pinnacle of creation. Christians believe in a God who imprints something of himself into humanity when he created them—a God who imparts something of his own glory into his sons and daughters. Human beings are created in such a way that God has "crowned them with glory and honor" (Ps 8:5). Humanity was made in glory, a royal glory no less, created to have dominion over creation as God's vice-regents.

---

4. See www.americanhumanist.org/Humanism/Humanist_Manifesto_I.

5. I have in mind Richard Wurmbrand's *Tortured For Christ* (Bartlesville, OK: Living Sacrifice, 1998); see also Catherine Mackenzie, *Richard Wurmbrand: A Voice in the Dark* (Fearn, UK: Christian Focus, 1997).

6. Cited in Dinesh D'Souza, *What's So Great about Christianity?* (Washington, DC: Regnery, 2007), 143.

The glory of humanity is a reflection of the glory of God. That is why Paul told the Corinthians that a man "is the image and glory of God" (1 Cor 11:7). The Dead Sea Scrolls contain a reference to Adam "our father, you fashioned in the likeness of your glory" (4Q508 frag. 8.4). That's a pretty good summary of the creation of humanity in Genesis 1 as the climax to creation. The Qumranites believed that a future salvation would be for those whom God elected, and "to them shall belong all the glory of Adam" (1QS 4.22–23). What we have in the Qumran scrolls is some basic exegesis of the Old Testament where salvation consisting of making the *Endzeit* the same as the *Urzeit*. In other words, the glory that Adam had with God in the beginning of creation (*Urzeit*) is to be restored in the saving work that God does for the elect at the end of all things (*Endzeit*). That is a good biblical theme: glory lost and glory regained.

While humanity was created in glory, it is also important to remember that they were created *for* glory. The first question of the Westminster Larger Catechism is, "What is the chief and highest end of man?" To which the answer is, "Man's chief and highest end is to glorify God, and fully to enjoy him forever." Contra Augustine, humanity was not created to populate heaven with rational creatures to make up for the number of the angels who decided to rebel against God. Humanity was created to glorify God—that is, to esteem God and enjoy his glory for all of eternity. God's purpose is to glorify himself by the effusion of his love. God achieves that by enabling humanity, his children, to enjoy the glory of his being. As John Piper puts it: "God created us for this: to live our lives in a way that makes him look more like the greatness and the beauty and the infinite worth that he really is."[7]

The gospel is thus the story of humanity regaining its stake in divine glory. While the gospel is theocentric and Christ-centered, and not about simply satisfying felt human needs for self-esteem and relational wholeness, even so, there is a significant amount of anthropocentrism in the gospel. God really is concerned with the fate of human beings, in spite of the fact that they have rejected his sovereignty, spurned his love, and mistreated his Son. It is the God-man Jesus Christ who reconciles fallen humanity to God. The saving work of Christ restores humanity to true humanness. The gospel declares the crucifixion of the "old self" and the enlivening of the "new self." Christ is the Savior of humanity, but in another sense he defines humanness, true humanness as God intended it to be. Christ and the Spirit renew humanity and lift them up to the throne of divine glory, where humanity was always intended to be.

Taking this altogether, humanity is not a mindless grouping of atoms or a

---

7. John Piper, *Don't Waste Your Life* (Wheaton, IL: Crossway, 2009), 33.

A LITERAL ADAM?

One topic that it is impossible to avoid when it comes to humanity is the historicity of Adam and Eve. In short, is it the case that "God directly created Adam and Eve, the historical parents of the entire human race"?[8] Put simply, is the story of Adam and Eve literal or metaphorical? This question is answered differently by (1) special creationists, who believe in a literal six-day creation with a literal Adam; (2) progressive creationists, who believe that God created new life forms over millions of years and that the first two homo sapiens were Adam and Eve; and (3) theistic evolutionists, who believe that God used evolution to create life and that Adam and Eve are chiefly symbolic.[9] What is so problematic is that in order to answer this question, one has to take into account cosmology, geology, biology, genetics, ancient Near Eastern creation stories, biblical theology, and hermeneutics.

Because I am convinced by cosmology and geology that the earth is old and find nothing in Scripture to contradict that, I lean toward progressive creationism as the most biblically and scientifically satisfying option.[10] Even so, I maintain belief in a literal Adam and Eve for several reasons:

1. The genetic similarities between chimpanzees and humans may be in the vicinity of 95 percent to 99 percent; but there is more than genetics that accounts for the differences between humans and chimps. In addition, similarity does not demand shared ancestry.
2. Though recent genetic studies have argued that humans emerged from a population pool of 10,000 people rather than two people, the actual rates of change in genetic diversity are ambiguous.
3. Genesis 1–11 contains a mixture of history and parable and oscillates between the literal and the figurative.[11] It was not intended to be a scientific account of human origins; rather, it is a creation story to be understood by all peoples, be they ancient or modern, that God is the Father of the entire human race. Genesis 1 is primarily about establishing a theistic worldview,

---

8. Wheaton College Statement of Faith. www.wheaton.edu/About-Wheaton/Statement-of-Faith-and-Educational-Purpose. Accessed 14 June 2013.

9. J. P. Moreland and John M. Reynolds, eds., *Three Views on Creation and Evolution* (Grand Rapids: Zondervan, 1999).

10. I also find the idea of amino acids randomly evolving into astronauts a bit farfetched and the notion of an Intelligent Designer seems far more believable than an atheistic account of evolutionism.

11. Henri Blocher, *In the Beginning: The Opening Chapters of Genesis* (trans. D. G. Preston; Leicester, UK: Inter-Varsity Press, 1984), 36–38.

> not refuting Darwinianism. The opening chapters of Genesis speak through a particular literary genre and a particular cultural context that saw humanity as formed immediately by God's creative act in opposition to competing creation stories about human origins. This literary rather than literal approach to Genesis 1–11 certainly opens up the possibility of a symbolic reading of Adam and Eve as the story of Israel's beginnings, not necessarily the beginnings of the human race. However, Genesis 1–3 has its poignancy and penetration as a historically rooted narrative of human beginnings. Even works of a literary or metaphorical nature can still have historical referents at their core. The story of Adam and Even is not a prescientific fable or a pious fiction of human origins. Rather, it is a theologically embedded story of God's creation of the human race; a story with characters as real as the earth they stand on, and yet they stand for more than being our primal parents, as their story testifies to the creative power of God over the world of human beings and explains how God's perfect paradise went wrong.
>
> 4. Paul clearly believed in a literal Adam, who was prototype and antitype to Christ, the second Adam (Rom 5:12–21; 1 Cor 15:21–22, 45). If there never was an original Adam, there never was an original sin; and if there was no original sin, that puts Jesus (risen or otherwise) into the realm of the unemployed.
>
> **FURTHER READING**
> Berkouwer, G. C. *Man: The Image of God*. Grand Rapids: Eerdmans, 1962.
> Jewett, Paul K. *Who We Are: Our Dignity as Human: A Neo-Evangelical Theology*. Grand Rapids: Eerdmans, 1996.
> Neil, Stephen. *What is Man?* London: Lutterworth, 1960.
> Sherlock, Charles. *The Doctrine of Humanity*. Leicester, UK: Inter-Varsity Press, 1996.

random mutation of matter into self-conscious existence. Human beings are right and royally glorious because they are created in the image of God. That is to say, human beings, as male and female, are the royal heirs of God's beautiful world. They were created to reign in glory and to enjoy God's glory.

But it is a glory that is spoiled and tarnished by the evil that has entered God's garden kingdom. The royal tenants of the garden have descended into little more than rational animals. The once-beautiful garden is now polluted with corruption at the physical, psychological, and spiritual levels. God's plan is to return humanity to its state of primal glory by uniting creation with the Logos. The end of all things in this world will include humanity returning to their glorious estate and glorifying God in an eternal state. The gospel is the story of human glory lost in evil, the gift of the glorious Lord Jesus, and the glorification of humanity in God's new world.

FURTHER READING

Caneday, Ardel B. "The Language of God and Adam's Genesis & Historicity in Paul's Gospel." *SWBTJ* 15 (2001): 26–49.

Collins, C. John. *Did Adam and Eve Really Exist? Who They Were and Why You Should Care.* Wheaton, IL: Crossway, 2011.

Collins, Francis. *The Language of God: A Scientist Presents Evidence for Belief.* New York: Free Press, 2006.

Enns, Peter. *The Evolution of Adam: What the Bible Does and Doesn't Say About Human Origins.* Grand Rapids: Brazos, 2012.

Ostling, Richard N. "The Search for the Historical Adam." *Christianity Today* 55.6 (2011): 22–27.

Walton, John. *The Lost World of Genesis One: Ancient Cosmology and the Origins Debate.* Downers Grove, IL: InterVarsity Press, 2009.

§7.2 IMAGE OF GOD

The central component in the doctrine of humanity is the affirmation that humans are created in the *imago dei*, that is, the "image of God." Reference to this theme persistently recurs throughout Scripture, both the Old and New Testament, where emphasis falls on humanity under God and humanity over creation. The gospel leads us to believe that the divine image is restored in humanity by Christ and the image is even defined by the humanity of Christ.

> Then God said, "Let us make mankind in our *image*, in our *likeness*, so that they may rule over the fish in the sea and the birds in the sky, over the livestock and all the wild animals, and over all the creatures that move along the ground."
>
> So God created human beings in his own *image*, in the *image of God* he created them; male and female he created them. (Gen 1:26–27)

> This is the written account of Adam's family line.
>
> When God created mankind, he made them in the *likeness of God*. He created them male and female and blessed them. And he named them "Mankind" when they were created. (Gen 5:1–2)

> Whoever sheds human blood,
>   by humans shall their blood be shed;
> for in the *image of God*
>   has God made mankind.
> As for you, be fruitful and increase in number; multiply on the earth and increase upon it. (Gen 9:6–7)

> A man ought not to cover his head, since he is the *image and glory of God*; but woman is the glory of man. For man did not come from woman, but woman from man; neither was man created for woman, but woman for man. (1 Cor 11:7–9)

> And just as we have borne the *image* of the earthly man, so shall we bear the *image* of the heavenly man. (1 Cor 15:49)

> For those God foreknew he also predestined to be conformed to the *image of his Son*, that he might be the firstborn among many brothers and sisters. (Rom 8:29)

> And we all, who with unveiled faces contemplate the Lord's glory, are being *transformed into his image* with ever-increasing glory, which comes from the Lord, who is the Spirit. (2 Cor 3:18)

> The god of this age has blinded the minds of unbelievers, so that they cannot see the light of the gospel that displays *the glory of Christ, who is the image of God*. (2 Cor 4:4)
>
> The *Son is the image of the invisible God*, the firstborn over all creation. (Col 1:15)
>
> [You] have put on the new self, which is being renewed in knowledge in *the image of its Creator*. (Col 3:10)

The crucial text here is Genesis 1:26–27, since it provides the preliminary snapshot of human beings as specially endowed with a particular quality that makes them more closely related to God than the other creatures of creation. Genesis shows humanity as bearers of the divine image, which specifically designates that which makes humanity like God. What this "image" actually is, however, is debated by theologians.[12]

1. *Substantive view.* This perspective identifies the image as some quality or characteristic within the makeup of humanity that is shared with God. That shared quality can be physical, psychological, or spiritual. Most often it is the capacity for reasoning and reflection, the ability to engage in rational discourse, or the possession of a soul that is considered the locus of the divine image in human beings.

In the patristic period, it was common to distinguish between "likeness of God" and "image of God." The "image" meant freewill and reason, while "likeness" meant a supernatural endowment. According to Irenaeus and Tertullian, humanity lost the "likeness of God" at the fall, but retained the "image of God." It was only through the renewing power of the Holy Spirit that the likeness was restored. Augustine focused on human capacity for reason; the Cappadocian Fathers identified the image with Adam's freedom from death and decay. In other words, for Augustine the image was marred by the fall, whereas for the Cappodicians the image was completely erased by the fall. The problem here is that the Hebrew of Genesis 1:26–27 uses parallelism, so that "image" and "likeness" are equivalent referents and not two separate things.

Luther and Calvin both propounded a unitary view of the image and maintained that a relic of the image remained in human beings after the fall albeit in a corrupted form. For Calvin, though, the retention of the image, even in a defaced form, was still the basis for our ability to know ourselves and to know God. Erickson defends a substantive view by regarding the image as that which is intrinsic to human nature. The image is not what a human *has*, or what a human *does*, but what a human *is*. He writes: "The image refers to the elements in the human makeup that enable the fulfillment of human destiny. The image is the powers of personality that make humans, like God, being capable of interacting with other persons, of thinking and reflecting, and of willing freely."[13]

---

12. Cf. Charles Sherlock, *The Doctrine of Humanity* (Leicester, UK: Inter-Varsity Press, 1996), 73–91.

13. Millard J. Erickson, *Christian Theology* (2nd ed.; Grand Rapids: Baker, 1998), 532.

2. *Relational view.* Many twentieth-century theologians focused on the image not as an aspect of God's character that humans share, but rather as a human capacity for relationships. For Brunner, the image has a formal aspect in human responsibility to respond to God, but it also has a material aspect in freedom, reason, and conscience.[14] Barth's mature theology identified the image as consisting of not only a vertical relationship with God but also a relationship with other human beings.[15] The image, then, is related to the fact that God brought into existence beings like himself who can love someone other than themselves. The image of God is the imaging of the Triune God in loving relationships. As the Godhead has fellowship within himself, so too are humans created to be in relationships with each other. To support this, Barth noted that in Genesis 1:27 and 5:1–2, Scripture mentions the image in the context of "male and female." It is *as male and female*, by possessing relationship with each other, that humans are image bearers. Thus, humans reflect this aspect of God's nature on two levels: in their relationship with God and in their relationship with each other.

Moreover, for Barth, we learn about humanity by knowing Christ's humanity, not vice versa. Jesus Christ is the true covenant partner who covenants with God and with humanity. *Ecce homo* means "behold the man," that is, behold the *true* man. The community of those "in Christ" reveals in the present age what it means to be in God's image. Jesus Christ defines humanity, and believers *become* authentically human in the corporate conformity to Jesus Christ. Thus, Barth integrates Christology and ecclesiology into his meaning of the *imago dei*.

3. *Functional view.* Another perspective regards the image not as a quality in humans, not as their capacity for relationships, but in terms of their function as exercising dominion over creation.[16] Both Genesis 1:28 and Psalm 8:5–6 emphasize humans as rulers of creation. The image then refers to humanity's dominion over the created order, which is a reflection of God's own dominion over the universe. God made humans to care for creation and to be representatives of God's lordship over the lower orders of creation.[17]

4. *Royal view.* A further view I want to put forward, a variation of the functional position, is the "royal view," whereby the "image" means that humanity is royal and is created to rule. In the ancient Near East, "image of God" was a throne name for monarchs. Kings were regarded as special servants of the gods and accordingly bore

---

14. Emil Brunner, *Man in Revolt* (trans. O. Wyon; New York: Scribner's, 1939), 510.

15. Karl Barth, *CD*, III/1:192–206.

16. Cf. Paul Sands, "The *Imago Dei* as Vocation," *EvQ* 82 (2010): 28–41.

17. Note that some theologians think that dominion is a consequence of the image and not its content (e.g., Erickson, *Christian Theology*, 532). Furthermore, many theologians define the image broadly as entailing all elements of relationality, substance, and dominion. For instance, Anthony Hoekema (*Created in God's Image* [Grand Rapids: Eerdmans, 1986], 69) writes: "Since the image of God includes the whole person, it must include both man's structure and man's functioning. One cannot function without a certain structure."

their image as rulers of the earth. The Egyptian Pharaoh was considered to be an incarnation of the sun god Ra. In a papyrus fragment from Egypt during the Ptolemaic period is a reference to a king as "a living image of Zeus, son of the Sun."[18] Rather than read the "image of God" as an ontological statement, if we take into account the ancient Near Eastern context, Genesis 1:26–27 may be saying no more than humanity is royal in God's eyes. Whereas the image was restricted to an elite few monarchs in oriental thought, the privilege of bearing God's image is democratized so that all humanity shares in it.[19] Humanity is thus royal and is made in order to rule over creation as God's vice-regent. The main *functions* of this royal reign in Genesis 1:26–28 include having dominion over the earth. On this perspective, God is a generous Creator who shares power with his creatures by inviting them and trusting them to participate in his reign over the world.[20]

Consequently, humanity is the cosmic media for expressing God's sovereignty and presence in the world. Ancient kings made iconic images of themselves and placed them all over their kingdom where people could see them. Think of Saddam Hussein, who filled Iraq with statues of himself to show his power and authority over the Arab nation. This proliferation of images was a form of media that marked out a king's territory by literally enfacing himself all over the realm with statues and paintings of himself. These images were reminders about just whose jurisdiction the people were living under. It was a royal sign of the king's presence and power over their subjects.

Similarly, then, God has set humanity in his creation as walking billboards of his own might and authority. Humans reflect the reign and goodness of God when they justly rule over the created order. The reign of humanity, at its best, is an advertisement for the sovereignty of God over the cosmos. C. S. Lewis beautifully captures God's intent to use humanity to radiate his image into the world when he wrote the fictive rant of a demon who abhors humanity with these words: "He [God] really does want to fill the universe with a lot of loathsome little replicas of Himself—creatures whose life, on its miniature scale, will be qualitatively like His own, not because He has absorbed them but because their wills freely conform to it."[21]

Furthermore, the "image of God" must be defined christologically. Now humans are little "icons" of God, and it is noteworthy that our English word "icon" comes from the Greek *eikōn*. The Sydney Opera House is an *eikōn* of Australia, the Eiffel Tower is an *eikōn* of France, and Big Ben is an *eikōn* of England. The building represents more than creative architecture; it evokes ideas and feelings that we associate with an entire country. By analogy, humans are an *eikōn* of God that signify and rep-

---

18. *NDIEC*, 9:36

19. Victor P. Hamilton, *The Book of Genesis* (NICOT; Grand Rapids: Eerdmans, 1990), 135.

20. J. Richard Middleton, *The Liberating Image: The Imago Dei in Genesis 1* (Grand Rapids: Brazos, 2005), 296–97.

21. C. S. Lewis, *The Screwtape Letters* (New York: Macmillan, 1961), 38.

resent something of God.²² But humans are cracked *eikōns*, tarnished in the beauty, diminished in authority, and darkened in the luminosity of their image-bearing.

Coming to the New Testament, we observe references to Jesus as the "image" of God, including his ruling function as the Lord over creation (Rom 8:29; 1 Cor 15:49; 2 Cor 3:18; 4:4; Col 1:15; 3:10). Jesus is the perfect *eikōn* of God, who radiates God's glory in his reign as the "firstborn" over creation and new creation (Col 1:15, 18). According to F. F. Bruce: "To say that Christ is the image of God is to say that in him the nature and being of God have been perfectly revealed—that in him the invisible has become visible."²³ Yet Christ's "imaging" of God is more than a revelation. It is also a representation of God and a rescuing of humanity. To see Christ as the "image of God" is to say that Jesus represents God to creation in a way that Adam and Eve were called to do, but failed. Moreover, Jesus enables other human beings to have a covenant relationship with God, of which their fallenness had deprived them.²⁴ Only the Son, who is the perfect *eikōn* of God, can rescue the cracked *eikōns* of creation.

Part of the meaning of salvation is that our *eikōnic* faculties are gradually restored to their Edenic state, but even better, they are conformed to the christological version of that *eikōnic* state.²⁵ Salvation means being conformed to the image of God's Son (Rom 8:29). Deliverance brings a gradual transformation into the glorious humanity of the Lord Jesus Christ (2 Cor 3:18; 4:4). In that renewed image we become immortal rather than mortal, heavenly rather than earthly (1 Cor 15:49). In the new creation, headed up by the new Adam, the new humanity reflects the original image of its Creator (Col 3:10). When we are seated with Christ, we are returned to our proper human state (Eph 2:6; Col 3:1; Rev 20:4). For God made human beings to rule with him and to rule for him. This return to our Adamic dominion over creation begins for the saints who are in Christ in both an embryonic (present) and eschatological (future) sense.

In sum, the *imago dei* is a function, a royal vocation for humanity to reflect the reign of God in their stewardship over creation. They pursue that royal task by protecting human life (Gen 9:5), resisting ideologies of power where brutal monarchs try to monopolize the image for themselves (Matt 20:25–28), and caring for the earth and the animal world (Gen 1:28).

---

22. Yes, I'm aware of the danger of the etymological fallacy of reading the meaning of our English word "icon" into the Greek word *eikōn*, but my point is that the words are conceptually connected; both share the idea of a visual representation of something else, even though they are definitely not synonymous terms.

23. F. F. Bruce, *Colossians, Philemon, Ephesians* (NICNT; Grand Rapids: Eerdmans, 1984), 57–58.

24. Colin Gunton, *Christ and Creation* (Grand Rapids: Eerdmans, 1992), 100.

25. But note that at regeneration we do not automatically go back to being exactly like Adam and Eve before the fall, because (as any woman will tell you) childbirth still hurts a lot, even for Christian women (see Gen 3:16 about labor pains as part of the curse of the fall)!

§7.3 WHAT IS HUMANITY? THE HUMAN CONSTITUTION

I know that little boys are made of frogs and snails and puppy dogs' tails. I know that little girls are made of sugar and spice and all things nice. But what are people *really* made up of concerning their material and immaterial constitution? We have heart, body, mind, spirit, and soul. What are these things? In particular, what and where is the "soul"?

Generally, Christians have maintained a dualistic view of humanity as containing material and immaterial elements. No one doubts that we all physically exist in bodies, but debate concerns our immaterial nature. Specifically, is there a difference between "spirit" and "soul"? In addition, what is the "heart," "mind," and "strength"? Consider these biblical texts:

> Love the LORD your God with all your *heart* and with all your *soul* and with all your *strength*. (Deut 6:5)

> Love the Lord your God with all your *heart* and with all your *soul* and with all your *mind* and with all your *strength*. (Mark 12:30)

> May your whole *spirit, soul and body* be kept blameless at the coming of our Lord Jesus Christ. (1 Thess 5:23)

> For the word of God is alive and active. Sharper than any double-edged sword, it penetrates even to dividing *soul and spirit*, joints and marrow; it judges the *thoughts and attitudes* of the *heart*. (Heb 4:12)

There are three main proposals that theologians have for the human constitution: dichotomism, trichotomism, and monism.

1. *Anthropological dichotomism*. This perspective is that humanity is made up of material and immaterial parts. It posits that "spirit" and "soul" are used interchangeably in Scripture to describe the immaterial element of human existence. Thus, humans are divided into two elements of "body" and "spirit/soul."

Dichotomism has been the main position in Christian thought over the centuries. It is the most biblical position because it accounts for several elements of the biblical teaching about human constitution. First, the "soul" and "spirit" are practically synonymous in Scripture. Job laments: "I will speak out in the anguish of my spirit, I will complain in the bitterness of my soul" (Job 7:11). Isaiah declares: "My soul yearns for you in the night; in the morning my spirit longs for you" (Isa 26:9).[26] Mary bursts out in praise: "My soul glorifies the Lord and my spirit rejoices in God my Savior" (Luke 1:46–47). In the gospel of John, Jesus is troubled in "soul" and troubled in "spirit" on different occasions (John 12:27; 13:21).[27]

Second, we are told that both the spirit and soul can survive death. Concerning Rachel's death we read in Genesis 35:18: "her soul was departing (for she was dying)" (ESV). Isaiah's Suffering Servant "poured out his soul to death" (Isa 53:12 ESV). In a Lucan parable the rich fool is admonished: "This night your soul is required of you" (Luke 12:20 ESV). Elsewhere, one gives up their spirit at death: "Dust returns to the ground it came from, and the spirit returns to God who gave it" (Eccl 12:7). Stephen at his martyrdom prayed: "Lord Jesus, receive my spirit" (Acts 7:59). All in all, soul and spirit covers the whole immaterial side of human existence (see Rom 8:10; 1 Cor 5:3; Col 2:5).[28]

2. Anthropological trichotomism. This perspective attributes to humanity three elements of body (physical element), soul (psychological element), and spirit (spiritual element). The classic text for this position is 1 Thessalonians 5:23, "May your whole spirit, soul and body be kept blameless at the coming of our Lord Jesus Christ." More likely, though, Paul is simply being emphatic by repetition. The spirit and soul here designate the interior nature of one's being, not separate compartments. Keep in mind that a similar telescoping of descriptors for the inner self is found in the Gospels, where Jesus taught that heart, soul, mind, and strength are basically the same thing, even if slightly different emphases are placed on each element (Matt 22:37; Mark 12:30; Luke 10:27). Similarly, Hebrews 4:12, with the word of God "dividing soul and spirit," is not envisaging a medical procedure like separating Siamese twins. Rather, it is more like "being pierced to the heart," which indicates conviction and emotion (e.g., Jer 4:18).

3. Anthropological monism. On this perspective, humans are regarded as an indivisible unity. The person comprises the "self," not three separate pieces of body, mind, and soul. In a materialistic/atheistic perspective, all of human constitution is physical, chemical, and electrical, where there is no immaterial part of one's being that can survive death. Christian monists argue that the human life cannot exist apart from the human body; thus, all "soul language" is metaphorical (e.g., Luke 2:35, "a sword

---

26. These passages use the Hebrew *nepeš* ("soul") and *rûaḥ* (spirit) respectively.

27. These passages use the Greek *psuchē* (soul) and *pneuma* (spirit) respectively.

28. Cf. Erickson, *Christian Theology*, 540–43; Wayne Grudem, *Systematic Theology* (Grand Rapids: Zondervan, 1994), 472–77; Michael Horton, *The Christian Faith* (Grand Rapids: Zondervan, 2011), 377–79.

will pierce your own soul"; Heb 6:19 "anchor for the soul"). According to Pannenberg: "When the life of the soul is conditioned in every detail by bodily organs and processes, how can it be detached from the body and survive without it?"[29]

Recently Joel Green has attempted to integrate the neurosciences into a Christian anthropology in favor of Christian monism.[30] Green claims that science shows that the differences between humans and animals are relative, not absolute. Animals also can have a sense of humanlike consciousness and make moral decisions. What separates humanity from the animal kingdom is our capacity to have a covenant relationship with God and a covenant relationship with other human beings that reflects the covenant love of God. Green also rejects a body/soul dualism and embraces the view of the unity of the human person, namely, that the soul is the self. Green, as a biblical scholar, has no problem with that because he surmises that the biblical view teaches that a person is a holistic and unified being. Much of what is attributed to the soul in terms of cognitive reasoning can be attributed to neurophysical processes in the brain, which means that soul and body might not always be able to be distinguished completely:

> If the capacities traditionally allocated to the "soul"—for example, consistency of memory, consciousness, spiritual experience, the capacity to make decisions on the basis of self-deliberation, planning and action on the basis of that decision, and taking responsibility for these decisions and actions—have a neural basis, then the concept of "soul," as traditionally understood in theology as a person's "authentic self," seems redundant.[31]

The monism view flounders, however, if we believe that Scripture clearly teaches a postmortem, disembodied intermediate state (see 2 Cor 5:1–10; Phil 1:23–24).[32] What is more, for all our acquired knowledge about the brain and how it works, there is still an explanatory gap as to how the physical correlates of phenomenal states are related to feelings of that state.[33]

I find the dichotomy position to be the most defensible. Humans have an immaterial and material aspect to their being. They have bodies that are united with the God-given, immortal, and immaterial "life" that is within them. That "life" is their soul or spirit.[34] The monist challenge from biology and neuroscience is certainly interesting, but I don't think it dissolves the material and immaterial distinction.

---

29. Wolfhart Pannenberg, *Systematic Theology* (3 vols.; trans. G. W. Bromiley; Edinburgh: T&T Clark, 1991), 2:182.

30. Joel Green, *Body, Soul, and Human Life: The Nature of Humanity in the Bible* (Grand Rapids: Baker, 2008).

31. Ibid., 45.

32. This is the clear weakness of Green's (ibid., 152–80) otherwise engaging book.

33. Joel B. Green, "Body and Soul, Mind and Brain: Critical Issues," in *In Search of the Soul: Four Views on the Mind-Body Problem* (ed. J. B. Green and S. L. Palmer; Downers Grove, IL: InterVarsity Press, 2005), 11–12.

34. I would surmise that the "heart" is the emotional intelligence that a person possesses, "mind" is their intellect and conscience, while "strength" is their sense of self-determination and will.

The question is: How does dualism relate to the unity of the human self at the biological, cognitive, and spiritual levels? I like Erickson's take, where he posits a "conditional unity" between body and soul/spirit (hereafter just "soul").[35] We could call this a psychosomatic unity between body and soul. This overarching unity of the self as materially and immaterially constituted means that the union of body and soul is intrinsic to our being.

In biblical teaching, a person is a unified being, not a soul trapped inside a body, not a mass of tissue that feels religious sensations when certain neurons fire in the brain. Yes, body and soul are often contrasted (e.g., Ps 31:9; Prov 16:24; Matt 10:28), but sometimes they are not distinguished (esp. in the Psalms, e.g., Ps 42:2–6; Luke 12:19). Yet there is an immaterial aspect of human existence that is separable from the physical existence apart in the body.[36] This immaterial part of the person survives death in what is called the "intermediate state" until it is reunited with the body at the resurrection (see 2 Cor 5:1–10; see discussion of this passage in §3.6). So on this view, the normal state of human existence is a materialized unity of body and soul. This unity is broken down at death, the immaterial element is preserved in the intermediate state, but body and soul are then reunified at the resurrection.

FURTHER READING

Green, Joel B., and Stuart L. Palmer, eds. *In Search of the Soul: Four Views on the Mind-Body Problem.* Downers Grove, IL: InterVarsity Press, 2005.

Swinburne, Richard. *The Evolution of the Soul.* Rev. ed. Oxford: Clarendon, 1997.

---

35. Erickson, *Christian Theology*, 554–57. Cf. Horton (*Christian Faith*, 377), who prefers to speak of a "psychosomatic holism" that emphasizes unity.

36. On the origins of the soul, the main views that are that souls are created by God *ex nihilo* at the moment of their infusion into the body (Lactantius, Aquinas, Lombard), souls and body are formed together (Tertullian), or souls are pre-existent (Origen).

§7.4 WHAT IS THE PROBLEM WITH HUMANITY?

The gospel *assumes* that something is horribly wrong in the relationship between God and human beings; consequently, something has also gone horribly wrong in men and women themselves. This horrible something is a relational rupture, a black hole in the human heart, and a state of perpetual hostility that characterizes human relationships. Praise God that the gospel *announces* that Jesus' death and resurrection is God's answer to heal that rupture, to bring light into the darkness, and to establish lasting peace. But just as the gospel gives us cause to celebrate the healing and restoration graciously bestowed by God, it also requires us to reflect on the deprived and depraved human state that required the deliverance that the Son of God brings.

Salvation happily implies the end of our ruination. But just what kind of ruination are we talking about? What we are saved *to* tells us much about what we are saved *from*! To give a short selection of answers, we could say that according to the gospel:

- since believers are *justified*, they were formerly *condemned*.
- since believers are *reconciled* to God, they were formerly *estranged* from God.
- since believers were *rescued* from darkness, they were formerly *trapped* in darkness.
- since believers were *cleansed* by Jesus' blood, they were formerly *defiled* by moral impurity.
- since believers are *redeemed*, they were formerly *enslaved*.
- since believers are *made alive*, they were formerly *dead*.

But what is it that left humanity condemned, estranged, trapped, defiled, enslaved, and dead? The answer to that question is "sin." Sin is the act that creates a broken relationship between God and humanity. The Scriptures speak much about sin, about its origins and its effect. Indeed, "the occasions by which this relationship breaks, the need to recognize this rupture, and the avenues for salvation are detailed in endless situations throughout the Scriptures."³⁷ The study of sin is called *hamartiology*, and we will examine now the nature of sin, the power of sin, the sources of sin, the effect of sin, and God's victory over evil.

7.4.1 THE NATURE OF SIN

What is sin? It's hard to be precise because there is a plethora of images for sin in Scripture. Among the most prominent are the following:

1. *Lawlessness* (Gk. *anomia*). The first picture we have of sin is that of lawlessness—that is, disobedience to divine commands. According to 1 John 3:4, "Everyone who sins breaks the law; in fact, sin is lawlessness." Sin is a willful violation of God's law. Sin and law have had an umbilical relationship since the power of sin is the law (1 Cor 15:56), the law identifies the existence of sin (Rom 7:7), and apart from law sin is dead (7:8). Originally sin entered the world apart from the law of Moses (5:13), and the law actually magnified the effect of sin (5:20). Even those without the law of Moses can still act contrary to the law written on their hearts (2:15).

2. *Transgression* (Heb.ʿābar; Gk. *parabasis*). The words for transgression denote the idea of crossing over a boundary or knowingly pressing beyond an established limit. The people of Israel were not to transgress the covenant or they would suffer its curses (Deut 26.13; Jer 34:18; Dan 9:11). In the New Testament, Adam's particular disobedience is called a "transgression" (Rom 4:15; 1 Tim 2:14). Transgression puts us into the deathly hallows of living in open defiance against God (Eph 2:1–6).

3. *Rebellion and disobedience* (Heb. *pāšaʿ, mārâ, mārad*; Gk. *apeithēs, apeitheō*). Sin is depicted as a form of rebellion typified by a deliberate rejection of God's designs for humanity in general and Israel in particular. In Ezekiel, Israel is called "a rebellious nation that has rebelled against me; they and their ancestors have been in revolt against me to this very day" (Ezek 2:3). In Isaiah, Yahweh raised up Israel like a child, "but they have rebelled against me" (Isa 1:2). The Suffering Servant was (lit.) "pierced for our rebellion" (53:5). In Lamentations we read: "The LORD is righteous, yet I rebelled against his command" (Lam 1:18). A further description of Israel in Psalm 78:8 is that of "a stubborn and rebellious generation, whose hearts were not loyal to God, whose spirits were not faithful to him."

The New Testament applies the same imagery to Gentiles: "As for you, you were dead in your transgressions and sins, in which you used to live when you followed the ways of this world and of the ruler of the kingdom of the air, the spirit who is now at work in those who are disobedient" (Eph 2:1–2). The Gentiles were even "sons of disobedience" (Eph 5:6; Col 3:6 ESV). Peter asks, "For it is time for

---

37. Clayton N. Jefford, "Sin," in *EDB*, 1224.

judgment to begin with God's household; and if it begins with us, what will the outcome be for those who do not obey the gospel of God?" (1 Pet 4:17). Ancient peoples are regarded as being disobedient to God from long ago (3:20; Heb 11:31). Disobedience implies a conscious walking away from God, away from privileges as much as responsibilities, a desire to walk apart from God.

4. *Perversion* (Heb. *'āwâ*; Gk. *diastrephō*). A further image for sin is that of something bent or twisted. Proverbs refers to people with twisted or warped minds (Prov 12:8). In the New Testament a similar series of images occurs when Jesus calls his contemporaries an "unbelieving and perverse generation" (Luke 9:41). Paul calls Christians to shine as stars amidst a "warped and crooked generation" (Phil 2:15). Note that the Nazi swastika is formed by twisting the Christian symbol of a cross out of shape. Perversion implies that something straight has been made crooked. Ultimately evil is the privation and ruin of something once originally good.

5. *Missing the mark* (Heb. *ḥāṭā'*; Gk. *hamartēma, harmatia, hamartanō*). Probably the most common and well-known concept for sin is "missing the mark." It is obviously analogous to missing a target in archery (e.g., Judg 20:16), though the archery metaphor breaks down because sin is not merely accidental, but a deliberate decision to fail, a voluntary and culpable mistake. Moses informed the Israelites: "Do not be afraid. God has come to test you, so that the fear of God will be with you to keep you from sinning [lit., 'missing the mark']" (Exod 20:20). The psalmist is penitent with the words: "Against you, you only, have I sinned ['missed the mark']" (Ps 51:4). The Suffering Servant "bore the sins ['misses'] of many" (Isa 53:12). In the New Testament this idea of sin as missing the mark is developed principally through the word *hamartia*, which signifies a departure from righteousness.[38] This sin is a failure to hit the mark of God's standard, his perfect love and his perfect law. This is highlighted by James: "If anyone, then, knows the good they ought to do and doesn't do it, it is sin for them" (Jas 4:17).

A full understanding of sin emerges not simply from word studies, but from the narrative of Scripture itself. Beginning with Genesis, we see that the concept of rebellion against God's commandments appears early in the biblical narrative. After the creation of the world and the formation of Adam and Eve, we encounter a scenario where humanity is presented with its first temptation — the choice between obedience to the divine command or the pursuit of human autonomy (Gen 3:1–7). No specific word for sin is used here, but the seeds of separation between God and humanity are clearly sown.

Curiously, this initial revolt against God finds no further mention in the Old Testament, yet its implications continue to dominate the actions of history's earli-

---

38. BDAG, 50.

est humans (Gen 1–11) and Israel's own dealings with God from the conquest of Canaan to the postexilic period. Later Christian interpreters of Genesis, from Paul to Augustine, make specific and extended usage of this episode of the "fall" of Adam in their construction of a doctrine of sin.

The core New Testament convictions concerning sin assume three basic tenets: (1) The world is inherently sinful. While "original sin" is never explicitly stated or defined by the Scriptures, its reality is strongly implied, since there is assumed to be an organic unity between Adam's sin and human sinfulness. (2) Sin is humanity's rebellious attitude toward God's will. The forms of this rebellion manifest themselves in numerous ways, climaxing in idolatry and immorality. (3) Salvation consists of the remission of sins, reconciliation to God, and redemption from sin's power through the work of Christ. Through the gospel message of Jesus, sinners are forgiven in the peacemaking work of the cross, and fallen humans are incorporated into the life-giving power of Christ's resurrection. The early Christian message stands as a direct answer to the problem of sin in the world, a message of hope for the hopeless and forgiveness for the condemned.[39]

In light of all this, a good definition of sin is given by Cornelius Plantinga: Sin is "any agential [acts and dispositions] evil for which some person (or group of persons) is to blame. In short, sin is culpable shalom-breaking ... shalom is God's design for creation and redemption; sin is blamable human vandalism of these great realities and therefore an affront to their architect and builder."[40] The strength of this definition is that it grasps the biblical vision of sin as bringing a ruptured relationship that needs the peace and healing that only the cross can bring.

That said, I think we can be even more precise about the nature and essence of sin. Sin means a despising of God and an attempt to dethrone God. The root of sin is the worship of the self in place of the worship of God. Sin breeds self-made men and women who love to worship their creator. Sinners want a theocracy where they are the "*theo*." Sin, in the end, is a form of cosmic treason. Sin is the foolish effort at deicide and the even more foolish belief in self-deification. It amounts to a pathetic attempt at a coup d'état against the Lord of the cosmos. We might even call sin the "Frank Sinatra Syndrome." Sinful humanity wants to raise and shake its puny fists against heaven and declare, "I did it my way."

A human being, addicted to the self-gratification of sin, engages in tirades against God, conscious or unconscious, to this effect: "I defy your authority and I declare my absolute independence of you." Sin is the act whereby these arrogant little *eikōns* grumble against their Maker as they strive to be free of his Word, his

---

39. Jefford, "Sin," 1224–26.
40. Cornelius Plantinga, *Not the Way It's Supposed to Be* (Grand Rapids: Eerdmans, 1995), 13–14.

will, his worship, and his world. Sin turns humanity into treasonous tyrants committed to any form of terror to gratify their lusts or to secure their own power. Sin is the quest to be free from God's authority and accountability and to replace it with a God-free autonomy. Sin is the evil that emerges in the absence of God.

Talking to people about sin is hard if people no longer believe in it. I cannot speak for America, but certainly in the United Kingdom and Australia, the words "sin" and "sinner" are no longer an affront. Sin means naughty, but fun. To be a sinner is to be hip and cool, a rebel who refuses to knuckle under any authority, especially not religious authority. For instance, not far from where I live is a tattoo parlor called "Sin the Skin," and close by there is an adult sex shop called "Sinsational" (yes, I know, I probably need to move to a better neighborhood!).

As we increasingly live in post-Christian societies, trying to convince people that they are "sinners" and it is this "sin" that separates them from God is becoming all the more difficult. We lose them simply in the terminology we use. Telling people that God rejoices over the repentance of one sinner is not going to penetrate their veil of irreligion (Luke 15:10). That is because "sin" and "sinner" sound like archaic, religious terms that only moralizing geriatrics use to describe young people having too much fun.

My suggestion, then, is that we drop the language of "sin" and instead use the language of "evil." While the word "sin" might have lost its shock value, the word "evil" has cultural currency and instantly conjures up thoughts of despicable inhumane acts from Auschwitz to 9/11. We know about evil from George Bush's famous "Axis of Evil" speech, and the motto of Google.com is "Don't Be Evil." Just saying the word "evil" will get people's attention. When I talk about sin to non-Christians (or even biblically illiterate Christians), I begin straightaway with the idea of evil. I talk about evil graphically to get their undivided attention. Then I discuss evil's origins, its consequences, our fear of it, and our hope for its defeat. But the big question I bring them to is this: Am I evil?

Now most people's gut reaction is to say, "No, of course not. There's seven billion people on this planet I haven't murdered, and I help my landlady take out her garbage." I then go for a quick tour of Romans 7:7–25 about the "wretched man" who is perplexed as to how to stop himself from doing "evil." I add to that a famous quote from Aleksandr Solzhenitsyn's *The Gulag Archipelago*: "If only there were evil people somewhere insidiously committing evil deeds, and it were necessary only to separate them from the rest of us and destroy them. But the line dividing good and evil cuts through the heart of every human being. And who is willing to destroy a piece of his own heart?"[41] Do you find the same struggle within yourself? What

---

41. See, e.g., www.goodreads.com/work/quotes/2944012-1918-1956.

are you really capable of? Are you both victim and perpetrator of evil? Thereafter, explaining God's plan to put the world to right and proclaiming the cross as God's solution to *our* evil, which is an offense against *him*, suddenly has more currency than telling unchurched people to repent of their sins.

7.4.2 THE EFFECT OF SIN

Sin (or evil) is obviously bad for humanity. It is dreadful for our well-being. It is divisive for our relationships with one another. It corrupts our natural environment. Sin deceives, entices, and enslaves. It perverts our psychological and spiritual make-up. Sin is positively fatal for our relationship with God. Indeed, sin is our "enemy" (1 Cor 15:26). Sin can even be likened to a malevolent personal power poised to strike at humanity (Gen 4:7; Rom 7:11). Even worse, sin is powerful because it is so pleasurable (Heb 11:25) as it gratifies our most insidious desires (Rom 6:12; Jas 1:15). The consequences of sin upon the self, our human relationships, and our standing with God are as tragic as they are terrible.

The most devastating consequence of sin is *death*. God told Adam that if he ate of the tree of the knowledge of good and evil, he would "certainly die" (Gen 2:17; 3:3). Through Satan's deception, Adam and Eve did eat, and the noetic transformation took them from innocence to guilt and then to death. This rebellious act terminated their relationship with God and marked their transformation from immortality to mortality. Adam and Eve died, and all of their sons and daughters died with them. As Paul said, "sin entered the world through one man, and death through sin, and in this way death came to all people" (Rom 5:12). The reality of death is emphasized in Genesis 5 with the genealogical list that follows the formula: "X lived a total of Y years, and then he died." The repetition is emphatic: Adam ... died, Seth ... died, Enosh ... died, and Kenan ... died. You see the point! Death enters the realm of God's creation and tyrannizes it. Death is physical (cessation of human life), spiritual (cut off from God), and eternal (perpetually removed from God's presence).

This sin–death nexus is emphasized at several points in Scripture. The warning of Ezekiel is that "the one who sins is the one who will die" (Ezek 18:4, 20). Paul told the Romans that "sin reigned in death" (Rom 5:21), "the wages of sin is death" (6:23), and sin "brought death" (7:10). In Hebrews, sin brings judgment: "People are destined to die once, and after that to face judgment" (Heb 9:27). James exhorts his readers that "sin, when it is full-grown, gives birth to death" (Jas 1:15).

If death is the penalty for our sins, then remission of our sins will mean deliverance from death. The good news of the gospel is that "through Christ Jesus the law of the Spirit who gives life has set you free from the law of sin and death" (Rom 8:2). The resurrection of believers at the end of the age means that "death has been swallowed up in victory" (1 Cor 15:54; cf. Isa 25:8). The gospel addresses the ugliest of ugliness in human existence: sin, evil, decay, and death. Jesus came to "free those who all their lives were held in slavery by their fear of death" (Heb 2:15). Those who are victorious "will not be hurt at all by the second death" (Rev 2:11). The gift of eternal life means that for believers there is no eternal death. Evil is not allowed the last word in God's world.

The gospel declares the victory of the Lord Jesus over death by deposing death of its power (i.e., evil) through the cross and by robbing death of its prize (i.e., human lives) through the resurrection. As a famous Greek hymn says: "Christ has risen, trampling down death by death, and giving life to those in the grave." Death, armed with evil and law, was no match for the Prince of Life. The gospel is not simply about how God deals with the individual's personal sins, a transaction of sin and righteousness to clean the slate; yes, that is true, but the gospel declares so much more, namely, God's victory over the personal and impersonal forces of evil: the world, the flesh, and Satan. The gospel is an invitation to live in fellowship with Christ rather than to suffer under the tyranny of evil. The gospel means emancipation from the slavery of evil to the freedom of a new and authentic humanity. The gospel of Christ blesses us with the news that a world ravaged with evil is not how it ought to be, nor how it can be, nor how it will be. The gospel whispers to us that Jesus means freedom.

There are several consequences that sin has on our relationship with God. First, there is *guilt*, as people are held liable for their sins.[42] Our own sin recapitulates and rehearses the sin of Adam and thus ratifies God's condemnation of Adam and his descendents. We show our family likeness by sinning, and we share in the corporate guilt of humanity by our own sin. Note how the Psalter laments: "My guilt has overwhelmed me like a burden too heavy to bear" (Ps 38:4). Elsewhere there is rejoicing because God "forgave the guilt of my sin" (32:5). The angel that touched Isaiah's lips with the tongs from the heavenly altar told him: "Your guilt is taken away and your sin atoned for" (Isa 6:7). Jesus indicted the Judean leaders because, though claiming to see, they were spiritually blind and thus guilty (John 9:41). Those who break one law are basically the same as someone who is guilty of breaking all of it (Jas 2:11). Because of sin we stand before God guilty with no prospect of reprieve.

Yet, the gospel announces that God removes our guilt by having Jesus take the guilt of our sin on himself. That is what the Suffering Servant of Isaiah does when the iniquity of the people is laid on him (Isa 53:5–6). For the writer to the Hebrews,

---

42. There are different types of guilt. There is psychological guilt, understood as feelings of regret and remorse. Then there is legal guilt, a forensic state of being in the wrong and worthy of punishment. The gospel frees us from both types of guilt.

on account of Jesus' sacrificial death we have "our hearts sprinkled to cleanse us from a guilty conscience" (Heb 10:22). Jesus releases us from the shame and blame of our guilt so that we again might be friends with God.

Second, a further result of sin is *estrangement*. Under this heading we can include many subaspects such as hostility and disfavor. Because of sin there is a mutual hostility between God and humanity. God hates corrupt religious practices, wickedness, and oppression of the poor (Pss 5:5; 11:5; Isa 61:8; Amos 5:21; Zech 8:17). God is hostile to the God-haters who despise him and his law (Exod. 20:5; Deut 7:10; Rom 1:30). Paul even wrote: "The mind governed by the flesh is hostile to God; it does not submit to God's law, nor can it do so" (Rom 8:7). The result is that God is "not pleased" with those who disobey him (Hos 8:13; 1 Cor 10:5; 1 Thess 2:15).

In the end, on account of our sin, we are alienated from God. Sin brings a disruption to the divine-human relationships. Because of sin, human beings are estranged from the God who made them and loves them. In the garden of Eden this meant no longer walking with God and instead being expelled from the garden. In the history of Israel this meant a physical exile from the land as the nation was exiled into Assyria and Babylon. The doctrine of reconciliation teaches that God overcomes this estrangement through the cross. In reconciliation, God does not count our sins against us (2 Cor 5:19), and he makes us his children instead of his enemies (Rom 5:10).

Sin also has a subjective effect on people in terms of what it does to them individually and corporately. Sin brings *degeneration*. Sin adversely impacts our inward disposition so that a person's mental and emotional life descends into godless and even subhuman behaviors. Sin makes us less human. That is why the psalmist likens his enemies who pursue him to "wild beasts" (Ps 74:19; cf. 57:4), and in Daniel 7 the pagan kingdoms that attack Israel are likened to ferocious and violent beasts (Dan 7:3–17). Rather than reflect the "image of God," people become a conglomerate mass of evil that makes up "the body ruled by sin" (Rom 6:6). Sin makes us degenerate from virtue to vice, from love to hate, and from kindness to malice. The only cure to the human cycle of degeneration is a God-wrought regeneration by the Holy Spirit.

Another consequence is *enslavement*. Paul tells the Romans that formerly they were "slaves to sin" (Rom 6:17, 20) and through the work of Christ they are set "free from the law of sin and death" (Rom 8:2). Freedom in Christ is the freedom to be fully and finally human. It is a freedom that means, ironically, slavery to God and righteousness (Rom 6:18, 22).

Sin also brings a *hardness of heart*. A heart absent of God is hostile to God. According to Proverbs, "whoever hardens their heart falls into trouble (Prov 28:14). Zechariah indicted the postexilic Judeans with the words: "They made their hearts as hard as flint and would not listen to the law or to the words that the LORD Almighty had sent by his Spirit through the earlier prophets. So the LORD Almighty was very angry" (Zech 7:12). Jesus was grieved at those who opposed or criticized his healing on the Sabbath because of the hardness of their hearts (Mark 3:5). The laws about divorce were only given because of the hardness of peoples' hearts (10:5), and Paul regards the unregenerate state as typified by ignorance and hardness of heart (Eph 4:18). The exhortation not to harden one's heart as the Israelites did in the wilderness is one of the main devices in Hebrews to warn people against sin (Heb 3:8, 15; 4:7; cf. Num 14:33; Deut 1:3; Ps 95:8; Acts 7:36). This hardness of heart can only be healed by a new and circumcised heart (Deut 30:6; Ezek 11:19; 18:31; 36:26).

The effect of sin also includes a *denial* of sin and its consequences. Sin, like all psychological defects, requires a denial of reality for it to continue. In order to remain alive, sin must deny God, suppress his Word written on our hearts, and rebuff the notion of his judgment. The first sin in the garden of Eden stemmed from a denial that God would hold Adam and Eve accountable for their disobedience—hence the words of the serpent, "You will not certainly die" (Gen 3:4). Paul's indictment of pagan immorality and idolatry in Romans 1:18–32 makes much of this theme of "denial." These human beings "suppress the truth by their wickedness" (1:18), with the net result that "their thinking became futile and their foolish hearts were darkened ... they became fools and exchanged the glory of the immortal God for images made to look like mortal human beings" (1:21–23).

Finally, sin manifests itself in *self-centeredness*. If sin denies God, then it deifies self in the place of God. Sin becomes the license and lord to whom gratification must be paid. Sin results in a desire to be esteemed above others by lessening the value of others. Sin arouses a conscious desire not to do to others as you would wish them do to you. Sin represses our ability to love and empathize with others. Sin makes us the opposite to the greatest and second greatest commandments by emptying our hearts of love for God and love for others, as we are consumed with love for self.

7.4.3 THE POWER OF SIN

Sin is bad, but exactly how bad? The English Puritan Ralph Venning wrote a book called *The Sinfulness of Sin*. That might sound like a silly tautology. Yet Venning's title is, I believe, well-chosen. He explains it this way: "sin is sinful, all sinful, only sinful, altogether sinful and always sinful."[43] This corresponds with the pervasive power of sin as underscored in Scripture: "The LORD saw how great the wickedness of the human race had become on the earth, and that every inclination of the

---

43. Ralph Venning, *The Sinfulness of Sin* (Edinburgh: Banner of Truth, 1965), 31.

thoughts of the human heart was only evil all the time" (Gen 6:5). Even our good deeds are tainted by sin and Isaiah hyperbolically likens them to "filthy rags" (Isa 64:6). According to Jeremiah, "the heart is deceitful above all things, and beyond cure. Who can understand it?" (Jer 17:9). And Paul remarks that we were even "dead in ... transgressions and sins" (Eph 2:1; Col 2:13). Let us be clear, sin is more than skin deep; it goes to the bone and even through to the heart.

In light of the devastating impact of sin, Reformed theologians are accustomed to speaking of "total depravity." That is not to say that human beings are as bad as they can possibly be. There is no denial that humans have a propensity for good and genuinely do good. There are, after all, virtuous atheists, Muslims, Hindus, and agnostics, who perform deeds that are genuinely benevolent. Such deeds will even be recognized as being good at the final judgment. God's common grace, his providential restraining of evil, and the human capacity to reflect God's character in the world mean that humanity is a vessel capable of love, peace, holiness, and goodness. The point affirmed in total depravity is not a denial of this human capacity for good; rather, it is an affirmation that sin *totally* permeates our intellect, wills, and hearts.[44] There is no cavern of our mind, no recess of our soul, and no room of our heart that is not infected with the deadly virus of sin.

A looming question has always been to what extent human beings are free to act and to determine their own destiny. What effect does sin have on their capacity to choose God and to do good? The first debates about human free will emerged in the fourth century between Augustine and Pelagius. Whereas Augustine said, "Grant unto us the ability to do what you command," Pelagius objected that if God has told us what we *ought* to do, then we obviously had the *ability* to do it. Otherwise God would be foolish to command it. In other words, Pelagius taught that "ought" means "can." If we ought to obey God, we have the ability to do so. He had a more optimistic view of human nature, believing that God created humanity with a capacity to obey him. For Pelagius, moral perfection was possible for humanity and therefore mandatory. Augustine, by contrast, believed that our free will has been weakened and incapacitated, though not completely destroyed, through sin. In order for free will to be restored, we need first the operation of divine grace. Here are Augustine's own words:

> I am, moreover, fully persuaded that the soul has fallen into sin, not through the fault of God, nor through any necessity either in the divine nature or in its own, but by its own free will; and that it can be delivered from the body of this death neither by the strength of its own will, as if that were in itself sufficient to achieve this, nor by the death of the body itself, but only by the grace of God through our

---

44. Cf. Calvin, *Institutes* 2.3.1–3.

Lord Jesus Christ, and that there is not one soul in the human family to whose salvation the one Mediator between God and men, the man Christ Jesus, is not absolutely necessary.[45]

Pelagianism did not win the day, though Semi-Pelagianism did. Semi-Pelagianism is the view that the human will *cooperates* with divine grace and thus produces salvation in tandem.

Similar debates occurred during the Reformation. Erasmus wrote a book called *The Free Will*, while Luther and Calvin both wrote responses with near-identical titles on *The Bondage of the Will*. The matter of contention was how free the human will was in light of sin and how efficacious God's grace needs to be in order to overcome sin. Inside the Protestant scheme the problem is that we are only free to do what we desire most. Our desire is for self-gratification, not for divine glory. As Martin Luther wrote: "The will of man without grace is not free, but is enslaved, and that too with its own consent."[46]

Human beings, in their fallen state, do not desire God or seek God (Rom 3:11). People desperately avoid God, lest their sins and evil deeds be exposed (Luke 5:8; John 3:19). If human beings have hearts that are deceitful and wicked (Jer 17:9), if they are slaves to sin (John 8:34; Rom 6:16–20), and if they are effectively dead in their sins (Eph 2:1–3), they cannot cooperate with divine grace. They need a gift of divine grace to make them alive (2:4–7) and to draw them to God (John 6:44; 12:32). Calvin wrote:

> We are all sinners by nature; therefore, we are held under the yoke of sin. But if the whole man is subject to the dominion of sin, surely the will, which is its principal seat, must be bound with the closest chains. And, indeed, if divine grace were preceded by any will of ours, Paul could not have said that, "it is God who works in us both to will and to do" [Phil 2:13].[47]

The Reformers are right. A dead corpse cannot cooperate with its own resuscitation. In order for us to choose God, God must choose to alter something in our desires so we can freely choose him! Our will is in bondage to evil, willingly no less, and no amount of altar calls or seeker sensitive services can overcome that. Unless our wills are set free from our sinful desires, we will never choose to believe in God. Ultimately, the gospel informs us that the only way to be free is to abandon our own freedom and come back to God's mercy.[48] That liberation occurs not by our own efforts, but by hearing the word of Christ and by receiving the gift of the Spirit.

---

45. Augustine, *Letters* 166.5.
46. Cited in J. H. Merle D'Aubigne, *History of the Reformation in the 16th Century* (New York: Carter, 1856), 78.
47. Calvin, *Institutes* 2.2.27.
48. Stephen Neil, *What Is Man?* (London: Lutterworth, 1960), 42.

7.4.4 THE ENTRANCE OF SIN

We know from the biblical story that God originally made the world good and that sin subsequently entered into the world through Adam and Eve's disobedience. After their sin, their progeny began to sin and incrementally increased in the depths of their depravity and the barbarity of their behavior. This Adamic sickness spread to all humanity as sinfulness appears in each and every creature descended from Adam. Paul says as much in Romans: "Therefore, just as sin entered the world through one man, and death through sin, and in this way death came to all people, because all sinned" (Rom 5:12). The two main issues raised by this passage are: (1) What impact did Adam's sin have on the sinfulness of humanity? (2) For which sin is humanity culpable—for Adam's sin, or each for their own sins?

This brings us naturally to the subject of "original sin." This term *original sin* has been used in the Western church to describe the inherited corruption and collective guilt that humanity received from Adam. The heuristic value of the doctrine of original sin is first, that it explains the universal and inevitable nature of sin. Second, that sin belongs to the nature of human beings in their fallen state. Third, it is inherited from our ancestors. Fourth, our disobedience has a historical beginning and a material cause in the disobedience of Adam.[49]

The way in which Adam's sin affects the moral state and forensic status of humanity can be understood in three main ways. According to Pelagius, the main thing we got from Adam was a bad example. Second, Semi-Pelagian theologians said that what we receive from Adam is a corrupted nature with a disposition toward sinning. Finally, Augustinian theologians have argued that we receive from Adam *both* a corrupted nature *and* his guilt imputed to us.

The ancient church rejected the Pelagian position that Adam was merely a bad example; likewise, they denied that humans enter the world with a blank slate. Human experience suggests otherwise; for instance, I'm amazed that I never had to teach my children how to lie; they picked it up like naturals! In the history of the church, it has been the Augustinian and Semi-Pelagian views that have captured the minds of most theologians at one time or another.

Note also that this is not strictly a problem posed by Christian theologians. Jewish authors reflected as to how the sin of Adam affected the subsequent sin of humanity.[50]

> For God created us for incorruption, and made us in the image of his own eternity, *but through the devil's envy death entered the world*, and those who belong to his company experience it. (Wis 2:23–24, italics added in all cases)

---

49. Henri Blocher, *Original Sin: Illuminating the Riddle* (NSBT 5; Downers Grove, IL: InterVarsity Press, 1997), 18.

50. Cf. John R. Levinson, *Portraits of Adam in Early Judaism: From Sirach to 2 Baruch* (JSPSup 1; Sheffield: JSOT Press, 1988).

> For the first Adam, burdened with an evil heart, transgressed and was overcome, *as were also all who were descended from him*. Thus the disease became permanent; the law was in the hearts of the people along with the evil root; but what was good departed, and the evil remained. (2 Esd. 3:21–22)
>
> O Adam, what have you done? For though it was you who sinned, *the fall was not yours alone, but ours also who are your descendants*. (2 Esd. 7:118).
>
> For, although Adam sinned first and has brought death upon all who were not in his own time, *yet each of them who has been born from him has prepared for himself the coming torment*. (2 Bar. 54.15).

Note how Wisdom attributes the entrance of sin to the devil, not directly to Adam. Second Esdras sees sin as a sickness that is shared by Adam and his descendents in a bond of solidarity. While *2 Baruch* identifies Adam as the first sinner and progenitor of human death, humans are ultimately responsible only for their own sin. Christian reflection on the impact of Adam's sin on the sin of humanity has been inherited from the Jewish tradition.

The primary text for discussion is Romans 5:12–21 (esp. v. 12). The problem is, as Wright notes: "'The Adam/Christ contrast of 5:12–21 is cryptic and elliptical: trying to read its Greek after the measured sentences of 5:1–11 is like turning from Rembrandt to Picasso."[51] In my estimation, the Adam/Christ typology that runs through 5:12–21 is really an extended commentary on 1 Corinthians 15:22 and 15:56: "For as in Adam all die, so in Christ all will be made alive … The sting of death is sin, and the power of sin is the law." In Romans 5:12–21, Paul tries to demonstrate how the law did not redeem Adam's fallen nature, but served only to antagonize the power of sin, to activate sinful desire, and to affirm the sentence of death due to Adam's progeny. Paul situates his argument about God's saving righteousness in the scope of humanity condemned and then justified, humanity enslaved in sin and set free in Christ; thus, justification creates not only a worldwide Abrahamic family but also a renewed humanity. Believers shift from the epoch of sin, death, and condemnation associated with Adam's transgression to the epoch of righteousness, life, and justification associated with the obedience of the new Adam.

> Therefore, just as sin entered the world through one man, and death through sin, and in this way death came to all people, *because all sinned*—
>   To be sure, sin was in the world before the law was given, but sin is not charged against anyone's account where there is no law. Nevertheless, death reigned from the time of Adam to the time of Moses, even over those who did not sin by breaking a command, as did Adam, who is a pattern of the one to come.

---

51. N. T. Wright, "The Letter to the Romans," in *NIB*, 10:508.

> But the gift is not like *the trespass. For if the many died by the trespass of the one man*, how much more did God's grace and the gift that came by the grace of the one man, Jesus Christ, overflow to the many! Nor can the gift of God be compared with the result of one man's sin: *The judgment followed one sin and brought condemnation*, but the gift followed many trespasses and brought justification. For if, *by the trespass of the one man*, death reigned through that one man, how much more will those who receive God's abundant provision of grace and of the gift of righteousness reign in life through the one man, Jesus Christ!
>
> *Consequently, just as one trespass resulted in condemnation for all people*, so also one righteous act resulted in justification and life for all people. For *just as through the disobedience of the one man the many were made sinners*, so also through the obedience of the one man the many will be made righteous.
>
> The law was brought in so that the trespass might increase. But where sin increased, grace increased all the more, so that, just as sin reigned in death, so also grace might reign through righteousness to bring eternal life through Jesus Christ our Lord. (Rom 5:12–21, italics added)

Augustine took issue with the Pelagians, who denied that there was any sin in newborn infants that needs to be removed by the grace of baptism. Augustine did not deny that fallen humanity imitates Adam in its sinning. But he argued that we are "in Adam" because we inherit our sinful nature from him. That sinful nature is transmitted seminally as we were biologically in Adam when he sinned (see Heb 7:10, where Levi was "in the body of his ancestor" Abraham when Melchizedek met him). As a result, "one man, Adam, has filled the whole wild world with his progeny. The human race, as if it were a single individual, is lying like a great big sick patient from the furthest east as far as the extreme west, and in need of a cure."[52]

For Augustine, humans are sinful in the sense of being caught up in Adam's "original sin," what he called *peccator originaliter*. Yet humans are also sinful for committing "actual sins," what he called *peccator actualiter*.[53] Augustine noted, "It is certainly clear that personal sins of each person by which they alone sinned are distinct from this one [original sin] in which all have sinned, when all were that one man"; but he adds, "from the one man all are born destined for condemnation, from which only the grace of Christ sets them free."[54] Thus, original sin is common to all people irrespective of the personal sins of each individual.[55]

Crucial for Augustine was that in his understanding of Romans 5:12, the prepositional phrase *eph' hō* (Greek) and *in quo* (Latin) meant "in whom" all sinned, with the "whom" being Adam. The verse allegedly teaches the propagation of sin from

---

52. Augustine, *Serm.* 374, cited in Bradley G. Green, "Augustine," in *Shapers of Christian Orthodoxy: Engaging with Early and Medieval Theologians* (ed. B. G. Green; Downers Grove, IL: InterVarsity Press, 2010), 251.

53. Green, "Augustine," 251.

54. Augustine, *Pecc. Merit.* 13, cited in Green, "Augustine," 251–52.

55. Augustine, *Adv. Jul.* 20.63.

Adam to humanity, not simply its imitation. So for Augustine, people sin like Adam because of a biological connection, and because they are "in Adam," they are born into the world condemned even before they have sinned themselves. His position is best summarized from the short remarks in *The City of God*: "Everyone, even little children, have broken God's covenant, not indeed in virtue of any personal action but in virtue of mankind's common origin in that single ancestor in whom all sinned."[56]

There are antecedents to Augustine. Origen believed that humans were either present in Adam's loins and expelled from Eden when Adam was expelled, or else, every human unexplainably experiences their own expulsion from Eden and subsequent condemnation.[57] Ambrosiaster commented: "For it is clear that all have sinned in Adam as though in a lump," which indicates a type of solidarity with Adam so that what is true of him is true of all humanity. Furthermore:

> For being corrupted by sin himself, all those whom he fathered were born under sin. For that reason we are all sinners, because we all descend from him.... We do not suffer this [second] death as a result of Adam's sin, but his fall makes it possible for us to get it by our own sins.... They were still bound by the sentence meted out in Adam, the seal of which was broken by the death of Christ. The sentence passed on Adam was that the human body would decompose on earth, but the soul would be bound by the chains of hell until it was released.[58]

In Ambrosiaster's thinking humans have solidarity with Adam in his sin, and they are condemned like Adam when they sin as Adam did.

In the medieval church many adopted a Semi-Pelagian position, whereby humanity received Adam's corrupt nature but did not receive his guilt credited to them. This is called "concupiscence," which refers to a habit or propensity toward sin. Advocates often appeal to texts that indicate that God does not punish people for someone else's sins: "Parents are not to be put to death for their children, nor children put to death for their parents; each will die for their own sin" (Deut 24:16; cf. 2 Kgs 14:6; 2 Chr 25:4). David Parker echoes the complaints of many that "it is ethically difficult to assign responsibility for a state or condition of existence and one over which the individual has no personal control." Instead Parker has an alternative:

> The terms "depravity" or "innate moral corruption" may be used to refer to the fact that, due to the absence of God's gracious presence and power resulting from the fall, man exists in a morally deprived condition. He is therefore unable to please God or to prevent himself from falling into sin.[59]

---

56. Augustine, *Civ.* 16.27.
57. Mark Reasoner, *Romans in Full Circle: A History of Interpretation* (Louisville: Westminster John Knox, 2005), 44.
58. Gerald Bray, ed. and trans., *Ambrosiaster: Commentaries on Romans and 1–2 Corinthians* (ACT; Downers Grove, IL: InterVarsity Press, 2009), 40–41.
59. David Parker, "Original Sin: A Study in Evangelical Theology," *EvQ* 61 (1989): 68.

§7.4 What Is the Problem with Humanity?

I should point out that a somewhat mediating view is advocated by Henri Blocher, who tries to forge a path between the Origenist and Augustinian conceptions of the nexus between Adam–sin–humanity. He splits the horns of the dilemma as to whether we are condemned by Adam's sin or by our own sin. On Blocher's account, humans are viewed through the legal identity of Adam, and Adam's sin efficaciously secures the condemnation of all people by virtue of their representation by him. Even so, beyond the federal headship of Adam over humanity, sin is both propagated by Adam and imitated from Adam. Blocher accordingly contends that we undergo the fact of death in solidarity with Adam like children who share in the sin of their father. Yet we do not undergo the penalty of Adam as if it were immediately ours. Rather, by sharing in the consequences of Adam's sin—in the spread of his corruption and death—our sinning certainly happens and our own guilt can be reckoned as originating with Adam. Hence Blocher's paraphrase of Rom 5:12: "Just as through one man, Adam, sin entered the world and the sin-death connection was established, and so death could be inflicted on all as the penalty of their sins."[60] Blocher's solution to the problem, balancing corporate identity and individual responsibility, should be judged a success.

Blocher's perspective is confirmed by a close reading of Romans 5:12–21. Beginning with 5:12, the train of thought can be broken down as follows:

a. Sin entered the world through Adam.
b. Death is the consequence of the sin of Adam.
c. Death has spread to the whole human race.
d. Human beings, because they enter the world alienated from God, sin.

The grammar of Romans 5:12d (*eph' hō pantes hēmarton*) can be translated in several different ways.[61] With the vast majority of modern English versions, I prefer the translation "because all sinned" for the reason that the conjunction *eph' hō* is best taken causally since it has that meaning elsewhere in Paul's letters (2 Cor 5:4; Phil 3:12; 4:10). Death spreads to all of humanity because all of humanity in their alienation from God engages in sin. The location of our sinning is the crux of the matter. Does it somehow occur "in" Adam's sin, or is it a sinning "in ourselves"? While I clearly favor the former, there is a sense in which both are true, so we do not have to choose absolutely between them.

First, there is a clear solidarity between Adam and his progeny so that what is true of the primal representative is true of those whom he represented. The primary cause of sin, its condemnation, and its punishment is ascribed to Adam. By

---

60. Blocher, *Original Sin*, 78.
61. Cf. Joseph A. Fitzmyer, *Romans* (AB; New York: Doubleday, 1993), 413–17.

the trespass of one man, many died (Rom 5:15). One sin brought condemnation (5:16). By the trespass of one man, death reigned over all people (5:17). By one trespass, condemnation fell on all people (5:18). Through the disobedience of one man, many were made sinners (5:19). It is not that we are guilty *for* Adam's sin; rather, we are guilty as sinners *in* Adam.[62] God sees us in and through Adam so that we are grafted into Adam's sin in Eden.[63] Ambrose captures perfectly this motif of our identification in and participation with Adam's sin: "In Adam I fell, in Adam I was cast out of paradise, in Adam I died. How shall God call me back, except he find me in Adam? For just as in Adam I am guilty of sin and owe a debt to death, so in Christ I am justified."[64]

Remember that Paul's primary point is the universal effect of Adam's disobedience as the author of death and condemnation, which is then reversed by Christ's righteous act leading to justification and life. It would be a floundering exegesis to regard 5:12 as teaching that all condemnation is solely due to individual personal sins. Paul plainly asserts that all people stand in a relationship to one of two men, Adam and Christ, and their relationship with them determines their eternal destiny. Either one belongs to Adam and is under the sentence of death because of his disobedience, or else one belongs to Christ and is assured of eternal life because of his obedience.[65]

Second, Romans 5 also affirms that because of Adam's sin, humanity subsequently engages in sin and transgression (see 5:13–14, 16). It is entirely true, then, that Paul envisages "Adam's baleful influence on humanity by the ratification of his sin in the sins of all individuals."[66] Adam creates a cycle of sin and transgression that rehearses the disobedience of the first man in all human beings (creating the "wretched man" in 7:7–25). It is right to regard Adam as causing sin as a "disease" (*4 Ezra* 3:22), an "inborn disease" (Augsburg Confession, art. 2), or even "sickness unto death" (Søren Kierkegaard) that makes humans sin. Adam originated the deadly sin pathogen that leads to infection and infirmity, for which there is no immunity.

Given both affirmations, we should heed the wise words of Larry Kreitzer:

> It is important to note that while Paul does turn to Adam as the means whereby sin enters the world, he does not tell us the means whereby that sin is transmitted from generation to another. The mechanics are left unexplained, beyond the simple declaration that "all humankind sinned." Adam's responsibility for the origin of sin's introduction in the world is affirmed by Paul alongside an affirmation of the individual's responsibility for the presence of sin in his or her life. For Paul, both

---

62. Horton, *Christian Faith*, 426.
63. Blocher, *Original Sin*, 77.
64. Ambrose, *Exc.* 2.6, cited in Gerald Bray, ed., *Romans* (ACCS; Downers Grove, IL: InterVarsity Press, 1998), 136.
65. Douglas J. Moo, *Romans* (NICNT: Grand Rapids: Eerdmans, 1996), 315; Thomas R. Schreiner, *Romans* (BECNT; Grand Rapids: Eerdmans, 1998), 275–77.
66. Fitzmyer, *Romans*, 416.

elements (personal guilt and responsibility as well as universal guilt and sin in Adam) are active.[67]

A doctrine of "original sin" is defensible on several grounds. (1) Genesis 1–5 portrays sin as originating in Adam's disobedience and spreading to all humanity, who share in the depravation, imitation, and condemnation of Adam's sin. (2) Elsewhere Scripture presents sin as something that is present in the human condition from the beginning, something inherited from one's parents.[68] (3) Romans 5:12–21 affirms Adam's influence on humanity through ingraining sin into them, but primarily it posits that Adam, as the federal head of humanity, is responsible for the guilt and condemnation of the human race universally. As such, the gospel tells us about salvation, whereas original sin tells us why we all need it.[69]

FURTHER READING

Blocher, Henri. *Original Sin: Illuminating the Riddle.* NSBT 5; Downers Grove, IL: InterVarsity Press, 1997.

Campbell, Iain D. *The Doctrine of Sin: In Reformed and Neo-Orthodox Thought.* Fearn, UK: Christian Focus, 1999.

Parker, David, "Original Sin: A Study in Evangelical Theology." *EvQ* 61 (1989): 51–69.

Plantinga, Cornelius. *Not the Way It's Supposed to Be: A Breviary of Sin.* Grand Rapids: Eerdmans, 1995.

Shuster, Marguerite. *The Fall and Sin: What We Have Become as Sinners.* Grand Rapids: Eerdmans, 2004.

---

67. Larry Kreitzer, "Adam and Christ," in *DPL*, 13.
68. Cf. Pss 51:5, 10; 143:2; Isa 64:6; Jer 17:9; John 1:13; 3:6; 5:42; 6:44; 8:34; 15:4–5; Jas 3:2; 1 John 1:8, 10; 5:12.
69. Concerning children, Erickson (*Christian Theology*, 654–56) argues for a "conditional imputation of guilt," whereby Adam's sin is only imputed once the condition of reaching an age of accountability and then voluntarily sinning takes place. So there is no condemnation until a child reaches an age of responsibility. This could be said to be a corollary of the view that all children are "elect" until reaching an account of accountability. If a child dies before the age of responsibility, the child would be received by the Lord as part of his grace and mercy to the "least of these."

§ 7.5 THE ODYSSEY OF THEODICY

The story of humanity cannot be told apart from the story of evil. It is evil that ravages the human heart with a mixture of self-worship and self-debasement. The world around us is infested by evils—individual and corporate, human, natural, and even supernatural. We are left angered and saddened at the grizzly and often gratuitous evil perpetrated in this world by persons. It often seems so needless, pointless, and utterly senseless; but it's there all the same. Our televisions and newspapers feature headlines of the latest evil deeds to hit our world. What philosophers and lawmakers have pondered is what evil is and how to defeat it. Theistic philosophers have also wondered more specifically how a good and loving God could allow evil to exist in the first place.

The Greek philosopher Socrates considered evil to be a matter of ignorance. Zoroastrian religion saw good and evil as two eternal and diametrically opposing forces in perpetual opposition. In Buddhist thought, evil is the product of desire, and by eliminating desire one destroys evil. The seventeenth-century philosopher Benedict de Spinoza was one of the first moral relativists who regarded evil as purely a matter of personal inclination and experience. Psychologist-philosopher Carl Jung called evil the "dark side of God" and interpreted the story of Jesus as God facing his own shadow. Yet in many ways, evil is reduced to something abstract, surreal, relative, or even illusory.

In contrast, Christianity takes evil more seriously than any other religion in the world.[70] In Christian thought, evil is not regarded as an illusion created by desire or a subjective construct, nor is it philosophized away; rather, evil is confronted in all of its brutal ugliness. The gospel is soberly concerned with evil: the reality of evil, the rescue from evil, and even the redemption of evil. Jesus taught his disciples to pray, "Our Father in heaven ... deliver us from evil" (Matt 6:9, 13 ESV), because he knew the power of evil and the fearful grip it had on people; he also knew that the only hope for humanity in the face of evil was God the Father.

The gospel presumes the biblical story line of a world gone wrong and presents us with a vision of a world that will be put to right through the Lord Jesus Christ. The

---

70. Neil, *What Is Man?* 33.

gospel declares that God's justice will triumph and evil will not have the last laugh. God's justice is a redemptive and restorative justice already at work in the world, entering through the evil-bearing cross and spreading like a viral contagion through the justice-seeking church. The final scene for humanity is not the wicked reigning in hell with some kind of spiteful delight at escaping any true recompense. Yes, judgment will happen, but the predominant vision for humanity in its final state is that of the saints ruling over a new creation in love, joy, and peace, and evil is no more.

In what follows, we will examine how an evangelical faith confronts evil. That involves a largely apologetic task, explaining how a good and gracious God can allow evil and suffering to exist in the world. But we will also engage in a preliminary examination of types of evil, and we will end this section by exploring how a gospel-driven faith leads us to respond to evil.

7.5.1 TYPES OF EVIL

There are various types of evil in the world. First, there is natural or physical evil. This type of evil refers to that which causes harm to people by bodily injury, by frustrating natural desires, or through the various social conditions under which humanity naturally exists. Natural evils can include sickness, natural disasters, death, famine, and mental suffering. It refers to that form of suffering and pain for which humanity is often not directly responsible.

Second, there are moral evils, which consist of that form of evil that refers to the harm one human being does to another. It is characterized by a desire to cause pain, harm, suffering, or prejudice against other human beings either willfully or by negligence. It is characterized by a depersonalization of a subject, hatred, greed, inequality, an inability to empathize, and a lust for power over others. In biblical terminology, evil is often equated as sin.

Third, social evil may be defined as that form of malice fostered by humans indirectly through the structures of societies. This can include things such as racism, poverty, discrimination, and caste systems. Human beings may not directly perpetrate this form of evil, but they can perpetuate it by their willing participation in social entities and values. For example, buying chocolate from companies that refuse to pay the African farmers for this ingredient is a participation in a social evil.

Fourth, there are metaphysical evils, which may be defined as the limitation exhibited in various parts of the natural world that prevents objects and creatures from reaching their ideal state. For example, animals and plant life are varyingly influenced by and dependent on climate; animals prey on other animals for food; and the natural order depends on a system of perpetual decay and renewal because of the interaction of its constituent parts.

Finally, there is supernatural evil. This form of evil attributes a high intensity of evil to the spiritual being known in Christian and Jewish tradition as "the Satan." The Satan is a created being, both personal and supernatural, and is identified in Scripture as the adversary of both God and humanity. In the biblical witness, the Satan is both a fallen angel and a hostile spiritual force. The primary work of the Satan is deception, temptation, and destruction.

7.5.2 THE PROBLEM OF EVIL

The experience of suffering and the observation of evil in the world are often said to count as reasons against a God who is both omnipotent (all-powerful) and omnibenevolent (all-good). How can such a God allow evil to exist? The Greek philosopher Epicurus (341–270 BC) put together a "paradox" that posed the question rather provocatively:

1. Is God willing to prevent evil, but not able? Then he is not all-powerful.
2. Is God able to prevent evil, but not willing? Then he is not all-good.
3. If God is both able and willing, then why is there evil?
4. If God is neither able nor willing to prevent evil, then why call him God?[71]

John L. Mackie has put it in a more sophisticated form:

1. A perfectly good being always prevents evil as far as he can.
2. An omnipotent and omniscient being can do anything possible.
3. So, if a perfectly good, omnipotent, and omniscient being exists, he prevents evil completely.
4. If God exists, then he is perfectly good, omnipotent, and omniscient.
5. So, if God exists, he prevents evil completely.
6. But evil exists.
7. Therefore, God does not exist.[72]

A further argument is not simply the existence of evil but the fact of gratuitous evil, that is, pointless and needless suffering. For example, even if God willed or permitted the Holocaust, why did so many people have to die? Why not one million Jews instead of six million? Did a person have to be stabbed with a knife twenty times instead of only once? It is the degree and not the fact of suffering that is said to be a problem here.

7.5.3 THEODICY

Theodicy is the task of explaining how an all-good and all-powerful God could allow evil and suffering. Constructing a defensible theodicy is a challenging task and

---

71. Cf. Kenneth Surin, "Evil, Problem of," in *The Blackwell Encyclopedia of Modern Christian Thought* (ed. A. E. McGrath; Oxford: Blackwell, 1995), 192.

72. Cited in Daniel Howard-Snyder, "God, Evil, and Suffering," in *Reasons for the Hope Within* (ed. M. J. Murray; Grand Rapids: Eerdmans, 1998), 83.

draws from theology, apologetics, and pastoral theology. Discussing the 9/11 tragedy in a university classroom or sitting beside a patient's bed in an oncology ward is no easy feat and no trivial matter. As humans we suffer, and we want to know why, what meaning it has, and what hope there is beyond it.

The Scriptures are filled with stories, proverbs, laments, prophetic oracles, psalms, discourses, and visions about evil and how it relates to God. Genesis and Job, Proverbs and Romans, as well as Jonah and Revelation—all have something to say about evil in our world and God's response to it. The biblical authors did not exist in a world remote from suffering or discuss it only in the abstract. Instead, Scripture presents to us an anthology of voices of the victims who have suffered, not least of all the Son of God himself. Indeed, the biblical accounts are uncensored and unsanitized accounts of the reality of suffering and evil. Also, the biblical authors point us to God as the only ultimate source of our hope to overcoming evil.

A philosophical solution to the logical problem of evil involves modifying one of three factors to defeat the purported logic of the argument that regards evil as proof counting against God's existence. One must redefine God's goodness, God's power, or the idea of evil itself, in order to dispel the inference that an all-good and all-powerful God is inconsistent with the existence of evil and suffering.[73]

I think it is possible, philosophically speaking, to cut down the logical problem at its existential knees. It is possible to demonstrate that the argument from evil against God's existence *presupposes precisely what it intends to refute*. In order to believe that "evil" exists, one needs an absolute standard by which evil is judged to be, or else we are simply left with competing views and voices about who or what is evil.

The argument from evil is only valid if we assume that evil is an objective moral quality; yet we can only have objective moral values if there is an absolute moral lawgiver in the first place (i.e., the moral argument for God's existence). In the absence of God, pushing an old lady in front of a bus is as equally meaningless as helping her walk across the street. We can collectively stipulate that such action is wrong, but this is no more than an opinion that has no power or value beyond the subscription of a collective will. After all, on what basis or on what authority does one describe one deed as "good" and another deed as "evil"? In the absence of God, ethics is reduced to aesthetics. To say that killing children is wrong describes a certain sociological position that ascribes relative value to human life, but it is not scientifically prescriptive. To say that "killing children is wrong" has no more truth value than saying, "I don't like cabbage-flavored ice cream." In itself killing a human being is a morally meaningless act. We can ascribe meaning to the deed if we wish, but this is nothing more than a language game, a sociological construct, with no objective or scientific quality. Jeffery B. Russell comments:

---

73. Erickson, *Christian Theology*, 439.

> The argument from evil, if it is valid, destroys the notion of all order and all cosmic principles, not just the one we call God. By destroying order and principle it renders all value judgments completely subjective.... If no order or purpose exists, then all human values and aspirations are absurd, and consequently good and evil are only subjective constructs. But since evil then cannot exist objectively, it cannot be adduced against the existence of God.[74]

In other words, to say that evil counts against God's existence must presume that evil is an objective entity. Yet if God does not exist, then neither does evil in the absolute sense. Without objective moral values, we are left only with actions and attitudes that individuals and societies consider undesirable—in other words, moral nihilism. Moral language becomes nothing more than an arbitrary system of values and beliefs that are completely ephemeral and without any ontological grounds for prescription.

Christians have long wrestled with the problem of evil. One of the first Christian responses was Gnosticism. Gnosticism probably emerged out of Jewish responses to the war with Rome and the defeat and suffering of the Jewish people. After the defeats of AD 70 and 135 some Jewish thinkers went in two directions. Some tried to turn their religion into a manufactured micro-piety to cope with the loss of the temple and expulsion from the land (i.e., Rabbinic Judaism). Others tried to turn Judaism into a pagan religion (i.e., Gnosticism). These Gnostics bought into Hellenistic cosmology and accepted Plato's idea of "the demiurge." In other words, the world with all of its evil and pain was not created by God, but by a wicked god, the demiurge. The problem is obviously that this is not the Christian view of creation and why Gnosticism was so resoundly rejected by the church fathers.

Probably the most popular response to the problem of evil has been the "free will defense" (FWD). Evil is attributed to God granting free will to human subjects, who use their freedom in such a way as to harm themselves and others. While God graciously grants free will, he cannot determine free will; otherwise it would not be free. The many sufferings in our world can be traced to human misuse of their free agency for malevolent ends. Alvin Plantinga summarizes his version of the FWD as follows:

> A world containing creatures who are significantly free (and freely perform more good than evil actions) is more valuable, all else being equal, than a world containing no free creatures at all. Now God can create free creatures, but He can't *cause* or *determine* them to do only what is right. For if He does so, then they aren't significantly free after all; they do not do what is right *freely*. To create creatures capable of *moral*

---

74. Jeffery B. Russell, *The Prince of Darkness: Radical Evil and the Power of Good in History* (Ithaca, NY: Cornell University Press, 1992), 139.

good, therefore, He must create creatures capable of moral evil; and He can't give these creatures the freedom to perform evil and at the same time prevent them from doing so. As it turned out, sadly enough, some of the free creatures God created went wrong in the exercise of their freedom; this is the source of moral evil. The fact that free creatures sometimes go wrong, however, counts neither against God's omnipotence nor against His goodness; for He could have forestalled the occurrence of moral evil only by removing the possibility of moral good.[75]

The same line of thought can be combined with a view of God's "middle knowledge" (i.e., his knowledge about all possibilities and possible worlds), so that God creates the world with the maximal amount of human freedom and the minimal degree of human suffering. Such an argument might run like this:

1. There are possible worlds that even an omnipotent being cannot actualize.
2. A world with morally free creatures producing only moral good is such a world.
3. Instead, God creates a world with maximal human freedom, which leads to maximal human good.
4. While this world is not the best possible world, it is the best possible way to achieve the best possible world, i.e., heaven on earth.

Plantinga's thesis has been so successful that it is safe to say the "logical" problem of evil has been solved. There are no logically valid arguments that indicate that evil is demonstrably incompatible with the existence of God. Therefore, atheist thinkers these days usually tend to pose more moderate claims, such as an inductive argument that the fact of gratuitous evil makes God's existence less probable than his actual existence.

At one level the FWD is entirely biblical since suffering is often attributed to the wicked hearts of people who conspire to do evil—hence the repeated refrain that some king or person "did evil in the eyes of the Lord" (e.g., Judg 6:1; 1 Kgs 11:6; 16:25). Elsewhere, evil is committed from the wicked desires that are stored up in the human heart (e.g., "a heart that devises wicked schemes, feet that are quick to rush into evil" [Prov 6:18]; "a good man brings good things out of the good stored up in his heart, and an evil man brings evil things out of the evil stored up in his heart" [Luke 6:45]).[76]

Scripture affirms that God is sovereign and that human beings are responsible for their actions. Yet the existence of evil and suffering is never accounted for *purely*

---

75. Alvin Plantinga, *God, Freedom, and Evil* (Grand Rapids: Eerdmans, 1978), 30.

76. The FWD can also be used to explain the existence of natural evil *if* one accepts the premise that natural evils (such as disease, earthquakes, volcanoes, etc.) are products of the fall, where human corruption infected the created order (see Gen 3; Rom 8).

on the basis of human freedom. Human freedom is the material cause of suffering, but it is not the ultimate cause. In Scripture the problem of suffering is always understood within the orbit of God's power and purpose. Think of the words that Joseph said to his brothers, "As for you, you meant evil against me, but God meant it for good, to bring it about that many people should be kept alive, as they are today" (Gen 50:20 [ESV]). In the book of Job, Job finally asks God why he allowed him to be so afflicted. The Lord responds by asking Job over sixty questions, such as:

> "Where were you when I laid the earth's foundation?
>   Tell me, if you understand.
> Who marked off its dimensions? Surely you know!
>   Who stretched a measuring line across it?
> On what were its footings set,
>   or who laid its cornerstone—
> while the morning stars sang together
>   and all the angels shouted for joy?" (Job 38:4–7)

God's response is in effect, "I am sovereign and I work in ways that you cannot ordinarily understand." Note Job's response to this:

> "I know that you can do all things;
>   no purpose of yours can be thwarted.
> You asked, 'Who is this that obscures my plans without knowledge?'
>   Surely I spoke of things I did not understand,
>   things too wonderful for me to know." (Job 42:2–3)

Even though God never actually answers Job's question, Job goes away satisfied, confident about God's sovereignty and goodness, and entrusting himself to the faithful goodness of his Maker.

A strong focus on God's sovereignty in the problem of evil can inevitably lead to making God the author of evil itself. While evil is the result of human freedom, it comes from a God-granted freedom. While evil is also the result of supernatural forces such as Satan, Satan was created by God. Is God then, directly or indirectly, the source of evil? As Paul would say, *mē genoito*, or "No way, dude"! I think the Westminster Confession 5.4 is on the right lines when it states:

> The almighty power, unsearchable wisdom, and infinite goodness of God so far manifest themselves in His providence, that *it extends itself even to the first fall*, and all other sins of angels and men; and that not by a bare permission, but such as has joined with it a most wise and powerful bounding, and otherwise ordering, and governing of them, in a manifold dispensation, to His own holy ends; yet so, as *the sinfulness thereof proceeds only from the creature, and not from God*, who, being most holy and righteous, *neither is nor can be the author or approver of sin*. (italics added)[77]

---

[77]. See www.reformed.org/documents/wcf_with_proofs/.

§7.5 The Odyssey of Theodicy

The Westminster divines do not pretend to offer an explanation as to why God permits evil and suffering, but they remained confident that nothing in the world, however tragic, is beyond the purview of God's power and providence. God remains sovereign over his creation, even over sin and suffering; God permits it and restrains it, within his divine design. God is not the author of evil; rather, its origins lie in the sinning creature, but God does use suffering to bring about the good of the world and good for his people. Paul writes to the Romans that "in all things God works for the good of those who love him" (Rom 8:28).

Let's be honest. It doesn't always feel that way. But the purposes of God are good and steadfast. Indeed, his promises are an anchor for the soul; we hold onto them and keep them precious. It is true that "Love Wins" in the end, but it's a sovereign love that was set in motion before eternity began. It is a holy love, a love that spares no expense in what it would pay to rescue those who, through their own inclination, would sell themselves into the bondage of suffering.

The recent theologies of open theism need some comment here, and it is notable that they are driven mainly by the task of theodicy.[78] For open theists, God is responsive and affected by the world he made; he shares in the suffering of his creatures. In open theism, God does not absolutely know the future, much less determine it. For if God knew the future, it would be determined precisely by his knowing it, rendering free agency impossible. As Clark Pinnock put it: "No being can know in advance exactly what a free agent will do, though he may predict it with high probability. God knows that whatever he wills and determines will come to pass, but if God is free and creatures are free, he cannot know in advance always exactly what will happen."[79] Instead, God sovereignly chooses not to know the future; he discovers with free agents the future as it comes to pass. Hence God's relationship to the future remains as it were "open."[80]

On such a perspective, God is not a grand controller who determines the future; rather, God is more like someone who joins us in the journey into the future. God remains trustworthy in this journey because he is an "omni-competent" companion who can handle anything that happens.[81] God genuinely empathizes with our suffering, he is equally surprised by it, but he is unable to overpower evil in this world without violating human freedom.

---

78. Cf., e.g., Gregory A. Boyd, *Letters from a Skeptic* (Wheaton, IL: Victor, 1994); William Hasker, *The Triumph of God over Evil: Theodicy for a World of Suffering* (Downers Grove, IL: InterVarsity Press, 2008).

79. Clark Pinnock, "There Is Room for us—A Reply to Bruce Ware," *JETS* 45 (2002): 216.

80. Cf. introduction in Gregory A. Boyd and Paul R. Eddy, *Across the Spectrum: Understanding Issues in Evangelical Theology* (Grand Rapids: Baker, 2009), 62–69.

81. John E. Sanders, "God as Personal," in *The Grace of God, The Will of Man: A Case for Arminianism* (ed. Clark H. Pinnock; Grand Rapids: Zondervan, 1989), 175; idem, "Historical Considerations," in *The Openness of God: A Biblical Challenge to the Traditional Understanding of God* (Downers Grove, IL: InterVarsity Press, 1994), 97.

Now in many ways, I resonate with the desire of open theists to depict God as relational, emotionally involved with his creatures, and supremely loving toward humanity. Open theism gains currency when classical theists overemphasize God's preordination of cosmic and human affairs without measured regard to God's interactive connection with his creatures. While God is indeed proactive in his plan (e.g., Eph 1:1–22), he is equally interactive (e.g., Exod 32:1–14), and in some sense even reactive (e.g., Jonah 3:10).[82] God's answer to prayer, after all, can be likened to a divine improvisation based on God's knowledge of all possibilities and the changelessness of his character where he genuinely responds to our petitions in his infinite wisdom and grace.

That said, the God of open theism does not remind me of the God of Job. It is not the Father of Jesus in Gethsemane. It is not the God of John the Seer and his vision of God's victory at Patmos. The God of open theists reminds me of the "Lord" in the Chris de Burgh song "Spanish Train," where the Devil defeats the Lord in a poker game and wins innocent souls to incarcerate in hell. The Lord and the Devil move on to playing games of chess for the souls of the dead; the Devil keeps winning because he cheats, and then the final stanza ends with the words: "And as for the Lord, well, he's just doing his best."[83] The image in the song is of God striving, but failing to stem the tide of evil in our world. Open theists genuinely believe that God will triumph over evil in the end; however, it would seem that the grounds for believing so, namely, the sovereignty of God, is eviscerated by their (re-)construction of the doctrine of God, whose relationship to the future remains "open."[84]

I don't get out of bed early every Sunday morning to worship a God who is "omni-competent" or "just doing his best." Christians have professed faith in a God who can sympathize with our suffering, yet never in such a way as to undermine his divine attributes, the maximality of his power—specifically, his knowledge, purposes, and love. The fact of the matter is, as C.S. Lewis himself recognized, that "everyone who believes in God at all, believes that he knows what you and I are going to do tomorrow." The foreknowledge of God is simply ingrained in classic orthodoxy and cannot be dispensed with even in order to protect a libertarian view of human freedom.[85]

The ultimate answer to evil is the story of the gospel. God made the world good, and evil is a tyrannical intrusion into God's city. God intends to cleanse this world

---

82. Graham Cole, "The Living God: Anthropomorphic or Anthropopathic?" *RTR* 59 (2000): 24–25.

83. Chris de Burgh, "Spanish Train," from the 1975 album *Spanish Train and Other Stories*. See complete lyrics at www.sing365.com/music/lyric.nsf/Spanish-Train-lyrics-Chris-De-Burgh/CF85030FF6BCCAEE48256968002F8851.

84. Cf. on the open theist view, William Hasker, *The Triumph of God over Evil: Theodicy for a World of Suffering* (Downers Grove, IL: InterVarsity Press, 2008).

85. C.S. Lewis, *Mere Christianity* (New York: Macmillan, 1960), 148.

of evil. He will expose evil for what it is, sentence the tyrants to punishment, and permanently partition evil away from his goodness. God solemnly covenants to unite himself to creation through the redemptive work of the Logos. Then God will fill creation with all his own glory that he shares with his people. God's answer to evil is not a syllogism, nor is it feigned sympathy; it is the cross of the Son of God. God in Christ Jesus participated in our humanity and shares in our grief, suffering, and sorrow. As Alister McGrath writes:

> God suffered in Christ. He knows what it is like to experience pain. He has travelled down the road of pain, abandonment, suffering and death — a road that is called Calvary. God is not like some alleged hero with feet of clay, who demands that others suffer, while remaining aloof from the world of pain himself. He has passed through the shadow of suffering himself. The God in whom Christians believe and hope is a God who himself suffered, and by doing so, transfigured the suffering of his people.[86]

The gospels tell the story of how Jesus went to his death in order to defeat evil — human, natural, supernatural — by undergoing the penalty for all the evil of the world. He allows the viper of death to strike him, but he drains the poison of sin from its mouth, so that although the serpent may yet still bite others, the venom of its attack is gone. Or as Paul said, because of Jesus Christ, the crucified and risen Lord, we have this confidence: "For I am convinced that neither death nor life, neither angels nor demons, neither the present nor the future, nor any powers, neither height nor depth, nor anything else in all creation, will be able to separate us from the love of God that is in Christ Jesus our Lord" (Rom 8:38–39).

FURTHER READING

Bolt, Peter G., ed. *Christ's Victory over Evil: Biblical Theology and Pastoral Ministry.* Nottingham, UK: Apollos, 2009.

Carson, D. A. *How Long O Lord? Reflections on Suffering and Evil.* Grand Rapids: Baker, 2006.

Howard-Snyder, Daniel. "God, Evil, and Suffering." Pp. 76–115 in *Reasons for the Hope Within.* Ed. M. J. Murray. Grand Rapids: Eerdmans, 1998.

Ware, Bruce A. *God's Lesser Glory: The Diminished God of Open Theism.* Wheaton, IL: Crossway, 2000.

Wright, N. T. *Evil and the Justice of God.* London: SPCK, 2006.

---

86. Alister E. McGrath, *Bridge-Building: Effective Christian Apologetics* (Leicester, UK: Inter-Varsity Press, 1993), 144.

WHAT TO TAKE HOME?

- God created humanity to share in his glory.
- The *imago dei* is the royal dominion given to humanity to rule over creation on God's behalf.
- Humanity consists of a psychosomatic unity of body and soul.
- The essence of sin is the desire to be free from God's sovereignty.
- Original sin is the entrance of sin and death into the human world through Adam's disobedience.
- Original sin consists of inheriting a corrupt nature and a receiving verdict of condemnation from Adam.
- The best theodicy is the Christian story of God's triumph over evil and suffering in the cross of Christ.

STUDY QUESTIONS FOR INDIVIDUALS AND GROUPS

1. What sets humanity apart from the animal world?
2. How does a Christian view of the image of God impact our understanding of human rights?
3. If someone said that salvation consists of the escape of the soul from the body, what would you say?
4. Describe the relationship between Adam's sin and our own sinning?
5. How would you explain the pastoral relevance of Christ's work on the cross to a grieving friend?

PART EIGHT

The Community of the Gospelized

Part Eight • The Community of the Gospelized

§8.1 The Evangelical Church
§8.2 Biblical Images of the Church
§8.3 The Shape of the Church
§8.4 The Marks of the Church
§8.5 Governance of the Church
§8.6 Emblems of the Gospel: Baptism and Lord's Supper

The study of the church is called "ecclesiology." Here we inquire as to the nature of the church as driven and defined by the gospel of Jesus Christ. Various images for the church are identified, and the general shape of the church in light of God's plan is set out. We will discuss the marks of the church, including oneness, holiness, catholicity, and apostolicity. This is followed by examining the contentious topics of church governance and the church sacraments.

"The true treasure of the Church is the Most Holy Gospel of the glory and the grace of God."[1]

Q. What do you believe concerning "the holy catholic church"?
A. I believe that the Son of God through his Spirit and Word, out of the entire human race, from the beginning of the world to its end, gathers, protects, and preserves for himself a community chosen for eternal life and united in true faith. And of this community I am and always will be a living member.[2]

"We exist as Christians by the Tradition of the Gospel ... testified in Scripture, transmitted in and by the Church through the power of the Holy Spirit."[3]

---

1. Martin Luther, Thesis 62 of the "Ninety-Five Theses."
2. Heidelberg Catechism, Question 54 (see www.crcna.org/welcome/beliefs/confessions/heidelberg-catechism).
3. "Scripture, Tradition and Traditions," Fourth World Conference on Faith and Order, Montreal, 1963, para 45.

§ 8.1 THE EVANGELICAL CHURCH

The evangelical churches are those that have the gospel at the center of their proclamation and practice. The evangelical church is a community created by the gospel, a church that promotes and preaches the gospel, that cultivates the gospel in its spirituality. Its members strive to live lives worthy of gospel, and at its center is Jesus Christ, the Lord announced in the gospel. This should be unsurprising because church and gospel go together like an egg and its shell. The spreading of the gospel into the world was concurrent with the expansion of the church into all areas of the world. The church is the custodian of the gospel that carries the gospel with her wherever she goes. In fact, where there is the true and authentic gospel, proclaimed in Word and embodied in sacraments, there one will find a true and authentic church.

The ancient Christian faith has always included an affirmation about the place of the church in God's redemptive project. The Apostles' Creed includes the confession, "I believe in ... the communion of the saints." To say such a thing is to identify the church as a communion, that is, a common-union of believers, united with each other by their love for God, their fellowship with Christ, and their life in the Spirit. It includes saints who have already entered heaven (the church triumphant) and the saints who still struggle on the earth (the church militant). They are a people believing in a single God, answering a common call, confessing a common gospel, receiving a common faith, sealed by a common baptism, and serving a common Lord, Jesus Christ. The communion of the saints is the living fellowship of all believers who participate in a shared worship, spiritual gifts, graces, material goods, and mutual edification.[4]

Our concern here is with that particular and sometimes peculiar people called the "evangelical church." Evangelicalism isn't an official entity as such but more like an interdenominational tribe or a shared theological ethos that traverses

---

4. Cf. Philip G. Ryken, ed., *The Communion of the Saints: Living in Fellowship with the People of God* (Phillipsburg, NJ: Presbyterian & Reformed, 2001), 9–10.

denominational lines. Evangelicals are not the only Christians in the world, but they are a significant portion of the world's Protestant population.

Evangelical ecclesiology has always been a bit of a conundrum. That is because there is no standard "evangelical ecclesiology," nor can there be in the strict sense. You can have an Anglican, Catholic, Baptist, Lutheran, Methodist, or Presbyterian ecclesiology. Such ecclesiologies prescribe the confession, order, structure, discipline, governance, worship, sacraments, and ministries of these respective denominations. But there is no prescriptive evangelical equivalent because evangelicalism is a *theological ethos*, not a *denominational entity*. While evangelicals might agree on certain ecclesiological principles, like Jesus Christ is the head of the church and the church is the body of Christ, the general agreements largely break down when it comes to the specific ordering and structures of the church. Yet this has not always been a negative thing. Precisely because evangelicalism has no prescriptive ecclesiology, it can accommodate itself to virtually any form of church order.[5]

Evangelicals have implied an ecclesiology more than worked one out. Evangelical convictions about ecclesiology have given birth to church planting ventures, parachurch ministries, cooperative missionary work, interdenominational seminaries, and joint conferences.[6] What is determinative for evangelicalism is the fact that people in the various denominations root themselves in the evangel and recognize the evangelical character of each other's ministries. This means that at a broad level, there is some sense of shared Christian identity and belief in a common mission that connects evangelicals together across the denominational spectrum. Evangelicalism is based on a mutual recognition that the gospel embodies a reality, an evangelical reality that binds us together in life and service to the Triune God, despite our differences on second order matters of doctrine.

To pursue an evangelical ecclesiology, then, is to set ourselves the task of identifying how the theological discourse within the evangelical "big tent" teaches us something about the church in our own denominational "little tents." An evangelical theology draws on the strengths of the various traditions of the church in order to enrich, strengthen, reform, and unify the ecclesiologies of our own respective denominations. An evangelical ecclesiology can never replace a denominational ecclesiology—not until the consummation, anyway—but as we all draw closer to Christ, so too our ecclesiologies will begin to be drawn closer together as well. Evangelical ecclesiology means coming together as Baptists, Presbyterians, Pentecostals, and Methodists, praying together, reading the Bible together, and learning what it means to be the people of God together.

---

5. Alister E. McGrath, *The Christian Theology Reader* (3rd ed.; Oxford: Blackwell, 2006), 121.

6. John G. Stackhouse, "Preface," in *Evangelical Ecclesiology: Reality or Illusion?* (Grand Rapids: Baker, 2003), 9.

§ 8.1 The Evangelical Church

Now it is no secret that evangelicals have not been known for their ecclesiology. John Stott comments:

> One of our chief evangelical blind spots has been to overlook the central importance of the church. We tend to proclaim individual salvation without moving on to the saved community. We emphasize that Christ died for us "to redeem us from all iniquity" rather than "to purify for himself a people of his own." We think of ourselves more as "Christians" than as "churchmen," and our message is more good news of a new life than of a new society.[7]

That rings true because evangelicals have traditionally been ecclesiology-lite. That is because a lite ecclesiology allows them flexibility in working with people from all denominations and because their own denominational structures are often controlled by liberals or bureaucrats. Why bother wasting time in committees when there are souls to save? Why bother painting the cathedral when you can preach to the folks at Walmart? While this ecclesiology-lite approach leads to wonderful opportunities to work with other Christians without denominational interference, it can also lead to a disinterest in the structure, organization, and visibility of the church.

I vividly remember at a luncheon how an Anglo-Catholic army chaplain accosted evangelicals on the grounds that "the problem with you evangelicals is that you have no ecclesiology." To which I promptly retorted, "No, the problem with us evangelicals is that we do not have *your* ecclesiology!" I stand by my original remark, for evangelicals believe in the church and are genuinely committed to it, but not in a way that Anglo-Catholics, liberals, and mainline Protestants are committed to the church. Still, I had to admit that something seems to be lacking in evangelical ecclesiology. I do not see anywhere near the same excitement, emotion, resolve, and passion for debates about ecclesiology as, for example, soteriology. I doubt that many American Presbyterians get riled over Tom Wright's ecclesiology as they do over his soteriology. So what is the problem here? I suggest three things.

A first problem is a radical Platonic dualism. Evangelicals have a tendency to seek spiritual unity rather than physical unity. They privilege the invisible church over the visible church. To give some examples, it is enough that I recognize that the Methodist church down the road contains genuine believers rather than to seek joint ways that I can work with them to further the kingdom in my neighborhood. Jesus' reign from heaven is limited to the hearts of believers, and this cannot or need not be extended to societies, institutions, or organizations as a whole. On this framework, the essence of Christianity becomes conceptual, cerebral, and

---

7. John Stott, *The Message of Ephesians: God's New Society* (Downers Grove, IL: InterVarsity Press, 1986), 9.

propositional—it is the ideas, not the tangible physicality that those ideas embody, that defines the church.

But this collapses Christianity into a Platonic idealism, where Christianity becomes a system of conceptual values that spasmodically penetrates into the real world, but the real world is merely the encrusted case that carries Christianity. Now Christianity has always had a propositional content to its truth claims; for example, you cannot get more propositional than "Jesus is Lord." But church unity, redemption, and sacraments are designed to carry forward the visible presence of God in our world. A thick description of the church must include saying something not just about the church as the people of God, but the church as the presence of God in the world.[8] As such, the visible nature of the church, the transformation of peoples by the gospel, and the encounter with God through Word and sacrament indicate that God meets people in the physical world and not just in the world of ideas.

A second problem in evangelicalism is anti-Catholicism. By that I do not mean a negative evaluation of the Roman Catholic Church. I'm a Protestant and I still have a protest against Rome. No, what I mean is that there is a negative disposition of the traditions, church fathers, and liturgy of the church prior to the Reformation. I've met some folks who really believe that the church disappeared about AD 100 and remained absent for the most part until 1517, when Martin Luther nailed his ninety-five theses to the door of Wittenberg Castle Church. However, the Reformation was about the recovery of the catholic (i.e., universal) faith of the church, not a denouncement of it in favor of sectarian innovations. Tradition is not the antiquated residue of a former generation that was mostly wrong about Scripture. Tradition is what our grandfathers and grandmothers in the faith learned from Scripture. Thus, I concur heartily with the words of J. Todd Billings:

> In our day, the Reformed tradition is in dire need of recovering the Catholic dimension of our heritage. Calvin and other Reformers did not, in fact, seek radical revision of a Nicene doctrine of the Trinity and a Chalcedonian Christology; moreover, the sacramental theology of Luther, Calvin, and even Zwingli was much closer to the patristic theology of Augustine, for example, than the highly cognitive memorialism that takes place in many of today's Reformed churches.[9]

We should see ourselves in a vertical relationship with the saints of the past, who have walked the life of faith ahead of us. They are our forefathers in the faith, and we are the torchbearers of their faith. We should also see ourselves in a horizontal relationship with other Christians in all corners of the world who together, like us,

---

8. Kevin Vanhoozer, *The Drama of Doctrine: A Canonical Linguistic Approach to Christian Theology* (Louisville: Westminster John Knox, 2002), 400.

9. J. Todd Billings, "The Promise of Catholic Calvinism," *Perspectives: Journal of Reformed Thought* (April 2006); see www.rca.org/Page.aspx?pid=2996&srcid=3466 (accessed 1 June 2011).

gather to call on the name of the Lord Jesus Christ. Wherever the gospel is preached faithfully and wherever God is worshiped as Trinity, there is the church.

A third problem is hyperindividualism. For some folks the gospel is an iGod app that enables a person to get a wifi connection with heaven (where the one mediator between God and Man is Apple Inc.). To use another metaphor, the church is reduced to the weekly meeting of Jesus' Facebook friends.[10] The locus of Christianity becomes God and me rather than God and us. One could contrast two slogans: "I believe, therefore I am saved" with "We believe, therefore we are God's people." Evangelicals tend to prefer the former rather than the latter as the default setting for their ecclesiology.

I do not think it possible, or even desirable, to eviscerate all and any type of individualism from theology. Individuals do have to respond to the gospel; individuals do have to cultivate obedience and holiness; and individuals are held accountable for their actions.[11] Even so, what evangelical ecclesiology has lacked is a notion of corporate identity. I am who I am only as I am someone who is a part of the church of Jesus Christ. The African theologian John Mbiti famously said: "I am because we are; since we are, therefore I am." The theological task is not to construct a list of ideas for individuals to assent to; rather, the theological task is to set out the faith of the Christian church and to profess what "we" believe. For it is in the church that theology is developed, confessed, proclaimed, and applied.

When we put this together, some basic tasks for evangelical theology should include:

- developing a practice of the church that implements the redemptive power of its physical presence, as opposed to a Platonic dualism that elevates spiritual ideas over physical embodiment
- recapturing the catholic vision of the Reformation to return the church to its catholic and apostolic faith by journeying into our past for treasures both theological and liturgical, as opposed to a sectarian view of the past that supposes that all who came before us were thieves and robbers
- construing our identity in a corporate sense as God's people who are united in Christ, as opposed to a crass individualism that focuses on just God and me

That is what an evangelical ecclesiology rooted in the gospel should set out to do. In brief, what is needed is a mixture of a thick catholicity, renewed Trinitarian theology, high sacramental theology, and historically informed revivalist preaching in order to renew the evangelical churches.

---

10. Nick Perrin, "Jesus' Eschatology and Kingdom Ethics: Ever the Twain Shall Meet," in *Jesus, Paul, and the People of God: A Theological Dialogue with N. T. Wright* (Downers Grove, IL: InterVarsity Press, 2011), 102.

11. Cf. Gary W. Burnett, *Paul and the Salvation of the Individual* (Leiden: Brill, 2001).

The ecclesiology I'm suggesting here is perhaps controversial, but I think there is solid justification for it. From a theological viewpoint, a high Christology and a high ecclesiology go together. If we think wonderfully high thoughts of Jesus, we should think wonderfully high thoughts about the church, which is, after all, "the body of Christ." In fact, the church may be the only advertisement for Christ that unbelievers ever see. Yes, I know that high ecclesiology can become a virtual ecclesiolatry, where the church replaces Jesus as the mediator of salvation. But if Colossians and Ephesians are anything to go by, a high Christology and a high view of the church go hand in glove. The New Testament views the Redeemer in the redemptive community, and redemption is effected by the message of grace and the means of grace that they possess. John Stott is correct: "The church is at the centre of the eternal and historical purpose of God."[12]

If what I've said above is true, the church is more than the Fed-Ex delivery boy leaving a package at people's door marked "gospel." Cyprian claimed that "he cannot have God for his Father who has not the church for his mother."[13] Similar were Augustine's memorable words written in the context of the Donatist controversy: "Outside the church there is no salvation."[14] To some this probably sounds a bit Romish. It is a common adage since the time of B. B. Warfield that the Reformation was about Augustine's doctrine of grace (salvation by grace alone) triumphing over Augustine's doctrine of the church (no salvation outside of the church).[15] The problem is that this claim is patently false. Just consider the Westminster Confession 25.2:

> The visible Church, which is also catholic or universal under the Gospel (not confined to one nation, as before under the law), consists of all those throughout the world that profess the true religion; and of their children: and is the kingdom of the Lord Jesus Christ, the house and family of God, *out of which there is no ordinary possibility of salvation.* (italics added)

That is Westminster, not the Vatican talking! Calvin said of the church that "there is no other means of entering into life unless she conceive us in the womb and give us birth, unless she nourish us at her breasts."[16] This is a stark contrast to popular notions of salvation that bypass the church completely. The church is not the savior, but it is the mother of the saved, who births and nurtures her children on the gospel.

I also want to assert that there is a symbiotic relationship between "gospel" and "church." To begin with, the church is created by the Word—not just any word, but

---

12. John Stott, *Evangelical Truth: A Personal Statement* (Leicester, UK: Inter-Varsity Press, 1999), 119.
13. Cyprian, *Unit. eccl.* 6; cf. Calvin, *Institutes* 4.1.1.
14. Augustine, *Bapt.* 4.17.
15. B. B. Warfield, "Augustine," in *Encyclopedia of Religion and Ethics* (ed. James Hastings; 12 vols.; New York: Scribner's, 1908–22), 2:224.
16. Calvin, *Institutes* 4.1.4.

the gospel word. The gospel creates a community to follow Jesus Christ, to know and love God, and to walk in the Spirit. The church is evangelically constituted, and so the evangel becomes the defining mark of its ethos. The gospel we preach shapes the kind of churches we create. The kind of churches we create in turn shapes the type of gospel we preach.[17] Belief in the gospel signifies our entry point into the faith. Baptism and the Lord's Supper are the chief emblems of the gospel, and they ensure that the gospel is remembered, visualized, and even experienced on a regular basis. Discipleship is a matter of learning to live out the realities that the gospel creates. And proclaiming the gospel is the mission of the church.

That is why we should think of the church as "the community of the gospelized"! When you magnetize a piece of metal, the metal becomes magnetic. When you sterilize a surgical tool, the tool becomes sterile. When you tenderize a piece of meat, the meat becomes tender. When a person or a church is gospelized, they ooze gospel, they bleed Jesus, they overflow with Spirit, they radiate the Father's glory. That is the goal of a gospelized community. Our *telos* is to be and become a church that knows the gospel, preaches the gospel, and lives according to the law of the gospel. We can expound this further.

1. *The church is the company of the gospel.* Kevin Vanhoozer has recently argued that doctrine helps individuals perform the theo-drama of the Christian life by enabling them to understand their identities as persons made new in Christ.[18] The church is like a company of actors who are cast to perform the redemptive drama of the gospel. The church gathers together scripted by Scripture, under the direction of the Holy Spirit, illuminated by our traditions, to be built up into Christ. We go to church to rehearse, to celebrate, and to better understand the drama of redemption that reaches us in the gospel of Jesus Christ.[19]

2. *The church is the public face of the gospel.* I've drawn this feature from a book written by J. L. Houlden.[20] The central thesis of the volume is that the history of Christian origins cannot be told apart from the history of the institution of the church. Houlden makes the point that Christology, however diversely expressed, was the driving force in most New Testament understandings of Christian community. The unity of Christians was not a collection of normative myths, nor a sacred book, but it was comprised of a unity of people whose reason for being together relates solely to Christ.[21] But the problem is that the institutionalization of the

---

17. Scot McKnight, *A Community Called Atonement* (Nashville: Abingdon, 2007), 5.

18. This can be contrasted with Karl Barth (*Epistle to the Romans* [trans. E. C. Hoskyns; Oxford: Oxford University Press, 1968], 36) who believed that the church's activity "is related to the Gospel only in so far as it is no more than a crater formed by the explosion of a shell and seeks to be no more than a void in which the Gospel reveals itself." The church is more than empty space in a theater; it is an actor called to faithfully perform on a stage!

19. Vanhoozer, *Drama of Doctrine*, 399–444.

20. J. L. Houlden, *The Public Face of the Gospel: New Testament Ideas of the Church* (London: SCM, 1997).

21. Ibid., 89.

church has tended to obscure the fundamental thrust of the gospel and become an unsatisfactory vehicle for the message.[22]

Ultimately the church is the house of Jesus Christ, and if people are to meet Jesus, they must walk through the cathedral door. General revelation will not establish a saving faith; rather, it pours oil on a bonfire of idolatries in the human mind. Even special revelation, Scripture no less, cannot lead to authentic faith apart from someone coming alongside the enquirer, much like Philip with the Ethiopian, and explaining the Scriptures to them (see Acts 8:30–40). The church is not a dispensable footnote in God's plan to repossess the world. The church is comprised of fishers of men (Matt 4:19); it is the salt of the earth (5:13), branches of the vine (John 15:5–10), an olive tree (Rom 11:13–24), a letter from Christ (2 Cor 3:2–3), God's building (1 Cor 3:9), ambassadors of reconciliation (2 Cor 5:20), wine and bread (1 Cor 5:7; 10:16–17), an ark of salvation (1 Pet 3:18–22), exiles in a foreign land (1 Pet 1:1; 2:11; cf. Heb 11:13), and a kingdom of priests (1 Pet 2:9; Rev 1:6; 5:10). Or to use an image from the *Epistle to Diognetus*, the church is to the world as a soul is to the body.[23]

These images have the qualities of reaching, finding, telling, and nourishing others. The church is a living monument to the gospel. Therefore, its lights, doors, windows, and occupants must reflect the gospel with all the energy and brightness of a Disney parade. The church is the only gospel that many people will hear, the only Bible some will ever read, and the only Jesus many will meet.

3. *The church is the hermeneutic of the gospel.* This point was fabulously made by missiologist Lesslie Newbigin.[24] Newbigin wondered how it would be possible that the gospel should become credible in a pluralistic society and that people would come to believe that the power of God over human affairs was manifested by a man killed on a cross. For Newbigin the answer, the "only hermeneutic of the gospel," is "a congregation of men and women who believe and live by it."[25] Jesus did not write a book, but he formed a community around him—a community that, at its heart, remembers and rehearses his deeds and words. Such a community has six characteristics: (1) It will be a community of praise. (2) It will be a community of truth. (3) It will be a community that does not live for itself but is deeply involved in local concerns. (4) It will be a community where men and women are prepared for and sustained in the exercise of the priesthood in the world. (5) It will be a community of mutual responsibility rooted in a new order. (6) It will be a community of hope. Newbigin concludes that if the gospel is to challenge our society and claim the high ground, it will not be by forming Christian political parties. Rather:

---

22. Ibid., 92, 100.
23. *Diogn.* 6.1–10.
24. Lesslie Newbigin, *The Gospel in a Pluralistic Society* (Grand Rapids: Eerdmans, 1989), 226–33.
25. Ibid., 227.

It will only be by movements that begin with the local congregation in which the reality of the new creation is present, known and experienced, and from which men and women will go into every sector of public life to claim it for Christ, to unmask the illusions which have remained hidden and to expose all areas of public life to the illumination of the gospel. But that will only happen as and when local congregations renounce an introverted concern for their own life, and recognize that they exist for the sake of those who are not members, as sign, instrument, and foretaste of God's redeeming grace for the whole life of society.[26]

An evangelical ecclesiology is, corny as it sounds, the attempt to be the gospel-driven church.[27] We are the community of the gospelized: the company of the gospel, the public face of the gospel, the hermeneutic of the gospel. The worship, mission, ethics, symbols, testimony, and spirituality of the church are shaped by what it thinks of and what it does with the gospel of Jesus Christ. The gospel is the mark and mission of the authentic church of Christ.

FURTHER READING

Belcher, Jim. *Deep Church*. Downers Grove, IL: InterVarsity Press, 2009.

Clapp, Rodney. *A Peculiar People: The Church as Culture in Post-Christian Society*. Downers Grove, IL: InterVarsity Press, 1996.

Ferguson, Everett. *The Church of Christ: A Biblical Ecclesiology for Today*. Grand Rapids: Eerdmans, 1996.

Harper, Brad, and Paul Louis Metzger. *Exploring Ecclesiology: An Evangelical and Ecumenical Introduction*. Grand Rapids: Brazos, 2009.

Husbands, M. A., and D. J. Treier, eds. *The Community of the Word: Towards an Evangelical Ecclesiology*. Downers Grove, IL: InterVarsity Press, 2005.

Kärkkäinen, Veli-Matti. *An Introduction to Ecclesiology: Ecumenical, Historical, and Global Perspectives*. Downers Grove, IL: InterVarsity Press, 2002.

Küng, Hans. *The Church*. London: T&T Clark, 2001.

Minear, Paul. *Images of the Church in the New Testament*. Louisville: Westminster John Knox, 2005.

Stott, John. *The Living Church: Convictions of a Life Long Pastor*. Downers Grove, IL: InterVarsity Press, 2011.

---

26. Ibid., 232–33.
27. Cf. Ian Stackhouse, *The Gospel-Driven Church: Retrieving Classical Ministries for Contemporary Revivalism* (Milton Keynes, UK: Paternoster, 2005).

ECCLESIOLOGY IN CONTENTION #1: KINGDOM OF GOD AND THE CHURCH OF GOD

How does the kingdom of God relate to the church of God? The answer obviously depends on what one means by "kingdom" (e.g., heaven, an experience, future millennium, etc.) and "church" (e.g., visible, invisible, institution, community, etc.). When I say "kingdom," I mean the redemptive reign of God to establish his rule among human beings, a kingdom that will appear as an apocalyptic act at the end of the age, but has already come into human history in the person and mission of Jesus to bring people under the power of God's reign.[28] Also, when I say "church," I take this to mean the people of God in the new age who are bonded together by their faith in God the Father, their union with Jesus Christ, and their partaking of the Holy Spirit, and they live according to the teachings, story, and symbols of Israel's Messiah. Given that clarification, what has "kingdom" to do with "church"?

One strand of Christian tradition has identified the kingdom with the visible institution of the church on earth. The church is an ecclesial kingdom that functions as a sign and symbol of God's visible rule on earth. The institution, hierarchy, and property of the church is the very embodiment of God's reign.[29] One can detect biblical materials to support this. The words of Jesus to Peter at Caesarea Philippi were, "And I tell you that you are Peter, and on this rock I will build my church, and the gates of Hades will not overcome it" (Matt 16:18). In this controversial text, Peter, the rock for the new community, is given great authority (i.e., keys) from which he is to exercise his ministry. In Hebrews, entering the "church" is described as coming "to Mount Zion, to the city of the living God, the heavenly Jerusalem" (Heb 12:22). Again, one can see the potential links between God's reign and church structure.

This model was teased out by Augustine: "Therefore, the Church even now is the Kingdom of Christ, and the Kingdom of heaven. Accordingly, even now His saints reign with Him, though otherwise than they shall reign hereafter."[30] This has been a popular image of the church wherever Christianity has had political influence and power. It has been the official Roman Catholic position since the Council of Trent. You could say that this model is also prevalent in conservative circles in the United States, where preachers aspire, as I heard one chap say, to get every soul "converted, baptized, and enrolled to vote."

---

28. George E. Ladd, *A Theology of the New Testament* (ed. and rev. D. A. Hagner; Grand Rapids: Eerdmans, 1993), 89–90.
29. Howard A. Snyder, *Models of the Kingdom* (Nashville: Abingdon, 1991), 67–76.
30. Augustine, *Civ.* 20.9, cited in ibid., 70.

The model that makes the church identical with the kingdom has several telling weaknesses. First, while it is recognized that the church is not completely identical to the kingdom, to say precisely what it is about the church that is the kingdom is difficult. Is it the sacraments? The clergy? Its influence over the people? Moreover, if we believe that the kingdom is both present and future, in what sense can the church be the kingdom?

Second, linking the church to the kingdom can lead to triumphalism and a lack of self-criticism. If the church is the kingdom, then to disagree with the church is to disagree with God! Yet anyone who has sat through a Baptist deacons' meeting or read any of the Vatican's official statements knows that the church says and does things that are far from perfect and not beyond scrutiny.

Third, this model yields a conception of the church as chiefly sacramental, hierarchical, institutional, and authoritarian.[31] The church loses its prophetic voice when its attention is focused on preserving its own position within a power-sharing agreement with the state.

Another strand of the Christian tradition (principally the Lutheran and Reformed varieties) has set forth a doctrine of two kingdoms: the secular and the sacred. Luther and Calvin, though clearly possessing their own distinctive views on the subject, do at least share a common view that the religious and civil are separate theaters:

> God has ordained the two governments: the spiritual, which by the Holy Spirit under Christ makes Christians and pious people; and the secular, which restrains the unchristian and wicked so that they are obliged to keep the peace outwardly.... The laws of worldly government extend no farther than to life and property and what is external upon earth. For over the soul God can and will let no one rule but himself. Therefore, where temporal power presumes to prescribe laws for the soul, it encroaches upon God's government and only misleads and destroys souls. We desire to make this so clear that every one shall grasp it, and that the princes and bishops may see what fools they are when they seek to coerce the people with their laws and commandments into believing one thing or another.[32]

> There are two governments: the one religious, by which the conscience is trained to piety and divine worship; the other civil, by which the individual is instructed in those duties which, as men and citizens, we are bound to perform. To these two forms are commonly given the not inappropriate names of spiritual and temporal jurisdiction, intimating that the former species has reference to the life of the soul, while the latter relates to matters of

---

31. Snyder, *Models*, 75.
32. Martin Luther, "Secular Authority: To What Extent It Should Be Obeyed (1523)," *Works of Martin Luther* (6 vols.; Philadelphia: Muhlenberg, 1930–43), 3:225–73.

the present life, not only to food and clothing, but to the enacting of laws which require a man to live among his fellows purely honorably, and modestly. The former has its seat within the soul, the latter only regulates the external conduct. We may call the one the religious, the other the civil kingdom. Now, these two, as we have divided them, are always to be viewed apart from each other. Let us now return to human laws. If they are imposed for the purpose of forming a religious obligation, as if the observance of them was in itself necessary, we say that the restraint thus laid on the conscience is unlawful. Our consciences have not to do with men but with God only. Hence the common distinction between the earthly forum and the forum of conscience.[33]

David VanDrunen summarizes the two kingdoms doctrine this way:

God is *not redeeming* the cultural activities and institutions of this world, but is *preserving* them through the covenant he made with all living creatures through Noah in Genesis 8:20–9:17. God himself rules this "common kingdom," and thus it is not, as some writers describe it, the "kingdom of man." This kingdom is in no sense a realm of moral neutrality or autonomy. God makes its institutions and activities honorable, though only for temporary or provisional purposes. Simultaneously, God *is redeeming people* for himself, by virtue of the covenant he made with Abraham and brought to glorious fulfillment in the work of the Lord Jesus Christ, who has completed Adam's original task once and for all. These redeemed people are citizens of the "redemptive kingdom," whom God is gathering now in the church and will welcome into the new heavens and new earth at Christ's glorious return. Until that day, Christians live as members of both kingdoms, discharging their proper duties in each.[34]

Michael Horton differentiates between the church's evangelistic mandate in the Great Commission and the cultural mandate of humanity to build society in their secular vocation. He contends that the New Testament nowhere fuses the two together.[35]

The strength of the two kingdoms doctrine is that the separation of religious institutions from secular government promotes religious liberty and rightly separates nature and grace. It safeguards the church from becoming a corrupted theocracy and also ensures that the church gets on with the business of the gospel rather than being distracted by worldly tasks. Amen!

However, despite all the apologies that the two kingdoms doctrine does not entail a retreat from surrounding culture and a detachment from social engagement, at the end of the day, that is precisely what it ends up doing. It results in a compartmentalization between the sacred and the secular, which diminishes the responsibility and ministry of

---

33. John Calvin, *Institutes* 3.19.15.
34. David VanDrunen, *Living in God's Two Kingdoms: A Biblical Vision for Christianity and Culture* (Wheaton, IL: Crossway, 2010), 15 (italics original).
35. Michael Horton, *The Christian Faith* (Grand Rapids: Zondervan, 2011), 712–14.

the church toward the public sphere. Moreover, the two kingdoms view is insufficiently christological, as it does not consistently apply the lordship of Christ to both salvation and creation. If Jesus is Lord, he is Lord over every square inch of the universe, and it is the church that points to and promotes the lordship of Jesus Christ over every sphere of human life.

In contrast, and more in line with the neo-Calvinist tradition, I would aver that where one finds God's priestly people, where the Spirit is working among them, and where allegiance to Christ is offered, there the reign of God is manifested. That applies as much to congregations as to charities and corporations. The church extends the kingdom by extending allegiance to Jesus, by engaging in redemptive acts that enhance the human condition, and by undertaking works that establish human custodianship over creation. By bringing church and kingdom into closer proximity, I do not mean outwardly Christianizing our culture with commitment to a vague religious tradition (i.e., civil religion) or establishing Christian ethics as the default setting for public values (i.e., so-called family values). I mean, rather, that the saving reign of God is manifested when the church, in Christ's name and with the Spirit's leading, establishes the divine purpose over theaters of public life for the good of humanity and for the glory of God.

Lest I be accused of conflating church and kingdom, I think it important to say that God builds the kingdom and Jesus builds the church. If we think of ourselves as kingdom builders through our social-cultural efforts, we will quickly learn that what we constructed was just another Tower of Babel. Yet in God's orchestration of the world, it is his human creatures, reflecting his image, whom he uses to accomplish his kingdom purposes. Remember that humanity is made for kingdom work. It was as a human being, Jesus of Nazareth, that God began inaugurating the kingdom on earth. To picture humanity as God's workers for the kingdom is perfectly apt because humans are made in the image of God, which means that they were designed to undertake the royal task of projecting God's reign on earth as an archetype of the kingdom that is in heaven.

Embedded in the gospel is the reality that, in the work of Jesus and through the power of the Spirit, God equips humans to get this task back on track. This is not building the kingdom with our own two hands. We are not building the kingdom, much less "Jerusalem," as the silly hymn says; instead we are building *for* the kingdom—a subtle difference but a crucial distinction. What we do on earth in our evangelism, social justice, deeds of mercy, politics, and public life will echo in eternity. The new creation will not obliterate the Christian work we do; no, it will enhance it.[36] Therefore, Christian churches should endeavor to fulfill the Great Commission

---

36. N. T. Wright, *Surprised by Hope* (New York: HarperOne, 2008), 218–24.

and simultaneously train believers to maintain a faithful presence in the world by witnessing and working toward that which displays the lordship of Jesus Christ. That is achieved by promoting the gospel with its allegiance to God, by seeking the welfare of cities, by performing redemptive works in deeds of mercy, by engaging in care for the world, and by enabling divinely appointed institutions like governments to act in accord with their assigned purpose.

In light of that, I propose six theses on church and kingdom:

1. The kingdom creates the messianic community, the church, the priesthood of believers, who bear God's Spirit and know God's salvation.
2. The church is not the kingdom, but it is the embassy for the kingdom on earth; it mediates allegiance to God.
3. The church is a witness to the kingdom by announcing the gospel of the kingdom.
4. The church, in public engagement, is a window into the life, hope, joy, and peace that the kingdom will finally bring.
5. The church builds toward the kingdom by projecting God's reign through the healing and restoration of peoples, steeples, places, spaces, and structures toward their divinely intended purpose.
6. It is the *basileia* coming through the *ecclesia* that will lead the redeemed people of God in the new creation to sing *alleluia*.

FURTHER READING

Doyle, Robert. "The Search for Theological Models: The Christian in his Society in the Sixteenth, Seventeenth and Nineteenth Centuries." Pp. 27–72 in *Christians in Society*, ed. Barry G. Webb. Explorations 3. Homebush West, NSW: Lancer, 1988.

Ladd, G. E. *Jesus and the Kingdom*. New York: Harper & Row, 1964, pp. 259–73.

Pannenberg, Wolfhart. *Systematic Theology*. 3 vols. Trans. G. W. Bromiley. Edinburgh: T&T Clark, 1988–91, 3:27–38.

Ridderbos, Herman. *The Coming of the Kingdom*. Trans. H. de Jongste. Philadelphia: Presbyterian and Reformed, 1962, pp. 334–96.

Torrance, T. F. *Kingdom and Church: A Study in the Theology of the Reformation*. Edinburgh: Oliver & Boyd, 1956.

VanDrunen, David. *Living in God's Two Kingdoms: A Biblical Vision for Christianity and Culture*. Wheaton, IL: Crossway, 2010.

§ 8.2 BIBLICAL IMAGES OF THE CHURCH

The church is the *ekklēsia*, a Greek word that means "gathering" or "assembly." This word is used in the LXX to translate the Hebrew word *qāhāl*, which often describes the assembling of Israel to hear the law, confess their sins, or renew the covenant (e.g., Deut 4:10, 33; Josh 8:33–55; 22:12; 2 Chr 24:6; Neh 8:1–3). The church is not a human institution or a social network. It is the people called by God into covenant with himself, and it exists as a consequence of the purpose of the Triune God. Its origins lie in God's desire to have a people of his own (Deut 7:6). It is unified by the one covenant of grace across the various dispensations of the Abrahamic, Mosaic, and new covenants. The church is formed by the Holy Spirit, who unites persons with Christ (1 Cor 3:16; Eph 4:4) and exists in a shared confession of the Lordship of Jesus Christ (Rom 10:9; 1 Cor 12:3).[37]

8.2.1 SHARED IMAGES BETWEEN THE TESTAMENTS

The church has its roots in the Old Testament, running from Adam to Israel. Contrary to dispensational theology, the church did not begin at Pentecost.[38] The new covenant is a renewal of the Mosaic covenant and the fulfillment of the Abrahamic covenant. God has one plan for one people, not two plans for two peoples. Jesus' aim to restore Israel resulted in the formation of a new community built around him, who would believe and receive the kingdom blessings that God had intended for the world through Israel (Matt 5:14; 10:1–6; 16:18; 28:19–20). Ephesians 2–3 makes sense only if the church, as the commonwealth of Jews and Gentiles united in Christ, constitutes the one people of God. Accordingly there are several images for the church that span across both Testaments.

1. *The people of God.* The term "people of God" refers to a constellation of images

---

[37] D. J. Tidball, "Church," in *NDBT*, 407 (407–11).
[38] Lewis S. Chafer, *Systematic Theology* (8 vols.; Dallas: Dallas Seminary Press, 1947), 4:36–53; Charles Ryrie, *Basic Theology* (Wheaton, IL: Victor, 1986), 466.

that denote the believing community as having its origin in God's covenantal call.[39] God's choice of Abraham to receive his special favor through a covenant was purposed to extend God's blessing to all the peoples of the earth (Gen 12:1–3). The covenant subsequently embraced by Israel was a further annunciation of the Abrahamic covenant. Israel was constituted as a redeemed people in their exodus from Egypt on the basis of God's remembering his promises to the patriarchs (Exod 3:15–17). Israel was chosen to be God's people on the basis of a gracious promise, not because of any merits of their own (Deut 7:7–8; 9:5–6). God would bless all people through the one people of Israel (Exod 19:6).

Paul writes of God's decision to make believers in Christ Jesus his people: "As God has said: 'I will live with them and walk among them, and I will be their God, and they will be my people'" (2 Cor 6:16). The apostle also applies Hosea 2:23 to believers in Romans 9:24–26:

> Even us, whom he also called, not only from the Jews but also from the Gentiles? As he says in Hosea:
> "I will call them 'my people' who are not my people;
> and I will call her 'my loved one' who is not my loved one,"
> and,
> "In the very place where it was said to them,
> 'You are not my people,'
> there they will be called 'children of the living God.'"

The point is that God, once again, has done an unlikely thing and made an unbelievable choice in whom he made his people. The church is the people of God who enter into a new covenant with God (2 Cor 3:4–18), a covenant initiated by God's grace (Eph 1:3–14; 2:1–10), instituted by Jesus' sacrifice as the great high priest (Heb 8–10), and sealed by the blood of Jesus (1 Cor 11:25).[40]

2. *Elect.* God's choice of Abraham and Israel to be the special objects of his covenant love is axiomatic for Israel's religious history. Reference to the nation as God's "chosen ones" is affirmed in multiple places. According to the Chronicler, David gave instructions about Israel's worship with the exhortation: "Remember the wonders he has done, his miracles, and the judgments he pronounced, you his servants, the descendants of Israel, *his chosen ones*, the children of Jacob" (1 Chr 16:12–13, italics added). This is similar to the words of the psalmist:

> Remember the wonders he has done,
> his miracles, and the judgments he pronounced,
> you his servants, the descendants of Abraham,
> his *chosen ones*, the children of Jacob....

---

39. Paul S. Minear, *Images of the Church in the New Testament* (Philadelphia: Westminster, 1960), 67.

40. Tidball, "Church," 407; Millard J. Erickson, *Christian Theology* (2nd ed.; Grand Rapids: Baker, 1998), 1045–46.

> He brought out his people with rejoicing,
>> his *chosen ones* with shouts of joy. (Ps 105:5–6, 43, italics added)

In the age of redemption, Isaiah prophesies:

> No longer will they build houses and others live in them,
>> or plant and others eat.
> For as the days of a tree,
>> so will be the days of my people;
> my *chosen ones* will long enjoy
>> the work of their hands. (Isa 65:22, italics added)

Israel's worship and hope for the future were determined by the fact that they had been specifically chosen by God. Jesus promised justice for his "chosen ones" (i.e., his followers) who call out to God day and night (Luke 18:7). The tribulation set to come in the future will be shortened for the sake of "the elect," probably referring to the escape of Jewish Christians from the sacking of Jerusalem in AD 70 (Mark 13:20). Paul refers to the "elect" as those *within* national Israel (Rom 11:7; cf. 9:7–8), but elsewhere it includes all those who believe in Jesus Christ (Rom 8:33; Col 3:12; 2 Tim 2:10). Peter, probably writing to Jewish Christians in Asia Minor, addresses them with the words: "To God's elect, exiles scattered throughout the provinces of Pontus, Galatia, Cappadocia, Asia and Bithynia" (1 Pet 1:1). In sum, the promise of a universal blessing made to Abraham and inherited by Israel is fulfilled in the church of Jesus Christ, which constitutes the elect from every nation.

3. *Flock.* God is repeatedly described as a shepherd who cares for Israel (Gen 49:24; 2 Sam 7:7; Ps 80:1; Jer 31:10; Ezek 34:16). A common refrain for Israel in the book of Psalms, in good old King James language, is that "we are thy people and the sheep of thy pasture" (Pss 79:13; 95:7; 100:3). Micah uses sheep and flock imagery to describe a restored Israel: "I will surely gather all of you, Jacob; I will surely bring together the remnant of Israel. I will bring them together like sheep in a pen, like a flock in its pasture" (Mic 2:12). The Davidic king was also called to be a shepherd over Israel, and God shepherds Israel through him (2 Sam 5:2; Ezek 34:23–24).

Jesus is the Davidic king who will "shepherd my people Israel" (Matt 2:6; cf. Mic 5:4). He addresses his disciples as "little flock" (Luke 12:32), he comes to restore the "lost sheep of the house of Israel" (Matt 10:5; 15:24), and he teaches that God intends there to be "one flock" (one people) and "one shepherd" (one messianic king; John 10:16). Paul told the Ephesian elders: "Be shepherds of the church of God, which he bought with his own blood" (Act 20:28). A similar exhortation to church leaders is given in 1 Peter 5:2: "Be shepherds of God's flock that is under your care, watching over them." Towards the end of Hebrews is the christological remark about "our Lord Jesus, that great Shepherd of the sheep" (Heb 13:20). In sum, "God is ultimately the shepherd-ruler of this flock; Jesus is the chief shepherd; Jesus appoints undershepherds, but the flock remains God's possession."[41]

4. *Priesthood.* Israel was nominated as God's "treasured possession" and "a kingdom of priests and a holy nation" (Exod 19:5–6; cf. Isa 61:6). As such, they were to worship God and live in holiness (Lev 19:1–2; 20:7–8). The New Testament likewise affirms the status of believers as priests and kings. Peter writes about the priestly role of Christians in the world: "But you are a chosen people, a royal priesthood, a holy nation, God's special possession, that you may declare the praises of him who called you out of darkness into his wonderful light" (1 Pet 2:9). The imagery of the church as a royal priesthood occurs also in Revelation (Rev 1:6; 5:10). As such, the church offers to God a sacrifice of praise (Heb 13:15), lives as living sacrifices (Rom 12:1), and engages in the priestly ministry of the gospel (15:16).

5. *Remnant.* Israel's disobedience of the law and their failure to uphold the covenant brought judgment on the nation. Yet even in the midst of judgment God preserved a remnant, who would form the germinal roots of a nation purified by judgment. The prophets appealed to the concept of a "remnant" who was faithful to God and in whom Israel's future would be found (e.g., Ezra 9:8–15; Isa 10:20–22; 28:5; 37:31–32; Amos 5:15; Mic 2:12; 5:7–8; Zeph 3:12–13; Zech 9:11–12). Paul adopts this terminology to describe a remnant of Jewish Christians within national Israel who have laid hold of the promise of God's Messiah (Rom 9:27; 11:1–6). The existence of the church, then, is not an abandonment of God's promises to Israel; rather, it is the remnant chosen by grace, which is first order proof of his faithfulness to Israel (11:5).

8.2.2 IMAGES UNIQUE TO THE NEW TESTAMENT

While a number of images are shared across both Testaments, indicating the continuity and oneness of God's people across redemptive history, there are also several images for the church unique to the New Testament.

1. *Body of Christ.* Arguably the foremost Pauline contribution to ecclesiology is his image of the church as the "body of Christ" (see esp. Rom 7:4; 1 Cor 10:16; 11:27; 12:27; Eph 4:12). It is rooted in the widely used Greco-Roman metaphor for the city-state as a body. It is a corollary of the christophany that Paul received on the Damascus Road, where he learned that by persecuting Christians he was persecuting Jesus (Acts 9:4; 22:7). The image of the church as the "body of Christ" implies that the church shares an organic unity with Christ, that Christ is head over the church, and that the members are mutually dependent in Christian service.

---

41. Minear, *Images of the Church*, 85.

Berkhof goes so far as to call this appellation the most "complete definition of the New Testament church."[42]

The picture of Christians as a "body" is applied to the participants in a cluster of house churches (Rom 12:4–5; 1 Cor 12:13) or universally to all believers (Eph 1:22–23). The church, as the body of Christ, is composed of different members who must grow the whole church (Rom 12:4–5; 1 Cor 10:16–17; 12:12–27; Col 1:24; 3:15; Eph 4:16). The visible unity of the church is established by a vertical unity with Christ created by the Spirit (1 Cor 12:12–13; Eph 4:4–5). Christ is the head of the church as both its source of life and the authority over its affairs (Eph 1:22–23; 4:15; 5:23; Col 1:18). The spiritual nourishment and physical unity of the body is contingent on growing up together in Christ (Eph 4:16; Col 2:19). The body is constituted sacramentally, since in baptism believers are baptized into the body of his death (Rom 6:4–6; 7:4; Col 2:11–12), and in the one loaf of the Eucharist they participate in his body surrendered in death (1 Cor 10:16–17). It is in "one loaf" and "one baptism" that believers share one faith in one Lord by one Spirit (1 Cor 10:17; Eph 4:4–5). Though the church is not an extension of the incarnation, its members form the physical and visible locus of Jesus' current activity on earth (Eph 1:22–23).[43]

2. *Temple of God.* In a specifically Trinitarian thrust, the church is the temple of the living God (2 Cor 6:16–18). The church is a temple of God's Spirit because believers, individually and corporately, are indwelt by the Holy Spirit (1 Cor 3:16; 6:19). The church is built on the foundations of the prophets and apostles, with Jesus Christ as the chief cornerstone. The building is joined together in Christ and grows into the temple of the Lord, where the Spirit of God dwells (Eph 2:20–23). The church is also described as a spiritual house (1 Pet 2:5), the household of God (1 Tim 3:15), and believers who persevere will be part of God's eschatological temple in the new heaven and new earth (Rev 3:12; 21:1–4). The Holy Spirit ensures that the church remains holy to the Lord and empowered in its mission from the Lord.

3. *New creation.* A unique facet of the church is that its members are regarded as new creations. Paul writes: "If anyone is in Christ, the new creation has come: The old has gone, the new is here!" (2 Cor 5:17). Here the image of glory that was defaced by the fall is restored anew in Christ. James uses an analogous image: "He chose to give us birth through the word of truth, that we might be a kind of firstfruits of all he created" (Jas 1:18). Believers are regarded as the first installment of God's creative word that brings spiritual new birth.

If I had to create my own "image" for the church, I would call the church *a living chapel of the gospel.* The church is a diverse body of people who proclaim and

---

42. Louis Berkhof, *Systematic Theology* (Grand Rapids: Eerdmans, 1958), 557.

43. R. K. Fung, "Body of Christ," in *DPL*, 76–82.

embody the good news that Jesus Christ is Lord. That means, among other things, inviting people to be reconciled to God through faith in the death and resurrection of Jesus Christ. While the invitation may be addressed to individuals, we are not simply handing out VIP passes for individuals to get into heaven; rather, we are drawing them into God's new covenant and into the covenantal life of the believing community. The offer of the gospel by the church means inviting people to wed themselves to the agent of the gospel and to join in its activities.

To believe in the gospel is to believe in the *Savior*, to experience the multifaceted elements of *salvation*, and to identify with those who number themselves among the *saved*. Understood this way, it becomes practically impossible to believe in the gospel without belonging to the gospel community. For as God draws us into his own triune life, he does that by drawing us into a community that praises the Father, imitates the Son, and follows the Spirit. Joining the church is not, then, an optional extra after one receives Christ. How can one receive Christ's promise and then reject Christ's own body? The church, as a living chapel of the gospel, enables those who believe the gospel to stay connected to Christ by inhabiting the community where the Spirit of Christ dwells most fully and where Christ's blessings are most present.

These images certainly do not exhaust the variety of ways that the church is presented in the Bible.[44] What appears to be the unifying element is that the one God of creation has one people, sharing in one Spirit, and united to one Lord Jesus; they represent God in the world, to the world, and for the world. God calls a people for himself, he redeems them, and he renews them, and they will dwell with him for all eternity.

---

44. Cf. Minear, *Images of the Church*, who lists ninety-six images for the church in the New Testament alone.

ECCLESIOLOGY IN CONTENTION #2: THE CHURCH AND ISRAEL

How does the church relate to Israel? This question has been a perennial one ever since Jewish Christian believers began sharing their faith with fellow Jews (Acts 2–5). It became more of an issue when Jewish Christians were persecuted, denounced, expelled from synagogues, and even cursed as "heretics" by Jewish leaders (John 9:22; 12:42; 16:2; Acts 8:1–3; 11:19; 12:1; 2 Cor 11:24; Rev 2:9; Justin, *Dial.* 16, 93, 95, 96, 123, 133). Christians who had been treated so might naturally ask, "Are we *really* one of them?" and "Are they *really* one of us?"

It was the degree of continuity and discontinuity between Israel and the church, between law and gospel, and between Christ and Moses that provided the catalyst for the theological and sociological chemistry of the early Christian movement. The debates that the Jewish Christian apostle Paul had with other Jewish Christians in Antioch and Galatia were stimulated by this very question: Is Jesus merely an add-on to the Mosaic covenant? What precisely is new in the new covenant?[45]

Historically speaking, the church began as a renewal movement within Judaism prior to AD 70, but after AD 70 it became a religious institution that had "parted ways" to some degree from common Judaism with a distinguishable set of beliefs and structures. What is more, Marcion's program of trying to de-judaize Christianity led many of the church fathers to think through the Israelite ancestry of their faith and to ponder how to relate to the Jewish people in the Roman empire. Much later, Reformed theology, with its penchant for "covenant" as the organic unity across the Bible, placed emphasis on the single, continuous plan for salvation that God had for his people. The problem was that it led to a view of supersessionism, whereby the church had effectively replaced Israel as God's people. A supersessionist theology, combined with European anti-Semitism, was the intellectual force that contributed to the Holocaust in the mid-twentieth century.

Christians have traditionally regarded the church as the "true Israel," "spiritual Israel," or "new Israel." For example, Justin Martyr informed a Jew named Trypho that Christians "are the true Israelite race, the spiritual one, that of Judah and Jacob and Abraham" (*Dial.* 11.5). Martin Luther declared: "The Jews are no longer Israel, for all things are to be new, and Israel must become new. Those alone are the true Israel who

---

45. Cf. Michael F. Bird, "New Testament Theology Reloaded: Integrating Biblical Theology and Christian Origins," *TynBul* 60 (2009): 161–87.

have accepted the new covenant, which was established and begun in Jerusalem."[46] Karl Barth wrote, "The Church is the historical successor to Israel."[47] These views in their diverse ways are arguing for a form of supersessionism.

However, the perspective whereby the church assumes the role, position, and blessings of Israel has been questioned on two fronts. First, dispensational theology has traditionally made a distinction between the church and Israel. Charles Ryrie went so far as to say that such a distinction was one of the essential elements of dispensational theology,[48] though in progressive dispensationalism the distinction is less prominent. In progressive dispensationalism, the Israel–church distinction is primarily a distinction between (1) the dispensation of Israel, in which divine blessings were poured on the nation, while the Gentiles were alienated or subordinated; and (2) the present dispensation of the church, where divine blessings are given to Jews and Gentiles, while national blessings are in abeyance. Accordingly, "Israel and the nations on the one hand and the church on the other are neither replacement peoples nor parallel, dual-track peoples but different redemptive dimensions of the same humanity."[49] Yet Bock and Blaising still maintain: "It is crucial to understand that promises made to Israel are to be fulfilled by Israel and not in something reconstituted to take its place."[50] Therein remains the point of contention, particularly with Reformed theology, which affirms that the church inherits the promises given to Israel, be they redemptive, spiritual, or national.

Second, several Pauline scholars insist that Paul regarded Jesus as Savior only for Gentiles and not for the Jews. The Jews are "saved" in their own *Sonderweg* ("special way") under the terms of the Mosaic covenant. As such, Paul envisaged Israel as a continuing entity with her own set of privileges and blessings that was still available for them. Jesus was to bring Gentiles into this heritage of Israel, and Israel's only problem was those who denied that Jesus was the instrument to redeem the Gentiles.[51] One scholar writes: "Paul nowhere addresses his churches as Israel. Nor does he transfer to them Israel's distinctive attributes."[52] In this case, the church is not "Israel"; instead, the church is a religious philosophy or *collegia* within the Roman world, built on a hybrid of Jewish-Hellenistic beliefs and values.

---

46. Martin Luther, in *Luther's Works* (ed. Jaroslav Pelikan; Minneapolis: Fortress, 1960), 35:287–88.
47. Karl Barth, *CD*, II/3:290.
48. Charles Ryrie, *Dispensationalism Today* (Chicago: Moody Press, 1965), 47.
49. Craig A. Blaising and Darrell L. Bock, "Conclusion," in *Dispensationalism, Israel and the Church* (Grand Rapids: Zondervan, 1992), 383–84.
50. Ibid., 392.
51. Cf. John Gager, *Reinventing Paul* (Oxford: Oxford University Press, 2000); Eung Chun Park, *Either Jew or Gentile: Paul's Unfolding Theology of Inclusivity* (Louisville: Westminster John Knox, 2003).
52. John Gager, *The Origins of Anti-Semitism* (New York: Oxford University Press, 1983), 228.

If the supersessionist and *Sonderweg* views are dissatisfying, we must contemplate several things in want of an alternative. A first factor is how the name "Israel" functioned in Judaism and early Christianity. The term denoted ancestry from "Jacob" (Gen 32:28), it came to signify the northern kingdom of the Hebrew people (e.g., 1 Kgs 12:20–21), and the name referred to the people apart from the priesthood (e.g., Deut 27:9). For the most part, "Israel" simply means a people, *coram Deo*, a people addressed by God.[53]

Furthermore, "Israel" was not just a term for an ethnic or national entity; it was also an honorific title, indicating a people in special relationship with God. Israel is the recipient of God's blessings, promises, and redemption (see 2 Sam 7:23; 1 Chr 17:21; Ps 25:22; Rom 9:4–5). Among Jewish authors writing approximate to the New Testament period, Philo refers to "Israel who sees God" as a philosophical category. Philo is careful to distinguish the Jewish people from Israel, so that "Israel" becomes a philosophical elite, those who discern the divine being.[54] Also, the Qumran sectarians appear to have regarded themselves as standing in continuity with the Babylonian remnant. As such they considered themselves to be the "congregation of Israel" of the last days; they saw themselves either as Israel or as its purest and holiest part.[55]

For Paul, the designations "Israel" and "Israelite" are evidently positive as they denote continuity with God's purposes announced to the patriarchs and fulfilled in the economy of God's action in Jesus Christ (Rom 11:1; Phil 3:5). Paul even considers Israelite history to be the ancestry of Jewish and Gentile Christians (1 Cor 10:1). Paradoxically Paul knows that not everyone descended from ethnic Israel is part of the Israel given the promises (Rom 9:6), and yet he looks forward to the salvation of national Israel in the eschatological future (11:26). Thus, for some Jews, what counted as Israelite identity seemed fluid and open to negotiation, especially in the Diaspora. For Paul, the church adopted the history of Israel as their own when God adopted Gentile believers in the Messiah into the family of the Abrahamic promises. If this is the case, then the logical corollary, precisely what Paul seems to claim, is that to be "in" Christ is to simultaneously be "in" Israel.

Another subject for consideration is the position of Jesus in relation to Israel. First, historically speaking, the best way to understand Jesus' ministry is in the context of Jewish restoration eschatology. Key prophetic hopes were focused on the return of the

---

53. Graham Harvey, *The True Israel: The Use of the Names Jew, Hebrew, and Israel in Ancient Jewish and Early Christian Literature* (Leiden: Brill, 1996), 267–73.
54. Michael F. Bird, *Crossing over Sea and Land: Jewish Missionary Activity in the Second Temple Period* (Peabody, MA: Hendrickson, 2010), 107–8.
55. Sigurd Grindheim, *The Crux of Election* (Tübingen: Mohr/Siebeck, 2005), 67–69.

twelve tribes to Judea from the Diaspora, the reconstitution of a new Israelite kingdom complete with a new Davidic king, the forgiveness of sins, a renewed covenant, a new temple, and the return of God to Zion. Now Jesus' announcement of the kingdom (Mark 1:14–15), his healings and exorcisms as signs of restoration (e.g., Matt 11:1–6), his call of twelve disciples (Mark 3:13–16), his ministry to the "lost sheep of the house of Israel" (Matt 10:5–6; 15:24), and even his death were all acts designed to bring about the restoration and redemption of Israel (see Luke 24:21; Acts 1:6). This was because Israel would be the cipher by which salvation would reach the rest of the world; a transformed Israel would transform the world! The community that Jesus created around himself was the beginnings of the restored Israel, united around their messianic leader, comprised of Judean and Galilean supporters, and claiming for itself continuity with Israel, even when the Judean leaders rejected the Messiah and the message about him.

Second, theologically speaking, Jesus is the embodiment of Israel. Israel was called to be a new Adam, a humanity ordained by God to be priests and regents of God's world, to spread the reign of God in their worship, law, and covenant. But they failed, and just as Adam was exiled from the garden for his disobedience, so Israel was exiled from Canaan for their disobedience. Jesus is the new Adam and the true Israel (Rom 5:12–21; 1 Cor 15:22). By his obedience and faithfulness to his messianic task, Jesus recapitulates the roles of Adam and Israel in himself, seen especially in his wilderness temptations (Matt 4:1–11). Jesus is the archetypal representative of Israel, and Israel's story, hopes, and destiny are summed up in him.

All of this means that it is impossible to view the church apart from the history and identity of Israel. In the early church, there is no hint that the church is some kind of redeemed humanity, sharing in Jewish salvation, albeit in a denationalized sense. Paul's speech to the Jews in Pisidian Antioch contains the proclamation: "Fellow citizens of Abraham and you God-fearing Gentiles, it is to us that this message of salvation has been sent.... We tell you the good news: *What God promised our ancestors he has fulfilled for us, their children, by raising up Jesus*" (Acts 13:26, 32–33, italics added). What God has "promised to our ancestors" does not include just spiritual and redemptive promises, excluding the promises specific to the nation. No, the form of fulfillment announced by Paul encompasses the whole sway of God's promises, from Abraham to Moses to the prophets—including cultic, covenantal, national, spiritual, and redemptive loci. All these promises find their singular and unified fulfillment in the cross, resurrection, and exaltation of Jesus.

Significant also is James's speech at the Jerusalem council, where James cites Amos 9:11 to prove that the restored Israel is the church made up of believing Jews and Gentiles:

Simon has described to us how God first intervened to choose a people for his name from the Gentiles. The words of the prophets are in agreement with this, as it is written:

"After this I will return
and rebuild David's fallen tent.
Its ruins I will rebuild,
and I will restore it,
that the rest of humanity may seek the Lord,
even all the Gentiles who bear my name,
says the Lord, who does these things"—
things known from long ago.

It is my judgment, therefore, that we should not make it difficult for the Gentiles who are turning to God. (Acts 15:14–19)

What James is effectively saying is that the hope for the reestablishment of the Davidic monarchy and Israel's national restoration are identified with the resurrection of Jesus and the formation of a messianic community of Jews and Gentiles.

In Paul the real hub of the debate on whether the church is the "new Israel" takes place. To begin with, we must acknowledge that most of Paul's references to "Israel" refer to his religious and ethnic compatriots who do not (yet) believe in Jesus the Messiah (e.g., 1 Cor 10:18; Eph 2:12; 3:6; Phil 3:5). Moreover, while several scholars try to take Romans 11:26 ("And in this way all Israel will be saved") as designating the church as the "Israel" who will be rescued at the end of history,[56] it seems clear from the wider context of Romans 9–11 (9:4, 6, 27, 31; 10:19, 21; 11:2, 7, 11, 25) that Paul is looking ahead to the eschatological salvation of national Israel.[57]

The central text in the debate is Paul's benediction at the end of Galatians: "And as for all who walk by this rule, peace and mercy be upon them, and upon the Israel of God" (Gal 6:16 ESV). The issues are: (1) Who are the "all" and "the Israel of God"? (2) Is there one blessing of peace for those who walk by this rule and another blessing of mercy for the Israel of God? (3) Is the "and" (*kai*) conjunctive, in the sense of a further addition, or explicative, in the sense of further description? A number of scholars argue that Paul's blessing here is for Jewish Christians who follow the rule that he lays down in the letter, and he offers a separate blessing for Israel because they are Israel![58]

---

56. Cf., e.g., N. T. Wright, "The Letter to the Romans," in *NIB*, 10:688–91.

57. Cf., e.g., Douglas J. Moo, *Romans* (NICNT; Grand Rapids: Eerdmans, 1996), 722–23; Thomas R. Schreiner, *Romans* (BECNT; Grand Rapids: Eerdmans, 1998), 614–15.

58. Cf. Susan Eastman, "Israel and Divine Mercy in Galatians and Romans," in *Between Gospel and Election: Explorations in the Interpretation of Romans 9–11* (eds. F. Wilk and J. R. Wagner; Tübingen: Mohr/Siebeck, 2010), 147–70.

I want to submit three arguments as to why Paul here must mean that the "Israel of God" is the church.

First, it is incredibly difficult to imagine Paul arguing so passionately in Galatians for the unity of Jews and Gentiles in one church, united in Christ, with everyone as equal sons and daughters of Abraham, and then at the very end of that letter pronouncing a benediction that serves to separate groups within his churches according ethnic categories.[59]

Second, Paul elsewhere takes language ordinarily used to describe Israel, like "circumcision" (Phil 3:3), "Jew" (Rom 2:28–29), and "God's chosen people" (Col 3:12), to designate Christians. These are prestige terms that demonstrate the incorporation of the church into a heritage that was once thought to be the exclusive property of ethnic Jews. Furthermore, in Romans Paul says that "a person is a Jew who is one inwardly; and circumcision is circumcision of the heart, by the Spirit" (Rom 2:29), which essentially redefines the identity of God's people around a new set of symbolic markers defined by Spirit, new creation, and obedience. Paul can also use Israel/Israelite in a fluid religious sense designating a privileged religious identity that is no longer defined ethnically (Eph 2:13; 3:6), and he even speaks of an Israel within Israel (Rom 9:6). Paul knows of two covenantal people: Israel "according to the flesh" and Israel "by the power of the Spirit" (Gal 4:29). The "Israel of God" (Gal 6:16) as an honorific title for God's people irrespective of ethnicity naturally contrasts with Israel "according to the flesh" (Rom 9:3 ESV) as a general designation for nonbelieving Jews.

Third, we might compare the benediction of Galatians 6:16 with the benediction in 1 Corinthians 16:22, "If anyone does not love the Lord, let that person be cursed! Come, Lord!" For Paul, there is no blessing for people *irrespective* of their relationship to Christ. The grace, peace, and mercy of God are from Christ for the elect in Christ.[60] For this reason, I concur with Calvin: "In a word, he gives the appellation *the Israel of God* to those whom he formerly denominated the children of Abraham by faith, (Gal. iii. 29,) and thus includes all believers, whether Jews or Gentiles, who were united into one church."[61]

It is axiomatic in the Catholic letters that the election of Israel is extended to include the church. In the latter part of the New Testament, there is a clear emphasis on the church as the "elect" people of God, who are partakers of the position and

---

59. Richard N. Longenecker, *Galatians* (WBC; Dallas: Word, 1990), 298.
60. Michael F. Bird, *A Bird's-Eye View of Paul: The Man, His Mission and His Message* (Nottingham, UK: Inter-Varsity Press, 2008), 50.
61. John Calvin, *Calvin's Commentaries: Romans—Galatians* (Wilmington, DE: APA, n.d.), 1932.

privileges of Israel. Peter writes to the "elect exiles of the Dispersion" (1 Pet 1:1 ESV), who are "a chosen people, a royal priesthood, a holy nation, God's special possession" (2:9) because they have come to Jesus Christ, "chosen by God" (1 Pet 2:4, 6). In 2 Peter 1:10, a godly character becomes sure proof of the surety of one's calling and election. In Hebrews, the new covenant to be made with the "people of Israel" is the covenant received by the church (Heb 8:8–10). In sum, the Old Testament correlation between "Israel" and the "elect" is continued in the New Testament with the same correlation between "church" and the "elect."[62]

The Revelation of John presents a visionary account of the church as an eschatological Israel comprised of people from among all the nations. In one vision, the 144,000 from the twelve tribes of Israel, who are sealed for salvation (Rev 7:4–8), are then described as "a great multitude that no one could count, from every nation, tribe, people and language, standing before the throne and before the Lamb" (7:9). The theme of the "twelve tribes" reappears later in the vision of the gates of the new Jerusalem, where the names of the twelve tribes are written on the gates, and the gates are wide open for the nations to enter (21:12, 24–26). Revelation appears not to have the replacement of national Israel by the church but the abolition of the national limits of the elect nation.[63]

In light of this I have five theses on the church and Israel. (1) The church does not replace Israel, but it is the representative of Israel in the messianic age. Ethnic or empirical Israel is not so much replaced as expanded in scope to become a renewed messianic Israel. God is not finished with national Israel, and salvation will yet avail for them. However, the locus of God's covenanting and electing activity is clearly the church made up of believing Jews and Gentiles.

(2) The church must be Israel because outside of Israel there is no salvation. Augustine, in response to the Donatist controversy, wrote *extra ecclesia nulla salus*, "outside of the church there is not salvation." The point is correct; God saves in, by, and for a community, and this community is called the church. However, this community is in historical and organic unity with the Israel who received the covenants, law, and prophetic promises. Outside of those covenants, laws, and promises it is impossible to attain salvation. Salvation came to Israel so that salvation would move through Israel to the world. Israel was called to be "a light for the Gentiles" (Isa 42:6; 49:6), and the church is called to fulfill that very role (Luke 2:32; Acts 13:47; 26:23).

---

62. Minear, *Images of the Church*, 81.
63. Richard Bauckham, *The Climax of Prophecy: Studies on the Book of Revelation* (Edinburgh: T&T Clark, 1993), 224–25.

According to Paul, the Gentiles are saved only by being grafted into Israel like a wild branch grafted into an olive tree (Rom 11:13–31), or like foreigners gaining citizenship in a commonwealth to which they did not naturally belong (Eph 2:11–22). Thus, we might say *extra Israel nulla salus*, "outside of Israel there is no salvation." The church carries forth the mission to be Israel-for-the-sake-of-the-world by bringing the Gentiles into the family of the Messiah. As such, "the Israel to whom the gospel comes and through whom the mission to the world is accomplished is the same Israel to whom the promise had been given."[64]

(3) The story of the church is the continuation of the story of Israel. There is no abrupt break between the history of Israel and the beginnings of the church in Acts. The hope for the "consolation of Israel" (Luke 2:25)—to "redeem Israel" (24:21), to "restore the kingdom to Israel" (Acts 1:6)—for the "times of refreshing" for Israel (3:19), and the reason why Paul was imprisoned for preaching about "the hope of Israel" (28:20), is because Jesus fulfills these hopes, and they have a present experience in the community created by the gospel. According to Acts, the church is not a *new Israel*, created *ex nihilo*, but a *renewed Israel*, living out the promises of the new covenant, comprised of a multiethnic people just as God promised Abraham. If that is the case, then the analogy between the church and Israel becomes a way of coordinating two stories, not two separate entities. The epic story of creation, the patriarchs, and Israel is integrated with the newer story of Jesus and his followers.[65] Berkhof was right: "The assumption of the entire New Testament is that Israel's way and the way of Jesus Christ are together the *one* way of the *one* God."[66]

(4) The unity of God's people is secured by the unity of his plan. The covenantal unity of salvation—both its macro-unity in the covenant of grace and its empirical unity in redemptive-history—shows that God has one purpose, one plan, one Messiah, and one people. Thus, the church is not a "parenthesis" or a "digression" in God's plan, as per dispensationalism, but the formation of the church, the renewed Israel, is one of the penultimate steps before the inauguration of a new creation.

(5) There remains an outstanding hope for Israel to one day respond to the gospel. That is Paul's hope in Romans 10 and 11. Luke grieves at Israel's disbelief in the gospel, but he holds out hope for the remnant of believing Jews to grow at the end of Acts 28. The church inherits *all* the promises given to Israel, but not in such a way that means

---

64. Minear, *Images of the Church*, 72.
65. Ibid., 77.
66. Hendrikus Berkhof, *Christian Theology: An Introduction to the Study of the Faith* (trans. S. Woudstra; Grand Rapids: Eerdmans, 1979), 222.

ethnic Israel has been written off by God. What we have here are not two parallel covenants, not two ways of salvation, but one tale of two Israels. There is an elect line that runs through the Scriptures, including Adam, Seth, Noah, Abraham, Isaac, Jacob, post-exodus Hebrews, postexilic Judeans, and Jesus. Yet John the Baptist warned his audience that ethnic descent from Abraham was no guarantee of salvation (Matt 3:9/ Luke 3:8). Paul taught that "for not all who are descended from Israel are Israel" (Rom 9:6), which implies a national election of the people and a special election of individuals within the nation. As Calvin wrote: "Yet, despite the great obstinacy with which they continue to wage war against the gospel, we must not despise them, while we consider that, for the sake of the promise, God's blessing still rests among them."[67]

FURTHER READING

Beale, G. K. "Peace and Mercy upon the Israel of God: The Old Testament Background of Galatians 6,16b." *Bib* 80 (1999): 204–23.

Blach, Michael J. *Has the Church Replaced Israel?: A Theological Evaluation.* Nashville: Broadman & Holman, 2010.

Campbell, W. S. "Israel." Pp. 441–46 in *DPL*.

Horner, Barry E. *Future Israel: Why Christian Anti-Semitism Must be Challenged.* Nashville: Broadman & Holman, 2007.

Köstenberger, Andreas. "The Identity of the *ISRAĒL TOU THEOU* (Israel of God) in Galatians 6:16." *Faith & Mission* 19 (2001): 3–24.

Ladd, G. E. "Israel and the Church." *EvQ* 36 (1964): 206–14.

Longenecker, Bruce W. "On Israel's God and God's Israel: Assessing Supersessionism in Paul." *JTS* 58 (2007): 26–44.

Motyer, Stephen. "Israel (Nation)," Pp. 581–87 in *NDBT*.

Voorwinde, Stephen. "How Jewish Is *Israel* in the New Testament?" *RTR* 67 (2008): 61–90.

---

67. Calvin, *Institutes* 4.16.15.

§ 8.3 THE SHAPE OF THE CHURCH

Ecclesiology normally focuses on the "marks" or "notes" of the church (we will discuss them in § 8.4). Here we will explore several features that broadly characterize the church as a gospel-shaped and gospel-serving community. There are factors that shape the nature, identity, and mission of the church, not shared by any other association in the world. I intend to show that the church is an eschatological, Trinitarian, diaconal, fellowshiping, and holistic community.

8.3.1 AN ESCHATOLOGICAL COMMUNITY

The church is the *new community* called out from the world into what is the beginning of the *new age*. The resurrection of Jesus and the gift of the Spirit mean that God's new world has begun, the future has partially invaded the present, the seeds of the new creation have already begun budding in the old garden, and God's victory on the cross is now beginning to claim back territory in a world enslaved by sin. The first Christians saw themselves as the vanguard of a new redeemed humanity that God was creating in Jesus Christ. For this reason, we can regard the church as an eschatological community.[68]

Stanley Grenz comments, "What the church is, in short, is determined by what the church is destined to become."[69] Who the church is *today* will impact who the church will be at the *eschaton*. The church, like a bride, waits for the day of her wedding and looks forward to her union with the bridegroom (Rev 19–20). We "wait eagerly" for the revelation of Jesus at the day of the Lord (Rom 8:23; cf. 1 Cor 1:7; Phil 3:20; Jude 21).

But we are not just waiting like old ladies at a bus stop for the P183 to Brunswick Terrace. The church, as the bride of Christ, actively endeavors to "make herself ready" for that festive occasion (Rev 19:7). That is seen chiefly in the preservation of her holiness and purity before the Lord. What is more, the eucharistic feast that the

---

68. Cf. Hans Küng, *The Church* (trans. Ray and Rosaleen Ockenden; London: SCM, 1971), 79–87; Brad Harper and Paul L. Metzger, *Exploring Ecclesiology: An Evangelical and Ecumenical Introduction* (Grand Rapids: Brazos, 2009), 47–77.

69. Stanley Grenz, *Theology for the Community of God* (Grand Rapids: Eerdmans, 1994), 479.

church celebrates at communion is not just a memorial looking back at Jesus' death; it also looks ahead to Jesus' return—hence the words, "whenever you eat this bread and drink this cup, you proclaim the Lord's death until he comes" (1 Cor 11:26). The bread and the wine of the Eucharist are the hors d'oeuvres of the messianic feast that celebrate in advance the eschatological joy still to come.

The church also announces the victory of the Lord Jesus in the gospel and attempts to make this victory a present experience as much like the future as possible. For a start, the bride and the Spirit invite others to come to the wedding feast and to drink from the free gift of the water of life (Rev 22:17). We also disempower the powers, moral or political, that enslave people and dehumanize them, precisely because this is what the Lord intends to do to them on the last day. Injecting eschatology into our ecclesiology, far from paralyzing church action with the inertia of waiting, is instead a primary motivation for the message and ministry that the church carries out.

8.3.2 A TRINITARIAN COMMUNITY

I often wonder: if believing in the Trinity were a crime, how much evidence would there be to convict most Christians? I'm guessing, probably not much. It should not be this way. The church belongs to the Triune God. It is called by the Father, redeemed by the Son, and indwelt by the Spirit. The tripersonal nature of God accordingly shapes the nature of the people of God.

First, the Triune God exists as a perfect community of persons in mutual interpenetration, unity, and reciprocal love. Humans, as "male and female," reflect the image of God when they replicate the intrapersonal relationships within the Godhead. John Zizioulas goes so far as to say that to be in a relationship is to be authentically human, as both Creator and creature are relational beings, so that relationality is what links God and humanity together.[70] The likeness between God and humanity is fundamentally a relational and covenantal communion, with God initiating and sustaining the relationship.[71] Hence, the quest for true humanity is the quest to be a community that reflects the characteristics of the Trinity.

Second, the Trinity does not remain within its own harmonious existence but attempts to express its *internal* love *externally*. The church can model this intra-Trinitarian love by loving "others" in the same way that the Triune God loves us.

Third, just as the Trinity is one-in-many, so too the church is called to be a unity-in-diversity. That is evident from Paul's analogy of the one body with many parts (Rom 12:4–5; 1 Cor 12:12–27). A common confession of the Triune God

---

70. John Zizioulas, *Being as Communion* (Crestwood, NY: St. Vladimir's Seminary Press, 1997), 106–7.

71. Harper and Metzger, *Exploring Ecclesiology*, 21.

should lead to a common communion with each other.[72] When the church, in all its magnificent diversity, remains as one, it models before the world the one-in-threeness of God.

Fourth, the prayers of the church are Trinitarian. That is evidence by the way we pray to God the Father (Matt 6:9; Rom 8:15; Gal 4:6), in the Spirit (Eph 6:18; Jude 20), and through the name of Jesus Christ the Son (John 15:15; 16:24; 2 Thess 1:12). Prayer can be likened to joining a great company of spiritual beings, centered in the Trinity and extending to the hosts of angels, wonderfully captured by the Celtic Prayer of St. Patrick's Breastplate:

> For my shield this day I call:
> A might power:
> The Holy Trinity!
> Affirming threeness,
> Confessing oneness,
> In the making of all
> Through love.[73]

As the church is called into being by the Triune God and called into communion with one another, the church is unlike any other institution on earth. It is not a cohort of faceless persons locked in the drudgery of a larger machine, nor a collective aggregate of individuals who retain only vague and incidental reasons for associating together. Like the Trinity, the church finds its identity in mutual, free, self-giving relationships. Like the Trinity, the church is called to a life in communion where persons flourish as mutually supported by one another.[74] Though human beings are individually the *imago dei*, the church is corporately the *imago trinitatis*.[75]

8.3.3 DIACONAL COMMUNITY

The church is the only organization that exists for the sake of others. The church is a servant community that ministers on behalf of God's name to both the members in the household of God and to the wider world around them. The words of Jesus enjoin us, "In the same way, let your light shine before others, that they may see your good deeds and glorify your Father in heaven" (Matt 5:16). Paul is hardly different: "Therefore, as we have opportunity, let us do good to all people, especially to those who belong to the family of believers" (Gal 6:10). Dietrich Bonhoeffer

---

72. Ibid., 35,

73. Cited in Kerry L. Dearborn, "Recovering a Trinitarian and Sacramental Ecclesiology," in *Evangelical Ecclesiology: Reality or Illusion?* (ed. John Stackhouse; Grand Rapids: Baker, 2003), 54.

74. Daniel Migliore, *Faith Seeking Understanding: An Introduction to Christian Theology* (Grand Rapids: Eerdmans, 1991), 264.

75. Miroslav Volf, *After Our Likeness: The Church as the Image of the Trinity* (Grand Rapids: Eerdmans, 1998).

wrote: "The church must share in the secular problems of ordinary human life, not dominating but helping and serving."[76]

The diaconate was established by the apostles (Acts 6:1–6) in order to make sure material needs and pastoral requirements were satisfied in the primitive messianic community. The danger, of course, with engaging in works of charity is that the church might abandon the rest of its calling and simply become a welfare industry or an instrument of political lobbying for various social causes. If the church forgets the basis and goal of its service—love for God, love for neighbor, and promotion of the gospel—ecclesiology becomes reduced to a social function.[77]

We offset that danger by remembering that mission is the proclamation of the gospel. Consequently, our urgent kingdom tasks in caring for the poor, looking after the outcast, and pleading the case for the oppressed are the vital business we do along the way, not a substitute for our work of preaching, administering the sacraments, and teaching. Such ministries of charity and justice reflect the character of God and actualize the reign of God in our midst. As we preach the boundless mercy and saving justice of God declared in the gospel, we are compelled to act in charity and to advocate for justice, lest we be accused of saying one thing and doing another.

8.3.4 FELLOWSHIPING COMMUNITY

What Christians share is beyond mutual interest and friendship, it is "fellowship." In Greek, the word *koinōnia* designates mutual interest, generosity, participation, sharing, and (I would add) partnership.[78] The gospel brings people into fellowship with the Son and with the Father (1 Cor 1:9; 1 John 1:3) as mediated by the Holy Spirit (2 Cor 13:13; Phil 2:1). The Eucharist celebrates our *koinōnia* with the blood and body of Christ in the sense of sharing in the benefits of Jesus' atoning death. The upshot is that we have a part in the Triune God and are partners with Christ in the mission of God.

However, this vertical "fellowship" spills out horizontally in the church, since the church, as the body of Christ, is the sphere of Christian *koinōnia*. The church is the place where the kingdom is proclaimed, revealed, and actualized in the new humanity that participates in Jesus Christ as the new Adam.[79] The church is a *koinōnia* because it possesses a "salvation we share" (Jude 3) and a "common faith" (Titus 1:4). Christian *koinōnia* is expressed in partnership in the promotion of the gospel (Gal 2:9; Phil 1:5; Phlm 6) and is tangibly demonstrated in meeting the physical needs of other believers (Acts 2:42; 2 Cor 8:4; Heb 13:16). Where believers share

---

76. Dietrich Bonhoeffer, *Letters and Papers from Prison* (New York: Macmillan, 1967), 204.

77. Migilore, *Faith Seeking Understanding*, 261.

78. BDAG, 552–53.

79. T. F. Torrance, *Incarnation* (Milton Keynes, UK: Paternoster, 2008), 166.

ECCLESIOLOGY IN CONTENTION #3: THE VISIBLE AND INVISIBLE CHURCH

The constitution of the church has been debated for most of history, but more so since the Reformation. In a nutshell, the point of contention revolves around whether one focuses on the church as a *visible* body of people identified with an ecclesial organization and its ministries, or focuses instead on the church as an *invisible* body of people who are regenerate and undetectable to the naked eye. Augustine developed the concept of the church as the company of the elect, known exclusively by God, who are invisible, yet exist in a mixed visible church of both sheep and goats. He distinguished between the invisible church as the communion of the elect and the visible church as the episcopacy. Augustine's debates with the Pelagians led him to emphasize the invisible church, while his debates with the Donatists led him to stress the importance of the visible church.[80] Calvin also distinguished between the visible church of those who profess to worship one God and Christ but is often filled with hypocrites, and the invisible church, which is the church as it really is before God, sanctified by the Spirit and true members of Christ.[81]

Popular level evangelicalism seems to eschew the visible church in favor of a purely invisible one. The visible church is purportedly the edifice of an entirely man-made institution, whereas true spirituality is found in the relationships and purity of the invisible church. But this is overly simplistic and unhelpful. The invisible church is the church in communion with God, partaking of his benefits, waiting to be glorified, and located in the visible church. The visible church is the invisible church manifested, nurturing the elect and calling the reprobate, and it constitutes what the invisible church will become at the eschaton.

What is needed in evangelicalism is a better appreciation of the visible church.[82] You cannot have a churchless Christianity any more than a Christless Christianity. In Acts, God did not save people and add them to a database; no, he added them to the church (Acts 2:47). Dietrich Bonhoeffer argued that "the Body of Christ can only be a visible Body, or else it is not a Body at all."[83] Christians are called to express their spiritual unity in visible forms (John 17:11, 21–22; Rom 15:6; 1 Cor 1:10; Phil 4:2), and

---

80. Horton, *Christian Faith*, 738.
81. Calvin, *Institutes* 4.1.7.
82. Cf. Kevin DeYoung and Ted Kluck, *Why We Love the Church: In Praise of Institutions and Organized Religion* (Chicago: Moody Press, 2009), 162–64.
83. Dietrich Bonhoeffer, *The Cost of Discipleship* (New York: Macmillan, 1959), 277.

> their ministries must be visible expressions of grace and service (2 Cor 8:24; Gal 5:13; 1 Tim 5:25; Heb 10:24; Jas 3:13). Only a visible church can preach in the marketplace, found schools, build orphanages, create hospitals, and administer the sacraments.[84]
>
> For Karl Barth, the visible and invisible nature of the church is based on the visible and invisible nature of divine grace in the incarnation.[85] The Lord invisibly rules the church, the Word has an invisible effect on believers, but a visible event brings them together and holds them in unity with each other.[86] The invisible and visible church are not two churches, one earthly and the other spiritual; instead, they are part of the one church. The visible form lives wholly by the invisible mystery. The invisible church can be found only by seeking out the visible church. The true church is the invisible becoming visible.[87]
>
> ---
>
> 84. Cf. Thomas C. Oden, *Systematic Theology* (3 vols.; Peabody, MA: Hendrickson, 2006), 3:333.
> 85. Cf. Kimlyn J. Bender, *Karl Barth's Christological Ecclesiology* (Aldershot, UK: Ashgate, 2005).
> 86. Barth, *CD*, I/2:219.
> 87. Ibid., IV/1:669.

and serve the cause of the gospel and the needs of their own community, there you find genuine *koinōnia*.

8.3.5 HOLISTIC COMMUNITY

If we take Act 2:42–47 as the ideal picture of the church, we can surmise that the ideal life of the church is one that is nurtured on Spirit, Word, and sacrament. We need a diet of all three to have a healthy and holistic Christian community.

Many churches are logocentric by having a heavy priority on the teaching and preaching of the Word, but at the neglect of the other means of grace. The problem is that if you have a church so fixated on the Word, with no room for the Spirit to move, and if you push the sacraments into a corner, you have effectively turned the church into a *mosque*. Islam is all about "word"; the *Qu'ran* is a dictated revelation and that is it. There is no symbol or sacrament of God to draw people closer, no Spirit of God to move in their midst; it is just word, word, word.

Alternatively, if you have a church that is all for the Spirit, seeking to be filled with the Spirit, trying to walk in the Spirit, yet reduces the Word to sound bites of cheesy advice and ignores the sacraments, you have effectively moved into *mysticism*. The emotional release of worship and the empowering of the Spirit for work become disconnected from instruction in the Word. Yet it is the Word that the spiritual life thirsts for. The Spirit binds together worship, word, and sacraments, so a healthy yearning for the Spirit should naturally leave us hungering for God's holy Word and the signs of his grace.

Then again, if you have a church focused almost exclusively on the sacraments, who explain away the Spirit on the grounds that it leads to volatile religious enthusiasm and pay lipservice to the Word, you've reduced the service to a *magic* show. Here God becomes a jack-in-the-box, who jumps out when the bread and the wine land on the table. The elements become substitutes for faith and obedience. The sacraments only have their power in the union of Word and Spirit, so feasting on the blood and body of Christ is possible only by the Spirit, who connects us together with Christ, and by the Word, by which the elements receive their true meaning.

A healthy church needs a steady diet of Spirit, Word, and sacrament. A church without the *Word*, without good biblically based preaching, will soon have a shriveled mind, then a wayward heart, next an unquiet soul, and finally a misdirected strength.[88] Without the Word you'll be starved of learning, you won't be challenged, and there will be no discipleship. A church without the *Spirit* will be boring and banal. You might even end up with a bibliolatrous Trinity of Father, Son, and Holy Bible. Such a church will degenerate into a tomb that is lush and pretty on the outside, but spiritually dead on the inside. Apart from the Spirit we are left to waver and work in our own insufficient strength that will quickly die out. Without the Spirit you'll be starved of spiritual vitality, devoid of divine empowerment, and end up in a lethargic spiritual wasteland. A church without the *sacraments* will be hungry for fellowship and lack the unity provided by the Lord's table. The church that eats together and prays together, stays together. Without the sacraments you'll be starved of godly fellowship and spiritual nourishment.

---

88. N. T. Wright, *Following Jesus: Biblical Reflections on Discipleship* (London: SPCK, 1997), xi.

§ 8.4 THE MARKS OF THE CHURCH

When you buy a new a computer or a new phone, you will often find an authenticating mark to indicate the product's genuineness. Similarly, you may need an authentication code to activate a new piece of software. Following such an analogy, what is the authenticating mark of the church? Traditionally this has been answered with a common set of descriptors going back to the Nicene Creed: "one holy, catholic, and apostolic church" (*ecclesia una, sancta, catholica, et apostolica*). The church is *one* because it shares in a single body, the body of Christ, the risen Lord. It is *holy* because it is called by God and sanctified by Christ through the Spirit. It is *catholic* because it is spread throughout the world and traverses geographic and ethnic boundaries. It is *apostolic* because it holds to the apostles' teachings and is sent out by Christ into the world.[89] We will explore these "marks" and then examine how they relate to the Reformed emphasis that the true church is marked out by proper preaching of the Word and administration of the sacraments. We will conclude that the gospel is the truest mark of the true church.

8.4.1 ONE

The *oneness* of the church derives from the one electing act of God, who calls a people to be his treasured possession. God chose the patriarchs and the Israelites, from above all the nations, to be his special people (Deut 7:6–9; 10:15; 14:2, 21; 26:19). Just as unity was vital for Israel (2 Chr 30:12; Ps 133), so it is also important for the church (John 17:23; Eph 4:12). The church has one head, Christ (1 Cor 11:3; Eph 4:15; 5:23; Col 2:10), and so it has only one body, (Eph 5:23; Col 1:18, 24). Jesus is one shepherd over one flock (John 10:16). Jesus prayed that his followers would be "one," just as the Father and the Son are one (17:11, 21). For Paul, the unity of the Spirit and the bond of peace are to be earnestly pursued because "there is one body and one Spirit, just as you were called to one hope when you were called; one Lord, one faith, one baptism; one God and Father of all, who is over all and through all

---

89. Cf. Oden, *Systematic Theology*, 3:297.

and in all" (Eph 4:4–6). The oneness of the church is beautifully symbolized in the one loaf of bread that we all share in the Eucharist (1 Cor 10:17).

Diversity in the church is a reality, and a good one, since diversity brings together a multiplicity of gifts and graces. The oneness of the church contains a unity-in-diversity, since what unites believers is infinitely stronger than anything that might divide them. We might even speak of an "irreducible plurality" to the church, as John Franke does. Franke does not laud an "anything goes" diversity; rather, he believes that "the plurality of the Christian community constitutes a faithful witness to God's intentions for the church."[90] The oneness of the church, then, is christological, with Christ as the head of one body; it is Trinitarian with church unity emulating the unity of Father, Son, and Spirit; it is kerygmatic as it is rooted in one evangelical faith; it is sacramental as it shares one baptism and partakes of one loaf; and it is visible since unity is expressed in tangible relationships with others.

8.4.2 HOLY

A further mark of the church is its *holiness*. This holiness does not mean the absence of sin or a purely regenerated membership.[91] Holiness is both a God-given status and an ethical state for the church to live up to. Holiness is created by God's consecration of the church for himself. Yet God also calls his people to live in holiness before him. A good example of this dual focus of holiness is found in the epistolary opening in 1 Corinthians, where Paul writes: "to the church of God in Corinth, to those *sanctified in Christ Jesus* and *called to be his holy people*" (1 Cor 1:2, italics added). The holiness Paul refers to here is both a position in Christ and a calling to be appropriately lived out.

Israel was made holy to the Lord as the firstfruits of God's harvest among the nations (Jer 2:3; Ezek 37:28); similarly believers are positionally sanctified by virtue of their union with Jesus Christ the Holy One (Acts 26:18; 1 Cor 1:30; 6:11; Eph 5:26; Heb 2:11; 10:29). Israel was called to walk in holiness before the Lord (Lev 19:2), and so are Christians by their ethical conduct (Eph 1:4; 1 Thess 4:3, 7; 2 Tim 1:9; Heb 12:14; 1 Pet 1:15–16). In addition, because law, prophecy, gospel, and exhortations are revealed from a holy God, the Word of God is always holy (Ezek 22:26; Rom 7:12; 2 Pet 3:2), and it makes its hearers become holy (Ps 19:7; Eph 5:26). The doctrine and beliefs of the church—rooted in Scripture, taught by the apostles, and transmitted by the faithful—are therefore part of the "most holy faith" (Jude 20).

Holiness is central to the mission of church. If the distinction between the

---

90. John R. Franke, *Manifold Witness: The Plurality of Truth* (Nashville: Abingdon, 2008), 8.

91. Cf. Calvin, *Institutes* 4.1.17.

church and the world is lost, the church forfeits its right to speak for God, and its members also risk coming under God's judgment. That is why, in Johannine tradition, the church is chosen from the world and hated by the world. Christians are the one fortress that won't surrender to the barbarian hordes who assail it (John 15:19). Christians must show love to the world, but without loving the world with all its sinful desires (1 John 2:15–17). Christians must imitate Christ, faithfully proclaim his gospel, and live holy cruciformed lives so they can truly say, "In this world we are like Jesus" (cf. 1 John 4:17).

Furthermore, the holiness of the church is rooted in the Trinity. The holy Father calls out a holy people for himself (Deut 7:6; Exod 19:5–6; 1 Pet 2:5). Jesus Christ sanctifies himself so that he can sanctify his followers (John 17:19). The Holy Spirit as the Spirit of holiness works holy living into the hearts, minds, and attitudes of God's people (Ps 143:10; Rom 8:1–11; 14:17; Gal 5:5; 6:8). Finally, the final state of redemptive history will be a holy God dwelling with his holy people in a holy place.

8.4.3 CATHOLIC

In the New Testament, the church is referred to mostly in the local sense, e.g., the "churches in Galatia" or the "church of God in Corinth" (Gal 1:2; 1 Cor 1:2); these expressions designate a local assembly or cluster of house churches in an area. Yet there are also references to "the church" as a *universal or catholic* entity spread across regions with Christ as its head (Eph 3:21; 5:23–25, 29; Col 1:18, 24).

One interesting thing about the primitive church is that they considered themselves to be a worldwide phenomenon through a network of assemblies spread throughout Palestine, Syria, Asia Minor, Greece, and Italy. When Paul addresses the Corinthians, he refers to them as one chapter among those "everywhere who call on the name of our Lord Jesus Christ—their Lord and ours" (1 Cor 1:2). He lauds the Romans because "your faith is being reported all over the world" (Rom 1:8).

There is much proof that the early churches took an interest in one another's affairs. For instance, the promulgation of the apostolic decree by the Jerusalem church to its daughter churches (Acts 15), Paul's letters to churches that he did not establish (e.g., Rome and Colossae), and Clement of Rome's first letter to the Corinthians all show that early Christian leaders took an interest in the affairs of other churches beyond their own regions. That is based on the conviction that the church is ultimately one body that extends into every place. This is what is meant by the catholic or universal church. The church universal is made up invisibly of the elect and visibly of the baptized. There is one church that exists in many places, and it adheres to one faith.

Common to the church everywhere, in all its diverse forms, is Jesus Christ, the head of the church, its source and authority (1 Cor 11:3; Eph 4:15; Col 2:10). Christ is made manifest in the churches through the preaching of the Word and the administration of the sacraments.[92] Because Jesus is with us until the end of the age, communicated by the Spirit, it is the presence of Christ in his community that seals its authenticity (Matt 28:20). Ignatius of Antioch rightly said, "Wherever Jesus Christ is, there is the catholic church."[93]

In the end, the catholicity of the church is an expression of its oneness. Believers are one in Christ and, therefore, one with each other. The concept of "independent" churches is an oxymoron. One cannot be "independent" of other churches any more than one can be independent of Christ. Calvin comments: "By the unity of the Church we must understand a unity into which we feel persuaded that we are truly ingrafted. For unless we are united with all the other members under Christ our head, no hope of the future inheritance awaits us. Hence the Church is called Catholic or Universal."[94]

The ecclesiological solipsism of many evangelical churches today needs to be countered with a healthy dose of catholicity. The communion of the saints is the fellowship that exists in a faith shared by all Christian believers, including even those departed saints who now dwell with Christ in heaven, as they are bound together in Christ through the bond of the Spirit. Catholicity is recognizing that God is at work in other places and in other churches, drawing men and women to himself and drawing them together under the banner of Jesus Christ.

8.4.4 APOSTOLIC

The *apostolicity* of the church can be defined differently. For Roman Catholics, it is chiefly the episcopacy that claims to stand in full and uninterrupted continuity with the apostles, especially Peter. Jesus appointed apostles, the apostles appointed bishops, and bishops baptized the people. The problem that Protestants have is that church history is full of "bishops behaving badly." Thus the episcopacy is no sure measure of authentic Christian faith, especially when so many bishops, ancient and modern, have taught things contrary to God's Word and done things contrary to God's law.[95]

Protestants, then, have preferred to define apostolicity, not in terms of episcopal succession, but in terms of the apostolic message. In other words, the mark of the church is holding to the true and authentic teaching of the apostles about the gospel. This is what Paul meant by the gospel and the pattern of instruction that he himself received and passed on (1 Cor 11:2; 15:1–3; 1 Thess 2:13; 2 Thess 2:15;

---

92. I would distinguish Christ's presence *with* the church from any view that implies the transubstantiation of the Christ *into* the church. Augustine's "whole of Christ" (*totus Christus*) led to an unhelpful conflation of Christ and church. The problem is that such a view identifies Christ with ecclesial hierarchy and replaces the Holy Spirit with the church as the mediator of salvation.

93. Ign. *Smyrn.* 8.2.

94. Calvin, *Institutes* 4.1.2.

95. I lament the fact that my namesake, Bishop Michael Bird of the Anglican Diocese of Niagara, has consented to bless same-sex unions, and I wish he would either change his theology or change his name.

3:6). Elsewhere in the New Testament there is a similar emphasis on receiving and transmitting apostolic tradition about Jesus (Luke 1:1–4; Phil 4:9; 2 Tim 1:13–14; Heb 10:32; Rev 3:3). The most lucid expression of this comes from Jude, where we hear about "the faith that was once for all entrusted to God's holy people" (Jude 3). Apostolicity entails that the church is built on the foundation of the apostles and prophets (Eph 2:20), it maintains the apostolic faith by guarding the good deposit of the gospel (2 Tim 1:14), and the church is constantly sending out messengers[96] to declare the good news of God (Matt 28:19–20; Luke 24:47–48; Acts 1:8).

8.4.5 THE MARKS OF THE CHURCH IN REFORMED THEOLOGY

The above-mentioned marks of the church were used by Roman Catholic apologists during the Reformation to criticize the Reformers for being schismatic. They argued that abandoning the Roman Catholic Church meant abandoning the Christian faith. For in what sense could the Reformed churches claim oneness, catholicity, holiness, and apostolicity apart from the structure and sacraments provided by the Roman church?

In response, many of the Reformers defined the "marks" of the church as the preaching of the Word, the proper administration of the sacraments, and (for some) the application of church discipline—though it was recognized by most of the magisterial Reformers that church discipline was not an essential mark of the church, but more properly, the mark of a healthy church.[97] Calvin believed that making discipline a mark of the church could lead to puritanical practices that stifled unity over matters not absolutely necessary to the faith.[98] Still, for the Reformers, Word and sacrament are the quintessential signs of the true church. Hence Calvin's description of the true church: "Wherever we see the word of God sincerely preached and heard, wherever we see the sacraments administered according to the institution of Christ, there we cannot have any doubt that the Church of God has some existence."[99]

This makes a lot of sense because Word and sacrament go naturally together, like beer and skittles, peanut butter and jelly, or cheese and wine.[100] Word and sacrament have an instant evangelical unity. The Word announces the gospel, while baptism

---

96. Or as I would call them, small "a" apostles.
97. Berkhof, *Systematic Theology*, 578.
98. Calvin, *Institutes* 4.1.12–15.
99. Ibid., 4.1.9.
100. See Michael S. Horton (*People and Place: A Covenant Ecclesiology* [Louisville: Westminster John Knox, 2008], 106): "Alongside preaching, the word that is delivered in baptism and the Supper creates the world of which it speaks. Preaching does not simply *refer to* an extra linguistic reality, but is indeed the linguistic means through which the Spirit *brings it about*. Even the sacraments, then, obtain their efficacy from the word that they ratify.... At the same time, they are also visual—indeed, tactile and edible, words. Since the word creates community beyond individual consumerism, it guarantees the efficacy of the sacraments not only as a means of grace, but also as a means of grace-enabled communion with human strangers. God does what he says. Because his word is no mere sign, but powerful ('living and active'), in the hands of the Spirit the sacraments also truly communicate God's saving grace" (italic original).

and Eucharist symbolize the gospel. The Word brings the gospel of grace, while the sacraments communicate grace by the energy of the Spirit.[101] When brought together, Word and sacrament create a synergy of memorial and mediation. The sacraments provide a dramatic recounting of the deeds of God in redemptive history, but also a real presentation of Christ who meets people as he is spiritually present in the Word, in the water, and even in a communion wafer. Word and sacrament are thus part of the single communicative action that draws the church into the drama of salvation by rehearsing the mighty deeds of God and by receiving the blessings of Christ's presence with his people. We have in Word and sacrament a divine script and holy props that nourish and strengthen our faith in the theo-drama in which we find ourselves.[102]

The benefit of emphasizing Word and sacrament is that the unity, catholicity, and apostolicity of the church are not rooted in corruptible institutions or in the subjectivity of human experience, but in the objective reality of the gospel. The apostolic gospel is the single determining mark of the true church. The authorizing insignia of a true church is the preaching of the gospel and the signification of the gospel by the sacraments.[103]

What is more, I do not think that the ancient view of the fourfold marks of the church (one, holy, catholic, and apostolic church) is at all incompatible with the twofold marks of the church according to the Reformers (preaching of Word and administration of the sacraments). That is because Word and sacrament are really an expression of the apostolicity on which unity, holiness, and catholicity depend. The Reformers' marks of the church demonstrate the importance of apostolicity for oneness, holiness, and catholicity, by defining how we can tell a true church from a false one. Where the Word is rightly preached and the sacraments rightly administered, there you will find the one, holy, catholic, and apostolic church.[104]

---

101. By "communicate grace" I don't mean an impartation of grace as per Roman Catholic sacramentalism; rather, I mean that the sacraments provide genuine blessings for the recipients. The grace of baptism and Eucharist is sanctifying and edifying, not salvific.

102. Vanhoozer, *Drama of Doctrine*, 410–13.

103. Horton, *Christian Faith*, 744.

104. Oden, *Systematic Theology*, 3:299.

ECCLESIOLOGY IN CONTENTION #4: THE UNITY OF THE CHURCH

There are currently over 30,000 Protestant denominations around the world. Denominations are a sign of lasting division, and the divisions are truly manifold. Sadly, divisions have plagued the church since the earliest days of the Jerusalem church, beginning with the complaint lodged by Greek-speaking believers that their widows were being neglected in the daily distribution of food (Acts 6:1–6). Other divisions in the New Testament are Paul's volatile confrontation with Peter at Antioch (Gal 2:11–14), the factions in Corinth (1 Cor 1:10–17), the ungodly libertines in Jude (Jude 4), and the departing believers in Ephesus recorded by John the Elder (1 John 2:19).

In the succeeding centuries, disunity was introduced through heresies like Gnosticism, the Donatist controversy, the schism between the Eastern and Western churches in 1054, the Protestant Reformation in the sixteenth century, the disagreement between Luther and Zwingli over the Lord's Supper, and an innumerable multiplicity of denominations with a thousand derivatives of those branches themselves. The state of the church is, to quote Samuel J. Stone's hymn, "Though with scornful wonder we see her sore oppressed, by schisms rent asunder, by heresies distressed."

There is ample biblical rationale for the unity of churches that call Jesus Lord. For a start, the unity of the twelve tribes of Israel was necessary for the integrity and survival of the Hebrew people in Canaan. It was Israel who came together in "one mind" to make David king (1 Chr 12:38). There is a wonderful celebration of unity among "God's people" in Psalm 133, which likens such unity to oil flowing down Aaron's beard. The unity of the twelve tribes, despite the Assyrian and Babylonian exiles, was a feature of Jewish eschatological hopes for a unified nation in a restored land (e.g., Ps 107; Isa 43:1–8; Zech 8:1–23). In his high priestly prayer Jesus prayed:

> My prayer is not for them alone. I pray also for those who will believe in me through their message, that all of them may be one, Father, just as you are in me and I am in you. May they also be in us so that the world may believe that you have sent me. I have given them the glory that you gave me, that they may be one as we are one—I in them and you in me—so that they may be brought to complete unity. Then the world will know that you sent me and have loved them even as you have loved me. (John 17:20–23)

The unity among believers should be like that between the Father and the Son. This unity will also be a sign to the world that God loves Jesus' followers just as God loves his Son.

The ideal picture of the church presented in Acts is that "all the believers were one in heart and mind" (Acts 4:32), which signifies a common cause and concern for each other (see also 1 Cor 1:10; Phil 2:2; 4:2). Paul makes a couple of poignant reminders about unity in Ephesians: "Make every effort to keep the unity of the Spirit through the bond of peace" (Eph 4:3), and the purpose of the various ministers in the church is to build up the church "until we all reach unity in the faith and in the knowledge of the Son of God and become mature, attaining to the whole measure of the fullness of Christ" (Eph 4:13). Note how Paul urges genuine effort and grit to keep the unity that the Spirit provides precisely because desire for unity is a sign of maturity in Christ.

Furthermore, the image of the church as the "body of Christ" is a powerful picture of a diverse people bonded together with Christ as the head, sharing the same Spirit and knowing that what unites them is infinitely stronger than anything that might divide them. To divide the body of Christ is to akin chopping up the body of the Messiah "in little pieces so we can each have a relic all our own" (1 Cor 1:13 [Message]).

The biblical exhortations in Scripture toward unity are important and are not negotiable. Christians must strive toward unity with their brothers and sisters. I lament the fact that in a recent denominational magazine that I subscribe to, a guest author said that "unity is overrated." The words made me gasp. Is Jesus' high priestly prayer overrated? Are Paul's words to the factions in the Corinthian church overrated? Granted, unity at any price is overrated. Unity at the expense of theological integrity and moral purity is overrated. But Christian unity itself is precious, purposeful, and powerful. There are several reasons why Christians should actively pursue unity with other believers.

First, unity is crucial to our Christian witness to the world. Jesus' high priestly prayer states that the oneness of church and unity with the Father and Son are purposed "so that the world may believe that you have sent me" (John 17:21). The world can look at Christians and see their oneness, mutual affection, and desire to safeguard each other's honor, and they will say with wonder, "See how these Christians love one another." Conversely, they can look at Christians with their rhetorical daggers, bad-mouthing blogs, needless divisions, and disruptive doctrines, and they will sneer in sarcastic contempt, "Oh, see how these Christians *love* one another." A house divided in half, into quarters, into small pieces is not going to attract people to take shelter in it from the storm of judgment.

Second, the church grows the most when it is united the most. The clearest example is the early Jerusalem church, where oneness of mind resulted in many being added to their number daily (Acts 2:47). There is strength in numbers, just like a cord of three strands is not easily broken (Eccl 4:12). Being united is a reason to get excited. Unity brings new energy to approach old tasks. The Spirit moves when there is consensus and concurrence on how to go about the business of being God's people in a world of darkness.

Third, unity means we can employ our limited resources more efficiently. A former colleague of mine noted that growing up in Orkney, there were two Lord's Day Observance Societies, one for conservative Presbyterians and the other one for ultraconservative Presbyterians. I have visited villages on the Isle of Skye where there are three Presbyterian churches of different forms within two hundred meters of each other, and the reasons for their original division have long been lost in the annals of ecclesiastical history. I am not a business consultant, but I know that avoiding duplication results in a better and smarter use of resources. Whether it is minimizing building costs, avoiding a multiplication of similar programs, securing larger attendances at key events, or being able to employ four pastors rather than just one, it makes good fiscal sense to minimize costs by working together. Obviously pure economics should not determine our ministry objectives, but if stewardship is part of any good ministry, not reinventing the wheel or replicating the church next door is a wise and godly option.

Of course, it is not all doom and gloom when it comes to unity. Many believers over the course of church history have worked together for church unity. The resolution of the Donatist controversy is one obvious example of a positive victory for Christian unity. After the Reformation, Jean-Alphonse Turretin (1671–1737) advocated the unity of Calvinists, Lutherans, and Anglicans, giving a speech at the University of Geneva about his distress at seeing the cloak of Christ torn to pieces.[105]

The modern impetus for unity came largely through the missionary movement that fostered cooperation on the mission field where Christians were able to work together largely away from the denominational politics of their sending countries. Unsurprisingly it was the watershed moment of the World Missionary Conference in Edinburgh in 1910 that gave rise to the modern ecumenical movement. The mutual anathemas between the Roman Catholic and Eastern Orthodox churches were repealed by the Bishop of Rome and the Patriarch of Constantinople in 1965. The World Evangelical Fellowship was established in 1951, and the various Lausanne Conferences have been drawing believers together since the 1970s.

---

105. William Baird, *History of New Testament Research—Volume One: From Deism to Tübingen* (Minneapolis: Fortress, 1992), 194.

If one were to envisage fresh ecumenical tasks for a new century, I would suggest something along these lines:

- creating a consensus about the gospel among evangelical, conservative mainline, and liturgical churches in the West
- riding the postdenominational wave in urban centers to synergize resources in largely secular cultures
- training and empowering leaders in the global south as the new leadership for the Christian faith
- working with Christians of all stripes to tackle the topics of Islam, social ethics, public theology, poverty, religious freedom, and "the welfare of the city"

§ 8.5 GOVERNANCE OF THE CHURCH

The administration, organization, and management of the church is not the most riveting subject in a systematic theology. Even so, it is a necessary and an important topic because it deals with matters of leadership and accountability. The day-to-day running of any church is impacted by its structures and strictures. Accordingly, an important task in evangelical theology is to inquire into the entailments of the gospel for church structure and to discern how to organize a community at whose center lies the gospel of Jesus Christ.[106]

Yet there are so many ways of organizing a church and its leadership. Which model should we employ: Episcopal, Presbyterian, or Congregationalist? Does the Bible have one single vision for church governance? Are we necessarily limited to Scripture when it comes to church management? Or can one develop an entirely new model based on corporate structures that seem to be effective? What I will do below is set forth the three main models for church government (Episcopalianism, Presbyterianism, and Congregationalism) and list the arguments used for justifying them. Readers can discern on their own which model is the most biblically sound and theologically coherent account of church leadership structures.

8.5.1 EPISCOPALIANISM

The Episcopalian form of church governance centers on the bishop as the fulcrum of faith, order, and ministry.[107] This form of church government is practiced by the Roman Catholic, Anglican, Orthodox, and Lutheran churches (in some Methodist churches too, but the bishop is not considered above the clergy and functions more like a superintendent). The diocese is the basic unit with a single bishop overseeing a number of priests and parishes. The bishop is distinct from and above the priests and

---

106. John Webster, *Word and Church: Essays in Church Dogmatics* (London: T&T Clark, 2001), 192.
107. Cf. Peter Toon, "Episcopalianism," in *Who Runs the Church? 4 Views on Church Government* (ed. S. B. Cowan; Grand Rapids: Zondervan, 2004), 21–41.

deacons, who serve in an individual congregation. A bishop can be subservient to an archbishop in charge of a large diocese. A bishop can also have a suffragan or assistant bishop in a larger diocese. Bishops are either appointed by Rome (Catholicism) or elected by a synod or committee, or the appointment can be a combination of the two (Anglicanism). Bishops in the Catholic and Orthodox traditions are not permitted to be married, while they are allowed to marry in the Anglican and Lutheran traditions.

Several arguments, biblical and historical, are often used to justify an Episcopalian form of church government. Catholic and Anglo-Catholic theologians argue for the establishment of an apostolic "college" in Jesus' appointment of the twelve (Mark 3:14–16). Peter was appointed by Christ to be leader in this college (Matt 16:17–19), and by tradition Peter was regarded as the founding bishop of Rome.[108] This tradition is considered the roots for the primacy of the bishop of Rome as the successor to Peter and his authority over the entire church. Although Orthodox and Anglican churches respect the bishop of Rome as the "Patriarch of the West," they reject his claim to the as vicar of Christ and supreme head of the church.

In terms of biblical arguments for Episcopalianism, one can point to the fact that the Jerusalem church, in addition to the apostles, appears to have developed a threefold ministry of deacons, elders, and a bishop.[109] Deacons were appointed by the apostles (Acts 6:1–6), as were elders (14:23). One should note the close relationship between "the apostles and elders" (15:2, 4, 6, 22–23; 16:4), with the apostles having the priority as former companions of Jesus and witnesses to his resurrection.

Within the next couple of decades all of the twelve apostles, through either martyrdom or mission, appear to have left Jerusalem. When Paul visited Jerusalem in the late AD 40s, only Peter, John, and James the brother of the Lord were there, functioning as a triumvirate of apostolic authority (Gal 2:9). It is probable that Peter subsequently journeyed to Rome and John went to Ephesus, so that only James was left in Jerusalem. When Paul returned to Jerusalem to deliver the collection in the late 50s, James appears to have been the sole apostolic authority among the elders and was for all intents and purposes the monarchial bishop (Acts 12:17; 21:18; Josephus, *Ant.* 20.200). For this reason, James is named as the first bishop of Jerusalem, who was succeeded by Symeon.[110]

---

108. Eusebius, *Hist. eccl.* 3.2.4.

109. In the Episcopal tradition, elders are also called priests. There is some warrant for this when considering: (1) the Old Testament priesthood was charged with serving God and God's people, which stands in a historic continuity with Christian ministry by analogy and typology; (2) Jesus Christ fulfills and abolishes the Levitical priesthood in terms of mediation and reconciliation, but a priestly role of service in worship of God and instruction in the Word is continued in the New Testament church; (3) a Christian priesthood is really an extension of the priesthood of all believers (1 Pet 2:5, 9) and a continuation of the priestly work of Christ by edifying and sanctifying the church of God (John 17; Heb 7–8); (4) Christian leaders have a sacred authority to bind and loose (Matt 16:19; 18:18); and (5) Paul can refer to his "priestly duty of proclaiming the gospel" (Rom 15:16). What a priesthood cannot be is: (1) an office of mediation since that is fulfilled by Christ alone (1 Tim 2:5; Heb 8:6); or (2) an absolute distinction from the laity since priesthood is universal.

110. Eusebius, *Hist. eccl.* 2.1; 3.11.

To this we might add that the Jerusalem church appears to have had authority over other churches in greater Palestine, since the church in Antioch looked to Jerusalem for authority and legitimacy (see Acts 15; Gal 2:1–10). Hence, the Jerusalem church evolved from an authority consisting of apostles with elders/deacons, to a monoepiscopacy with the bishop acting as first among equals with the elders and possessing a jurisdiction that extended as far as Syria.

On this paradigm, bishops are the successors of the apostles. The apostles were regarded as special authorities, who were above overseers/elders in local congregations. The mantle was passed from the apostles to others who received their office from them through the laying on of hands (1 Tim 5:22; 2 Tim 1:6; Heb 6:2). The appointment of the apostles by Christ (Mark 3:14–16; 1 Tim 2:7; 2 Tim 1:11), the apostles' appointment of certain persons to overseeing ministries (2 Tim 1:6), and the subsequent appointment of elders by these apostolary ordinands (1 Tim 5:22; Titus 1:5), provide a chain of succession and contribute to the formation of a historical episcopate.

In the early second century, amidst the threat of heresy and the dangers of persecution, there arose a concerted focus on the authority of the bishop as the lynchpin for church unity and gospel integrity. The letters of Ignatius, the bishop of Antioch, underscore the importance that the episcopacy came to have in some quarters.

- "Let us, therefore, *be careful not to oppose the bishop*, in order that we may be obedient to God." (Ign. *Eph.* 5.3)
- "For everyone whom the Master of the house sends to manage his own house we must welcome as we would the one who sent him. It is obvious, therefore, that *we must regard the bishop as the Lord himself*." (Ign. *Eph.* 6.1)
- "Be eager to do everything in godly harmony, *the bishop presiding in the place of God* and the presbyters in the place of the council of the apostles and the deacons ... since they have been entrusted with the ministry of Jesus Christ." (Ign. *Magn.* 6.1)
- "Let there be nothing among you that is capable of dividing you, but *be united with the bishop* and with those who lead." (Ign. *Magn.* 6.2)
- "Therefore, as the Lord did nothing without the Father, either by himself or through the apostles (for he was united with him), so *you must not do anything without the bishop* and the presbyters." (Ign. *Magn.* 7.1, italics added in all cases)

The role of the bishop became increasingly elevated as a symbol of unity in the early church. By the late second century, Irenaeus and Hippolytus were clear advocates of Episcopal authority, as they saw the bishop as the key means of retaining the purity of the gospel and the unity of the church. The bishop was the historic link with the apostles as well as the conveyer and preserver of the apostolic message.

Thus, the historical Episcopate (i.e., apostolic succession) can be defined either as the physical and unbroken succession of bishops in a given diocese, or, perhaps better, as the succession of overseers and ministers in the church across the ages by means of formal ordination and consecration. On this second view (a universal succession by ordination), each and every bishop represents a symbolic link between the church of his place, the churches in other places, and the churches of generations gone by. The historical Episcopate is meant to be an embodiment of the gospel in the church as an effectual sign of unity and as providing guardianship to both Word and sacrament.[111]

Several criticisms and concerns can be registered against the Episcopal form of church governance. (1) The Roman Catholic claims of the primacy and infallibility of the Pope are extravagant and lacking in biblical support. (2) The fact that the New Testament regards the offices of *episkopos* and *presbyteros* as synonymous seriously damages the claims for the superiority and authority of a single *episkopos* over a plural of *presbyteroi* (Acts 20:17, 28; Titus 1:5–7; 1 Pet 5:1–2). (3) Even if one accepts the pattern of the Ignatian letters for church government, there the bishop functions more like a senior pastor, since he is with the congregation every week in the breaking of bread, which is hardly identical to a metropolitan bishop; he is more like a resident pastor with seniority (Ign. *Eph.* 20.2). (4) It is also more likely that the monoepiscopacy emerged from within a plurality of elders, as a first among equals, rather than an apostolic order of ordination. (5) One could object that the Episcopacy, especially one that is not elected by a synod, is the hardest form of church authority to reform and hold accountable by the clergy and the laity.[112]

8.5.2 PRESBYTERIANISM

The Presbyterian form of church government focuses on a plurality of elders constituting a "session" as the head of a congregation.[113] The session includes "teaching elders" (i.e., ordained pastors) and "ruling elders" (i.e., lay folks who lead). The elders from a number of local churches then comprise a presbytery, which has ruling authority over the churches in its region. The presbyteries in turn are part of a synod or general assembly, which governs the entire denominational body. Churches that practice this form of governance are naturally called "Presbyterian"; it includes examples like the Church of Scotland, Free Church of Scotland, Dutch Reformed,

---

111. Toon, "Episcopalianism," 38.
112. Although Calvin clearly preferred Presbyterian government, he was apparently willing to allow an Episcopal government for Reformed churches for the sake of unity.
113. L. Roy Taylor, "Presbyterianism," in *Who Runs the Church? 4 Views on Church Government* (ed. S. B. Cowan; Grand Rapids: Zondervan, 2004), 73–98; Horton, *Christian Faith*, 744–47; Robert L. Reymond, *A New Systematic Theology of the Christian Faith* (2nd ed.; Nashville: Nelson, 1998), 895–910.

> ## SOME COMIC BELIEF
>
> A young Anglican ordinand goes off to see a retired bishop in search of some pastoral wisdom before he is formally ordained to the priesthood and takes charge of his first parish. He asks the wise old bishop a question:
> "How can I be a good pastor?"
> "Make good decisions!" came the reply from the old bishop.
> "Okay, but um, well, how do I learn how to make good decisions then?" the young man asked.
> "Easy, you learn that from experience; that's how you learn to make good decisions."
> "Okay, that's all well and good, but how do I get the experience to make good decisions?"
> "By making bad decisions!" the bishop replied with a grin.

Reformed Church of America, Presbyterian Church of the USA, Evangelical Presbyterian Church, and Australian Presbyterian Church.

In Presbyterian church governance, the centerpiece of leadership revolves around the office of the elder. This office appears across both Testaments, where it represents a form of leadership for a "biblical church," not just a "New Testament church."[114] Moses was instructed to gather the elders of Israel together to tell them of God's plan to deliver the Hebrews from Egypt (Exod 3:16–17). Moses and the elders approached Pharaoh with their demand to be set free to worship God (3:18). After the giving of the law at Sinai, seventy elders were summoned to worship the Lord and to feast in his presence (24:1, 9–11). In the wilderness wanderings, seventy elders were again summoned to share in the leadership of the nation alongside Moses (Num 11:16–17). These elders were charged with urging the people to obey God's commands (Deut 27:1).

Even with the advent of the offices of prophet, priest, and king, the role of the elders in Israelite society remained prominent during the united and divided monarchies. Later, the elders became the locus of authority in the Jewish communities in exile, as demonstrated by Jeremiah and Ezekiel (Jer 29:1; Ezek 8:1; 14:1; 20:1, 3). In New Testament times, the Jewish elders were important in the leadership of Judean

---

114. Taylor, "Presbyterianism," 76.

society (e.g., Matt 21:23; 26:3; 26:47, 57; Acts 4:5, 8, 23; 5:21; 6:12) and Diaspora communities (cf. Acts 13:15; 18:17).[115]

The New Testament consistently demonstrates the prevalence of a plurality of elders in the churches. The Jerusalem church had a plurality of elders (Acts 11:30; 15:2, 4, 22–23; 16:4). Paul and Barnabas appointed elders in the churches throughout Asia Minor (Acts 14:23). Paul addressed his letter to the Philippians to the "overseers and deacons" (Phil 1:1). The church in Ephesus, established by Paul and later pastored by Timothy, had a group of elders (Acts 20:17; 1 Tim 5:17–20). Paul commanded Titus to appoint elders in the towns of Crete (Titus 1:5). In James 5:14, those who are sick should call the elders to anoint them with oil. In 1 Peter 5:1–5, Peter exhorts elders to be good shepherds, and congregations should submit to the eldership. The author of Hebrews refers to the leaders who keep watch over the congregation (Heb 13:17).

Presbyterianism also differentiates between elders who teach and elders who have only governing responsibilities. This is rooted in Paul's instructions in 1 Timothy: "The elders who direct the affairs of the church well are worthy of double honor, especially those whose work is preaching and teaching" (1 Tim 5:17). Though elders are for the most part not differentiated in role, and all had to be able to teach (1 Tim 3:2; 2 Tim 2:24), there are inklings that some elders had a special teaching ministry (Acts 13:1; 1 Cor 12:28–29; Eph 4:11; Jas 3:1).

The notion of a Presbytery is often justified by way of reference to Acts 15. There the Antiochene church appealed to the Jerusalem church to help resolve a contentious theological matter about Gentiles and circumcision. The matter was settled by an embassy from the Antiochene church and the elders of the Jerusalem church (Acts 15:4, 22). The resolution was then considered binding on both churches (Acts 15:23–33). Thus, a college of elders effectively governed a collective body of churches.

The Presbyterian system is also not without its detractions. (1) The division between teaching and ruling elders seems somewhat artificial. All elders were supposed to be able to teach (1 Tim 3:2; 2 Tim 2:24). The lone teaching elder could be said to resemble a localized bishop who is first among equals with fellow elders, but he had a didactic and moral authority above them by virtue of his role. (2) Acts 15 does not appear to be a "presbytery meeting" of two equal churches. The Jerusalem church was in a position of ascendency over the Antiochene church. James was not just a spokesman for the elders in Jerusalem, but was a primary leader in some regard. Acts 15 looks more hierarchical than a form of representative government.

---

115. On epigraphical evidence from inscriptions about the role of elders in Jewish synagogues, see J. B. Frey, ed., *Corpus Inscriptionum Iudaicarum* (2 vols. New York: Ktav, repr. 1975), § 663, 735, 739.

(3) There is little biblical warrant for the courts, consistories, synods, and assemblies that make up the Presbyterian system. In practice, Presbyterianism can become litigious, with doctrinal disputes forever filling the courts with accusations about who is or is not theologically sound. (4) The emergence of the monoepiscopacy, even if arising from an eldership and in the postapostolic era, is still a development that needs to be wrestled within the history of the church and as an outworking of the apostolic churches. (5) To restrict preaching and administration of the sacraments to an eldership could be judged to deny the implications of the priesthood of all believers.

8.5.3 CONGREGATIONALISM

Congregationalist churches are those governed by the democratic rule of the congregation and who elect officers such as deacons, elders, and pastors. The key element is the independence and autonomy of the local congregation from all other ecclesial authorities. Although congregational churches can join associations, they are free and independent from interference. There are a variety of congregational models. The two most popular varieties are those with (1) a single elder, a diaconate, and a congregation; (2) those with plurality of elders (of which the pastor is but one), a diaconate, and a congregation. This form of church governance is practiced by Baptists, Anabaptists, Church of Christ, Pentecostal, and Independent Bible Churches.[116]

The biblical rationale for this model is that, on the one hand, the early Christians established churches that were in close fellowship with one another (Rom 1:8; Eph 1:15; Col 1:4; Phlm 5). On the other hand, these churches also appear to be local, self-governing, and free from outside interference by other authorities. That is, the early congregations were visibly independent of each other, but spiritually interdependent on each other. The model found in Acts and the epistles makes a plurality of elders and deacons the norm (Acts 14:23; Phil 1:1), with one particular individual set apart for the ministry of teaching and preaching (1 Tim 5:17–18).

The officers of the church are selected by a common vote. The replacement for Judas Iscariot was chosen by lot after the disciples had put forward Joseph Barsabbas and Matthias as the candidates (Acts 1:23). The first deacons to serve the Greek-speaking congregations were chosen from "seven men from among you" to serve the community (6:3). The church in Antioch appointed Paul and Barnabas to be their delegates to the Jerusalem council (15:2). The Jerusalem church chose some men to

---

116. Paige Patterson, "Single-Elder Congregationalism," in *Who Runs the Church? 4 Views on Church Government* (ed. S. B. Cowan; Grand Rapids: Zondervan, 2004), 131–52; and Samuel E. Waldron, "Plural-Elder Congregationalism," in ibid., 185–221; Wayne Grudem, *Systematic Theology* (Grand Rapids: Zondervan, 1995), 928–36.

accompany Paul and Barnabas back to Antioch to convey the decision of the council and to deliver the apostolic decree (15:25). Paul recounts how Titus was "chosen by the churches to accompany us as we carry the offering" (2 Cor 8:19; cf. 1 Cor 16:3).

It is also pointed out that disciplining members appears to be a matter for the entire church to take authority for when it occurs. A person is disciplined if they "refuse to listen even to the church" (Matt 18:17), and a person is excluded only when the church is properly "assembled" (1 Cor 5:4). If one takes seriously the view of the priesthood of all believers and the Spirit's role in speaking through the body of Christ, it makes sense to allow all faithful and fellowshiping members a say on who is elected to leadership and how the church is to be administered. Finally, one might suggest that, following Old Testament precedent (e.g., Exod 4:29–31; 1 Sam 7:5–6; 10:24; Neh 8:1–18), leadership functions best when it operates with the consent of the governed.

Naturally it is possible to criticize the Congregationalist model on several fronts. (1) In some cases it looks as if officers were externally appointed by men like Paul and Barnabas (Acts 14:23) and Titus (Titus 1:5). The words for "appoint" (*cheirotoneō, kathistēmi,*) do not mean install by means of a free and open vote.[117] (2) Though many may prefer a "biblical" idea of church as opposed to an Episcopal hierarchy, the irony is that it was the bishops of the third century whom God used to ratify the canon and determine which books should be in the Bible. (3) One must also wonder if an "independent church" is an oxymoron. The churches are meant to be in gospel partnership and eucharistic fellowship with each other. The danger of the Congregationalist model is that it can lead to an ecclesiology where everyone does what is right in their own eyes and acts with a deliberate disregard for the wider body of Christ (Judg 17:6; 21:25).[118] Though a democratic church government may provide accountability of the church leaders to the laity, an independent church lacks accountability to anyone else.[119] (4) Parishioners in the Episcopal and Presbyterian systems still have a voice and vote through parish councils, committees, and representative lay bodies. No sensible bishop or presbytery would normally impose or depose a minister without first consulting the church. (5) My own experience has been that pastors of congregational churches suffer higher rates of burnout than in any other form of church government. Don't get me wrong; I know that there are pastors who have long-term and fruitful ministries in Congregationalist churches, but Congregationalist churches are more conducive to pastors being stressed to breaking point and unfairly sacked.

---

117. Contra Grudem, *Systematic Theology*, 921–22.

118. Though see William L. Pitts, "The Relation of Baptists to Other Churches," in *The People of God: Essays on the Believers' Church* (ed. P. A. Basen and D. S. Dockery; Nashville: Broadman & Holman, 1991), 235–50 and Steve R. Harmon, *Towards Baptist Catholicity: Essays on Tradition and the Baptist Vision* (SBHT 27; Milton Keynes, UK: Paternoster, 2006).

119. We might comically say that "In those days Israel had no bishop; everyone did as they saw fit" (hat tip to my student Yarran Johnston).

8.5.4 SOME REFLECTIONS AND A CONCLUSION

The primitive church looks as if it adopted a number of models for its leadership and structures, depending on the location and circumstances. Households, synagogues, philosophical schools, and associations all provided templates that various churches used at some time or other. Churches independent of synagogues might well follow a household pattern, with the *paterfamilias* functioning as the lead figure. Elsewhere, something like a synagogue model with a plurality of elders and a president appears to have been the norm. Complicating matters is that in some letters Paul identifies the church leaders by their office (e.g., Phil 1:1), but in other places he makes no specific mention of leaders when we would expect him to appeal to the officers of the church to resolve a controversial matter (e.g., Galatians, 1–2 Corinthians).

We are also beset with the problem that all models of church government can be anchored in the biblical material to some degree, and all models of church government have clearly undergone postbiblical developments as they attained their current form. The questions are: Which model is the most biblically rooted, and which trajectory of development coheres with the leadership paradigm of Scripture? Taking together Acts and the Pastoral Epistles, the New Testament writings that speak most directly to the issue of offices and structures, one could legitimately infer a threefold office of a senior leader selected from among the elders, an eldership, and a diaconate is the most primitive and pervasive form of church governance.

The matter of church governance needs to be put into perspective. Ultimately a church is a gospel community, and its leadership is elected for the purpose of promoting the gospel and preparing the saints for living gospel-driven lives. There is no single way to do that. I have had the pleasuring of attending a number of Baptist, Pentecostal, Anglican, and Presbyterian churches, each of which had a wonderful cohort of gifted and tireless workers for the gospel. I have thus been involved in a variety of church governance models and their ministries. One thing I have learned is this: the single most important factor in the governance of the church is not the structure or model it is based on, but the Christian character of the folks who lead it.

I honestly believe that any form of ecclesial government can foster a healthy church with a kingdom vision, a gospel focus, a hunger for holiness, and a passion for God's glory ... *if* the men and women entrusted with authority are genuinely committed to loving God and loving God's people. The most determinative factor for church leadership is a Godward passion, spiritual depth, and Christlike attitudes. We still need shepherds after God's own heart. The structure of the pen for the sheep is not insignificant, but subservient to this is a stronger need for godly bishops, overseers, elders, pastors, priests, and deacons over the flock.

ECCLESIOLOGY IN CONTENTION #5: THE PURPOSE OF THE CHURCH

What is the purpose of the church? On the safe assumption that we are not meant to sit around and read Left Behind novels until the second coming, what is it that God expects us to do in the interim? Several things probably should feature in our understanding of the church's purpose.

1. *Evangelism and mission.* Erickson rightly calls the gospel the "heart of the ministry of the church."[120] Evangelicals are people excited about promoting the evangel! Evangelicals get busy proclaiming the good news about salvation through the Lord Jesus Christ. The Gospels portray Jesus in the Olivet Discourse prophesying that "the gospel must first be preached to all nations" before the end comes (Mark 13:10; cf. Matt 24:14). In the itinerant preaching ministry of the seventy(-two) disciples, Satan fell like lightning as their work of proclamation, exorcism, and healing struck a powerful blow against the kingdom of darkness (Luke 10:18).

The Great Commission is a cornerstone text with the risen Jesus' command to "go and make disciples of all nations" (Matt 28:19). Further instruction is given to the apostles that they "will be my witnesses in Jerusalem, and in all Judea and Samaria, and to the ends of the earth" (Acts 1:8). Mission is an eschatological event that continues the ministry of Jesus and builds toward the ultimate victory of God over rebellion in this world.

2. *Make disciples.* The Great Commission does not urge us to get people to make decisions or even to get conversions, but to "make disciples" through "teaching them to obey everything I have commanded you" (Matt 28:19–20). The ministry of "the apostles, the prophets, the evangelists, the pastors and teachers ... [should operate] so that the body of Christ may be built up until we all reach unity in the faith and in the knowledge of the Son of God and become mature, attaining to the whole measure of the fullness of Christ" (Eph 4:11–13). The role of teachers is to ensure that believers are edified by instruction in Scripture, abiding in the words of Jesus, holding to apostolic testimony, and introduced to the wisdom of the fathers (Acts 13:1; Rom 12:17; 1 Cor 12:28; Eph 4:11). Practically, that takes the form of preaching, catechisms, Sunday school classes, family devotions, Bible study, and seminary training. This is why we need biblically trained pastors, scholars, and theologians.

3. *Administer the sacraments.* The proper administration of the sacraments is more of a feature of the church than merely part of its primary purpose. Nonetheless, a church will

---

120. Erickson, *Christian Theology*, 1069–76.

need to purposefully integrate the sacraments into its diet of worship and fellowship in order to be spiritually nourished and unified. Baptism is a symbolically rich image of the gospel that tells of our dying and rising with Christ. It is the mark of entrance into the church, which binds us together so that we share one faith, one Lord, and one baptism. We can exhort each other with the words "remember your baptism" as a slogan for holding fast to the faith. The Lord's Supper brings us to sober introspection, spiritual accountability, and joyous celebration at Jesus' death and return. The sacraments are effective signs of the community that remembers Jesus, worships God, and is filled with the Holy Spirit.

4. *Kingdom work.* The church is the custodian of the kingdom and commits itself to kingdom ministry that brings salvation, deliverance, and redemption to all of God's creation. That requires acts of compassion, mercy ministry, public engagement, and social justice. Jesus made no distinction between his kingdom mission in proclamation to the lost and in healing the sick. Preaching good news to the poor, setting captives free, giving sight to the blind, and offering deliverance for the oppressed were part of the signs that Israel's restoration was dawning with the explosive aftereffect of a salvation for Israel and the Gentiles (Isa 61:1; Matt 11:5/Luke 7:22; Luke 4:18). Concern for the vulnerable and rejection of greed are among the basic elements of covenantal justice (e.g., Exod 22:22; Deut 10:17–19; Prov 21:15; Amos 5:24).

The New Testament is full of exhortations for the saints to help others in practical ways as a means of sharing the love of God with others. James says, "Religion that God our Father accepts as pure and faultless is this: to look after orphans and widows in their distress and to keep oneself from being polluted by the world" (Jas 1:27). John the Elder writes: "If anyone has material possessions and sees a brother or sister in need but has no pity on them, how can the love of God be in that person?" (1 John 3:17). In summary we can say that a messianic community should make every effort "to act justly and to love mercy and to walk humbly with your God" (Mic 6:8), to "let justice roll on like a river, righteousness like a never-failing stream!" (Amos 5:24), and to "not love with words or speech but with actions and in truth" (1 John 3:18). The reign of God is a dynamic reality that can be demonstrated in loving action to those suffering and in the justice that is brought on the wicked.

5. *Worship.* A definition of worship is notoriously difficult to set out without fault. Evidently it is more than just singing songs to the Lord on Sunday. The essence of worship is often reduced to "obedience" or "religious affections," depending on who is arguing the case. More probably it consists of both of these. Worship is drawing near to God in service, thanksgiving, and joyful praise.[121] This interlocking nature of praxis

---

121. Cf. D. A. Carson, "'Worship the Lord Your God': The Perennial Challenge," in *Worship: Adoration and Action* (ed. D. A. Carson; Eugene, OR: Wipf & Stock, 2002), 13–18.

and praise for worship is highlighted in Hebrews: "Through Jesus, therefore, let us continually offer to God a sacrifice of praise—the fruit of lips that openly profess his name. And do not forget to do good and to share with others, for with such sacrifices God is pleased" (Heb 13:15–16).

According to Miroslav Volf, authentic Christian worship expresses itself in action and adoration. Through action, the church anticipates a world devoid of evil and suffering, where God's *shalom* is the state of order. Christian worship leads to a summit of adoration that anticipates our enjoyment of God in the new creation, where God's people dwell in perfect communion with each other and with their Lord.[122] There is also a deep sense in which "worship" is the real purpose and goal of the church. Worship drives mission, as John Piper has famously said: "Missions is not the ultimate goal of the church. Worship is. Missions exists because worship [does."][123] We make disciples so that they can properly worship God and live a life that is worthy of him. The sacraments help us in worship by reminding us what God has done for us in the past, by bringing us closer to God in the present, and by turning our minds toward our future life with God in eternity. The consummation of all kingdom work will be worshiping the king in his new creation.

FURTHER READING

Basden, Paul A., and David S. Dockery, eds. *The People of God: Essays on the Believers' Church*. Nashville: Broadman & Holman, 1991.

Bradshaw, Tim. *The Olive Branch: An Evangelical Anglican Doctrine of the Church*. Carlisle, UK: Paternoster, 2006.

Dulles, Avery. *Models of the Church*. Garden City, NY: Doubleday, 1974.

Ryken, Philip Graham, ed. *The Communion of the Saints: Living in Fellowship with the People of God*. Phillipsburg, NJ: Presbyterian & Reformed, 2001.

Webster, John. *Word and Church: Essays in Church Dogmatics*. London: T&T Clark, 2001, pp. 191–210.

---

122. Miroslav Volf, "Worship as Adoration and Action: Reflections on a Christian Way of Being-in-the-World," in *Worship: Adoration and Action*, 203–11 (esp. 207–8).

123. John Piper, *Let the Nations Be Glad* (3rd ed.; Grand Rapids: Baker, 2010), 15.

§ 8.6 EMBLEMS OF THE GOSPEL: BAPTISM AND LORD'S SUPPER

In the Protestant tradition, which evangelicals share, the two recognized sacraments are those instituted by Jesus Christ himself: baptism and the Lord's Supper. I prefer to call these "sacraments" rather than "ordinances." An "ordinance" is a ritual ordained by Christ and repeated by the church that is chiefly symbolic in character. A "sacrament," by contrast, is defined as a visible sign of an invisible grace.[124] The Latin *sacramentum* pertained to something sworn in dedication and devotion to the gods. It meant a shift from the secular to the sacred. The difference is that whereas an ordinance remembers God's grace toward us, a sacrament is a means by which God's divine presence is actualized in the midst of the believing community.

These two are not necessarily mutually exclusive. Baptism and the Lord's Supper are obviously symbolic to some extent, but the Protestant confessions have largely affirmed that they are also a means of grace, a communication of God to his people; thus they are ordinarily referred to as sacraments. According to the Westminster Confession 27.1:

> Sacraments are holy signs and seals of the covenant of grace, immediately instituted by God, to represent Christ and His benefits; and to confirm our interest in Him: as also, to put a visible difference between those that belong unto the Church and the rest of the world; and solemnly to engage them to the service of God in Christ, according to His Word.[125]

They are a means of grace by virtue of the "work of the Holy Spirit" and the "word of institution" (WCF 27.3). The sacraments are *sacred* events, richly laden with symbolic meanings, but they are effective symbols that impart grace to the recipients.

---

124. Augustine (*Tract. Ev. Jo.* 50.3) famously wrote that the sacraments are "visible signs that represent an invisible reality."

125. The Westminster Confession of Faith can be found at www.reformed.org/documents/wcf_with_proofs/.

Importantly, the sacraments of baptism and the Lord's Supper are christocentric and gospel freighted. For Karl Rahner, Jesus is a type of "primal sacrament" as the sign and reality of God's redemptive grace. The church itself becomes a sacrament for Rahner because it has the abiding presence of God's eschatological grace.[126] I don't agree with Rahner on everything here, but he's right about one thing: Jesus is Holy God and Holy Man. Accordingly, the power, grace, and holiness of the sacraments are rooted in him. What makes one *holy* catholic church is the holiness of its Lord—not the holiness of its doctrines or clerical orders, but the holy Lord cleaved and united with his people, partly through the sacraments he ordained for them. Jesus is the God of all holiness and boundless grace, whom we remember and meet in baptism and the Lord's Supper. Because Christ is indelibly connected to the church, he both authorizes and sanctifies the sacraments as a means of grace that communicates himself to his people.

Concerning the gospel, the sacraments of baptism and Lord's Supper serve as "virtual realities" of the gospel, which draw the believing community into the story of redemption and into Christ's presence through the Spirit.[127] The sacraments are portals that bring us into the promises that the gospel declares: the experience of divine grace and fellowship with his Son. The sacraments remember, realize, and rehearse the central promise of the gospel—we died and rose with Christ, Jesus is with us, and Jesus is coming again to take us into eternal fellowship with himself in his kingdom.

The rituals of baptism and Lord's Supper are recollections of the work of the Lord Jesus as recounted in the gospel; they are confessions of our faith about Jesus as narrated in the gospel; and they identify the believing community with the story of the gospel that centers on Christ Jesus. That is why whenever there is a baptism or a Lord's Supper, there should also be preaching of the gospel. Sacrament and preaching mutually reinforce each other and doubly edify the body of Christ. To quote the Heidelberg Catechism (Q 66), the sacraments are a means by which God "may the more fully declare and seal to us the promise of the gospel." We explore now these emblems of the gospel in the church of the Lord Jesus.[128]

8.6.1 A BRIDGE OVER TROUBLED WATERS: BAPTISM

Rites of passage are important for communities. They indicate inclusion, acceptance, and membership. I remember vividly being handed my maroon beret on

---

126. Karl Rahner, *The Church and the Sacraments* (New York: Herder & Herder, 1963), 15–24. Similarly, Donald Bloesch (*The Church: Sacraments, Worship, Ministry, Mission* [Downers Grove, IL: InterVarsity Press, 2002], 172) calls Jesus Christ the "*Ursacrament* of the church, the visible sign of invisible grace."

127. Harper and Metzger, *Exploring Ecclesiology*, 124.

128. On baptism and the Lord's Supper in some contemporary evangelical theologies, see Erickson, *Christian Theology*, 1098–134; Grudem, *Systematic Theology*, 950–1002; Horton, *Christian Faith*, 751–827.

my qualification as a paratrooper. It signified that I was no longer just your average "grunt" (i.e., light infantry), but I was now a full-fledged airborne warrior! We can think of countless other examples. For a lawyer, passing exams and being admitted to the bar to practice law is a big deal. Giving new clergy a license of ordination and perhaps even handing them their clerical garb is a big event in the life of a new minister. Graduating from months of training at a police academy and receiving one's own police badge is equally climactic. Rites of passage are ubiquitous because they meet a universal need to mark entrance into a new body of people.

In the Christian faith, across its many forms, the rite of passage for entry into the church is baptism. Baptism is a symbol of the gospel; it marks entry into the gospelizing community and creates a bond of unity with all those in every place who are baptized into Christ Jesus. Tertullian called baptism a *sacramentum* because he believed it resembled the solemn and sacred oaths that soldiers undertook when they enlisted in the army.[129] But here is where the debates start. Who should be baptized, how should people be baptized, and what does baptism do for the recipient? These are questions we will engage, and I hope the discussion will prove to be far from "dry"!

Acts of the Apostles	Epistles
When the people heard this, they were cut to the heart and said to Peter and the other apostles, "Brothers, what shall we do?" Peter replied, *"Repent and be baptized, every one of you, in the name of Jesus Christ for the forgiveness of your sins. And you will receive the gift of the Holy Spirit. The promise is for you and your children* and for all who are far off—for all whom the Lord our God will call." (2:37–39) But when they believed Philip as he proclaimed the good news of the kingdom of God and the name of Jesus Christ, *they were baptized*, both men and women. (8:12) Then Philip began with that very passage of Scripture and told him the good news about Jesus. As they traveled along the road, they came to some water and the eunuch said, *"Look, here is water. What can stand in the way of my being baptized?"* And he gave orders to stop the chariot. Then both Philip and the eunuch went down into the water and Philip baptized him. (8:35–38)	Or don't you know that all of us who were *baptized into Christ Jesus were baptized into his death*? We were therefore buried with him *through baptism* into death in order that, just as Christ was raised from the dead through the glory of the Father, we too may live a new life. (Rom 6:3–4) Is Christ divided? Was Paul crucified for you? *Were you baptized into the name of Paul?* I thank God that I did not baptize any of you except Crispus and Gaius, so no one can say that you were baptized into my name. (Yes, I also *baptized the household of Stephanas*; beyond that, I don't remember if I baptized anyone else.) For Christ did not send me to baptize, but to preach the gospel—not with wisdom and eloquence, lest the cross of Christ be emptied of its power. (1 Cor 1:13–17) For I do not want you to be ignorant of the fact, brothers and sisters, that our ancestors were all under the cloud and that they all passed through the sea. *They were*

---

129. Tertullian, *Spect.* 4; *Scorp.* 4; *Mart.* 3.

Then Ananias went to the house and entered it. Placing his hands on Saul, he said, "Brother Saul, the Lord—Jesus, who appeared to you on the road as you were coming here—has sent me so that you may see again and be filled with the Holy Spirit." Immediately, something like scales fell from Saul's eyes, and he could see again. *He got up and was baptized.* (9:17–18)

While Peter was still speaking these words, the Holy Spirit came on all who heard the message. The circumcised believers who had come with Peter were astonished that the gift of the Holy Spirit had been poured out even on Gentiles. For they heard them speaking in tongues and praising God. Then Peter said, *"Surely no one can stand in the way of their being baptized with water. They have received the Holy Spirit just as we have." So he ordered that they be baptized in the name of Jesus Christ.* Then they asked Peter to stay with them for a few days. (10:44–48)

One of those listening was a woman from the city of Thyatira named Lydia, a dealer in purple cloth. She was a worshiper of God. The Lord opened her heart to respond to Paul's message. *When she and the members of her household were baptized,* she invited us to her home. (16:14–15)

At that hour of the night the jailer took them and washed their wounds; *then immediately he and all his household were baptized.* (16:33)

Crispus, the synagogue leader, and his entire household believed in the Lord; and *many of the Corinthians who heard Paul believed and were baptized.* (18:8)

While Apollos was at Corinth, Paul took the road through the interior and arrived at Ephesus. There he found some disciples and asked them, "Did you receive the Holy Spirit when you believed?" They answered, "No, we have not even heard that there is a Holy Spirit." So Paul asked, "Then what baptism did you receive?" "John's baptism," they replied. Paul said, "John's baptism was a baptism of repentance. He told the people to believe in the one coming after him, that is, in Jesus." *On hearing this, they were baptized into the* *all baptized into Moses in the cloud and in the sea.* (1 Cor 10:1–2)

So in Christ Jesus you are all children of God through faith, *for all of you who were baptized into Christ have clothed yourselves with Christ.* (Gal 3:26–27)

In him you were also circumcised with a circumcision not performed by human hands. Your whole self ruled by the flesh was put off when you were circumcised by Christ, *having been buried with him in baptism,* in which you were also raised with him through your faith in the working of God, who raised him from the dead. (Col 2:11–12)

In that state he went and made proclamation to the imprisoned spirits—to those who were disobedient long ago when God waited patiently in the days of Noah while the ark was being built. In it only a few people, eight in all, were saved through water, and *this water symbolizes baptism that now saves you* also—not the removal of dirt from the body but the pledge of a clear conscience toward God. It saves you by the resurrection of Jesus Christ. (1 Pet 3:19–21)

This is the one who came by water and blood—Jesus Christ. He did not come by water only, but by water and blood. And it is the Spirit who testifies, because the Spirit is the truth. For there are three that testify: the Spirit, the water and the blood; and the three are in agreement. (1 John 5:6–8, italics added in all cases)

> *name of the Lord Jesus.* When Paul placed his hands on them, the Holy Spirit came on them, and they spoke in tongues and prophesied. (19:1–6)
>
> You will be his witness to all people of what you have seen and heard. And now what are you waiting for? Get up, *be baptized and wash your sins away*, calling on his name. (22:15–16)

8.6.1.1 WHO SHOULD BE BAPTIZED?

Let's cut to the chase. Do we baptize babies or only believing adults? The three positions we can analyze here are paedobaptism, credobaptism, and dual baptism.

1. *Paedobaptism.* The baptizing of infants is known as paedobaptism; it is practiced by Catholic, Orthodox, Lutheran, Anglican, Methodist, and Reformed churches. It does not mean that they only baptize infants, for adults may be baptized too; but parents are encouraged to present their children for baptism. Infant baptism functions to initiate children into the new covenant and to incorporate them into the visible church. Several arguments for infant baptism have been put forward. Due to my own theological pedigree, I'll focus mostly on arguments from the Reformed tradition.[130]

First, there are biblical-theological arguments for justifying infant baptism. Reformed advocates see a single covenant of grace administered through two historic covenants symbolized first by circumcision (Abrahamic covenants) and later by baptism (new covenant). Circumcision was a sign of God's promise, and that promise is made good in the gospel of Christ, which is symbolized by baptism. What circumcision anticipates, baptism celebrates. The covenant sign of circumcision in the Abrahamic covenant is replaced with baptism as the symbol for the new covenant.

The fruit of the covenant promise emblematized in circumcision consisted of regeneration (Deut 30:6), cleansing (cf. Isa 52:1; Ezek 44:6–7), and repentance (Deut 10:16; Jer 4:4). It is precisely these things that are said to be the fruit of Christ's work and are represented in baptism (Acts 2:38; 22:16; Eph 5:26; Col 2:12; Titus 3:5–7; Heb 10:22). This is why Paul writes to the Colossians: "In him you were also circumcised with a circumcision not performed by human hands. Your whole self ruled by the flesh was put off when *you were circumcised by Christ, having been buried with him in baptism*, in which you were also raised with him through your faith in

---

130. Cf. Sinclair B. Ferguson, "Infant Baptism View," in *Understanding Four Views on Baptism* (ed. J. H. Armstrong; Grand Rapids: Zondervan, 2007), 77–111; Richard L. Pratt, "Reformed View: Baptism as a Sacrament of the Covenant," in *Baptism: Three Views* (ed. D. F. Wright; Downers Grove, IL: InterVarsity Press, 2009), 59–72; Reymond, *New Systematic Theology*, 923–55; Horton, *Christian Faith*, 788–98.

the working of God, who raised him from the dead" (Col 2:11–12, italics added). Here believers undergo a circumcision by Christ when they are buried with him in baptism. The Colossians, then, have undergone the true circumcision defined as their baptism.

George Beasley-Murray, a Baptist scholar, regarded circumcision as replaced by baptism: "Baptism, then, did away with the need for circumcision because it signified the union of the believer with Christ, and in union with Him the old nature was sloughed off.... Baptism differs from circumcision as the new aeon differs from the old; the two rites belong to different worlds."[131] Following this logic the Belgic Confession (sec. 34) states: "Having abolished circumcision, which was done with blood, Christ established in its place the sacrament of baptism.... Baptism does for our children what circumcision did for the Jewish people."[132]

Given this parallelism between circumcision and baptism as markers of covenant initiation, baptism points to God's promises with Abraham eschatologically fulfilled by the work of Jesus Christ. Baptism testifies to an external promise of grace, not the subjective experience of that grace. Baptism is not a sign and seal of faith (i.e., the believers' response to the gospel); rather, it is a sign for faith (i.e., the gospel that elicits faith). Thus, baptism is a "sign and seal" of God's grace in the context of the new covenant (WCF 28.1; cf. Rom 4:11). Just as circumcision was a sign of the promise for children in the covenant family of Israel, so now baptism is the sign of the promise for the children of the covenant family in the church. To quote the Belgic Confession (sec. 34) again: "We believe our children ought to be baptized and sealed with the sign of the covenant, as little children were circumcised in Israel on the basis of the same promises made to our children. And truly, Christ has shed his blood no less for washing the little children of believers than he did for adults."

What is more, if the new covenant is the eschatological fulfillment of the Abrahamic covenant and if the Abrahamic covenant had a place for children, how much more so should the new covenant have a place for children. God has always covenanted with families; hence God's covenant with Noah was between "you and ... your descendants" (Gen 9:9–10). God's covenant with Abraham included "you and your descendents" (17:7–8). Thus, when Peter says that the gospel promise "is for you and your children" (Acts 2:39), we should not be surprised. God calls and covenants with families, who are all part of the covenant promise. If we see baptism as a symbol of God's promise of grace given to the covenant family in the Messiah, we will move away from seeing baptism as simply an outward display of one's own inward experience. Baptism is a sign and symbol for everyone in the messianic fam-

---

131. George R. Beasley-Murray, *Baptism in the New Testament* (London: Macmillan & Co., 1962), 341–42.

132. Quotes from the Belgic Confession can be found at: www.crcna.org/welcome/beliefs/confessions/belgic-confession.

ily. The Church of Scotland's *Book of Common Order* has a fine address to the parents of a child after baptism:

> Your child belongs to God in Christ. From this day she will be at home in the Christian community, and there will always be a place for her. Tell her of her baptism, and unfold to her the treasure she has been given today, so that she may know she is baptized, and, as she grows, make her own response in faith and love, and come in due time to share in the communion of the body and blood of Christ.[133]

Second, the fact that Jesus received children and blessed them when they were brought to him by their parents is believed to overture infant baptism (e.g., Matt 19:13–15/Luke 18:15–17). If the "kingdom of heaven belongs to such as these," they must also belong to the covenant since the new covenant is the legal constitution for the kingdom community. Some also argue that Jesus' command in the Great Commission to make disciples of "all nations" includes children. Furthermore, what it means to "go and make disciples" is defined by the participles "baptizing" and "teaching"—but note which comes first, baptizing! When Peter preached to the Jerusalemites at Pentecost, he told them, "Repent and be baptized, every one of you, in the name of Jesus Christ for the forgiveness of your sins. And you will receive the gift of the Holy Spirit"; then he adds the words, "The promise is for you and your children" (Acts 2:38–39). This was a promise of inclusion in the new covenant for children, not simply predicting an opportunity on a future day for children to decide for themselves to receive Christ.

Paul also points out that in the exodus the Israelites "were all baptized into Moses in the cloud and in the sea" (1 Cor 10:2). This baptism into Moses experienced by the Israelites included children, and it prefigures union with Christ. Peter appeals to the deliverance of Noah and his family through the waters of judgment as a precursor to baptism (1 Pet 3:20–21).

Another matter supporting infant baptism is the narrations about the baptism of entire households in Acts. When the head of a household was converted, the entire household was baptized (see Acts 16:14–15, 33; 18:8). Now a "household" (*oikos*) usually included the *paterfamilias* or male head, his wife, their children, dependent relatives, retainers like employees, freedmen, and slaves. The house was under the authority of the *paterfamilias*, and his religion was their religion. So most likely all were baptized and incorporated into the faith of the *paterfamilias*.

Third, the church fathers contain another resource for supporting the practice of infant baptism. To set the record straight, the church fathers are a mixed bag on baptism. Both paedobaptists and credobaptists can find church fathers to support

---

133. *Book of Common Order of the Church of Scotland* (Edinburgh: Saint Andrews Press, 1994), 90.

their view, but they seldom take time to look at some of the erroneous theological reasons given by the fathers as to why they held their views. So, yes, aha, the church baptized babies, but only because some of them believed in baptismal regeneration. Then, yes, aha, the church baptized believers, but only because people delayed baptism on account of their thinking that there was no remission for postbaptismal sins.

That caveat aside, we can note the following. Infant baptism emerges in funeral inscriptions from the third century for children who died in infancy or childhood and who had a "clinical" baptism applied shortly before death. Irenaeus (ca. 115–202) might allude to infant baptism when he wrote: "He [Christ] came to save all through his own person; all that is, who through him are reborn to God; infants, children, boys, young men and old."[134] When Tertullian (ca. 160–220) opposed infant baptism, he did not do it on the grounds that it was a recent innovation; instead, he thought baptism was a kind of trump card to play at the end of one's life. Origen (ca. 185–254) regarded infant baptism as a tradition received from the apostles when he wrote: "It is on this account as well that the Church has received the tradition from the apostles to give baptism even to little children."[135] When Cyprian (ca. 200–258) wrote to Fidus on the subject of infant baptism, Fidus's main problem with baptizing babies was that they were still impure after childbirth. Cyprian responded that the grace of God avails for everyone irrespective of age:

> [Therefore,] no one ought to be hindered from baptism and from the grace of God, who is merciful and kind and loving to all. Which ... we think is to be even more observed in respect of infants and newly-born persons, who on this very account deserve more from our help and from the divine mercy, that immediately, on the very beginning of their birth, lamenting and weeping, they do nothing else but entreat.[136]

The *Apostolic Tradition*, possibly written by Hippolytus in Rome in the late second or early third century, mentions the process of candidacy for baptism, and it includes a liturgical order for the baptism of children:

> At the hour in which the cock crows, they shall first pray over the water. When they come to the water, the water shall be pure and flowing, that is, the water of a spring or a flowing body of water. Then they shall take off all their clothes. The children shall be baptized first. All of the children who can answer for themselves, let them answer. If there are any children who cannot answer for themselves, let their parents answer for them, or someone else from their family.[137]

It seems, then, that by AD 175 infant baptism was practiced in Lyon (Irenaeus), Carthage (Tertullian, Cyprian), Alexandria (Origen), and Rome (Hippolytus).

Fourth, there are said to be several problems with the credobaptist view accord-

---

134. Irenaeus, *Haer.* 2.22.4.
135. Origen, *Comm. Rom.* 5.9.11.
136. Cyprian, *Sent.* 58.5.
137. *Trad. Ap.* 21.1–5.

ing to paedobaptist advocates. Perhaps the most compelling objection is that it leaves the children of believing parents in a kind of spiritual limbo. On the credobaptist scheme, children have no positive status before God other than being providentially blessed by growing up in a Christian household, where they receive instruction in the Christian faith. Children are pagans at worst and potential Christians at best. However, if we keep thinking in terms of covenant and family, which is how God has always done business with his people, there must be some positive position for children in the church family. It is impossible to regard children as covenantally holy in their family if their entire family is not in fact integrated into the covenant of grace (see 1 Cor 7:14).

In fact, credobaptists sense this covenantal and familial pressure, which is precisely why they invented the ritual of infant dedications. They want to show that children brought into the believing home are holy and cherished by God, but the problem is that they lack the theological framework to do so consistently with their own beliefs about baptism, covenant, and church.

2. *Credobaptism.* The baptism of persons upon a profession of faith is known as "credobaptism." It is practiced by Anabaptist, Baptist, Pentecostal, Independent, and Free churches. In some cases, they do baptize children, but generally only upon a confession of faith and after questioning by the pastor. The important thing to remember about credobaptism is that it is not so much based on the absence of infant baptism in the New Testament. Instead, it is based on their doctrine of the church. The hub of the credobaptist position is the conviction that the church consists entirely of a regenerate membership. Therefore, since baptism is the means of initiation into the church, they only baptize those who show signs of regeneration and make a profession of faith. Baptism is for believers and is an outward sign of an inward experience. In historic Baptist doctrine: "Those who do actually profess repentance towards God, faith in, and obedience to, our Lord Jesus Christ, are the only proper subjects of this ordinance [of baptism]" (1689 LBC 29.2).[138]

A vast array of biblical evidence is assembled in defense of credobaptism. First, one may observe that there is a recurrent pattern in Acts where people "believed" and then get "baptized": "Repent and be baptized" (Acts 2:38); "those who accepted his message were baptized" (2:41); "when they believed Philip as he proclaimed the good news of the kingdom of God and the name of Jesus Christ, they were baptized, both men and women" (8:12); "Simon himself believed and was baptized" (8:13); "surely no one can stand in the way of their being baptized with water. They have

---

138. For an online version of the London Baptist Confession, see www.1689.com/confession.html. Cf. also Bruce A. Ware, "Believer's Baptism View," in *Understanding Four Views on Baptism* (ed. J. H. Armstrong; Grand Rapids: Zondervan, 2007), 19–50; Thomas J. Nettles, "Baptist View: Baptism as a Symbol of Christ's Saving Work," in *Baptism: Three Views* (ed. D. F. Wright; Downers Grove, IL: InterVarsity Press, 2009), 25–41; Erickson, *Christian Theology*, 1098–1114; Grudem, *Systematic Theology*, 966–87.

received the Holy Spirit just as we have" (10:47); "many of the Corinthians who heard Paul believed and were baptized" (18:8); "'[John] told the people to believe in the one coming after him, that is, in Jesus.' On hearing this, they were baptized in the name of the Lord Jesus" (19:4–5). Undoubtedly conversion and baptism go hand in hand in the New Testament.

Second, many of the standard texts used to prop up infant baptism are said to be misinterpreted by paedobaptists. It is possible to take Peter's word that "the promise is for you and your children" as a promise that they too can receive the Holy Spirit if they believe and are baptized (Acts 2:39). Also, Paul's remark about circumcision and baptism in Colossians 2:11–12 ("Your whole self ruled by the flesh was put off when you were circumcised by Christ, having been buried with him in baptism") is misconstrued by paedobaptists. What replaces circumcision here is not baptism but regeneration, the circumcision of the heart.[139]

Third, baptism frequently signifies the believer's death to their old way of life and their entrance into new life in Christ. Hence Paul's remarks about "having been buried with [Christ] in baptism, in which you were also raised with him through your faith in the working of God, who raised him from the dead" (Col 2:12), and "we were therefore buried with him through baptism into death in order that, just as Christ was raised from the dead through the glory of the Father, we too may live a new life" (Rom 6:4). Baptism, then, is a symbolic way of identifying a shift from a former life of slavery in sin to the new life in Christ. On a few occasions baptism is linked with the Spirit (1 Cor 12:13; Titus 3:5); however, the Spirit is received by faith (Acts 2:38–39; Gal 3:2, 5). If baptism externally symbolizes an inward experience of faith, then one must have faith in order to be baptized.

Fourth, concerning household baptisms, Scripture is admittedly unclear as to who was baptized, but two things call for comment. To begin with, some think that "household" means slaves and retainers, not children. This is suggested by Paul's commendation of the household of Stephanus: "You know that the household of Stephanas were the first converts in Achaia, and they have devoted themselves to the service of the Lord's people" (1 Cor 16:15).[140] The whole "household" contained converts who were dedicated to Christian service. Also, some argue that it was those who believed within the household who were baptized, not necessarily everyone en masse. At the house of the Philippian jailer, Paul and Silas "spoke the word of the Lord to him and to all the others in his house," and from them people were baptized (Acts 16:32). Similarly, concerning Crispus in Corinth, "his entire household

---

139. Cf. Michael F. Bird, *Colossians and Philemon* (NCCS; Eugene, OR: Cascade, 2009), 78; J. P. T. Hunt, "Colossians 2:11–12, The Circumcision/Baptism Analogy, and Infant Baptism," *TynBul* 41 (1990): 227–44.

140. James D. G. Dunn, *The Theology of Paul the Apostle* (Edinburgh: T&T Clark, 1998), 457–58.

believed in the Lord; and many of the Corinthians who heard Paul believed and were baptized" (18:8). James Dunn concludes:

> For it has to be recognized that *infant baptism can find no real support in the theology of baptism which any NT writer can be shown to espouse*. And the more we recognize the primary function of baptism throughout the first decades of Christianity was to serve as a means of expressing the initiate's faith and commitment, the less justified in terms of Christian beginnings would the practice of infant baptism appear to be.[141]

Fifth, credobaptists argue that the baptism of believers was the dominant position in the first three hundred years of the church. Tertullian's work *Baptism* is the earliest extended theological discussion of baptism in the early church, and it is clearly in favor of baptism upon profession of faith.[142] For Tertullian, "preaching comes first, baptizing later, when preaching has preceded."[143] Elsewhere he comments, "Baptismal washing is a sealing of faith, which faith is begun and commended by the faith of repentance."[144] He vigorously opposed baptizing children and stated that they should come "when they are learning, when they are being taught what they are coming to: let them be made Christians when they have come competent to know Christ."[145] For Tertullian this "believer's baptism" is far from just symbolic, for it is associated with the forgiveness of sins and new birth. In the first chapter of *Baptism* he writes, "Happy is our sacrament of water, in that, by washing away the sins of our early blindness, we are set free and admitted into eternal life!" Tertullian even describes Christians as little fishes "born" in the water: "But we, little fishes, after the example of our *icthys*, Jesus Christ, are born in water, nor have we safety in any other way than by permanently abiding in water." Everett Ferguson in his magisterial and exhaustive study of baptism in the early church concludes:

> There is general agreement that there is no firm evidence for infant baptism before the latter part of the second century.... Arguments against the originality of baby baptism, in addition to its lack of early attestation, include: the essential nature ascribed to verbal confession and repentance; the liturgy designed for persons of responsible age; size of baptisteries; and the lack of an agreed theology to support it.[146]

Sixth, from a theological horizon, Karl Barth and Markus Barth argued against infant baptism. They rejected any sacramental position and any concept of mediation of grace in baptism. Markus Barth successfully changed his father's mind on

---

141. James D. G. Dunn, *Unity and Diversity in the New Testament* (2nd ed.; London: SCM, 1990), 160 (italics original).
142. Cf. Everett Ferguson, *Baptism in the Early Church: History, Theology, and Liturgy in the First Five Centuries* (Grand Rapids: Eerdmans, 2009), 336–50.
143. Tertullian, *Bapt.* 14.
144. Tertullian, *Paen.* 6.16–17.
145. Tertullian, *Bapt.* 18.
146. Ferguson, *Baptism*, 856–57.

baptism by an exegetical argument for believer's baptism.[147] The younger Barth wrote: "Baptism will be understood only as proclamation, thanks, and praise of that which has already occurred in Christ and was also appropriated—as also a 'burial' among Christians is confirmed—and proclaimed in thanks and praise as the already commencing death and certainty of resurrection."[148]

Karl Barth saw baptism as uniting a divine action (Spirit baptism) with a human action (faith). These actions are united together because Jesus died on our behalf, and his death is a promise for everyone to experience the Spirit and the final resurrection. The human action moves toward the divine action in Christ, who achieves this for us. Barth's key objection is that infant baptism does not reflect this unity between the divine and human action.[149] For Barth:

> Baptism takes place in active recognition of the grace of God which justifies, sanctifies and calls. It is not itself, however, the bearer, means, or instrument of grace. Baptism responds to a mystery, the sacrament of the history of Jesus Christ, of His resurrection, of the outpouring of the Holy Spirit. It is not itself, however, a mystery or sacrament.[150]

Barth is driven in his view by the fact that Christian discipleship cannot be inherited.[151]

3. *Dual baptism.* A third position is for churches to permit both views of baptism, credo- and paedo-, to be practiced side by side.[152] This policy of dual baptism is held by the Nazarene Church, American Evangelical Covenant Church, Evangelical Free Church, French Reformed Church, and Presbyterian Church (USA). John Bunyan, the Baptist Puritan and author of *Pilgrim's Progress*, accepted paedobaptists into fellowship. As far as I know, most paedobaptist churches do not force congregants to baptize their children but only refuse to rebaptize adults, so they are technically open to believer's baptism. There are a number of reasons why this is a defensible and even desirable theological stance.

First, we should recognize that baptism in the New Testament is not "believer's baptism," but "convert's baptism." George R. Beasley-Murray has pointed out that baptism and conversion are "inseparable" and one demands the other; neither is complete without the other. Yet he also notes that the child growing up in a Chris-

---

147. Markus Barth, *Die Taufe—ein Sakrament?: Ein exegetischer Beitrag zum Gespräch über die kirchliche Taufe* (Zollikon-Zürich: Evangelische Verlag, 1951); idem, "Baptism and Evangelism," *SJT* 12 (1959): 32–40. See his lectures available online at http://cruciality.wordpress.com/2010/04/05/markus-barth-on-baptism-in-the-new-testament-and-today/.

148. Markus Barth and Helmut Blanke, *Colossians: A New Translation with Introduction and Commentary* (AB; trans. A. B. Beck; New York: Doubleday, 1994), 369.

149. Barth, *CD*, IV/4:102–7. For a response to Barth, see Horton, *People and Place*, 118–19.

150. Barth, *CD*, IV/4:102.

151. John Webster, *Barth's Ethics of Reconciliation* (Cambridge: Cambridge University Press, 1995), 163.

152. Anthony N. S. Lane, "Dual-Practice Baptism View," in *Baptism: Three Views* (ed. D. F. Wright; Downers Grove, IL: InterVarsity Press, 2009), 139–71.

tian family is in a different position from one growing up in an unbelieving home. A Christian child lives in a converted home, not a pagan one.[153] Even if children in converted "households" are not baptized, their conversion and baptism may be regarded as being done by *proxy* through their parents. That may sound strange to those accustomed to a free, libertarian, and individualist society, but the households of the ancient world were an extended family unit with a shared identity and a sense of corporate personhood.

Moreover, neither Acts nor Paul shows a clear affirmation for the need to baptize second-generation Christians whose parents were themselves baptized. While technically the children were unbaptized, yet the conversion-baptism ritual undergone by their parents included them by proxy in virtue of their parent's representative position as heads of the house. If we grant this conversion-initiation link and if we accept the representative significance of the *paterfamilias* in a family unit, we should not ask if the early church baptized babies. Rather, we should ask if they ever thought to baptize the children of converts at all. I suspect that eventually this practice of proxy baptism for the children of converts was abandoned and the church diverged along two paths: believer's baptism and infant baptism.[154]

Second, continuing on from my first point, I think this explains why both believer's baptism and infant baptism were practiced by Christian communities concurrently up to the third century. The fact that Tertullian and Gregory of Nazianzus opposed infant baptism proves the existence of people who both practiced it and questioned it. It appears that the early church had divergent opinions on the subject, yet this was never thought to be a threat to the unity and oneness of the church. There was a frank acceptance of diversity of opinion on the matter.[155]

Third, one can acknowledge that there is much to learn from both paedobaptism and credobaptism. Paedobaptism warns against individualism and highlights that God deals with families, not just individuals. Infant baptism showcases the prevenient nature of God's grace and the operation of this grace in the believing community. Credobaptism warns against nominal belief and highlights the need for a personal experience of God. Believer's baptism brings to the surface the vital importance of proclaiming the gospel to our children and teenagers to bring them to a point of personal faith.[156]

Fourth, another factor for us to consider is that baptism itself is a doctrine of secondary importance. Beyond the foundational Christian beliefs about repentance and faith, the author of Hebrews knows of a second tier of elementary Christian beliefs

---

153. Beasley-Murray, *Baptism*, 393–95.

154. The idea of baptism by proxy may explain why some in Corinth were performing baptisms on behalf of the dead (see 1 Cor 15:29).

155. Lane, "Dual-Practice," 154.

156. Ibid., 167–68.

concerning "baptisms" (Heb 6:2).[157] In a theological triage we can classify Christian beliefs into three categories: (1) essential beliefs, things without which one cannot claim to be a Christian, such as belief in the gospel, Trinity, incarnation, return of Christ, inspiration of Scripture; (2) important beliefs, either significant for church order or doctrinally disputed areas, but not of salvific import, such as church government, can women be preachers, covenant theology versus dispensational theology, schemes of eschatology, Lord's Supper, and baptism; and (3) indifferent matters, things that are a matter of conscience and conviction, such as whether Christians should drink alcohol, home schooling versus public schooling, and preferred Bible translations. If baptism is a second order doctrine, it should not be a barrier to unity and fellowship in churches that proclaim the gospel and profess Jesus as Lord.

Fifth, it seems to me that there is a deep need in the church to do something to acknowledge that a child has entered into the home of believing parents and to acknowledge a time when this child has made this faith his or her own. So credobaptists hold "infant dedications" to signify the entrance of the child into a believing home and to make a corporate promise by parents and parishioners to raise up the child in the instruction of the Lord. Later, should the child come to a decision of personal faith later in life, he or she is baptized. For paedobaptists, they baptize their children as a sign and seal of the covenant of grace, and a later time when the child is older and wishes to formally make an affirmation of their baptismal promises, they become "confirmed" as a member of the church.

Simply from a sociological view, it looks as if (1) we need some ritual or event to show publicly that a child has been brought into a believing family and to commit ourselves to raise this child "as" or "to be" a Christian, all in the context of the wider body of Christ; and (2) we also need some ritual or ceremony to show that this parents' child has appropriated their parents' faith and taken their own place in the community of the gospelized. The million dollar question is: Where do you put the water? At the initiatory ritual or at the confirming ritual? I want to tentatively suggest that if you have a public initiation of the child into God's family and if you have a public declaration of the child's own faith later, then where you put the water isn't the most important part! That will dissatisfy most credobaptists and paedobaptists, but I find it gospelically satisfying.[158] Brad Harper and Paul Metzger hold to

---

157. Cf. the NIV translation of "cleansing rites," where the ESV has "washings" and the NRSV uses "baptisms."

158. I should point out that this is not strictly possible in an ecclesiology that holds that the local church consists exclusively of the regenerate. I believe that the church in fact consists of an *ecclesia mixta* (i.e., a mix of the regenerate and unregenerate). That is because: (1) I've been in churches where they think that everyone who is a member is regenerate, but clearly everyone who was a member was not regenerate; and (2) the warning passages in Heb 6:4–6 and Jesus' teaching about the wheat and weeds in Matt 13:34–40 only make sense if the church is a mixed community of authentic and inauthentic believers. Simon Magus "believed and was baptized," qualifying for church membership, but in Christian tradition he was regarded as the founder of Gnosticism (see Acts 8:12–24).

§ 8.6 Emblems of the Gospel: Baptism and Lord's Supper

credobaptism, but they go so far as to suggest that "a theology of unity supersedes a particular theology of infant or believer baptism; thus, we honor the baptism of infants and do not feel it necessary for those baptized as infants to be rebaptized unless it is a matter of conscience."[159]

Sixth, it might be possible also to construct a definition of baptism that paedobaptists and credobaptists might be able to accept. J. I. Packer, an Anglican paedobaptist, offers a definition of baptism along these lines:

> Christian baptism ... is a sign from God that signifies inward cleansing and remission of sins (Acts 22:16; 1 Cor 6:11; Eph 5:25–27), Spirit-wrought regeneration and new life (Titus 3:5), and the abiding presence of the Holy Spirit as God's seal testifying and guaranteeing that one will be kept safe in Christ forever (1 Cor 12:13; Eph 1:13–14). Baptism carries these meanings because first and fundamentally it signifies union with Christ in his death, burial, and resurrection (Rom 6:3–7; Col 2:11–12); and this union with Christ is the source of every element in our salvation (1 John 5:11–12). Receiving the sign in faith assures the persons baptized that God's gift of new life in Christ is freely given them.[160]

Although I started out as a credobaptist and moved to becoming a paedobaptist, it is this dual-baptism view that I admittedly gravitate to because I think it allows us to hold together two competing theologies on a nonessential matter of the faith. A dual-baptism position enables us to make sure that baptism, a symbol of the gospel, becomes a means of gospel unity, rather than an occasion for division in the already-all-too-much divided churches.

8.6.1.2 HOW SHOULD PEOPLE BE BAPTIZED?

I've heard some energetic Baptist preachers passionately thump their pulpits that "*baptizō* means 'immerse,' not 'sprinkle.'" From a linguistic standpoint they are right as the nouns *baptisma* and *baptismos* mean "plunging, dipping, washing," while the verb *baptizō* means "to submerge, immerse" (often cited is 2 Kgs 5:14 [LXX], "So he went down and dipped himself [*ebaptisato*] in the Jordan seven times").[161] Such language was also used for the dyeing of fabrics that were washed in a new color. By analogy, in baptism by immersion, Christians are dipped and dyed into the death of Christ (Rom 6:3), they rise from the waters like Christ in his resurrection (Rom 6:4), and thereafter they are clothed with Christ in following his example (Rom 13:11–14; Gal 3:27). Baptism by full immersion would seem to

---

159. Harper and Metzger, *Exploring Ecclesiology*, 141.
160. J. I. Packer, *Concise Theology* (Wheaton, IL: Tyndale, 1993), 212. Note the approving comments of Bruce Ware, "Believer's Baptism View," 41 n.34.
161. Cf. BDAG, 164–65; Ferguson, *Baptism*, 38–59; Eckhard J. Schnabel, "The Language of Baptism: The Meaning of βαπτίζω in the New Testament," in *Understanding the Times: New Testament Studies in the 21st Century* (ed. A. J. Köstenberger and R. W. Yarbrough; Festschrift D. A. Carson; Wheaton, IL: Crossway, 2011), 217–46.

be the natural choice of means that speaks to the reality of dying and rising with Christ.[162] Baptism by full immersion was also practiced widely in the early church, and the liturgical handbooks often prescribe immersion three times—in the name of Father, the Son, and the Holy Spirit.[163]

However, this does not mean that baptism by immersion is required or necessary for a baptism to be valid. While immersion in water evokes the image of dying and rising with Christ, pouring water over someone evokes the image of being baptized by the Holy Spirit. Both images—union with Christ and Spirit baptism—indicate the initiatory element of salvation and emblematize the gospel. Moreover, John Smyth, the founder of the Baptists, was apparently self-baptized by pouring water over himself.[164] The *Didache* gives some instruction about baptism that prescribes baptism in a stream (presumably by immersion), but permits baptism by pouring if no such water is nearby.[165]

I would suggest that these two modes of baptism, by immersion or by affusion, should be retained because they both point to Jesus as the baptized and the baptizer. Immersion calls to mind Jesus' own "baptism," which is his death (Mark 10:38–39; Luke 12:50), while affusion is a moving picture of Jesus as the dispenser of the Holy Spirit (Matt 3:11; John 15:26; 16:7; Acts 2:1–4; 1 Cor 12:13).

8.6.1.3 WHAT DOES BAPTISM DO FOR THE RECIPIENT?

The blessing of baptism is varyingly understood. On the one hand, some (mainly credobaptists) see baptism as an external sign of an inward experience. Baptism is a public testimony of an invisible grace that one believes in Christ and has received the gift of the Holy Spirit. There is no real spiritual benefit to baptism; the only blessing is that of obedience, and afterward a person can be formally admitted into membership in a local church.[166] A key passage used to support this practice is Galatians 3:26–27: "So in Christ Jesus you are all children of God through faith, for all of you who were baptized into Christ have clothed yourselves with Christ." According to Karl Barth, this text

> is looking back to the divine change, to the putting on of Christ which in Jesus Christ Himself has been effected objectively and subjectively for the recipients of the epistle by His Holy Spirit, and that baptism is recalled as the concrete moment

---

162. Cf. Beasley-Murray, *Baptism*, 133; Erickson, *Christian Theology*, 1113–14; Nettles, "Baptist View," 26–27; Ware, "Believer's Baptism View," 21–23.

163. Cf. Timothy George, *Galatians* (NAC; Nashville: Broadman & Holman, 1994), 280–81.

164. Jason K. Lee, *The Theology of John Smyth: Puritan, Separatist, Baptist, Mennonite* (Macon, GA: Mercer University Press, 2003), 71–74.

165. *Did* 7.1–4.

166. Cf. Erickson, *Christian Theology*, 1105–6, 1110; but see Grudem, *Systematic Theology*, 980–81, who sees baptism as a means to enjoying God's favor, fostering joy in the believer, reassurance in Christ's work, and a means to strengthen and encourage faith.

in their own life in which they for their part confirmed, recognized and accepted their investing with Christ from above, their ontic relationship to Him, not only in gratitude and hope, but also in readiness and vigilance.[167]

Baptism is a gospel picture of conversion portrayed in the descending into and rising from the water.

Another position locates baptism as the moment of new birth; this is called "baptismal regeneration." It is a view held by Catholics, Lutherans, Anglo-Catholics, and even Churches of Christ. For example, the Catechism of the Catholic Church teaches that baptism brings the forgiveness of sins, new creation, and incorporation into the church.[168] The Augsburg Confession (art. 9) declares that baptism "is necessary to salvation and that through Baptism is offered the grace of God"; they condemn the Anabaptists, "who reject the Baptism of children, and say that children are saved without Baptism." Similar is the Anglican Thirty-Nine Articles (art. 27):

> Baptism is not only a sign of profession, and mark of difference [from the world] ... but is also a sign of Regeneration or new Birth, whereby, as by an instrument, they that receive Baptism rightly are grafted into the Church; the promises of the forgiveness of sin, and of our adoption to be the sons of God by the Holy Ghost, are visibly signed and sealed; Faith is confirmed, and Grace increased by virtue of prayer unto God.[169]

Though the Catholic tradition regards baptismal regeneration as occurring *ex opere operato*, automatically effective in and through itself, irrespective of the faith of the baptizer or baptizee, other traditions have urged the necessity of faith by either the baptizee or by the parents who present their children for baptism. The sacramentalist position is argued on several biblical grounds.

First, baptism is regarded as a means of reception of the Spirit. Jesus received the Spirit at his own baptism, which sets a precedent for his followers (Matt 3:16). Jesus told Nicodemus, "Very truly I tell you, no one can enter the kingdom of God unless they are born of water and the Spirit" (John 3:5). Given the earlier contrast in the Fourth Gospel between John the Baptist, who baptizes in water (John 1:26, 31), and Jesus, who will baptize in the Spirit (John 1:33), here "born of water and the Spirit" could have something to do with water baptism and baptism in the Spirit. The two go together by association, or maybe water baptism is the means to the Spirit baptism.[170] The *locus classicus* for baptismal regeneration is Peter's speech at Pentecost:

---

167. Barth, *CD*, IV/4:116.
168. *CCC*, 1262–74.
169. The Westminster Confession (27.5) protests: "Although it [baptism] is a great sin to condemn or neglect this ordinance, yet grace and salvation are not so inseparably annexed unto it, as that no person can be regenerated, or saved, without it: or, that all that are baptized are undoubtedly regenerated."
170. Cf. J. Ramsey Michaels, *The Gospel of John* (NICNT; Grand Rapids: Eerdmans, 2010), 182–85.

"Repent and be baptized, every one of you, in the name of Jesus Christ for the forgiveness of your sins. And you will receive the gift of the Holy Spirit" (Acts 2:38). Though this is admittedly only one conversion-baptism account of many in Acts, it shows that baptism was a means to reception of the Spirit for the Jerusalemites.

Second, baptism is an instrument of union with Christ. Romans 6:3–4 ("all of us who were baptized into Christ Jesus were baptized into his death ... we were therefore buried with him through baptism into death") and Galatians 3:27 ("all of you who were baptized into Christ have clothed yourselves with Christ") regard baptism as a means to being united, identified, and incorporated into the crucified and risen Lord. Here the baptismal water is a type of conductor that unites us to Christ through the electrifying power of the Holy Spirit.

Third, baptism is connected with several salvific blessings, such as forgiveness of sins, new birth, sanctification, and even justification. After Paul's christophany on the road to Damascus, Ananias told him "Get up, be baptized and wash your sins away" (Acts 22:16). It is interesting how this same language of "washing" occurs elsewhere. Paul wrote to Titus that God "saved us, not because of righteous things we had done, but because of his mercy. He saved us through the washing of rebirth and renewal by the Holy Spirit" (Titus 3:5). There are probable echoes of baptism when Paul writes to the Corinthians: "But you were washed, you were sanctified, you were justified in the name of the Lord Jesus Christ and by the Spirit of our God" (1 Cor 6:11). Even more provocatively, Peter tells Christians in Asia Minor that just as Noah and his sons were saved through the floodwaters, so too "this water symbolizes baptism that now saves you also—not the removal of dirt from the body but the pledge of a clear conscience toward God. It saves you by the resurrection of Jesus" (1 Pet 3:21). Did you hear that? "Baptism ... now saves you"!

These passages collectively indicate that baptism is more than a symbol.[171] The biblical language includes images of rebirth, renewal, forgiveness, salvation, and union with Christ, all intimately associated with baptism.[172] Ferguson comments: "The New Testament and early Christian literature are virtually unanimous in ascribing a saving significance to baptism."[173]

Now I would contest a strict view of baptismal regeneration because experience tells me that people get regenerated apart from baptism, and this is confirmed by other conversions in the book of Acts that take place before baptism. Yes, Acts 2:38 ties baptism to the Spirit, but most likely it was to make it emphatic to the Jerusa-

---

171. Note the words of David Wright (*What Has Infant Baptism Done to Baptism? An Enquiry into the End of Christendom* [Milton Keynes, UK: Paternoster, 2005], 91): "There is not a single text which prima facie ascribes to baptism only a symbolic or representational or significatory function"; see also Beasley-Murray (*Baptism*, 262): "The idea that baptism is a purely symbolic rite must be pronounced not alone unsatisfactory but out of harmony with the New Testament itself."

172. Pratt, "Reformed View," 61.

173. Ferguson, *Baptism*, 854.

lemites that Jesus' *name* brings the forgiveness of sins and Jesus' *name* bequeaths to them the Spirit—all the more important if people in this audience included those who had chanted for Jesus' execution only a few weeks earlier.

John 3:3–5 is an opaque text, certainly open to a baptismal interpretation, but it looks like a general affirmation that God gives life and new birth to believers.[174] Concerning 1 Peter 3:21, yes, baptism "saves you," but only in conjunction with the subjective response of the pledge of a clear conscience and objectively in the resurrection of Jesus Christ. So now that we have put the baptismal sacramentalist to the exegetical sword, we might relax and content ourselves with the view that baptism is purely symbolic for dying and rising with Christ and anything more than that is engaging in a liturgical legalism.

But not so fast! Baptism is indeed symbolic, but it's no empty symbol. Baptism is not simply a witness to God's grace or an expression of someone's faith experience. It is essential to note that the New Testament knows of no divorce between the reception of the Spirit and the confession of Christ in baptism. The New Testament will not permit us to divide Christ and the Spirit from baptism. The early church did not believe in a baptism that merely symbolized the work of saving grace. Instead, they believed in the experience of grace given by the Spirit, yet intrinsically bound up with baptism, faith, union with Christ, and the life of the age to come.[175] Baptism is part of the salvific drama with a chorus of actors chanting their lines in solos, duets, counterpoints, and chorales. The result is not a cacophony of noise, but a sweet harmony of sound. Spirit, baptism, faith, and union with Christ are all indelibly connected together in one dramatic movement.

In what order? Well, there is none; they are just there. You don't have to look at pictures in a picture book in any particular order. The Spirit goes where he wishes. Sometimes he likes to take a dip with believers; other times he sits by the pool. What we can say is that baptism is a means of symbolically rehearsing Christ's death and resurrection, it's one way of receiving the Spirit, it marks our transference to live under the lordship of Jesus Christ, it places us on the breast of our mother the church, it initiates us into the community of the gospelized, it's a key element in the journey of our own salvation from spiritual death to new birth to life in the new creation, and it reinforces our identity with Christ. So much so that when we go into the waters of baptism, we never come out the same person as we went in! When we come away from the baptismal waters, we are stained with Christ. From that moment we are most definitely clothed with Christ, and we can exhort ourselves to holiness and good works by remembering, as Martin Luther did, "I am a baptized Christian."

---

174. D. A. Carson, *The Gospel according to John* (PNTC; Grand Rapids: Eerdmans, 1991), 194.

175. Beasley-Murray, *Baptism*, 277.

8.6.1.4 CONCLUSION

When Paul said that there was "one Lord, one faith, one baptism" (Eph 4:5), I wonder which baptism he had in mind? Did he mean believer's baptism or infant baptism? I think he simply meant Christian baptism—baptism that is performed in obedience to Christ's command, in the name of the Triune God, and which initiates the recipient into the church of Jesus Christ.

Debates about baptism are not going to go away. The outstanding issue is how we in the evangelical churches, who hold different views on this matter, intend to get along with each other. One strategy could be to simply acknowledge that baptism is a second order issue, to engage in polite banter on the subject here and there, but get on with the business of being Baptists, Anglicans, or Presbyterians, each in our own setting. We might politely demur from recognizing each other's baptismal theology, but we should still treat one another in a gracious fashion at conferences, at seminaries, or in parachurch organizations.

Still, I have a bold proposal for you. If we base our doctrine of baptism not on the doctrine of the church (credobaptism) or on the doctrine of the covenant (paedobaptism), but on the doctrine of the gospel, then perhaps we can reach a point of "equivalent alternatives" regarding baptism.[176] On such a view, we are compelled to recognize any baptism that is tied to the message of the gospel and to a gospel-proclaiming community. Take heed as to how Paul prioritizes his gospel ministry over his baptizing activities, all in the context of addressing church divisions drawn partly over baptism! He writes: "I thank God that I did not baptize any of you except Crispus and Gaius, so no one can say that you were baptized in my name.... For Christ did not send me to baptize, but to preach the gospel—not with wisdom and eloquence, lest the cross of Christ be emptied of its power" (1 Cor 1:14–17).

If a similar priority invades our divisions over baptism, what might the outcome be? Well, perhaps we will be compelled to provide a generous recognition of the genuine "Christianness" of any baptism administered in the name of the Triune God, in obedience to Christ, and which showcases the gospel, even if we disagree as to its mode and occasion. We are not baptized into a denomination; we are baptized into Christ. Thus, we receive all other believers as fellow baptized Christians, believing that baptism is a bond that unites us together as we are all baptized into the Lord Jesus and we are all baptized by one Spirit into one church.

FURTHER READING

Beasley-Murray, George R. *Baptism in the New Testament*. London: Macmillan, 1962.

---

176. Lane, "Dual-Practice," 164.

Bird, Michael F. "Re-Thinking a Sacramental View of Baptism and the Lord's Supper for the Post-Christendom Baptist Church." Pp. 61–76 in *Baptist Sacramentalism 2* (ed. Anthony R. Cross and Philip E. Thompson; SBHT 25; Milton Keynes, UK: Paternoster, 2008).

Ferguson, Everett. *Baptism in the Early Church: History, Theology, and Liturgy in the First Five Centuries.* Grand Rapids: Eerdmans, 2009.

Hyde, Daniel R. *Jesus Loves the Little Children: Why We Baptize Infants.* Grand Rapids: Reformed Fellowship, 2006.

Kline, Meredith G. *By Oath Consigned: A Reinterpretation of the Covenant Signs of Circumcision and Baptism.* Grand Rapids: Eerdmans, 1968.

Murray, John. *Christian Baptism.* Phillipsburg, NJ: Presbyterian & Reformed, 1980.

Schreiner, Thomas R., and Shawn D. Wright, eds. *Believer's Baptism: The Sign of the New Covenant.* Nashville: Broadman & Holman, 2006.

Strawberry, Greg, ed. *The Case for Covenantal Infant Baptism.* Phillipsburg, NJ: Presbyterian & Reformed, 2003.

Wright, David F. *What Has Infant Baptism Done to Baptism? An Enquiry at the End of Christendom.* Milton Keynes, UK: Paternoster, 2005.

8.6.2 A FEAST OF MEANINGS: THE EUCHARIST

For two thousand years one of the most visible emblems of historical Christianity has been that believers have ordinarily met together to share an extraordinary meal to celebrate the death and resurrection of Jesus Christ. The meal goes by many names: "the breaking of bread," "communion," "the Lord's Table," the "Lord's Supper," an "Agape feast," and my favorite term, the "Eucharist."[177] It is genuinely sad that this meal, which is intended as a sign of unity within the church, has been a point of fierce and enduring divisions. It has separated Catholics and Protestants from each other. It has also separated Lutheran, Free, and Reformed churches from each other. Many pressing questions arise: In what way is Jesus present in the bread and wine? What benefit does one get in partaking? Who can preside at communion? How often should communion be held, and who can attend? These are hard questions, and we cannot shy away from them. We cannot retreat into a meal-less and symbol-less Christianity because too much is at stake in the Eucharist.

The Eucharist is ultimately a microcosm of our theology since what we think about the gospel, salvation, Christ, and community surfaces in our theology of the Eucharist. The meaning of the Eucharist is ultimately anchored in a story, in fact, *the story*. It is a snapshot of the grand narrative about God, creation, the fall, Israel, the

---

177. The word *Eucharist* comes from the Greek *eucharistia*, meaning "thanksgiving."

exile, the Messiah, the church, and the consummation. The bread and the wine tell a story about God, redemption, Jesus, and salvation. Tom Wright suggests, "The question for us must be: How can we, today, get in on this story? How can we understand this remarkable gift of God and use it properly? How can we make the best of it?"[178]

I propose that the Eucharist is the gospel meal for the gospelizing community. It is the celebration of the new covenant, the new exodus, and our new hope in the Lord Jesus. The Eucharist is essentially *remembering* Jesus' death, *reinscribing* the story of Jesus' passion with paschal imagery, *restating* the promises of the new covenant, *rehearsing* the victory of Jesus over sin and death, and *refocusing* our attention towards the *parousia* of the Lord Jesus. It is with a renewed understanding of the Eucharist that we may propose a radical praxis for the way we perform this meal with our brothers and sisters in Messiah Jesus. Yet before we start thinking how we can maximize gospel unity in the gospel meal, we must first trek through much desert.

8.6.2.1 DIFFERENT VIEWS ON EUCHARIST

All the major traditions agree that the Eucharist was instituted by Jesus, it is to be repeated by his followers, it is a form of proclamation about his death, and it is a means to the unity of the church. The different views of the Eucharist emerge from divergent understandings of the biblical texts that refer to Jesus' *presence* in the Eucharist, the *profit* of the Eucharist, and *presidency* over the Eucharist.

Gospel of John	Synoptic Gospels	Apostle Paul
[32] Jesus said to them, "Very truly I tell you, it is not Moses who has given you the bread from heaven, but it is my Father who gives you the true bread from heaven. [33] For the bread of God is the bread that comes down from heaven and gives life to the world." [34]"Sir," they said, "always give us this bread." [35]Then Jesus declared, *"I am the bread of life. Whoever comes to me will never go hungry,*	[22]While they were eating, Jesus took bread, and when he had given thanks, he broke it and gave it to his disciples, saying, *"Take it; this is my body."* [23]Then he took the cup, and when he had given thanks, he gave it to them, and they all drank from it. [24]*"This is my blood of the covenant,* which is poured out for many," he said to them. [25]"Truly I tell you, I will not drink again of the fruit of the vine	[16]Is not the cup of thanksgiving for which we give thanks a participation in the blood of Christ? And is not the bread that we break a participation in the body of Christ? [17]Because there is one loaf, we, who are many, are one body, for we all partake of the one loaf. [18]Consider the people of Israel: Do not those who eat the sacrifices participate in the altar? [19] Do I mean then that food sacrificed to

---

178. N. T. Wright, *The Meal Jesus Gave Us: Understanding Holy Communion* (Louisville: Westminster John Knox, 2002), 34.

§ 8.6 Emblems of the Gospel: Baptism and Lord's Supper

and whoever believes in me will never be thirsty.... [47]Very truly I tell you, whoever believes has eternal life. [48]*I am the bread of life.* [49]Your ancestors ate the manna in the wilderness, yet they died. [50]But here is the bread that comes down from heaven, *which people may eat and not die.* [51]*I am the living bread that came down from heaven. Whoever eats of this bread will live forever. This bread is my flesh, which I will give for the life of the world."* [52]*Then the Jews began to argue sharply among themselves, "How can this man give us his flesh to eat?"* [53]*Jesus said to them, "Very truly I tell you, unless you eat the flesh of the Son of Man and drink his blood, you have no life in you.* [54]*Whoever eats my flesh and drinks my blood has eternal life, and I will raise them up at the last day.* [55]*For my flesh is real food and my blood is real drink.* [56]*Whoever eats my flesh and drinks my blood remains in me, and I in them.* [57]*Just as the living Father sent me and I live because of the Father, so the one who feeds on me will live because of me.* [58]*This is the bread that came down from heaven. Your ancestors ate manna and died, but whoever feeds on this bread will live forever."* (John 6:32–59)

until that day when I drink it new in the kingdom of God." (Mark 14:22–25)

[26]While they were eating, Jesus took bread, and when he had given thanks, he broke it and gave it to his disciples, saying, *"Take and eat; this is my body."* [27]Then he took the cup, and when he had given thanks, he gave it to them, saying, "Drink from it, all of you. [28]*This is my blood of the covenant,* which is poured out for many for the forgiveness of sins. [29]I tell you, I will not drink of this fruit of the vine from now on until that day when I drink it new with you in my Father's kingdom." (Matt 26:26–29)

[15]And he said to them, "I have eagerly desired to eat this Passover with you before I suffer. [16]For I tell you, I will not eat it again until it finds fulfillment in the kingdom of God." [17]After taking the cup, he gave thanks and said, "Take this and divide it among you. [18]For I tell you I will not drink again of the fruit of the vine until the kingdom of God comes." [19]And he took bread, gave thanks and broke it, and gave it to them, saying, *"This is my body given for you; do this in remembrance of me."* [20]In the same way, after the supper he took the cup, saying, *"This cup is the new covenant in my blood,* which is poured out for you. (Luke 22:15–20)

Then they told what had happened on the road, and how he was known to them in the breaking of the bread (Luke 24:35 [ESV])

an idol is anything, or that an idol is anything? [20]No, but the sacrifices of pagans are offered to demons, not to God, and I do not want you to be participants with demons. [21]You cannot drink the cup of the Lord and the cup of demons too; you cannot have a part in both the Lord's table and the table of demons. (1 Cor 10:16–21)

[23]For I received from the Lord what I also passed on to you: The Lord Jesus, on the night he was betrayed, took bread, [24]and when he had given thanks, he broke it and said, *"This is my body, which is for you; do this in remembrance of me."* [25]In the same way, after supper he took the cup, saying, *"This cup is the new covenant in my blood; do this, whenever you drink it, in remembrance of me."* [26] For whenever you eat this bread and drink this cup, *you proclaim the Lord's death until he comes.* [27]So then, whoever eats the bread or drinks the cup of the Lord in an unworthy manner will be guilty of **sinning against the body and blood of the Lord**. [28]Everyone ought to examine themselves before they eat of the bread and drink of the cup. [29] *For those who eat and drink without discerning the body of Christ eat and drink judgment on themselves.* (1 Cor 11:23–29, italics added in all cases)

8.6.2.2 ROMAN CATHOLIC VIEW

The Roman Catholic view on the Eucharist is spelled out in the Council of Trent and in the official Catechism of the Catholic Church.[179] According to the Catechism 1322: "Those who have been raised to the dignity of the royal priesthood by Baptism and configured more deeply to Christ by Confirmation participate with the whole community in the Lord's own sacrifice by means of the Eucharist." For Catholics the Eucharist is "the source and summit of the Christian life."[180] In Catholic tradition, the Eucharist is a memorial of Jesus' passion and resurrection, a holy sacrifice that re-presents the one sacrifice of Christ's body, a holy communion that unites recipients to Christ and to each other, and a holy mass that ends with a sending out of the faithful to live godly lives.[181]

Catholic teaching sees a prefiguring of the Eucharist in several biblical stories: in Melchizedek, who brought out "bread and wine" to bless Abraham (Gen 14:18); the Passover lamb, who was sacrificed to protect the firstborn of the Hebrews (Exod 12), and even in Jesus' feeding miracles (e.g., Mark 6:34–44; 8:1–10).[182] The sacrificial nature of the Eucharist is argued on the basis that the Eucharist was instituted during the Passover festival (e.g., Matt 26:17–19), Jesus is the Passover Lamb who is sacrificed (1 Cor 5:7), Paul contrasts the Lord's Table with the "sacrifice of pagans" as different sacrifices offered to a different God (1 Cor 10:20), and a sacrificial understanding of the Eucharist seems to have emerged fairly quickly in the early church.[183] Accordingly, "in the Eucharistic sacrifice the whole of creation loved by God is presented to the Father through the death and the resurrection of Christ. Through Christ the Church can offer the sacrifice of praise in thanksgiving for all that God has made good, beautiful, and just in creation and in humanity."[184]

In regards to Christ's presence, in Catholic teaching the bread and wine *become* the body and blood of Christ when solemnly consecrated by the priest. This is rooted in the eucharistic discourse of the Fourth Gospel, where Jesus tells the Judeans that they must eat his flesh and drink his blood (John 6:53–56). Also, the words of institution state, "This is my body"—words that are taken literally (e.g., Matt 26:26).

The belief in a literal and physical presence of Jesus in the bread and wine was pervasive in the early church. Ignatius criticized certain false believers for having

---

179. Cf. Thomas A. Baima, "Roman Catholic View: Christ's True, Real, and Substantial Presence," in *Understanding Four Views on the Lord's Supper* (ed. J. H. Armstrong; Grand Rapids: Zondervan, 2007), 119–36; Jeffrey Gros, "The Roman Catholic View," in *The Lord's Supper: Five Views* (ed. G. T. Smith; Downers Grove, IL: InterVarsity Press, 2008), 13–32.

180. *CCC* 1324.

181. Ibid., 1330–32.

182. Cf. Brant Pitre, *Jesus and the Jewish Roots of the Eucharist* (New York: Doubleday, 2011).

183. See *Did* 14.1–3: "On the Lord's own day gather together and break bread and give thanks, having first confessed your sins so that your sacrifice may be pure. But let no one who has a quarrel with a companion join you until they have been reconciled, so that your sacrifice may not be defiled. This is the sacrifice concerning which the Lord said, 'In every place and time offer me a pure sacrifice, for I am a great king, says the Lord, and my name is marvelous among the nations.'"

184. *CCC* 1359.

a Docetic view of the Eucharist: "They abstain from Eucharist and prayer because they refuse to acknowledge that the Eucharist is the flesh of our savior Jesus Christ, which suffered for our sins and which the Father by his goodness raised up."[185] Irenaeus wrote: "For as the bread, which is produced from the earth, when it receives the invocation of God, is no longer common bread, but the Eucharist, consisting of two realities, earthly and heavenly; so also our bodies, when they receive the Eucharist, are no longer corruptible, having the hope of the resurrection to eternity."[186]

The obvious problem for the Catholic view is that the elements still will taste like bread and wine. To explain this, the Council of Trent affirmed the doctrine of *transubstantiation*, which reaches "a change of the whole substance of the bread into the substance of the body of Christ our Lord and of the whole substance of the wine into the substance of his blood." This is based on Aquinas's distinction between "accidents" (what something outwardly is) and "substance" (what something inwardly is) developed from Aristotle. While the accidents of the bread remain the same, the substance is transformed into the body and blood of Christ.[187] Christ remains present in the elements as long as they endure or until they are consumed.[188] What is more, because the elements contain the body and blood of Christ, the Eucharist is therefore worshiped.[189]

In regard to efficacy, the Eucharist benefits recipients in several ways. According to Roman Catholic teaching, the Eucharist facilitates intimate union with Christ Jesus; it "preserves, increases, and renews the life of grace received at Baptism," separates communicants from sin by infusing them with grace that strengthens them, and enables communicants to perform works of love.[190] In addition, the Eucharist is effective even for departed saints: "Eucharistic sacrifice is also offered for *the faithful departed* who 'have died in Christ but are not yet wholly purified,' so that they may be able to enter into the light and peace of Christ."[191] As a pledge of glory to come, "there is no surer pledge or dearer sign of this great hope in the new heavens and new earth 'in which righteousness dwells,' than the Eucharist."[192]

In regards to presidency, the head of the Eucharist is Christ himself as the high priest of the new covenant. Christ presides invisibly over every eucharistic celebration. But only a validly ordained bishop or priest, "acting in the person of Christ as the head," may consecrate the Eucharist, though in missional contexts deacons are

---

185. Ign. *Smyrn.* 6.2.
186. Irenaeus, *Haer.* 4.18.5.
187. In the Eastern Orthodox tradition, they acknowledge that the elements are the body and blood of Christ, but rather than appeal to transubstantiation, they simply call it a "mystery." The Orthodox identify the Eucharist as a bringing together of two realities, the Creator and the creaturely, fused together by the energies of God.
188. *CCC* 1377.
189. *CCC* 1378.
190. *CCC* 1391–1401.
191. *CCC* 1371 (italics original).
192. *CCC* 1405.

allowed to distribute the elements.[193] The presidency over the Eucharist is strictly priestly and clerical.

8.6.2.3 LUTHERAN VIEW

The Lutheran position is largely a response to the Catholic view insofar as the Lutheran position rejects the notion of the Eucharist as a sacrifice and similarly rejects the idea of transubstantiation. But the Lutheran perspective on the Lord's Supper retains the idea of a real physical presence of Jesus in the elements, and the Eucharist is still regarded as a means of grace.[194] In Lutheran sacramental theology, in baptism one is joined to the body of Christ. In the Eucharist, the recipient receives that body. The sacrament is a sign of God's grace effected by the preaching of Word. Lutherans also call the Eucharist a sacrament of the "altar" because Lutherans traditionally have a particular place in their sanctuaries with a table and a crucifix above it to symbolize Christ's atoning death.

Lutheran eucharistic theology is differentiated from Roman Catholic teaching (esp. in Luther's *Babylonian Captivity of the Church*), but also from the various Reformers like Zwingli, who denied a real physical presence. In the Marburg Colloquy between Luther and Zwingli in October 1529, Zwingli used John 6:63 ("The Spirit gives life; the flesh counts for nothing") to interpret the Eucharist in spiritual rather than physical terms. Luther responded by replying with the words of institution and focusing on the word "is" ("This *is* my body; the cup *is* the new covenant in my blood"). Luther famously etched the German word "est" for "is" onto the table during the discussion. It was failure to agree on this subject that prevented full unity between the Lutheran and Reformed churches.

Lutherans hold to a real presence of Christ in the elements in what is called *consubstantiation*. According to this teaching, Christ's body and blood are understood as being "in, with, and under" the bread and wine. Consubstantiation entails the coexistence and substantial union of the body and blood of Christ with the Eucharistic elements after their consecration. Christ's presence is not identical to the elements, but it is contained within them, much like a nut in a cookie. Accordingly, the Augsburg Confession (art. 10) states: "Of the Supper of the Lord they teach that the Body and Blood of Christ are truly present, and are distributed to those who eat the Supper of the Lord."[195]

Concerning the efficacy of the Eucharist, the Augsburg Confession (art. 13) affirms that "the Sacraments were ordained, not only to be marks of profession

---

193. *CCC* 1348.
194. Cf. David P. Scaer, "Lutheran View," in *Understanding Four Views on the Lord's Supper* (ed. J. H. Armstrong; Grand Rapids: Zondervan, 2007), 87–101; John R. Stephenson, "The Lutheran View," in *The Lord's Supper: Five Views* (ed. G. T. Smith; Downers Grove, IL: InterVarsity Press, 2008), 41–58.

among men, but rather to be signs and testimonies of the will of God toward us, instituted to awaken and confirm faith in those who use them." So there is an inward and edifying benefit to partaking of the Eucharist. But there is more to it as well for Lutherans, as Luther himself taught in his Small Catechism:

What is the benefit of such eating and drinking?

That is shown us in these words: *Given, and shed for you, for the remission of sins*; namely, that in the Sacrament forgiveness of sins, life, and salvation are given us through these words. For where there is forgiveness of sins, there is also life and salvation.

How can bodily eating and drinking do such great things?

It is not the eating and drinking, indeed, that does them, but the words which stand here, namely: *Given, and shed for you, for the remission of sins*. Which words are, beside the bodily eating and drinking, as the chief thing in the Sacrament; and he that believes these words has what they say and express, namely, the forgiveness of sins.

Importantly for Luther, the union of Word and Eucharist provides what is stated by the repetition of the words of institution: we receive the forgiveness of sins. This means, "In other words, we go to the sacrament because we receive there a great treasure [the Lord's body and blood] through and in which we obtain the forgiveness of sins."[196]

In regards to presidency, the Augsburg Confession also commands that teaching the Word and administering the sacraments be restricted to those who are "regularly called," i.e., ordained clergy.

8.6.2.4 ZWINGLIAN VIEW

The extent to which Ulrich Zwingli actually held to what we call the "Zwinglian" view of the Lord's Supper is a disputed matter for historians of the Reformation. Zwingli may have altered his position over time.[197] That said, Zwingli is closely associated with the view that the Eucharist is symbolic and commemorative of Jesus' death.[198] This view is popular in the Free churches, especially Baptist churches, and is probably the majority position in evangelicalism.[199]

---

195. The Augsburg Confession is widely available on the Internet; see, e.g., www.stpaulskingsville.org/pdf/boc/augsburgconfession.pdf.

196. Luther's Large Catechism, art. 5.22.

197. Cf. G. W. Bromiley, ed., *Zwingli and Bullinger* (London: SCM, 1953); Bruce A. Ware, "The Meaning of the Lord's Supper in the Theology of Ulrich Zwingli," in *The Lord's Supper: Remembering and Proclaiming Christ Until He Comes* (ed. Matthew R. Crawford and Thomas R. Schreiner; NACSBT 10; Nashville: Broadman & Holman, 2010), 229–47.

198. Russell D. Moore, "Baptist View," in *Understanding Four Views on the Lord's Supper* (ed. J. H. Armstrong; Grand Rapids: Zondervan, 2007), 29–44; Roger E. Olson, "The Baptist View," in *The Lord's Supper: Five Views* (ed. G. T. Smith; Downers Grove, IL: InterVarsity Press, 2008), 91–108; Matthew R. Crawford and Thomas R. Schreiner, eds., *The Lord's Supper: Remembering and Proclaiming Christ Until He Comes* (NACSBT 10; Nashville: Broadman & Holman, 2010).

199. Though it should be recognized that a Baptist like Wayne Grudem (*Systematic Theology*, 995–96) believes in a spiritual presence in the Eucharist.

The commemorative nature of the Eucharist is a defensible position considering two things. First, the Eucharist is based largely on the Jewish Passover meal, which was itself symbolic and commemorative of the deliverance of the Hebrews from Egypt in the Exodus. The Passover meal was a solemn reminder of the bitterness of their life in Egypt, a partial reenactment of the deliverance by killing a lamb, and a joyful demonstration of their hope for a new exodus in the future. Second, Jesus' own words of institution highlight the commemorative aspect with these words: "Do this in remembrance of me" (Luke 22:19; 1 Cor 11:24–25).

It must be noted that many Baptist theologians do not reduce the Eucharist to a "mere symbol," as they often prefer to regard it as an "effective sign" of God's grace in the past and God's triumph in the future. Christ is always present with his people, and in the Lord's Supper the presence of Christ is identified in the proclamation that Christ is united to his people (Matt 28:20). The Lord's Supper reminds believers that the church is the temple of God, where God dwells with his people. Millard Erickson contends that "it is not so much that the sacrament brings Christ to the communicant as that the believer's faith brings Christ to the sacrament."[200]

In regards to the benefits of partaking of the Supper, the 1689 LBC (following WCF 27, 29) states that there is a "spiritual nourishment," a "growth in him [Christ]," a further "bond and pledge" to Christ and to other believers, and in the Supper believers "spiritually receive, and feed upon Christ crucified, and all the benefits of his death." That is stated in the context of regarding the Lord's Supper as a "perpetual remembrance" and regarding the elements as "figurative," not really the body and blood of Jesus (LBC 30.1–7). The chief blessings of the Supper are that it narrates a sacred event instituted by Christ. It is a support and guide to faith. There is a blessing for the obedient who faithfully administer and receive it.

In regards to presidency, the 1689 LBC states that the Supper can be "administered by those only who are qualified and thereunto called, according to the commission of Christ" (LBC 28.2; 30.3). However, for the most part, Baptist and Anabaptist churches have strongly emphasized the priesthood of all believers, with the implication that presidency of the Lord's Supper is not restricted to clergy. Other officers of the church, such as elders, deacons, or members in good standing, can preside over the supper.

8.6.2.5 REFORMED VIEW

The problem with providing the "Reformed view" of the Lord's Supper is that there was a wide diversity of opinion among the Reformers. Zwingli, Bucer, Bullinger, and Calvin all held different views, not always unrelated, but different all the same.

---

200. Erickson, *Christian Theology*, 1128–29.

§8.6 Emblems of the Gospel: Baptism and Lord's Supper

For the sake of simplicity, I will major on Calvin and the WCF as the exemplars of the Reformed approach to the Eucharist.[201] In the Reformed tradition, sacraments and gospel go together, as signs of the true church, but also because they are mutually interpreting. What the gospel proclaims, the Eucharist embodies: Christ given for our salvation and received through faith. Calvin begins his introduction to the Eucharist with the words:

> After God has once received us into his family, it is not that he may regard us in the light of servants, but of sons, performing the part of a kind and anxious parent, and providing for our maintenance during the whole course of our lives. And, not contented with this, he has been pleased by a pledge to assure us of his continued liberality. To this end, he has given another sacrament to his Church by the hand of his only-begotten Son—viz. *a spiritual feast*, at which Christ testifies that he himself is living bread (John 6:51), *on which our souls feed, for a true and blessed immortality.*[202]

Concerning presence, Calvin is adamant that one cannot divorce the sign (bread and wine) from what it signifies (Christ). As such, "the Lord was pleased, by calling himself the bread of life, not only to teach that our salvation is treasured up in the faith of his death and resurrection, but also, by virtue of true communication with him, his life passes into us and becomes ours, just as bread when taken for food gives vigor to the body."[203] Similarly, Calvin taught in his Geneva Catechism that just as wine "strengthens, refreshes, and rejoices a man physically, so [Christ's] blood is our joy, our refreshing, and our spiritual strength."[204] Calvin even repeats the idea of a real "feeding" on Christ in conjunction with the motif of a heavenly "ascent" to Christ.[205] He writes:

> But if we are carried to heaven with our eyes and minds, that we may there behold Christ in the glory of his kingdom, as the symbols invite us to him in his integrity, so, under the symbol of bread, we must feed on his body, and, under the symbol of wine, drink separately of his blood, and thereby have the full enjoyment of him. For though he withdrew his flesh from us, and with his body ascended to heaven, he, however, sits at the right hand of the Father; that is, he reigns in power and majesty, and the glory of the Father. This kingdom is not limited by any intervals of space, nor circumscribed by any dimensions. Christ can exert his energy wherever he pleases, in earth and heaven, can manifest his presence by the exercise of his power, can always be present with his people, breathing into them his own life, can live in them, sustain, confirm, and invigorate them, and preserve them safe, just as if he

---

201. John Hesselink, "Reformed View," in *Understanding Four Views on the Lord's Supper* (ed. J. H. Armstrong; Grand Rapids: Zondervan, 2007), 59–71; Leanne Van Dyk, "The Reformed View," in *The Lord's Supper: Five Views* (ed. G. T. Smith; Downers Grove, IL: InterVarsity Press, 2008), 67–82; Reymond, *New Systematic Theology*, 955–67; Horton, *Christian Faith*, 798–827.
202. Calvin, *Institutes* 4.17.1 (italics added).
203. Ibid., 4.17.5.
204. Geneva Catechism, Q. 341.
205. Calvin, *Institutes* 4.17.2, 15, 16, 18, 31.

were with them in the body; in fine, can feed them with his own body, communion with which he transfuses into them. After this manner, the body and blood of Christ are exhibited to us in the sacrament.[206]

The Westminster divines acknowledged the symbolic nature of the Eucharist in that it was instituted to "represent Christ" (WCF 27.1); it's a "perpetual remembrance" (WCF 29.1) and a "commemoration" of Jesus' offering of himself as an atoning sacrifice (WCF 29.2). However, they root the Eucharist in a more sacramental theology bound up with their covenant theology. As such, Eucharist and baptism are "signs and seals of the covenant of grace" (WCF 27.2). In the Eucharist there is even a "sacramental union, between the sign and the thing signified" (ibid.). Therefore, there is a movement beyond symbol into a real presence of Christ through the Spirit and in the faith of the believer. In the Eucharist believers spiritually "receive and feed upon, Christ crucified, and all benefits of His death" (WCF 29.7).

Concerning the efficacy of the meal, the benefits accrued to the believer are principally an intense experience of God's grace and spiritual nourishment for the soul. In the words of the Belgic Confession: "We believe and confess that our Savior Jesus Christ has ordained and instituted the sacrament of the Holy Supper to nourish and sustain those who are already born again and ingrafted into his family, his church." Furthermore, "at that table he makes us enjoy himself as much as the merits of his suffering and death, as he nourishes, strengthens, and comforts our poor, desolate souls by the eating of his flesh, and relieves and renews them by the drinking of his blood."[207] The Eucharist creates a bond between the communicant and Christ as well as unity among believers as they joyously feast together on Christ. Calvin put it this way:

> The Lord there communicates his body so that he may become altogether one with us, and we with him. Moreover, since he has only one body of which he makes us all to be partakers, we must necessarily, by this participation, all become one body. This unity is represented by the bread which is exhibited in the sacrament. As it is composed of many grains, so mingled together, that one cannot be distinguished from another; so ought our minds to be so cordially united, as not to allow of any dissension or division.[208]

The crucial aspect of the Reformed view of the Eucharist is the Holy Spirit as the instrument of communicating Christ's presence and conferring grace on the participant. Hence, for the Westminster Confession, the realities in the Eucharist depend on the "work of the Spirit," which sources our spiritual nourishment (WCF 27.3). For Calvin, "the sacraments profit not a whit without the power of the Holy Spirit."[209] In his Geneva Catechism (Q. 313), he said: "The power and efficacy of a sacrament does

---

206. Ibid., 4.17.18.
207. Belgic Confession, art. 35.
208. Calvin, *Institutes* 4.17.38.

not lie in the external elements, but wholly emanates from the Spirit of God." This means that the benefits of the sacrament "are conferred through the Holy Spirit, who makes us partakers in Christ; conferred, indeed, with the help of outward signs."[210]

Finally, in regards to presidency, the Westminster Confession 27.4 states that the sacraments may be administered only by a "minister of the Word lawfully ordained."

In light of these summaries, I want to revisit the presence of Jesus in the Eucharist, comment on the spiritual profit of the Eucharist, and offer some thoughts on presidency and participation in the Eucharist.

8.6.2.6 IT'S ALL ABOUT PRESENCE

I don't know if you've seen the movie *Monster's Inc.*, but there is a charming scene where the head monster in the monster energy factory tells his crew of monsters that scaring children is "all about presence" (the children's screams are harvested and used for energy in Monstropolis). Eucharist is all about presence! The debates about Christ's presence are not esoteric or needless debates about the mere meaning of a ritual. One's eucharistic theology of "presence" is derivative of wider beliefs about the nature of God, human salvation, God's communication of himself, and how God is found.[211] What one believes about incarnation, gospel, and redemption is expressed in what one thinks of the presence of Christ in the bread and wine. In evaluating the various proposals about the presence of Christ, I find the Catholic, Lutheran, and Zwinglian views not entirely false in everything they say, but highly dissatisfying in the end.

Against the Catholic view, it appears to have gone beyond "presence" to a virtual "mutation" of Jesus in the elements. Though Thomas Aquinas and the Council of Trent deployed the resources of Aristotelian thought and the arsenal of their eucharistic tradition to explain the real presence, in the end, transubstantiation still sounds "weird." The Catholic magisterium has not fashioned a satisfactory answer as to how the elements are both bread and wine and Jesus' body and blood at the same time. If you have to invoke Aristotle and some kookie distinction between substance and accidents, then you are pretty much grasping at straws.

I eminently prefer the Eastern Orthodox Church's explanation for the real presence of Christ in the elements. I once asked an Orthodox priest: "Nickos, mate, how can the bread and wine be bread and wine and be Christ at the same time?" After a brief paused, he looked me in the eye and replied, "Stuffed, if I know, mate; it's just a mystery!" At least he's honest: we don't know and we can't know. The Catholic tradition acknowledges the paschal mystery, but it would be better off dropping transubstantiation and just running with the mystery theme.

---

209. Ibid., 4.14.9.
210. Ibid., 4.14.16.
211. Thomas J. Davis, *This Is My Body: The Presence of* *Christ in Reformation Thought* (Grand Rapids: Baker Academic, 2008), 13–14.

On top of that, one can grant the clearly eucharistic subtext to John 6, with its references to eating Jesus' flesh and drinking his blood (esp. vv. 51–58). However, John's gospel is decidedly a-sacramental since Jesus is never baptized and never institutes the Eucharist in the narrative. The big emphasis in the Fourth Gospel is on faith, believing, and trusting in the Father and the Son (e.g., John 5:24; 20:31). The discourse in John 6 is largely metaphorical for believing in Jesus Christ as the one who takes away the sins of the world.

Still, it's hard not to think about the Eucharist when one reads this passage. Calvin saw an "intimation" of the Eucharist in John 6 because it teaches that Christ is the bread of life, we believe in him for that, and we express our faith in him by feeding on him at the Eucharist. For Calvin, Jesus is teaching that our salvation is treasured up in our faith, but there is also a real communication of him that takes place in his body and blood.[212] So I would say that John 6 is not about the Eucharist, but it certainly foreshadows it. Consequently, "this means that if John 6 is not about the eucharist, the eucharist is undoubtedly about John 6."[213]

Against the Lutheran view, one feels as if they are still groping after an explanation that retains Christ's real presence, but is somehow sufficiently distanced from the Catholic view of transubstantiation. The problem as I see it is that the difference between consubstantiation and transubstantiation looks to be mostly semantic rather than ontological. Furthermore, the Lutheran claim that the Reformed churches believe in only a "spiritual presence," like an illusory or fictive apparition of Christ around the elements, is a caricature. That is unfair because the Reformed generally believe in a real, genuine presence, but without the confusion of consubstantiation.

The other thing to remember is that when Paul says, "For whenever you eat this bread and drink this cup, you proclaim the Lord's death until he comes" (1 Cor 11:26), the meal looks forward to the Lord's bodily return and thus presupposes his bodily absence in the interim. So whatever "presence" we have in the Eucharist, it is not Jesus' physical body that is present, since his glorified body is exclusively located in heaven. According to Richard Hays: "Thus, the meal acknowledges the *absence* of the Lord and mingles memory and hope, recalling his death and awaiting his coming again."[214]

Against the Zwinglian view, I have to profess that most Baptist churches I have visited believe in the doctrine of the "real absence" of Jesus from the Eucharist. Wherever Jesus is, he is nowhere near the bread and the wine (whoops, make that grape juice). In fact, it is probably better for Jesus to wait outside the church during our communion services, because if he came too close to the bread and grape juice, we might end up turning Catholic! There is no denying by anyone, including Catholic

---

212. Calvin, *Institutes* 4.17.5.
213. Cf. David Gibson, "Eating Is Believing? On Midrash and the Mixing of Metaphors in John 6," *Them* 27.7 (2002): 15.

214. Richard B. Hays, *First Corinthians* (Interpretation; Louisville: Westminster John Knox, 2011), 199 (italics original).

and Orthodox, that the Eucharist is a memorial meal (see "do this in remembrance of me" in Luke 22:19; 1 Cor 11:24–25). The Eucharist commemorates and celebrates the sacrificial death of Jesus Christ. However, on the Zwinglian view, there is still a gaping gap between the sign and the one who is signified by the elements.

The problem is that symbols tend to be effective signs and evocative indicators of certain states of affairs. Symbols activate realities even if they do not fully include those realities in their own makeup. G. B. Caird argued that symbols are more than metaphors; like a kiss or a handshake, they are a means of conveying what they represent.[215] So I think there is clearly more to the Eucharist than the memory of Jesus' death and reminding us that Christ is with us.

Consider the following. The two travelers to Emmaus told the disciples how they met Jesus on their journey and how he was made known "to them *in the breaking of the bread* [*en tē klasei tou artou*]" (Luke 24:35). The eucharistic echoes are transparent here. Luke is evidently pointing ahead to Acts 2, where the disciples were dedicated to "breaking bread" together in their fellowship (Acts 2:42, 46). When the disciples met together to break bread, they also met with Jesus in the bread.

In addition, Paul teaches about a real encounter with Christ through the elements. Through the wine there is a real "participation" in the blood of Christ and through the bread a real "participation" in the body of Christ (1 Cor 10:16). The word for "participation" is *koinōnia*, meaning "fellowship" or "sharing." Plain as day, through bread and wine, we actually commune with Christ, and this communion requires an exclusive allegiance that forbids us from partaking of pagan sacrifices. The bread and wine of the Eucharist actually fosters a vertical communion with the risen Christ and facilitates a closer horizontal relationship with fellow believers.

I remain concerned that the Zwinglian position is reducible to a quasi-docetic view of the Lord's Supper, based on an aversion to the possibility of physical presentations of Jesus Christ to the church. But if one believes that the Word became flesh, then why cannot one believe that the Word meets us afresh in the bread of a meal that Jesus himself instituted?[216]

Stepping back for a minute, one thing we have to say is that the early church

---

215. G. B. Caird, *The Language and Imagery of the Bible* (London: Duckworth, 1980), 101–2.

216. The "sacramental principle" of some Catholic and Anglo-Catholic theologies asserts that an invisible divine presence is disclosed through created realities that function as symbols for the divine. The divine mystery is conveyed through the symbols of everyday and ordinary life so that persons may intuit something of the mercy and goodness of God. This explains why it is that things like paintings, statues, music, clothing, the landscape, and so forth can excite religious feelings and meditations about God. That is part of God's common grace to us. Of course, what happens in the Eucharist is a special grace, a specific application of the sacramental principle, whereby the incarnate Lord is present with his people in the eucharistic meal. One might say that in the eucharistic is an intrinsic connection of gospel, Word, and sacrament so that the presence of Christ is experienced in the word and symbolic world created by the eucharistic event. The sacramental principle allows us to attribute a real ontology to the Eucharist, but without a purely immanentist view of God's presence. See further Christopher J. Cocksworth, *Evangelical Eucharistic Thought in the Church of England* (Cambridge: Cambridge University Press, 1993).

quickly developed a notion of a real presence of Jesus at the Eucharist. Ignatius wrote: "I want the bread of God, which is the flesh of Christ who is of the seed of David; and for drink I want his blood, which is incorruptible love."[217] Similarly, Justin Martyr said:

> For we do not receive these things as common bread or as common drink; but as Jesus Christ our Savior being incarnate by God's word who took on flesh and blood for our salvation, so also we have been taught that the food consecrated by the word of prayer which comes from him, from which our flesh and blood are nourished by transformation, is the flesh and blood of that incarnate Jesus.[218]

The early church probably arrived at this conclusion of a "real presence" by reading Jesus' words of institution (Matt 26:26–29) in light of the Johannine eucharistic discourse (John 6:26–65). The question is: What kind of presence is found in the Eucharist, and by what instrument is that presence communicated to us?

In the end, I think the Reformed position is the one that has the most explanatory power for understanding Jesus' presence in the Eucharist. The Reformed view is that it is the Holy Spirit who makes Christ present in the Eucharist, and it is the same Spirit who communicates benefits to partakers of the Eucharist. The presence of Christ is *not* mediated through the *Church's mutation* of the elements into Christ's body and blood (i.e., transubstantiation or consubstantiation). The presence of Christ is *not* restricted to the *believer's faith*, reducing the bread and wine to a memorial. It is the Holy Spirit who draws Christ downward and the believer upward to meet Christ in the gospel meal.[219]

The Reformed view of the Eucharist is thoroughly Trinitarian as it highlights the gracious character of the Father in giving us Christ. The sacrament presents us to Christ and unites us with him as food for our soul. The Holy Spirit is the instrument of our union with Christ and perichoretically energizes the elements to convey the presence of Christ and the grace that accompanies his work.[220]

Moreover, I would maintain that the presence of Christ in the meal, a real "participation" in Christ, is essential for the meal to have any efficacy or value. Calvin's words from his *Short Treatise on the Lord's Supper* are robust on this matter:

> We begin now to enter on the question so much debated, both anciently and at the present time — how we are to understand the words in which the bread is called the body of Christ, and the wine his blood. This may be disposed of without much difficulty, if we carefully observe the principle which I lately laid down, viz., *that all the benefit which we should seek in the Supper is annihilated if Jesus Christ be not there given*

---

217. Ign. *Rom.* 7.3.
218. Justin, *1 Apol.* 67.
219. Strongly recommended on this point is Horton, *People and Place*, 124–52.
220. Van Dyk, "Reformed View," 79.

to us as the substance and foundation of all. That being fixed, we will confess, without doubt, that *to deny that a true communication of Jesus Christ is presented to us in the Supper, is to render this holy sacrament frivolous and useless—an execrable blasphemy unfit to be listened to.* (italics added)[221]

You read him right! No presence means there is no point and no purpose to this meal. If there is no communication of Christ in and through the bread and wine, then this meal is an exercise in futility. But if Christ is present in the bread and the wine through the Spirit, we have here a means of grace, a harvest of blessings, and a real communion with Christ.

The Anglican tradition has emphasized the element of "participation" or "partaking" with Christ in the bread and wine from 1 Corinthians 10:16. Thus, "it is a Sacrament of our Redemption by Christ's death: insomuch that to such as rightly, worthily, and with faith, receive the same, the Bread which we break is a partaking of the Body of Christ; and likewise the Cup of Blessing is a partaking of the Blood of Christ."[222] For the Anglican Divine Richard Hooker, Christ is encountered in the Eucharist as fully human and divine; this is accomplished by the Spirit, by whom communicants are transformed as they partake of Christ's holiness and virtue. He wrote that in the Eucharist is "a true and a real participation of Christ, who thereby imparteth himself even his whole Person as a mystical Head unto every soul that receiveth him, and that every such receiver doth thereby incorporate or unite himself unto Christ as a mystical member of him, yea of them also whom he acknowledgeth to be his own."[223]

Some are reticent to take Paul's remarks on "participation" in the literal sense. They point out that this participation with Christ through the bread and wine parallels the participation of Judeans in the altar of the cultus and the participation of pagans with demons in their temples (1 Cor 10:18–21). The meat in those altars did not convey the real presence of Yahweh, much less the real presence of a demon; so by parallel, the eucharistic elements of bread and wine do not contain the real presence of Jesus.[224]

I demur for two reasons. First, there is a real fellowshiping with either Yahweh or demons, depending on the altar. So already we are beyond mere memorialism as one fellowships with the deity in the meat consumed from the altar. Thus, the Christian Eucharist, at a minimum, is a fellowshiping with Christ qualitatively different from the fellowship you have with Christ anywhere else. Second, Paul does not say we meet Christ through the bread and wine that symbolically represent his

---

221. William S. Johnson, John H. Leith, George W. Stroup, eds., *Reformed Reader: A Sourcebook in Christian Theology* (Louisville: Westminster John Knox, 1993), 317.
222. Thirty-Nine Articles §38.
223. Richard Hooker, *Laws of Ecclesiastical Polity: Books 1–5* (New York: De Capo, 1971), 5.lxvii.7.
224. Cf., e.g., Moore, "Baptist View," 40.

metaphorical presence; rather, Paul says that we participate with Christ's *body* and with Christ's *blood*. There is a direct fellowshiping with Christ's body and blood as the elements in a sense become what they proclaim. One can only fellowship with Christ's body and blood if Christ is somehow present in the bread and wine. You cannot fellowship, partake, share, or commune with one who is entirely absent.

In light of all this, we need some eucharistic charity, as all Christian traditions share something in common by affirming the memory, proclamation, and presence of Jesus with his people in the Eucharist. As a possible consensus statement, the Leuenberg Agreement, a joint ecumenical statement between Lutheran and Reformed churches composed in 1973, states: "In the Lord's Supper the risen Jesus Christ imparts himself in his body and blood, given for all, through his word of promise with bread and wine. He thus gives himself unreservedly to all who receive the bread and wine; faith receives the Lord's Supper for salvation, unfaith for judgment" (III.1.18).[225]

If we can all agree that the Lord's Supper is a gospel meal, it makes perfect sense that, irrespective of how we understand presence, we will eat and drink together precisely to remember the Lord of the gospel. Ultimately it is beyond our understanding as to how we meet Jesus in bread and wine through the Spirit. We would do well to be like Calvin and insist that the operation of the Spirit in the Eucharist is something we would "rather experience than understand."[226]

8.6.2.7 BLESSING OF THE MEAL

I enjoy posing this question to students: "What do you get from this meal that you don't get from anywhere else? What is available at the Lord's Table that is not on the menu at Sizzler? What is the efficacy and blessing of the Eucharist?" Traditionally the Protestant churches have confessed that the Eucharist is a means of grace. Indeed, the question is not whether Eucharist is a means of grace, but *how* it is a means of grace.[227] Sadly, I lament that so many evangelical churches have abandoned the notion that the Eucharist is a means of grace. Instead, they are so paranoid about sacramentalism that they devote an inordinate amount of time in their eucharistic messages explaining what Eucharist does not do, why it is nothing special, and why it is no big deal.

Many evangelicals have such low expectations about what they get out of the Eucharist. I've read one story where an old man once took communion in church next to his granddaughter. When the loaf of bread was brought to him, he ripped off a big piece of bread, nudged his granddaughter with his elbow, and told her

---

225. See this agreement at www.leuenberg.net/node/642.
226. Calvin, *Institutes* 4.17.32.
227. Moore, "Baptist View," 35.

§ 8.6 Emblems of the Gospel: Baptism and Lord's Supper

that, "This is more than I had for breakfast."[228] The old man was right, but for the wrong reason. The Eucharist is more than what he had for breakfast, not because of the portion size, but because of the benefit that accrues to the participant who receives the elements in faith. The Eucharist is grace food, gospel food, Jesus food, Trinitarian food. But what does it feed us?

The first thing to consider is that food and fellowship are part of God's blessing of his people for the future. If the Israelites remained obedient to God, ideally, they were promised to "dwell secure in a land of grain and new wine, where the heavens drop dew" (Deut 33:28). Isaiah prophesied about a day when God would lay out a banquet for all peoples that includes a "feast of rich food for all peoples, a banquet of aged wine—the best of meats and the finest of wines" (Isa 25:6). Amos referred to the end of exile for the nation where "new wine will drip from the mountains and flow from all the hills" (Amos 9:13). A similar image of national restoration is given by Zechariah: "The seed will grow well, the vine will yield its fruit, the ground will produce its crops, and the heavens will drop their dew. I will give all these things as an inheritance to the remnant of this people" (Zech 8:12).

All of these promises point ahead to the messianic feast (Matt 8:11; Luke 13:29; Rev 19:9, 17–18). In light of that, we could say that Eucharist is the hors d'oeuvres of the coming messianic feast. As such, churches should attempt to move beyond guilt-tripping sermons and focus on the joy and victory that this feast points to. It is a celebratory feast of our redemption, our inclusion in God's covenant, and our victory over evil. We should get away from the all-too-common "funereal atmosphere, complete with somber droning organ music," and replace it with paschal festivity.[229] We should introduce Eucharist as the joyful feast of the people of God.[230]

The Eucharist is a genuine recollection of Jesus' death through the rehearsal of his words as Paul repeats them in 1 Corinthians 11:24–26. Notably, when Jesus wanted his disciples to understand his death and to remember what he did for them, he didn't give them a textbook or a lecture; instead, he gave them a meal. This meal is fundamentally a way of thanking the Lord Jesus for what he has done for us. Part of that thanksgiving should be expressed in our worship at the Eucharist. The ascended Christ is presented to us in the elements by the Holy Spirit. We are quickened by our memory of Christ and our membership in Christ. At the Lord's Table, we have participation in Christ's benefits and an anticipation of the glorious wedding supper of the Lamb. We remember, rejoice, and refocus our attention on Christ, who came and is yet to come.

There is clearly a spiritual benefit to partaking of the Eucharist. The Eucharist is often called nourishment for the soul. Ignatius of Antioch even called the Eucharist

---

228. Davis, *This Is My Body*, 13.
229. Moore, "Baptist View," 33.
230. Davis, *This Is My Body*, 17.

the "medicine of immortality," and Calvin labeled it a "taste of immortality."[231] One feeds on Christ in the Eucharist and so shares in his presence and fellowship and receives fresh grace. The wine and bread are tokens of Jesus' love designed to empower us to service, obedience, and faithfulness.

If I may paraphrase Richard Hooker: The very letter of the word of Christ gives us plain assurance that this mystery of the Eucharist, like nails that fasten us to his cross, draws us to experience the efficacy, force, and virtue of the blood that he has shed for us. In the wounds of our Redeemer, we dip our tongues, we are dyed red, both within and without, our hunger is satisfied, and our thirst is quenched. Such are the wonderful things that one experiences, majestic to sight and sound, whose soul is possessed by our Paschal Lamb. There we are made joyful in the strength of this new wine; this bread has in it more than the substance that our eyes observe, since this sacred cup with a solemn prayer brings us to the endless life and salvation of both our soul and body. The Eucharist serves as medicine to heal our infirmities and to cleanse our sins as a sacrifice of thanksgiving. In coming to the Eucharist we learn that it sanctifies us in the heart, enlightens our faith, and genuinely conforms us into the image of Jesus Christ. What these elements are in themselves is not fully understood by anyone. How can they be! Yet it is enough for one who partakes of the elements to know that they are the body and blood of Christ; in them his promise and grace is found sufficient, and his Word makes himself fully known. The faithful communicant should rest on this thought at the Eucharist, "My God, you are faithful. My soul is happy and satisfied in you."[232]

A further blessing of the Eucharist is unity. Paul labors the fact that the "one loaf" is representative of the unity of one people with their one Lord (1 Cor 10:17). The rich in Corinth were sinning against the body of Christ by introducing divisions and discriminating against the poor (11:17–24). The bread and the wine symbolize the body and blood of Christ given, not just for *me*, but for *us*. The family that takes the Eucharist together and prays together stays together.

Interestingly, the *Didache* 9.4 interprets the Eucharist as embodying a hope for the gathering of the church into God's eschatological kingdom: "Just as this broken bread was scattered upon the mountains and then was gathered together and became one, so may your church be gathered together from the ends of the earth into your kingdom; for yours is the glory and the power through Jesus Christ forever." It's a wonderful image of the Eucharist as the kingdom meal, for kingdom people, confirming their kingdom hope. The Eucharist symbolizes our unity with all believers in God's kingdom, but in another sense the Eucharist proleptically achieves it when

---

231. Ign. *Eph.* 20.2; Calvin, *Institutes* 4.17.17.
232. Hooker, *Laws of Ecclesiastical Polity*, 5.lxvii.12.

we eat and drink together in the presence of the Lord Jesus Christ. The unity of God's people in the kingdom gets a preview in the unity we experience at Eucharist.

8.6.2.8 WHO CAN PRESIDE OVER AND PARTAKE OF COMMUNION?

I regard the presidency issue as fairly straightforward. Though the developing church restricted Eucharist to presidency by the bishop,[233] if we really believe in the priesthood of all believers, in theory any believer can stand up and lead the people in the Eucharist. In practice, though, I would suggest that the only qualifications we make for one to lead communion is that he or she be theologically informed about Eucharist, be a person whose walk matches their talk, and be spiritually mature enough to be respected by their fellow believers. I would not randomly select people from the pew to lead the Eucharist, but neither should it be restricted to sacred orders or even elders.

The question of participation is more complex and disputed. Since the *Didache* and Justin Martyr, the Eucharist has been restricted to believers.[234] Most churches practice some form of restriction in regard to the Lord's Supper. Hence, the Westminster Confession 29.8 advocates that "ignorant and wicked men" cannot be admitted to the supper. Many Lutherans do not allow non-Lutherans to partake of the Eucharist if they do not believe in consubstantiation. According to Vatican II, a Catholic priest can only offer the Eucharist to a person from one of the separated churches if he or she agrees with Roman Catholic teaching about the Eucharist and if a member of their own faith tradition is not available to minister to them. In the USA, some Baptist leaders like Mark Dever and Al Mohler do not give communion to paedobaptists like Ligon Duncan or Tim Keller. Thus, for some, church discipline requires that unbelievers, "carnal" Christians, and members of different denominations be excluded from the celebration of the Eucharist. I confess that I think such exclusions simply miss the point, and the Scriptures overwhelmingly favor an open communion table.

The antecedent to the Eucharist is obviously Jesus' institution of the common meal for his disciples to remember him by. The meal that Jesus had with his followers the night he was betrayed was itself a continuation of his earlier ministry, where meals and fellowship were a big part of his praxis and preaching. Jesus was known for banqueting with the bad. He ate with tax collectors and sinners (Matt 9:10–11)—so much so that Jesus acquired a reputation for being "a glutton and a drunkard [and] a friend of ... sinners" (Matt 11:19/Luke 7:34). This brought great offense to the Pharisees, who could not understand why an otherwise learned rabbi,

---

233. Ign. *Smyrn.* 8.1–2.
234. *Did.* 9.5; Justin, *Dial.* 66.

whom God used to do miraculous deeds, would be so unscrupulous and scandalous in the company he kept.

The Pharisees were basically a religious dining club. For them shared meals were a symbol of the cultic purity and religious propriety that defined the holiness of Israel, the way it was meant to be done (you can see the link between holiness and food as far back as Pentateuchal laws about unclean foods [e.g., Deut 14] and Dan 1:5–16). Moreover, it was a holiness defined by exclusion. Yet Jesus shows no fear of impurity or contamination when coming into contact with sinners. For Jesus it is holiness that is a contagion, and divine holiness spreads and infects everything that comes into contact with it.[235] In Jesus' ministry, the open meals that he shared with "outsiders" were acted parables of the open invitation of the kingdom of God.[236] Jesus told the parable of the prodigal son to explain to the Pharisees why he "welcomes sinners and eats with them" (Luke 15:2).

If the "Lord's Table" is anything like Jesus' practice of table fellowship, it should exhibit the same shocking openness as to who can attend. All who are willing to come to Jesus are invited. They may come as they are, but they are not allowed to stay as they are. That is because God's grace is scandalous. It is not the table for the righteous who use the table to publicly show that they are "holy"; it is the table for sinners who know they are unworthy. This table is for the poor in spirit who need spiritual food and yearn for a banquet of grace.[237]

Another thing I find interesting is that when Paul was on his voyage to Rome, in the midst of a terrifying storm that scared the heebie-jeebies out of all the passengers, he interrupts their panicked behavior with a communion service:

> Just before dawn Paul urged them all to eat. "For the last fourteen days," he said, "you have been in constant suspense and have gone without food—you haven't eaten anything. Now I urge you to take some food. You need it to survive. Not one of you will lose a single hair from his head." After he said this, he took some bread and gave thanks to God in front of them all. Then he broke it and began to eat. They were all encouraged and ate some food themselves. Altogether there were 276 of us on board. (Acts 27:33–37)

Paul seems to be doing more than offering to make some peanut butter and jelly sandwiches and to say grace. In Acts, breaking bread has clear eucharistic echoes of a shared meal among disciples in the name of Jesus Christ (Acts 2:42, 46; 20:7, 11). The description of what Paul does is unmistakably reminiscent of Jesus' own table practice, including the Last Supper (Luke 9:16; 22:19; 24:30). Paul did not hand out the food to the Roman soldiers and prisoners and then slink off into the corner for a

---

235. Cf. Craig L. Blomberg, *Contagious Holiness: Jesus' Meals with Sinners* (Leicester, UK: Apollos, 2005).

236. Cf. Michael F. Bird, *Jesus and the Origins of the Gentile Mission* (LNTS 331; London: T&T Clark, 2006), 104–8.

237. The chronology of the institution of the Lord's Supper is difficult to determine as to precisely when Judas Iscariot left the house (see Matt 26; John 13), but Judas was probably at the meal when Jesus instituted the Supper. If so, what does that mean for our theology of who can come to the Lord's table?

§ 8.6 Emblems of the Gospel: Baptism and Lord's Supper

closed service with the Christians. No, Paul gave thanks "in front of them all," and all ate together with the ship's company. Consider also the effect of Paul's actions, "they were all encouraged" (Acts 27:37). Sounds like Eucharist to me!

In regards to 1 Corinthians 11:17–34, much is made of Paul's warnings about partaking in an "unworthy manner," with the result that one sins "against the body and blood of the Lord," and also those who partake without "discerning the body of Christ eat and drink judgment on themselves." I've heard endless communion devotionals where the leader warns the congregation about not partaking if you have some unconfessed sin in your heart, abstaining if you don't know Jesus as your personal Savior, letting the elements pass you by if you're not baptized as a believer—I've heard them all; in fact, I've even said this stuff myself at times. So I say repentantly now that warnings like these have absolutely nothing to do with what Paul was talking to the Corinthians about.

The problem at the Corinthian meals was serious, and Paul makes the point that whatever meal they think they are having, it sure ain't the Lord's Supper (1 Cor 11:20). It's become just another meal at Corinth that reinforces social divisions between rich and poor. The problem is that the practice of the Corinthians fostered "divisions" between the classes because the rich members "despise the church of God by humiliating those who have nothing" (11:18, 22). Basically, the wealthier members went ahead and ate a meal in full festivity in the triclinium of a house, leaving no food for the poorer members. These poorer folks—probably slaves, artisans, day laborers—who turned up later, were given the scraps and were probably made to dine in an adjacent area like an atrium.

Let me illustrate this further. Imagine I held a communion service at my house where I invited the doctors, lawyers, professors, and bankers to feast on Italian herb bread and an Argentinean pinot noir in the dining room, and then rudely told the factory workers, waitresses, brick layers, and the unemployed to eat some stale bread and watered-down grape juice on the porch. That is the kind of offensive behavior that infuriated Paul. This is what it means to partake in an unworthy manner. Discriminating like this is a sin against the body and the blood of the Lord. To create divisions based on occupation, social status, patronage, and education—and to stratify participation in the Eucharist along those lines—is to fail to discern the unity of the body of Christ in the meal. Judgment here is threatened for the rich who despise the poor by treating them the same way the poor get treated at every other meal in ancient Corinth. Brian Rosner and Roy Ciampa summarized 1 Corinthians 11:17–34 this way: "Wealthy believers should honor the Lord and their poorer brothers and sisters in the way they practice the Lord's Supper."[238]

---

238. Roy E. Ciampa and Brian S. Rosner, *The First Letter to the Corinthians* (PNTC; Grand Rapids: Eerdmans, 2010), 541.

So when Paul says that "everyone ought to examine themselves" (1 Cor 11:28), he does not mean they must make sure that you've got Jesus' flag flying in your heart, that your conscience is 100 percent pure, and that your name is on the membership rolls. No, he means to make sure you are not one of those rich folks oppressing the poor through the meal, because you are bringing judgment on yourself, as Jesus has a special concern for the poor. The Eucharist should be marked by a manifestation of unity and common concern for each other that is worthy of the Lord. Moreover, note also that people are called to examine *themselves*. We are not called to be a pharisaic police force going around and determining who is and who is not worthy to come to this table. Note the wise words of John Calvin:

> Those who think it sacrilege to partake the Lord's bread with the wicked, are in this more rigid than Paul. For when he exhorts us to pure and holy communion, he does not require that we should examine others, or that everyone should examine the whole church, but that each should examine himself.[239]

It is common in the Reformed tradition to "fence" the communion table. That entails warning people about the danger of drinking judgment on themselves if they harbor sin in their hearts, lack full assurance, or are not accredited members in good standing. The problem is that the Lord's Table is exactly that—Jesus' own table; he invites and qualifies people to come, and if you try to fence the table to keep people out, Jesus will knock your fence down. Jesus did it to the Pharisees (Luke 15:1–2), and Paul did it to Peter (Gal 2:11–14). Rather than make the folks in our churches somberly wrestle with whether they are truly worthy to come to this table, we should be telling them that the good news is that Jesus had made them worthy to come and the only condition is faith. Calvin warned of the dangers of teaching that the Lord's Table is only for the righteous:

> Certainly the devil could have no shorter method of destroying men than by thus infatuating them [with their sinfulness], and so excluding them from the taste and savour of this food with which their most merciful Father in heaven had been pleased to feed them. Therefore, lest we should rush over such a precipice, let us remember that this sacred feast is medicine to the sick, comfort to the sinner, and bounty to the poor; while to the healthy, the righteous, and the rich, if any such could be found, it would be of no value.[240]

There is a story I heard while in Scotland about how Rev. "Rabbi" Duncan noticed a young girl troubled by a lack of assurance who let the cup pass her by.

---

239. Calvin, *Institutes* 4.1.15 (see also 4.17.41, where Calvin warns about the view that no one may partake of the Supper except the righteous and the innocent).
240. Ibid., 4.17.42.

§ 8.6 Emblems of the Gospel: Baptism and Lord's Supper

He stepped down from the pulpit and handed the cup back to her. He told her something like, "Take it, lassy; it is meant for sinners such as you and I." That's the point. The Eucharist is the gospel meal for all who come to Jesus. Moltmann is right when he insists that given the open invitation of the Lord to sup with him, the restrictive measures of churches must be justified before the eyes of the crucified one.[241] Open communion is the tradition received from Jesus and transmitted by Paul, but unfortunately has turned into a ritual reserved for the righteous in many evangelical churches today.

Don't get me wrong. I don't believe that communion should be offered indiscriminately. Personally, I would not receive communion from or give communion to someone I knew to be an outright apostate. It is possible to abuse the Lord's Table, like those churches that give communion to cats and dogs.[242] Sadly, in church history some pretty disgusting things have been done at communion. According to Epiphanius, heretical groups such as the Borborites, Coddians, and Phibionites engaged in erotic group sex and then used semen and menstrual blood as eucharistic materials.[243] Furthermore, contra Moltmann, I do not think that the invitation to the crucified one extends to the world at large.[244] After all, the invitation of the Lord's Supper is for fellowship with one who is confessed as "Lord" by the invitees; it's not a rite for religious tourists. We cannot reduce this meal to a cheap grace that divorces gospel, discipleship, and fellowship from each other.[245]

However, although the Eucharist is not a meal designed for unbelievers, Paul knows about unbelievers attending worship services, yet he makes no ruling as to regards their participation in the Eucharist itself (1 Cor 14:24–25). My gut feeling is that the Eucharist is not a designated means of evangelism; it probably strikes unchurched people as a rather peculiar ritual. Even so, there is a sense in which the Eucharist offers us the gospel, a chance to "taste and see that the LORD is good" and to learn that "blessed is the one who takes refuge in him" (Ps 34:8). The Eucharist is a place where the journey of faith can finally cross the threshold into the pastures of assent to the gospel, attachment to Christ, and assurance in the God who saves. It is for pilgrims on the path from unfaith to faith. I have a friend who grew up in a Christian home and who came to faith through a communion service. Should we be surprised? With the gospel being preached in word and symbol, I would expect it to happen more often!

---

241. Jürgen Moltmann, *Church in the Power of the Spirit: A Contribution to a Messianic Ecclesiology* (London: SCM, 1992), 246.

242. Read the story about St. Peter's Anglican church in Toronto (www.care2.com/causes/dog-receives-communion-at-church.html).

243. Epiphanius, *Pan.* 25–26.

244. Moltmann, *Church in the Power of the Spirit*, 246.

245. Cf. Wolfhart Pannenberg, *Systematic Theology* (3 vols.; trans. G. W. Bromiley; Edinburgh: T&T Clark, 1991), 3:329–30.

ECCLESIOLOGY IN CONTENTION #6: PAEDOCOMMUNION

The matter of paedocommunion, children participating in the Eucharist, is a disputed matter in the Reformed churches. It's not an issue in Baptist churches, who generally only administer communion to professing baptized members. Generally speaking, Reformed, Anglican, Lutheran, and Catholic churches have only administered the Eucharist to people who are baptized and have made an open profession of faith, often in conjunction with confirmation.

However, a number of Reformed theologians have argued that the logic of covenant theology requires that covenant children participate in the covenant meal. My reckoning is that if one admits a child to the covenant family through baptism and then omits them from the covenant meal, one has basically capitulated to the Baptist position that children are only potential Christians and not de facto members of the covenant family. How can one accept them into the household of faith through baptism and then exclude them from the Eucharist as you would a pagan or an apostate?

Unsurprisingly, a number of ex-Baptists turned Reformed have been among the main advocates for paedocommunion. I think they have sensed the logical pressure of covenant theology and campaigned for covenant children to participate in the covenant feast. What is more, if children shared in the Passover meal celebrated by Israel in the Mosaic covenant (Exod 12:26–27; 13:8, 14), should they not share in the mystery of the Paschal Lamb in the new covenant? Paul regarded all who were baptized as part of the body of Christ (1 Cor 12:13), and he regarded the children of believers as holy (7:14). Did children participate in communal Agape meals? I imagine so, especially if that was the only meal that their family ate that day!

There is good evidence that in the early church, sometimes at least, infants partook of communion. Augustine argued that Jesus is pro-infant! The African bishop wrote: "Yes, they're infants, but they are his members. They're infants, but they receive his sacraments. They are infants, but they share in his table, in order to have life in themselves."[246] Though much has been written on the subject, especially in relation to the "Federal Vision," the best case I've heard for it comes from the Anglican bishop of North Sydney, Glenn Davies. I quote him *in extenso*:

> The Lord's Supper is for the Lord's people. It is a meal in celebration of the redemption he has won for us. All those to whom this salvation belongs are appropriate guests at the

---

246. Augustine, *Serm.* 174.7.

Lord's Table. Participation in the Lord's Supper is participation in Christ. To deny this meal to those who participate in Christ is a travesty of the one body in which we all share. Our covenant children are members of Christ's body and share in Christ. They should therefore share in the one bread and drink the same cup of blessing which we drink. However this is not to suggest that the warnings [of] 1 Cor 11:27–30 have no relevance for children. Participants in the covenant meal are required to be in covenantal fellowship, and that covenantal fellowship is evidenced, through God's grace, by covenantal obedience.

Yet it is a mistake to judge the faithfulness of an individual solely in terms of mature self-understanding or an articulate profession of faith. Evidence of covenant standing is not correlative to one's age. An understanding appropriate to the age, however, does not necessarily imply that children have the ability to articulate the meaning of the sacrament in adult thought forms. Conversely, an inability to give an articulate explanation of the relationship a child sustains to his or her parents does not mean that they have an incorrect understanding of their relationship to them. There is much that may be deficient about our own understanding of the Lord's Supper, as indeed there was for the twelve apostles who first took of it with their Master. Yet the immaturity of their understanding did not prevent their participation in that Supper.

The importance of Paul's warnings, however, is whether or not the child is remaining faithful to the covenant in which he or she stands. To deny them the Lord's Supper is to effectively discipline them in the same way we would do a covenant breaker. Their exclusion is tantamount to identifying them with the world, unworthy to eat and drink the body and blood of the Lord. Yet our children belong to God, by the sure promise of his Word signed and sealed in baptism. Let us then feed them with the blessing of Christ, and teach them through the Supper that the privilege of union and communion with Christ belongs to them. The Lord's Supper is for the Lord's Children.[247]

I would suggest that children at an appropriate age of intellectual capacity, with due instruction from their parents about the significance of the meal, should partake in the Lord's Supper.

FURTHER READING

Davies, Glenn. "The Lord's Supper for the Lord's Children." *RTR* 50.1 (1991): 12–20.

Gallant, Tim. *Feed My Lambs: Why the Lord's Table Should be Restored to Covenant Children*. Grande Prairie, AL: Pactum Reformanda, 2002.

Venema, Cornelis P. *Children at the Lord's Table: Assessing the Case for Paedocommunion*. Grand Rapids: Reformed Heritage, 2009.

---

247. Glenn Davies, "The Lord's Supper for the Lord's Children," *RTR* 50 (1991): 19–20.

8.6.2.9 THE EUCHARIST AS DINNER THEATER

The Eucharist is the gospel in sight, smell, and taste. The gospel is proclaimed so we know what the elements mean. The drama of the gospel comes alive as we feed on the Christ who saved us by his death, resurrection, and ascension. We are participants in the eucharistic drama, where Christ is spiritually presented to us and we in turn fellowship with him. But what can we do to heighten our gratitude, increase our unity, and maximize the experience of grace?[248] I have one suggestion: make a real meal of it!

It was because of the type of abuses that occurred in Corinth that the "meal" became separated from the liturgical celebration of Christ's death and resurrection. However, it seems clear that in the beginning the early Christian Agape or "love feast" (Gk. *agapē*) was combined with the eucharistic celebration. According to Robert Jewett, "the purely symbolic meal of modern Christianity, restricted to a bit of bread and a sip of wine or juice, is tacitly presupposed for the early church, an assumption so preposterous that it is never articulated or acknowledged."[249] Bo Reicke has demonstrated that the early eucharistic meals took place in the context of a common meal through to the fourth century (see Jude 12, "These people are blemishes at your *love feasts*" [italics added]; Ign. *Smyrn.* 8.2, "It is not permissible either to baptize or to hold a love feast without the bishop").[250]

I want to suggest a return to the love feast for our Eucharist—a proper meal, which climaxes in a eucharistic celebration. This may not be practical in a church of several hundred people. In such cases, I wonder if the best place for a love feast is a cell group, a home Bible study meeting, or a small fellowship of families that meet on a regular week night to study the Scriptures, pray, worship, and hold a love feast. I've seen churches that hold alternative services in which the meal is the main part of the service and is accompanied by testimonies, prayer, teaching, and Eucharist. We might retain the usual practice of having the Eucharist when the whole church meets, but we should strive to bring back the love feast into our eucharistic worship.

As to how often one should celebrate the Eucharist we are given no clear instruction in Scripture.[251] One gets the impression from Acts 2:46 ("Every day they continued to meet together ... [and] broke bread in their homes and ate together") that it was a daily occurrence, though in Acts 20:7 ("On the first day of the week we came together to break bread") I suspect that it was weekly. The Reformed worship manuals counsel to do it "frequently." What "frequently" entails is a matter of

---

248. From a Baptist perspective see Ray Van Neste, "The Lord's Supper in the Context of the Local Church," in *The Lord's Supper: Remembering and Proclaiming Christ Until He Comes* (ed. Matthew R. Crawford and Thomas R. Schreiner; NACSBT 10; Nashville: Broadman & Holman, 2010), 364–90.

249. Robert Jewett, "Tenement Churches and Pauline Love Feasts," *QR* 14 (1994): 44.

250. Bo Reicke, *Diakonie, Festfreude und Zelos: in Verbindung mit der altchristlichen Agapenfeier* (Uppsala: Lundequist, 1951), 21–149.

251. Cf. Calvin, *Institutes* 4.17.44–46.

conscience and preference. I would prefer weekly, in the setting of a love feast in a home group, but perhaps monthly in a Sunday worship service.

The common complaint I hear is that holding the Lord's Supper too frequently can make the event stale, robotic, repetitive, and boring. However, that is only true if we put little to no preparation into it. If we prepare our eucharistic celebration with the same planning and effort that we use to prepare worship and sermons, we can make the Eucharist the penultimate climax of the service, second only to the preaching of the Word.

FURTHER READING

Barth, Markus. *Rediscovering the Lord's Supper*. Eugene, OR: Cascade, 2006.

Marshall, I. Howard. *Last Supper and Lord's Supper*. Grand Rapids: Eerdmans, 1980.

Moloney, Francis J. *A Body Broken for a Broken People: Eucharist in the New Testament*. Melbourne: Collins Dove, 1990.

Witherington, Ben III. *Making a Meal of It: Rethinking the Theology of the Lord's Supper*. Waco, TX: Baylor University Press, 2007.

WHAT TO TAKE HOME?

- Evangelical ecclesiology needs to better appreciate the value of the visible church, recover a vision for catholicity, and to be less individualistic.
- The church is not the kingdom of God, and the church does not build the kingdom; rather, the church builds for the kingdom.
- There is a diverse array of biblical images for the church from the "body of Christ" to "new creation."
- The church does not replace Israel; instead, the church is the representative of Israel in the messianic age.
- The church is shaped by the fact that it is an eschatological, Trinitarian, diaconal, fellowshiping, and holistic community.
- The marks of the church are "one, holy, catholic, and apostolic church," and the signs of the apostolic church are the faithful preaching of the Word and the proper administration of the sacraments.
- The main forms of church governance are Episcopal, Presbyterian, and Congregational.
- The purpose of the church is evangelism, discipleship, sacraments, kingdom work, and worship.
- The three main views of baptism are paedobaptism, credobaptism, and dual-practice baptism.
- Baptism has a key part in the salvific drama and is integral to our faith, union with Christ, and reception of the Spirit.
- The main views of the Eucharist are Catholic, Lutheran, Zwinglian, and Reformed.
- Christ is present in the Eucharist by the work of the Holy Spirit.
- The blessing of the Eucharist is its memorial of Christ, a participation with Christ, and a means of unity with other believers.
- The most biblical model for the Eucharist is an open table (perhaps even including children).

STUDY QUESTIONS FOR INDIVIDUALS AND GROUPS

1. To what extent do you demonstrate your membership and fellowship with believers outside of your own church?
2. Which biblical image for the church do you prefer and why?
3. In what way is the church called to the same vocation as Israel?
4. How does an evangelical view of apostolicity differ from Roman Catholic views?
5. Explain which model of church government you find most preferable.
6. What are your thoughts concerning the dual-baptism view?
7. What blessing or grace is there to be received by baptism?
8. Describe what the Eucharist symbolizes.
9. Explain your understanding of the presence of Christ in the Eucharist.

EPILOGUE: URGENT TASKS FOR EVANGELICAL THEOLOGY IN THE 21ST CENTURY

In some closing comments I want to suggest three urgent tasks for the future of evangelical theology for the next half century.

1. *Recapturing a gospel-centered faith.* I have labored the point at length, that the center and boundary of evangelical theology must be the evangel, the gospel. The gospel has the singular claim to be our theological center because it is indelibly connected to all of the doctrinal loci. Even more convincing, at least to me, is that the gospel is the theological center because it is the gospel that brings us to Christ.

If that is the case, then let us keep asking one question: so what? What does that the gospel have to do with my prayers and my preaching? What does gospel teach me about humility, dying to self, and being crucified to the world? How does gospel impact my approach to soteriological controversies about justification and whether I should cooperate with the local Orthodox Church in setting up a shelter for women and children escaping domestic violence? We must believe and live as if the gospel—with the Triune God as its epicenter—really makes a difference to all that we think, do, and say.

Let us never forget that evangelicals are called to be in the business of the evangel and all that pertains to it. I want to make it clear that being an evangelical is not about fractious theological polemics or schmoozing to the latest cultural fad. We are in the business of gospelizing, proclaiming the good news, and discipling men and women in a gospel-driven faith. Our task is to make sure that our spirituality, mission, worship, preaching, ministry, social concern, prayer, and counseling are characteristically evangelicalesque. We must become vessels of the gospel and carry the good news of Jesus Christ with us wherever we go; otherwise, we have no right to call ourselves evangelicals.

I'm all too conscious that I have only scratched the surface here of developing a gospelized theology. I think there needs to be further exploration as to exactly how

Epilogue: Urgent Tasks for Evangelical Theology in the 21st Century

the gospel holds the evangelical ship together at both the theological and practical levels. Attention needs to be paid in our seminaries and churches to plotting the intersection between gospel, doctrine, ethics, and praxis.

To give a few examples: one task that comes immediately to mind is pursuing how the gospel shapes approaches to engaging culture. Or else imagine a fully worked out doctrine of pneumatology built on the gospel as the cornerstone for its construction. Or one can envisage using the gospel to plot the relationship between the work of Christ and the imitation of Christ and so provide a helpful integration between faith and obedience without confusing "law" and "gospel," and without relaxing Jesus' strenuous commands to his followers. The development of a distinctively evangelical view of ecumenism in a post-Christian society commends itself as another avenue of study. Some brave soul is also welcomed to kick off a conversation on how the gospel impacts our attitudes toward suffering and practicing pastoral care. The possibilities are endless!

Constantly steering our churches, parachurch ministries, and families toward the gospel—and to the Lord, whom the gospel presents to us as both Judge and Savior—is probably the single most important factor for ushering in genuine evangelical renewal in our churches and giving the Holy Spirit more to work with in terms of ushering in a period of spiritual revival. The church that is thoroughly gospelized in its theology and praxis will never run the danger of assuming the gospel, nor will it be easily assuaged from it.

2. *Restoring an apocalyptic worldview.* The task of liberal theology has always been the de-apocalyptizing of theology. This is observable from Marcion to Schleiermacher to Harnack to Bultmann. The Christian hope for the displacement of this world with a new heaven and a new earth is often substituted with religious poetry, social ethics, or the cultural domestication of the faith—these are the marks of a compromised Christianity. According to liberal theologians, evangelical believers have, to use the words of Judas in *Jesus Christ Superstar*, "Too much heaven on their minds." Many self-confessed "progressive Christians" believe that in order to save Christianity, one must crucify its hope for the supernatural transformation of this world in favor of a this-worldly social transformation through utilitarian means. In fact, John Gager, an "unbelieving Christian" by his own profession, argues that the way the apostle Paul can be made relevant to society is to strip away the apocalyptic framework from his thinking.[252]

Let me be clear. This de-apocalypticizing agenda must be put to the eschatological sword. The church has confessed that it lives within an invasive story. God, the

---

252. John Gager, *Re-Reading Paul* (New York: Oxford University Press, 2000), 151–52.

kingdom, and a new creation have burst into our world, bringing with it the incipient transformation of our age by the Son and the Spirit, which is a foretaste of a world to come. I've tried to express this by leaning on Ernst Käsemann's refrain that God intends to "recapture the world for himself" and N. T. Wright's catch phrase about God "putting the world to rights." We look at God's justice to be declared and enacted on the world, not immanently, but by a supernatural and transcendent act. For only in light of the eschatological narrative of God's forthcoming victory over death and the devil does Christian hope have any currency. We maintain hope in a God who holds our future in his hand, and we entrust ourselves to his faithfulness.

Apocalyptic theology flows through Christian doctrine like blood in the veins of our body. Our worldview and worship are inspired by the invasion of heavenly forces upon the earth and the eventual redemption of our bodies in a new cosmos. Our present identity and mission are determined by who Jesus is and who he will be revealed to be at the end of history. The gospel we announce is fundamentally a declaration of victory to those who do not even believe there is a battle going on. The triumph of the Lamb over the powers and principalities of this world authorizes us to bring redemption to the men and women who live under the tyranny of death, sin, evil, and injustice. Thus, an apocalyptic theology, far from stifling social action and cultural engagement, in fact spurs us on toward it because we understand ourselves as engaging in a struggle against the world, the flesh, and the devil at every corner that we walk.

By restoring an apocalyptic worldview, I do not mean giving legitimacy to certain end-time schemes that for some mystifying reason continue to attract attention in some quarters. I mean, rather, orientating our theology and discipleship to the triumphant Lamb and ensuring that theology retains a focus on the mystery and majesty of God, his otherness, and his plan to turn this sin-ridden earth into a new garden of Eden. A healthy dose of apocalypticism means that theology can never be undertaken as an exercise in intellectual curiosity. A theology textbook should be more like a manual for warfare, guiding the soldiers of Christ in how to take every thought captive to Christ and instructing them on how to act as peacekeepers in a world that knows no peace.

3. *Rethinking an evangelical ecclesiology.* It is evident to me that we live in a time of post-denominationalism in the west. We are witnessing a worn-out ecumenical movement in the mainline churches and are contemporaries to a dramatic growth of Christianity in the global south. These are significant factors that shape the global church scene. This means that there has been no other time in history when evangelicals really need to beef up their doctrine of the church to deal with these issues.

First, I write this volume at a time when many evangelicals are leaving their liberal denominations because of unorthodox teachings, leaving their conservative denominations because of bureaucracy, and are busy planting independent churches all over English-speaking countries. I understand the attraction, and I genuinely applaud the efforts of this generation of church planters. My concern, however, is whether their newfound freedom from the fetters of ecclesial structure is won at the price of catholicity. It takes more than attending gospel conferences like "The Gospel Coalition" and "Together for the Gospel" to count oneself in communion with a wider body of Christians.

If one really believes that they stand in a relationship with "all those everywhere who call on the name of our Lord Jesus Christ—their Lord and ours" (1 Cor 1:2), they are going to have to find a way to prove it. Spiritual unity must be expressed visibly. A communion based entirely on invisible unity is a bit like an online marriage, where husband and wife never actually come into physical contact with each other, but simply trade comments via emails and love each other from the safe distances of their laptops. Marriage is hard work and risky business, and so is striving for visible, sacramental, and ministerial unity with other Christians. Since we live in a post-denominational age, where people's loyalty to denominations is at an all-time low, we can either make this a time when everyone does what is ecclesiologically right in his or her own eyes, or we can seize on this fluid movement across denominational boundaries and accept it as an opportunity for building visible networks, shared ministries, and common industries of gospelizing, the likes of which have never been seen before.

Second, the great optimism that the ecumenical movement ushered in at the dawn of the 1960s died around the same time that Elvis did. Evangelicals have traditionally been suspicious towards ecumenism, with some justification I would say, and evangelicals have never been terribly excited about working with groups whom they largely regard either with disdain or with distrust. It is worth pointing out that the Reformation was primarily about returning the medieval Roman Catholic Church to its own apostolic gospel. A lot of water has passed under the bridge since Martin Luther posted his ninety-five theses, but the need for reformation, renewal, and revival in other churches still remains. I would say that the Reformed or Protestant churches still have the charge of bringing the "catholic church" (by which I mean all historic Christ-confessing churches) into a phase of spiritual and evangelical renewal by teaching and showing them the doctrine of the gospel.

In many ways, this is already happening in segments of Africa and South America. In many places evangelicals are influencing the religious culture and theological texture of the landscape. But if we are going to do that more widely, we need to be better informed about other Christian traditions, we need to build bridges over which the gospel can travel, and we must develop a much greater appreciation of the need for Christian unity. In a post-Christian West and a post-Arab Spring East, it will be vital to the health of our churches, evangelical or nonevangelical, that we at least begin talking to each other and finding ways to move beyond old debates and work together for the oneness of Christ's body.

The evangelical churches of the West must also add a new factor into their ecclesiology: the global church. We are at a stage where Christianity is growing radically in the global south and stagnating in Europe and North America. A point is coming when the global south will be the major population centers of Christianity. Thus, we need to take greater account of voices in the global church in the development of theology and also ensure that we no longer act toward the global church with an attitude of colonial condescension.

While ecclesiology has been a typical evangelical blind spot, it is time to bring it to the forefront of our thinking. Theology is for the church, and all ministry is to and through the church. Thus, a renewed doctrine of the church should trickle down into our theology and ministry as well. I submit that reloading our ecclesiology with new gospel software will give us a greater appreciation for the catholicity of the church, propel us toward bold, new, gospel-driven ventures in Christian unity, and move us to listen to and train leaders in the global churches.

SELECT BIBLIOGRAPHY

Abasciano, Brian J. "Corporate Election in Romans 9: A Reply to Thomas Schreiner." *JETS* 49 (2006): 351–71.
Achard, Robert Martin. *A Light to the Nations: A Study of the Old Testament Concept of Israel's Mission to the World*. Trans. J. P. Smith. Edinburgh: Oliver & Boyd, 1962.
Allen, R. Michael. *Reformed Theology*. London: T&T Clark, 2010.
Allert, Craig D. *A High View of Scripture: The Authority of the Bible and the Formation of the New Testament Canon*. Grand Rapids: Baker, 2007.
Allison, Dale C. *The Historical Christ and the Theological Jesus*. Grand Rapids: Eerdmans, 2009.
———. *Resurrecting Jesus*. London: T&T Clark, 2005.
Anderson, Allan. *An Introduction to Pentecostalism: Global Charismatic Christianity*. Cambridge: Cambridge University Press, 2004.
Armstrong, J. H., ed. *Understanding Four Views on Baptism*. Grand Rapids: Zondervan, 2007.
———. ed. *Understanding Four Views on the Lord's Supper*. Grand Rapids: Zondervan, 2007.
Ashby, Stephen M. "A Reformed Arminian View." Pages 137–87 in *Four Views on Eternal Security*. Edited by J. Matthew Pinson. Grand Rapids: Zondervan, 2002.
Aulen, Gustaf. *Christus Victor*. London: SPCK, 1953.
Aune, David E. "Eschatology (Early Christian)." *ABD*, 2:594–609.
———. *Revelation*. WBC. 3 vols. Dallas: Word, 1997–98.
———. *Rereading Paul Together: Protestant and Catholic Perspectives on Justification*. Grand Rapids: Baker, 2006.
Avis, Paul, ed. *Divine Revelation*. London: Darton, Longman and Todd, 1997.
Baddeley, Mark. "Does God Feel Our Pain?" *The Briefing* 384 (2010): 12–17.
Bahnsen, Greg L. *Van Til's Apologetic: Readings and Analysis*. Philipsburg, NJ: Presbyterian & Reformed, 1998.
Bailey, Daniel P. "Concepts of *Stellvertretung* in the Interpretation of Isaiah 53." Pages 223–50 in *Jesus and the Suffering Servant: Isaiah 53 and Christian Origins*. Edited by W. H. Bellinger and W. R. Farmer. Harrisburg, PA: Trinity Press International, 1998.

Select Bibliography

Balmer, Randall. *The Making of Evangelicalism: From Revivalism to Politics and Beyond.* Waco, TX: Baylor University Press, 2010.

Balthasar, Hans Urs von. *The Scandal of the Incarnation: Irenaeus against the Heresies.* San Francisco: Ignatius, 1990.

———. *Theodrama: The Last Act.* San Francisco: Ignatius, 1998.

Barbour, Ian. *Issues in Science and Religion.* New York: Harper & Row, 1971.

Barnett, Paul. *Jesus and the Logic of History.* NSBT. Downers Grove, IL: InterVarsity Press, 1997.

Barr, James. *The Bible in the Modern World.* London: SCM, 1973.

———. *Biblical Faith and Natural Theology.* Oxford: Clarendon, 1993.

Barrett, C.K. *Acts 1–14.* ICC. Edinburgh: T&T Clark, 1994.

———. *The Epistle to the Romans.* BNTC. 2nd ed. London: Black, 1991.

———. *The Second Epistle to the Corinthians.* London: Harper & Row, 1957.

Barth, Karl. *Church Dogmatics.* 4 vols. Trans. G. W. Bromiley. London: Continuum, 2004.

———. *Evangelical Theology: An Introduction.* New York: Holt, Rinehart, & Winston, 1963.

———. *The Göttingen Dogmatics: Instruction in the Christian Religion.* Edited by H. Reiffen. Trans. G. W. Bromiley. Grand Rapids: Eerdmans, 1991.

———. *The Humanity of God.* Richmond: John Knox, 1960.

Barth, Markus. "Baptism and Evangelism." *SJT* 12 (1959): 32–40.

———. *Justification.* Trans. A. M. Woodruff III. Eugene, OR: Wipf & Stock, 2006.

———. *Rediscovering the Lord's Supper.* Eugene, OR: Cascade, 2006.

———. *Die Taufe—ein Sakrament?: Ein exegetischer Beitrag zum Gespräch über die kirchliche Taufe.* Zollikon-Zürich: Evangelische Verlag, 1951.

Barth, Markus., and Helmut Blanke. *Colossians: A New Translation with Introduction and Commentary.* AB. Trans. A. B. Beck. New York: Doubleday, 1994.

Barth, Markus and Verne H. Fletcher. *Acquittal by Resurrection.* New York: Holt, Rinehard and Winston, 1964.

Basden, Paul A., and David S. Dockery, eds. *The People of God: Essays on the Believers' Church.* Nashville: Broadman & Holman, 1991.

Bateman Herbert W., ed. *Four Views on the Warning Passages in Hebrews.* Grand Rapids: Kregel, 2007.

———. ed. *Three Central Issues in Contemporary Dispensationalism.* Grand Rapids: Kregel, 1999.

Bauckham, Richard. "The Delay of the Parousia." *TynBul* 31 (1980): 3–36.

———. "The Future of Jesus Christ." Pages 265–80 in *The Cambridge Companion to Jesus.* Edited by M. N. Bockmuehl. Cambridge: Cambridge University Press, 2001.

———. "Hades, Hell." *ABD*, 3:14-15.

———. *Jesus and the God of Israel: "God Crucified" and Other Studies on the New Testament's Christology of Divine Identity*. Milton Keynes: Paternoster, 2008.

———. "Jesus the Revelation of God." Pages 174–200 in *Divine Revelation*. Edited by P. Avis. Grand Rapids: Eerdmans, 1997.

———. *Jude, 2 Peter*. WBC. Waco, TX: Word, 1983.

———. *The Theology of the Book of Revelation*. Cambridge: Cambridge University Press, 1993.

Bavinck, Hermann. *Reformed Dogmatics. Volume 1: Prolegomena*. Edited by J. Bolt. Trans. by J. Vriend. Grand Rapids: Baker, 2003.

———. *Reformed Dogmatics. Volume 2: God and Creation*. Edited by J. Bolt. Trans. by J. Vriend. Grand Rapids: Baker, 2004.

Beale, Greg K. *The Book of Revelation*. NIGTC. Grand Rapids: Eerdmans, 1999.

———. "The Eschatological Conception of New Testament Theology." Pages 11–52 in *The Reader Must Understand: Eschatology in Bible and Theology*. Edited by M. Elliott and K. E. Brower. Leicester, UK: Apollos, 1997.

———. "Peace and Mercy upon the Israel of God: The Old Testament Background of Galatians 6,16b." *Bib* 80 (1999): 204–23.

———. *The Temple and the Church's Mission*. NSBT 17. Downers Grove, IL: InterVarsity Press, 2004.

Beasley-Murray, George R. *Baptism in the New Testament*. London: Macmillan, 1962.

———. *John*. WBC. Dallas: Word, 1999.

Bebbington, David. *Evangelicalism in Modern Britain: A History from the 1730s to the 1980s*. Grand Rapids: Baker, 1989.

———. "The Gospel in the Nineteenth Century." *VE* 13 (1983): 19–28.

Bell, Richard H. *No One Seeks God: An Exegetical and Theological Study of Romans 1.18–3.20*. WUNT 1.106. Tübingen: Mohr/Siebeck, 1998.

———. *Provoked to Jealousy: The Origin and Purpose of the Jealousy Motif in Romans*. WUNT 2.63. Tübingen: Mohr/Siebeck, 1994.

Bell, Rob. *Love Wins: A Book about Heaven, Hell, and the Fate of Every Person Who Ever Lived*. New York: Harper, 2011.

Bender, Kimlyn J. *Karl Barth's Christological Ecclesiology*. Aldershot, UK: Ashgate, 2005.

Berding, Kenneth, and Jonathan Lunde, eds. *Three Views on the New Testament Use of the Old Testament*. Grand Rapids: Zondervan, 2008.

Berkhof, Hendrikus. *The Christian Faith: An Introduction to the Study of the Faith*. Grand Rapids: Eerdmans, 1979.

Berkhof, Louis. *The History of Christian Doctrines*. Grand Rapids: Baker, 1975.

———. *Systematic Theology*. Grand Rapids: Eerdmans, 1949.

Berkouwer, G. C. *Divine Election*. Grand Rapids: Eerdmans, 1960.

———. *Faith and Sanctification*. Grand Rapids: Eerdmans, 1952.

———. *General Revelation*. Grand Rapids: Eerdmans, 1955.

———. *Man: The Image of God*. Grand Rapids: Eerdmans, 1962.

———. *The Triumph of Grace in the Theology of Karl Barth*. Grand Rapids: Eerdmans, 1956.

Bilezikian, Gilbert. "Hermeneutical Bungee-Jumping: Subordination in the Trinity." *JETS* 40 (1997): 57–68.

Billings, J. Todd. *Calvin, Participation, and the Gift*. Oxford: Oxford University Press, 2007.

———. *The Word of God for the People of God: An Entryway to the Theological Interpretation of Scripture*. Grand Rapid: Eerdmans, 2010.

Bird, Michael F. *Are You the One Who Is to Come? The Historical Jesus and the Messianic Question*. Grand Rapids: Baker, 2009.

———. *A Bird's-Eye View of Paul: The Man, His Mission and His Message*. Nottingham, UK: Inter-Varsity Press, 2008.

———. "Birth of Jesus." Pages 71–75 in *Encyclopedia of the Historical Jesus*. Edited by C. A. Evans. New York: Routledge, 2008.

———. *Colossians and Philemon*. NCCS; Eugene, OR: Cascade, 2009.

———. "The Crucifixion of Jesus as the Fulfilment of Mark 9:1." *TrinJ* 24 (2003): 23–36.

———. "From Manuscript to MP3." Pages 1–18 in *The Sacred Text: Excavating the Texts, Exploring the Interpretations, and Engaging the Theologies of the Christian Scriptures*. Edited by M. Bird and M. Pahl. Piscataway, NJ: Gorgias, 2010.

———. "Is There Really a 'Third Quest' for the Historical Jesus?" *SBET* 24 (2006): 195–256.

———. *Jesus and the Origins of the Gentile Mission*. LNTS 331. London: T&T Clark, 2006.

———. "John the Baptist." Pages 61–80 in *Jesus among His Friends and Enemies*. Edited by L. Hurtado and C. Keith. Grand Rapids: Baker, 2011.

———. "Judgment and Justification in Paul: A Review Article." *BBR* 18 (2008): 299–313.

———. "Justification: A Progressive Reformer View." Pages 131–57 in *Five Views of Justification*. Edited by P. R. Eddy and J. Beilby. Downers Grove, IL: Inter-Varsity Press, 2011.

———. "New Testament Theology Reloaded: Integrating Biblical Theology and Christian Origins." *TynBul* 60 (2009): 161–87.

———. "The Peril of Modernizing Jesus and the Crisis of Not Contemporizing the Christ." *EvQ* 78 (2006): 291–312.

———. "Progressive Reformed Response to Theosis." Pages 249–53 in *Five Views of Justification*. Edited by P. R. Eddy and J. Beilby. Downers Grove, IL: InterVarsity Press, 2011.

———. "Re-Thinking a Sacramental View of Baptism and the Lord's Supper for the Post-Christendom Baptist Church." Pages 61–76 in *Baptist Sacramentalism 2*. Edited by Anthony R. Cross and Philip E. Thompson. SBHT 5. Milton Keynes, UK: Paternoster, 2008.

———. *The Saving Righteousness of God: Studies in Paul, Justification and the New Perspective*. PBM. Carlisle, UK: Paternoster, 2007.

———. "Should Evangelicals Participate in the 'Third Quest for the Historical Jesus'?" *Them* 29 (2004): 4–14.

———. "What If Martin Luther Had Read the Dead Sea Scrolls? Historical Particularity and Theological Interpretation in Pauline Theology: Galatians as a Test Case." *JTI* 3 (2009): 107–25.

Bird, Michael F., and James G. Crossley. *How Did Christianity Begin? A Believer and Non-Believer Examine the Evidence*. London: SPCK, 2008.

Bird, Michael F., and Robert Shillaker. "The Son Really, Really Is the Son: A Response to Kevin Giles." *TrinJ* 30 (2009): 257–68.

———. "Subordination in the Trinity and Gender Roles: A Response to Recent Discussion." *TrinJ* 29 (2008): 267–83.

Bird, Michael F., and Preston M. Sprinkle, eds. *The Faith of Jesus Christ: Exegetical, Biblical, and Theological Studies*. Milton Keynes, UK: Paternoster, 2009.

Blaising, Craig A. "Dispensationalism: The Search for a Definition." Pages 13–34 in *Dispensationalism, Israel and the Church: The Search for a Definition*. Grand Rapids: Zondervan, 1992.

Blaising, Craig A., and Darrell L. Bock, eds. *Dispensationalism, Israel and the Church: The Search for a Definition*. Grand Rapids: Zondervan, 1992.

Blocher, Henri. "*Agnus Victor*: The Atonement as Victory and Vicarious Punishment." Pages 67–91 in *What Does It Mean to Be Saved?* Edited by J. G. Stackhouse. Grand Rapids: Baker, 2002.

———. "God and the Cross." Pages 125–41 in *Engaging the Doctrine of God: Contemporary Protestant Perspectives*. Edited by B. L. McCormack. Grand Rapids: Baker, 2008.

———. "Helpful or Harmful? The 'Apocrypha' and Evangelical Theology." *EJTh* 13 (2004): 81–90.

———. *In the Beginning: The Opening Chapters of Genesis*. Trans. D. G. Preston; Leicester, UK: Inter-Varsity Press, 1984.

———. "Justification of the Ungodly (*Sola Fide*): Theological Reflections." Pages 465–500 in *Justification and Variegated Nomism: Volume 2—The Paradoxes of Paul*. Edited by D. A. Carson, Mark A. Seifrid, and Peter T. O'Brien. Grand Rapids: Baker, 2004.

———. *Original Sin: Illuminating the Riddle*. NSBT 5. Downers Grove, IL: InterVarsity Press, 1997.

———. "The Sacrifice of Jesus Christ: The Current Theological Situation." *EJTh* 8 (1999): 23–36.

Bloesch, Donald G. *The Church: Sacraments, Worship, Ministry, Mission*. Downers Grove, IL: InterVarsity Press, 2002.

———. *God the Almighty: Power, Wisdom, Holiness, Love*. Downers Grove, IL: InterVarsity Press, 1995.

———. *Holy Scripture: Revelation, Inspiration and Interpretation*. Downers Grove, IL: InterVarsity Press, 1994.

———. *The Holy Spirit: Works and Gifts*. Downers Grove, IL: InterVarsity Press, 2000.

———. *Jesus Christ: Savior and Lord*. Downers Grove, IL: InterVarsity Press, 2005.

———. *The Last Things: Resurrection, Judgment, Glory*. Downers Grove, IL: InterVarsity Press, 2004.

———. *A Theology of Word and Spirit: Authority and Method in Theology*. Downers Grove, IL: InterVarsity Press, 1992.

Bock, Darrell L. *Recovering the Real Lost Gospel*. Nashville: Broadman & Holman, 2010.

Bock, Darrell L., and Robert L. Webb, eds. *Key Events in the Life of the Historical Jesus: A Collaborative Exploration of Context and Coherence*. Grand Rapids: Eerdmans, 2010.

Bockmuehl, Markus. *This Jesus: Martyr, Lord, Messiah*. London: T&T Clark, 1994.

———. *Seeing the Word: Refocusing New Testament Study*. Grand Rapids: Baker, 2006.

Boersma, Hans. *Violence, Hospitality, and the Cross: Reappropriating the Atonement Tradition*. Grand Rapids: Baker, 2004.

Boettner, Loraine. *The Millennium*. Philadelphia, PA: Presbyterian & Reformed, 1957.

———. *The Reformed Doctrine of Predestination*. Philadelphia: Presbyterian and Reformed, 1932.

———. "Postmillennialism." Pages 115–41 in *The Meaning of the Millennium: Four Views*. Edited by R. G. Clouse. Downers Grove, IL: InterVarsity Press, 1977.

Boff, Leonardo. *Trinity and Society: Theology of Liberation*. Marynoll, NY: Orbis, 1988.

Bolt, Peter G. *The Cross from a Distance: Atonement in Mark's Gospel*. NSBT. Downers Grove, IL: InterVarsity Press, 2004.

———. "Three Heads in the Divine Order: The Early Church Fathers and 1 Corinthians 11:3." *RTR* 64 (2005): 147–61.

———. ed. *Christ's Victory over Evil: Biblical Theology and Pastoral Ministry*. Nottingham: Apollos, 2009.

Bonda, Jan. *The One Purpose of God: An Answer to the Doctrine of Eternal Punishment*. Grand Rapids: Eerdmans, 1998.

Bonhoeffer, Dietrich. *The Cost of Discipleship*. New York: Macmillan, 1959.

———. *Letters and Papers from Prison*. New York: Macmillan, 1967.

Borland, James. *Christ in the Old Testament*. Fearn, UK: Christian Focus, 2010.

Bornkamm, Günther. *Jesus of Nazareth*. Trans. I. Mcluskey, F. Mcluskey, and J. Robinson. New York: Harper & Row, 1960.

Bowles, Ralph G. "Does Revelation 14:11 Teach Eternal Torment? Examining a Proof-text on Hell." *EvQ* 73 (2001): 21–36.

Bowman, Robert M., and J. Ed Komoszewski. *Putting Jesus in His Place: The Case for the Deity of Christ*. Grand Rapids: Kregel, 2007.

Boyd, Gregory A. *Letters from a Skeptic*. Wheaton, IL: Victor, 1994.

———. *God at War: The Bible and Spiritual Conflict*. Downers Grove, IL: InterVarsity Press, 1997.

———. "Christus Victor View." Pages 23–49 in *The Nature of the Atonement: Four Views*. Edited by J. Beilby and P. R. Eddy. Downers Grove, IL: InterVarsity Press, 2006.

Boyd, Gregory A., and Paul R. Eddy. *Across the Spectrum: Understanding Issues in Evangelical Theology*. Grand Rapids: Baker, 2009.

Bradshaw, Tim. *The Olive Branch: An Evangelical Anglican Doctrine of the Church*. Carlisle, UK: Paternoster, 2006.

Bray, Gerald L. *The Doctrine of God*. Downers Grove, IL: InterVarsity Press, 1993.

———. "The Double Procession of the Holy Spirit in Evangelical Theology Today: Do We Still Need It?" *JETS* 41 (1998): 415–26.

———. "The *Filioque* Clause in History and Theology." *TynBul* 34 (1983): 91–144.

———. ed. and trans. *Commentaries on Romans and 1–2 Corinthians by Ambrosiaster*. ACT; Downers Grove, IL: InterVarsity Press, 2009.

Bromiley, Geoffrey W. "Atone." *ISBE*, 1:352–59.

———. "The Authority of Scripture." Pages 15–23 in *The New Bible Commentary*. Edited by F. Davidson, A. M. Stibbs, and E. F. Kevan. London: Inter-Varsity Fellowship, 1954.

———. *An Introduction to the Theology of Karl Barth*. Grand Rapids: Eerdmans, 1979.

Select Bibliography

Brown, David. "Anselm on Atonement." Pages 279–302 in *The Cambridge Companion to Anselm*. Edited by B. Davies and B. Leftow. Cambridge: Cambridge University Press, 2005.

Brown, Raymond. *The Birth of the Messiah*. ABRL. New York: Doubleday, 1993.

Bruce, F. F. *The Canon of Scripture*. Downers Grove, IL: InterVarsity Press, 1988.

———. *The Epistle to the Hebrews*. NICNT, rev. ed. Grand Rapids: Eerdmans, 1990.

Brueggemann, Walter. *Isaiah 40–66*. Louisville: Westminster John Knox, 1998.

———. *Theology of the Old Testament: Testimony, Dispute, Advocacy*. Minneapolis: Fortress, 1997.

Brunner, Emil. *The Christian Doctrine of God*. 2 vols. Trans. O. Wyon. London: Lutterworth, 1949.

———. *Dogmatics: The Christian Doctrine of Creation and Redemption*. Philadelphia: Westminster, 1980.

———. *Man in Revolt*. Trans. O. Wyon. New York: Scribner's, 1939.

Bullinger, Heinrich. *Werke Dritte Abteilung: Theologische Schriften—Band 2: Unveröffentlichte Werke aus der Kappeler Zeit*. Zürich: Theologischer Verlag Zürich, 1991.

Bultmann, Rudolf. *The Gospel of John: A Commentary*. Trans. G. R. Beasley-Murray. Philadelphia: Westminster, 1971.

———. "New Testament and Mythology." Pages 1–44 in *New Testament and Mythology and Other Basic Writings*. Trans. S. M. Ogden. Philadelphia: Fortress, 1984.

———. *Theology of the New Testament*. 2 vols. Trans. K. Grobel. London: SCM, 1952.

Burge, Gary M. *Who Are God's People in the Middle East?* Grand Rapids: Zondervan, 1993.

———. *Whose Land? Whose Promise? What Christians Are Not Being Told about Israel and the Palestinians*. Cleveland: Pilgrim, 2003.

Burgess, Stanley M. *The Holy Spirit: Eastern Christian Traditions*. Peabody, MA: Hendrickson, 1989.

Burke, Trevor. *Adopted into God's Family: Exploring a Pauline Metaphor*. Downers Grove, IL: InterVarsity Press, 2006.

Burnett, Gary W. *Paul and the Salvation of the Individual*. Leiden: Brill, 2001.

Burridge, Richard A., and Graham Gould. *Jesus Now and Then*. Grand Rapids: Eerdmans, 2004.

Cadbury, Henry. *The Peril of Modernizing Jesus*. London: SPCK, 1962.

Campbell, Iain D. *The Doctrine of Sin: In Reformed and Neo-Orthodox Thought*. Fearn, UK: Christian Focus, 1999.

Caneday, Ardel B. "The Language of God and Adam's Genesis & Historicity in Paul's Gospel." *SWBTJ* 15 (2001): 26–49.

Carnell, Edward J. *The Case for Christian Orthodox Theology*. Eugene, OR: Wipf & Stock, 2005.

Carson, D. A. "The Apocryphal/Deuterocanonical Books: An Evangelical View." Pages xliv–xlvii in *The Parallel Apocrypha*. Edited by John Kohlenberger. Oxford: Oxford University Press, 1997.

———. "Atonement in Romans 3:21–26." Pages 117–39 in *The Glory of the Atonement*. Edited by C. E. Hill and F. A. James. Downers Grove, IL: InterVarsity Press, 2005.

———. "The Biblical Gospel." Pages 75–85 in *For Such a Time as This: Perspectives on Evangelicalism, Past, Present, and Future*. Edited by S. Brady and H. Rowdon. London: Evangelical Alliance, 1996.

———. *Christ and Culture Revisited*. Grand Rapids: Eerdmans, 2008.

———. *Evangelicalism: What Is It and Is It Worth Keeping?* Wheaton, IL: Crossway, 2010.

———. *The Gagging of God: Christianity Confronts Pluralism*. Grand Rapids: Zondervan, 1996.

———. *The God Who Is There: Finding Your Place in God's Story*. Grand Rapids: Baker, 2010.

———. *The Gospel according to John*. PNTC. Grand Rapids: Eerdmans, 1991.

———. *Holy Sonnets of the Twentieth Century*. Grand Rapids: Baker, 1994.

———. *How Long O Lord? Reflections on Suffering and Evil*. Grand Rapids: Baker, 2006.

———. "Reflections on Assurance." Pages 247–76 in *Still Sovereign: Contemporary Perspectives on Election, Foreknowledge, and Grace*. Edited by T. R. Schreiner and B. A. Ware. Grand Rapids: Baker, 2000.

———. "The Vindication of Imputation: On Fields of Discourse and Semantic Fields." Pages 46–78 in *Justification: What's at Stake in the Current Debates*. Edited by M. Husbands and D. J. Treier. Downers Grove, IL: InterVarsity Press, 2004.

———. "'Worship the Lord Your God': The Perennial Challenge." Pages 13–18 in *Worship: Adoration and Action*. Edited by D. A. Carson. Eugene, OR: Wipf & Stock, 2002.

Carson, D. A., and Greg Beale, eds. *Commentary on the New Testament Use of the Old Testament*. Grand Rapids: Baker, 2007.

Carson, D. A., and Tim Keller. *Gospel-Centered Ministry*. Wheaton, IL: Crossway, 2011.

Chafer, Lewis Sperry. *Systematic Theology*. 8 vols. Dallas: Dallas Seminary Press, 1947.

Select Bibliography

Chan, Mark L. Y. *Christology from Within and Ahead: Hermeneutics, Contingency, and the Quest for the Transcontextual Criteria in Christology*. BIS 49. Leiden: Brill, 2000.

Chalke, Stephen, and Alan Mann. *The Lost Message of Jesus*. Grand Rapids: Zondervan, 2003.

Charlesworth, James H. *The Historical Jesus: An Essential Guide*. Nashville: Abingdon, 2008.

Chester, Andrew. *Messiah and Exaltation*. Tübingen: Mohr/Siebeck, 2007.

Chester, Tim. *From Creation to New Creation: Understanding the Bible Story*. Carlisle, UK: Paternoster, 2003.

Childs, B. S. *Biblical Theology of the Old and New Testaments: Theological Reflection on the Christian Bible*. Minneapolis: Fortress, 1992.

Christensen, Michael J., and Jeffery A. Wittung, eds. *Partakers of the Divine Nature: The History and Development of Deification in the Christian Traditions*. Grand Rapids: Baker, 2007.

Chung, Sung Wook. "A Bold Innovator: Barth on God and Election." Pages 60–76 in *Karl Barth and Evangelical Theology: Convergences and Differences*. Edited by S. W. Chung. Grand Rapids: Baker, 2006.

———. "Toward the Reformed and Covenantal Theology of Premillennialism: A Proposal." Pages 133–46 in *A Case for Historic Premillennialism*. Edited by C. L. Blomberg and S. W. Chung. Grand Rapids: Baker, 2009.

Ciampa, Roy E. "Paul's Theology of the Gospel." Pages 180–91 in *Paul as Missionary: Identity, Activity, Theology, and Practice*. Edited by T. J. Burke and B. S. Rosner. LNTS 420. London: T&T Clark, 2011.

Clark, David K. *To Know and Love God: Method for Theology*. Wheaton, IL: Crossway, 2003.

Clark, Kelly James. "Reformed Epistemologist's Response." Pages 255–63 in *Five Views on Apologetics*. Edited by Steven B. Cowan. Grand Rapids: Zondervan, 2000.

Clifford, Ross, and Philip Johnson. *The Cross Is Not Enough: Living as Witnesses to the Resurrection*. Grand Rapids: Baker, 2012.

Cocksworth, Christopher J. *Evangelical Eucharistic Thought in the Church of England*. Cambridge: Cambridge University Press, 1993.

Cohick, Lynn H. *Ephesians*. NCCS. Eugene, OR: Cascade, 2010.

Cole, Graham. *God the Peacemaker: How Atonement Brings Shalom*. NSBT. Downers Grove: InterVarsity Press, 2009.

———. *He Who Gives Life: The Doctrine of the Holy Spirit*. Wheaton, IL: Crossway, 2007.

———. "The Living God: Anthropomorphic or Athropopathic?" *RTR* 59 (2000): 16–27.

Colijn, Brenda B. *Images of Salvation in the New Testament*. Downers Grove, IL: InterVarsity Press, 2010.

Collins, C. John. *Did Adam and Eve Really Exist? Who They Were and Why You Should Care*. Wheaton, IL: Crossway, 2011.

Collins, Francis. *The Language of God: A Scientist Presents Evidence for Belief*. New York: Free Press, 2006.

Copan, Paul. "Is *Creatio Ex Nihilo* a Post-Biblical Invention? An Examination of Gerhard May's Proposal." *TrinJ* 17 (1996): 77–93.

Copan, Paul, and William Lane Craig. *Creation out of Nothing: A Biblical, Philosophical, and Scientific Exploration*. Grand Rapids: Baker, 2004.

Corduan, Winfried. *Handmaid to Theology: An Essay in Philosophical Prolegomena*. Grand Rapids, Baker, 1981.

Craig, William Lane. *Reasonable Faith: Christian Truth and Apologetics*. Wheaton, IL: Crossway, 1994.

———. *The Son Rises: The Historical Evidence for the Resurrection of Jesus*. Chicago: Moody, 1981.

Cranfield, C. E. B. "Some Reflections on the Subject of the Virgin Birth." Pages 151–66 in *On Romans: And Other New Testament Essays*. Edinburgh: T&T Clark, 2001.

Crisp, Oliver. *God Incarnate: Explorations in Christology*. London: T&T Clark, 2009.

———. *Revisioning Christology: Theology in the Reformed Tradition*. Surrey, UK: Ashgate, 2011.

Crockett, William V., ed. *Four Views on Hell*. Grand Rapids: Zondervan, 1992.

Crockett, William V., and James G. Sigountos, eds. *Through No Fault of Their Own: The Fate of Those Who Have Never Heard*. Grand Rapids: Baker, 1991.

Cross, Anthony R., and Philip E. Thompson, eds. *Baptist Sacramentalism*. SBHT 5; Milton Keynes, UK: Paternoster, 2003.

———. *Baptist Sacramentalism 2*. SBHT 25. Milton Keynes, UK: Paternoster, 2008.

Crossan, J. D. *The Historical Jesus*. San Francisco: Harper, 1991.

Cullmann, Oscar. *Christ and Time*. Trans. Floyd V. Filson. Philadelphia: Westminster, 1950.

Culpeppar, Robert. *Interpreting the Atonement*. Grand Rapids: Eerdmans, 1966.

Culver, Robert. *Systematic Theology: Biblical and Historical*. Fearn, UK: Mentor, 2005.

Davids, Peter H. *The First Epistle of Peter*. NICNT. Grand Rapids: Eerdmans, 1990.

Davies, Glenn. "The Lords' Supper for the Lord's Children." *RTR* 50 (1991): 12–20.

Davis, Stephen T. *Risen Indeed: Making Sense of the Resurrection.* Grand Rapids: Eerdmans, 1993.

Dawson, Gerrit. *Jesus Ascended: The Meaning of Christ's Continuing Incarnation.* London: T&T Clark, 2001.

D'Aubigne, J. H. Merle. *History of the Reformation in the 16th Century.* New York: R. Carter, 1856.

Demarest, B. A. "Amyraldianism." *EDT,* 41–42.

Denny, James. *The Christian Doctrine of Reconciliation.* Piscataway: Gorgias, 2010.

deSilva, David A. "Hebrews 6:4–8: A Socio-Rhetorical Investigation (Part 1)." *TynBul* 50 (1999): 33–57.

DeYoung, Kevin, and Ted Kluck. *Why We Love the Church: In Praise of Institutions and Organized Religion.* Chicago: Moody Press, 2009.

Di Beradino, Angelo., ed. *We Believe in One Holy Catholic and Apostolic Church.* Downers Grove, IL: InterVarsity Press, 2010.

Dickson, John. *The Best Kept Secret of Christian Mission: Promoting the Gospel with More than Our Lips.* Grand Rapids: Zondervan, 2009.

Dodd, C. H. *According to the Scriptures: The Substructure of New Testament Theology.* London: Nisbet, 1953.

———. *The Founder of Christianity.* New York: Macmillan, 1970.

———. "*Hilastērion*, Its Cognates, Derivatives and Synonyms in the Septuagint." *JTS* 32 (1931): 352–60.

———. *The Parables of the Kingdom.* New York: Scribner, 1961.

Doyle, Robert. "The Search for Theological Models: The Christian in his Society in the Sixteenth, Seventeenth and Nineteenth Centuries." Pages 27–72 in *Christians in Society.* Edited by B. G. Webb. Explorations 3. Homebush West, NSW: Lancer, 1988.

D'Souza, Dinesh. *What's So Great about Christianity?* Washington, DC: Regenery, 2007.

Dulles, Avery. *Models of the Church.* Garden City, NY: Doubleday, 1974.

———. *Models of Revelation.* Dublin: Gill & MacMillan, 1983.

Dumbrell, William J. *Covenant and Creation.* Nashville: Thomas Nelson, 1984.

Dunn, James D. G. *Baptism in the Spirit.* London: SCM, 1970.

———. *Did the First Christians Worship Jesus? The New Testament Evidence.* Louisville: Westminster John Knox, 2010.

———. *Jesus Remembered.* CITM 1. Grand Rapids: Eerdmans, 2003.

———. *The New Perspective on Paul.* Rev. ed. Grand Rapids: Eerdmans, 2008.

———. *Romans 1–8.* WBC. Dallas: Word, 1988.

———. *The Theology of Paul the Apostle*. Edinburgh: T&T Clark, 1998.

———. *Unity and Diversity in the New Testament*. 2nd ed. London: SCM, 1990.

Eastman, Susan. "Israel and Divine Mercy in Galatians and Romans." Pages 147–70 in *Between Gospel and Election: Explorations in the Interpretation of Romans 9–11*. Edited by F. Wilk and J. R. Wagner. Tübingen: Mohr/Siebeck, 2010.

Edgar, Brian. "Biblical Anthropology and the Intermediate State." *EvQ* 74 (2002): 27–45, 109–21.

Edwards, Jonathan. *The Works of Jonathan Edwards*. 2 vols. Edinburgh: T&T Clark, 1974.

Ellis, E. Earle. *The Old Testament in Early Christianity: Canon and Interpretation in the Light of Modern Research*. WUNT 54. Tübingen: Mohr/Siebeck, 1991.

Enns, Peter. *Inspiration and Incarnation: Evangelicals and the Problem of the Old Testament*. Grand Rapids: Baker, 2005.

Erickson, Millard J. *Christian Theology*. 2nd ed. Grand Rapids: Baker, 1998.

———. *God in Three Persons: A Contemporary Interpretation of the Trinity*. Grand Rapids: Baker, 1995.

———. *How Shall They Be Saved? The Destiny of Those Who Do Not Hear of Jesus*. Grand Rapids: Baker, 1996.

———. "Second Coming of Christ." *EDT*, 992–95.

———. *Who's Tampering with the Trinity: An Assessment of the Subordination Debate*. Grand Rapids: Kregel, 2009.

Eskola, Timo. *Messiah and the Throne: Jewish Merkabah Mysticism and Early Christian Exaltation Discourse*. WUNT 2.142. Tübingen: Mohr/Siebeck, 2001.

Fairburn, Donald. "Contemporary Millennial/Tribulational Debates: Whose Side Was the Early Church On?" Pages 105–31 in *A Case for Historic Premillennialism*. Edited by C. L. Blomberg and S. W. Chung. Grand Rapids: Baker, 2009.

Farrow, Douglas B. *Ascension and Ecclesia: On the Significance of the Doctrine of the Ascension*. Grand Rapids: Eerdmans, 1999.

Fee, Gordon D. *God's Empowering Presence: The Holy Spirit in the Letters of Paul*. Peabody, MA: Hendrickson, 1994.

———. "Paul and the Trinity: The Experience of Christ and the Spirit for Paul's Understanding of God." Pages 49–72 in *The Trinity: An Interdisciplinary Symposium on the Trinity*. Edited by S. T. Davis, D. Kendall, and G. O'Collins. Oxford: Oxford University Press, 2002.

———. *Revelation*. NCCS; Eugene, OR: Wipf & Stock, 2011.

Feinberg, John S. *No One Like Him: The Doctrine of God*. Wheaton, IL: Crossway, 2001.

Feinberg, Paul D. "The Case for the Pretribulation Rapture Position." Pages 45–86 in *The Rapture*. Grand Rapids: Zondervan, 1984.

Ferguson, Everett. *Baptism in the Early Church: History, Theology, and Liturgy in the First Five Centuries.* Grand Rapids: Eerdmans, 2009.

Ferguson, Sinclair. *The Holy Spirit.* Downers Grove, IL: InterVarsity Press, 1997.

Fesko, J. V. "Sanctification and Union with Christ: A Reformed Perspective." *EvQ 82* (2010): 197–214.

Finlan, Stephen, and Vladimir Kharlamov, eds. *Theōsis: Deification in Christian Theology.* Eugene, OR: Pickwick, 2006.

Fishbane, Michael. *Biblical Interpretation in Ancient Israel.* Oxford: Clarendon, 1985.

Fitzmyer, Joseph A. *Romans: A New Translation with Introduction and Commentary.* AB. New York: Doubleday, 1993.

Forsyth, Peter T. *The Cruciality of the Cross.* London: Hodder & Stoughton, 1909.

Fowl, Stephen E. *Engaging with Scripture.* Oxford: Blackwell, 1998.

Frame, John. *The Doctrine of God.* Phillipsburg, NJ: Presbyterian & Reformed, 2002.

———. "Presuppositional Apologetics." Pages 207–31 in *Five Views on Apologetics.* Edited by Steven B. Cowan. Grand Rapids: Zondervan, 2000.

France, R. T. *The Gospel of Matthew.* NICNT. Grand Rapids: Eerdmans, 2007.

Franke, John R. *Manifold Witness: The Plurality of Truth.* Nashville: Abingdon, 2008.

Fretheim, Terence. *The Suffering of God: An Old Testament Perspective.* Minneapolis: Fortress, 1984.

Fredericks, Daniel C., and Daniel T. Estes. *Ecclesiastes and the Song of Songs.* AOTC. Nottingham: Apollos, 2010.

Fuller, Daniel P. *The Unity of the Bible: Unfolding God's Plan for Humanity.* Grand Rapids: Zondervan, 2000.

Fung, R. K. "Body of Christ." *DPL,* 76–82.

Gaffin, Richard B. *The Centrality of the Resurrection: A Study in Paul's Soteriology.* Grand Rapids: Baker, 1978.

———. *Resurrection and Redemption: A Study in Paul's Soteriology.* Grand Rapids: Baker, 1987.

Gager, John. *The Origins of Anti-Semitism.* New York: Oxford University Press, 1983.

———. *Reinventing Paul.* New York: Oxford University Press, 2000.

Gallant, Tim. *Feed My Lambs: Why the Lord's Table Should be Restored to Covenant Children.* Grande Prairie, Alberta: Pactum Reformanda, 2002.

Garcia, Mark A. *Life in Christ: Union with Christ and Twofold Grace in Calvin's Theology.* Carlisle, UK: Paternoster, 2008.

Garland, David E. *1 Corinthians.* BECNT. Grand Rapids: Baker, 2003.

Gathercole, Simon. "The Cross and Substitutionary Atonement." *SBET* 21 (2003): 152–65.

———. *The Preexistent Son: Recovering the Christologies of Matthew, Mark, and Luke*. Grand Rapids: Eerdmans, 2006.

Gaventa, Beverly R., and Richard B. Hays. "Seeking the Identity of Jesus." Pages 1–24 in *Seeking the Identity of Jesus: A Pilgrimage*. Edited by B. R. Gaventa and R. B. Hays. Grand Rapids: Eerdmans, 2008.

Geisler, Norman. *Chosen but Free: A Balanced View of God's Sovereignty and Free Will*. Minneapolis: Bethany, 2010.

Gelpi, Donald. *The Divine Mother: A Trinitarian Theology of the Holy Spirit*. Lanham, MD: University of America Press, 1984.

Gench, Frances Taylor. "Repentance in the NT." *NIB*, 4:762–74.

Gentry, Kenneth L. "Postmillennialism." Pages 11–57 in *Three Views on the Millennium*. Edited by D. L. Bock. Grand Rapids: Zondervan, 1999.

George, Timothy. *Galatians*. NAC. Nashville: Broadman & Holman, 2001.

Gibson, David A. "Eating Is Believing? On Midrash and the Mixing of Metaphors in John 6." *Them* 27/7 (2002): 5–15.

———. *Reading the Decree: Exegesis, Election, and Christology in Calvin and Barth*. London: T&T Clark, 2009.

Gibson, David N., and Daniel Strange, eds. *Engaging with Barth: Contemporary Evangelical Critiques*. New York: T&T Clark, 2008.

Gibson, Jim, and Michael Bird. "Quest for an Evangelical Prolegomena to Theology." Pages 95–106 in *Proclaiming Truth, Pastoring Hearts: Essays in Honour of Deane J. Woods*. Edited by R. T. Stanton and L. J. Crawford. Adelaide: SCM, 2003.

Gilbert, Greg. *What is the Gospel?* Wheaton, IL: Crossway, 2010.

Giles, Kevin. *The Eternal Generation of the Son: Maintaining Orthodoxy in Trinitarian Theology*. Downers Grove, IL: InterVarsity Press, 2012.

———. *Jesus and the Father: Modern Evangelicals Reinvent the Doctrine of the Trinity*. Grand Rapids: Zondervan, 2006.

———. "Michael Bird and Robert Shillaker: The Son Is Not Eternally Subordinated in Authority to the Father." *TrinJ* 30 (2009): 237–56.

———. *The Trinity and Subordinationism*. Downers Grove, IL: InterVarsity Press, 2002.

Gleason, R.C. "The Old Testament Background of the Warning in Hebrews 6:4–6." *BSac* 155 (1998): 62–91.

Goldingay, John. *Models for Interpretation of Scripture*. Grand Rapids: Eerdmans, 1994.

Goldsworthy, Graeme. *According to Plan: The Unfolding of God in the Bible*. Leicester, UK: Inter-Varsity Press, 1991.

———. *Gospel-Centered Hermeneutics: Foundations and Principles of Evangelical Biblical Interpretation*. Downers Grove, IL: InterVarsity Press, 2007.

———. "Kingdom of God." *NDBT*, 615–20.

Gombis, Timothy. *The Drama of Ephesians: Participating in the Triumph of God*. Downers Grove, IL: InterVarsity Press, 2010.

Goppelt, Leonhard. *A Commentary on I Peter*. Trans. J. E. Alsup. Grand Rapids: Eerdmans, 1993.

———. *Typos: The Typological Interpretation of the Old Testament in the New*. Grand Rapids: Eerdmans, 1982.

Gorday, Peter, ed. *Colossians, 1–2 Thessalonians, 1–2 Timothy, Titus, Philemon*. ACCS 9. Downers Grove, IL: InterVarsity Press, 2000.

Gorman, Michael J. *Cruciformity: Paul's Narrative Spirituality of the Cross*. Grand Rapids: Eerdmans, 2001.

———. *Inhabiting the Cruciform God: Kenosis, Justification, and Theosis in Paul's Narrative Soteriology*. Grand Rapids: Eerdmans, 2009.

Grant, Jamie A., and Alistair I. Wilson, eds. *The God of Covenant: Biblical, Theological, and Contemporary Perspectives*. Leicester: Apollos: 2005.

Green, Bradley G. "Augustine." Pages 235–92 in *Shapers of Christian Orthodoxy: Engaging with Early and Medieval Theologians*. Edited by B. G. Green. Downers Grove, IL: InterVarsity Press, 2010.

Green, Joel B. "Body and Soul, Mind and Brain: Critical Issues." Pages 7–32 in *In Search of the Soul: Four Views on the Mind-Body Problem*. Edited by J. B. Green and S. L. Palmer. Downers Grove, IL: InterVarsity Press, 2005.

———. *Body, Soul, and Human Life: The Nature of Humanity in the Bible*. Grand Rapids: Baker, 2008.

———. "Kaleidoscopic View" Pages 157–85 in *The Nature of the Atonement*. Edited by J. Beilby and P. R. Eddy. Downers Grove, IL: InterVarsity Press, 2006.

———. *Salvation*. UBT. St Louis: Chalice, 2003.

Greidanus, Sidney. *Preaching Christ from the Old Testament*. Grand Rapids: Eerdmans, 1999.

Grenz, Stanley E. *Renewing the Centre: Evangelical Theology in a Post-Theological Era*. Grand Rapids: Baker, 2000.

———. *Theology for the Community of God*. Grand Rapids: Eerdmans, 1994.

Grenz, Stanley J., and Roger E. Olson. *Who Needs Theology? An Invitation to the Study of God*. Downers Grove, IL: InterVarsity Press, 1992.

Grubbs, Norris C., and Curtis Scott Drumm, "What Does Theology Have to Do with the Bible? A Call for the Expansion of the Doctrine of Inspiration." *JETS* 53 (2010): 65–79

Grudem, Wayne. *1 Peter*. TNTC. Grand Rapids: Eerdmans, 1988.

———. ed., *Are Miraculous Gifts for Today? Four Views*. Grand Rapids, MI: Zondervan, 1996.

———. "He Did Not Descend Into Hell: A Plea for Following Scripture Instead of the Apostle's Creed." *JETS* 34 (1991): 107–12.

———. *Systematic Theology: An Introduction to Biblical Doctrine*. Grand Rapids: Zondervan, 1994.

Gruenler, R.G. *The Trinity in the Gospel of John: A Thematic Commentary on the Fourth Gospel*. Grand Rapids: Baker, 1986.

Gulley, Philip, and James Mulholland. *If Grace Is True: Why God Will Save Every Person*. San Francisco: Harper San Francisco, 2003.

Gundry. Robert H. *Church and the Tribulation: A Biblical Examination of Posttribulationism*. Grand Rapids: Zondervan, 1973.

———. *Mark: A Commentary on His Apology for the Cross*. Grand Rapids: Eerdmans, 1993.

———. "Pastoral Pensées: The Hopelessness of the Unevangelized." *Them* 36 (2011).

Gundry-Volf, Judith. "Apostasy, Falling Away, Perseverance." *DPL*, 39–45.

———. *A Brief Theology of Revelation*. Edinburgh: T&T Clark, 1995.

———. *Paul and Perseverance: Staying In and Falling Away*. Louisville: Westminster John Knox, 1990.

Gunton, Colin E. *The Actuality of Atonement*. Grand Rapids: Eerdmans, 1989.

———. *A Brief Theology of Revelation*. Edinburgh: T&T Clark, 1995.

———. *Christ and Creation*. Grand Rapids: Eerdmans, 1992.

———. *Father, Son, and Holy Spirit: Essays towards a Fully Trinitarian Theology*. London: T&T Clark, 2003.

———. *The One, the Three and the Many*. Cambridge: CUP, 1999.

———. *The Promise of Trinitarian Theology*. Edinburgh: T&T Clark, 1991.

Guthrie, Shirley C. *Christian Doctrine*. Rev. ed. Louisville: Westminster John Knox, 1994.

Habermas, Gary. *The Risen Jesus and Future Hope*. Lanham, MD: Rowman & Littlefield, 2003.

Hagner, D. A. "Gospel, Kingdom, and Resurrection in the Synoptic Gospels." Pages 99–121 in *Life in the Face of Death: The Resurrection Message of the New Testament*. Edited by R. N. Longenecker. Grand Rapids: Eerdmans, 1998.

Hahn, Scott A. *Justification: Becoming a Child of God* (Cassette Recording). Saint Joseph Communications, 1995.

Haire, James, Christine Ledger, and Stephen Pickard, eds. *From Resurrection to Return: Perspectives from Theology and Science on Christian Eschatology*. Adelaide, AU: ATF Press, 2007.

Hamid-Khani, Saeed. *Revelation and Concealment of Christ: A Theological Inquiry into the Elusive Language of the Fourth Gospel*. WUNT 2.120. Tübingen: Mohr/Siebeck, 2000.

Select Bibliography

Hamilton, James M. *God's Glory in Salvation through Judgment: A Biblical Theology.* Wheaton, IL: Crossway, 2010.

———. *God's Indwelling Presence: The Holy Spirit in the Old & New Testaments.* NACSBT. Nashville: Broadman & Holman, 2006.

———. "The Messianic Music of the Song of Songs: A Non-Allegorical Interpretation." *WTJ* 68 (2006): 331–45.

———. "Old Covenant Believers in the Indwelling Spirit: A Survey of the Spectrum of Opinion." *TrinJ* 24 (2003): 37–54.

———. "The Skull Crushing Seed of the Woman: Inner-Biblical Interpretation of Genesis 3:15." *SBJT* 10 (2006): 30–54.

———. "The Virgin Will Conceive: Typological Fulfillment in Matthew 1:18–23." Pages 228–47 in *Built upon the Rock: Studies in the Gospel of Matthew*. Edited by J. Nolland and D. Gurtner. Grand Rapids: Eerdmans, 2008.

Hamilton, Victor P. *The Book of Genesis*. NICOT. Grand Rapids: Eerdmans, 1990.

Hanson, A.T. *Jesus Christ in the Old Testament*. London: SPCK, 1965.

Harmon, Steve R. *Towards Baptist Catholicity: Essays on Tradition and the Baptist Vision*. SBHT 27. Milton Keynes, UK: Paternoster, 2006.

Harnack, Adolf von. *What is Christianity?* 3rd ed.. London: Williams and Norgate, 1904.

Harper, Brad, and Paul Louis Metzger. *Exploring Ecclesiology: An Evangelical and Ecumenical Introduction*. Grand Rapids: Brazos, 2009.

Harris, Murray. *Jesus as God: The New Testament Use of Theos in Reference to Jesus*. Grand Rapids: Baker, 1992.

Harrison, E. F. "Soul Sleep." *EDT*, 1037–38.

Harrison, R. K. "Creation." Pages 1020–25 in vol. 1, *The Zondervan Pictorial Encyclopedia of the Bible*. Edited by M. C. Tenney. 5 vols. Grand Rapids: Zondervan, 1975.

Hart, David Bentley. *In the Aftermath: Provocations and Laments*. Grand Rapids: Eerdmans, 2009.

———. "The Lively God of Robert Jenson." *First Things* 156 (2005): 15.

Harvey, Graham. *The True Israel: The Use of the Names Jew, Hebrew, and Israel in Ancient Jewish and Early Christian Literature*. Leiden: Brill, 1996.

Hasker, William. *The Triumph of God over Evil: Theodicy for a World of Suffering*. Downers Grove, IL: InterVarsity Press, 2008.

Hauerwas, Stanley. *With the Grain of the Universe: The Church's Witness and Natural Theology*. London: SCM, 2002.

Hays, Richard. *First Corinthians*. Interpretation. Louisville: John Knox, 1997.

———. "'Why Do You Stand Looking Up toward Heaven?' New Testament Eschatology at the Turn of the Millennium." Pages 113–33 in *Theology at the*

Turn of the Millennium. Edited by L. G. Jones and J. J. Buckley. Oxford: Blackwell, 2001.

Helm, Paul. *The Divine Revelation: The Basic Issues*. Vancouver, BC: Regent College Publishing, 2004.

———. *Faith and Understanding*. Edinburgh: Edinburgh University Press, 1997.

———. *The Providence of God*. Nottingham, UK: Inter-Varsity Press, 1993.

Hengel, Martin. *The Cross of the Son of God*. Trans. J. Bowden. London: SCM, 1976.

———. *The Septuagint as Christian Scripture: Its Prehistory and the Problem of Its Canon*. Trans. M. E. Biddle. London: T&T Clark, 2002.

———. *Studies in Early Christology*. Edinburgh: T&T Clark, 1995.

Henry, Carl F. *God, Revelation, and Authority*. 6 vols. Wheaton, IL: Crossway, 1999.

Hill, Charles E. "Paul's Understanding of Christ's Kingdom in 1 Corinthians 15.20–28." *NovT* 30 (1988): 297–320.

———. *Regnum Caelorum: Patterns of Millennial Thought in Early Christianity*. 2nd ed. Grand Rapids: Eerdmans, 2001.

Hill, Charles E., and Frank A. James, eds. *The Glory of the Atonement*. Downers Grove, IL: InterVarsity Press, 2005.

Hobbes, Thomas. *Leviathan: Parts I and II*. Edited by A. P. Martinich. Petersborough, ON: Broadview, 2005.

Hodge, A. A. *Outlines of Theology*. London: Banner of Truth, 1860.

Hodge, Charles. *Systematic Theology*. 3 vols. London: James Clarke & Co., 1960 [1841].

Hoekema, Anthony. "Amillennialism." Pages 155–87 in *The Millennium: Four Views*. Edited by R. G. Clouse. Downers Grove, IL: InterVarsity Press, 1977.

———. *The Bible and the Future*. Grand Rapids: Eerdmans, 1979.

———. *Created in God's Image*. Grand Rapids: Eerdmans, 1986.

Horner, Barry E. *Future Israel: Why Christian Anti-Semitism Must be Challenged*. Nashville: Broadman & Holman, 2007.

Horrell, J. Scott. "Towards a Biblical Model of the Social Trinity: Avoiding Equivocation of Nature and Order." *JETS* 47 (2004): 399–421.

Horton, Michael S. *The Christian Faith*. Grand Rapids: Zondervan, 2011.

———. "A Classical Calvinist View." Pages 23–42 in *Four Views on Eternal Security*. Edited by J. Matthew Pinson. Grand Rapids: Zondervan, 2002.

———. *God of Promise: Introducing Covenant Theology*. Grand Rapids: Baker, 2006.

———. *People and Place: A Covenant Ecclesiology*. Louisville: Westminster John Knox, 2008.

Houlden, J. L. *The Public Face of the Gospel: New Testament Ideas of the Church*. London: SCM, 1997.

Howard-Snyder, Daniel. "God, Evil, and Suffering." Pages 76–115 in *Reasons for the Hope Within*. Edited by M. J. Murray. Grand Rapids: Eerdmans, 1998.

Hubbard, Moyer V. *New Creation in Paul's Letters and Thought*. SNTSMS 119. Cambridge: Cambridge University Press, 2002.

Hunsinger, George. *How to Read Karl Barth*. Oxford: Oxford University Press, 1993.

Hunt, J. P. T. "Colossians 2:11–12: The Circumcision/Baptism Analogy, and Infant Baptism." *TynBul* 41 (1990): 227–44.

Hunter, A. M. *The Gospel according to Paul*. Philadelphia: Westminster, 1966.

Hurtado, Larry. *Lord Jesus Christ*. Grand Rapids: Eerdmans, 1998.

Husbands, M. A, and D. J. Treier, eds. *The Community of the Word: Toward an Evangelical Ecclesiology*. Downers Grove, IL: InterVarsity Press, 2005.

Hyde, Daniel R. *Jesus Loves the Little Children: Why We Baptize Infants*. Grand Rapids: Reformed Fellowship, 2006.

Jackson, T. Ryan. *New Creation in Paul's Letters: A Study of the History and Social Setting of a Pauline Concept*. WUNT 2.272. Tübingen: Mohr/Siebeck, 2010.

Jeffery, Stephen, Michael Ovey, and Andrew Sach. *Pierced for Our Transgressions: Rediscovering the Glory of Penal Substitution*. Wheaton, IL: Crossway, 2007.

Jefford, Clayton N. "Sin." *EDB*, 1224–26.

Jensen, Peter. *The Revelation of God*. Downers Grove, IL: InterVarsity Press, 2002.

Jenson, Robert. *Creed and Canon*. Louisville: Westminster John Knox, 2010.

Jeremias, Joachim. *The Parables of Jesus*. New York: Scribners, 1963.

Jewett, Paul K. *Election and Predestination*. Grand Rapids: Eerdmans, 1985.

———. *God, Creation, and Revelation: A Neo-Evangelical Theology*. Grand Rapids: Eerdmans, 1991.

———. *Who We Are: Our Dignity as Human: A Neo-Evangelical Theology*. Grand Rapids: Eerdmans, 1996.

Jewett, Robert. *Romans*. Hermeneia. Minneapolis: Fortress, 2007.

———. "Tenement Churches and Pauline Love Feasts." *QR* 14 (1994): 43–58.

Jobes, Karen H. *1 Peter*. BECNT. Grand Rapids: Baker, 2005.

Johnson, Luke Timothy. "Learning the Human Jesus: Historical Criticism and Literary Criticism." Pages 153–77 in *The Historical Jesus: Five Views*. Edited by J. K. Beilby and P. R. Eddy. Downers Grove, IL: InterVarsity Press, 2009.

———. *The Real Jesus: The Misguided Quest for the Historical Jesus and the Truth of the Gospels*. San Francisco: Harper One, 1996.

———. *Religious Experience in Early Christianity*. Philadelphia: Fortress, 1998.

Juel, Donald H. "The Trinity and the New Testament." *Theology Today* 54/3 (1997): 312–24.

Jüngel, Eberhard. *Justification: The Heart of the Christian Faith*. Edinburgh: T&T Clark, 2001.

Kähler, Martin. *The So-Called Historical Jesus and the Historic, Biblical Christ*. Trans. Carl E. Braaten. Philadelphia: Fortress, 1964.

Kärkkäinen, Veli-Matti. *Christology: A Global Introduction*. Grand Rapids: Baker Academic, 2003.

———. *An Introduction to Ecclesiology: Ecumenical, Historical, and Global Perspectives*. Downers Grove, IL: InterVarsity Press, 2002.

———. *Pneumatology: The Holy Spirit in Ecumenical, International, and Contextual Perspective*. Grand Rapids: Baker, 2002.

Käsemann, Ernst. "The Beginnings of Christian Theology." Pages 82–107 in *New Testament Questions of Today*. London: SCM, 1969.

———. "The Problem of the Historical Jesus." Pages 15–47 in *Essays on New Testament Themes*. SBT 41. Trans. W. J. Montague; London: SCM, 1964.

Kasper, Walter. *The God of Jesus Christ*. Trans. J. J. O'Connell; New York: Crossroad, 1984.

Keck, Leander E. "Towards the Renewal of NT Christology." *NTS* 32 (1986): 362–77.

———. *Who Is Jesus? History in Perfect Tense*. Columbia: University of South Carolina, 2000.

Keener, Craig S. "Is Subordination within The Trinity Really Heresy? A Study of John 5:18 in Context." *TrinJ* 20 (1999): 39–51.

Kelly, J. N. D. *Early Christian Doctrines*. London: Adam and Charles Black, 1958.

Kendall, R. T. *Calvin and English Calvinism to 1649*. Carlisle, UK: Paternoster, 1997.

Kennard, Douglas. *Messiah Jesus: Christology in His Day and Ours*. New York: Peter Lang, 2008.

Kinlaw, Dennis F. *Let's Start with Jesus: A New Way of Doing Theology*. Grand Rapids: Zondervan, 2005.

Kirk, J. R. Daniel. "The Sufficiency of the Cross." *SBET* 24 (2006): 35–39.

Kistemaker, Simon J. *Exposition of the Acts of the Apostles*. NTC. Grand Rapids: Baker, 1990.

Kittel, Gerhard, G. K. A. Bell, and A. Deissman, eds. *Mysterium Christi*. London: Longmans & Green, 1930.

Klein, William H. *The New Chosen People: A Corporate View of Election*. Grand Rapids: Zondervan, 1990.

Kline, Meredith G. *By Oath Consigned: A Reinterpretation of the Covenant Signs of Circumcision and Baptism*. Grand Rapids: Eerdmans, 1968.

Klooster, F. H. "Elect, Election." *EDT*, 348–49.

Knox, D. B. *Justification by Faith*. London: Church Book Room, 1959.

———. "Some Aspects of the Atonement." Pages 253–66 in *Selected Works: Volume 1—The Doctrine of God*. Kingsford, Aus.: Matthias Media, 2000.

Knox, John. *The Humanity and Divinity of Christ*. Cambridge: Cambridge University Press, 1967.

Knoll, Mark A., David W. Bebbington, and George A. Rawlyk, eds. *Evangelicalism: Comparative Studies of Popular Protestantism in North America, the British Isles, and Beyond 1700—1900*. Oxford: Oxford University Press, 1994.

Köstenberger, Andreas J. "The Identity of the *ISRAĒL TOU THEOU* (Israel of God) in Galatians 6:16." *Faith & Mission* 19 (2001): 3–24.

———. *John*. BECNT. Grand Rapids: Baker, 2004.

———. *A Theology of John's Gospel and Letters*. Grand Rapids: Zondervan, 2008.

Köstenberger, Andreas J., and Scott R. Swain. *Father, Son and Spirit: The Trinity in John's Gospel*. NSBT 24. Downers Grove, IL: InterVarsity Press, 2008.

Kovach, Stephen, and Peter Schemm. "A Defense of the Doctrine of the Eternal Subordination of the Son." *JETS* 42 (1999): 461–76.

Kovacs, Judith L. *1 Corinthians: Interpreted by Early Christian Commentators*. Grand Rapids: Eerdmans, 2005.

Kreitzer, Larry. "Adam and Christ." *DPL*, 9–15.

Kroeger, R. C., and C. C. Kroeger, "Subordinationism." *EDT*, 1058.

Kung, Hans. *The Church*. London: T&T Clark, 2001.

Laato, Timo. "Paul's Anthropological Considerations: Two Problems." Pages 343–59 in *Justification and Variegated Nomism: Volume 2—The Paradoxes of Paul*. Edited by D. A. Carson, Mark A. Seifrid, and Peter T. O'Brien. Grand Rapids: Baker, 2004.

Labooy, Guus. "The Historicity of the Virginal Conception. A Study in Argumentation." *EJTh* 13 (2004): 91–101.

LaCugna, Catherine Mowry. "The Trinitarian Mystery." Pages 149–92 in *Systematic Theology: Roman Catholic Perspectives*. Vol. 1. Edited by Francis Schüssler Fiorenza and John P. Calvin. Minneapolis: Fortress, 1991.

Ladd, G. E. "Historic Premillennialism." Pages 15–40 in *The Millennium: Four Views*. Edited by R. G. Clouse. Downers Grove, IL: InterVarsity Press, 1977.

———. *A Theology of the New Testament*. Edited and rev. by D. A. Hagner. Grand Rapids: Eerdmans, 1993.

Lane, Anthony N. S. "B. B. Warfield on the Humanity of Scripture." *VE* 16 (1986): 77–94.

———. "Dual-Practice Baptism View." Pages 139–71 in *Baptism: Three Views*. Edited by D. F. Wright. Downers Grove, IL: InterVarsity Press, 2009.

———. *Justification by Faith in Catholic-Protestant Dialogue: An Evangelical Assessment*. London: T&T Clark, 2002.

Lash, Nicholas. "Up and Down in Christology." Pages 31–46 in *New Studies in Theology*. Edited by S. Sykes and D. Holmes. London: Duckworth, 1980.

Law, R. "Glory." Pages 451–53 in *Hastings Dictionary of the Apostolic Church*. Edited by J. A. Hastings. Los Angeles: University of California Press, 1916.

Lee, Aquila H. I. *From Messiah to Preexistent Son: Jesus' Self-Consciousness and Early Christian Exegesis of Messianic Psalms*. WUNT 2.192; Tübingen: Mohr/Siebeck, 2005.

Lee, Jason K. *The Theology of John Smyth: Puritan, Separatist, Baptist, Mennonite*. Macon, GA: Mercer University Press, 2003.

Letham, Robert. *The Work of Christ*. Leicester, UK: Inter-Varsity Press, 1993.

———. *The Holy Trinity: In Scripture, History, Theology, and Worship*. Phillipsburg, NJ: Presbyterian & Reformed, 2004.

Levinson, John R. *Portraits of Adam in Early Judaism: From Sirach to 2 Baruch*. JSPSup 1. Sheffield: JSOT Press, 1988.

Lewandowski, Joseph D. *Interpreting Culture: Rethinking Method and Truth in Social Theory*. Lincoln: University of Nebraska Press, 2001.

Lewis, Gordon R., and Bruce A. Demarest. *Integrative Theology*. 3 vols. Grand Rapids: Zondervan, 1987–94.

Lewis, C. S. *The Problem of Pain*. New York: Macmillan, 1962.

———. *The Screwtape Letters*. New York: Macmillan, 1961.

Licona, Michael R. *The Resurrection of Jesus: A New Historiographical Approach*. Downers Grove, IL: InterVarsity Press, 2010.

Lincoln, Andrew. "'Born of the Virgin Mary': Creedal Affirmation and Critical Reading." Pages 84–103 in *Christology and Scripture: Interdisciplinary Perspectives*. Edited by A. T. Lincoln and A. Paddison. London: T&T Clark, 2008.

Lints, Richard. The *Fabric of Theology: A Prolegomenon to Evangelical Theology*. Grand Rapids: Eerdmans, 1993.

Lunde, J. M. "Repentance." *NDBT*, 726–27.

MacDonald, Gregory. *The Evangelical Universalist*. Eugene, OR: Cascade, 2006.

———. ed. *"All Shall Be Well": Explorations in Universalism and Christian Theology from Origen to Moltmann*. Eugene, OR: Cascade, 2011.

Machen, J. G. *The Virgin Birth of Christ*. New York: Harper, 1930.

Mackenzie, Catherine. *Richard Wurmbrand: A Voice in the Dark*. Fearn, UK: Christian Focus, 1997.

MacLeod, Donald. "How Right Are the Justified? Or, What is a *Dikaios*?" *SBET* 22 (2004): 191–95.

Macquarrie, John. *Jesus Christ in Modern Thought*. London: SCM, 1990.

———. *Principles of Christian Theology*. London: SCM, 2003.

Marshall, I. Howard. *Aspects of the Atonement: Cross and Resurrection in the Reconciling of God and Humanity.* London: Paternoster, 2007.

———. "The Christian Millennium." *EvQ* 72 (2000): 217–36.

———. "Is Apocalyptic the Mother of Christian Theology?" Pages 33-42 in *Tradition and Interpretation in the New Testament.* Edited by G. F. Hawthorne and O. Betz. Grand Rapids: Eerdmans, 1987.

———. *Kept by the Power of God: A Study of Perseverance and Falling Away.* Minneapolis: Bethany, 1969.

———. *Last Supper and Lord's Supper.* Grand Rapids: Eerdmans, 1980.

———. "The New Testament Does *Not* Teach Universal Salvation." Pages 55–76 in *Universal Salvation?: The Current Debate.* Edited by R. Parry and C. Partridge. Carlisle, UK: Paternoster, 2003.

———. *New Testament Theology: Many Witnesses, One Gospel.* Nottingham, UK: Apollos, 2004.

———. "Universal Grace and Atonement in the Pastoral Epistles." Pages 51–70 in *The Grace of God, the Will of Man.* Edited by C. Pinnock. Minneapolis: Bethany, 1995.

Martin, Ralph P. *2 Corinthians.* WBC. Dallas: Word, 1986.

———. *Reconciliation: A Study of Paul's Theology.* Atlanta: John Knox, 1981

Martyn, J. L. "The Apocalyptic Gospel in Galatians." *Int* 54/3 (2000): 246–66.

Mathews, K. A. *Genesis 1–11:26.* NAC. Nashville: Broadman & Holman, 2001.

McCartney, D. J. "*Ecce Homo*: The Coming of the Kingdom as the Restoration of Human Viceregency." *WTJ* 56 (1994): 1–21.

McCormack, Bruce. "The Ontological Presuppositions of Barth's Doctrine of the Atonement." Pages 346–66 in *The Glory of the Atonement.* Edited by C. E. Hill and F. A. James. Downers Grove, IL: InterVarsity Press, 2004.

———. "Participation in God, Yes, Deification, No: Two Modern Protestant Responses to an Ancient Question." Pages 347–74 in *Denkwürdiges Geheimnis: Beiträge zur Gotteslehre. Festschrift für Eberhard Jüngel zum 70. Geburtstag.* Edited by I. U. Dalferth, J. Fischer, and H.-P. Grosshans. Tübingen: Mohr/Siebeck, 2004.

———. "Union with Christ in Calvin's Theology: Ground for a Divinisation Theory?" Pages 504–29 in *Tributes to John Calvin.* Edited by David W. Hall. Phillipsburg, NJ: Presbyterian & Reformed 2010.

McCormack, Bruce, and Clifford Anderson, eds. *Karl Barth and American Evangelicalism.* Grand Rapids: Eerdmans, 2011.

McCready, Douglas. *He Came Down from Heaven: The Preexistence of Christ and the Christian Faith.* Downers Grove, IL: InterVarsity Press, 2005.

McDonald, Lee Martin. *The Biblical Canon: Its Origins, Transmission, and Authority.* Peabody, MA: Hendrickson, 2007.

McDonough, Sean. *Christ as Creator: Origins of a New Testament Doctrine.* Oxford: Oxford University Press, 2010.

McGinn, Sheila E., ed. *Celebrating Romans: Template for Pauline Theology.* Grand Rapids: Eerdmans, 2004.

McGowan, A. T. B. "Amyraldianism." Pages 12–13 in *The Dictionary of Historical Theology.* Edited by T. Hart and R. Bauckham. Grand Rapids: Eerdmans, 2000.

———. "In Defence of 'Headship Theology.'" Pages 178–99 in *The God of Covenant: Biblical, Theological, and Contemporary Perspectives.* Edited by J. A. Grant and A. I. Wilson. Leicester, UK: Apollos: 2005.

———. *Divine Spiration of Scripture.* Nottingham, UK: Apollos, 2007.

———. "Justification and the *Ordo Salutis*." Pages 147–63 in *Justification in Perspective: Historical Developments and Contemporary Challenges.* Edited by B. L. McCormack. Grand Rapids: Baker, 2006.

———. *The New Birth.* Fearn, UK: Christian Focus, 1999.

McGrath, Alister E. *Bridge-Building: Effective Christian Apologetics.* Leicester, UK: Inter-Varsity Press, 1993.

———. *A Brief History of Heaven.* Oxford: Blackwell, 2003.

———. *Christian Theology: An Introduction.* Oxford: Blackwell, 2001.

———. *The Christian Theology Reader.* 3rd ed. Oxford: Blackwell, 2006.

———. *Evangelicalism and the Future of Christianity.* Leiceste, UK: Inter-Varsity Press, 1995.

———. *Heresy: A History of Defending the Truth.* San Francisco: Harper One, 2009.

———. *Iustitia Dei: A History of the Christian Doctrine of Justification: The Beginnings to the Reformation.* Cambridge: Cambridge University Press, 1986.

———. "Justification." *DPL*, 517–23.

———. *Luther's Theology of the Cross: Martin Luther's Theological Breakthrough.* Oxford: Blackwell, 1995.

———. "The Moral Theory of the Atonement: An Historic and Theological Critique." *SJT* 38 (1985): 205–20.

———. *A New Vision for Israel: The Teachings of Jesus in National Context.* Grand Rapids: Eerdmans, 1999.

———. *The Open Secret: A New Vision for Natural Theology.* Oxford: Blackwell, 2008.

———. *The Passionate Intellect: Christian Faith and Discipleship of the Mind.* Downers Grove, IL: InterVarsity Press, 2010.

———. *A Scientific Theology: Volume 1—Nature.* Grand Rapids: Eerdmans, 2001.

———. *A Scientific Theology: Volume 2—Reality.* Grand Rapids: Eerdmans, 2001.

———. *A Scientific Theology: Volume 3—Theory*. Grand Rapids: Eerdmans, 2003.

———. *T. F. Torrance: An Intellectual Biography*. Edinburgh: T&T Clark, 1999.

McGuckin, John Anthony. *We Believe in One Lord Jesus Christ*. ACD 2. Downers Grove, IL: InterVarsity Press, 2009.

McIntyre, John. *The Shape of Pneumatology*. Edinburgh: T&T Clark, 1997.

McKnight, Scot. *A Community Called Atonement*. Nashville: Abingdon, 2007.

———. *Embracing Grace: A Gospel for All of Us*. Brewster, MA: Paraclete, 2005.

———. *Jesus and His Death: Historiography, the Historical Jesus, and Atonement Theory*. Waco, TX: Baylor University Press, 2005.

———. *The King Jesus Gospel: The Original Good News Revisited*. Grand Rapids: Zondervan, 2011).

———. *The Real Mary: Why Evangelical Christians Can Embrace the Mother of Jesus*. Brewster, MA: Paraclete, 2007.

———. "The Warning Passages of Hebrews: A Formal Analysis and Theological Conclusions." *TrinJ* 13 (1992): 21–59.

McLaren, Brian. *A New Kind of Christianity: Ten Questions That Are Transforming the Faith*. San Francisco: Harper One, 2010.

———. *The Story We Find Ourselves in: Further Adventures in a New Kind of Christian*. San Francisco: Jossey-Bass, 2003.

Meier, John P. *Matthew*. NTM 3. Delaware: Liturgical, 1980.

———. "The Present State of the 'Third Quest' for the Historical Jesus: Loss and Gain." *Bib* 80 (1999): 459–87.

Metzger, Bruce M. "The Meaning of Christ's Ascension." Pages 118–28 in *Search the Scriptures: New Testament Studies in Honor of Raymond T. Stamm*. Edited by J. M. Myers, O. Reimherr, and H. N. Bream. Leiden: Brill, 1969.

———. *A Textual Commentary on the Greek New Testament*. 2nd ed. Stuttgart: Deutsche Bibel Gesellschaft, 1994.

Michaels, J. Ramsey. *The Gospel of John*. NICNT. Grand Rapids: Eerdmans, 2010.

Middleton, J. Richard. *The Liberating Image: The Imago Dei in Genesis 1*. Grand Rapids: Brazos, 2005.

Migilore, Daniel. *Faith Seeking Understanding: An Introduction to Christian Theology*. Grand Rapids: Eerdmans, 1991.

Mikkelsen, Hans Vium. *Reconciled Humanity: Karl Barth in Dialogue*. Grand Rapids: Eerdmans, 2010.

Milne, Bruce. *Know the Truth*. 3rd ed. Downers Grove, IL: InterVarsity Press, 2009.

Minear, Paul S. *Images of the Church in the New Testament*. Philadelphia: Westminster, 1960.

Moloney, Francis J. *A Body Broken for a Broken People: Eucharist in the New Testament*. Melbourne: Collins Dove, 1990.

Moltmann, Jürgen. *The Coming of God*. Trans. M. Kohl. London: SCM, 1996.

———. *Jesus Christ for Today's World*. Minneapolis: Fortress, 1994.

———. *The Spirit of Life: A Universal Affirmation*. Trans. M. Kohl. Minneapolis: Fortress, 1992.

———. *Theology of Hope*. New York: Harper & Row, 1967.

Moo, Douglas J. "The Case for the Post-Tribulation Rapture Position." Pages 169–211 in *Three Views of the Rapture: Pre-, Mid-, Or Post-Tribulation?* Edited by S. N. Gundry. Grand Rapids: Zondervan, 1984.

———. *The Epistle to the Romans*. NICNT. Grand Rapids: 1996.

———. "Nature in the New Creation: New Testament Eschatology and the Environment." *JETS* 49 (2006): 449–88.

Moreland, J. P., and John M. Reynolds, eds. *Three Views on Creation and Evolution*. Grand Rapids: Zondervan, 1999.

Morris, Leon. *Apocalyptic*. Grand Rapids: Eerdmans, 1972.

———. *Apostolic Preaching of the Cross*. Grand Rapids: Eerdmans, 1955.

———. *The Atonement: Its Meaning and Significance*. Leicester, UK: Inter-Varsity Press, 1983.

———. *The Cross in the New Testament*. Grand Rapids: Eerdmans, 1965.

———. *The Epistle to the Romans*. PNTC. Grand Rapids: Eerdmans, 1988.

———. *The Gospel according to John*. NICNT. Rev. ed. Grand Rapids: Eerdmans, 1995.

———. *I Believe in Revelation*. Grand Rapids: Eerdmans, 1976.

Mugridge, Alan. "'Warning in the Epistle to the Hebrews': An Exegetical and Theological Study." *RTR* 46 (1987): 74–82.

Murray, John. "The Adamic Administration." Pages 47–59 in vol. 2, *Collected Writings of John Murray*. Edinburgh: Banner of Truth, 1977.

———. *Christian Baptism*. Philipsburg, NJ: Presbyterian & Reformed, 1980.

———. *Redemption Accomplished and Applied*. Grand Rapids: Eerdmans, 1955.

Naselli, Andrew D. "John Owen's Argument for Definite Atonement in *The Death of Death in the Death of Christ*: A Summary and Evaluation." *SBJT* 14 (2010): 60–83.

Needham, Nick. "Justification in the Early Church Fathers." Pages 25–53 in *Justification in Perspective: Historical Developments and Contemporary Challenges*. Edited by B. L. McCormack. Grand Rapids: Baker, 2006.

———. *The Triumph of Grace: Augustine's Writings on Salvation*. London: Grace Publications Trust, 2000.

Neil, Stephen. *What is Man?* London: Lutterworth, 1960.

Newbigin, Lesslie. *The Gospel in a Pluralistic Society*. Grand Rapids: Eerdmans, 1989.

———. *The Trinitarian Faith and Today's Mission*. Pennsylvania: John Knox, 1963.

Nicole, Roger. "C. H. Dodd and the Doctrine of Propitiation." *WTJ* 17 (1954–55): 117–57.

———. "Moyse Amyraut (1596–1664) and the Controversy on Universal Grace, First Phase (1634–1637)." PhD diss., Harvard University, 1966.

Niebuhr, Richard. *Christ and Culture*. New York: Harper, 1951.

———. *The Kingdom of God in America*. New York: Harper, 1937.

O'Brien, Peter T. *The Letter to the Ephesians*. PNTC. Grand Rapids: Eerdmans, 1999.

———. *The Letter to the Hebrews*. PNTC. Grand Rapids: Eerdmans, 2010.

———. "Was Paul a Covenantal Nomist?" Pages 249–96 in *Justification and Variegated Nomism: Volume 2—The Paradoxes of Paul*. Edited by D. A. Carson, Mark A. Seifrid, and Peter T. O'Brien. Grand Rapids: Baker, 2004.

O'Collins, Gerald. *Jesus Our Redeemer: A Christian Approach to Salvation*. Oxford: Oxford University Press, 2007.

———. *The Tripersonal God: Understanding and Interpreting the Trinity*. London: Geoffrey Chapman, 1999.

Oden, Thomas C. "The Death of Modernity and Postmodern Evangelical Spirituality." Pages 19–33 in *The Challenge of Postmodernism: An Evangelical Assessment*. Edited by D. S. Dockery. Wheaton, IL: Victor, 1995.

———. *Systematic Theology*. 3 vols. Peabody, MA: Hendrickson, 2006.

O'Donovan, Oliver. *Resurrection and the Moral Order: An Outline for Evangelical Ethics*. Leicester, UK: Inter-Varsity Press, 1986.

Olson, Roger E. *Arminian Theology: Myths and Realities*. Downers Grove, IL: Inter-Varsity Press, 2006.

———. *The Story of Christian Theology: Twenty Centuries of Tradition and Reform*. Downers Grove, IL: InterVarsity Press, 1999.

———. *The Westminster Handbook to Evangelical Theology*. Louisville: Westminster John Knox, 2004.

Olson, Roger E., and Christopher Hall. *The Trinity*. Grand Rapids: Eerdmans, 2002.

O'Neil, M. "Karl Barth's Doctrine of Election." *EvQ* 76 (2004): 311–26.

The Orthodox Study Bible: Ancient Christianity Speaks to Today's World. Nashville: Nelson, 2008.

Oropeza, B. J. *Paul and Apostasy: Eschatology, Perseverance, and Falling Away in the Corinthian Congregation*. WUNT 2.115; Tübingen: Mohr/Siebeck, 2000.

Ortberg, John. "The Shyness of God." *Christianity Today* 45/2 (2001): 66–67.

Ortlund, Dane C. "Justified by Faith, Judged according to Works: Another Look at a Pauline Paradox." *JETS* 52 (2009): 323–39.

Ostling, Richard N. "The Search for the Historical Adam." *Christianity Today* 55/6 (2011): 22–27.

Owen, John. *The Death of Death in the Death of Christ*. London: Banner of Truth, 1959.

Packer, J. I. *Concise Theology*. Wheaton, IL: Tyndale, 1993.

———. *Evangelism and the Sovereignty of God*. Downers Grove, IL: InterVarsity Press, 1961.

———. *"Fundamentalism" and the Word of God: Some Evangelical Principles*. Grand Rapids: Eerdmans, 1958.

———. *Keep in Step with the Spirit: Finding Fullness in Our Walk with God*. Downers Grove, IL: InterVarsity Press, 2005.

———. "The Logic of Penal Substitution." *TynBul* 25 (1974): 3–45.

———. "Regeneration." *EDT*, 924–26.

———. What Do You Mean When You Say God?" *Christianity Today* 30 (September 1986): 27–31.

Packer, J. I., and Thomas C. Oden. *One Faith: The Evangelical Consensus*. Downers Grove, IL: InterVarsity Press, 1999.

Pannenberg, Wolfhart. *Jesus: God and Man*. 2nd ed. Philadelphia: Westminster John Knox, 1968.

———. *Systematic Theology*. 3 vols. Trans. G. W. Bromiley. Edinburgh: T&T Clark, 1991.

Parker, David. "Original Sin: A Study in Evangelical Theology." *EvQ* 61 (1989): 51–69.

———. "Evangelicals and Mary: Recent Theological Evaluations." *ERT* 30 (2006): 121–40.

Parry, Robin, and Chris Partridge, eds. *Universal Salvation?: The Current Debate*. Carlisle, UK: Paternoster, 2003.

Partner, Daniel, ed. *Essential Works of Charles Spurgeon*. Uhrichsville, OH: Barbour, 2009.

Pascal, Blaise. *Pensées and Other Writings*. Oxford: Oxford University Press, 2008.

Patterson, Paige. "Single-Elder Congregationalism." Pages 131–52 in *Who Runs the Church? 4 Views on Church Government*. Edited by S. B. Cowan. Grand Rapids: Zondervan, 2004.

———. "The Work of Christ." Pages 545–602 in *A Theology for the Church*. Edited by D. L. Atkin. Nashville: Broadman & Holman, 2007.

Payton, James R. *Getting the Reformation Wrong: Correcting Some Misunderstandings*. Downers Grove, IL: InterVarsity Press, 2010.

Peacock, Arthur. *Creation and the World of Science*. Oxford: Clarendon, 1979.

Pelikan, Jaroslav. *Acts*. BTCB. Grand Rapids: Brazos, 2005.

———. *The Christian Tradition: A History of the Development of Doctrine*. Chicago: University of Chicago Press, 1971.

Perriman, Andrew. *The Coming Son of Man: New Testament Eschatology for an Emerging Church*. Milton Keynes, UK: Paternoster, 2005.

Perrin, Nick. "Jesus' Eschatology and Kingdom Ethics: Ever the Twain Shall Meet." Pages 92–114 in *Jesus, Paul, and the People of God: A Theological Dialogue with N. T. Wright*. Edited by N. Perrin and R. Hays. Downers Grove, IL: InterVarsity Press, 2011.

Perry, Tim. *Mary for Evangelicals: Toward an Understanding of the Mother of our Lord*. Downers Grove, IL: InterVarsity Press, 2006.

Peters, George W. *A Biblical Theology of Missions*. Chicago: Moody Press, 1974.

Peterson, David. *Possessed by God: A New Testament Theology of Holiness and Sanctification*. NSBT. Downers Grove, IL: InterVarsity Press, 1995.

———, ed. *Where Wrath and Mercy Meet*. Waynesboro, GA: Paternoster, 2001.

Peterson, Eugene. *Reversed Thunder: The Revelation of John and the Praying Imagination*. San Francisco: Harper & Row, 1988.

Peterson, Robert A. *Calvin's Doctrine of the Atonement*. Phillipsburg, NJ: Presbyterian & Reformed, 1983.

Peterson, Robert, and Christopher W. Morgan, eds. *Faith Comes by Hearing: A Response to Inclusivism*. Downers Grove, IL: InterVarsity Press, 2008.

Phillips, Timothy R, and Dennis L. Okholm. *A Family of Faith: An Introduction to Evangelical Christianity*. Grand Rapids: Baker, 2001.

Pinnock, Clark H. "From Augustine to Arminius: A Pilgrimage in Theology." Pages 15–30 in *The Grace of God and the Will of Man*. Edited by C. H. Pinnock. Grand Rapids: Bethany, 1995.

———. *The Scripture Principle*. Vancouver, BC: Regent College Publishing, 2002.

———. "There Is Room for Us—A Reply to Bruce Ware." *JETS* 45 (2002): 213–20.

Pinson, J. Matthew, ed. *Four Views on Eternal Security*. Grand Rapids: Zondervan, 2002.

Piper, John. *Don't Waste Your Life*. Wheaton, IL: Crossway, 2009.

———. *God Is the Gospel: Meditations on God's Love as the Gift of Himself*. Wheaton, IL: Crossway, 2005.

———. *Let the Nations Be Glad*. 3rd ed. Grand Rapids: Baker, 2010.

Pitts, William L. "The Relation of Baptists to Other Churches." Pages 235–50 in *The People of God: Essays on the Believers' Church*. Edited by P. A. Basen and D. S. Dockery. Nashville: Broadman & Holman, 1991.

Plantinga, Alvin. *God, Freedom, and Evil*. Grand Rapids: Eerdmans, 1978.

———. "Reason and Belief in God." Pages 16–93 in *Faith and Rationality*. Edited by A. Plantinga and N. Wolterstorff. Notre Dame, IN: University of Notre Dame Press, 1983.

———. "Two Dozen (or so) Theistic Arguments." Pages 203–28 in *Alvin Plantinga*. Edited by Deane-Peter Baker. Cambridge: Cambridge University Press, 2007.

———. *Warranted Christian Belief*. Oxford: Oxford University Press, 2000.

———. *Warrant: The Current Debate*. Oxford: Oxford University Press, 1993.

———. *Warrant and Proper Function*. Oxford: Oxford University Press, 1993.

Plantinga, Cornelius. "The Fourth Gospel as Trinitarian Source Then and Now." Pages 303–21 in *Biblical Hermeneutics in Historical Perspective*. Edited by M. S. Burrows and P. Rorem. Grand Rapids: Eerdmans, 1991.

———. *Not the Way It's Supposed to Be*. Grand Rapids: Eerdmans, 1995.

Porter, Stanley E. *Idioms of the Greek New Testament*. Sheffield: Sheffield: Sheffield Academic Press, 1992.

———. Καταλλάσσω *in Ancient Greek Literature, with Reference to the Pauline Writings*. Cordoba: Ediciónes El Almendro, 1994.

———. "Reconciliation as the Heart of Paul's Misionary Theology." Pages 169–79 in *Paul as Missionary: Identity, Activity, Theology, and Practice*. Edited by T. J. Burke and B. S. Rosner. LNTS 420. London: T&T Clark, 2011.

Powell, Mark Allan. *The Jesus Debate: Modern Historians Investigate the Life of Christ*. Louisville: Westminster John Knox, 1998.

———. *Loving Jesus*. Minneapolis: Fortress, 2004.

Powys, David. *"Hell": A Hard Look at a Hard Question: The Fate of the Unrighteous in New Testament Thought*. PBM. Milton Keynes, UK: Paternoster, 2007.

Rahner, Karl. *The Church and the Sacraments*. New York: Herder & Herder, 1963.

———. "Observations on the Problem of the 'Anonymous Christian.'" Pages 390–98 in *Theological Investigation*. Baltimore: Helicon, 1979.

Ramm, Bernard. *Special Revelation and the Word of God*. Grand Rapids: Eerdmans, 1961.

Rauschenbusch, Walter. *Theology for the Social Gospel*. New York: Abingdon, 1917.

Reasoner, Mark. *Romans in Full Circle: A History of Interpretation*. Louisville: Westminster John Knox, 2005.

Reicke, Bo. *Diakonie, Festfreude und Zelos: In Verbindung mit der altchristlichen Agapenfeier*. Uppsala: Lundequist, 1951.

Reymond, Robert L. *A New Systematic Theology of the Christian Faith*. 2nd ed. Nashville: Nelson, 1998.

Reynolds, Benjamin E. "Faith/Faithfulness." Pages 627–29 in *EDEJ*. Edited by J. J. Collins and D. C. Harlow. Grand Rapids: Eerdmans, 2010.

Riddelbarger, Kim. *A Case for Amillennialism*. Grand Rapids: Baker, 2003.

Ritschl, Albrecht. *The Christian Doctrine of Justification and Reconciliation*. Edinburgh: T&T Clark, 1902.

Roberts, Vaughan. *God's Big Picture: Tracing the Storyline of the Bible*. Nottingham, UK: Inter-Varsity Press, 2002.

Robinson, James M. *A New Quest for the Historical Jesus*. SBT 25. London: SCM, 1959.

Rowe, C. Kavin. "Biblical Pressure and Trinitarian Hermeneutics." *ProEccl* 11 (2002): 295–312.

Russell, Jeffery B. *The Prince of Darkness: Radical Evil and the Power of Good in History*. Ithaca, NY: Cornell University Press, 1992.

Ryken, Philip G., ed. *The Communion of the Saints: Living in Fellowship with the People of God*. Philipsburg, NJ: Presbyterian & Reformed, 2001.

Ryle, J. C. *Expository Thoughts on the Gospels*. Grand Rapids: Baker, 1979.

Ryrie, Charles. *Basic Theology*. Wheaton, IL: Victor, 1986.

———. *Dispensationalism Today*. Chicago: Moody Press, 1965.

Sanders, E. P. *The Historical Figure of Jesus*. London: Penguin, 1993.

———. *Paul and Palestinian Judaism*. London: SCM, 1977.

Sanders, Fred. *The Deep Things of God: How the Trinity Changes Everything*. Wheaton, IL: Crossway, 2010.

Sanders, John E. "God as Personal." Pages 165–80 in *The Grace of God, The Will of Man: A Case for Arminianism*. Edited by C. H. Pinnock. Grand Rapids: Zondervan, 1989.

———. "Historical Considerations." Pages 59–100 in *The Openness of God: A Biblical Challenge to the Traditional Understanding of God*. Downers Grove, IL: InterVarsity Press, 1994.

———. "Inclusivism." Pages 21–55 in *What About Those Who Have Never Heard? Three Views on the Destiny of the Unevangelised*. Ed. John E. Sanders. Downers Grove, IL: InterVarsity Press, 1995.

Satterthwaite, P. E. "Biblical History." *NDBT*, 43–51.

Sands, Paul. "The *Imago Dei* as Vocation." *EvQ* 82 (2010): 28–41.

Saucy, Robert. " 'Sinners' Who Are Forgiven or 'Saints' Who Sin? " *BSac* 152 (1995): 400–412.

Sawyer, John F. A. *The Fifth Gospel: Isaiah in the History of Christianity*. Cambridge: Cambridge University Press, 1996.

Schaeffer, Francis A. *The God Who Is There*. Downers Grove, IL: InterVarsity Press, 1968.

Schleiermacher, Friedrich. *The Christian Faith*. Trans. H. R. Mackintosh and J. S. Steward. Edinburgh: T&T Clark, 1928.

Schmiechen, Peter. *Saving Power: Theories of Atonement and Forms of the Church.* Grand Rapids: Eerdmans, 2005.

Schnabel, Eckhard J. "The Language of Baptism: The Meaning of βαπτίζω in the New Testament." Pages 217–46 in *Understanding the Times: New Testament Studies in the 21st Century.* Edited by A. J. Köstenberger and R. W. Yarbrough. Festschrift D. A. Carson. Wheaton, IL: Crossway, 2011.

Schreiner, Thomas R. "Corporate and Individual Election in Romans 9: A Response to Brian Abasciano." *JETS* 49 (2006): 373–86.

———. "Does Romans 9 Teach Individual Election unto Salvation?" Pages 89–106 in *Still Sovereign: Contemporary Perspectives on Election, Foreknowledge, and Grace.* Edited by T. R. Schreiner and B. A. Ware. Grand Rapids: Baker, 2000.

———. *New Testament Theology: Magnifying God in Christ.* Grand Rapids: Baker, 2008.

———. *Paul: Apostles of God's Glory in Christ: A Pauline Theology.* Downers Grove, IL: InterVarsity Press, 2001.

———. "Penal Substitution View." Pages 67–98 in *The Nature of the Atonement.* Edited by J. Beilby and P. R. Eddy. Downers Grove, IL: InterVarsity Press, 2006.

———. *Romans.* BECNT. Grand Rapids: Baker, 1998.

Schreiner, Thomas R., and Ardel Caneday. *The Race Set before Us: A Biblical Theology of Perseverance and Assurance.* Downers Grove, IL: InterVarsity Press, 2001.

Schreiner, Thomas R., and Shawn D. Wright, eds. *Believer's Baptism: The Sign of the New Covenant.* Nashville: Broadman & Holman, 2006.

Schweitzer, Albert. *The Quest of the Historical Jesus.* Trans. W. Montgomery. London: Adam and Charles Black, 1911.

Scobie, Charles. *The Ways of our Lord: An Approach to Biblical Theology.* Grand Rapids: Eerdmans, 2003.

Seifrid, Mark A. "In Christ." *DPL,* 433–36.

Sell, A. P. F., J. J. Hall, and D. W. Bebbington. *Protestant Non-Conformist Texts: The Eighteenth Century.* Aldershot, UK: Ashgate, 2006.

Sherlock, Charles. *God on the Inside: Trinitarian Spirituality.* Wanniassa, AU: Acorn, 1991.

———. *The Doctrine of Humanity.* Leicester, UK: Inter-Varsity Press, 1996.

Shuster, Marguerite. *The Fall and Sin: What We Have Become as Sinners.* Grand Rapids: Eerdmans, 2004.

Smith, Gordon T. *Beginning Well: Christian Conversion and Authentic Transformation.* Downers Grove, IL: InterVarsity Press, 2001.

———, ed. *The Lord's Supper: Five Views*. Downers Grove, IL: InterVarsity Press, 2008.

Smith, S. M. "Hope, Theology of." *EDT*, 532–34.

Snodgrass, Klyne. "The Gospel in Romans: A Theology of Revelation." Pages 288–314 in *Gospel in Paul*. Edited by L. Ann Jervis and Peter Richardson. JSNTSup 108. Sheffield: Sheffield Academic Press, 1994.

Snyder, Howard A. *Models of the Kingdom*. Nashville: Abingdon, 1991.

Sproul, R. C. *Faith Alone: The Evangelical Doctrine of Justification*. Grand Rapids: Baker, 1999.

Sproul, R. C., John H. Gerstner, and Arthur Lindsley, eds. *Classical Apologetics: A Rational Defense of the Christian Faith*. Grand Rapids: Zondervan, 1984.

Stackhouse, John G., ed. *Evangelical Futures: A Conversation on Theological Method*. Grand Rapids: Baker, 2000.

———. "Preface." Pages 9–11 in *Evangelical Ecclesiology: Reality or Illusion?* Grand Rapids: Baker, 2003.

Stanley, Alan P. *Salvation Is More Complicated Than You Think: A Study on the Teaching of Jesus*. Colorado Springs, CO: Authentic, 2007.

Stott, John. *The Cross of Christ*. Downers Grove, IL: InterVarsity Press, 1986.

———. *Evangelical Truth: A Personal Statement*. Leicester, UK: Inter-Varsity Press, 1999.

———. *The Living Church: Convictions of a Life Long Pastor*. Downers Grove, IL: InterVarsity Press, 2011.

———. *Why I Am a Christian*. Leicester, UK: Inter-Varsity Press, 2003.

Strauss, Mark. *Four Portraits, One Jesus: An Introduction to Jesus and the Gospels*. Grand Rapids: Zondervan, 2007.

Strawberry, Greg, ed. *The Case for Covenantal Infant Baptism*. Phillipsburg, NJ: Presbyterian & Reformed, 2003.

Strom, Mark. *The Symphony of Scripture: Making Sense of the Bible's Many Themes*. Downers Grove, IL: InterVarsity Press, 1990.

Stuhlmacher, Peter. *Biblische Theologie des Neuen Testaments*. 2 vols. Göttingen: Vandenhoeck und Ruprecht, 1992–1999.

———. *Revisiting Paul's Doctrine of Justification: A Challenge to the New Perspective*. Downers Grove, IL: InterVarsity Press, 2001.

Sudduth, Michael. *The Reformed Objections to Natural Theology*. Farnham, UK: Ashgate, 2009.

Surin, Kenneth. "Evil, Problem of." Pages 192–99 in *The Blackwell Encyclopedia of Modern Christian Thought*. Edited by A. E. McGrath. Oxford: Blackwell, 1995.

Sweet, Leonard I., ed. *The Evangelical Tradition in America*. Macon, GA: Mercer University Press, 1984.

Swinburne, Richard. *The Evolution of the Soul*. Rev. ed. Oxford: Clarendon, 1997.

Taylor, Iain, ed. *Not Evangelical Enough: The Gospel at the Centre*. Carlisle, UK: Paternoster, 2003.

Taylor, L. Roy "Presbyterianism." Pages 73–98 in *Who Runs the Church? 4 Views on Church Government*. Edited by S. B. Cowan. Grand Rapids: Zondervan, 2004.

Taylor, S. S. "Faith, faithfulness." *NDBT*, 487–93.

Tennent, Timothy C. *Theology in the Context of World Christianity: How the Global Church Is Influencing the Way We Think about and Discuss Theology*. Grand Rapids: Zondervan, 2007.

Theissen, Gerd, and Annette Merz. *The Historical Jesus: A Comprehensive Guide*. Trans. John Bowden; Minneapolis: Fortress, 1998.

Thiessen, Henry C. *Lectures in Systematic Theology*. Grand Rapids: Eerdmans, 1977 [1949].

Theobald, Michael. Pages 226–40 in "Rechtfertigung und Ekklesiologie nach Paulus: Anmerkungen zur 'Gemeinsamen Erklärung zur Rechtfertigungslehre.'" In *Studien zum Römerbrief*. WUNT 136. Tübingen: Mohr/Siebeck, 2001.

Thompson, Mark D. *A Clear and Present Word: The Clarity of Scripture*. NSBT. Downers Grove, IL: InterVarsity Press, 2006.

Thorsen, Donald A. *The Wesleyan Quadrilateal: Scripture, Tradition, Reason, and Experience as a Model for Evangelical Theology*. Lexington, KY: Emeth, 1990.

Tidball, Derek. "Church." *NDBT*, 407–11.

———. *Skillful Shepherds: Explorations in Pastoral Theology*. Leicester, UK: Apollos, 1997.

Tiessen, Terence L. *Irenaeus on the Salvation of the Unevangelized*. ATLAMS 31. Metuchen, NJ: Scarecrow, 1993.

———. *Who Can Be Saved? Reassessing Salvation in Christ and World Religions*. Downers Grove, IL: InterVarsity Press, 2004.

Tilley, Terence W. "Remembering the Historic Jesus—a New Research Program?" *TS* 68 (2007): 3–35.

Tillich, Paul. *Systematic Theology*. 3 vols. London: SCM, 1951–63.

Toon, Peter. *The Ascension of Our Lord*. Nashville: Nelson, 1984.

———. "Episcopalianism." Pages 21–41 in *Who Runs the Church? 4 Views on Church Government*. Edited by S. B. Cowan. Grand Rapids: Zondervan, 2004.

Torrance, T. F. *The Christian Doctrine of God: One Being Three Persons*. Edinburgh: T&T Clark, 1996.

———. *Incarnation*. Milton Keynes, UK: Paternoster, 2008.

———. *Kingdom and Church: A Study in the Theology of the Reformation*. Edinburgh: Oliver & Boyd, 1956.

———. *The Trinitarian Faith*. Edinburgh: T&T Clark, 1995.
Travis, Stephen H. *Christ and the Judgment of God: The Limits of Divine Retribution in New Testament Thought*. 2nd ed. Milton Keynes, UK: Paternoster, 2008.
Treier, Daniel J. "Scripture and Hermeneutics." Pages 35-49 in *The Cambridge Companion to Evangelical Theology*. Edited by Timothy Larsen and Daniel J. Treier. Cambridge: Cambridge University Press, 2007.
Turner, Seth. "The Interim, Earthly Messianic Kingdom in Paul." *JSNT* 25 (2003): 323–42.
Tyrrell, George. *Christianity at the Crossroads*. London: Longman Green, 1909.
Updike, John. "Seven Stanzas at Easter." *Christian Century* 78/8 (1961): 236.
Van Driel, Edwin. *Incarnation Anyway: Arguments for Supralapsarian Christology*. Oxford: Oxford University Press, 2008.
VanDrunen, David. *Living in God's Two Kingdoms: A Biblical Vision for Christianity and Culture*. Wheaton, IL: Crossway, 2010.
VanGemeren, Willem. *The Progress of Redemption: The Story of Salvation from Creation to the New Jerusalem*. Grand Rapids: Zondervan, 1988.
Vanhoozer, Kevin J. "The Apostolic Discourse and Its Developments." Pages 191–207 in *Scripture's Doctrine and Theology's Bible: How the New Testament Shapes Christian Dogmatics*. Edited by M. Bockmuehl and A. J. Torrance. Grand Rapids: Baker, 2008.
———. *The Drama of Doctrine: A Canonical Linguistic Approach to Christian Theology*. Louisville: Westminster John Knox, 2002.
———. *First Theology: God, Scripture, and Hermeneutics*. Downers Grove, IL: InterVarsity Press, 2002.
———. *Is There a Meaning in This Text? The Bible, the Reader, and the Morality of Literary Knowledge*. Grand Rapids: Zondervan, 1998.
———. "The Voice and the Actor: A Dramatic Proposal about the Ministry and Minstrelsy of Theology." Pages 61–106 in *Evangelical Futures: A Conversation on Theological Method*. Edited by J. G. Stackhouse. Vancouver, BC: Regent College Publishing, 2000.
———. "Wrighting the Wrongs of the Reformation? The State of the Union with Christ in St. Paul and Protestant Soteriology." Pages 236–61 in *Jesus, Paul and the People of God: A Theological Dialogue with N.T. Wright*. Downers Grove, IL: InterVarsity Press, 2011.
Van Til, Cornelius. *Christian Theory of Knowledge*. Phillipsburg, NJ: Presbyterian and Reformed, 1969.
———. *In Defense of the Faith*. 3rd ed. Philadelphia, NJ: Presbyterian and Reformed, 1967.
Venema, Cornelis P. *Children at the Lord's Table: Assessing the Case for Paedocommunion*. Grand Rapids: Reformed Heritage, 2009.

Venning, Ralph. *The Sinfulness of Sin*. Edinburgh: Banner of Truth, 1965.

Vickers, Brian. *Jesus' Blood and Righteousness: Paul's Theology of Imputation*. Wheaton, IL: Crossway, 2006.

Vlach, Michael J. *Has the Church Replaced Israel?: A Theological Evaluation*. Nashville: Broadman & Holman, 2010.

Volf, Miroslav. *After Our Likeness: The Church as the Image of the Trinity*. Grand Rapids: Eerdmans, 1998.

———. *Exclusion and Embrace: A Theological Exploration of Identity, Otherness, and Reconciliation*. Nashville: Abingdon, 1996.

———. "Worship as Adoration and Action: Reflections on a Christian Way of Being-in-the-World." Pages 203–11 in *Worship: Adoration and Action*. Edited by D. A. Carson. Eugene, OR: Wipf & Stock, 2002.

Von Campenhausen, H. *The Virgin Birth in the Theology of the Ancient Church*. Trans. F. Clarke. London: SCM, 1964.

Walton, John. *The Lost World of Genesis One: Ancient Cosmology and the Origins Debate*. Downers Grove, IL: InterVarsity Press, 2009.

Walvoord, John F. *The Rapture Question*. Findlay, OH: Dunham, 1957.

Warfield, B. B. *Inspiration and Authority of the Bible*. London: Epworth, 1956.

Ward, Timothy. *Words of Life: Scripture as the Living and Active Word of God*. Nottingham, UK: Apollos, 2009.

Ware, Bruce A. *Father, Son, and Holy Spirit: Relationships, Roles, and Relevance*. Wheaton, IL: Crossway, 2005.

———. *God's Lesser Glory: The Diminished God of Open Theism*. Wheaton, IL: Crossway, 2000.

Waters, Guy Prentiss. *Justification and the New Perspective on Paul: A Review and Response*. Phillipsburg, NJ: Presbyterian & Reformed, 2004.

Watson, Francis. "An Evangelical Response." Pages 285–89 in *The Trustworthiness of God: Perspectives on the Nature of Scripture*. Edited by C. Trueman and P. Helm. Grand Rapids: Eerdmans, 2002.

———. "Not the New Perspective." Unpublished paper delivered at the British New Testament Conference in Manchester in September 2001. www.abdn.ac.uk/divinity/watsonart.shhtml. Accessed 9 March 2011.

———. *Paul, Judaism, and the Gentile: Beyond the New Perspective*. Grand Rapids: Eerdmans, 2006.

Wax, Trevin. "The Justification Debate: A Primer." *Christianity Today* 53/6 (2009): 34–35.

———. *Counterfeit Gospels: Rediscovering the Good News in a World of False Hope*. Chicago: Moody Press, 2011.

Webb, Barry. *Five Festal Garments: Christian Reflections on the Song of Songs, Ruth,*

Lamentations, Ecclesiastes, Esther. NSBT 10. Downers Grove, IL: InterVarsity Press, 2000.

Webber, Robert. *The Church in the World*. Grand Rapids: Zondervan, 1986.

Webster, John. *Barth's Ethics of Reconciliation*. Cambridge: Cambridge University Press, 1995.

———. "Biblical Reasoning." *ATR* 90 (2008): 733–51.

———. *Confessing God: Essays in Christian Dogmatics II*. London: T&T Clark, 2005.

———. "'It Was the Will of the Lord to Bruise Him': Soteriology and the Doctrine of God." Pages 15–35 in *God of Salvation: Soteriology in Theological Perspective*. Edited by I. J. Davidson and M. Rae. Farnham, UK: Ashgate, 2011.

———. "Providence." Pages 203–26 in *Mapping Modern Theology: A Thematic and Historical Introduction*. Edited by Kelly M. Kapic and Bruce L. McCormack; Grand Rapids: Baker, 2012.

———. *Scripture: A Dogmatic Sketch*. Cambridge: Cambridge University Press, 2003.

———. *Word and Church*. London: T&T Clark, 2001.

Welker, Michael, and Cynthia A. Jarvis, eds. *Loving God with Our Minds: The Pastor as Theologian*. Grand Rapids: Eerdmans, 2004.

Wells, David F., and John D. Woodbridge, eds. *The Evangelicals: What They Believe, Who They Are, Where They Are Changing*. Nashville: Abingdon, 1975.

Wenham, John. "The Case for Conditional Immortality." Pages 161–91 in *Universalism and the Doctrine of Hell*. Edited by Nigel Cameron. Grand Rapids: Baker, 1992.

Williams, D. H. *Evangelicals and Tradition: The Formative Influence of the Early Church*. Grand Rapids: Baker, 2005.

———. "Justification by Faith: A Patristic Doctrine." *JEH* 57/6 (2006): 649–67.

———. *Retrieving the Tradition and Renewing Evangelicalism: A Primer for Suspicious Protestants*. Grand Rapids: Eerdmans, 1999.

Williams, David J. *Acts*. NIBC. Peabody, MA: Hendrickson, 1985.

———. *Paul's Metaphors: Their Context and Character*. Peabody, MA: Hendrickson, 1999.

Williams, J. Rodman. *Renewal Theology: Systematic Theology from a Charismatic Perspective*. Grand Rapids: Zondervan, 1996.

Williams, Michael. *Far as the Curse Is Found: The Covenant Story of Redemption*. Phillipsburg, NJ: Presbyterian & Reformed, 2005.

Williams, Rowan. *Arius: Heresy and Tradition*. London: SCM, 1987.

Williams, S. N. "Providence." *NDBT*, 710-15.

Williamson, Paul R. *Sealed with an Oath: Covenant in God's Unfolding Purpose*. NSBT 23. Downers Grove, IL: InterVarsity Press, 2007.

Witherington, Ben III. "Jesus as the Alpha and Omega of New Testament Thought." Pages 25–46 in *Contours of Christology in the New Testament*. Edited by R. N. Longenecker. Grand Rapids: Eerdmans, 2005.

———. *The Jesus Quest: The Third Search for the Jew of Nazareth*. 2nd ed. Downers Grove, IL: InterVarsity Press, 1997.

———. *Letters and Homilies for Hellenized Christians: A Socio-Rhetorical Commentary on 1–2 Peter*. Downers Grove, IL: InterVarsity Press, 2007.

———. *Letters and Homilies for Jewish Christians: A Socio-Rhetorical Commentary on Hebrews, James and Jude*. Nottingham, UK: Apollos, 2007.

———. *Making a Meal of It: Rethinking the Theology of the Lord's Supper*. Waco, TX: Baylor University Press, 2007.

———. *The Problem with Evangelical Theology: Testing the Exegetical Foundations of Calvinism, Dispensationalism, and Weslyanism*. Waco, TX: Baylor University Press, 2005.

———. *Revelation*. CGNTC. Cambridge: Cambridge University Press, 2003.

Wolters, Albert. *Creation Regained: Biblical Basics for a Reformational Worldview*. 2nd ed. Grand Rapids: Eerdmans, 2005.

Woodbridge, John. *Biblical Authority: A Critique of the Rogers/McKim Proposal*. Grand Rapids: Zondervan, 1982.

Wright, Christopher J. H. *Knowing Jesus through the Old Testament*. Downers Grove, IL: InterVarsity Press, 1992.

———. *Salvation Belongs to Our God: Celebrating the Bible's Central Story*. Downers Grove, IL: InterVarsity Press, 2008.

Wright, David. *What Has Infant Baptism Done to Baptism? An Enquiry into the End of Christendom*. Milton Keynes, UK: Paternoster, 2005.

———, ed. *Baptism: Three Views*. Downers Grove, IL: InterVarsity Press, 2009.

Wright, N. T. *The Challenge of Jesus*. London: SPCK, 2000.

———. *Climax of the Covenant: Christ and the Law in Pauline Theology*. Edinburgh: T&T Clark, 1991.

———. *Evil and the Justice of God*. London: SPCK, 2006.

———. *Following Jesus: Biblical Reflections on Discipleship*. London: SPCK, 1997.

———. *Hebrews for Everyone*. London: SPCK, 2004.

———. *Jesus and the Victory of God*. COQG 2. London: SPCK, 1996.

———. *Justification: God's Plan and Paul's Vision*. Downers Grove, IL: InterVarsity Press, 2009.

———. *The Last Word*. San Francisco: Harper One, 2005.

———. "The Letter to the Romans." *NIB*, 10:395–770.

———. *The Meal Jesus Gave Us: Understanding Holy Communion*. Louisville: Westminster John Knox, 2002.

Select Bibliography

———. *New Testament and the People of God*. COQG 1. London: SPCK, 1992.

———. "Paul in Different Perspective: Lecture 1: Starting Points and Opening Reflections." Unpublished lecture delivered at Auburn Avenue Presbyterian Church, Monroe, LA (3 January 2005). www.ntwrightpage.com/Wright_Auburn_Paul.htm. Accessed 1 Dec 2010.

———. "Power to Become Children: Isaiah 52.7–10 and John 1.1–18." Sermon preached at Cathedral Church of Christ, 25 December 2007. http://www.ntwrightpage.com/sermons/Christmas07.htm. Accessed 24 Dec 2010.

———. "Quest for the Historical Jesus." *ABD*, 3:796–802.

———. *The Resurrection of the Son of God*. COQG 3; London: SPCK, 2003.

———. *Surprised by Hope*. New York: Harper One, 2008.

———. *What Saint Paul Really Said*. Oxford: Lion, 1997.

Wurmbrand, Richard. *Tortured for Christ*. Bartlesville, OK: Living Sacrifice, 1998.

Yarbrough, Robert W. "Divine Election in the Gospel of John." Pages 47–62 in *Still Sovereign: Contemporary Perspectives on Election, Foreknowledge, and Grace*. Edited by T. R. Schreiner and B. A. Ware. Grand Rapids: Baker, 2000.

———. "Forgiveness and Reconciliation." *NDBT*, 498–503.

Yinger, Kent L. *The New Perspective on Paul: An Introduction*. Eugene, OR: Cascade, 2011.

Zannoni, Arthur E. *Tell Me Your Name: Images of God in the Bible*. Chicago: Liturgy Training Publication, 2000.

Ziep, Arie W. *The Ascension of the Messiah in Lukan Christology*. Leiden: Brill, 1997.

Zizioulas, John. *Being as Communion*. Crestwood, NY: St. Vladamir's Seminary Press, 1997.

SCRIPTURE AND APOCRYPHA INDEX

GENESIS

1–11 . . . . . 498, 654–55, 669
1–5 683
1–3 . . . . . .310, 311, 466, 655
1–2 . . . . .223, 497
1 . . . . .158, 467
1:1–2 . . . . .148, 159, 160, 621
1:1 . . . . . .100, 128, 327, 472
1:2 . . . . . .104, 171, 616, 622
1:4 157
1:10 157
1:12 157
1:18 157
1:20 572
1:21 157
1:25 157
1:26–28 . . . . . 286, 510, 660
1:26–27 . . . . . 137, 143, 144,
   285, 657, 658, 660
1:26 . . . . 101, 104
1:27–28 282
1:27 659
1:28 . . . . . . .442, 455, 500,
   505, 659, 661
1:31 . . . . 133, 157
2–3 144
2:7 . . . . 572, 627
2:8–10 . . . . 319, 497
2:15 162
2:16–17 283
2:16 319
2:17 . . . . .310, 497, 671
3–11 498–500
3 . . . . 498, 689
3:1–7 668
3:3 . . . . 310, 671
3:4 . . . . 591, 674
3:14–19 498
3:15 . . . . . 44, 207, 219, 222,
   227, 282, 359,
   414–415, 496, 499, 500

3:16 661
3:19–24 310
3:19 311
3:20 499
3:21 499
3:22–23 499
3:22 101
4:1–14 498
4:7 671
4:15 499
4:23–24 498
4:25–26 . . . . 499, 500
4:26 499
5 . . . . 310, 498
5:1–2 . . . . 657, 659
5:24 . . . . 323, 450
5:29 500
5:32–10:32 498
6–9 222
6–8 499
6:5 675
6:6 129
6:9 . . . . 499, 500
6:18 500
8:20–9:17 500
8:20–21 500
9:1–17 140
9:1–3 499
9:5 661
9:6–7 657
9:9–17 499
9:9–11 . . . . 227, 762
9:9–10 134
9:18–29 498
9:26–27 500
9:29 498
10 499
11:1–9 . . . . 498, 501
11:7 101
11:27–32 . . . . 498, 499
12 500

12:1–10 168
12:1–4 538
12:1–3 . . . . . . 103, 227, 496,
   501, 502, 714
12:2–3 500
12:2 503
12:3 501
14:18 780
14:19–22 142
15–22 . . . . 501, 538
15–21 222
15:3–4 359
15:6 . . . . 51, 538
15:18 . . . . 134, 501
16:5 472
16:7–13 . . . . 103, 360
17:1 503
17:4–5 140
17:7–8 762
17:15–21 369
18:14 133
18:19 503
18:25 . . . . 492, 594
21:17–21 360
21:17–18 103
22 . . . . 502, 538
22:11–18 103
22:18 501
24:3 142
26:4 501
26:5 . . . . 503, 538
31:10–13 . . . . 103, 360
32:24–32 168
32:28 721
35:18 663
37:35 323
49:10 . . . . . . .260, 360, 496
49:24 715
50:17 552
50:20 690

Scripture and Apocrypha Index

EXODUS
1–2 . . . . 369, 502
2:23–24 502
3 503
3:2–6 . . . . 103, 360
3:7–8 502
3:8 555
3:14 . . . . 105, 126, 616
3:15–17 714
3:15 168
3:16–17 749
3:17 555
3:18 749
4:21–22 102
4:22–23 198
4:22 571
4:29–31 752
6:3 168
6:6 . . . . 553, 555
6:7 603
12 . . . . 50, 780
12:13 403
13:3 555
13:15 555
13:21–22 503
14:4 137
14:30 555
15:2 555
15:13 . . . . 135, 555
15:26 420
19 503
19:4–6 502
19:4–5 . . . . 227, 502
19:5–6 . . . . . 140, 286, 503,
539, 716, 737
19:5 134
19:6 . . . . . 136, 153, 285, 714
20:4 103
20:5 673
20:7 471
20:20 668
21:28–32 553
22:22 755
23:7 566
24 503
24:1 749
24:9–11 749
25–26 503
29:45 219
31:1–3 637
31:3 204
32 146
32:9–14 129
32:34 503
33–34 206
33:7–11 503
33:19 133
33:20 103
34:6 . . . . 135, 504
34:9 550
35:30–35 637
35:31 204
40:35 366

LEVITICUS
4 405
4:20 550
4:26 550
4:35 550
5:10 550
5:13 550
5:16 550
6:7 550
10:22–26 539
11:44 136
16:1–15 407
16:21–22 424
17:11 . . . . 403, 573
17:14 573
18:4–5 503
18:5 227
19:1–2 . . . . 502, 716
19:2 . . . . 539, 542
19:12 471
19:20 404
19:22 550
20:7–8 716
20:7 . . . . 136, 542
20:26 542
22:32 471
25 553
25:26 404
25:51–52 404
26:11–12 332
26:12 603

NUMBERS
11:16–17 749
11:25 632
13–14 602
14:33 674
19:13, 20 332
23:19 . . . . 129, 393, 471
24:2 631
27:18 . . . . 104, 628
32:14–15 599

DEUTERONOMY
1–29 504
1:3 674
1:31 . . . . 105, 571
3:24 142
3:25 139
4:10 713
4:15–28 539
4:23 539
4:29–30 539
4:33 713
4:35 142
4:37 . . . . 515, 516
4:39 . . . . 142, 327
5:11 471
6:2 573
6:4–6 101
6:4–5 469
6:4 . . . . 101, 464, 469
6:5 662
7:6–9 735
7:6–8 516
7:6–7 515
7:6 . . . . 136, 713, 737
7:7–8 714
7:8 553
7:9 135
7:10 673
9 211
9:1–29 516
9:1–19 223
9:1–6 503
9:5–6 714
9:6 496
9:26 553
10:12–19 503
10:15 . . . . 515, 516, 735
10:16 . . . . 534, 761
10:17–19 755
10:17 472
11:16–17 539

Scripture and Apocrypha Index

13:5	553
14:2	516, 735
14:21	735
15:15	553
18:15	360
18:18	51
21:8	424
21:23	406
22:7	573
24:18	553
24:26	680
25:1	566
26:1–10	223
26:5–9	516
26:13	667
26:16–19	504
26:16	136
26:17–18	502
26:19	735
27:1	749
27:9	721
28	503
29:29	167, 219
30:6	534, 674, 761
30:15	573
30:19	573
32:4	130
32:15	472
32:18	138
32:36	241
32:43	306
33:25–28	143
33:28	793
34:5–7	322
34:9	196, 204, 628

JOSHUA

2:11	142
3:5	136
8:30–35	504
8:33–55	713
22:12	713
24:1–28	504
24:19–20	136
24:19	551

JUDGES

2:1	103, 360
3:10	104, 622, 628, 632
5:11	419
6:1	689
6:12	103
6:23–24	103
6:24	568
6:34	622, 628
11:29	622, 628
13:2–7	369
13:25	628
14:6	622, 628
14:19	622, 628
15:14–15	622
15:14	628
17:6	752
20:16	668
21:25	752

RUTH

2:20	553

1 SAMUEL

1–3	369
2:6–9	143
2:6	323
2:10	143
3:7	195
6:13	104
7:5–6	752
10:24	752
11:6	628
15:10	195
15:29	471
16:7–12	515
16:13	623, 628
16:14	104
18:12	104
28:7–25	322

2 SAMUEL

5–6	330
5:2	715
7:7	715
7:11–14	360
7:12–16	222, 496, 505
7:12	314
7:23	553, 721
12:23	594
22:3	472, 555
23:2	196, 639

1 KINGS

2:10	314
2:11–12	323
3:8	515
3:29	137
8:10–11	330
8:23	142
8:27	132
8:33–35	539
8:48	539
8:60	142
9:4–8	330
11:6	689
11:43	314
12:20–21	721
16:25	689
18	146
22:19	143
22:50	314
24:4	551

2 KINGS

2	629
2:11–12	322
2:11	450
5:14	771
11:17–18	504
14:6	680
16:3	334
19:15	142
21:4	332
21:7	332
22–23	504

1 CHRONICLES

6:49	424
12:38	741
16:12–13	714
16:13	515
16:25	139
16:35	557
17:21	553, 721
22:8	195

2 CHRONICLES

1:11	137
2:12	162
6:14	142

Reference	Page
6:18	132
6:41	133
7:14	539
12:12	143
14–15	504
18:18	143
23:19	332
24:6	713
25:4	680
29:16	332
30:12	735

EZRA

Reference	Page
1:2	143
3:11	135
5:11	101
7:16–17	332
9:1–15	504
9:7	539
9:8–15	716
9:11–12	542
10:1–5	504

NEHEMIAH

Reference	Page
1:10	553
8–10	504
8:1–18	752
8:1–3	713
9:6	142, 143, 472
9:7–8	538
10:33	424

JOB

Reference	Page
5:10	143, 162
7:8–9	311
7:9	317, 323
7:11	663
7:21	311
8:12	311
9:33–35	456
11:7	204
12:23	143
14:12	314
17:13	317
17:16	311
19:25–26	311
19:25	168
26:12–13	148, 621
26:13	616
33:4	104, 148, 155, 572, 616, 621
33:6	104
33:24	554
33:28	553
34:14	104
36:26	128
37:5	143
37:10	143
37:13	143
37:16	134
38:4–7	690
41:11	128
42:2–3	690
42:2	133

PSALMS

Reference	Page
2	286, 473, 474
2:6	330, 473
2:7	473
2:9	373
4:6	461
5:5	673
6:5	311, 317
8:1–3	142
8:4–6	143
8:4–5	650
8:5–6	455, 659
8:5	652
8:6	50
9:11	330
9:14	555
11:5	673
11:9	553
12:6	642
13:3	314
14:1–2	535
16	51
16:10	317, 433
16:11	573
17	51
18:2	555
18:25	135
18:46	472
19	184
19:1–14	176
19:1–8	171
19:1–6	190
19:1–4	173
19:1–2	70
19:7–14	190
19:7	642, 736
19:14	168, 553
20	416
21	416
21:4	573
22	51, 405, 416
22:1	301
22:28	143
22:29	311
23:6	133, 573
24	449
25:11	550
25:22	721
27:13	133
28:8	555
29:11	568
30:9	311
31:5	135
31:9	665
31:19	133
32:1	550
32:5	672
33:4	135, 642
33:5	143
33:6–9	104
34:8	799
37:2	311
38:4	672
42:2–6	665
44:25–26	311
45:6	102
46:4–7	330
47	449
48:1–8	330
49:7–9	573
49:14–15	311
49:14	317
49:15	553
51	492
51:1–14	549
51:1	135, 550
51:4	668
51:5	683
51:7	315
51:10	556, 683
55:15	317

55:19. 129	98:3 . . . . 135, 139	133. . . . . 735, 741
57:4 673	99:1 379	134:3 142
57:5 123	100:3 . . . . 472, 715	135:6 143
57:11. 123	102:11. 311	135:7. 143
58:11. 492	102:25–27. 470	135:21. 330
61:6 573	102:26–28. 129	136:3 472
62:2 130	103:2–10. 549	139:7–10. . . . . 132, 616
62:12 302	103:3–4 . . . . 553, 573	139:14. 652
65:5 492	104:2 461	139:16. 515
67:2–7. 153	104:14. 143	142:7. 133
68. 449	104:21. 143	143:2 683
68:18 641	104:24 136	143:8. 573
69:16. 133	104:28 143	143:10. . . . . 632, 737
69:28 574	104:29–31. 104	143:11. 573
69:34 162	104:30–32. . . . . . . 148, 622	144:14. 330
71:20 573	104:30 . . . . 155, 616	145:7. 133
72:8–14. 284	105:5–6 715	145:12. 510
74:2 330	105:6 515	145:13. . . . . 135, 210
74:19. 673	105:43. . . . . 515, 715	
77:15. 553	106:5 515	
78:8 667	106:13. 218	# PROVERBS
78:35 168	106:47. . . . . 139, 557	
78:42 553	107 741	2:19 573
79:1 332	107:11. 218	3:2 573
79:9 . . . . 216, 550, 557	109:21 133	3:16 573
79:13 715	110 . . . . 286, 331, 449,	4:10 573
80:1 715	453, 454, 474	4:22 573
82. 104	110:1–2. 260	6:18 689
82:6 102	110:1. . . . . 265, 453, 454,	8. 104
82:8 492	472	8:1–12. 138
85:8 155	111:10 136	8:22 114
85:10. . . . . 306, 568	115:1. . . . . . 139, 216, 217	8:35 573
86:9 216	115:15. 142	9:10 136
86:17. 133	115:16. 510	10:16. . . . . 311, 575
87:1–3. 330	116:3. 317	12:8 668
89. . . . . 360, 505	116:12–13. 133	16:4 219
89:20 106	117:1. 153	16:24 665
90:2 128	118:14. 555	17:15. 566
90:4 128	118:22. 332	19:21 219
91:16. 573	119 645	21:15. 755
93:1 379	119:40. 573	21:18. 554
95. 602	119:50. 573	25:26 542
95:5–7 472	119:64. 143	28:14. 673
95:7 715	119:88. 573	
95:8 674	119:159. 573	# ECCLESIASTES
96:3–10. 153	121:2 142	
96:10 472	124:8 142	3:17 492
96:13 472	130:8 553	4:12 743
97:1 379	131:2. 138	5:18 311
98. 492	132. . . . . 360, 505	7:20 544
		12:7 663

SONG OF SONGS

1–8 361

ISAIAH

1:2 667
1:4 136
1:26–27 329
2:2–5 378
2:2–4 . . . . 153, 284, 329, 504
4:4–5 636
5:19 218
5:23 566
5:24 136
6 . . . . 147, 168
6:1–10 471
6:3 . . . . 88, 135
6:4 167
6:7 672
6:8 101
7 369
7:9 588
7:14 . . . . . . 366, 369, 462, 471
9 568
9:2 461
9:6–7 568
9:7 . . . . 260, 306
10:20–22 716
11 505
11:1–10 284
11:1–6 153
11:1–5 505
11:2–3 629
11:2 . . . . 204, 624
11:3–4 472
11:4 492
11:6–9 279
11:6 155
11:11–16 504
12:2 555
14:26 . . . . 218, 219
14:27 219
16:5 360
22:11 219
23:9 219
24:23 379
25:1 218
25:6–8 . . . . 249, 270
25:6 793
25:8 . . . . 311, 671
26:1 330
26:3 . . . . 273, 556
26:9 663
27:13 269
28:29 . . . . 218, 219
28:5 716
30:15 555
31:1 136
32:14–18 250
32:17 306
33:2 555
33:22 472
33:24 . . . . 550, 551
34:10 378
35:4 272
37:16 142
37:26 515
37:31–32 716
38:1–6 129
38:4 195
40–66 152
40–55 . . . 153, 403, 504, 505
40:3 469
40:5 . . . . 215, 272
40:7–8 311
40:9 152
40:12–13 . . . . 149, 622
40:21–22 160
41:4 . . . . 128, 472
41:8–9 516
41:14 . . . . 136, 168
41:27 152
42:1 . . . . 106, 515, 624
42:6 . . . . 140, 153, 285,
                                    505, 725
42:8 139
42:9 155
42:18–19 153
43 554
43:1–8 . . . . 553, 741
43:3 . . . . 136, 472
43:4 573
43:5–7 215
43:5 378
43:7 143
43:12 169
43:14 . . . . 136, 168
43:19 155
43:25 . . . . 134, 550
44:1–2 515
44:3 379
44:6–8 101
44:6 . . . . 160, 168, 472
44:7–8 134
44:8 142
44:9–20 146
44:22 550
44:23 . . . . 139, 215, 557
44:24 168
44:25–28 134
44:28 332
45:5 142
45:14 142
45:22 142
45:23 . . . . 464, 470
46:9 . . . . 127, 142
46:10–11 219
47:4 168
47:21 492
48:9–11 215
48:11 139
48:12 472
48:17 . . . . 136, 168
48:20 553
49:3 505
49:6 . . . . 140, 153, 285,
                                    505, 725
49:7 . . . . 136, 168
49:15 138
49:26 168
51:10–11 553
52 . . . . 360, 416, 454
52:1 761
52:7 . . . . . 47, 152, 155, 227,
                          494, 496, 568, 571
52:14 301
53 . . . . . 51, 360, 403–4, 416,
                          423, 505, 554
53:4–5 . . . . 403, 406
53:5–6 . . . . 505, 672
53:5 . . . . 403, 420, 570,
                                    571, 667
53:6 404
53:7–12 404
53:8 505
53:9 404
53:10–12 573
53:10 404
53:11–12 . . . . 404, 505
53:11 . . . . . 311, 403, 404, 425

53:12 . . . . . . 403, 404, 663
54. . . . . 330, 504
54:5 168
55–56 492
55:1–13 505
55:5 378
55:7 539
55:12 570
56:8 378
57:15 128
59:20 . . . . . . 168, 241, 539
60 378
60:16 168
61 . . . . 51, 504, 505
61:1–4 624
61:1–2 . . . . 53, 624
61:1 . . . . . . 104, 613, 629, 755
61:6 716
61:8 673
62:12 553
63:1 555
63:10 . . . . 106, 616
63:15 143
63:16 . . . . 105, 168
64:6 . . . . 675, 683
64:8 105
65 . . . . 140, 153, 328,
329, 378
65:1 168
65:9 515
65:15 515
65:16–17 101
65:17–25 332
65:17 . . . . 153, 155, 250,
285, 329
65:22 . . . . 515, 715
65:25 155
66 . . . . . . 140, 153, 219, 328,
329, 378, 510
66:1 143
66:12 570
66:13 138
66:18–19 215
66:20 332
66:22–24 . . . . 219, 329
66:22 . . . . 153, 155, 250, 285

JEREMIAH

1:4 195
1:11 195
1:13 195
2:1 195
2:3 736
3:18 504
4:4 761
4:18 663
5:7 551
7:4 330
7:23 603
7:31 334
7:32 334
10:11–12 146
10:12 138
11:10 539
13:3 195
13:8 195
16:14–15 553
17:9 . . . . . 491, 675, 676, 683
18:1 195
18:5 195
18:18 196
18:23 550
21:8 573
23:24 132
26:3 539
29:1 749
30:1–11 504
30:22 603
31:10 715
31:11–12 553
31:18–20 504
31:31–40 141
31:31–34 . . . . 153, 405, 504
31:31–24 222
31:31 504
31:33 534
31:34 550
32:27 133
32:40 534
33:1–34 504
33:8 551
33:17–26 360
33:20–21 . . . . 497, 505
33:20 510
33:25–26 497
33:25 143
34:18 667
39:18 538
49:20 218
50:34 168
51:15 138

LAMENTATIONS

1:18 667
3:22–24 162
3:22 307

EZEKIEL

1 . . . . 147, 168
2:3 667
3:14 104
8:1–3 104
8:1 749
10:18 330
11:1 624
11:5–14 624
11:5 631
11:16–21 504
11:18–19 379
11:19–20 154
11:19 . . . . 534, 674
12:1 195
12:8 195
12:17 195
12:21 195
12:26 195
14:1 749
16 . . . . 211, 503
16:1–63 223
16:60–63 141
18:4 671
18:20 . . . . 491, 671
18:23 423
18:30 539
18:31 . . . . 534, 674
20:1 749
20:3 749
22:26 736
28:13 319
31:8–9 319
33:8 311
33:11 584
34 496
34:16 715
34:23–24 . . . . 360, 715
34:23 153
34:25 570

36:25–27 534	9:11–14 539	9:13 793
36:26–27 . . . . 154, 379	9:11 667	
36:26 674	9:19 550	**OBADIAH**
36:27 543	9:24–27 . . . . 292, 297	15 260
36:28 . . . . 219, 603	9:24 261	21 379
36:35 319	9:25 261	
37 . . . . 504, 624	9:26 261	**JONAH**
37:1 104	9:27 262	3:10 . . . . 129, 692
37:5 627	11:31 262	
37:7–10 624	12:1–2 . . . . . . 154, 262, 440	**MICAH**
37:15–23 504	12:1 291	2:12 . . . . 715, 716
37:24–25 360	12:2–3 . . . . 311, 573	3:8 . . . . 196, 624, 637
37:26–27 141	12:2 . . . . 280, 314, 336	4:1–4 . . . . 378, 504
37:26 570	12:3 326	4:1–3 . . . . 153, 284
37:27 332	12:11 262	4:10 553
37:28 736		4:12 218
40–48 . . . . 329, 330	**HOSEA**	5:1–8 505
40–43 504	1:1 195	5:1–5 153
44:6–7 761	1:6 551	5:1–4 360
45:17 424	2:14–23 . . . . . 496, 504, 516	5:4 715
47 504	2:23 714	5:7–8 716
48:1–29 504	6:7 223	6:4 553
	8:13 673	6:8 . . . . 53, 755
DANIEL	11:1 . . . . 102, 198, 360,	7:18–20 551
1:5–16 796	388, 571	7:18 306
1:20 204	11:9 136	
2:21 204	13:14 . . . . 311, 317, 553	**NAHUM**
2:26–27 204		1:15 . . . . 568, 571
2:28–45 284	**JOEL**	
2:44 . . . . 260, 379	1:1 195	**HABAKKUK**
3:25 103	2:1 269	2:3 246
4 641	2:27 142	2:4 . . . . 538, 588, 641
5:11, 14 204	2:28–32 . . . . 624, 641	3:18 472
6:26 . . . . 260, 379	2:28–29 629	
7 . . . . 262, 266, 363,	2:28 . . . . 379, 452	**ZEPHANIAH**
454, 505, 554		1:7, 14 260
7:1–8 261	**AMOS**	1:14–16 269
7:3–17 673	3:2 . . . . 515, 518	1:14–15 291
7:8 . . . . 261, 262	3:7 219	3:9–13 504
7:11 . . . . 261, 262	4:13 167	3:12–13 716
7:13–14 . . . . . . 261, 286, 455	5:15 716	3:15 379
7:13 . . . . 261, 265, 266,	5:18 260	
472, 505	5:20 260	**HAGGAI**
7:18 . . . . 261, 455, 505	5:21 673	2:9 330
7:20–21 . . . . 261, 262	5:24 755	2:20 195
7:27 . . . . 260, 286, 505	9:11–15 379	
8:9 262	9:11–12 505	
9 211	9:11 722	
9:9–19 504		
9:9 551		

ZECHARIAH

1:1 195
3:4 397
3:9 550
4:8 195
6:11–12 496
7:12 . . . . 624, 631, 674
8:1–23 741
8:8 219
8:12 793
8:17 673
8:23 . . . . 153, 378, 504
9 362
9:10 570
9:11–12 716
9:11 405
10:1 143
10:8 553
12:4 260
14 504
14:5–17 284
14:5 269
14:9 379

MALACHI

2:5 573
3:1 469
3:6 . . . . 129, 471
3:17 105
4:2 420

MATTHEW

1 355
1:1–17 209
1:1 . . . . 366, 501
1:16 366
1:18–25 366
1:18–23 360
1:18 . . . . 171, 365, 366, 624
1:20–23 366
1:20 . . . . . 171, 365, 366, 624
1:21–23 365
1:21 . . . . 366, 425, 462,
            548, 551, 556
1:23 . . . . . 106, 369, 462, 471
1:24–25 366
2:1 . . . . 366, 478
2:6 715

2:15 . . . . 359, 360, 388
2:17–18 359
2:22–23 366
2:23 359
3:7 296
3:9 . . . . 501, 727
3:11–12 539
3:11 . . . . 378, 625, 634, 772
3:13–17 . . . . 378, 624
3:16 . . . . 106, 156, 773
3:17 123
4:1–11 . . . . . . 360, 389, 390,
            393, 625, 722
4:1 106
4:4 197
4:17 248
4:19 706
4:23 . . . . 48, 239
5–7 380
5:5 501
5:13 706
5:14 713
5:16 730
5:17 468
5:18 . . . . 327, 640
5:20 . . . . 249, 379
5:21–22 . . . . 249, 469
5:22 . . . . 334, 616
5:24 559
5:27–28 469
5:29–30 . . . . 334, 585
5:33–34 469
5:34 143
5:38–39 469
5:43–44 469
5:45 . . . . 143, 162
5:48 . . . . 136, 544
6:8–9 105
6:8 458
6:9–13 . . . . 101, 468
6:9 . . . . 138, 327, 471,
            684, 730
6:10 . . . . 249, 287
6:12 . . . . 551, 552
6:13 . . . . 245, 292, 684
6:14–15 551
6:15 551
6:19–21 327
6:24 469
6:25–28 162

6:26 143
6:33 509
7:9–11 138
7:11 458
7:13 585
7:14 573
7:21 . . . . 105, 249, 379
8:10–12 378
8:11–12 . . . . . . 249, 270, 501
8:11 793
8:12 335
9:2–6 551
9:10–11 795
9:18 281
9:22 . . . . 493, 588
9:24 314
9:29–30 588
9:35 . . . . 48, 235, 239
10:1–6 713
10:5–6 . . . . 209, 378, 722
10:5 715
10:15 . . . . 249, 585
10:16–25 245
10:18–20 452
10:22 556
10:23 . . . . 244, 245, 262,
            263–264
10:28 . . . . 311, 334, 665
10:29 143
11:1–6 722
11:4–5 379
11:5 755
11:12 249
11:15 53
11:16 265
11:19 795
11:22–24 585
11:23 317
11:25 142
11:28 . . . . 432, 531
12:18 515
12:28–31 616
12:28 . . . . 48, 106, 156, 239,
            249, 379, 625
12:29 . . . . 394, 416
12:31–32 616
12:31 626
12:32 316
12:36–37 569
12:40 433

12:41–42 . . . . 249, 585
12:41–32 265
12:45 265
12:47–50 367
13:1–32 245
13:1–23 603
13:14–16 359
13:21 292
13:31–32 277
13:34–40 770
13:35 . . . . 129, 359
14:24 404
15:6 197
15:24 . . . . 209, 378, 715, 722
15:30–32 594
16:18 . . . . . 317, 434, 708, 713
16:19 746
16:21–17:13 263
16:25–27 245
16:25 556
16:27–28 . . . . 262, 263
16:27 . . . . 264, 569
16:28 263
17:1–8 322
18:1–4 594
18:3 249
18:8–9 . . . . 573, 585
18:8 337
18:9 334
18:15–25 551
18:17 752
18:18 746
19:13–15 763
19:16–24 574
19:16 556
19:21 327
19:23–24 249
19:25 556
19:26 133
19:28 . . . . . . 267, 287, 378,
456, 627
19:29 574
20:25–28 661
20:28 . . . . 404, 421, 425, 554
21:23 750
21:25 327
21:42 332
22:13 585
22:16 212
22:23–33 311

22:29 204
22:30 . . . . 255, 332
22:32 574
22:36–39 135
22:37 663
22:44–45 454
22:44 453
23:8–10 382
23:13 249
23:15 334
23:22 143
23:27 381
23:33 . . . . 267, 334, 585
23:36 265
23:37–39 . . . . 209, 421
23:37 . . . 138, 302, 400, 404
24 . . . . . . 262, 295, 296, 297
24:1–36 264
24:13 556
24:14 . . . . 48, 239, 271
24:15 262
24:21–29 298
24:21 . . . . 291, 296
24:22–24 515
24:31 269
24:36 245
24:40–41 293
24:41 585
24:43 296
25:1–26 249
25:1–13 271
25:31–46 569
25:31–36 304
25:31 262
25:34 129
25:41 . . . . 335, 337, 584
25:46 . . . . 335, 336, 574
26 796
26:3 750
26:17–19 780
26:26–29 . . . . 779, 790
26:26 780
26:28 . . . 134, 400, 403, 421,
550, 551, 552
26:29 . . . . 245, 270, 510
26:31 400
26:47 750
26:53–56 362
26:54–56 359
26:57 750

26:64–65 472
26:64 . . . 262, 266, 453, 454
27 385
27:37 416
27:45–46 301
27:46 405
27:51 456
27:52–53 433
27:57–61 437
28:1–8 437
28:9 . . . . 106, 448, 452
28:13 437
28:17 452
28:18 . . . . 440, 480, 646
28:19–20 . . . . . 123, 276, 425,
592, 713, 739, 754
28:19 754
28:20 . . . . 270, 784

MARK

1:1–5 209
1:1 . . . . 48, 357
1:4 . . . . 539, 551
1:7–8 539
1:8 . . . . 625, 634
1:9–15 196
1:9–11 378
1:11 473
1:12 106
1:14–15 . . . . 468, 540, 722
1:15 . . . . . . 48, 51, 235, 246,
248, 364, 538, 580
1:22 469
1:27 469
2:5–12 551
2:17 468
3:5 674
3:13–16 . . . . 378, 722
3:14–16 747
3:23–27 379
3:27 394
3:29 106
4:1–32 245
4:11–12 . . . . 204, 646
4:30–32 380
5:23 493
6 379
6:3 365
6:14–17 266

6:34–44 780	13:26 . . . . 264, 266	2:4–7 366
7:13 197	13:28 265	2:4 366
8. 379	13:30 . . . . 245, 265	2:5 366
8:1–10. 780	13:32–37. 264	2:7 372
8:12 265	13:32 245	2:11 366
8:35–38 245	14:22–26. 381	2:14 155
8:35 494	14:22–25. . . . . 385, 421, 779	2:16 319
8:38 265	14:24 405	2:25 . . . . 632, 726
9:1 . . . . . 245, 262, 263, 385	14:25 . . . . . . 245, 270, 510	2:26 168
9:2–9 123	14:27 381	2:29–32 365
9:12 421	14:36 . . . . 138, 468	2:32 725
9:43–47 334	14:62 . . .245, 262, 265, 266,	2:35 663
9:43 335	304, 381, 453	2:38 . . . . 421, 553
9:45–47 267	15. 385	2:39 366
9:47–48. 585	15:34 405	3:3 539
9:47 249	15:38 456	3:7 296
10:5 674	15:42–47. 437	3:8 . . . . 501, 727
10:14–16. 594	16:1–8. 437	3:16–17. 539
10:15. . . . . 249, 379	16:19. 453	3:16 . . . . 378, 625, 634, 636
10:23–25. 379		3:31 388
10:28 585	## LUKE	3:38 388
10:35–45. 445	1:1–4 . . . . 353, 739	4:1–13. . . . . 389, 390, 393,
10:38–39. 772	1:1–2. . . . . 64, 209	479, 625
10:41–45. 123	1:1 362	4:1 . . . . , ...106
10:45 . . . . . 391, 404, 421,	1:5 366	4:14–21. 196
425, 554	1:15–16. 629	4:14 . . . . 106, 625, 629
11–13 304	1:15 . . . . 196, 637	4:18–21. 379
11:1–10. 381	1:17. 629	4:18–19. 629
11:12–23. 265	1:26–35 366	4:18 . . . . 53, 613, 755
11:15–17. 381	1:27 366	4:21 362
11:27–33. 469	1:31 366	4:43 . . . . 48, 219, 239
12:1–12. 380	1:32 366	5:1–11. 168
12:18–27. 311	1:34 366	5:1 197
12:29–30. . . . . 101, 469	1:35 . . . . .171, 366, 616, 624	5:8 676
12:30 . . . . 662, 663	1:37 133	5:32 540
12:35–37. 381	1:41 631	6:12–16. 515
12:36 453	1:46–55 365	6:45 689
13. . . . . .262, 266, 295,	1:46–47 . . . . 196, 663	7:22 . . . . 53, 379, 755
296, 297, 381	1:47 367	7:30 218
13:1–37. 264	1:48 367	7:34 795
13:1–5. 264	1:67 632	7:41–43. . . . . 551, 552
13:5–23 264	1:68–79. 365	7:47–50. 551
13:9–11. 452	1:68 421	7:47 399
13:10. 754	1:69 555	7:50 . . . . 538, 588
13:14. 262	1:76 469	8:1 . . . . 48, 239
13:19–25. 298	1:77 . . . . 421, 551	8:11 197
13:19. 291	2:1–20. 50	8:15 271
13:20 715	2:1–14. 506	8:17 302
13:24–28 264	2:1 297	8:48 588
13:24–25. 266		9:16 796

9:22 165
9:23–24 387
9:23 . . . . 435, 445
9:24–26 245
9:26 262
9:35 515
9:41 668
9:51 . . . . 327, 451
10–11 280
10:15. 317
10:18. . . . . . .280, 303, 394,
416, 754
10:21 . . . . . . 106, 142, 625
10:27 663
11:1–26. 280
11:1–4. 468
11:2 . . . . . . .249, 287, 471
11:4 . . . . .245, 292, 551, 552
11:13. 451
11:20 . . . .48, 239, 249, 379
11:28 197
11:49–50. 245
12:5 . . . . 267, 334
12:11–12. 452
12:12 . . . . 451, 632
12:19. 665
12:20 663
12:32 715
12:40 262
12:49 468
12:50 772
13:18–19. 245
13:23–25 591
13:28–30. 378
13:28–29. . . . .249, 270, 501
13:29 793
13:34–35. 209
13:34 . . . 302, 381, 400, 404
15:1–32. 380
15:1–2. 798
15:2 796
15:10. . . . . 540, 670
15:11–32. 551
16:13. 469
16:14–18. 318
16:16. . . . . .48, 239, 249
16:19–31 . . . . .317, 318, 320
16:23–31. 584
16:23 317
17:3–4 . . . . .540, 551

17:20–21. 379
17:21. . . . . 246, 249
17:22. 262
17:34–35. 293
18:3 306
18:5 306
18:7 . . . . . . 245, 515, 715
18:8 262
18:9–14. . . . . 559, 561
18:14. 561
18:15–17. 763
18:31–34. 165
18:31. 362
19:9–10. 506
19:10. 556
19:11–27 245
19:42–44. 264
20:27–39. 311
20:36 . . . . .154–55, 311, 447
20:42 453
21. 262
21:5–36. 264
21:24 266
21:27 262
21:28 553
21:30 264
21:35 266
22:15–20. 779
22:18 . . . . . . 245, 270, 510
22:19 . . . .419, 784, 789, 796
22:20 . . . . 413, 457
22:22 . . . . 165, 219
22:29–30 267
22:29. 456
22:30 . . . . . .287, 378, 456
22:31 280
22:32 596
22:37 362
22:53 280
22:69 . . . . 266, 453
23. 385
23:24 421
23:34 551
23:35 515
23:42 319
23:43 . . . .319, 320, 433, 450
23:45 457
23:46 . . . . 319, 320
23:50–55 437
24:1–10. 437

24:7 165
24:8 204
24:11. 437
24:21 . . . . . . 553, 722, 726
24:26–27 . . . . 51, 219
24:26 . . . . 48, 219, 634
24:27 . . . . 165, 359
24:29–53 450
24:29 615
24:30 796
24:31–32. 204
24:35 . . . . . . 204, 779, 789
24:44–47 165
24:44 . . . . 51, 166, 362
24:45 . . . . 204, 363
24:46–48 453
24:47–49. 592
24:47–48. 739
24:47 . . .471, 540, 550, 552
24:49 629
24:52 452

JOHN

1:1–18. . . . . . . 105, 209, 364
1:1–14. 507
1:1–3. 156
1:1–2. 361
1:1 . . . . . .128, 353, 460, 471
1:2–3 149
1:3–4 249
1:3 160
1:4 574
1:5 516
1:10 472
1:11–12. 571
1:12–13. . . . . .138, 514, 534, 628
1:12 . . . . 137, 588
1:13 . . . . 533, 683
1:14. . . . .137, 205, 206, 208,
249, 352, 375, 460,
471, 478, 503
1:16 . . . . 211, 223
1:17. 212
1:18 . . . . 168, 206
1:23 469
1:26 773
1:29 . . . . 427, 507
1:31 773

1:33 . . . . 625, 634, 773	5:39 359	10:30 . . . . 111, 469
1:36 507	5:42 683	10:34–36. . . . . . . 102, 104
2:1–4 634	5:43 468	10:35–36. 640
2:12–25. 381	6. . . . . 379, 788	10:35 . . . . 197, 642
2:21 332	6:26–65 790	10:36 111
3:3–8 155	6:27 574	10:44–48 634
3:3–5 . . . . . . .250, 533, 537, 613, 775	6:32–59 779	11:11. 314
3:3 627	6:33 575	11:23–26. 249
3:5–7 627	6:35 574	11:24 . . . . 249, 440
3:5–6 516	6:37 516	11:25–26. 249
3:5 . . . . 204, 379, 773	6:39 249	11:25 574
3:6–7 628	6:40 249	11:26 280
3:6 683	6:44 . . . . . . 111, 249, 516, 676, 683	11:41–42. 468
3:7 533	6:48 574	11:51–52. 421
3:13 468	6:51–58. 788	11:52. 571
3:14–15. 219	6:51 . . . . 426, 785	12:16. . . . . 214, 634
3:15–16. 574	6:53–56 780	12:23 . . . . 214, 634
3:16 . . . . 135, 211, 420, 423, 426, 428, 516, 525, 531, 636	6:54 249	12:24 400
	6:57 111	12:27–41. 471
	6:63 . . . . . . .155, 196, 613, 627, 782	12:27 663
3:17 556		12:28 . . . . 123, 214
3:19–20. 304	6:65 516	12:31 . . . . . . 249, 250, 416
3:19 . . . . .491, 516, 535, 676	6:68 574	12:32 . . . . . . .516, 535, 676
3:27 327	6:70 515	12:37–40. 516
3:31 249	7:38 . . . . 206, 613	12:41 214
3:35 . . . . 135, 139	7:39 . . . . . 451, 537, 613, 634	12:42 719
3:36 . . . . 296, 574	8–9. 212	12:44–50 250
4:14 574	8:1–13. 634	12:46 516
4:23–24 204	8:12 574	12:49 111
4:42 472	8:14–17. 634	13. 796
5. 375	8:15–16. 249	13:1–17. 123
5:17 111	8:16–18. 111	13:21 663
5:18 . . . . .111, 467, 469	8:34 . . . . .516, 535, 676, 683	13:31–32. . . . . 123, 214
5:19 120	8:40 478	13:31 634
5:20 . . . . 135, 139	8:41 365	13:34–35. . . . . 135, 568
5:21 574	8:42 111	14–16 111
5:22 . . . . 249, 472	8:47 516	14:1–3. 250
5:23 470	8:54 123	14:2–3. . . . . 328, 510
5:24 . . . . .302, 574, 588, 604, 788	8:58 . . . . 105, 126	14:3 . . . . 259, 267, 324
	9:22 719	14:6 . . . . . . .210, 212, 363, 574, 591, 616
5:25 . . . . 249, 250, 280, 446	9:39 249	
5:26–27 111	9:41 672	14:7–10. 471
5:26 574	10:10. . . . . . . .169, 574, 613	14:7–9. 469
5:27 . . . . 249, 301	10:11. 127	14:9–10. . . . . 111, 118
5:28–29 . . . . . 249, 280, 569	10:14–15. 425	14:13–14. . . . . . 122, 458, 471
5:29 585	10:16. 735	14:13. . . . . 111, 214
5:30 249	10:25–26. 516	14:16–17. . . . . 204, 451
5:36–39 206	10:27–29. 598	14:16. . . . . . . 111, 112, 155, 613, 616
5:39–40 . . . . 84, 574	10:28 574	14:17. . . . . 111, 204, 516, 537

14:24 111
14:26 . . . 111, 112, 155, 204, 367, 451, 613, 620, 632, 635
14:27 570
14:28 . . . . 120, 473
15:4–5 683
15:5–10 706
15:5–6 598
15:13 . . . . 399, 400, 425
15:15 730
15:16 . . . . 458, 471, 515, 516, 521, 535
15:19 737
15:24 516
15:26–27 . . . . 453, 616
15:26 . . . 111, 112, 155, 204, 367, 451, 613, 620, 635, 772
16:2 719
16:7 . . . . 112, 155, 451, 537, 613, 616, 620, 635, 772
16:8–15 616
16:8–11 631
16:8–9 516
16:8 516
16:11 . . . . 394, 416
16:13–16 204
16:13–14 112
16:13 . . . . 63, 111, 204, 632, 645
16:14 123
16:17 111
16:23–26 . . . . . 122, 458, 471
16:24 730
16:27 139
16:28 111
16:33 . . . . . . 219, 292, 298, 416, 570
17 . . . . 111, 457, 746
17:1–5 214
17:1 . . . . 112, 123
17:2–3 . . . . 112, 574
17:2 516
17:3 249
17:4–5 112
17:5 . . . . 128, 468, 634
17:6–8 112
17:9–12 112

17:9 425
17:11 . . . . 111, 732, 735
17:15 297
17:17 112
17:19 136
17:20–23 741
17:21–23 . . . . 111, 112
17:21–22 732
17:21 . . . . 111, 735, 742
17:23 735
17:24 128
17:25 111
19 385
19:1–7 634
19:19 416
19:26–27 367
19:28 362
19:38–42 437
20 355
20:1–2 437
20:17 . . . . 319, 327
20:19 570
20:21–22 614
20:21 . . . . 111, 123
20:22–23 111
20:22 . . . . 620, 625, 634
20:23 . . . . 550, 551
20:28 . . . . 105, 471
20:31 . . . . 353, 574, 588, 788
21:23 267

ACTS

1:2 451
1:5 634
1:6 . . . . 553, 722, 726
1:8 . . . . 123, 452, 453, 614, 615, 629, 634, 739, 754
1:9–11 450
1:11 . . . . 242, 267, 269, 327, 458
1:16 639
1:23 751
2–5 719
2 . . . . 464, 537
2:1–11 625
2:1–4 . . . . 615, 634, 772
2:4 629
2:17–21 641

2:17 452
2:21 . . . . 471, 494
2:22–36 . . . . 359, 377
2:22–24 49
2:22 477
2:23 . . . . 214–15, 218, 219, 518
2:24 616
2:25–28 127
2:27–32 433
2:27 . . . . 317, 319, 449
2:31 . . . . 317, 319, 433, 436, 449
2:32 616
2:33–35 453
2:33 . . . . 120, 452
2:34–36 454
2:34 436
2:36–38 540
2:36 . . . . . 49, 440, 464, 473
2:37–39 759
2:38–39 . . . . 763, 766
2:38 . . . . . 44, 105, 155, 421, 452, 471, 535, 551, 552, 613, 635, 761, 765, 774
2:39 . . . . 762, 766
2:40 . . . . 337, 494
2:41 765
2:42–47 733
2:42 . . . . . 56, 731, 789, 796
2:44–47 633
2:46 . . . . 789, 796, 802
2:47 . . . . 494, 732, 743
3 382
3:6 452
3:13 137
3:15 575
3:16 452
3:18–21 . . . . 385, 421
3:19–26 504
3:19 . . . . 539, 540, 726
3:20–25 382
3:21 267
3:26 . . . . 436, 616
4:2 436
4:5 750
4:8 . . . . . . 196, 614, 637, 750
4:10 616
4:11 332

4:12 . . . . 142, 210, 471, 494, 556, 591	9:15 515	14:21. 190
4:18 452	9:17–18 . . . . 629, 760	14:22 . . . . 236, 292, 509
4:20 80	9:17 637	14:23 . . . . 746, 750, 751, 752
4:23 750	9:31 616	15 . . . . 737, 747, 750
4:25 616	10:26 420	15:2 . . . . 746, 750, 751
4:28 . . . . 219, 515	10:34–43 357	15:4 . . . . 746, 750
4:30 452	10:36–48 49	15:6 746
4:31 . . . . . 196, 614, 616, 637	10:36 . . . . 570, 571	15:7 . . . . 45, 515, 539
4:32 742	10:38 106	15:14–19 723
4:33 436	10:40 616	15:22–23 . . . . 746, 750
5:3–4 . . . . 106, 616	10:41 436	15:22 750
5:20 572	10:42 301	15:23–33 750
5:21 750	10:43 . . . . .421, 551, 552	15:25 752
5:30 616	10:44–48 . . . . 635, 760	15:28 632
5:31 . . . . 120, 421, 453, 472, 540, 551, 552	10:44–46 535	16:4 . . . . 746, 750
5:32 616	10:47 766	16:7 . . . . 616, 632
5:40 452	10:48 . . . . 105, 471	16:14–15 . . . . 760, 763
6:1–6 . . . . . . .731, 741, 746	11:14 494	16:14. . . . . 531, 536
6:3 751	11:17 535	16:31. . . . . . 494, 538, 588
6:5 629	11:18 . . . . 536, 540	16:32 766
6:8 629	11:19 719	16:33 . . . . 760, 763
6:10 614	11:24 . . . . 614, 629	17–28 641
6:12 750	11:28 297	17:7. 50
7:1–53. 504	11:30 750	17:14–34 141
7:26 557	12:1 719	17:18. 436
7:36 674	12:17 746	17:22–32 . . . . 70, 176
7:38 363	13:1 . . . . 632, 750, 754	17:22–31 . . . . 173, 174
7:49 143	13:2 616	17:22–29 190
7:51 631	13:9 . . . . 614, 637	17:23. 169
7:53 457	13:13–39 49	17:24–25 128
7:55–60 . . . . 319, 320	13:15. 750	17:24. 132
7:55 . . . . .196, 614, 629	13:17. 515	17:26. . . . . 143, 515
7:56 485	13:23 472	17:28. 132
7:59 . . . . 105, 319, 663	13:24–30 385	17:30–31 190
7:60 314	13:25–29 421	17:31. . . . . 301, 472, 590
8:1–3. 719	13:26 722	17:32. 313
8:12–24. 770	13:30 616	18:8 . . . . . 760, 763, 766, 767
8:12 . . . . .48, 236, 239, 452, 765	13:32–33. . .51, 362, 507, 722	18:17. 750
8:13 765	13:33–34 . . . . 166, 221	19:1–6 761
8:14–17 . . . . 535, 636	13:33 436	19:2 636
8:16 . . . . 105, 452, 471	13:36 . . . . 218, 314	19:4–5 766
8:22 . . . . 540, 552	13:37 616	19:4 636
8:25 165	13:38–39 552	19:5–6 635
8:29 632	13:38 . . . . 421, 552	19:5 . . . . 105, 471
8:30–40 706	13:39 561	19:8 . . . . 236, 509
8:35–38 759	13:47 725	20:7 . . . . 796, 802
9:1–22. 168	13:48 . . . . 515, 517	20:11 796
9:4 716	13:52 637	20:17 . . . . 748, 750
	14:15–17 . . . . . . 70, 141, 173, 176, 190	20:21 . . . . 51, 221, 509, 538, 540
	14:15. 142	

20:22–23 632
20:25 509
20:27 218
20:28 . . . . 413, 425, 715, 748
20:32 541
21:10 632
21:18 746
22:7 716
22:15–16 761
22:16 . . . . 761, 771, 774
24:15 280
24:25 585
26:17–19 394
26:18 . . . . 421, 736
26:20 . . . . 539, 540
26:23 725
27:33–37 796
27:37 797
28 726
28:18 552
28:20 726
28:23 . . . . 48, 236
28:25–27 616
28:31 . . . . 48, 236

ROMANS

1–11 542
1–10 578
1:1–4 . . . . 107, 208
1:1–3 561
1:1 . . . . 44, 89
1:2–4 50
1:2–3 51
1:2 . . . . 166, 359
1:3–4 . . . . 45, 209, 343,
         436, 465, 473
1:3 44
1:4 . . . . . 250, 440, 443, 556
1:5 538
1:6–7 531
1:7 541
1:8 . . . . 105, 737, 751
1:9 44
1:16–18 175
1:16 . . . . 44, 52, 132,
         165, 494
1:17 . . . . 135, 641
1:18–3:20 407
1:18–32 . . . . 184, 491, 674

1:18–31 146
1:18–25 . . . . 71, 174, 176, 184
1:18–23 548
1:18–19 175
1:18 . . . . 175, 296, 407,
         535, 593, 674
1:19–23 175
1:19–20 . . . . . . 70, 171, 593
1:20 . . . . 70, 142, 175
1:21–23 674
1:23 128
1:24–31 548
1:25 162
1:30 673
2:5 . . . . 296, 407
2:6 302
2:7 593
2:8 407
2:13 546
2:15 667
2:16 . . . . 165, 259, 301,
         302, 472, 590
2:28–29 724
2:29 . . . . 534, 724
3:1 535
3:5 407
3:8 567
3:10–18 491
3:11 676
3:21–4:25 561
3:21–26 . . . . 127, 567
3:21 . . . . 169, 567
3:23–25 561
3:23–24 559
3:23 491
3:24–25 . . . . 443, 554
3:24 . . . . 391, 421
3:25–26 399
3:25 . . . . . 198, 403, 407, 585
3:26 492
3:27–4:25 514
3:29 567
3:30 101
4 . . . . 57, 135, 501
4:1–25 . . . . 501, 520
4:4–5 . . . . 563, 564
4:5 559
4:7–8 552
4:7 551
4:11 762

4:15 667
4:16 501
4:17–18 140
4:17 161
4:19–21 . . . . 538, 539
4:25 . . . . . 49, 155, 385, 404,
         436, 443, 561, 568
5 586
5:1–11 . . . . 558, 678
5:1 . . . . . 420, 538, 561, 570
5:2 . . . . 326, 457
5:5 . . . . 44, 135, 399, 613
5:6 559
5:8 . . . . . . 127, 135, 211, 399
5:9–10 541
5:9 . . . . 296, 421, 443
5:10–11 . . . . 421, 557, 558
5:10 . . . . . 423, 443, 556, 673
5:12–21 . . 226, 311, 360, 389,
         390, 491, 581, 655,
         678, 679, 681,
         683, 722
5:12 . . . . 311, 671, 677,
         679, 681, 682
5:13–14 682
5:13 667
5:15–21 311
5:15 . . . . 211, 477, 682
5:16 . . . . 564, 566, 682
5:17–19 . . . . 563, 564
5:17 . . . . 211, 564, 575,
         586, 682
5:18–21 561
5:18 . . . . 479, 586, 587,
         590, 682
5:19 . . . . 479, 546, 563, 682
5:20 667
5:21 . . . . 311, 575, 671
6 401
6:1–7 408
6:1–2 . . . . 444, 542, 567
6:3–7 771
6:3–4 . . . . 385, 759, 774
6:3 771
6:4–8 302
6:4–6 717
6:4 . . . . . 251, 445, 534, 766
6:5 561
6:6–7 401
6:6 . . . . 554, 673

6:7 561	8:18–22. 442	9:24–26 714
6:12 671	8:19–20. 288	9:27 . . . . 716, 723
6:13 401	8:19 137	9:30–10:21 519
6:14 627	8:20–23 . . . . 153, 251	9:30 520
6:16–20. 676	8:20 541	9:31 723
6:17–22. 627	8:21 . . . . 137, 545	10. . . . . 535, 726
6:17 . . . . 64, 673	8:23 . . . . 391, 421, 445,	10:4 . . . . 362, 363
6:18 673	545, 553, 572,	10:9–13. 520
6:19 542	615, 622, 728	10:9–11. . . . . 509, 536
6:20 673	8:24–25 446	10:9–10. 436
6:22 . . . . 169, 542, 673	8:26–27 122	10:9 . . . . . 105, 455, 616, 713
6:23 . . . . . 311, 337, 575, 671	8:26 616	10:10. . . . . 538, 541, 588
7:4 . . . . . 401, 534, 716, 717	8:27 616	10:14–15. 592
7:6 169	8:28 . . . . 256, 531, 691	10:16–21 301
7:7–25. . . . . 670, 682	8:29–30 . . . . . 215, 513, 514,	10:16–18. 590
7:7 667	518, 519, 532,	10:16. . . . . 364, 471
7:8 667	533, 544, 545	10:17–21. 520
7:10. 671	8:29 . . . . 134, 250, 441,	10:17. . . . . 63, 520, 535, 592
7:11 671	509, 518, 543,	10:19. 723
7:12 736	576, 657, 661	10:21 723
7:14. 535	8:30 . . . . . 137, 211, 531, 603	11 . . . . 221, 726
7:25 535	8:31–39 519	11:1–32. . . . . 519, 597
8. . . . . 155, 417, 518,	8:31–35. 604	11:1–6. 716
519, 567, 689	8:32 502	11:1–5. 520
8:1–14. 542	8:33 . . . . 568, 715	11:1. 721
8:1–11. 737	8:34 . . . . 49, 120, 453,	11:2 723
8:1 . . . . 561, 564, 566	457, 568	11:5–6. 520
8:2 . . . . 155, 575, 613,	8:35–39 211	11:5 716
671, 673	8:37 . . . . 304, 416	11:7. . . . . 515, 715, 723
8:3 . . . . 405, 468, 480	8:38–39 . . . . . 324, 598, 693	11:11. . . . . 519, 723
8:7 673	9–11 . . . . . 519, 520, 558, 586	11:13–31 726
8:9–11. 367	9. 519	11:13–24. 706
8:9 . . . . 118, 156, 561	9:1–29. 519	11:15. 558
8:10–11. . . . . 444, 627	9:1–5 . . . . 515, 519	11:25 . . . . . . 256, 587, 723
8:10 . . . . 575, 663	9:3 724	11:26 . . . . 269, 295, 587, 721
8:11 . . . . 155, 156, 250,	9:4–5 721	11:32. 586
481, 616, 625	9:4 . . . . 501, 723	11:36 . . . . 160, 471, 472, 569
8:12 542	9:5 . . . . 106, 471	12 542
8:13–17. 138	9:6–8 519	12:1–2. 542
8:13 631	9:6 . . . . 519, 597, 721,	12:1 716
8:14–17. 635	723, 727	12:4–5 . . . . 717, 729
8:14 . . . . 137, 569, 616	9:7–8 715	12:6–8 630
8:15–16. . . . . . 105, 514, 572	9:8–9 519	12:10. 123
8:15 . . . . 138, 572, 730	9:9–18 519	12:12 292
8:16–17. 137	9:10–13. 520	12:17. 754
8:16 . . . . 604, 616	9:16 520	12:19. 306
8:17 . . . . 545, 571, 572	9:17–18 520	13:11–14 771
8:18–39. 514	9:19–29. 519	14–15 56
8:18–30. 434	9:23 520	14:1–23. 56
8:18–23. 243	9:24–29 531	14:9 . . . . 281, 444

14:10–12 569
14:10 . . . . 288, 301, 303, 585
14:14 357
14:17 . . . . 251, 509, 570, 631, 737
15:6 732
15:7–8 167
15:8 212
15:13 637
15:16 . . . . 44, 89, 107, 136, 716, 746
15:19 . . . . 44, 196, 614, 629, 637
15:30 107
15:33 570
16:20 . . . . 288, 570
16:25–27 217
16:25–26 166
16:26 . . . . 169, 538, 575
16:27 . . . . 101, 105, 136, 471

1 CORINTHIANS

1–4 . . . . 254, 445
1:1–3 208
1:2 . . . . 136, 541, 542, 631, 736, 737
1:4–6 546
1:4 211
1:7–8 546
1:7 . . . . 250, 260, 270, 630, 728
1:8–9 598
1:8 . . . . . 251, 254, 260, 546
1:9–10 321
1:9 . . . . . 135, 210, 531, 731
1:10–17 741
1:10 . . . . 546, 732, 742
1:13–17 759
1:13 742
1:14–17 776
1:15–16 641
1:18–2:5 385
1:18–25 185
1:18–21 107
1:18 585
1:21 . . . . 176, 538, 588
1:24 531
1:30 . . . . 136, 316, 391, 421, 541, 543, 554, 563, 567, 736

2:1–4 107
2:2 . . . . 413, 435
2:4 . . . . 196, 629
2:7 219
2:8 137
2:9–13 204
2:9 . . . . 167, 256
2:10–14 635
2:10–12 63
2:10–11 616
2:11 616
2:12 632
2:14–15 627
2:14 204
2:16 382
3 315
3:2 56
3:9 706
3:10–15 569
3:11 344
3:15 316
3:16–17 . . . . 509, 616
3:16 . . . . . 106, 332, 713, 717
4:1 219
4:2 135
4:5 . . . . 270, 302
4:8–13 254
4:8 254
4:14 321
4:16–17 542
4:16 481
4:17 481
4:20 236
5:1 321
5:3 663
5:4 752
5:5 . . . . 251, 260
5:7 . . . . 50, 706, 780
6:2 303
6:3 . . . . 288, 515
6:9–10 251
6:11 . . . . 108, 136, 156, 316, 420, 568, 631, 736, 771, 774
6:14 . . . . 127, 446
6:17 546
6:19–20 . . . . 554, 616
6:19 717
6:20 391
7:11 557

7:12–13 357–358
7:14 . . . . 136, 765
7:23 . . . . 421, 554
7:29 271
8:1 84
8:3 518
8:4–6 361
8:4–5 146
8:5–6 469
8:6 . . . . . 101, 149, 161, 184, 464, 471, 472
9:12 44
9:16 271
9:27 598
10:1–11 360
10:1–2 760
10:1 721
10:2 763
10:4 . . . . 364, 467
10:5 673
10:9 467
10:11 . . . . 248, 250
10:12 598
10:13 135
10:16–21 779
10:16–17 . . . . 706, 717
10:16 . . . . . 385, 716, 789, 791
10:17 . . . . 717, 736, 794
10:18–21 791
10:18 723
10:20–21 146
10:20 780
10:31 123
11:1 . . . . 481, 542
11:2 . . . . 64, 739
11:3 . . . . 120, 735, 737
11:7–9 657
11:7 653
11:17–34 797
11:17–24 794
11:18 797
11:20 797
11:22 797
11:23–29 779
11:23–25 . . . . 49, 64, 105
11:24–26 793
11:24–25 . . . . 419, 784, 789
11:25 714
11:26 . . . . 254, 270, 729, 788
11:27 716

Reference	Pages
11:28	798
12–14	635
12	630
12:3–7	108
12:3	105, 536, 713
12:7	630
12:8–10	630
12:8	204
12:11	616, 630
12:12–27	717, 729
12:12–13	717
12:12	561
12:13	633, 635, 717, 766, 771, 772
12:27	716
12:28–30	630
12:28–29	632, 750
12:28	754
12:30	635
12:31	630, 637
13:13	135, 538
14:1	637
14:12	630, 637
14:24–25	799
14:31	273
15	254, 320, 321, 394, 417, 447
15:1–3	64, 739
15:2–4	465
15:2–3	56
15:2	165, 494, 548, 587
15:3–8	209, 436, 438
15:3–5	49, 201, 343, 385
15:3–4	50, 166, 358, 359
15:4	437
15:12–58	313
15:17	155, 443
15:19	194, 446
15:20–23	154, 269
15:20	250, 441, 481
15:21–22	226, 311, 655
15:22–24	288
15:22	389, 581, 587, 590, 678, 722
15:23–27	288
15:23	250, 260, 441, 481, 509
15:24–28	269
15:24–26	234
15:24	251, 283
15:25	436, 453
15:26	671
15:27	50
15:28	120, 155, 219, 240, 243, 270, 473, 510, 587, 590
15:29	769
15:35–38	242, 324
15:43	127
15:45–49	226, 389
15:45	655
15:47–48	468
15:48–58	250
15:49	545, 657, 661
15:50	251
15:51–54	155
15:51–52	288, 294
15:51	314
15:52	269
15:53–54	575
15:54–57	394, 416
15:54	671
15:56	667, 678
15:58	255, 447
16:3	752
16:13	539
16:15	766
16:17	260
16:22	105, 270, 471, 724

2 CORINTHIANS

Reference	Pages
1:4	559
1:6–22	271
1:14	251, 260
1:18–20	109, 210
1:18	135
1:20	166, 221
1:21–22	109
1:22	250, 509
1:24	604
2:10–12	168
2:12	44
3–5	156
3:1–4:6	109
3:2–3	706
3:4–18	714
3:4	604
3:6–8	156
3:6	155, 575, 627
3:9	564, 566
3:12	605
3:17–18	104
3:17	156, 613, 616
3:18	543, 545, 576, 631, 657, 661
4:1–6	165
4:4	280, 658, 661
4:6	156, 471, 627
4:14	446
4:16	446
5	321, 324
5:1–10	320, 664, 665
5:1–9	289
5:4	303, 681
5:5	155, 250, 509
5:7	539, 587
5:8	314
5:10	288, 301, 303, 569, 585, 587
5:11–6:2	242
5:11	587
5:14–21	558
5:14–15	426, 427
5:14	587
5:15	49, 385, 432, 436
5:16	347
5:17–21	156
5:17	155, 251, 442, 534, 543, 717
5:18–21	557
5:18–20	421
5:18–19	427, 558
5:19	343, 673
5:20	587, 706
5:21	210, 302, 405, 432, 563, 564
6:1	598
6:16–18	717
6:16	714
6:18	133
7:1	542
7:6–7	260
7:9–10	540
8:4	731
8:9	358, 468
8:19	752
8:24	733
9:6	569
9:13	44
10:10	260
10:14	44
11:4	52

11:7 . . . . 44, 89
11:15 569
11:24 719
12 147
12:4 319
12:21 540
13:4 281
13:5 605
13:11 135
13:13 731
13:14 . . . . 97, 105, 109, 616, 633

GALATIANS

1–4 542
1:1–4 208
1:1 . . . . 105, 616
1:2 737
1:4–5 471
1:4 . . . . . 394, 418, 421, 556
1:6 . . . . 52, 531
1:7 44
1:11–12 164
1:12 168
1:15 531
1:23 539
2:1–10 747
2:7–10 53
2:9 . . . . 731, 746
2:11–21 567
2:11–14 . . . . 741, 798
2:15–21 561
2:17 563
2:19–21 385
2:19–20 408
2:20 . . . . 302, 387
2:21 421
3 . . . . 57, 501
3:1–5 613
3:1 . . . . 49, 385, 413
3:2–3 635
3:2 766
3:3 631
3:5 766
3:8 . . . . 51, 166, 227, 364
3:10–14 561
3:13–14 . . . . 167, 391
3:13 . . . . 226, 385, 390, 405, 406, 421, 554
3:14 . . . . 155, 514, 567
3:16 501
3:17–18 222
3:19 457
3:24 227
3:26–29 509
3:26–28 514
3:26–27 . . . . 760, 772
3:26 . . . . 137, 138, 514
3:27 . . . . 771, 774
3:28 . . . . 385, 567
3:29 . . . . 572, 724
4 330
4:4–6 . . . . 109, 514
4:4–5 . . . . 358, 507, 572
4:4 . . . . . 219, 365, 377, 468
4:5 . . . . 421, 554, 572
4:6–7 572
4:6 . . . . 137, 138, 613, 730
4:8–9 176
4:9 169
4:24 361
4:26 331
4:29 724
5–6 542
5 155
5:1–6 567
5:4 598
5:5 . . . . 546, 567, 737
5:6 539
5:13 733
5:15 637
5:16–26 542
5:21 251
5:22–23 . . . . 631, 637
5:22 543
5:25 . . . . 543, 631, 637
6:2 227
6:7–8 569
6:8 737
6:10 730
6:14–16 242
6:14 435
6:15 . . . . . 155, 251, 442, 534
6:16 . . . . 221, 723, 724

EPHESIANS

1–3 542
1–2 514
1 527
1:1–22 692
1:1–14 . . . . 517, 519
1:1 541
1:3–14 . . . . 109, 714
1:3–4 547
1:4–6 598
1:4–5 517
1:4 . . . . . 129, 139, 219, 736
1:5 . . . . 432, 514, 572
1:7 . . . . 391, 421, 443, 551, 552, 554
1:9 219
1:10 . . . . 166, 328
1:11–12 . . . . 214, 216
1:11 . . . . 129, 218, 517
1:13–14 . . . . 250, 771
1:13 . . . . 44, 52, 155, 165, 494, 547, 613, 615
1:14 . . . . 155, 421, 509, 553, 557, 615
1:15 751
1:17 . . . . 58, 204
1:18 . . . . 204, 531
1:20–22 453
1:20–21 472
1:21 251
1:22–23 717
1:22 480
2–3 713
2 416
2:1–10 714
2:1–6 667
2:1–3 676
2:1–2 667
2:1 . . . . 311, 535, 675
2:4–7 676
2:4–5 445
2:4 594
2:5–10 219
2:5–6 . . . . 251, 253
2:5 . . . . 311, 534
2:6 . . . . 281, 445, 453, 456, 661
2:7 456
2:8–10 557
2:8–9 . . . . 561, 567, 592
2:8 . . . . 536, 538
2:10 569
2:11–3:21 221
2:11–3:12 567
2:11–22 . . . . 507, 726

Reference	Pages
2:11–18	571
2:12	723
2:13	169, 403, 724
2:14–17	420, 557
2:14	570
2:16	421, 559
2:17	570
2:18	457
2:19–21	332
2:20–23	717
2:20	332, 631, 632, 739
3:3–6	166
3:5	632
3:6	723, 724
3:9–11	129
3:9	160, 204
3:10	136
3:11	219
3:12	457, 605
3:16–17	543
3:20–21	216
3:21	105, 215, 737
4–6	542
4:3	633, 742
4:4	531, 713
4:4–6	736
4:4–5	633, 717
4:5	539, 776
4:8–10	323
4:8	641
4:9	433
4:11–13	754
4:11	629, 630, 632, 750, 754
4:12	630, 716, 735
4:13	742
4:15	717, 735, 737
4:16	717
4:18	674
4:24	534, 543
4:27	280
4:30	106, 553, 616
4:32	553
5:1	134, 481, 542
5:6	667
5:8	169
5:18	543, 637
5:19–20	637
5:20	105
5:23–25	737
5:23	717, 735
5:25–27	771
5:25–26	401
5:25	425
5:26	736, 761
5:29	737
6:8	569
6:15	570, 571
6:17	629
6:18	730
6:19	166

PHILIPPIANS

Reference	Pages
1:1	750, 751, 753
1:5	731
1:6	260, 604
1:9–11	80
1:10	260
1:16	44
1:19	156, 367
1:20–24	320
1:23–24	664
1:23	289, 314, 324, 328
1:26	260
1:27	44
1:29	135, 536
2	467
2:1–2	633
2:1	731
2:2	742
2:3	123
2:5–11	105, 123, 343, 358, 385, 387, 401, 445, 464, 466, 467, 481, 542, 564
2:5–10	421
2:5–7	120
2:5	382
2:6–11	466
2:6–8	361
2:8	563
2:9–11	242, 453, 454, 470
2:10–11	137
2:11	105
2:12–13	543
2:12	260, 569
2:13	598, 604, 627, 676
2:15	137, 326, 668
2:16	260, 598

Reference	Pages
3:3	221, 724
3:5	721, 723
3:7–9	563
3:8	135
3:9	210, 563, 564
3:10–12	446
3:10–11	250
3:12	681
3:14	446
3:17	542
3:20–21	268, 294
3:20	270, 288, 327, 472, 728
3:21	155, 269, 288, 544
4:1	604
4:2	732, 742
4:3	574
4:7	571
4:9	739
4:10	681
4:20	471

COLOSSIANS

Reference	Pages
1–2	542
1	467
1:3	105
1:4	751
1:5	135, 165, 310, 326, 327, 539
1:6–7	41
1:6	58
1:9	204, 637
1:13	251, 421, 532
1:14	391, 421, 551, 552, 554
1:15–20	105, 466, 467
1:15–17	361
1:15	156, 250, 441, 471, 526, 658, 661
1:16–17	149
1:16	143, 151, 286, 472
1:17	144
1:18	154, 156, 250, 441, 481, 509, 661, 717, 735, 737
1:20–22	557, 558
1:20	156, 420, 421, 571
1:22–23	580, 598
1:22	169, 421

Scripture and Apocrypha Index

1:23 . . . . .310, 539, 598	2:13 . . . . . 165, 196, 517, 739	2:9 280
1:24 . . . . .298, 717, 735, 737	2:14 . . . . 481, 542	2:13 . . . . .109, 542, 556, 631
1:27 . . . . 166, 326	2:15 673	2:14 . . . . . 137, 259, 531, 545
2:5 663	2:16 296	2:15 . . . . 64, 604, 739
2:10 . . . . 735, 737	2:18 280	2:16 135
2:11–12 . . . . . .717, 760, 762, 766, 771	2:19 . . . . 137, 260, 268	3. 256
2:11 534	3:2 44	3:3 . . . . 135, 211
2:12 . . . . .251, 253, 445, 761, 766	3:4 292	3:6–15 256
2:13–15 . . . . 394, 418	3:5 598	3:6 . . . . 56, 739
2:13 . . . . 534, 675	3:13 . . . . 260, 268, 269, 297	3:7–9 542
2:15 . . . . 395, 571	4:3 . . . . 136, 736	3:9 481
2:17 362	4:4–5 176	
2:18 103	4:7 . . . . 136, 736	### 1 TIMOTHY
2:19 717	4:13–17 . . . . 288, 297	1:16 575
2:20 . . . . 302, 408	4:13 . . . . 256, 314	1:17 575
3–4. 542	4:14–17 . . . . 269, 293	1:19 599
3. 446	4:14 . . . . . 49, 294, 385, 436	2:3–6 427
3:1–2 446	4:15–17 273	2:3–5 423
3:1 . . . . .120, 251, 253, 281, 445, 453, 456, 661	4:15 . . . . 260, 358	2:4 . . . . 525, 584, 586
3:2 456	4:16 . . . . 268, 269, 294, 327	2:5–6 456
3:3 . . . . 302, 310	4:17 . . . . .294, 295, 299, 510	2:5 . . . . . 122, 210, 367, 390, 425, 480, 746
3:4 . . . . 268, 545	4:18 273	2:6 . . . . 425, 426, 554
3:5–6 296	5:1–10 297	2:7 747
3:6 667	5:1–4 288	2:14 667
3:10 . . . . .442, 534, 543, 627, 658, 661	5:2–12 298	3:2 750
3:11 . . . . 385, 567	5:2 . . . . 251, 260, 296	3:15 717
3:12 . . . . 515, 715, 724	5:8 538	3:16 . . . . .196, 440, 443, 449, 478, 561
3:13 . . . . 421, 553	5:9 295	4:6 56
3:15 717	5:23 . . . . 105, 260, 662, 663	4:10 . . . . 426, 427
3:16 . . . . 56, 204	5:24 . . . . 135, 211	5:17–20 750
3:17 . . . . 105, 471		5:17–18 751
3:25 569	### 2 THESSALO- NIANS	5:17 750
4:11 236		5:21 515
4:12 58	1:4–5 271	5:22 747
	1:5 251	5:24–25 569
### 1 THESSALO- NIANS	1:7 . . . . 260, 327	5:24 585
	1:8 . . . . 301, 590	5:25 733
1:3 . . . . 271, 538	1:9 584	6:3 56
1:4–5 . . . . 517, 531	1:12 730	6:12 . . . . 531, 575
1:5 . . . . . .165, 196, 614, 637	2. 292	6:14 260
1:6 . . . . 481, 542	2:1–12 . . . . 278, 299	6:15 472
1:10 . . . . .270, 295, 327, 556, 585	2:1–2 253	6:16 . . . . 128, 575
2:8–9 . . . . 44, 89	2:1 . . . . 260, 293, 299	6:20 43
2:12 . . . . 251, 510	2:2–3 262	
	2:2 . . . . 251, 260	### 2 TIMOTHY
	2:3–17 253	1:6 747
	2:3 . . . . 292, 299	1:7 543
	2:8 260	
	2:9–10 298	

1:9–10. 218
1:9 . . . . .219, 561, 736
1:10 . . . . 165, 169, 260,
310, 494
1:11. 747
1:12–14. 43
1:13–14. . . . . 57, 739
1:13 . . . . .56, 64
1:14. 739
2:8 . . . . .50, 253, 343,
436, 465
2:10 . . . . 515, 545, 547,
575, 715
2:11 253
2:12 . . . . 287, 456
2:17–18. 253
2:19 . . . . 129, 423
2:21 541
2:22 135
2:24 750
2:25 536
2:26 280
3:1–13. 278
3:16–17. 639
3:16 . . . . 63, 171
4:1 . . . . 251, 260, 301,
472
4:8 260
4:14 569
4:18 251

TITUS
1:1 515
1:2 575
1:4 731
1:5–7 748
1:5 . . . . .747, 750, 752
2:11 . . . . 427, 587
2:13 . . . 106, 220, 260, 268,
270, 471, 545
2:14 . . . . 391, 401, 420,
421, 554
3:3–7 628
3:4–7 109
3:4–6 . . . . 169, 472
3:5–7 761
3:5 . . . . .534, 561, 627,
631, 766, 774
3:7 575

PHILEMON
5. 751
6. 731

HEBREWS
1–12. 542
1–2. 363
1:1–3. . . . . 149, 361
1:1–2. . . . . 200, 206–207
1:1 80
1:2 . . . . . 168, 436, 440, 472
1:3 . . . . . 144, 331, 420, 436,
453, 454, 471, 472
1:5–11. 455
1:5 436
1:8 129
1:10–12. 470
1:10 156
1:13 . . . . 120, 331, 453
1:14. 602
2:1–5. 602
2:1–4. 599
2:1 601
2:3–4. 601
2:4 . . . . 629, 630
2:6–10 285
2:8–9. 256
2:9 427
2:10 143
2:11 736
2:14–18. 479
2:14–17. 462
2:14–15. . . . . 395, 416, 446
2:14 478
2:15 . . . . 602, 672
2:17 . . . . 210, 382, 478
3–4. 602
3:1–6. 564
3:1 601
3:5–6 135
3:6 . . . . .210, 326, 603,
604, 605
3:7–4:13 599
3:8 674
3:12 601
3:15 674
4:1 331
4:2 364
4:7 674
4:12 . . . . 662, 663
4:14–5:10 507
4:15–16. 481
4:16 . . . . 457, 603, 605
5:6 . . . . 129, 453
5:8–9. 563
5:9 . . . . 129, 557
5:11–6:12 599
5:12–14. 56
6:1–2. 56
6:1 540
6:2 . . . . .585, 747, 770
6:4–9 600
6:4–6 . . . . 601, 602, 770
6:4–5 601
6:4 601
6:6 601
6:9 603
6:10 127
6:11 557
6:12 . . . . 481, 542, 602
6:14 575
6:17–18. 604
6:17 218
6:19–20. 457
6:19 . . . . 130, 393, 664
6:20 129
7–8. 746
7:10. 679
7:17. . . . . 129, 453
7:21 . . . . 129, 453
7:24–25 129
7:25 . . . . 122, 458, 602
7:28 . . . . 129, 363
8–10. 714
8–9. 507
8:1 . . . . 331, 405, 453
8:5 362
8:6 . . . . . . 210, 367, 457, 746
8:8–10. 725
8:12 . . . . 551, 552
9:5 407
9:12 . . . . .129, 391, 421, 554
9:14–22. 420
9:14–15. 602
9:14 . . . . 129, 156, 198,
316, 403, 616
9:15 . . . . 210, 226, 367,
457, 532, 554
9:22 . . . . 421, 552

875

9:24 327
9:27–28 . . . . 422, 585
9:27 . . . . .310, 491, 671
9:28 . . . . 268, 270, 602
10:1–22. 316
10:1 362
10:2 421
10:6 405
10:8 405
10:10. . . . . 541, 602
10:12–13. 453
10:12. 120
10:18. 552
10:19–39. 599
10:19–23. 457
10:19. . . . . 601, 603
10:22 . . . . 421, 601, 673, 761
10:23 . . . . 135, 603
10:24–25. 273
10:24. 733
10:25 . . . . 256, 602
10:26–39. 600
10:27 585
10:29 . . . . . . 601, 616, 736
10:32 739
10:35 603
10:36 . . . . 601, 602
10:39 . . . . 538, 603
11. 135
11:1. 539
11:3 161
11:5 602
11:6 588
11:7. 538
11:8–19. 501
11:8–11. 538
11:10–16. 602
11:10. 331
11:13. . . . . 602, 706
11:16. . . . . 311, 331
11:25 671
11:28 602
11:31. 668
11:33. 419
12. . . . . 331, 542
12:1–29. 599
12:1–4. 421
12:1–2. 446
12:1 323
12:2 . . . . .120, 331, 453, 602

12:3–4 401
12:3 . . . . .387, 481, 542, 563
12:4 542
12:10. 542
12:11. 306
12:14. . . . . .136, 541, 542, 736
12:15 602
12:22–24. . . . . 323, 331
12:22 . . . . 311, 708
12:23 . . . . 325, 441
12:24 . . . . 122, 210, 367, 457
12:28 509
13. 542
13:6 603
13:7 51
13:8 . . . . 129, 471
13:11. 405
13:14. . . . . 331, 602
13:15–16. . . . . 603, 756
13:15. 716
13:16. 731
13:17. . . . . 481, 750
13:20–21. 471
13:20 . . . . 226, 715
13:22 601

JAMES

1:5 137
1:15 . . . . 311, 671
1:17. . . . . 129, 471
1:18 . . . . .155, 535, 717
1:21 535
1:27 . . . . 542, 755
2:11 672
2:13 307
2:14 538
2:15–17. 53
2:21–23. . . . . 501, 538
2:24 569
3:1 . . . . 84, 750
3:2 683
3:6 334
3:13 . . . . 204, 733
4:7 . . . . 280, 542
4:17 668
5:3–5 248
5:7 260
5:8 270
5:11 307

5:14 750

1 PETER

1:1–2. 518
1:1 . . . . . .515, 706, 715, 725
1:2 . . . . 110, 403, 541
1:3 . . . . . .105, 155, 444, 533
1:4–5 327
1:4 501
1:7 260
1:9–11. 166
1:9 . . . . 403, 538
1:11. . . . . 118, 367
1:12 . . . . 166, 196, 637
1:13 260
1:15–16. 736
1:18–19. 554
1:18 . . . . 391, 421
1:20 . . . . .129, 248, 468,
 515, 518
1:21 . . . . 137, 616
1:23 . . . . 155, 535
1:24 311
2:4 725
2:5–9 332
2:5 . . . . 717, 737, 746
2:6 725
2:9–10 . . . . 221, 518
2:9 . . . . 286, 515, 532, 706,
 716, 725, 746
2:10 169
2:11 706
2:21 . . . . 387, 401, 421,
 481, 542
2:22–25 404
2:24 . . . . .198, 401, 406,
 420, 481
3:15 56
3:18–22. 706
3:18–21. 433
3:18 155
3:19–21. . . . . 319, 760
3:19–20. . . . . .317, 323, 364
3:20–21. 763
3:20 . . . . 592, 668
3:21 . . . . . .385, 444, 556,
 774, 775
3:22 . . . . 453, 472
4:11 471

Scripture and Apocrypha Index

4:13 . . . . 260, 545
4:14 . . . . 471, 545
4:17 . . . . 89, 165, 301,
                 585, 590, 668
4:19 135
5:1–5 750
5:1–2 748
5:2 715
5:8–9 542
5:8 280
5:10 . . . . 211, 273, 545,
                     556, 575

2 PETER

1:1 471
1:3 . . . . 133, 532
1:4 . . . . 576, 578
1:5–7 542
1:9 . . . . 316, 421
1:10 725
1:11 471
1:16 . . . . 194, 260
1:17 139
1:20–21 . . 171, 196, 638, 640
1:21 . . . . 63, 631
2:4 . . . . 303, 515
2:20 599
3:2–14. 278
3:2 736
3:3 248
3:4–5 254
3:4 260
3:8 128
3:9 . . . . 423, 525, 540, 586
3:11 136
3:12 260
3:18 . . . . 105, 471

1 JOHN

1:1–3. . . . . 80, 208
1:1 572
1:2 574
1:3 731
1:7 421
1:8 . . . . 533, 544, 683
1:9 . . . . 421, 551, 552
1:10 683
2:2 . . . . . . 426, 427, 525, 552
2:6 481

2:12 . . . . 471, 551, 552
2:14 416
2:15–17. 737
2:15–16. 542
2:15 74
2:18 248
2:19 . . . . 603, 741
2:20 63
2:24–25 574
2:28 . . . . 260, 604
2:29 . . . . 155, 543
3:1 135
3:2 . . . . 268, 481
3:4 667
3:8 395
3:9 . . . . 155, 533, 543
3:10 137
3:14 574
3:16 481
3:17 755
3:18 755
3:21 457
4:2–3 110
4:2 478
4:3 299
4:4 416
4:6 204
4:7 . . . . 155, 543
4:8 . . . . 123, 135
4:14 . . . . 427, 472
4:17 . . . . 585, 737
5:1 . . . . 155, 533
5:2 137
5:4 . . . . 155, 219, 416,
                     539, 543
5:6–8 760
5:6 403
5:7 100
5:11–13 574
5:11–12 771
5:12 683
5:14 457
5:16 574
5:18 . . . . . 155, 533, 543, 598
5:20 574

2 JOHN

3. 477
7. . . . . 299, 478
9. 56

3 JOHN

11. 481

JUDE

1. 597
3. . . . . 57, 539, 578, 731, 739
4. 741
5. 468
6. . . . . 303, 515, 584
7. 337
9. 641
12. 802
13. 335
14–15 641
14. 269
20. . . . . . . 122, 539, 730, 736
21. . . . . . 270, 575, 597, 728
24. 597
25. . . 101, 105, 471, 472, 557

REVELATION

1:4 126
1:5–6 252
1:5 . . . . . 135, 154, 415, 441,
                   481, 509, 564
1:6 . . . . . 286, 421, 706, 716
1:7 . . . . 268, 403
1:8 . . . . . . 128, 133, 160, 472
1:9 . . . . 273, 299
1:13 485
1:17–18. 472
1:18 . . . . . 281, 317, 318, 322
2–3 297
2:5 . . . . 268, 269, 540
2:7 . . . . 252, 319, 574
2:8 . . . . 281, 472
2:9–10 292
2:9 719
2:10 . . . . 297, 574
2:11 . . . . 252, 311, 672
2:13 280
2:16 . . . . 268, 269, 540
2:17 . . . . 252, 514
2:21–22. 540
2:26–27 456
2:26 252
3:1 281
3:3 . . . . 268, 540, 739

877

Reference	Pages
3:5	252, 574
3:7	643
3:10	252, 292, 295, 296
3:11	269, 297
3:12	252, 329, 331, 332, 333, 717
3:14	643, 644
3:19	540
3:21	120, 252, 453, 456, 480
4–5	147, 327, 472
4:8	126
4:9–10	281
4:11	128, 160, 162, 471
5	367, 416
5:6	507
5:9–10	252, 421
5:9	299, 415, 421, 554
5:10	286, 287, 456, 706, 716
5:12–13	471
5:13	471
6	289, 294, 299
6:8	317, 322
6:9–11	289, 322
6:10–11	328
6:10	306, 472
6:11	270
6:16–17	295
7	294, 299
7:1–8	299
7:2	281
7:4–8	725
7:9–17	299
7:9	299, 725
7:10	473
7:13–17	322, 328
7:14	292, 299, 300, 421
7:15	332
7:17	473
8	294, 299
9	294, 299
9:1–2	335
9:11	335
10	294, 299
10:6	281
10:7	166
11	294, 299
11:15–19	251
11:15	269
11:18	295
11:19	332
12	280, 292, 294, 299, 415
12:1–11	373
12:7–9	303
12:9	252
12:10	397, 418
12:11	252, 415, 507
13	262, 294, 299
13:8	129, 226, 507, 526, 574
13:10	252, 273, 298
13:14	281
14	294, 299
14:3	553
14:4	554
14:6	44
14:10–11	335
14:10	295, 335
14:12	252, 273, 298
14:15–17	332
15	294, 299
15:1	295
15:2	252
15:3	643
15:5–8	332
15:7	295
16	294, 299
16:1	295, 332
16:7	399
16:9	540
16:15	269
16:17	332
16:19	295
17:1–19:5	251
17	294, 299
17:8	574
17:14	472
18	294
19	287, 289, 297, 728
19:1–2	307
19:7	728
19:9	270, 644, 793
19:10–21	268
19:10	103
19:11–21	269, 290, 307
19:14	297
19:16	472
19:17–18	793
19:20	251, 323, 335
20	280, 282, 287, 287–90, 297, 728
20:1–6	280, 307
20:2–3	280
20:3	281
20:4–8	275
20:4–6	277, 278, 288, 290
20:4–5	574
20:4	269, 281, 287, 289, 294, 661
20:5	281
20:6	280, 283, 311, 456
20:7–15	290
20:10	251, 323, 335
20:11–15	304, 307, 569
20:12	574
20:13–14	317, 322
20:14–15	323
20:14	323
20:15	574
21:1–22:5	251, 329
21	219, 259, 307, 328, 503, 510, 645
21:1–4	717
21:1–3	330
21:1	155, 329, 331
21:2–3	155
21:2	311, 329
21:3	219, 283–284, 331, 332
21:4–6	331
21:4	155, 311, 332
21:5	155, 642, 644
21:6	128, 472, 574
21:7–8	331
21:7	252
21:8	323, 335
21:10–27	331
21:10–21	329
21:10	330, 331
21:12	725
21:24–26	725
21:27	332, 574
22	259, 307, 328, 503, 510, 645
22:1–5	322
22:1–3	332
22:1	473
22:2–4	332

22:3 . . . . 332, 473
22:5 . . . . 287, 456
22:6 . . . . 269, 642, 644
22:8–9 103
22:12 . . . . 269, 303
22:13 . . . . 128, 472
22:17 . . . . .531, 574, 729
22:20 . . . . 269, 270
22:21 282

APOCRYPHA
2 ESDRAS
3:21–22 678
7:118 678

2 MACCABEES
1:5 558
6:23 317
7 291
7:1–29 311
7:14 154
7:33 558
9:12 467
12:43–45 . . . . 315, 316
12:43 . . . . 154, 311

4 MACCABEES
17:22 407

SIRACH
24:1–17 136
45:1 313
46:11 313
49:1 313

WISDOM OF SOLOMON
2:23–24 . . . . 677, 678
13 146
16:13 318

SUBJECT INDEX

a priori, 113
Abraham in redemptive history, 500–501
Abrahamic covenant, 501–2, 713–14, 761–62
action as worship, 756
activism, 20
Acts of Paul and Thecla, 253
Acts of Philip, 365
"actual sins" versus "original sin," 679
Adam
    atonement and, 388–90, 401
    historicity of, 654–55
    humanity of Jesus and, 480
    image of God and, 661
    impact of sin of, 677–83
    Jesus as second/new, 384, 562–63
    new creation and, 442–43
    in redemptive history, 491–92, 497–99
    virgin conception and, 371–72
Adam-Christ typology, 581, 586, 587, 655
Adam-Christology, 466–67
Adamic covenant, 223–24, 226–27
adoption in salvation, 571–72
adoptionism, 96, 474
adoration as worship, 756
advocacy of Jesus. *See* mediation of Christ
Advocate (Holy Spirit), 451, 616, 635
"Agape feast." *See* Eucharist
Age of Reason, prolegomena in, 34–38
"all people," salvation and, 587–88
allegory, biblical use of, 361
Alpha and Omega, 472
American Evangelical Covenant Church, 768
Amidah, Jewish, 440
amillennialism, 278–81
Amyraldian view of atonement, 429–32, 434
Anabaptists, 314, 564, 751, 765, 784
"anastasity" (neologism), 445
"angel of the Lord," 102–3
Anglican tradition
    on atonement, 430–31
    description of, 23
    on election, 522
    governance model of, 745

on sacraments, 761, 773, 789n216, 791–92, 800
    See also Thirty-Nine Articles of Religion (Anglican)
animal kingdom versus humanity, 664
answers.com, 651
anthropocentrism, 653
anthropological dichotomism, 662–63, 664
anthropological monism, 663–64
anthropological trichotomism, 663
anthropology, 650
anti-Catholicism, 702
Antiochus IV Epiphanes, 261–62, 291, 299
Antipas of Pergamum, 278
apocalypse defined, 257
Apocalypse of Moses, 319
apocalyptic eschatology, 241–43, 257, 808–9
apocalypticism, 257, 809
Apocrypha, authority/canonicity of, 316–17
apokalypsis, 260
apokatastasis, doctrine of, 582, 583
Apollinarianism, 117, 368, 482, 483, 484
apologetic theology, 32, 44, 80
apostasy, warnings against, 528, 596–97, 600–602, 603n243
apostle, office of, 631, 746
Apostles' Creed
    on ascension of Jesus, 449
    biblical canon and, 66
    on communion of saints, 699
    on *descendit ad inferos*, 433–34
    on forgiveness, 550
    on judgment, 301
    on life of Jesus, 357
    on virgin conception, 374
apostolic "college," 746
apostolic testimony/teachings, 67–68, 357–58
Apostolic Tradition, 764
apostolicity of Scripture/church, 65, 69, 738–39
"appointed," the, 517
archbishop, office of, 746
Arian Christology, 111
Arianism, 118, 119, 619

Aristotle, influence of, 33, 181, 305, 781, 787
Arius/Arians, 96, 116, 117, 474–76, 617
Arminian, The, 522
Arminianism
    on atonement, 402, 420, 429, 431
    on election, 528–29
    on salvation, 586, 589, 594, 595, 596
ascension of Jesus, 449–59
Assumption of Moses, 641
assurance of salvation, 595–96, 598–99, 602–5
Athanasian Creed, 98, 99, 449
atheists
    authoritative sources for, 37
    depravity and, 675
    eschatology and, 274
    on existence of God, 689
    on historicity of Jesus, 437
    on humanity, 651, 654n10, 663
    natural revelation and, 176
Athenians, 540n90
atonement
    achievement of, 388, 421
    Amyraldian view of, 429–32, 434
    Christus Victor model of, 393–97, 410
    defined, 388
    exemplary model of, 401–2, 410
    extent of (for whom), 420–22
    governmental theory of, 402, 410
    limited/general views of, 422–27, 528
    moral influence model of, 398–400, 410
    pejorative criticism of, 411–12
    penal substitution model of, 402–10
    ransom model of, 391–93, 410
    recapitulation model of, 388–90, 410
    satisfaction model of, 397–98, 410
    universal, view of, 427–29
    See also cross of Christ; salvation
Augsburg Confession, 682, 773, 782–83
Australian Presbyterian Church, 749
authority
    in church governance, 746–48, 753
    exaltation of Jesus and, 453–55, 473
    of Jesus Christ, 469
    primary sources of, 62
    in prolegomena, 33–34
    of Scripture, 639
    sin of humanity and, 669–70
autobasileia, 240
autotheos, 120–21

Babel, tower of, in redemptive history, 498–99
Babylonian Captivity of the Church (Luther), *The*, 782
baptism
    about, 758–59
    biblical accounts of, 759–60
    gospel and, 776
    Holy Spirit and, 633–37, 766, 772–75
    by immersion/affusion, 771–72
    as mark of church, 740
    purpose of church and, 755
    resurrection of Christ and, 444
    spiritual benefits of, 772–76
    Trinity and, 106–7
    who should have, 761–71
    See also sacrament
baptismal regeneration, 634, 764, 773–74
Baptist Faith and Message, 198n205
Baptists
    on baptism, 765, 771–72
    on Eucharist, 783, 784, 788, 795, 800
    governance model of, 751
    view on theology of, 23
Barnabas, 538
Barth, evangelicals on Karl, 191–93
2 Baruch, 288, 291n105, 317, 678
"Bebbington Quadrilateral," 20
"begotten/proceeding," eternally, 96
Belgic Confession, 70, 171–72, 762, 786
belief
    baptism and, 765–67, 768–70
    divine enabling of, 536
    scope of salvation and, 588
    See also Christian beliefs
"believing criticism," 69
Benedictus, 365
Bible
    defined, 63
    systematic theology and, 60–61
    tradition and, 65
    as Word of God, 63
    See also New Testament; Old Testament; Scripture
biblical studies/exposition, 21–22, 25
biblicism, 20, 77–80
Bill and Ted's Excellent Adventure, 310
binitarianism, 105, 623
bishop, office of, 745–48
Blanchard, Jonathan, 276n75
blessings of God

Subject Index

baptism and, 772–76
covenantal, 537, 543, 550, 568, 570, 573, 636
in redemptive history, 501, 503
security of salvation and, 596, 601n235, 602

blood of Christ
atonement and, 415, 573
Eucharist and, 780–92, 794, 797
forgiveness and, 551–52
redemptive shedding of, 401, 403, 404–9
redemptive significance of, 391, 392, 395–96, 554–55

body (flesh), the
eschatology and, 242
humanity of Jesus and, 478, 481
new creation and, 154–55
soul and, 312–14, 665

"body of Christ"
the church as, 716–17, 742
Eucharist and, 780–94, 797, 800–801

Bondage of the Will (Luther/Calvin), *The*, 521–22, 676

Book of Common Order of the Church of Scotland, 763

Book of Common Prayer, 23, 358

Book of Concord, The, 536n78

Book of Discipline of the United Methodist Church, The, 81n94

Brazos Theological Commentary on the Bible series, 25

"breaking of bread," 777, 789. *See also* Eucharist

"breath of life," 572, 621–22, 624, 627–28. *See also* vivification

Buddhism, 194, 684

burnout, 752

Cain in redemptive history, 498–99
calling in *ordo salutis*, 531–32, 533
Calminians, 589
Calvinism/Calvinists
on atonement, 402, 420, 422, 431
description of, 23–24
on election, 522, 527–29
on salvation, 588–89, 594, 596, 599

Calvin's Christology, 578

canon of scripture
criteria for inclusion in, 65–66
defined, 63
evangelical theology and, 22
inspiration and, 638
prolegomena and, 44
tradition and, 68, 69

"canon of truth," 66

Catechism of the Catholic Church, 150n114, 157, 315, 367, 560, 773, 780–82

Catholic Church. *See* Roman Catholic Church

"catholic evangelical," 24

catholicity of church, 19, 25, 737–38, 810

Center of Theological Inquiry (Princeton), 352

Chalcedonian Creed, 68, 463, 464

changelessness of God, 129

charismata, 635

charismatic movement, 611

charity, gospel proclamation and, 731

Chicago Statement on Biblical Inerrancy, 643

child abuse, divine, 411–12

children
baptism of, 761–71
dedication of, 770
Eucharist and, 800–801
salvation of, 593–94
sins of, 677, 680, 681, 683n69

chiliasm, 289–90

chiliasts, 275

"chosen," the, 515, 516–17

"Christ Alone Is Our Salvation," 490

Christ Pantocrator, 583

Christian beliefs
categories of, 769–70
gospel and, 43, 44
Scripture and, 64
systematic theology and, 60–61
theology for interconnectedness of, 57
See also belief

Christian community
ascension of Jesus and, 453
baptism and, 635
Holy Spirit's work in, 632–33
image of God and, 659
inspiration of Scripture and, 638n49, 639
sacraments and, 758
Scripture and, 64, 80
teaching in, 56
theology and, 41
Trinity and, 124, 134

Christian life/practice
church governance and, 753

Subject Index

eschatology and, 236
Holy Spirit's work in, 631
resurrection of Christ and, 446
return of Christ and, 271, 273
Scripture and, 64
social action and, 53
theology and, 56, 82–83
Christian Origins and the Question of God (Wright), 350
Christian theology
    eschatology in, 236, 238–40, 241
    evangelical theology and, 21
    goal of, 84
    gospel and, 44
    prolegomena to (*see* prolegomena)
Christianity
    in evangelical ecclesiology, 701–2
    resurrection of Christ and, 438
Christification, 545
christological revelation, 172, 205–12
Christology
    defined, 342
    eschatology/pneumatology and, 452
    in evangelical ecclesiology, 704
    functional versus titular, 356n39
    gospel-driven, 343–45
    identity of Jesus in, 464, 473–74
    methods in, 346
    Powell on, 84
    preexistence of Christ in, 466–67
    prolegomena to, 43, 383
    resurrection of Christ and, 441
Christology from Above, 351–56
Christology from Below
    about, 349–50
    versus Christology from Above, 354–56
    quests for historical Jesus in, 346–49
Christophany, 103, 360
christotokos, 482
Christus Victor, 393–97, 414–20, 578
Christus Victor (Aulen), 396
church, the
    biblical images of, 713–18
    as global, 811
    gospel-driven goals for, 704–7
    gospel-shaped features of, 728–34
    Holy Spirit and, 625–33
    Israel and, 719–27
    Jesus Christ and, 344
    judgment and, 308
    kingdom of God and, 708–12

    marks of, 735–40
    mission of (see mission of church)
    purpose of, 754–56
    in redemptive history, 508–9
    the state of, 741
    unity of, 735–36, 741–44, 811
    as visible/invisible, 701–2, 732–33, 810
    See also community of faith; gospelized community
church administration, 745–53
church discipline, 739, 752, 795
Church Dogmatics (Barth), 38, 387
church governance, 745–53
church growth, unity and, 742–43
church leadership, 745–53
church management, 745–53
Church of Christ, 751
Church of Scotland, 748
church organization, 745–53
Churches of Christ, 773
circumcision, 761–62
City of God (Augustine), *The*, 680
classical premillennialism, 281
Clement (epistles), 273, 408, 618
Comforter (Holy Spirit), 616
Coming of God (Moltmann), *The*, 272
Comma Johannaeum, 100n17
"communion." *See* Eucharist
community
    church as holistic, 733–34
    consensus of, 69
    in diversity, 57, 238, 729
    reconciliation in, 559
    security of salvation and, 601–3
    Trinity in, 123
    See also Christian community; covenant community; gospelized community
community of faith
    forgiveness and, 550, 552–53
    gospel and, 43
    new creation and, 157
    revelation and, 170–71, 196
    theology and, 30, 74
concupiscence, 680
confessions of the church
    evangelical theology and, 22
    nature and, 70
    tradition and, 64, 68, 69
    See also specific confessions

Subject Index

Congregationalism (model of governance), 751–52
consciousness
  of humanity, 664
  revelation and, 170
  state of (*see* postmortem state)
consent of the governed, 752
consistent eschatology model, 244–46
consubstantial, 96, 115
consubstantiation, 782, 790
contentions in ecclesiology. *See* ecclesiology contentions
conversion
  baptism and, 768–69
  millennium and gradualistic, 276
conversionism, 20
Cooper, Anthony Ashley, example of, 481–82
cosmological argument for existence of God, 181
Council of Chalcedon, 117, 482, 484–85
Council of Ephesus, 117, 482, 521
Council of Florence, 315
Council of Nicaea, 117, 474, 482
Council of Toledo, 117, 118
Council of Trent
  on church/kingdom, 708
  on justification, 560
  on purgatory, 315
  on sacraments, 780, 781, 787
  on salvation, 604
Councils of Constantinople (First/Second)
  on deity/humanity of Jesus, 464, 482, 483
  on Holy Spirit, 617
  on salvation, 582
  on Trinity, 117, 118
covenant community, 154, 531, 601, 603
covenant initiation, 761–62
covenant theologies, 222–28
covenantal monotheism, 144
covenantal nomism, 565
covenants
  church and, 710, 713–14, 718, 719–27, 755
  creation and, 140–41, 155
  Holy Spirit and, 636
  humanity and, 661, 664, 667, 680, 692
  Jesus Christ and, 49, 405, 421, 457, 659
  in redemptive history, 496–97, 500, 502–6, 508–11

  sacraments and, 757, 761–63, 765, 770, 778, 781, 782, 786
  salvation and, 492, 537, 543, 550, 567–68, 570, 593
creatio ex nihilo, 158–62, 665n36
creation
  God/Jesus shared role in, 472
  goodness of, 157–58
  of humanity, 652–53, 655
  humanity of Jesus and, 480
  preexistence of Christ and, 468
  in redemptive history, 497–500
  triune act of, 148–52, 621–22
  See also new creation
creational monotheism, 142–48
creationists, special/progressive, 654
credobaptism, 765–68. *See also* dual baptism view
creeds
  Christology and, 353
  evangelical theology and, 22
  tradition and, 66, 68, 69
  See also specific creeds
cross of Christ
  abandonment cry on, 405
  achievement of, 388, 421
  Christus Victor and, 416
  eschatology and, 241–42
  judgment and, 301–2
  pejorative criticism of, 411–12
  problem of evil and, 693
  resurrection of Christ and, 436
  scope of salvation and, 592–93
  for whom it avails, 420–22
  worship and, 435
  See also atonement
crucicentrism, 20
cruciformity, 435
culpability, sinfulness and, 677–83
cultural progress in prolegomena, 35, 38–39
culture, theology and, 22, 56, 73–76
"curse," Jesus, 554

danger of apostasy, 528
Darby, J. N., 300
Darwinianism, 655
David in redemptive history, 504–5
Davidide, Jesus as, 473, 715, 723
Day of Atonement, 407, 424
"day of the Lord"
  eschatology and, 251, 253, 567, 728

gospel and, 47
return of Jesus Christ as, 260, 269, 291n105
deacon, office of, 746, 751
Dead Sea Scrolls. *See* Qumran texts
death
Christ and, 324–25
Christus Victor and, 393, 414–15, 418
as effect of sin, 310–12, 671
eschatology and, 242–43, 309
gospel and, 310
of Jesus Christ, 48–49, 380–81, 385–88 (*see also* cross of Christ)
physical versus second, 311–12
in redemptive history, 498
representative versus substitutionary, 403, 407–8
Scripture/writings on, 317–24
understanding state upon, 309
views on state upon, 312–17
See also cross of Christ
Death of Death in the Death of Christ (Owen), The, 423
Death Studies, 310
debt forgiveness, 552n123
Decalogue in redemptive history, 503
dedication of infant, 770
Defensio Fidei Catholicae de Satisfactione Christi (Grotius), 402
degeneration, sin and, 673
deification, 575–78
deism, 35, 145
deity of Holy Spirit, 616–18
deity of Jesus
affirming/identifying, 460–65
early church on, 473–76
human nature and, 482–85
Jesus/disciples on, 468–69
New Testament on, 470–73
Old Testament on, 469–70
preexistence and, 465–68
delay of *parousia*, 244–46
deliberate redemption view, 422–27
denial of sin, 674
denominations
Eucharist participation and, 795
versus theological ethos, 700–701
unity of church and, 741–44
depravity
scope of salvation and, 589–90
sin of humanity and, 666, 680

total, 528, 675
deprived ability, 528
descendit ad inferos, 433–34
diaconate
in biblical church governance, 753
ecclesiology and, 730–31
dialectic encounter, revelation through, 169–70
dialectic theology, 81
dichotomism, anthropological, 662–63, 664
dictation theory of inspiration, 640
Didache, 65, 270, 291n105, 772, 780n183, 794, 795
diocese, 745
Diognetus, Epistle to, 225, 385, 408, 706
disciples
of Christ, 378
making, 754
discipleship
cross of Christ and, 435
evangelical church and, 705
gospel's call for, 51
humanity of Jesus and, 480–81
resurrection of Christ and, 445–46
theology to prepare for, 56
discipline, church, 739, 752, 795
"disease," sin as, 682
"disobedience"
Adam's, 677, 683
as sin, 667–68
dispensational premillennialism, 281
dispensational theology, 220–21, 720
ditheism, 116
diversity
in the church, 736
ecclesiology and, 729
in postmodernity, 238
theological, 57
divine attributes
communicable, 134–37
incommunicable, 127–34
divine nature
humanity of Jesus and, 482–85
participating in, 576–78
divinization, 575–78
Docetism, 354, 374, 382, 478, 781, 789
Doctor Faustus (Marlowe), 335
doctrine
evangelical prolegomena and, 45
evangelical theology and, 22
experience and, 73

Subject Index

dogmatics
    methodology and, 80
    revelation through, 169
dogmatics
    evangelical prolegomena and, 44
    prolegomena to, 29–30, 38
DOGOD (Arminianism), 528
dominion over creation, 659–60
Donatists, 704, 725, 732, 741, 743
dreams, 73
dual baptism view, 768–71
dualism
    in evangelical ecclesiology, 701–2
    in view of humanity, 662, 665
Dutch Reformed, 748
dynamic theory of inspiration, 640, 641–42

Early High Christology Club (EHCC), 355
Eastern Orthodox tradition/churches
    governance model of, 745
    on Holy Spirit, 619
    on justification, 564
    Roman Catholic Church and, 742
    on sacraments, 761, 781, 787
    on theosis, 575
Ebionism, 354
Ebionite Christology, 473
ecce homo, 659
ecclesia mixta, 770n158
ecclesiastical authority, 34
ecclesiology
    defined, 698
    eschatological complacency in, 242
    evangelicals and, 700–707
    gospel-shaped church in, 728–34
    prolegomena to, 43
    rethinking evangelical, 809–11
ecclesiology contentions
    church/Israel, 719–27
    church/kingdom, 708–12
    paedocommunion, 800–801
    purpose of church, 754–56
    unity of church, 741–44
    visible/invisible church, 732–33
ecology/environment
    creation and, 163
    new creation and, 442–43
    sin and, 671
economic justice, gospel and, 52–54
ecumenical movement, 743–44
Editio Critica Maior, 468
effort, salvation and, 542

elder, office of
    in biblical church governance, 749–50, 753
    in Congregationalism, 751
    in Episcopalianism, 746, 747
    teaching/ruling, in Presbyterianism, 748, 750–51
elect, the
    biblical references to, 714–15
    Israel/church and, 724–25
election
    atonement and, 420, 422, 425, 429, 430n204, 432, 434
    Barth's doctrine of, 192, 387, 526–27, 583
    evangelicalism on, 522, 524–25, 527–29
    God's purpose in, 153, 216
    Israel and, 727
    justification and, 562n149
    in New Perspective on Paul, 565
    in *ordo salutis*, 532, 547
    in redemptive history, 503, 508
    Scripture references to, 514–20
    security of salvation and, 597, 603
    types of, 515n23
    unconditional/open views of, 528
emotions of God, 130–31
empiricism in prolegomena, 35
empowerment by Holy Spirit
    about, 104, 628–31
    Christ's life and, 111, 411, 452, 624–25
    eschatology and, 242
    gospel and, 610, 612, 614
    of leadership/church, 622, 626–27
    See also power of God
encouragement, return of Christ and, 273
endurance, return of Christ and, 271, 273
Enlightenment, the
    eschatology and, 237–38
    prolegomena in, 34–38
Enoch, First/Second Books of, 245, 288, 317, 319, 334, 454, 505, 641
enslavement to sin
    about, 673
    free will and, 676
    redemption from, 553–55
environment/ecology
    creation and, 163
    new creation and, 442–43
    sin and, 671
epiphaneia, 260

Subject Index

Episcopalianism (model of governance), 745–48
epistemology in prolegomena, 33, 40
error, theology and, 57, 60–61
Eschantillon de la doctrine de Calvin touchant la predestination (Amyraut), 430
eschatology
    biblical elements of, 247–51
    Christology/pneumatology and, 452
    cosmic versus individual, 309
    defined, 234, 257
    ecclesiology and, 728–29
    gospel and importance of, 235–41
    historical positions on, 244–47
    interpretations of, 251–56
    Israel/church and, 725
    justification and, 567
    need for, 241–43, 272
    prolegomena to, 43
    restoring apocalyptic worldview in, 808–9
    resurrection of Christ and, 441
    salvation and, 545–46
estrangement, sin and, 673
"eternal life" versus "life," 572–75
eternalness of God, 127–28
ethics, Christian
    defined, 344
    evangelical ecclesiology and, 707
    evangelical prolegomena and, 44
    evangelical theology and, 22
    humanity of Jesus and, 481
    resurrection of Christ and, 446
    salvation and, 542
Eucharist
    blessings of, 792–95
    children partaking of, 800–801
    controversy over, 741
    frequency of, 802–3
    Jesus' presence and, 787–92
    as mark of church, 740
    meal/feast for, 793, 795–97, 802
    meanings of, 777–78
    participation in, 795–99
    purpose of church and, 755
    return of Christ and, 269–70
    views on, 778–79
    See also sacrament
Eutychians, 483
evangel, 21, 22, 41

evangelical church defined, 699
evangelical ecclesiology
    description of present, 700–701
    problems identified in, 701–3
    suggestions for, 703–7
Evangelical Free Church, 768
Evangelical Presbyterian Church, 749
evangelical theology
    authoritative sources for, 62
    definition/purpose of, 21, 30–31
    ecclesiology and, 700
    methodology for, 81–83
    prolegomena to, 41, 42–45
    tasks for, 703, 807–11
    tradition and, 68–70
Evangelical Universalist (MacDonald), *The*, 584
evangelicalism
    cardinal points of, 20–21
    cross-centered, 435
    description of, 19, 699–700
    ecclesiology and, 700–707
    formation of modern, 19–20
    on Holy Spirit, 611–12
    on Karl Barth, 191–93
    problems identified in, 701–2
    prolegomena to, 41
    tradition and, 64–65
evangelism, 271, 754. *See also* witness, Christian
Eve
    historicity of, 654–55
    Mary and, 368
    in redemptive history, 497–99
evil
    Christian response to, 688–91
    Christus Victor and, 393, 418
    entrance of, 655
    philosophical solutions to, 684, 687–88
    problem of, 686
    recent theologies on, 691–92
    theodicy of, 686–87
    trinity of, 542
    triumph of God over, 372–74, 685, 692–93
    types of, 685–86
"evil" (the word) versus the word "sin," 670–71
evolutionist, theistic, 654
ex nihilo, 158–62, 665n36
ex opere operato, 773
exaltation of Jesus
    about, 449–59

887

Subject Index

apostolic emphasis on, 413
Christology and, 464
God's throne and, 472–74
gospel and, 48–49
having perspective of, 446, 447
new creation and, 155–56
return of Jesus and, 262–63, 266–67
exclusive monotheism, 143
exclusivism, 591–95
exemplary model of atonement, 401–2, 410
exodus
    Eucharist and, 784
    Jesus Christ and, 360, 388
    in redemptive history, 502–3, 553, 571
    See also new exodus
experience, religious
    evangelical prolegomena and, 42–43
    in prolegomena, 35
    revelation through, 169
    theology and, 72–73
expiation, 407
4 Ezra, 285–86, 288, 317, 678, 682

failure to hit mark as sin, 668
fait accompli, 583
faith
    baptism and, 766
    cross-centered, 435
    election and, 520
    gospel's call for, 51
    Jesus' life and, 382
    in *ordo salutis*, 534–36, 537–40
    recapturing gospel-centered, 807–8
    resurrection of Christ and, 444
    scope of salvation and, 586–87, 588
    security of salvation and, 604, 605
    theology for integrity of, 56–57
    works and, 569–70
"faithfulness," 538–39
faithfulness of God, 134–35, 597–98, 603
fall of humanity
    early church on, 669
    gospel and, 491–92
    incarnation and, 523–27
    in redemptive history, 497–500
"falling away," 597–601
fatherhood, depiction of God and, 138
feast, Eucharist as, 793, 802
Feast of Tabernacles, 451
Federal Vision, 564

feelings, religious. See experience, religious
fellowship
    in community, 633 (*see also* community of faith)
    ecclesiology and, 731, 733
    Eucharist and, 793
    within Godhead, 659
female, male and, 659
femaleness, depiction of God and, 137–38
feminine imagery depicting Godhead, 138, 623
fideism, 187
filioque, 118, 619–20
"filled with the Spirit," 637
"flock" image of church, 715–16
Flood in redemptive history, the, 498–99
foederus gratiae, 222
foederus naturae, 222
food, Eucharist and, 793, 796
foreknowledge, God's, 134, 518–19
forgiveness, human/divine, 550–53
"formless," earth as, 159
Forty-Two Articles of Religion, 314
foundationalism in prolegomena, 39
Fourth World Conference on Faith and Order (1963), 698
Free Church of Scotland, 748
Free churches, 765, 783
"free will defense" (FWD), 688–89
Free Will (Erasmus), The, 676
free will, human, 675–76
freedom
    problem of evil and human, 689–91
    from slavery to sin, 553–55, 613–14
French Reformed Church, 768
functional view of "image," 659
fundamentalism, 19, 43

gender issues, 119–20, 137–38, 623
general atonement view, 528
general revelation. See natural revelation
genetic studies, 654
Geneva Catechism, 785, 786
Gentiles and Jews, salvation and, 720, 722–26
gifts of the Spirit, 629–31
glorification in *ordo salutis*, 544–45
glory of God
    about, 137, 139
    humanity created for, 653
    Jesus shares in, 470–71
    judgment and, 307–8

Subject Index

glossolalia, 634
Gnosticism
 about, 96
 on creation, 146–47, 161
 on deity of Jesus, 474, 475
 founder of, 770n158
 Jesus' life and, 382
 on problem of evil, 688
 on Scripture, 64–65
 on Trinity, 115
 unity of church and, 741
 on virgin conception, 371
goals. See purpose of God; telos (goal)
God
 attributes of, 126–37, 471
 blessings of (*see* blessings of God)
 as Creator, 140–49, 151, 472
 doctrine of, 88
 essence of, 139
 existence of, 180–83, 687–88
 gender and, 137–38
 goodness of, 133–34, 687
 gospel of, 89–91
 Holy Spirit as, 616–18
 Jesus Christ and, 343–44, 460–65
 Jesus Christ as, 468–76 (*see also* Trinity)
 judgment by (*see* judgment, divine)
 justice of (*see* justice, divine)
 names of, 471–72
 oneness of, 100–101
 plan of (redemptive), 218–28
 prolegomena and, 30, 40, 44
 purpose of, 214–18
 self-disclosure of, 167–71 (*see also* revelation)
 sovereignty of (*see* sovereignty of God)
 theology and, 57–58
 throne of, Jesus and, 472
 triumph of, over evil, 372–74
 two wills of, 586
 wrath of, 296
 See also glory of God; kingdom of God; Word of God
"God-breathed," 63, 639
Godhead. *See* Trinity
"Godspell" (Schwarz), 30
goodness of God, 133–34, 687
gospel, the
 baptism and, 776
 biblical features of, 47–52
 the "call" and, 531–32
 church as living chapel of, 717–18
 church/kingdom and, 711–12
 Creator and, 140–41
 death and, 310
 definitions of, 23, 47, 52
 distorted/false, 52–54
 emblems of, 757–58
 evangelical church and, 699, 704–7
 God of, 89–91, 460
 Holy Spirit and, 612–14
 hope and, 326–27
 humanity and, 653, 657
 Israel and, 726–27
 Jesus Christ central to, 343–45, 460
 judgment and, 301
 kingdom of God and, 235–41
 logical working of, 513–14
 as mark of church, 740
 in methodology, 81–83
 preaching, need for, 593
 problem of evil and, 692–93
 in prolegomena, 41–45
 in redemptive history, 496–97
 return of Christ and, 258–59
 revelation and, 164–67
 sacraments and, 758
 of salvation, 491–95
 salvation images in, 548–49
 sin of humanity and, 666, 669, 671–72
 as theological center, 807–8
 universalism and, 591
 Word of God and, 63
gospel food, Eucharist as, 793
"gospel meal," 778. *See also* Eucharist
Gospel of Peter, 436
Gospel of the Ebionites, 623
Gospel of Thomas, 348, 365
gospelized community
 church as, 44, 705–7
 church governance and, 753
 Eucharist for, 778
 features that characterize, 728–34
gospelizing, 30–31, 807
Gospels, theological significance of, 357–58
Goths, 619
governance of the church, 745–53
governmental theory of atonement, 402, 410
grace
 covenant of, 222, 226–28
 election of, 526

889

gospel of, 740
irresistible/opposable views of, 528
judgment and, 306–7
in redemptive history, 499
sacraments and, 757
security of salvation and, 604
grace food, Eucharist as, 793
Great Commission, 710, 711, 754, 763
Greek philosophy. *See* Hellenistic thought
guardian-redeemer, 553
guidance by Holy Spirit, 632
guilt
atonement and, 400
forgiveness and, 550
sin of humanity and, 672–73, 677–83
The Gulag Archipelago 1918–1956 (Solzhenitsyn), 670

Hades, death and, 317–24
handicapped, salvation of intellectually, 593–94
HANDS (deity of Jesus), 470–73
heart, hardness of, 673–74
"heart" of humanity, 662, 663, 664n34
heaven and earth
new creation and, 326–33
in redemptive history, 510–11
relationship between, 147
Hebrew Bible, tradition and, 65
Heidelberg Catechism, 45, 302, 536n76, 547n116, 698, 758
Heidelberg Disputation, 386
hell
about, 333–37
descendit ad inferos and, 433–34
intermediate state and, 317, 323
scope of salvation and, 584, 585, 591
Hellenistic thought
on death, 313, 317
on historical Jesus, 348
monotheism and, 476
on problem of evil, 688
in prolegomena, 32–33
Helper (Holy Spirit), 616
Helvetic Confessions/Consensus, 432n210
henotheism, 145–46
hermeneutic of gospel, 706–7
historical premillennialism, 281
history
of Israel/church, 719, 726
models of atonement and, 413–16
revelation through, 169, 193–95

theology and church, 22
history, redemptive
the church in, 508–9
consummation of, 510–11
creation/fall in, 497–500
defined, 496
God's plan and, 218–19, 226, 228, 496–97
holiness and, 737
Jesus in, 506–8
patriarchs/Israel in, 500–506
holiness, 135–36, 139, 541–43, 736–37
holiness movement, 611
Holiness tradition, 544n101
Holy Spirit
baptism and, 633–37, 766, 772–73, 774–75
blasphemy against, 626
church and, 625–33, 752
creation/new creation and, 152, 155–56, 621–22
deity of, 616–18
evangelicals and, 611–12
filioque controversy and, 619–20
gender and, 623
gospel and, 52, 612–14
grieving the, 106, 616, 626
Israel and, 622–25
Jesus Christ and, 344, 451–52, 624–25
in *ordo salutis*, 531, 533, 535, 537, 542–43, 546–47
as personal being, 615–16
prolegomena and, 44
revelation and, 196, 199, 203, 623–24, 638–46
scope of salvation and, 592
tradition and, 69
understanding, 612
Word of God and, 63, 642, 645
work of, 367, 621–46 (*see also* empowerment by Holy Spirit)
homoousious, 119
honor given to Jesus, 470–71
hope
death and, 310, 311–12
Eucharist and, 778, 794
gospel and, 326–27
heaven and, 328
Jesus' life and, 382
resurrection of Christ and, 446
sin of humanity and, 669
See also parousia

house churches, 109, 271, 717, 737, 753
household baptisms, 763, 766–67, 769
human constitution, theological proposals on, 662–65
human nature, sinful, 676
Humanist Manifesto I, 652
humanity
    doctrine of, 657
    dualistic view of, 662
    existence/condition of, 651–52
    fall of (see fall of humanity)
    royal glory in creation of, 652–53, 655
    sin of (see sin)
    study of, 650
humanity of Jesus
    affirming/identifying, 460–65
    divine image restored in, 657, 661
    divine nature and, 482–85
    New Testament on, 476–79
    permanency of, 485
    significance of, 479–82
Hymenaeus and Philetus, 252–54
hypostasis/hypostases, 96, 100, 118, 477, 484
hypostatic union of Christ's natures, 482–85

"icons" and image of God, 660–61
idealism in evangelical ecclesiology, 702
identity
    with Christ and baptism, 774–75
    corporate, evangelical, 703
    of Israel/church, 722
    of Jesus Christ, 383, 440–41
"Identity of Jesus Project" (Princeton), 352
idolatry as sin, 669
If Grace Is True: Why God Will Save Every Person (Gulley/Mullholland), 583–84
illumination, divine, 203–5, 631–32
image of Christ, 544–45
image of God
    biblical references to, 657–58
    Christ's ascension and, 455
    "equal with God" versus, 466
    God's gender and, 137
    humanity created in, 655
    natural revelation and, 176
    new creation and, 442
    sin and marring of, 498
    theological views on, 658–61
    Trinitarian communion and, 124
imago dei, 657, 659, 661

imago trinitatis, 730
imitation of Christ, 481
immaculate conception, 371. *See also* virgin conception
"Immanuel," 471
immorality as sin, 669
immortality of the soul, 312–14
immutability of God, 129–30
impassibility of God, 130–31
imputation of righteousness, 552n121, 562–64
"In Christ Alone" (Townshend/Getty), 397, 435
"in Christ," meaning of, 546–47
in nuce, 526
inaugurated eschatology position, 247
incarnation
    Christology of, 350, 353
    exaltation of Jesus and, 455
    fall of humanity and, 523–27
    humanity of Jesus and, 478–79
    of Jesus Christ, 172, 205–12
    preexistence of Christ and, 465, 468
    redemption and, 461–65
    scope of salvation and, 581
Independent Bible Church, 751, 765
"independent church," 752
individualism, hyper-, 703
inerrancy, 643–44
infallibility, 643–44
infant baptism, 761–69, 771
infant dedication, 770
infant salvation, 593–94
inscripturation, inspired
    Holy Spirit and, 638–46
    as revelation, 196–202, 631
    as source for theology, 62–63
inspiration by Holy Spirit, 638–42
Institutes of the Christian Religion (Calvin), 26, 33, 80, 514, 546n111, 628
integrating motif in prolegomena, 43–44
intellectual authority in prolegomena, 34
intellectual progress in prolegomena, 35, 38–39
intellectually handicapped, salvation of, 593–94
intelligent design, 182, 654n10
intercession of Christ. *See* mediation of Christ
intermediate state
    Christ and, 324–25
    gospel and, 310

891

Subject Index

heaven and, 328
human constitution and, 664, 665
importance of understanding, 309
options of, 312–17
Scripture/writings on, 317–24
Internet access, Christianity and, 20
intuition theory of inspiration, 640
irresistible grace, 528
Islam/Muslims, 476, 482
Israel
    adoption as coheirs with, 571
    choosing of, 515n23, 516, 519–20
    Christology and, 353–55
    the church and, 508–9, 713–16, 719–27, 735–36, 741
    covenant theology and, 223–24, 226–27
    dispensationalism and, 221
    eschatology and, 241, 247–51
    Holy Spirit and, 622–25
    Jesus and God of, 468–76
    Jesus and Old Testament, 360–64
    Jesus' ascension and, 454
    Jesus' birth and, 369, 371–72
    Jesus' death and, 385, 403, 408, 421, 425, 434
    Jesus' identity and, 464, 467
    Jesus' ministry and, 378–84
    Jesus' recapitulation of, 388–90
    Jesus' resurrection and, 438, 440–41, 447
    Jesus' return and, 263, 269
    justification and, 563, 565, 567
    premillennialism and, 281, 285–87
    redemption/rescue of, 553, 555
    in redemptive history, 502–8
    repentance by, 539–40
    restoration of, 570
    sacraments and, 762–63, 793, 796, 800
    security of salvation and, 593, 597–99
    sin of, 667–69, 673–74
    tribulationism views of, 295, 298
"Israel/Israelite" (names), 721
"It Is Well With My Soul" (Bonar), 544

Jehovah's Witnesses, 314, 476
Jerusalem
    about the new, 329–33
    destruction of, 291, 296
Jerusalem, Creed of, 68
"Jesus," meaning of, 556
Jesus Christ
    Adam and (*see* Adam)
    ascension of, 449–59
    baptism of, 377–78
    birth of, 365–66, 369–75 (*see also* incarnation; virgin conception)
    as Creator, 149–50, 151, 154–57
    culture and, 74–76
    death of, 48–49, 380–81, 385–88 (*see also* cross of Christ)
    after death of, 433–34, 438
    deity of (*see* deity of Jesus)
    as eschatological prophet, 247
    exaltation of (*see* exaltation of Jesus)
    as God, 468–76
    gospel and, 48–50, 343–45
    as head of church, 735, 737–38
    Holy Spirit and, 344, 624–25
    humanity of (*see* humanity of Jesus)
    identity of, 383, 440–41
    incarnation of (*see* incarnation)
    Israel and, 721–23
    as Judge, 301
    life of, theological significance of, 357–58
    mediation of (*see* mediation of Christ)
    as Messiah (*see* Messiah)
    ministry of, 375, 377–84
    Old Testament and, 359–64
    our representative, 403
    as place of rest, 324–25
    preexistence of, 465–68
    priestly office of, 481–82 (*see also* mediation of Christ)
    prolegomena and, 41–42, 44, 383
    quests for the historical, 346–49
    in redemptive history, 506–8
    reign of, 455–56 (*see also* exaltation of Jesus)
    resurrection of (*see* resurrection of Jesus)
    salvation only through, 591–93
    Satan and, 372–74
    second coming of (*see* return of Jesus Christ)
    session of, 450–59
    as Shepherd (*see* Shepherd, the Good; Shepherd King/ruler)
    sonship of, 477
    teaching/preaching of, 378–80
    tomb of, 437
    tradition and, 67
    vindication of, 303–4

See also blood of Christ; "body of Christ"
"Jesus died for our sins," meaning of, 406–7
Jesus food, Eucharist as, 793
"Jesus Quest Episode III: A New Hope," 349
Jewish Antiquities, 313, 557
Jewish Scriptures, tradition and, 65
Jewish War, 313, 558
Jews and Gentiles, salvation and, 720, 722–26
Joint Declaration on the Doctrine of Justification, 560–61
Joseph of Arimathea, 437
Jubilees, 245
Judaism (Palestinian), 564–65
judgment, divine
    atonement and, 405–6, 408
    the church and, 308
    God/Jesus' shared role in, 472
    intermediate state and, 323
    Jesus' message of, 379
    meaning of, 301–8
    millennium and, 275–76, 279, 282, 288, 289
    in redemptive history, 499, 504–5
    salvation and, 491–92
    scope of salvation and, 583, 584–85, 590–91
    tribulation and, 295, 298
justice, divine
    atonement and, 399, 402
    judgment and, 305–6
    judging versus saving, 492
    scope of salvation and, 582, 584, 589–90, 591
justice, social/economic
    depiction of God and, 137
    gospel and, 52–54
    gospel proclamation and, 731
    purpose of church and, 755
justification
    biblical teaching on, 559, 566–68
    church teachings on, 560–66
    faith and works in, 569–70
    in *ordo salutis*, 514n21, 540–41
    resurrection of Christ and, 443–44

kalam cosmological argument, 181
kenotic Christology, 467
kerygma, 64, 347, 351
kingdom of God
    biblical references to, 247–51
    Christus Victor and, 416
    church of God and, 708–12
    gospel and, 47–48, 235–41, 258–59
    historical scholarship on, 244–47
    interpretations of, 247–56
    Jesus' ministry and, 379, 381
    millennium and, 276, 279, 282
    resurrection of Christ and, 446, 447–48
kingdom work, 755
kingship of Jesus Christ. *See* exaltation of Jesus
kinsman redeemer, 555
knowledge
    gifts of, 73
    of God, theology for, 58
    God's absolute, 134, 692
    God's middle, 689
    in prolegomena, 33, 39, 40
    scope of salvation and, 593
kosmos, 74

"Lamb of God," 418, 472–73, 526, 554
language used to depict God, 137–38
lapsarianism (infra-/supra-/sub-), 524
"last day/days," 250, 252
Last Supper, the, atonement and, 405
Lateran Council, Fourth, 158
Lausanne conferences, 743
Lausanne Covenant, 258, 259, 357
law, the
    atonement and curse of, 406
    in redemptive history, 502–3
"lawlessness" as sin, 667
leadership accountability, 745
"left behind," 256
legalism, gospel and, 52
Leuenberg Agreement, 792
Leviathan (Hobbes), 200
liberal theology/liberalism
    Barth and, 191–92
    on death of Christ, 386
    prolegomena and, 35, 43
    on Scripture veracity, 644
    social gospel and, 52, 54
"life"
    versus "eternal life," 572–75
    of humanity, 664
    See also "breath of life"
"Light from Light," 114
limited atonement view, 422–27, 528

Subject Index

litigation in church governance, 751
liturgies, tradition and, 69
logic, evangelical prolegomena and, 42–43
logical order of God's decree, 524
logos, 30
Logos, the
    Christology of, 353
    creation and, 149, 151
    God's plan and, 219, 226
    incarnation and, 209–10, 526
    judgment and, 307
    kingdom of God and, 236, 240
    new creation and, 156, 328
    Trinity and, 114, 116, 117
Logos Christology, 96, 474
London Baptist Confession of Faith, 643, 646n69, 765n138, 784
"Lord," 471
"Lord of Israel," 454, 464, 470
"Lord's Supper"
    controversy over, 741
    purpose of church and, 755
    return of Christ and, 269–70
    See also Eucharist
"Lord's Table," 777, 796. *See also* Eucharist
love, divine
    about, 135, 139
    atonement and, 399, 428
    ecclesiology and, 729
    problem of evil and, 691
    scope of salvation and, 584, 591
    unity of church and, 742
Love Wins (Bell), 584
Luther (movie), 342
Lutherans
    on atonement, 420
    on church/kingdom, 709–10
    on deity/humanity of Jesus, 463, 485
    governance model of, 745
    on justification, 560–61
    on sacraments, 761, 773, 782–83, 788, 792, 795, 800
Luther's Small/Large Catechisms, 783

Maccabean period, 261–62
Macedonianism, 118
Magnificat, 365
Magus, Simon, example of, 770n158
male and female, 659
male headship, 119–20
maleness, depiction of God and, 137–38
marana tha, 270
Marburg, Colloquy of, 782
Mariolatry, 376
marriage, 119, 255, 271
Martyrdom of Polycarp, 90
martyrs, scope of salvation and, 589–90
Mary (mother of Jesus), 367–68
maternal language depicting Godhead, 138, 623
mediation of Christ
    humanity of Jesus and, 479, 480
    Mary and, 367
    preexistence of Christ and, 468
    session of Jesus and, 456–58
medicine, Eucharist as, 794
mentally handicapped, salvation of, 593–94
Mere Christianity (Lewis), 183
merits, justification and, 562–63
Messiah
    baptism and role of, 634, 636
    exaltation of Jesus and, 453–54, 456
    gospel and, 460
    Holy Spirit and, 624–25
    Jesus as Old Testament, 359–60
    resurrection of Christ and, 440–41
    Satan and birth of, 373–74
    See also "Lord of Israel"; Shepherd King/ruler; "Son of David/Adam/Israel's God"; "Son of God"
messianic administration, 226
messianic community, 373, 415, 517, 625, 712, 723, 755
messianic feast, 793
messianic interregnum, 282, 288
metaphysical evil, 685
Methodists, 745, 761
methodology, 77
Middle Ages, 33, 35, 39, 53, 68, 237, 521, 582
middle knowledge of God, 689
millennium
    defined, 257, 275
    Internet resources on, 291
    post-, 275–78
    pre-, 281–91
    present to future, 278–81
"mind" of humanity, 662, 664n34
ministerial offices, 629–31
ministry, 123, 447–48
"missing the mark" as sin, 668

Subject Index

mission of church
    charity and proclamation in, 731
    eschatology and, 242
    evangelical ecclesiology and, 707
    holiness and, 737
    Holy Spirit and, 629–31
    ministry of Jesus and, 383
    new creation and, 156–57
    purpose of church and, 754, 756
    in redemptive history, 508
    return of Christ and, 271, 273
    theology and, 44
missions/mission service, 123, 447, 590
Modal Monarchianism, 117
modalism, 97, 115
modernity, 34–38, 237–38
monad, 97
Monarchianism, 97, 117, 474
monergism, 589
monism, anthropological, 663–64
monoepiscopacy, 748, 751
Monophysitism, 117, 483, 484–85
monotheists/monotheism, 142–48, 468–69, 476
Monothelites, 483
moral argument for existence of God, 183, 687–88
moral decision-making, 664
moral evils, 685
moral influence model of atonement, 398–400, 402n133, 410
moral state in justification, 566
Mosaic covenant, 223–24, 227, 508, 713–14, 720
Mother Mary. *See* Mary (mother of Jesus)
motivation, resurrection of Christ and, 446
munus triplex Christi, 364
Muslims/Islam, 476, 482

naive biblicism, 77–80
natural revelation
    about, 70, 172, 173–78
    scope of salvation and, 592, 593
natural theology, 70–72, 178–93
Natural Theology (Paley), 182
naturalism in prolegomena, 35
natural/physical evil, 685
nature
    revelation and, 70–72, 171–78
    sinful human, 676

"Nature and Domain of Sacred Doctrine" (Thomas Aquinas), 33
Nazarene Church, 768
"Nazareth Manifesto," the, 379
neoorthodoxy, 192, 386–88
Nero, 292, 299
Nestorianism, 482–85
"new awareness," 170
new birth
    baptism and, 634
    Holy Spirit and, 627, 631
    in *ordo salutis*, 533–37
    resurrection of Christ and, 444
    security of salvation and, 605
new covenant. *See* covenants
new creation
    biblical references to, 152–54
    Christians as, 544–45
    church member as, 717
    heaven and, 326–33
    Holy Spirit and, 622
    image of God and, 661
    in redemptive history, 510–11
    resurrection of Christ and, 441–43
    security of salvation and, 604
    stages of, 154–57
    view of, 152–57
new exodus
    Eucharist and, 778, 784
    Jesus Christ and, 360, 378, 380–81, 388, 403–4, 418, 479
    new creation and, 152
    redemption and, 504, 507, 553, 555, 571
new Israel
    the church and, 719, 722–23
    covenants and, 224, 492
    Jesus Christ and, 378, 380, 472
    millennium and, 286
    new creation and, 329
    redemption and, 507–8
    salvation and, 563, 571
    Trinity and, 134
New Perspective on Paul (NPP), 564–66
"New Quest" for the historical Jesus, 348
New Testament
    experience and, 72
    gospel and, 43–44, 52
    images of the church in, 713–18
    tradition and, 65–66, 69
    as Word of God, 63

Subject Index

Niceans, 474
Nicene Creed
    on ascension of Jesus, 449
    on Christology, 353
    on the church, 735
    on creation, 141
    on deity/humanity of Jesus, 461–62, 463, 464
    on Holy Spirit, 612, 617–18
    on intermediate state, 313
    on return of Christ, 258
    on Trinity, 118
Niceno-Constantinopolitan Creed
    on authority of Scripture, 68
    on deity/humanity of Jesus, 461
    on Holy Spirit, 619–20
    on Trinity, 118
nihilism in prolegomena, 39
Noah in redemptive history, 498–99
novum, 272
NPP. See New Perspective on Paul (NPP)
nuda scriptura, 68
Nunc dimittis, 365

obedience
    Jesus' representative, 479–80
    purpose of church and, 755
obligation
    atonement and, 398, 431
    covenantal, 224, 227
    redemptive history and, 503
    salvation and, 598
offices of church, 629–31
Old Testament
    gospel's fulfillment of, 50–51
    images of the church in, 713–16
    Jesus Christ and, 359–64, 469–70
    scope of salvation and, 592–93
    tradition and, 65
    as Word of God, 63
    See also Scripture
omnibenevolence of God, 133–34
"omni-compentence" perspective of God, 691
omnipotence of God, 132–33, 689
omnipresence of God, 132
omniscience of God, 134, 689
On Baptism (Tertullian), 767
On "Not Three Gods" (Gregory), 116
On the Holy Spirit (Basil), 618

oneness of church, 735–36
ontological argument for existence of God, 180
open communion, 799
opposable grace, 528
oral tradition versus *regula fidei*, 67
"ordinances," 757
ordo evangelium, 190
ordo salutis (listed in order)
    defined, 513–14
    predestination in, 514–22, 526–30
    calling in, 531–32
    regeneration in, 532–37
    faith/repentance in, 537–40
    glorification in, 544–45
    justification in, 540–41
    qualifications to, 545–47
    transformation in, 541–44
"original sin," 669, 677, 679, 683
Orthodox Study Bible, The, 575
Orthodox tradition/churches, 745, 761. *See also* Eastern Orthodox tradition/churches
orthodoxy, 23, 65, 84
orthokardia, 84
orthopraxy, 23, 84
ousia, 118
overseer, office of, 747

pactum salutis, 112, 222
paedobaptism, 761–65. *See also* dual baptism view
paedocommunion, 800–801
pagan culture/mythology
    eschatology and, 242
    virgin conception and, 369–70
paganism, 145–46
panentheism, 132, 145
pantheism, 145
parables of Jesus, 379–80
Paradise Regained (Milton), 393
parallelism, Semitic, 635, 658
parousia
    ascension of Jesus and, 458
    biblical references to, 261–69, 273
    biblical scholarship on, 272
    death and, 320–22
    defined, 259–60
    delay of, 244–46
    eschatology and, 243, 250, 252–54, 256

Eucharist and, 778
humanity of Jesus and, 481
millennium and, 274, 279, 280, 287–88
tribulation and, 292, 293–94, 297, 298, 299
particular redemption, view of, 422–27
Paschal homily, 419, 448
Passover, Jewish
Eucharist and, 780, 784, 800
Jesus Christ and, 50, 403, 425
redemption and, 516, 553
pastor, 751, 752
paterfamilias, 753, 763, 769
patriarchalism, depiction of God and, 137–38
patriarchs in redemptive history, 500–506
Patristic Era, Trinity in, 113–18
peace, salvation and, 568, 570–71
peccator originaliter/actualiter, 679
Pelagianism, 224, 401, 520–21, 528, 544n101, 563, 594, 675–76, 677, 679, 732. See *also* Semi-Pelagianism
penal substitutionary view of atonement
about, 402–10
evangelicals and, 413–14
pejorative criticism of, 411–12
Pentecost, 248, 452, 633–35
Pentecostal Church, 751, 765
Pentecostal soteriology, 628
Pentecostalism, 544n101, 611, 612, 633–34
"people of God," 713–14
perfectionism, 544n101
perichoresis, 118–19
persecution of Christians, 292
perseverance, 528, 595–99, 603
personal/propositional revelation, 198–202
Personhood of Holy Spirit, 615–16
"perversion" as sin, 668
Phaedo (Plato), 313
Philadelphian Church, 296–97
Philetus and Hymenaeus, 252–54
philosophy
in prolegomena, 32–33, 39
systematic theology and, 61
Pietism, 420
Pilgrim's Progress (Bunyan), 768
plan of God
elements of, 218–19
redemptive history and, 496–97
theologies of unity in, 219–28
See *also ordo salutis*

Platonic dualism/idealism, 701–2
Platonism
Christian apologists on, 32
creation and, 158–59, 161
on immortality of the soul, 313
Logos Christology and, 96
on problem of evil, 688
pluralism, 22, 238, 344
pneumaphobia, 611
pneumatology, 109, 196, 452, 610, 808
"point of contact" (Brunner), 188
Pope, office of, 748
positional sanctification, 541, 631
post-Christianity, 22, 75, 670, 808, 811
post-denominationalism, 809–10
"postfoundationalist," 39
postmillennialists, 275–78
postmodernity, 22, 38–40, 238
postmortem state
heaven and, 328
human constitution and, 664
judgment and, 305
millennium and, 289n100
Scripture/writings on, 311, 320–21, 324
views on, 254, 313–14, 316
See *also* intermediate state
posttribulationism, 297–300
poverty, gospel and, 52–54
power
of Christ's resurrection, 445–46
of God, 114, 132–33, 687
See *also* empowerment by Holy Spirit
praise, 755
prayer, 122–23, 692, 730
preaching of the Word, 738, 739–40, 755. See *also* proclamation
predestination
in church history, 520–22, 526–30
debate over, 514–15
scope of salvation and, 586
Scripture references to, 515–20
preexistence of Christ, 465–68
premillennialism, 275, 281–91
preparatio evangelium, 190
Presbyterian Church of the USA, 23, 749, 768
Presbyterianism (model of governance), 748–51
Presbytery, 750
presence of God, 132

897

Subject Index

preterism, 257
pre-theology. See prolegomena
pretribulationism, 292, 294–97
price of redemption, 553–55
priest, office of, 746n109
priesthood, church as royal, 716
priesthood of believers
    church and, 712, 746n109, 751, 752
    Eucharist and, 784, 795
priestly office of Christ, 481–82. *See also* mediation of Christ
primacy, Godhead and, 120–22
"Problem of the Historical Jesus" (Käsemann), "The," 347–48
proclamation
    charity and gospel, 731
    purpose of church and, 754
    revelation through, 195–96
    Word of God and, 64
    See also preaching of the Word
profession of faith, baptism upon, 765–68
progressive creationist, 654
prolegomena
    to Christology, 383
    in church history, 33–40
    definition/task of, 28, 32–33
    evangelical, 42–45
    need for, 40–42
proleptic eschatology position, 247
Prologium (Anselm), 180
promises of God
    covenantal, 224, 227
    Holy Spirit as, 613
    problem of evil and, 691
    in redemptive history, 500, 501–3, 506, 508, 509, 510–11
    security of salvation and, 597–98, 602, 604
prophet, office of, 631
prophetic eschatology, 257, 266
prophetic word
    God's plan and, 217, 234
    gospel and, 166–67
    Holy Spirit's work of, 631–32
    inspiration and, 638
    Jesus Christ and, 359–60
    revelation and, 195–96, 209, 212
propitiation, 402, 407
propositional/personal revelation, 198–202
propter Christum, 587
Protestant Reformation/Reformers
    on centrality of cross, 386
    on deity/humanity of Jesus, 463, 485
    evangelical theology and, 22
    evangelicalism and, 702
    on human free will, 676
    on justification, 560–61, 569
    on marks of church, 738–39
    on mediation of Christ, 367
    on predestination, 521–22
    prolegomena in, 33–34, 41
    on scope of salvation, 582
    tradition and, 69–70
    unity of church and, 741
    on visible/invisible church, 732
Protevangelium of James, 365
providential monotheism, 144
psychological well-being, sin and, 671
psychopannychy, 314
purgatory, doctrine of, 315–17
purpose of God
    about, 214–18
    humanity of Jesus and, 480
    problem of evil and, 691
    redemptive history and, 496–97
    See also ordo salutis; telos (goal)
purpose of the church, 754–56

Q source, 348
Quakers, 582, 583
Quest for the Historical Jesus, 346–47
Qumran texts, 246, 285, 312–13, 454, 564, 653
Qumranites as remnant of Babylon, 721

"ransom," Jesus as, 554
ransom model of atonement, 391–93, 410
rapture, 293–94, 295, 297
rationalism in prolegomena, 34, 35, 39
realized eschatology, 246–47
reason
    eschatology and, 237–38
    in prolegomena, 35, 37
rebellion
    existence of, 147
    as sin, 667–68, 669
recapitulation, doctrine of, 581
recapitulation model of atonement, 388–90, 410
reconciliation
    in *ordo salutis*, 541

in salvation, 557–59
scope of salvation and, 583
redemption
covenant of, 222
God/Jesus shared role in, 472
God's plan and, 218–19, 226, 228
incarnation and, 461–65
preexistence of Christ and, 468
revelation and, 212–13
salvation as, 553–55
See also history, redemptive; salvation
Redemption: Accomplished and Applied (Murray), 514
Reformation. *See* Protestant Reformation/Reformers
Reformed Church of America, 749
"Reformed epistemology," 186
Reformed theology/tradition
on atonement, 429, 431–32
on church/kingdom, 709–11
covenant theology in, 222
on deity/humanity of Jesus, 463, 485
on *descendit ad inferos*, 434
description of, 23–24
on Holy Spirit, 628
on incarnation/sin, 524
on justification, 552n121, 561–64
on marks of church, 735, 739–40
on predestination, 527
on sacraments, 761, 784–87, 788, 790, 792, 798, 800
on salvation, 586, 589, 595, 603, 604
on total depravity, 675
regal monotheism, 143
regeneration
baptism and, 634, 764, 773–74
Holy Spirit and, 627
image of God and, 661n25
in *ordo salutis*, 532–37
security of salvation and, 604
regula fidei, 21n7, 66–68, 80, 115, 624n24
reign of Jesus Christ. *See* exaltation of Jesus
relational view of "image," 659
relationality of God, 134
relationships
ecclesiology and, 729
effects of sin on, 666–67, 671, 673
forgiveness and, 550
Holy Spirit and, 631
reconciliation and, 557
unity of church and, 742

relevance in prolegomena, 38, 39
"religious affections," 755
religious authority in prolegomena, 34
remnant, the, 716
Remonstrants, 522, 527, 529n56, 596n226
Renaissance prolegomena in European, 34
repentance
baptism and, 765–67
gospel's call for, 51
in *ordo salutis*, 537–40
reprobation, 515, 524
rescue from/for salvation, 555–57
resources, unity and church, 743
response to Christ, scope of salvation and, 592–93
resurrection, eschatological
about, 242, 243, 253–54
emphasis of atonement versus, 413
first/second, 275, 281, 298
intermediate state and, 323
millennium and, 275–76, 279, 280, 281, 282, 288, 289
tribulation and, 295, 298
resurrection of Jesus
apostolic emphasis on, 413
cross of Christ and, 436
gospel and, 48–49
historicity of, 437–40
meaning of, 440–48
new creation and, 154–55
return of Jesus Christ
ascension of Jesus and, 458–59
biblical references to, 259–69
creation and, 155–56
emphasis of atonement versus, 413
eschatology of, 253–54, 269
gospel and, 258–59
implications of, 271, 273
intermediate state and, 323
looking forward to, 269–71
millennium and, 275–76, 279, 282
rapture and, 293–94, 295, 297
secret (*see* rapture)
tribulation and, 295
See also parousia
revelation
Christ's incarnation as, 172, 205–12
divine illumination as, 203–5
Dulles' models of, 169–70
as God's self-disclosure, 167–71

Subject Index

gospel and, 164–67
history and, 193–95
Holy Spirit's work of, 631–32
methodology and, 79–80
modes of, 171–72
nature as, 70–72, 172, 173–78 (*see also* natural theology)
proclamation as, 195–96
prolegomena and, 34–35, 40–41
redemptive nature of, 212–13
Scripture as, 62–63, 196–202, 638
"right hand of God." *See* exaltation of Jesus; session of Jesus
righteousness, 401–2, 416
Roman Catholic Church
    on church/kingdom, 708
    Eastern Orthodox churches and, 742
    evangelicalism and, 702
    governance model of, 745, 748
    on Holy Spirit, 619, 628
    on incarnation/sin, 523–24
    on justification, 560–61
    on marks of church, 735, 738–39
    prolegomena in, 34, 36
    on purgatory, 315
    on sacraments, 761, 773, 780–82, 787–88, 789n216, 795, 800
    on salvation, 589, 594, 595–96
    tradition and, 68
Roman empire, eschatology and, 237
royal view of "image," 659–60
royalty of Jesus. *See* exaltation of Jesus
"rule of faith/truth," 21n7, 66, 69
rule over creation, 660

Sabellian Christology, 111, 117
sacrament
    about, 757–58
    holistic community with, 733–34
    as mark of church, 738, 739–40
    purpose of church and, 754–55
    See also baptism; Eucharist
sacramentum, 757, 759
sacrifice
    Christus Victor and, 417
    Jesus' substitute, 480
    redemption and, 554
sacrificial system (OT), 403, 550
"Saint Patrick's Breastplate" prayer, 730
salvation
    availability of, 420–22, 434
    baptism and, 774–75
    center of, 578–79
    Christology and, 443–45, 480–81
    eschatology and, 270
    exclusive view of, 591–95
    gospel of, 44, 48, 52, 491–95
    images of, 548–49
    Israel/church and, 720, 725–26
    scope of, 580–81
    security of, 595–605
    sequence of, 513–14, 524 (*see also ordo salutis*)
    sin of humanity and, 666, 669
    universal view of, 581–91
    visible church and, 704
    See also atonement; election; redemption
salvation history. *See* history, redemptive
sanctification, 541, 631
sanctuary, heavenly, 457
Satan
    Christ's ransom and, 391–93
    Jesus Christ and, 372–74
    problem of evil and, 690
    supernatural evil and, 686
    victory over, 393–94, 414–15
satisfaction theory of atonement, 397–98, 410
"saved," meaning of, 493–94, 546, 548
"Savior," 471, 472
science
    creation and, 163
    human constitution and, 664
    in prolegomena, 36–38, 40
Scripture
    defined, 63
    inspiration of, 638–42
    in prolegomena, 33–34, 36–37, 43, 45
    revelation through, 196–202, 638
    as source for theology, 62–64, 77–80
    theology for unity of, 55–57
    tradition and, 64–70
    veracity of, 642–46
    See also Bible; Word of God
"second coming," 259. *See also* return of Jesus Christ
Second Helvetic Confession, 93n10, 119
"Second Quest" for the historical Jesus," 348–49
seed of Abraham, 372
"self," 663

self-centeredness, 674
self-deification, 669
self-gratification, 669, 676
self-sufficiency of God, 128–29
Semi-Pelagianism, 521, 560, 676, 677, 680. See also Pelagianism
sensus divinitatis (Calvin), 71, 177, 186, 189
Sermon on the Mount, 380
"Servant of the Lord," 505
service, ecclesiology and, 730–31
"session" in Presbyterianism, 748
session of Jesus, 450–59
Seventh-day Adventists, 314
shalom
    judgment and, 306
    justification and, 568
    new creation and, 155, 329
    purpose of church and, 756
shalom-breaking, culpable, 669
Shema, 101, 161, 468, 470
Sheol, death and, 317–24
Shepherd, the Good, 127, 167, 312, 322, 381, 384, 400, 425, 605, 715
Shepherd King/ruler, 362, 381, 715–16, 735
Shepherd of Hermas, 65, 116, 286
Short Treatise on the Supper of Our Lord (Calvin), 790–91
sin
    atonement and, 405–7
    as broken relationship, 666–67
    Christus Victor and, 394–95, 418
    effects of, 671–74
    entrance of, 311, 677–83
    Eucharist and unconfessed, 797
    forgiveness of, 551
    incarnation and, 523–27
    as moral evil, 685
    nature/essence of, 667–71
    "noetic effects of," 175–76
    power of, 674–76
    in redemptive history, 499
    salvation images for, 548
    transformation and, 544
"sin" (the word) versus the word "evil," 670–71
Sinaitic covenant, 502–6
Sinfulness of Sin (Venning), The, 674
slavery to sin
    about, 673
    free will and, 676
    redemption from, 553–55

Smyth, John, example of, 772
social classes, Eucharist and, 797
social evil, 685
social gospel, 52–54
Socinians, 314
sola fide, 587
sola gratia, 587
sola scriptura, tradition and, 68, 69–70
solipsism, 738
solus Christus, 367
"Son of David/Adam/Israel's God," 372, 388, 473, 476
"Son of God"
    deity/humanity of Jesus as, 461
    preexistence of Christ and, 465–68
    recapitulation and, 388
    Trinity and, 102
    virgin conception and, 376
"Son of Man"
    atonement and, 404
    biblical references to, 261–69
    deity/humanity of Jesus as, 461, 476, 486
    enthroned with God, 472
    eschatology and, 244–45
    new creation and, 154
    in redemptive history, 505
"sons" of God, believers as, 571
sonship of Jesus, 477
soteriology, 84, 490, 545, 557, 628, 701
"soul"
    of humanity, 662–65
    immortality of the, 312–14
soul nourishment (Eucharist), 793–94
soul sleep, 314
sovereignty of God
    in creation, 140–41
    image of God and, 660
    in regeneration, 627–28
    theodicy and, 690–91
"Spanish Train" (de Burgh), 692
special creationist, 654
special revelation
    defined, 172
    divine illumination as, 203–5
    history as, 193–95
    inscripturation as, 196–202
    proclamation as, 195–96
    redemptive nature of, 212–13
Spirit baptism, 633–36
Spirit filling, 637, 733–34
"spirit" of humanity, 662–63, 665

"Spirit of the Lord," 102, 104
spiritual gifts, 629–31
spiritual Israel, 719. *See also* new Israel
spiritual well-being, sin and, 671
spirituality
    evangelical ecclesiology and, 707
    resurrection of Christ and, 445–46
St. Peter's Anglican Church (Toronto), 799n242
stewardship, unity and, 743
Stoicism, 32
"strength" of humanity, 662, 664n34
subordination, functional, 119–20
subordinationism, 97, 116, 473
substance/consubstantial, 97, 115, 118
substantive view of "image," 658
substitutionary view of atonement, penal
    about, 402–10
    evangelicals and, 413–14
    pejorative criticism of, 411–12
suffering
    Christian response to, 688–91
    eschatology and, 242–43
    existence of, 147
    by God, 131
    as natural evil, 685
    philosophical solutions to, 687–88
    problem of, 686
    recent theologies on, 691–92
    scope of salvation and, 589–90
    theodicy of, 686–87
    ultimate answer to, 692–93
Suffering Servant, 154, 384, 403–4, 505
"sufficient for all, but efficient for only the elect," 434n223
Summa Theologica (Thomas Aquinas), 80
summum bonum, 183
supernatural evil, 685–86
synergism, 589
Synod of Constantinople, 582
Synod of Dort, 522
Synod of Mainz, 521
Synods of Orange, 521
systematic theology
    biblical studies and, 21–22, 25
    inherent obstacles to, 60–61
    methodology and, 78–80
Systematic Theology (Grudem), 78
Systematic Theology (Hodge), 36
Targum Isaiah, 505

teleological argument for existence of God, 182
telos (goal), 243, 414, 446, 705. *See also* purpose of God
"temple of God," 717
temptation, tribulation and, 292
Testament of Abraham, 318
Testament of Moses, 291n105
testimony, biblical
    to the gospel, 47–52
    to Scripture itself, 63
testimony of church/forefathers, tradition and, 69. *See also* apostolic testimony/ teachings
Tetrapolitan Confession, 569
thanksgiving, Eucharist and, 793
theism, 36, 181, 684, 691–92
theistic evolutionist, 654
theodicy
    about, 686–87
    Christian response in, 688–91
    philosophical solutions in, 687–88
    recent theologies in, 691–92
    ultimate answer in, 692–93
theological methods
    author's preferred, 81–83
    usual, described, 77–81
"Theological Sausage Maker 3000," 77
theology
    authoritative sources for, 62, 64, 70, 72, 73, 76, 81
    caveat on, 84
    definition of, 29–31
    eschatology and, 272, 808–9
    goal of, 58
    Jesus' life and, 381–82
    necessity of, 55–58
    pre-theology of (*see* prolegomena)
    requirements to study, 26
    See also Christian theology; evangelical theology; systematic theology
theophany, 360
theopneustos, 63, 639
theos, 30
theosis in salvation, 575–78
theotokos, 368, 482
"There Is a Green Hill Far Away" (Alexander), 401
Thinker (Rodin), *The*, 333–34
Third Chimpanzee (Diamond), *The*, 652
"Third Quest" for the historical Jesus, 349

Subject Index

Thirty-Nine Articles of Religion (Anglican)
    on Apocrypha, 316
    on atonement, 430
    on creation, 141
    on deity/humanity of Jesus, 463
    on Holy Spirit, 615
    on sacraments, 773, 791n222
    on Trinity, 97–98
"thousand years," 275
throne of God, Jesus and, 472
timelessness of God, 128
tolerance, in postmodernity, 238
Tome (Leo I), 117
tongues, speaking in, 634
Torah. *See* law, the
total depravity, 528, 675
tradition
    evangelical theology and, 68–70
    evangelicalism and, 702
    in prolegomena, 36
    theology and, 64–70
"tradition of the truth," 66
traditionalism, 70
"Transcendental Argument" (Van Til), 185
transformation
    image of God and, 661
    justification and, 561, 567–68
    in *ordo salutis*, 541–44
    theosis and, 576–78
"transgression" as sin, 667
transubstantiation, 781, 790
Treatise on the Resurrection, 253–54
trials, eschatological, 292, 300. *See also* tribulation
tribulation
    defined, 257
    judgment and, 304
    mid-, 294
    post-, 297–300
    pre-, 292, 294–97
trichotomism, anthropological, 663
Trinitarian food, 793
Trinitarian theology, 122
Trinitarianism
    discussions within, 118–22
    incipient, 106–10, 124
    monotheism and, 476
    proto, 111–12, 124
Trinity
    the "call" and the, 532
    confronting the, 92–95
    creation by, 148–52, 622
    creeds/confessions of, 95, 97–98
    doctrine of, 88, 98, 100, 121
    ecclesiology and, 729–30
    holiness and, 737
    Holy Spirit in, 611, 617, 619–20, 623
    justification and, 568
    New Testament roots of, 105–12
    Old Testament roots of, 100–104, 112–13
    in Patristic era, 113–18
    practical implications of, 122–24
    preexistence of Christ and, 465
    a priori argument for, 113
    resurrection of Christ and, 444–45
    salvation and, 556
Trinity in Unity (Athanasian Creed), 99
tritheism, 116
triumphalism, eschatology and, 242
truth, absolute/relative, in prolegomena, 39
TULIP (Calvinism), 422, 528, 599
Two Horizons series, 25
typology, Jesus Christ and, 360

unbelief, in prolegomena, 40
unclean food, Eucharist and, 796
Unitarians, 582
unity
    of biblical materials, 55–56
    of body/soul, 313–14, 324, 665
    of Christian beliefs, 60
    in Christology, 355, 416, 436, 458, 462, 464, 469, 475–76, 485
    of the church, 735–36, 741–44, 811
    covenantal, and eschatology, 279, 282, 284, 297, 307
    in creation, 156
    ecclesiology and, 729
    Eucharist and, 794–95
    of God's decree, 524, 525n48
    of God's plan, 214, 219–28
    of the gospel, 90–91
    Holy Spirit's work in, 632–33
    of Israel/church, 724, 726
    new creation and, 328, 332
    in redemptive history, 496, 507, 548
    in revelation, 164, 166, 184n170, 196, 202, 212
    spiritual versus physical, 701
    in the Trinity, 95–96, 98, 121
Unity in Trinity (Athanasian Creed), 99
universal atonement view, 427–29

Subject Index

universalism, 581–91
Universalists, Christian, 582

vengeance, judgment and divine, 306
veracity of Scriptures, 642–46
verbal theory of inspiration, 640–42
victory model of atonement
    about, 393–97, 410
    Bird on centrality of, 414–20
violence, judgment and, 306
virgin conception
    Barth/Pannenberg on, 376–77
    biblical references to, 365–66
    historicity of, 366, 369–70
    theological significance of, 370–75
Virgin Mary. See Mary (mother of Jesus)
visions, 73
vivification, 104, 155, 572, 627–28
voice and vote, 752
Vulgate, Latin, 317

water baptism, 635
"wedding supper of the Lamb," 270–71
Wesleyan Quadrilateral, 81
Wesleyanism/Wesleyans
    on atonement, 420
    on election, 522, 529n56
    on justification, 564
    on perfectionism, 544n101
Westminster Confession of Faith
    on Apocrypha, 316
    on atonement, 423
    on calling, 532n66
    on creation, 141, 158
    on deity/humanity of Jesus, 463
    description of, 23
    on life of Jesus, 357
    on problem of evil, 690–91
    on revelation, 200
    on sacraments, 757, 762, 773n169, 784–87, 795
    on salvation, 595, 604
    on Scripture, 64, 199, 638, 646n69
    on Trinity, 100
    on veracity of Holy Spirit, 645
    on the visible church, 704
Westminster Larger Catechism, 498, 653
Westminster Shorter Catechism, 201, 215, 562
Wheaton College, 276, 654

"When I Survey the Wondrous Cross" (Watts), 435
wisdom of God (attribute), 136–37
Wisdom of God (entity), 102, 104, 114
"Without the Gospel," 16–18
witness, Christian
    ascension of Jesus and, 452–53
    Holy Spirit and, 614
    theology to prepare for, 56
    unity of church and, 742
    See also evangelism
women in ministry, 119–20
"Word," the
    Eucharist and, 783, 789
    Jesus named as, 471
    Trinity and, 102, 104, 114
Word of God
    forms of, 62–63
    gospel as, 165
    holistic community with, 733–34
    preaching, as mark of church, 738, 739–40
    in prolegomena, 30, 37, 38
    tradition and, 66, 69
    veracity of, 642, 645
    See also Scripture
"word of the Lord"
    gospel proclamation as, 165, 195
    Holy Spirit and, 104, 624, 642
works
    covenant of, 222
    faith and, 569–70
World Evangelical Fellowship (1951), 743
World Missionary Conference (Edinburgh, 1910), 743
worldview, creation and Christian, 162
worship
    ascension of Jesus and, 452–53
    creation and, 162
    cross-centered, 435
    evangelical ecclesiology and, 707
    purpose of church and, 755–66
    resurrection of Christ and, 447–48
    Trinity and, 122–23

Zoroastrianism, 684
Zwinglian view on Lord's Supper, 783–84, 788–90

AUTHOR INDEX

Abasciano, Brian J., 520
Abelard, Peter, 398–99
Achard, Robert M., 153
Achtemeier, Elizabeth, 184
Allen, R. Michael, 433
Allert, Craig, 639
Allison, Dale C., 244, 349, 590
Ambrose, 682
Ambrosiaster, 109, 680
Amyraut, Moyse, 429–30
Anderson, Allan, 634
Anselm, 58
Anselm of Canterbury, 40, 180, 397, 399, 409, 413–14, 463
Apollinarius, 117
Aquinas. *See* Thomas Aquinas
Archer, Gleason L., 292
Ardo, Theodor W., 234
Arminius, Jacob, 522, 596
Ashby, Stephen M., 596
Athanasius, 108, 116, 209, 210, 462, 475–76, 576
Augustine, 29, 88, 95, 159, 332, 333, 361, 362, 392, 395–96, 408–9, 485, 520–21, 521, 576, 587, 619–20, 633, 644, 653, 658, 675–76, 677, 679–80, 704, 708, 725–26, 732, 738, 757, 800
Aulen, Gustaf, 396–97
Aune, David E., 244, 288, 296, 561

Baddeley, Mark, 131
Bahnsen, Greg L., 185
Bailey, Daniel P., 408
Baima, Thomas A., 780
Balmer, Randall, 19
Balthasar, Hans Urs von, 151, 209, 390, 444
Barbour, Ian, 159
Barclay, John, 586–87
Barnett, Paul, 321, 438
Barr, James, 197
Barrett, C. K., 107, 517
Barth, Karl, 28, 29, 38, 40, 43–44, 55–56, 61, 71, 81–82, 120, 135, 139, 150, 162, 179, 184, 191, 194, 202, 203, 207–8, 236, 272, 347, 352, 375, 376, 387, 409, 490, 525, 526–27, 536, 557, 564, 583, 613, 632, 636, 659, 705, 720, 733, 767–68, 772–73
Barth, Markus, 436, 767–68
Basil of Caesarea, 159, 422, 428, 618, 658
Bateman, Herber W., 220
Bauckham, Richard, 211, 243, 246, 290, 318, 319, 433, 469, 597, 725
Bavinck, Hermann, 127–28, 162, 525
Beale, Gregory K., 248, 278, 283, 290, 292, 308, 329, 332, 359
Beasley-Murray, George R., 206, 266, 288, 762, 768–69, 772, 774, 775
Bebbington, David W., 19, 20, 387, 596
Bell, G. K. A., 383
Bell, Richard H., 184–85, 587
Bell, Rob, 336, 584
Ben Sirach. *See* Jesus ben Sirach
Bender, Kimlyn J., 733
Benedict VIII, 619
Benedict XVI, 28. *See also* Ratzinger, Joseph
Berding, Kenneth, 359
Berkhof, Hendrikus, 353–54, 355, 375, 726
Berkhof, Louis, 127, 168, 274–75, 513, 522, 547, 717, 739
Berkouwer, G. C., 177–78, 432, 542
Bernard, J. R. L., 29
Beza, Theodore, 522
Bilezikian, Gilbert, 119
Billings, J. Todd, 68, 199, 577, 578, 702
Bird, Michael F., 25, 106, 120, 153, 156, 244–45, 251, 260, 261, 263, 271, 298, 348, 349, 350, 359, 365, 378, 436, 437, 443, 446, 467, 505, 514, 554, 557, 559, 561, 564, 566, 568, 570, 571, 575, 645, 719, 721, 724, 766, 796
Blaising, Craig A., 220, 720
Blanke, Helmut, 768
Blocher, Henri, 306, 317, 397, 411, 418, 566, 654, 677, 681, 682
Bloesch, Donald G., 43, 69, 100, 118, 122, 137, 189, 202, 306, 342, 610, 615, 620, 623, 638, 644, 758
Blomberg, Craig L., 289, 296, 300, 796

Author Index

Bock, Darrell L., 220, 221, 636, 720
Bockmuehl, Markus, 25, 325, 370, 379
Boersma, Hans, 414
Boettner, Loraine, 275, 642
Boff, Leonardo, 124
Boice, James M., 424
Bolt, Peter G., 119, 404, 405
Bonar, Horatio, 544
Bonda, Jan, 586
Bonhoeffer, Dietrich, 730–31, 732
Bornkamm, Günther, 348
Bowles, Ralph G., 336
Bowman, Robert M., 470
Boyd, Gregory A., 393, 414, 691
Bray, Gerald L., 96, 109, 121, 475, 680, 682
Bromiley, Geoffrey W., 192, 400, 643, 783
Brown, David, 397
Bruce, F. F., 66, 294, 603, 661
Brueggemann, Walter, 329, 555
Brunner, Emil, 71, 81–82, 162, 188, 194, 358, 381, 387, 400, 527, 562, 659
Bucer, Martin, 562
Bullinger, Heinrich, 225
Bultmann, Rudolf, 73, 81–82, 194, 347, 351–52
Bunyan, John, 768
Burge, Gary M., 221
Burke, Trevor, 572
Burnett, Gary W., 703
Burridge, Richard A., 348

Cadbury, Henry, 247
Caird, George B., 266–67, 293, 327, 789
Calvin, John, 16, 25, 33, 43, 71, 80, 121, 142, 177, 186, 188, 364, 396, 409, 415–16, 422, 433, 434, 485, 514, 521, 523–25, 531, 540, 543, 544, 546, 552, 562, 569, 577, 596, 605, 628, 658, 675, 676, 704, 709–10, 724, 727, 732, 736, 738–39, 748, 785–86, 788, 790–92, 798, 802
Camus, Albert, 651
Cappadocian Fathers. *See* Basil of Caesarea; Gregory of Nazianzus; Gregory of Nyssa
Carnell, Edward, 201
Carson, D. A., 19, 35, 75–76, 93, 102, 190, 206, 263, 296, 317, 359, 407, 541, 564, 588, 603, 650, 755, 775
Casey, P. M., 261
Chafer, Lewis S., 220, 713
Chalke, Stephen, 411

Chan, Mark L. Y., 352
Charlesworth, James H., 346
Chester, Tim, 122
Childs, Brevard S., 557
Christensen, Michael J., 575
Chung, Sung Wook, 282, 283–84, 527
Ciampa, Roy E., 546, 797
Clark, Kelly James, 186
Clement of Alexandria, 159, 388, 576
Clement of Rome, 113, 618, 737
Clifford, Ross, 436
Cocceius, Johannes, 222, 415
Cochrane, Arthur C., 570
Cocksworth, Christopher J., 789
Cohick, Lynn H., 515
Cole, Graham A., 226, 387, 398, 412, 418–19, 444, 537, 539, 545, 546, 564, 571, 619, 621, 622, 629, 692
Colijn, Brenda B., 529, 552, 555, 556, 572
Copan, Paul, 158
Corduan, Winfried, 38
Craig, William L., 71
Crawford, Matthew R., 783
Crisp, Oliver D., 22, 430, 432
Cross, Anthony R., 23
Crossan, J. D., 246
Crossley, James G., 365, 437, 645
Cullmann, Oscar, 252
Culpeppar, Robert, 399
Culver, Robert, 29
Cyprian, 436, 555, 704, 764
Cyril of Jerusalem, 68, 385–86, 428, 476, 477

D'Aubigne, J. H. Merle, 676
Davids, Peter H., 518
Davies, Glenn, 800–801
Davies, W. D., 320
Davis, Thomas J., 787, 793
de Burgh, Chris, 692
Dearborn, Kerry L., 730
Deissmann, Gustav A., 259, 383
Delbridge, Arthur, 29
Demarest, B. A., 430
Derrida, Jacque, 39
deSilva, David A., 602
DeYoung, Kevin, 732
Diamond, Jared, 652
Dickson, John, 47, 49
Dodd, C. H., 246, 359, 407
Drumm, Curtis S., 638

D'Souza, Dinesh, 652
Dulles, Avery, 169–70
Dumbrell, William J., 227, 501–3
Dunn, James D. G., 44, 72, 103, 105, 286, 407, 466, 473, 546, 561, 566, 625, 636, 766–67

Eastman, Susan, 723
Eddy, Paul R., 691
Edgar, Brian, 123
Edwards, James R., 264
Edwards, Jonathan, 113
Eliot, T. S., 274
Ellis, E. Earle, 359
Enns, Peter, 205, 359, 363
Ephraem the Syrian, 106
Epicurus, 686
Epiphanius Of Salamis, 799
Erasmus, Desiderius, 676
Erickson, Millard J., 43, 111–12, 120, 124, 172, 194, 219, 269, 281, 282, 294, 328, 432, 519, 524, 534, 550, 584, 594, 640, 658, 659, 663, 665, 683, 687, 714, 754, 758, 765, 772, 784
Eriugena, Johannes Scotus, 521
Eskola, Timo, 473, 474
Estes, Daniel T., 361
Eusebius, 364, 746
Eutyches, 117

Fairburn, Donald, 300
Fee, Gordon D., 28, 110, 290, 629, 631, 635
Feinberg, John S., 537, 619
Feinberg, Paul D., 295–96
Ferguson, Everett, 106, 767, 771, 774
Ferguson, Sinclair B., 616, 761
Fesko, J. V., 541
Finlan, Stephen, 575
Fishbane, Michael, 360
Fitzmyer, Joseph A., 560, 681, 682
Fletcher, Verne H., 436
Forsyth, Peter T., 386
Fosdick, Harry E., 42
Foucault, Michel, 39
Fowl, Stephen E., 73
Frame, John, 186
France, R. T., 264, 266, 425
Franke, John R., 736
Fredericks, Daniel C., 361
Frei, Hans, 40

Fretheim, Terence, 132
Frey, J. B., 750
Fulbert Of Chartres, 342
Fuller, Daniel P., 537
Fung, R. K., 717

Gaffin, Richard, 547
Gager, John, 720, 808
Garcia, Mark A., 577
Garland, David E., 403
Gathercole, Simon G., 245, 377, 468
Gaunilo of Marmoutiers, 180
Gaventa, Beverly R., 353
Gelpi, Donald, 623
Gench, Frances T., 540
Gentry, Kenneth L., 275, 276
George, Timothy, 406, 772
Gerstner, John H., 186
Getty, Keith, 397, 435
Gibson, David, 788
Gibson, James, 25
Giles, Kevin, 78, 119, 120
Gill, John, 596
Gleason, R. C., 602
Goldingay, John E., 261, 360, 363
Goldsworthy, Graeme, 45, 195, 235, 247–48, 497
Gombis, Timothy, 416–17
Goodwin, Thomas, 415
Goppelt, Leonhard, 360, 534
Gorday, Peter, 395
Gorman, Michael J., 387, 568, 575
Gottschalk, 521
Gould, Graham, 348
Green, Bradley G., 679
Green, Joel B., 319, 324, 380–81, 552, 664
Gregory of Nazianzus, 112–13, 368, 393, 428, 462, 658, 769
Gregory of Nyssa, 116, 391, 393, 582, 658
Grenz, Stanley E., 40–41, 43, 62, 74, 151, 314, 622, 728
Grindheim, Sigurd, 721
Gros, Jeffery, 780
Grotius, Hugo, 402
Grubbs, Norris C., 638
Grudem, Wayne, 41, 78, 119, 129, 222, 266, 281, 282, 288, 303, 323, 412, 424, 426, 433, 434, 443, 450, 451, 458, 479, 530, 533, 550, 562, 630, 637, 663, 751, 752, 758, 765, 772, 783

Author Index

Gruenler, R. G., 111
Gulley, Philip, 583–84
Gundry, Robert H., 266, 293, 294, 298, 337, 404, 563
Gundry-Volf, Judith, 598–99
Gunton, Colin E., 118–19, 158, 168, 398, 461, 661
Guthrie, Shirley C., 138

Habermas, Gary, 435
Hagner, D. A., 155
Hahn, Scott A., 560
Hall, Christopher, 100, 113
Hall, D. J., 596
Hamid-Khani, Saeed, 204
Hamilton, James M., 291, 308, 360, 361, 415, 537
Hamilton, Victor P., 660
Hanson, A. T., 361
Harmon, Steve R., 23, 752
Harnack, Adolf von, 346
Harper, Brad, 728, 729, 758, 770–71
Harris, Murray J., 321, 470
Harrison, E. F., 314
Harrison, R. K., 160
Hart, David B., 26, 493
Harvey, Graham, 721
Hasker, William, 692
Hauerwas, Stanley, 189
Hays, Richard B., 57, 241, 254–55, 331, 353, 788
Helm, Paul, 188, 201, 645
Hengel, Martin, 355, 363
Henry, Carl F., 188, 199
Hesselink, John, 785
Hill, Charles E., 288, 289, 403
Hippolytus of Rome, 115–16, 747, 764
Hobbes, Thomas, 200
Hodge, A. A., 277, 278
Hodge, Charles, 36–37, 422, 432, 547
Hoekema, Anthony A., 260, 279, 659
Honorius Of Autun, 523
Hooker, Richard, 791, 794
Hopko, Thomas, 623
Horrell, J. Scott, 120
Horton, Michael S., 222, 266, 279, 281, 313–14, 324, 424, 463, 527, 530, 532, 546, 547, 562, 566, 593, 603, 604, 663, 682, 710, 732, 739, 740, 748, 758, 761, 768, 785, 790

Houlden, J. L., 705
Howard-Snyder, Daniel, 686
Hubbard, Moyer V., 153
Hunsinger, George, 184
Hunt, J. P. T., 766
Hunter, A. M., 546
Hurtado, Larry W., 105, 359, 413, 433, 452, 460, 467

Ignatius of Antioch, 58, 113–14, 205, 362, 461, 538, 738, 747, 748, 780–81, 790, 793–94, 795, 802
Irenaeus, 45, 57, 66–67, 106, 115, 148, 161, 206–7, 218, 253, 368, 389–90, 462, 474, 555, 576, 581, 589, 619, 624, 658, 764, 781

Jackson, T. Ryan, 154
James, Frank A., 403
Jeffery, Stephen, 402, 404, 406, 424
Jefford, Clayton N., 667, 669
Jensen, Peter, 42–43, 49, 73, 164, 170, 201, 213, 239
Jenson, Robert W., 25, 465
Jeremias, Joachim, 247, 319, 324, 334
Jerome, 316
Jesus ben Sirach, 135
Jewett, Paul K, 156, 519
Jewett, Robert, 586, 802
Jobes, Karen H., 110
John Chrysostom, 386, 395, 419–20, 448, 559
Johnson, Luke T., 72, 350, 352
Johnson, Philip, 436
Johnson, William S., 791
Josephus, Flavius, 313, 407, 557–58, 746
Jung, Carl, 684
Jüngel, Eberhard, 561
Justin Martyr, 32, 103, 114, 116, 158, 259, 313, 361, 364, 370, 374, 437, 474, 592, 719, 790, 795

Kähler, Martin, 350
Kant, Immanuel, 39, 180, 183
Kärkkläinen, Veli-Matti, 43
Käsemann, Ernst, 236, 347, 809
Kasper, Walter, 90, 112, 210
Keck, Leander E., 346, 441
Keener, Craig S., 119, 271, 280
Keller, Tim, 93
Kelly, J. N. D., 392

Kendall, R. T., 423
Kennard, Douglas, 357
Kevan, E. F., 643
Keynes, Milton, 23
Kharlamov, Vladimir, 575
Kierkegaard, Søren, 682
Kirk, J. R. Daniel, 563
Kittel, Gerhard, 383
Klauber, Martin I., 432
Klink, Edward W., 25
Klooster, F. H., 515
Kluck, Ted, 732
Knox, D. B., 397, 426, 430–31, 539
Knox, John, 465
Koester, Craig R., 250
Komoszewski, J. Ed, 470
Köstenberger, Andreas J., 111, 112, 206, 516, 598
Kovach, Stephen, 119
Kovacs, Judith L., 108
Kreitzer, Larry, 682–83
Kristemaker, Simon J., 174
Kroeger, C. C., 119
Kroeger, R. C., 119
Küng, Hans, 728

Laato, Timo, 564
Lactantius, 665
LaCugna, Catherine M., 122
Ladd, George E., 239, 280, 282, 288, 379, 561, 708
Lane, Anthony N. S., 69, 561, 639, 768, 769, 776
Larsen, Timothy, 276
Law, R., 218
Lee, Aquila H. I., 453
Lee, Jason K., 772
Leith, John H., 791
Leithart, Peter J., 224
Leo I, 342
Letham, Robert, 113, 547
Levinson, John R., 677
Lewandowski, Joseph D., 234
Lewis, C. S., 24, 133, 183, 269, 307, 591, 660
Lewis, Gordon R., 295
Lindbeck, George, 40
Lindsley, Arthur, 186
Lockett, Darian R., 25
Lombard. *See* Peter Lombard
Longenecker, Richard N., 321, 724

Lorein, Geert W., 299
Lucas, Ernest C., 261
Lunde, Jonathan M., 359, 539
Luther, Martin, 33, 43, 49, 314, 365, 386, 485, 521, 536, 542, 658, 676, 698, 709, 719–20, 782–83

Macaskill, Grant, 319
MacDonald (pseudonym), Gregory, 584
Macedonius I of Constantinople, 117, 617
Machen, J. Gresham, 375
Mackenzie, Catherine, 652
Mackie, John L., 686
MacLaren, Brian, 53, 54
MacLeod, Donald, 566
Macquarrie, John, 197, 198, 465
Mann, Alan, 411
Marcion, 156, 719
Marlowe, Chritopher, 335
Marshall, I. Howard, 236, 280, 404, 406, 557, 584, 586, 590, 596–97, 601, 603
Martin, Ralph P., 156, 557
Martyn, J. L., 536
Mathews, K. A., 102
Mathison, Keith, 275
Maximus the Confessor, 523
Mbiti, John, 703
McCormack, Bruce, 191, 411, 578
McCready, Douglas, 465
McDonald, Lee M., 66
McDonough, Sean, 149–50
McGinn, Sheila E., 44
McGowan, Andrew T. B., 41, 93, 196, 226, 430, 534, 541, 547
McGrath, Alister E., 20–21, 29, 40, 72, 178, 189, 199, 332, 368, 386, 399, 400, 476, 523, 550, 560, 619, 693, 700
McGuckin, John A., 464
McKnight, Scot, 47, 265, 408, 412, 420, 448, 557, 568, 601, 705
McLaren, Brian, 411
Meier, John P., 107, 247, 349
Melanchthon, Philipp, 208, 562
Merz, Annette, 247, 348
Metzger, Bruce M., 100, 459
Metzger, Paul L., 728, 729, 758, 770–71
Michaels, J. Ramsay, 534, 773
Middleton, J. Richard, 660
Migilore, Daniel, 730, 731
Mikkelsen, Hans V., 352

Author Index

Milne, Bruce, 616
Milton, John, 393
Minear, Paul S., 714, 716, 718, 725, 726
Moltmann, Jürgen, 234, 236, 272, 583, 615, 623, 799
Moo, Douglas J., 266, 298, 443, 545, 566, 682, 723
Moore, Russell, D., 783, 791, 792, 793
Moreland, J. P., 654
Morris, Leon, 164, 198, 201, 407, 409, 533, 564, 571
Mounce, Robert H., 288
Mugridge, Alan, 601
Mullholland, James, 583–84
Murray, John, 223, 418, 514, 530, 535, 546, 547, 588
Myers, Benjamin F., 349, 527

Naselli, Andrew D., 419, 424
Needham, Nick, 520, 560
Neil, Stephen, 480, 676, 684
Nestorius, 117
Nettles, Thomas J., 765, 772
Newbigin, Lesslie J., 123, 156–57, 706–7
Nicole, Roger, 407, 430
Niebuhr, H. Richard, 74
Nietzsche, Friedrich, 39
Noll, Mark A., 19

O'Brien, Peter T., 129, 216–17, 517, 566, 603
O'Collins, Gerald, 104, 114, 116, 413
Oden, Thomas C., 24, 34, 127, 733, 735, 740
O'Donovan, Oliver, 44, 442
Okholm, Dennis L., 19
Olson, Roger E., 20, 100, 113, 523, 529, 596, 783
Origen, 116–17, 240, 370, 391, 474, 576, 577, 581–82, 665, 680, 764
Ortberg, John, 123
Ortlund, Dane C., 570
Osborne, Grant R., 296
Osiander, Andreas, 523, 578
Outler, Albert, 81
Ovey, Michael, 402, 404, 406, 424
Owen, John, 423, 431–32

Packer, J. I., 24, 129, 131, 358, 403, 530, 534, 627, 639, 640, 643, 771
Paley, William, 182
Pannenberg, Wolfhart, 120, 135–36, 195, 208, 324, 349–50, 368, 376–77, 436, 482, 527, 664, 799
Park, Eung C., 720
Parker, David, 680
Parry, Robin. *See* MacDonald (pseudonym), Gregory
Pascal, Blaise, 650
Patterson, Paige, 429, 751
Paul of Samosata, 117
Payton, James R., 562
Peacock, Arthur, 159
Pelagius, 224, 401, 520–21, 594, 675, 677
Pelikan, Jaroslav, 30, 70, 210, 422, 517, 576, 586
Pennington, Jonathan T., 248
Perkins, William, 514
Perriman, Andrew, 265, 266
Perrin, Nick, 703
Peter Lombard, 665
Peters, George W., 343
Peterson, David, 403, 541
Peterson, Eugene, 374
Peterson, Robert A., 416, 529
Phillips, Timothy R., 19
Philo, 96, 467
Pinnock, Clark H., 168, 529, 597, 691
Pinson, J. Matthew, 595
Piper, John, 88, 432, 435, 626, 653, 756
Pitre, Brant, 780
Pitts, William L., 752
Plantinga, Alvin, 71, 186–88, 688–89
Plantinga, Cornelius, 111, 669
Plato, 158, 313
Plevnik, Joseph, 268
Polhill, J. B., 636
Polycarp, 454
Porter, Stanley E., 545, 558, 559
Powell, Mark A., 84, 349
Pratt, Richard L., 761, 774

Rahner, Karl, 315, 582–83, 758
Ramm, Bernard, 201, 202, 203, 208, 213
Ratzinger, Joseph, 315. *See also* Benedict XVI
Rauschenbusch, Walter, 53
Rawlyk, George A., 19
Reasoner, Mark, 680
Reddish, M. G., 289
Reicke, Bo, 802
Reiser, Marius, 334
Reymond, Robert L., 562, 748, 761

Reynolds, Benjamin E., 538
Reynolds, John M., 654
Rice, Timothy ("Tim") M. B., 348
Richardson, Peter, 165
Riddelbarger, Kim, 279
Ridderbos, Herman, 239
Ritschl, Albrecht, 566
Robinson, James M., 348
Rosner, Brian S., 546, 797
Rowe, C. Kavin, 111
Russell, Jeffery B., 687–88
Ryken, Philip G., 424, 699
Ryle, J. C., 60
Ryrie, Charles, 29, 41, 220, 221, 261, 428, 534, 713, 720

Sabellius, 117
Sach, Andrew, 402, 404, 406, 424
Sanders, E. P., 349, 438, 564–65
Sanders, Fred, 92, 122, 124
Sanders, John E., 592, 691
Sands, Paul, 659
Satterthwaite, P. E., 501, 504
Saucy, Robert, 544
Sawyer, John F. A., 152
Sayers, Dorothy L., 94
Scaer, David P., 782
Schaeffer, Francis A., 190
Schemm, Peter, 119
Schleiermacher, Friedrich, 474, 615
Schmiechen, Peter, 413
Schnabel, Eckhard J., 771
Schreiner, Thomas R., 167, 175–76, 217, 240, 252, 291, 379, 397, 413–14, 520, 531, 682, 723, 783
Schwarz, Stephen, 30
Schweitzer, Albert, 244, 346–47
Scobie, Charles, 403
Scofield, C. I., 220
Seifrid, Mark A., 546
Sell, A. P. F., 596
Shepherd, Norman, 562
Sherlock, Charles, 122, 658
Shillaker, Robert, 120
Smail, Tom, 305
Smith, Gordon T., 198, 780
Snodgrass, Klyne, 165
Snyder, Howard A., 708–9
Socinus, Faustus, 399
Socrates, 684

Solzhenitsyn, Alexsandr I., 670
Son, Kiwong, 331
Spinoza, Benedict de, 684
Sproul, R. C., 186
Spurgeon, Charles, 424
Stackhouse, Ian, 706
Stackhouse, John G., 700
Stephenson, John R., 782
Stone, Samuel J., 741
Storms, Sam, 291
Stott, John, 387, 402, 419, 435, 701, 704
Strauss, Mark, 370, 371
Strong, Augustus H., 432
Stroup, George W., 791
Stuckenbruck, Loren, 290
Stuhlmacher, Peter, 458, 557
Sudduth, Michael, 179, 189
Suetonius, 369
Surin, Kenneth, 686
Swain, Scott R., 111, 112
Sweet, Leonard I., 19

Taylor, Justin, 16
Taylor, L. Roy, 748, 749
Taylor, S. S., 538
Tennent, Timothy C., 20, 344
Tertullian, 67, 93–94, 115, 365, 592, 610, 658, 665, 759, 764, 767, 769
Theissen, Gerd, 247, 348
Theobald, Michael, 566
Theodoret of Cyrus, 422
Thiessen, Henry C., 79
Thiselton, Anthony, 566
Thomas Aquinas, 33, 80, 152, 178, 180, 182, 315, 521, 523, 665, 781, 787
Thompson, Mark D., 646
Thompson, Philip E., 23
Tidball, Derek J., 44, 713, 714
Tiessen, Terence L., 581, 592
Tillich, Paul, 80, 350, 355
Toon, Peter, 449, 450, 745, 748
Torrance, Thomas F., 122, 141, 150–51, 355, 400, 477, 731
Towner, Philip H., 253
Townshend, Stuart, 397, 435
Travis, Stephen H., 305
Treier, Daniel J., 644
Trueman, Carl, 645
Turner, Seth, 288
Turretin, Francis, 432

Author Index

Turretin, Jean-Alphonse, 743
Tyrrell, George, 347

Updike, John, 439
Ursinus, Zacharias, 222

van Driel, Edwin Chr., 524, 525
Van Dyk, Leanne, 785, 790
Van Neste, Ray, 802
Van Til, Cornelius, 185–86
VanDrunen, David, 710
Vanhoozer, Kevin J., 24–25, 30–31, 40, 42, 67, 78–79, 92, 100, 164, 201, 532, 564, 568, 646, 702, 705, 740
Venning, Ralph, 674
Vickers, Brian, 552, 564
Volf, Miroslav, 306, 557, 730, 756

Waldron, Samuel E., 751
Walvoord, John F., 220, 295
Ward, Timothy, 93, 196, 203, 205, 642
Ware, Bruce A., 120, 765, 771, 772, 783
Warfield, B. B., 628, 639, 640, 704
Waters, Guy P., 566
Watson, Francis, 45, 565, 566
Watts, Isaac, 142, 435
Wax, Trevin, 47
Webb, Barry, 361
Webster, John, 28, 41–42, 61, 89, 93, 144, 170, 196, 202, 205, 490, 638, 644, 745, 768
Webster, Robert, 414
Weiss, Johannes, 244
Wellhausen, Julius, 153
Wells, David F., 19
Wenham, John, 336
Wesley, John, 24, 43, 81, 522, 529, 544, 596

Westcott, B. F., 546
Williams, D. H., 560
Williams, David J., 517, 554
Williams, J. Rodman, 625, 633
Williams, Michael D., 61, 78, 141, 228, 497, 503, 507–8, 529
Williams, Rowan, 475
Williams, S. N., 144
Williamson, Paul R., 224, 497
Wilson, Doug, 291
Winter, Paul, 245
Witherington, Ben, III, 72–73, 161, 245, 288, 300, 349, 406, 428, 529, 544
Wittung, Jeffery A., 575
Wolters, Albert, 140
Woodbridge, John D., 19, 642
Woodbridge, Paul, 321
Wooden, R. Glenn, 261
Wright, David, 774
Wright, G. Ernest, 194
Wright, N. T., 47, 140, 145, 205, 239, 246, 262, 267, 285, 315, 327–28, 332, 336, 337, 346, 350, 357, 372, 390, 405–6, 442, 443, 455, 467, 514, 531, 539, 564, 566, 591, 646, 678, 711, 723, 734, 778, 809
Wurmbrand, Richard, 652

Xenophon, 319, 540

Yarbrough, Robert W., 516, 552
Yinger, Kent L., 564

Zannoni, Arthur E., 148
Ziep, Arie W., 458
Zizioulas, John, 729
Zwingli, Huldrych (*also*, Ulrich), 485, 562, 782, 783